Contents

Criollo culture colour section following p.216

Sports and outdoor activities colour section following p.456

The legendary Ruta 40 colour section following p.696

◄◄ Street musicians, Buenos Aires ◄ Paprikas drying, Cachi

Metres
5000
4000
3000
2000
1500
1000
400
200
0
BOLIVIA
BRAZIL
PARAGUAY
BRAZIL
URUGUAY
CHILE
PACIFIC OCEAN
ATLANTIC OCEAN
CORDILLERA DE LOS ANDES
La Quiaca
Jujuy
Salta
Cafayate
Tucumán
Santiago del Estero
Catamarca
La Rioja
Laguna Mar Chiquita
Córdoba
San Juan
Mendoza
San Luis
San Rafael
Santa Fe
Rosario
Formosa
Resistencia
Corrientes
Posadas
Puerto Iguazú
Concordia
Gualeguaychú
Colonia del Sacramento
San Antonio de Areco
BUENOS AIRES
La Plata
Santa Rosa
Mar del Plata
Bahía Blanca
Neuquén
Río Negro
San Martín de los Andes
Carmen de Patagones
Bariloche
El Bolsón
Esquel
Río Chubut
Península Valdés
Puerto Madryn
Trelew
Comodoro Rivadavia
Perito Moreno
Puerto Deseado
Puerto San Julián
El Calafate
Puerto Santa Cruz
Puerto Natales
Río Gallegos
Punta Arenas
Straits of Magellan
Ushuaia
Cape Horn
FALKLAND ISLANDS (ISLAS MALVINAS)
Argentine Antarctic Territory
Río Paraná
Río Uruguay
RN-49
RN-34
RN-81
RN-16
RN-12
RN-11
RN-14
RN-40
RN-9
RN-7
RN-188
RN-35
RN-3
RN-2
RN-22
RN-25
RP-43
N
0
200 km

The **Rough Guide** to

Argentina

written and researched by

Danny Aeberhard, Andrew Benson, Rosalba O'Brien and Lucy Phillips

with additional contributions by

Keith Drew and Paul Smith

ROUGH GUIDES

NEW YORK • LONDON • DELHI

www.roughguides.com

Introduction to Argentina

Argentina is a vast land: even without the titanic wedge of Antarctica that the authorities like to include in the national territory, it ranks as one of the world's largest countries. The mainland points down from the Tropic of Capricorn like a massive stalactite, tapering towards the planet's most southerly extremities. Consequently, the country encompasses a staggering diversity of landscapes, ranging from the hot and humid jungles of the Northeast and the bone-dry highland steppes of the Northwest, via the fertile Pampas and windswept Patagonia, to the end-of-the-world archipelago of Tierra del Fuego.

Argentina is, for the most part, less obviously "exotic" than most of its neighbours to the north, and its inhabitants will readily, and rightly, tell you how great an influence Europe has been on their nation. It was once said that Argentina is actually the most American of all European countries, but even that clever maxim is wide of the mark. It's a country with a very special character all of its own, distilled into the national ideal of **Argentinidad** – an elusive identity that the country's utopian thinkers and practical doers have never really agreed upon.

In terms of identity, there are lots of sweeping generalizations about the people of Argentina, who generally get bad press in the rest of the continent for being arrogant. Though such a characterization isn't entirely without merit, it's more the exception than the rule – you're bound to be wowed by Argentines' zeal for so many aspects of their culture. On this score there is a lot of truth in the clichés – their passions are dominated by **football**, politics and living life in the fast lane (literally, when it comes to driving) – but not everyone dances the **tango**, or is obsessed with **Evita** or gallops around on a horse. The locals will help to make any trip to their country memorable.

Fact file

• Argentina is the world's eighth largest nation by area, with 2.75 million square kilometres, though with a population of just under 39 million – one-third of whom live in the capital Buenos Aires – it is one of the least densely populated of the ten biggest countries.

• Argentina not only produces the finest beef on earth, but it also is one of the world's leading producers of lemons, wheat, wine and genetically modified soya. Around half of the country's arable land (over 100,000 square kilometres) is planted with the latter crop.

• Five Argentines have been honoured with Nobel Prizes, including three in the sciences: Bernardo A. Houssay (Medicine and Physiology, 1947), Luis F. Leloir (Chemistry, 1970) and César Milstein (Medicine and Physiology, 1984). Two Argentines have been awarded the Nobel Peace Prize: Carlos Saavedra Lamas (politician, 1936) and Adolfo Pérez Esquivel (architect, sculptor and human-rights activist, 1980).

• Independent environmental organizations have declared that Argentina's cities enjoy some of the world's cleanest urban air – despite the decrepit buses – but Buenos Aires has also been voted one of the noisiest capitals – again, the buses being largely to blame.

• Just over one-third of Argentina's parliament is female – the ninth highest ratio in the world, according to the Inter-Parliamentary Union.

▼ Floralis Genérica, Buenos Aires

In addition to the people, there are loads of reasons to visit Argentina. Perhaps the most obvious is **Buenos Aires**, one of the most fascinating of all Latin American capitals. It's an immensely enjoyable place just to wander about, people-watching, shopping or simply soaking up the unique atmosphere. Its many barrios, or neighbourhoods, are startlingly different – some are decadently old-fashioned, others thrustingly modern – but all of them ooze character. Elsewhere in the country, cities aren't exactly the main draw, with the exception of beautiful **Salta** in the Northwest, beguiling **Rosario** – the birthplace of Che Guevara – and **Ushuaia**, which, in addition to being the world's most southerly city, enjoys a fabulous setting on Tierra del Fuego.

The vastness of the **land** and the varied **wildlife** inhabiting it are the country's real attractions outside the capital. In theory, by hopping on a plane or two you could spot howler monkeys and toucans in northern jungles in the morning, then watch the antics of penguins tobogganing into the icy South Atlantic in the afternoon. There are hundreds of bird species – including the Andean Condor and three varieties of flamingo – plus pumas, armadillos, llamas, foxes and tapirs, to be found in the country's forests, mountainsides and the dizzying heights of the altiplano, or *puna*. Lush tea plantations and parched salt-flats, palm groves and icebergs, plus the world's mightiest waterfalls, are just some of the sights that will catch you unawares if you were expecting Argentina to be one big cattle ranch. Dozens of these biosystems are protected by a network of national and provincial **parks and reserves**.

As for **getting around** and seeing these wonders, you can generally rely on a well-developed infrastructure inherited from decades of domestic tourism. Thanks in part to an increasing number of boutique hotels, the range and quality of **accommodation** have improved noticeably in recent years. A special treat are the beautiful ranches, known as **estancias** – or *fincas* in the north – that have been converted into luxury resorts. In most places, you'll be able to rely on the services of top-notch tour operators, who will not only show you the sights but also fix you up with all kinds of **outdoor adventures**: horse-riding, trekking, white-water rafting, kayaking, skiing, hang-gliding, along with

Pre-Columbian Argentina

Of all South American countries, superficially, at least, Argentina has the least marked pre-colonial culture. During the nineteenth century in particular, whole indigenous peoples were wiped out by various waves of newcomers, their superior weapons and their deadly diseases. Yet drinking *mate* – now a quintessentially Argentine custom – was learned from the native peoples, while a good many traditional festivals and prevailing superstitious beliefs were inherited from those who lived on Argentine soil long before the Europeans arrived. Though no Machu Picchu, the pre-Columbian – and mostly pre-Inca – ruins at Quilmes, Tilcara and Shinkal are nevertheless marvellous archeological sites, while fine rock drawings can be admired at accessible locations across the country.

▼ Ruins at Quilmes

more relaxing pursuits such as wine-tasting, bird-watching or photography safaris. Argentina is so huge and varied it's hard to take in all in one go – don't be surprised if you find yourself longing to return to explore the areas you didn't get to see the first time around.

▼ Parque Nacional Los Glaciares

Where to go

Argentina has many attractions that could claim the title of natural wonders of the world: the majestic waterfalls of **Iguazú**; the spectacular **Glaciar Perito Moreno**; fascinating whale colonies off **Península Valdés**; or the mountains around the holiday resort of **Bariloche** – indeed, **Patagonia** in general. Yet many of the country's most noteworthy sights are also its least known, such as the **Esteros del Iberá**, a huge reserve of floating islands offering close-up encounters with all sorts of birds and mammals; or **Antofagasta de la Sierra**, a remote village set amid frozen lagoons mottled pink with flamingoes; or **Laguna Diamante**, a high-altitude lake reflecting a wondrous volcano. In any case, weather conditions and the sheer size of the country will rule out any attempt to see every corner; it's more sensible and rewarding to concentrate on a particular section of the country.

Other than if you're visiting Argentina as part of a South American tour, **Buenos Aires** is likely to be your point of entry, as it has the country's only *bona fide* international airport, Ezeiza. Only inveterate city-haters will be able to resist the capital's charms. Buenos Aires is one of the world's greatest urban experiences, with an intriguing blend of architecture and a vernacular flair that includes houses painted in the colours of a legendary football team. The city's museums are eclectic enough to suit all interests – Latin American art, colonial silverware, dinosaurs and ethnography are just four subjects on offer – and you can round off a day's sightseeing with a tango show, a bar tour or a meal at one of the hundreds of fabulous restaurants.

Due north stretches the **Litoral**, an expanse of subtropical watery landscapes that shares borders with Uruguay, Brazil and Paraguay. Here are the photogenic **Iguazú waterfalls** and Jesuit missions whose once-noble ruins are crumbling into the jungle – with the exception of well-preserved **San Ignacio Miní**. Immediately west of the Litoral stretches the **Chaco**, one of Argentina's most infrequently visited regions, a place for those with an ardent interest in **wildlife**. Be prepared for fierce heat and a poor tourism infrastructure here. Up in the country's landlocked **Northwest** is the **Quebrada de Humahuaca**, a fabulous gorge lined with rainbow-hued rocks; it winds up to the oxygen-starved altiplano, where llamas and their wild relatives graze. In the **Valles Calchaquíes**, a series of stunningly scenic valleys, high-altitude vineyards produce the delightfully flowery torrontés wine along with some subtle reds.

Stretching across Argentina's broad midriff to the west and immediately south of Buenos Aires are **the Pampas**, arguably the country's most archetypal landscape. Formed by horizon-to-horizon plains interspersed with low sierras, this subtly beautiful scenery is punctuated by small towns, the odd ranch and countless clumps of pampas grass (*cortaderas*). Part arid, part wetland, the Pampas are grazed by millions of cattle and planted with soya and wheat fields the size of whole European countries. The Pampas are also where you'll glimpse signs of traditional **gaucho culture**, most famously in the charming town of **San Antonio de Areco**. Here, too, are some of the classiest estancias, offering a combination of luxury and horseback

Tango

Tango is not only a dance, or even an art form, but it is also a powerful symbol, perhaps what people associate with Argentina more than anything else. Essentially and intrinsically linked to Buenos Aires and its history, it nonetheless has fans all around the country. Rosario and to a lesser extent, Córdoba, the country's two biggest cities after the capital, have a strong tango culture, complete with *milongas* (dance halls) and shops to buy the right footwear. And don't be surprised to find humble folk in some remote village, hundreds of miles from Buenos Aires, listening to a scratchy recording of Carlos Gardel – still the leading figure of tango as song. Perhaps it is because tango depicts the Argentine psyche so well: a unique blend of nostalgia, resignation and passion.

adventures. On the Atlantic Coast are a string of fun beach resorts, including longstanding favourite **Mar del Plata**.

The further west you go, the larger the Central Sierras loom: the mild climate and bucolic woodlands of these ancient mountains have attracted Argentine tourists since the late nineteenth century, and within reach of **Córdoba**, the country's vibrant second city, are some of the oldest resorts on the continent. In the **Cuyo**, further west still, with the highest Andean peaks as a backdrop, you can discover one of Argentina's most enjoyable cities, the regional capital of **Mendoza**, also the country's **wine capital**. From here, the scenic **Alta Montaña** route climbs steeply to the Chilean border, passing **Cerro Aconcagua**, now well established as a fantasy challenge for mountaineers. Just south, **Las Leñas** is a winter resort where skiers sometimes end up on the pages of the continent's glamour magazines, while the nearby black-and-red lava wastes of **La Payunia**, one of the country's hidden jewels, are all but overlooked. Likewise, **San Juan** and **La**

Península Valdés

The Patagonian headland, Península Valdés, offers unrivalled opportunities for seeing the world's most endangered large cetacean, the southern right whale. Every year as many as a thousand of these gigantic mammals come to breed and give birth in the sheltered waters nearby. Nineteenth-century whalers named them "right whales" because their curious nature meant they swam close to passing ships, making them the right whales – in other words, the easiest – to harpoon. That same curiosity leads them to approach whale-watching boats – sometimes so close you can smell their breath. You don't even need to go out in a boat: take an evening stroll along the beaches of Golfo San José or Golfo Nuevo and you'll often see and hear the creatures.

▲ Lago Belgrano, Parque Nacional Perito Moreno

Rioja provinces are relatively uncharted territories, but their marvellous mountain and valley landscapes reward exploration, along with their under-rated wineries. Their star attractions are a brace of parks: **Parque Nacional Talampaya**, with its giant red cliffs, and the nearby **Parque Provincial Ischigualasto**, usually known as the **Valle de la Luna** on account of its intriguing moonscapes.

Argentina has the lion's share of the wild, sparsely populated expanses of **Patagonia** and boasts by far the more interesting half of the remote archipelago of **Tierra del Fuego**. These are lands of seemingly endless arid steppe hemmed in for the most part by the southern leg of the Andes, a series of volcanoes, craggy peaks and deep glacial lakes. An almost unbroken chain of national parks along these Patagonian and Fuegian cordilleras makes for some of the best trekking anywhere on the planet. Certainly include the savage granite peaks of the Fitz Roy massif in **Parque Nacional Los Glaciares** in your itinerary, but also the less frequently visited araucaria, or monkey puzzle, forests of **Parque Nacional Lanín** or the trail network of **Parque Nacional Nahuel Huapi**. For wildlife enthusiasts, **Peninsula Valdés** is a must-see (see box opposite). If you have a historical bent, you may like to trace the region's associations with Fitzroy and Darwin in the beautiful **Beagle Channel** off Ushuaia, or track down the legacy of Butch Cassidy, who lived near Cholila, or of the Welsh settlers whose influence can still be felt in communities like **Gaiman** and **Trevelin**.

When to go

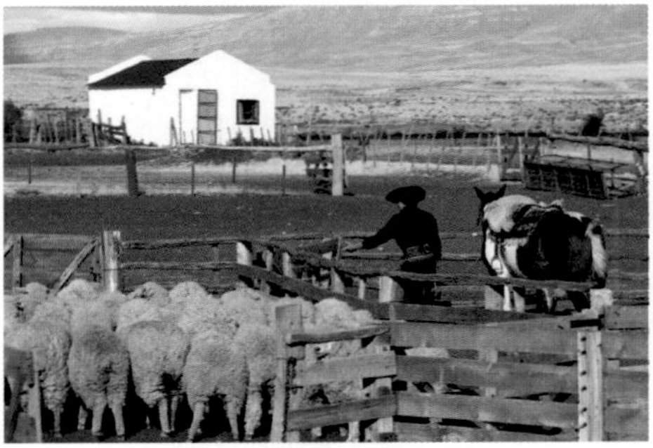

▲ Gaucho on an estancia, Patagonia

Given the size of Argentina, you're unlikely to flit from region to region, and, if you can, you should try and visit each area at the optimal time of year. Roughly falling from September to November, the Argentine spring is perfect just about everywhere, although in the far south icy gales may blow. Avoid the southern half of the country in the coldest months (May–Oct), when deep snow can cut off towns and villages; likewise with the Chaco and most other lowland parts of the North in the height of summer (Dec–Feb), as temperatures can be scorching. Midsummer's the only time, however, to climb the highest Andean peaks (Aconcagua is accessible from Dec to Feb), and it is also the most reliable time of year to head for Tierra del Fuego, though it has been known to snow there in December. Buenos Aires can get very hot and sticky in December and January but it can also come across as somewhat bleak in midwinter (July and Aug). The winter months of June, July and August, on the other hand, are obviously the time to head for the ski resorts. Autumn (late March and April) is a great time to visit Mendoza and San Juan provinces for the wine harvests, and Patagonia and Tierra del Fuego to enjoy the eye-catching red and orange hues of the beeches. A final point to bear in mind: the national holiday seasons are roughly January, Easter and July, when transport and accommodation can get booked up and rates are hiked, sometimes as much as seventy percent.

Average temperatures and rainfall

	Jan	Mar	May	July	Sept	Nov
Bahía Blanca						
Av High (°C)	30	25	16	12	17	24
Av Low (°C)	17	13	6	2	6	11
Av High (°F)	86	77	61	54	63	75
Av Low (°F)	63	55	43	36	43	52
Rainfall (mm)	50	76	34	28	42	54
Rainfall (in)	1.9	3	1.3	1.1	1.7	2.1
Bariloche						
Av High (°C)	21	18	9	5	10	16
Av Low (°C)	8	5	1	1	1	5
Av High (°F)	70	64	48	41	50	61
Av Low (°F)	46	41	34	34	34	41
Rainfall (mm)	26	41	149	144	63	29
Rainfall (in)	1.0	1.6	5.9	5.7	2.5	1.1
Buenos Aires						
Av High (°C)	29	26	18	14	18	24
Av Low (°C)	17	15	8	5	7	12
Av High (°F)	84	79	64	57	64	75
Av Low (°F)	93	117	77	59	78	89
Rainfall (mm)	2.2	1.4	2.2	2.3	2.2	2.0
Rainfall (in)	3.7	4.6	3.0	2.3	3.1	3.5
Jujuy						
Av High (°C)	29	26	21	18	24	28
Av Low (°C)	16	14	8	4	10	13
Av High (°F)	84	79	70	64	75	83
Av Low (°F)	61	57	46	39	50	55
Rainfall (mm)	200	145	14	6	11	76
Rainfall (in)	7.9	5.7	0.6	0.2	0.4	3.0
Mendoza						
Av High (°C)	31	26	18	14	20	27
Av Low (°C)	18	16	6	2	7	15
Av High (°F)	88	79	64	57	68	81
Av Low (°F)	64	61	43	36	45	59
Rainfall (mm)	30	27	10	7	13	18
Rainfall (in)	1.2	1.1	0.4	0.3	0.5	0.7
Posadas						
Av High (°C)	32	30	23	21	24	29
Av Low (°C)	22	20	14	12	13	18
Av High (°F)	90	86	74	70	75	84
Av Low (°F)	72	68	57	54	55	64
Rainfall (mm)	137	138	147	100	134	135
Rainfall (in)	5.4	5.5	5.8	3.9	5.3	5.3
Ushuaia						
Av High (°C)	13	12	6	3	7	12
Av Low (°C)	5	3	-1	-3	0	2
Av High (°F)	55	54	43	37	45	54
Av Low (°F)	41	37	30	27	32	36
Rainfall (mm)	52	54	50	42	39	42
Rainfall (in)	2.0	2.1	1.9	1.7	1.5	1.7

29

things not to miss

It's not possible to see everything Argentina has to offer in one trip – and we don't suggest you try. What follows, in no particular order, is a selective taste of the country's highlights: vibrant cities, dramatic landscapes, spectacular wildlife and more. They're arranged in five colour-coded categories to help you find the very best things to do and experience. All highlights have a page reference to take you straight into the guide, where you can find out more.

01 **Ruta de los Siete Lagos** Page **616** • Seven Patagonian lakes – their sparkling waters emerald, ultramarine, cobalt, turquoise, cerulean, sapphire and indigo – linked by a rugged mountain road: a magical route best explored in a 4WD.

02 Bookstores in Buenos Aires Page **177** • As befits one of the world's most literate cities, Buenos Aires is a bookworm's paradise – outlets range from palatial megastores selling glossy coffee-table publications to dusty basements stacked with well-leafed secondhand tomes.

03 Carnival in the Litoral Page **322** • Like their neighbours across the river in Uruguay and Brazil, the people of the Northeast do know how to party, not least in Gualeguaychú in the lead-up to Lent.

04 Winter sports Pages **541**, **631** & **755** • Las Leñas for the jet-set après-ski, Cerro Catedral for traditional pistes and Tierra del Fuego for the world's most southerly resorts – winter sports in Argentina combine great snow with a lot of showing off.

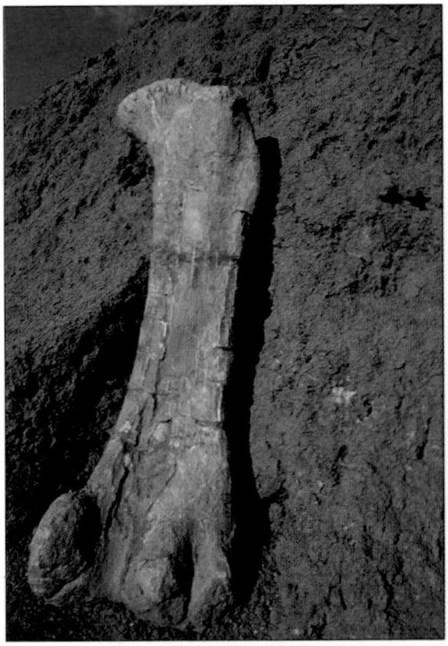

05 Dinosaur fossils in Neuquén Page **588** • The world's biggest dinosaurs once roamed Neuquén Province – nothing will convey their immensity more than standing underneath their skeletons or seeing their giant footprints in the rock.

06 Andean camelids Page **818** • Shaggy llamas and silky-fleeced alpacas, imposing guanacos and delicate vicuñas – all four of these distant relatives of the camel can be spotted the whole length of Argentina's cordillera.

07 Ushuaia Page **750** • Once Argentina's most feared penal colony, now vaunted as the world's southernmost city, Ushuaia sits proudly on the Beagle Channel, backed by serrated peaks and a bijou glacier.

08 Asados Page **43** • The local answer to the barbecue, and inseparable from Argentinidad (the national identity), these meat-roasting rituals are prepared with the utmost pride and devoured in a carnivorous bliss.

09 La Recoleta Page **135** • The prestigious resting-place of Argentina's great and good – even Evita sneaked in – this cemetery is one of the world's most exclusive patches of real estate.

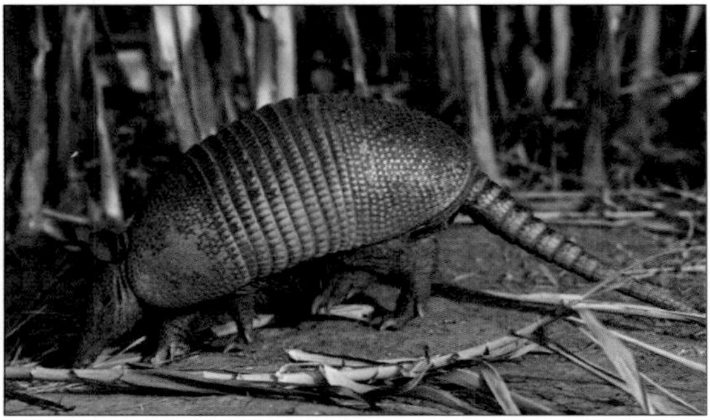

10 Chaqueño flora and fauna Page **401** • Brave the scorching heat, hammam-like humidity and persistent mosquitoes of the Gran Chaco in the hope of spotting jaguars, armadillos and monkeys – or, an easier bet, a giant waterlily.

11 **The Pampas** Page **234** • Rugged gauchos, nodding pampas grass and herds of contented cattle are the famous inhabitants of Argentina's most archetypal landscape – fertile plains stretching for as far as the eye can see.

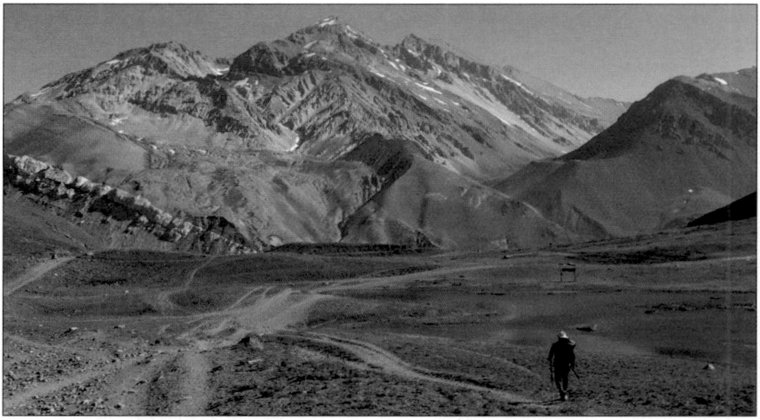

12 **Climbing Aconcagua** Page **532** • Despite frigid temperatures and extreme altitude – 6959m – the highest peak outside the Himalayas can be climbed with the right preparation and a knowledgeable guide, making for a world-class mountaineering experience.

13 **Evita** Page **150** • Perón's "rags to riches" First Lady, loved and loathed, but never forgotten – monuments and museums, musicals and Madonna have preserved her memory.

14 Colonia del Sacramento, Uruguay Page **190** • Treated by Porteños as the quietest barrio of Buenos Aires, this immaculate colonial gem across the Río de la Plata is a haven of peace; it also competes with Havana for exhibiting the best-preserved vintage automobiles.

15 Wines of Mendoza Pages **510** & **524** • What better to accompany a juicy grilled *bife de chorizo* than one of the province's award-winning malbecs or syrahs?

16 The ombú Page **209** • "If Buenos Aires owes its beauty to the great Pampa, then the Pampa owes its to the ombú" – Luis Domínguez (1948), about the beautiful tree.

17 Estancias Pages **294**, **346**, **395**, **438** & **689** • Try your hand at cattle-herding or sheep-shearing at a working estancia – one of the great Argentine institutions – and get an authentic taste of the gaucho way of life.

18 Cueva de las Manos Pintadas Page **694** • A prehistoric mural, an early finger-printing exercise or ancient graffiti? Whatever it is, this delicate tableau of many hands is one of the continent's most enchanting archeological sites.

19 Tigre and the Paraná Delta Page **183** • Take a boat or paddle a kayak around the swampy islets and muddy creeks of Tigre – a subtropical Venice right on the capital's doorstep.

20 Iguazú Falls Page **355** • Known simply as the Cataratas, the world's biggest, most awe-inspiring set of waterfalls is set among dense jungle, home to brightly coloured birds and butterflies.

21 San Telmo, Buenos Aires Page **119** • Take a stroll down the cobbled streets of this bohemian neighbourhood full of tango bars and antique shops, talented street performers and decaying grandeur.

22 Sierras de Córdoba Page **296** • The cool, clean air of these ancient highlands lie within easy reach of Córdoba, Argentina's second city; even Che Guevara came here to cure his asthma.

23 Glaciar Perito Moreno Page **723** • Standing before, or even trekking on, one of the world's last advancing glaciers is a treat for the eyes, and for the ears; compare impossible shades of blue as you listen to a chorus of cracks, thuds and whines.

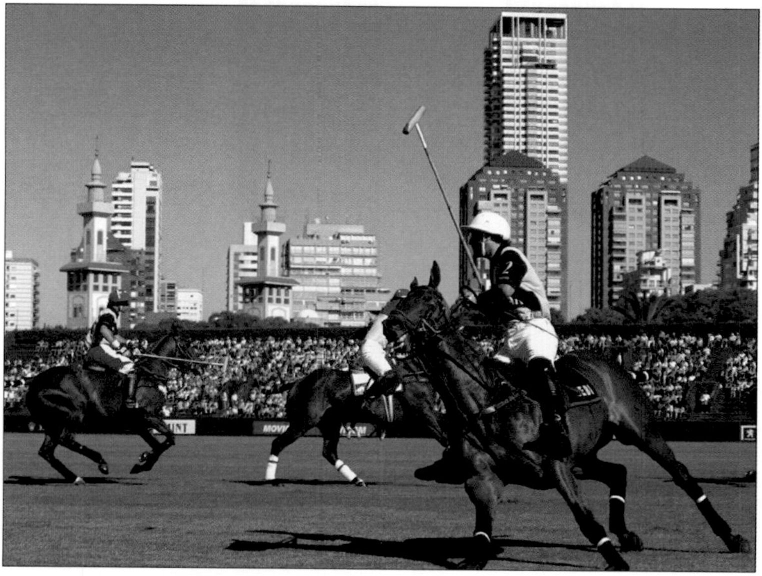

24 Polo Page **51** • One of the country's most idiosyncratic sports is also one of its most thrilling to watch, as galloping hooves tear across a manicured lawn.

25 Teatro Colón, Buenos Aires Page **112** • Versailles and La Scala rolled into one, the Colón is one of the world's truly great historic opera houses – Caruso and Callas once thrilled its audiences.

26 Birdlife at the Esteros del Iberá Page **340** • Hundreds of varieties to excite ornithologists, delight photographers and entertain every visitor – the shimmering lagoons of these vital wetlands mirror myriad birds, from tiny hummingbirds to majestic herons.

27 Traditional handicrafts Page **491** • Argentina's looms, kilns and workshops produce some of the finest ponchos, pots and silverware you could wish for, as well as world-class leatherware, jewellery and, great for souvenirs, *mate* paraphernalia.

28 Football Page **50** • It wouldn't be a stretch to say that nothing else quite holds a grip on Argentine society like football – for some no trip to the country is complete without attending a match.

29 Quebrada de Humahuaca Page **455** • Polychrome mountains and whiter-than-white salt-flats, bottle-green valleys and spiky cactus forests, expanses of windswept steppe and deep gorges – some of the planet's most incredible scenery.

Basics

Basics

Getting there

Though some visitors reach Argentina overland from a neighbouring country and a handful arrive by ship, the overwhelming majority of travellers first set foot on Argentine soil at Buenos Aires' international airport, Ezeiza.

In general, airfares to Argentina tend to be quite high, but they do vary widely depending on the routing and the **season**. The highest fares are charged between December and February, around Easter and in July and August. You'll get the best prices during the low season, March to June and September. Note also that flying on weekends often hikes return fares; price ranges quoted in this section assume midweek travel. You can often reduce costs by going through a **discount flight agent** (see p.30). Also, many airlines and travel websites offer you the opportunity to book your ticket online, cutting out the costs of agents and middlemen entirely.

The cheapest deals around are generally the **APEX** (Advanced Purchase Excursion) fares offered by airlines. They're not particularly flexible, though, and come with several restrictions: you need to book and pay for your ticket at least 21 days before departure, your trip needs to be a minimum of seven days and a maximum of three months and you are likely to be penalized heavily if you change your schedule at all.

It's worth remembering that most cheap return fares offer no refunds or only a very small percentag'e refund if you need to cancel your journey, so make sure you have travel insurance (see p.67) before you pay for your ticket.

From the US and Canada

Several airlines, including American Airlines, United and Aerolíneas Argentinas, offer daily nonstop **flights from the US** to Buenos Aires. Typical **fares** start at US$900 from New York in low season, US$1000 from Chicago or Washington, and rise by US$400 or so from November to January. Flying **times** to Buenos Aires are around eleven hours from New York and Chicago, and nine from Miami.

There's less choice if you're flying **from Canada**, with Air Canada offering the only direct flight into the country – from Toronto via São Paulo (with connections from other major Canadian cities). You'll be able to put together a considerably more flexible itinerary if you look for connecting flights with a US carrier. Direct flights from Toronto take around thirteen hours and **prices** start at CAN$1625 in low season; via Vancouver the journey time is around eighteen hours, and fares start from around CAN$1865.

From the UK and Ireland

Most visitors travelling from the UK or Ireland choose to come **by plane**, though anyone with loads of time and good sea legs might like to arrive the old-fashioned way, **by ship**. However, this is usually very expensive and much less glamorous than it sounds.

By air

About a dozen airlines offer regular scheduled flights **from the UK** to Buenos Aires. As a rule, you'll have to choose between flying **via another European city** or **via the US** (the latter trips can be marginally less expensive, but are usually longer). It's nearly always cheaper to book your flight through a specialized or discount flight agent. We've listed several on p.30, but it's also worth checking the travel sections of London's *Time Out* and the national Sunday newspapers, or phoning the Air Travel Advisory Bureau (☎020/7636 5000) for a list. Non-student adult **fares** from London to Buenos Aires usually start at around £650 in the low season, rising to over £900 in the high season.

There are no direct flights **from Ireland** to Argentina. If you're trying to keep costs down, consider flying to London with an

Fly less – stay longer! Travel and climate change

Climate change is the single biggest issue facing our planet. It is caused by a build-up in the atmosphere of carbon dioxide and other greenhouse gases, which are emitted by many sources – including planes. Already, flights account for around three to four percent of human-induced global warming: that figure may sound small, but it is rising year on year and threatens to counteract the progress made by reducing greenhouse emissions in other areas.

Rough Guides regard travel, overall, as a global benefit, and feel strongly that the advantages to developing economies are important, as are the opportunities for greater contact and awareness among peoples. But we all have a responsibility to limit our personal "carbon footprint". That means giving thought to how often we fly and what we can do to redress the harm that our trips create.

Flying and climate change

Pretty much every form of motorized travel generates CO_2, but planes are particularly bad offenders, releasing large volumes of greenhouse gases at altitudes where their impact is far more harmful. Flying also allows us to travel much further than we would contemplate doing by road or rail, so the emissions attributable to each passenger become truly shocking. For example, one person taking a return flight between Europe and California produces the equivalent impact of 2.5 tonnes of CO_2 – similar to the yearly output of the average UK car.

Less harmful planes may evolve but it will be decades before they replace the current fleet – which could be too late for avoiding climate chaos. In the meantime, there are limited options for concerned travellers: to reduce the amount we travel by air (take fewer trips, stay longer!), to avoid night flights (when plane contrails trap heat from Earth but can't reflect sunlight back to space) and to make the trips we do take "climate neutral" via a carbon offset scheme.

Carbon offset schemes

Offset schemes run by Ⓦwww.climatecare.org, Ⓦwww.carbonneutral.com and others allow you to "neutralize" the greenhouse gases that you are responsible for releasing. Their websites have simple calculators that let you work out the impact of any flight. Once that's done, you can pay to fund projects that will reduce future carbon emissions by an equivalent amount (such the distribution of low-energy light bulbs and cooking stoves in developing countries). Please take the time to visit our website and make your trip climate neutral.

Ⓦwww.roughguides.com/climatechange

economy airline such as Ryanair (Ⓦwww.ryanair.com) and making a connection there. For less hassle, though, and only a fraction more money, you're better off flying direct to New York or Miami and catching an onward flight from there.

In addition to fares, it's worth paying attention to the **routings** used by different airlines — in particular, check how many stops are involved, and how long you'll have to spend in transit. The shortest and most convenient routings from London, often via São Paulo or Madrid, entail a total travelling time of around sixteen hours. Apart from trying to minimize the length of the flight, another reason to scrutinize the routings is that many airlines allow you to break your journey and take stopovers on the way — sometimes for free, sometimes for a surcharge of around ten percent. Potential stopovers include Bogotá, Rio and São Paulo in South America; Newark, Boston, Chicago, Dallas, Houston, Miami and Washington DC in the US; and Frankfurt, Madrid, Milan, Rome and Paris in Europe.

By sea

You can still reach Buenos Aires from Europe **by sea**, though it's not as alluring a trip as it once was and the possibilities are extremely limited. Passenger-carrying cargo vessels of the Grimaldi Line (Ⓣ020/7839 1961, Ⓦwww.grimaldi.co.uk) sail about every eleven days from Tilbury to Brazil via Hamburg, Antwerp, Le Havre and Bilbao, then on to Buenos Aires for £1000 or more (outbound only). German shipping lines – often container ships with room for passengers – also sail to various South American ports, including Buenos Aires, from Felixstowe, Hamburg, Antwerp, Le Havre and Bilbao, and cost around £1700 one way. Another route sails from Southampton to Buenos Aires (£2000). For information call Strand Voyages, Charing Cross Shopping Concourse, Strand, London WC2N 4HZ (Ⓣ020/7836 6363, Ⓦwww.strandtravel.co.uk).

From Australia, New Zealand and South Africa

The best flight deals to Argentina from Australia and New Zealand are offered by Aerolíneas Argentinas and LAN in conjunction with Qantas and Air New Zealand, either direct to Buenos Aires or via a stopover in Santiago. **In Australia**, flights to Argentina leave from Sydney, plus a couple a week that depart from Brisbane and Melbourne. The most direct route to Buenos Aires **from New Zealand** is via Auckland and takes about seventeen hours. Flights **from South Africa** to Argentina leave from Cape Town and Johannesburg and go via São Paulo, taking sixteen or seventeen hours. Malaysia Airlines flights between Kuala Lumpur and Buenos Aires stop over in Cape Town, from where the last leg takes around ten hours direct.

Airfares depend on both the season and duration of stay. Seat availability on most international flights out of Australia, New Zealand and South Africa is increasingly limited, so book several weeks ahead. **Fares** from Australia start normally start around A$2000 in low season, with flights from New Zealand costing around NZ$2100. The lowest return fares from Cape Town cost around ZAR8000.

Round-the-world flights

If Argentina is only one stop on a longer journey, you might want to consider buying a **round-the-world (RTW)** ticket. Some travel agents can sell you an "off-the-shelf" RTW ticket that will have you touching down in about half a dozen cities (Buenos Aires is on many itineraries). Alternatively, you can have a travel agent assemble a RTW ticket for you; in this case the ticket can be tailored to your needs but is apt to be more expensive.

Airlines, agents and operators

Online booking

Ⓦ**www.expedia.co.uk** (in UK)
Ⓦ**www.expedia.com** (in US)
Ⓦ**www.expedia.ca** (in Canada)
Ⓦ**www.lastminute.com** (in UK)
Ⓦ**www.opodo.co.uk** (in UK)
Ⓦ**www.orbitz.com** (in US)
Ⓦ**www.travelocity.co.uk** (in UK)
Ⓦ**www.travelocity.com** (in US)
Ⓦ**www.travelocity.ca** (in Canada)
Ⓦ**www.zuji.com.au** (in Australia)
Ⓦ**www.zuji.co.nz** (in New Zealand)

Airlines

Aerolíneas Argentinas US Ⓣ1-800/333-0276, Canada Ⓣ1-800/688-0008, UK Ⓣ0800/096 9747, Australia Ⓣ02/9234-9000, New Zealand Ⓣ09/379 3675, Ⓦwww.aerolineas.com.ar.
Air Canada US & Canada Ⓣ1-888/247-2262, UK Ⓣ0871/220 1111, Republic of Ireland Ⓣ01/679 3958, Australia Ⓣ1300/655 767, New Zealand Ⓣ0508/747 767, Ⓦwww.aircanada.ca.
Air France US Ⓣ1-800/237-2747, Canada Ⓣ1-800/667-2747, UK Ⓣ0870/142 4343, Australia Ⓣ1300/390 190, South Africa Ⓣ0861/340 340, Ⓦwww.airfrance.com.
Air New Zealand Australia Ⓣ13 24 76, New Zealand Ⓣ0800/737 000, Ⓦwww.airnz.com.au or Ⓦwww.airnz.co.nz.
Alitalia US Ⓣ1-800/223-5730, Canada Ⓣ1-800/361-8336, UK Ⓣ0870/544 8259, Republic of Ireland Ⓣ01/677 5171, New Zealand Ⓣ09/308 3357, South Africa Ⓣ11/721 4500, Ⓦwww.alitalia.com.
American Airlines US & Canada Ⓣ1-800/433-7300, UK Ⓣ0845/7789 789 Republic of Ireland Ⓣ01/602 0550, Australia Ⓣ1800/673 486, New Zealand Ⓣ0800/445 442, Ⓦwww.aa.com.
Avianca US Ⓣ1-800/284-2622, UK Ⓣ0870/576 7747, Republic of Ireland Ⓣ01/280 2641, Ⓦwww.avianca.com.

British Airways US & Canada ⓣ1-800/AIRWAYS, UK ⓣ0870/850 9850, Republic of Ireland ⓣ1890/626 747, Australia ⓣ1300/767 177, New Zealand ⓣ09/966 9777, South Africa ⓣ114/418 600, ⓦwww.ba.com.
Continental Airlines US & Canada ⓣ1-800/523-3273, UK ⓣ0845/607 6760, Republic of Ireland ⓣ1890/925 252, Australia ⓣ02/9244 2242, New Zealand ⓣ09/308 3350, International ⓣ1800/231 0856, ⓦwww.continental.com.
Delta US & Canada ⓣ1-800/221-1212, UK ⓣ0845/600 0950, Republic of Ireland ⓣ1850/882 031 or 01/407 3165, Australia ⓣ1300/302 849, New Zealand ⓣ09/9772232, ⓦwww.delta.com.
Iberia US ⓣ1-800/772-4642, UK ⓣ0870/609 0500, Republic of Ireland ⓣ0818/462 000, South Africa ⓣ011/884 5909, ⓦwww.iberia.com.
LAN US & Canada ⓣ1-866/435-9526, UK ⓣ0800/977 6100, Australia ⓣ1300/361 400 or 02/9244 2333, New Zealand ⓣ09/977 2233, South Africa ⓣ11/781 2111, ⓦwww.lan.com.
Lufthansa US ⓣ1-800/3995-838, Canada ⓣ1-800/563-5954, UK ⓣ0870/837 7747, Republic of Ireland ⓣ01/844 5544, Australia ⓣ1300/655 727, New Zealand ⓣ0800-945 220, South Africa ⓣ0861/842 538, ⓦwww.lufthansa.com.
Malaysia Airlines South Africa ⓣ11/880 9614 or 11/19 7607, ⓦwww.malaysiaairlines.com.
Qantas US & Canada ⓣ1-800/227-4500, UK ⓣ0845/774 7767, Republic of Ireland ⓣ01/407 3278, Australia ⓣ13 13 13, New Zealand ⓣ0800/808 767 or 09/357 8900, South Africa ⓣ11/441 8550, ⓦwww.qantas.com.
United Airlines US ⓣ1-800/UNITED-1, UK ⓣ0845/844 4777, Australia ⓣ13 17 77, ⓦwww.united.com.

Discount agents

Adventure World Australia ⓣ02/8913 0755, ⓦwww.adventureworld.com.au; New Zealand ⓣ09/524 5118, ⓦwww.adventureworld.co.nz. Agents for a vast array of international adventure travel companies that operate trips to South America.
Airtech US ⓣ212/219-7000, ⓦwww.airtech.com. Standby seat broker; also deals in consolidator fares and courier flights.
Airtreks US & Canada ⓣ1-877/247-8735 or international ⓣ415/977-7100, ⓦwww.airtreks.com. RTW and Circle Pacific tickets. The website features an interactive database that lets you build and price your own RTW itinerary.
Bridge the World UK ⓣ0870/443 2399, ⓦwww.bridgetheworld.com. Specializing in RTW tickets, with good deals aimed at backpackers.
Ebookers UK ⓣ0870/010 7000, ⓦwww.ebookers.com. Low fares on an extensive selection of scheduled flights.
Flight Centre UK ⓣ0870/499 0040, ⓦwww.flightcentre.co.uk; Australia ⓣ13 13 13, ⓦwww.flightcentre.com.au; New Zealand ⓣ0800/24 35 44, ⓦwww.flightcentre.co.nz. Specializes in discount international airfares and holiday packages.
Joe Walsh Tours Republic of Ireland ⓣ01/241 0800, ⓦwww.joewalshtours.com. General budget fares agent.
Major Travel UK ⓣ020/7393 1070, ⓦwww.majortravel.co.uk. Reliable discount agent.
North South Travel UK ⓣ&ⓕ01245/608 291, ⓦwww.northsouthtravel.co.uk. Recommended travel agency offering competitive discounted fares worldwide. All profits are used to support projects in the developing world, especially the promotion of sustainable tourism.
Premier Travel Northern Ireland ⓣ028/7126 3333, ⓦwww.premiertravel.uk.com. Discount flight specialists.
South America Travel Centre Australia ⓣ1800/655 051 or 03/9642 5353, ⓦwww.satc.com.au. Big selection of tours and city accommodation packages throughout the region.
South American Experience UK ⓣ020/7976 5511, ⓦwww.southamericanexperience.co.uk. Mainly a discount flight agent, but also offers a range of tours, plus a very popular "soft landing package", designed to make arrivals pain-free.

STA Travel US & Canada ⓣ1-800/781-4040, ⓦwww.sta-travel.com; UK ⓣ0870/160 0599, ⓦwww.statravel.co.uk; Australia ⓣ1300/733 035, ⓦwww.statravel.com.au; New Zealand ⓣ0508/782 872, ⓦwww.statravel.co.nz. Worldwide specialists in independent travel. Also provides student IDs, travel insurance, car rental, railpasses etc.

Top Deck UK ⓣ020/8879 6789, ⓦwww.topdecktravel.co.uk. Long-established agent dealing in discount flights.

Trailfinders UK ⓣ020/7938 3939, ⓦwww.trailfinders.com; Republic of Ireland ⓣ01/677 7888, ⓦwww.trailfinders.ie; Australia ⓣ1300/651900, ⓦwww.trailfinders.com.au. One of the best-informed and most efficient agents for independent travellers.

Travel Cuts US ⓣ1-800/592-CUTS, Canada ⓣ1-888/246-9762, ⓦwww.travelcuts.com. Popular, long-established student-travel organization, with worldwide offers.

Specialist tour operators

Abercrombie & Kent UK ⓣ0845/070 0614, ⓦwww.abercrombiekent.co.uk. Upmarket tours staying in the plushest hotels, such as the *Llao Llao* in Bariloche, as well as fifteen-day tours of the Lake District and Torres del Paine.

Adventure Center US ⓣ1-800/228-8747, ⓦwww.adventurecenter.com. Hiking and "soft adventure". Offers a few Argentina tours, including a 23-day "Patagonian Dreaming" Buenos Aires-to-Ushuaia trip.

The Adventure Travel Company New Zealand ⓣ09/379 9755, ⓦwww.adventuretravel.co.nz. NZ agent for Peregrine Adventures (see p.32).

Adventures Abroad US & Canada ⓣ1-800/665-3998, ⓦwww.adventures-abroad.com. Adventure specialists offering two-week tours to Patagonia.

Adventures on Skis US ⓣ1-800/628-9655 or 970/925-9500, ⓦwww.advonskis.com. Offers trips to Las Leñas and Cerro Catedral resorts.

Austral Tours UK ⓣ020/7233 5384, ⓦwww.latinamerica.co.uk. Especially good at organizing special-interest holidays based around wine, fishing, trekking or archeology. Six-day Puerto Varas-to-Bariloche trek.

Australian Andean Adventures Australia ⓣ02/9299 9973, ⓦwww.andeanadventures.com.au. Trekking specialist offering cross-country skiing and an explorers' trek in Patagonia.

British Airways Holidays UK ⓣ0870/243 4224, ⓦwww.baholidays.co.uk. Offers an exhaustive range of package and custom holidays, including a tour of Patagonia.

Contours Australia ⓣ1300/135 391, ⓦwww.contourstravel.com.au. Specialists in tailored city stopover packages and tours, including self-drive tours through the Lake District and a ten-day budget tour of Patagonia.

Dragoman UK ⓣ0870/499 4478, ⓦwww.dragoman.co.uk. Extended overland journeys; shorter camping and hotel-based safaris, too. Thirty-day mostly camping trip from Santiago to Rio de Janeiro via Bariloche, Buenos Aires.

Exodus UK ⓣ0870/240 5550, ⓦwww.exodus.co.uk. Adventure-tour operator taking small groups for specialist programmes, including walking, biking, overland, adventure and cultural trips. Among its tours is a three-week Fitz Roy and Torres del Paine trip.

Explore Worldwide UK ⓣ01252/760 000, ⓦwww.explore.co.uk. Small-group tours, treks, expeditions and safaris. Offers three-week tours of the fjords and Patagonia.

Holidaze Ski Tours US ⓣ1-800/526-2827, ⓦwww.holidaze.com. Skiing in South America during the northern summer.

Journeys International US ⓣ1-800/255-8735, ⓦwww.journeys-intl.com. Runs a fifteen-day "Pure Patagonia" tour for US$3600.

Journey Latin America UK ⓣ020/8747 3108, ⓦwww.journeylatinamerica.co.uk. Specialists in flights, packages and tailor-made trips to Latin America. Two-week Salta hiking and biking trip.

Mountain Travel-Sobek US ⓣ1-888/687-6235, ⓦwww.mtsobek.com. Seventeen-day "Patagonia Explorer" adventure package.

Nature Expeditions International ⓣ1-800/869-0639, ⓦwww.naturexp.com. The fifteen-day Argentina nature tour with lectures takes in the Atlantic coast and glaciers.

Peregrine Adventures Australia ⓣ03/9662 2700 or 02/9290 2770, ⓦwww.peregrine.net.au; New Zealand, see Adventure Travel Company (see p.31).

REI Adventures US ⓣ1-800/622-2236, ⓦwww.rei.com/travel. Fourteen-day hiking, biking and rafting trip in the northern Lake District.

South American Experience UK ⓣ020/7976 5511; ⓦwww.southamericanexperience.co.uk. Organizes flights, custom packages, local excursions (such as to tango shows) and estancia holidays.

Tailored Expeditions in Argentina ⓦwww.tailoredexpeditions.com. Organizes custom packages and local excursions with emphasis on the Northwest, cultural activities and luxury accommodation.

Tucan Travel UK ⓣ020/8896 1600, ⓦwww.tucantravel.com. Group holidays in Argentina, plus a range of overland expeditions in the rest of South America.

Wild Frontiers UK ⓣ020/7736 3968, ⓦwww.wildfrontiers.co.uk. Offers horse-riding trips in Patagonia.

Wilderness Travel US ⓣ1-800/368-2794, ⓦwww.wildernesstravel.com. Specialists in hiking, cultural and wildlife adventures. Offers an eleven-day tour in the Lake District.

Wildlife Worldwide UK ⓣ020/8667 9158, ⓦwww.wildlifeworldwide.com. Tailor-made trips for wildlife and wilderness enthusiasts. Seventeen-day southern Patagonia and Iguazú trip.

World Expeditions UK ⓣ020/8870 2600, ⓦwww.worldexpeditions.co.uk; Australia ⓣ1300/720 000, ⓦwww.worldexpeditions.com.au. Australian-owned adventure company offering a two-week Jesuit-route trip and fifteen days in Torres del Paine. Challenging trips, such as a three-week Aconcagua ascent, available for hardcore adventurers. Special offerings for over-50 travellers.

Getting around

Distances are immense in Argentina, and you are likely to spend a considerable portion of your budget on travel. Ground transport (mostly bus) is best for giving a true impression of the scale of the country and for appreciating the landscape. However, you may want to cover some big legs, particularly to and around Patagonia, in which case travelling by domestic flights can often save a day or more. Also, though the inter-city bus network is extensive, services in remote areas can be poor and infrequent; in these places, it is worth considering car rental. Finally, boat trips and ferry crossings are well worth working into your itinerary if possible.

By bus

By far the most common and straightforward method of transport in Argentina is the **bus** (*omnibus, bus* or *micro*). There are hundreds of private companies, most of which concentrate on one particular region, although a few, such as TAC and Cruz del Sur, run essentially nationwide.

Many buses are modern, plush Brazilian-built models designed for long-distance travel. Replacement of stock and maintenance suffered following the 2001 crisis, so breakdowns do happen, but in general your biggest worry will be what movie the driver has chosen to "entertain" you with (usually subtitled Hollywood action flicks of the Stallone/Seagal/Schwarzenegger type, played with the sound either turned off or at thunderous volume). On longer journeys, snacks, and even hot meals, are served (included in the ticket price), although these vary considerably in quality and tend towards sweet-toothed tastes. *Coche cama, ejecutivo* and *pullman* services are the luxury services, with wide, fully reclinable seats; *semi-cama* services are not far behind in terms of seat comfort. These services usually cost twenty to forty percent more than the *común* (regular) services, but are well worth the extra, particularly over long distances. On minor routes, you'll have less choice of buses, but most are decent with plenty of legroom. Many services turn the air-conditioning up beyond most people's levels of endurance; take a sweater onboard.

Buying tickets (*boletos*) is normally a simple on-the-spot matter, but you must plan in advance if travelling in the high season (mid-Dec to Feb), especially if you're taking a long-distance bus from Buenos Aires or any other major city to a particularly popular holiday destination. In these cases you should buy your ticket two to three days beforehand; note that prices rise during peak times. Note, too, that some destinations have both direct (*directo* or *rápido*) and slower services that stop at all intermediary points, and though virtually all services call into the bus terminal (*terminal de omnibus*), this is not always the case: some drop you on the road outside the centre. Similarly, when heading to Buenos Aires, check that the bus goes to **Retiro**, the central bus terminal (see p.93).

There's usually some kind of **left-luggage office** (*guardamaleta* or *guardaequipaje*) at terminals, or, if you have a few hours to kill between connections, the company with whom you have your onward ticket will usually store your pack free of charge, enabling you to look around town unencumbered.

By air

Argentina's most important domestic **airport** is Buenos Aires' Aeroparque Jorge Newbery, which has **flights** to all the country's provincial capitals and major tourist centres. People who want to get an overview of Argentina's tremendous variety in a limited time may rely heavily on domestic flights to

Special deals for domestic flights

Note that two of the companies offering domestic flights in Argentina, Aerolíneas Argentinas and LAN, offer special **discount fares** for flights within the country as long as you buy your international ticket with them. You can either book the domestic flights at the same time or show your international ticket when booking inside the country. More details are given on the airlines' websites, Ⓦwww.aerolineas.com.ar and Ⓦwww.lan.com.

combat the vast distances involved – what takes twenty or more hours by bus might take only one or two by plane. As a rule, you'll find **prices** are the same whether you buy your ticket direct from the airline office or from the plentiful travel agencies in most towns and cities. Airlines' websites normally have schedules and prices, often in English. Availability can be a problem on tourist routes such as those around Patagonia or at popular times (the summer), and if these feature in your itinerary you are advised to book as far in advance as possible. Some deals booked in advance are good value, although non-residents usually pay a considerably higher tariff than Argentine residents. Domestic **departure taxes** are usually only $20 or so, but check to see whether or not this has been included in the price before buying your ticket.

Aerolíneas Argentinas (Ⓣ0810/222-86527, Ⓦwww.aerolineas.com.ar) is the national flag carrier, with the biggest destination network and including flights operated nominally by Austral. It increasingly faces criticism for its poor in-flight service, long delays and unreliability, but in many places it may be your only option, especially since the majority of its rivals hung up their wings during the economic crisis. You should be able to get a discount on Aerolíneas's internal flights if you book them at the same time as you book your international flights, with a bigger discount if you use Aerolíneas for the international flight (see box above).

Chilean flag carrier **LAN** (Ⓣ0810-9999-526, Ⓦwww.lan.com) has an Argentine subsidiary (LAN Argentina) operating flights to the country's major tourist destinations. The airline is part of the oneworld alliance, but the best promotions within the country are open only to residents.

The military also provides civilian services – the Air Force's **LADE** (Ⓣ0810/810-5233, Ⓦwww.lade.com.ar) is one of the cheapest methods of travel in the country and flies to isolated, often unexpected places, including many destinations in Patagonia. However, routings can be convoluted, and you might find a flight stops four or five times between its original departure point and final destination. There are rarely flights anywhere more than a couple of times a week, timetables change frequently (up to once a month) and services can be cancelled at the last moment if the Air Force needs the plane. That said, it's worth asking at LADE offices as you travel round just in case they've something useful.

Other small airlines in operation include Salta-based Andes (Ⓣ0810-777-26337, Ⓦwww.andesonline.com), which connects the city with Buenos Aires and Puerto Madryn, and Sol (Ⓣ0810-444-765), a Rosario-based low-cost airline that serves destinations in the centre of the country such as Córdoba and Santa Fe as well as some coastal and Uruguayan destinations.

By car

You are unlikely to want or need a **car** for your whole stay in Argentina, but you'll find one pretty indispensable if you want to explore some of the more isolated areas of Patagonia, Tierra del Fuego, the Northwest, Mendoza or San Juan. If possible, it makes sense to get a group together, not just to keep costs down but also to share the driving, which can be arduous and potentially dangerous, especially on unsealed roads. Approximately thirty percent of roads are paved in Argentina, but some of the less important of these routes are littered with potholes. Unsealed roads can be extremely muddy after rain, and may be impassable, even to 4WDs, after prolonged wet spells. 4WD is not usually necessary, but can be useful on minor roads in mountainous areas, when you're likely to encounter snow, or on Ruta 40 in Patagonia. Outside major cities, most accidents (often the most serious ones) occur on unsurfaced gravel roads (*ripio*) – for information about safe driving on these, see *The legendary Ruta 40* colour section.

Altitude can also be a problem in the high Andes – you may need to adjust the fuel intake (see p.66) – while in rural areas it's common to see livestock in the road. One thing worth noting: flashing your lights when driving is a warning to other vehicles *not* to do something, as opposed to the British system, where it is used to signal concession of right of way. You can be fined for not wearing **seatbelts** (both in the front and back), although most Argentines display a cavalier disregard of this law.

To **rent a car**, you need to be over 21 (25 with some agencies) and hold a driver's licence – an international one is not usually necessary. Bring a credit card and your passport for the **deposit**. Before you drive off, check that you've been given insurance, tax and ownership papers, check carefully for dents and paintwork damage and get hold of a 24-hour emergency telephone number. Also, pay close attention to the small print, most notably what you're liable for in the event of an accident: the list of people with grievances after renting a car and spending considerably more than they intended is a long one. Your insurance will not normally cover you for flipping the car, or smashed windscreens or headlights – a particularly common occurrence if driving on unsurfaced roads. Another frequent type of damage is bent door hinges – be careful when opening doors that they're not wrenched off by high winds.

Car rental **costs** are relatively high in Argentina, though rates between different agencies can vary considerably. Small, local firms often give very good deals – up to half the price of the global rental names – and it doesn't necessarily hold that the local branch of an international agency will be up to the standards you expect. The main cities offer the most economical prices, while costs are highest in Patagonia; **unlimited mileage** deals are usually your best option, as per-kilometre charges can otherwise exceed your daily rental cost many times over. Unfortunately, there are relatively few places in Argentina where you can rent a vehicle and drop it in another specified town without being clobbered with a high relocation fee. Book as early as possible if you're travelling in high season to popular holiday destinations, as demand usually outstrips supply. It's fairly straightforward to take a vehicle into **Chile** but it is essential to have the correct paperwork from the rental firm. Many provide this free of charge, particularly those in towns near the border.

If you plan to do a lot of driving, consider a membership with the **Automóvil Club Argentino (ACA)**, which has a useful **emergency breakdown** towing and repair services and offers discounts at a series of lodges across the country (many of which are in need of an overhaul). You can join in Buenos Aires at Av del Libertador 1850 (Mon–Fri 10am–6pm; ⓣ011/4808-4000, ⓦwww.aca.org.ar), or at any of the ACA service stations.

Addresses

Addresses are nearly always written with the street name followed by the street number – thus, San Martín 2443; with avenues (*avenidas*), the abbreviation "**Av**" or "**Avda**" appears before the name – thus, Av San Martín 2443. The relatively rare abbreviation "**c/**" for *calle* (street) is used only to avoid confusion in a city that has streets named after other cities: thus c/Tucumán 564, Salta or c/Salta 1097, Tucumán. If the name is followed by "**s/n**" (*sin número*), it means the building is numberless, frequently the case in small villages and for larger buildings such as hotels or town halls. Sometimes streets whose names have been officially changed continue to be referred to by their former names, even in written addresses. In most cities, **blocks** (*cuadras*) go up in 100s, making it relatively easy to work out on a map where a hotel at no. 977 or a restaurant at no. 2233 is located.

For more on driving in Buenos Aires, see p.96.

Car rental agencies

Alamo US ⓣ1-800/462-5266, ⓦwww.alamo.com.
Apex New Zealand ⓣ3/379 2647, ⓦwww.apexrentals.co.nz.
Auto Europe US & Canada ⓣ1-888/223-5555, ⓦwww.autoeurope.com.
Avis US & Canada ⓣ1-800/331-1212, UK ⓣ0870/606 0100, Republic of Ireland ⓣ021/428 1111, Australia ⓣ13 63 33 or 02/9353 9000, New Zealand ⓣ09/526 2847 or 0800/655 111, ⓦwww.avis.com.
Budget US ⓣ1-800/527-0700, Canada ⓣ1-800/268-8900, UK ⓣ0870/156 5656, Australia ⓣ1300/362 848, New Zealand ⓣ0800/283 438, ⓦwww.budget.com.
Dollar US ⓣ1-800/800-3665, Canada ⓣ1-800/229 0984, UK ⓣ 0808/234 7524, Republic of Ireland ⓣ1800/575 800, ⓦwww.dollar.com.
Enterprise US ⓣ1-800/261-7331, ⓦwww.enterprise.com.
Europcar US & Canada ⓣ1-877/940 6900, UK ⓣ0870/607 5000, Republic of Ireland ⓣ01/614 2800, Australia ⓣ393/306 160, ⓦwww.europcar.com.
Europe by Car US ⓣ1-800/223-1516, ⓦwww.europebycar.com.
Hertz US & Canada ⓣ1-800/654-3131, UK ⓣ020/7026 0077, Republic of Ireland ⓣ01/870 5777, New Zealand ⓣ0800/654 321, ⓦwww.hertz.com.
Holiday Autos UK ⓣ0870/400 4461, Republic of Ireland ⓣ01/872 9366, Australia ⓣ299/394 433, US ⓣ866-392/9288, South Africa ⓣ11/2340 597, ⓦwww.holidayautos.co.uk.
National US ⓣ1-800/CAR-RENT, UK ⓣ0870/400 4581, Australia ⓣ0870/600 6666, New Zealand ⓣ03/366 5574, ⓦwww.nationalcar.com.
SIXT US ⓣ1-877/347-3227, UK ⓣ0800/4747 4227, Republic of Ireland ⓣ1850/206 088, ⓦwww.irishcarrentals.ie.
Suncars UK ⓣ0870/500 5566, Republic of Ireland ⓣ1850/201 416, ⓦwww.suncars.com.
Thrifty US & Canada ⓣ1-800/847-4389, UK ⓣ01494/751 500, Republic of Ireland ⓣ01/844 1950, Australia ⓣ1300/367 227, New Zealand ⓣ09/256 1405, ⓦwww.thrifty.com.

By boat

Boat services in Argentina fall into two broad categories: those that serve as a functional form of transport, and (with some overlap) those that you take to enjoy tourist sights. The two **ferry services** you are most likely to use are the comfortable ones from Buenos Aires to Colonia del Sacramento in Uruguay (also served by the speedier hydrofoil) and the much more spartan Chilean ones that transport foot passengers and vehicles across the Magellan Straits into Tierra del Fuego at Punta Delgada and Porvenir. There are also several practical river crossings throughout the Litoral region, connecting towns such as Concordia with Salto in Uruguay; Rosario with Victoria in Entre Ríos; Goya in Corrientes with Reconquista in Santa Fe; as well as numerous crossings from Misiones to neighbouring Paraguay and Brazil. Tigre, just northwest of the capital, tends towards the pleasure-trips end of the market, and offers boat trips around the Delta and to Isla Martín García.

In Patagonia, most **boat trips** are designed purely for their scenic value, including ones that give access to the polar scenery of the Parque Nacional Los Glaciares, trips on the lakes of Chilean Torres del Paine, and the Three Lakes Crossing from Bariloche to Chile, a trip that can be truncated so as to access the Pampa Linda area of Parque Nacional Nahuel Huapi.

By rail

Argentina's **train network**, developed through British investment in the late nineteenth century and nationalized by the Perón administration in 1948, collapsed in 1993 when government subsidies were withdrawn. The railways are now in a pitiful state, with very little in the way of long-distance services – just a handful in Buenos Aires Province (see p.129), which are cheaper than the bus but considerably less savoury. However, the government has announced a plethora of measures and licences intended to reinvigorate the system and introduce new, modern services, most notably a high-speed train connecting Buenos Aires, Rosario and Córdoba. This service, Latin America's first bullet train, is due to open in 2010.

You're far less likely to want to use Argentine trains as a method of getting from place to place, however, than you are to try one of the country's **tourist trains**, where the aim is simply to travel for the fun of it. There are two principal lines: *La Trochita* (see p.641), the Old Patagonian Express from Esquel; and the *Tren a las Nubes* (see p.440), one of the highest railways in the world, climbing through the mountains from Salta towards the Chilean border. At the time of writing the latter was out of action but due to be reactivated at any time.

Cycling

Most towns with a tourist infrastructure have at least one place that rents **bicycles** for half- or full-day visits to sights at very reasonable prices. These excursions can be great fun, but remember to bring spare inner tubes and a pump, especially if you're cycling off sealed roads, and check that the brakes and seat height are properly adjusted. There are almost no places that rent **motorbikes**.

Argentina is also a popular destination for more serious cyclists, and expeditions along routes such as the arduous, partly unsurfaced RN-40 attract mountain-biking devotees who often value physical endurance above the need to see sights (most points of interest off RN-40 lie a good way west along branch roads, which deters most people from visiting more than one or two). Expeditions such as these need to be planned thoroughly. You should buy an extremely robust mountain bike and the very best **equipment** you can afford. Bring plenty of high-quality spares with you, as they can be hard to come by out of the major centres; punctures and broken spokes are extremely common on unsealed roads. Be prepared to get extremely dusty, and pay particular attention to how much **water** you're going to need per stage. Wind is a big problem in places like Patagonia, and if you get the season wrong, your progress will be cut to a handful of kilometres a day. High altitude can have a similar effect. Keep yourself covered as best you can to protect from wind and sun (especially your face), and do not expect much consideration from other vehicles on the road.

For more **information**, see *Latin America by Bike: A Complete Touring Guide*, by Walter Sienko (Mountaineers Books, US; 1993).

Hitchhiking

Hitchhiking always involves an element of risk, but it can also be one of the most rewarding ways to travel, especially if you can speak at least elementary conversational Spanish. It is getting trickier to hitchhike in Argentina: some truck drivers are prohibited by company rules from picking you up, others are reluctant as it often invalidates car insurance or you become the liability of the driver. And in general, it is not advisable for women travelling on their own to hitchhike, or for anyone to head out of large urban areas by hitchhiking: you're far better off catching a local bus out to an outlying service station or road checkpoint and trying from there. In the south of the country, hitching is still generally very safe. In places such as Patagonia, where roads are few and traffic sparse, you'll often find yourself part of a queue, especially in summer. If you do try to hitchhike, always travel with sufficient reserves of water, food, clothes and shelter: you can get stranded for days in some of the more isolated spots.

Local transport

There are two main types of taxi in Argentina: regular **urban taxis** that you can flag down in the street; and **remises**, or minicab radio taxis, that you must book by phone or at their central booking booth. Urban taxis are fitted with meters – make sure they use them – and each municipality has its own rates. *Remises* operate with rates fixed according to the destination and are less expensive than taxis for out-of-town and long-distance trips. Often, it makes more sense to hire a *remise* for a day than to rent your own car: it can be more economical, you save yourself the hassle of driving and you'll normally get the sights pointed out for you along the way.

In some places, **shared taxis** (*taxis colectivos*) also run on fixed routes between towns: they wait at a given collection point, each passenger pays a set fee and the *colectivos* leave when full (some carry destination signs on their windscreen, others don't, so always ask around). They often drop you at a place of your choice at the other end. *Taxi colectivos* also drive up and down fixed routes within certain cities: flag one down and pay your share (usually posted on the windscreen).

Accommodation

Accommodation in Argentina runs the gamut from campsites and youth hostels to fabulously luxurious estancias (ranches) and opulent hotels offering every conceivable amenity. Between these two extremes you'll find a whole variety of establishments, including charming old colonial houses with balconies and dark and seedy hotels that lack so much as a window. Informal room rental is also common in towns with seasonal influxes of tourists but too few hotels to cope.

Prices vary considerably depending on where you are in the country. Areas receiving large numbers of foreign visitors, particularly Buenos Aires and Patagonia, have seen prices rise sharply in recent years; less-visited areas offer less variety but also much better bargains. Even in the capital, however, you can expect to pay rather less for comparable accommodation than you would in most European countries, Australasia or North America. Single travellers on a budget and seeking more privacy than is available at a youth hostel will find things harder, although the number of places offering per-person prices appears to be on the rise, especially at resorts and estancias where meals or activities are included. Discounts can sometimes be negotiated, particularly if you are staying for a longer period. Bear in mind the practice of dual pricing, and that taxes are often not included in quoted prices (see "Costs", p.59).

Hotels

Most towns in Argentina will have at least one **hotel**, though in many places these are unimaginative, rather drab places. If you are on a budget, and the option is available, you might do better to head for a hostel. Posadas and bed-and-breakfasts (B&Bs; see opposite) can be more attractive in the middle of the range, while small boutique or designer hotels – which have popped up in significant numbers in Argentina in the last few years – often have a lot more individuality than the standard plush but monotonous five-star places aimed at business travellers.

Few hotels in Argentina are downright dangerous, although as a general rule those around bus terminals can be somewhat sleazy; women travelling alone may feel uncomfortable at these places. Also, at the lower end of the market, particularly in larger towns, a handful of places calling themselves hotels are actually more accustomed to

Accommodation price codes

All the **accommodation** listed in this guide has been sorted according to the **price codes** below, which account for the cost of the **least expensive double or twin room in high season**, in Argentine pesos. Prices of beds in shared hostel dorms are specified in the text; they tend to cost about $15–30. As a general rule, categories ❶ and ❷ will be a budget hotel or private hostel rooms outside tourist areas; ❸ and ❹ the same in a tourist area; ❺ and ❻ more comfortable, mid-range hotels; ❼ and ❽ upmarket rooms with all modern conveniences and attractive decor; and category ❾ will take in most luxury hotels, estancias and boutique hotels. Places that cater mainly to foreigners – usually either youth hostels or, at the other end, top-range hotels – sometimes quote prices in US dollars (US$); these are specified in the text, as are half-board, full-board and all-inclusive deals.

❶ under $30	❹ $75–90	❼ $210–300
❷ $30–45	❺ $90–150	❽ $300–450
❸ $45–75	❻ $150–210	❾ over $450

dealing with prostitutes and their clients than tourists: this is usually quite clear from a look around the lobby and the reaction to your request for a room.

Most tourist offices carry a list of all the hotels in town that are **licensed** (*habilitado*); but new places may not appear and the quantity of stars that a place has been awarded should be taken with a pinch of salt. Many times places classified as *sin estrella* (no stars) can have more character than one- or two-star joints.

Posadas, hosterías and B&Bs

The use of the term **posada** usually denotes a fairly characterful place, often with a slightly rustic feel, but generally comfortable or even luxurious. In a similar vein, the term **hostería** is frequently used for smallish, upmarket hotels – oriented towards tourists rather than businessmen.

A similar type of accommodation, particularly common around Buenos Aires, are **B&Bs** (the English term is used), which tend to be chic, converted townhouses with an exclusive but cosy atmosphere – price-wise they tend to be mid-range to top-range options, and generally offer far more attractive surroundings than standard hotels at the same price.

Hostels

Youth hostels are known as *albergues juveniles* or *albergues de la juventud* in Argentina, though the term "*(youth) hostel*" is frequently used instead – *albergue* is normally taken to mean *albergue transitorio* (short-stay hotels where rooms are rented by the hour). There is an extensive chain of mostly reliable hostels in Argentina affiliated with Hostelling International (see below), as well as a growing number of independent hostels. The latter vary more in quality, but when they are good – particularly in Buenos Aires, Mendoza and Salta – they are among the country's best. Accommodation is generally in **dormitories**, though most places also have several double **rooms**, often en suite. Facilities vary, too, from next to nothing to swimming pools, Internet access, washing machines, cable TV and patios with barbecue equipment.

Note you sometimes see the term "**hostal**" used as a seemingly general term for hotels – both youth hostels and high-rise modern hotels call themselves *hostales*, though the former often prefer the English term, "hostel".

Youth hostel associations

The local office of Hostelling International is in Buenos Aires, at Florida 835 (Ⓣ011/4511-8723; Ⓦwww.hihostels.com/argentina). Associated hostels give discounts – usually a few pesos a night – to holders of HI cards but they rarely require that you possess a card in order to stay there.

US and Canada

Hostelling International Canada Ⓣ1-800/663-5777, Ⓦwww.hihostels.ca.
Hostelling International–American Youth Hostels US Ⓣ1-301/495-1240, Ⓦwww.hiayh.org.

UK and Ireland

Irish Youth Hostel Association Republic of Ireland Ⓣ01/830 4555, Ⓦwww.irelandyha.org.
Hostelling International Northern Ireland Ⓣ028/9031 5435, Ⓦwww.hini.org.uk.

Scottish Youth Hostel Association ⓣ01786/891 400, ⓦwww.syha.org.uk.
Youth Hostel Association (YHA) England and Wales ⓣ0870/770 8868, ⓦwww.yha.org.uk.

Australia and New Zealand

Australia Youth Hostels Association Australia ⓣ02/9565 1699, ⓦwww.yha.com.au.
Youth Hostelling Association New Zealand ⓣ0800/278 299 or 03/379 9970, ⓦwww.yha.co.nz.

Residenciales and hospedajes

Basic **hospedajes** and **residenciales** have low prestige in Argentina and often are not recommended by tourist offices, but again, they can be far more welcoming, clean and secure than one-star hotels; a few of them stand out as some of Argentina's best budget accommodation. Furnishings tend to the basic, with little more than a bed, perhaps a desk and chair and a fan in each room – though some are far less spartan than others and there is even the odd *one* with cable TV. Most places offer private bathrooms. There's little difference between *residenciales* and *hospedajes* – indeed, the same establishment may be described in different accommodation lists as both, or even as a hotel or hostel. The only real difference is that *hospedajes* tend to be part of a family house.

Estancias

A very different experience to staying in a hotel is provided by Argentina's many **estancias** (ranches, or **fincas** as they are known in the North) that are open to visitors. Guests usually stay in the *casco*, or farmhouse, which can be anything from a simple family home to an extravagant castle-like residence. Estancias are nearly always family-run, the income from tourism tending to serve as a supplement to the declining profits earned from the land itself. Accommodation is generally luxurious, with bags of character, and a stay is a mini-vacation in itself; for about $300–900 a day you are provided four meals, invariably including a traditional *asado,* with activities such as horse-riding and swimming also usually part of the price. Many places offer experiences that reflect the local area, from cattle herding and branding in the pampas to wine tasting at Mendoza to observing caymans in the Litoral.

You can **book** your estancia accommodation either by approaching individual estancias directly or through certain travel agencies; a comprehensive one in Buenos Aires is Estancias Argentinas, Roque Sáenz Peña 616, 9th floor (ⓣ011/4343-2366, ⓦwww.estanciasargentinas.com).

Cabañas

Popular in resort towns, self-catering **cabañas** are small, chalet-style buildings that can resemble miniature suburban villas with cable TV and microwaves, but are far more likely to be pleasingly simple and rustic wooden constructions. *Cabañas* can be very good value for money for small groups, and if you have been staying in a lot of hotels or doing some hardcore camping, they can be fun and relaxing places to take a break for a few days. A few of the simpler ones can also be surprisingly affordable options for couples or even single travellers. They are usually grouped together in outfits of between two and ten cabins; many campsites also offer basic ones as an alternative to tents.

Camping

There are plenty of places to camp throughout Argentina, with most towns and villages having their own municipal **campsites** (*campings*), but standards vary wildly. At the major resorts, there are usually plenty of privately owned, well-organized sites, with facilities ranging from provisions stores to volleyball courts and TV rooms. Some are attractive, but mostly they seem to take the fun out of camping and you're more likely to wake up to a view of next door's 4WD than the surrounding countryside. They are, however, good places to meet other travellers and generally offer a high degree of security. There are also simpler campsites, though at nearly all of them showers, electric light and barbecue facilities are standard. A campsite with no, or very limited, facilities is referred to as a *camping libre*. Municipal sites can be rather desolate and sometimes not particularly safe: it's usually a good idea to check with locals as to the security of the place before pitching a tent. Expect to pay at least $5 per person plus $5 per tent, and more in touristy locations, though some basic (or more remote) places still charge a couple of pesos only.

Food and drink

Argentine food can be summed up by one word: beef. And not just any beef, but the best in the world – succulent, cherry-red, healthy and certainly not mad, meat raised on some of the greenest, most extensive pastures known to cattle. The *asado*, or barbecue, is an institution, every bit a part of the Argentine way of life as football, fast driving and tango.

Where to eat

Apart from generic *restaurantes* (or *restoranes*), you will come across *parrillas* (for steak and beef), *marisquerías* (for seafood), *confiterías* (cafés for coffee, cakes, snacks or simple meals), *comedores* (simple local eateries), *pizzerías, bodegones* (unpretentious restaurants that theoretically serve a house wine) and *cantinas* (neighbourhood places often dishing up Italian food, such as home-made pasta). By South American standards the quality of restaurants is high, and by international standards the exchange rate makes them unbelievable value. If you're on a tight budget make lunch your main meal, and take advantage of the **menú del día** or **menú ejecutivo** – usually good-value set meals for $15–30 – and in the evening try **tenedor libre** restaurants where you can eat as much as you like for a set price (around $10–20) at self-service buffets. Up your budget to $40 a head and you can dine à la carte at most mid-range restaurants, wine included. The country also has a fair sprinkling of gourmet locales (*restaurantes de autor*), concentrated in, but by no means limited to, Buenos Aires. In these your per-head bill will push into triple figures, but this still compares well with European or North American cities and you get fabulous food, wine, ambience and service. You should splash out at least once during your visit.

When to eat

Breakfast is usually served up until around 10am, and **lunch** from around noon until 3pm. Hardly any restaurant opens for **dinner** before 8pm, and in the hotter months – and all year round in Buenos Aires – few people turn up before 10 or even 11pm. Don't be surprised to see people pouring into restaurants well after midnight: Argentines, and Porteños in particular, are night owls. If you think you're going to be starving by 7pm, do like the locals and either eat a big, cooked lunch or have **merienda** – tea and snacks – at a café in the late afternoon.

What to eat

While beef is the most prominent feature on many menus, it's not the whole story. In general, you seldom have a bad meal in Argentina. That said, imagination, innovation and a sense of subtle flavour are sometimes lacking, with Argentines preferring to eat the wholesome but often bland dishes their immigrant forebears cooked. At the other end of the spectrum, there is some inventive *cordon bleu* cooking being concocted by daring young chefs across the country. Fast food is extremely popular, but you can also snack on delicious local specialities if you want to avoid the ubiquitous multinational chains.

Breakfast

Cheaper hotels and more modest accommodation often skimp on **breakfast**: you'll be lucky to be given more than tea or coffee and some bread, jam and butter, though **medialunas** (small, sticky croissants) are sometimes also served. More upmarket hotels will go all out with their "American-style" buffet breakfast: an array of cereal, yogurt, fruit, breads and even eggs, bacon and sausages, making it worthwhile to wake up early and get down to the restaurant. The sacred national delicacy **dulce de leche** (see box, p.45) is often provided for spreading on toast or bread, as is top-notch honey.

Snacks

If you're feeling peckish during the day there are plenty of **minutas** (snacks) to choose from. The **lomito** (as opposed to *lomo* – the name of the steak cut itself) is a nourishing sandwich filled with a juicy slice of steak, often made with delicious **pan árabe** (*pitta bread*); the **chivito** (originally Uruguayan) refers to a similar kind of sandwich made with a less tender cut, though it literally means "kid", or baby goat. Other street food includes the **choripán**, a local version of the hot dog made with natural meaty sausages (*chorizos*), while at cafés a popular snack is the **tostado** (*mixto*), a toasted cheese and ham sandwich, usually daintily thin and sometimes (in the provinces) called a **carlitos**. **Barrolucas** are beef and cheese sandwiches, a local variant on the cheeseburger, and very popular around Mendoza. **Milanesas**, in this context, refer to breaded veal escalopes (also called *milanesas*) served in a sandwich, hamburger-style. **Empanadas** are small pasties (pastries with savoury fillings) usually stuffed with beef, cheese and/or vegetables, although the fillings are as varied as the cook's imagination.

Parrillas, pizza and pasta

Parrillas, pizza and pasta are the mainstays of Argentine cuisine, both at home and in restaurants. **Parrillas** are simply barbecues (or the restaurants that employ them) where

Asado basics

The term **asado** (from *asar*, to roast) originally referred specifically to a particular cut of beef, the brisket, meant to be slowly grilled or roasted, but now is applied to any **barbecued meat**. Since barbecues are an integral part of life in Argentina, it's good to know your way around the vocabulary of beef-eating, especially as beef in Argentina isn't cut in the same way as in the rest of the world – cuts are sliced through bone and muscle rather than across them.

Argentines like their meat **well done** (*cocido*), and indeed, some cuts are better cooked through. If you prefer your meat medium, ask for *a punto*, and for rare – which really requires some insistence – *jugoso*. Before you get to the steaks, you'll be offered **achuras**, or offal, and different types of sausage. **Chorizos** are excellent beef sausages, while **morcilla**, blood sausage, is an acquired taste. Sometimes **provoletta**, sliced provolone cheese, grilled on the barbecue till crispy on the edges, will be on the menu. Otherwise, it's beef all the way.

After these "appetizers" – which you can always skip, since Argentine *parrillas* are much more meat-generous than their Brazilian counterparts – you move on to the **asado** cut, followed by the **tira de asado** (ribs; aka *costillar* or *asado a secas*). There's not much meat on them, but they explode with a meaty taste. Next is the muscly but delicious **vacío** (flank). But save some room for the prime cuts: **bife ancho** is entrecôte; **bife angosto** or **lomito** is the sirloin (referred to as **medallones** when cut into slices); **cuadril** is a lump of rumpsteak, often preferred by home barbecue masters; **lomo**, one of the luxury cuts and often kept in reserve, is fillet steak; **bife de chorizo** (not to be confused with *chorizo* sausage) is what the French call a *pavé*, a slab of meat, cut from either the sirloin or entrecôte. The **entraña**, a sinewy cut from inside the beast, is a love-it-or-hate it cut; aficionados claim it's the main delicacy. Rarely barbecued, the **peceto** (eye round steak) is a tender lump of flesh, often braised (*estufado*) and served on top of pasta, roasted with potatoes (*peceto al horno con papas*) or sliced cold for *vittel tonne* – a classic Argentine starter made with tuna and mayonnaise.

Mustard (*mostaza*) may be available, but the lightly salted meat is usually best served with nothing on it but the traditional condiments of **chimichurri** – olive oil shaken in a bottle with salt, garlic, chile pepper, vinegar and bayleaf – and **salsa criolla**, similar but with onion and tomato as well; everyone jealously guards their secret formulas for both these "magic" dressings.

you can try the traditional *asado* (see box, p.43). Usually there's a set menu, the **parrillada**, but the establishments themselves vary enormously. At many, especially in big cities, the decor is stylish, the staff laid-back, the crockery delicate and the meat served tidily. Elsewhere, especially in smaller towns, *parrillas* are more basic, and you're likely to be served by burly, sweaty waiters who spend all their time grilling and carving hunks of flesh and hurling them onto plates. Traditionally, you eat the offal before moving on to the choicer cuts, but don't be put off – you can choose to skip these delicacies and head straight for the steaks and fillets. Either way, *parrillas* are not for the faint-hearted: everything comes with heaps of salads and mountains of chips (ordered separately), unadorned with sauces and in huge portions, meant for sharing. But the meat is invariably fabulous.

Mass immigration from Italy since the middle of the nineteenth century has had a profound influence on Argentine food and drink – the abundance of **fresh pasta** (*pasta casera*) is just one example. The fillings tend to be a little unexciting (lots of cheese, including ricotta, but seldom meat), the sauces are not exactly memorable (mostly tomato and onion) and the pasta itself cooked beyond *al dente*, yet it's a reliable staple and rarely downright bad. Very convincing parmesan- and Roquefort-style cheeses are both produced in Argentina, and are often used in sauces.

Pizzas are very good on the whole, though the toppings tend to lack originality, especially away from the capital. One popular ingredient regularly used as a garnish may be unfamiliar to visitors: the **palmito**, a sweet, crunchy vegetable resembling something between asparagus and celery. Argentine pizzas are nearly always of the thick-crust variety, wood-oven baked and very big, meant to be divided between a number of diners.

Other cuisines

In addition to the authentic **Italian** cooking available all over the country, **Spanish** restaurants serve tapas and familiar dishes such as *paella*, while specifically Basque restaurants are also fairly commonplace; these are often the places to head for fish or seafood. **Chinese** and, increasingly, **Korean** restaurants are found in many Argentine cities, but they rarely serve anything remotely like authentic Asian food and specialize in *tenedor libre* buffet diners. **Japanese**, **Indian** and **Thai** restaurants have become fashionable in Buenos Aires, where nearly every national cuisine from Armenian to Vietnamese via Mexican and Polish is also available, but such variety is almost unheard of in the provinces.

Arab and **Middle Eastern** food, including specialities such as kebabs and *kepe*, seasoned ground raw meat, is far more widespread, as is **German** fare, such as sauerkraut (*chucrút*) and frankfurters, along with Central and Eastern European food, often served in *choperías*, or beer-gardens. **Welsh tearooms** are a speciality of Patagonia.

For more on other Argentine (*criollo*) cooking, see the *Criollo culture* colour section.

Vegetarian food

Your experience as a **vegetarian** in Argentina will depend on where in the country you are. You shouldn't have too many problems in the capital, the larger cities or the Patagonian resorts, all of which are relatively cosmopolitan. While there aren't many **restaurants** completely dedicated to non-meat eaters, they do exist and many places have a few good non-meat alternatives. The exceptions are the *parrillas*, though the sight and smell of entire animals roasting on the grill is unlikely to appeal to vegetarians anyway.

In the smaller provincial towns, however, vegetarian fare tends to be a lot simpler and you will likely have to adjust to a diet of pizza, pasta, empanadas and salads, with very little variety in the toppings and fillings. The good news is that these fillings are often options such as spinach, **acelga** (Swiss chard – similar to spinach, but slightly more bitter) and ricotta. Other foods to keep an eye out for are **fainá**, a fairly bland but agreeable Genovese speciality made with chickpea dough and **milanesas de soja** (breaded and fried soya) – **a la napolitana** means it comes with cheese and tomato – while **milanesas** of vegetables like **berenjena** (eggplant/aubergine) and **calabaza** (pumpkin) are also quite popular.

Dulce de leche

Dulce de leche, a sticky, sweet goo made by laboriously boiling large quantities of vanilla-flavoured milk and sugar until they almost disappear, is claimed by Argentines as a national invention, although similar concoctions are made in Brazil, France and Italy. Something called *manjar* is produced in Chile, but Argentines rightly regard it as far inferior. The thick caramel is eaten with a spoon, spread on bread or biscuits, used to fill cakes, biscuits and fritters or dolloped onto other desserts. Some of the best flavours of ice cream are variations on the *dulce de leche* theme. Although some people still make their own, most people buy it ready-made, in jars. While all Argentines agree that *dulce de leche* is fabulous, there is no consensus on a particular brand: the divisions between those who favour Havanna and those who would only buy Chimbote run almost as deep as those between supporters of Boca Juniors and River Plate. Foreigners are advised to maintain a diplomatic neutrality on the issue.

When all the cheese gets a bit much, look out for the popular Chinese-ish *tenedor libres*, which usually feature a good smattering of veggies, as do Middle Eastern restaurants. Another possibility would be to self-cater – supermarkets are usually fairly well stocked with vegetables, seasonings and soya products.

You should always check the ingredients of a dish before ordering, as the addition of small amounts of meat is not always referred to on menus. Don't be surprised if your "no como carne" (I don't eat meat) is dismissed with a glib "no tiene mucha" (It doesn't contain much) and be particularly on your guard for the seemingly ever-present **jamón** (ham).

Vegans will have a hard time outside of Buenos Aires, as pretty much everything that doesn't contain meat contains cheese or pastry. Waiters will rarely be familiar with veganism, but will usually try to accommodate your requests.

Desserts

Argentines have a fairly sweet tooth and love anything with sugar, especially, *dulce de leche* (see box above). Even breakfast tends to be dominated by sweet things such as sticky croissants (*medialunas*) or **chocolate con churros**, Andalucian-style hot chocolate with fritters, sometimes filled with *dulce de leche*. All kinds of cakes and biscuits, including *alfajores* (maize-flour cookie sandwiches, filled with jam or *dulce de leche*, sometimes coated with chocolate), pastries called **facturas** and other candies and sweets are popular with Argentines of all ages.

However, for dessert you'll seldom be offered anything other than the tired trio of **flan** (a kind of crème caramel, religiously served with a thick custard or *dulce de leche*), **budín de pan** (a syrupy version of bread pudding) and fresh fruit salad (*ensalada de fruta*). In Andean regions, or in *criollo* eateries, you'll most likely be served **dulce vigilante**, a slab of neutral, pallid cheese called *quesillo* eaten with candied fruit such as sweet potato (*batata*), quince (*membrillo*), (*al*)*cayote* (a kind of spaghetti squash), pumpkin (*zapallo*) or lime (*lima*). *Panqueques*, or crepes, are also popular.

With such a large Italian community it is not surprising that superb **helado** (ice cream) is easy to come by in Argentina. Even the tiniest village has at least one *heladería artesanal*. Cones and cups are usually prominently displayed, with the price clearly marked. If you're feeling really self-indulgent you might like to have your cone dipped in chocolate (*bañado*). Some of the leading ice-cream makers offer an overwhelming range of flavours (*sabores*). Chocolate chip (*granizado*) is a favourite, and raspberry mousse (*mousse de frambuesa*) is also delicious.

Drinks

Fizzy drinks (*gaseosas*) are popular with people of all ages and often accompany meals. All the big brand names are available, along with local brands such as Paso de los Toros, who make tonic water and fizzy grapefruit (*pomelo*) drinks. You will often be asked if you want **mineral water** – either still (*agua sin gas*) or carbonated – (*agua con gas* or *soda*) – with your meal, but you can ask for **tap water** (*agua de la llave*), which is safe to drink in most places, though this may raise eyebrows. Although little is grown in the country, good **coffee** is easy to come by. You will find very decent espressos, or delicious *café con leche*, in most cafés; instant coffee is mercifully rare. **Tea** is usually made from teabags; Argentine tea is strong rather than subtle, and is served with either milk or lemon. **Herbal teas** (*infusiones*) are all the rage, camomile (*manzanilla*) being the most common. **Mate** is a whole world unto itself and is explained, along with the etiquette and ritual involved, on pp.392–393. **Fruit juices** (*jugos*) and **milkshakes** (*licuados*) can be excellent, though freshly squeezed orange juice is often sold at ridiculously high prices.

Argentina's **beer** is more thirst-quenching than alcoholic and mostly comes as fairly bland lager, with Quilmes dominating the market and Heineken producing a frequently sold beer in the country; imported brands are fairly common in the cities, though more expensive. Regional brews are sometimes worth trying: in Mendoza, the Andes brand crops up all over, while Salta's own brand is also good, and a kind of stout (*cerveza negra*) can sometimes be obtained in the Northwest. **Home-brewed beer** (*cerveza artesanal*) is increasingly available, often coming in a surprising array of flavours. Usually when you ask for a beer, it comes in large litre bottles, meant for sharing; a small bottle is known as a *porrón*. If you want draught beer ask for a *chopp* (or a *liso* in Santa Fe province).

The produce of Argentina's **vineyards,** ranging from gutsy plonk to some of the world's prize-winning **wines**, is widely available both in the country and abroad; Most vintages are excellent and not too expensive. Unfortunately, many restaurants still have limited, unimaginative wine lists, which don't reflect Argentina's drift away from mass-produced table wines to far superior single or multi-varietals (for more on wine, see box, p.510). It is also quite difficult to get wine by the glass, and half-bottles too are rare. Cheaper wine is commonly made into **sangria** or its fruitier, white wine equivalent, **clericó**.

Don't be surprised to see home-grown variants (*nacionales*) of whisky, gin, brandy, port, sherry and rum, none of which is that good; familiar imported brands (*importados*) can be very dear, however. It's far better to stick to the locally distilled **aguardientes**, or firewaters, some of which (from Catamarca, for example) are deliciously grapey. There is no national alcoholic drink or cocktail, but a number of Italian vermouths and digestives are made in Argentina. **Fernet Branca** is the most popular, a demonic-looking brew the colour of molasses with a medicinal taste, invariably combined with Coke and consumed in huge quantities – it's generally regarded as the gaucho's favourite tipple. Indigenous peoples still make **chicha** from fermented *algarrobo* fruit or *piñones* (monkey puzzle nuts) but this is very difficult to obtain.

The media

In terms of newspaper circulation, Argentina is Latin America's most literate nation, and it has a diverse and generally high-quality press. Its television programming is a rather chaotic amalgam of light-entertainment shows and sports, and its radio services tend to fall into one of two categories: urban mainstream commercial channels or amateur ones designed to serve the needs of local rural communities.

Newspapers and magazines

In the past, the fortunes of the print **press** in Argentina have varied greatly, depending on the prevailing political situation. Overbearing state control and censorship characterized much of the twentieth century, but the current situation is much more dynamic, and a resilient streak of investigative journalism provides a constant stream of stories revolving around official corruption. Self-censorship, though, is fairly widespread, and deep criticism of the country's institutions is pretty muted in favour of a generally patriotic stance.

The *Buenos Aires Herald* (Ⓦwww.buenosairesherald.com) is South America's most prestigious **English-language daily** and dates back to 1876. Although the quality of the writing and editing is a little inconsistent, the *Herald* is useful for getting the low-down on current events in Argentina and for catching up on international news and sports, as it features the main stories from the wires as well as syndicated articles from the likes of the *New York Times* and Britain's *Independent*. In recent years, it has been headed by author and commentator Andrew Graham-Yooll, and is notable for its critical take on many aspects of Argentine politics and society. Perhaps not surprisingly, it is still associated in many minds with the old-style Anglo-Argentine elite, but it won international plaudits for its stand on human rights issues in the years of the military dictatorship. The *Herald* is easily available in the capital, but don't expect to find it outside major cities and tourist centres.

If you have some Spanish, the most accessible of the **national dailies** is *Clarín* (Ⓦwww.clarin.com.ar), the paper with the highest circulation; its website is one of the most popular Spanish-language sites on the Net. Despite its mass-market appeal, it remains, by British and even American standards, pretty highbrow, with politics on page three, followed by a fair-sized economics section. It's not unusual to see football on the front page, but celebrities are usually kept in their place – that is, the "Espectáculos" supplement, which also has good listings of what's on. The paper's clear format makes it easy to read, although it has a reputation for a somewhat uncritical stance. The *Clarín* media group has a stake in several leading provincial dailies, such as the *Río Negro*, which are to a large extent reproductions of the mother paper but with a more local focus. *Clarín* also owns *Olé*, a paper dedicated solely to sports, with football taking up the lion's share.

The country's major **broadsheet** is *La Nación* (Ⓦwww.lanacion.com.ar), founded in 1870. The favoured reading of the upper and educated classes, it is conservative in some ways, but is also the most international, outward-looking and arguably best written of the Spanish-language newspapers. It's worth keeping an eye out for its bumper Sunday edition, full of supplements with articles on travel, columns by the likes of Paulo Coelho and Tomás Eloy Martínez and a large classified section. At the other extreme, the unabashedly anti-establishment *Página 12* (Ⓦwww.pagina12.com.ar) is a left-leaning paper founded in 1987 with a distinct, trenchant style, a strong tradition of investigative journalism and a particular penchant for harrying ex-members of Latin military juntas, especially the Argentine ones, who are guilty of crimes against humanity. In the 1990s the *Clarín* group bought a stake in it, though, and some think it has lost its teeth a little since then; in recent years it has been the only paper that has consistently supported President Kirchner. Popular with students and intellectuals, it requires a pretty good knowledge of Spanish and Argentine politics, although certain features – such as the photos of *desaparecidos* on the anniversary of their disappearance – need little explanation.

Argentina's **regional press** is also strong, though the quality varies enormously across the country. A handful of local dailies, such as Mendoza's *Los Andes* (Ⓦwww.losandes.com.ar), Córdoba's *La Voz del Interior* (Ⓦwww.lavozdelinterior.com.ar) and Rosario's *La Capital* (Ⓦwww.lacapital.com.ar), are every bit as informative and well-written as the leading national newspapers, and they contain vital information about tourist attractions, cultural events and travel news. The other advantage is that they're often on the newsstands before the Buenos Aires-based titles arrive. The capital itself does not have a local paper as such, but in the evenings look out for *La Razón* (Ⓦwww.larazon.com.ar), once an august broadsheet but now relaunched by Clarín as a freebie given out at subte stations and toll-booths. *Hecho en Buenos Aires* and Córdoba's *La Luciernaga* are similar in idea to London's *Big Issue*; homeless vendors buy copies of the magazines – dealing mostly with social and cultural topics – and sell them in the street for a couple of pesos' profit per issue.

As far as **magazines** go, the Argentine market is mostly a mix of Spanish-language versions of well-known international titles – often produced in Madrid – and home-grown enterprises. Popular gossip magazines include *Gente* (Ⓦwww.gente.com.ar) and *Caras* (Ⓦwww.caras.uol.com.ar), as well as *Noticias* (Ⓦwww.noticias.uol.com.ar), which also breaks a lot of investigative exclusives. Fashion magazines *El Planeta Urbano* (Ⓦwww.elplanetaurbano.com) and *D-Mode* (Ⓦwww.d-mode.com) are good for finding out which clubs and restaurants young, hip Porteños are heading to, while *Lugares* is a magazine about Argentine travel destinations. The writing in the latter tends to be of the puff variety, but it does have good photos and ideas and provides an English translation.

Newspapers and magazines are sold at **pavement kiosks** (*kioskos*), usually found near a town's main square and at bus terminals. Outside Buenos Aires, you pay a supplement, and dailies often don't arrive till late in the day. International publications such as *Time*, *Newsweek*, *The Economist*, the *Miami Herald* and the *Daily Telegraph* are sold at the kiosks on Calle Florida and in Recoleta in Buenos Aires, and at the capital's airports, as are some imported European and US magazines. However, check the cover as they can often be long past their publication date; they are also usually so expensive that unless you're really desperate you're probably better off with the *BA Herald*.

Radio

Argentina's most popular **radio** station, Cadena 100 (99.9FM), plays a fairly standard formula of Latin pop, whereas Rock y Pop (95.9FM) veers, as its name would imply, toward rock and blues. Dance music can be heard on X4 (106.7FM) and classical on Radio Clasica (96.7FM). WBAT (Ⓦwww.wbat.com.ar) is an English-language Argentine station that is currently confined to the Web, but with ambitions to hit the airwaves. Neither the **BBC World Service** nor the Voice of America now broadcast on shortwave to Argentina.

Towns are blessed with a remarkable number of small-time radio stations, which are listened to avidly by locals, though they're rarely likely to appeal to foreign visitors. In rural areas, local amateur radio stations form a vital part of the community fabric, providing a message service that relays every conceivable type of salutation, appeal and snippet of gossip. You will hear everything from news of births and deaths to people asking to be given lifts along little-transited routes. Messages normally go out twice a day (noon is a common time), and it is sometimes amazing how effective this seemingly rudimentary system can be. Should you ever lose anything or have documents stolen, these services are normally all too pleased to put out an appeal for you; indeed, this is usually your best chance of recovering your property.

Television

There are five national **television stations**, mostly showing a mix of football, soap operas (*telenovelas*) and chat shows.There have been Argentine versions of international hits such as *Big Brother* and *Popstars,* although on the whole there is less interest in "reality TV" than in Europe or the US. The channels also show syndicated foreign programmes, but they are almost always dubbed. Even if you can't understand much, however, Argentine TV can provide a fascinating glimpse into certain aspects of society, from the almost freakish plastic surgery of some presenters to the bouncy Saturday afternoon cumbia show *Pasion de Sabado*. There are also some worthwhile news documentary shows, such as *Punto Doc*. Cable TV is common in many mid-range and even budget hotels; the channels you get depend on the cable provider, but they generally include CNN and BBC World in English, with a myriad of channels playing movies and (mostly American) TV shows, usually subtitled. Where they are dubbed, you can sometimes turn the dubbing off by pressing the SAP (Second Audio Protocol) button on your remote. Fox and ESPN cover worldwide sports, including baseball, the NBA and English Premiership football. Argentine cable news channels include Clarín's TN (*Telenoticias*) and the unique Crónica, a budget Buenos Aires-based news channel that provides live, unedited coverage of anything that happens in the city; indeed, it is said that the Crónica vans often arrive before the police do.

Festivals

Festivals of all kinds, both religious, celebrating local patrons, and secular, showing off produce such as handicrafts, olives, goats or wine, are good excuses for much partying and pomp in Argentina, particularly the closer you get to the country's northern neighbours, with their strong festival traditions.

In the Northwest, for example, there is probably a feast every day of the year somewhere (see box, pp.456–457), and the nearer you get to Brazil, the more gusto you will see **Carnaval** celebrated with, although Argentina's premier parades are found at Gualeguaychú (see p.322). Other major festivals are November's celebration of pampas culture, the **Fiesta de la Tradición**, in San Antonio de Areco and elsewhere (see p.239), September's religious **Fiesta del Milagro** in Salta (see p.429) and Mendoza's wine-inspired **Fiesta de la Vendimia** in March (see p.522).

On the whole, **holidays** such as Christmas and Easter are more religious, family-focused occasions than they are in Europe and the US. Although some traditions – such as the European custom of eating chocolate eggs at Easter – are starting to take off, the festivals are generally a lot less commercial, and the run-up to them doesn't start two months beforehand. Christmas is celebrated more on Christmas Eve evening than during Christmas Day – midnight on December 24 (and again on December 31) is a great time to be in Buenos Aires, particularly if you have a high vantage point from which to watch the sky explode with fireworks. Imported festivals such as St Valentine's and Halloween are also becoming increasingly popular, while more home-grown festivals include the **Día de las Malvinas** (June 10), the day the South Atlantic conflict ended, remembered with ceremonies, and the **Día de la Primavera** (September 21), when young people gather in parks to picnic and drink cheap wine.

For a list of public holidays, see the box on p.73.

Sports

Argentines suffer an incurable addiction to sport; many go rigid at the thought of even one week without football (soccer), and you'll hear informed and spirited debate in bars on subjects as diverse as tennis, rugby, basketball and the uniquely Argentine equestrian sport of pato.

The following are some practical hints on spectator sports. For more on these, see *Sports and outdoor activities* colour section.

Football

Attending a **football** (soccer) match is one of the highlights of many people's visits to Argentina, and it is certainly worth setting aside time to do so, even if you're not normally a fan of the sport. The domestic league's year is split into two **seasons** – allowing for two champions and two sets of celebrations. The first season runs from August to December and is known as the *apertura* (opening); the second, from February to June, is the *clausura* (closing); fixtures are mostly played on Sunday afternoons. In addition, there are two South American club championships – the Copa Libertador and Copa Sudamericana, roughly equivalent to the European Championship and UEFA cup, respectively. These are generally dominated by teams from Argentina, Brazil and Colombia, with a leg played in each country, usually a midweek fixture. If you're lucky, you may even get the chance to see the national side (*la selección*) strutting their stuff in a friendly or World Cup qualifier.

You can usually buy **tickets** at the grounds on match day, although some games sell out in advance, notably the *clásico* derbys between the big five (Boca Juniors, River Plate, Racing, Independiente and San Lorenzo, all in Buenos Aires) and top-of-the-table clashes. For these, you can get tickets two days before the game at the stadium (be prepared for a scrum) or further in advance for some games from Ticketek (Ⓣ011/5237-7200, Ⓦwww.ticketek.com.ar). Alternatively, many tour agencies, hotels and hostels have caught on to visitors' interest in attending games and, for a premium, provide a service of ticket and transfer. The Museo de la Pasión Boquense at Boca's Bombonera (see p.124) also arranges match-day visits – its website (Ⓦwww.museoboquense.com) has a list of upcoming fixtures.

Tickets for spectators are either in the *popular* or the more expensive *platea*, with the price depending on your vantage point and the game's importance, although it always compares favourably with the cost of European match tickets. The *popular* are the standing-only **terraces**, where the young men, the hardcore home fans, sing and swear their way through the match. This is the most colourful part of the stadium, but it's also the area where you're most likely to be pickpocketed, charged by police or faced with the wrath of the equally hardcore away fans (in the *visitantes* section, where you can often buy the cheapest tickets, though it's standing room only). Unless you're pretty confident, or with someone who is, you may be better off heading to the relative safety of the *platea* **seats**, from where you can photograph the *popular* and enjoy the match sitting down. Don't be surprised if someone's in the seat allocated to you on the ticket – locals pay scant regard to official seating arrangements. After major wins, the Obelisco in central Buenos Aires is the epicentre of raucous **celebrations**.

It's advisable to turn up forty minutes or so before the match in order to avoid the rush, and not to hang around the stadium afterwards, when trouble sometimes brews. Dress down, avoid flaunting the colours of either side and take the minimum of valuables.

For the season's **fixture list**, head to Ⓦwww.uol.com.ar/uolfutbol.

Polo and pato

Although it's mainly a game for *estancieros* and wealthy families from Barrio Norte, **polo** is nonetheless far less snobbish or exclusive in Argentina than in Britain or the US; there are some 150 teams and 5000 club members nationwide. You don't need an invitation from a member or a double-barrelled surname to see the world's top polo players; simply turn up and buy a ticket during the open championship in November and December, played at the **Campo de Polo** in Palermo, Buenos Aires. Even if the rules go over your head, the game is exciting and aesthetically pleasing, with hooves galloping over impeccably trimmed grass.

The sport is at least as hard as it looks, but if you're confident on horseback and determined to have a go, many estancias (listed throughout the text) offer lessons as part of their accommodation and activity packages. Alternatively, contact the Asociación Argentina de Polo at Arévalo 3065, Buenos Aires (ⓣ011/4777-6444, ⓦwww.aapolo.com), which can also provide match information.

The curious sport of **pato**, a sort of lacrosse on horseback, also has its national tournament in November and December each year, played at the **Campo Argentino de Pato** in San Miguel, just outside the city limits. If you don't catch a live match, you may see a televised game on one of the otherwise eminently missable rural farming channels. For more information on pato, see the national federation's website, ⓦwww.fedpato.com.ar, and the *Sports and outdoor activities* colour section.

Rugby

Argentina's national **rugby** squad, the Pumas (founded in 1965), is currently ranked sixth in the world. It does not yet take part in any major tournament, though it may be admitted to the southern hemisphere Tri Nations at some point in the near future. In the meantime, you can catch the burly Pumas playing test series at home or in World Cup qualifiers. These games are played all over the country – in 2006 the Pumas played Wales in Puerto Madryn. See the website of the Unión Argentina de Rugby (ⓦwww.uar.com.ar) for upcoming fixtures.

Outdoor activities

Argentina is a highly exciting destination for outdoors enthusiasts: world-class fly-fishing, horse-riding, trekking and rock-climbing opportunities abound, as do options for white-water rafting, skiing, ice climbing and even – for those with sufficient stamina and preparation – expeditions onto the Southern Patagonian Icecap.

The following are some practical hints on Argentina's outdoor pursuits. For more on these, see the *Sports and outdoor activities* colour section.

Trekking

Argentina offers some truly marvellous **trekking**, and it is still possible to find areas where you can trek for days without seeing a soul. Trail quality varies considerably, and many are difficult to follow, so always get hold of the best map available and ask for information as you go. Most of the best treks are in the national parks – especially the ones in Patagonia – but you can often find lesser-known but equally superb options in the lands bordering them. Most people head for the savage granite spires of the **Fitz Roy** region around El Chaltén, an area whose fame has spread so rapidly over the last ten

Trekking routes

Please refer to the following pages in the guide for further information on specific treks and trails:

El Bolsón region, p.633.
La Cueva de las Manos Pintadas, p.694.
Fitz Roy sector, Parque Nacional Los Glaciares, p.708.
Parque Nacional Los Alerces, p.643.
Parque Nacional Baritú, p.472.
Parque Nacional Calilegua, p.470.
Parque Nacional Lanín, p.595.
Parque Nacional Nahuel Huapi, p.613.
Parque Nacional Perito Moreno, p.698.
Parque Nacional El Rey, p.470.
Parque Nacional Tierra del Fuego, p.760.
Parque Provincial Talampaya, p.561.
Torres del Paine, p.736.

years that it now holds a similar status to Chile's renowned Torres del Paine. Tourist pressures are starting to tell, however, at least in the high season (late Dec to Feb), when campsites are packed. The other principal trekking destination is the mountainous area of **Parque Nacional Nahuel Huapi**, south of Bariloche. This area has the best infrastructure, with a network of generally well-marked trails and mountain refuges. In the north of the country, some of the best trekking is in **Jujuy Province**, especially in Calilegua, where the habitat ranges from subtropical to bald, mountain landscape. **Salta Province** also offers a good variety of high mountain valley and cloudforest trails.

You should always be well prepared for your trips, even for half-day hikes. Good quality, **water- and windproof clothing** is vital: temperatures plummet at night and often with little warning during the day. Keep spare dry layers of clothing and socks in a plastic bag in your pack. **Boots** should provide firm ankle support and have the toughest soles possible (Vibram soles are recommended). Gore-Tex boots are only waterproof to a degree: they will not stay dry when you have to cross swampland. A **balaclava** is sometimes more useful than a woollen hat. Make sure that your **tent** is properly waterproofed and that it can cope with high winds (especially if you're trekking in Patagonia). You'll need a minimum of a three-season sleeping bag, to be used in conjunction with a solid or semi-inflatable foam mattress (essential, as the ground will otherwise suck out all your body heat). Also bring high-factor **sunblock** and lipsalve, plus good **sunglasses** and headgear. Park authorities often require you to carry a **stove** for cooking. The Camping Gaz models that run on butane cylinders (refills are fairly widely available in *ferretería* hardware shops) are not so useful in exposed areas, where you're better off with a high-pressure petrol stove such as an MSR, although these are liable to clog with impurities in the fuel, so filter it first. Telescopic hiking poles save your knees from a lot of strain and are useful for balance. Miner-style head **torches** are preferable to regular hand-held ones, and gaffer tape makes an excellent all-purpose emergency repair tool. Carry a **first-aid kit** and a **compass**, and know how to use both. And always carry plenty of **water** – aim to have at least two litres on you at all times. Pump-action **water filters** can be very handy, as you can thus avoid the hassle of having to boil suspect water.

Note also that, in the national parks, especially on the less-travelled and overnight routes, you should inform the **park ranger** (*guardaparque*) of your plans, not forgetting to report your safe arrival at your destination – the ranger will send a search party out for you if you do not arrive. You'd be advised to buy all your camping equipment before you leave home: quality gear is expensive and hard to come by in Argentina, and there are still relatively few places that rent decent equipment, even in some of the key trekking areas.

Climbing

For **climbers**, the Andes offer incredible variety. You do not have to be a technical expert, but you should always take preparations seriously. You can often arrange a climb close to the date – though it's best to bring as much high-quality gear with you as you can. The climbing season is fairly short – November to March in some places, though December to February is the best time. The best-known challenge is South America's highest peak, **Aconcagua** (6962m), accessed from the city of Mendoza (see p.532). Not considered the most technical challenge, this peak nevertheless merits top-level expedition status, as the altitude and storms claim several victims a year. Only slightly less lofty are nearby Tupungato (6750m), just to the south; Mercedario (6770m), just to the north; Cerro Bonete (6872m) and Pissis (6779m) on the provincial border between La Rioja and Catamarca; and Ojos del Salado, the highest active volcano in the world (6885m), a little further north into Catamarca. The last three can be climbed from Fiambalá, but Ojos is most normally climbed from the Chilean side of the border. The most famous volcano to climb is the elegant cone of **Lanín** (3776m), which can be ascended in two days via the relatively straightforward northeastern route. Parque Nacional Nahuel Huapi, near Bariloche, offers the **Cerro Catedral** massif and **Cerro Tronador** (3554m). Southern Patagonia is also a highly prized climbing destination. One testing summit is **San Lorenzo** (3706m), which, from the Argentine side, can best be approached along the valley of the Río Oro, although the summit itself is usually climbed from across the border in Chile. Further south are the inspirational granite spires of the Fitz Roy massif and Cerro Torre, which have few equals on the planet in terms of technical difficulty and scenic grandeur.

On all of these climbs, but especially those over 4000m, make sure to acclimatize thoroughly, and be fully aware of the dangers of *puna*, or altitude sickness (see p.66).

Useful climbing contacts

In Argentina

Centro Andino Buenos Aires Rivadavia 1255, Buenos Aires ⓣ 011/4381-1566, ⓦ www.caba.org.ar. Offers climbing courses, talks and slideshows.

Club Andino Bariloche (CAB) 20 de Febrero 30, Bariloche, Río Negro ⓣ 02944/422266, ⓦ www.clubandino.com.ar. The country's oldest and most famous mountaineering club, with excellent specialist knowledge of guides and Patagonian challenges.

In the US

American Alpine Club 710 Tenth St, Suite 100, Golden, CO 80401 ⓣ 303/384-0110, ⓦ www.americanalpineclub.org. Annual membership includes free rescue insurance for peaks up to 6000m, and access to its comprehensive library.

In the UK

British Mountaineering Council 177–179 Burton Rd, Manchester M20 2BB ⓣ 0161/445-6111, ⓦ www.thebmc.co.uk. Produces regularly updated expedition reports. Excellent insurance services and book catalogue.

Fishing

As a destination for **fly-fishing** (*pesca con mosca*), Argentina is unparalleled, with Patagonia drawing in professionals from around the globe. Trout, introduced in the early twentieth century, are the sport's mainstay, but there is also fishing for landlocked and even Pacific salmon. The most famous places to go are those where the world's largest sea-running brown trout (*trucha marrón*) are found: principally the **Río Grande** and other rivers of eastern and central Tierra del Fuego, and the Río Gallegos on the mainland. The reaches of the Río Santa Cruz near Comandante Luis Piedra Buena have some impressive specimens of steelhead trout (sea-running rainbows, or *trucha arco iris*), and the area around Río Pico is famous for its brook trout. The Patagonian **Lake District** – around Junín de los Andes, San Martín de los Andes, Bariloche and Esquel – is the country's most popular trout-fishing destination, offering superb angling in delightful scenery.

The trout-fishing season runs from mid-November to Easter. Regulations change slightly from year to year, but **permits** are valid countrywide. They can be purchased at national park offices, some *guardaparque* posts, tourist offices and at fishing equipment shops, which are fairly plentiful – especially in places like the north Patagonian Lake District. With your permit, you are issued a **booklet** detailing the regulations of the type of fishing allowed in each river and lake in the region, the restrictions on catch-and-release and the number of specimens you are allowed to take for eating. Argentine law states that permit holders are allowed to fish any waters they can reach without crossing private land. You are, in theory at least, allowed to walk along the bank as far as you like from any public road, although in practice you may find that owners of some of the more prestigious beats try to obstruct you in this.

For more **information** on fly-fishing in Argentina, contact the Asociación Argentina de Pesca con Mosca, Lerma 452 (1414) Buenos Aires (Ⓣ011/4773 0821, Ⓦwww.aapm.org.ar).

Skiing

Argentina's **ski resorts** are not on the same scale as those of Europe or North America and attract mainly domestic and Latin American tourists (from Chile and Brazil), as well as a smattering of foreigners who are looking to ski during the northern summer. However, infrastructure is constantly being upgraded, and it's easy to rent gear. The main skiing months are July and August (late July is peak season), although in some resorts it is possible to ski from late May to early October. Snow conditions vary from year to year, but you can often find excellent powder.

The most prestigious resort for downhill skiing is modern **Las Leñas** (see p.541), which also offers the most challenging skiing and once hosted the World Cup. Following this are **Chapelco**, near San Martín de los Andes, where you also have extensive cross-country options (see p.612), and the Bariloche resorts of **Cerro Catedral** and **Cerro Otto** (see p.631), which are the longest-running in the country, with wonderful panoramas of the Nahuel Huapi region, albeit with rather too many people. **Ushuaia** (see p.750) is an up-and-coming resort, with some fantastic cross-country possibilities and expanding – if still relatively limited – downhill facilities; the resort's right by the scenic town, so it's a good choice if you want to combine skiing with sightseeing. Bariloche and Las Leñas are the best destinations for those interested in après-ski. Other, more minor resorts include the mountain bowl of La Hoya near Esquel (traditionally a late-season resort and good for beginners; see p.639); the tiny Cerro Bayo near Villa La Angostura; and isolated Valdelén near Río Turbio, with gentle runs on wooded hillsides right on the Chilean border. If you can afford it, consider hopping over the border to Chile, where resorts such as Portillo (Ⓦwww.skiportillo.com) and El Colorado (Ⓦwww.elcolorado.cl) offer a sophisticated and varied skiing experience that nowhere in Argentina can really match.

Rafting

Though it does not have the same range of extreme options as neighbouring Chile, Argentina nevertheless has some beautiful **white-water rafting** possibilities, ranging from grades II to IV. Most of these are offered as day-trips, and include journeys through enchanting monkey puzzle tree scenery on the generally sedate Río Aluminé; along the turbulent and often silty Río Mendoza; on the Río Manso in the Alpine-like country south of Parque Nacional Nahuel Huapi; and along the similar but less-visited Río Corcovado, south of Esquel. Esquel can also be used as a base for rafting on Chile's fabulous, world-famous Río Futaleufú, a turquoise river that flows through temperate rainforest and tests rafters with rapids of grade V. You do not need previous rafting experience to enjoy these, but you should obviously be able to swim. Pay heed to operators' safety instructions, and ensure your safety gear (especially helmets and life-jackets) fits well. Recommended individual operators are listed in the guide.

National parks and reserves

Argentina's national parks are some of the country's principal lures, encompassing the variety of ecosystems and scenery that exist here. Though some parks were established purely for their fabulous scenery, many others – especially the newer ones – were created to protect examples of different ecosystems. In addition, some protect important archeological or geological sites. The parks also vary in size, from the minuscule botanical reserve of Colonia Benítez in Chaco Province, less than a tenth of a square kilometre, to the grand and savage Parque Nacional Los Glaciares in Santa Cruz, which covers some six thousand square kilometres.

These national protected areas fall into four different categories – **parques nacionales**, **reservas naturales**, **reservas naturales estrictas** and **monumentos naturales** – but the distinctions between them matter little to the tourist, although it is as well to be aware that "*monumento natural*" is used to refer to individual species, such as the *huemul* (the native Patagonian Andean deer), and the southern right whale, as well as to places. More relevant to the visitor are the different degrees of protection within the parks: strict scientific zones (*zonas intangibles*) that are not open to the general public, zones with routes of public access that are otherwise under full protection and buffer zones where locals engage in limited forms of sustainable exploitation (such as forestry and the hunting of introduced species). The situation is complicated by the presence of indigenous communities in some parks, while in others there are enclaves of private land that even *guardaparques* (rangers) must ask permission to enter.

The most famous park of all is the subtropical **Iguazú**, with its breathtaking waterfalls (see p.355), followed by the great Patagonian parks that protect the lakes and subantarctic forests of the mountainous border with Chile – most notably **Nahuel Huapi**, in Río Negro (see p.613), and **Los Glaciares** in Santa Cruz, with the Perito Moreno Glacier and the Fitz Roy trekking sector (see p.703). **Lanín**, with its famous volcano and monkey puzzle forests (see p.595), **Los Alerces** (see p.643) and **Perito Moreno** (distinct from the glacier; see p.698) are three other mighty Patagonian Andean parks, while in **Parque Nacional Tierra del Fuego** the Andes meet the Beagle Channel (see p.760). One of the easiest national parks to access from Buenos Aires is **El Palmar**, in the province of Entre Ríos, a savannah plain studded with graceful native palms (see p.332). Famous for its cloudforest are the northwestern mountain parks of **Baritú** (see p.472), **Calilegua** (see p.470) and **El Rey** (see p.470), while geologically fascinating are the spectacular canyons of **Talampaya** in La Rioja Province (see p.561), and the **Bosques Petrificados** (petrified forests) in Santa Cruz (see p.681).

In addition to the national parks, Argentina has an array of provincial nature reserves and protected areas, the most exceptional of which is the **Península Valdés**, on the coast of Chubut near Puerto Madryn (see p.664). Marine mammals are the star attractions here, principally southern right whales and orcas. It is also one of the finest places to see the animals of the Patagonian steppe, as is **Punta Tombo**, also in Chubut Province (see p.675). This reserve is most famous for sheltering the largest colony of Magellanic penguins on the continent. The **Esteros de Iberá** swampland, in Corrientes Province (see p.335), is good for spotting caymans and capybaras as well as a remarkable variety of birdlife. In Mendoza, the **Parque Provincial Aconcagua** (see p.532) was set up to protect the western hemisphere's highest peak, while **Ischigualasto** in San Juan (see p.559) protects a lunar landscape with bizarrely eroded geological formations.

Information and visits

The **National Park Headquarters** is in Buenos Aires at Santa Fe 690 (Mon–Fri 10am–5pm; ⓣ011/4311-0303, ⓦwww.parquesnacionales.gov.ar). There is an underfunded and not terribly helpful information office on the ground floor that may be able to provide some introductory leaflets. A wider range of free material is available at each individual park, but these are of variable quality – many only have a basic map and a brief park description.

Nature enthusiasts will gain more from a visit to the **Fundación Vida Silvestre**, located at Defensa 251, 6o (1065) Buenos Aires (Mon–Fri 10am–1pm & 2–6pm; ⓣ011/4343-4086 or 4331-3631, ⓦwww.vidasilvestre.org.ar), a committed and highly professional environmental organization, and an associate of the WWF. Visit its shop for back issues of its beautiful magazine and for books and leaflets on wildlife and ecological issues, as well as for information on its nature reserves. Bird-watchers should visit the headquarters of the country's well-respected birding organization, **Aves Argentinas/Asociación Ornitológica del Plata**, at 25 de Mayo 749, 2o "6" (1002) Buenos Aires (Mon–Fri 3–8pm; ⓣ011/4312-1015, ⓦwww.avesargentinas.org.ar). They have an excellent library and a shop, and organize regular outings to the capital's prolific Costanera Sur marshland reserve, as well as **birding safaris** around the country. The $65 annual membership (US$75 outside Argentina) entitles you to their high-quality quarterly magazine, discounts on bird safaris, free access to the library and the possibility of getting involved in scientific and conservation work.

Each national park has its own **intendencia**, or park administration, although these are often in the principal access town, not within the park itself. An information office or visitors' centre is often attached, and you can usually buy fishing licences. Parks are frequently subdivided into more manageable units, the larger divisions of which are called **seccionales**, often with some sort of small information office of their own in the main building.

Argentina's **guardaparques**, or national park rangers, are some of the most professional on the continent: generally friendly, they are well trained and dedicated to jobs that are demanding and often extremely isolated. All have a good grounding in the wildlife of the region and are happy to share their knowledge, although don't expect them all to be professional naturalists – some are, but ranger duties often involve more contact with the general public than the wildlife. It's a good idea to register with the *guardaparque* before heading out on treks.

All national parks have routes of public access, though many of the ones in more isolated areas – Baritú, Perito Moreno and Santiago del Estero's Copo, for example – are not served by any public transport or even tour vehicles, and the only way to visit is to have your own transport. Some parks are **free**, but in the more touristy ones, there's often a **fee**, which is charged at the park gate. Scenic attractions thus serve to generate funds for less commercial parks that are still vitally important from an ecological perspective.

Camping is possible in many parks, and sites are graded according to three categories: *camping libre* sites, which are free but have no or very few services (perhaps a latrine and sometimes a shower block); *camping agreste* sites, which are run as concessions and usually provide hot water, showers, toilets, places for lighting a campfire and some sort of small shop; and *camping organizado* sites, which have more services, including electricity and often some sort of restaurant. In some areas, Bariloche being the most obvious example, local climbing clubs maintain a network of **refuges** for trekkers and climbers. These range from simple places with space for sleeping bags but no services to those that provide mattresses, meals and a shop.

Always try to be **environmentally responsible**. Stick to marked trails, camp only at authorized sites, take all litter with you (don't burn it), bury toilet waste at least 30m away from all water sources and use detergents and toothpastes as sparingly as possible, choosing biodegradable options such as glycerine soap. Above all, pay particular respect to the **fire risk**. Every year, fires destroy huge swathes of forest, and virtually all of these are started by hand: some deliberately, but most because of unpardonable negligence. As ever, one of the prime culprits is the cigarette butt, often casually tossed out of a car window, but just as bad are campfires, both those that are poorly tended and those that are poorly extinguished. Woodland becomes tinder-dry in summer droughts, and, especially in places such as Patagonia, it is vulnerable to sparks carried by the strong winds. Once started, winds, inaccessibility and limited water resources can turn fires into infernos that blaze for weeks on end, and much fire-damaged land never regenerates its growth. Many parks have a complete ban on lighting campfires and trekkers are asked to take **stoves** upon which to do their cooking; please respect this. Others ban fires during high-risk periods. The most environmentally responsible approach is to avoid lighting campfires at all: even dead wood has a role to play in often-fragile ecosystems. If you do need to light one, never choose a spot on peaty soil, as peat, once it has caught, becomes virtually impossible to put out. Choose a spot on stony or sandy soil, use only fallen wood and always extinguish the fire with water, not earth, stirring up the ashes to ensure all embers are quenched.

Culture and etiquette

Argentina's mores reflect its overwhelmingly European ancestry, and, apart from the language barrier, most foreigners will have little trouble fitting in.

Argentine society generally displays a pleasing balance between formal politeness and casual tolerance. When it comes to dress, Argentines are quite conservative, and take great pride in their appearance, but in the bigger cities in particular you will see examples of many different styles and subcultures. Outlandish clothing might raise eyebrows out in the provinces, but probably no more than it would in, say, deepest Wisconsin or Wiltshire.

Rules, regulations and bureaucracy

Argentines' rather cavalier attitude towards **rules** and considerations of health and safety is probably the biggest culture shock many foreigners have to deal with; the most obvious example of this is the anarchy you'll see on the roads, but you will also likely come across things such as loose wiring in hotels or wobbly cliff-top fencing. A complaint will probably get you no more than a shrug of the shoulders, though there are signs of a change in attitudes. Many visitors actually find the lack of regulations liberating.

Another difference is the Kafka-esque **bureaucracy** that you will bump up against if you're in the country for any length of time – when obtaining a visa, say, or picking up a parcel from the post office. Do not lose your temper if faced with a red-tape kind of situation – it will have absolutely no benefit and quite possibly hinder your cause. Take a book, and go submissively through whatever the process may be one step at a time; you are not going to change something that was inherited from Europe and has evolved over centuries through sheer force of will.

Sexual harassment and discrimination

Women planning on travelling alone to the country can do so with confidence. Some **machista** attitudes do persist – men usually pay in restaurants, and it is relatively unusual for groups of girls to go out drinking the way they might in Europe or the US – but the next generation seems to be shedding these inhibitions with alacrity and few people will find it strange that you are travelling unaccompanied. You will probably find you are the target of comments in the street and chat-up lines more frequently than you are accustomed to, but those responsible will not persist if you make it clear you're not interested. Such attentions are almost never hostile or physical – Italian-style bottom pinching is very rare here.

Greetings

When **greeting** people or taking your leave, it is normal to kiss everyone present on the cheek (just once, always the right cheek), even among men, who may emphasize their masculinity by slapping each other on the back. Shaking hands tends to be the preserve of businessmen or formal situations; if in doubt, watch the locals. One area of etiquette that will probably be new to you is the very Argentine custom of drinking *mate*, which comes with its own set of rules (see box, pp.392–393), but foreigners will be given lots of leeway here, as in other areas of social custom – *faux pas* are more likely to cause amusement than offence.

Drinking and smoking

Argentine attitudes to **drinking** tend to be similar to those in southern Europe: alcohol is fine in moderation, and usually taken with food. Public drunkenness is rare and frowned upon, though it occurs more frequently among the young than it used to. **Smoking** is fairly common among both sexes and all classes, although a number of areas, including Buenos Aires and Córdoba, have recently passed statutes making it illegal to smoke in enclosed public areas. Whether enforcement of this will continue remains to be seen – Argentine history is littered with laws that are obeyed patchily at best before being quietly disposed of.

Shopping

You will find no real tradition of **haggling** in Argentina, although you can always try it when buying pricey artwork, antiques, etc. Expensive services such as excursions and car rental are also obvious candidates for bargaining sessions, while hotel rates can be beaten down off season, late at night or if you're paying cash (*efectivo*). But try and be reasonable, especially in the case of already low-priced crafts or high-quality goods and services that are obviously worth every centavo.

Tipping

Tipping is not very common in Argentina, with a couple of exceptions. It's normal to round up taxi fares to the nearest 25 centavos (though not expected), and you should add a small gratuity to restaurant bills if service is not included. The kids who hang around taxi ranks to open and close doors also appreciate a coin.

Travel essentials

Costs

After a decade of peso-to-dollar parity the authorities bowed to international pressure at the beginning of 2002 and devalued the currency. The **Argentine peso** has remained stable at just over three to the US dollar ever since, with only slight fluctuations. All prices in this book are quoted in Argentine pesos ($) unless noted otherwise.

Argentina is one of the best-value destinations on the continent. Although a luxury holiday is still no giveaway anywhere in the country, it is possible to get by on a remarkably limited budget, and the top quality of just about everything, from wine to clothes and books to adventure trips, makes the occasional bitter pill of stiff prices much sweeter to swallow than in many other countries.

Student cards

These are not as useful as they can be in some countries, as museums and the like often refuse to give **student discounts**. Some bus companies, however, do give a ten- to fifteen- percent discount for holders of **ISIC cards**, as do certain hotels, laundries and outdoor gear shops, and even one or two ice-cream parlours. ASATEJ, Argentina's student travel agency, issues a booklet that lists partners throughout the country. The international student card often suffices for a discount at youth hostels in the country, though membership of the Youth Hostelling Association may entitle you to even lower rates.

Adhering to a reasonable **daily budget** is not impossible, but there are considerable regional variations. As a rule of thumb, the further south you travel the more you will need to stretch your budget. Roughly speaking, on average you'll need to plan on spending at least $370/US$120/£60 a week on a tight budget (sharing a dorm, eating snacks, limiting other spending), $1000/US$320/£160 staying in budget accommodation but not stinting and $7500/US$2400/£1200 or more a week to live in the lap of luxury. If you're **travelling alone**, reckon on adding up to fifty percent to these prices. For advice on tipping, see opposite.

Camping and self-catering are good ways of saving money, though the now-extensive network of youth hostels enables you to pay little without sleeping rough. **Accommodation** remains more expensive than in Peru or Bolivia, but is also rather more luxurious on the whole.

Eating out is extremely good value for money, as the quantities are generous and the quality reliable; you can save even more money by having your main meal at lunch time – especially by opting for the set menu (usually called *menú ejecutivo*). Home-grown fast-food equivalents tend to be better – healthier and cheaper, in any case – than the international chains. Picnicking is another option; local produce is often world-class and an alfresco meal of bread, cheese, ham or salami with fresh fruit and a bottle of table wine in a great location is a match for any restaurant feast.

Long-distance **transport** will eat up a considerable chunk of your expenses. The enormous distances to cover are obviously an important factor to bear in mind, and you may have to budget for some internal flights, so look out for special deals once you're there. Buses vary greatly in condition and price from one category to another. Some companies give student discounts, while others promote given destinations with special fares, so it's worth asking around. Remember, too, that the better companies usually give you free food and drink (of varying quality) on lengthy journeys, more than compensating for a slightly higher fare. Spacious and modern buses offering *coche cama* comfort overnight enable you to save the price of a room and are worthwhile options for covering the longest distances over less interesting terrain. City transport – including taxis and *remises* (radio taxis) – is extremely inexpensive, despite a series of government-authorized price rises, but then most cities are compact enough to walk around anyway.

Hotels, restaurants and big stores may ask for a hefty handling fee for credit-card payments (as high as twenty percent), while many businesses – and hotels in particular – will give you a fair-sized **discount for cash payments** (*efectivo* or *contado*) on the quoted price, though they may need prompting. Out of season, at weekends and during slow periods it is a good idea to bargain hotel prices down.

Be aware that many services, especially air travel (mainly with Aerolíneas Argentinas and LAN) and hotels, operate **dual pricing** – one price for Argentine residents (including foreigners) and another, often as much as three times more, for non-residents. Hotels and other types of commerce, especially at the luxury end of the market, may charge foreigners in US dollars, rather than Argentine pesos, as a covert but perfectly legal way of charging more. This practice is mostly found in more touristy locations such as Ushuaia and Bariloche, as well as the capital.

Crime and personal safety

With the effects of the recent economic crisis still lingering, Argentina has lost the reputation it enjoyed for many years as a totally safe destination. However, any concern you have should be kept in perspective – the actual likelihood of being a victim of crime remains small, and Argentina is still one of South America's safest countries in which to travel.

The more rural parts of the country should present no problems, but the usual precautions should be taken in large cities and some of the northern border towns, where poverty and easily available arms and drugs make opportunistic crime a more common occurrence. In Buenos Aires, incidents of violence and armed robbery have dramatically increased in recent years; this includes the wave of much-publicized "express kidnappings", where victims are bundled into cars and forced to get money out at ATMs or held for ransom. This unpleasant practice has affected locals more than tourists, and fortunately seems to be on the wane. Some potential pitfalls are outlined here, not to induce paranoia, but on the principle that to be forewarned is to be forearmed.

There are some **basic precautions** you should take to reduce the likelihood of being a victim of crime. First, only carry what you need for that day, and conceal valuable items such as cameras and jewellery. Be cautious when withdrawing cash from ATMs. Avoid bumbags (fanny packs), which are the equivalent of announcing that you are carrying valuables; for similar reasons, money belts are useful when travelling, but you should avoid pulling wads of cash out of them when out and about in the city. It's also worth packing a casual outfit for city days, if you have room – nothing announces that you are a tourist more definitely than hiking boots and trek clothing. Whatever you wear, you should always try to look like you know what you're doing or where you're going, even if you don't: muggers and con artists tend to pick on less confident-looking tourists. If you're not sure about the wisdom of walking somewhere, play it safe and take a cab – but call radio taxis or hail them in the street, rather than taking a waiting one. Don't wander around quiet areas, particularly after dark and on your own. At all times, keep your bag secure – across your shoulders, rather than over just one – and wrap the strap round your leg in bars and restaurants. Remember that pickpockets most commonly hang around markets, busy subway stations and bus terminals (particularly Retiro in the capital), and on crowded trains and buses. Finally, in the rare event of being held up at gunpoint, don't play the hero – your belongings are replaceable, but you're not.

Theft from **hotels** is rare, but do not leave valuables lying around. Use the hotel safe if there is one. Some hostels have lockers (it's worth having a padlock of your own), but in any case, reports of theft from these places are rare. Compared with other Latin American countries, you're unlikely to have things stolen on long-distance **buses**, but it makes sense to take your daypack with you when you disembark for meal stops, and, particularly at night, to keep your bag by your feet rather than on the overhead rack. However, pilfering from checked-in luggage on **flights** is quite common – don't leave anything of value in outside pockets, and lock your bag where possible. Airports have machines that will cover bags in plastic, for a small fee. **Car theft** has become a ridiculously common occurrence; if you are renting a car, check that the insurance will cover you, and always park in a car park or where someone will keep an eye on it. When driving in the city, keep windows closed and doors locked.

Noisy street demonstrations have long been a part of the fabric of Argentine urban life, even more so since the 2001 crisis. However, the chance of getting caught up in

Emergency numbers

Ambulance ☎107
Fire ☎100
Police ☎101
Tourist police in Buenos Aires ☎0800/999-5000

this kind of thing is very rare indeed – tourists are not targets and none has been hurt as a result of a demonstration. Though usually peaceful, demonstrations have turned violent in the past, however, and if so the police do not hesitate to use tear gas, so it is best to keep your distance. Roadblocks by unemployed *piqueteros*, particularly in the capital, are more of an annoyance in terms of traffic flow, and you should always allow plenty of time to arrive at your destination for this reason.

As elsewhere in Latin America, you should be aware of the possibility of **scams**. A popular one, especially in the tourist areas of Buenos Aires, is having mustard, ice cream or some similar substance "spilt" over you. Some person (or persons) then offers to help clean it off – cleaning you out at the same time. If this happens to you, push them off, get away from them fast and make as much noise as possible, shouting "thief!" ("*ladrón*!"), "police!" ("*policia*!") or for help ("*Socorro*!"). Note, too, that, though the police are entitled to check your documents, they have no right to inspect your money ortraveller's cheques: anyone who does is a con artist, and you should ask for their identification or offer to be taken to the police station (*gendarmería*). If you ever do get "arrested", never get into a vehicle other than an official police car.

Drugs are frowned upon, although perhaps not as much as in other parts of South America. Drug use, particularly of marijuana and cocaine, is fairly common amongst the younger generation, and quite openly celebrated in some popular song lyrics. However, despite a flirtation with marijuana decriminalization in the early 1990s (a ruling that has since been reversed), Argentine society at large doesn't draw much of a line between soft drugs and hard drugs and the penalties for either are stiff if you get caught. You're very much advised to steer clear of buying or openly partaking. As everywhere else, there are many slang words for drugs: common ones for marijuana include *porro, maconia* and *yerba;* for cocaine, *merca* and *papa.*

It's always advisable to take photocopies of important **documents** (passport with entrance stamp and entry card, airline tickets, insurance policy certificate and telephone numbers) in case of theft of the original: keep one with you, separate from the documents themselves, and leave another copy at home. You could also send yourself an email with the pertinent details. If you are unlucky enough to be the victim of a robbery (*asalto*) or lose anything of value, you will need to make a report at the nearest police station for insurance purposes. This is usually a time-consuming but fairly straightforward process. Check that the report includes a comprehensive account of everything lost and its value, and that the police add the date and an official stamp (*sello*). These reports do not cost anything.

Electricity

220V/50Hz is standard throughout the country. The sockets are two-pronged with round pins, but are different to the two-pin European plugs. **Adapters** will probably be needed and can be bought at a string of electrical shops along Calle Talcahuano, in Buenos Aires. Some, but not all, of the multi-adaptors on sale at airports will do the trick, so check the instructions.

Entry requirements

Citizens of the US, Canada, the UK, Ireland, Australia and New Zealand do not currently need a **visa** for tourist trips to Argentina of up to ninety days, but always verify this in advance with your local consulate. All visitors need a valid **passport** and will have to fill in a landing card (*tarjeta de entrada*) on arrival, when you will be given a stamp. In theory, this could be for thirty, sixty or ninety days, but in practice it's almost always ninety. If you are travelling alone with a child you may be requested to show a notarized document certifying both parents' permission for the child to travel. Keep your landing card safe, as you'll need to show it to leave the country. If you do lose it, it's rarely a serious problem, but you'll have to fill in a new form at the border control.

On entering the country, you will also be given a **customs declaration form**. Duty is not charged on used personal effects, books and other articles for non-commercial purposes, up to the value of US$300. Make sure you declare any valuable electronic items such as laptop computers, as customs

Government travel advisories

Australian Department of Foreign Affairs Ⓦwww.dfat.gov.au/zw-cgi/view/Advice/Argentina
British Foreign & Commonwealth Office Ⓦwww.fco.gov.uk.
Canadian Department of Foreign Affairs Ⓦwww.dfait-maeci.gc.ca.
Irish Department of Foreign Affairs Ⓦwww.irlgov.ie/iveagh.
New Zealand Ministry of Foreign Affairs Ⓦwww.mft.govt.nz.
US State Department Ⓦhttp://travel.state.gov/argentina.html.

officers can be suspicious that you may be bringing them into the country to sell.

You can **extend your stay** for a further ninety days by presenting your passport to the main immigration department, Dirección de Migraciones in Buenos Aires, at Av Antártida Argentina 1350, Retiro (Ⓣ011/4317-0237 or 4317-0238). This costs $100 and must be done on weekdays between 8am and 1pm; be prepared for a possible lengthy wait. You can do this extension, called a *prórroga,* once only. Alternatively, you could try leaving the country (the short hop to Colonia del Sacramento in Uruguay is a good option) and returning to get a fresh stamp. This usually works, but may be frowned upon if done repeatedly, and the provision of an extra stamp is totally at the discretion of the border guards. Some people manage to stay for a year or more on tourist visas, using a combination of brief trips abroad and an extension. If you do overshoot your stay, you can pay a $50 fine at Migraciones, who will give you a form that allows you to leave the country within ten days. This was a fairly common practice at the time of publication, but bear in mind that if you do this your stay in the country will be illegal and could potentially cause you problems. If you are crossing into **Chile**, make sure your papers are in order, as Chilean officials are considerably more scrupulous than their Argentine counterparts.

When leaving the country, you must obtain an **exit stamp**. At certain border controls, particularly in the north of the country, it is often up to you to ensure that the bus driver stops and waits while you get this – otherwise drivers may not stop, assuming that all passengers are Argentine nationals and don't need stamps. In some places (for example, Clorinda), your Argentine exit stamp is actually given on the far side of the border, but check this with the driver beforehand.

Visas for work or study must be obtained in advance from your consulate. Extensive paperwork, much of which must be translated into Spanish by a certified translator, is required; allow plenty of time before departure to start the process. The websites listed above have the details of what documentation is needed, or contact the consulate directly.

Although checks are rare, visitors are legally obliged to carry their passport as ID. You might get away with carrying a photocopy, but don't forget to copy your entrance stamp and landing card as well. In the majority of cases, this is acceptable to police, but getting a copy certified by a public notary increases its credibility.

Argentine embassies and consulates abroad

Australia

Embassy John McEwan House, Level 2, 7 National Circuit, Barton ACT 2600 Ⓣ02/6273-9111, Ⓦwww.argentina.org.au.
Consulate 44 Market St, Piso 20, Sydney, NSW Ⓣ02/9262-2933, Ⓦwww.argentina.org.au/consulado.

Canada

Embassy 90 Sparks St, Suite 910, Ottawa, Ontario K1P 5B4 Ⓣ613/236-2351, Ⓦwww.argentina-canada.net.
Consulates 2000 Peel St, 7th floor, Suite 600, Montréal, Québec H3A 2W5 Ⓣ514/842-6582, Ⓦwww.consargenmtl.com; 5001 Yonge St, Suite 201, Toronto, Ontario M2N 6P6 Ⓣ416/955-9190, Ⓦwww.consargtoro.ca.

New Zealand

Embassy Sovereign Assurance Building, Level 14, 142 Lambton Quay, PO Box 5430, Wellington Ⓣ04/472-8330, Ⓦwww.arg.org.nz.

UK

Embassy 65 Brook St, London W1K 4AH Ⓣ020/7318 1300, Ⓦwww.argentine-embassy-uk.org.

Consulate 27 Three Kings Yard, London W1K 4DF ⓣ020/7318 1340, ⓔfclond@mrecic.gov.ar.

US

Embassy 1600 New Hampshire Ave, NW, Washington DC 20009 ⓣ202/238-6401, ⓦwww.embajadaargentinaeeuu.org.
Consulates 245 Peachtree Center Ave, Suite 2101, Atlanta, Georgia 30303 ⓣ404/880-0805, ⓦwww.consuladoargentinoatlanta.org; 205 N Michigan Ave, Piso 42, Suite 4209, Chicago, IL 60601 ⓣ312/819-2610, ⓔargchic@aol.com; 3050 Post Oak Blvd, Suite 1625, Houston, TX 77056 ⓣ713/871-8935, ⓔchous_ar@hotmail.com; 5055 Wilshire Blvd Suite 210, Los Angeles, CA 90036 ⓣ323/954-9155, ⓦwww.consuladoargentino-losangeles.org; 800 Brickell Ave, Penthouse 1, Miami, FL 33131 ⓣ305/373-1889, ⓦwww.consuladoargentinoenmiami.com; 12 West 56th St, New York, NY 10019 ⓣ212/603-0400, ⓦwww.congenargentinany.com.

Embassies in Argentina

Australia

Buenos Aires Villanueva 1400, C1426BMJ ⓣ011/4779-3500.

Canada

Buenos Aires Tagle 2828, C1425EEH ⓣ011/4808-1000.

New Zealand

Buenos Aires Carlos Pellegrini 1427, 5th floor, CP1011 ⓣ011/4328-0747.

UK

Buenos Aires Dr Luis Agote 2412, C1425EOF ⓣ011/4808-2200.

US

Buenos Aires Av Colombia 4300, C1425GMN ⓣ011/5777-4533.

Gay and lesbian travellers

Despite remarkable progress in recent years, the attitude in Argentina towards gay men and lesbians is generally ambivalent. **Discreet relationships** are tolerated, but in this overwhelmingly Roman Catholic nation any "deviance", including any explicit physical contact between members of the same sex (let alone transvestism or overtly intimate behaviour) will be almost universally disapproved of, to say the least. Violent manifestations of **homophobia** are rare, however, especially now that the Church and the military have less influence, and homosexual acts between consenting adults have long been legal.

Gay and lesbian **associations** are springing up in the major cities, notably in Buenos Aires, where nightlife and meeting places are increasingly open (see p.166), but rural areas still do their best to act as if homosexuality doesn't exist. Psychotherapy enjoys the status of a pseudo-religion in Argentina, so don't be surprised to see analysts and "parapsychologists" advertising their "cures" – even in the pink press. Yet, one of the first pieces of legislation passed by parliament in 2003 afforded all citizens protection from discrimination, making a specific reference to sexual orientation. In the same year, the city of Buenos Aires legalized non-marriage unions for hetero-sexuals and homosexuals alike, with several gay couples tying the knot in highly publicized ceremonies.

Contacts for gay and lesbian travellers

You'll find listed below some of the main companies and organizations catering for gay and lesbian travellers, in a number of countries including Argentina itself; English is widely spoken in the country's well-travelled gay community.

In Argentina

Adia Turismo Av Córdoba 836, 9th floor, Office 907, Buenos Aires ⓣ011/4393-0531, ⓦwww.adiatur.com. Dynamic tour operator organizing tours for gays and lesbians in Buenos Aires, the Cuyo, Mesopotamia, the Northwest and Patagonia.
Bue Gay Argentina Pueyrredón 2031, 1st floor, B, Buenos Aires ⓣ011/4805-1401, ⓦwww.buegay.com.ar. Young company concentrating on city tours and activity vacations around the country, accompanied by gay tour guides.
Calu Travel Service Paraguay 946, Buenos Aires ⓣ011/4325-5477, ⓦwww.calutravel.com.ar. Versatile, professional company offering all kinds of travel services and running its own gay beach resort (Calu Beach) – the only one in the country – at Mar del Plata.

Pride Travel Paraguay 523, 2nd floor, E, Buenos Aires ⓣ011/5218-6556, ⓦwww.pride-travel.com. Argentine travel agent offering air tickets, day-trips, tours and adventure tourism aimed at gay and lesbian travellers.

In the US and Canada

Ferrari Publications PO Box 37887,
International Gay & Lesbian Travel Association 4331 N Federal Hwy, Suite 304, Ft Lauderdale, FL 33308 ⓣ1-800/448-8550, ⓦwww.iglta.org. Trade group that can provide a list of gay- and lesbian-owned or -friendly travel agents, accommodation and other travel businesses.
Out and About Travel Providence, RI ⓣ1-800/842-4753, ⓦwww.outandaboutravel.com. Gay- and lesbian-oriented cruises, tours and packages.

In the UK

ⓦwww.gaytravel.co.uk Online gay and lesbian travel agent offering good deals on all types of holidays. Also lists gay- and lesbian-friendly hotels around the world.
Madison Travel 118 Western Rd, Hove, East Sussex BN3 1DB ⓣ01273/202 532, ⓦwww.madisontravel.co.uk. Established travel agents specializing in packages to gay- and lesbian-friendly mainstream destinations.

In Australia and New Zealand

Gay and Lesbian Travel PO Box 208, Darlinghurst, NSW 1300 ⓣ02/9380 4115, ⓦwww.galta.com.au. Directory and links for gay and lesbian travel worldwide.
Silke's Travel 263 Oxford St, Darlinghurst, NSW 2010 ⓣ02/9380 6244 or 1800/807 860, ⓔsilba@magna.com.au. Long-established gay and lesbian specialist, with the emphasis on women's travel.

Gay resources on the Web

Gay Argentina ⓦwww.ar.gay.com. Directory and links for gay and lesbian travel in Argentina.
Gay Information in Argentina ⓦwww.nexo.org. Perhaps the most comprehensive gay info website in the country, with latest news on gay life, the gay community, culture, politics and what's going on in the rest of the world, too.
Gay Places to Stay ⓦwww.gayplaces2stay.com. Information about gay-friendly accommodation worldwide.
Gay Travel ⓦwww.gaytravel.com. The most helpful site for trip planning, bookings and general information about international travel.
Nexo ⓦwww.nexo.org. The best site for finding out latest news and venues in Argentina.
Out and About ⓦwww.outandabout.com. Gay travel newsletter with back issues on gay life in Argentina and Brazil.
Viajar Travel ⓦwww.viajartravel.com. Adventure travel specialists with lots of information about South America.

Health

Travel to Argentina doesn't raise any major **health** worries and with a small dose of precaution and a handful of standard vaccinations (tetanus, polio, typhoid and hepatitis A) you are unlikely to encounter any serious problems. A bout of **travellers' diarrhoea**, as your body adjusts to local micro-organisms in the food and water, is the most you're likely to have to worry about. It's best to ease yourself gently into the local diet – the sudden ingestion of generous quantities of red meat, beefy wine, strong coffee and sweet pastries can be very unsettling for a stomach used to gentler repasts. The tap water in Argentina is generally safe to drink, if sometimes heavily chlorinated, but you may prefer to err on the side of caution in rural areas in the north of the country. Mineral water is good and widely available.

Argentine **pharmacies** are plentiful, well-stocked and a useful port of call for help with minor medical problems; the staff may offer simple diagnostic advice and will often help dress wounds, but if in doubt consult a doctor. You'll find a wider range of medicines available without **prescription** here than in many other countries and, while the brand names will undoubtedly be different, if you have the packaging of the product you're looking for, take it along so the pharmacist can find you the local equivalent. Medicines and cosmetic products are fairly expensive, however, as they are mostly imported, so if you have room, take plenty of supplies.

The easiest way to get treatment for more serious ailments is to visit the outpatient department of a **hospital**, where treatment will usually be free. In Buenos Aires, the Hospital de Clínicas, José de San Martín, Av Córdoba 2351 (ⓣ011/4961-6001), is a particularly efficient place to receive medical advice and prescriptions; you can simply walk in and, for a small fee, make an on-the-spot appointment with the relevant specialist department – English-speaking doctors can usually be found. For a list of English-speaking doctors throughout the country, contact the British, Australian, New Zealand, Canadian or US embassy in Buenos Aires. For emergencies or ambulances in Argentina, dial ⓣ107.

Though your chances of contracting any of the following **diseases** are very low, they are sufficiently serious that you should be aware of their existence and of measures you should take to avoid infection. For up-to-date information on current health risks in Argentina check ⓦwww.cdc.gov and ⓦwww.medicineplanet.com.

Chagas' disease is transmitted by a microscopic parasite, the *Trypanosoma cruzi*, which is transported by a small beetle, the vinchuca or chinche gaucha. The parasite-bearing beetle bites its "victim" and then defecates next to the wound. Scratching of the bite then causes the parasite to be borne into the bloodstream. The immediate symptoms – a fever, a hard swelling on the skin and occasionally around the eyes – last two to three weeks, are mild and may even be imperceptible. The disease is treatable at this stage. In around twenty percent of untreated cases, however, potentially fatal cardiac problems caused by a gross enlargement of the heart can appear twenty or thirty years later, with no other symptoms suffered in between. Though it can be extremely serious, the disease isn't widespread and travellers should be aware of, but not unduly worried about, catching it. Contact is most likely to occur in poorer rural regions, particularly in dwellings with adobe walls. Where possible you should avoid camping in such areas, but if you do sleep in an adobe hut, you should use a mosquito net and sling your hammock as far away from the walls as possible. If you suspect you have been bitten by a vinchuca, avoid scratching the wound; instead, bathe it with alcohol and get a blood test as soon as possible.

Cholera outbreaks are very rare, but there have been sporadic cases in the Northwest. If travelling in an area where there is an outbreak, you should exercise extreme caution with food, particularly shellfish (though this is pretty rare, anyway, in the main areas concerned), and drinking water. There is an immunization for cholera, but it's so ineffective as to be considered worthless by the World Health Organization.

Dengue fever is a viral disease transmitted by mosquitoes. The symptoms are a high fever, headache and eye and muscular pain; it can be very debilitating but is rarely fatal. Dengue fever occurs in urban areas in the north of Argentina, especially close to the Paraguayan border; there are regular public health campaigns aimed at avoiding outbreaks, principally by making sure that stagnant water cannot collect. There is no vaccination against dengue fever, though the disease is treatable, and the best way to avoid the slim chance of infection is by covering up during the day (unlike malarial mosquitoes, dengue mosquitoes bite during the day) and using mosquito repellent.

Hantavirus is a rare, incurable viral disease transmitted by long-tailed wild mice. The virus is present in the excrement, urine and saliva of the mouse, and is transmitted to humans through breathing in contaminated air, consuming contaminated food or water or by being bitten by or handling a virus-bearing mouse. The disease occurs throughout the Americas (though not in the far south of Patagonia) and produces haemorrhagic fever and severe respiratory problems. Initial symptoms are similar to influenza – with fever, headache, stomach-ache and muscle pain – but the fatality rate is around fifty percent. The disease cannot survive sunlight, detergent or disinfectant: the best way to avoid contamination is by being scrupulously clean when camping, particularly in rural areas. Recommended precautions include using tents with proper floors, good fastenings and no holes; keeping food in sealed containers and out of reach of mice (hanging a knotted carrier bag from a tree is a standard precaution) and cleaning up properly after eating. If staying in a *cabaña* that looks as if it hasn't been used for a while, let the place ventilate for a good thirty minutes before checking (while covering your mouth and nose with a handkerchief) for signs of mouse excrement. If any is found, all surfaces should be disinfected, then swept and aired. Despite the severity of Hantavirus, you should not be unduly worried about the disease. In the unlikely case that there is an outbreak in the area you are visiting you will be informed by the local authorities of the virus's presence.

HIV and AIDS cases have been climbing steadily in Argentina in recent years; according to national statistics, around two percent of the adult population between 15 and 49 years carry HIV. Note that some of the condoms sold in Argentina are of pretty poor quality, so it's wise to bring a reliable brand with you.

Malaria is a minor risk in Argentina, confined to (mostly off-the-beaten-track) parts of Salta and Jujuy provinces (the low-lying bits of Iruya, San Martín, Santa Victoria, Ledesma, San Pedro and Santa Bárbara departments), and the far northern borders of Corrientes and Misiones (not Iguazú) from October to May. Though the risk is low, it's certainly worth taking anti-malarial precautions if you are visiting these regions. Fortunately, resistance to the standard anti-malarial drug Chloroquine has not yet been reported. Guard against mosquito bites by covering up after dusk, using insect repellent and, where possible, mosquito nets and anti-mosquito coils or plug-ins, both of which are widely available in Argentina and often provided in hotels.

Rabies is theoretically present throughout Argentina, though the last known case of transmission to humans dates back to the 1960s. If you are planning on travelling in areas where you are likely to come into contact with wild animals, you might consider getting vaccinated before you go if doing so will put your mind at rest. The vaccine doesn't make you immune to the disease, but does buy you more time if you are bitten – though you will still need to receive a second jab.

Yellow fever is a very serious mosquito-borne viral disease occurring in subtropical and tropical forested regions, particularly where there are monkeys. It's a minor risk in the northeast of Argentina, but it is a wise precaution to invest in a ten-year vaccination for longer trips – and essential if you are travelling elsewhere in Latin America.

Puna (altitude sickness)

Altitude sickness is a potentially – if very rarely – fatal condition encountered at anything over 2000m, but likeliest and most serious at altitudes of 4000m and above. It can cause severe difficulties, but a little preparation should help you avoid the worst of its effects. In many South American countries it is known by the Quichoa word *soroche*, but in Argentina it is most commonly, and confusingly, called *puna* (the local word for altiplano, or high Andean steppes). You'll also hear the verb *apunar* and the word *apunamiento*, referring to the state of suffering from *puna*, whether affecting humans or vehicles (which also need to be adjusted for these heights).

First, to avoid the effects of the *puna*, don't rush anywhere – walk slowly and breathe steadily – and make things easier on yourself by not smoking. Whenever possible, **acclimatize**: it's better to spend a day or two at around 2000m and then 3000–3500m before climbing to 4000m or more rather than force the body to cope with a sudden reduction in oxygen levels. Make sure you're fully **rested**; an all-night party isn't the best preparation for a trip up into the Andes. Alcohol is also best avoided both prior to and during high-altitude travel; the best thing to **drink** is plenty of still water – never fizzy because it froths over and can even explode at high altitudes – or tea. **Eating**, too, needs some consideration: digestion uses up considerable quantities of oxygen, so snacking is preferable to copious meals. Carry supplies of high-energy cereal bars, chocolate, dried fruit (the local raisins, prunes and dried apricots are delicious), walnuts or cashews, crackers and biscuits, and avoid anything that ferments in the stomach, such as milk, fresh fruit and juices, vegetables or acidic food – they're guaranteed to make you throw up if you're affected. The best form of sugar to ingest is honey, because it's the least acidic. Grilled meat is fine, so *asados* are all right, but don't over-indulge. If you're **driving** into the altiplano make sure that your vehicle's engine has been properly adjusted. All engines labour because of the low oxygen levels, so don't try to force the pace: stay in low gears and go easy on the air-conditioning. Take care also with items such as ink pens and screw-top tubes and bottles of shampoo or creams – the low pressure at these altitudes may cause them to burst or leak.

Minor symptoms of the *puna*, such as headaches or a strange feeling of pressure inside the skull, nausea, loss of appetite, insomnia or dizziness, are nothing to worry about, but more severe problems, such as persistent migraines, repeated vomiting, severe breathing difficulties, excessive fatigue and a marked reduction in the need to urinate are of more concern. If you suffer from any of these, return to a lower altitude and seek out medical advice at once. Severe respiratory problems should be treated immediately with oxygen, carried by tour operators on excursions to 3000m or more as a legal requirement, but you're unlikely ever to need it (see more information relating to Aconcagua on p.532).

Sunstroke and sunburn

You should take the sun very seriously in Argentina. The north of the country, especially the Chaco region and La Rioja Province, is one of the hottest regions of Latin America in summer – temperatures regularly rocket above the forty-degree mark; the extended siestas taken by locals are wise precautions against the debilitating effects of the midday heat. Where possible, avoid excessive activity between about 11am and 4pm and when you do have to be out in the sun, wear sunscreen and a hat. You should also drink plenty of liquids – but not alcohol – and always make sure you have a sufficient supply of water when embarking on a hike. Throughout the country, the sun can be extremely fierce and even people with darker skin should use a much higher factor sunscreen than they might normally: using factor 15 or above is a sensible precaution. Remember that the cooler temperatures in the south are deceptive – ozone depletion and long summer days here can be more hazardous than the fierce heat of the north.

Medical resources for travellers

Up-to-date information about travel-related health issues can be obtained from the organizations listed below.

US and Canada

CDC ⓣ1-877/394-8747, ⓦwww.cdc.gov/travel. Official US government travel health site.

International Association for Medical Assistance to Travellers (IAMAT) 417 Center St, Lewiston, NY 14092 ⓣ716/754-4883; 1287 St. Clair Avenue West, Suite #1, Toronto, Ontario M6E 1B8 ⓣ416/652-0137; ⓦwww.iamat.org. A nonprofit organization supported by donations, it can provide a list of English-speaking doctors in Argentina, climate charts and leaflets on various diseases and inoculations.

International Society for Travel Medicine ⓣ1-770/736-7060, ⓦwww.istm.org. Has a full list of travel health clinics.

Canadian Society for International Health ⓦwww.csih.org. Extensive list of travel health centres.

UK and Ireland

British Airways Travel Clinics ⓣ0845/600 2236, ⓦwww.britishairways.com/travel/healthclinintro/public/en_gb.

Hospital for Tropical Diseases Travel Clinic ⓣ0845/155 5000 or ⓣ020/7387 4411, ⓦwww.thehtd.org.

MASTA (Medical Advisory Service for Travellers Abroad) ⓣ0870/606 2782 for the nearest clinic, ⓦwww.masta.org.

Travel Medicine Services ⓣ028/9031 5220.

Tropical Medical Bureau Republic of Ireland ⓣ1850/487 674, ⓦwww.tmb.ie.

Australia, New Zealand and South Africa

Travellers' Medical and Vaccination Centre ⓣ1300/658 844, ⓦwww.tmvc.com.au. Lists travel clinics in Australia, New Zealand and South Africa.

Insurance

It is a good idea to take out an insurance policy before travelling abroad to cover against theft, loss and illness or injury. Before paying for a new policy, however, it's worth checking whether you are already covered: some home insurance policies may cover your possessions when overseas, and many private medical schemes include cover when abroad. In Canada, provincial health plans usually provide partial cover for medical mishaps overseas, while holders of official student/teacher/youth cards in the US and Canada are entitled to meagre accident coverage and hospital in-patient benefits. Students will often find that their student health coverage extends during the vacations and for one term beyond the date of last enrollment.

After checking out the possibilities above, you might want to contact a specialist travel insurance company, or consider the travel insurance deal we offer (see below). A typical travel insurance policy usually provides cover for the loss of baggage, tickets and – up to a certain limit – cash or cheques, as well as cancellation or curtailment of your journey. Most of them exclude so-called dangerous sports unless an extra premium is paid: in Argentina this can mean scuba-diving, white-water rafting, windsurfing and trekking, though probably not kayaking or jeep safaris. Many policies can be chopped and changed to exclude coverage you don't need – for example, sickness and accident benefits can often be excluded or included at will. If you do take medical coverage, ascertain whether benefits will be paid as treatment proceeds or only after you return home, and if there is a 24-hour medical emergency number. When securing baggage cover, make sure that the per-article limit – typically under £500/$750 and sometimes as little as £250/$400 – will cover your most valuable possession. If you need to make a claim, you should keep receipts for medicines and medical treatment, and in the event you have anything stolen, you must obtain an official statement from the police.

Rough Guides has teamed up with Columbus Direct to offer you **travel insurance** that can be tailored to suit your needs. Products include a low-cost **backpacker** option for long stays; a **short break** option for city getaways; a typical **holiday package** option; and others. There are also annual **multi-trip** policies for those who travel regularly. Different sports and activities (trekking, skiing, etc) can be usually be covered if required.

See our website (ⓦwww.roughguides.com/insurance) for eligibility and purchasing options. Alternatively, UK residents should call ⓣ0870/033 9988; Australians should call ⓣ1300/669 999 and New Zealanders should call ⓣ0800/55 9911. All other nationalities should call ⓣ+44 870/890 2843.

Internet

Most villages in Argentina have public places where you can access the **Internet**. There's the odd cybercafé, but you'll mostly find access is via the *locutorios* (see p.74). Rates vary considerably, from $1 to $9 an hour, with the highest rates in Patagonia. In Buenos Aires, most places have fast cable modems, but out in the sticks it can be painfully slow. The Spanish **keyboard** is prevalent; if you have problems locating the "@" symbol (called *arroba* in Spanish), try holding the "Alt" key down and type 64.

Laundry

Most towns and cities have a plentiful supply of **laundries** (*lavanderías* or *lavaderos*), especially since not everyone has a washing machine. Laverap is a virtually nationwide chain of laundries and is mostly dependable. Some of them also do dry-cleaning, though you may have to go to a *tintorería*. Self-service places are almost unheard of; you normally give your name and leave your washing to pick it up later. Laundry is either charged by weight or itemized, but **rates** are not excessive, especially compared with the high prices charged by hotels. Furthermore, the quality is good and the service is usually quick and reliable. One important word of vocabulary to know is **planchado** (ironed).

Living and working in Argentina

More and more foreigners are choosing to **stay** in Argentina long term, and if you want to take the plunge, you will be in good company. Organizations that cater to expats include YesBA (the Young Expatriates Society of Buenos Aires; ⓦwww.yesba.org), who meet up in the capital on a regular basis and organize club nights etc; the South American Explorers' Club, which now has a Buenos Aires clubhouse (see p.94); and the website/online forum at ⓦwww.livinginargentina.com. Remember that tourist visas are usually valid for ninety days; visa renewal means an encounter with immigration services, as does the often-frustrating process of trying to obtain some form of **residence permit** (usually granted only if you have an Argentine spouse or make a sizeable investment In the national economy). Many medium-term residents simply leave the country from time to time (classically hopping across to Colonia, in Uruguay), to get a new three-month stamp, but this approach might not be tolerated over many years.

As far as **working** is concerned, remember Argentines themselves compete for the few jobs on offer and your entry into the employment market may not be looked upon kindly; also, unless you are on a contract with an international firm or organization, you will be paid in pesos, which will inevitably add up to a pretty low salary by global standards, though of course it will stretch a lot further. If you're determined anyway, many English-speaking foreigners do the obvious thing and **teach** English. Training in this is an advantage but by no means necessary; the demand for native English-speaking teachers is so high that many soon build up a roster of students via the odd newspaper ad and word of mouth. Working in **tourism** is another possibility – a fair proportion of agencies and hotels are run by foreigners; consider also translation if you have the language ability.

If you need a **place to stay**, look out for *pensiones*, which offer monthly rates. Try the notice boards at the Universidad de Buenos Aires' language faculty at 25 de Mayo 221 or the Asatej travel agency at Florida 835, 3rd floor, where Porteños offering rooms to foreigners often advertise, or the classified sections of the daily papers *Clarín* and the *Buenos Aires Herald*. There are also **websites** – one is Ⓦwww.alojargentina.com – offering information in English on alternative accommodation in Buenos Aires, primarily in shared apartments, university residences and B&B-type establishments, as well as reservations. Otherwise, renting can be difficult, as you need somebody who owns property to be your guarantor; two-year contracts are the norm.

Study and work programmes

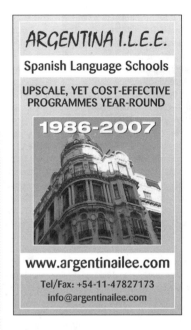

AFS Intercultural Programmes US Ⓣ1-800/AFS-INFO, Canada Ⓣ1-800/361-7248 or 514-288-3282, UK Ⓣ0113/242 6136, Australia Ⓣ1300/131 736 or Ⓣ02/9215 0077, New Zealand Ⓣ0800/600 300 or 04/494 6020, South Africa Ⓣ11/447 2673, international enquiries Ⓣ1-212-807-8686, Ⓦwww.afs.org. Intercultural exchange organization with programmes in over fifty countries.

American Institute for Foreign Study US Ⓣ1-866/906-2437, Ⓦwww.aifs.com. Language study and cultural immersion, as well as au pair programmes.

Council on International Educational Exchange (CIEE) US Ⓣ1-800/40-STUDY or Ⓣ1-207/533-7600, UK Ⓣ020/8939 9057, Ⓦwww.ciee.org. Leading NGO offering study programmes and volunteer projects around the world.

Earthwatch Institute US Ⓣ1-800/776-0188 or 978-461/0081, UK Ⓣ01865/318 838, Australia Ⓣ03/9682 6828, Ⓦwww.earthwatch.org. Scientific expedition project that spans over fifty countries with environmental and archeological ventures worldwide.

Mail

Argentina's rather unreliable privatized **postal service**, Correo Argentino, is the *bête noire* of many a hapless expat. Not only is it costly to send post to North America or Europe (starting at $4 for a postcard), but many items also never arrive. If you want to **send mail abroad**, always use the *certificado* (registered post) system, which costs about

$11 for a letter, but increases chances of arrival. The smaller OCA company is more reliable than Correo Argentino but also more expensive ($10 is the cheapest tariff for an international letter). Safer still is Correo Argentino's *encomienda* system (around $100 for a package under 1kg to Europe or the US), a **courier-style** service; if you are sending something important or irreplaceable, it is highly recommended that you use this service or a similar international one such as UPS (☎0800/2222-877) or DHL (☎0810/222-345). For regular airmail, expect delivery times of one to two weeks – the quickest deliveries, unsurprisingly, are those out of Buenos Aires. You are not permitted to seal envelopes with sticky tape: they must be gummed down (glue is usually available at the counter). The good news is that as well as post offices, many *locutorios*, lottery kiosks and small stores deal with mail, which means you don't usually have to go very far to find somewhere open.

Receiving mail is generally even more fraught with difficulties than sending it. Again, a courier-style service is your best bet; if not, make sure the sender at least registers the letter or parcel. All **parcels** go to the international office at Retiro, in Buenos Aires, and you will receive a card informing you that it is there; you will have to pay customs duties and should expect a long wait. If you are elsewhere in the country you may be able to have the parcel sent on to the main post office near you. All post offices keep **poste restante** for up to a year. Items should be addressed clearly, with the recipient's surname in capital letters and underlined, followed by their first name in regular script, then "Poste Restante" or "Lista de Correos", Correo Central, followed by the rest of the address. Buenos Aires city is normally referred to as Capital Federal to distinguish it from its neighbouring province. Bring your passport to collect items ($4 fee per item).

For sending **packages within Argentina**, your best bet it to use the *encomienda* services offered by bus companies (seal boxes in brown paper to prevent casual theft by tampering). This isn't a door-to-door service like the post: the recipient must collect the package from its end destination (bring suitable ID). By addressing the package to yourself, this system makes an excellent and remarkably good-value way of reducing the weight in your pack whilst travelling, but be aware that companies usually keep an *encomienda* for only one month before returning it to its original sender. If sending an *encomienda* to Buenos Aires, check whether it gets held at the Retiro bus station (the most convenient) or at a bus depot elsewhere in the capital. Non-local letters take a week to arrive.

Maps

There are a number of **country maps** available outside Argentina, including the **Rough Guides'** detailed, indestructible Argentina map, complete with comprehensive gazetteer. Other than the maps in this book, the best city map of Buenos Aires is the brilliant **Insight Fleximap**, which is clear, reliable and easy to fold.

Within Argentina, **road maps** can be obtained at bookshops and kiosks in all big towns and cities or at service stations. Many maps aren't up to date or contain a surprising number of errors: it's often a good idea to buy a couple of maps and compare them as you go along, always checking with the locals to see whether a given road does exist and is passable, especially with the vehicle you intend to use. The most reliable maps are those produced by **ACA** (Automóvil Club), which does individual maps for each province, to varying degrees of accuracy. These are widely available at ACA offices, kiosks on Calle Florida in the capital and service stations. Glossy and fairly clear – but at times erratic – regional road maps (Cuyo, Northwest, Lake District, etc) are produced by **AutoMapa** and are often available at petrol stations and bookshops. Slightly more detailed but a tad less accurate is the mini-atlas *Atlas Vial* published by **YPF**, the national petrol company and sold at their service stations. For Buenos Aires, there's an excellent series by **Mapa de Dios** (Ⓦwww.dediosonline.com), sold in bookshops, with themes such as restaurants, tango and shopping.

For 1:100,000 **ordnance survey-style maps**, the Instituto Geográfico Militar at Av Cabildo 381 in Buenos Aires is the place to go (Mon–Fri 8.30am–4pm; Ⓦwww.igm.gov.ar). These topographical and colour satellite maps are great to look at and very detailed, but they're not really very practical unless you're used to maps of this type.

Map outlets

As well as over-the-counter sales, most of the outlets listed below allow you to order and pay for maps by mail, over the phone and via the Internet. These are specialist outlets rather than the bigger, more general bookstores.

In the US and Canada

Distant Lands 56 S Raymond Ave, Pasadena, CA 91105 Ⓣ1-800/310-3220, Ⓦwww.distantlands.com.
Longitude Books 115 W 30th St #1206, New York, NY 10001 Ⓣ1-800/342-2164, Ⓦwww.longitudebooks.com.
Travel Bug Bookstore 3065 W Broadway, Vancouver, BC, V6K 2G9 Ⓣ604/737-1122, Ⓦwww.travelbugbooks.ca.
World of Maps 1235 Wellington St, Ottawa, ON, K1Y 3A3 Ⓣ1-800/214-8524 or Ⓣ613/724-6776, Ⓦwww.worldofmaps.com.

In the UK and Ireland

Stanfords 12–14 Long Acre, London WC2E 9LP Ⓣ020/7836 1321, Ⓦwww.stanfords.co.uk. One of the best travel bookshops in the world, with a global catalogue, expert knowledge and worldwide mail order. Also at 39 Spring Gardens, Manchester Ⓣ0161/831 0250, and 29 Corn St, Bristol Ⓣ0117/929 9966.
Easons Bookshop 40 O'Connell St, Dublin 1 Ⓣ01/858 3881, Ⓦwww.eason.ie.
National Map Centre Ireland 34 Aungier St, Dublin Ⓣ01/476 0471, Ⓦwww.mapcentre.ie.

In Australia and New Zealand

Mapland 372 Little Bourke St, Melbourne Ⓣ03/9670 4383, Ⓦwww.mapland.com.au.
Map World (Australia) 371 Pitt St, Sydney Ⓣ02/9261 3601, Ⓦwww.mapworld.net.au. Also at 900 Hay St, Perth Ⓣ08/9322 5733, Jolimont Centre, Canberra Ⓣ02/6230 4097 and 1981 Logan Road, Brisbane Ⓣ07/3349 6633.
Map World (New Zealand) 173 Gloucester St, Christchurch Ⓣ0800/627 967, Ⓦwww.mapworld.co.nz.

Money

The Argentine peso, divided into one hundred centavos, is represented in this book by "$".

Since mid-2002 the exchange rate against the US dollar has fluctuated slightly around or just above the three-peso mark. Notes come in 2, 5, 10, 20, 50 and 100 denominations, while 1 peso and 1 (rare), 5, 10, 25 and 50 centavo coins are in circulation. Sometimes people are loath to give change, as coins can be in short supply, so it's a good idea to have plenty of loose change on your person; otherwise insist that they find change if they want to do business. Ask for small denomination notes at banks if possible, break bigger ones up at places where they obviously have plenty of change (busy shops, supermarkets and post offices), and withdraw odd amounts from ATMs ($190, $340, etc) to avoid getting your cash dispensed in $100 bills only – trying to buy a drink, an empanada or a postcard with a crisp $100 note can be a frustrating ordeal and won't make you many friends. Argentine money is difficult to change outside the country, except in Uruguay and border areas of Bolivia, Brazil and Paraguay, where it may even be used as legal tender.

You can check current **exchange rates** and convert figures on Ⓦwww.xe.net/currency.

Taxes

IVA (*Impuesto de Valor Agregado*) is the Argentine equivalent of VAT or **sales tax** and is usually included in the price displayed or

Currency notation

When you see the $ sign in Argentina – and throughout this book – you can safely assume that the currency being referred to is the Argentine peso. Where a price is quoted in US dollars, the normal notation in Argentina – and the notation we use – is US$.

quoted for most goods and services. The major exceptions are some hotels, which quote their rates before tax, plus airfares and car rental fees. IVA is currently a hefty **21 percent** and is added to everything except food and medicines. It is worth knowing that foreigners can often get IVA reimbursed on many purchases, though this is practical only for bigger transactions (over $100) and subject to all kinds of limits and complications. Shops in the more touristy areas will volunteer information and provide the necessary forms, but finding the right place to go to have the final paperwork completed, signed and stamped and to get your money back, at your point of exit (international airports), is a much taller order; ask for instructions when you check in, as you must display your purchases before check-in and then go through the often frustratingly slow formalities once you've been given your boarding pass.

ATMs and credit and debit cards

ATMs (*cajeros automáticos*) are plentiful in Argentina. It's rare that you'll find a town or even a village without one, though you can sometimes be caught out in very remote places, especially in the Northwest, so never rely completely on them. Most machines take all credit cards or display those that can be used: you can nearly always get money out with Visa or Mastercard, or with any cards linked to the Plus or Cirrus systems. Most ATMs are either Banelco or LINK – test the networks to see which works best with your card. Machines are mostly multilingual though some of them use Spanish only, so you might need to have a phrase book or a Spanish-speaker handy.

Credit cards (*tarjetas de crédito*) are a very handy source of funds, and can be used either in the abundant ATMs or for purchases. Visa and Mastercard are the most widely used and recognized, with American Express and Diners Club less likely to be accepted. Be warned that you might have to show your ID when making a purchase with plastic, and, especially in small establishments in remote areas, the authorization process can take ages and may not succeed at all. Using your **debit card**, which is not liable to interest payments like credit cards, is usually the best method to get cash and the flat transaction fee is generally quite small – your bank will able to advise on this. Make sure you have a card and personal identification number (PIN) that are designed to work overseas.

Traveller's cheques

Unfortunately, **traveller's cheques** are not really a viable option in Argentina. They can almost never be used like cash and fewer and fewer banks seem to accept them. Those places that do accept them charge exorbitant commission and take quite a while to fill out all the paperwork. If you do take a stock of traveller's cheques (as a precaution in case your credit card goes astray) make sure they're in US dollars and are one of the main brands, such as American Express – their own, not those issued by a bank with the Amex logo – and that your signature is 100 percent identical to that in your passport, down to the colour of the ink. Be scrupulously careful when countersigning the cheques – you will be watched like a hawk as you do so. **Casas de cambio** tend to be the best bet for changing the cheques; the opening hours for these vary from region to region but on the whole they are open from 9am to 6pm, perhaps closing for lunch or siesta. A few are open on Saturday mornings but Sunday opening is virtually non-existent. Tourist offices should be able to tell you where you can changetraveller's cheques, but be prepared for blank looks. Banks may also be able to give you a **cash advance** on your credit card, though again this may be expensive.

Wiring money

Having money **wired from home** using one of the companies listed below is never convenient or cheap, and should be considered a last resort. It's possible to have money wired directly from a bank in your home country to a bank in Argentina, although this is somewhat less reliable because it involves two separate institutions. If you go this route, your home bank will need the address of the branch bank where you want to pick up the money and the address and telex number of the Buenos Aires head office, which will act as the clearing house; wiring money this way normally takes two working days.

Money-wiring companies

Travelers Express/MoneyGram US ☎1-800/444-3010, Canada ☎1-800/933-3278, UK, Ireland and New Zealand ☎00800/6663 9472, Australia ☎0011800/6663 9472; Ⓦwww.moneygram.com.
Western Union US & Canada ☎1-800/CALL-CASH, Australia ☎1800/501 500, New Zealand ☎0800/005 253, UK ☎0800/833 833, Republic of Ireland ☎66/947 5603; Ⓦwww.westernunion.com (customers in the US and Canada can send money online). Works through all post offices in Argentina.

Opening hours

Most **shops and services** are open Monday to Friday 9am to 7pm, and Saturday 9am to 2pm. Outside the capital, they may close at some point during the afternoon for between one and five hours. As a rule, the further north you go the longer the siesta – often offset by later closing times in the evening. Supermarkets seldom close during the day and are generally open much later, often until 8 or even 10pm, and on Saturday afternoons. Large shopping malls don't close before 10pm and their food and drink sections (*patios de comida*) may stay open as late as midnight. Many of them open on Sundays, too. **Banks** tend to be open only on weekdays, from 10am to 4pm, but *casas de cambio* more or less follow shop hours. However, in the Northeast, bank opening hours tend to be more like 7am to noon, to avoid the hot, steamy afternoons.

The opening hours of **attractions** are indicated in the text; however, bear in mind that these often change from one season to another. If you are going out of your way to visit something, it is best to check if its opening times have changed. **Museums** are a law unto themselves, each one having its own timetable, but all commonly close one day a week, usually Monday. Several Buenos Aires museums are also closed for at least a month in January and February. **Tourist offices** are forever adjusting their opening times, but the trend is towards longer hours and opening daily. However, don't bank on finding them open late in the evening or at weekends, especially in the low season or off the beaten track. **Post offices'** hours vary; most should be open between 9am and 6pm on weekdays,

Public holidays

On the most important national **public holidays**, such as Christmas Day, just about everything closes. On most holidays you will find lots of places stay open. Bear in mind that some of these holidays (marked with an *) move to the nearest Monday, and that there are several local public holidays, specific to a city or province, throughout the year. Many offices close for the whole of Semana Santa (Holy Week), the week leading up to Easter, while the Thursday is optional, as is New Year's Eve. Oddly, Easter Monday is not a holiday.

January 1	New Year's Day
Good Friday	Friday before Easter
March 24	Commemoration of the 1976 coup
April 2*	Malvinas Veterans' Day
May 1	Labour Day
May 25	Day of the Revolution
June 20*	Day of the Flag
July 9	Independence Day
August 17*	San Martín
October 12*	Columbus Day
December 8	Immaculate Conception
December 25	Christmas Day

with siestas in the hottest places, and 9am to 1pm on Saturdays. Outside these hours, many *locutorios* will deal with mail.

Phones

Privatization of the telephone system in the 1990s improved the quality and extent of the service, which is now generally very good, but raised prices hugely. Except in very remote areas, you should not have any problem making local or international calls.

By far the most common and straightforward way to make **calls** and send **faxes** is from the ubiquitous public call centres known as **locutorios**. You'll be assigned a cabin with a meter with which you can monitor your expenditure. Make as many calls as you want and then pay at the counter. Check all rates before committing yourself to a chat, and ask for details of special international and domestic rates: there is often a period of an hour or so in the day when calls are substantially **discounted**. Better still, buy one of the pre-paid phonecards sold at *locutorios* by companies such as Hablemás or Colibri – in Buenos Aires, the chemist chain Farmacity also sells them. They usually come in denominations of $5 or $10 and involve calling a local or toll-free number and typing in a PIN before making your call. With these, calls to landlines in Europe or the US from the capital fall to as little as $0.20 a minute.

Faxes are charged per sheet. Phone boxes on the street take coins or phonecards (which you can buy at kiosks), but this is more expensive and less convenient than using the *locutorio* system; in addition, the boxes are often out of order.

Calling within Argentina

Once in Argentina, **to make a call to another part of the country**, dial: ⓣ0 + area or city code + the number.

Calling home from abroad

One of the most convenient ways of phoning home from abroad is via a **telephone charge card** from your phone company back home. Using a PIN, you can make calls from most hotel, public and private phones. Since most major charge cards are free to obtain, it's certainly worth getting one at least for emergencies; enquire first though whether your destination is covered, and bear in mind that rates aren't necessarily cheaper than calling from a public phone.

In the **US and Canada**, companies such as AT&T, Sprint and Canada Direct enable their customers to make credit-card calls while overseas. This includes Argentina; call them to check the toll-free access code. In **the UK and Ireland**, British Telecom (ⓣ0800/345 144) will issue the BT Charge Card free to all BT customers, which can be used in Argentina. To call **Australia and New Zealand** from Argentina, telephone charge cards such as Telstra Telecard (ⓣ1800/038-000) or Optus Calling Card (ⓣ1300/300-937) in Australia, and Telecom NZ's Calling Card (ⓣ04/801-9000) can be used to make calls abroad.

Note that the initial zero is omitted from the area code when dialling the UK, Ireland, Australia and New Zealand from abroad.

Calling Argentina from abroad

To **call Argentina from abroad**, dial your country's International Direct Dialling prefix then:

+ ⓣ54 (Argentina's country code)
+ area or city code
+ destination phone number

Area and city codes are provided with all numbers throughout the guide.

International phone codes

Australia ⓣ0061 + city code.
New Zealand ⓣ0064 + city code.
Republic of Ireland ⓣ00353 + city code.
UK ⓣ0044 + city code.
US and Canada ⓣ001 + area code.

Mobile phones

If you want to use your **mobile phone** in Argentina, you'll need to check with your phone provider whether it will work there, and what the call charges are. Most UK, Australian and New Zealand mobiles use GSM and Argentina operates a GSM 1900 network so, in theory, you should be able to use your phone. US phones use a different system and unless you have a tri-band phone it is unlikely to be usable in Argentina. You are also likely to be charged extra for incoming calls when abroad, as the people calling you will be paying the usual rate.

The economic crisis slowed down take-up of mobiles (*celulares*) among Argentines, but with prices falling to an almost reasonable level they are now undergoing a boom. Argentine mobile numbers have a rather confusing array of codes depending on where you're calling them from, but they are usually prefixed by ⓣ15 and use area codes, like fixed lines.

Photography

Photographic **film** is not cheap in Argentina. Black-and-white and fast films, especially slides, are not always easy to lay your hands on, though standard film, of all brands, is widespread and reliable. Since slower film (for example, 100 ASA) is recommended in places like the altiplano, bring a plentiful supply with you, and the same goes for all camera spares and supplies, which sell for exorbitant prices here, even in the rare duty-free zones. **Developing** and printing are usually of high quality but are also quite expensive and outside Buenos Aires the situation is extremely erratic. A constant, however, is that you should watch out where you take photos: sensitive border areas and all military installations, including many civilian airports, are camera **no-go areas**, so watch out for signs and take no risks.

Public toilets

An everyday minor frustration is the general lack of **public toilets** (*baños*; men: *caballeros*, *hombres*, *varones* or *señores*; women: *damas*, *mujeres* or *señoras*). The toilets in modern shopping malls tend to be spick and span, however, and are often the best place to head for. In bars and cafés the toilets are usually of an acceptable standard and not all establishments insist that you buy a drink, though you may be made to feel you should. Outside Buenos Aires, toilet paper, hot water and soap (*jabón*) are frequently missing. In bus stations, airports and large shops there is often an attendant who keeps the toilets clean and dispenses **toilet paper** (*papel higiénico*), sometimes for a small fee, usually $0.50. Note that in rural areas or small towns, toilet paper must often be left in a bin rather than flushed, to avoid blocking the narrow pipes.

Time

After some confusing experiments with daylight saving and even different time zones within the country, Argentina now applies a standard time nationwide throughout the year: three hours behind GMT.

Tourist information

The main **national tourist board** is in Buenos Aires (see p.94), and is a fairly useful stop for maps and general information. Piles of leaflets, glossy brochures and maps are dished out at provincial and municipal **tourist offices** (*oficinas de turismo*) across the country, which vary enormously in terms of quality of service and quantity of information – often the smaller the place, the better the service, though in the tiniest and remotest places you will find information only at the municipalidad. Don't rely on staff speaking any language other than Spanish, or on the printed info being translated into foreign languages. The majority of local governments also have a website (indicated in the text of the relevant chapter), which, on the whole, are not terribly useful – being aimed mostly at residents – but they are worth checking out, especially those that are popular tourist destinations, as some provide transport and accommodation lists.

In addition, every province maintains a **casa de provincia** (provincial tourist office) in Buenos Aires, where you can pick up information about what there is to see or do prior to travelling there. The standard of information you'll glean from them again varies, often reflecting the comparative wealth of a given province. Some of the *casas* have fairly in-depth archives and the busier of them should be able to provide you with detailed printouts of accommodation and transport to various destinations under their jurisdiction. Getting the information you need can sometimes be a question of finding the right person – the *casas de provincia* are staffed by people from the various provinces and if you persist you may well be rewarded with some real insider knowledge. As well as the *casas de provincia* there are also several **shop-window tourist offices** in Buenos Aires run by major resorts, mostly those on the Atlantic seaboard (see below).

Argentina has taken to the **Internet** more enthusiastically than any other South American country, with most businesses and organizations having a Web presence. The sites are often quite sophisticated, albeit with a tendency to put in lots of flash graphics. Sometimes rudimentary translation into English is included, although you may find it just as easy to pick your way over the Spanish. Wherever pertinent, websites are listed in the guide, including sites for accommodation (reservations are usually possible via email), local tourist information and attractions. The national newspapers also have websites that can be very useful sources of information – see "The media", p.47. Unless otherwise indicated, all the sites below have a version in English.

Casas de provincias in Buenos Aires

Buenos Aires Av Callao 237 (Mon–Fri 9.30am–7pm; ⓣ011/4373-2636).
Catamarca Av Córdoba 2080 (Mon–Fri 8am–6pm; ⓣ011/4374-6891).
Córdoba Av Callao 232 (Mon–Fri 8am–7.30pm; ⓣ011/4372-8859).
Corrientes San Martín 333, 4th floor (Mon–Fri 10am–6pm; ⓣ011/4394-7418).
Chaco Av Callao 322 (Mon–Fri 10am–6pm; ⓣ011/4372-0961).
Chubut Sarmiento 1172 (Mon–Fri 10.30am–5.30pm).
Entre Ríos Suipacha 844 (Mon–Fri 9am–6pm).
Formosa H. Yrigoyen 1429 (Mon–Fri 9am–3pm; ⓣ011/4381-2037).
Jujuy Av Santa Fe 967 (Mon–Fri 9.30am–6.30pm; ⓣ011/4393-6096).
La Pampa Suipacha 346 (Jan & Feb Mon–Fri 9am–3.30pm; rest of year same days 8am–6pm; ⓣ011/4326-0511).
La Rioja Callao 745 (Mon–Fri 9.30am–6.30pm; ⓣ011/4813-3417).
Mendoza Av Callao 445 (Mon–Fri 10am–6pm; ⓣ011/4371-0835).
Misiones Santa Fe 989 (Mon–Fri 9am–6pm; ⓣ011/4393-1211).
Neuquén Pte Perón 685 (Mon–Fri 9.30am–4pm).
Río Negro Tucumán 1916 (Mon–Fri 10am–6pm; ⓣ011/4371-7273).
Salta Av Pte Roque S. Peña 933 (Mon–Fri 10am–6pm; ⓣ011/4326-2456).
San Juan Sarmiento 1251 (Mon–Fri 9am–5pm; ⓣ011/4382-9241).
San Luis Azcuénaga 1087 (Mon–Fri 10am–6pm; ⓣ011/4822-0426).
Santa Cruz Suipacha 1120 (Mon–Fri 9.30am–5.30pm; ⓣ011/4325-3098).
Santa Fe Montevideo 373, 2nd floor (Mon–Fri 9.30am–3.30pm; ⓣ011/4375-4570).
Santiago del Estero Florida 274 (Mon–Fri 9am–3pm; ⓣ011/4322-1389).
Tierra del Fuego Marcelo de T. Alvear 190 (Mon–Fri 10am–5pm; ⓣ011/4311-0233).
Tucumán Suipacha 140 (Mon–Fri 9.30am–5.30pm; ⓣ011/4322-0010).

Resort tourist offices in Buenos Aires

Mar del Plata Av Corrientes 1660 (ⓣ011/4384-5658).
Pinamar Florida 930.
San Clemente del Tuyú Bartolomé Mitre 1135.
Villa Carlos Paz Lavalle 623 (ⓣ011/4322-0053).
Villa Gesell Bartolomé Mitre 1702 (ⓣ011/4374-5199).

Useful websites

National

Argentina – LANIC ⓦlanic.utexas.edu/la/argentina. The most complete resource of links to every imaginable aspect of life in Argentina, invaluable both to travellers and researchers.

Argentina National Tourism ⓦ www.turismo.gov.ar. The government's official tourism website; eye candy rather than practical, although the section on the country's World Heritage sites is good.

Directorio de museos Argentinas ⓦ www.museosargentinos.org.ar. Useful searchable database of most of the country's museums, including descriptions as well as practicalities.

Literatura Argentina Contemporánea ⓦ www.literatura.org. Site dedicated to Argentine writers, with a biography and bibliography for all the major authors. Mostly Spanish, but with some useful English links.

El portal del tango ⓦ www.elportaldeltango.com. Lots of background on the national dance.

Proyecto Desaparecidos ⓦ www.desaparecidos.org/arg. An interface for finding out more about the human side of this harrowing episode in Argentina's history. Contains links to other relevant sites, including those of the Madres and Hijos and the site with the contents of the Nunca Más report.

Rough Guides ⓦ www.roughguides.com. Featuring both guidebook text and an extensive collection of readers' travel journals, as well as links to buy the guides and maps.

South American Explorers ⓦ www.saexplorers.org. Useful site set up by the experienced nonprofit organization South American Explorers aimed at scientists, explorers and travellers to South America. Includes travel-related news, descriptions of individual trips, a bulletin board and links to other websites

Regional

Argentina Travel Net ⓦ www.argentinatravelnet.com.

Argentina on View ⓦ www.argentinaonview.com. Two of the best of the country's many travel information websites, divided by region or province.

Inter Patagonia ⓦ www.interpatagonia.com. All about Patagonia, dividing it by region or by category (museums, adventure tourism, etc).

Mercotour ⓦ www.mercotour.com. Reliable region-by-region site full of information of interest to tourists, with pretty comprehensive accommodation information.

Buenos Aires

Xsalir ⓦ www.xsalir.com. All the places to go out to in and around the capital: bars, discos, restaurants, concerts and theatres, all searchable by genre and area. Spanish only.

The outdoors

Argentina Parques Nacionales ⓦ www.parquesnacionales.gov.ar. Spanish-only site for the country's national park system, with information and news on all the parks.

Planeta Argentina ⓦ www.planeta.com/argentina.html. Articles and advice relating to ecotourism in Argentina.

Great Outdoor Recreation Page ⓦ www.gorp.com. Covers outdoor pursuits throughout the world, particularly strong on hiking advice and locations.

General information

DolarPeso ⓦ www.dolarpeso.com. Features the day's exchange rate, for both dollars and euros.

Las páginas amarillas ⓦ www.paginasamarillas.com.ar. Argentina's Yellow Pages, the place to find addresses and phone numbers of businesses, including hotels, taxis, laundries, etc.

Travellers with disabilities

Argentina does not have a particularly sophisticated infrastructure for travellers with disabilities, but most Argentines are extremely willing to help anyone experiencing problems and this helpful attitude goes some way to making up for deficiencies in facilities. There are also a couple of organizations based in the capital that can help you once you arrive, and several that can help you plan your trip before you leave home.

Things are beginning to improve, and it is in Buenos Aires that you will find the most notable changes: a recent welcome innovation has been the introduction of wheelchair **ramps** on the city's pavements – though unfortunately the pavements themselves tend to be narrow, are often littered with potholes or loose slabs and, especially in the microcentro, can become almost impassable due to the volume of pedestrians during peak hours. Public transport is less problematic, with many of the new buses that now circulate in the city offering low-floor access. Laws demand that all new hotels now provide at least one room that is accessible for those in wheelchairs, but the only surefire option for those with severe mobility problems is at the top end of the price range: most five-star hotels, including the *Marriott Plaza* and the *Sheraton* have full wheelchair access, including wide doorways and roll-in showers. Those who have some mobility problems, but do not require full wheelchair access, will find most mid-range hotels are adequate, offering spacious accommodation and lifts. In all cases, the only way of finding out if a place meets your particular requirements is to ring the hotel in person and make specific enquiries.

Outside Buenos Aires, finding facilities for the disabled is pretty much a hit-and-miss affair, although there have been some notable improvements at major **tourist attractions** such as the Iguazú Falls, where new ramps and catwalks have been constructed, making the vast majority of the falls area accessible by wheelchair. The **hostel associations**, Red Argentina de Albergues Juveniles and the Asociación Argentina de Albergues de la Juventud, can offer information on access at their respective hostel networks.

Useful contacts

In the US and Canada

Directions Unlimited 720 N. Bedford Rd, Bedford Hills, NY 10507 ⓣ914/241-1700. Travel agency specializing in customized tours for people with disabilities.

Mobility International USA PO Box 10767, Eugene, OR 97440. Voice and TDD: ⓣ541/343-1284. Information and referral services, access guides, tours and exchange programmes. Annual membership US$25 (includes quarterly newsletter).

Twin Peaks Press Box 129, Vancouver, WA 98666 ⓣ360/694-2462 or 1-800/637-2256. Publisher of the *Directory of Travel Agencies for the Disabled* (US$19.95), listing more than 370 agencies worldwide; *Travel for the Disabled* (US$19.95); and *Wheelchair Vagabond* (US$14.95), loaded with personal tips.

In the UK and Ireland

Disability Action Group 2 Annadale Ave, Belfast BT7 3JH ⓣ01232/491011. Information about access for disabled travellers abroad.

RADAR (Royal Association for Disability and Rehabilitation) 12 City Forum, 250 City Rd, London EC1V 8AF ⓣ020/7250 3222, minicom ⓣ020/7250 4119, ⓦwww.radar.org. Provides brief lists of accommodation in Argentina; also offers good general advice for travellers with disabilities.

In Australia and New Zealand

ACROD (Australian Council for Rehabilitation of the Disabled) PO Box 60, Curtin, ACT 2605 ⓣ02/6282-4333, and 24 Cabarita Rd, Cabarita, NSW 2137 ⓣ02/9743-2699. Provides lists of travel agencies and tour operators for people with disabilities.

Barrier Free Travel 36 Wheatley St, North Bellingen, NSW 2454 ⓣ02/6655-1733. Independent travel consultant, who will draw up individual itineraries catering for your particular needs.

Disabled Persons Assembly PO Box 10, 138 The Terrace, Wellington ⓣ04/472-2626. Provides lists of travel agencies and tour operators for people with disabilities.

Websites

ⓦ**www.access-able.com** US-based site with scant information on Argentina but good general tips for travellers plus a forum where travellers can exchange information. Also links to other organizations and specialist tour operators.

ⓦ**www.sath.org** The home pages of the US-based society for the advancement of travellers with handicaps, with plenty of tips on specific issues such as wheelchair access, visual impairment and arthritis, though no specific information on Argentina.

Travelling with children

Argentines love children and you will generally find them accommodating and understanding if you're travelling as a family.

There are some **hotels** that have a no-child rule; these are fairly few and far between, but check when you reserve. Most have triple rooms or suites with connecting rooms to accommodate families; apartment hotels and *cabañas*, which also contain small kitchens, are particularly good. Many hotels will be able to provide a cot if you have a small child (ask when you reserve), but be aware that though perfectly adequate these may be pretty old and are unlikely to confirm to exacting European or US safety standards. Top hotels will often provide babysitting services, too.

When it comes to **eating** out, only the very snotty top-of-the-range restaurants will turn children away or look pained when you walk in; the vast majority will do their best to make sure you and your offspring are comfortable and entertained. Highchairs are sometimes, but not always, provided. It is quite normal to see children out with their parents until late – you may well see families strolling home at 1 or 2 am, especially in summer.

To **entertain** them during the day, Argentina's **natural attractions** may be your best bet – the country has little in the way of amusement parks or specific family destinations, and the ones that do exist are generally rather poor. Buenos Aires has enough to keep them amused for a couple of days, although its somewhat sophisticated attractions will mostly appeal more to adults. Rosario is a particularly good city destination for children (see p.379), and fun for their parents, too. Other than that, consider the waterfalls and jungle critters at Iguazú, the boat rides and glaciers of Parque Nacional Los Glaciares or the whales and penguins near Península Valdés. If they're old enough, Northern hemisphere children may enjoy the novelty of going skiing during their summer vacation, while the simple beach pleasures of Mar del Plata will appeal to younger children. Wherever you go, do not be too ambitious in planning your itinerary and avoid the summer heat unless you will be spending most of your time in Patagonia.

International brands of **nappies** (diapers), **wipes** and **baby milk** are widely available, as are **dummies** (pacifiers). Also bring any **children's medicine** with you that you are likely to need, as it can be difficult to work out what the local equivalent is. Many people who work in pharmacies have little medical training and give incorrect advice so if your child does get sick, go to a private hospital, preferably in one of the larger cities, where you will be attended by a paediatrician rapidly and professionally. **Baby food** is usually only sold in large supermarkets, and the range is very limited, but waiters will usually be happy to provide mashed potatoes, pumpkin and so on. Discreet **breastfeeding** in public is fine. Changing facilities are practically non-existent (large city malls being the only exception), so you will have to get used to changing on the move.

Guide

Guide

1

Buenos Aires and around

CHAPTER 1

Highlights

* **Teatro Colón** World-class acoustics and sumptuous decor make the national opera house a monument to Argentina's golden age. See p.112

* **San Telmo** Of all the city's barrios, San Telmo is perhaps the most traditional – go on a Sunday for the Porteño ambience at its most exuberant. See p.119

* **Recoleta Cemetery** Wander around one of the world's most exclusive cemeteries, where Evita's resting place is hidden away among ostentatious tombs and elaborate sculptures. See p.135

* **MALBA** Visit this museum of contemporary Latin American art for its collection of paintings, photos and sculptures, for its cinema, for its cutting-edge architecture – or for its modish café. See p.146

* **Palermo Viejo** Borges and Cortázar loved it, the glitterati flock to it and you can enjoy its tree-lined streets, fashionable boutiques and fantastic restaurants and guesthouses. See p.146

* **Tango** Listen to *bandoneón* players, watch couples show off their prowess in the street, choose between showcase extravaganzas or humble *milongas* – and maybe learn the basic steps. See p.169

* **Tigre and the Paraná Delta** The equivalent of having the Everglades on the doorstep of Manhattan – a vivid reminder that Buenos Aires is a subtropical city. See p.183

△ Teatro Colón

1

Buenos Aires and around

Of all South America's capitals and major cities, **Buenos Aires** – aka Capital Federal, Baires, BsAs or simply **BA** – has by far the most going for it. Seductive and cultured, beguilingly eclectic and in constant flux, it never bores, seldom sleeps and invariably exerts a mesmerizing power over its visitors. Repeatedly described as a hybrid of Paris, Madrid, Milan and London, with an admixture of Manhattan, it is in fact a city that is totally *sui generis:* thanks in part to its deeply entrenched **traditions**, such as drinking tea-like *mate* (see box, pp.392–393), and its proud and hospitable, extravagant and attractive inhabitants – known as **Porteños** – but also to its location. To the north and east of the city flows the caramel-hued **Río de la Plata** (River Plate), the world's widest river estuary, while to the south and west extend the **Pampas**, a horizon-defying plain of verdant grasslands, punctuated by sleepy towns, clumps of pampas grass (*cortaderas*) and the odd ombú tree, in whose broad shade the gauchos traditionally rested. Away from its extensive **harbour** facilities, stacked high with containers, and ever-busier cruise-ship docks, the city has tended to shun the river, while its outer suburbs seem to meld seamlessly into the Pampas beyond.

Rio may have a more striking topography, and Quito undoubtedly boasts a finer colonial heritage, but by Latin American standards Buenos Aires enjoys an incomparable **lifestyle**. Restaurants, bars, cafés and nightclubs to suit every taste and pocket, a world-class opera house, myriad theatres, cinemas and galleries and splendid French-style palaces underscore both its attachment to the arts and its sense of style. Another boon are its countless **parks and gardens**, many coming complete with outstanding sports facilities. Yet another noteworthy feature of Buenos Aires is the abundance of **trees** lining the streets – around one-fifth of which are still picturesquely cobbled – and providing shade in the many lively **plazas** that dot the huge conurbation; they add welcome splashes of colour, particularly when they blaze with yellow, pink and mauve blooms in spring and early summer. The squadrons of squawky parrots that populate them help visitors forget that this is the world's twelfth largest city: there are nearly fourteen million inhabitants in the Greater Buenos Aires (**Gran Buenos Aires**) area, which spills beyond the **Ciudad Autónoma**'s defining boundary of multi-lane ring roads into Buenos Aires Province.

Indeed, on the map and from the air, the metropolis looks dauntingly huge, stretching over 40km from north to south and more than 30km from west to east. Yet, BA's compact centre and the relative proximity of all the main sights mean that you don't have to travel that much to gain a sense of knowing the city. Of the city's 47 **barrios**, you will most probably be visiting only the half-dozen most central. **Retiro**, **Recoleta** and **Palermo** are the leafiest and wealthiest – you may well opt to stay in one of their boutique hotels or guest-houses, or head there to shop or dine. The bulk of the city **museums** lie within their boundaries, too, with themes as varied as science and Spanish-American

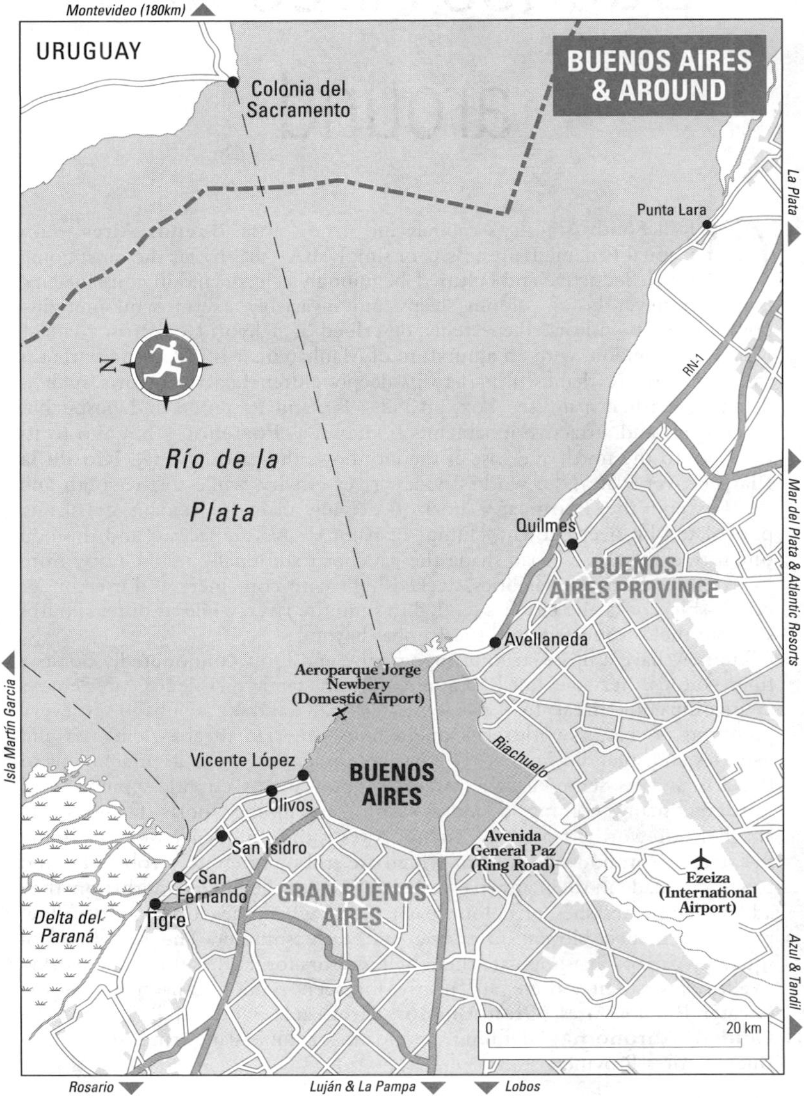

art, immigration and Eva Perón. Downtown Buenos Aires takes in the tiny but historic barrios of **San Nicolás** and **Monserrat** – busy and smoke-choked on weekdays, spookily quiet on Sundays, when all the office workers and public officials have gone home. Once seedy, but increasingly gentrified, **San Telmo** is primarily known for its avant-garde artists, its antiques fair and its tango haunts, while resolutely working-class **La Boca**, further south still, is so inextricably and fanatically linked with its football team, Boca Juniors – whose main rivals, River Plate, have their stadium in middle-class **Belgrano** – that many of its buildings are painted blue and yellow. **Puerto Madero**, the newest barrio, runs along the former **dockside**, where disused warehouses and wharves have been transformed into five-star hotels and even a private university.

Few major cities enjoy such easy access to their hinterlands as BA, but the Atlantic resorts, magnificent estancias (farmsteads or ranches) and traditional Pampean villages are distant enough to warrant at least one overnight stay, and are therefore covered in Chapter 2. Closer to the city, the **northern suburbs** are primarily residential but still boast a curiosity or two, including a tourist train and, above all, **Tigre**, a kind of cross between Venice and the Everglades, at the edge of the **Paraná Delta**. **Colonia del Sacramento** (or, Colonia, for short) is regarded by many Porteños as a forty-eighth barrio, somewhat to the locals' annoyance, but this former Portuguese colony lies on a protuberance of the Uruguayan coast directly opposite the Argentine capital. It's a peaceful haven, with carefully preserved **colonial buildings** and idyllic river **beaches**; transport is convenient and enjoyable, making it a perfect choice for a short break from the hurly-burly of BA.

Buenos Aires

Though vast, **BUENOS AIRES** lends itself perfectly to aimless wandering, and its mostly ordered grid pattern makes it fairly easy to orient yourself. The boundaries of the Capital Federal are marked by the **Río de la Plata** to the northeast and by its tributary, the **Riachuelo**, to the south, while **Avenida General Paz** forms a semi-circular ring around the west of the city, connecting the two. Cutting right across the middle, **Avenida Rivadavia**, an immensely long street (Porteños claim it is the world's longest) runs east–west for nearly two hundred blocks from Plaza de Mayo to Morón, outside the city limits. The other main east–west thoroughfares are avenidas Corrientes, Córdoba and Santa Fe, while north–south the major routes are Avenida L.N. Além – which changes its name to Avenida del Libertador as it swings out to the northern suburbs – Avenida Callao and **Avenida 9 de Julio** – a car-oriented conglomeration of four multi-lane roads.

The **city centre** is bounded approximately by Avenida de Mayo to the south, Avenida L.N. Além to the east, Avenida Córdoba to the north and Avenida Callao to the west. The narrow streets in its eastern half form the so-called microcentro, enclosing the financial district, **La City**, and major shopping, eating and accommodation destinations. The centre is a hectic place, particularly during the week, but from the bustle of **Calle Florida**, the microcentro's pedestrianized artery, to the *fin-de-siècle* elegance of **Avenida de Mayo** and the café culture of **Corrientes**, the area is surprisingly varied in both architecture and atmosphere. Providing a quiet counterpoint, the converted dock area of **Puerto Madero** runs alongside it to the east, beyond which is the unexpectedly wild **Reserva Ecológica**, one of the city's most unusual green spaces.

The **south** of the city, containing its oldest parts, begins just beyond Plaza de Mayo. Its narrow, often cobbled streets are lined with some of the capital's finest architecture, typified by late nineteenth-century townhouses with ornate Italianate facades, sturdy but elegant wooden doors and finely wrought iron railings. From the cultivated charm of **San Telmo**, the setting of the city's Sunday antique market, to the boisterous passion of **Boca** on match days, the south offers an appealing mix of tradition and popular culture.

The **north** of Buenos Aires is generally regarded as beginning at Avenida Córdoba. The area is home to four of the city's wealthiest neighbourhoods – **Retiro** and **Recoleta**, **Palermo** and **Belgrano** – which are renowned for their palaces, plazas and parks. This is also where you'll find some of the city's finest **museums**, as well as **La Recoleta**, one of the world's most astonishing cemeteries. Further north, wide avenues sweep past enormous parks, such as Parque 3 de Febrero, and some of the country's major sports venues. Pockets of mid-nineteenth-century Buenos Aires remain, the most beguiling of all being **Palermo Viejo**, whose cobbled streets and single-storey houses contrast with the grandiose mansions and high-rise apartment blocks that populate much of this side of the city. This is also where you'll find many of the city's best restaurants and nightlife.

Although the above neighbourhoods contain most of the obvious attractions, the immense residential neighbourhoods that stretch west of Avenida Callao hold gems of their own for those with a bit more time to explore, notably the shrine-like tomb of Carlos Gardel, the godfather of tango, in the huge cemetery of **Chacarita**. Then there is the weekend gaucho fair in the barrio of **Mataderos**, which offers the unforgettable sight of dashingly dressed horsemen galloping through the city streets, as well as providing an authentic brew of regional cooking and live folk music.

Some history

Nuestra Señora de Santa María del Buen Aire, provider of the *buen aire*, or good wind, was the patron saint of the Spanish and Portuguese sailors who first landed on the banks of the Río de la Plata estuary in 1516. The city was eventually named in her honour: Ciudad de la Santísima Trinidad y Puerto de Santa María de los Buenos Ayres, or "the City of the Most Holy Trinity and Port of St Mary of the Fair Winds" – hence Porteño, from *puerto*, the name given to anyone born in the city. Twenty years would pass, however, before any attempt was made to establish a settlement here. In 1536, around the time Francisco Pizarro was subjugating the Inca, Spanish aristocrat **Pedro de Mendoza** arrived at the site of present-day Buenos Aires with a group of 1600 or so would-be colonists. Lacking adequate supplies, Mendoza tried to co-opt the native population, the **Querandíes**, into gathering provisions for the settlers, but this proved unsuccessful, and with little foodstuff available, the venture failed horribly – a mere eighteen months after its arrival, the party's size had been reduced by two-thirds. Within five years the remaining settlers had fled to Asunción del Paraguay, upriver.

The second attempt to settle the area came in 1580, when an expedition by **Juan de Garay** came downriver from Asunción to refound the city. This time around the enterprise was better prepared: provisions were now available from

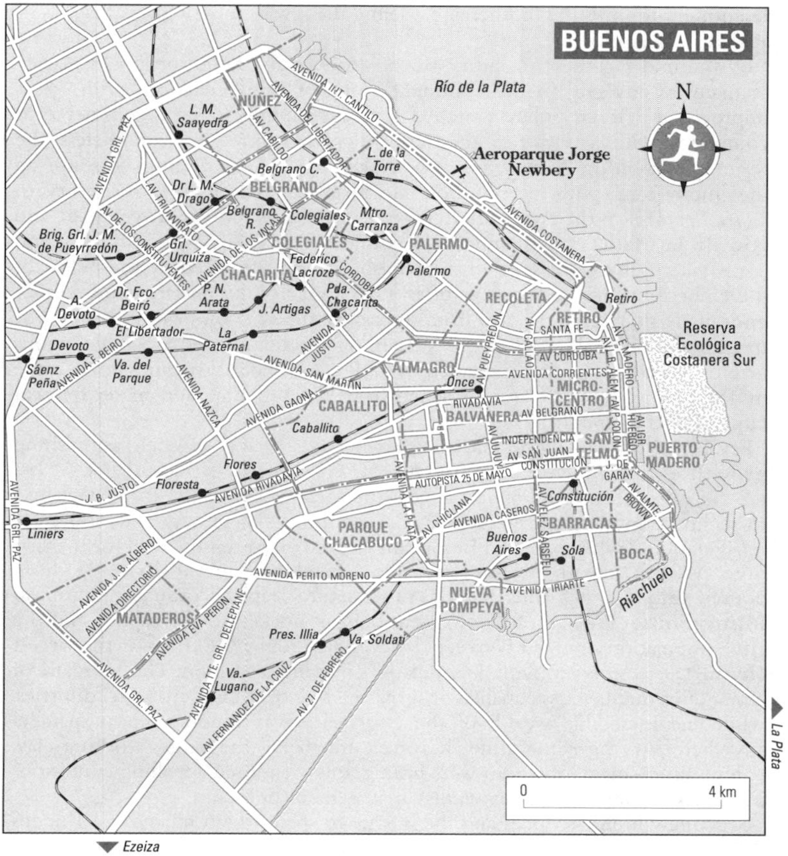

Asunción and Santa Fe, founded by Garay on his way downriver. Furthermore, the horses brought over by Mendoza had reproduced rapidly in the Pampas; the cattle that Garay introduced also soon grew in number. The fact that this land was absolutely ideal for agriculture at first made little impression on the Spanish, who were more interested in precious metals: they named the settlement's river the Plata (silver) in the belief that it flowed from the lands of silver and gold in the Andes.

Expansion was slow – Buenos Aires remained a distant outpost of the Spanish-American empire for the next two centuries. Although the Pampas proved fertile, the settlement seemed destined to remain poor and tiny once the Spanish discovered the area had no silver after all. Any possibility of growth was checked by Spain, which did not want Buenos Aires – the logical point of entry for commerce from Europe – to flourish as an independent port. All **trade**, the Crown dictated, must pass through Lima, although this entailed a much longer, more expensive journey. The ruling had two far-reaching effects. First, it forced the colony to turn to **smuggling**: silver from the mines of Potosí, in Alto Peru (now Bolivia), and locally produced leather were exchanged for slaves and manufactured items from Portugal. Second, it bred resentment towards the motherland, fueling the revolutionary fever that was to appear in the years to come.

By the mid-eighteenth century, Buenos Aires had 12,000 inhabitants, twice as many as any city in the continent's interior. Trade relations with Spain improved as Crown policy switched from attempting to stifle commerce to competing with its rivals by drastically increasing imports. Nonetheless, the Spanish grip on the New World was weakening. The last attempt to shore up the empire came with the Bourbon reforms of the late eighteenth century; in 1776, Spain gave the Argentine territories the status of **Viceroyalty of the Río de la Plata**, with Buenos Aires as the capital. This was the fourth – and last – viceroyalty to be created in Spanish America. Boosted by the defeat of the embryonic British invasions of 1806, the Viceroyalty declared **independence** in 1810, freeing the area from the last vestiges of colonial hindrance. For the next bloody half-century or so, Buenos Aires maintained a rather tenuous grip over a country bitterly divided by civil wars. The real turning point came in 1880, when the city was detached from the province and made **federal capital** of the republic.

Few cities in the world have experienced a period of such astonishing **growth** as that which spurred Buenos Aires between 1870 and 1914. At last the city was able to exploit and export the great riches of the Pampas, thanks to techno-logical advances such as the steamship, the railway and, above all, refrigeration – which enabled Europeans to dine on Argentine beef for the first time. Massive foreign investment – most notably from the British – soon poured into the city and Buenos Aires' stature leapt accordingly. European **immigrants**, over half of whom were Italians, flocked to the capital, and the city's population doubled between 1880 and 1890; by 1900 it was the largest city in Latin America, with a population nearing a million. The standard of living of its middle class equalled or surpassed that of many European countries, while the incredible wealth of the city's elite was almost without parallel anywhere. At the same time, however, much of the large working-class community – many of whom were immigrants – endured appalling conditions in the city's overcrowded *conventillos*, or tenement buildings.

Seemingly limitless riches and the energy to spend them meant that Buenos Aires' grand ambitions could be realized at last. Most of the old town was razed and an eclectic range of new buildings went up in a huge grid pattern, a perfect implementation of the orderly, square *urbs americana* city plan. Remodelled in the 1880s (some of the inspiration was Haussmann's Paris), and interconnected by trams, buses and, later, Latin America's first underground railway, Buenos Aires had little cause to envy the capitals of the old continent. In 1926, both horrified and impressed by Buenos Aires' incredible dynamism, visiting French architect Le Corbusier felt compelled to describe the city as "a gigantic agglomeration of insatiable energy".

By the mid-twentieth century the period of breakneck development had come to a close: the country as a whole was sliding into a long period of political turmoil and economic **crisis** and the capital's growth ground to a halt. In September 1945, Buenos Aires saw the first of what was to become a regular fixture – a massive **demonstration** that filled the city centre; in this case, it was called to demand an end to the military government. The following month, union members who had benefited from former Work Minister **Juan Perón**'s pro-worker policies descended on the Plaza de Mayo to protest his imprisonment. Rallies of almost religious fervour in support of Perón and his wife **Evita**, who came out onto the balcony of the Casa Rosada to deliver their speeches, followed at regular intervals until Evita's death and Perón's deposition. In 1953, one demonstration was bombed by upper-class anti-Peronists, which led to retaliatory arson attacks on places such as the opposition party headquarters and the Jockey Club. In June 1954 the armed forces, planning a coup, bombed a pro-Perón demonstration in the Plaza de Mayo, killing some three hundred people but leaving Perón untouched. Shortly afterwards, Perón resigned and went into exile, leaving a polarized country in his wake.

The dark times of the 1976–83 military **dictatorship** came to the attention of the world through the silent protests of the Mothers of the Disappeared in the capital's Plaza de Mayo. Feigning ignorance as to the fate of the disappeared – anyone considered to be opposed to the regime's idea of "Western and Christian values" – the military was in fact torturing and killing them behind closed doors throughout the city. The most notorious detention centre was the ESMA, or Navy Mechanics School, in the northern suburb of Núñez; the controversy surrounding President Kirchner's announcement in 2004 that it would become the Museo de la Memoria illustrates how the scars from those bitter years are still fresh.

Although the legacy of European immigration, which once gave the city a cosmopolitan tinge, remains, since the 1970s most of the city's new arrivals have come from Argentina's poorer provinces and neighbouring countries (Peru, Bolivia and Paraguay), and settled in the capital's growing number of **shanty-towns**. Euphemistically termed *villas de emergencia* in reference to their supposed temporary status, they are more commonly and accurately known as *villas miseria*, or settlements of abject poverty. In stark contrast to these pockets of deprivation, the temporary **stabilization** of the country's currency in the 1990s brought a new upsurge in spending by those who could afford it – and an infrastructure to match. Smart new shopping malls, restaurants and cinema complexes sprung up around the city, changing the way many Porteños lived. The good times rolled, and sushi bars and drive-in fast-food outlets became part of the city's identity, as did secure private housing estates (known as *countrys*) on the outskirts of the city.

But Buenos Aires entered the twenty-first century in retreat. Its new-found prosperity was built on the shakiest of foundations – huge loans from the IMF and the pawning-off of all national industry in a series of badly handled and often corrupt privatizations. If Porteños suspected it couldn't last, they chose to look the other way, hanging on to the mantra of the dollar-peso peg and enjoying cheap imports while the country and its economy spiralled downwards. When the bubble finally burst, it did so with a bang. Weeks of mostly peaceful demonstrations, and the odd bout of supermarket looting, came to a horrendous head on December 20, 2001, when widespread rioting was brutally suppressed by the police, leading to dozen of deaths. Since then, demonstrations and roadblocks by unemployed *piqueteros* have become part of the fabric of everyday life in the city, although fortunately violence is very rare. The grinding **recession**, followed by a messy devaluation of the currency in 2002, took their toll on the city; even now the sad sight of broken pavements and *cartoneros* rooting through rubbish are just two obvious examples of the economic problems. To add to the city's woes, a fire broke out during a rock concert at **República Cromañón** in December 2004, resulting in 194 deaths and hundreds of injuries – the worst tragedy of its kind in Argentine history. All nightclubs and similar establishments were shut down for some time after the incident, pending rigorous safety checks (many were not allowed to reopen), but the public was not reassured and the disaster cost mayor **Aníbal Ibarra** his office; criminal investigations and the trial of those responsible, including the disco's owner, are still ongoing.

However, as Argentina approaches its 2010 bicentennial celebrations, things are definitely looking up for the city, with **international tourism** one of the main engines of recovery. Dozens of new gourmet restaurants have sprung up, and mostly stayed; boutique hotels have mushroomed, even in parts of the city where foreigners previously never ventured; the world's biggest **cruise liners** drop anchor offshore; and Buenos Aires has become the self-proclaimed leading **gay and lesbian** destination in Latin America. All the candidates for the mayoral election in June 2007, including winner Mauricio Macri, outlined plans for a more modern city, with improved transport, less pollution, more enterprise and an eco-friendly approach to urban life. Globally familiar city problems (traffic, crime, social inequity) linger, but much has been done, at least superficially to improve the quality of life – work has even begun on mending those broken pavements.

Arrival

Buenos Aires is well served by numerous international and domestic **flights**. It is also a transport hub for the rest of the country, with frequent daily **bus** services to and from most towns and cities. Additionally, there are **ferry** services to and from Uruguay (see p.191).

By air

All **international flights**, with the exception of a few from neighbouring countries, arrive 35km west of the city centre at Ministro Pistarini Airport or – as it is actually referred to by everyone – **Ezeiza**, in reference to the outlying neighbourhood in which it is situated. In comparison with some Latin American airports, arriving at Ezeiza is relatively stress-free: touting for taxis has been banned and the tourist information stand (Mon–Fri 10am–5pm) has good information on accommodation in the city. Ignore the privately run exchange booths strategically placed before you exit arrivals – instead **change money** at the small branch of Banco Nación in the airport arrivals hall, where you will get a much better rate.

If you want to take a **taxi** into the city ($60 and up), ask at one of the official taxi stands immediately outside the arrivals exit. Less expensive are the **tourist buses** operated by Manuel Tienda León (Ⓣ011/4314-3636, Ⓦwww.tiendaleon.com.ar). Running every thirty minutes 24/7 between Ezeiza and the centre, these nonstop buses cost about $25 and take approximately forty minutes, making them a quick and secure way to reach the centre of town. They drop you at the company's main terminal at San Martín and Madero, from where you can pick up a taxi. If you are transferring to a domestic flight (for some destinations these also leave from Ezeiza; check first), you could get a Manuel Tienda León bus ($28; 9am–midnight) to the Aeroparque Metropolitano Jorge Newbery; if you are staying in a part of the city near the domestic airport, such as Palermo or Belgrano, you might consider using this service and taking a taxi for the final stretch, though be aware that queues for taxis at Aeroparque can be long at busy arrival times (early in the morning and in the evening). Alternatively, there's the **local bus** #86, which runs between Ezeiza and Boca, entering the city via Rivadavia and continuing past Congreso, Plaza de Mayo and San Telmo; it takes about two hours, and leaves just beyond the entrance to the airport. Make sure you have change for the ticket machines, as notes are not accepted, and be warned that it can become very full and bulky suitcases or backpacks may cause serious inconvenience for other passengers and yourself.

Buenos Aires' other airport is **Aeroparque Metropolitano Jorge Newbery**, usually known as Aeroparque, on the Costanera Norte, around six kilometres north of the city centre. Most **domestic flights** and some flights from Brazil and Uruguay arrive here. Manuel Tienda Léon also runs a bus service from here to Terminal Madero in the centre ($9; 9am–midnight); the price is a few pesos less than a taxi and a few pesos more than the local bus (the #33 will take you to Paseo Colón). Aeroparque also has a tourist information booth (Mon–Sun 10am–5pm).

By bus

If you are travelling to Buenos Aires by **bus** from other points in Argentina, or on international services from neighbouring countries, you will arrive at Buenos Aires' huge long-distance bus terminal, known as **Retiro** (it is located in the barrio of that name), at the corner of Avenida Antártida and Ramos Mejía. There are good facilities at the terminal, including toilets, shops, cafés and left luggage. Unlike the majority of the country's bus terminals, Retiro is very centrally located and nobody with a reasonable amount of energy will find it too strenuous to walk to hotels in the Florida/Retiro area of the city (although at night or in bad weather this is not recommended – the pavements often get waterlogged when it rains and, as often in station districts, there is a seedy feel to the immediate surroundings). Taxis are plentiful and the Retiro subte station is just a block away, outside the adjoining train station (see below). There are also plenty of local buses leaving from stands along Ramos Mejía, though actually finding the one you want might be a rather daunting first taste of local bus transport. Buses #5 or #50 will take you to Congreso and the upper end of Avenida de Mayo, a promising hunting ground for accommodation if you haven't booked ahead.

By train

Few tourists arrive in Buenos Aires by **train** these days; although plans are afoot to reinstate long-distance services (possibly with high-speed connections), currently most trains are suburban only. The main exceptions are: trains from the Atlantic coast, Tandil and Carmen de Patagones, which arrive at **Constitución**, in the south of the city at General Hornos 11 (Ferrobaires ⓣ011/4304-0028); trains from Mercedes and Lobos, which arrive at **Once**, in the west of the city at Avenida Pueyrredón and Bartolomé Mitre (TBA ⓣ0800/333-822); and trains from Rosario and Zarate, which arrive at **Retiro** on Avenida Ramos Mejía (TBA ⓣ0800/333-822). All three terminals have subte stations (Constitución, Plaza Miserere and Retiro, respectively) and are served by numerous local bus routes.

Information

For **information**, head to one of the city's numerous tourist kiosks; the staff do not generally have much specialist knowledge but they can usually provide maps and a few leaflets. The most central kiosk is in the microcentro at Avenida Diagonal Roque Sáenz Peña and Florida (Mon–Fri 9am–6pm, Sat 10am–4pm). There are other kiosks in the Retiro bus terminal, at Calle 10 local 83

(Mon–Sat 7.30am–1pm); in Recoleta, on avenidas Quintana and Ortíz, near the cemetery (Mon–Sun 11am–7pm); in Puerto Madero, by dock 4, also offering information on Montevideo (Mon–Sun 10am–6pm); and in San Telmo at Defensa 1250 (Sat & Sun 10am–6pm only). There's also a free telephone line designed to offer tourist and transport information, as well as aid, in the event you are robbed or ripped off (daily 9am–9pm; ⓣ0800/999-BUETUR), and a comprehensive website with ideas of where to go and what to do (ⓦwww.bue.gov.ar). The city government also organizes free walking tours, in English and Spanish, usually around a given barrio, but sometimes with themes such as Evita or Carlos Gardel – ask for the current schedule.

You can also pick up local and countrywide information from the **National Tourist Office** at Santa Fe 883 (Mon–Fri 9am–5pm; ⓣ011/4312-2232 or toll-free ⓣ0800/555-0016). Especially worth seeking out is the *Viva Bue* booklet, which has extensive theatre and exhibitions listings as well as a good, clear fold-out map of the central barrios. Published bi-monthly, it's usually given out free at all the tourist information booths.

Another excellent source of English-language information is the ever-reliable South American Explorers, which has set up a clubhouse in San Telmo at Estados Unidos 577 (Mon–Tues 1–6pm, Wed–Sun 1–7pm; ⓣ011/4307-9625, ⓦwww.saexplorers.org). Membership of US$50 a year gets you access to this and all their other clubhouses, where you can store gear, use their computers, consult trip reports, chat with their knowledgeable staff, borrow books, find out about local volunteer opportunities, obtain discounts on hostels and other services and generally chill out. The clubhouse also holds events such as movie showings, cookery classes and the odd party, and produces a newsletter – sign up at the website.

If you are planning to stay in the city a while and make use of the public transport, a combined **street map and bus guide** such as *Guía Lumi* or *Guía "T"* is a useful accessory. Both are widely available from central kiosks and occasionally, at knockdown prices, from hawkers on the buses or trains.

City transport

Buenos Aires may seem like a daunting city to get around, but it's actually served by an extensive, inexpensive and generally efficient **public transport** service – albeit not the world's cleanest, quietest or most modern. The easiest part of this system to come to grips with is undoubtedly the underground rail system, or **subte**, which serves most of the city centre and the north of the city. You may also want to familiarize yourself with a few bus routes, as **buses** are the only form of public transport that serve the outlying barrios and the south of the city. That said, with **taxis** being plentiful and cheap, despite repeated post-crisis price hikes, you'll likely find them the most convenient means to get you where you want to go.

The subte

The oldest in Latin America, the southern hemisphere and the Spanish-speaking world (inaugurated in 1913), Buenos Aires' underground rail system, or **subte** (short for *subterráneo*), was also one of the first in the world to be privatized: the network was taken over by Metrovías in 1994. It's a reasonably efficient system – you shouldn't have to wait more than a few minutes during peak periods – and certainly the quickest way to get from the centre to outlying points such as

Caballito, Plaza Italia (Palermo) or Chacarita. Many of the stations are beautifully decorated with tile murals, depicting anything from famous battles to Gaudí masterpieces, but they are also often dirty, unprepossessing and very hot in the summer. The trains themselves are noisy and not especially comfortable. The other main flaw in the subte's design is that it's shaped like a fork, meaning that journeys across town involve going down one "prong" and changing at least once before heading back up to your final destination. This is destined to improve, as the network is being extended, with work underway on new north–south lines as well as extensions to the existing lines.

Using the subte is a fairly straightforward business. There are at present **five lines**, plus a "premetro" system which serves the far southwestern corner of the city, linking up with the subte at the end of line E. Lines A, B, D and E run from the city centre outwards, while line C, which runs between Retiro and Constitución, connects them all. Check the name of the last station on the line you are travelling on in order to make sure you're heading in the right direction; directions to station platforms are given by this final destination. Tickets can be purchased from the *boleterías* (ticket booths) at each station. A single *viaje* ticket ($0.70) will take you anywhere on the system. You can also buy multi-trip tickets, but the only thing you will save is time – there are no discounts for multiple trips. The ticket booths usually have good, free maps of the system, available on request.

Even if you use the subte only once during your stay in Buenos Aires, you really shouldn't miss the chance to travel on **Line A**, which runs between Plaza de Mayo and Caballito. It's the only line to preserve the network's original carriages, and travelling in one of the rickety and elegantly lit wood-framed interiors is like being propelled along in an antique wardrobe. They may not, however, be operative for much longer – for some time the city government has been announcing plans to replace the beloved old carriages with more modern ones.

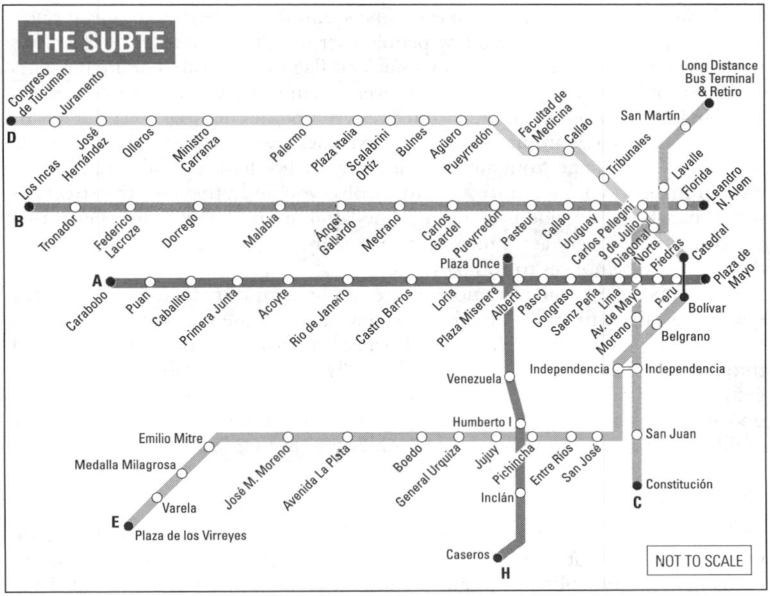

THE SUBTE

Buses

Peak hours aside, when traffic is increasingly gridlocked, Buenos Aires' **buses** (*colectivos*) are a useful way of getting to many of the outlying barrios for those on a limited budget. This said, they can also be something of a plague: they are quite noisy, prone to belching out clouds of exhaust and they are driven crazily, making them the main culprits in the city's traffic accidents – standing, or even sitting, can be an ordeal, and is certainly an experience. From a visitor's point of view, possibly the most daunting thing about them is the sheer number of routes – almost two hundred wend their way around the vast capital. Invest in a combined street and bus-route map (see p.94), however, and you shouldn't have too much trouble. Very short journeys cost $0.75; all other trips within the city cost $0.80. Tickets are acquired on board from a machine, which gives change for coins, though not for notes: as you get on you need to state your fare (or your destination if you are unsure of the fare) to the driver before inserting your money in the ticket machine. Be forewarned, though: do not expect the driver to be helpful if you're not sure where you're going, or to wait for you to take your seat before accelerating. Once in Gran Buenos Aires fares increase slightly, so if you're travelling beyond the city boundaries (to San Isidro, for example, or Ezeiza) it is easier just to state your destination.

Despite accidents involving buses, the system is a generally safe way of getting around the city – though, as always, keep your eyes on your belongings, especially when buses are crowded. Many services run all night, notably the #5 and the #86. Argentines are generally very courteous bus passengers and never hesitate in giving up their seat to someone who looks like they need it more – don't be shy of doing the same.

Taxis and remises

The sheer volume of black and yellow **taxis** touting their business on Buenos Aires' streets is one of the city's most characteristic sights and – other than during sudden downpours, when everyone seems to decide to take one at once, or in the outer barrios, where few people ever use them – it's rare that it takes more than a few minutes, or even seconds, to flag down a cab. The meter starts at $2.60 and clocks up 26 centavos every couple of blocks, representing a sizeable increase over recent years, but still resulting in fares that rival the bus or metro in many cities around the world. Taxi rides are sometimes white-knuckle affairs – drivers range from amiable characters who drive carefully and like to chat to maniacs who seem to want to involve you and others on the streets in some road-borne suicide pact, though the latter are mercifully rare. Regardless of road skills, drivers are generally trustworthy, despite occasional reports of their using accomplices to rob passengers.

Radio taxis are regarded as more secure and better quality than the unaffiliated type – they are distinguished by the company name on the side and can be hailed in the street or ordered by telephone. **Remises** are plain cars that can also booked through an office. They're cheaper and usually more comfortable than taxis for getting to the airport (they tend to have larger boots) and you may prefer to book one for early-morning starts to either the bus terminal or Aeroparque. For numbers of radio taxi and remise companies see "Listings", p.180.

Driving

Make no mistake: **driving** in Buenos Aires demands nerves of steel to negotiate the traffic, which at times feels like a Formula One race, with high-speed weaving common and even a split-second hesitation punished by a fusillade of honking. The good news is that the city is a straightforward place to navigate once you've got the hang of the street system. With a few exceptions – notably avenidas 9 de Julio and Del Libertador – the streets are one way, with the direction (which mostly alternates street by street) marked on the street signs with an arrow. Some streets within the centre, mostly around the financial district, are closed to private traffic during the day.

The local technique for crossing the city's numerous traffic-light-less intersections at night is to slow down and flash your lights to warn drivers of your approach. In theory the vehicle coming from the right has the right of way, at all times, but be prepared to give way if the other driver looks more determined and never take it for granted that a speeding bus will respect your trajectory: accidents involving buses regularly make the headlines. Parking in the street, wherever the curb is not painted yellow, is allowed. However, car theft has risen sharply in recent years and you may prefer the relative security of a *playa de estacionamiento* (car park; not a beach). There are numerous ones throughout the city centre that charge three or four pesos an hour; look out for the flag-waving dummies or scantily clad ladies marking the entrance.

Many of the world's major **car rental** companies and several national companies (see "Listings", p.179) operate in Buenos Aires, offering a range of vehicles, of which the most economical is usually a Fiat Uno, Suzuki Fun or Daewoo Tico. Be prepared to book some time ahead if you're planning to rent a car over a long weekend or holiday period. Given the excellent public transport system and the abundance of taxis, however, there's really little point in renting a car simply to tour the city.

Accommodation

Buenos Aires' recent rise in popularity with international visitors means that many of the city's best **accommodation** – at all levels – is frequently full. With around half of all the country's hotels in the capital, you should always be able find somewhere to stay, but if you are fussy about where you lay your head, you are advised to reserve in advance. At the budget end, the number of **hostels**, which are mostly of a high quality, has mushroomed in recent years. Indeed, a cheerful hostel or costlier but homely **B&B** tends to be a better deal than the city-centre **hotels**, which can be grim, especially at the middle and lower end of the market. The city has also seen a surge in upmarket **boutique hotels**, altogether more pleasant (though naturally more expensive) places to stay, catering principally to international visitors and scattered throughout the central neighbourhoods. Wherever you spend the night, a fan or air-conditioning is really a requirement in summer, and heating a big plus in winter. **Discounts** can sometimes be negotiated, particularly if you are staying for more than a few days, but note that credit cards may entail a surcharge. **Breakfast** is not always included at the budget hotels, but in any case you'll probably get a better start to the day in a nearby *confitería*.

For advice on long-term accommodation, see "Living in Argentina", p.68.

The city centre

The biggest concentration of accommodation is to be found in the **city centre**, mostly hostels and budget to mid-range hotels on and around Avenida de Mayo and Congreso, plus a sprinkling of top-range places in the streets surrounding busy but pedestrianized Florida. It is not a laid-back area in which to stay, and in many of the more traditional hotels you face a choice of internal windowless rooms, or front rooms where it can be hard to escape the noise of the city-centre traffic. However, there are plenty of exceptions, and the area has excellent transport links and is handy for its abundance of shopping and banks.

Hostels

Milhouse Hipólito Yrigoyen 959 ⓣ011/4345-9604, ⓦwww.milhousehostel.com. Large, popular hostel, part of the HI chain, in a three-storey nineteenth-century house a block from Av de Mayo. As well as providing a big communal area, the hostel regularly arranges both in-house events such as tango lessons as well as trips to football matches and nightclubs. Dorms $30, doubles with private bath ❺

V&S Youth Hostel Viamonte 887 ⓣ011/4322-0994, ⓦwww.hostelclub.com. The most luxurious hostel in Buenos Aires, the *V&S* is centrally located in a 1910 French-style mansion. A bar and giant TV top the list of amenities, as well all kinds of interesting organized excursions to keep you occupied. In addition to dormitory accommodation (US$10 per person) there are three great-value double rooms (❺) with private bathrooms and balconies.

Hotels

725 Buenos Aires Roque Sáenz Peña 725 ⓣ011/4131-8000, ⓦwww.725buenosaireshotel.com. A swish bar, trendy restaurant, spa and swimming pool are just some of the attractions at this fabulous hotel, in an equally remarkable 1920s building; the decor combines dark wood with vibrant colour schemes, with gorgeous results. ❾

Castelar Av de Mayo 1152 ⓣ011/4383-5000, ⓦwww.castelarhotel.com.ar. A Buenos Aires institution, this pleasant, old-fashioned hotel, where Spanish poet Federico García Lorca stayed when he was in town, offers attractive and soundproof, if slightly over-priced, rooms with big comfortable beds. There's also a glamorous bar downstairs and a sauna/spa. ❼

Chile Av de Mayo 1297 ⓣ011/4383-7877. Well-known Art Deco hotel; some rooms have balconies overlooking a side street and others have great views of Av de Mayo. All are spacious, with central heating, a/c and TV. ❺

Concept Santiago del Estero 186 ⓣ011/4383-3473. The angular, rather 1980s design of this place is quite different from the traditional hotels in the neighbourhood, but the brightly coloured rooms are good value for money and even have digital panels to control the a/c and TV. ❺

Esplendor San Martín 780 ⓣ011/5256-8800, ⓦwww.esplendorbuenosaires.com. In this boutique hotel belonging to the Fën group (ⓦwww.grupofen.com) 52 rooms, including very spacious suites (US$232 plus tax), are arranged around a luminous atrium, on a corner of the beautiful late-nineteenth-century building mostly occupied by Galerías Pacífico (see p.114). Avant-garde works adorn the immaculate walls and each room has its own luxurious decor. There is a decent restaurant that offers a reasonable *menú ejecutivo* for lunch. ❾

Gran Hotel España Tacuarí 80 ⓣ011/4343-5541. Good budget option in central yet quiet location, with clean, basic rooms, helpful staff and a lovely antique, manually operated elevator. It's worth paying a few pesos more for the front rooms with little balconies. ❸

Hotel de los Dos Congresos Rivadavia 1777 ⓣ011/4371-0072, ⓦwww.hoteldoscongresos.com. Well-maintained hotel in a late-nineteenth-century building. The best rooms at the front overlook the Congreso building and have a spiral staircase and mezzanine within them. All are decorated in a clean, modern style with a/c, TV and mini-bar, although the interior rooms can be on the stuffy side. ❻

Ibis Buenos Aires Hipólito Yrigoyen 1592 ⓣ011/5300-5555, ⓦwww.ibishotel.com. Part of the Accor chain, the *Ibis* is a good-value hotel, offering clean, simple comfort and a friendly welcome in the city centre, near the Congreso building. ❻

Jousten Av Corrientes 280 ⓣ011/4321-6750, ⓦwww.nh-hoteles.com. High-end accommodation in a beautiful early twentieth-century building popular with business travellers but with appeal for all; also has an excellent restaurant serving modern Spanish cuisine. One of four central hotels ran by the Spanish NH designer hotel chain. ❾

Lyon Riobamba 251 ⓣ011/4372-0100, ⓦwww.hotel-lyon.com.ar. Elegant hotel on a relatively quiet street one block from Callao, with exceptionally large suites. ❻

Nuevo Hotel Callao Callao 292 ⓣ011/4374-3861, ⓦwww.hotelcallao.com.ar. Pleasant hotel with light, clean and attractive rooms, some with great balconies overlooking Callao and all with a/c and TV. ❻

Nuevo Mundial Av de Mayo 1298 ⓣ011/4383-0011, ⓦwww.hotel-mundial.com.ar. Beautifully old-fashioned hotel (vertigo sufferers might wish to avoid looking down on the stunning central stairwell), with some rooms boasting decent-sized balconies; the more expensive "Comfort" rooms have been renovated recently and are more modern. ❸–❺

O'Rei Lavalle 733 ☎011/4393-7186. The high-ceilinged rooms are a bit gloomy and basic, but the *O'Rei* has two things really going for it – it's very central, and very cheap. ❸

Obelisco Center Roque Sáenz Peña 991 ☎011/4326-0909, ⓦwww.obeliscohotel.com.ar. Large, comfortable rooms in a hotel overlooking the Obelisco monument – you won't have any trouble finding your way back after a late night. Apartments with kitchenettes also available. ❽

Roma Av de Mayo 1413 ☎011/4381-4921. A good deal, given its pleasant and central location, the *Roma* has some nice, if slightly noisy, rooms with balconies looking onto Av de Mayo, and a fabulous antique elevator. ❹

Sportsman Rivadavia 1425 ☎011/4381-8021, ⓦwww.hotelsportsman.com.ar. Popular budget hotel in a rambling old building with lots of character, though the interior is beginning to show its age. There's a range of rooms available, all with fans and some with shared bathrooms; the nicest ones are the en-suite doubles at the front, which have balconies. ❸–❹

San Telmo, Monserrat, Puerto Madero and Constitución

Most accommodation in the south is in the barrio of **San Telmo**, a magnet for travellers as much for its cobbled streets and prettily crumbling buildings as for its budget hotels and youth hostels; much of **Monserrat**, technically a separate neighbourhood, comes under its wing both in terms of geography and personality. Newcomer **Puerto Madero** now has a handful of upmarket places to stay, while the area around **Constitución** station, while not the most desirable part of the city, has some interesting accommodation options, as well as plenty of less salubrious budget joints.

Hostels

Antico Hostel Boutique Bolivar 893, San Telmo ☎011/4363-0123, ⓦwww.anticohostel.com. New, above-average hostel, with a lovely open central patio where guests share breakfast around a large table; it also has a bar and comfy chairs. There's another bar on the roof, where the fire is lit for a *parrilla* at weekends. Rooms are well kept, and all have a/c and lockers. Shared rooms are US$12 per person (discount for stays of more than five days) and there is one en-suite double (❻).

Che Lagarto Youth Hostel Venezuela 857, Monserrat ☎011/4304-7618, ⓦwww.chelagarto.com. Long-running, laid-back hostel popular with a younger (and sometimes rather noisy) crowd; recently moved to the edges of San Telmo. $25 per person, or ❸ for a double with private bath.

El Hostal de San Telmo Carlos Calvo 614, San Telmo ☎011/4300-6899, ⓦwww.elhostaldesantelmo.com. In one of the prettiest parts of San Telmo, this small hostel is friendly and well kept, with laundry facilities, a terrace and a barbecue area. Rooms have two, four or eight beds costing US$6 a night.

Tango City Hostel Inn Piedras 680, Monserrat ☎0800/666-4678 or 011/4300-5764, ⓦwww.hostel-inn.com. Wildly popular with young backpackers – expect significant alcohol consumption, if less than snappy service – this hostel is now something of an institution. Beds start at US$10, which includes Internet access and extras such as Spanish and tango lessons. Its smaller, slightly quieter sister establishment, the *Hostel Inn*, is nearby at Humberto Primo 820. Advance reservation essential Dec–March.

Hotels

La Cayetana México 1330, Monserrat ☎011/4383-2230, ⓦwww.lacayetanahotel.com.ar. Beautifully renovated nineteenth-century townhouse, with a huge sun-lit central patio and much of the original furniture worked harmoniously into the rooms, each of which is individually decorated. The only drawback is the location near Constitución – a good seven blocks away from anywhere of interest – but taxis are always available. Reservations essential; the hotel won't accept anyone who just turns up. ❽

Faena Hotel & Universe Marta Salotti 445, Puerto Madero Este ☎011/4010-9000, ⓦwww.faenahotelanduniverse.com. Buenos Aires' hotel for the in-crowd, this former grain-storage building has been given a serious Philippe Starck makeover and now has a *belle époque* jazz bar, a café stuffed with kitsch antiques, a floor-to-ceiling white restaurant with unicorn heads on the walls, an oriental spa and, of course, swish rooms. It's the kind of place that's too cool for a reception – you get an "experience manager" – and where the movie producers and celebrities that stay here certainly don't talk about anything as crude as money; count on US$500 and up for a room. 9

Gran Hotel América Bernardo de Irigoyen 1608, Constitución ⓣ011/4307-8785, ⓦwww.granhotelamerica.com.ar. A stone's throw from Constitución station, this reasonably priced hotel was where famous tango composer Angel Villoldo entertained his lady friends. Some of the rooms are a bit gloomy and noisy but the large, airy triples are a good deal at $70. 3

Lugar Gay Defensa 1120, San Telmo ⓣ011/4300-4747, ⓦwww.lugargay.org. Behind an unmarked green door and flanked by two antique stores, this exclusively male B&B provides a welcoming atmosphere for single gay men and couples. 6

Los Tres Reyes Brasil 425 ⓣ011/4300-9456. Just half a block from Parque Lezama, the simple but comfortable rooms and spotless private bathrooms are excellent value for the money. Breakfast included. 4

Youkali Kultur-Hotel Estados Unidos 1393, Constitución ⓣ011/4381-6064, ⓦwww.youkali.com.ar. An ordinary-looking building in a rather run-down neighbourhood is the surprising home to a small offbeat hotel, where each of the five rooms is decorated differently, with an artist's touch; all guests have use of the flower-filled sun terrace, and there's a modern German restaurant and bar downstairs. 6–7

Retiro and Recoleta

These two barrios, jointly known as Barrio Norte, are where the city's top-flight luxury hotels tend to be located, although some cheaper options exist too. The central area of **Retiro** around Plaza San Martín contains a limited smattering of hotels. As you move northwards into **Recoleta**, the possibilities increase, although so does the distance from the city centre. Nonetheless, Recoleta has plenty to offer *per se* – restaurants, bars and shops – and is still within walking distance (about 20min) of the microcentro, but with less hustle and bustle.

Hotels and hostels

Alvear Palace Hotel Av Alvear 1891, Recoleta ⓣ011/4804-7777, ⓦwww.alvearpalace.com. Once the choice of wealthy landowners and now the favourite of politicians, royalty, musicians and film stars, this is the most stylish and traditional of all Buenos Aires' luxury hotels. It offers fabulously refurbished decorated rooms in Louis XV style and all the extras you would expect, including a personal butler. If you can't afford the US$450 price tag (for a standard, that is – the "Royal Suite" goes for ten times that), you can still enjoy the pool for $35 during the day – a tempting option in the dead of summer. 9

Ayacucho Palace Ayacucho 1408, Recoleta ⓣ011/4806-1815, ⓦwww.ayacuchohotel.com.ar. Though housed in a smart French-style building, the rooms in this hotel are rather dowdy. That said, they are clean, comfortable and come with a/c. 7

Design Suites and Towers Marcelo T. de Alvear 1683, Recoleta ⓣ011/4814-8700, ⓦwww.designsuites.com. One of the first modern design hotels to open in the city (they now have branches open or planned in Bariloche, Calafate, Salta and Ushuaia), it has maintained its sky-high standards, with enormous apartment-like rooms and some even more gigantic suites (US$175 plus tax), plus a designer goods shop and art gallery. 9

Etoile Pres. Ortíz 1835, Recoleta ⓣ011/4805-2626, ⓦwww.etoile.com.ar. Modern, glitzy hotel with very large rooms and its own health club. The slightly more expensive front rooms have fantastic bird's-eye views of Recoleta Cemetery. 8

Four Seasons Posadas 1086, Retiro ⓣ011/4321-1200, ⓦwww.fourseasons.com/buenosaires. Part of the international chain, this fantastically luxurious hotel is divided between a modern tower-block and the *belle époque* Alazaga Unzué mansion (see p.134), which looks like a French chateau inside and out. Sun brunch, open to the public, is served in the latter; rates around US$350. 9

Gran Dorá Maipú 963, Retiro ⓣ011/4312-7391, ⓦwww.dorahotel.com.ar. Airy, if rather old-fashioned, rooms and spotless marble bathrooms, in a central, business-oriented establishment. 7

Guido Palace Guido 1780, Recoleta ⓣ011/4812-0341, ⓦwww.guidopalace.com.ar. Not exactly a palace, more a functional, typical mid-range hotel. Its big advantage is its location in the heart of Recoleta. 6

Lion d'Or Hotel Pacheco de Melo 2019, Recoleta ⓣ011/4803-8992, ⓦwww.hotel-liondor.com.ar. Homely, friendly place, with a variety of appealing rooms mercifully free of the tasteless decor found in similar places nearby. Rooms vary considerably in size, style and price, ranging from $50 for an internal single with shared bath to $220 for a lovely, spacious triple with a fireplace and balcony. 4–6

Marriott Plaza Hotel Florida 1005, Retiro ⓣ011/4318-3000, ⓦwww.marriottplaza.com.ar. Long-established luxury hotel now run by the Marriott chain, which has given it a slightly corporate feel. Rooms are plush but rather bland; the nicest ones have a stunning view over Plaza San Martín. Elegant 1930s-style bar and good restaurant. 9

Palacio Duhau-Park Hyatt Av Alvear 1661, Recoleta ⓣ011/5171-1234. The Duhau family home on the city's most desirable street (see p.135) is now a hyper-luxury hotel, with huge rooms decorated with soothing woods and marble baths; the top-floor Duhau suite has a wrap-around terrace, among its many enticing features. The giant, superbly lit swimming pool, restaurant, vinoteca and *Oak Bar* mean you never need to leave the building. Rack rates US$400–1000. 9

Plaza Francia E. Schiaffino 2189 and Av del Libertador, Recoleta ⓣ011/4804-9631, ⓦwww.hotelplazafrancia.com. Immaculate hotel with handsome but somewhat cramped rooms, plus some roomy suites affording panoramic views of Recoleta (US$280). Avoid the noisy rooms overlooking Avenida Libertador, though. 8

Recoleta Youth Hostel Libertad 1216, Recoleta ⓣ011/4812-4419, ⓦwww.trhostel.com.ar. Smart hostel in an attractively modernized and spacious old mansion. Accommodation is in a mixture of dormitories (US$8 per person) and double rooms (2), and there is a large terrace area and good facilities including TV and Internet access.

Palermo and Belgrano

Away from the blasting horns and spluttering buses of the centre, **Palermo** is a greener, more relaxed neighbourhood in which to stay. There are some fabulous, if expensive, small hotels, a handful of extremely agreeable B&Bs and some fun hostels, all with the added benefit of being close to the city's most interesting bars, restaurants and boutiques. It's also worth bearing in mind that the streets here tend to be cleaner and safer than in more southerly districts, though some in Palermo Viejo suffer from a surfeit of dogs. There are very few accommodation options in adjacent **Belgrano**, but this calm barrio does have a couple of outstanding boutique hotels and a quirky B&B.

B&Bs and hostels

Casa Amarilla El Salvador 4586, Palermo ⓣ011/4832-0680, ⓦwww.laamarillita.com.ar. Newish, small and attractive hostel in trendy Palermo Soho, with shared cooking facilities, comfortable living room and terrace. There's also a room with a kitchen area refurbished especially for wheelchair users. Beds from US$7 per person, with discounts for extended stays.

Casa Bloody Mary Volta 1867, Belgrano ⓣ011/4777-7106, ⓦwww.casabloodymary.com. This Tudor-style house – hence the name, with a twist of irony, nothing to do with cocktails – on the edge of trendy Las Cañitas has a handful of comfortable rooms done out in a restrained style, and serves a typical Porteño breakfast based on scrumptious *medialunas*. 6–8

Casa Esmeralda Honduras 5765, Palermo ⓣ011/4772-2446, ⓦwww.casaesmeralda.com.ar. Wonderful Franco–Argentine-run guest-house smack in the middle of Palermo Hollywood, with a green garden and friendly service. Shared rooms for US$8, and some doubles (3).

Garufa Fitz Roy 1925, Palermo ⓣ011/4771-6431, ⓦwww.garufabuenosaires.com. Tiny, unpretentious B&B in Palermo Hollywood with a *quincho* for *asados* and owners with an interest in tango; note that it is due for refurbishment in late 2007 and plans to go more upmarket, with prices to match. 7

La Otra Orilla Julián Álvarez 1779, Palermo ⓣ011/4867-4070, ⓦwww.otraorilla.com.ar. Lovely, quiet little B&B in Palermo Viejo, with seven rooms of varying sizes, all comfortably, brightly and tastefully decorated, and some with balconies. Prices, including buffet breakfast and free Internet, range from $105 for the smallest single with shared bath to $435 for the suite with a/c and TV. 5–7

Posada Palermo Salguero 1655, Palermo ⓣ011/4826-8792, ⓦwww.posadapalermo.com. Wonderful B&B in a more residential corner of Palermo, away, but not far, from the nerve centre of Soho; this typical *casa chorizo* (kind of elongated townhouse found in most Argentine cities), offers smart rooms, a homely atmosphere and a great breakfast, including home-made preserves. 7

So Hostel Charcas 4416, Palermo ⓣ011/4779-2949, ⓦwww.sohostel.com.ar. Excellent Palermo Soho hostel with accommodation ranging from dorms at $22 per person to rooms with private bath and TV (❸); all rooms have a/c and there is a decent café serving breakfast.

Hotels

Alpino Cabello 3318, Palermo ⓣ011/4802-5151, ⓦwww.hotel-alpino.com.ar. The *Alpino*, located in a residential sector of Palermo near the Parque Las Heras, has appealing, spacious rooms with baths; they also rent rooms for around $100 from 9am to 6pm, which can be useful for rest between flights. ❻

Bo Bo Guatemala 4882, Palermo ⓣ011/4774-0505, ⓦwww.bobo hotel.com. In addition to its own refined restaurant, this stylish but friendly boutique hotel offers rooms done out in different styles from classical to pop – which basically means lots of yellow. ❾

Costa Petit Hotel Costa Rica 5141, Palermo ⓣ011/4776-8296, ⓦwww.costapetithotel.com. An outdoor swimming pool sets this stunning Palermo Soho establishment apart from its rivals; the hotel can also arrange activities such as polo or shopping. Just four handsomely decorated rooms, all with a retro look but modern conveniences. ❾

Finisterra Báez 248, Belgrano ⓣ011/4773-0901, ⓦwww.248finisterra.com. A garden, terrace and outdoor Jacuzzi are some of the extras justifying the high prices at this converted Belgrano townhouse, furnished with early twentieth-century antiques from the same period as the building. ❾

Home Honduras 5860, Palermo ⓣ011/4778-1008, ⓦwww.homebuenosaires.com. Owned and run by a British record producer and his Irish–Argentine wife, this masterpiece of modern architecture and hotel design is simply incredible: from the wallpaper in each room to the swimming pool and deck, the attention to detail is breathtaking. Every Fri night a DJ adds further coolness to the restaurant/bar. For the outstanding "Garden" suite you'll have to fork out US$320 plus tax. ❾

Krista Bonpland 1665, Palermo ⓣ011/4771-4697, ⓦwww.kristahotel.com.ar. This exquisitely elegant mansion in Palermo Hollywood functions as a fine boutique hotel, where the rooms each have their own character thanks to details such as wood panelling, stained-glass windows and mouldings. ❼–❽

My BA Zabala 1925, Belgrano ⓣ011/4787-5765, ⓦwww.mybaahotel.com.ar. Magnificent 1940s-style house in a smart part of Belgrano, with rooms ranging from a superb "standard" to a luxurious suite decorated with retro Argentine design furnishings and fittings – the bathrooms are exemplary. Modern bistro restaurant attached. ❾

Vain Thames 2226, Palermo ⓣ011/4776-8246, ⓦwww.vainuniverse.com. A complimentary drink and massage let you know what you have to look forward to at one of the most pleasurable boutique hotels in the city: gorgeous decor, designer furniture, a beguiling interior patio and a wine bar all lurk behind a fabulous Neoclassical facade. ❽–❾

The city centre

A sometimes chaotic mix of cafés, grand nineteenth-century public edifices, high-rise office blocks and tearing traffic, the **city centre** exudes both energy and elegance. Its heart is the spacious, palm-dotted **Plaza de Mayo**, a good place to begin a tour of the area, perhaps more for its historical and political connections than for its somewhat mismatched collection of buildings, which includes the famous **Casa Rosada**, or government house. If you head north from the plaza, you reach **La City**, where financial institutions jostle for space with a handful of modest museums. A gentler introduction to the area, however, would be to amble westwards from the plaza along **Avenida de Mayo**, with its impressive selection of Art Nouveau and Art Deco architecture. At its western end, Avenida de Mayo opens onto the **Plaza del Congreso**, presided over by the **Congreso** building, the seat of the senate.

From Plaza del Congreso, the route north along Avenida Callao will take you to **Avenida Corrientes**. Now a busy shopping street, Corrientes was famous in the past as the hub of the city's left-leaning café society. Though there's less plotting going on here today, it's still the place to get some culture, lined as it is with bookstores, music shops, cinemas, theatres and cafés. A short detour north from Corrientes will take you to **Plaza Lavalle**, a long grassy square most notable for its opera house, the regal **Teatro Colón**.

East from Plaza Lavalle, you'll hit the jarring and enormous **Avenida 9 de Julio** – the city's multi-lane central nerve. Presiding at its heart is the stark white **Obelisco**, a 67-metre stake through the intersection between 9 de Julio and Corrientes. Crossing east over the avenue, you could head down pedestrianized **Lavalle**, which will bring you to the central section of **Calle Florida**, where you'll be swept along by a stream of human traffic past elegant *galerías* (arcades) and stores of every kind. East of Florida lies a grid of much quieter streets – commonly referred to as "El Bajo" and home to some of the centre's best bars and restaurants – which lead down to Avenida L.N. Além. East of El Bajo is the city's newest barrio, **Puerto Madero**, a swanky assemblage of restaurant, loft and office space in converted docks. On the eastern side of the docks, the spectacularly wild **Reserva Ecológica**, a reclaimed park filled with pampas grass and birds, runs along the city's old riverside avenue, the **Costanera Sur**.

Plaza de Mayo

The one place that can lay claim to most of Buenos Aires' historical moments and monuments is the **Plaza de Mayo**. It's been bombed, filled by Evita's *descamisados* (literally "the shirtless ones", or manual workers) and was for many years the site of the Madres de Plaza de Mayo's weekly demonstration (see box below). Towering palm trees give the plaza a wonderfully tropical

Madres de Plaza de Mayo

Many of those arrested, tortured and executed during the **1976–83 dictatorship** (see Contexts, p.799) were **young dissidents**, who vanished without a trace. Their mothers, frustrated by the authorities' intimidating silence when they tried to find out what had happened to their children, in 1976 started what would become the **Madres** movement.

At first just a handful of women, the Madres met weekly in the **Plaza de Mayo**, the historical centre of the city, as much to support each other as to embarrass the regime into providing answers; the wearing of white headscarves emerged as a means of identification. As their numbers grew, so did their defiance – standing their ground and challenging the military to carry out its threat to fire on them in front of foreign journalists, for instance. Some disappeared themselves after the notorious "Angel of Death" Alfredo Astiz infiltrated the group, posing as the brother of a *desaparecido* (disappeared).

In 1982, during the Malvinas/Falklands crisis, the Madres were accused of being anti-patriotic for their stance **against the war**, a conflict that they claimed was an attempt by the regime to divert attention away from its murderous acts. With the return to democracy in 1983, the Madres were disappointed by the new government's reluctance to delve too deeply into what had happened during the "Dirty War", as well as by the later granting of immunity to many of those accused of kidnap, torture and murder. The group rejected economic "compensation" and both it and the respect in which it is held were key in finally getting the amnesty laws overturned in 2005. The Madres continued to protest at the Pirámide de Mayo weekly until January 2006, when, after around 1500 protests, the Madres finally brought their long vigil to an end, citing confidence in President Kirchner. Now some of the Madres have branched into other areas of social protest: the emblem of the white headscarf was at the forefront of the movement to demand the **non-payment of the country's foreign debt**, among other issues.

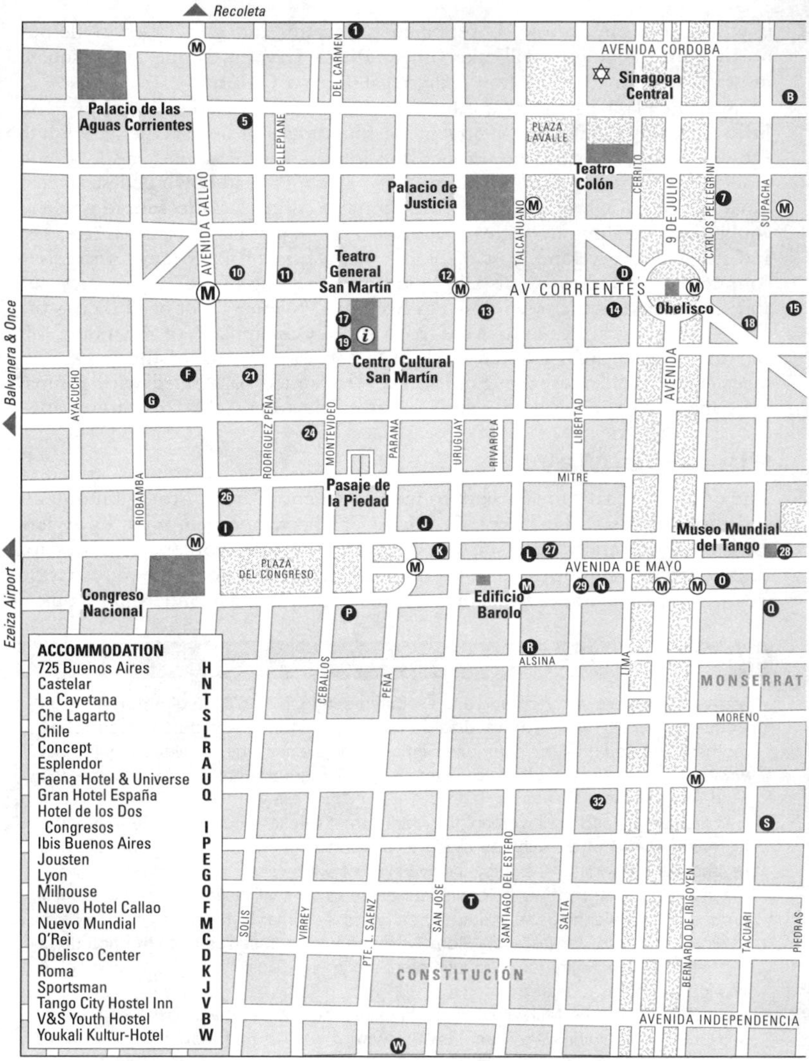

EATING & DRINKING

A222	16	Brasserie Petanque	33	Cancun	34	El Claustro	3	La Esquina de las Flores	1
La Americana	26	Cabaña Las Lilas	23	Celta Bar	21	Confitería Ideal	18	Fin del Mundo	35
Arturito	14	Cadore	10	Chiquilín	19	Crizia	8	La Giralda	12
Bice	6	Café Tortoni	28	La Cigale	4	Las Cuartetas	15	Los 36 Billares	27

feel. At its centre stands the **Pirámide de Mayo**, erected in 1811 to mark the first anniversary of the May 25 Revolution, when a junta overthrew the Spanish viceroy, declared Buenos Aires' independence from Spain and set about establishing the city's jurisdiction over the rest of the territory. The headscarves painted on the ground around the pyramid echo those worn by the Madres.

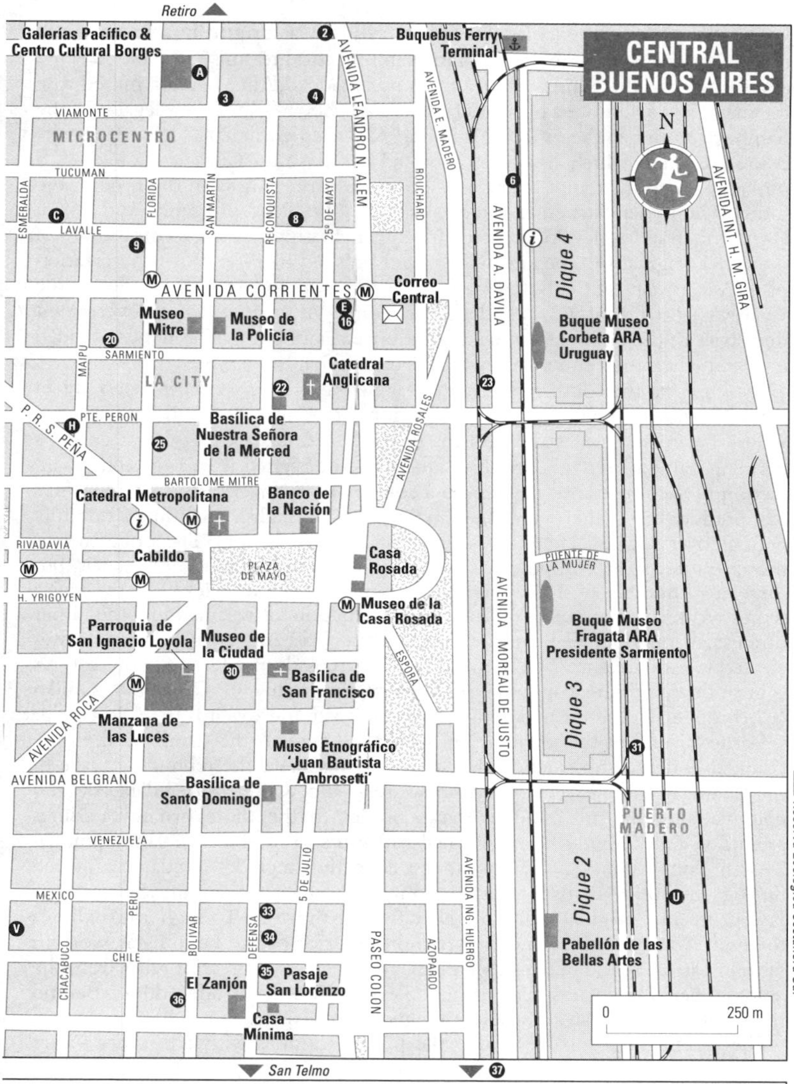

El Globo	29	Laurak-Bat	32	Patio San Ramón	22	Richmond	9	Winery	2
Granix	25	Medio y Medio	24	La Paz	11	El Retortuño	36		
Güerrin	13	New Brighton	20	Pippo	17	Siga La Vaca	37		
"i" Fresh Market	31	Parrilla Peña	5	La Puerto Rico	30	Tomo 1	7		

Evita, Maradona, Galtieri and Perón have all addressed the crowds from the balcony of the unmissable **Casa de Gobierno**, otherwise known as the **Casa Rosada** (enquire at Museo de la Casa Rosada, see p.106, about the possibility of guided tours; take your passport), the pink governmental palace that occupies the eastern end of the square. The practice of painting buildings pink was common during the nineteenth century, particularly in the countryside, where you'll still see many estancias this colour, which was originally achieved with the use of ox blood, for both decorative and practical reasons – the blood acted as a fixative for the whitewash to which it was added. After being a muted rose for many years, followed by a brief phase in a shocking pink – a legacy of the flamboyant Menem years – the building was restored in 2007 to a deep rose colour, a shade which has been patented as "Casa de Gobierno pink" in a probably fruitless attempt to prevent any more tampering with the tone in the future. The present structure, a typically Argentine blend of French and Italian Renaissance styles, developed in a fairly organic fashion. It stands on the site of the city's original fort, begun in 1594 and finished in 1720. With the creation of the Viceroyalty of the Río de la Plata in 1776, the fort was remodelled as the viceroy's palace. In 1862, President Bartolomé Mitre moved the government ministries to the building, remodelling it once again. The final touch was added in 1885, when the central arch was added, unifying the facade.

Visits are via the south side entrance, which also leads to the **Museo de la Casa Rosada**, Hipólito Yrigoyen 219 (Mon–Fri 10am–6pm, Sun 2–6pm; free), whose basement houses the remains of the old Aduana de Taylor, a customs building named after the British engineer who designed it in 1855. The main section of the museum is devoted to a collection of objects used by Argentina's past presidents, together with panels in Spanish and English providing a carefully neutral overview of Argentina's turbulent political history. The collection is mostly rather staid, composed largely of official photographs and medals, but there are a number of slightly more idiosyncratic exhibits – look for the tango scores written in honour of political parties and politicians, including the rather unmusical-sounding *El Socialista*, written for socialist Alfredo Palacios, who was elected to Congress in 1904. Behind the Casa Rosada, the Plaza Colón features a gigantic Argentine flag and a Carrara marble statue of **Cristóbal Colón** (Christopher Columbus), looking out to the river and towards the Old World.

At the far end of the square from the Casa Rosada is the **Cabildo**, the only colonial-era civil construction that managed to survive the rebuilding craze of the 1880s. Its simple, unadorned lines, green and white shuttered facade and colonnaded front still stand in stark contrast to the more ornate buildings around it. The Cabildo houses a small **museum** (Tues–Fri 11.30am–6pm, Sat 2–6pm, Sun 1–6pm; $2) whose modest collection includes standards captured during the 1806 British invasion, some delicate watercolours by Enrique Pellegrini and original plans of the city and the fort. Though the exhibits themselves are of only minor interest, the interior of the building is worth a visit, in particular the upper galleries lined with an assortment of relics from the colonial period onwards, such as huge keys and sturdy wooden doors. Behind the Cabildo, a patio area houses a café and small artisans' fair.

The architectural mix pervading the plaza continues with the rather severe Neoclassical facade of the **Catedral Metropolitana** (daily 9am–7pm; free guided tours to the cathedral Mon–Fri 11.30am & 4pm, Sat & Sun 4pm, guided visits of the crypt Mon–Fri 1.15pm, Sat & Sun 10am), which, despite its location, is far from being the most impressive cathedral in the city, let alone the country. Like so many of Buenos Aires' churches, the cathedral assumed its final form over many years; built and rebuilt since the sixteenth century, the present building was completed in the mid-nineteenth century. The twelve columns that front the entrance represent the twelve apostles; above them sits a carved tympanum whose bas-relief depicts the arrival of Jacob and his family in Egypt. The interior features Venetian mosaic floors, gilded columns and a silver-plated altar, though by far the most significant item is the solemnly guarded **mausoleum** to Independence hero San Martín.

△ Plaza de Mayo

La City

Immediately north of the Plaza de Mayo, **La City**, Buenos Aires' financial district, takes up the southeastern quarter of the grid of streets known as the microcentro, bounded to the west by Calle Florida, to the north by Corrientes and to the east by Avenida L.N. Além. La City's atmosphere serves as a barometer of the country's economic ups and downs – from frantic money changing in the 1980s to the noisy pot-banging demonstrations that followed the savings withdrawal freeze of the early twenty-first century – so its current busy but ordered scenes of bank workers going about their business must come as a relief for the government. The tight confines and endless foot traffic make it difficult to look up, but if you do you'll be rewarded with an impressive spread of grand facades crowned with domes and towers.

La City was once known as the *barrio inglés*, in reference to the large number of British immigrants who set up business here. Indeed, the first financial institutions were built in a rather Victorian style; it seems that the Porteño elite thought their houses should be French and their banks British. There's also an Anglican church, the Doric-style **Catedral Anglicana de San Juan Bautista**, three blocks north of Plaza de Mayo, at 25 de Mayo 276: the church was built on land donated by General Rosas in 1830. Around the corner, at Reconquista and Perón, there's the **Basílica de Nuestra Señora de la Merced**, one of the most beautiful and least visited churches in Buenos Aires, although it has been favoured by important political and military figures through the ages. The facade has been recently restored, while every inch of the sombre interior is ornamented with gilt or tiles. Next door, at Reconquista 269, is one of the city's best-kept secrets, the **Convento de San Ramón** (Mon–Fri 10.30am–6pm; free). At its heart is a charming courtyard where you can eat in the restaurant under the arches, or just take a break from elbowing your way through the crowds outside.

One block west, at San Martín 336, you'll find the small **Museo Mitre** (closed for refurbishment at time of writing), housed in a discreet colonial residence and still bearing the old street number 208. Once the residence of Bartolomé Mitre, who founded the newspaper *La Nación* and was president in the 1860s, the rooms are grouped around a central patio and have been restored using the house's original contents. They give a good insight into nineteenth-century living; look out for the opium pipe in the study. More drug paraphernalia is on display opposite, at the **Museo de la Policía** at San Martín 353, with entrance on 7th floor (Mon–Fri 2–6pm, closed Jan & Feb; free). Here you can inspect old police uniforms, including one that's pure gaucho, right down to the *boleadoras* (lasso balls). Spookier exhibits include cases of detection equipment, an embalmed police dog and a whole array of devices used by thieves, drug dealers and anarchists. A black-magic section includes the cape belonging to José López Rega, Isabel Perón's sinister adviser and founder of the Triple A death squad, and you can also see the box where Juan Perón's hands were kept after they were mysteriously removed from his body. The gratuitously gory forensic medicine display is best avoided unless you have a very strong stomach.

Avenida de Mayo

Heading west from Plaza de Mayo takes you along one of the capital's grandest thoroughfares, **Avenida de Mayo**, a wide, tree-lined boulevard flanked with ornamental street lamps and offering a stunning ten-block vista between Plaza de Mayo and Plaza del Congreso. Part of a project to remodel the city along the lines of Haussmann's Paris, Avenida de Mayo is notable for its architectural melange; many of its buildings are topped with decorative domes and ornamented with elaborate balustrades and sinuous caryatids. Unimpressed with the city's European pretensions, Borges called it one of the saddest areas in Buenos Aires, yet even he couldn't resist the charm of its **confiterías** and traditional restaurants, a handful of which remain open.

Just half a block west of Plaza de Mayo, at Avenida de Mayo 567, there's the magnificent, French-influenced **La Prensa** building, with grand wrought-iron doors, curvaceous lamps and a steep mansard roof. The building now houses the city's culture secretariat but was originally built as the headquarters of the national newspaper *La Prensa*, which first went into circulation in 1869. You can pop in to take a peek at the opulent interior – all ornamental glass and elaborate woodwork – or take advantage of one of the free guided tours organized by the city government (Sat 4pm & 5pm, Sun hourly 11am–4pm). Open tango classes for beginners also take place in the central patio (Sat 3pm).

The splendour of Buenos Aires' golden age is visible underground as well – on the corner of Perú and Avenida de Mayo, **Perú station**, the second stop on Line A of the subte (you'll need a ticket to enter), has been refurbished with old advertisements and fittings by the imaginative Museo de la Ciudad (see p.117), to reflect the history of the line. Two and a half blocks west, at Avenida de Mayo 829, you'll find the **Café Tortoni** (Ⓣ011/4342-4328, Ⓦwww.cafetortoni.com.ar). Its presence on every tourist's must-visit list – some days you even have to line up to get in – has spoilt the atmosphere a little and hiked the prices a lot, but the *Tortoni*, which has existed in some form for over 150 years, is still worth stopping by for a *cafecito*. Famous for its literary and artistic connections – notable habitués included poets Alfonsina Storni and Rubén Darío – its heavy brown columns and Art Nouveau-mirrored walls create an elegant ambience. Next door, at Avenida de Mayo 833, the fine **Palacio Carlos Gardel** is home to the Academia Nacional del Tango, with year-long courses in elements of tango, and the **Museo Mundial del Tango**, on the first floor and accessed from the building's back entrance at Rivadavia 830 (Mon–Fri 2–6pm; $5). The museum traces the history of tango (in Spanish, though an English-speaking guide may be available) through displays such as Tita Merello's glittering dress and a photo of men dancing tango together in 1910 – women were rarely available to dance in those days, except in brothels.

Cross Avenida 9 de Julio – said to be one of the world's widest avenues –and you'll pass a stunning black statue of **Don Quixote** on a white base that represents the fictional knight's home La Mancha. Parallel to it on Hipólito Yrigoyen, memorial slabs recall those who died during the disturbances on December 20, 2001 (see Contexts, p.805). A further couple of blocks west there's another famous café, but one with a very different atmosphere from the *Tortoni*. The cavernous and rather spartan **36 Billares**, Av de Mayo 1265, introduced the game of billiards to Argentina in 1882. There's still a popular billiards salon downstairs, as well as a games room at the back of the café where an almost exclusively male crowd passes the day playing chess, dice, pool and *truco*, Argentina's favourite card game.

Edificio Barolo

On the south side of the street, at no. 1370, stands the avenue's most fantastical building, the **Edificio Barolo** – named after the extremely wealthy farmer of Italian origin who had it built. Designed by the Italian architect Mario Palanti and constructed between 1919 and 1923, its unusual top-heavy form is an example of the eclectic style popular at the time. Created as a monument to Dante's *Divine Comedy* (of which Barolo was a great admirer) it is full of references to the epic poem – its different sections represent Hell, Purgatory and Heaven, its height in metres equals the number of songs (100) and it has 22 floors, the same as the number of stanzas in each canto. Moreover, in early June, the roof's tip aligns with the Southern Cross constellation – the "entrance to heaven". Rather prosaically, the building is used mostly for offices, but there is also a sumptuous ground-floor café/restaurant, *Palacio Barolo* (see p.163). On Mondays and Thursdays (2–7pm; $15; Ⓦwww.pbarolo.com.ar/visitasguiadas) there are fascinating guided tours of the building, explaining its details and symbolism.

Plaza del Congreso

At its western extremity, Avenida de Mayo opens up to encircle the **Plaza del Congreso**, a three-block-long wedge of grass dotted with statues, a fountain, swooping pigeons and a number of benches. Its western end is presided over by the Greco-Roman **Congreso** building (guided visits in English Mon, Tues, Thurs & Fri 11am & 4pm at Hipólito Yrigoyen 1846; free), inaugurated in 1906 and designed by Vittorio Meano, who was also the architect of the Teatro Colón (see p.112). The northern wing, is where the Lower Chamber sits, while the southern wing is used by the Upper Chamber of senators. The semicircular rooms where debates take place are an interesting mixture of traditional and modern – as the politicians take their seats, a sensor under each chair indicates if the chamber has reached quorum. Each member's fingerprint is read by a computer in the back of each seat before he or she votes, while the public peeps from behind the velvet curtains of theatrical-looking boxes. Especially diverting is the marble Salon Azul; look up to see the giant 2000kg chandelier featuring figures representing the Republic and its provinces.

The square's most striking monument is the exuberant **Monumento a los dos Congresos**, a series of sculptural allegories atop heavy granite steps and crowned by the triumphant figure of the Republic, erected to commemorate

Argentine party politics

As with most Western democracies, **Argentine politics** have been dominated for as long as anyone can remember by **two major political parties**, with a host of smaller outfits coming and going. The major political force is undoubtedly the party officially called **the Partido Justicialista (PJ)**, but usually referred to as the **Peronists**. This was the party created as the machine behind Juan Domingo Perón. Its political bent can best be described as a sort of **national socialism**, mixing conservative social policy and avid patriotism with protectionist economics and all-out encouragement of trade unions – the latter form the backbone of the party, whose support mostly comes from the working class, especially in the countryside. However, in recent years its ideology has seemingly encompassed just about every conceivable strand of political thought, and factional in-fighting has somewhat inevitably followed. It put up several candidates in the 2003 presidential elections, including former President Menem, the neo-liberal who sold the country's industry and services into foreign hands, and the left-of-centre victor, Néstor Kirchner.

Argentina's other major party is the **Unión Cívica Radical (UCR)**, or the **Radicals**. Formed in 1891, it's the oldest party, and the one favoured by university-educated, city-dwelling professionals. Its politicians usually avoid the populism of the Peronists and tend towards liberal social policy, but despite the name there's nothing especially radical about them. It's hard to pinpoint any kind of clear Radical economic policy, which may be the reason the party made a bad situation worse when it was last in power (1999–2001); President De la Rúa's short term in office was utterly disastrous. As a result, their power waned in the 2003 elections, where they were beaten not just by the Peronists but also by defectors from the party who had formed their own distinct alliances. They remain a weak and fragmented force, with a dissident Radical bloc even supporting current President Kirchner.

the 1813 Assembly and the 1816 Declaration of Independence, made at the Congress of Tucumán. The plaza has traditionally been the final rallying point for many political demonstrations, with the monument acting as a magnet for graffiti – it was recently cleaned and has been fenced off. At the centre of the square stands a greening bronze statue, a somewhat rain-streaked version of Rodin's *The Thinker*. This is *kilómetro cero* – the point from which all roads that lead from Buenos Aires are measured. On the northeastern corner, where Rivadavia crosses Paraná, stands the **Teatro Liceo**, one of the city's oldest theatres still in use.

Avenida Corrientes and around

Running parallel to Avenida de Mayo, four blocks north of Plaza Congreso, **Avenida Corrientes** is another of the city's principal arteries, sweeping down to the lower grounds of El Bajo. Unlike other thoroughfares, it's not the architecture along here that is of note – rather, its the atmosphere generated by its mix of cafés, bookstores, cinemas, theatres and pizzerias. For years, cafés such as *La Paz*, on the corner of Corrientes and Montevideo, and the austere *La Giralda* two blocks west, have been the favoured meeting places of left-wing intellectuals and bohemians – and good places to spot the Porteño talent for whiling away hours over a single tiny coffee.

Corrientes' **bookstores**, many of which stay open till the wee hours, have always been as much places to hang out in as to buy from – in marked contrast to almost every other type of shop in the city, where you'll be accosted by sales assistants as soon as you cross the threshold. The most basic places are simply one long room open to the street with piles of books slung on tables with huge handwritten price labels. There are more upmarket places, too, such as the very swish Gandhi at no.1743 and the leftish, alternative Liberarte at no.1555. Almost as comprehensive as the bookstores are the street's numerous pavement kiosks, proffering a mind-boggling range of newspapers, magazines and books on subjects from psychology to sex to tango.

On the southern side of Corrientes at no.1660, **La Plaza** is a pleasant, winding, tree-lined pedestrian arcade with a handful of cafés, shops and performance spaces, all named after poets such as Pablo Neruda and Alfonsina Storni. One block east, at Corrientes 1530, you'll find the glass front of the **Teatro General San Martín** (see p.173 for booking details), one of the city's most important cultural spaces. As well as the theatre itself, there's an arthouse cinema and a small free gallery that often has some worthwhile exhibitions showcasing Argentine photographers, among other subjects. Adjoining the theatre at the back is a large and rather shabby 1960s building that is home to the eclectic **Centro Cultural General San Martín** (see p.172), a space for cutting-edge art, theatre and dance and also a major venue for conventions and academic debates. Its front entrance is at Sarmiento 1551, but it can also be accessed via the Teatro San Martín.

Just off Bartolomé Mitre, three blocks south of Corrientes (between Montevideo and Paraná), the **Pasaje de la Piedad** is a late nineteenth-century pedestrian street with arched street lamps and grand three-storey houses with elegant porches and stately wooden doors. Currently gated off to the public and with a lot of building work going on, you might not think it worth of a detour, unless you also wish to visit the **Basílica de la Piedad** opposite, one of the oldest religious sites in the city. The twin steeples of the current church date from 1895; it is attractive and airy inside, with an unusual fresco featuring Adam and Eve frolicking in the Garden of Eden.

The iconic 67-metre tall **Obelisco** dominates the busy intersection between Corrientes and Avenida 9 de Julio and is the centrepiece of a breathtaking cityscape. Its giant scale and strategic location also make it a magnet for carloads of celebrating fans after a major football victory. Erected in 1936 in just 31 days, it commemorates four key events in the city's history: the first and second foundings; the first raising of the flag in 1812; and the naming of Buenos Aires as Capital Federal in 1880.

Plaza Lavalle and the Teatro Colón

One block north of Corrientes, between Libertad and Talcahuano, you will emerge in **Plaza Lavalle**. Although less famous than the Plaza de Mayo, Plaza Lavalle can nonetheless lay a claim to its own share of the city's history. It began life as a public park, inaugurated in 1827 by British immigrants. The following year it was the site of the city's first funfair. In 1857, the plaza was the departure point for the first Argentine train journey, made by the locomotive *La Porteña* to Floresta in the west of the capital; the original locomotive can still be seen in the Complejo Museográfico in Luján (see p.243). Just over thirty years later, the plaza was the scene of confrontations during the 1890 revolution, also known as the Revolución del Parque. Nowadays it's practically synonymous with the law courts; the whole area is often referred to as Tribunales. Stretching for three blocks, the plaza is a pleasant green space at the heart of the city – though somewhat marred by an underground garage. It is notable for its fine collection of native and exotic trees, many of them over a hundred years old. Amongst the pines, magnolias and jacarandas stands an ancient *ceibo Jujeño*, planted by then-mayor Torcuato de Alvear in 1870. The stretch of Roque Sáenz Peña that connects the plaza with 9 de Julio is paved over, and its fountains and row of patio cafés are pleasant and popular places to take a coffee break or eat lunch.

The southern end of the square is dominated by the grimy **Palacio de Justicia**, which houses the Supreme Court. In a loose and heavy-handed interpretation of Neoclassicism, heavily adorned with pillars, the building stands as a monument to architectural uncertainty. The needs of the lawyers who rush to and from the court are catered for by numerous stallholders who set up tables spread with pamphlets and secondhand books explaining every conceivable aspect of Argentine law.

On the eastern side of the square, between Viamonte and Tucumán, resides the handsome **Teatro Colón**, with its grand but restrained French Renaissance exterior. Most famous as an opera house – though it also hosts ballet and classical recitals – the Teatro Colón is undoubtedly Argentina's most prestigious cultural institution and is considered to have some of the best acoustics in the world. Most of the twentieth century's major opera and ballet stars appeared here, from Caruso and Callas to Nijinsky and Nureyev, while classical music performances have been given by the likes of Toscanini and Rubinstein. The interior features an Italian Renaissance-style central hall, the beautiful gilded and mirrored Salón Dorado (allegedly inspired by Versailles) and the stunning auditorium itself, whose five tiers of balconies culminate in a huge dome decorated with frescoes by Raúl Soldi. Closed for an extensive refurbishment at the time of writing, the theatre is scheduled to reopen on May 25, 2008, with a performance of Verdi's *Aida*, the same opera staged when the theatre originally opened in 1908. Once the theatre reopens, enquire at the box office for both guided visits and tickets for performances; it's in the passageway that cuts sideways through the building.

At the far northern end of the plaza, at Libertad 785, lies the **Sinagoga Central de la Congregación Israelita de la República Argentina**, the central synagogue of Argentina's Jewish population; visits are possible (Tues &

Jewish Buenos Aires

Perhaps one of the most surprising facts about Argentina is that it's home to one of the largest **Jewish communities** in the world, currently estimated at around 250,000, although this is around half the size it was at its peak in the mid-twentieth century. Around eighty percent live in Buenos Aires; the more well-to-do in Belgrano, and the lower middle classes in Once, the city's version of New York City's Lower East Side. The latter is where you'll find most of the city's kosher restaurants, especially on the streets around Pueyrredón between Córdoba and Corrientes. Approximately eighty synagogues dot the city, including the huge non-Orthodox Central Synagogue (see opposite), along with more than seventy Jewish educational institutions.

The first Jewish **immigrants** arrived in Argentina from Western European countries around the middle of the nineteenth century; later Jewish refugees fled here in large numbers from pogroms and persecution in Russia and Eastern Europe, and were commonly known as "rusos", a term still often used erroneously to refer to all Jews. Perón's government was one of the first to recognize the State of Israel, but he also halted Jewish immigration and infamously allowed Nazi war criminals to settle in Argentina, including Adolf Eichmann, the SS officer who masterminded the systematic massacre of Jews. Eichmann was later abducted from a Buenos Aires suburb by Israeli secret agents and whisked off for trial and execution in Jerusalem. Jews suffered particularly harshly during the 1976–83 dictatorship, often because they were artists, intellectuals, left-wing sympathizers or anti-junta militants rather than for overtly religious reasons, although many junta members and torturers were openly anti-Semitic; it is estimated that over 1000 of the disappeared were Jewish.

More recently, the Jewish community was the target of two of the country's most murderous **terrorist attacks**: a bomb explosion at the Israeli Embassy in 1992, in which around thirty people died, and another at the headquarters of AMIA, the Argentine Jewish association, in 1994. At least 86 people were killed, more than 200 wounded and the community's archives destroyed; not all the victims were Jewish and the atrocities triggered a reassuring demonstration of solidarity in society at large. No one has ever claimed responsibility and the perpetrators have yet to be found, with locals who had been accused of complicity, including police, cleared in 2004. In 2006, Argentine prosecutors officially accused the Iranian government and Hezbollah of the crime, a charge Teheran adamantly denies.

Thurs 3.30–6pm only; free) but security is strict – take your passport. Guides (English speakers available) will take you around the synagogue and small museum of religious artefacts, many imported from Europe, and explain the history of the Jewish community in Argentina. Just over the road, at Libertad 815, the **Teatro Nacional Cervantes** has an intricate exterior which is an example of Plateresque ornamentation, a richly adorned Spanish architectural style common in the early sixteenth century and named for its supposed similarity to fine silversmith's work. Inside, a small **museum** (Mon–Fri 10am–6pm; free) features models of stage sets, photos of local actors and some rather woebegone costumes.

Calle Florida and around

Pedestrianized **Calle Florida** bisects the lower reaches of Corrientes, running between Avenida de Mayo and Plaza San Martín. At the beginning of last century, Florida was one of the city's most elegant streets – the obligatory route for a stroll following tea at Harrods (see p.114). Nowadays over one million people a day tramp its length, and cutting your way through its stream of north–south foot traffic requires considerable determination. That said, this traffic is probably Florida's most appealing quality; there's always a lively buzz, and a handful of street performers doing their best to charm passers-by.

Florida commences at Plazo de Mayo and, save for the elegant facade of the **Banco de Boston** at no. 99, which is particularly impressive when lit up at night, its initial blocks are mostly taken up with bookstores, clothes stores and exchange offices. There are also lots of fast-food outlets, packed with office workers at lunch time, but at least one vestige of Florida's more sophisticated past remains in the shape of the almost anachronistic **Richmond confitería** at Florida 468. Famed for its cakes, hot chocolate and large leather armchairs, it also has a chess and billiards room downstairs. Across Florida, one block north of Corrientes, lies **Lavalle**, also partly pedestrianized, and a sort of cheap and cheerful version of Florida, noted for its cinemas and stores selling fake football tops.

Towards the northern end of Florida, the crowds become thinner and the stores more upmarket – at no. 877 you'll see there was once a **Harrods**. Until the 1960s, this operated as the South American branch of the famous department store, with visitors flocking to marvel at its full-size London bus and live Indian elephant. Despite occasional rumblings that it is to be reopened, and its intermittent use as an exposition hall and arts venue, it has been sadly shuttered for years, and is no longer linked to the London store – a glimmer of hope was kindled when it served as the site for musical gigs during the 2007 Film Festival, but so far to no avail. You can still find traces of the street's old-world glamour in Florida's *galerías* – shopping arcades – some of which sell a bit of everything, some of which specialize in goods such as computers or leatherware and many of which are of architectural interest in their own right. The most notable is the **Galerías Pacífico** shopping centre at Florida 753, which offers a glitzy bit of retailing within a vaulted and attractively frescoed building constructed by Paris department store Bon Marché at the end of the nineteenth century. On the first floor, you'll find the entrance to the **Centro Cultural Borges** (see p.172), a large space offering a worthwhile selection of photography and painting exhibitions from both Argentine and foreign artists. Florida's last two blocks, before it spills into Plaza San Martín, are filled with leather and handicraft stores; look out also for the fine decorative facade and door of the **Centro Naval** on the corner of Córdoba.

Puerto Madero

Parallel to Florida, some seven blocks east and running north–south from Avenida Córdoba to Avenida Juan de Garay, **Puerto Madero** is the only barrio to the east of the city centre. Constructed in 1882, the port consists of four enormous docks that run along the Río de la Plata and are lined by brick warehouse buildings that once housed the grain from the Pampas before it was shipped around the world. By the time the port was closed in 1898 it was already insufficient in scale to cope with the volume of maritime traffic, and a new port was constructed to the north. For most of the twentieth century, Puerto Madero sat as an industrial relic, but in the 1990s it began to be transformed into a voguish mix of restaurants, luxury apartments and offices. It is a pleasant place to stroll – boats bob on the water, while on the dockside much of the original brickwork and iron girders shipped over from Middlesbrough, England have been preserved. The development is upmarket and a bit lacking in colour, but the quality of the restaurants – though they are not the city's cheapest or most inventive – has improved of late, and there are far worse ways to spend a sunny afternoon than sitting on one of the verandahs, sipping a *clericó* and enjoying the breeze off the river.

The northern end of Puerto Madero starts just opposite the Buquebus terminal at *dique* (dock) four. The **Opera Bay** nightclub (see p.166), which looks like a sort of squashed, scaled-down Sydney Opera House, will likely catch your attention first, though it is Spanish architect Santiago Calatrava's striking white bridge known as the **Puente de la Mujer** (the "women's bridge") that is the area's focal point. Unveiled in 2001, its modernist curves are very new-millennium; it's about halfway along dock three. Docks four and three

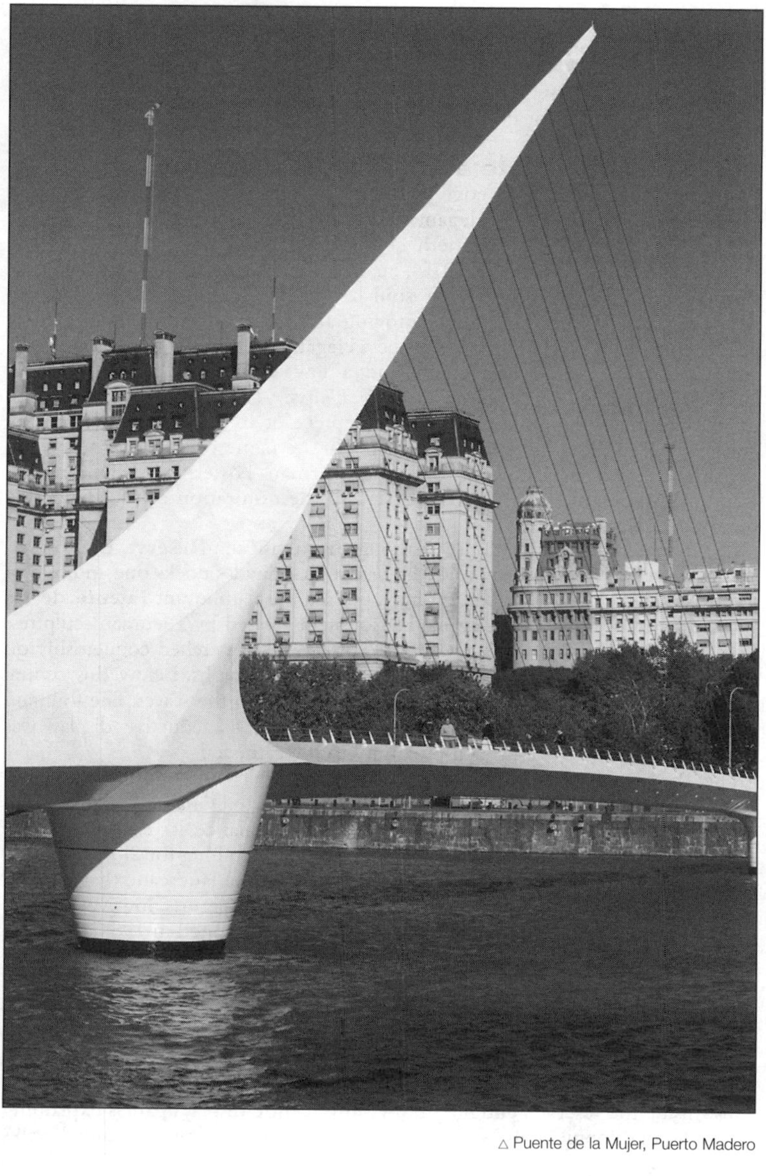

△ Puente de la Mujer, Puerto Madero

are the most interesting – in addition to hosting the pick of the restaurants, the west bank is also home to two **museum ships**. At dock four sits the well-maintained *Buque Museo Corbeta ARA Uruguay* (daily 9am–9pm; $1), built in British shipyards in 1874 and the Argentine navy's first training ship. Its finest hour came in 1903 when it rescued a Swedish scientific expedition stuck in Antarctic ice. At dock three you'll find the *Buque Museo Fragata ARA Presidente Sarmiento* (daily 9am–8pm; $2), also built in British shipyards, and the Argentine navy's flagship from 1899 to 1938. Dock two belongs to the city's prestigious (and expensive) Catholic university, which has opened a **Pabellón de las Bellas Artes** (Tues–Sun 11am–7pm; free), a small, permanent collection of Argentine art. Dock one is still in the early stages of development, and just beyond it in the Dársena Sur harbour floats the city's lone casino: a neon-lit faux steamship, with slot machines and card tables open around the clock.

Puerto Madero Este and the Costanera Sur

Running along the eastern edge of Puerto Madero, the **Costanera Sur** is a sweeping avenue flanked by elegant balustrades, built as a riverside promenade at the beginning of the twentieth century. A landfill project separated the avenue from the river in the 1970s, an area now home to the city's newest, shiniest and in some ways rather soul-less barrio-within-a-barrio, **Puerto Madero Este**. With development moving at a smart pace, the small grid of streets consists of elegant apartments, less elegant but equally expensive high-rise monoliths, chi-chi restaurants and a few neighbourhood stores. The landmark site here is the *Faena Hotel & Universe* (see p.99), in a converted grain warehouse; the building is the centrepiece of an ongoing cultural, retail and residential development called El Aleph, the name of a Borges story and the first project in Latin America for Norman Foster, most famous for London's "Gherkin" at 30 St Mary Axe, and the restoration of the Reichstag building in Berlin.

The main reason to cross the river, though, is to visit the **Reserva Ecológica**, the entrance of which lies opposite the bridge that divides docks one and two of Puerto Madero. Just before you go in, you'll see the flamboyant **Fuente de las Nereidas**, a large and elaborate marble fountain created by Tucumán sculptress Lola Mora in 1902. The fountain depicts a naked Venus perched coquettishly on the edge of a shell supported by two straining sea nymphs. Below this central sculpture three Tritons struggle to restrain horses among the waves. The fountain was originally destined for the Plaza de Mayo, but its seductive display was thought too risqué to be in such proximity to the cathedral.

The Reserva Ecológica itself (Tues–Sun April–Oct 8am–6pm, Nov–March 8am–7pm; free; ⓣ011/4315-4129) offers an unexpectedly natural environment just minutes from the fury of the city centre. At first glance, it's easy to imagine this sizeable fragment of wild and watery grassland, stretching for 2km alongside the Costanera, to be an oddly neglected remnant of the landscape that greeted Pedro de Mendoza as he sailed into the estuary. Its origins, however, are far more recent. When the Costanera Sur landfill was abandoned in 1984, the seeds present in the silt dredged from the river and borne by the wind took root, and before long the area was covered in vegetation and teeming with wildlife. Nowadays, the Reserva Ecológica is a strange and wonderful place where the juxtaposition of urban and natural is a recurring theme, whether it is factory chimneys glimpsed through fronds of pampas grass or the city skyline over a lake populated by ducks and herons.

Just inside the reserve's entrance, the visitors' centre displays panels explaining the park's development and serves as the starting point for ranger-guided walks on some of the park's many trails (Sat & Sun 10.30am & 3.30pm); keep a look out also for the full-moon nocturnal tours, when, weather permitting, you can spot all manner of creatures, mainly birds, that keep a low daytime profile. There is a surprising diversity of flora and fauna in the park, with over two hundred species of birds visiting during the year. Aquatic species include ducks, herons, elegant Black-necked Swans, skittish coots, the Common Gallinule and the Snail Hawk, a bird of prey that uses its hooked beak to pluck freshwater snails out of their shells. The park is also home to small mammals, such as the easily spotted coypu, an aquatic rodent, and reptiles such as monitor lizards. The reserve's vegetation includes the ceibo, a tall tree with a twisted trunk whose bright red blossom is Argentina's national flower, but the most dominant plant is the *cortadera*, or pampas grass.

The south

Described by Borges as "an older, more solid world", **the south** is Buenos Aires' most traditional quarter. Immediately south of the Plaza de Mayo lies the barrio of **Monserrat**, packed with historic buildings, churches and a couple of noteworthy museums. Heading south through Monserrat, you'll emerge amongst the cobbled streets and alleyways of **San Telmo**, where grand nineteenth-century mansions testify to the days when the barrio was home to the wealthy landowners. San Telmo is most commonly visited on a Sunday, when its central square, Plaza Dorrego, is the scene of a fascinating **antiques fair**, although there are plenty of antiques stores also open during the week. At the southern end of the barrio, there's the tranquil **Parque Lezama** – a good spot for observing local life, and home to an important history museum. Beyond Parque Lezama, and stretching all the way to the city's southern boundary, the Río Riachuelo, the quirky barrio of **La Boca** is a great place to spend a morning, wandering its colourful streets and soaking up its idiosyncratic atmosphere.

Monserrat

Monserrat, also known as Barrio Sur, is the city's oldest district and, together with neighbouring San Telmo, is one of the most beguiling areas to explore on foot. A good starting point for delving into its grid of narrow streets and historic buildings is **Calle Defensa**, named in honour of the barrio's residents, who, during the British invasions of 1806 and 1807, impeded the British troops by pouring boiling water on them as they marched down the street.

On the corner of Alsina and Defensa stands the Neo-Baroque **Basílica de San Francisco** (Mon–Fri 8.30am–7pm), one of the churches burnt by angry Peronists in March 1955 in reaction to the navy's bombing of an anti-Church, pro-Perón trade union rally in the Plaza de Mayo. The basilica was eventually restored, reconsecrated and officially reopened in 1967. An oak column from the original altarpiece, destroyed by the fire, is preserved in the adjoining Franciscan monastery, where monks sell bee-derived products, including honey and soap.

Half a block west of the church at Defensa 219, on the first floor of a handsome private residence, is the imaginative **Museo de la Ciudad** (Mon–Fri 11am–7pm, Sat & Sun 3–7pm; $5). There is a permanent display of children's toys through the ages here, but the majority of the small museum is devoted to regularly changing exhibitions designed to illustrate everyday aspects of Porteño life, such as holidays or shopping. The objects are wittily displayed, although sadly the tongue-in-cheek descriptions are in Spanish only. Downstairs, a salon open to the street holds larger items, such as rescued doors and a traditional barrow from which an *ambulante* would have sold his or her wares, decorated in the *filete* style (see box below). Just by the museum on the corner, it's worth popping into the **Farmacia de la Estrella**, a beautifully preserved old pharmacy. Founded in 1834, it boasts an opulent interior of heavy walnut fittings, quirky old-fashioned medical murals and mirrors, finished off with a stunning frescoed ceiling.

Continuing south along Defensa, you'll find the **Basílica de Santo Domingo**, an austere twin-towered structure on the corner of Avenida Belgrano whose glory is somewhat overshadowed by the elevated mausoleum to General Belgrano that dominates the tiled patio at its front. The square on which the basilica stands was taken by the British on June 27, 1806, on which date Catholicism was outlawed. In the corner to the left of the altar as you enter you can see the flags from British regiments captured by General Liniers when the city was retaken two months later.

Taking up the block bounded by Alsina, Perú, Moreno and Bolívar – one block west of Defensa – is the complex of buildings known as the **Manzana de las Luces**, or "block of enlightenment" (guided visits Mon–Fri 3pm, Sat & Sun 3pm, 4.30pm & 6pm from entrance at Perú 272; $5). Dating from 1662, the complex originally housed a Jesuit community, and has been home to numerous official institutions throughout its history. The forty-minute tour (in Spanish, with summary explanations given in English if needed) visits the inner patio, a series of tunnels, constructed to connect the churches, some of the surrounding chambers, including one that was the scene of a nineteenth-century political assassination, and the reconstructed **Sala de Representantes**, a semicircular chamber similar to those in Congreso (see p.110) where the first provincial legislature once sat. Opposite the statue of General Roca at Av Julio Roca 600, the **Mercado de las Luces** (Mon–Fri 10am–7.30pm, Sun 2–7pm) has a number of stalls set up in one of the Jesuit corridors, selling antiques, crystals, candles and other artisan products. The block also encompasses the elite Colegio Nacional as well as Buenos Aires' oldest church, **San Ignacio**, begun in 1675, on the corner of Bolívar and Alsina. As with many of the city's churches, various later additions have modified San Ignacio's original construction, the most recent being the tower at the northern end of the church, erected in 1850. Apart from the

Filete art

As you wander around Monserrat and San Telmo, look out for examples of **filete art**, particularly on shop signs. Characterized by ornate lettering, heavy shading and the use of scrolls and flowers entwined with the azure and white of the national flag, this distinctive art form first made its appearance on the city transport system in the early twentieth century. Often associated with tango, its actual origins are a little murky, but it seems to have been introduced by Italian immigrants. Banned from public transport in 1975 – the authorities felt bus destinations and numbers should be unadorned – it moved onto signs above stores and cafés as well as more traditional canvases. Today it is synonymous with Porteño identity, particularly in the south. As well as tango stars, a popular subject is the pithy saying, including the classic *si bebe para olvidar paga antes de tomar* ("if you drink to forget, pay first") and the more obscure *si querés la leche fresca, atá la vaca a la sombre* ("if you want fresh milk, tie the cow up in the shade").

rather Baroque Altar Mayor, the church's interior is fairly simple, which serves to make one of its most notable icons, the beautiful seventeenth-century Nuestra Señora de las Nieves, all the more arresting.

Museo Etnográfico Juan Bautista Ambrosetti

Part of the Universidad de Buenos Aires, the fascinating **Museo Etnográfico Juan Bautista Ambrosetti** lies at Moreno 350 (Tues–Fri 1–7pm, Sat & Sun 3–7pm, guided visits Sat & Sun 4pm; closed Jan; $2 voluntary). Although the museum has some international anthropological exhibits, its real interest lies in its well-displayed collection from pre-Columbian South America. The ground-floor rooms display the impressive jewellery, pots and tools of the few native groups who lived on what is now Argentine territory – chiefly, the Araucanas and the Mapuche, but also the Yámana and other peoples of Tierra del Fuego. Panels (and pamphlets in English) recount stories such as that of Jemmy Button, one of four Yámana Indians taken to England by Fitzroy in 1830, where he lived for a period in the unlikely surroundings of Walthamstow, a borough of London. The initial interest in "civilizing" Fueginos was later replaced by a tendency to exhibit them in circuses in Europe: in 1882 the Karl Hagenbeck Circus displayed a family of Alacalufs in a cage in Berlin and Paris.

The upper floor deals with different themes relating to the culture, religion and trade of various pre-Columbian South American peoples, including the Inca. Of particular note are a fine Huari tunic covered in the symbols that they used in place of a written language and religious costumes from Bolivia made of jaguar skin. There are many fascinating examples of the gradual Hispanicization of the indigenous people, where Christian motifs and European materials were added to native American beliefs – look out for the wooden statue of Jesus wearing a jaguar pelt.

San Telmo

It's impossible not to be seduced by the crumbling facades and cobbled streets of **San Telmo**, a neighbourhood that is proud of its reputation as the guardian of the city's traditions. A small, almost square-shaped barrio, San Telmo is bounded to the north by Avenida Chile, six blocks south of Plaza de Mayo, to the west by **Calle Piedras**, to the east by Paseo Colón and to the south by Parque Lezama. Like neighbouring Monserrat, its main artery is **Calle Defensa**, once the road from the Plaza de Mayo to the city's port. The barrio's appearance of decaying luxury is the result of a kind of gentrification. When the city's grand mansions were abandoned by their patrician owners after a yellow fever epidemic in 1871, they were soon converted into *conventillos* (tenements) by landlords keen to make a quick buck from newly arrived immigrants. This sudden loss of cachet preserved many of the barrio's original features: whereas much of the north, centre and west of the city was variously torn down, smartened up or otherwise modernized, San Telmo's inhabitants simply adapted the neighbourhood's buildings to their needs. It's still largely a working-class area, and well-heeled Palermo-dwellers may warn you off coming here, but the area's superb architecture also attracts bohemians, students, backpackers and artists. Together with rising rents, the recent appearance of designer clothing and homewares stores amongst the traditional antiques shops is an indication that San Telmo may once again be going up in the world – and this new gentrification is not a development that everyone welcomes.

The barrio is one of Buenos Aires' major tourist attractions, particularly for its Sunday antiques market, the **Feria de San Telmo**, which takes place in the

neighbourhood's central square, Plaza Dorrego; there is also now a smaller version on Saturdays. It's also the barrio most associated with **tango**, and the place where many of the best-known tango shows and bars have their home. At the southern end of the barrio, the small, palm-lined Parque Lezama, containing the city's well-organized **Museo Histórico Nacional**, makes a restful spot to end a tour of the neighbourhood.

Defensa and around

Leading south from Plaza de Mayo to Parque Lezama, **Defensa** runs through the heart of San Telmo. On weekends, vehicles are replaced with human traffic as visitors wend their way past performance artists and buskers to visit the cobbled lane's antiques stores and bars. Just off Defensa, half a block south of Avenida Chile, you'll find one of the barrio's most charming streets, the **Pasaje San Lorenzo**, a small alley running for just two blocks. On it, at no. 380, stands the narrowest building in Buenos Aires: the **Casa Mínima**, a tiny two-storey house – its 2.17m front is just wide enough to accommodate a doorway. The house was constructed by liberated slaves on a sliver of land given to them by their former masters. At the bottom of Pasaje San Lorenzo you'll find a cluster of **tango bars**, of which the most famous is *El Viejo*

Almacén, founded in 1968 by Edmundo Rivero, one of Argentina's most revered tango singers, on the corner of Independencia and Balcarce. From here, looking down to Paseo Colón, you can see the massive bronze *Canto al Trabajo*, sculpted by Rogelio Yrurtia (see p.153) in 1907. Composed of a heaving mass of bodies hauling a huge rock, it is executed in a more expressionistic style than the majority of Yrurtia's rather academic works. Back on Defensa, at no.755, **El Zanjón** (guided visits daily hourly 11am–6pm; $20; reservations advisable on ⓣ011/4361-3002) is the newest addition to San Telmo's attractions, a very handsome, though perhaps overdone, reconstruction of the site of both a pre-yellow-fever-era mansion and a *conventillo*. A visit to the tastefully lit tunnels, where the city's water once flowed, is the highlight of the site, though the tour price is a bit steep to see what are essentially little more than foundations and cisterns. Don't, however, miss the **Mercado Municipal** (Mon–Sat 7am–2pm & 4.30–9pm, Sun 7am–2pm) on Defensa between Carlos Calvo and Estados Unidos, a thriving city-centre food market.

Plaza Dorrego and the Feria de San Pedro Telmo

At the heart of San Telmo on the corner of Defensa and Humberto 1°, **Plaza Dorrego** is a tiny square surrounded by elegant mansions, most of them now converted into bars and antiques shops. During the week, cafés set up tables in the square, and on Sunday it becomes the setting for the city's long-running antiques market, the **Feria de San Pedro Telmo** (10am–5pm). Overflowing with antique *mates*, jewel-coloured soda syphons, watches and old ticket machines from the city's buses, the stalls make for fascinating browsing, albeit occasionally heavy crowds. There are no real bargains to be had – the stallholders and habitués are far too canny to let a gem slip through their fingers – but among the jumble you may find your own souvenir of Buenos Aires. The market's pickpockets are also very canny – one famously swiped the bag of US President Bush's daughter despite the presence of six security guards – so be careful with your belongings. After the stallholders pack away their wares on Sunday evenings, Plaza Dorrego becomes – weather permitting – the setting of a free outdoor **milonga** (tango dance; see box, p.170). There's a refreshing informality to this regular event, frequented by tourists, locals and tango fanatics alike, which might encourage even those with only a rudimentary knowledge of tango to take the plunge. The bars and restaurants surrounding the plaza are tempting, too, but prices can be steep. Just around the corner from Plaza Dorrego, at Humberto 1° 340, stands the **Iglesia de San Pedro Telmo**, whose prettily eclectic facade is a melange of post-colonial, Baroque and Neoclassical influences.

Heading south from Plaza Dorrego along Defensa, you'll come to the **Pasaje de la Defensa** at no.1179, a converted nineteenth-century residence, home to a café, and stairs leading up to a gallery and more antiques shops. Half a block south, the old-world appeal of San Telmo's most charming quarter is rather abruptly curtailed by busy Avenida San Juan, where you'll find the **Museo de Arte Moderno de Buenos Aires** (MAMBA) at no. 350, housed in an old tobacco factory, with a permanent collection of mostly Argentine art from the 1940s to 1960s. It was closed for refurbishment at the time of writing – in the meantime, exhibitions from its collection have been given a temporary home on the second floor of the main post office building, the Correo Central, at Corrientes 172 (Tues–Fri 10am–8pm, Sat & Sun 11am–8pm). The small **Museo del Cine**, around the corner at Defensa 1220, also being renovated, has temporary exhibitions on Argentine cinema.

Parque Lezama and the Museo Histórico Nacional

Heading south for another three blocks along Defensa will bring you to **Parque Lezama**, an inviting green expanse. On a bluff overlooking Paseo Colón, the park is generally regarded as the site of Buenos Aires' founding by **Pedro de Mendoza** in 1536. The conquistador's statue looms over visitors as they enter the park from the corner of Defensa and Brasil; a bronze of the man himself thrusts his sword into the ground, while behind him a bas-relief shows an indigenous man, throwing up his hands in surrender. On the eastern side, a bust of **Ulrich Schmidl**, a German mercenary soldier who accompanied Mendoza, overlooks Paseo Colón. Schmidl's chronicles of the trip, published as *Log of a Journey to Spain and the Indies* (1567), recount how the would-be settlers had to resort to eating rats, snakes, shoe leather and, in a few extreme cases, corpses of hanged men. The park is best visited in early evening, when the sun filters through its trees, children run along its paths and groups of old men play cards or chess at stone tables.

Within the park, though entered via Defensa 1600, the **Museo Histórico Nacional** (Tues–Sun 11am–6pm; $3), founded in 1887, is housed in a magnificent colonial building painted a startling deep red and covered with elaborate white mouldings that look very much like piped icing. The museum takes a chronological tour through Argentina's history, concentrating mainly on the tumultuous nineteenth century. You'll find portraits of all the big names from the formative years of Argentina (and further afield), from Christopher Columbus and Ferdinand Magellan to José de San Martín and Admiral William Brown, as well as the maps and tools they used, down to San Martín's *mate* gourd. A high point of the collection is the absolutely stunning **Tarja de Potosí**, an elaborate silver and gold shield given to General Belgrano in 1813 by the women of Potosí (a silver-mining town in Upper Peru, now Bolivia) in recognition of his role in the struggle for independence from Spain. Over a metre tall, it's a delicately worked and intricate piece complete with tiny figures symbolizing the discovery of America. The section on the abortive British invasions is interesting – look out for the satirical cartoons published in London at the time, one of which mocks, "suppose for fun we just knock down this town of Buenos Aires". There are also a number of important paintings of historical, rather than specifically artistic, interest, including a huge one by Uruguayan master Juan Manuel Blanes that occupies an entire wall and shows a pensive General Roca leading his troops during the Conquest of the Desert.

Looking rather out of place among all the French- and Italian-influenced architecture and cobbled streets, the exotic **Iglesia Ortodoxa Rusa** (Ⓣ011/4361-4274) lies opposite the northern end of the park, at Brasil 313. A mass of bright blue curvaceous domes, it was the first Russian Orthodox Church in Latin America. Built in 1899, it contains many valuable icons donated by Tsar Nicolas II and brought from Russia as that empire was falling into decline.

Boca

More than any other barrio in Buenos Aires, **Boca** (or "La Boca") and its inhabitants seem to flaunt their idiosyncrasies. Located in the capital's southeastern corner, this working-class riverside neighbourhood has been known as the "República de la Boca" since 1882, when a group of local youths declared that the barrio was seceding from the country. Even today its residents have a reputation for playing by their own rules and are most famous for their brightly coloured wooden and corrugated-iron houses. The district was the favoured destination for many Italian immigrants, and the colours of the houses derive

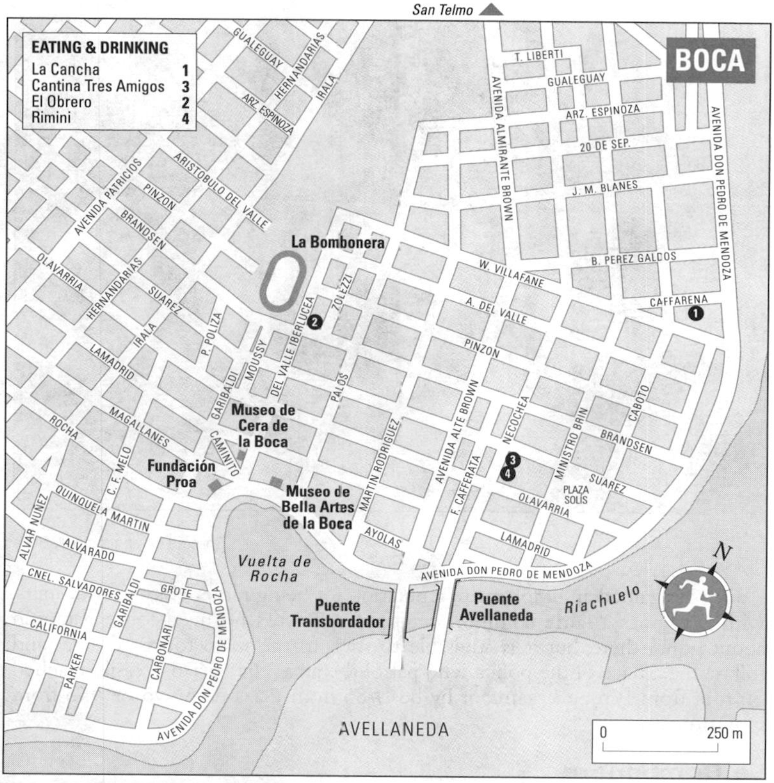

from the Genoese custom of painting homes with the paint left over from boats. Boca's other most characteristic emblem is its football team, **Boca Juniors**, the country's most popular club and probably the most famous one abroad.

Named after the *boca*, or mouth, of the Río Riachuelo, which snakes along its southern border, Boca is an irregularly shaped barrio, longer than it is wide. Its main thoroughfare is Avenida Almirante Brown, which cuts through the neighbourhood from Parque Lezama to the towering iron **Puente Transbordador** that straddles the Riachuelo. Apart from some excellent pizzerias, there's little to detain you along the avenue: the majority of Boca's attractions are packed into the grids of streets on either side. Even then, there's not a great deal to see as such, and unless you plan to visit all the museums an hour or two will suffice; morning is the ideal time to go, when the light best captures the district's bright hues and before the tour buses arrive. By far the most visited area is the huddle of three or four streets around the **Vuelta de Rocha**, an acute bulge in the river's course, which includes the ba rrio's most famous street, the **Caminito**. Lined with the most pristine examples of Boca's coloured houses, it's very photogenic but not very lived-in – a life-size museum or a tourist trap, depending on your point of view. A couple of blocks north of Caminito, there's the equally famous **Bombonera**, the Boca Juniors' football stadium. Alongside the river, cafés line Avenida Don Pedro de Mendoza, also home to an excellent art gallery, the **Fundación Proa**.

△ Children playing football, Boca

Boca has gained an unfortunate reputation for being rather risky for outsiders, with muggings a fairly common occurrence. There's no need to be paranoid about going there, but it is advisable to stick to the main tourist district and follow the advice of the police who patrol the area. The barrio is easily reached on foot from Parque Lezama or by bus #86 from Plaza de Mayo or #53 from Constitución.

La Bombonera

The true heart of Boca is **La Bombonera**, at Brandsen 805. Built in 1940, the Boca Juniors' stadium was remodelled in the 1990s by the club's millionaire president and city mayor Mauricio Macri. The stadium's name, literally "the chocolate box", refers to its particularly compact structure; although Boca has more fans than any other Argentine team, the stadium's capacity is less than several of its city rivals. Seeing a game here is an incredible experience, even for non-soccer fans, and it's worth arranging your itinerary around one – see Basics, p.50, for more details. If you don't get the opportunity to watch a match, at least head for the **Museo de la Pasión Boquense** and its **stadium tour** (daily 10am–6pm; $12 for museum visit only or tour only, $20 for both; Ⓦwww.museoboquense.com). The museum is a modern audio-visual experience, with a 360-degree film that puts you in the boots of a Boca player, and a charming model of how the barrio would have looked and sounded in the 1930s. The tour not only includes the stands, pitch and press conference room, but even the players' Jacuzzi and dressing room, complete with statues of the Virgin Mary. Just inside the stadium entrance, there's a large painting by famous local artist Benito Quinquela Martín (see opposite) entitled *Orígen de la bandera de Boca* ("the origin of Boca's flag"), which illustrates one of the club's most famous anecdotes. Though the exact date and circumstances of the event are disputed, all agree that Boca chose the colours of its strip from the flag of the next ship to pass through its then busy port. The boat was Swedish, and thus the distinctive blue and yellow strip was born.

Around the stadium, a huddle of stalls and shops sell Boca souvenirs while, on the pavement outside the stadium, stars with the names of Boca players past and present, some featuring their footprints, were laid as part of the club's centenary celebrations in 2005. Some of the neighbouring houses have taken up the blue and yellow theme, too, with facades painted like giant football shirts. From the stadium it's a short walk southwards to La Boca's other nerve centre: Calle Caminito.

Caminito and around

A former train siding now transformed into a pedestrian street and open-air art museum, **Caminito**, which runs diagonally between the riverfront and Calle Olavarría, draws tourists in droves. It contains the greatest concentration of Boca's vibrantly painted houses, whose appearance on postcards and brochures is the reason why the street will likely look familiar. The street was "founded" by the barrio's most famous artist, **Benito Quinquela Martín**, who painted epic and expressive scenes of the neighbourhood's daily life. Quinquela Martín rescued the old siding from oblivion after the rail company removed the tracks in 1954. He encouraged the immigrants' tradition of painting their houses in bright colours and took the name for the street from a famous 1926 tango by Gabino Coria Peñaloza and Juan de Dios Filiberto.

There's something of the pastiche about Caminito: locals refer to it as the best example of "Buenos Aires for export". Nonetheless, the bold blocks of rainbow-coloured walls, set off with contrasting window frames and balconies, are still an arresting sight. Down the middle of the street, there's an **arts and crafts fair**, dominated by garish paintings of the area. Tango musicians frequently perform along the street too, accompanied by the sound of cameras clicking. At the western end of Caminito, Calle Garibaldi runs past and on south, a charmingly ramshackle street with a slew of coloured corrugated iron buildings, less done up than those of Caminito, and currently being renovated by the city government.

The eastern end of Caminito leads to Avenida Pedro de Mendoza and the river, where the gaudy trinkets sold the length of the street seem to have overflowed into the harbour and aboard the *Nicolas Mihanovich*, a floating **market**. The Riachuelo bulges dramatically at this point, creating an inlet known as the **Vuelta de Rocha**. A wide pedestrian walkway stretches alongside it in a rather ambitious attempt to draw passers-by closer to the notoriously polluted and foul-smelling river. Some of the pollution is caused by the fact that approximately 3.5 million people live close to the river, though the vast majority is caused by the hundreds of factories that empty their waste directly into it. Mention La Boca to any Porteño outside the barrio – particularly River Plate fans – and they'll hold their nose.

The view from Pedro de Mendoza is of a jumbled but majestic mass of boats, factories and bridges: directly south, across the river, there's the suburb of Avellaneda (a working-class area that was the setting for one of Argentina's best movies of recent years, *Luna de Avellaneda*) while to your left there's one of Buenos Aires' major landmarks, the massive iron **Puente Transbordador**, or transport bridge, built in the early years of the twentieth century and now out of use, though there is talk of getting it up and running again. Next to the transport bridge is Puente Nicolás Avellaneda – a very similar construction built in 1939. This functioning bridge is one of the major causeways in and out of the city. Far below it, small rowing boats ferry passengers to and from Avellaneda. Around the corner from the southern end of Caminito, there's a wax museum, the **Museo de Cera de la Boca**, Del Valle Iberlucea 1261 (Mon–Fri 10am–6pm, Sat & Sun 11am–8pm; $5), an old-fashioned and rather Gothic place that is great fun to visit.

Away from the riverbank, the area around the bottom of Caminito has a number of pleasant outdoor cafés on the corner of Del Valle Iberlucea and Pedro de Mendoza, where you can soak up a bit of local colour. Half a block south of the intersection between Caminito and Pedro de Mendoza at no.1929 you'll find one of Buenos Aires' best art galleries, the **Fundación Proa** (Tues–Sun 11am–7pm, guided visits Sat & Sun noon–6pm in Spanish, enquire in advance for English; $3; Ⓣ011/4303-0909, Ⓦwww.proa.org). Housed in a converted mansion – all Italianate elegance outside and modern, angular galleries within – Proa has no permanent collection but hosts some fascinating and diverse exhibitions, usually with a Latin American theme, ranging from 1980s Argentine art to pre-Columbian Aztec sculptures.

Further east along Pedro de Mendoza at no. 1835 there's the long-established **Museo de Bellas Artes de La Boca** (Tues–Fri 10.30am–5.30pm, Sat & Sun 11am–5.30pm, closed Mon; free). It was founded in 1938 by Benito Quinquela Martín on the site of his studio (now also a school) and houses many of his major works, as well as those of contemporary Argentine artists. It's the perfect setting for a display of Quinquela Martín's work, since you can actually see much of his subject matter simply by peering out of the windows of the gallery or climbing up to the viewpoint on the roof. More than anyone, Quinquela Martín conveyed the industrial grandeur of La Boca, dedicating himself to painting scenes of everyday life. He was so associated with the city's least salubrious neighbourhood that, like the tango, he only garnered respect at home once he had become famous abroad.

Further east along Pedro de Mendoza and running parallel to Avenida Almirante Brown, the high pavements of **Calle Necochea** are home to the area's famous *cantinas*, fantastically gaudy and rowdy restaurants where the food is less important than the unlimited wine and lively entertainment that accompany it. Although they had their heyday in the 1970s, some – such as *Rimini* and *Cantina 3 Amigos* – remain open. The streets around here also contain less pristine examples of Boca's colourful architecture as well as authentic (and cheap) Italian restaurants, but remember this is a very poor neighbourhood – don't wander in quiet areas and keep valuables out of sight.

The north

A combination of extravagant elegance and an authentic lived-in feel pervades **the north** of Buenos Aires, whose four residential barrios – Retiro, Recoleta, Belgrano and Palermo – each retain a distinctive character. Parts of the two northern barrios nearest to the centre, **Retiro** and **Recoleta**, known jointly as **Barrio Norte** (though this sometimes refers only to the northwestern reaches of Recoleta, on the border with Palermo), have chic streets lined with boutiques, art galleries and smart cafés. However, the dockside fringes and the highly insalubrious bits near the city's biggest train station, also called Retiro, are just as down-at-the-heel as parts of the southern barrios, if not more so. Recoleta is associated primarily with its magnificent **cemetery** where, among other national celebrities, Evita is buried. Both barrios also share an extraordinary concentration of French-style **palaces**, tangible proof of the obsession of the city's elite at the beginning of the twentieth century with established European cities. Many of these palaces can be visited and some of them house the area's opulent museum collections, but they are also sights in themselves.

Palermo and **Belgrano**, further north, are large districts composed of a mixture of tall apartment buildings, tree-lined boulevards, little cobbled streets and grandiose Neocolonial houses. An inordinate number of Buenos Aires' best **restaurants** and **shops** are here, so you should plan a visit in this direction at least once. It's worth making a day of it to check out the beautiful **parks** and **gardens**, attend a game of polo or pato – Argentina's most idiosyncratic national **sport** – or to see another beguiling side of the city in, for example, Palermo Soho, a district of lively cafés-cum-art galleries.

Retiro

Squeezed between the city centre to the south, Recoleta to the west and mostly inhospitable docklands to the north and east, **Retiro** gets its name from a hermit's *retiro* (retreat) that was hidden among dense woodland here in the sixteenth century, when Buenos Aires was little more than a village. Today it's surprisingly varied for such a small barrio: commercial **art galleries** and airline offices outnumber other businesses along the busy streets around the end of Calle Florida near the barrio's focal point, Plaza San Martín, while west of busy Avenida 9 de Julio lies a smart, quiet residential area.

The rather sleazy northernmost swathe of the barrio is chiefly of interest for the **Museo Nacional de Inmigración**, a sort of Argentine equivalent of New York's Ellis Island. Lying at Retiro's aristocratic heart, meanwhile, **Plaza San Martín** is one of the city's most enticing green spaces, flanked by opulent patrician buildings. More outstanding examples of the barrio's palaces, which reflect how wealthy Porteños of the late nineteenth century yearned for their city to be a New World version of Paris, are clustered around **Plaza Carlos Pellegrini**, undeniably one of the city's most elegant squares. In between the two plazas, the **Museo Isaac Fernández Blanco**, a gem among the city's museums, contains an impressive collection of colonial silverware, furniture and paintings.

For most Porteños, the barrio's name has become synonymous with the once grand but now mostly decrepit **Estación Retiro**, on Avenida Dr Ramos Mejia, which still retains original Edwardian features, such as porcelain tiles and wrought-iron lamps. Next to it is the city's major bus terminal, a modern and fairly efficient complex, and beyond that urban wasteland and a shanty-town. You can reach the barrio by subte; both San Martín and Retiro stations are on Line C.

Museo Nacional de Inmigración

Between 1911 and 1920 just under half a million immigrants passed through the Gran Hotel de los Inmigrantes, Av Antártida Argentina 1355, now home to the **Museo Nacional de Inmigración** (Mon–Fri 10am–5pm, Sat & Sun 11am–6pm; free; Ⓣ011/4317-0285, Ⓦwww.mininterior.gov.ar/migraciones/museo/index.html), next to Dársena Norte (northern wharf). They were encouraged to come by an Argentine government keen to populate the country's vast territory with "industrious" Europeans. For some, the state-run hotel was their first taste of life in the New World. The hall that once functioned as the dining area houses a display of hospital equipment and panels – informative, but in Spanish only – describing the history of the hotel and its antecedents as well as wider information on the immigration phenomenon. The *microcine* room is most interesting, with its collection of photos and descriptions of daily life. Writ large are the words of a pamphlet given to Italian immigrants, informing them of the rules of social etiquette – don't spit, walk on the

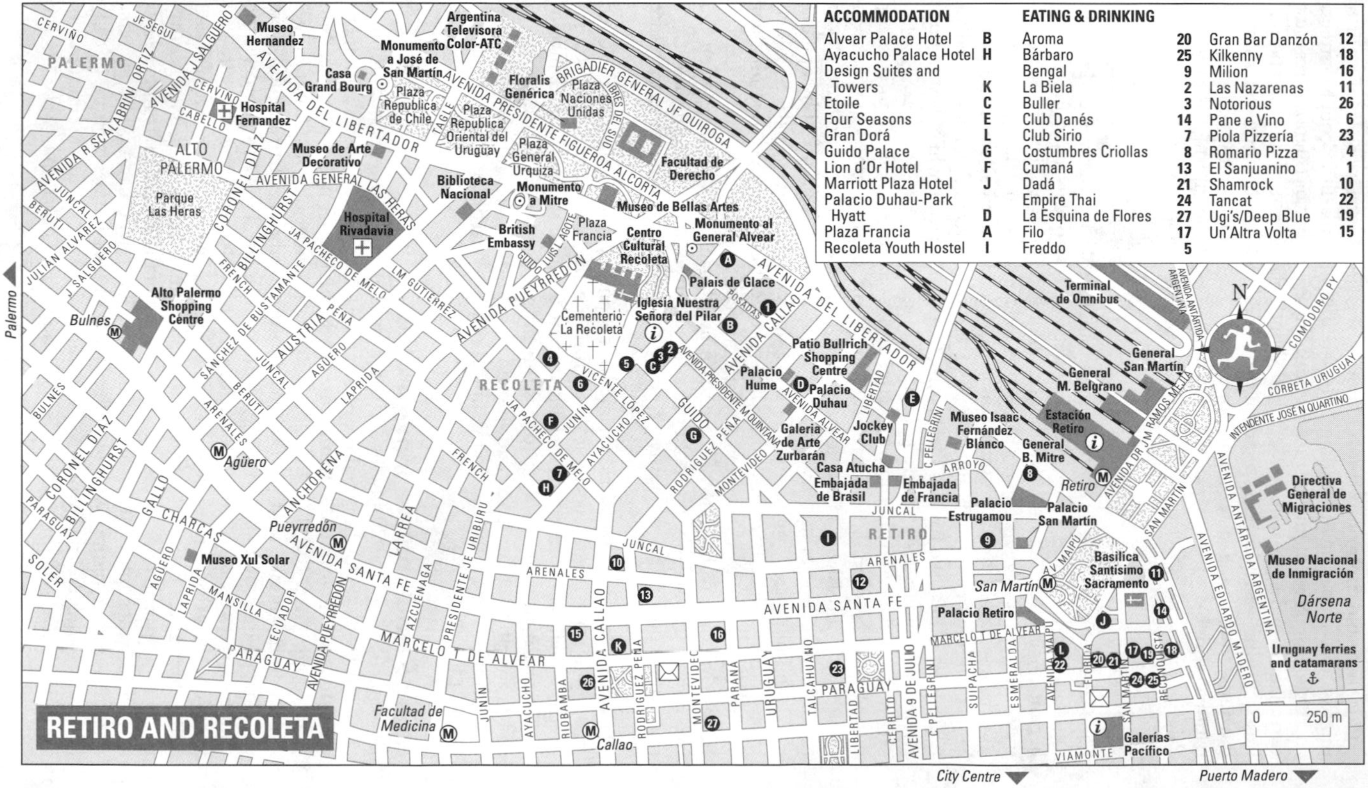
RETIRO AND RECOLETA
ACCOMMODATION
Alvear Palace Hotel B
Ayacucho Palace Hotel H
Design Suites and Towers K
Etoile C
Four Seasons E
Gran Dorá L
Guido Palace G
Lion d'Or Hotel F
Marriott Plaza Hotel J
Palacio Duhau-Park Hyatt D
Plaza Francia A
Recoleta Youth Hostel I
EATING & DRINKING
Aroma 20
Bárbaro 25
Bengal 9
La Biela 2
Buller 3
Club Danés 14
Club Sirio 7
Costumbres Criollas 8
Cumaná 13
Dadá 21
Empire Thai 24
La Esquina de Flores 27
Filo 17
Freddo 5
Gran Bar Danzón 12
Kilkenny 18
Milion 16
Las Nazarenas 11
Notorious 26
Pane e Vino 6
Piola Pizzería 23
Romario Pizza 4
El Sanjuanino 1
Shamrock 10
Tancat 22
Ugi's/Deep Blue 19
Un'Altra Volta 15
PALERMO
ALTO PALERMO
RECOLETA
RETIRO
Museo Hernandez
Hospital Fernandez
Casa Grand Bourg
Monumento a José de San Martín
Argentina Televisora Color-ATC
Floralis Genérica
Plaza Naciones Unidas
Facultad de Derecho
Museo de Arte Decorativo
Biblioteca Nacional
Hospital Rivadavia
Parque Las Heras
Alto Palermo Shopping Centre
Bulnes
Agüero
Pueyrredón
Museo Xul Solar
Monumento a Mitre
Museo de Bellas Artes
British Embassy
Centro Cultural Recoleta
Monumento al General Alvear
Palais de Glace
Iglesia Nuestra Señora del Pilar
Cementerio La Recoleta
Patio Bullrich Shopping Centre
Palacio Hume
Palacio Duhau
Galeria de Arte Zurbarán
Jockey Club
Casa Atucha
Embajada de Brasil
Embajada de Francia
Museo Isaac Fernández Blanco
Terminal de Omnibus
General San Martín
General M. Belgrano
Estación Retiro
General B. Mitre
Retiro
Palacio Estrugamou
Palacio San Martín
Basilica Santisimo Sacramento
San Martín
Palacio Retiro
Galerias Pacífico
Directiva General de Migraciones
Museo Nacional de Inmigración
Dársena Norte
Uruguay ferries and catamarans
Facultad de Medicina
Callao
0 250 m
N
AVENIDA DEL LIBERTADOR
AVENIDA SANTA FE
AVENIDA CALLAO
AVENIDA 9 DE JULIO
AVENIDA PUEYRREDÓN
AVENIDA ANTÁRTIDA ARGENTINA
AVENIDA EDUARDO MADERO
MARCELO T DE ALVEAR
Palermo
City Centre
Puerto Madero

pavement so you're not taken for a beggar, take your hat off at the theatre and, whatever you do, don't call a lady *donna*. Modern Argentines can check their surname against the computer database of immigration records. A panel states: "Argentina gave them lodging and they bequeathed us their children and their children's children." Given the bearing immigration has had in shaping Argentina, it's a shame that more hasn't been done with the displays, though more ambitious plans are in the works. The building is in the port area, behind the modern Migraciones headquarters, so it's advisable to take a taxi rather than negotiate the labyrinth of roads and their heavy traffic on foot.

Estación Retiro

A massive complex of rail terminals looming to the west of the museum, **Estación Retiro** is in fact three train stations in one: General San Martín, General Belgrano and General Mitre. The third of these is also by far the most impressive, a massive stone and metal structure completed in 1915 by Charles John Dudley, a British constructor based in Liverpool. Decorated with Royal Doulton porcelain tiles, it is a majestic, airy edifice with an iron roof that, at the time, was the largest of its kind in the world. Recently restored to its former glory, it's worth a visit for its splendid café, *Café Retiro*. From here, too, suburban rail lines lead out into the northern suburbs and onwards to Tigre.

Plaza San Martín

Immediately southeast of the stations, the leafy **Plaza San Martín** plays many roles: romantic meeting-place, picnic area for office workers, children's playground and many people's arrival point in downtown Buenos Aires, owing to the main train and bus terminals nearby. The more open, northern half of the plaza, facing the train stations, slopes down to Avenida del Libertador, which runs through northern Buenos Aires all the way to Tigre. The **Monumento a los Héroes de la Guerra de las Malvinas** stands on the brow of the slope, a sombre cenotaph comprising 25 black marble plaques inscribed with the 649 names of the country's fallen during the conflict, its eternal flame partly symbolizing Argentina's persistent claim over the South Atlantic islands. It is permanently guarded by a rotation of the army, navy and air force, and is the scene of both remembrance ceremonies and demonstrations on April 2 each year, the day on which Argentina began its brief occupation of the islands in 1982. Ironically, and deliberately, the monument is opposite the former Plaza Británica – called the Plaza Fuerza Aérea Argentina since 1982. At the centre of the plaza, there are echoes of London's Big Ben in the seventy-metre **Torre de los Ingleses**, the Anglo-Argentine community's contribution to the 1910 centenary celebrations. During and after the 1982 conflict there was talk of demolishing the tower, and it was officially renamed Torre Monumental. It was closed indefinitely at the time of writing, but should it be open you can climb to the sixth floor for great views.

Plaza San Martín was designed by Argentina's most important landscape architect, Frenchman **Charles Thays** (see box, p.130), and created especially for a monument to **General San Martín** that was moved to its southwestern corner in 1910 for the country's centenary. Aligned with Avenida Santa Fe, the imposing bronze equestrian statue – cast in 1862, and Argentina's first – stands proudly on a high marble pedestal decorated with scenes representing national liberation. The Libertador points west, showing the way across the Andes. The plaza's lush lawns are a favourite sunbathing spot in the warmer months, but when it gets baking hot you can always cool down on a bench beneath the luxuriant palms, ceibos, monkey puzzles, lime trees and acacias.

Charles Thays: Buenos Aires' landscape artist

In the 1880s, French botanist and **landscape architect Charles Thays** (1849–1934) travelled to South America to study its rich flora, particularly the continent's hundreds of endemic tree species. He initially settled in Argentina, where his services were in great demand as municipal authorities across the country sought to smarten their cities up. They, like their European and North American counterparts, were spurred by the realization that the country's fast-growing urban sprawls needed parks and gardens to provide vital breathing spaces and recreational areas.

In 1890, Thays was appointed director of parks and gardens in Buenos Aires, in no small part due to his adeptness at transforming open plazas formerly used for military parades, or *plazas secas*, into shady *plazas verdes*, or green squares, such as Plaza San Martín. He also designed the capital's botanical garden and the zoo – which he planted with dozens of tipas – as well as Palermo's Parque 3 de Febrero, Belgrano's Barrancas, Córdoba's Parque Sarmiento and Parque San Martín, Tucumán's Parque 9 de Julio and, most impressive of them all, Mendoza's Parque General San Martín. Thays received countless private commissions, too, including the garden of Palacio Hume, on Avenida Alvear in Recoleta, and the layout of the exclusive residential estate known as Barrio Parque, in Palermo Chico.

Despite his French origins, he preferred the informal English style of landscaping, and also experimented with combinations of native plants such as jacarandas, tipas and *palo borracho* with Canary Island palms, planes and lime trees. Oddly enough, given the high regard in which he was held and his contributions to the greening of Buenos Aires, the lone plaza named in his honour, Plaza Carlos Thays, in Palermo, is disappointingly barren, and definitely not the best example of landscaping the city has to offer.

Basílica del Santísimo Sacramento and Edificio Kavanagh

The **Basílica del Santísimo Sacramento**, at San Martín 1039, lurks east of the Plaza San Martín, at the end of a narrow *pasaje* and rather dwarfed by the skyscrapers surrounding it. It was built with some of the vast fortune of Mercedes Castellanos de Anchorena, a matriarchal figure who married into one of Argentina's wealthiest and most influential landowning clans (hence the Argentine expression "as rich as an Anchorena"). Consecrated in 1916, the basilica is still regarded as the smartest place to get married in Buenos Aires. Not surprisingly, it was designed by French architects, with a white marble dome and five slender turrets; it's no coincidence that it looks so much like Paris's Sacré Coeur. Inside, no expense was spared: red onyx from Morocco, marble from Verona and Carrara, red sandstone from the Vosges, glazed mosaic tiles from Venice and bronze from France were imported to decorate her monument to devotion. Down in the crypt and behind a protective grille, is Mercedes Castellanos de Anchorena's **mausoleum**, an ostentatious yet doleful concoction of marble angels guarded by a demure Virgin Mary. The basilica was undergoing extensive renovation work at the time of writing, and may be closed to the public at times.

The **Edificio Kavanagh**, next to the basilica at San Martín and Florida 1065, similarly sums up the social – and architectural – evolution in twentieth-century Buenos Aires. It is rumoured that Corina Kavanagh sold most of her property in the country to erect what, when it went up in 1935, was to be the tallest building (120m) in South America. It is also rumoured that she deliberately built it in front of the basilica to conceal her bitter rival's masterpiece. It was the first structure on the continent to use reinforced concrete and the first building in Latin America to integrate air-conditioning. The two facades of its distinctive flat-iron shape – it's built in a wedge formed by the two streets – were hailed at the time by the American Institute of Architects as the world's best example of Rationalist architecture, and the building was inhabited in the early years by many of the city's rich and famous, including Enrique Larreta (see p.152). Although still impressive, it long ago lost its title as the city's tallest building; that honour currently belongs to the Faro "twin towers" in Puerto Madero (170m).

Palacio Retiro

Press baron José Paz, founder of daily newspaper *La Prensa* and related by marriage to the Anchorenas, wanted his Buenos Aires home to look like the Louvre, so he commissioned the **Palacio Retiro** (guided visits in English Tues & Fri 4pm, $18; in Spanish Tues–Fri 11am & 3pm, Wed & Thurs 4pm, Sat 11am, $8) – previously known as the Palacio Paz – to be built by a French architect between 1902 and 1914, but he died in 1912, without ever seeing the finished product. The palace runs along the southwest side of Plaza San Martín, and access is via magnificent wrought-iron gates at Av Santa Fe 750. It remains the largest single house ever built in Argentina, and its main facade is an uncanny replica of the Sully wing of the Parisian palace, with steeply stacked slate roofs, a double row of tiny windows and a colonnaded ground floor.

Inside, the eighteen rooms open to the public – less than one sixth of the whole building – are decorated in an eclectic range of French styles, from Gothic to Empire, including a scaled-down copy of the Hall of Mirrors in Versailles, but the *pièce de résistance* is the great Hall of Honour, a cavernous, circular room lined with several types of European marble and crowned with a stained-glass dome from which the Sun King beams down. Artur Rubinstein entertained guests in the little music room and the Prince of Wales dined here during his visit to the city in 1925, but the Paz family fell on hard times in the late 1930s, most of the original furniture was sold off and the palace was divided between the Círculo Militar, an officers' club, and the **Museo de Armas de la Nación** (Mon–Fri 1–7pm; $2); the latter now houses an exhibition of armour, weapons and military uniforms, some dating back to the Wars of Independence.

Palacio San Martín

Just north of the Palacio Retiro and northwest of Plaza San Martín, at Arenales and Esmeralda, **Palacio San Martín** (free guided visits in English and Spanish Thurs 11am, Fri 3pm, 4pm & 5pm; ⓣ011/4819-8092) is a particularly extravagant example of the city's ostentatious palaces. Built in 1905 for the **Anchorena** family, it was originally known as the Palacio Anchorena. Mercedes Castellanos de Anchorena (see opposite) lived here with her family for twenty years, until the Great Depression left them penniless. The enormous building is actually divided up into three subtly different palaces, all sharing a huge Neoclassical entrance and ceremonial courtyard. Its overall structure is based on a nineteenth-century Parisian banker's mansion, with slate mansard roofs, colonnades and domed attics, while the Neo-Baroque interior is inspired by the eighteenth-century Hotel de Condé, also in Paris. Fashionable Art Nouveau details, such as ornate stained-glass windows and wrought-iron staircases, were also incorporated.

After the palace and its accumulated treasures were hurriedly sold off in 1927, the government turned it into the Ministry of Foreign Affairs, International Trade and Worship, and renamed it Palacio San Martín. Since the 1980s, when the ministry moved into the larger plate-glass building across Calle Esmeralda, the palace has been reserved for state ceremonies, and is open to the public for tours. Some of the original furniture and paintings have been recovered, but the guided visits are above all a rare opportunity to witness the opulent interior of a Porteño palace. The gilt mirrors, marble fireplaces and chandeliers are all on a grandiose scale, yet they still look lost in the cavernous rooms, with their polished parquet floors, inlaid wooden panelling and ceilings richly decorated with oil paintings. The outside of the building was being restored at the time of writing, so visits were suspended; call ahead to check times, as they may have changed.

Museo de Arte Hispanoamericano Isaac Fernández Blanco

Two blocks north and one west of Palacio San Martín, at Suipacha 1422, the **Museo de Arte Hispanoamericano Isaac Fernández Blanco** (Tues–Sun & holidays 2–7pm; $3, free Thurs; ⓣ011/4327-0272, ⓦwww.museos.buenosaires.gov.ar), is one of the city's undisputed cultural highlights. The museum occupies the **Palacio Noel**, a stunning Neocolonial house built in the 1920s by architect Martín Noel, who later donated it to the city. Its style imitates eighteenth-century Lima Baroque, a backlash against the slavish imitation of Parisian palaces fashionable at the time. With plain white walls, lace-like window-grilles, dark wooden bow windows and wrought-iron balconies, it's the perfect residence for the superb collection of **Spanish-American art** on display inside. Several private holdings, including the Noel brothers' own collection of colonial art, were merged to form the museum's current assortment. Most of the artefacts on display, all favourably presented, were produced in the seventeenth and early eighteenth centuries, in Peru or Alto Peru (present-day Bolivia).

The collection is spread across three floors and divided into three principal parts – the influence of the Conquest in the Andes, Buenos Aires as the port to the continent and the mix of Jesuit and indigenous cultures in the jungle. One of the most striking pieces is a fantastic eighteenth-century silver sacrarium, embellished with a portrait of Christ on a copper plaque, just to the right of the entrance. Other high points of this huge and varied collection include a Luso-Brazilian silver votive lamp, polychrome furniture – the work of Bolivian craftsmen – and fine Jesuit/Guaraní statues, all carved from wood. There's also an extensive display of anonymous paintings from the **Cusqueña School** – one of the most prodigious in colonial South America. Its masters, based in the Peruvian city of Cusco and especially active in the eighteenth century, produced subtle oil paintings, mostly of religious, devotional subjects, which somehow combined sombre understatement with a startling vitality and mixed traditional Catholic imagery with indigenous motifs. Particularly of note are a *Virgin of Mercy Crowned by the Holy Trinity* and a startling naked Mary Magdalene in a delicately coloured seventeenth-century painting by Antonio Bermejo. Upstairs, impressive temporary exhibits showcase different themes, while the new display in the basement is on the symbolic power of silver and features some fine wrought-silver *mate* vessels. There are also examples of the huge, ornate tortoiseshell combs that were the fashion for *nouveaux riches* Porteñas in the 1820s until someone pointed out how vulgar they were.

Though now fully restored, the Palacio Noel was badly damaged in 1992 by a terrorist bomb that tore apart the Israeli Embassy that stood just opposite the museum (see box, p.113) and killed thirty people. Today, the site is named **Plaza Embajada de Israel**, and the scarred, bare white wall, which stands in stark contrast to the ornate palaces of the district, bears plaques commemorating those who lost their lives.

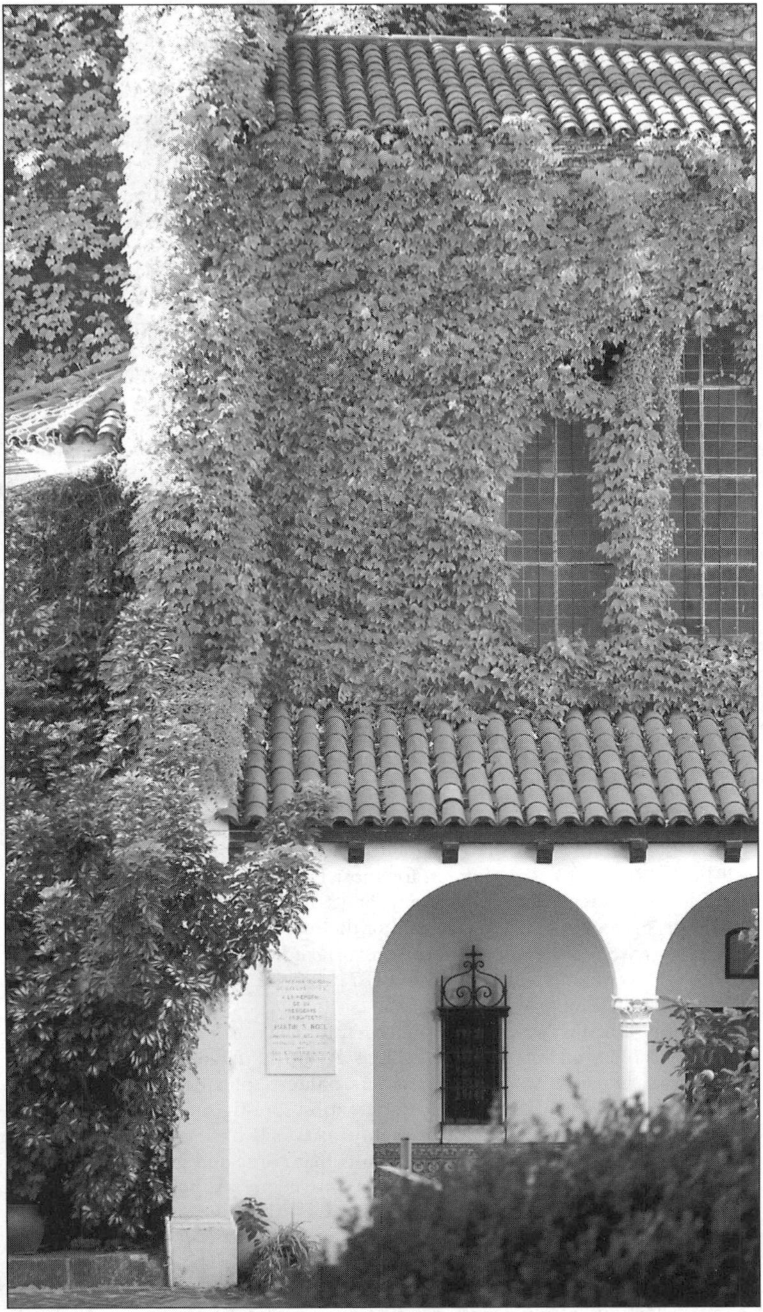

△ Museo de Arte Hispanoamericano Isaac Fernández Blanco

Plaza Carlos Pellegrini and around

The elegant triangle of **Plaza Carlos Pellegrini** is a centre of Retiro's well-heeled residential streets west of Avenida 9 de Julio, and near it you'll find a variety of spectacular buildings that share a common theme: their meticulous French style. Between 1910 and 1925, the obsession with turning Buenos Aires into the "Paris of the South" reached a fever pitch in this part of the city, making this neighbourhood one of the more exclusive, something it remains to this day. The many feats of **Carlos Pellegrini**, president in the 1890s and the plaza's namesake, include founding both the Banco Nación and Argentina's influential **Jockey Club**; the latter's national headquarters occupies the massive honey-coloured **Palacio Unzué de Casares**, on the north side of the plaza at Av Alvear 1345. Built in the severely unadorned *style académique*, it's alleviated only by its delicate wrought-iron balconies. Opposite, on the south side of the plaza, stands the **Palacio Celedonio Pereda**, named after a member of the oligarchy who wanted a carbon copy of the Palais Jacquemart-André in Paris. The Porteño palace, now occupied by the Brazilian Embassy, is a uniformly successful replica, classical columns and all.

Directly east of the plaza, at the corner of Calle Cerrito, ivy-clad **Casa Atucha** presides, a soberly stylish Second Empire mansion by René Sergent, a French architect who never set foot in Argentina but designed dozens of houses here. Half a block north, at Cerrito 1455, the **Mansion Alzaga Unzué** now forms a luxurious annexe of the *Four Seasons* hotel (see p.100). It's a faultless duplicate of a Loire chateau, built in attractive red brick and cream limestone and topped with a shiny slate mansard roof. Back up on the other side of Arroyo, the Louis XIV-style **Palacio Ortiz Basualdo** has been the location of the French Embassy since 1925. This magnificent palace with slightly incongruous detailing, including Art Nouveau balconies, monumental Ionic pilasters and bulging Second Empire corner-turrets, mercifully escaped demolition in the 1950s when Avenida 9 de Julio was widened, though it did have to be altered considerably to accommodate the highway. From Plaza Carlos Pellegrini, Avenida Alvear leads due northwest to Recoleta.

Recoleta

Northwest of Retiro and stretching all the way to Avenida Coronel Díaz, the well-heeled barrio of **Recoleta** is, for most Porteños, intrinsically tied to the magnificent **La Recoleta Cemetery** at its heart. Recoleta wasn't always a prestigious place, though: until the end of the seventeenth century, its groves of Barbary figs were hideouts for notorious brigands. It wasn't until the cholera and yellow fever epidemics of 1867 and 1871 that the city's wealthy moved here from hitherto fashionable San Telmo.

Even though many of its residents have left for the northern suburbs in recent years, a Recoleta address still has cachet. **Avenida Alvear** is Buenos Aires' swankiest street: along it you'll find stately **palaces**, plus designer **boutiques**, swish art galleries and one of the city's most prestigious hotels. Scattered throughout the barrio are a host of **restaurants** and bars, ranging from some of the city's most traditional to trendy joints that come and go.

There's more to Recoleta than the fabulous cemetery, beginning with the gleaming white **Basílica Nuestra Señora del Pilar**, one of the capital's few remaining colonial buildings. Also close by are two arts centres, the **Centro Cultural de Recoleta**, housed in a disused convent, and the **Palais de Glace**, a former skating-rink and tango hall. Not far away, the country's biggest and richest collections of nineteenth- and twentieth-century art are on display at the **Museo Nacional de Bellas Artes**.

On every scrap of grass around Recoleta it seems there's a monument or **sculpture** of some description, such as the giant, hydraulic aluminium flower, the **Floralis Genérica**. Tucked away in the southwestern corner of the barrio is the **Museo Xul Solar**, the former home of one of Argentina's most original artists – it contains a large collection of his intriguing paintings.

The subte skirts the southern edge of Recoleta, but the barrio is walking distance (or a short cab ride) from the city centre.

Avenida Alvear

Only five blocks in length, stretching from Plaza Carlos Pellegrini – technically in Retiro – to Plaza San Martín de Tours, Avenida Alvear is one of the city's shortest but most exclusive avenues, lined with expensive **art galleries** – selling mostly conventional portraits and landscapes but also some avant-garde pieces – and international designer **fashion boutiques** like Louis Vuitton and Emporio Armani. At the corner of Ayacucho lies the city's most famous and traditional luxury hotel, the French Art Deco **Alvear Palace** (see p.100), built in 1932 and recently restored. Two blocks south, opposite elegant apartment buildings between Montevideo and Rodriguez Peña, are three palaces that were home to some of Argentina's wealthiest families at the beginning of the twentieth century. Although none is open to the public, the exteriors are worth a peek for their splendid architecture. The northernmost, behind a Charles Thays-designed garden, is the **Palacio Hume**. This perfectly symmetrical Art Nouveau creation, embellished with intricate wrought-iron-work, now looks a little the worse for wear. It was originally built for British rail-engineer Alexander Hume, but was sold to the Duhau family in the 1920s, who staged the city's first-ever art exhibition inside. The Duhau family also built the middle palace, the **Palacio Duhau**, now the *Park Hyatt*. This austere imitation of an eighteenth-century French Neoclassical *palais* has been converted into another of the city's leading hotels. The third palace, the severely Neoclassical **Nunciatura Apostólica**, on the corner of Montevideo, was designed by a French architect for a member of the Anchorena family. Nowadays it's the seat of the Vatican's Argentina representative, and was used by Pope John Paul II during his visits to the country.

La Recoleta Cemetery

In around 1720, drawn to the area's tranquillity, which was deemed perfect for meditation or "recollection" (hence the name), Franciscan monks set up a monastery in present-day Recoleta. A hundred years later, after the monks had been ejected by the city governor, **La Recoleta Cemetery**, at Avenida Quintana and Junín (daily 7am–6pm; guided tours last Sun of month March–Nov at 2.30pm; free), was created in the monastery's gardens. One of the world's most remarkable burial grounds, it presents an exhilarating mixture of architectural whimsy and a panorama of Argentine history. It is an awe-inspiring place, exerting a magnetic attraction on locals and foreigners alike. The giant vaults, stacked along avenues inside the high walls, resemble the rooftops of a fanciful Utopian town from above. The necropolis is a city within a city, a lesson in architectural styles and fashions. In his 1923 poem *La Recoleta*, Borges eulogized the cemetery and its beautiful graves, with their Latin inscriptions and fateful dates. Another Argentine writer, Martín Cáparros, was even more melancholy: for him, La Recoleta was a magnificent tribute to many great civilizations of the past – from Babylonian and Egyptian, to Roman and Byzantine – and its flamboyant architecture embodied the grandiose hopes of Argentina's heroes and historians that their country would become just as great. But in the end, he concluded, the only fatherland they managed to build was the cemetery itself.

The burial ground is a great place to wander, exploring its narrow streets and wide avenues of yews and cypress trees. The tombs themselves range from simple headstones to bombastic masterpieces built in a variety of styles including Art Nouveau, Art Deco, Secessionist, Neoclassical, Neo-Byzantine and even Neo-Babylonian. The oldest monumental grave, dating from 1836, is that of **Juan Facundo Quiroga**, the much-feared La Rioja *caudillo* (local leader) and General Rosas' henchman. It stands straight ahead of the gateway, along with the marble statue of the *Virgen Dolorosa*, said to be a likeness of his widow. Next to it, inscribed with a Borges poem, stands the solemn granite mausoleum occupied by several generations of the eminent Alvear family, including **Torcuato de Alvear** who, as city mayor, had the ceremonial portico of Doric columns added to the cemetery's entrance. As well as individual tombs and family vaults, La Recoleta contains a number of monuments, such as the magnificent **Panteón de los Guerreros del Paraguay**; up against the far-west corner of the cemetery, this is the mass grave of Argentine heroes of the late nineteenth-century War of the Triple Alliance against Paraguay, and is guarded by two bronze infantrymen. Over by the northwest wall, due west of the central plaza, is the **Monumento a los Caídos en la Revolución de 1890**, a huge granite slab smothered in commemorative plaques, beneath a centenarian cypress tree. It's the tomb of several Radical Party leaders, including founding father Leandro Além and Hipólito Yrigoyen, two-time president of Argentina. Three aisles south, there's an incongruous statue of a boxer – the final resting place of **Angel Firpo**, who fought Jack Dempsey for the world heavyweight title in 1923.

The cemetery's most famous resident, though, is **Evita**. Given the snobbishness surrounding the cemetery – the authorities who preside over it treat it more like a gentlemen's club than a burial ground – it's hardly surprising that Porteño high society tried to prevent Evita's family from laying her to rest here. Even President Perón himself had to make do with second-best Chacarita Cemetery (see p.154) – and he has since been moved to San Vicente. Nevertheless, her family's plain, polished black granite vault – pithily marked **Familia Duarte** – has been her resting place since the 1970s (until, as is rumoured, her remains are also moved to San Vicente). Unlike many other graves, it's not signposted – the cemetery authorities are still uneasy about her presence – but you can locate it by following the signs to President Sarmiento's, over to the left when you come in, then counting five alleyways farther away from the entrance, and looking out for the pile of bouquets by the vault. Some poignant quotes from her speeches are inscribed on bronze plaques, including a tribute from the union of taxi drivers.

Despite La Recoleta's tradition for coffins to be stacked up in multi-generation family vaults rather than buried under separate gravestones, there's a long waiting list for a plot, and money and status count less than family ties. Most of the great artists, scientists, financiers and politicians buried here would not have been granted a space without a resoundingly patrician surname like San Martín or Dorrego, Anchorena or Pueyrredón, Mitre or Hernández. The main exception is that of the military heroes, many of them Irish or British seafarers, who played a key part in Argentina's struggle for independence, such as **Admiral William Brown**, an Argentine hero of Irish origins, who at the beginning of the nineteenth century decimated the Spanish fleet near Isla Martín García (see p.189). An unusual monument decorated with a beautiful miniature of his frigate, the *Hercules*, is a highlight of the cemetery's central plaza.

To find out more about the cemetery's history and the individual tombs, and find your way around, try and get hold of Robert Wright's comprehensive colour map with its "Top 50 Tombs and Mausoleums" ($20; Ⓦwww.urbex.com.ar).

Basílica Nuestra Señora del Pilar

Just north of the cemetery gates is the stark white silhouette of the **Basílica Nuestra Señora del Pilar** (Mon–Sat 10.30am–6.15pm, Sun 2.30–6.15pm; free). Built in the early eighteenth century by Jesuits, it's the second oldest church in Buenos Aires and effectively the parish church for the Recoleta elite, although it was allowed to decline until the 1930s. The sky-blue Pas-de-Calais ceramic tiles atop its single slender turret were then painstakingly restored, along with the plain facade. The interior was also remodelled, and the monks' cells turned into side-chapels, each decorated with a gilded reredos and polychrome wooden saints. These include a statue of San Pedro de Alcántara, the Virgen de la Merced and the Casa de Ejercicios, all attributed to a native artist known simply as "José". The magnificent Baroque silver altarpiece, embellished with an Inca sun and other pre-Hispanic details, was made by craftsmen from Alto Peru. Equally admirable is the fine altar crucifix allegedly donated to the city by King Carlos III of Spain. It is possible to visit the cloisters above the church (Tues–Sat 10.30am–6.15pm, Sun 2.30–6.15pm; Tues–Fri $2, Sat & Sun $1.50) via the staircase three altars to the left. The rooms, once home to Franciscan monks, now hold a collection of religious paintings and artefacts, including some impressive colonial and *criollo* silverware. From the windows you get a good view over Recoleta Cemetery.

Centro Cultural Recoleta and around

Immediately north of Basílica Nuestra Señora del Pilar, at Junín 1930, the **Centro Cultural Recoleta** (Tues–Fri 2–9pm, Sat & Sun 10am–9pm; $1; Ⓦwww.centroculturalrecoleta.org) is one of the city's leading **arts centres**, a good deal bigger and more impressive inside than its modest front suggests. The building, which dates from the 1730s, is one of Buenos Aires' oldest, and originally housed Franciscan monks. The building was extensively, but tastefully, remodelled in the 1980s and retains its former cloisters. These cool, white, arched hallways and simple rooms make an excellent setting for the changing art, photography and audio-visual exhibitions that the centre hosts. Straight on from the entrance and to the right, the **Museo Participativo de Ciencias** (Tues–Fri 10am–5pm, Sat & Sun 3.30–7.30pm; $6), is a small but colourful hands-on interactive science museum that's popular with local children. Back outside there's a series of attractive cobbled patios that lead to "El Aleph" auditorium, a converted chapel painted garish pink. Facing it, a simple board lists the places "that should never be forgotten" which were used by the military dictatorship for torturing dissidents, such as ESMA and Pozo de Quilmes; it echoes a similar list erected in Berlin to remember the Nazi concentration camps. Further on, the roof terrace affords views of the surrounding plazas. The centre also has a mini **hotel** (Ⓣ011/4803-4223) for visiting artists, with rooms beautifully bedecked in original artwork – contact the centre directly for prices and reservations. Finally, the **Sala Villa Villa**, opposite the terrace, puts on contemporary theatre and dance; it's the occasional home of, among others, the internationally renowned De La Guarda, the anarchic theatre troupe who swing on trapezes above the audience.

Directly east of the cultural centre, at Posadas 1725, is the **Palais de Glace** (Tues–Sun 2–8pm; $1), a distinctive circular *belle époque* building that started life as an ice rink. It's more famous, however, for being the home of tango, or rather the place where tango crossed over from being considered a sordid feature of brothels to a fashionable society dance, when Porteño trendsetter Barón de Marchi staged tango soirées here in the 1920s. The Palais' vast hall is now used for a variety of **art exhibitions**, often with a political tinge – many deal with themes related to the military dictatorship and the disappeared – and trade shows, including popular wine tastings.

Between the two arts centres, **Plaza San Martín de Tours**, a grassy slope at the northern end of Avenida Alvear (see p.135), is shaded by three of the biggest rubber trees in the city, an impressive sight with their huge buttress-roots, contorted like arthritic limbs. Another 100-year-old rubber tree, the famous Gran Gomero, shelters the terrace of nearby *La Biela*, on the corner of Avenida Quintana, 100m west. One of the city's most traditional *confiterías*, it gets its name, which means "connecting-rod", from being the favourite haunt of racing drivers in the 1940s and 50s. Nearby, on the parkland next to the cemetery, buskers, jugglers and groups practising the fluid Brazilian martial art of *capoeira* entertain crowds during the **Fería Hippy** at weekends (9am–7pm; free), while artisans sell hand-crafted wares including *mate* gourds, jewellery and ceramics at stalls arranged along the wide paths.

Museo Nacional de Bellas Artes

Argentina's principal art museum, the **Museo Nacional de Bellas Artes** (Tues–Fri 12.30–7.30pm, Sat & Sun 9.30am–7.30pm; free; Ⓦwww.mnba.org.ar) is housed in an unassuming, slightly gloomy, brick-red Neoclassical building at Av del Libertador 1473, half a kilometre due north of Recoleta Cemetery. Like the barrio's architecture, the museum's contents, comprising mostly nineteenth- and twentieth-century paintings and some sculpture, are resoundingly European, while the Old World influences on the Argentine art on display are clearly evident.

The museum's collection is large (around 11,000 pieces) and only about a tenth of it is on display at any time. The selection is always changing, but certain key paintings, such as Degas's *Two Yellow and Pink Dancers*, are usually on view. In the ground-floor galleries, there is a modest collection of mainly **European art**. Degas and fellow **Impressionists** Monet, Pissarro and Renoir are given pride of place, while El Greco, Goya and Rubens get a couple of paintings each, as do later masters as varied as Chagall, Modigliani, Pollock and Picasso. There is also an impressive collection of **Rodin** sculptures – one study of his (*Study of Hands for The Secret*) mysteriously disappeared recently, and was found by a *cartonero* who sold it to an antiques store for $50. Two untitled pieces by Argentine-born artist Lucio Fontana, just to the right of the main entrance, are not his best works, but their position is a recognition of his international status. In a room by itself, the wide-ranging **Hirsch bequest** – left to the nation by the wealthy Belgrano landowners and art-collectors – includes some fabulous paintings, sculptures, furniture and other art objects spanning several centuries from all over Europe, including a retable from Spain and a Hals portrait.

The upper-floor galleries are an excellent introduction to **Argentine art**, containing a selection of the country's major artists, many of them influenced by European masters. *The Bath* by Prilidiano Pueyrredón clearly takes its lead from Bouguereau's *Toilette de Vénus*, while Xul Solar's masterpiece *Preacher* could easily be mistaken for a Klee (see p.140). Raquel Forner, who painted *Tableau of Pain*, was actually a pupil of Othon Friesz, whose *In the Emir's Garden* is hanging downstairs. Later Argentine artists also on display here, such as Guillermo Kuitca and Juan Carlos Distéfano, managed to break away from this imitative tendency and create a movement of their own.

The monuments and statues of northern Buenos Aires

Much of **northern Buenos Aires** has the feel of an open-air museum, with dozens of **monuments** and **statues** dominating the green spaces throughout Retiro, Recoleta, Palermo and Belgrano. Some of the sculptures were created by renowned artists, including Rodin and Bourdelle, and others are lesser works, but they almost all relate the history of Argentina. When northern Buenos Aires was being landscaped at the beginning of the twentieth century, the fashion was for great open squares to be presided over by the statue of a famous person, but this was not to everyone's liking. Borges once complained that "there wasn't a single square left in the city that hadn't been ruined by a dirty great bronze statue of someone or other".

The belligerent equestrian statue of **General San Martín** on Plaza San Martín started this trend when it was moved here in 1910. In 1950, another, more placid bronze of the national hero was erected to mark the centenary of his death. It's opposite the Instituto Sanmartiniano, and depicts the Libertador serenely seated on a granite plinth, surrounded by his grandchildren. In front of Recoleta's Palais de Glace stands another equestrian statue, this one of a hatless **General Carlos M. de Alvear**, on a grey- and red-granite pedestal. An acutely elegant creation by Emile-Antoine Bourdelle, it's considered both one of the city's and the artist's finest works. Further north, Plaza Mitre is dominated by a monument to **Bartolomé Mitre**, who founded the influential broadsheet *La Nación* in the mid-nineteenth century. A bronze Mitre sits astride a majestic mount on a solid granite pedestal decorated with an extravagant set of white marble figures. Behind the square, next to the British Embassy, is a very green statue of **George Canning**. Lord Canning was British Foreign Secretary in the 1820s and instrumental in getting the South American nations' independence from Spain recognized by the rest of Europe. Previously next to the Torre de los Ingleses (see p.129), the tonne of bronze was chucked into the Río de la Plata at the height of the South Atlantic conflict, then fished out several years later and moved to this "safer" position.

Further west, the plazas named after Uruguay and Chile also have statues of their respective national heroes as their focal points. The sandstone monument to Uruguay's **General Artigas** has an unfortunate fascist look about it, while a majestic bronze of Chile's **Bernardo O'Higgins** sits astride a rearing mount in a pastoral setting of huge tipas, pines and a spreading ombú tree. At the corner of Plaza Sicilia, in Palermo, a marble and bronze statue of **President Sarmiento** by Rodin stands on the exact location of his arch-enemy Rosas's mansion. Opposite is a far more dramatic equestrian statue of **Juan Manuel de Rosas** himself. A surprisingly diminutive statue of **Manuel Belgrano** stands at the centre of Plaza Belgrano, in the barrio named after the inventor of the national flag.

One of the most recent additions is a statue of **Pope John Paul II**, funded by the city's Polish community, and positioned next to the Biblioteca Nacional in 1999. Below, in Plaza Evita, is a bronze statue of **Eva Perón** – but not a very good likeness – the only one to a famous woman in the whole city.

For Argentina's 1910 **centenary** celebrations, the country's major ethnic communities each donated a monument to their adoptive country. At the middle of Recoleta's Plaza Francia, a very Baroque marble monument represents Liberty, while Plaza Alemania is dominated by a huge monument that juxtaposes an effete white-marble youth, not unlike Michelangelo's *David*, standing coyly next to a sturdy ox, with three embarrassed-looking youths posing by a plough. On Plaza Italia, aptly at the heart of Palermo, is a pompous equestrian monument to **Garibaldi,** Italy's national hero and South American freedom fighter. The busy rotunda at the junction of Avenida del Libertador and Avenida Sarmiento, due north, is taken up by the most glorious monument in the city, the **Monumento de los Españoles**, whose fine bronze sculptures symbolize the Andes, the Chaco, the Pampas and the Río de la Plata. Its allegorical figures, including the dainty angel at the top, are sculpted from Carrara marble and are so dazzlingly white that the monument is often blamed for road accidents.

Floralis Genérica

At the Plaza de las Naciones Unidas, next to the massive Doric columns of the Facultad de Derecho (Law Faculty), which in turn lurks behind the Museo Nacional de Bellas Artes, it's hard to miss the 25-metre-high aluminium and steel bloom named **Floralis Genérica**, one of the city's newest sculptures. Argentine architect **Eduardo Catalano** donated this work to the city as a tribute to all flowers and a symbol of "hope for the country's new spring". A system of light sensors and hydraulics closes the petals at sunset and opens them again at 8am, but they stay open on May 25, September 21 (the beginning of spring), Christmas Eve and New Year's Eve.

Biblioteca Nacional

About half a kilometre west of the Museo de Bellas Artes, standing back from Avenida del Libertador at the top of a steep slope, is the futuristic **Biblioteca Nacional**, Agüero 2502 (Mon–Sat 9am–9pm, Sat & Sun noon–9pm; guided visits Mon–Sat 3pm; free; ⓦwww.bibnal.edu.ar), Argentina's copyright library. It's built on the site of Quinta Unzué, the elegant palace where the Peróns lived when they were in power and where Evita died. After the so-called Revolución Libertadora, which overthrew Perón in 1955, Argentina's leaders were petrified that the residence would become a shrine to Evita and had it razed. The government decided to build a library on the site, but political upheavals, financial scandals and disagreements over the design held up construction for over three decades; the library was finally inaugurated in 1992. Designed in the 1960s by a trio of Argentina's leading architects, it's a kind of giant cuboid mushroom perched on four hefty stalks. Inside, what you see is but a small sampling of the library's extensive collection, since most of the five million tomes and documents – including a first edition of *Don Quixote*, a 1455 Gutenberg Bible and the personal collection of General Belgrano – are tucked away in huge underground rooms.

Attractively landscaped gardens, a café and terrace stretch out from the Biblioteca Nacional's southwest corner, while on the other side, along Avenida del Libertador, the park adjoining the library has been symbolically renamed Plaza Evita. The park is overlooked by a statue of Eva Perón unveiled by President Menem less than a week before his mandate ended in 1999; Peronists saw the placement of this monument as a way of avenging Evita's ill-treatment at the hands of the oligarchy even after her death.

Museo Xul Solar

A dozen blocks west of the library, the **Museo Xul Solar** (Tues–Fri noon–8pm, Sat noon–7pm, closed Jan; $3) is at Laprida 1212, near the corner of Mansilla. The museum is in the "Fundación Pan Klub", an early twentieth-century townhouse where, for the last twenty years of his life, eccentric Porteño artist Xul Solar (1888–1963) lived. The house was remodelled in the 1990s, and its award-winning design is as exciting as the display of Solar's paintings and other works. The space contains work spanning nearly five decades and is on several different levels, built of timber and glass, each dedicated to a specific period in the artist's career.

Solar's preferred media were watercolour and tempera, though in addition to the very Klee-like paintings, there's a set of "Pan Altars," multicoloured mini-retables designed for his "universal religions" – Solar once told Borges that he had "founded twelve new religions since lunch". Other curiosities include a piano whose keyboard he replaced with three rows of painted keys with textured surfaces, created both for blind pianists and to implement his notion of the correspondence of colour and music. In some of the later works you can detect Solar's passion for linguistics and his plans for universal understanding based on his versions of Esperanto. His "Neocreole" – mixing Spanish, Portuguese, Guaraní and English – was to be a common language for all Americans, while "Panlengua" was a set of monosyllables based on arithmetic and astrology. Texts written in these languages inspired the more child-like paintings.

Palermo

Much of **Palermo**, Buenos Aires' largest barrio, is vibrantly green and appealingly well-kempt: ornate balconies overflow with jasmine and roses, grand apartment blocks line wide avenues, and plane trees, palms and jacarandas shade older, cobbled streets; its beautifully landscaped parks, some of the biggest in the world, come alive with locals practising in-line skating, playing football or walking their dogs. Given its sizeable proportions – it stretches all the way from Avenida Coronel Díaz, on the border with Recoleta, to Colegiales and Belgrano, to the north – it's not surprising that the barrio isn't completely homogeneous. It's really several distinctive sub-neighbourhoods rolled into one: Palermo Chico, Barrio Parque, Alto Palermo, Villa Freud, Palermo Viejo, Palermo Soho, Palermo Hollywood and Las Cañitas.

Palermo takes its name from an Italian farmer, Giovanni Domenico Palermo, who in 1590 bought the flood plains to the north of Buenos Aires, drained them and turned them into vineyards and orchards, soon known as the "campos de Palermo." In the early nineteenth century, President Juan Manuel de Rosas bought up the farmland and built a mansion, La Quinta, where he lived until his overthrow. The barrio began to take on its present-day appearance at the end of the nineteenth century, when its large parks and gardens were laid out. At that time it was rather insalubrious, but it gradually gentrified throughout the twentieth century, and is now regarded as a distinctly classy place to live, despite the conspicuous lines of prostitutes in parts of Palermo Soho.

The bit of Palermo around Plaza República de Chile that juts into Recoleta is known as **Palermo Chico** and contains some significant museums, including the **Museo de Arte Decorativo**, while immediately to the north **Barrio Parque** is an oasis of private mansions laid out by Charles Thays. The nearby **Museo de Arte Latinoamericano de Buenos Aires (MALBA)** is a must for fans of modern art, while popular crafts are the order of the day at the **Museo de Arte Popular**. About ten blocks west, **Palermo Viejo** is a traditional neighbourhood with lovely old houses along cobbled streets, but it's become such a trendy place, full of funky cafés and avant-garde art galleries, that

Dog walkers

Along the wide avenues and in the many parks of Barrio Norte and Palermo, you'll often be treated to one of Buenos Aires' more characteristic sights: the *paseaperros*, or professional **dog walkers**. Joggers holding seven or eight prized pedigrees on leashes are surprising enough, but these dilettantes are rightly held in contempt by the beefy specialists who confidently swagger along towed by twenty to thirty dogs – you can't help wondering how it is they don't get tangled up or lose one of the pack. These invariably athletic young men (and, occasionally, women) are not paid just to take all manner of aristocratic breeds for a stroll, with the inevitable pit stops along the way, but must brush and groom them and look out for signs of ill-health; many dog walkers have veterinary training. They perform these vital duties every weekday – the dogs' owners usually manage such chores themselves on the weekends.

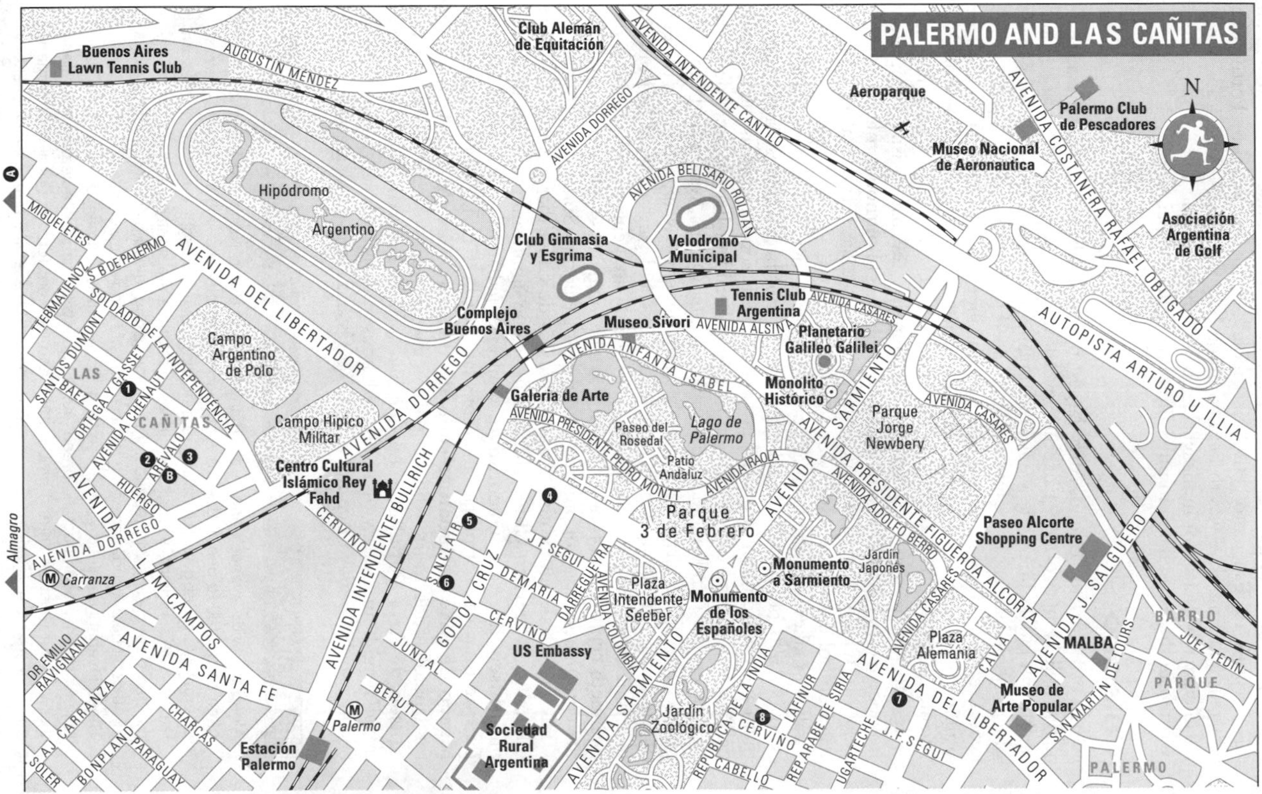
PALERMO AND LAS CAÑITAS
N
Buenos Aires Lawn Tennis Club
Club Alemán de Equitación
Aeroparque
Palermo Club de Pescadores
Museo Nacional de Aeronautica
Asociación Argentina de Golf
Hipódromo Argentino
Club Gimnasia y Esgrima
Velodromo Municipal
Tennis Club Argentina
Complejo Buenos Aires
Museo Sívori
Planetario Galileo Galilei
Monolito Histórico
Galeria de Arte
Campo Argentino de Polo
Campo Hipico Militar
Centro Cultural Islámico Rey Fahd
Paseo del Rosedal
Lago de Palermo
Patio Andaluz
Parque Jorge Newbery
Parque 3 de Febrero
Paseo Alcorte Shopping Centre
Jardín Japonés
Monumento a Sarmiento
Plaza Intendente Seeber
Monumento de los Españoles
Plaza Alemania
MALBA
Museo de Arte Popular
US Embassy
Sociedad Rural Argentina
Jardín Zoológico
Estación Palermo
Palermo
Carranza
Almagro
LAS CAÑITAS
BARRIO PARQUE
PALERMO
AUGUSTIN MÉNDEZ
AVENIDA INTENDENTE CANTILO
AVENIDA COSTANERA RAFAEL OBLIGADO
AUTOPISTA ARTURO U ILLIA
AVENIDA DORREGO
AVENIDA BELISARIO ROLDÁN
AVENIDA DEL LIBERTADOR
AVENIDA CASARES
AVENIDA ALSINA
AVENIDA INFANTA ISABEL
AVENIDA PRESIDENTE PEDRO MONTT
AVENIDA IRAOLA
SARMIENTO
AVENIDA SARMIENTO
AVENIDA PRESIDENTE FIGUEROA ALCORTA
AVENIDA ADOLFO BERRO
AVENIDA J. SALGUERO
JUEZ TEDÍN
SAN MARTIN DE TOURS
CAVIA
AVENIDA INTENDENTE BULLRICH
CERVIÑO
J.F. SEGUI
DEMARIA
DARREGUEYRA
AVENIDA COLOMBIA
SINCLAIR
GODOY CRUZ
JUNCAL
BERUTI
AVENIDA SANTA FE
L M CAMPOS
CHARCAS
PARAGUAY
BONPLAND
CARRANZA
DR EMILIO RAVIGNANI
A J SOLER
MIGUELETES
TEBMATIENZO
S B DE PALERMO
SOLDADO DE LA INDEPENDENCIA
SANTOS DUMONT
BAEZ
ORTEGA Y GASSET
AVENIDA CHENAUT
ARÉVALO
HUERGO
REPUBLICA DE LA INDIA
LAFINUR
REPARABE DE SIRIA
UGARTECHE
CABELLO
1
2
3
4
5
6
7
8
A
B

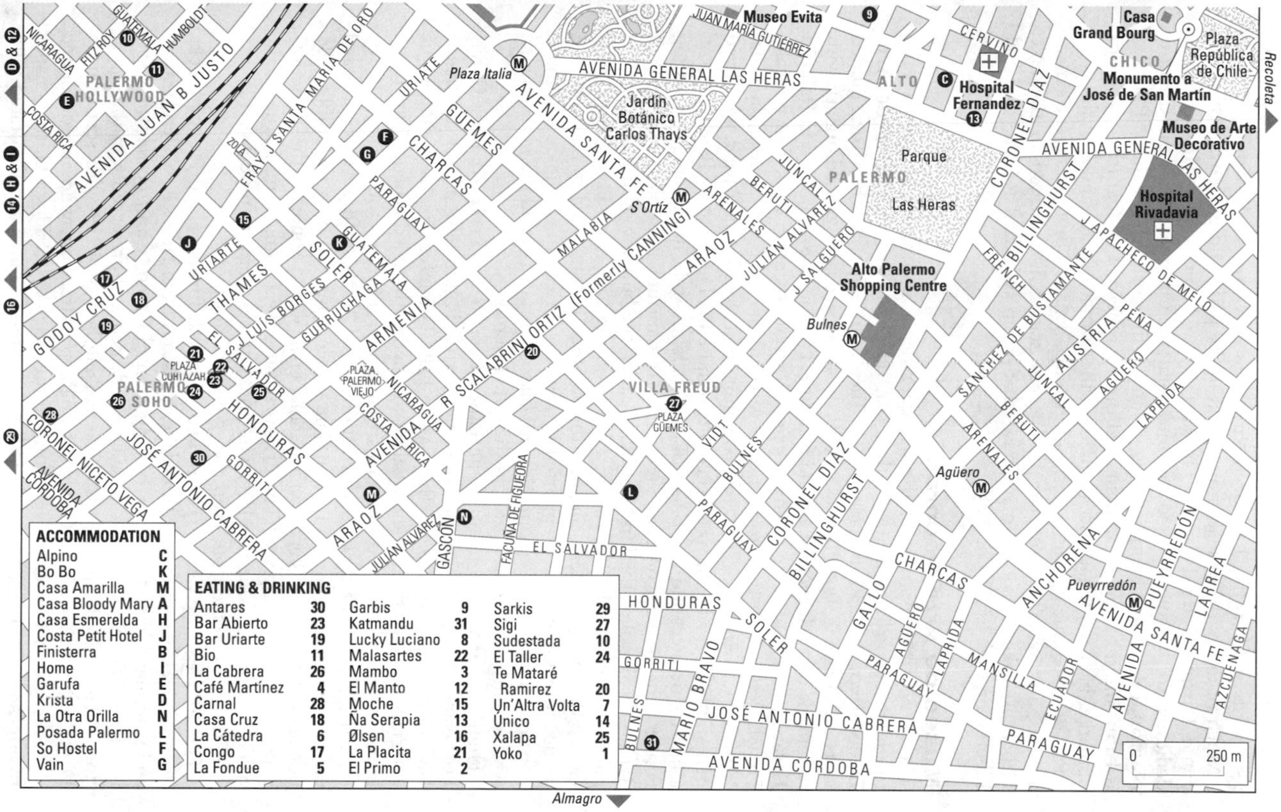

ACCOMMODATION

Alpino	C
Bo Bo	K
Casa Amarilla	M
Casa Bloody Mary	A
Casa Esmerelda	H
Costa Petit Hotel	J
Finisterra	B
Home	I
Garufa	E
Krista	D
La Otra Orilla	N
Posada Palermo	L
So Hostel	F
Vain	G

EATING & DRINKING

Antares	30	Garbis	9	Sarkis	29
Bar Abierto	23	Katmandu	31	Sigi	27
Bar Uriarte	19	Lucky Luciano	8	Sudestada	10
Bio	11	Malasartes	22	El Taller	24
La Cabrera	26	Mambo	3	Te Mataré Ramírez	20
Café Martínez	4	El Manto	12	Un'Altra Volta	7
Carnal	28	Moche	15	Único	14
Casa Cruz	18	Ña Serapia	13	Xalapa	25
La Cátedra	6	Ølsen	16	Yoko	1
Congo	17	La Placita	21		
La Fondue	5	El Primo	2		

the area around Plaza Cortázar is now known as **Palermo Soho**. Across the rail tracks, people in the media work, eat and drink in a cluster of TV studios, restaurants and bars that have been christened **Palermo Hollywood**.

Much of the north of Palermo is taken up by parks and gardens, such as the grand **Parque 3 de Febrero**. The area is also home to the **Museo Evita**, dedicated to the country's most famous daughter. On one side of the **Campo Nacional de Polo**, or national polo ground, at the northern reaches of Palermo, is Latin America's biggest mosque, and on the other is **Las Cañitas**, a zone of upmarket bars and restaurants, focused on the corner of Báez and Arévalo.

Part of subte Line D runs underneath Avenida Santa Fe, one of Palermo's main arteries, and where appropriate the nearest station is indicated in the text. Otherwise, take one of the many buses that go up avenidas Las Heras and Del Libertador, such as #10 or #38.

Museo de Arte Decorativo

There's no finer example of the decadent decor money could buy in early twentieth-century Buenos Aires than that on display in the **Museo de Arte Decorativo**, Av del Libertador 1902 (Tues–Sun 2–7pm; $2, free Tues; guided visits in English 2.30pm Tues ($3) & Wed–Sun ($5); Ⓦwww.mnad.org.ar), with its remarkable collection of art and furniture. The museum is housed in **Palacio Errázuriz**, one of the city's most original private mansions, albeit of typically French design. The two-storey palace was built in 1911 for Chilean diplomat Matías Errázuriz and his patrician Argentine wife, Josefina de Alvear, who lived here until 1937, when it was turned into a museum. Designed by René Sergent, a French architect and proponent of the Academic style, it has three contrasting facades. The western one, on Sanchez de Bustamante, is inspired by the Petit Trianon at Versailles; the long northern side of the building with its Corinthian pillars, on Avenida del Libertador, is based on the palaces on Paris's Place de la Concorde; and the eastern end, near the entrance, is dominated by an enormous semicircular stone porch, supported by four Tuscan columns. The coach house, now a restaurant and tearoom, *Croque Madame*, sits just beyond the monumental wrought-iron and bronze gates, in the style of Louis XVI.

High society was frequently entertained here in the Errázuriz days; García Lorca and Blasco Ibáñez gave readings, Artur Rubinstein played and Anna Pavlova danced *Swan Lake* in the massive halls. The interior is as French as the exterior, especially the Regency ballroom, lined with gilded Rococo panels and huge mirrors, all stripped from a Parisian house. This was the location of the city's first private charity ball, which fittingly had the theme of seventeenth- and eighteenth-century French fashion. The whole house is on an incredible scale, not least the French Renaissance Grand Hall, where some of the museum's prize artworks are displayed. The Errázuriz and Alvear family arms feature in the hall's magnificent stone fireplace, while next to it is a bronze model of a Rodin sculpture they desired, but even they couldn't afford.

The couple's extravagant taste in **art** – Flemish furniture and French clocks, Sèvres porcelain, bronzes by Bourdelle, tapestries from Brussels, Gallé glassware and paintings, old and modern, ranging from El Greco (*Christ Bearing the Cross*) to Manet (*The Sacrifice of the Rose*) – is reflected and preserved. On the upper floor, Matías Errázuriz's boudoir was embellished in 1919 with scenes from Dante's *Divine Comedy* by Catalan artist Josep Maria Sert, who also decorated the Rockefeller Center in New York. In the basement resides a Gothic chapel, transferred from the Château de Champagnette in France and decorated with a French polychrome wooden chancel, an early sixteenth-century Spanish alabaster effigy of a knight and seventeenth-century Swiss stained-glass

△ Statue, Museo de Arte Decorativo

windows. Temporary exhibitions of ancient and contemporary art are also held down here, or in the garden in the summer, as are classical concerts, notably a Christmas carol service towards the end of Advent.

Barrio Parque and around

Across Avenida del Libertador, the **Instituto Nacional Sanmartiniano**, at Plaza Gran Bourg (Ⓣ011/4801-0848, Ⓦwww.i-n-sanmartiniano.com.ar), is housed in the **Casa Grand Bourg**, a reproduction – on a slightly larger scale – of the Parisian villa where José de San Martín lived in exile from 1838 to 1848. It occasionally holds special events, such as lectures and book presentations, usually free of charge. Immediately to the north lies the unordered anomaly of **Barrio Parque**, a maze of winding and curving streets laid out in 1912 by Charles Thays (see box, p.130). It's worth taking a leisurely stroll around here if you're in the area, to admire the variety of architectural styles – Art Deco, Neocolonial, Tudor, Secessionist, Flemish and Italian Renaissance – of the opulent houses lining the neighbourhood's arteries. Oval Calle Ombú is the barrio's hub, from which several streets radiate like spokes; the two finest houses are the manor at Ombú 2994 and the curious circular building at no. 3088.

About 200m west of the Instituto Sanmartiniano, a rambling Neocolonial house at Avenida del Libertador 2373 houses the small **Museo de Arte Popular**, also known as Museo Hernández (Wed–Fri 1–7pm, Sat, Sun & holidays 10am–8pm; $3, free Sun; guided tours on request; ⓣ011/4803-2384, ⓦwww.museohernandez.org.ar). José Hernández, after whom the museum is officially named, wrote the great gaucho classic *Martín Fierro* (1872), a revolutionary epic poem that made *campo* (peasant) culture respectable, and in this vein the museum's purpose is to highlight the value of **popular crafts**. It has a permanent exhibition about Argentine folk heritage housed in two buildings separated by a shady patio. The first section is an impressive but unimaginatively presented display of mostly nineteenth-century rural silverware; spurs, stirrups, saddles, knives and gaucho weaponry stand side by side with a large collection of fine silver *mate* ware, including a particularly splendid and unusual *mate* vessel in the shape of an ostrich. The second part, across the courtyard, comprises a number of beautiful Mapuche hand-woven ponchos displayed alongside factory-made competition.

Museo de Arte Latinoamericano de Buenos Aires (MALBA)

Buenos Aires' newest, and arguably best, art museum, the **Museo de Arte Latinoamericano de Buenos Aires** (MALBA; Mon & Thurs–Sun noon–8pm, Wed noon–9pm; $10, free Wed; ⓦwww.malba.org.ar) is at Avenida Figueroa Alcorta 3415, between Barrio Parque and the Paseo Alcorta shopping centre. The modern, glass-fronted building is an attraction in its own right and its airy, spacious galleries contrast with the dark nooks and crannies of the city's more traditional art museums. The collection concentrates purely on Latin American art, with important twentieth-century works and impressive temporary exhibitions.

The **Constantini collection**, on the first floor up, is arranged chronologically, beginning with the 1910s and 1920s, when the Modernist movement in Latin America heralded the start of a real sense of regional identity. This is exemplified in paintings such as a series by Argentine master Xul Solar, a Frida Kahlo self-portrait and Brazilian Tarsila Do Amaral's very much Mexican-influenced *Abaporu*. Dark political undercurrents run through the 1930s to 1950s and the work of Antonio Berni and the Chilean Roberto Matta, while Catholic traditions are given a Surrealist twist in Remedios Varo's votive box *Icono*. Things get more conceptual from the 1960s on, with the moving installations of Julio Le Parc and the LSD-splashed "end of art" collages by the "Nueva Figuración" movement.

Upstairs, temporary exhibitions generally feature the collected works of a prominent modern or contemporary artist, often an Argentine. The MALBA also has its own small art house cinema (see website for programme) and a gift shop.

Palermo Viejo and around

Bounded by avenidas Santa Fe, Córdoba, Juan B. Justo and Raúl Scalabrini Ortíz, **Palermo Viejo** is the only area of Palermo that still has an old-fashioned

Borges and Buenos Aires

This city that I believed was my past,
is my future, my present;
the years I have spent in Europe are an illusion,
I always was (and will be) in Buenos Aires.

Jorge Luis Borges, "Arrabal," from *Fervor de Buenos Aires* (1921)

There's no shortage of literary works inspired by Argentina's capital city, but no writer has written so passionately about it as **Jorge Luis Borges**. Though he was born in the heart of Buenos Aires, in 1898, it was the city's humbler barrios that most captivated Borges' imagination. His early childhood was spent in **Palermo**, now one of Buenos Aires' more exclusive neighbourhoods, but a somewhat marginal barrio at the start of the twentieth century. Borges' middle-class family inhabited one of the few two-storey houses on their street, **Calle Serrano**, and, though his excursions were strictly controlled, from behind the garden wall Borges observed the colourful street life that was kept tantalizingly out of his reach. In particular, his attention was caught by the men who gathered to drink and play cards in the local *almacén* (a sort of store-cum-bar) at his street corner. With their tales of knife fights and air of lawlessness, these men appeared time and again in Borges' early short stories, and, later, in *Doctor Brodie's Report*, a collection published in 1970.

Borges' writing talent surfaced at a precocious age: at 6 he wrote his first short story as well as a piece in English on Greek mythology, and in 1910, when he was 11, the newspaper *El País* published his translation of Oscar Wilde's *The Happy Prince*. However, it was not until he returned from Europe in 1921, where he had been stranded with his family during World War I, that Borges published his first book, *Fervor de Buenos Aires*, a collection of **poems** that attempted to capture the essence of the city. Enthused by his re-encounter with Buenos Aires at an age at which he was free to go where he wanted, Borges set out to explore the marginal corners of the city which, during his seven-year absence, had grown considerably. His wanderings took him to the city's outlying barrios, where streets lined with simple one-storey buildings blended with the surrounding Pampas, or to the poorer areas of the city centre with their tenement buildings and bars frequented by prostitutes. With the notable exception of La Boca, which he appears to have regarded as too idiosyncratic – and perhaps, too obviously picturesque – Borges felt greatest affection for the **south** of Buenos Aires. His exploration of the area that he regarded as representing the heart of the city took in not only the traditional houses of San Telmo and Monserrat, with their patios and decorative facades, but also the humbler streets of Barracas, a largely industrial working-class neighbourhood, and Constitución, where, in a gloomy basement in Avenida Juan de Garay, he set one of his most famous short stories, *El Aleph*.

For a writer as sensitive to visual subtlety as Borges – many of his early poems focus on the city's atmospheric evening light – it seems particularly tragic that he should have gone virtually blind in his fifties. Nonetheless, from 1955 to 1973, Borges was **Director of the National Library**, then located in Monserrat (see p.140), where his pleasure at being surrounded by books – even if he could no longer read them – was heightened by the fact that his daily journey to work took him through one of his favourite parts of the city, from his apartment in Maipú along pedestrianized Florida. As Borges' fame grew, he spent considerable periods of time away from Argentina, travelling to Europe, the United States and other Latin American countries – though he claimed always to return to Buenos Aires in his dreams. Borges died in 1986 in Geneva, where he is buried in the Plainpalais cemetery.

Porteño feel to it, although it's also the most fashionable place to live, shop or have an evening out. The part of the city most closely linked to Borges, where he lived and began writing poetry in the 1920s, its architecture has changed little since then. It's a compact oblong of quiet streets, most of them still cobbled and lined with brightly painted one- or two-storey Neocolonial villas and townhouses, many of them recently restored, some of them hidden behind luxuriant gardens full of bougainvillea and jasmine. Part run-down, part gentrified, it's a leafy district with a laid-back bohemian ambience, and many of its stylish houses have been converted into bars, cafés and boutiques. Large communities from Poland, Ukraine, Lebanon and Armenia live here, alongside a larger Italian contingent and some old Spanish families, and they all have their shops, churches and clubs, adding to the district's colour. The area also boasts a dazzling blend of outstanding **restaurants**, serving cuisines as varied as Armenian and Vietnamese, and has succeeded in luring the city's residents and visitors alike away from more superficial districts such as Puerto Madero and Las Cañitas.

Palermo Viejo's official epicentre is **Plaza Palermo Viejo**, a wide, park-like square dominated by a children's playground and some huge lime trees, but the barrio's cultural and social focal point is nearby **Plaza Serrano**. The plaza's official name (used on maps but unknown by most taxi drivers) is Plaza Cortázar, after Argentine novelist Julio Cortázar, who frequented this part of the city in the 1960s and set his Surrealist novel *Hopscotch* here. This lively plaza is crowded with makeshift craft stalls, although the city authorities have controversially been trying to expel them, so as to clean the plaza up; it is more permanently surrounded by trattorias, cafés and bars, some of them doubling as arts centres and galleries. Among them, a rash of independent designer shops sell upmarket bohemian clothes, jewellery and furnishings, hence the new name for this neighbourhood – **Palermo Soho**, really a sort of sub-barrio of Palermo Viejo. The stretch of Serrano leading due east from this plaza, to Avenida Santa Fe, has been officially renamed Calle J.L. Borges, although many signs still read Serrano. The writer spent part of his childhood in a two-storey villa at no. 2135, and Borges pilgrims should try and make one of the guided tours held most days at 3pm (Spanish only). A commemorative plaque at no. 2108 is inscribed with a stanza from *Mythical Foundation of Buenos Aires*, a poem where the colonial beginnings of Buenos Aires are narrated with a typical Borgesian twist: in it the city is founded not in San Telmo, its historical starting point, but here in the middle of Palermo.

North of Palermo Viejo, centred around Honduras and Fitzroy, the so-named **Palermo Hollywood** is the current hip evening destination, home to an ever-changing pantheon of restaurants, bars and clubs (see pp.164–166), which range from lively and fun to painfully trendy.

The nearest subte stations to Palermo Viejo are Scalabrini Ortíz and Plaza Italia.

Jardin Botánico and Jardín Zoológico

The entrance to Buenos Aires' charming **botanical garden** (daily 8am–6pm; free; guided visits Sat, Sun & holidays 10.30am & 4.30pm) is at Plaza Italia, east of Palermo Viejo and near the Plaza Italia subte station. Established at the end of the nineteenth century by Schubeck, the gardener to the royal courts of Bavaria, who died before getting very far, the layout was handed over to Charles Thays, who completed work in 1902. He divided the garden into distinct areas representing the regions of Argentina and further afield, but few of the labels on the shrubs and trees are now legible. The garden is officially named after Thays, and he is honoured with a bronze bust alongside the city's Headquarters of Parks and Gardens, inside the garden. Next to this stands a large glasshouse brought back from the 1900 Universal Exhibition in Paris, where it was part of

Argentina's pavilion: this ethereal Art Nouveau construction of wrought-iron and crystal shelters the garden's less hardy specimens such as orchids and cacti. Sadly, its age is beginning to show. In fact, the park in general is rather overgrown and teeming with feral cats, but its brighter grassy spots are popular with sunbathers, and it has been renovated with some success.

Upon entering, you'll be greeted by a lush waterlily pool around an elegant stone statue of *Ondina de Plata*, a demure river-nymph from a legend about the Río de la Plata. This Italianate section is dotted with a number of sculptures, including a white marble Venus copied from a Roman statue in the Louvre, a bronze she-wolf with heavy dugs being suckled by Romulus and Remus – a centenary gift to the city from its Italian community – and *Saturnalia*, an enormous, fun ensemble of a Roman orgy, intended to warn cityfolk against debauchery. As with bronzes elsewhere in the city, you may notice some are missing parts – the rising price of scrap metal coupled with high unemployment in recent years has resulted in the prising-off of plaques and the decapitation of busts throughout Buenos Aires.

Next door on Plaza Italia, Buenos Aires' **zoo** (Jan & Feb daily 10am–6pm, March–Dec Tues–Sun 10am–5.30pm; $4, or $8.50 for the "pasaporte", entitling you to all the attractions and activities) was also landscaped by Thays and is of considerable architectural, as well as zoological, interest. Its monumental pavilions and cages, built around 1905, include a fabulous replica of the temple to the goddess Lakshmi in Mumbai, a Chinese temple, a Byzantine portico and a Japanese pagoda. A popular place for kids, especially during the school holidays, it's home to an aquarium, a mock rainforest and some 2500 animals. The big cat area – pumas, lions, jaguars – is a highlight. Borges fondly wrote that the zoo "smelled of toffee and tiger", a description that still holds true. Fauna from throughout the world, ranging from apes to zebras, is represented, while a Himalayan snow leopard is a proud newcomer. It's also the place to learn the difference between guanacos, llamas, vicuñas and alpacas – the four camelids native to South America.

Outside the zoo, traditional **mateos** (horse and carriages), decorated with the ribbons and swirls of *filete* art (see box, p.118), cart off the romantically minded on trips around Palermo's parks ($20–50, depending on trip length).

Jardín Japonés

Taking up part of Plaza Sicilia, immediately north of the zoo, the **Jardín Japonés** has its entrance on Plaza de la República Islámica de Irán (daily 10am–6pm, free guided visits Sat & Sun 3pm; Mon & Wed–Fri $3, Sat, Sun & holidays $4, free Tues; Ⓦ www.jardinjapones.org.ar). The garden was donated to the city by Buenos Aires' small Japanese community in 1979, in readiness for a state visit by the Japanese imperial family. The purr of traffic on all sides undermines Zen transpiring within the garden's walls, but it's still relatively peaceful. The beautifully landscaped gardens, including a bonsai section and standing stones, and planted with handsome black pines and ginkgos, are at their best in the springtime, when the almond trees are in blossom and the azaleas are out. Great shoals of huge koi carp, in lakes crossed by typical red-lacquer bridges and zigzagging stepping-stones, kiss the air with their pouting mouths. A temple-like **café** serves green tea, sushi and some Argentine dishes, while the Japanese cultural centre next door, puts on regular dance, music, theatre, martial arts and craft displays.

Parque 3 de Febrero

A short way northwest, at the corner of Avenida del Libertador and Avenida Sarmiento, **Parque 3 de Febrero** is one of the biggest and most popular parks in the city. Another Palermo fixture designed by Thays, it was originally envisioned by President Sarmiento, who believed that parks were a civilizing influence and wanted something for Buenos Aires that would be on the scale of New York's Central Park or London's Hyde Park. Named in honour of the date in 1852 when his arch-rival General Rosas was defeated, the park is a wonderful place to stroll on a sunny afternoon. With its beautifully tended trees, lawns and patios, it's at its most serene during the week. Although the wide pathways running along the banks of the boating lake become rather crowded with joggers, cyclists and in-line skaters on weekends and public holidays, that's also the time to see Porteños at play. You'll see typical scenes of families drinking *mate* under the shade of palms or rubber trees, but perhaps also less expected sights, such as tai chi classes, or transvestite volleyball games. The park's most interesting features, such as the **Jardín de los Poetas**, dotted with stone and bronze busts of major Argentine and international poets, including Borges, Federico García Lorca and Shakespeare, are at its centre near the boating lake. Nearby is an **Andalucian patio**, decorated with vibrant ceramic tiles and donated by the city of Seville, while alongside it an immaculate **Rosedal** (rose garden; summer 8am–8pm, winter 9am–6pm) showcases new and colourful varieties of the flower. At the northern end of the rose garden, an Edwardian-style bridge delicately arches over the boating lake. On the other side of the bridge, at Avenida Infanta Isabel 555, you'll find the **Museo de Artes Plásticas Eduardo Sívori** (Tues–Fri noon–7pm; Sat & Sun 10am–7pm; $3, free Wed; Ⓦwww.museos.buenosaires.gov.ar), which regularly holds exhibitions of homegrown artists. Named for the Argentine painter (1847–1918) who helped found the National Academy of Fine Art, the museum has a collection of some five thousand works and its own small sculpture garden and café. The far eastern tip of the park, at Avenida Sarmiento, serves as the setting for the UFO-shaped **Planetario Galileo Galilei** (Mon–Fri 9am–6pm, Sat & Sun 2.30–9pm, guided visits Sat & Sun 4pm, 5.30pm, 6pm & 7pm; free, shows $4; Ⓣ001/4772-9265). In the entrance hall, you can see an alarmingly huge metal meteorite, discovered in the Chaco in the 1960s (see p.408) and every Sunday at 7pm (weather permitting) local astronomy enthusiasts cluster around telescopes to peer at the night sky; the shows, not suitable for young children, and in Spanish only, include images taken by the Hubble telescope.

Museo Evita

A block from the Botanical Garden, at Lafinur 2988, the **Museo Evita** (Tues–Sun 2–7pm; $6), was, for many Argentines, a long time coming. Housed in an attractive early twentieth-century building that was once a hotel, it was bought in 1948 by Evita's Social Aid Foundation to be set up as an emergency temporary home for families with no homes to go to. The well-laid-out museum traces Evita's life and passions, as well as the daily life of the families who were given shelter here, with helpful info sheets in English in each room. The walls are adorned with quotes from her speeches and autobiography *La Razón de mi Vida* (My Mission in Life), such as the succinct and apt: "The two greatest conditions to which a woman of the people can aspire: love of the humble and the hatred of the oligarchs." Despite its uncritical stance and glossing over of the less salubrious facts in Evita's life, including her Nazi sympathies, the museum has some interesting pieces, including magazines featuring her when she was Eva Duarte the radio star and videos of the extraordinary scenes in the city after she died.

Campo Argentino de Polo and the mosque

The **Campo Argentino de Polo**, home to the country's **polo** tournaments, most of which take place in November and December (see p.51), is at Avenida del Libertador and Dorrego. It's a perfect piece of turf. You can admire thoroughbreds of a different kind on the other side of Avenida del Libertador at the **Hipódromo Argentino**, the country's major **racecourse** (free for women, $3 for men). To the right as you enter, there are the stables where you can see close-up the horses stamping and snorting prior to the race. To the left are the stands – both simple benches and the Old World elegance of the main grandstand. Races generally take place from around 4pm to 10pm; you can obtain a calendar of race days from Ⓦwww.palermo.com.ar.

In 2000, the two minarets and fifty-metre-high blue and white dome of the **Centro Cultural Islámico Rey Fahd**, Latin America's largest mosque and Islamic school complex, went up near the polo ground at Avenida Libertador and Avenida Bullrich. The cost of the building (estimated at twenty million dollars) was met entirely by the King of Saudi Arabia, but the land, prime real estate, was donated, controversially, by President Menem. Argentina has a Muslim community estimated at between one and two million, spread across the north of the country, but the overwhelming majority, like Menem, are from a secular Syrio-Lebanese background.

Belgrano

North of Palermo, **Belgrano**, like most of the northern barrios, is largely residential, apart from the lively shopping streets on either side of its main artery, Avenida Cabildo. Named after General Manuel Belgrano, hero of Argentina's struggle for independence, it was founded as a separate town in 1855. Over the next decade or two lots of wealthy Porteños built their summer or weekend homes here, and it was incorporated into Buenos Aires during the city's whirlwind expansion in the 1880s. Many Anglo-Argentines settled in the barrio in those years, and it became popular with the city's sizeable Jewish community in the 1950s. More recently Taiwanese and Korean immigrants have settled in **Barrio Chino**, or Chinatown.

Parts of Belgrano still have a rural feel, like western **Belgrano R**, whose cobbled streets are lined with huge trees, mock-Tudor villas and Neocolonial mansions. **Belgrano C** is the central part of the barrio, whose nucleus lies at

the junction of avenidas Cabildo and Justamento. As well as stores, cafés and galleries, it's where the barrio's museums are situated. The chief reason to visit Belgrano is to take in two of the city's major art collections: the **Museo de Arte Español**, and the **Museo Casa de Yrurtia**, in a Neocolonial house that once belonged to leading Argentine sculptor Rogelio Yrurtia. Nearby **Museo Histórico Sarmiento** is full of the memorabilia of one of Argentina's key historical figures.

Juramento station, one stop before the end of subte Line D, is close to all of the museums, while plenty of buses run along Avenida Cabildo, including #41, #57, #59 and #60.

Museo de Arte Español

On the northern side of Plaza Belgrano, the **Museo de Arte Español**, Juramento 2291 (Mon & Wed–Fri 2–8pm, Sat, Sun & holidays 3–8pm, guided visits Sun 4pm & 6pm; $3, free Thurs; Ⓦwww.museos.buenosaires.gov.ar), a well-restored, whitewashed colonial building, is home to a priceless collection of **Spanish art**. Amassed by an aristocratic Uruguayan exile, **Enrique Larreta**, the collection comprises pieces from the Renaissance to the early twentieth century. In 1900, Larreta married Josefina Anchorena, daughter of Mercedes Castellanos de Anchorena (see p.130), and her dowry was a Greco-Roman villa, built in 1882. Larreta had the house transformed into an Andalucian-style mansion, now the museum. From around 1900 to 1916, the dandyish Larreta spent many of his days in Spain; during that time he visited churches and monasteries, buying up artwork for his Belgrano home, most of them from the Renaissance – statues and paintings of saints, but also furniture, porcelain, silverware and tapestries, all of which are displayed in this house, which he bequeathed to the city.

Greeting visitors is a Munch-like portrait of the novelist, painted in 1912 by Spanish artist Ignacio de Zuloaga. The five rooms of the single-storey building, arranged around the original Roman-style atrium, contain several masterpieces, including an immaculate early sixteenth-century retable, *La Infancia de Cristo*, delicately painted and decorated with gold leaf; it's thought to have once belonged to William Randolph Hearst. Equally marvellous is Correa de Vivar's *Adoration of the Magi*, a sixteenth-century painting from Toledo, in which a fine-featured Mary is adorned with a gold-leaf halo. Also notable is an altarpiece dedicated to St Anne, dating from 1503 and painted for a church near Burgos, Spain. Its painstaking detail, vibrant colours and the haunting expressions of the Holy Family and other figures, with their fabulous headdresses, make it the finest work in the collection.

Behind the museum, with its entrance around the corner at Vuelta de Obligado 2155, a serene Andalucian **garden** (Mon–Fri 9am–1pm; free), dominated by a huge ombú tree and surrounded by a profusion of magnolias, hydrangeas and agapanthus, makes for a lovely respite before heading back out into the barrio. Note that classical concerts are held at the museum from time to time.

Museo Histórico Sarmiento

Nearby, on the northeast corner of Plaza Belgrano, the **Museo Histórico Sarmiento**, Juramento 2180 (Mon–Fri 2–6pm; $1, free Thurs), a Neoclassical construction with a splendid portico, was built in 1870 as Belgrano's city hall and served briefly as the seat of Argentina's government in 1880. In 1938, it was turned into a museum dedicated to **Domingo Sarmiento**, president of Argentina from 1868 to 1874 and also a highly regarded writer. His best-known and controversial work, *Facundo: Civilisación y Barbarismo* (1845), is considered one of the most important Latin American works of the nineteenth century. In it, he crystallizes the great debate of the day – the conflict between "civilization" and "barbarism". His belief that for Argentina to progress it must adopt the urban culture of Europe, had far-reaching consequences in the country – such as the encouragement of immigration. He took part in overthrowing President Rosas – the very embodiment of the feudal interior – and emphasized the importance of education, introducing North American schooling methods he discovered while serving as a diplomat in the United States. The rather musty and highly eclectic display of Sarmiento memorabilia includes a large collection of Delft china, a bizarre articulated armchair he took with him into exile in Asunción and a first edition of *Facundo*.

Museo Casa de Yrurtia and Barrio Chino

Three blocks north, at O'Higgins 2390, the **Museo Casa de Yrurtia** (Tues–Fri 1–7pm, Sun 3–7pm; $1) is a beautiful single-storey Spanish-style house built in 1923 by sculptor **Rogelio Yrurtia**. His work, along with that of other artists, and furniture and decorations from around the world, is displayed in the naturally appointed rooms. The artist intended the Baroque-inspired building to be the home for him and his Dutch wife, but she died shortly after they moved in. He lived here for over twenty years with his second wife, **Lía Correa Morales**, herself an important painter. Behind the house, the courtyard, luxuriant with grapevines, plane trees and a tall Canary Island palm, serves as the setting for a Yrurtia bronze of two men boxing.

The eleven rooms contain several of Correa Morales' still lifes, landscapes and portraits, including many of her husband, and a large number of pieces by Yrurtia. The ceilings are just high enough to take the full-sized trial moulds of his monumental sculptures, some of which are city landmarks. These include the strangely homoerotic *Mausoleo Rivadavia* on Plaza Miserere, Once, *La Justicia* at the Palacio de Justicia and the statue of Manuel Dorrego on Plazoleta Suipacha. Mostly, the couple's work fits well with the Kashmiri shawls, Chinese vases and Spanish cabinets that decorate the rooms, while a Picasso, *Rue Cortot*, hangs discreetly on the wall of the entrance hall.

The small **Barrio Chino**, Buenos Aires' **Chinatown**, is three blocks to the east of the Museo Yrurtia, stretching along Arribeños between Juramento and Olazábal. As well as Chinese supermarkets and shops, a small oriental art gallery and the Chuan Kuan Tse Buddhist temple at Montañeses 2175, it's also home to the most authentic Far Eastern food in the city (see p.161), and regular street fairs.

El Monumental

Out on the eastern edge of Belgrano, on the border with residential barrio Nuñez at Avenida Pte Figueroa Alcorta 7597, rise the huge concrete stands of the northern counterpart to the Bombonera, the **Monumental** (☎011/4323-7600). Home to the River Plate football club, it can seat 70,000 and is the country's largest stadium. The original structure dates from 1938, but it was remodelled for the controversial 1978 World Cup. Matches at the Monumental are a glorious riot of red and white shirts, banners and streamers. Bus #130 from Boca via Paseo Colon and Avenida del Libertador goes there, filling with River's good-humoured fans on match days.

The west

West of central Buenos Aires a vast, mostly residential area spreads out for over a dozen kilometres towards Avenida General Paz. Northwest of Palermo, the barrio of **Chacarita** is best known for its namesake **cemetery**, where the remains of Juan Domingo Perón used to rest and tango singer Carlos Gardel is buried. **Caballito**, right in the heart of the city, makes a pleasant half-day trip for the **book and record market** held in the barrio's central park, Parque Rivadavia, and its entertaining natural history museum. Architecture fans shouldn't miss the stunning **Palacio de las Aguas Corrientes** in the barrio of **Balvanera**, the neighbourhood just west of Congreso and Avenida Callao, where you will also find a museum devoted to **Carlos Gardel**. Finally, right out at the city edges, the hugely enjoyable gaucho fair, the **Feria de Mataderos**, is held on Saturdays or Sundays in the barrio of the same name and provides one of the best days out in the city.

Chacarita

Dominated by railway lines, **Chacarita** takes its name from the days when the barrio was home to a small farm (*chacra*) run by Jesuits. Nowadays, the neighbourhood is synonymous with the enormous **Cementerio de Chacarita** (daily 7am–6pm; free). Less aristocratic than Recoleta's cemetery, but impressive nonetheless, it contains one of the city's two most-visited tombs, that of **Carlos Gardel**, Argentina's most famous ever tango singer (see p.825). Note, however, that **Juan Domingo Perón**'s remains are no longer in Chacarita (see box below).

Lying at the northern end of Avenida Corrientes (subte station Federico Lacroze, Line B), with the monumental main entrance at Avenida Guzmán 780, the cemetery covers a good third of the barrio; at one square kilometre, it's Argentina's largest. Much of it is dominated by numbered streets, unremarkable graves and crosses and, to the right of the entrance, enormous pantheons. Immediately facing the entrance, however, a section of grand mausoleums comes quite close to the Baroque splendour of Recoleta. There is also a greater feeling of space. A grid of streets intersected by diagonals, it's flanked by marble and polished granite tombs, often with decorative glass fronts. By far the best

The remains of President Perón

When **Juan Domingo Perón** (president 1946–55 and 1973–74) died in Olivos on July 1,1974, he was buried in **Chacarita Cemetery**, and remained there until October 2006. This resting place never proved entirely safe, however – in 1987, his grave was opened, the hands of his corpse cut off and removed, and his sword and other personal effects stolen; the culprits have never been found, though a murky Italian organization was widely blamed. Understandably, his family was always uneasy about leaving his remains in Chacarita, and so amid much ceremony and controversy, what was left of his body was removed to a more secluded location in **October 2006**. The riots that plagued him when alive broke out once more, as violent clashes, mostly involving Peronist trade unionists barred from the ceremony, led to several injuries. His new resting place is a mausoleum at his former summer residence, near **San Vicente**, 50km south of the city. There are rumours that **Evita's** remains will be moved there, too, from Recoleta. The judicial authorities took the opportunity to carry out DNA tests on his cadaver, at the request of **Martha Holgado**, who claimed to be his illegitimate daughter. According to the septuagenarian, her mother had an affair with Perón while he was still married to his first wife. The tests proved negative.

sight in the cemetery, however, is Gardel's tomb, on the corner of streets 6 and 33, a brisk five-minute walk to the left of the entrance and a little towards the middle. It is topped by a life-sized statue of the singer in typical rakish pose: hand in pocket, hair slicked back and characteristic wide grin. Every inch of the surrounding stonework is plastered with plaques of gratitude and flowers placed there by the singer's devotees. There is a pilgrimage to his graveside every year on the anniversary of his death (June 24). Many visitors also light a cigarette and place it between the statue's fingers; you will often see a dog-end still dangling between his index and forefinger.

Not far from Gardel's grave, slightly nearer the entrance, is one of the most majestic mausoleums in the whole cemetery, that of aviation pioneer **Jorge Newbery**, after whom Buenos Aires' domestic airport is named. He died near Mendoza while preparing for the first flight across the Andes and is honoured with a tomb that somehow manages to be magnificent, sinister and camp all at once: four hungry-looking condors overlook a supine nude male form who is outstretched in a melodramatic pose like some latter-day Prometheus. At the centre of the graveyard, the **Recinto de Personalidades** is a collection of rather kitsch statues adorning the graves of some of Argentina's most popular figures, including tango composer Aníbal Troilo, pianist Osvaldo Pugliese, poet Alfonsina Storni and painter Quinquela Martín. Also buried here is Agustín Magaldi, who at the height of his popularity was second only to Gardel as the nation's most-loved singer and is also famous for being Evita's first lover and the man she left her home town of Junín with to move to Buenos Aires. You may be able to pick up a free map of the grounds at the cemetery's administrative offices, to the right of the entrance.

Caballito

An unassuming, mostly middle-class barrio, **Caballito** lies at the very centre of the metropolis. Narrow Plaza Primera Junta, the last stop on Line A of the subte, is the barrio's core, while Avenida Rivadavia, flanked by high-rise apartment blocks and shopping malls, runs east–west through it. Southwest of the avenue, the neighbourhood takes on a different feel, all quiet cobbled streets lined with acacias and small, ornate villas; it's home to the humanities faculty of the University of Buenos Aires. A 1950s tram, the **Tranvía Histórico**, leaving from Emilio Mitre and Bonifacio (Emilio Mitre subte), does a twenty-minute spin around part of the neighbourhood at weekends (Sat 5–8.30pm, Sun 10am–1pm & 5–8.30pm, closed Jan; free; Ⓣ011/4431-1073, Ⓦwww.tranvia.org.ar); it's only really of interest if you, or the children with you, have never been in a tram before. Five blocks east of Plaza Primera Junta, you'll find **Parque Rivadavia**, wedged between avenidas Rivadavia and Rosario. There is an excellent secondhand **book market** here at weekends.

Caballito is also home to the **Museo Argentino de Ciencias Naturales**, at Angel Gallardo 490 (daily 2–7pm; $3) in the circular Parque del Centenario. The museum is of note for its impressive paleontological collection, including a spiky-necked amargasaurus from Neuquén and fifteen-metre patagosaurus sauropod from Chubút, along with a host of surprisingly recent beasts that once lived on what is now Argentine territory, such as sabre-tooth tigers, giant sloths and glyptodonts (giant armadillos). Otherwise there are lots of shells, fish and, upstairs, a host of musty insects, stuffed birds and other beings. The ground-floor bijou "planetarium" offers a brief illustrated and narrated history of the universe aimed at kids (Spanish only). Popular with young and older alike, the museum is housed in an attractive purpose-built 1930s edifice, an interesting variant on Art Deco, embellished with sculptures of all manner of creatures, from owls to spiders.

Balvanera

Just west of the city centre, **Balvanera** is a commercial, somewhat downmarket barrio, home to many of the city's recent South American immigrants. It has two focal points: **Once**, a noisy shopping area around the Once (de Septiembre) train station, traditionally patronized by the city's less well-heeled Jewish community; and **Abasto**, focused on what is now the Abasto shopping centre (see p.177). The train station is named after the date in 1852 when the revolution against *caudillo* Justo T. de Urquiza was declared. As for the whole barrio, it takes its name from a place in La Rioja, Spain, linked to one of many miracles involving the Virgin Mary – Nuestra Señora de Balvanera.

For the visitor, the main points of interest are the spectacular **Palacio de las Aguas Corrientes**, right on the Recoleta border at Córdoba and Riobamba, and a museum in Abasto dedicated to Carlos Gardel. The former is every bit as palatial as the name suggests and has been described quite accurately as a cross between London's Victoria and Albert Museum and the Uffizi in Florence. Somewhat incongruously, it is home to twelve giant tanks that supplied Buenos Aires with water from 1894 until 1978. An impressive feat of engineering, it was planned and built in Europe, down to the glazed coloured ceramics that dot the facade, all manufactured by Royal Doulton of London, but painted in Buenos Aires. Inside, there is a small museum (Mon–Fri 9am–1pm; guided tours Mon, Wed & Fri 11am; free) explaining the building's history.

The **Museo Casa Carlos Gardel**, meanwhile, at Jean Jaurès 735 (Mon & Wed–Fri 11am–6pm; $3, free Wed), is dedicated to the life of the great tango singer. Known as the *zorzal criollo* (creole songbird), Gardel popularized tango abroad in the early twentieth century, inspiring devotion for his distinctive voice and charismatic personality. The museum is housed in his home, which has been lovingly restored to capture his life here. Although the collection is a bit limited and out of the way for general interest, tango aficionados will enjoy the old photos and tango scores and the temporary exhibits on themes relating to Gardel, such as his passion for racehorses. At one point it gets quite postmodern, with a collection of photos of pictures of Gardel from around Buenos Aires, as photographer Luis Martin points out: "wherever you go in the city, he is always watching you." As if to confirm this, some of the houses in the immediate area have murals on the sides of a grinning Gardel. Appropriately, the nearest subte station is Carlos Gardel on line B – exiting the station, head north up Corrientes two blocks to reach Jean Jaurès.

Mataderos

Lying just inside the boundary of Capital Federal, around 6km southwest of Caballito, **Mataderos** is a barrio with a gory past. For many years, people came to Mataderos to drink the fresh blood of animals killed in the slaughterhouses from which the area takes its name, in the belief that this would cure such illnesses as tuberculosis. The slaughterhouses have long gone, but Mataderos is still home to the **Mercado Nacional de Hacienda**, or livestock market, set back from the intersection of Lisandro de la Torre and Avenida de los Corrales, whose faded pink walls and arcades provide the backdrop for one of Buenos Aires' most fabulous events: the Sunday **Feria de Mataderos** (from 11am; buses #92 & #126; ⓣ011/4687-5602 on Sun, 4374-9664 Mon–Fri, Ⓦwww.feriademataderos.com.ar). A celebration of Argentina's rural traditions, this busy fair attracts thousands of locals and tourists for its blend of folk music, traditional crafts and regional food such as *locro*, empanadas and *tortas fritas*, mouthwatering fried cakes. You can also try your hand at regional dances such as the *chamamé* and *chacarera*. The undoubted

△ Folk dancing, Feria de Mataderos

highpoint, however, is the display of **gaucho skills** in which riders participate in events such as the *sortija*, in which, galloping at breakneck speed and standing rigid in their stirrups, they attempt to spear a small ring strung on a ribbon. Take plenty of cash – the artisan wares here are good quality and considerably cheaper than in the central stores – and make sure the fair is actually on before setting out, as it sometimes closes or moves to Saturdays, especially during the summer months; the city's main tourist office (see p.94) should be able to advise.

Eating

Buenos Aires is Latin America's **gastronomic capital** and, with most places very good value indeed, eating out here must count as a highlight of any visit to Argentina. In addition to the excellent and ubiquitous **pizza** and **pasta** restaurants common to the country as a whole, the capital offers a number of **cosmopolitan** cuisines, ranging from Armenian and Basque via Japanese and Peruvian to Thai and Vietnamese. The city's crowning glory, however – though you have to be a meat eater – are its **parrillas**, whose top-end representatives offer the country's choicest beef cooked on an *asador criollo* – staked around an open fire. There are plenty of humbler places, too, where you can enjoy a succulent *parrillada* in a lively atmosphere.

Though most restaurants open in the evening at around 8pm, it's worth bearing in mind that most Porteños don't go out to eat until a couple of hours later; many restaurants suddenly go from empty to full between 9.30pm and 10pm. Most kitchens close around midnight during the week, though at weekends many keep serving till the small hours. There are also plenty of *confiterías* and pizzerias open throughout the night, so you shouldn't have trouble satisfying your hunger at any time. Prices in the upmarket end of the range have rocketed in the past few years, but remain noticeably lower than in comparable places in, say, North America or Europe

Restaurants

Excellent meals can be had throughout Buenos Aires but, with some exceptions, the **centre** and the **south** are best for the city's most traditional restaurants, while the **north** is the place for more innovative or exotic cooking. **Puerto Madero**, the recently renovated port area, is knee-deep in big, glitzy themed restaurants, though – a couple of decent places notwithstanding – these are hardly the capital's most exciting eating options. You'll find a far more original crop of restaurants in **Palermo**, in three clusters – Palermo Soho around Plaza Cortázar/Serrano; Palermo Hollywood around Honduras and Fitzroy; and Las Cañitas around Báez and Chenaut.

The city centre

Arturito Corrientes 1124 ☎011/4382-0227. An old-fashioned haven reigned over by courteous white-jacketed waiters, *Arturito* is a Corrientes landmark, and its *bife de chorizo con papas* (rump steak and chips) is an unquestionably good deal.

Chiquilín Sarmiento 1599 ☎011/4373-5163. A classic Porteño restaurant serving traditional dishes at moderate prices in a friendly and stylish atmosphere. The *pollo al verdeo* (chicken with spring onions) is good, but it's the revered *bife* that brings most people in.

El Claustro San Martín 705 ☎011/4312-0235. The vaulted dining room was part of the Santa Catalina convent, making it a haven of peace and quiet amid the frantic financial district. Considering the inventiveness of the cuisine – including a tajine-like lamb dish or pears with lemongrass – the two-course lunch served every weekday is quite reasonably priced.

Crizia Lavalle 345. Elegant first-floor restaurant with varied, moderate-to-expensive menu featuring lots of seafood dishes, including sushi and salmon ceviche, as well as goats' cheese and meat grilled over *quebracho* wood. Lunch Mon–Fri, dinner Tues–Sat, plus after-office drinks on Wed.

Las Cuartetas Corrientes 838. A pared-down pizza and empanada joint where you can grab a slice of pizza at the counter and while away a few hours after the cinema over a cold Quilmes.

El Globo Hipólito Yrigoyen 1199 ☎011/4381-3926. One of several Spanish restaurants in the area, *El Globo* has a gorgeously old-fashioned interior and serves classic dishes such as *gambas al ajillo* (spicy prawns) and *puchero* that are perfectly acceptable, if a little lacking in Mediterranean flair.

Granix Florida 165, Galería Güemes, Entrada Mitre, 1st floor. You pay on entry ($20) at this large, airy, self-service vegetarian restaurant located in one of Florida's magnificent shopping arcades, and then eat as much as you want. Salads are straight-from-the-market fresh and the variety of soft drinks, warm dishes and delicious desserts, including some unusual options, is overwhelming.

Güerrín Corrientes 1368. A quintessential Porteño pizza experience, the traditional order here is a portion of *muzzarella* and *fainá* eaten at the counter and accompanied by a glass of sweet moscato. Some locals hold that the pizzas served in the proper dining area are a notch above the counter versions; however, all are inexpensive.

Parrilla Peña Rodriguez Peña 682. Knowledgeable liveried waiters serve up some of the juiciest meat in town, as well as fine wines and mouthwatering salads, but no coffee, at this great-value no-nonsense *parrilla*; when it closed for "renovation" locals' hearts sank, but to their relief all they did was add more tables on the ground floor and smarten the paint.

Patio San Ramón Reconquista 269. Generously portioned, well-cooked and inexpensive food with daily specials such as *pollo al horno con puré de batata* (roast chicken with sweet potato puree). The real attraction, however, is the stunning location – the patio of an old convent where, among palm trees and birdsong, you might even forget that you're at the heart of Buenos Aires' financial district. Lunch only, closed weekends.

Pippo Montevideo 341 ☎011/4374-0762. Despite its fairly indifferent pasta and *parrillada*, Pippo has established itself as a Buenos Aires institution. You may be blinded by its bright lights, but it's worth a visit just to catch a glimpse of Porteño dining in all its noisy, gesticulating glory. The thick *vermicelli mixto*, with Bolognese sauce and pesto, is a good bet.

Tomo 1 Carlos Pellegrini 525, in *Hotel Panamericano* ☎011/4326-6695. Considered by many to be Buenos Aires' best haute cuisine restaurant, this is an elegant but refreshingly unpretentious place where the emphasis is squarely placed on the exquisitely cooked food, such as chilled melon soup and quail with pistachios. Not cheap, but good value, particularly if you go for the set menus, available both at lunch times and evenings.

Winery Av Alem 880 ⓣ011/4314-2639. As well as a store that holds regular tastings of all the best Argentine wines, *Winery* has a restaurant serving cheeses, gourmet sandwiches and unusual specialities such as braised goat.

Puerto Madero

Bice Av Alicia M. de Justo 192 ⓣ011/4315-6216. Style often triumphs over content in Puerto Madero, but the excellent pasta and gnocchi at this highly regarded, if expensive, Italian restaurant will not disappoint.

Cabaña Las Lilas Av Alicia M. de Justo 516 ⓣ011/4313-1336. The place to head if you want to splurge on just about the finest steak you'll find anywhere; an *ojo de bife*, best savoured from a shaded verandah on the waterfront, will set you back over $60. Very popular with tourists; reservations advisable.

"i" Fresh Market Azucena Villaflor and Olga Cossenttini, Puerto Madero Este. By Dique 3, the pick of the chic new places in Puerto Madero Este. A great place for lunch or *merienda*, with a selection of inventive sandwiches, salads and bruschettas, plus a range of yummy *licuados* (fruit shakes) and herbal teas to accompany; meals such as pasta and steak are also available.

Siga La Vaca Av Alicia M. de Justo 1714 ⓣ011/4315-6801. At this upmarket *tenedor libre* you can eat till you drop for a reasonable sum; the fixed rate includes a carafe of wine, a dazzling choice of salads and, of course, a mountain of meat.

San Telmo, Monserrat and Boca

Brasserie Petanque Defensa and Mexico, Monserrat. Classic French food such as *boeuf bourguignon*, *moules*, steak tartare and crème brulée, with a particularly good lunch-time *menu du jour*, at times, slightly uppity classic French service to match.

La Cancha Brandsen 697, Boca ⓣ011/4362-2975. In the shadow of La Bombonera, *La Cancha* is open daily for lunch and dinner, but is an especially ideal locale for a weekend lunch, with fresh seafood, including excellent squid and *pejerrey* (kingfish).

Cancún Defensa 680, San Telmo. Unusual informal Mexican restaurant, famed for its margaritas, which serves up generous portions of tacos and nachos adapted to Argentine tastebuds – they go easy on the jalapeño.

El Desnivel Defensa 855, San Telmo ⓣ011/4399-9081. This popular, no-frills *parrilla* offers good meat-laden dishes at rock-bottom prices.

Laurak-Bat Belgrano 1144, Monserrat ⓣ011/4381-0682. A moderately priced Basque restaurant within *Club Vasco* boasting specialities such as *bacalao al pil-pil* (salt cod in a garlic sauce).

El Obrero Caffarena 64, Boca ⓣ011/4362-9912. With Boca Juniors souvenirs decorating the walls and tango musicians sauntering from table to table at weekends, the atmosphere at the hugely popular and moderately priced *El Obrero* is as much a part of its appeal as the simple home-cooked food, including great *milanesas*. Closed Sun.

El Retortuño Bolivar 747, San Telmo. Friendly community locale with a limited but inexpensive menu of food from the Cuyo region of Argentina, including dishes such as *locro* and *pastel de humita*, and attractive regional decor, with earthenware jugs for the house wine. Some evenings there is also folk music from around 11pm, for a small surcharge.

Retiro and Recoleta

Bengal Arenales 837, Retiro ⓣ011/4314-2926. Although, as the name suggests, this smart restaurant offers Indian specialities, including a perfectly passable *rogan josh*, it really excels in its Mediterranean Italian dishes, with a strong focus on fish. The decor and ambience are decidedly posh but the highly attentive service is not snobbish, and the wine and food, albeit not budget-priced, are impeccable, down to all the nibbly bits they serve before and after. Closed Sat dinner & Sun.

Club Danés Alem 1074, 12th floor, Retiro ⓣ011/4312-9266. This lunch-only Danish restaurant serves a mean *smörrebrod* – lots of herrings, anchovies and blue cheese – and other specialities in a suitably airy dining room with great river views. Brown ale brewed in Buenos Aires Province is available. Closed Sat & Sun.

Club Sírio Ayacucho 1496, Recoleta ⓣ011/4806-5764. Every major Argentine city has its Syrian club/restaurant, and this palatial place is one of the best, with an excellent and varied menu of starters. Closed Sun.

Empire Thai Tres Sargentos 427, Retiro ⓣ011/4312-5706. Unbeatable cocktails and a trendy ambience (very gay-friendly) make up for the slight lack of authenticity in the cuisine – the red and green curries are not quite right, but they are very palatable nonetheless. Closed Sat lunch & Sun.

La Esquina de las Flores Avenida Córdoba 1587, Recoleta ⓣ011/4813-3630. Reliable vegetarian and macrobiotic restaurant serving up a variety of hot (including a good *carbonada de vegetales* – a vegetarian version of the popular *criollo* stew) and cold dishes. Closed Sat dinner & Sun.

Filo San Martín 975, Retiro ⓣ011/4311-0312. Some of the centre's best salads, featuring less common ingredients such as rocket, radishes and sultanas soaked in wine, imaginative pizza and pasta and Italian-inspired fusion dishes such as Venetian mussel soup with Patagonian clams.

Milion Paraná 1048, Recoleta ☎4815-9925. Cocktails and modern Argentine cuisine served in a beautifully converted mansion, with dozens of candlelit rooms.

Las Nazarenas Reconquista 1132, Retiro ☎011/4312-5559. *Parrillada* cooked gaucho-style on the *asador criollo*, where meat is staked around an open barbecue. Superb, but expensive.

Pane e Vino Vincente López 2036, Recoleta ☎011/4801-0550. A great place to lunch along this street lined with tourist traps; it has an outdoor seating area.

Piola Pizzería Libertad 1078, Recoleta. Dozens of toppings to choose from at this huge, hip, gay-friendly pizza joint, where thin crusts meet the upper crust.

Romario Pizza Vicente López 2102, Recoleta. A young crowd savours *Romario's* great pizzas in a small, outdoor seating area from where Recoleta in full swing can be observed; part of an excellent chain that also delivers.

El Sanjuanino Posadas 1515 ☎011/4805-2683. The place to try *empanadas*, this inexpensive restaurant also has other regional fare such as *locro* and *humitas*, as well as more exotic dishes like pickled *vizcacha*. Closed Mon.

Tancat Paraguay 645, Retiro ☎011/4312-5442. A beautifully decorated and lit Spanish–Catalan *tasca*, where the *cañas* (small glasses of draught beer), varied tapas and other mainstays, like grilled baby squid, are totally genuine; the service is brisk, it gets very busy at lunch times (bookings recommended) and can be noisy, but that only adds to the authenticity. Moderately priced (unless you opt for seafood, which will push the bill through the ceiling).

Palermo

Bar Uriarte Uriarte 1572 ☎011/4834-6004. This luxurious and pricey restaurant serves toothsome food, mostly with a Mediterranean touch, in a bright, airy dining room, decorated with ethnic art and dominated by a northern-style adobe oven used to cook meat- and dough-based dishes. You pass the kitchen on the way in, so it is strictly what-you-see-is-what-you-get. Weekend brunch is a big draw.

Bio Humboldt 2199 ☎011/4774-3880. Stylish vegetarian restaurant, more inventive than most but still wholesome, with dishes incorporating ingredients such as quinoa and tofu, with of course lots of vegetables. Organic wine and beer are also served. Closed Mon dinner & Sun.

La Cabrera Cabrera 5099 & 5127. This fabulous down-to-earth *parrilla* serves hard-to-beat *bifes de chorizo* (the half portion can feed two) with an array of delicious *tapa* garnishes; so popular they had to open a second restaurant just up the road, and they refuse bookings, so just turn up and grit your teeth until a table is free (try going early). Closed for lunch Tues–Fri.

Casa Cruz Uriarte 1658 ☎011/4833-1112. You may need to book ahead to experience this mind-bogglingly trendy restaurant – the doormen and dressed-to-kill receptionists tell you on arrival this is somewhere special. The glossy red mahogany panelling and perfect portions make you feel as if you are dining inside a Chinese lacquered box, while the dining room is separated from the open-plan kitchen by a glass-fronted vertical cellar. The food is eclectic, sumptuously presented and, surprisingly for somewhere so fashionable, absolutely delicious. Warm oysters are served with tapioca caviar and a pear salad; grilled octopus comes with passion-fruit sauce and chorizo juice; a brain and ham tart is garnished with shallots and pistachios. Faultless service and subdued lighting, but the bill is steep by local standards.

La Cátedra Cerviño 4699 ☎011/4777-4601. Traditional Argentine restaurant in a beautiful Neocolonial house, with some unusual sauces in an otherwise standard menu. Popular with the polo crowd.

La Fondue J.F. Segui 4674 ☎011/4778-0110. A small, friendly side-street bistro that uses home-made ingredients to make unbeatable pasta and fondue. Be sure to leave room for the excellent tiramisu.

Garbis Scalabrini Ortiz 3190 ☎011/4511-6600. A stand-out diner in the local Armenian community, *Garbis* prepares a delicious and very different *picada*, as well as a range of shish-kebabs.

Katmandu Av Córdoba 3547 ☎011/4963-1122. Indian cuisine is not the city's strongest culinary point, but *Katmandu* prepares a respectable sampling, including a very reasonable *rogan josh*, amid Indian antiques.

Lucky Luciano Cerviño 3948 ☎011/4802-1262. So popular that it had to leave its old, smaller confines round the corner, *Lucky* has made the move without losing the authentic Italian atmosphere and food that earned it its reputation.

El Manto Costa Rica 5801 ☎011/4774-2409. Lamb, yogurt and mint dominate the menu at this authentic and atmospheric Armenian restaurant, where a Carrara marble statue of the Virgin presides over lunch and dinner. Closed Sun.

Moche Nicaragua 5091 ☎011/4772-4160. The Peruvian chef here used to work for his country's embassy, so he knows how to make ceviche and other national dishes, plus inventive concoctions such as pisco sour mousse – try the Peruvian beer or the refreshing home-made lemonade. Moderate prices. Closed Mon dinner & Sun.

Ña Serapia Las Heras 3357. An unexpectedly traditional and rustic restaurant in the heart of upmarket Palermo, *Ña Serapia* styles itself as a *pulpería* and bar and serves delicious regional dishes including *locro* and *tamales* at very reasonable prices.

Ølsen Gorriti 5870 ⓣ011/4776-7677. This large, modern restaurant serves exciting cuisine with a Scandinavian touch, such as salmon pizza or goat-cheese ravioli. There are around forty different kinds of vodka and all manner of cocktails to kick things off, as well as an admirable wine cellar. The decor alone is worth seeing – you will want to take the grandiose stove back to your own home, if it only it fitted – and, weather permitting, there are tables in the shady, secluded garden, which would look more like a tiny patch of Swedish forest if it weren't for the exuberant bamboo.

La Placita Borges 1636. Filling home cooking at this traditional *cantina*, a counterpoint to the trendy bars across Plaza Serrano, though it is a bit marred by the glaring fluorescent-strip lighting.

Sarkis Thames 1101 ⓣ011/4772-4911. Spartan decor, but excellent tabbouleh, *keppe crudo* (raw meat with onion – much better than it sounds) and falafel at this popular restaurant serving a fusion of Armenian, Arab and Turkish cuisine.

Sudestada Guatemala and Fitzroy ⓣ011/4776-3777. Smart noodle bar with a Vietnamese chef who prepares tasty curries and other Southeast Asian food at reasonable prices, all in modern, minimalist surroundings. Closed Sun.

Te Mataré Ramirez Paraguay 4062 ⓣ011/4831-9156. Self-styled "aphrodisiac" restaurant, perfect for those eager to indulge in rich food, including such heavenly delights as chicken in passion-fruit sauce, oysters with champagne cream and a chocolate fondue to share, all with risqué names and accompanied by "sensual jazz".

Xalapa Gurruchaga and El Salvador ⓣ011/4833-6102. Argentines usually shy away from hot and spicy food, but this place, which has the most authentic and tasty Mexican fare in the city, is packed even mid-week. Proceed with caution, lest you torch your taste buds, especially when sampling the stuffed chiles. Dinner only.

Belgrano and Las Cañitas

Hsiang Ting Tang Arribeños 2245 ⓣ011/4786-0371. An upmarket Chinatown restaurant offering a wide range of Taiwanese dishes, including a scrumptious pork sautéed in ginger, in soothing surroundings.

Keum Kang Sang Mendoza 1650, 1st floor. Genuine, fairly expensive Korean fare with some Japanese dishes thrown in, are served in a choice of four menus, ranging from classic to deluxe. If you don't like hot spice, avoid the *kuchukaru*. Closed Tues.

El Pobre Luis Arribeños 2393 ⓣ011/4780-5847. A classic Uruguayan *parrilla* in Bajo Belgrano, famed for its suckling pig and defiantly refusing to serve brunch. Closed Sun.

El Primo Báez 302 ⓣ011/4775-0150. This popular *parrilla* in Las Cañitas offers traditional Porteño dishes with a bit of flair; the steak is especially savoury.

Sucre Sucre 676 ⓣ011/4782-9082. Belgrano Chico is chic as well as *chico*, and this haute-cuisine restaurant, housed in an avant-garde concrete edifice fits into its surroundings perfectly. The food is truly amazing – the swordfish in a tomato, caper and olive sauce transports you to the Mediterranean – and the decor, service and wine list are impeccable, although late-night music can make it noisy. Expect high prices to match the quality.

Todos Contentos Arribeños 2177. One of the best places to eat in Belgrano's Chinatown, a cheap and cheerful Chinese and Taiwanese establishment with a good selection of very filling noodle soups. Closed Mon lunch.

Yoko Ortega and Gasset 1813. Sushi with a personal touch in Las Cañitas – try the salmon *ceviche*, a dish made with raw marinated fish, popular on South America's Pacific coast.

The western barrios

Madremasa Olleros 3891 and Fraga, Chacarita (Federico Lacroze subte station). This restaurant serving mouthwatering dishes with an exotic touch is just a couple of blocks from the famous Chacarita Cemetery, in a barrio where otherwise a decent pizza is regarded as gastronomy. In an unpretentious, slightly bohemian decor – simple wooden tables with paper sheets – you can try chicken tajine with cheese, spinach and mint or even a tasty sandwich, such as a pumpkin and coriander chapatti with apple chutney. Wine by the glass, unbeatable-value set lunches and efficient service are welcome bonuses.

La Piurana Av Corrientes 3362, Balvanera (Carlos Gardel subte). One of a small enclave of simple Bolivian and Peruvian eateries near Abasto, La Piurana is a friendly, family-run restaurant offering specialties such as ceviche and chifles (fried plantains) at reasonable prices.

Los Sabios Av Corrientes 3733, Almagro (Medrano subte). This extremely inexpensive vegetarian Chinese *tenedor libre* is well worth the journey out to Almagro for non-meat eaters: all the fake duck and assorted takes on tofu noodles you can eat for next to nothing.
Tuñin Rivadavia 3902, Almagro (Castro Barros subte). One of the city's best and most popular pizzerias, serving up huge *milanesas* as well as a tasty *fugazzeta* and other classics within walls adorned by a curious mix of boxing photos and *filete* art.
Urondo Bar Beauchef 1207 and Estrada, Parque Chacabuco ⓣ011/4922-9671. Open only in the evening from Wed to Sat (best take a taxi), this laid-back family-run joint is another oasis of fine cuisine in an otherwise unremarkable barrio, just south of Chacarita. Rabbit, tuna and *osso buco* are just some of the ingredients cooked with an unusual flare.

Cafés, confiterías and snacks

You can learn a lot about Porteños from a little discreet people-watching in the city's **cafés**. People stream through all day, from office workers grabbing a quick *medialuna* in the morning to ladies of leisure taking afternoon tea to students gossiping over a beer or juice in the evenings. They're not quite the hotbed of revolutionary activity they were in the 1970s, but they're still in many ways where you'll find authentic Buenos Aires – over an excellent espresso, usually served with a welcomingly hydrating glass of water. **Confiterías** are traditional tearooms that also specialize in biscuits, cakes and pastries to accompany the tea and coffee, although the dividing line between these, regular cafés and even restaurants (many serve full-blown meals, especially at lunch time) can be quite blurred.

A222 Corrientes 222, 19th floor, in the city centre. For breathtaking views of Puerto Madero and its surroundings, have a tea or coffee at one of the window tables; stay for a glass of wine and watch the same scene turn into a sea of lights as dusk turns to night. Pass on dinner, though: it is overpriced and the service is poor. This fabulous viewpoint is near the top of one of the most sumptuous Rationalist towers in the city, the CoMeGa building dating from 1932, and the lifts alone are worth a visit.
Abuela Pan Bolívar 707, San Telmo. Homely vegetarian café and whole-food store offering a daily menu with options such as tofu burgers, stuffed aubergines and vegetarian sushi. Mon–Fri 8am–7pm.
La Americana Callao 83–99, in the city centre. A Callao landmark, serving up juicy empanadas – some say they're the city's best – to be consumed standing up at metal counters.
Aroma Florida 980, Retiro, plus several other branches. Inside its characterless, a/c interior filled with office workers fuelling up on cappuccino and paninis, you could easily be in any European city. But if you're missing lattes or *macchiatos*, this is where you'll find them.
La Biela Quintana 600, Recoleta. Institutional *confitería* famed for its *lomitos* and coffee, served in the elegant bistro interior or, with a surcharge, in the shade of a gigantic gum tree on the terrace.
Café Martinez Libertador 3598, Palermo. One of several branches of this 70-year-old, upmarket café. Its enticing speciality drinks include the "Cappuccino Martinez", a rich mix of chocolate, honey, steamed milk, cream, cinnamon – and a little coffee.
Café Tortoni Av de Mayo 825, in the city centre ⓣ011/4342-4328. Buenos Aires' most famous café (see p.109) exudes pure elegance, but it is in grave danger of turning into a tourist trap. Some evenings it hosts live jazz or tango in *La Bodega* downstairs, but there are many far more authentic venues around.
Costumbres Criollas Esmeralda 1392 at Av Libertador, Retiro. A small restaurant specializing in excellent *empanadas tucumanas* and regional dishes such as *locro* and *tamales*. Worth seeking out for a snack if you have an hour or two to kill in the vicinity of Retiro.
Cumaná Rodriguez Peña 1149, Recoleta. Popular with students and office workers, this is a good place to try *mate*, served from 4 to 7.30pm with a basket of crackers. It also offers a selection of provincial food, such as empanadas and *cazuelas* (casseroles).
La Giralda Corrientes and Uruguay, in the city centre. Brightly lit and austerely decorated Corrientes café famous for its *chocolate con churros*. A perennial hangout for students and intellectuals and a good place to experience the Porteño passion for conversation.
Confitería Ideal Suipacha 384, in the city centre. It's not quite as famous as the *Tortoni*, and therefore less frequented, though it is just as beautiful, if a little worn at the edges, with a great tango salon upstairs. Do not be put off by the dusty, smelly entrance.

Medio y Medio Montevideo and Perón, in the city centre. Named after Montevideo market's famous drink, *Medio y Medio* serves *chivitos* (Uruguayan beef sandwiches) and, of course, *mate* from behind its ornate facade.

New Brighton Sarmiento 645, in the city centre. The classic Anglo–Porteño *Brighton*, which first opened its doors in 1908, has now been renovated and reopened after several years of being closed, and retains many of its original features, including its long wooden bar and row of stools. Wood panelling and stained glass help recreate a *belle époque* atmosphere, with a café area at the front and expensive but quality restaurant at the back.

Palacio Barolo Av de Mayo 1380, in the city centre. Open since early 2007, this fabulous *confitería*-cum-restaurant on the ground floor of the emblematic Barolo building (see p.109), already oozes atmosphere and its pricey cakes, *medialunas* and coffees are well above average – try the special "Café Barolo", laced with Cointreau and sprinkled with cinnamon. The meals are also excellent and unusual – this may be the only the place in the city where you can eat native creatures such as ñandú (rhea), capybara, vizcacha, cayman, *pacú* (a river fish), llama and guanaco, which come in sauces flavoured with herbs, mustard and red berries.

La Paz Av Corrientes 1599, in the city centre. The classic Corrientes (and Porteño) café; less sumptuous but also with fewer tourists than the *Tortoni*. Until the military all but wiped it out, *La Paz* was the favourite hangout of left-wing intellectuals and writers and it's still a good place to meet a friend or read a book over a coffee, especially when it's raining outside and the windows steam up.

La Puerto Rico Alsina 420, Monserrat. Simple and elegant, one of the city's classic *confiterías*, famous for its outstanding espressos; now serving meals too.

Sigi Plaza Güemes, Palermo. Coffee and introspection go hand in hand at this café in the centre of Villa Freud that also prepares a range of *supremas de pollo* (breaded chicken fillets) with inventive sauces.

Ugi's Paraguay and San Martín, plus numerous other branches throughout the city. The ubiquitous *Ugi's* offers a quarter of a fast and very reasonable cheese and tomato pizza for a few coins.

Las Violetas Av Rivadavia 3899 and Medrano, Almagro. Wonderfully restored in 2001 – having been rescued from closure by popular demand – this *confitería*/restaurant is a monument to the Porteño heyday of the 1920s, with its fine wood panelling, gorgeous stained glass, Carrara marble table-tops and impressive columns; it was a favourite hangout of writers such as Roberto Arlt. The *confitería* is justly famed for its breads, cakes and pastries, while the restaurant combines attentive service with copious and refined cuisine – try the delicious *agnelottis* (pasta) filled with ricotta, ham and walnuts.

Heladerías

More than anything else, one institution in Buenos Aires, and indeed the rest of the country, serves as a constant reminder of Argentina's strong Italian inheritance: the **heladería**, or ice-cream parlour. Ubiquitous, varied, extremely popular and the subject of fierce debate as to which is the best, these minefields of temptation serve millions of cones and cups daily, and dispatch hundreds of boys on motorbikes to satisfy the needs of those who cannot be bothered to go and out and buy in person.

Cadore Corrientes 1695, in the city centre. Some experts have declared *this* the best place for ice cream in the city – despite much competition – and the *dulce de leche* flavour above all.

Freddo Guido and Junín, Recoleta. Arguably Buenos Aires' best ice-cream chain – *dulce de leche* aficionados will be in heaven, and few will fail to be seduced by the banana split or *sambayon*. You get to choose two flavours with your cone, but almost inevitably you'll want to try more. One of many branches throughout the city (see ⓦwww.freddo.com.ar for others).

Persicco Vuelta de Obligado 2092, Belgrano, and other branches. Stylish parlours – part modern, part retro – dishing out fabulous ice creams and sorbets, with emphasis on chocolate flavours; excellent cakes, croissants, coffees and ice-cream *gateaux*, too.

Un'Altra Volta Libertador 3060 (Palermo Chico), Echeverría 2302 (Belgrano), Santa Fe 1826 (Recoleta), Callao and Melo (Recoleta) and Ayacucho and Quintana (Recoleta). Fighting it out with *Freddo* and *Persicco* to be the city's number-one ice-cream chain, *Volta*, as it is usually known, produces delicious desserts rivalling those in Italy, clearly the inspiration for its gourmet *gelato;* fabulous cakes, pastries and coffee, too.

Drinking and nightlife

If you've come to Buenos Aires eager to experience the city after dark you will not leave disappointed. Porteños are consummate night owls and though nightlife peaks from Thursday to Saturday, you'll find plenty of things to do during the rest of the week too.

Worthwhile venues are spread all over the city, but certain areas offer an especially large selection of night-time diversions. The city's young and affluent head to **Palermo Soho** and **Palermo Hollywood** to strut their stuff year-round, and **Costanera Norte** as well in the summer. **El Bajo**, as the streets around Reconquista and 25 de Mayo are known, offers a walkable circuit of bars and restaurants as well as the odd Irish pub, while **San Telmo** harbours some eclectic and charismatic bars in amongst the tango spectacles. With that in mind, if you really want to sample the full range of Buenos Aires' nightlife you'll have to follow the locals' lead and move around a bit.

On Fridays, *La Nación*, with its *Vía Libre* supplement, provides topical listings, as does the *Buenos Aires Herald* via its useful, if more limited, *Get Out!*. Also worth looking out for is the tiny magazine *wipe*, given out in some bars or on sale in kiosks, which is particularly good for the trendy end of the city's cultural events and nightlife. *El Tangauta* and *Buenos Aires Tango* are the listings magazines for, of course, **tango**. Websites with worthwhile listings include Ⓦwww.xsalir.com, Ⓦwww.adondevamos.com and Ⓦwww.wipe.com.ar; for dance clubs, the best listings website is Ⓦwww.buenosaliens.com.

Bars and pubs

Buenos Aires has no shortage of great **bars**, ranging from noisy Irish **pubs** to eminently cool places where the young and chic sip wine, cocktails and imported beers. Most of the former and their ilk are clustered in Bajo Retiro, the lower streets situated where the barrio slopes down to the waterside, or in San Telmo; while the latter variety are easiest to find – there are dozens – in any part of Palermo Viejo, Soho or Hollywood. Note that smoking is now banned in public spaces, including bars and restaurants, a rule that Porteños seem to be more or less sticking to – at least for the time being.

Antares Armenia 1447, Palermo. Home-brewed kölsch, porter, stout and barley beer, to name just a few, to accompany tapas and simple dishes, in a roomy, converted storehouse; jazz, blues and Irish music add to the ambience.

Bar Abierto J.L. Borges 1613, Palermo. Pizzas, snacks, drinks and coffee come accompanied by live music, lectures and performances in this converted *almacén* with contemporary paintings on the walls.

Bar Británico Defensa and Brasil, San Telmo. Long-established bohemian bar overlooking Parque Lezama, reopened in 2007 after a sustained neighbourhood campaign to save it from closure. It has been freshly renovated, but retains both the table where Ernesto Sábato wrote *On Heroes and Tombs* and its 24-hour opening policy.

Bárbaro Tres Sargentos 415, Retiro. This cosy bar, a long-standing institution tucked down a side street, regularly puts on live jazz.

Buller Pres. Ortíz 1827, Recoleta. The shiny stainless-steel vats and whiff of malt tell you that this brasserie brews its own excellent beer, which runs the gamut from pale ale to creamy stout, all served with hot and cold dishes.

Carnal Niceto Vega 5511, Palermo. This bar, right opposite *Niceto* (see p.166), has a large upstairs terrace that fills quickly during the warmer months, when a DJ plays laid-back dance grooves for a young, trendy crowd.

Celta Bar Sarmiento 1702, in the city centre. Popular with a friendly and relaxed crowd, this attractive bar with big wooden tables is a good place for an early-evening drink. Also live music, including Argentine rock, Brazilian MPB and jazz, in the basement.

La Cigale 25 de Mayo 722, in the city centre. Renowned for its long-running lively Tues nights, when it offers French cocktails at ridiculously cheap prices. Popular with students.

Congo Honduras 5329, Palermo. One of the places to go of the moment, not least for its massive garden area at the back, which allows those wedded to their cigarettes to indulge and for everyone to enjoy the stars. Get there early – very early by local standards (around 8pm) to get an outdoor booth, where you can sample the food – and expect to queue if you arrive after 10pm.
Dadá San Martín 941, Retiro. Small, hip and attractive bar, playing jazz soundtracks, serving reasonable food and offering a laid-back alternative to the nearby Irish joints.
Deep Blue Reconquista 920, Retiro. A popular, modern bar, done out in vibrant blue, with the funkiest pool tables in the city downstairs; also has a branch at Ayacucho 1240.
Fin del Mundo Chile and Defensa, San Telmo. The epicentre of San Telmo's burgeoning bar scene, flagged by a number of other bars and restaurants, all with outdoor seating and all full on summer's evenings.
Gibraltar Peru 895, San Telmo. Popular both with expats and locals who like to hang out with expats, *Gibraltar* is a British-style pub that's a bit more relaxed than *Kilkenny*, with a friendly atmosphere, bar service and great bar food, including fish and chips and Thai curry.
Gran Bar Danzón Libertad 1161, 1st floor, Retiro. Fashionable after-office bar and restaurant with sharply dressed staff and a very comprehensive wine list. Elegant and popular, even mid-week.
Kilkenny Reconquista and Paraguay, Retiro. The boisterous *Kilkenny* is one of the few bars heaving well before midnight and is an established favourite of both visiting foreigners and Guinness-drinking Porteños, though these days it can be a bit on the sleazy side. The bar – one of several Irish-themed pubs in the area – is the focus for the uproarious St Patrick's Day celebrations in the microcentro.
Malasartes Honduras 4999, Palermo. Funky Plaza Serrano hangout with avant-garde art on the walls and serving reasonably priced drinks and snacks.
Plaza Dorrego Bar Defensa 1098, San Telmo. Most traditional of the bars around Plaza Dorrego, a sober wood-panelled place where the names of countless customers have been etched on its wooden tables and walls, and piles of empty peanut shells adorn the tables.
Shamrock Rodríguez Peña 1220, Recoleta. Irish bar with a Porteño touch. A good place to meet foreigners, with a small club downstairs.
El Taller Borges 1595, Palermo ⓣ011/4831-5501. Bars and restaurants have sprouted around it, but *El Taller* still has the best outside seating in one of Buenos Aires' liveliest evening plazas. It also hosts regular jazz events.
Único Honduras and Fitzroy, Palermo. At the very centre of Palermo Hollywood, a lively crowd is always guaranteed at this well-known bar, which also does reasonable food; it fills early but is more laid-back after 1am or so.

Nightclubs

In terms of **nightclubs**, Buenos Aires stands head and shoulders above any other city in Argentina and, arguably, Latin America. A typical Porteño night out might begin with a pizza with friends around 10pm, followed by a few hours spent in a bar or *confitería*. Not until at least 2am, or frequently an hour or two later, would anyone dream of hitting a nightclub – from when it might take a good hour or so for your average clubber actually to ease him or herself onto the dancefloor. There has, however, been a slight tendency to go out earlier in recent times, in an effort to beat the rush caused by a mix of a booming economy (and so bigger crowds) with a fall in the number of nightspots open since the *República Cromañón* fire (see p.91). The ensuing crackdown by the city government on health and safety in discos and clubs has also included the stricter enforcement of closing times, another spur to going out earlier. Drunkenness is also more common than it used to be in the past, but the levels of alcohol you will see being consumed are still below the Western European or North American norms; drugs, particularly cocaine, are quite common, though obviously illegal.

Music in clubs is usually either commercial dance or more cutting-edge, mixed by DJs of international standing. Although Buenos Aires has some great home-grown DJs, trends in dance music tend to follow those of Europe and the US (particularly London) and clubbers are almost always young and affluent. At the other end of the spectrum, **bailantas** are events where the predominant music is *cumbia villera* – a version of Colombia's famous, repetitive rhythm that's the Argentine equivalent of gangsta rap, glorifying drugs and crime. Cheap, alcoholic and rowdy, *bailantas* are not really recommendable unless you go in the company of a regular.

Admission prices range wildly from free (particularly for women) to $60 or more, with prices sometimes including a free drink. And if you haven't had enough by the time the club finally closes, you could go on to one of the increasingly popular **after-hours clubs** (referred to simply as *afters*), which principally operate on Sundays, usually from around 9am until noon.

For more information and listings on **gay nightlife**, see below.

Bahrein Lavalle 345, in the city centre ⓦwww.bahreinba.com. Sharing the same building as the *Crizia* restaurant (see p.158), this über-cool new club is in a beautifully renovated townhouse dripping with antique furnishings. Drum 'n' bass on Wed, house and techno on Fri and Sat.

Big One Alsina 940, Palermo ⓦwww.bigoneclub.com.ar. A very lively crowd combined with its majestic setting in a converted nineteenth-century industrial building have made this club deservedly popular. Less emphasis on posing and more on the music, which is mostly house and trance on Sat. The venue, Alsina, is gay/gay-friendly on Fri, with more commercial dance music.

Buenos Aires News Paseo de la Infanta Isabel, Palermo. Large and flashy complex of bars, dance-floors and a restaurant. Mainstream dance music and a smartly dressed clientele.

Caix Costanera Norte ⓦwww.caix-ba.com.ar. For some years the most noteworthy after-hours club, attracting an inevitably motley bunch on Sun from 8am.

Fantástico Bailable Rivadavia and Sánchez de Loria, Once (Loria subte). The best known *bailanta* – and a good place to try the heady mix of non-stop dancing and full-on flirting that goes with the territory.

Maluco Beleza Sarmiento 1728, in the city centre ⓦwww.malucobeleza.com.ar. Long-running Brazilian club, playing a mix of lambada, afro, samba and reggae to a lively crowd of Brazilians and Brazilophiles. Wed is Brazilian music only, with a *feijoado* (traditional stew) served.

Mambo Báez 243, Las Cañitas ⓣ011/4778-0115. Extravagantly tropical Club Latino with dinner-shows and disco – runs Thurs–Sun; book ahead. Rather overpriced and limited menu. Salsa classes Wed, Fri and Sat 8.30pm.

Niceto Niceto Vega 5510, Palermo ⓦwww.nicetoclub.com. For many years the home of *Club 69* (see below), *Niceto* now hosts Zizek urban beats – hip-hop and its cousins – on Wed, house on Thurs, indie on Fri and bands on Sat.

Opera Bay Commercial dance music in an impressive setting in Puerto Madero, with great views over the docks. Wed's rather seedy after-office parties are best avoided, though.

Pacha Costanera Norte and La Pampa ⓦwww.pachabuenosaires.com. The club scene in Buenos Aires changes fast but "Clubland" nights at *Pacha* just keep on going. Big and glitzy like its Ibiza namesake, Pacha attracts a lively crowd, including a sprinkling of Argentine celebrities. Dance DJs of international standing often play here. Sat from 1am.

Roxy Lacroze and Alvaro Thomas, Palermo ⓦwww.club69.com.ar. In their new, bigger, home, Thurs's (in) famous *Club 69* "fiestas" are the ones to hit to for a friendly, diverse crowd, outlandish podium dancers and house music played by the city's most acclaimed resident DJs.

Gay and lesbian nightlife

Buenos Aires is increasingly considered the major urban gay tourist destination in Latin America, a fact even publicized by the city authorities. However, there seem to be fewer bars and nightclubs for gays and lesbians than a decade ago, and the scene can be a disappointment for those looking for specifically gay and lesbian locales. In fact, for a lot of gay and lesbian tourists the very attraction is a lack of any "ghetto", although San Telmo is the nearest the city comes to such a phenomenon. As in many Latin American cities, exclusively gay places are not always the best places to go out in any case, especially when it comes to restaurants; anywhere fashionable, with a "mixed" crowd, will most likely prove a better option. Remember that in terms of nightlife almost nothing gets going in this city much before 1, 2 or even 3am, although there are a couple of places that come to life at a more reasonable hour.

Few other Argentine cities have much of a **gay scene**, with the possible exceptions of Córdoba, Rosario and Mendoza; Buenos Aires, with its anonymity and trendiness, exercises the same centripetal effect that most capitals do. There is also an increasing open-mindedness on the part of its inhabitants and authorities – in 2002 it was the first city in Latin America to legalize gay civil unions. The streets, plazas and parks of Buenos Aires can be very cruisy, making them likelier places to meet people than bars or discos, where people tend to go out in groups of friends. News of events and venues can be gleaned from *La Otra Guía*, the main pink publication (ⓦwww.nexo.org), along with the monthly *Queer* newspaper. *Gay Buenos Aires* (ⓦwww.gay-ba.com) is a suitably pink booklet in English and Spanish, available at most bookshops; it carries comprehensive details of meeting-points, clubs, restaurants, hotels, travel agencies, gay-friendly shops and so forth. Most venues will also hand out a free gay city map, *BSASGay* (ⓦwww.mapabsasgay.com.ar), with all the latest locales. Women are far less well catered for than men, but information about events and venues for lesbians can be found at the website ⓦwww.lafulana.org.ar.

The long-established heart of gay Buenos Aires is the corner of avenidas Pueyrredón and Santa Fe, where nondescript *Confitería El Olmo* is still the place to hang out on Friday and Saturday evenings for free entrance flyers or discount vouchers, and to find out where to go. Palermo has increasingly become the main magnet, especially Palermo Hollywood, while San Telmo has ambitions to become the Porteño "Village", or Chueca. One interesting newcomer is *La Marshall* at Av Córdoba 4185, where a **gay milonga** takes place every Wednesday at 10pm, preceded by classes at 8.30pm.

Alsina Buenos Aires Alsina 934, in the city centre. This palatial venue – the same converted industrial building that hosts the mixed "Big One" on Sat – stages a welcome, and extremely popular, matinee "tea dance" on Sun (starting at 9pm), attracting some of the most beautiful people in the city. All ages and tastes come to dance to varied music, everything from house to 70s disco.

Amerika Gascón 1040, Almagro. One of the biggest and best-known gay discos, especially since the demise of the famed *Bunker*. Three dancefloors playing house and Latin music, Fri–Sun.

Angel's Viamonte 2168, Recoleta. Extremely popular club, frequented by drag queens Thurs–Sun.

Bach Bar Cabrera 4390, Palermo. Fairly mixed bar, with shows on Fri and Sat and karaoke on Sun, all starting very late, even though it is a pre-disco venue. Closed Mon.

Bulnes Class Bulnes 1250, Palermo. Laid-back bar frequented by professional types and open after office hours on Thurs (6pm), later Fri & Sat.

Chueca Soler 3283, Palermo. Arguably the city's best gay restaurant, doubling up as a bar, and staging shows and events. The food tends towards the nouvelle cuisine, to match the trendy decor. Open Wed–Sat from 9pm.

Contramano Rodríguez Peña 1082, Recoleta. One of the longest-running discos, attracting an older crowd, with an earlier start (8pm) on Sun, and shows on Sat. Open Wed–Sun.

Inside Restobar Bartolomé Mitre 1571, in the city centre. Located in a beautiful setting in the Pasaje de la Piedad. Functions as a restaurant, wine bar and show, hosting strippers, singers and dancers.

Sitges Av Córdoba 4119, corner of Pringles, Palermo. Large, bright trendy bar, frequented by a mixed but invariably young crowd. Bursting at the seams from 6pm Thurs to Sun, with late-night weekend shows.

Titanic Cabaret Av Santa Fe 2516, Palermo. Late-night weekend shows Sat, including strippers and other raucous fun.

Titanic Club Av Callao 1156, Recoleta. Basement bar, club and meeting-place, with strippers and female impersonators delighting the public from the bar-top catwalk. Mon–Fri 10pm till late.

The arts and entertainment

There's a superb range of **cultural events** on offer in Argentina's capital, ranging from avant-garde theatre to blockbuster movies and grand opera with a wealth of options in between. One of the best features of Porteño cultural life is the strong tradition of free or very cheap events, including film showings at the city's museums and cultural centres, tango and a series of enthusiastically attended outdoor events put on by the city government every summer; street performers are also of very high quality.

A plethora of listings are given in the entertainment sections of both *Clarín* and *La Nación*. Numerous independent listings sheets are also available in bars, bookshops and kiosks throughout the city; it's always worth trying the tourist

△ Tango in La Boca

kiosks for pamphlets and magazines. *Arte al Día* (☎011/5031-0023, Ⓦwww.artealdia.com) is a monthly newspaper with details of art exhibitions at galleries and arts centres available from newspaper stands.

You can buy tickets at discounted prices for theatre, cinema and music events at the various centralized *carteleras* (ticket agencies) in the centre, such as Cartelera Baires, Av Corrientes 1382, local 24 (Mon–Thurs 10am–10pm, Fri 10am–11pm, Sat 10am–midnight, Sun 2–10pm; ☎011/4372-5058). Alternatively Ticketek (☎011/5237-7200, Ⓦwww.ticketek.com.ar) sells tickets to many upcoming concerts, plays and sporting events, bookable over the phone or online with a credit card. The most central of their outlets is at Viamonte 560 (Mon–Sat 9am–8.30pm).

Tango

The most obvious face of **tango** in Buenos Aires is that of the tango *espectáculos* offered by places such as *El Viejo Almacén*. Often referred to by Porteños as "tango for export", these generally rather expensive *cena shows* (dinner followed by the show) are performed by professionals who put on a highly skilled and choreographed display. Many visitors seek something less touristy, but the problem with this is that locals who are tango fans tend to go to either music recitals or to *milongas* (see box, p.170) to dance. If you want to dance yourself – or would prefer to see tango as a social phenomenon – you should also head to a *milonga*, although note the days, times and locations of these change frequently – a *milonga* refers to a moveable event rather than a specific venue. The best place to go for information on the week's *milonga* schedule and the availability of tango lessons is the specialist information desk and website (Ⓦwww.tangodata.com.ar) run by the city government in the Teatro General San Martín at Corrientes 1530. Both have detailed literature on every aspect of tango in the city. There are also two free tango magazines with listings, *El Tangauta* and *Buenos Aires Tango*, which can generally be picked up at tourist kiosks, hotels, cultural centres and record stores.

Many hotels and hostels offer excursions to dinner shows. There are also regular tango festivals, with a host of free shows and hundreds of classes and *milongas* – the biggest are the October and March World Tango Festivals, the competitive World Championships in August and the **Día del Tango**, celebrated on and around December 11 (Carlos Gardel's birthday).

Bar Sur Estados Unidos 299, San Telmo ☎011/4362-6086. One of San Telmo's more reasonably priced tango shows ($120 upwards). The quality of the shows can vary but it's an intimate space where audience participation is encouraged towards the end of the evening. Daily 8pm–4am.

La Calesita Av Rivadavia 1350, Nuñez ☎011/4743-3631. During the summer, this popular weekly *milonga* takes place outdoors at a park on the Costanera Sur under strings of fairy lights. Sat at 11pm with class at 9.30pm. Dec–March only.

Central Cultural del Sur Caseros & Baigorri, Barracas ☎011/4305-6653, Ⓦwww.centrodelsur.com.ar. Wonderful arts centre housed in a well-preserved nineteenth-century stables and inn, with outdoor stages and a patio for folklore on Sat nights and tango on Sun (6.30pm lesson, 9pm show).

El Chino Beazley 3566, Pompeya ☎011/4911-0215. This bar and *parrilla* in traditional Pompeya in the southwest of the city is probably the most authentic place to hear tango sung by the talented staff and a crowd of locals and regulars. It's even been the subject of a movie, *Bar El Chino*. Fri and Sat from 10pm.

Club Gricel La Rioja 1180, San Cristóbal (Urquiza subte) ☎011/4957-7157. Small, friendly club holding *milongas* on Fri and Sat from 11pm and Sun from 9pm. Also daily classes.

Confitería Ideal Suipacha 384, 1st floor, in the city centre ☎011/5265-8069, Ⓦwww.confiteriaideal.com. An oasis of elegance just a few blocks from busy Corrientes, the *Ideal* has a stunning salon, which is undoubtedly one of the most traditional and consistently popular places to dance. Classes Mon, Wed, Thurs & Fri noon, Sat

3.30pm; *milongas* Mon, Wed & Sun 3pm, Tues & Sat 10pm.

Niño Bien Centro Región Leonesa, Humberto 1° 1462, Constitución (San José subte) ⓣ011/4147-8687. Popular with both locals and foreign "tango tourists", and with a great atmosphere. Thurs from 10.30pm, with a class at 9pm.

Parakultural ⓦwww.parakultural.com.ar. Young, bohemian organization that puts on the coolest *milongas* and shows in town at a

Milongas

Tango, the dance once regarded as the preserve of older couples, or merely a tourist attraction, has gained a whole new audience in recent times, with an increasing number of young people filling the floors of social clubs, *confiterías* and traditional dancehalls for regular events known as **milongas.** While the setting for a *milonga* can range from a sports hall to an elegant salon, the structure – and etiquette – of the dances varies little. In many cases, classes are given first. Once the event gets underway, it is divided into musical sets, known as *tandas*, which will cover the three subgenres of tango: tango "proper"; *milonga* – a more uptempo sound; and waltz. Each is danced differently. Occasionally there will also be an isolated interval of salsa, rock or jazz. Even if you don't dance, it's still worth going: the spectacle of couples slipping almost trance-like around the dancefloor, as if illustrating the oft-quoted remark "tango is an emotion that is danced", is a captivating sight. Apart from the understated skill and composure of the dancers, one of the most appealing aspects of the *milonga* is the absence of class – and, especially, age – divisions; indeed, most younger dancers regard it as an honour to be partnered by older and more experienced dancers.

The invitation to dance comes from the man, who will nod towards the woman whom he wishes to dance with. She signals her acceptance of the offer with an equally subtle gesture and only then will her new partner approach her table. Once on the dancefloor, the couple waits eight *compases*, or bars, and then begins to dance, circulating in a counter-clockwise direction around the dancefloor. As the floor of a *milonga* will inevitably be full of couples, it's unlikely that you'll see the spectacular choreography of the shows, but what you will see is real tango, in which the dancers' feet barely seem to leave the ground. The woman follows the man's lead by responding to *marcas*, or signs, given by her partner to indicate the move he wishes her to make. The more competent she is, the greater number of variations and personal touches she will add. Though the basic steps of the tango may not look very difficult, it entails a rigorous attention to posture and a subtle shifting of weight from leg to leg, essential to avoid losing balance. The couple will normally dance together until the end of a set, which lasts for four or five melodies. Once the set is finished, it is good tango etiquette for the woman to thank her partner who, if the experience has been successful and enjoyable, is likely to ask her to dance again later in the evening.

Watching real tango danced is the kind of experience that makes people long to do it themselves. Unfortunately, a *milonga* is not the best place to take your first plunge; unlike, say, salsa, even the best partner in the world will find it hard to carry a complete novice through a tango. In short, if you can't bear the thought of attending a *milonga* without dancing, the answer is to take some classes – you should reckon on taking about six to be able to hold your own on the dancefloor. There are innumerable places in Buenos Aires offering dance classes, including cultural centres, bars and *confiterías* and, for the impatient or shy, there are private teachers advertising in *El Tangauta* and *Buenos Aires Tango* (see p.169). If you're going to take classes, it's important to have an appropriate pair of shoes with a sole that allows you to swivel (rubber soles are useless). For women, it's not necessary to wear heels but it is important that the shoes support the instep. At a *milonga*, however, a pair of supportive and well-polished heels is the norm, and will act as a signal that you are there to dance. Any woman going to a *milonga*, but not intending to dance, should make that clear in her choice of dress and footwear; go dressed to kill and you'll spend the night turning down invitations from bemused-looking men.

rotating eclectic set of venues. See the website for schedule; also classes.

Piazzola Centro de Artes Galería Güemes, Florida 165, in the city centre. One of the most central tango show locations, with a dinner and show daily at 8.30pm for around $250.

Señor Tango Vieytes 1655, Barracas ⓣ011/4303-0231, ⓦwww.senortango.com.ar. Large and very professional *tanguería* in the quiet southern barrio of Barracas. Daily dinner and a real spectacle of a show that traces the history of tango and incorporates trapezes, 1980s tango fusion and even horses. From 8.30pm; $150 upwards.

Taconeando Balcarce 725, San Telmo ⓣ011/4307-6696, ⓦwww.taconeando.com. Smaller, more informal *tango cena* show; a good option if you want to see a show rather than a *milonga* but also want to avoid the larger, more commercial options; prices from $100.

El Tasso Defensa 1575, opposite Parque Lezama, San Telmo ⓣ011/4307-6506, ⓦtangotassa.com.ar. Friendly San Telmo neighbourhood cultural centre with free *milongas*, renowned for the quality of their orchestras. Sun from 10pm.

El Viejo Almacén Av Independencia and Balcarce, San Telmo ⓣ011/4307-6689. Probably the most famous of San Telmo's *tanguerías*, housed in an attractive nineteenth-century building. Occasionally hosts nationally famous tango singers, otherwise slickly executed dinner and dance shows daily from 8pm. $165 upwards.

La Viruta Armenia 1366, Palermo ⓣ011/4779-0030, ⓦwww.lavirutatango.com. Huge, long-running institution with regular *milongas* that mix tango with folklore, salsa and even rock 'n' roll. Fri, Sat & Sun from midnight; classes also available.

Cinemas

Porteños are keen and knowledgeable cinema-goers and there are dozens of **cinemas** in the city showing everything from the latest Hollywood releases to Argentine films and foreign art house cinema. Foreign films are usually subtitled, though occasionally the original language soundtrack is slightly or completely muted; movies that appeal to children are usually dubbed, though tend to be shown in both versions. Traditionally, cinemas showing purely mainstream stuff were concentrated on Calle Lavalle, while art house flicks were more common on Avenida Corrientes. However, both are increasingly losing out to the multiplex cinemas in the city's various shopping malls, which offer excellent visuals and acoustics, though in a blander atmosphere. Numerous free film showings are held at the city's cultural centres and museums. In April, Buenos Aires holds an **International Festival of Independent Cinema** (ⓦwww.bafici.gov.ar), with an excellent selection of national and foreign films at venues throughout the city – it's a good idea to book ahead where possible as Buenos Aires turns into a city of cinephiles during this popular event.

The more interesting or unusual cinemas are listed below; for what's on, consult the listings sections of *Clarín* or *La Nación*, or visit ⓦwww.pantalla.com.ar, which features all the city's cinemas and all the movies showing, complete with reviews.

Abasto Shopping Av Corrientes 3200, Balvanera. Enormous modern cinema at the Abasto shopping centre, featuring a good mix of international and local movies; usually one of the main hosts of April's film festival.

Arteplex Centro Av Corrientes 1145, in the city centre ⓣ011/4382-7934. One of the few art house cinemas still operating on Corrientes.

Complejo Tita Merello Suipacha 442, in the city centre ⓣ011/4322-1195. Another central art house cinema, named after one of the great names of the history of tango, who appeared in dozens of films as of 1933.

Cosmos Av Corrientes 2046, Balvanera ⓣ011/4953-5405, ⓦwww.cinecosmos.com. Many locals' favourite art house cinema, usually one of the venues of the film festival.

Gaumont Rivadavia 1633, Balvanera ⓣ011/4371-3050. One of several "Espacio INCAA" showcase cinemas run by the Instituto Nacional de Cine y Artes Audiovisuales, the Argentine national cinema institute. If your Spanish is up to it, this is the place to catch the best examples of the country's strong national film industry.

Sala Leopoldo Lugones Av Corrientes 1530, in the city centre. Part of the Teatro San Martín complex, this pioneering screening locale puts on outstanding cycles dedicated to given directors, actors, countries or themes.

Village Recoleta Vicente López and Junín, Recoleta ⓣ011/4805-2220. The most modern place to watch movies in the city, with big screens and comfortable seats. Its sixteen *salas* show all the big movies plus many lesser-known Latin American ones too.

Cultural centres and art galleries

Buenos Aires' numerous **cultural centres** are one of the city's greatest assets. Every neighbourhood has its own modest centre – good places to find out about free tango classes and generally offering a mixture of art exhibitions, film and cafés – while the major institutions such as the Centro Cultural Borges and the Centro Cultural Recoleta put on some of the city's best exhibitions. Buenos Aires also has some prestigious commercial **art galleries**, the majority of which are based in Retiro and Recoleta, particularly around Plaza San Martín and nearby Suipacha and Arenales. During May or June, the art fair **ARTE BA** (ⓦwww.arteba.com), held in La Rural exhibition centre in Palermo, showcases work from Buenos Aires' most important galleries.

British Arts Centre (BAC) Suipacha 1333, Retiro ⓣ011/4393-2004. The place to head for if you're nostalgic for a bit of Hitchcock – regular film and video showings, as well as English-language plays by playwrights such as Harold Pinter. Closed for remodelling at time of writing.

Carlos Regazzoni Sculpture Park Av Libertador 405, Retiro ⓣ011/4315-3663. Identifiable by the rusting iron giraffe outside, this sculpture collection is definitely something different. Regazzoni works in Paris and Buenos Aires, recycling old railway junk and making it into figures of animals and vehicles, among other objects – one of his most impressive pieces is a full scale twin-prop plane, complete with pilot. Most of the work is scattered inside a railway shed, which also holds occasional cultural events, mostly with a recycling theme. Mon–Fri 9am–6pm; $5.

Centro Cultural Borges Viamonte and San Martín, Retiro ⓣ011/5555-5359, ⓦwww.ccborges.org.ar. Large space above the Galerías Pacífico shopping centre. Several galleries show a mixture of photography and painting, as well as a theatre and art house cinema. Mon–Sat 10am–9pm, Sun noon–9pm; $4.

Centro Cultural General San Martín Sarmiento 1551, in the city centre ⓣ011/4374-1251, ⓦwww.teatrosanmartin.com.ar. Tucked behind the Teatro General San Martín, with a varied selection of free painting, sculpture, craft and photography exhibitions and an art house cinema.

Centro Cultural Recoleta Junín 1930, Recoleta ⓣ011/4803-1040. One of the city's best cultural centres – see p.137.

Centro Cultural Ricardo Rojas Corrientes 2038 ⓣ011/4954-5521. Affiliated with the University of Buenos Aires, this friendly cultural centre and gallery space offers free events including live music and bargain film showings, usually alternative/art house.

Espacio Fundación Telefónica Arenales 1540, Recoleta ⓣ 011/4333-1300, ⓦwww.fundacion.telefonica.com.ar/espacio. A new, high-tech art centre that lays emphasis on communications media, as you would expect for a foundation run by a telecoms company. This sleek, modern space stages small, mostly avant-garde exhibitions of work by contemporary Argentine artists, and houses an excellent *mediatheque*. Tues–Sun 2–8.30pm; free.

Fundación Federico J. Klemm Marcelo T. de Alvear 626, Retiro. The late Argentine art maverick Federico Klemm was a kind of self-fashioned Andy Warhol, producing bizarre portraits of modern-day Argentine celebrities in mythic and homoerotic poses. Klemm was also a collector of modern art with a serious collection of works by Picasso, Dali, Mapplethorpe and Warhol himself – to name just a few – as well as major Argentine artists such as Berni and Kuitca. Mon–Fri 11am–8pm.

Goethe Institut Corrientes 319, in the city centre ⓣ011/4311-8964, ⓦwww.goethe.de/hs/bue. Smart German cultural institute that has a good library for German and English books, as well as German movies and plays on offer. Mon–Fri 9am–6pm; closed during summer.

Museo de la Shoá Montevideo 919, Recoleta. Dynamic institute that holds excellent exhibitions of Jewish art, mostly relating to the Holocaust; also organizes seminars. Mon–Thurs 11am–7pm, Fri 10am–5pm. Bring ID.

Ruth Benzacar Gallery Florida 1000, Retiro ⓣ011/4313-8480. Rather unexpectedly reached through an underground entrance at the end of Florida, this prestigious gallery has temporary exhibitions featuring international artists as well as Argentines. Mon–Fri 11.30am–8pm.

Theatre

Theatre is very strongly represented in Buenos Aires, with Avenida Corrientes standing up well in comparison to New York's Broadway and London's West End – although obviously almost all plays are in Spanish. Away from the major theatrical venues – where you'll find a good spread of international and Argentine theatre, both classic and contemporary, ranging from serious drama to reviews and musicals – the city is dotted with innumerable independent venues, with stages in bars and tiny auditoriums at the back of shopping centres; the terms "Off Corrientes" and "Off Off Corrientes" found in press listings are based on those used in New York and London. The standard of productions at smaller venues varies wildly, but they're invariably enthusiastically attended and can be fun. You'll find many independent theatres in the streets around Corrientes and in San Telmo, well publicized by flyers given out in the street, in bars and in bookshops. Argentine playwrights to look out for include Roberto Cossa, whose plays deal with themes of middle-class Porteño life and immigration, in a somewhat similar vein to Arthur Miller; Griselda Gambaro, whose powerful works often focus on the ambiguous power relations between victims and victimizers (with a clear reference to Argentina's traumatic past); and the idiosyncratic Roberto Arlt, who offered a darkly humorous and sometimes surreal vision of modernity. The website Ⓦwww.alternativateatral.com is a mine of information about Off and Off Off Corrientes shows.

Andamio 90 Paraná 660, in the city centre ⓣ011/4373-5670, Ⓦwww.andamio90.org. Long-established theatre school run by actress and director Alejandra Boero. Two auditoriums put on a range of classics by playwrights such as Eugene O'Neill.

Teatro Concert Corrientes 1218, in the city centre ⓣ011/4381-0345. An Off Corrientes theatre that puts on plays with a difference, such as the multimedia work of Alfredo Casero. Shows Fri & Sat only.

Teatro General San Martín Corrientes 1500, in the city centre ⓣ011/4371-0111, Ⓦwww.teatrosanmartin.com.ar. Excellent modern venue with several auditoriums and a varied programme that usually includes one or two Argentine plays as well as international standards such as Pinter or Brecht. Also hosts contemporary dance events, ballet, children's theatre and art house cinema in the Sala Leopoldo Lugones (see p.111).

Teatro Nacional Cervantes Libertad 815, Retiro Ⓦwww.teatrocervantes.gov.ar. This grand old-fashioned theatre, superb inside and out, presents a broad programme of old and new Argentine and foreign works.

Teatro Ópera Corrientes 860, in the city centre. Fabulous Art Deco theatre, which in its heyday billed Edith Piaf and Josephine Baker, has undergone a recent revival focusing on a music and dance programme, usually of a very high quality.

Teatro El Vitral Rodríguez Peña 344, in the city centre ⓣ011/4371-0948. An attractive old mansion off Corrientes is the setting for this small independent theatre putting on alternative plays and some whacky musical comedies.

Live music

Places offering **live music**, including folk, jazz, tango and rock, are scattered all over the city and differ enormously in style and ambience, though the quality is invariably high. For recitals by local bands, check the *Sí* supplement in *Clarín* on Fridays and the oppositionally named *No* supplement in *Página 12* on Thursdays. International stars are beginning to come back to the city, after the lean crisis years, and usually play at one of the mega-venues, including the football stadiums, such as the Bombonera (see p.124) or Monumental (see p.153). Some of the bars listed on pp.164–165 also have live music from time to time. The website Ⓦwww.mundoteatral.com.ar is an excellent source of information about venues, gigs and shows going on around the city, though with a focus more on off-beat stuff. If folk music is your thing, check out Ⓦwww.folkloreclub.com.ar. Classical music and opera are accounted for on pp.174–175.

Blues Special Club Av Almirante Brown 102, Boca ⓣ011/4854-2338 The name says it all: special blues acts, including those from the US, perform Fri–Sun, while most Fri there is also a *zapada blusera*, or jam session. Tickets are cheaper if you book in advance.
Estadio Luna Park Bouchard 465, in the city centre. ⓣ011/4311-5100, ⓦwww.lunapark.com.ar. Wonderful Art Deco edifice whose huge capacity lends itself to big sell-out events like boxing fights, but also to concerts by big names. In early 2007, it packed in fans to see Tom Jones, Julio Iglesias and the Pet Shop Boys, who performed a song called "Luna Park". Make sure you don't get a "poor visibility" seat.
Estadio Obras Sanitarias Av Libertador 73955, Núñez ⓣ011/4702-3223, ⓦwww.estadioobras.com. Seating over five thousand, this leading venue for rock bands – both home grown and world-famous – has seen the likes of Iggy Pop, the Red Hot Chili Peppers, Duran Duran and even the Sex Pistols grace its stage.
Mitos Argentinos Humberto 1° 489, San Telmo ⓣ011/4362-7810, ⓦwww.mitosargentinos.com.ar. Dinner on Fri and Sat and lunch on Sun (empanadas, steak, etc), are accompanied by live music, but the main attraction is the offbeat nature of the bands playing Thurs–Sat in this old mansion; they have names like Los Melones and Camisa de Fuerza ("straitjacket").
ND/Ateneo Paraguay 918, Recoleta ⓣ011/4328-2888, ⓦwww.ndateneo.com.ar. Folk, rock, tango, jazz, modern classical – all the big national and South American names play here at some point. The medium-sized theatre also hosts film screenings and recitals.
No Avestruz Humboldt 1857, Palermo Viejo ⓣ011/4771-1141, ⓦwww.noavestruz.com.ar. Outstanding venue hosting emerging and established artists focusing on jazz and Latin sounds from Buenos Aires and further afield. Delicious food, too.
Notorious Av Callao 966, Recoleta ⓣ011/4816-2888, ⓦwww.notorious.com.ar. Friendly bar selling CDs that you can listen to on headphones. There's also a great garden at the back where you can chill out over a cold beer. Interesting intimate concerts given – blues, jazz, tango, Latin – throughout the year.
Pan y Teatro Muñiz and Las Casas, Boedo ⓣ011/4924-6920, ⓦwww.panyteatro.com.ar. Open every day except Mon, this beautifully restored grocer's shop serves an original blend of Italian and *criollo* food and puts on shows, including tango, classical music and jazz.
Peña del Abasto Anchorena 571, Abasto ⓣ011/5076-0148. Another wonderful folk venue, with some of the county's leading performers, and a dancefloor; shows Wed–Sun 10pm.
Peña del Colorado Güemes 3657, Palermo ⓣ011/4822-1038, ⓦwww.delcolorado.com.ar. Famed for its past-midnight *guitarreadas* (bring your guitar, play and sing) that "finish when the candles burn out", the *Colorado* is the city's most traditional folk venue – there is also a *mate* bar, a restaurant and occasional folk and even tango shows.
Teatro Gran Rex Corrientes 855, in the city centre. Seating over three thousand, this gigantic edifice is one of the major venues for musicals and gigs by national and international groups, such as Coldplay, plus theatre groups, such as the Black Theatre of Prague.
Thelonius Club Salguero 1884, Palermo ⓣ011/4342-7650, ⓦwww.thelonius.com.ar. The odd soul or blues concert is given here, but as the name implies, this is a jazz club, and generally regarded as the top; the music is always mesmerizing, the acoustics are faultless and the food isn't bad, but the barstools and metal chairs are not that comfortable – the only downside.
La Trastienda Balcarce 460, San Telmo ⓣ011/4342-7650, ⓦwww.latrastienda.com. Trendy live music in a late nineteenth-century mansion, with a wide-ranging roster of acts including rock, jazz, salsa and tango.
Vaca Profana Lavalle 3683, Abasto ⓣ011/4867-0934, ⓦwww.vacaprofana.com.ar. Groundbreaking joint serving a delicious vegetarian *picada* (mixed platter) and all manner of food and drinks, but more interesting for its avant-garde music and occasionally theatre – new South American sounds including neo-ethnic.

Classical music, opera and ballet

Argentina has a number of world-class classical performers, including **opera** singers, such as tenors Marcelo Álvarez and José Cura, and soprano María Cristina Kiehr, and the **classical music** on offer in the city has seen a revival over the past couple of years, as the post-crisis doldrums have worn off. Some of the best concerts are small-scale affairs held at museums, churches and the like, in particular the **Museo de Arte Hispanoamericano Isaac Fernández Blanco** (see p.132). An evening at the world-class **Teatro Cólon** is a memorable experience, both for the opulent decor and the enthusiastic audience – the 2006–2007 renovation work should make things even better. Internationally renowned Argentine **ballet** star Julio Bocca retired in 2007, though come-backs are always possible; meanwhile a younger Argentine ballet star has come to dominate world stages: La Plata-born Iñaki Urlezaga, a member of London's Royal Ballet, also delights crowds in his native land from time to time. Perhaps the most famous Argentine classical musician alive is pianist and conductor Daniel Barenboim, who has dual Argentine and Israeli citizenship and makes occasional visits to his city of birth; at the end of 2006 he memorably conducted a free open-air New Year's Eve concert on Avenida 9 de Julio with a classical and tango repertoire that was attended by tens of thousands despite the sweltering heat. Keeping a much lower media profile, but equally acclaimed, is multiple Grammy Award winner Martha Argerich; also a concert pianist, she presides over her own international piano competition in Buenos Aires. For news of concerts, consult Ⓦwww.musicaclasicaargentina.com, Ⓦwww.mozarteumargentino.org and Ⓦwww.festivalesmusicales.org.ar, all of which are packed with information.

Casa de la Cultura Av de Mayo 575, in the city centre. Free classical concerts, mostly chamber music, are given from time to time in the marvellous Salón Dorado; look out for flyers and posters.

Manufactura Papelera Bolívar 1582, San Telmo Ⓦwww.papeleracultural.8m.com. This fabulous recycled paper factory in the heart of San Telmo puts on highly intellectual shows and, from time to time, classical music concerts.

La Scala de San Telmo Pasaje Giuffra 371 (Defensa 800), San Telmo Ⓣ011/4362-1187, Ⓦwww.lascala.com.ar. Not Milan, but this sumptuous bijou theatre hosts tango, jazz and other music genres, plus some excellent operas and classical concerts, including ancient music.

Teatro Avenida Av de Mayo 1222, Monserrat Ⓣ011/4381-0662, Ⓦwww.balirica.org.ar. This stylish theatre, opened only a few months after the Colón in 1908, is the home to Buenos Aires Lírica, which puts on a limited number of operas here every season.

Teatro Coliseo Marcelo T. de Alvear 1125, Retiro Ⓣ011/4816-3789. The most important venue for ballet, musicals and classical music after the Colón, which it replaced during the latter's renovation; also offers occasional free recitals.

Teatro Colón Libertad 621, in the city centre Ⓣ011/4378-7344, Ⓦwww.teatrocolon.org.ar. Buenos Aires' most glamorous night out and one of the world's great opera houses – acoustically on a par with La Scala in Milan, showcasing opera, ballet and classical music, including the Buenos Aires Philharmonic, from March to Dec. Due to reopen May 2008 after an overhaul, including the installation of silent a/c. Tickets must be bought at the box office in person (foreigners were being charged far higher prices than locals when it closed in 2006; if that policy continues when it reopens try and go with an Argentine).

Teatro Margarita Xirgu Chacabuco 875, San Telmo Ⓣ011/4300-8817, Ⓦwww.mxirgu.com.ar. Named after a leading Catalan actress, this opulent theatre was opened by the city's Catalan community, and now stages spectacles in a gamut running from children's theatre to serious operas and classical recitals.

Shopping

Shopping in Buenos Aires is a pleasure unmatched elsewhere in South America. While goods tend to be more Western and familiar than those you will come across in, say, Bolivia or Peru, you can nonetheless count on finding some highly original items to take home. The combination of inventive designers and the devalued peso has made Buenos Aires a great place to expand your wardrobe. Although the days of astonished and delighted foreign currency-earning visitors buying stuff in bulk may have passed, you can still find some decent deals. **Fashions** tend to echo those of Europe, albeit a season behind, though there are certain Argentine chains, with branches in most of the major malls, that produce some fairly unique off-the-peg designs – names to look out for include Kosiuko, Paula Cahen d'Anvers, Ummo and Ossira – which rub shoulders with stores selling more understated, classic clothing.

Buenos Aires prides itself on being a literary city, and its dozens of new and secondhand **bookstores** are a real treat, and lingering is both encouraged and almost unavoidable. A succession of shops selling books and music – with an enormous selection of tango, jazz, classical, folk and rock – are strung along Avenida Corrientes between 9 de Julio and Callao. Others stretch out on Florida north of Avenida Córdoba, together with a bevy of craft, T-shirt and leather stores aimed at tourists, many of them in covered arcades or *galerías*. Contemporary **art**, including some intriguing landscapes and "gaucho art", is on sale at the scores of smart galleries – *galerías de arte* – that line Retiro. More galleries are scattered across Recoleta, with several along Avenida Alvear, but anyone looking for colonial paintings and antiques should head for San Telmo.

The city's markets, along with some of the *casas de provincia* (see p.76), are also where you'll find **handicrafts**, sometimes at lower prices than at the specialized craft centres or *ferias*. Here you'll come across beautiful, unique ceramics, wooden masks or alpaca-wool items at far better value than the mass-produced alternatives; note that the word *alpaca* also means pewter in Spanish. Other typically Argentine goods include *mate* paraphernalia, polo wear, wine and world-class leatherware. A box of widely available Havanna *alfajores* (see p.45) makes a good present, or take a jar or two of *dulce de leche* away with you to satisfy cravings.

On a practical note, visitors can get even better bargains by claiming back tax on certain purchases of domestically produced goods – look out for the "Tax Free Shopping" signs, usually on luxury-goods stores, and ask for the relevant document when you spend the minimum amount (currently $70). You can then get this stamped at the airport and exchanged for hard cash of around fifteen percent of what you paid – make sure you also have the receipts and, prior to check-in, the goods themselves – to hand.

△ Polo shop, Recoleta

Shopping malls

Over the past decade or two, shopping malls have partly superseded small shops and street markets, but those in Buenos Aires are among the most tastefully appointed in the world – and lots of the good old-fashioned stores have survived as well. Several of the malls, like Abasto, are housed in revamped buildings of historical and architectural interest. On a practical level, the malls are air-conditioned and the places where you'll find that rarity in Buenos Aires, public toilets.

Abasto Av Corrientes 3200, Balvanera. This grand building, dating from the 1880s, was once the city food market; now it's the daddy of all the central malls. As well as a ten-screen cinema, it has hundreds of designer and cheaper stores, an enormous food hall, an amusement arcade and a museum for children, the Museo de los Niños (museum Tues–Sun 1–8pm; $12).

Bond Street Av Santa Fe 1670, Recoleta. The alternative mall, full of local teenagers skulking around skate stores and tattoo parlours; there's also a few surf shops in the surrounding streets. A good place to pick up flyers for live music and clubs.

Buenos Aires Design Center Plaza Intendente Alvear, Recoleta. Right next to the Centro Cultural de Recoleta, this mall is dedicated to shops selling the latest designs, mostly for the home, from Argentina and elsewhere.

Galerías Pacifico Florida 750, in the city centre. Fashion boutiques and bookshops in a beautiful building decorated with murals by leading Argentine artists, plus the Centro Cultural Borges at the top and a food court, children's play area and baby changing room (nappies/diapers provided) in the basement. The most central mall.

Paseo Alcorta Figueroa Alcorta and Salguero, Palermo. A huge shopping complex, with several cinemas and the large Carrefour supermarket.

Patio Bullrich Libertador 750, Retiro. Once a thoroughbred horse market, this is one of the most upmarket malls, and a good place to find designer clothes and leather.

Books and music

Corrientes is the traditional place to head for **books and music**, though there are also a number of secondhand stores on Avenida de Mayo, and various upmarket bookstores, with good foreign-language and glossy souvenir book sections, around Florida, Córdoba and Santa Fe. If you're in town during April, don't miss Buenos Aires' hugely popular **Feria del Libro** (Ⓦwww.el-libro.com.ar), held at the Centro de Exposiciones on avenidas Figueroa Alcorta and Pueyrredón, which attracts staggeringly large numbers of people and provides a good opportunity for some serious browsing plus the chance to meet famous authors or attend special events such as lectures on Borges or poetry recitals.

Ateneo Grand Splendid Santa Fe 1860, Recoleta. A strong contender for the most beautiful bookshop in the world – and easily the largest in Latin America – this major branch of the Ateneo/Yenny chain is housed in a former cinema, built in 1919 and inspired by the Opéra Garnier in Paris. It is particularly strong on art and architecture books, with an array of collectable albums of photos of Buenos Aires and the rest of the country. There is a small café on the ground floor, from where you can admire the sumptuousness of it all and browse before you buy.

Gandhi Av Corrientes 1743, in the city centre. Upmarket bookstore offering an excellent range of fiction, non-fiction and periodicals, plus a coffee shop where you can browse your purchases.

Kel Ediciones Marcelo T. de Alvear 1369, Recoleta. This all-English bookstore has mostly fairly mainstream stock but it's big enough for anyone to find that perfect accompaniment to a long-distance bus journey; they also stock *Rough Guides*.

Liberarte Av Corrientes 1555, in the city centre. An emporium of the assorted interests of the Porteño left-wing intelligentsia. Loads of offbeat periodicals.

Librería de Ávila Alsina 500, Monserrat. Sprawling antique bookshop, well worth a visit as much for the ambience as the books, which include a great selection on Argentina.

Librerías ABC Maipú 866, Retiro. Good foreign-language section (mostly in German and English) and loads of travel books and guides.

Musimundo Florida 267, in the city centre, and branches throughout the city. Argentina's major record chain, stocking everything from techno to tango.

Walrus Books Estados Unidos 617, San Telmo. Excellent English-language new and secondhand bookstore, with the emphasis on quality literature and non-fiction from around the world. Tues–Sun 10am–8pm. Restricted opening hours during the summer.

Zival's Av Callao 395, in the city centre Ⓦwww.tangostore.com. Small but well-stocked music store, particularly good for tango. There's a strong selection of CDs and DVDs as well as books and sheet music, and the staff are very knowledgeable on the best tango recordings.

Arts and crafts

The best craftsmen display their wares at the Sunday fairs in Recoleta, San Telmo and Mataderos, but local **arts and crafts** are also available at a number of central stores.

El Boyero Florida 953, Retiro. Usual leather and *campo* (countryside) artefacts, but also with some more interesting, less garish designs than in many of the surrounding stores.

Kelly's Paraguay 431, Retiro. Colourful store selling a variety of ponchos from different provinces, ceramics and, of course, *mates*.

Plata Lappas Florida 740, in the city centre. The city's most renowned silverware and kitchenware have been sold here for years. Some of it is imported, but there's still plenty of local stuff, including gorgeous goblets.

Puro Diseño Buenos Aires Design, Av Pueyrredón 2501, Recoleta. Tucked away next to the Centro Cultural Recoleta, this store showcases Argentine designs, with everything from lamps and ashtrays to handbags and shoes.

Leather goods

The cattle of the Pampas not only provide the world's best beef, they also offer up their hides to be turned into top-class shoes, jackets, bags and belts, among other products. Classy city-centre shops will not disappoint when it comes to quality, but prices are not necessarily that low by international standards; try and track down factory outlets in further-flung barrios.

Casa López Marcelo T. de Alvear 640, Retiro. Regarded as the city's very best exporter of classic leather goods, it has prices to match, starting at around $60 for a wallet.

Centro del Cuero Murillo 500–700, Villa Crespo. With around thirty warehouse stores selling leather clothing wholesale and direct to the public, this is the place to go for a bargain. Prices are mostly unmarked so be prepared to haggle, although there are some boutiques here, too. Three blocks west from Malabia station on subte line B.

Charles Calfun Florida 918, Retiro. Purveyor of leather jackets and bags for half a century, along with the fur coats beloved by Recoleta's socialites.

Fortín Santa Fe 1245, Retiro. High-quality handmade leather goods, principally boots, jackets and bags.

Outdoor equipment

In addition to the outlets listed here, there is a whole row of **camping** and **fishing** shops along the 100 to 200 block of Calle Paraná, just off Corrientes. Ushuaia and many Patagonian towns are just as well stocked as Buenos Aires, so you avoid the transport, although prices may be higher down there.

Deporcamping Santa Fe 4830, Palermo Ⓣ011/4772-0534. Limited but decent quality range of trekking clothes and boots, tents, mats and sleeping bags; also Maglites and stoves.

Ecrin Mendoza 1679, Belgrano Ⓣ011/4784-4799, Ⓦwww.escalada.com. The place for technical climbing and mountaineering gear, plus crampons and ropes. The store also stocks both imported and much cheaper Argentine outdoor jackets.

Explorer Lavalle 423, in the city centre. Central store stocking good-quality clothing and reasonable boots, along with an impressive range of penknives.

Listings

ACA (Automóvil Club Argentino) Main office at Libertador 1850 ⓣ011/4808-4000, ⓦwww.aca.org.ar.

Airlines Aerolíneas Argentinas, Perú 2 ⓣ011/4340-7777 or 0810/222-86527; Aeroméxico, Esmeralda 1063 ⓣ011/4315-1936; Air Canada, Av Córdoba 656 ⓣ011/4327-3640; Air France, San Martín 334, 23rd floor ⓣ011/4317-4700; Alitalia, Suipacha 1111, 28th floor ⓣ011/4310-9999; American Airlines, Suipacha 1111, 28th floor ⓣ011/4318-1111; Andes, Av Córdoba 966, 8th floor ⓣ011/4328-9700; Avianca, Carlos Pellegrini 1163, 4th floor ⓣ011/4322-2731; British Airways, Carlos Pellegrini 1163, ground floor ⓣ011/4320-6600; Copa Airlines, Carlos Pellegrini 989, 2nd floor ⓣ0810/222-2672; Delta, Reconquista 737, 3rd floor ⓣ011/4312-1200; Gol ⓣ0810/266-3131; Iberia, Carlos Pellegrini 1163, 1st floor ⓣ011/4131-1000; KLM, San Martín 334, 23rd floor ⓣ0880/333-0390; LADE, Perú 714 ⓣ011/5129-9001; LAN, Cerrito 866 ⓣ011/4378-2222; Lloyd Aéreo Boliviano (LAB), Carlos Pellegrini 137 ⓣ011/4323-1900; Lufthansa, Marcelo T. de Alvear 590, 6th floor ⓣ011/4319-0600; Mexicana, Av Córdoba 755, 1st floor ⓣ011/4000-6300; Pluna, Florida 1 ⓣ011/4342-4420; Qantas, Av Córdoba 673, 13th floor ⓣ011/4114-5800; South African Airways, Carlos Pellegrini 1141, 5th floor ⓣ011/5556-6666; TAM, Cerrito 1026 ⓣ011/4819-6950; United Airlines, Av Madero 900, 9th floor ⓣ0810/777-8648.

Airport enquiries Ezeiza and Aeroparque ⓣ011/5480-6111.

American Express Arenales 707. Changes its own cheques commission-free Mon–Fri 10am–3pm.

Banks and exchange Commission is rarely charged when exchanging cash and increasingly the more central places will exchange pounds sterling and other currencies, although your safest bet is to have US dollars or euros. There is an entire street of bureaux de change in the financial district, near the corner of San Martín and Sarmiento – rates are similar and opening hours are generally Mon–Fri 9am–6pm. This is also where you'll find the central bank branches, with similar hours. At other times, look out for the branches of exchange company Metropolis at Corrientes 2557, Florida 506 and Quintana 576, which are also open at weekends. Buenos Aires is the only city in the country where you will find it relatively easy to change travellers' cheques, though it can still be difficult. American Express (see above) changes its own cheques. More convenient are ATMs, which are widespread for Visa and Mastercard and generally reliable, although they are usually only stocked with pesos, not US dollars (despite what the screen may say).

Buses Retiro bus terminal is at Av Antártida and Ramos Mejía (ⓣ011/4310-0700). It's almost impossible to get through on the station's general number, but their website (ⓦwww.tebasa.com.ar) will let you check companies and destinations and gives you the individual phone numbers (and, where they exist, websites), so you can call to check times and, in most cases, make a reservation. Alternatively, visit the terminal itself, where the 150 or so companies all have ticket booths and there is a useful information booth.

Car rental Al Rent a Car International, Maipu 965 ⓣ011/4311-1000, ⓦwww.airentacar.com.ar; Avis, Cerrito 1527 ⓣ011/4326-5542, ⓦwww.avis.com.ar; Dollar, San Martín 945 ⓣ011/4315-8800, ⓦwww.dollar.com.ar; Localiza, Cerrito 1080 ⓣ011/4813-3184, ⓦwww.localiza.com/argentina; Thrifty, Carlos Pellegrini 1576 ⓣ011/4326-0338, ⓦwww.grupoexpress.com.ar.

Embassies and consulates Australia, Villanueva 1400 (Mon–Thurs 8.30am–5pm; ⓣ011/4779-3500); Brazil, Cerrito 1350 (Mon–Fri 10am–1pm; ⓣ011/4515-2400); Canada, Tagle 2828 (Mon–Thurs 2–6pm; ⓣ011/4808-1000); Chile, San Martín 439, 9th floor (Mon–Fri 9am–1pm; ⓣ011/4394-6582); Ireland, Libertador 1068, 6th floor (Mon–Fri 9.30am–3.30pm; ⓣ011/5787-0801); New Zealand, Carlos Pellegrini 1427, 5th floor (Mon–Thurs 9am–1pm & 2–5.30pm, Fri 9am–1pm; ⓣ011/4328-0747); Peru, Las Heras 2545 (Mon–Fri 8am–1pm; ⓣ011/4802-3826); South Africa, Marcelo T. de Alvear 590, 8th floor (Mon–Fri 8.30am–noon; ⓣ011/4317-2900); UK, Dr Luis Agote 2412 (Mon–Fri 9am–3pm; ⓣ011/4808-2200); US, Av Colombia 4300 (Mon–Fri 8.30am–noon & 2.30–4pm; ⓣ011/5777-4533); Uruguay, Ayacucho 1616 (Mon–Fri 9.30am–4.30pm; ⓣ011/4807-3040).

Hospitals Consultorio de Medicina del Viajero, Hospital de Infecciosas F.J. Muñiz, Uspallata ⓣ011/4305-0357; Hospital Británico, Perdriel 74 ⓣ011/4309-6400; Hospital Italiano ⓣ011/4959-0200. The Argentine medical emergency number is ⓣ107.

Internet access It's not difficult to find a place to check your email in Buenos Aires – cybercafés are absolutely everywhere and many *locutorios* also have a few machines; quality of connection, keyboard, console, seating and general comfort vary enormously. Prices keep going up but are still very cheap by international standards (mostly a peso or two an hour) and access is usually via cable modems. Practically all upmarket hotels, plus many cafés, some *locutorios* and all of Calle Florida are Wi-Fi enabled.

Laundry Laverap, Suipacha 722 ⓣ011/4322-3458 or Av Córdoba 466 ⓣ011/4312-5460, plus many others across the city. Most Laveraps will also pick up and deliver free of charge.

Pharmacies Farmacia Center Callao 1180; Salud Global, Cerviño 4716 ⓣ011/4776-0868, free delivery.

Police Tourist police Corrientes 436 ⓣ011/4346-5748. emergencies ⓣ101.

Post office Correo Central, Sarmiento 189 (Mon–Fri 10am–8pm). In addition to standard post and parcel facilities, there is a *poste restante* office on the first floor (small charge). There are numerous smaller branches throughout the city, open from 10am to 6pm. Outside these hours, there are many post office counters within stationery shops (*papelerías*), at *locutorios* and at kiosks.

Taxis and remises Ordinary taxis are plentiful throughout the city (see p.96), though it's recommended to call a radio-taxi firm for longer trips: Premium (ⓣ011/4374-6666, ⓦwww.taxipremium.com) has good-quality cars, all with a/c, at the same price as other taxis; Ciudad (ⓣ011/4923-7444) is generally reliable and has "mini-vans" (people carriers) that are useful if you are several and/or have a lot of luggage. They cost the same as ordinary taxis but have a minimum charge; reserve ahead. Otherwise, for longer journeys, booked ahead of time, a *remise* is a good option: try Del Sol (ⓣ011/4702-8070) or Tres Sargentos (ⓣ011/4312-0057).

Travel agents and tour operators Fuegos del Sur, Maipú 812 1°K (ⓣ011/4311-1376, ⓦwww.fuegosdelsur.com), run by the dependable Tomás Lorenz, is the place to go for deals on domestic and Brazilian trips. ASATEJ, Florida 835, 3rd floor (ⓣ011/4114-7595, ⓦwww.asatej.com), is a young and dynamic travel agency, offering cheap flight deals, particularly for students, ISIC cardholders etc – be prepared to wait as the office gets very busy. Agreste, Viamonte 1636 (ⓣ011/4373-4442, ⓦwww.agreste.cjb.net), offers adventurous camping trips across the country to destinations such as the Saltos de Moconá and the Valle de la Luna. Buenos Aires Tur, Lavalle 1444, Office 10 (ⓣ011/4371-2304, ⓦwww.buenosairestur.com), offers city tours of Buenos Aires and visits to tango shows, Tigre and nearby estancias. Say Hueque, Viamonte 749, 6th floor (ⓣ011/5199-2517/20, ⓦwww.sayhueque.com), is a highly commendable outfit with English-speaking staff, geared to the independent traveller and offering trips all over the country.

Around Buenos Aires

For all its parks and tree-lined avenues, Buenos Aires is nonetheless predominantly urban, and it can be nice to get away from the hectic tumult for a day or two. The **northern suburbs**, particularly San Isidro, have preserved their villagey charm, and are less than forty minutes away from central Buenos Aires by train. Further north, the steamy swamps and traditional stilted houses of the **Paraná Delta** could not be a more radical change from the capital – it's as if the Everglades extended just beyond Manhattan. This intriguing watery landscape, which lends itself to kayak explorations and water-skiing, is right by **Tigre**, a riverside resort with historical significance, a fabulous art museum and a colourful market. Tigre also serves as the departure point for launches to **Isla Martín García**, a sparsely populated island at the mouth of the Río Uruguay, once a political penal colony but now a nature reserve. The beautifully preserved Uruguayan town of **Colonia del Sacramento**, a former Portuguese colony and a short ferry ride across the Río de la Plata from Buenos Aires, is another popular day-trip destination. However, like the Delta, it really deserves at least an overnight stay in order to appreciate it to the fullest.

The northern suburbs

As you cross Avenida General Paz, the peripheral highway that separates the Federal Capital from the northern part of Greater Buenos Aires, you enter a leafier suburban world, where residents enjoy cleaner air and live at a more relaxed pace. Here, the subtropical heart that lies beneath Buenos Aires' European veneer starts to show through. **San Isidro**, the suburb of most interest, has a picturesque historic quarter perfect for whiling away a lazy afternoon. Skirting the Río de la Plata, the **Tren de la Costa** (see box, p.182) allows you to make a leisurely trip to Tigre and is an attraction in its own right.

San Isidro

Wealth and tradition ooze from the streets of **SAN ISIDRO**, one of Buenos Aires' most beautiful suburbs. Even the mighty Avenida Libertador, a multi-lane highway stretching northward from the city centre, acquiesces to the barrio's old-fashioned elegance and winds past its luxurious residences as a cobbled street. San Isidro's most interesting section is the **Casco Histórico**, centred on Plaza Mitre, where there's a small **Museo del Rugby** (Tues–Sat 10am–6pm, Sun 10am–8pm; free; Ⓦwww.museodelrugby.com) and rugby-themed bar, with a collection of memorabilia for fanatics of the sport; questions concerning its ongoing viability hang over its future, however.

The plaza itself is on a slope, with two levels. On its upper level, the soaring Neo-Gothic **cathedral** (Mon–Sat 7.30am–8pm, Sun 8am–10pm), built in 1898, merits popping into for its striking French stained-glass windows. Behind it, winding, villa-lined Beccar Varela leads to the viewpoint **Mirador Los 3 Ombúes**. From here you can see glimpses of the Río de la Plata, steadily being overtaken by the islands of the Paraná Delta. The lovely pink and green facade of the nineteenth-century villa, **Quinta Los Naranjos**, is opposite the viewpoint, while **Quinta Los Ombúes**, a simple whitewashed building with red-tiled roof and green shutters at Beccar Varela 774, has been recently opened to the public as the **Museo Municipal de San Isidro Dr Horacio Beccar Varela** (Jan & Feb Tues & Thurs 8am–3pm, Sat & Sun 3–7pm, March–Dec Tues & Thurs 8am–noon & 2–6pm, Sat & Sun 2–6pm; free). This nineteenth-century villa is filled with the wealthy Beccar Varela family's art and furniture and has a garden with views over the river.

Claiming the title of the oldest house in the north of Buenos Aires, the **Casa del General Pueyrredón**, Rivera Indarte 48 (Tues & Thurs 2–6pm, Sat & Sun 3–7pm; free; Ⓣ011/4512-3131), stands in the remnants of lots distributed in 1580, when San Isidro was the site of numerous small farms. The house itself was built in 1790, and was bought by General Pueyrredón – Supreme Director of the United Provinces of the Río de la Plata from 1816 to 1820. His son, Prilidiano Pueyrredón, a painter and architect, inherited the house and added the beautiful Doric-columned gallery that runs along its northern side. Now a Monumento Histórico Nacional and housing San Isidro's **Museo Histórico Municipal**, the building's classic colonial lines, punctuated by green shutters and centred around a patio, are enhanced by its splendid location: there are fantastic views of the river estuary from the garden. The garden's enormous carob tree (known as the *algarrobo histórico*), with its sprawling branches propped up on sticks, was the location of Pueyrredón's discussions with General San Martín on Latin American independence. The museum has a display of historical documents relating to the general's achievements but also features a series of rooms furnished in period style. To get to the house, follow Avenida del Libertador past the

Tren de la Costa

The **Tren de la Costa** (daily; $6 for a *boleto turístico* one way, which means you can get off and on as many times as you like – tickets can be bought onboard; every 20min 7am–11pm; ⓣ011/4002-6000) runs north from Olivos to Tigre, a 25-minute trip if you do it in one go. It's one of the most attractive options for getting to Tigre – it runs parallel to the waterfront, mostly through green parkland and past grandiose suburban mansions and villas – and also presents a number of enticing stop-offs, with eleven restored or purpose-built stations along the route. Originally part of the state-run Tren del Bajo line, which was built in 1891 and ran northwards from Retiro station, the service fell into disuse in the 1960s. In 1995, the northernmost section reopened as this privately run scenic railway, with luxurious mock-Victorian carriages running smoothly and silently along electrified tracks.

To get to the Olivos terminus, known as **Estación Maipú**, first take a commuter train from Retiro (see p.93) to Olivos's Estación Mitre, a thirty-minute journey. From here, take the walkway across Avenida Maipú to the red-brick station (many of the stations are modelled on those of the British Victorian era).

As well as hopping-off points for Olivos and San Isidro, many of the Tren de la Costa's stations hold their own appeal. **Estación Borges**, the nearest to Olivos's marina, is referred to as the "station of the arts" – it's home to an art café with open-air sculptures. **Libertador** station has a shopping centre comprised of outlets for many of the most popular Argentine designer stores, while **Anchorena** station has been christened "Estación Tango" and sits alongside a cultural centre that puts on tango shows and classes; it's also the station closest to the river, and borders a riverside park. **Estación Barrancas** hosts an antiques fair (Sat & Sun 10am–6pm) and provides access to a cycling path, which runs north to San Isidro. **Estación San Isidro**, with its upmarket shopping mall, is located conveniently near the suburb's historic quarter. North of here, you pass through four more riverside stations – Punta Chica, Marina Nueva, San Fernando and Canal – before arriving at the northern terminus, **Estación Delta**, close to Tigre's fruit market and opposite the entrance to the Parque de la Costa.

cathedral but turn left into Roque Sáenz Peña, some five blocks away; it's on the right towards the end of the street.

Down on the riverfront, the **Parque de la Ribera**, north of the Tren de la Costa station, is the place where San Isidro's affluent go to talk politics, drink *mate* and take in the view of the city from the tranquillity of deckchairs under palm trees. Further along the waterfront, where the Camino de la Ribera crosses Planes y Almafuerte, there's a small **ecological reserve** (Mon–Fri 9am–6pm, Sat & Sun 9am–7pm; free; guided visits daily at 5pm in summer and 4pm rest of year), home to 55 bird species.

Practicalities

The barrio is a worthwhile diversion from the Tren de la Costa, which brings you right to the foot of Plaza Mitre. Though surrounded by a shopping centre, the revamped station has somehow managed not to detract too much from San Isidro's charm. As well as the train, buses #60 (bajo) from Constitución, via Callao, and #168 from Boca, go to San Isidro. For the energetic, an excellent cycling path runs alongside the rail tracks north from Barrancas station to San Isidro; it's also popular with in-line skaters. Bikes, skates and other equipment can be rented at various outlets en route. The **tourist office** on the plaza (Mon–Fri 8am–5pm, Sat & Sun 10am–6pm; ⓣ011/4512-3209, ⓦwww.sanisidroturismo.gov.ar) hands out plenty of maps and information on places of interest.

Should you wish to take a longer break from the hustle and bustle, there are some limited **accommodation** options in San Isidro. In front of the cathedral, the smart *Hotel Del Casco*, Av del Libertador 16170 (Ⓣ011/4732-3993, Ⓦwww.hoteldelcasco.com.ar; ❾), is in a late nineteenth-century mansion, which has been renovated but retains much of its original features, including an elegant central patio. Less expensive is the *Posada de San Isidro* (Ⓣ011/4732-1221, Ⓦwww.posadasanisidro.com.ar; ❺), which has modern, slightly characterless rooms with basic cooking facilities three blocks from the main train station at Maipú 66. Good **food**, with the emphasis on fish, can be found upstairs at *La Cartuja*, on the corner of Plaza Mitre, which also boasts a gourmet ice-cream parlour downstairs, or try *Placeres Patagónicas* at the Tren de la Costa complex, which does Patagonian-style *tablas* of smoked boar, trout, cheese and salami as well as a range of teas and *torta galesa*. Further inland, Boulevard Dardo Rocha, which lines the Hipódromo de San Isidro (a huge racecourse – see Ⓦwww.hipodromosanisidro.com.ar for race details), has a renowned selection of upmarket *parrillas* and other, mainly evening, restaurants – *Rosa Negra* at no. 1918 is particularly good.

The Paraná Delta

One of the world's most beautiful and unusual landscapes, the exotic **Paraná Delta** lies just a few kilometres north of Buenos Aires' Avenida General Paz. Constantly changing due to sediment deposits by the Río Paraná, the Delta region is a wonderfully seductive maze of lush, green islands separated by rivers and streams. Lining the banks, traditional houses on stilts peep out from behind screens of subtropical vegetation. The Delta actually begins at the port of Diamante in Entre Ríos Province, some 450km northwest of the city, and its one thousand square kilometres are divided into three administrative sections. By far the most visited area is the first section, most of which lies within an hour and a half's boat trip from the picturesque town of **Tigre**, around 20km northwest of Capital Federal. A favourite weekend destination for Porteños, this section is also home to around three thousand islanders; the area's infrastructure includes petrol stations along the riverbanks, schools, floating shops and even a mobile library, as well as a number of restaurants and hotels. Travel beyond the first section into the wide Río Paraná de las Palmas, however, and you may be forgiven for thinking that you've stumbled onto a tributary of the Amazon. At this point the Delta widens and inhabitants and amenities are much more dispersed.

The Delta can be visited on a day-trip, but it's worth taking it in on an overnight stay. Though for many the Delta's biggest attraction is that it offers the chance to do not much at all, its numerous waterways are also popular with watersports enthusiasts, as well as devotees of more traditional rowing and fishing. **Isla Martín García**, a former penal colony close to the Uruguayan coast some 40km to the northeast of Tigre, is reachable by a regular boat service and makes for an interesting day or overnight trip (see p.188). Lots of water and a warm climate unfortunately mean that mosquitoes are a real problem in and around the Delta, so come prepared.

Tigre and around

TIGRE owes its poetic name to the jaguars – popularly known as *tigres* in Latin America – that inhabited the Delta region until the beginning of the twentieth century. The town sits on an island bounded by the Río Luján, the Río Reconquista and the Río Tigre and was first documented in 1635 under the name of El Pueblo de las Conchas, a small settlement that functioned as a defensive outpost against Portuguese invasions. A favoured summer retreat of the Porteño elite in the late nineteenth and early twentieth centuries, the town's sumptuous mansions and palatial rowing clubs date from this period. Back then social life revolved around events at the Tigre Club, home to Argentina's first casino, and the grand *Tigre Hotel*, whose clientele included Enrico Caruso and the Prince of Wales. The town's decline as a glamorous destination was in part a result of the closure of the casino (shut in 1933 through a law which prohibited casinos in the vicinity of the capital) and in part a result of the growing popularity of Mar del Plata. The *Tigre Hotel* was demolished in 1940, although the elegant Tigre Club still stands, and has now been reinvented as the excellent Museo de Arte Tigre.

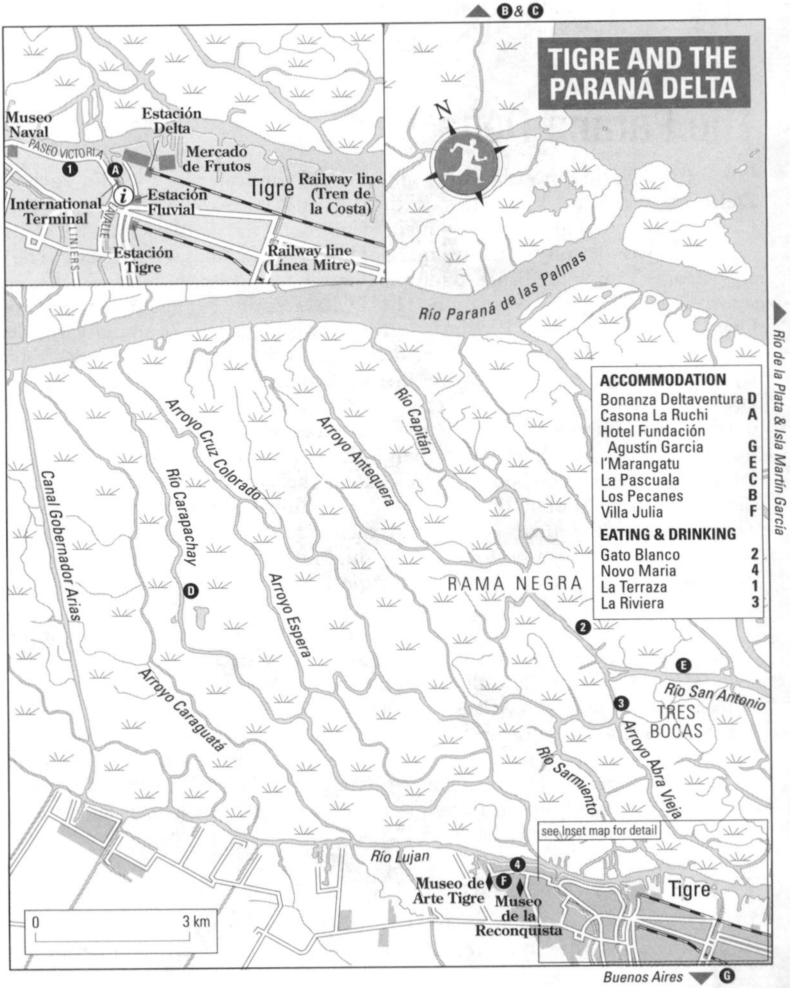

As a departure point for excursions to the Delta and Isla Martín García (see p.188), the town itself is sometimes overlooked by tourists. At first glance, it's a bit of a hotchpotch: a recent upsurge in investment in the area has brought new development; many sites – such as a slightly twee train station and the mega amusement park **Parque de la Costa** – seem to have been built with scant regard for Tigre's distinctive architectural heritage. Don't be put off by initial impressions, however – Tigre offers an appealing mix of faded glamour and day-trip brashness and the bars and restaurants around its refurbished riverside area provide perfect vantage points for an unhurried contemplation of the comings and goings of Delta life.

Arrival and information

Trains depart regularly for Tigre from Retiro station (Línea Mitre); the hour's journey costs $1 and terminates at Tigre's train station on the riverbank, just a block south of the **Estación Fluvial**, where you'll find Tigre's tourist office, a number of kiosks representing assorted hotels and restaurants and various boat companies' ticket offices. For a few pesos more, you can transfer to the Tren de la Costa at Olivos, which drops you at the portals of the Parque de la Costa. There are so many ways of seeing the Delta that it can seem slightly bewildering, and not surprisingly the excellent **tourist office** (daily 9am–5pm; ⓣ011/4512-4498, ⓦwww.tigre.gov.ar) is often busy, especially at weekends. It's worth the wait, though, as they have good maps and can help you find your way through the labyrinth of trips available and make reservations if you do not yet have anything booked.

Accommodation

There are some attractive **accommodation** options both in Tigre and on the Delta itself. However, getting to most Delta destinations requires a bit of forward planning, so you should ring ahead to make a reservation and obtain transport details. One of the most accessible places to stay is the area known as **Tres Bocas**, at the confluence of the Abra Vieja, Capitán and San Antonio rivers, a thirty-minute boat trip from the Estación Fluvial. However, to really appreciate the wild charm of the Delta, you need to head further out to the more isolated places in the second section. In addition to the hotels detailed below, there are plenty of houses and *cabañas* available to rent for weekends or longer stays – see ⓦwww.tigre.gov.ar for a list.

Bonanza Deltaventura ⓣ011/4728-1674, ⓦwww.deltaventura.com. At an isolated spot on the Carapachay River, *Deltaventura* is the place to go for serious peace and quiet, with only three rooms and around 6km worth of trails, where you can trek, bird-watch and canoe. It can also be visited as a day-trip ($95, including lunch). ❻

Casona La Ruchi Lavalle 557, Tigre ⓣ011/4749-2499, ⓦwww.casonalaruchi.com.ar. A fabulous old family house with enormous wood-floored bedrooms, huge balconies, a swimming pool in the garden and exceptionally friendly owners, though only shared bathrooms are available. ❺

Hotel Fundación Agustín García Av Liniers 1547, Tigre ⓣ011/4749-0140, ⓔfundaciongarcia@yahoo.com.ar. Simple town hotel with good views over the river. ❸

I'Marangatu ⓣ011/4728-0752, ⓦwww.i-marangatu.com.ar. Well-known place on the Río San Antonio close to the Tres Bocas part of the Delta, complete with swimming pool, sports pitches and even a heliport. ❼, half-board

La Pascuala ⓣ011/4728-1253, ⓦwww.lapascuala.com. In the second, quieter section on Arroyo Las Canas, these thoroughly luxurious bungalows are the Delta's closest approximation to a jungle lodge. ❽, all-inclusive

Los Pecanes ⓣ011/4728-1932, ⓦwww.hosterialospecanes.com. An appealing, family-run *hostería* out on the Arroyo Felicaria in the second section of the Delta, away from the roar of the jet skis. ❻

Villa Julia Paseo Victoria 800 ⓣ011/4749-0242, ⓦwww.villajulia.com.ar. A 1910

house carefully converted into a luxury hotel, using many of the original floors, fittings and furniture alongside modern comforts such as soft pillows and a/c. The rooms' wide balconies look out over the river, and the hotel has its own elegant restaurant, the *Acacia*. 9

The Town

Tigre lies along the western bank of the Río Luján, one of the Delta's main arteries, and the town is divided in half by the smaller Río Tigre, which runs north–south through its centre. Riverside avenues flank both sides of the Río Tigre, while the broad Paseo Victorica runs along the Río Luján on the western side of town. A good place to begin a tour of the area is around the **Estación Fluvial**, immediately north of the bridge over the Río Tigre. The point of contact between island and mainland life, the Estación bustles with activity, particularly at weekends, when holidaymakers and locals pass their luggage to the crew of waiting boats. Many Porteños have weekend houses on the islands, and a typical Sunday will see them departing en masse, loaded with the ingredients for the obligatory barbecue, and returning in the evening with a large sack of freshly picked oranges.

On the same side of the river as the Estación Fluvial you'll find the **Parque de la Costa**, Vivanco 1509 (summer Tues–Sun 11am–9pm, rest of year Sat & Sun 11am–8pm; $33; ⓣ011/4002-6000), one of Latin America's largest amusement parks, with roller coasters, carousels and arcades. A couple of blocks to the west, alongside the Río Luján, there's a rather more serene attraction, the **Puerto de Frutos** (daily 10am–7pm). A Tigre institution, the Puerto de Frutos – or fruit port – has declined somewhat in importance since the days when fruit cultivation was the region's main source of income, but it is still a working port, and you can watch boats being unloaded with wood, wicker – which grows in abundance in the Delta – and other goods. The Puerto also operates as a craft market, with country-style furniture and wickerwork the chief products.

The most enjoyable part of Tigre to explore on foot is on the western side of the Río Tigre. Once over the bridge, follow riverside Avenida Lavalle north to the confluence of the river with the Río Luján, where Lavalle merges with **Paseo Victorica**, a delightful road with plenty of bars and restaurants. The **Museo Naval**, Paseo Victorica 602 (Mon–Fri 8.30am–5.30pm, Sat & Sun 10.30am–6.30pm; $2), is housed in the old naval workshops and holds exhibits – such as scale models and navigational instruments – relating to general maritime history as well as to Argentine naval history. At the end of Paseo Victorica, you will find the former casino, the Tigre Club, now the **Museo de Arte Tigre** (Wed–Fri 9am–7pm, Sat & Sun noon–7pm; guided tours hourly; $5). A vast turreted and balustraded structure dating from 1900, the building was influenced by grand European hotels of the same period. Inside, the opulent mansion – with its marble staircase, wrought-iron bannisters, gigantic chandeliers and ceiling frescoes – is a setting to rival any of the capital's art museums. The art itself – mostly by Argentines or on Argentine subjects, with many gauchos in evidence – is arranged into themes such as Tigre, the human figure and architecture. The largest salon, previously the ballroom, takes ports as its theme, with works by Quinquela Martín (see p.125) and Oscar Vaz, who uses light to great effect in his busy Boca scenes. In the landscapes room, look out for two gaucho scenes by the wonderful Florencia Molino Campos.

From the end of Victorica, the road curves round, merging with Avenida Liniers, which leads back towards the bridge. The avenue is flanked by fine, if sometimes slightly decaying, examples of the town's grand nineteenth-century mansions, interspersed with equally luxurious modern residences. Almost as

△ Museo de Arte Tigre

impressive as the street's architecture are its giant trees whose powerful roots have turned the narrow pavement into a kind of pedestrian roller coaster. At no.818, you'll find reconstructed colonial **Casa de Goyechea**, housing the **Museo de la Reconquista** (Wed–Sun 10am–6pm; free), surrounded by a lovely verandah and garden. The building was used as a base by General Liniers and his troops before they launched their counter-attack against the British invasions in 1806. The museum has an interesting display of documents and objects relating to the recapture of Buenos Aires, such as a number of British caricatures from the time satirizing the poor performance of British troops. There's also a section devoted to local history, including the rise and fall of the Tigre Club and *Hotel*.

Eating and drinking

There are plenty of **restaurants** in Tigre; the pick of them are along Paseo Victorica. The best options include *La Terraza* at no.135, a classy *parrilla* with an outside seating area both on the pavement and on the first floor, and *Novo Maria* at no. 611, Tigre's most upmarket restaurant, situated in an elegant dining room on the riverbank. *Via Toscana* at no.470, meanwhile, has a lovely Victorian-style garden area from where you can enjoy its ice cream and watch river life. There are lots of cheap and cheerful *parrillas* near the entrance to the Parque de la Costa, while the above-average café at the Estación Fluvial prepares imaginative sandwiches with flavoured mayonnaises for eating in or take-away. On the **Delta** itself, there are a number of eating options, including the rather swanky *Gato Blanco*, on the Río Capitán (Ⓣ011/4728-0390), which does a mean *lenguada a la citron vert* (tongue with green lemon); the Germanic *Alpenhaus* (Ⓣ011/4728-0422) at Rama Negra; and the simple and pretty *La Riviera* (Ⓣ011/4728-0177) just by the jetty at Tres Bocas, one of the Delta's oldest restaurants, with a typical *parrilla* menu. There's not much in the way of **nightlife** in the Delta – which is kind of the point – although some restaurants, including *La Riviera*, double up as a bar if you fancy a contemplative beer or two.

Boat trips and activities

There are myriad ways to go messing about on the river delta; but again you should plan ahead and make reservations when at all possible. Remember the summer months see more options, but also more visitors.

First, there are companies offering **paseos**, or round-trip tours. They generally last around an hour and inevitably don't go far into the Delta, but if you're pressed for time they do at least give a taste of river life. Rather touristy catamarans as well as the better, smaller *lanchas* (launches) run regular *paseos* (11am–5pm; $11–20), some from the Estación Fluvial and some from around the international terminal opposite at Lavalle 520. A second option are the frequent **passenger services**, known as *lanchas colectivas*, run by three companies – Interisleña, Delta and Jilgüero. These are used by Delta residents to go about their daily business – picking up supplies, taking children to school – and go to all points in it. If you have a specific destination in mind, phone the tourist office (not the companies themselves) for the timetable. Most routes are one way, but all three companies also do round trips to the Paraná de las Palmas in the second section, lasting about four hours (Delta 10.30am; Jilgüero 12.30pm; Interisleña 2.15pm and 3.30pm). All cost around $15–20; if possible, avoid the weekends, when the boats are packed and the trips take much longer. If you want to do some **walking**, you will need to take one of the regular services to Rama Negra and/or Tres Bocas ($12 return), where you can disembark and wander for a considerable distance thanks to a public riverside path and wooden footbridges that cross from island to island.

As far as activities are concerned, there are various places around Tigre where you can practise **watersports**. Parana Ecoturismo (Ⓣ011/4797-1143, Ⓦwww.paranaecoturismo.com.ar) does guided tours in **kayaks**, while Puro Remo, Lavalle 945 (Ⓣ011/4731-2924, Ⓦwww.puroremo.com.ar), gives you the choice of kayaks or more old-fashioned rowing boats with wooden oars. Note that you must take a guide or instructor with you for safety reasons and should ring ahead and reserve. There's also a **wake-boarding** school run by South American champion Gabriela Díaz (Ⓣ011/4728-0031, Ⓦwww.wakeschool.com.ar).

Isla Martín García

With its quirky historical buildings, abandoned prison, uninhabited forest and permanent population of only two hundred, **ISLA MARTÍN GARCÍA** seems to have walked off the pages of a children's adventure story. First discovered by Portuguese navigator **Juan de Solís** on his pioneering trip to the Río de la Plata in 1516, the island has a rich history and unexpectedly varied terrain that make it a compelling excursion from Buenos Aires.

The island is best known for being used as a **prison**, principally as the place where Perón was kept before he was president in 1945 by members of the military who were jittery about his popularity. Other presidents incarcerated here include Hipólito Yrigoyen, Marcelo T. de Alvear and Arturo Frondizi. In the winter, which is bleak, the island's former role seems appropriate, but in the summer its green plazas and lush vegetation make it seem more of a tropical retreat than a place for punishment. The heads of state were given their own houses (now commemorated with plaques) and were allowed life's little luxuries – Alvear's flowery English china toilet is preserved in the island's museum (see opposite). Life was harder for common prisoners, especially during colonial times, when they were more or less abandoned to their fate. Though only a few kilometres from the Uruguayan coast, Martín García is separated from the mainland by a channel known as the **Canal del Infierno** (Hell's Channel) whose seven currents would have been a daunting prospect for any prisoner foolhardy enough to try to swim to freedom. In fact, most died of disease or were killed by other inmates within a short time of arriving. The island's penal status dates back to 1765, when the first prisoners were moved here from Buenos Aires' Cabildo, as their habit of shouting obscenities at passing women there made their complete removal from society desirable.

Martín García's location between Uruguay and Buenos Aires has also given it an important **strategic** role historically. Most notably, it was used as a source of supplies by forces loyal to the Spanish Crown in Montevideo in 1814. The loyalists were finally defeated by a naval squadron commanded by William Brown, an Irish-born lieutenant-colonel, who knew the waters around Martín García and led the loyalist boats onto the sand banks surrounding it. In 1886, the island came under the jurisdiction of the Argentine Navy, who remained in control until 1974. A pact signed by the Argentine and Uruguayan governments agreed that, despite being much closer to the Uruguayan coast, Martín García should remain Argentine on the condition that it functioned as a **nature reserve** rather than a military base.

The Island

With a surface area of less than two square kilometres, Martín García can easily be seen in a day or two. The island has an underlying rock formation, giving it a greater height above the river (some 27m) than the low-lying sediment-formed islands of the Delta. Many of Buenos Aires' cobbles came from the old *canteras*, or quarries, in the southwest of the island. Given the island's small size, the terrain is surprisingly varied, ranging from sandy beaches and reedbeds to jungly areas of thick subtropical vegetation. Of the island's equally varied fauna, which includes herons, deer and coypu, the most surprising inhabitants are perhaps the large monitor lizards that amble lazily about, occasionally losing a tail in scraps with local dogs.

Walking up from the dock, the unsealed road leads straight to the sloping, leafy **Plaza Almirante Brown**. Here, you'll find the island's civic centre, a small collection of attractive buildings housing administrative offices and a tiny post office. On the northeastern corner of the square, you'll see the crumbling ruins of a prison building. Along the street to the east of the square, the **Cine Teatro** is a gem of decorative architecture with an original and elaborate facade. Opposite it, the **Museo Histórico** (Tues, Thurs, Sat & Sun 9am–5pm; free), which relates the island's history through displays and in-character testimonials, is housed in an old *pulpería*. Down the street and to the left is the **Casa de Rubén Darío**, where the Nicaraguan poet stayed for a short time when the building functioned as a hospital in the early part of the twentieth century. This was also where Argentine doctor **Luis Agote**, who developed modern blood transfusion techniques just in time for World War I, worked for a while; it now houses a modest ecological exhibition.

A number of unsealed roads and paths lead around the island, which can be explored on foot or by renting one of the bicycles occasionally available near the port. Around the perimeter, **gun batteries**, constructed on President Sarmiento's orders at the beginning of the War of the Triple Alliance (see Contexts, p.791) but never used, overlook the river. On the northern side of the island the so-called **Barrio Chino**, towards the old jetty, is a small collection of abandoned houses that seem to be in danger of being devoured by the surrounding forest. Nothing to do with Asia, the *chinas* were actually area prostitutes visited by sailors in the eighteenth century. Beyond the island's airstrip, which runs north–south across the island, there is a small protected area, off-limits to visitors and inhabited only by the odd hermit. The rules of the reserve limit the population numbers in the rest of the island to two hundred, all of who rent their houses from the state.

Practicalities

Boats and tours to Isla Martín García are operated by Cacciola Turismo (Tues, Thurs, Sat & Sun at 8.30am, return 5pm; journey time 3hr; $50–60, including guided tour; $60–90 for the full tour and lunch). Boats depart from the international terminal at Tigre, Lavalle 520; arrive at least half an hour ahead of departure. Tickets are best bought in advance from their Buenos Aires office at Florida 520, 1st floor (Ⓣ011/4393-6100, Ⓦwww.cacciolaviajes.com). The first part of the journey to the island passes through the Delta region and itself is a highlight of the trip. For most people, a day-trip will probably be enough, but if you want to enjoy the island at a more relaxed pace you can spend the night at the island's **hostería** (packages arranged through Cacciola; $190 per person including return trip and all meals). There's also a campsite where you can pitch a tent, and some basic cabins – you'll need your own sheets and towels (reservations advisable during busy periods; Ⓣ011/4225-6908). There are a couple of simple restaurants on the island and you may be able to buy fish from locals to cook yourself. The bright pink *panadería* just off the plaza dates from 1913 and is famous for its *pan dulce* – for Porteños, a visit to the island isn't complete without taking back brown-paper packages filled with this fruit cake.

Note that Martín García's mosquitoes are possibly even more ferocious than the Delta's and a good repellent is a must, particularly if you venture into the forested region around the Barrio Chino.

Into Uruguay: Colonia del Sacramento

The historic Uruguayan town of **COLONIA DEL SACRAMENTO** feels a universe apart from the hustle and bustle of Buenos Aires, but it's only a short boat ride away across the Río de la Plata, and is a popular Porteño day-trip or weekend destination. A visit here offers an introduction, albeit fairly atypical, to Argentina's small neighbour, along with an enticing blend of colonial history, museums and a laid-back ambience. The colonial legacy is not wholly Spanish, for it was the Portuguese Manoel Lobo who founded Nova Colonia do Sacramento in 1680. Although officially ceded to Spain in 1750, its Portuguese settlers resisted the transfer of power and the Spanish Viceroyalty took possession only in 1777, destroying part of the town in the process and leaving some overgrown ruins as testimony. Meanwhile, Colonia was established as a smuggling centre, exploited mainly by the British, while the Spanish were busy building up Buenos Aires. A stop was put to this when Uruguay was created in 1828 as a buffer state between Argentina and Brazil.

Colonia enjoys a superb location 180km west of Montevideo, perched on a promontory jutting into the great expanse of the Río de la Plata opposite Buenos Aires. The warm light reflects off the bronze water, especially at dusk, further enhancing the town's remarkable beauty. While its detractors complain that Colonia has been over-restored or that this once sleepy old town is now a playground for wealthy Porteños, it has in fact managed to cling to its charisma thanks to the sheer quality of its architecture, both old and modern. With its immaculate yet luxuriant parks and gardens, quiet cobbled streets and miles of beaches nearby, Colonia is a relaxing and well-tended place, without being sterile. Although fewer and further between these days, and nothing like as numerous as in, say, Havana, well-preserved vintage automobiles are still a common sight around the town's streets; you will also witness the local addiction to *mate*, and it is not infrequent to see a whole family perched on a motor-scooter, each member clutching a thermos flask and other *mate* paraphernalia. Shopping is definitely an interesting activity – the historic town is packed with a huge array of shops and galleries selling everything from leather *mate* gourds to oil paintings, via woollens and leather goods, but prices often reflect the area's upmarket nature. Finally, another asset is the warm welcome of the inhabitants: Uruguayans are among Latin America's friendliest peoples.

Arrival and information

With so many people in Buenos Aires wanting to enjoy the attractions of Colonia, **getting there** from the Argentine capital is no problem. The downside is that river crossings, especially in the high-speed catamarans, are not cheap and seats tend to fill up quickly at weekends and during holidays. If you can, go during the week, when there are fewer visitors and hotel rooms are considerably cheaper. Ideally, you should try to go on a **ferry**, as you can go out on deck for some fresh air and views of the Buenos Aires skyline and the Uruguayan coast. However, if you're going as a day-trip it's probably better to plump for the more expensive but considerably faster **catamarans**.

Boats to Colonia depart from the modern **terminal** at Dársena Norte, Av Antártida Argentina 821, at the bottom of Avenida Córdoba, in Buenos Aires – a newer, more efficient terminal, due to be completed by early 2008, was under construction next door at the time of writing. The ferry companies can arrange a hotel transfer for $10; otherwise take a taxi to or from the rank just outside the terminal buildings. Reaching the terminal on foot involves jay-walking across a rather bewildering skein of busy roads and overgrown rail-tracks in between the ferry terminals and downtown Buenos Aires – not an advisable place to linger, especially after dark. The crossing takes just under an hour on the catamaran or hydrofoil and three hours on the ferry, and a return fare (Dec–March) costs between around $100 and $200, or $70 and $120 respectively, including tax. Crossings may be cheaper in winter, but also much less frequent. Buquebus/Ferrytur (Ⓣ011/4315-6500, Ⓦwww.buquebus.com) is the main company that operates the services and they also have offices at Avenida Córdoba 879 and at Posadas 1452. Their new rivals, Colonia Express (Ⓣ011/431-5100, Ⓦwww.coloniaexpress.com.ar), have their offices at Av Córdoba 753. Book tickets in advance during high season, either directly at the terminal or offices or by phone with a credit card (in which case arrive even earlier at the terminal, see above). Note that the ferry companies often have *paquetes*, which can be good value, comprising ferry trip, city tour and lunch and/or a night in a hotel. When you travel on the high-speed ferries, your luggage has to be checked in, and there's a charge for excess baggage (usually over 30kg). With this and customs to clear, it's sensible to arrive at least half an hour before departure; have your **passport** with you when buying tickets and checking in. And be sure to hold on to the insignificant-looking Uruguayan tourist card, marked "Mercosur", for your return journey: people have been fined when leaving Uruguay if they can't produce one.

There is a national **tourist office** at the port, on the right as you exit, run by the Ministry of Tourism and covering all of Uruguay. It opens during the day when the boats come in and can ply you with maps and various other pamphlets on Colonia and locales further afield. If you want more details on Colonia, the city tourist office is at the corner of General Flores and Rivera

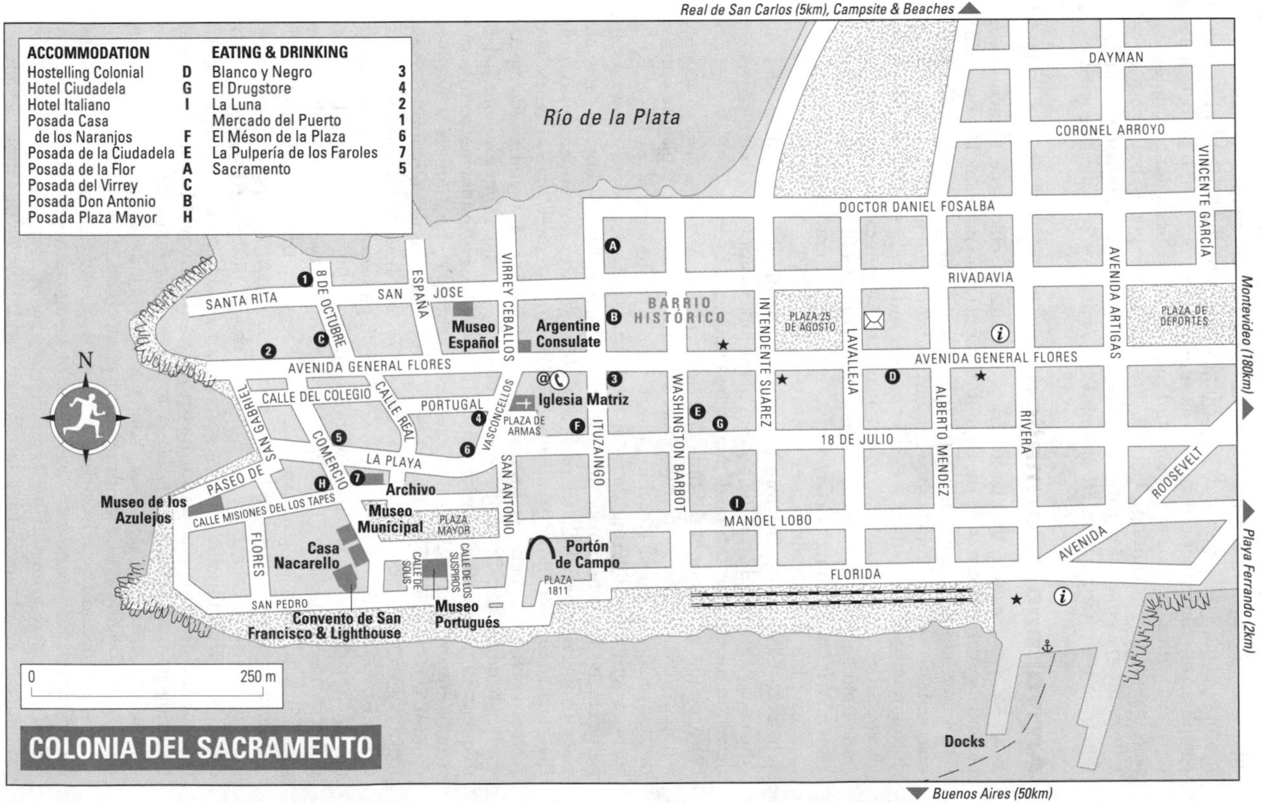
COLONIA DEL SACRAMENTO
ACCOMMODATION
Hostelling Colonial D
Hotel Ciudadela G
Hotel Italiano I
Posada Casa de los Naranjos F
Posada de la Ciudadela E
Posada de la Flor A
Posada del Virrey C
Posada Don Antonio B
Posada Plaza Mayor H
EATING & DRINKING
Blanco y Negro 3
El Drugstore 4
La Luna 2
Mercado del Puerto 1
El Méson de la Plaza 6
La Pulpería de los Faroles 7
Sacramento 5
Real de San Carlos (5km), Campsite & Beaches
Montevideo (180km)
Playa Ferrando (2km)
Buenos Aires (50km)
Río de la Plata
BARRIO HISTÓRICO
DAYMAN
CORONEL ARROYO
VINCENTE GARCÍA
DOCTOR DANIEL FOSALBA
RIVADAVIA
AVENIDA ARTIGAS
PLAZA DE DEPORTES
PLAZA 25 DE AGOSTO
AVENIDA GENERAL FLORES
INTENDENTE SUAREZ
LAVALLEJA
ALBERTO MENDEZ
RIVERA
18 DE JULIO
WASHINGTON BARBOT
ITUZAINGO
MANOEL LOBO
ROOSEVELT
AVENIDA
FLORIDA
VIRREY CEBALLOS
SAN JOSE
ESPAÑA
8 DE OCTUBRE
SANTA RITA
CALLE DEL COLEGIO
CALLE REAL
PORTUGAL
VASCONCELLOS
PLAZA DE ARMAS
SAN ANTONIO
SAN GABRIEL
COMERCIO
LA PLAYA
PASEO DE
CALLE MISIONES DEL LOS TAPES
FLORES
SAN PEDRO
CALLE DE SOLIS
CALLE DE LOS SUSPIROS
PLAZA MAYOR
PLAZA 1811
Museo Español
Argentine Consulate
Iglesia Matriz
Archivo
Museo Municipal
Museo de los Azulejos
Casa Nacarello
Convento de San Francisco & Lighthouse
Museo Portugués
Portón de Campo
Docks
N
0
250 m

(Mon–Fri 8am–7pm, Sat & Sun 10am–6pm; ⓣ598/052-26141, ⓦwww.colonianet.com). Pick up the highly informative booklet *güear*, in Spanish and English; it is packed full with all manner of useful data about the town and its surroundings. While you can easily **change money** on arrival in Colonia, or at the Buquebus terminal in Buenos Aires, you'll really only need Uruguayan pesos to buy stamps or make a telephone call – elsewhere you can pay with Argentine pesos or US dollars. One US dollar was worth around 24 Uruguayan pesos at the time of writing (in other words, the Uruguayan peso is worth on eighth of an Argentine peso). The Uruguayan currency is also depicted by the $ sign (but in this guide as UR$, to avoid confusion), but many prices are quoted and displayed in US dollars or even Argentine pesos.

Accommodation

The devaluation of the Argentine peso made Uruguay, like every other foreign country, relatively expensive for Argentine travellers. Previously the bread and butter of the Uruguayan tourism industry (see box, p.194), they are choosing to save their money and vacation at home, leading Colonia **hotels** to drop their prices in an attempt to woo them back. This means that although budget options are a bit thin on the ground, relative bargains are easier to find than in the past. You should, however, calculate on spending more than you would in Argentina for the same level of comfort. Alternatively, you can pitch your tent at the privately run *Brisas del Plata* **campsite** (ⓣ598/520-2207), 8km north of the town centre. If you can, though, it's worth splashing out for at least one night in a colonial-style hotel with some charm, a reason in itself for coming to Colonia. If rooms run out in the historic centre (consult ⓦwww.hotelesencolonia.com) there are more modern hotels, even a couple belonging to major international chains, in the new town, but these obviously lack the charm and convenience of the old quarter. Most places include breakfast in the price.

Hostelling Colonial General Flores 440 ⓣ598/052-30347, ⓔhostelling_colonial@hotmail.com. With two storeys of rooms looking out onto a courtyard, Colonia's very decent youth hostel resembles an old inn. It charges US$7 a night for a bed, with free Internet and bike rental.

Hotel Ciudadela 18 de Julio 315 ⓣ598/052-21183, ⓔciudadela@internet.com.uy. The rooms are a little sad-looking, especially downstairs, but the bathrooms are spotless, and the owners are friendly and knowledgeable. ④

Hotel Italiano Intendente Suarez and Manuel Lobo ⓣ598/052-22103, ⓦwww.hotelitaliano.com.uy. This laid-back family-run hotel is handily located between the port, the Plaza 25 de Agosto and the historic town. The rooms are small, but there are extras, such as a swimming pool, garage and restaurant. ⑥

Hotel Perla del Plata Washington Barbot 121 ⓣ598/052-25848. Simple, modern, but appealingly bright hotel outside the historic centre. ⑤

Posada Casa de los Naranjos 18 de Julio 219 ⓣ598/052-24630, ⓦwww.posadalosnaranjos.com. Some of the rooms in this converted historic home are rather gloomy, but the rooms overlooking the leafy garden and pool are a delight. ⑥

Posada de la Ciudadela Washington Barbot 164 ⓣ598/052-22683. A bit dog-eared, but with character, this posada is not a bad budget option and has a flexible check-out time. ③

Posada de la Flor Ituzaingó 268 ⓣ598/052-30794. Each room in this tastefully decorated colonial house, located on a quiet street near the waterfront, is named after a flower, but the temptation to overdo the floral theme has been resisted. ⑤

Posada del Virrey España 217 ⓣ598/052-22223, ⓦwww.posadadelvirrey.com. Elegant place with all modern conveniences – a/c, cable TV, Jacuzzis in some rooms, plus great river and bay views and a delicious buffet breakfast. ⑥

Posada Don Antonio Ituzaingó 232 ⓣ598/052-25344, ⓦwww.posadadonantonio.com. Pleasant surroundings, a swimming pool and country-home-style decor make this relatively new posada very good value for money. ⑥

Posada Plaza Mayor Calle del Comercio 111 ⓣ598/052-23193, ⓦwww.posadaplazamayor.com.uy. Housed in a colonial-style building, the *Plaza Mayor* combines atmosphere with comfort, plus sea views from upstairs rooms, and an attractive fountain-cooled patio. It's a favourite with Argentine honeymooners. ⑦–⑧

The Town

It's not difficult to find your way around Colonia's **Barrio Histórico**, confined to the far western end of the headland and bounded by the Río de la Plata on three sides. It is best seen early in the morning, before the day-trippers arrive, or at dusk, especially when there's a good sunset (arm yourself with mosquito repellent, however). By opting for aimless wandering around the roughly cobbled streets, you'll get different perspectives of the old town, with its well-restored colonial and Neocolonial buildings, mostly clustered around the lush Plaza Mayor. Providing an interesting contrast, sleek-lined modern villas, many of them weekend retreats for rich Porteños, have been harmoniously slotted into vacant plots of land, where colonial houses had been allowed to collapse.

A brief overview of Uruguay

A piece of land smaller than Buenos Aires province, **Uruguay** inevitably lives in the shadow of Argentina. Though it shares a longer land border with Brazil (985 km) than it does with Argentina (579 km), there's no doubt that culturally, historically and linguistically it has far more in common with its Río de la Plata neighbour. Uruguayans, however, resent being treated as a mere satellite of Argentina, for they have much that distinguishes them. Most notably, apart from a disastrous dictatorship from 1973 to 1985, Uruguayans have known **democracy** for longer than most Latin American nations, and the country also has some of the region's freest conditions of politics and labour.

That said, the country is very reliant on the other members of the Mercosur community for its trade and has suffered a crushing recession in recent years, in tandem with Argentina's and Brazil's own economic problems. Similarly, **tourism** from neighbouring countries was an important earner – in addition to Colonia and Carmelo on the Río de la Plata border, the coastal area around trendy Punta del Este was very popular with Argentines until devaluation took it out of the financial reach of all except the wealthiest. Uruguay is taking longer to recover from its recession than Argentina, and although it has enjoyed a smoother relationship with the IMF there is much scepticism about this within the country.

Geographically, Uruguay is very flat – its highest point, Cerro Catedral, is just 514 metres above sea level – and is mostly **pampas**, given over to grazing cattle. Its approximately 3.5 million people – over eighty percent of them descendants of European immigrants – live in the capital Montevideo and a host of smaller towns clustered in the south of the country, including Fray Bentos, famous for its meat-packing factory.

Culturally, Uruguayans are most famous for their obsessive drinking of **mate**, even more so than Argentines. Thermoses and gourds are touted around everywhere – keep a lookout for the leather satchels created especially for the purpose. Uruguayans are also known for their distinctive celebration of **carnival**, which features *murgas*, bands of singers in fancy dress. The *murgas'* songs have sharply satirical lyrics, accompanied by *candombe* (®www.candombe.com), a drum-based rhythm that originated in the music brought over by African slaves in the eighteenth century. While the beef-eating gaucho culture and Italian-inflected Spanish familiar from Argentina hold sway over most of Uruguay, the closer you get to the Brazilian border and its more subtropical climate, the more you can detect a Portuguese influence.

Websites with more general information on the country include ®www.uruguaytotal.com and ®www.visit-uruguay.com.

There are seven **museums** in all, none of which takes very long to see, and in any case a multi-entry pass entitling you to visit all of them costs only UR$10, while the climb to the top of the lighthouse for a bird's-eye view won't break the bank either. Out of town, in either direction, are miles of sandy **beaches**, though the best one is 2km east at Playa Ferrando. Along the sweeping bay to the north of Colonia, 5km away, is the white-elephant curiosity of **Real de San Carlos**, a dilapidated tourist complex built at the beginning of the twentieth century.

Barrio Histórico

The best approach to the **Barrio Histórico** from the port and the nineteenth-century "new" town – focused on Plaza 25 de Agosto – is via Calle Manoel Lobo, which steers you through the ornately carved **Portón de Campo**, the only remaining colonial gateway in the fortified walls, rebuilt in the 1960s. Just beyond lies the **Plaza Mayor**, the heart of the Barrio Histórico, which effectively doubles as a botanical garden: its age-old fig trees, palms and cycads, draped with jasmine and bougainvillea, are enjoyed by birds and humans alike. Since Colonia started out as a Portuguese settlement, it's logical to begin with the **Museo Portugués** (daily 11am–4.45pm), housed in an early eighteenth-century house on the southern side of the square, at the corner of Calle de los Suspiros ("Street of Sighs") – one of Colonia's most photographed streets. Inside the museum an early colonial ambience has been recreated, with a modest display of domestic items, clothes and jewellery from Manoel Lobo's times. The town's beginnings are well explained, but in Spanish only. A Colonia landmark, and the first thing you see when approaching by sea, is the pristine white lighthouse, **El Faro** (summer: daily 9am–8pm; winter: daily 12.30–6pm; UR$15), a few metres towards the waterfront from this corner of the plaza, and with views from the top that take in the whole town. The sturdy lighthouse somehow looks as if it is shored up by the ruined walls of the late seventeenth-century **Convento de San Francisco**, never rebuilt after the Spanish bombardments in the early eighteenth century.

The two well-restored stucco-facaded colonial buildings on the west side of the plaza are the **Casa Nacarello**, on the corner of San Francisco (daily 11am–4.45pm), which transports you to seventeenth-century Portugal, complete with a rustic kitchen, four-poster bed and garlic-strings, and the **Museo Municipal** (daily 11am–4.45pm), adjoining it to the north and home to an eclectic collection ranging from dinosaur remains to an array of fancy lace fans once used by Colonia's society ladies. In the northwest corner of the plaza is the flinty facade of the **Archivo Regional** (Mon–Fri 11am–4.45pm), with a small but informative collection of maps and parchments. A discreetly restored colonial building at the far western end of Calle Misiones de los Tapes houses the **Museo de los Azulejos** (daily 11am–4.45pm). *Azulejos*, decorative glazed wall-tiles inspired by Moorish designs, are incorporated into Colonia's street signs and some of its facades; the museum's small collection comprises varied and colourful samples of different styles.

From the eastern end of the Plaza Mayor, Calle San Antonio leads to the **Plaza de Armas** (or Plaza Manoel Lobo), dominated to the north by the gleaming white mass of the **Iglesia Matriz**, which dates from 1680 and is Uruguay's oldest church. Faithfully restored to the original design – it was severely damaged by an explosion in 1823, when gunpowder stored inside by the occupying Brazilian army went off – its immaculate facade and interior are stark but elegant. The whitewashed, blue-lit nave and arched aisles are set off by the dark jacaranda wood of the pews and doors and museum pieces of religious art, including a seventeenth-century Portuguese retable simply decorated with scenes of the Crucifixion. Next to the church, in the square, the ruins of the Portuguese Governor's house have been landscaped into a garden, with a walkway and signs explaining the original positions of the rooms. Across Colonia's main artery, Avenida General Flores, 100m northwest of Iglesia Matriz on the corner of Calle de España and Calle San José, is the **Museo Español** (daily 11am–4.45pm). A logical follow-on from the Museo Portugués, it contains a limited collection of furniture, paintings and costumes from the mid-eighteenth century, with detailed panels in Spanish only, explaining Colonia's role in the eighteenth-century rivalry between Portugal and Spain, with the British occasionally throwing a spanner into the works.

Real de San Carlos

The **Real de San Carlos**, 5km to the north of the centre, is all that remains of a once-grandiose entertainment complex named for King Carlos III of Spain and built in the early twentieth century by Nicolas Mihanovic, an Argentine immigrant. It cost him a fortune to construct the racecourse, now overgrown and used as a paddock, a Basque *pelota frontón* (still an impressive building, albeit rusting and crumbling away), a hotel/casino that lost its patrons when Argentina started levying prohibitive taxes on river crossings and a Moorish-looking bullring that became useless when the Uruguayan government banned bullfights only two years after it was built. Though the eerie, abandoned buildings are apparently doomed to remain empty shells, the high quality of their original architecture makes them worth seeing.

To get there, it's a pleasant stroll along the waterfront, or rent a bike from one of the myriad of bike-rental places just outside the ferry terminal. Alternatively take one of the COTUC or ABC buses that leave from Avenida General Flores every fifteen minutes (UR$12).

The beaches

Another of Colonia's assets is its set of long sandy **beaches**, fringed with eucalyptus and pines. Ignore the water's unappealing muddy colour; it's perfectly clean and safe on this side of the estuary. From the Muelle Viejo, a rickety jetty at the end of Calle de España, you can sometimes charter boats to the furthest beaches at the other side of the 10km arc of coastline that sweeps to the north. Some of these beaches are deserted during the week and remain quiet at weekends and, on the way, you can take a closer look at the wooded islets out in the estuary. Alternatively, take the COTUC Real de San Carlos bus that returns along the waterfront, stopping at one of the popular beaches, such as Playa Oreja de Negro, which has toilets, restaurants and kiosks. The best bathing areas within easy reach of Colonia are at Playa Ferrando, in a wooded setting 2km beyond the ferry port to the east; *Alagua*, right on the beachfront, serves ice-cold beers and very decent food.

Eating and drinking

Colonia is all very low-key, so while the restaurants and bars are fine, there's not much to do later in the evening. The **food** is mostly traditional Uruguayan fare: *parrilladas*, pasta or pizza – the same familiar trio you find in Argentina. That said, more adventurous new places are cropping up all the time, and often a good atmosphere, with live music, makes up for the unimaginative cuisine.

Blanco y Negro General Flores and Ituzaingó. Stylish wooden interior and live music form the backdrop to a menu of home-made pastas, plus the standard beef dishes.
El Drugstore Vasconcellos 179. Funky decor, smiling waitresses, live music at weekends, combined with fresh food at decent prices – with a view of the Iglesia Matriz thrown in. A couple of surprises on the menu include sushi and glazed chilli chicken.
La Luna General Flores 43. You can enjoy a great panoramic view over the river from the upstairs terrace while sampling reasonable seafood, such as popular *rabas* (fried squid rings, traditionally accompanied by champagne).
Mercado del Puerto Santa Rita 40. No-nonsense food – snacks, pasta and steaks – served on a terrace by the harbour, as the name suggests.
El Mesón de la Plaza Vasconcellos 153 ⓣ598/052-24807. The elegance of the decor and the attentive service are backed up by a wide-ranging menu and excellent wine list. A favourite haunt of upwardly mobile Porteños.
La Pulpería de los Faroles Misiones de los Tapes 101. The surroundings are pleasant and the staff friendly at this place, which, in addition to the usual Río de la Plata fare, has some more unusual veggie dishes, such as palm hearts on spinach.
Sacramento Comercio and La Playa Fabulous food in postmodern surroundings – and even a couple of tables outside, weather permitting – includes juicy steak with potatoes and bacon, ultra-fresh salads and unforgettable desserts. Uruguayan wine served by the glass, charming service and live music on Fri and Sat eve. Avoid the fish dishes, though.

Listings

Car rental Multicar, Manoel Lobo 505 ⓣ598/052-24893; Thrifty, General Flores 172, with an office at the port ⓣ598/052-22939.
Consulate Argentina, General Flores 350 ⓣ598/052-22093.
Exchange Cambio Colonia, dockside, and at Flores 401. Cambio Viaggio, Rivera and Florida.
Ferry companies Offices at the port: Buquebus ⓣ598/052-22975 or 23365; Colonia Express ⓣ598/052-29676.
Left luggage At the ferry terminal (7am–9pm); free if you have a ticket to or from Buenos Aires.
Police ⓣ598/052-23347 and 23348.
Post office Lavalleja 226 (Mon–Fri 9am–6pm).
Taxis Plaza 25 de Agosto ⓣ598/052-22920 or 22556.
Telephones *Locutorio*, Flores and Mendez.

Travel details

Buses

Buenos Aires to: Asunción, Paraguay (hourly; 18–22hr); Bahía Blanca (every 2hr; 9hr); Bariloche (7 daily; 21–23hr); Carmen de Patagones (4 daily; 12hr); Catamarca (8 daily; 15hr); Chilecito (2 daily; 20hr); Clorinda (3 daily; 17hr); Comodoro Rivadavia (daily; 26hr); Córdoba (hourly; 11hr); Corrientes (6 daily; 12hr); Florianapolis, Brazil (4 daily; 26hr); Formosa (5 daily; 14–15hr); Jujuy (hourly; 22hr); La Rioja (4 daily; 17hr); Las Grutas (3 daily; 14–15hr); Lima, Peru (2 weekly; 72hr); Mar del Plata (hourly; 7hr); Mendoza (hourly; 17hr); Merlo (6 daily; 12hr); Neuquén (4 daily; 15hr); Paraná (8 daily; 7hr); Posadas (8 daily; 13hr); Puerto Iguazú (7 daily; 14hr 30min–19hr); Resistencia (every 2hr; 13hr); Rio de Janeiro, Brazil (daily; 40hr); Rio Gallegos (daily; 36hr); Rosario (every 45min; 4hr); Salta (hourly; 22hr); Santiago de Chile, Chile (daily; 19hr); Santiago del Estero (11 daily; 13hr); San Juan (10 daily; 16hr); San Luis (9 daily; 12hr); San Rafael (4 daily; 13hr); Santa Rosa (every 2hr; 8–10hr); Trelew (daily; 20hr); Tucumán (every 2hr; 15hr); Zapala (3 daily; 17–18hr).

Ferries

Buenos Aires to: Colonia, Uruguay (4–5 daily; 55min–2hr 45min); Montevideo, Uruguay (2 daily; 2hr 35min).

Trains

Buenos Aires to: Bahía Blanca (1 daily; 13hr); La Plata (every 30min; 1hr); Mar del Plata (3 daily; 6hr); Rosario (1 daily; 4hr); Tandil (1 weekly; 6hr).

Flights

Buenos Aires to: Bahía Blanca (2 daily; 1hr);

Bariloche (10 daily; 2hr 20min); Catamarca (1 daily; 2hr 30min); Comodoro Rivadavia (2 daily; 2hr 30min); Córdoba (10 daily; 1hr 15min); Corrientes (1 daily; 1hr 20min); El Calafate (4 daily; 3hr 20min); Formosa (1 daily; 1hr 45min); Jujuy (1 daily; 2hr 10min); La Rioja (1 daily; 3hr); Mar del Plata (3 daily; 1hr 15min); Mendoza (7–9 daily; 1hr 50min); Neuquén (4 daily; 1hr 40min); Posadas (3 daily; 1hr 30min); Puerto Iguazú (7–10 daily; 1hr 50min); Puerto Madryn (1 daily; 2hr); Resistencia (1–2 daily; 1hr 30min); Rio Gallegos (3 daily; 3hr 15min); Rosario (2 daily; 1hr); Salta (4–5 daily; 2hr); San Juan (1–2 daily; 1hr 50min); San Luis (1 daily; 1hr 30min); San Martín de los Andes (1 daily; 2hr 20min); San Rafael (1 daily; 2hr 35min); Santa Fe (2 daily; 1hr); Santa Rosa (2 weekly; 1hr 20min); Santiago del Estero (2 weekly; 1hr 40min); Trelew (2 daily; 2hr); Tucumán (5 daily; 1hr 50min); Ushuaia (6 daily; 3hr 40min).

2

The Atlantic resorts and the Pampas

CHAPTER 2

Highlights

* **Small beach resorts** The small and fashionable resorts of Cariló, Mar de las Pampas and Mar del Sud have an intimate feel as well as quiet sands, pine forests and long walks. See p.214, p.218 & p.228

* **San Antonio de Areco** An attractive riverside pampas town that's a magnet for those interested in gaucho culture and crafts. See p.235

* **Estancias** The fertile pampas are home to many of the country's best-appointed and best-known estancias, easily accessible from Buenos Aires for a taste of country living. See p.239, p.246 & p.259

* **Luján** Home to Argentina's patron saint, with an enormous basilica and thousands of pilgrims that are a testimony to the country's still strong Catholic traditions. See p.240

* **Pulperías** A sprinkling of *pulperías*, the traditional bars-cum-stores that were the hangout of many a gaucho and the scene of many a fight, are still going, albeit more peacefully these days. See p.244

* **Sierra de la Ventana** The flat pampas fold into the craggy Sierra de la Ventana range in the west of the province, an area known for good walking, pretty chalets and delicious *picada* platters. See p.252

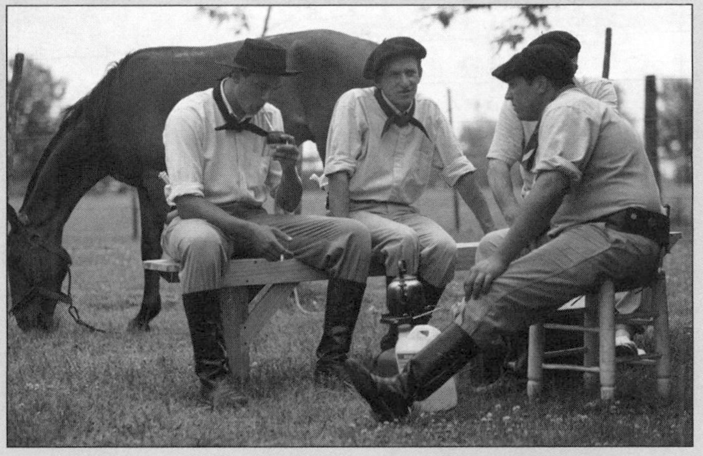

△ Fiesta de la Tradición, San Antonio de Areco

2

The Atlantic resorts and the Pampas

Attractive a city though Buenos Aires is, you may wish to escape the urban mêlée for a few days. The country's big-ticket destinations tend to be in its far corners, but closer to the capital there are plenty of less obvious (and, in the case of foreign tourists, less visited) possibilities that are well worth considering; you should certainly try to make time in your schedule to see something of the famous Pampas, Argentina's heartland. The country's beaches are less renowned, but you will find that there are some thirty resorts fringing the **Atlantic coast** of Buenos Aires Province, stretching from San Clemente in the north to Bahía Blanca, nearly 700km south of the capital. They are generally characterized by wide, sandy beaches edged by dunes, and little else, although Mar del Plata has some interesting historical buildings and is a thriving city in its own right.

The coastal route south starts at **La Plata**, the capital of Buenos Aires Province on the Río de la Plata, which is often taken as a day-trip from Buenos Aires. Another 260km southwest, the river flows out into the cool waters of the Atlantic Ocean, and the **resorts** that line the coast – all popular with local families in the summer – begin. **Pinamar** and **Villa Gesell** are the younger, more upmarket destinations, while **Mar del Plata** is the liveliest, with crowds that pack its beaches by day, then move to the city's numerous clubs and restaurants at night. If you hanker after peace and quiet, there are more isolated spots, though, such as exclusive **Cariló**, forested **Mar de las Pampas** or sleepy **Mar del Sud**.

Moving inland, Buenos Aires Province – covering 307,000 square kilometres south and west of the capital – is dominated by the vast expanse of the **Pampas**, a region almost synonymous with Argentina itself. This is the birthplace of the **gaucho** and source of much of Argentina's wealth – the grain and beef produced by this incredibly fertile farmland constitute the bulk of the country's exports. Though agriculture rather than tourism is the province's main business, one major exception is **San Antonio de Areco**, lying just over 100km west of the capital. A charmingly old-fashioned town of cobbled streets and well-preserved nineteenth-century architecture, it is a must if you're interested in the Pampas' distinctive culture; **Tandil**, further south, is another noted centre of pampas culture, with some great little cafés and museums, and is a worthwhile detour if you're headed to Patagonia overland. The quiet and

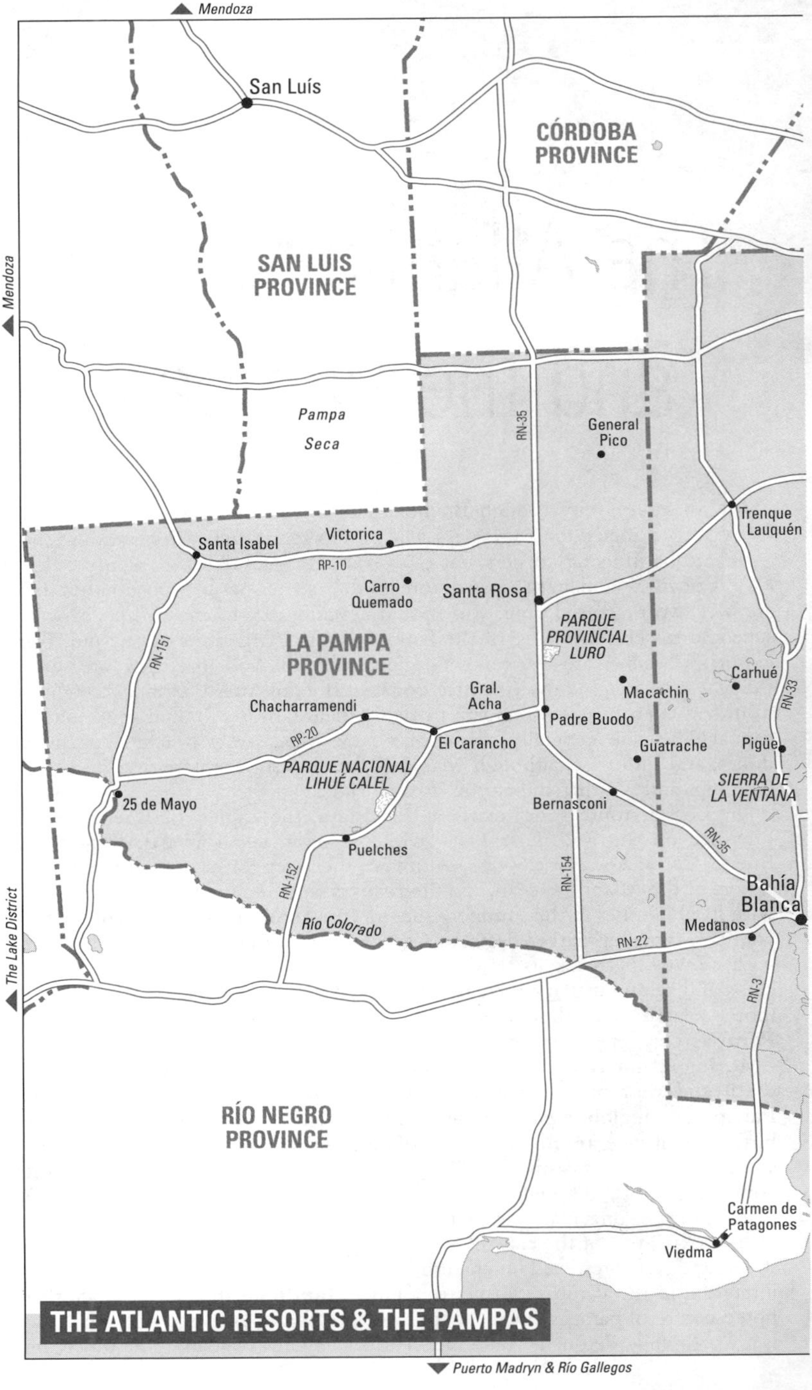
Mendoza
San Luís
CÓRDOBA PROVINCE
SAN LUIS PROVINCE
Mendoza
Pampa Seca
RN-35
General Pico
Trenque Lauquén
Santa Isabel
Victorica
RP-10
Carro Quemado
Santa Rosa
PARQUE PROVINCIAL LURO
LA PAMPA PROVINCE
RN-151
Carhué
Macachin
RN-33
Gral. Acha
Chacharramendi
Padre Buodo
RP-20
El Carancho
Guatrache
Pigüe
PARQUE NACIONAL LIHUÉ CALEL
SIERRA DE LA VENTANA
25 de Mayo
Bernasconi
Puelches
RN-35
RN-154
RN-152
Bahía Blanca
The Lake District
Río Colorado
Medanos
RN-22
RN-3
RÍO NEGRO PROVINCE
Carmen de Patagones
Viedma
THE ATLANTIC RESORTS & THE PAMPAS
Puerto Madryn & Río Gallegos

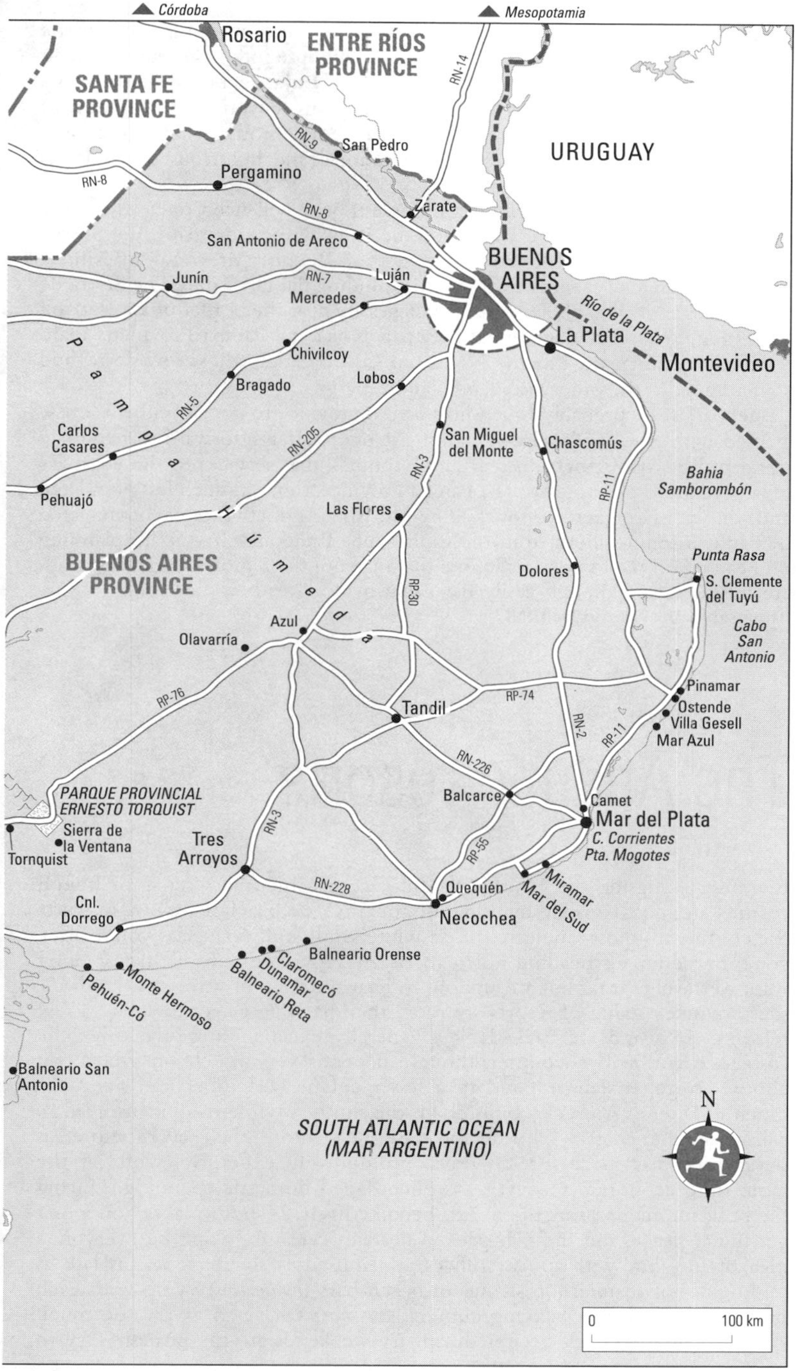
Córdoba
Mesopotamia
Rosario
ENTRE RÍOS PROVINCE
SANTA FE PROVINCE
URUGUAY
RN-14
RN-9
San Pedro
RN-8
Pergamino
RN-8
Zarate
San Antonio de Areco
BUENOS AIRES
Junín
RN-7
Luján
Mercedes
Río de la Plata
La Plata
Montevideo
Chivilcoy
Pampa Húmeda
Bragado
Lobos
RN-5
Carlos Casares
RN-205
San Miguel del Monte
Chascomús
RN-3
RP-11
Bahia Samborombón
Pehuajó
Las Flores
BUENOS AIRES PROVINCE
Dolores
Punta Rasa
S. Clemente del Tuyú
RP-30
Azul
Olavarría
Cabo San Antonio
Pinamar
RP-76
RP-74
Ostende
Tandil
Villa Gesell
RN-2
RP-11
Mar Azul
RN-226
PARQUE PROVINCIAL ERNESTO TORQUIST
Balcarce
Camet
Sierra de la Ventana
Mar del Plata
Tornquist
RN-3
C. Corrientes
Pta. Mogotes
Tres Arroyos
RP-55
Miramar
RN-228
Quequén
Mar del Sud
Cnl. Dorrego
Necochea
Balneario Orense
Claromecó
Dunamar
Balneario Reta
Monte Hermoso
Pehuén-Có
Balneario San Antonio
N
SOUTH ATLANTIC OCEAN (MAR ARGENTINO)
0
100 km

attractive town of **Mercedes** is less visited but has an authentic *pulpería* (a traditional bar-cum-store) that also offers a glimpse into Argentina's gaucho past. On the way to Mercedes, the small city of **Luján** exposes the country's spiritual heart, with a mass display of religious devotion in honour of Argentina's patron saint, the Virgin of Luján. And throughout the province, you'll find some of Argentina's most traditional and luxurious **estancias** – great places to spend a night or two.

To reach anything approaching a mountain, you will need to head for the west of the province, where you'll find the Pampas' most dramatic, the **Sierra de la Ventana** range, 550km southwest of Buenos Aires and offering a welcome change of scenery from the surrounding flat farmlands. The Sierra de la Ventana and its two chocolate-box villages are near the border of **La Pampa Province**, whose modest capital is **Santa Rosa**. La Pampa Province's main tourist attraction is the **Parque Nacional Lihué Calel**, whose low sierras add some drama to the otherwise gentle landscape.

Buenos Aires is probably Argentina's easiest province to get around: it is criss-crossed with roads and railways, making it pretty straightforward to negotiate using **public transport**. Bear in mind, though, that services to the coast are greatly reduced out of season. La Pampa Province, though much less populated and still with large areas untouched by tourism, is nonetheless well connected by routes running south from the capital into Patagonia. If you are planning on heading off the beaten track, note that many of the region's secondary roads are unsealed, and though easily navigable in dry weather, they may become impassable after heavy rainfall.

The Atlantic resorts

Running alongside the South Atlantic Ocean, Argentina's score of **beach resorts** are mostly visited by domestic tourists. The beaches are not, in truth, the continent's most fabulous – if it's white sands and warm seas you're after, you'd be better off heading north to Brazil. However, if you can't or don't want to travel that far but are anxious to hear the thud of waves on the shore, the province's string of resorts are more than passable places to spend a few relaxing days, and are backed by a generally excellent infrastructure. The ambience you will encounter, though, depends very much on when you choose to go. In January, and to a lesser extent December and February, much of Buenos Aires city pulls down the shutters while its citizens head *en masse* for the coast – this is the case now more than ever before, as devaluation has made foreign travel prohibitively expensive, while at the same time economic recovery has encouraged domestic spending. During the peak summer season, the resorts become lively, 24-hour places. You won't get much peace, and the jam-packed beaches certainly won't be everyone's idea of fun, but with tourist offices and museums staying open as late as midnight, not to mention strings of beach bars (*balnearios*) vying with each other to draw in the partying punters, you won't have to worry too much about keeping yourself occupied. January weekends are the busiest – try to avoid setting out during these times, especially if travelling by road, as there is the very real possibility of long tailbacks. If, on the other hand, you visit out of season, you will have less choice of hotels and restaurants and are likely to need thermals more often than swimsuits. The upside is that accommodation is cheaper – often, half the cost that it would be in summer – and, during spring and autumn, the coast can be pleasant and quiet, although you should probably avoid winter unless you like your beaches windblown and desolate.

Heading southeast from the capital on the Buenos Aires–La Plata Autopista, the first major settlement you come to is not strictly speaking a coastal town at all, but the province's tidy capital, **La Plata**, a university town that is situated, like the national capital, on the Río de la Plata estuary. The river finally fans out into the ocean around 150km southwest of Buenos Aires city – directly opposite Uruguay's capital, Montevideo. On the Argentine side, the province concaves into the huge bay, the Bahía Samborombón, and it is at its furthest tip that the Atlantic coast proper starts, with **San Clemente del Tuyú**. The stretch of road between here and Mar del Plata, known as the **Interbalnearia**, is lined with resorts, of which the best are the trendy pair **Pinamar** and **Villa Gesell** and their smaller satellites **Cariló** and **Mar de las Pampas**. Further along the highway, now RP-11, about 400km from the capital, you come to the daddy of all Argentine resorts – **Mar del Plata**. After "Mardel", as the coast bends around to the west, it becomes less frequented. The coastal road ends at **Necochea**, and with it the bulk of Porteño tourism. After this, the rows of small resorts are more down-to-earth, local places, visited mostly by provincial day-trippers. The port city of **Bahía Blanca** no longer has a beach – and nor are you likely to wish to take a dip next to the country's largest petrochemical complex – but it has a charming port area and is an important transport hub, connecting you to destinations further south in Patagonia or west to La Pampa.

La Plata

We have named the new capital after the magnificent river that flows past it, and beneath this stone we deposit – in the hope that they remain eternally buried here – the rivalries, the hatred, the rancour and all the passions that have, for so long, impeded the prosperity of our country.

Dardo Rocha, founder of La Plata, 1882

With the declaration of Buenos Aires as the federal capital in 1880, Buenos Aires Province – already by far the wealthiest and most powerful in the republic – was left without a centre of government. A year later, the province's newly named governor, Dardo Rocha, proposed that a provincial capital be created fifty kilometres east of the federal capital. The new city's layout, based on rationalist concepts and characterized by an absolutely regular numbered street plan sitting within a five-kilometre square, was designed by the French architect Pedro Benoit. An international competition was held to choose designs for the most important public buildings, and the winning architects included Germans and Italians as well as Argentines, a mix of nationalities reflected in the city's impressive civic architecture.

The country's first entirely planned city, **La Plata** was officially founded on November 19, 1882. Electric streetlights were installed in 1884 – the first in Latin America. Unfortunately, much of La Plata's carefully conceived architectural identity was lost during the twentieth century, as anonymous modern constructions replaced many of the city's original buildings. On a brighter note, there have been some successful attempts to preserve what's left – most notably the old train station, now the wonderful setting for the **Pasaje Dardo Rocha** arts centre – and the 1990s saw the final completion of the city's grandiose Neo-Gothic cathedral, over a hundred years after its foundation stone was laid.

La Plata was essentially conceived as an **administrative centre**, and one might argue that it shows: indeed, for many Argentines the city is little more than a place you visit in order to carry out the dreaded and complicated *trámites*, bureaucratic procedures in which Argentine public bodies seem to specialize. In terms of identity, the city suffers somewhat through its proximity to Buenos Aires, whose seemingly endless sprawl now laps at its outskirts, practically turning the city that was created as a counterbalance to the capital into its suburb. But it has a rich cultural life, partly because it is an important **university town**, with three major institutes that attract students from all over the country. La Plata's chief attractions are its pleasant park, the **Paseo del Bosque**, and – even though it is struggling to live up to its self-proclaimed reputation as one of the world's major natural history museums – the **Museo de Ciencias Naturales**. Note that the majority of the city's museums and galleries are closed for the entire month of January.

Arrival and information

Theoretically, the nicest place to arrive in La Plata is at the beautiful *fin-de-siècle* **train station**, on the corner of avenidas 1 and 44, around ten blocks northwest of the town centre; the train itself, however, which leaves from Constitución in the capital, is unfortunately not so beautiful, being dirty and, at times, downright dangerous. The nearby **bus terminal**, on the corner of calles 4 and 42, has frequent, quicker and safer buses to and from the capital (around $6) and most major cities throughout the country. You could also get a *remise* from Buenos Aires city.

La Plata's **tourist office** (Mon–Fri 9am–5pm; ⓣ0221/422-9764, ⓦwww.laplata.gov.ar) is in the Palacio Campodónico on Diagonal 79 between calles 5 and 56; there's also an information centre in the Pasaje Dardo Rocha (daily 10am–5pm; ⓣ0221/427-1535). The staff can provide maps and information on the city, as well as lists of hotels.

Ironically (for a place designed along ultra-rational lines), La Plata can be quite a challenge to navigate. The prevalence of streets cutting across the blocks is very disorienting, and you won't need to walk around for very long to see why it's known as the "**city of diagonals**". On paper, or from the air, its numbered grid layout looks incredibly logical – the city is basically a kind of *mega cuadra*, or block divided into smaller blocks, punctuated at absolutely regular intervals by diagonals and green spaces. In practice, however, the sudden convergence of similar-looking streets can be confusing. Fortunately, the city is small enough that you're unlikely to go too far off track. If you grow tired of walking, there are plenty of reasonably priced taxis available.

Accommodation

La Plata's **hotels** mostly cater to a business clientele and politicians. As a result, they are somewhat overpriced and rather uninspiring. Other than some rather seedy joints near the stations, real budget accommodation is practically non-existent. The *Roga*, Calle 54 no. 334 (ⓣ0221/421-9553, ⓦwww.hotelroga.com.ar; ❺), is reasonably priced, however, and pleasantly located near the Paseo del Bosque, with adequate if rather old-fashioned rooms – the newer rooms are more attractive and cost about $20 more. More upmarket is the central *San Marco*, Calle 54 no. 523 (ⓣ0221/422-9322, ⓦwww.sanmarcohotel.com.ar; ❻), which has comfortable rooms with cable TV and a/c. Offering bigger rooms and apartments is the modern *Argentino*, Calle 46 no. 536 (ⓣ0221/423-4111, ⓦwww.hotelargentino.com; ❻), while La Plata's highest-end hotel is the four-star *Corregidor*, Calle 6 no. 126 (ⓣ0221/425-6800, ⓦwww.hotelcorregidor.com.ar; ❼). Part of the Howard Johnson chain, this has a standard level of comfort and service, although the rooms are perhaps a touch on the gloomy side. Its best feature is its location, right on the Plaza San Martín.

The City

La Plata's major points of interest lie along avenidas 51 and 53. At the very centre of the city, **Plaza Moreno** is dominated by the city's monumental **cathedral**, while ten blocks northeast the **Paseo del Bosque** hosts the city's zoo, planetarium and the **Museo de Ciencias Naturales**. Cultural activity centres around **Plaza San Martín**, halfway between the two; on the eastern side of this plaza, the city's arts centre, the **Pasaje Dardo Rocha**, is notable not only for its contemporary art museum but also for its stunning interior.

Plaza Moreno and around

La Plata's official centre is **Plaza Moreno**, a vast open square covering four blocks. The city's foundation stone was laid in the centre of the square in 1882, together with a time capsule containing documents and medals relating to the founding of the city. Over the years, a handful of theories circulated claiming the buried documents offered proof that La Plata was founded according to a secret Masonic scheme. When the capsule was unearthed on the city's centenary, however, the papers were too damaged to bear out the theory. The contents of the exhumed time capsule can be viewed in the **Museo y Archivo Dardo Rocha** (Mon–Fri 9am–1pm; free; ⓣ0221/421-1689), which is housed in the residence once occupied by La Plata's founder on the western side of the square at Calle 50 no. 933.

On the northern end of the square is the Germanic **municipalidad**, a broad white edifice dominated by a lofty central clock tower and elegant arched stained-glass windows. At the southern end you can't miss the gigantic, slightly forbidding **Catedral de la Inmaculada Concepción** (daily 9am–7.30pm), South America's largest Neo-Gothic church. Designed by Pedro Benoit, it features a pinkish stone facade and steep slate roofs. The foundation stone was laid in 1884 but the cathedral was not finally completed until 1932, with its two principal towers not finished until 1999. If the cathedral doesn't strike you as exactly beautiful, it is certainly tremendously imposing, with its soaring, vertigo-inducing interior punctuated by austere ribbed columns, while its high windows make it surprisingly light and airy. The **museum in the crypt** (same hours; $4) has some excellent photographs documenting the cathedral's construction; the entrance fee also allows you to visit the crypt and a *mirador* (viewpoint), 63 metres high and accessed by a lift, which gives a good view of La Plata's distinctive city plan.

Two blocks northeast of Plaza Moreno is the site where the grand Italianate **Teatro Argentino**, second in national importance after Buenos Aires' Teatro Colón, once stood. Sadly, it was razed to the ground after a suspicious fire in the 1970s and has been rebuilt as an octagonal concrete monolith. However, the structure is still impressively big inside and puts on a decent selection of operas and plays – contact the box office (Tues–Sun 10am–8pm; ⓣ0221/427-1732, ⓦwww.teatroargentino.ic.gba.gov.ar) for details of the current programme.

Plaza San Martín and around

Avenidas 51 and 53 lead from Plaza Moreno to **Plaza San Martín**, the real hub of city life. This square is smaller and less stately than Plaza Moreno, though it too is flanked by government buildings. At the northern end there's the **Casa de Gobierno**, a sturdy Flemish-Renaissance building with a central slate-roofed dome; to the south you'll find the **Palacio de la Legislatura**, designed in the style of the German Renaissance – its grand Neoclassical entrance sitting slightly awkwardly on a more restrained facade. More interesting than these civic edifices, however, is the **Pasaje Dardo Rocha**, on the western side of the square. This elegant pitched-roof building, whose three-storey facade mixes French and Italian influences, was built in 1883 as the city's first train station. After the station moved to its current site, the Pasaje was remodelled and it now functions as an important **cultural centre** comprising a small cinema and various art museums, including the very worthwhile **Museo de Arte Contemporáneo Latinoamericano**, or MACLA (Tues–Fri 10am–8pm, Sat & Sun 2–10pm; free). The galleries are located around a stunning Doric-columned central hall, in which natural light (enhanced by a discreet modern lighting system) filters down through a high glass roof onto a vast sweep of black and white tiled floor, nicely setting off the geometric designs of many of the works on display.

Five blocks west of Plaza San Martín, along Avenida 7, is the circular, cobbled **Plaza Italia**, where a small **crafts fair** is held at weekends.

Paseo del Bosque and around

From Plaza San Martín, Avenida 53 heads north past the Casa de Gobierno. After four blocks you come to Plaza Rivadavia, next to the **Paseo del Bosque**, La Plata's major green space.

Before entering the park, take a small detour along Boulevard 53, a short diagonal road branching off to the right of the plaza. Halfway along the street at no. 320 stands the angular **Casa Curutchet**, the only Le Corbusier-designed residence built in Latin America. Commissioned by local surgeon Pedro Curutchet in 1949, the house is a typical Le Corbusier construction, combining functionality with a playful use of colour and perspective. The building now houses the Colegio de Arquitectos of Buenos Aires Province and is open to visitors (Mon–Fri 10am–2.30pm; ⓣ0221/482-2631; $5).

The park itself covers just over half a square kilometre. It's an attractive open space, dissected by various roads and with a pretty artificial lake. Aside from the famous Museo de Ciencias Naturales (see below), the park's attractions include the city's old-fashioned **zoo** (Tues–Sun 9am–6pm; $4), complete with original enclosures dating from its foundation in 1907. These enclosures are a little small for the larger exotic species like the rhinoceros, but seem more appropriate for smaller native fauna such as the endangered grey fox. Within the zoo, a **botanical garden** offers examples of most of Argentina's most typical trees, such as the ombú, the araucaria (monkey puzzle) and the ceibo. The park is also home to an **astronomical observatory** (guided visits Feb–Mar & Oct–Dec Fri 8.30pm & Sat 8pm, Apr–Sept Fri 8pm & Sat 7pm; $3) and the **Teatro Martín Fierro**, an open-air theatre located just to the west of the lake – schedules of what's showing are available from the Pasaje Dardo Rocha. Passing either side of the park will take you past two **football stadiums** – the homes of Gimnasia y Esgrima and Estudiantes – great rivals, both in the top division. Estudiantes won the Argentine league in December 2006 for the first time in over two decades, with the team built around one-time Manchester United player Juan Sebastián Verón and impressively managed by Diego Simeone, who is best known for his theatrics after being kicked by David Beckham during the 1998 World Cup.

Museo de Ciencias Naturales

The first purpose-built museum in Latin America, and something of a relic in itself, the **Museo de Ciencias Naturales** (Tues–Sun 10am–6pm; $12), housed in the Universidad Nacional de La Plata's natural science faculty, is a real treat for anyone with a fondness for old-fashioned museums. It is gradually being remodelled, and modern audio-visuals make a brief appearance in the first rooms. However, later rooms, such as the six dedicated to zoology, are being preserved to look just as they did when the museum was first opened in 1888, with the embalmed animals exhibited in glass cases with hard-to-read labels.

The museum has 21 rooms, all chronologically ordered, including a **paleontological section** that contains a reproduction of a diplodocus skeleton, and the original skeleton of a neuquensaurus, or titanosaurus, a herbivorous dinosaur common in northern Patagonia towards the end of the Cretaceous Period. Room VI is dedicated to the beginnings of the **Cenozoic Period**, also known as the Age of Mammals, which extends from around 65 million years ago to the

△ Museo de Ciencias Naturales, La Plata

present day. It houses the museum's most important collection: the megafauna, a group of giant herbivorous mammals that evolved in South America at the time when the region was separated from the other continents. The room's striking collection of skeletons includes the creepy gliptodon, forerunner of today's armadillo; the enormous megatherium, largest of the megafauna, which, when standing upright on its powerful two hind legs, would have reached almost double its already impressive six metres; the toxodon, somewhat similar to the hippopotamus, though unrelated; and the camel-like macrauchenia. These megafauna were wiped out around three million years ago after South America reconnected with North America and smaller and more successful fauna such as the sabre-toothed tiger – and, later, humans – arrived. Upstairs, a **Latin American archeology** section showcases items used by the main indigenous groups that once inhabited Argentine territory, from the colourful, feathered headdresses of the Amazonicos to the simple wood and leather articles of Tierra del Fuego's Onas, alongside a large collection of pre-Columbian ceramics from the Peruvian region. The most notable pieces are the **suplicantes** from the Condorhuasi-Alamito culture that thrived in Central Catamarca between about 200 and 500 AD. These fascinating stone sculptures combine animal- and human-like elements with more abstract details and represent fantastic, stylized beings. While their exact use is unknown, it is thought that they had some kind of ceremonial or ritual function – perhaps being used for some kind of funerary practice, since the upturned faces are similar to those of the corpses found in funerary urns. Highly sophisticated and unique to the Condorhuasi, the *suplicantes* are among the most valuable pieces in the museum's collection.

Eating and drinking

La Plata is large and cosmopolitan enough to have a bit of culinary breadth. There are some quite decent **restaurants**, mostly aimed at businessmen, although you'll find local hangouts more convivial – the bulk of these are located around the intersection of calles 10 and 47, such as *La Trattoria*, a restaurant and café that gives great views of the to and fro of La Plata life. The city's best-known and most appealing bar and restaurant is the *Cervecería Modelo*, at calles 5 and 54, whose vast wood-panelled interior is hung with hams; the seemingly endless menu includes everything from hamburgers and liverwurst sandwiches to *bife de chorizo* and seafood. Diagonally opposite, *La Nueva Alternativa* is a smart *parrilla*, set up as an alternative to the *Modelo* (hence the name). For something a bit different, head to *Zoco*, a great little restaurant bar that does delicious Arab food and drinks on Diagonal 74 between 49 and 50. The menu includes good vegetarian options, such as falafel and Lebanese vegetables.

Listings

Exchange Banco de Galicia, Av 7 no. 875.
Hospital Hospital Italiano, Av 51 between calles 29 and 30.
Internet access There is a *locutorio* in the bus terminal with Internet and Wi-Fi.
Laundry Marva, Av 7 no. 1239.
Post office At the corner of calles 4 and 51.

The Interbalnearia

The busiest section of the Atlantic coast lies between **San Clemente del Tuyú**, 260km southeast of La Plata, and Mar del Plata, another 200km or so south. The many resorts in this section are connected by RP-11, or the **Interbalnearia**. The route from La Plata runs southeast along RP-36, which takes you through flat pampas landscape, dotted with cows and divided at intervals by tree-lined drives leading to estancias. Tall metal wind pumps, which extract water from beneath the surface of the land, inject a little drama into the scene, while giant cardoon thistles – a desiccated brown in summer – sprout in clusters like outsize bouquets. The RP-36 joins up with RP-11 around 90km southeast of La Plata; RP-11 then continues due south for another 100km before swinging east to San Clemente and then south, hugging the coast. This first stretch of rather drab, flat resorts has little to offer, other than in the environs of San Clemente itself, where you'll find the important natural reserves of the **Bahía Samborombón** and **Campos del Tuyú**. As you hit **Pinamar** and **Villa Gesell**, where sand dunes predominate, you will encounter Argentina's most exclusive and in many ways most attractive beach destinations, now growing fast and encompassing several smaller places on their outskirts.

San Clemente del Tuyú and around

The sudden and somewhat incongruous appearance of tower blocks on the otherwise bare horizon of the Pampas marks the site of **SAN CLEMENTE DEL TUYÚ**. Argentina's first beach resort – but not its best – is just south of the point at which the Río de la Plata officially ends and the Atlantic Ocean begins. The main reason to come to San Clemente is not to see the town itself, but for its use as a base for visiting the nearby nature reserves of **Bahía Samborombón** and the **Reserva Campos del Tuyú**. It is a family-oriented resort whose pedestrianized main street, Calle 1, is lined with numerous cheap restaurants and amusement arcades where visitors zap away until the early hours. Those with children to entertain are drawn to San Clemente for its **Mundo Marino** (Jan & Feb daily 10am–8pm, March–Dec various days 10am–6pm; ticket office closes 2hr before park; $43; ⓣ02252/430300, ⓦwww.mundomarino.com.ar), South America's largest oceanarium. Ten kilometres from town, it is one of the few oceanariums in the world to have a killer whale. However, its self-proclaimed conservation mission sits uneasily with the circus-like shows that constitute its primary attraction, while the sight of the majestic orca enclosed in a large swimming pool is frankly depressing. Just outside Mundo Marino, San Clemente's charmingly ramshackle **port area** is little more than a modest quay and gaggle of fishing boats. You can try freshly caught grey mullet at any one of the port's congenial local restaurants, most of which have outside seating where you can watch your dinner being cooked on the barbecue.

Practicalities

San Clemente's **bus terminal** is on Avenida Naval, between San Martín and Calle 25, eight blocks west of the centre. You should be able to pick up a map of the town from the terminal's tourist information kiosk and are strongly advised to do so, as San Clemente's web of numbered streets appears to have little logic to it. If you can find it, there is also a small **tourist office** (daily Dec–Feb 9am–9pm, March–Nov 9am–noon & 3–9pm; ⓣ02252/430718) that carries basic maps and info housed in a wooden cabin one block from the beach at the corner of calles 2 and 63.

Most of the town's plentiful **accommodation** options are within easy walking distance of the centre and the beach. One of the best is the friendly *Bellini*, Calle 21 no. 111 (ⓣ02252/421043; ❹), with bright hallways and decent rooms, as well as its own parking. The *Sur*, Calle 3 no. 2194 (ⓣ02252/521137, ⓦwww.hotelsursanclemente.com.ar; ❹), offers comfortable, good-value rooms; the best is at the front, with a large balcony overlooking the street. It seems a little extravagant to go four-star in such a down-to-earth place, though you can do so at the rather floral *Fontainebleau*, which has its own swimming pool and is right on the beachfront at Calle 3 no. 2290 (ⓣ02252/421187, ⓦwww.fontainebleau.com.ar; ❼). There are many cheap pasta, *parrilla* and pizza **restaurants** on Calle 1.

Bahía Samborombón, Termas Marinas and the Reserva Campos del Tuyú

Some 20km northeast of San Clemente is the southern end of the **Bahía Samborombón**, an immense bay bordered by protected wetlands. Visited by over 190 species of migrating birds on their epic journeys between North America and Patagonia, the bay's most easterly point, **Punta Rasa**, is home to an Estación de Investigaciones Biológicas, where birds are ringed and their patterns of migration tracked. An excellent spot for bird-watching, Punta Rasa is easily reached by taxi from town.

To the west of Punta Rasa is **Termas Marinas** (daily 10am–6pm, with some later closings in the summer; $43; ⓦwww.termasmarinas.com.ar). Previously a nature theme park called Bahía Aventura, the park – run by the same outfit responsible for Mundo Marino – now essentially consists of five giant hot tubs. The water is natural, bubbling up from the earth and said to have all kinds of medicinal properties. There are also excellent views over Punta Rasa and the Bahía Samborombón from the top of the Faro San Antonio lighthouse inside the park.

The bay area is home to one of the few remaining groups of pampas deer, whose numbers were severely reduced with the introduction of agriculture in the region, as well as by hunting. A hundred or so of these deer are protected in the **Reserva Campos del Tuyú**, to the west of Termas Marinas. For many years the reserve has been run by the Fundación Vida Silvestre in Buenos Aires (ⓦwww.vidasilvestre.org.ar), and entry has been restricted to those with conservation credentials, but in 2009 Campos del Tuyú will become the province's first national park and should open to the public – contact the tourist office in San Clemente or the provincial headquarters in Buenos Aires for visiting information.

Pinamar and around

PINAMAR, 80km south of San Clemente, takes its name from the surrounding pine forests that were planted amongst dunes by the town's founder, Jorge Bunge, in the 1930s. This attractive setting is now somewhat overwhelmed, however, by the town's mix of high-rise buildings and ostentatious chalet-style constructions. Long the favourite resort of the Porteño elite, in the 1990s the town became almost synonymous with the high-living lifestyle of the Menem era, and the exploits of the politicians and celebrities who holidayed here were staples of the gossip mags. Pinamar fell out of popularity for while following the high-profile murder of a journalist here in 1997 and the economic recession, but it has bounced back with a vengeance, and you now once again stand a good chance of bumping into senators in shorts.

To the south, Pinamar stretches out along the coast, swallowing up the neighbouring resorts of **Ostende**, **Valeria del Mar** and **Cariló**. Generally speaking, the further away you get from the centre, the quieter and more upmarket your surroundings become; these resorts can be easily reached as a day-trip, but they also have their own, interesting accommodation options.

Arrival and information

All long-distance **buses** arrive in Pinamar at the terminal at Jason 2250, several blocks west of the town centre, just off Avenida Bunge. The **train station**, served by Ferrobaires (Ⓣ011/4305-0157), which runs trains from Buenos Aires (Constitución), is a couple of kilometres west of town, a short taxi ride away. Pinamar shares an **airport** with Villa Gesell (see p.215). With glossy brochures advertising golf courses, spas and estate agencies, the **tourist office**, Bunge 654 (Jan & Feb daily 8am–10pm, March–Dec Mon–Sat 8am–8pm, Sun 10am–6pm; Ⓣ02254/491680, Ⓦwww.pinamar.gov.ar), is heavily geared towards Pinamar's wealthy visitors, but it does provide decent maps and guides of the resort.

Accommodation

Hotels in Pinamar and its satellite resorts are plentiful, if generally expensive, with little in the way of decent budget accommodation, particularly in Cariló. As in all resorts, reservations are advisable in high season. There are only a handful of **campsites**: *Quimey Lemú*, just 250m north of the entrance to town along RP-11 (Ⓣ02254/484949, Ⓦwww.quimeylemu.com.ar; ❶), is set in attractive wooded grounds with plenty of facilities. It also has some small cabins for rent (❸). More convenient if you don't have your own transport is the small but well-located *Camping Saint Tropez* (Ⓣ02254/482498, Ⓦwww.sainttropezpinamar.com.ar; ❶), on the border with Ostende at Quintana 138.

Algeciras Hotel Av del Libertador 75 Ⓣ02254/485550, Ⓦwww.algecirashotel.com.ar. A large and rather ugly building houses this luxurious, top-of-the-range place, which has a swimming pool, sauna and nursery. ❽

La Hostería Avuturda and Jacarandá, Cariló Ⓣ02254/570704, Ⓦwww.hosteriacarilo.com.ar. One of only a handful of hotels in upmarket Cariló, *La Hostería* features attractive, wood-panelled rooms with balconies, TV and video, as well as a host of spa facilities. ❽

Hotel Casablanca Av de los Tritones 258 Ⓣ02254/482474, Ⓔhotelcasablanca@telpin.com.ar. A block from the beach, the *Casablanca* offers light, airy rooms with balconies. ❺

Playas Hotel Av Bunge 250 Ⓣ02254/482236, Ⓦwww.playashotel.com.ar. Pinamar's longest-established hotel, attracting an older clientele, with elegant rooms and bar as well as its own swimming pool. ❻

Posada Pecos Odiseo and Silenios ⓣ02254/484386, ⓦwww.posadapecos.com.ar. Charming *hostería*-style place, whose tiled floors and whitewashed walls lend an attractive, slightly rustic feel. ❺

Talara Laurel 29, Cariló ⓣ02254/470304, ⓦwww.talarahotel.com.ar. Friendlier and less plush than most of the Cariló hotels, *Talara* still has spacious, comfortable rooms and services including a sauna, gym, heated pool and beach tent. ❼

Viejo Ostende Biarritz 799, Ostende ⓣ02254/486081, ⓦwww.hotelostende.com.ar. A beautifully preserved reminder of the days when this pioneer resort hosted literary figures such as Argentine authors Adolfo Bioy Casares and Silvina Ocampo as well as Antoine de St-Exupéry. The rooms are quite simple and you do pay rather over the odds for the ambience, but the price includes breakfast and dinner, access to the hotel swimming pool, a beach tent at the *balneario* and a nursery. ❼

The Town

With its burgeoning popularity, Pinamar is no longer quite as exclusive as it once was, although by Argentine standards it remains fairly expensive. Its main street, **Avenida Bunge**, is a wide avenue flanked by restaurants and branches of the same boutiques that make up most of the capital's malls. Bunge runs east to west through the town centre, ending at beachfront Avenida del Mar. Though the town itself has little to detain you, the **beach** is attractive, its pale sands dotted with delicate shells and, to the north and south of the centre, bordered by high dunes. Various companies offer excursions by jeep to the most dramatic section of dunes, where, during the summer, you can try **sandboarding**; ask at the tourist office for details.

Eating, drinking and nightlife

The majority of Pinamar's **restaurants** are around Avenida Bunge and along the seafront. There are a number specializing in freshly caught seafood, such as the bustling *Viejo Lobo* at Avenida del Mar and Bunge. The *Tulumei*, Bunge 64, is a small, friendly and prettily decorated place with a laid-back atmosphere, good music and imaginative seafood dishes. Next door, *Pasta Nostra* does a good-value Italian menu, including three courses and a glass of wine. However, the best of Pinamar's cooking is undoubtedly found at the teahouse and restaurant *Tante*, De las Artes 35 (ⓣ02254/482735). The wide-ranging menu offers elaborate, mostly Germanic, dishes, including some good vegetarian options, and at *merienda* time there's a number of exotic tea blends with which to wash down *Tante*'s exceptionally good cakes. **Nightlife** is mostly centred on a handful of bars along Avenida Bunge and the seafront. One of the most consistently cool, *UFO Point*, on the beachfront at Avenida del Mar and Tobías, is where you'll find the best DJs, while **Paco Bar**, Av de las Artes 156, is a more traditional place, its walls and counters stuffed with years' worth of memorabilia. Pinamar's biggest nightclubs are the *Ku* and *El Alma*, on Quintana and Nuestras Malvinas, which play everything from dance to rock and salsa.

Ostende, Valeria del Mar and Cariló

Pinamar merges seamlessly with **OSTENDE**, **VALERIA DEL MAR** and **CARILÓ**, all to the south. Ostende and Valeria del Mar effectively act as quieter barrios of Pinamar, but Cariló has more of a separate personality, a fact made clear as Calle Bathurst, the paved main street of Valeria del Mar, abruptly turns into Cariló's sandy Calle Divisadero. Cariló jealously guards its reputation as the most exclusive of all Argentina's resorts, with bijou shopping malls and luxury holiday homes set back tastefully in the forest. Development in the village is very tightly controlled, with all hotels (mostly self-catering apartments) being restricted to one defined area. If you can afford it, and don't mind the rather snooty attitude of some of its regulars, Cariló's varied and thick vegetation, quiet, sandy streets and gourmet restaurants can make it a very agreeable destination. Stressed-out professional Porteños come to Cariló to *desenchufarse* (literally, unplug themselves), but if you fancy some activity, **horse-riding** and **polo** lessons are possible at the Estancia Dos Montes (ⓣ02254/480045), just west of the village.

The local Montemar **bus** from the corner of Bunge and Libertador in Pinamar connects all four resorts, or you can simply stroll along the beach, which runs for 10km or so without interruptions past all of them.

Villa Gesell and around

Separated from Cariló by a strictly off-limits nature reserve, **VILLA GESELL** is reached by taking RP-11 a further 20km or so south. After posh Pinamar, the more relaxed feel of Gesell may come as something of a relief. The resort has a carefully cultivated reputation as Argentina's laid-back alternative, although the bohemian vibes of yesteryear have been pretty much developed out of it. Nonetheless, it remains an enjoyable place to sample Argentine beach life.

The town is named after its founder, Carlos Gesell, a mildly eccentric outsider of German descent. In 1931, Gesell bought a stretch of coastal land, largely dominated by still-moving sand dunes. His aim was to get trees to grow in order to provide wood for the family's furniture business. After some experimentation, Gesell managed to stabilize the dunes by planting a mixture of vegetation including tamarisks, acacias and esparto grass. He sold lots, many of which were bought by Germans and Central Europeans escaping World War II. In the 1960s, the small resort became a particular favourite of nature-loving middle-class youngsters, and remains popular today with parties of Argentine youth holidaying away from the family.

Something of the bohemian feel that once distinguished Gesell can still be discerned in the small but fast-growing double resort of **Mar de las Pampas** and **Mar Azul**, 10km down the coast. Although the outskirts of Gesell now nearly lap at Mar de las Pampas' edge, it remains a more tranquil, less developed getaway, albeit one with a buzzing atmosphere in the summer. Beyond Mar Azul lies the **Faro Querandí**, a lighthouse set amongst a reserve of dunes that can be visited as a half-day trip from Villa Gesell.

Arrival and information

The town's main **bus terminal** (ⓣ02255/477253) is some distance west of the centre, at Avenida 3 and Paseo 140; you'll probably want to get a local bus (#504, which will drop you off close to Avenida 3) or taxi to the centre. Villa Gesell's **airport** (ⓣ02255/460418) is 3km south from the turn-off to town on RP-11, with regular flights during the summer from Buenos Aires with Sol (ⓣ0810/444-4765, ⓦwww.sol.com.ar). A shuttle runs from the airport to the town, dropping off at central hotels.

The popularity of Gesell is reflected by the fact that the resort is served by five **tourist offices**. The most central one is at Av 3 no. 820 (daily 8am–midnight; ⓣ02255/478042, ⓦwww.gesell.gov.ar). Other useful ones are at the bus terminal (5am–1pm & 5pm–1am), and further out on the road towards Mar de las Pampas at Av 3 and Paseo 174 (Fri–Sun 10am–5pm). All have good maps and numerous leaflets on current events in the resort.

Accommodation

As with the other coastal resorts, the cost of **accommodation** varies considerably according to the season. Many places cut prices by up to fifty percent out

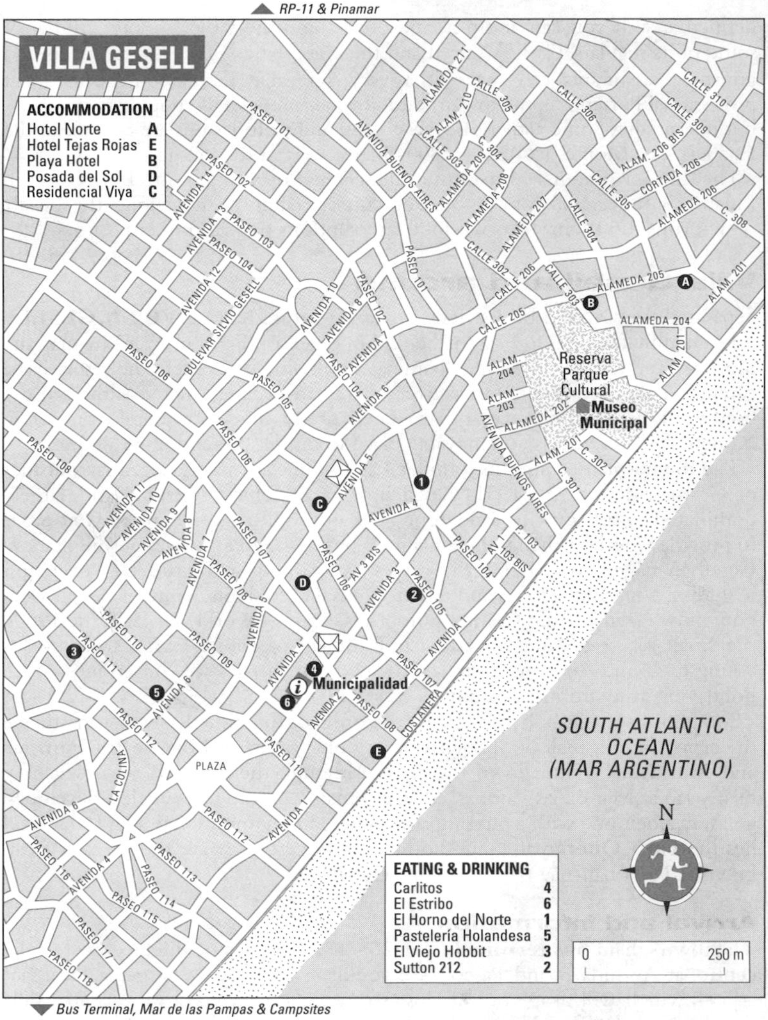

of season; others close altogether. It is easier to find budget accommodation here than it is in Pinamar, with plenty of *hospedajes* on Avenida 5, between paseos 104 and 107. The tourist office holds a complete list of these as well as Villa Gesell's numerous **campsites**, all of which are some distance from the centre. Some of the nicest sites lie among the dunes at the southern end of town: try *Mar Dorado*, Av 3 and Paseo 170 (ⓣ02255/470963, ⓦwww.mardorado.com.ar; ①), or *Monte Bubi*, Av 3 and Paseo 168 (ⓣ02255/470732, ⓔmontebubi@gesell.com.ar; ①).

Hotel Norte Alameda 205 no. 644 ⓣ02255/458041, ⓔnortehotel@gesell.com.ar. Light, airy and comfortable rooms and a wooded garden in a quiet neighbourhood about 1km northeast of the centre. ⑤

Hotel Tejas Rojas Costanera no. 848 ⓣ02255/462565, ⓦwww.hoteltejasrojas.com.ar. This beachfront hotel is in a cool, tiled and spacious building and has a swimming pool. Rooms with sea views cost slightly more. Closed Easter–Oct. ⑦

Criollo culture

The meaning of the word *criollo* – the English-language equivalent is "creole" – changes across the Americas, although fundamentally it refers to a way of life born there, but with European or African roots. In Argentina, *criollo* (pronounced cree-osh-oh) has become a byword for that which is absolutely Argentine – the traditional culture of the countryside, and the antithesis of Buenos Aires' sophisticated elite. Ironically, even the richest Porteño is usually keen to prove that he or she is just a *criollo*, never happier than when sipping a *mate* by the fire.

▲ Traditional parrilla

Criollo cuisine

The distinctive *criollo* **cuisine** has developed over the years, as indigenous ingredients such as maize, beans, peppers and squash have been added to the country's ever-present beef, and adapted by the Spanish and other immigrant groups. This is not food you will find in elegant city restaurants – it's cheap and filling peasant fare, served in humble *pulperías*, stores and cafés. Classics include the **empanada**, a small pasty either baked or fried, and filled with anything at hand, often minced beef or cheese; **humita**, steamed creamed sweet corn, sometimes served in neat parcels made from the husk of corn cobs; and **locro**, a substantial stew based on maize, with onions, beans and meat thrown in. Then, of course, there's the **asado** – the barbecue that takes place year-round, come sunshine or snow (or, as the *criollo* saying would have it, *llueve o truene* – rain or thunder). Usually held on Sunday, the *asado* is a sacrosanct male preserve, the pride of the true host and a chance to show off his *criollo* credentials. For more on *asados*, see p.43.

▼ Locro

Spending time with your mate

Over 90 percent of Argentine households are regular imbibers of **mate**, the unofficial national drink. Bitter and with a sort of grassy aftertaste, it has been used in rituals since pre-Hispanic times, although nowadays it's more of a simple and spontaneous act that brings people together. The word *mate* (often spelled *maté* in English) comes from the Quichoa *mati,* or "vessel", referring to the native calabash from which it's traditionally drunk. In early colonial times the Church and Spanish Crown banned *mate*, but the colonizers went on drinking it regardless and, as often happens with prohibited substances, it became even more popular. For more on *mate* and how to drink it, see the box on pp.392–93.

▲ Tirador

Gaucho gear

Clothing is another important indicator of *criollo* status, rooted in the dress of the gaucho. The basic gaucho uniform included **bombachas** and a **poncho**. The former are flared trousers, buttoned at the bottom (ideal for riding); the latter needs little introduction, although originally it was an all-purpose garment, used for shielding the wearer from wind and rain, as a blanket and, wrapped around the arm, as a shield in knife fights. *Bombachas* are still worn in the pampas, ponchos less so, although you will see them on sale in many places, typically featuring geometric designs. The outfit is finished off with **alpargatas** – canvas and rope-sole shoes, similar to espadrilles. The gaucho's wide **belt** (*tirador*), usually decorated with coins and used as a tool belt, his **knife** (*facón*), his ornate **spurs** and riding **whips** and his **boleadoras** – a sort of lasso finished with heavy balls designed to trip running game – do not have much practical application today, but are used for decorative purposes, as are leather artefacts of all kinds.

Pride before fall: criollo philosophy

A profound attachment to *criollo* culture affects daily life at all levels of Argentine society. It is characterized by a great **pride** – gauchos, despite suffering poverty and discrimination, were never humble, and looked down on many people, including city-dwellers and recent immigrants. Come crisis or catastrophe, *llueve o truene*, this pride is rarely dented and today is sometimes perceived – particularly in other Latin American countries – as arrogance. Other gaucho qualities include a fierce **independence** and a decidedly anti-authoritarian streak, also still in clear evidence today, even from authority figures: Argentine politicians win popular plaudits by thumbing their noses at other countries and international institutions. And of course, Argentina produced the twentieth-century's ultimate rebel in the figure of Che Guevara.

▼ Ornate facón

▲ Gaucho horse skills

A kingdom for a horse

Introduced by the Spanish in the early years of the colonial period, **horses** flourished on the pampas' pastures and quickly became crucial as a means of covering the region's vast distances and for working the developing cattle ranches. The beast was as common and disposable as fallen fruit, to the astonishment of nineteenth-century European travellers, who considered horses high-value goods. They reported that everybody – Porteños included – did practically all tasks on horseback, with even beggars asking for alms from the saddle. Today the horse is not so omnipresent as it once was, but it remains a key feature of *criollo* culture. You'll find evidence of this all over Argentina, from the country's world-class polo ponies, to the popular *hipódromos* (racecourses) that skirt many towns, to the countryside from Salta to Patagonia, where the estancia worker trots home at the end of the day, alone except for his dog, his cattle and his mount.

▼ Gaucho with horses, La Pampa Province

Playa Hotel Alameda 205 and 303 ⓣ02255/458027, ⓦwww.playahotelgesell.com.ar. Villa Gesell's oldest hotel is set in wooded grounds near the Reserva Parque Cultural, far from the bustle of the centre. The pretty whitewashed building has pleasant, simply decorated rooms. Closed April–Oct. ⑥

Posada del Sol Av 4 no. 642 ⓣ02255/462086, ⓦwww.gesell.com.ar/posadadelsol. Definitely the most unusual place in town, this very friendly posada has a mini-zoo in its garden in which parrots, flamingoes and rabbits wander freely. Rooms are small but comfortable and well equipped. Closed April–Oct. ⑤

Residencial Viya Av 5 no. 582 ⓣ02255/462757, ⓦwww.gesell.com.ar/viya. The best of the town's budget places, this charming *residencial* has a pleasant garden and seating area and plain but very well-kept rooms. ⑤

The Resort

Villa Gesell is an amiable resort whose winding streets – many of them unsealed – do their best to defeat the order imposed by a complex system of numbered avenidas (which run parallel to the sea), paseos, calles and alamedas, designed by Gesell to follow the natural course of the land. The town's main street is Avenida 3, the centre of its lively nightlife. At the northern end of town, and entered from Alameda 202, lies the **Reserva Parque Cultural**. Also designed by Gesell, the park's wooded walkways offer welcome shade on hot days, and the dunes which separate it from the beach to the east are particularly good for sunbathing or picnicking. The house used by Gesell has been turned into a small **museum** (daily 10am–8pm; $1) dedicated to this pioneering family, who also own a famous Argentine chain of baby equipment.

If you fancy something a bit livelier, head for one of Villa Gesell's popular **balnearios**, such as *Amarelo*, *Pleno Sol* or *Playa 13 al sur*, which vie with each other every year to become the season's in spot. The *balnearios* are spread out along the length of the beach and lure regulars with the music from their bars. There are also various places to rent **bikes** in town; try Casa Macca, on Avenida Buenos Aires between Paseo 101 and Avenida 5 (ⓣ02255/468013), or Rodados Luis, on Paseo 107 between avenidas 4 and 5 (ⓣ02255/463897).

Gesell has been a magnet for artisans since the 1960s, and there's a good **artisan fair**, selling a mixture of locally made crafts, jewellery and leather goods, every evening from about 8pm on Avenida 3 between paseos 112 and 113, in front of the ACA building. The town has a lively cultural life, with numerous mini-**festivals**; these include the German winter beer festival, the Winterfest, on the third weekend in August, and the Spanish community's Fiesta de la Raza en el Mar, celebrated in mid-October with a procession, concerts and a giant paella the size of a swimming pool.

Eating, drinking and nightlife

For **places to eat**, *El Estribo*, Av 3 and Paseo 109, is the best traditional *parrilla* in town, while *Sutton 212*, Paseo 105 no. 212, is the eatery of the moment – its funky decor gives it the feeling of a laid-back bar, but the kitchen serves up great food, including a very good *lomo* with red wine sauce. You can get pints of home-brew and delicious platters of farmhouse cheeses in the enjoyable faux-Middle Earth surroundings of *El Viejo Hobbit*, on Avenida 8 between paseos 111 and 112, or juicy *empanadas tucumanas* at *El Horno del Norte*, on Avenida 4 at Paseo 104, which bakes them to order in a traditional oven outside. Don't miss Gesell fast-food institution *Carlitos*, Av 3 no. 814 – you'll come across branches of *Carlitos* all over the province, but this one is the original and best. The self-styled "King of Pancakes" makes them with an exhaustive range of savoury and sweet fillings; try *mendicrim y palta* (cream cheese and avocado). There are a number of European-style **teahouses**, such as the lovely *Pastelería Holandesa*, on the corner of Avenida 6 and Paseo 111, where the Dutch owner does *Uitsmijter*, a kind of high tea of eggs, bacon, potatoes and salad, in the evenings.

You'll have no problem finding **nightlife** in Gesell; just follow the crowds to the area around Avenida 3 and paseos 104 and 105, where bars such as *Chauen* and *New Rock* are clustered. And no self-respecting Argentine beach resort would be without its disco complex: Gesell's, called *Pueblo Límite*, is out on Avenida Buenos Aires, opposite the Secretaría de Turismo.

Mar de las Pampas and Mar Azul

The evocatively named **MAR DE LAS PAMPAS**, just south of Villa Gesell, is a haven of tranquil pine forests and pampas grass. The beach is not as deserted as you might expect, since it is easily accessible from Gesell, but inland you can lose yourself along sandy tracks that meander around dunes and woody valleys, where the only sounds comes from birds. There is no real gap between it and **MAR AZUL**, distinguished from its neighbour only by its more regular lanes. The two are currently enjoying a reputation for maintaining the bohemian spirit of Villa Gesell, with blues musicians playing at local pub *Mr Gone* on Mar Azul's main drag, Avenida Mar del Plata, and *Blue Beach*, a *balneario*, cultivating a chilled-out atmosphere to a reggae soundtrack, although the resorts are all a bit too VIP to be truly counterculture.

Accommodation is mostly in small, luxurious *cabaña* outfits distributed amongst the trees, such as *Brugge* (Ⓣ02255/455685) or *Aqui me quedo* (Ⓣ02255/479884). There are dozens more – enquire at Gesell's tourist offices, which can also provide maps of the two resorts. The only hotel is the friendly *Hostería Alamos*, at Av Mar del Plata and Calle 35 in the centre of Mar Azul (Ⓣ02255/479631, Ⓦwww.gesell.com.ar/alamos; ❺); all the rooms are comfortable and have large balconies. There are a couple of **campsites**, the best of which is *Camping del Sur*, on Av Mar del Plata and Calle 47, two blocks from Mar Azul's beach (Ⓣ02255/479502, Ⓦwww.campingdelsur.com.ar; ❶).

The resorts can be reached on foot from Villa Gesell, either along the beach or via Avenida 3, but it's a pretty hefty walk. Alternatively, you could take the local bus, which leaves every half-hour from behind the bus terminal on Avenida 4 and passes through both villages.

Faro Querandí

Thirty kilometres south of Villa Gesell lies the Reserva Dunícola, a wild landscape of shifting dunes and pampas grass, whose soaring centrepiece is the 56-metre high **FARO QUERANDÍ**. An elegant stone staircase spirals to the top of this lighthouse, from where there are stunning views of the surrounding coast. You can visit the Faro on an excursion run by El Ultimo Querandi, on Av 3 and Paseo 110 bis in Gesell (Ⓣ02255/468989); the half-day excursions run daily.

Mar del Plata and around

Big, busy and brash, **MAR DEL PLATA** towers above all other resorts on Argentina's Atlantic coast. Around six million tourists holiday here every year, drawn by its bustling beaches and lively entertainment. If the thought of queuing for a restaurant or seeking an unoccupied scrap of sand makes you shudder, you're better off avoiding the resort in the height of summer, but if you prefer to mix your trips to the beach with a spot of culture, nightlife or shopping, you may find this seaside town has a certain cheeky charm for you.

Despite some haphazard development, Mar del Plata is a solid and attractive city, favoured by the gentle drama of a sweeping coastline and hilly terrain, and while its rather urban beaches may lack the wild charm of less developed strips of sand, they are fun places to hang out – good for people-watching as well as swimming and sunbathing.

Mar del Plata is also the only resort really worth visiting out of season – while the city may breathe a sigh of relief when the last of the tourists leave at the end of the summer, it certainly doesn't close down. The city has around 600,000 inhabitants, a rich cultural life that includes a number of modest but interesting

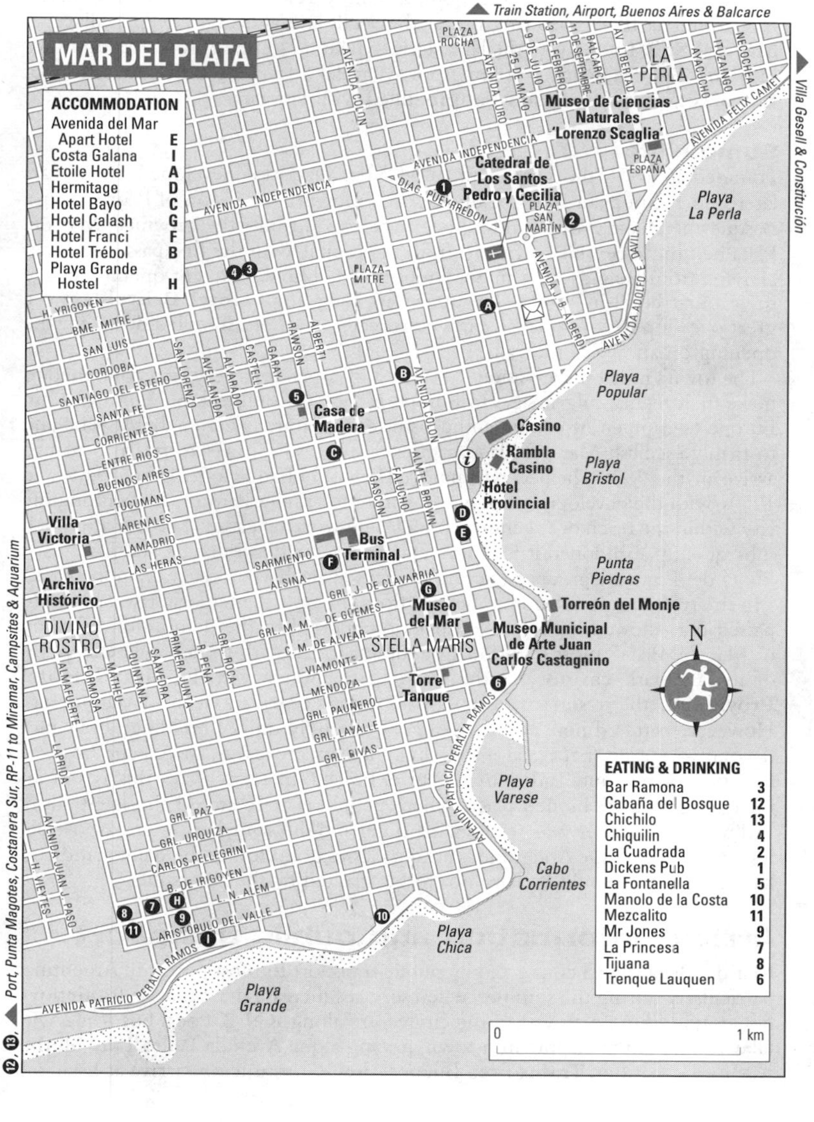

museums and **galleries**, and one of Argentina's most important **ports**, appealing not only for its colourful traditional fishing boats and seafood restaurants, but also for a close encounter with the area's noisy colony of sea lions. Mar del Plata is home to some excellent bars as well, and, once the sun goes down at the height of the summer, a nonstop **nightlife**. Working off all the steaks and *churros* won't be a problem – catering to so many tourists, the city also provides the opportunity to pursue a vast range of sports and other **activities** during the day.

South of Mar del Plata, RP-11 continues through a subdued landscape of wooded reddish-brown cliffs and the creamy aquamarine waters of the Atlantic and arrives, after 40km, at the popular family resort of **Miramar**, with the Interbalnearia finally petering out at the small and alluringly sleepy village of **Mar del Sud**. To the west, the land starts to take on some contours as you move into the Tandilia Range; 60km from Mar del Plata, the chief attraction of **Balcarce** is its large **Museo Fangio**, filled with fast cars.

Some history

Founded in 1874, the settlement of Mar del Plata was developed three years later into a European-style bathing resort, following the vision of Pedro Luro, a Basque merchant. As the railway began to expand into the province, Mar del Plata became accessible to visitors from the capital, with the first passenger train arriving from Buenos Aires in September 1886. The subsequent opening of the town's first hotel in 1888 – the luxurious, long-gone **Hotel Bristol** – was a great occasion for the Buenos Aires elite, many of whom travelled down for the opening on an overnight train.

The town's initial success aside, the richest of Argentina's very rich continued to make their regular pilgrimages to Europe. It took the outbreak of World War I in Europe to dampen Argentine enthusiasm for the journey across the Atlantic and to firmly establish Mar del Plata as an exclusive resort. **Mass tourism** began to arrive in the 1930s, helped by improved roads, but took off in the 1940s and 1950s, with the development of union-run hotels under Perón finally putting the city within the reach of Argentina's middle and working classes. The horrified rich subsequently abandoned it for more chic resorts such as Pinamar and Uruguay's Punta del Este and, groups of young students apart, have never really gone back.

In the rush to reap maximum benefit from the resort's meteoric rise, laws were passed that allowed high-rise construction and led to the demolition of many of Mar del Plata's most traditional buildings. Today, with the notable exception of its landmark **casino** and the building that once was the **Grand Hotel Provincial**, the resort's coastline is dominated by modern developments. However, scattered here and there are wonderfully quirky buildings, built in a decorative – even fantastical – style known as **pintoresco**, an eclectic brew of mostly Norman and Tudor architecture. Indeed, in many ways this is still an intriguingly old-fashioned place, where people eagerly attend the latest show and return, year after year, to the same hotel and the same beach tent. Above all, it's a place where the Argentine working classes go to forget the daily grind and have fun, and it would be hard not to be affected by the atmosphere.

Arrival, information and public transport

Mar del Plata is well connected by public transport to most points in Argentina, particularly during the summer, when services increase dramatically. Its **airport** lies around 8km northwest of the city centre along RN-2. Local bus #542 will take you from the airport into town, passing along Avenida Pedro Luro all the way to the seafront. **Trains** from Buenos Aires (Constitución) arrive at Estación

Norte, to the northwest of the town centre at Luro and Italia, where you can still see the first train that brought passengers to Mar del Plata. Current trains include the relatively stylish Pullman services *El Marplatense* and *Expreso del Atlántico* (both operated by Ferrobaires, ⓣ011/4306-7919), which run from the capital on Fridays, returning on Sundays; services are more frequent during the summer. Various local buses, including the #542, run between the station and the town centre. The **bus terminal** is right in the centre of things at Alberti 1602, and is a good point from which to start looking for reasonably priced accommodation if you haven't booked. If you are **travelling by car** from Buenos Aires, you have a choice of three routes. Mind-numbingly straight RN-2 is the most direct of these, but is also by far the busiest route during the summer. The RP-29 via Balcarce and coastal RP-11/RP-56 are quieter, have lower tolls and meander through more attractive landscape, but add 80km or so to your journey.

The main office for Emtur, Mar del Plata's **tourist information** service, is centrally located on the northwest corner of the old *Hotel Provincial* on the Boulevard Marítimo, on the inland side by Avenida Colón (Mon–Sat 8am–8pm, Sun 10am–5pm; ⓣ0223/495-1777, ⓦwww.mardelplata.gov.ar). They can provide you with a map of the resort and leaflets on things to do; listings also appear in the local *La Capital* newspaper.

Though the majority of Mar del Plata's attractions are within reasonable walking distance of each other, the combination of summer heat and hilly streets will probably make you want to grab a **taxi** or hop on a bus from time to time. Taxis are easy to come by and cheap; **local buses** are efficient and routes are well marked at bus stops. Useful routes include #551, #552 and #553, all of which run between Avenida Constitución – the centre of the city's nightlife – downtown and the port.

Accommodation

It's advisable to book ahead if you plan to stay in Mar del Plata during high season. Most of the **budget accommodation** is to be found around the bus terminal, although you can also find some good deals in La Perla, a pleasant barrio with hilly streets just to the north of the town centre. There are a score of **campsites**, many of them just out of town along the Costanera Sur/RP-11 that heads south to Miramar. The pick of these is the large *Del Faro*, Costanera Sur 400, near the lighthouse and some of the best beaches (ⓣ0223/467-1168, ⓦwww.autocampingdelfaro.com.ar; ❶). The site is well equipped with pool, store, laundry, restaurant and shower blocks, and there are also simple *cabañas* and bungalows (❺). You can reach the Costanera Sur via local bus #511, which passes by the bus and train terminals.

Avenida del Mar Apart Hotel Las Heras 2128 ⓣ0223/451-2125, ⓔreservas@apart-avenidadelmar.com.ar. One of many *apart hotels* (hotels with self-catering apartments) along the seafront. All apartments come kitted with large kitchens, cable TV and eating areas, and some have big balconies with excellent sea views. One, two or three rooms – the latter sleep up to six. ❼–❽

Costa Galana Blvd Marítimo 5725 ⓣ0223/410-5000, ⓦwww.hotelcostagalana.com. Modern luxury hotel overlooking Playa Grande, and with a private tunnel running to the beach. Large, attractively decorated rooms with a/c; all with sea views. ❾

Etoile Hotel Santiago del Estero 1869 ⓣ0223/493-4968, ⓔhoteletoile@hotmail.com. Three-star hotel with five-star pretensions. The comfortable, spacious, if slightly dog-eared rooms are very reasonably priced, the hotel is in a central spot and facilities include a gym and a pool. ❻

Hermitage Hotel Av Colón 1643 ⓣ0223/451-9081, ⓦwww.hermitagehotel.com.ar. A classically elegant hotel, almost lost amid the surrounding modern buildings. Popular with visiting celebrities, the *Hermitage* has suitably luxurious rooms, a pool and spa, and an excellent location. ❽

Hotel Bayo Alberti 2056 ⓣ0223/495-6546. This pretty hotel stands out from its rather dingy neighbours near the bus terminal. Private bathrooms and breakfast are included. Open Jan & Feb only. ④
Hotel Calash Falucho 1355 ⓣ0223/451-6115, ⓔcalash@copetel.com.ar. On a quiet street near the centre, this friendly, mock-Tudor hotel has rambling hallways, a wooden staircase and simple but light and attractive rooms. There's also a café and a shady seating area outside. ⑤
Hotel Franci Sarmiento 2742 ⓣ0223/486-2484. Right by the bus terminal, this is a good-value hotel. Rooms have TV and private bathroom, and there's a 24hr bar. ④
Hotel Trébol Corrientes 2243 ⓣ 0223/495-7251. Centrally located hotel with simple but pleasant rooms, all with private bathrooms (singles half-price) and breakfast included. Open Jan & Feb only. ④
Playa Grande Hostel Quintana 168 ⓣ0223/451-7307, ⓦwww.hostelplayagrande.com.ar. In a large, bright house a couple of blocks from the sea, this is one of Mar del Plata's most reliable hostels. Shared dorms ($35 per person) are decent, and there's an on-site surf school. Private doubles (④) available as well.

The City

Mar del Plata's centre is **Plaza San Martín** but on summer days its true heart lies further southeast in the area surrounding central **Playa Bristol** and the **Rambla Casino**, a pedestrian promenade flanking the grand casino and *Hotel Provincial*. Aside from the beach itself, there's little in the way of sightseeing in the city centre, other than the quietly attractive neighbourhood of **La Perla**. Culture vultures will want to head south to the steep streets of **Loma Stella Maris**, where they'll find the Museo de Arte Juan Carlos Castagnino, or to the quiet residential area of **Divino Rostro**, where the main attractions are the Villa Victoria cultural centre and the Archivo Histórico Municipal. South along the coast, a visit to the **port** makes a fine way to end the day – both for the lively bustle of returning fishermen and for the majestic sea lions who have made their home at the port's southern end.

Plaza San Martín and the microcentro

Plaza San Martín, Mar del Plata's spacious central square, covers four blocks and is bounded by calles San Martín, 25 de Mayo, H. Yrigoyen and San Luis. The square's statue of San Martín, executed by sculptor Luis Perlotti, is slightly unusual in that it shows the general in his old age. At the southern end of the square, the **Catedral de los Santos Pedro y Cecilia** was designed by Pedro Benoit, chief architect of La Plata (see p.205). A fairly unremarkable example of late nineteenth-century Neo-Gothic, the exterior is not particularly eye-catching, but it's worth taking a quick spin round the interior for its beautiful and decorative stained-glass windows.

Immediately south of the square lies the hectic **microcentro**, dominated by pedestrianized Calle San Martín, which becomes so packed on summer evenings that it can be difficult to weave your way through the assembled mass of holidaymakers and street performers. Alternatively, follow Avenida Luro eight blocks northwest of Plaza San Martín to reach **Plaza Rocha**, where there is a small **green fair** (Thurs & Sat 9am–1pm) selling organic vegetables, honey, jams and other goods from local orchards.

La Perla

Heading north from Plaza San Martín takes you through the much quieter neighbourhood of **La Perla**. Just one block from the plaza on Mitre and 9 de Julio, you'll find the lovely *La Cuadrada* café (see p.227), and following Mitre another two blocks will bring you to La Perla **beach**, almost as busy as the central beaches but regarded as slightly more upmarket. Inland is La Perla's main square, the Plaza España, where you can visit the **Museo de Ciencias**

Naturales Lorenzo Scaglia (Mon–Fri 9am–5pm, Sat & Sun 4–8pm; $2), which has a good collection of fossils from all over the world, including Patagonian dinosaurs, as well as a salt- and freshwater aquarium.

Playa Bristol and around

Playa Bristol, Mar del Plata's most famous beach, is nine blocks southeast of Plaza San Martín. Together with neighbouring Playa Popular, just to the north, these are the city's busiest beaches and in high season their blanket coverage of beach tents and shades suggests a strange nomadic settlement. At the centre of the bay formed by these two beaches the **Rambla Casino**'s monumental red

△ Beach, Mar del Plata

and white buildings, the casino and the former *Hotel Provincial*, form one of Argentina's most recognizable cityscapes. Right by them, two stone statues of sea lions flank a flight of steps going down to the beach; for years, it has been *de rigueur* for holidaymakers to have their photo taken beside these well-known sculptures. Follow the bay round to the southeast and you will come to a promontory known as Punta Piedras, crowned by another of the city's landmark buildings, the **Torreón del Monje**. This "monk's tower" is a perfect example of Mar del Plata's peculiar brand of fantasy architecture, which at times makes the city look like a toy village. Built as a folly in 1904 by Ernesto Tornquist, the tower is a little overwhelmed by its neighbours these days, but you can still get a great view of Playa Bristol and the Rambla Casino from its *confitería*.

Loma Stella Maris

One block inland from Playa Bristol, wide Avenida Colón begins to climb to the hill known as **Loma Stella Maris**. The area provides some good views over the city, particularly from the crest of the hill back down the impeccably straight Avenida Colón, while Güemes, which branches off Colón, has some of the city's most upmarket **shopping**. The barrio is also a pleasant place to wander if you're interested in Mar del Plata's *pintoresco* architecture – most of the major examples are in this neighbourhood, including the Villa Magnasco at Brown 1300 and the Villa Tur at Güemes 2342. At Colón 1189, the imposing Villa Ortiz Basualdo, an exuberantly turreted and half-timbered Anglo-Norman mansion, houses the **Museo Municipal de Arte Juan Carlos Castagnino** (Mon & Wed–Fri 2–8pm, Sat & Sun 1–7pm; $2). Local artist Castagnino was born in 1908 and painted colourful Expressionist scenes of Mar del Plata. His work forms the basis of the permanent collection, which has also been boosted in recent years by a growing number of contemporary Argentine works. The museum is also notable for its interesting temporary exhibitions and elegant Art Nouveau interior designed by Belgian Gustave Serrurier-Bovy.

Opposite, the **Museo del Mar**, Colón 1114 (Mon–Thurs 10am–6pm, Fri–Sun 10am–8pm; $8; ⓦwww.museodelmar.org), is a modern complex built around the sea-shell obsession of Benjamin Sisterna, who spent over sixty years amassing 30,000 shells, which the museum claims is one of the world's largest such collections on display. It's certainly impressively varied, spread, along with other attractions, over four floors. The shells are divided geographically, with the most striking section being the examples from the Indopacific; Sisterna's pride was a giant, undulating Tridacna shell from the Philippines, gifted to him after years of pestering its owners. There's also an aquarium, with specimens from Mar del Plata's waters and Patagonian sharks.

Three blocks south, you can climb to the top of the bizarre, castle-like **Torre Tanque**, Falucho 995, an Anglo-Norman water tower, from where there are great views over the city (Mon–Fri 8am–2.45pm; free).

Divino Rostro

Some 3km south of Plaza San Martín is the leafy and well-heeled neighbourhood of **Divino Rostro**. The area is almost exclusively residential, with little in the way of cafés or bars, but is worth the detour to Matheu 1851 to see the **Villa Victoria**, which houses the **Centro Cultural Victoria Ocampo** (Mon & Tues–Sun noon–6pm; $3; ⓣ0223/492-0569). The site of some lively exhibitions and events, the villa is an architectural curiosity in its own right. Built of Norwegian wood, it is a fine example of the prefabricated housing which the English took with them to their colonial outposts. It was shipped to the country in 1911 by the great-aunt of one of Argentina's most famous authors, Victoria

Ocampo. Ocampo inherited the house in the 1930s and it became a kind of cultural retreat, visited by the various Argentine and foreign writers courted by her. In 1973, six years before her death, Ocampo donated the house to UNESCO – who promptly auctioned off most of its furnishings – and in 1981 it was purchased by the municipalidad. The bedroom is now the only room containing original furniture, donated back to the house by a private individual who had bought it at auction. However, the beautiful, airy rooms still hint at the gracious lifestyle enjoyed by Argentina's elite at the beginning of the last century.

The excellent **Archivo Histórico Municipal** (Mon–Fri 8am–5pm, Sat & Sun 2–6pm; $2; ⓣ0223/495-1200), at Lamadrid 3870, one block southeast of Villa Victoria, has plenty of interesting information on Mar del Plata's history. Within the archives are some wonderful photos of the resort's early days when the cognoscenti from Buenos Aires flocked to the *Hotel Bristol*, as well as copies of the strict rules enforced on bathers: single men could be fined or arrested for approaching within thirty metres of women bathers or for using opera glasses. The museum also has a permanent exhibition on Alfonsina Storni (see box below), who committed suicide here in 1938.

To reach the Archivo Histórico and Villa Victoria, take bus #591 from Avenida Luro or the Boulevard Marítimo and get off on the corner of Las Heras and Matheu.

The Port and Costanera Sur

After the Rambla Casino, Mar del Plata's favourite postcard image is the striking deep yellow fishing boats that depart daily from its **port**, about 4km south of the city centre. In the early evening you can watch them returning to the Banquina de los Pescadores full of crates bursting with bass, sole and squid, which are hauled onto the quayside by the fishermen, mostly first- and second-generation Italians. At the far end of the wharf there is a colony of around eight hundred **sea lions** – all males, with their distinctive giant manes and loud bark. These can be observed from an incredibly close (and smelly) distance – only one metre or so – all year round, though the colony is much smaller in summer, as large numbers head for the Uruguayan coast to mate. There are also a number of good **seafood restaurants** around the port, mostly grouped around the Centro Comercial. Various buses head to the area, including #551 and #553, which can be caught along Avenida Luro.

Alfonsina Storni

One of Latin America's most important poets, **Alfonsina Storni** reached prominence in the 1920s when she joined a group of intellectuals known as **La Peña**, which gathered in Buenos Aires' famous *Café Tortoni* and included writers such as Jorge Luis Borges and Roberto Arlt, painters Benito Quinquela Martín and Molina Campos and various musicians. During his stay in the city, she met the great Spanish poet Federico García Lorca, of whom she wrote *Portrait of García Lorca,* one of her best works.

In addition to being a feminist, Storni was concerned with themes relating to nature, the city and death, with many of her poems having a dark, even apocalyptical edge. In 1935, Storni was operated on for cancer and this, plus a subsequent series of suicides of close friends, including writers Horacio Quiroga and Leopoldo Lugones, appears to have precipitated her own descent into depression. In October 1938, Storni booked into a quiet hotel in Mar del Plata, one of her favourite cities, sent a poem entitled *Voy a dormir* (I am going to sleep) to *La Nación* newspaper and, three days later, threw herself into the sea.

Following the coastal road round southeast of the port will take you along the **Costanera Sur**, via an area known as **Punta Magotes** – easy to locate, with the city's red and white striped lighthouse, the Faro de Punta Magotes, at its head. Here you'll find quieter beaches and *balnearios*, including several popular with the surf crowd and a naturist beach, as well as most campsites. It's also home to the **Mar del Plata Aquarium**, Costanera 5600 (Jan & Feb daily 10am–8pm, March daily 10am–7pm, April–Oct Fri–Sun 9.30am–6.30pm, Nov & Dec Mon–Fri 9.30am–7.30pm; $39; ⓣ0223/467-0700, ⓦwww.mdpaquarium.com.ar), reopened in 2006 after several years of closure. There are the inevitable sea lion and dolphin shows, but the aquarium's foundation carries out conservation and educational work to try and ensure it's not just a theme park. If you won't be heading to Patagonia you might take this opportunity to see Magellanic and Emperor penguins. There are also crocs, fish of every stripe and a *balneario* to allow human visitors to take a dip.

Mar del Plata gradually peters out along the Costanera – RP-11 – which leads eventually to Miramar.

Eating, drinking and nightlife

There's a huge number of reasonable **restaurants** in the microcentro, though in high season if you want to avoid standing in line you may prefer to head for the otherwise quiet streets around Castelli and Yrigoyen, southwest of the microcentro, where there are some attractive small bars and restaurants.

For many visitors, Mar del Plata's summer **nightlife** is at least as important as its beaches – and if you want to keep up with the locals, you'll need both stamina and transport. The densest concentration of **bars** is along lively Calle Além, which also has a good selection of late-night restaurants and is swamped by a young crowd, intent on showing off their tan, during the summer. Their next port of call is likely to be Constitución, an enormous avenue 4km north of the town centre, housing numerous **clubs**, none of which really gets going till well after 2am.

Restaurants and cafés

Cabaña del Bosque El Cardenal, Bosque Peralta Ramos ⓣ0223/467-3007. Mar del Plata's most famous café is in a wooden building set in lush grounds within a residential district around 10km south of the city centre. The wildly exotic and rambling interior, decorated with fossils, carved wooden sculptures and stuffed animals, is worth a visit on its own, though the café's fantastic cakes are a pretty enticing attraction, too. Bus #526 gets you there.

Chichilo Centro Comercial Puerto, Local 17. One of a clutch of cheap and excellent seafood restaurants that serve up the fresh catch of the day in the port's Centro Comercial; try local *rabas* (squid rings), *lenguada* (sole) or *langostinos* (shrimp).

Chiquilin Castelli and H. Yrigoyen. Attractive oak-panelled pub with an eclectic menu that gives an inventive twist to standard dishes, such as Russian-style pasta stuffed with beef, as well as offering less common options, such as tacos. There's live music some evenings, too.

La Fontanella Rawson 2302 ⓣ0223/494-0533. Named for its pretty fountain, *La Fontanella* specializes in *pizza a la piedra* as well as fish and pasta.

Manolo de la Costa Castelli 15. Offering good sea views, *Manolo de la Costa* is a Mar del Plata institution that does upmarket fast food such as pizzas and a delicious *brochette mixto* (kebab), but it is for its fabulous range of filled *churros* (fried dough) that it is best known. The sister branch at Rivadavia 2371 is busy, too, and a popular spot for *chocolate con churros* after a hard night's clubbing.

Mezcalito Além 3926. One of Além's resto/bars, which do food as well as drinks – in this case, Mexican, with authentic stuff such as *pollo con mole* (chicken in *mole* sauce) mixed with the usual Tex Mex burritos and fajitas.

Trenque Lauquen Colón 891 ⓣ0223/486-5262. Mar del Plata's most famous restaurant, recently moved to a new, larger location. Good value – this is some of the best meat you're ever likely to eat. Book ahead.

Bars and nightclubs

Bar Ramona Castelli and H. Yrigoyen. A slightly posey but attractive bar, popular with the young and well-to-do.

Chocolate Constitución 4445. Large, glossy club, consistently one of Mar del Plata's most highly rated dance destinations.

La Cuadrada 9 de Julio and Mitre. A café/bar and theatre that's worth a visit for its decor alone. The interior is covered with paintings, sculptures and antiques, and with a basement that is a rabbit warren of tiny rooms filled with wooden tables and stone seats. It's a mesmerizing place to while away an hour over a beer or a cup of their extensive range of teas. The food is also excellent and served with great style.

Dickens Pub Diagonal Pueyrredón 3017. Pub that holds regular jazz evenings; popular with foreign visitors.

Extasis Corrientes 2044. Lively bar in the Constitución area that's the city's most popular for gay residents and visitors. Open Fri & Sat only.

Mr Jones Além, between Matheu and Quintana. One of Além's most popular bars, heaving with bronzed bodies on summer evenings. Next to it is the softer lit, sit-down *Mr Lounge*.

Pinar de Rocha Constitución 5470 ⓣ0223/476-4710. The city's newest big dance club, with three floors, each featuring a different style of music, and a *cena-show* (dinner with show).

La Princesa B. de Irigoyen 3820. Long-running, hip surfer bar and restaurant, with a good range of *milanesas* (both meat and soya), pizzas and salads to accompany your margarita.

Sobremonte Constitución. Constitución's most popular club complex, featuring bars and dance-floors ranging from a mock-Mexican *cantina* to the laid-back Velvet chillout room. The music is generally mainstream dance, although international DJs of the stature of Sasha and Deep Dish have played here.

Tijuana B. de Irigoyen 3966. Alternative hangout to *Mr Jones* around the corner – and in a very similar vein.

Entertainment

Mar del Plata is also well catered for as far as **theatres** and **cinemas** are concerned; most of them are in the downtown area, such as the Teatro Colón, H. Yrigoyen 1665 (ⓣ0223/499-6555), and the Cine Ambassador, Córdoba 1673 (ⓣ0223/495-7271). In March, Mar del Plata hosts a major international **film festival** (ⓦwww.mardelplatafilmfest.com), one of South America's most important, in which movies from around the world compete, with an emphasis on Latin American works. **Live music** concerts are a part of the fabric of summer too, with some popular national acts playing outdoors at the *balnearios*, as well as indoors in the theatres. Regular **folk music shows** take place at the Casa de Folklore, San Juan 2543 (ⓣ0223/472-3955).

In addition, Mar del Plata is the host of a **football** mini-tournament during the summer, in which the country's five major teams – Boca Juniors, River Plate, San Lorenzo, Racing and Independiente – decamp from their Buenos Aires homes to battle it out by the sea. Other sports tournaments are held throughout the season, including everything from backgammon to surfing – the tourist office can provide you with details.

Listings

Airlines Aerolíneas Argentinas, Moreno 2442 (ⓣ0223/496-0101); LADE, Blvd M.P.P. Ramos 2158 (ⓣ0223/493-8211).

Banks and exchange There are many banks on avenidas Independencia, Luro and San Martín. Jonestur, Luro 3185 (Mon–Fri 10am–7pm, Sat 10am–1pm), exchanges currency and travellers' cheques.

Bike rental H. Yrigoyen 2249 ⓣ0223/494-1932.

Hospitals Hospital Interzonal Mar del Plata, Juan B. Justo 6800 ⓣ0223/477-0265.

Laundry Laverap, Falucho 1572.

Post office The main office is at Luro 2460, on the corner of Santiago del Estero, offering all the usual facilities; there are numerous other offices throughout the city.

Taxis Plus Ultra ⓣ0223/492-3766; Tele Taxi ⓣ0223/475-8888.

Travel agents and tour operators You'll find several travel agents in Galería de las Américas at San Martín 2648. Surf school: Paseo Victoria Ocampo ⓣ15/4002072. Paragliding: Arcángel

ⓣ0223/463-1167, suitable for beginners. Horse-riding: Playa Los Lobos, Costanera Sur ⓣ0223/460-5548. Fishing trips are possible from the Banquina de Pescadores in the port (ⓣ0223/489-1612 or 480-1648).

Miramar and Mar del Sud

Heading south from Mar del Plata, the first resort you come to is **MIRAMAR**, 40km further down RP-11. A largely modern town, it sells itself very much as a family-oriented resort and consequently most visitors tend to be those with children in tow. Miramar's beachfront is dominated by some rather grim high-rise buildings and, though it's not a bad place to entertain children for a couple of days, has little really to recommend it. A more interesting choice than Miramar if you want a complete break from the bustle of places like Mar del Plata is tiny **MAR DEL SUD**, a further 16km south. One of Argentina's least-developed beach resorts, Mar del Sud is in many ways one of its most appealing. It is becoming increasing popular with in-the-know Porteños looking for something a little different, but the atmosphere remains tranquil, with a friendly, community feel and the occasional party. Its beaches are far less frequented than those further north and, if you venture a few hundred metres away from the small clutch of beachgoers grouped around the bottom of the grandly named Avenida 100, you won't have much trouble finding a stretch of soft sand to yourself. The town's pleasantly unassuming buildings are dominated by the crumbling faded-pink walls and steeply pitched roof of the ex-**Boulevard Atlantic Hotel**, an elegant, French-influenced construction built in 1886. It's now a wonderfully creepy old building, its once glamorous rooms taken over by doves and scattered with chunks of plaster. Guided visits are possible during the day on request from Eduardo Gambo, who runs the place and is something of a local personality. Eduardo shows scary movies in the evening in the old dining room; however, he sometimes cuts them short to tell the audience the ending himself. If you're lucky, you may even get to see the film set in the hotel in which he himself played the vampire.

Practicalities

Buses to Miramar arrive at different terminals/offices in the town centre – most are along Diagonal Fte de la Plaza, which leads south to Plaza General Alvarado. El Rápido del Sur, which serves Mar del Plata, and Expreso Mar del Sud, for Mar del Sud, leave from Avenida 23 and Calle 34, four blocks northwest of the plaza. There's a helpful **tourist office** (Mon–Fri 7am–midnight, Sat & Sun 8am–midnight; ⓣ02291/420190, ⓦwww.miramar-digital.com.ar) on the northern corner of Plaza General Alvarado, which also covers Mar del Sud. **Accommodation** is easy to find, with a wide choice of places in the streets surrounding Plaza General Alvarado. The seafront is taken up by apartment buildings; the closest hotel to the sea is the *Marina*, Av 9 no. 744 (ⓣ02291/420462, ⓦwww.miramar-digital.com/hotelmarina; ❻), one block back from the beach, which has some attractive rooms with balconies and sea views; these cost a few pesos more than the internal rooms but are worth it. **Eating** options are plentiful, too, with most places again around Plaza General Alvarado and the seafront.

In Mar del Sud, though the main section of the *Boulevard Atlantic* is uninhabitable, there are some slightly musty but well-equipped apartments adjoining the hotel, with a definite Gothic appeal as well as cooking facilities (ⓣ02291/491135; ❸). The only hotel on the seafront itself is the *Hostería Villa del Mar* on the corner of Avenida 100 (ⓣ02291/491141; ❹; closed Feb–Nov), which has small rooms overlooking the sea and a lovely breakfast area with a hearth. *La Posada*, at calles 15 and 98 (ⓣ02291/491274; ④), is two blocks from the beach and has comfortable, simple rooms with shared bath; it's one of the few places open year round. **Campsite** *La Ponderosa*, 400 metres from the beach and to the west of the town centre, on the corner of Avenida La Playa (ⓣ02291/491118), is well equipped, with showers, a restaurant and shops. The town's few **places to eat** are mostly around the bottom of Avenida 100; the best is Croat restaurant *Makarska*, which does goulash as well as a tasty vegetable and ricotta strudel. The *JR Café* is a family-friendly bar that also houses the town's *locutorio*.

Balcarce and the Museo Fangio

Around 60km northwest of Mar del Plata on RN-226, the agricultural town of **BALCARCE**, near the tabletop foothills of the Tandilia Range, does not, at first glance, appear to have much to distinguish it from other provincial towns. This modest place, however, was the hometown of legendary Formula One driver **Juan Manuel Fangio**, and it now houses a spectacular museum that is certainly worth the detour if cars and racing are your thing. The **Museo Fangio** (daily Jan & Feb 10am–7pm, March–Dec 10am–5pm; $13; ⓣ02266/425540, ⓦwww.museofangio.com) was built to honour the man who won the Formula One World Championship five times in the 1950s, a record not equalled until the twenty-first century. The five floors of the museum are connected by a spiral ramp and tell Fangio's story in words, pictures and trophies. There are also displays on other prominent drivers, but the car's the star here – around thirty of them, in fact, including a 1927 Ford model-T, a red 1954 Maserati 250 and the Brabham BT36 driven by Argentine ex-Formula One driver Carlos Reutemann, now a politician. The most impressive, though – and saved for the top floor – is the Mercedes-Benz Silver Arrow that Fangio drove to victory in 1954.

Buses run between Mar del Plata and Balcarce every two hours and take ninety minutes; you will need to take a taxi (Teletaxi: ⓣ02266/425076) from the terminal to the museum. If you need to spend the night in the town, there's a basic **hotel**, the *Alberghini* (ⓣ02266/431397; ④), at Av Kelly 688, near the museum.

The southern beach resorts

Beyond the Interbalnearia, the coast slopes round to the west and the resorts are more widely spaced. Porteños and foreigners rarely venture this far south – most tourists come from southern Buenos Aires Province, and as a result the resorts here have an unpretentious and relaxed feel, with simple, unsophisticated eating and entertainment options; **fishing** is a popular activity. The area is an important cereal-producing region and, away from the coast, vast fields of sunflower, wheat and linseed mirror the immensity of the pampas sky, while grain elevators cluster around the edge of towns. The three main resorts are **Necochea**, favoured by families and surfers, the twin town of sandy **Claromecó** and wooded **Dunamar** and lively **Monte Hermoso**. There is no direct coast road linking the three; if you want to travel between them you'll have to make a detour inland via the agricultural town of Tres Arroyos, from where buses run to them all. The final coastal stop before hitting the Patagonian seaboard is **Bahía Blanca**, an important provincial city. Of limited appeal, its strategic location means you may well nevertheless find yourself passing through; if so, it's worth visiting its colourful port area, home to the excellent and unusual Museo del Puerto.

Necochea and around

NECOCHEA is a sprawling resort town popular with families, thanks to its much-publicized wide beaches, as well as surfers – it is home to some of the country's best waves. The town has a disjointed layout: the town centre proper, known as the **centro viejo**, sits 3km inland, but most tourist activity is packed into a grid of streets down by the seafront known as the **centro nuevo**. The enormous **Parque Miguel Lillo** lies immediately west of the centro nuevo, alongside Calle 89, and contains, among other things, a lake, an amphitheatre, a go-kart track and a small regional history museum. Necochea's beachfront is a typically regimented and busy stretch of sand dominated by tents and sunshades and lined with restaurants. To the north, close to the mouth of the Río Quequén, lies the quieter **Playa de los Patos**, flanked by low dunes and popular for fishing and surfing. To the south, the beaches extend for over 30km; the most accessible of these undeveloped rocky stretches is known as **Las Grutas**, backed by low cliffs and lying around 10km from the centre.

Just 3km east of Necochea, much quieter and smaller **QUEQUÉN** has a tranquillity disturbed only by the lorries that rumble to and from its busy port. Quequén can seem a bit desolate – it's certainly not the place to be if you seek excitement – but in many ways it has more character than its brasher neighbour, with a quirky charm given it by a sprinkling of grand but rather dilapidated mansions standing on grassy lots. Quequén's best-known feature is the huge **Monumento a las Malvinas**, at the end of Diagonal Almirante Brown nearest the coast, which has *La Libertad*, Argentina's lady liberty, bearing up a dying soldier and looking in the direction of the disputed islands; the area is home to a large number of ex-combatants from the 1982 conflict. An unsealed road hugs the coast, taking you past the central beaches, such as **Playa Bonita**, less wide than Necochea's but still popular, and on to the aptly named **Bahía de los Vientos** ("Bay of winds"), where the hulks of shipwrecked boats rest on rocky outcrops. The beaches here are narrower and wilder and are a good place to head for aimless strolling along the coast.

Practicalities

Necochea's **bus terminal** is at Avenida 58 and Jesuita Cardiel, in the centro viejo. The **tourist office** (Mon–Sat 8.30am–9pm, Sun 9am–7pm; ⓣ02262/425983), in a cabin on the seafront at the corner of Avenida 79, has limited information. Accommodation-wise, at all but the height of the summer season it shouldn't be difficult to find somewhere to stay in Necochea – and prices are generally lower here than they are further north. Most hotels are in the centro nuevo, with the pick being the *Hostería del Bosque*, Calle 89 no. 350 (ⓣ02262/420002, ⓔjfrigerio@telpin.com.ar; ❻), a charming *hostería* with elegantly decorated rooms, big, comfortable beds and a lovely shady courtyard that is set with tables and chairs for breakfast. The best of the town's budget options is *La Casona*, Calle 6 no. 4356 (ⓣ02262/423345, ⓔlacasonahlc@yahoo.com.ar; closed Apr–Nov; ❸), a friendly place with rooms around a central garden, while the new, upmarket *Nikén*, Calle 87 no. 335 (ⓣ02262/432323, ⓦwww.hotelniken.com.ar; ❻), is one of the few to offer a pool. There are many **campsites**, the nicest is in Quequén: *Monte Pasubio* (ⓣ02262/451482; ❶), off Calle 502 and named after a nearby shipwreck, is right by the sea. Equipped with a restaurant and store, it offers shady camping spots on the beach, has a laid-back atmosphere and is popular with surfers. Both tents and bungalows are also available to rent. When it comes to **eating**, Necochea is the place to take a break from beef – try some fish. Many restaurants are centred on Plaza San Martín and the surrounding streets, the best one being the friendly *Taberna Española*, Calle 89 no. 366, opposite the park. A nice spot to sit on a summer evening, it has a menu including paella and *cazuela de mariscos*. Fish is also available in the port, for example at long-established and popular *Cantina Venezia*, Calle 59 no. 259. The majority of **bars** are on the pedestrianized streets between Plaza San Martín and the seafront; many have outdoor seating and the area fills with musicians, performance artists and artisan stalls in the evening.

Claromecó and Dunamar

Warm currents from Brazil bring both exotic shells and stinging jellyfish to the waters of tranquil **CLAROMECÓ**. A small resort 140km south of Necochea, Claromecó is known for its fishing activity, and if you go down to the beach in the evening you may see fishermen going out with horses, which they use to take nets out into the sea. Claromecó's main, ample beach and seafront are rather flat and barren; the central section, overlooked by a spindly lighthouse, is the most popular with swimmers. Some 8km west there is a more interesting stretch of beach known as the *caracolero* – a kind of graveyard of large and beautiful shells, washed up from Brazil. Excursions there in the ubiquitous 4WDs are available – enquire at Four Turismo Aventur, Av 26 and 15 (Ⓣ02982/480135), which also rents out bikes.

Much more attractive than Claromecó is its neighbour **DUNAMAR**, on the western side of the Claromecó stream and run by the same municipalidad. Dunamar's sandy lanes were planted with pines and other trees in the 1940s by Ernesto Gesell, from the same family who created the better-known Villa Gesell (see p.215). This greener environment gives the village a distinct, altogether more appealing character, and it's a good choice if you want some quiet, self-catering days in one of the pretty houses that are available to rent or if you'd like to camp in more natural surroundings.

Practicalities

Buses arrive at the terminal on Claromecó's main plaza, where there are a *confitería* and left-luggage facilities. There are one or two direct services a day from Buenos Aires but if you are coming from elsewhere you will normally have to make a connection at Tres Arroyos. The town's small and friendly **tourist office** (daily 7am–noon & 3–9pm; Ⓣ02982/480467; Ⓦwww.claromeconet.com) is next to the bus terminal. There are only a handful of **hotels** here, all unfortunately located in Claromecó centre. Brightly coloured *Hostal Su-Yay*, on Calle 11 just to the right of the bus terminal (Ⓣ02982/480319, Ⓔhostalsuyay@celcla.com.ar; ❺), is the best place in town, offering a snack bar, a pretty patio and big rooms, some with a balcony overlooking the plaza. The nicest **campsites** are in Dunamar, such as *Los Troncos*, on the banks of the Claromecó stream (Ⓣ02982/480297; ❶), a simple, fairly rustic site with hot water, shops and barbecue facilities. Most visitors to Claramecó and Dunamar **rent** a house or apartment. Enquire directly at places advertising with signs saying "se alquila", or check the tourist office website. Calculate on rentals costing around $100 per day; many are only available December to March. As far as **eating and drinking** go, you will always find *parrillas* along the beach in the summer, or you could try the pasta at *La Gallina Turuleca*, Av 26 no. 555. A popular choice in the evenings is *La Barra*, an upmarket bar on the seafront at the foot of Calle 26. In Dunamar, the *Barlovento* is a lovely beach bar which serves *Frikadeller*, a Danish meatball dish, sells home-made preserves and has a small library.

Monte Hermoso

Lying 280km southwest of Necochea, **MONTE HERMOSO** is the major resort for the far south of Buenos Aires Province. While there is little about it that it is remarkable, it is not a bad option if you fancy a mid-sized resort well off the gringo (and Porteño) trail. Those keen on archeology will be intrigued by **El Pisadero**, a site that consists of a series of human footprints dating from around 5000 BC as well as older giant sloth prints that have been embedded in the sediment of the beach – formerly the site of a lake – 6km west of town, next to the *Camping Americano* (see below). They are only visible at low tide; the helpful staff at the otherwise rather dry **Museo de Ciencias Naturales**, on Avenida Costanera between avenidas Patagonia and Dufaur (March–Nov Sat & Sun 4–7pm, Dec–Feb Mon–Fri 8am–8pm, Sat & Sun 4–7pm; free), can provide you with directions and tide times. The other main sight in Monte Hermoso is the town's unusual lighthouse, the **Faro Recalado** (March–Nov Fri–Sun 8am–6pm; Dec–Feb daily 8am–8pm; $2), an openwork structure towering seventy metres above the resort, making it the tallest in South America. If you have the energy you can climb the 327 steps to the top for panoramic views.

A couple of **buses** a day, run by Plusmar and Cóndor Estrella, connect Monte Hermoso directly with Buenos Aires. **Accommodation** in the resort is plentiful, although it tends to be rather uninspiring. Top marks go to the lovely *Appart Italia*, Faro Recalado 250 (ⓣ02921/481598, ⓔappartitalia@uol.com.ar; ⑤), which is a good deal with its high-ceilinged apartments and kitchen areas – rooms are either spacious and include a dining area, or small but sweet, with balconies and Italian-style wooden shutters. There are a number of campsites, including the highly organized *Camping Americano* (ⓣ02921/481149, ⓦwww.campingamericano.com.ar; ❶), with numerous facilities including a pool, restaurant and beach bar, around 5km west from the centre; take the bus from Avenida Faro Recalado. **Restaurants** include the *Marfil*, on Valle Encantado 91, which features unusual and tasty combinations of pasta and seafood, such as squid ink *sorrentinos* stuffed with prawns, while trendy *Margarita* is a pretty **bar** perched up on a hill on the corner of Faro Recalado and Dorrego.

Bahía Blanca

Sprawling out into the empty pampas like a disjointed patchwork quilt, **BAHÍA BLANCA** is not the most immediately appealing of cities. Though it's the economic and industrial centre of the south of Buenos Aires Province, with nearly 300,000 inhabitants, it has a rather subdued feel and many Argentines regard it as synonymous with the military: the country's largest naval base, Puerto Belgrano, lies 20km southeast of town. However, the city shouldn't be written off altogether; its transport links with Sierra de la Ventana, resorts of the Pampas region and major Patagonian cities are a practical plus, and you'll find it has a spread of handsome – if fairly typical – early twentieth-century architecture and enough modest attractions among its parks, museums and galleries to fill a day or so.

The City

Despite its straggling outskirts, Bahía's centre is compact, walkable and easy to navigate. The main square is the distinguished Plaza Rivadavia, covering four blocks and bordered by an array of grand public edifices, largely constructed in the slightly ponderous vein of French Second Empire architecture favoured in Argentina at the beginning of the twentieth century – note the sharply pitched roofs and heavy ornamentation characteristic of this style. Three blocks north,

Avenida Além leads off to the left. A pleasant, tree-lined avenue flanked by an interesting mix of architectural styles, which hint at English, French and Italian influence but remain defiantly Argentine, it is frequented by students from the nearby university. For a more idiosyncratic piece of architectural history, head southwest from Plaza Rivadavia along Avenida Colón about ten blocks; over the bridge to your left lies the dourly named **Calle Brickman**. Known as the Barrio Inglés, the street's semi-detached dwellings were built by the English railway companies to house their workers. Their red-brick facades stand out among the more traditionally Argentine whitewashed and stuccoed buildings and, though their rather French shutters mean that they can scarcely be called typically English, the houses would not look entirely out of place in a south London suburb.

Continuing along Colón will take you to **Puerto Ingeniero White**, 10km from the city centre. In the 1880s, this was a major port that exported grain to Europe. It declined in consequence during the twentieth century, although it remains the country's most important deep-water harbour and you can still watch the trucks unloading huge piles of grain and seed onto giant forklifts. Here, too, you'll find the truly original **Museo del Puerto**, on Calle Guillermo Torres (Mon–Fri 9am–noon, Sat & Sun 5–8pm; free; Ⓣ0291/457-3006). Housed in the Great Southern Railway's old customs building, a brightly painted corrugated-iron construction, the museum takes as its theme the everyday life of the port and its inhabitants, with the avowed aims of telling the stories of common people and preserving immigrant traditions. The collection is composed of a wonderfully eclectic mix of objects, all donated by locals and displayed with verve and humour by the museum's enthusiastic staff. The themed rooms include one dedicated to the sea, where the lights suddenly dim for an impromptu simulation of a storm, and a reconstruction of a traditional barber's, with a background recording of Carlos Gardel, Argentina's famous tango singer. At weekends the kitchen here becomes a centre of the community when it is transformed into a **confitería**, where you can try out the cakes made from recipes passed on by local residents, mostly Italian in origin. Sundays are generally the port's liveliest time, with locals ending a stroll along its streets in the museum *confitería* or in one of the neighbouring *cantinas*. During the week it can seem a bit desolate, though its wooden and corrugated-iron buildings and cobbled streets give it the air of a faded Boca, and thus a certain charm. To get to Puerto Ingeniero White and the museum, take bus #500 from Avenida Colón in the centre of Bahía Blanca and get off at the corner of Mascarello and Belgrano, two blocks west of Guillermo Torres.

Practicalities

Bahía's **airport** is about 15km east of the city, and its **bus terminal** is on Estados Unidos and Almirante G. Brown, also a couple of kilometres east. Taxis (Ⓣ0291/455-0003) are readily available. The **tourist office** (daily 8am–7pm; Ⓣ0291/459-4007, Ⓦwww.bahiablanca.gov.ar) is in the basement of the building just to the right of the municipalidad on Plaza Rivadavia, the main square. The staff are helpful, but there isn't much printed information.

There's a pretty unexceptional and slightly overpriced selection of **hotels** in town, largely catering to business travellers. One of the better ones is the *Italía*, Brown 181 (Ⓣ0291/456-2700, Ⓔhitalia@rcc.com.ar; ④), two blocks southwest of Plaza Rivadavia. Unusually for the town, each room has a window, a TV and a private bathroom, and many have balconies looking out onto the bustle below. Just around the corner, the *Muñiz*, O'Higgins 23 (Ⓣ0291/456-0060, Ⓦwww.hotelmuniz.com.ar; ⑤), is a similar, slightly more elegant hotel. There are no hostels and only one **campsite**: *Camping Balneario Maldonado*, Parque Marítimo Almirante Brown (☎0291/455-1614; bus #514 from bus terminal); facilities include a saltwater swimming pool.

Eating and drinking options include *Gambrinus*, Arribeños 174, a well-established German restaurant specializing in cold cuts, liverwurst with pickled cucumber sandwiches and sausages served with potatoes or sauerkraut. The elegant *Pavarotti*, meanwhile, at Belgrano 272, has a good à la carte menu with fresh fish, paella and risotto. For traditional *cantinas*, head to Ingeniero White, where you can get excellent seafood at places such as the long-established *Cantina Royal*, Guillermo Torres 4133 (☎0291/457-0348), or the newer *Micho*, Guillermo Torres 3875 (☎0291/457-0346; closed Mon), on the site of an old Greek taverna, which does delicious rustic fish soup. As far as **nightlife** is concerned, the town is a bit on the quiet side. However, there are a number of **bars** on Fuerte Argentino on the other side of the Napostá stream north of the city centre, including popular *La Chacarera*, Fuerte Argentino 707, which also serves food.

The Pampas

The vast expanse of flat pampas grassland that radiates out from Buenos Aires is one of the country's most famous features, just as the **gaucho** who once roamed on horseback, knife clenched between teeth, leaving a trail of broken hearts and gnawed steak bones behind him, is as important a part of the collective romantic imagination as the Wild West cowboy is in the US. The popular depiction of this splendid, freedom-loving figure – whose real life must actually have been rather lonely and brutal – was crystallized in José Hernández' epic poem *Martín Fierro*, from which just about every Argentine can quote. It's a way of life whose time has passed, but the gaucho's legacy remains. You're not likely to witness knife fights over a woman, but you can still visit well-preserved *pulperías* (traditional bars), stay at estancias and watch weather-beaten old *paisanos* (countrymen) playing cards and chuckling behind their huge handlebar moustaches. Shrines to the semi-mythical Gauchito Gil (see box, p.337), one of the most famous gauchos of all, are often seen by the roadside in the Pampas.

The best area for this kind of visit is the **Eastern Pampas**, in a radius of a couple of hundred kilometres around Buenos Aires city. This is where you'll find the *pampa húmeda* (wet pampa), land that is the country's most fertile – and most valuable. There are several sites of interest here, most notably **San Antonio de Areco**, which has retained a remarkably authentic feel despite its popularity. As you move into the **Western Pampas**, and towards the border with La Pampa Province, the scenery starts to change. The unremitting flat landscape is given welcome relief by the modest mountain range of **Sierra de la Ventana**, while the drier, more desert-like features of the *pampa seca* (dry pampa) herald the start of the long route south through Patagonia.

The Eastern Pampas

The eastern part of Buenos Aires Province is home to a clutch of towns that embody the spirit of the Pampas while each retaining their own, individual character. The closest are potential day-trips from the capital, although spending a night – perhaps at a nearby estancia – will give you a better feel for the much slower pace of life in the interior. Others are useful as stopping-off points. The charming town of **San Antonio de Areco** is the main site of interest to the capital's northwest, on RN-8; if you visit only one pampas town during your stay in Argentina, this is the one to head for. The recognized centre of pampas tradition, San Antonio puts on a popular gaucho festival in November and has some highly respected artisans and an extremely attractive and unusually well-preserved town centre. At the very beginning of RN-5, **Luján**, 68km west of the capital, is Argentina's most important religious site, thanks to its vast basilica, built to house the country's patron saint, the Virgin of Luján. Further along RN-5, **Mercedes** stands out thanks to its authentic *pulpería*, largely untouched since the nineteenth century, and the nearby village **Tomás Jofré**, stuffed with good restaurants. The small town of **Lobos**, to the capital's southwest, is a popular weekend destination for Porteños, primarily for its lakeside setting, as well as a couple of particularly attractive estancias in the surrounding countryside. Moving further south, **Azul**'s low-lying hills are home to Latin America's first Trappist monastery, while **Tandil** is an appealing town of cobbled streets and traditional pampas culture.

San Antonio de Areco and around

Delightful **San Antonio de Areco** is considered the home of gaucho traditions and hosts the annual **Fiesta de la Tradición** (see box, p.239), the country's most important festival celebrating pampas culture. Despite its modest promotion as a tourist destination, San Antonio has retained a surprisingly genuine feel, augmented by its setting on the banks of a tranquil river, the Río Areco. You may not find the town full of galloping gauchos outside festival week, but you still have a good chance of spotting estancia workers on horseback, sporting traditional berets and rakishly knotted scarves, or of coming across *paisanos* propping up the bar of a traditional *boliche* establishment. San Antonio has a prestigious literary connection: the town was the setting for Ricardo Güiraldes' Argentine classic *Don Segundo Sombra* (1926), a novel that was influential in changing the image of the gaucho from that of an undesirable outlaw to a symbol of national values.

The town's only real sights are a couple of museums, the most important of which is the **Museo Gauchesco Ricardo Güiraldes**. But what really makes San Antonio memorable is the harmonious architectural character of the town's centre; all cobbled streets and faded Italianate and colonial facades punctuated by elaborate wrought-iron grilles and delicately arching lamps. There are also some excellent **artisans** working in the town in *talleres* (workshops). Weaving and leatherwork are well represented, but the silversmiths are the highlight.

The town's traditional gaucho atmosphere also extends to the surrounding area, where you will find some of Argentina's most famous **estancias**, offering a luxurious accommodation alternative to staying in Areco itself.

Arrival and information

Most **buses** from Buenos Aires and Rosario stop at the pink Chevallier terminal at General Paz and Avenida Dr Smith, six blocks east of Areco's town

SAN ANTONIO DE ARECO
Pergamino & Rosario
El Ombu, La Pampa & Buenos Aires
A
0 200 m
N
ACCOMMODATION
Los Abuelos B
Antigua Casona D
Club River A
Hostal de Areco C
EATING & DRINKING
Almacén de Ramos Generales 5
Barril 990 9
Café de las Artes 3
La Costa 2
La Esquina de Marti 6
La Olla de Cobre 4
Posada de la Ribera 1
Puesto La Lechuza 7
La Vieja Sodería 8
Posta El Triunfo
Museo Gauchesco Ricardo Güiraldes
Parque Criollo
Río Areco
Puente Viejo
Puente Gabino Tapia
Zoo
Centro Cultural Usina Vieja
Centro Cultural y Taller Draghi
La Cinacina
Los Principios
PLAZA RUIZ DE ARELLANO
Iglesia Parroquial San Antonio de Padua
Chevallier Bus Terminal
RN-8
AVENIDA SMITH
CAMINO J.A. GÜIRALDES
RICARDO GÜIRALDES
V. TABOADA
SOSA
E. PEREYRA
CIRIACO DÍAZ
V. NOGUEIRA
G LOPEZ
ZERBONI
MATHEU
LAVALLE
MITRE
SEGUNDO SOMBRA
G. PAZ
SAN MARTÍN
ALEM
ALVEAR
MARTINEZ
GÜIRALDES
PELLEGRINI
ITALIA
A. DEL VALLE
MORENO
BELGRANO
ALSINA
ARELLANO
ZAPIOLA
BOLIVAR
RIVADAVIA
SAMIENTO
ALBERDI

centre. It's an easy and enjoyable stroll into town along Calle Segundo Sombra, which brings you to Areco's main square, Plaza Ruiz de Arellano. If you're carrying a lot of luggage – or heading for an estancia – take a *remise* (Ⓣ02326/456225).

The **tourist office** on the corner of Arellano and Zerboni (daily 8am–8pm; Ⓣ02326/453165) has useful information, including maps and lists of hotels and artisan workshops. There's also a kiosk (Sat & Sun 11am–8pm) in Plaza Ruiz de Arellano, to cope with the extra influx of Porteños on weekends.

Accommodation

San Antonio is easily visited as a day-trip from Buenos Aires, but many museums and workshops close during the afternoon, so this can be a frustrating experience. Although **hotels** are thin on the ground, staying overnight gives you the chance to explore the town at a more leisurely pace and enjoy it as its best, in the morning and evening. One of the most attractive accommodation options is the *Hostal de Areco* at Zapiola 25 (Ⓣ02326/456118, Ⓦwww.hostaldeareco.com.ar; ❹), a traditional rose-coloured building with farmhouse-style decor. **Antigua Casona**, Segunda Sombra 495 (Ⓣ02326/456600, Ⓦwww.antiguacasona.com; ❺), is a B&B in an old townhouse, renovated lightly – a bit too lightly, in places – but the odd damp patch is made up for by a lovely tiled patio where a good breakfast is served, and a large garden that ensures you hear crickets and birdsong rather than traffic. *Los Abuelos*, on Zapiola and Zerboni (Ⓣ02326/456390; ❸), is a reasonable option if you prefer a more modern hotel – there is a TV and fan in each room, and some rooms have balconies with views over the Río Areco. Several cafés also double up as simple *hospedajes* – see p.239 for details. If you plan on visiting during the Fiesta de la Tradición celebrations, book at least two weeks in advance; once the hotels are full, the tourist office can provide information on staying with families. There are one or two **campsites** within easy reach of San Antonio, with the best being *Club River* (Ⓣ02326/452744; ❶), reached by following Zerboni west out of town. It includes a swimming pool.

The Town

Areco's main square, the leafy **Plaza Ruiz de Arellano**, six blocks west of the bus terminal, is named after José Ruiz de Arellano, whose estancia stood on the site now occupied by the town and who built San Antonio's founding chapel, the **Iglesia Parroquial San Antonio de Padua**, on the south side of the square. The original chapel, a simple adobe construction, was declared a parish church in 1730, and was rebuilt in 1792 and then again in 1870 in keeping with the town's growing importance. Of no great architectural note, the current version is nonetheless a pleasingly simple white construction, with clear Italian influences. The exterior is dominated by a sculpture of San Antonio himself, who stands within a niche clad with blue and white tiles that echo those of the church's small bell-shaped dome. The inside is impressive, with a high vaulted ceiling.

Among the elegant *fin-de-siècle* residences that flank the plaza, there is the Italianate **municipalidad**, to the north; originally a private residence, it is painted a particularly delicate version of the pink that characterizes so many of Areco's buildings. On the northwest corner of the square stands a typically colonial two-storied construction known as the **Casa de los Martínez**, after the local family who once inhabited it. The building's handsome but rather plain green and white exterior is dominated by the original railings of a balcony, which runs all the way around the first floor.

Right opposite the church, at Lavalle 387, one of San Antonio's most renowned silversmiths runs the **Centro Cultural y Taller Draghi** (Mon–Sat

9am–1pm & 3.30–8pm, Sun 10am–1pm; free guided visits 11am, noon, 4pm, 5pm & 6pm; $5). The centre displays pieces made in the style of *platería criolla*, which first emerged around 1750 when local craftsmen, who had previously been working according to Spanish and Portuguese tradition, began to develop their own style. Fantastically ornate yet sturdy, in keeping with the practical use to which the items are – at least in theory – put, the style is still commonly used to produce gaucho knives (*facones*), belts (*rastras*), *mates* and stirrups. The museum/workshop mixes the creations of Juan José Draghi – who has produced pieces for various international figures, including the king and queen of Spain – with a collection of nineteenth-century silver spurs, bridles and swords that have been his inspiration; however, there's little in the way of labels, so it's hard to tell which is antique and which modern. Among Draghi's finest work are the *mates*, which come in their original chalice shape (based on those used in churches) with finely wrought silver stems of cherubs and flowers. Such *mates* are now for decoration only, being expensive – not to mention likely to scald your fingers if filled with hot water. The Draghi family also has elegant rooms available in a *parador* (inn) a block away in Matheu – enquire at the workshop (Ⓣ02326/455583).

A block north of Plaza Ruiz de Arellano, at Alsina 66, is the **Centro Cultural Usina Vieja** (Tues–Sun 11.15am–4.45pm; $1.50). The restored building originally housed Areco's first electrical generator and has been declared a national industrial monument. Now housing a cultural centre, the building also contains the **Museo de la Ciudad**, an eclectic collection – mainly supplied through local donations – of everyday items, from clothing to record-players and even the town's old telephone switchboard, plus occasional temporary exhibitions, focusing mainly on subjects related to rural Argentine life. There's also a good display of the famous gaucho cartoons of Florencia Molino Campos, first published in almanacs and now adorning hotel walls the length of the country.

Beyond the cultural centre, wide Calle Zerboni separates the town centre from the grassy banks of the Río Areco, popular for picnics and *asados* during good weather. Zerboni is home to a small **zoo** (summer 11am–1pm & 3–6pm, winter 11am–5pm; $2), chiefly of interest for its pleasant green surroundings. Crossing the simple brick **Puente Viejo** opposite leads to the rather scrubby **Parque Criollo**, less a park than a kind of exhibition ground, used during the Fiesta de la Tradición as the setting for the main displays of gaucho skills. It also houses the **Museo Gauchesco Ricardo Güiraldes** (Wed–Mon 11am–5pm; $3). The entrance to the park and the museum is via the *Pulpería La Blanqueada*, once a staging post on the old Camino Real, which linked Buenos Aires with Alto Peru. It was the setting for the first encounter between Fabio, the young hero of Güiraldes' novel – a sort of South American Huckleberry Finn – and his mentor, Don Segundo Sombra. The *pulpería* was closed in the 1930s but its original features have been retained, including the traditional grille that separated the owner from his customers and their knives and light fingers. For a *pulpería* that's still serving, head to Moreno and Mitre, where you'll find *Los Principios*, an authentic store that also sells groceries to locals from its high wooden shelves.

The museum, a short distance away across the park, is housed in a 1930s reproduction of an old estancia. Its collection mixes gaucho paraphernalia – *mate* gourds, silverware and *boleadoras* (lasso balls) – with objects deemed to be interesting largely because of their famous owners – General Rosas' bed, W.H. Hudson's books, and so on. Of particular interest are the black and white photos of the original gauchos who were the inspiration for Güiraldes, and the branding irons they used – each landowner had his own, somewhat cabalistic symbol, worn in various forms as a badge of pride by his men as well as his cattle.

The Fiesta de la Tradición

One of Argentina's most original and enjoyable festivals, San Antonio de Areco's **Fiesta de la Tradición,** began in 1939, on an initiative of then-mayor José Antonio Güiraldes. The actual Día de la Tradición is November 10 – the date of birth of José Hernández, author of Argentina's gaucho text par excellence, *Martín Fierro* – but the celebrations last for a week and are organized to run from weekend to weekend, either the first or second week in November, depending on the weather forecast. Activities, including exhibitions, dances, music recitals and shows of gaucho skills, go throughout the week, although the highpoint is the final Sunday, which begins with dancing and a procession of gauchos dressed in their traditional loose trousers (*bombachas*), ornamented belts and wide-brimmed hats or berets. An *asado con cuero*, at which meat – primarily beef – is cooked around a fire with its skin on, takes place at midday in the Parque Criollo ($5 for gauchos, $40 for everyone else) and is followed by an extensive display of gaucho skills, including *jineteadas*, or Argentine bronco riding.

At the end is an impressive collection of works by Pedro Figari, a Uruguayan artist who worked with Güiraldes on the literary journal *Martín Fierro*. His paintings, with their characteristic intense blue skies and flat mottled surfaces, seem to capture the almost hypnotic quality of the pampas landscape perfectly. In the park, beyond the museum, it is possible to take a spin in a horse and cart; enquire at the *Posta El Triunfo*, which also offers simple food and lodging.

Eating, drinking and nightlife

San Antonio de Areco has an excellent selection of **restaurants**, cafés and bars that ooze character. *La Esquina de Marti*, on the main plaza at Lavalle and Arellano, has walls adorned with old signs, ads and bottles and is a tasteful recreation of a *pulpería* serving straightforward Argentine classics. A similar ambience is found at *Almacén de Ramos Generales*, Zapiola 143, with *parrilla*, *picadas* and specials such as trout in Roquefort sauce. The owners also run the wonderful *La Vieja Sodería* café/bar at Bolivar and General Paz, whose walls are lined with coloured soda bottles; it does a wide range of teas and beers. At Bolivar 68, the pretty *Café de las Artes* does tasty home-made pasta, while the length of Calle Zerboni, which skirts the park, is thick with the smoke of *parrillas* – *La Costa*, on the corner of Zerboni and Belgrano, is especially popular with locals. On the riverside at the far end of Calle Martínez, the jack-of-all trades *Posada de la Ribera* does local food such as empanadas and *picadas*, has basic rooms available and also rents out *piraguas* (boats) and mountain bikes. If you've got a sweet tooth, don't miss *La Olla de Cobre*, a small chocolate factory and sweet shop at Matheu 433 (closed Tues), where you can try handmade chocolates and particularly delicious *alfajores* before buying.

The best **bars** in Areco are *boliches* – traditional places where estancia workers drink Fernet and play cards. Some of the best include *Bar San Martín*, on Moreno and Alvear, and *Puesto La Lechuza*, at Segundo Sombra and Bolivar, which can also be good places to catch folklore music and dancing. *Barril 990*, San Martín 381, is a more modern pub, where there is occasional live music. *Boliches* in the modern sense of the word – nightclubs – are out on Avenida Dr Smith, such as *La Loca Cubana* next to the bus terminal (Fri & Sat only).

Estancias in and around San Antonio de Areco

The countryside around San Antonio is home to a couple of the province's most traditional **estancias**. Arguably the most luxurious is **El Ombú**,

Cuartel 4 (☎011/4710-2795, Ⓦwww.estanciaelombu.com; ❾, or US$50 as a day visit). Its rooms are sumptuously decorated and a lovely tiled and ivy-covered verandah runs round the exterior of the building. As well as offering horse-riding, the estancia has a small but well-maintained swimming pool and a games room. Other activities include helping out with – or at least observing – farm tasks such as cattle herding and, of course, eating delicious *asados*, sometimes served under the shade of the large ombú tree that gives the estancia its name. Directions are on the website; the estancia will arrange a transfer from Buenos Aires for around US$60.

The nearby **La Bamba** (☎02326/456293, Ⓦwww.la-bamba.com.ar; ❾) was used in Maria Luisa Bemberg's film *Camila* – the story of the ill-fated romance between Camila O'Gorman and a priest – and is one of Argentina's most distinctive estancias. The elegantly simple deep-rose facade of the *casco*, presided over by a watchtower, is a particularly beautiful example of early eighteenth-century rural architecture. The Río Areco runs through the grounds, so guests can fish as well as ride, although the "shows" in the recently built *pulpería* and immaculate living rooms do make the place seem a bit like a Disney version of an estancia experience at times.

La Cinacina estancia in Areco itself has more affordable "days in the country"; follow Bartolomé Mitre five blocks west of the main plaza to the end of the street (☎02326/452773, Ⓦwww.lacinacina.com.ar). It offers a full day of *asado*, horse-riding and a display of gaucho skills for $90, or $150 as a day-trip from Buenos Aires with transport included (Tues, Fri & Sun). Staying the night is also possible, in pretty, light, country-style rooms (❽).

Luján

Officially founded in 1755 on the site of a shrine containing a tiny ceramic figure of the Virgin Mary, **Luján**, about 70km west of Buenos Aires, is now one of the major religious centres in Latin America. The **Virgin of Luján** is the patron saint of Argentina, Paraguay and Uruguay and the epic basilica erected in her honour in 1887 in Luján attracts around five million visitors a year. This Neo-Gothic edifice is one of the most memorable – though not really the most beautiful – churches in Argentina. Its main interest lies in its role as a machine dedicated to perpetuating the cult of the Virgin, the centrepiece of a town that seems designed as a kind of antechamber to her sanctuary. The town's other major attraction, the vast **Complejo Museográfico Enrique Udaondo**, is a multiplex museum with an important historical section, as well as Argentina's largest transport museum. Away from the museums and the basilica, all grouped around the central square, Luján is pretty much like any other provincial town, with elegant, early twentieth-century townhouses and slightly less elegant modern buildings. The town is actually quite large, with around 90,000 inhabitants, but its identity seems strangely subsumed by the Goliath in its midst.

If you want to get a real flavour of Luján in full religious swing, you should visit at the weekend, when seven or eight Masses are held a day – but, unless you want to take part, try to avoid visiting during the annual **pilgrimages**, when the town becomes seriously full. These take place on October 5, when up to a million young people walk here from Buenos Aires; May 8, the day of the Coronation of the Virgin; and December 8, when smaller, informal pilgrimages mark the Day of the Immaculate Conception.

Arrival and information

There are regular buses to Luján from Buenos Aires, arriving at the **bus terminal** on Avenida Nuestra Señora de Luján 600 (☎02323/420044), a couple of blocks north of the town's central square, Plaza Belgrano. There are also frequent trains from the capital (Once station), terminating at Luján's **train station**, a couple of kilometres southeast of the centre at Avenida España and Belgrano. The **tourist office** (Mon–Fri 8am–2pm; ⓣ02323/420453, ⓦwww.lujanargentina.com) is in a building known as the Casa de la Cúpula, which stands in a park area on the riverbank between Lavalle and San Martín, one block west of Plaza Belgrano. In addition to maps and hotel lists, they have detailed info on the phenomenon of the Virgin and the basilica's history and importance.

Accommodation

There is plenty of accommodation in the city – mostly fair, mid-range **hotels**. The ones around the bus terminal are on the whole pretty seedy and not a very good deal. An exception is the *Biarritz*, on Lezica and Torrezuri 717 (ⓣ02323/435988; ❺), one block south of the terminal. The simple but reasonable rooms all have a/c and cable TV; breakfast is included. In general, though, you're probably better off heading to the streets to the east of the basilica. At 9 de Julio 1054, *La Paz* (ⓣ02323/424034; ❺) is one of Luján's oldest hotels, offering airy rooms and a pretty garden overlooked by the basilica's towers. Two blocks east of Plaza Belgrano, there's *Los Monjes*, at Francia 981 (ⓣ02323/420606, ⓦwww.hotellosmonjes.com.ar; ❺), with attractive decent-sized a/c rooms, a good breakfast and a swimming pool. The *Hoxon*, at 9 de Julio 760 (ⓣ02323/429970, ⓦwww.hotelhoxon.com.ar; ❺), also offers comfortable rooms, if rather lacking in character; the hotel has an outdoor pool, a sunbathing area and a gym.

Some visitors set up camp informally around the river, but there are also a couple of organized **campsites** on the way out of town. Just outside the town, *El Triángulo*, on RN-7 at Km69.50 (ⓣ02323/430116; ❶), is a reasonable wooded site that has showers, security and a picnic area. Follow Avenida Nuestra Señora de Luján out of town and turn left at the main access point – the campsite is just over the bridge, on the banks of the Río Luján.

The Town

At busy times, all you need to do to visit the Virgin is go with the flow. The town's main drag, Avenida Nuestra Señora de Luján, rolls up like a tarmac carpet to the door of the **Basílica de Nuestra Señora de Luján** (daily 8am–8pm; Mass Mon–Sat 8am, 9am, 10am, 11am, 5pm & 7pm, Sun 8am, 9am, 10am, 11am, 12.30pm, 3.30pm, 5pm & 7pm), at the far end of Luján's main square, Plaza Belgrano. Begun in 1887 but not actually finished until 1937, the basilica is a mammoth edifice, built using a pinkish stone quarried in Entre Ríos. A heavy, some might say heavy-handed, French influence is evident – reflecting the nationality of the basilica's architect, Ulderico Courtois. In true Neo-Gothic style, everything about the basilica points heavenwards, from its remarkably elongated twin spires, which stand 106 metres tall, to the acute angles of the architraves surrounding the three main doors. At the very centre of the facade there is a large circular stained-glass window depicting the Virgin. The basilica's nineteen bells were cast in Milan from the bronze of World War I cannons.

Despite its grand exterior, it's what goes on inside the basilica that's most likely to catch your attention. Composed of a large central nave, thirty metres long, and two lateral naves, the relatively restrained interior simmers with hushed activity. On busy days, entering the place through one of the heavy bronze doors is a bit like stepping onto a religious conveyor belt, as you get caught up in a seemingly endless stream of pilgrims, some on their knees, others in wheelchairs, making their way to the **Camarín de la Virgen**. Up to eight Masses a day take place in the basilica and the aisles are lined with confessional boxes,

△ Basílica de Nuestra Señora de Luján

where privacy seems to have been abandoned as priests sit expectantly with their doors open, bathed in a pool of light. To visit the Virgin herself, head up the stairs to the chamber behind the main altar. Positioned several feet off the ground and swathed in robes and adornments, the statue at the centre of all the fuss is rather hard to see – luckily, the **crypt** below the basilica holds a replica and explains the history. It also harbours reproductions of Virgins from all over the world, but particularly from Latin America and Eastern Europe.

A tiny miracle: the Virgin of Luján

In 1630, a Portuguese ship docked in Buenos Aires on its way back from Brazil. Among its cargo was a simple terracotta image of the **Virgin** made by an anonymous Brazilian craftsman. The icon had been brought to Argentina at the request of a merchant from Sumampa, Santiago del Estero, and, after unloading, it was transported by cart along the old Camino Viejo (now RN-8) towards the estancia of its new owner. The cart paused on the outskirts of **Luján**, from where, the story goes, it could not be moved. Various packages were taken down from the cart in an attempt to lighten the load – all to no avail, until the tiny package containing the Virgin was removed. In the time-honoured tradition of miracles, this was taken as a sign that the Virgin had decided on her own destination. A small chapel was built and the first pilgrims began to arrive.

The Virgin has actually been moved over the centuries, although according to legend it took three attempts and several days of prayer the first time. In 1872, Luján's Lazarist order – a religious body founded in Paris in 1625 with the emphasis on preaching to the rural poor – was entrusted with the care of the Virgin by the archbishop of Buenos Aires. In 1875, a member of the order, **Padre Jorge María Salvaire**, was almost killed in one of the last Indian raids on Azul. Praying to the Virgin, he promised that if he survived he would promote her cult, write her history and, finally, build a huge temple in her name. He survived, and the foundation stone to the basilica was laid on his initiative in 1887.

The original terracotta Virgin is now barely recognizable: a protective bell-shaped silver casing was placed around the image in the late nineteenth century. Sky-blue and white robes were also added, reflecting the colours of the Argentine flag, as well as a Gothic golden surround, in keeping with the style of the new basilica; these were replaced in 2006. The face of the original statue can now just about be seen, peering out a small gap in the casing. Even if you don't visit Luján itself, you're likely to have seen the Virgin: she is the patron saint of public transport, and stickers with her image can be seen on almost every bus rear windscreen in Argentina.

Back outside, stalls selling Virgin paraphernalia line the otherwise rather bare Plaza Belgrano. West of the plaza in a cluster of mustard and white colonial buildings is the **Complejo Museográfico Enrique Udaondo** (Wed–Fri 3–6pm, Sat & Sun 10am–6pm; $1; ⓣ02323/420245). It claims to be the most important museum complex in South America; this is debatable, but it's certainly one of the continent's biggest. Its principal collections are those within the Museo Histórico Colonial, housed in the Casa del Virrey and the cabildo on the western side of Plaza Belgrano, and the Museo de Transportes, on the northern end of the plaza, between Avenida Nuestra Señora de Luján and Lezica y Torrezuri.

The **Museo Histórico Colonial** is rather misleadingly named, since its exhibits actually cover a much wider period. There's a small display on Luján's history in the Casa del Virrey, but the museum's principal collection is accessed via the **Cabildo** next door, a two-storey galleried building dating from 1772. The leaders of the short-lived British invasion, General William Beresford and Colonel Dennis Pack, were held here after their surrender in August 1806. Trophies captured during the quashing of the invasion, notably the staff of the 71st Highland Regiment, are prominently displayed. An internal door leads onto a pretty courtyard with a marble well in the centre and an elegant wooden balustrade around the first floor of its green and white walls. No doubt it all looked a little less idyllic when the courtyard's cells, to the left as you enter, were actually occupied. Other rooms here feature displays on the gaucho – including some fine silver *mate* vessels – nineteenth-century fashion and the disastrous and bloody War of the Triple Alliance.

The **Museo de Transportes**, Argentina's largest transport museum, offers less a chronology of the evolution of transport than a display of some of Argentina's most historically significant planes, trains and carriages. The museum's two most important exhibits are *La Porteña*, Argentina's first steam locomotive, whose maiden journey between Plaza Lavalle and Floresta in Buenos Aires took place in 1857, and *Plus Ultra*, the hydroplane with which Ramón Franco, brother of General Franco, made the first crossing of the South Atlantic in 1926. Two of the museum's more unusual exhibits are Gato and Mancha, the Argentine horses used by Tschiffely, a Swiss explorer who rode from Buenos Aires to New York in the 1930s, and preserved – albeit in a rather moth-eaten state – for posterity. Gato and Mancha were *caballos criollos*, Argentina's national breed, descended from the first horses brought by the conquistadors and characterized by a sturdy elongated body, a smooth gait and – as Tschiffely's trip demonstrated – an amazing hardiness.

Eating and drinking

There are plenty of **eating** options, mainly *parrillas* geared up to feed hungry pilgrims, on Avenida San Martín, while next to the tourist office you'll find *La Recova*, a restaurant offering pleasant outdoor seating and a simple, reasonably priced menu that focuses on pasta. Luján's most famous restaurant is a long way out of the centre: *L'Eau Vive* at Constitución 2112 (ⓣ02323/421774; open for lunch and dinner Tues–Sat) is fifteen blocks east along Avenida San Martín from Plaza Colón and most easily reached by taxi. The restaurant's main claim to fame is that it is run exclusively by nuns. The cooking – a traditional European menu with an emphasis on rich meat dishes – is generally excellent.

Mercedes and around

Tranquil and cultured **MERCEDES**, 30km southwest of Luján along RN-5, was founded in 1752 as a fortress to protect that city from Indian attacks. It's a well-preserved provincial town and easy to find your way around – the main drag is Avenida 29, which crosses central **Plaza San Martín**. The plaza is not especially remarkable, despite its grand Italianate **Palacio Municipal** and large Gothic **Basílica Catedral Nuestra Señora de Mercedes**. It is, however, a real hub of activity – especially in the evening, when locals fill the tables that spill out of its various inviting *confiterías*.

Aside from just wandering around the town itself, Mercedes' main draw is its **pulpería**, twenty or so blocks north of Plaza San Martín, at the end of Avenida 29. *Pulperías*, essentially provisions stores with a bar attached, performed an important social role in rural Argentina and enjoy an almost mythical status in gaucho folklore. The sign outside *Mercedes' pulpería*, known locally as "*lo de Cacho*" (Cacho's place), claims it to be the last *pulpería*, run by the last *pulpero* – quite possibly a justifiable claim. The gloomy interior, which has hardly changed since it opened its doors in 1850, harbours a collection of dusty bottles, handwritten notices – included an original wanted poster for the biggest gaucho outlaw of them all, Juan Moreira – and gaucho paraphernalia: it doesn't require much imagination to conjure up visions of the knife fights that the friendly and talkative Cacho claims to have witnessed in his youth. To get to the *pulpería*, best visited in the evening for a beer and a *picada* featuring some of the renowned local salami, when you may also catch some impromptu singing and guitar playing, take the local bus which runs towards the park from Avenida 29.

A couple of blocks beyond the last stop, the road becomes unsealed and on the left-hand corner you'll see the simple white building, a sign saying "*pulpería*" painted on its side.

Practicalities

Mercedes' **bus terminal**, served by regular buses from the capital, is south of the town centre, from where it's a twenty-minute walk to Plaza San Martín. There's an infrequent local bus from the terminal to the centre, so if you don't fancy the walk you may be better off taking one of the terminal **taxis** (Ⓣ02324/420651). There are also regular trains from Once station in the capital; the **train station** is along Av España, eight blocks north of the centre. The **tourist office**, on the corner of Avenida 29 and Calle 26 (Mon–Fri 7.30am–8pm, Sat & Sun 9am–7pm; Ⓣ02324/421080, Ⓦwww.mercedes.gba.gov.ar), doesn't have much in the way of printed information, but the staff are enthusiastic and knowledgeable, and can provide you with a map of the town.

Accommodation is not plentiful, and what exists is rather lacking in character. The *Gran Hotel Mercedes*, on the corner of Avenida 29 and Calle 16 (Ⓣ02324/425987; ➎), looks stern and unpromising from the outside, but inside the rooms are quite comfortable and have a/c and TV, while facilities include a restaurant and bar area. Otherwise, try the *Hostal del Sol*, on the edge of town at avenidas 2 and 3 (Ⓣ02324/433400; ➎), which has large, smart rooms. There's a municipal **campsite** in the park on the edge of town; take any local bus from Avenida 29. Note that Mercedes hosts a motorbike rally at the end of March, which is the only time you might have trouble finding space to pitch your tent here.

Eating and **drinking** options in the centre include *La Vieja Esquina*, a charming traditional bar on the corner of calles 25 and 28, which also sells delicatessen produce. Mercedes is the national capital of **salami** and even hosts a salami festival in September. You should certainly try some while you are here – the *picado grueso* is favoured by locals, although its high fat content might be off-putting. Of the *confiterías* around the plaza, good for coffee, sandwiches and snacks, one of the nicest is *La Recova*, the only building in the square to retain an old-fashioned arcade.

Tomás Jofré

Some 15km back up RN-5 towards Luján, follow the signposted turn-off for 7km along the pretty, vegetation-lined RN-42 to reach the small village of **TOMÁS JOFRÉ**. This tiny settlement of unsealed, unnamed roads is a popular weekend day-trip for Porteños, primarily for its traditional restaurants, including the long-established *Silvano* (Ⓣ02324 432035; closed Mon & Tues), with a huge set menu of traditional food, and *Fronteras* (Ⓣ02324/424477, Ⓦwww.comedorfronteras.com.ar; advisable to book ahead; closed Mon), which does delicious home-made pastas, such as *sorrentinos* filled with mozzarella, ricotta and ham. There's also another *pulpería*, *La Colorada* (closed Sun), named after a particularly bloody fight that took place here soon after it opened in 1869.

If hankering for a starry sky and birdsong, you may want to consider spending the night in Tomás Jofré. The typical pampas architecture of the *Cua Cua* (Ⓣ02324/433328, Ⓦwww.cuacua.com.ar; ➎), as well as containing a restaurant doing the usual delicious countryside trio of *picada*, *asado* and home-made pasta, has very attractive country-style rooms, a lovely garden, use of a pool and a no-children rule.

Lobos and around

About 100km southwest of the capital on RN-205 – you can also reach it from Mercedes via RP-41 – **LOBOS** is an old-fashioned country town with pretty, slightly crumbling houses and a famous son – Juan Domingo Perón, who was born here in 1895 at the house which now bears the address Perón 482, and where an archive of his letters and photos is stored.

Lobos sits on a series of lakes known as the **Lagunas Encadenadas** ("chained lakes"), the area's main attraction. To get to Lobos's quiet lakeside area, around 15km southwest of town – where there are picnic spots shaded by pines and eucalyptus – take the local bus that runs every couple of hours from the corner of Além and 9 de Julio, opposite the train station. Fishing, boating and windsurfing are all possible; equipment can be rented from several spots around the lake.

Those who fancy something more active will find Lobos is something of a centre for **parachuting** and **polo**. For the former, there is a large and well-equipped skydiving school, CEPA (T 02227/1561-3722; W www.paracaidismolobos.com.ar), on RP-205 at Km105, just outside Lobos. All levels are catered for, and tandem jumps with instructors are available. Polo is taught at a number of ranches that also double as estancias. The most notable is **La Martina Polo Ranch** (T 02226/430777, W www.lamartinapolo.com.ar), a prestigious school attended by Argentina's top players, although they will also teach beginners. La Martina is about 40km northeast of Lobos just outside the tiny settlement of Vicente Casares, off RN-3 just past the RN-205 junction. You can visit it as a day-trip or stay in the comfortable rooms of the nineteenth-century estancia building (9, full board). For more on estancias around Lobos see below.

Practicalities

Lobos's **bus** and **train** terminals face each other on the corner of Hiriart and Além, around six blocks east of the town's central square, Plaza 1810. The municipalidad is at the southern end of the plaza and contains a small but useful **tourist office** (Mon–Fri 7.30am–2pm, Sat & Sun 10am–6pm; T 02227/422275, W www.lobos.gov.ar). There's not much **accommodation** in town; in the centre there's the *Class Hotel*, Belgrano and Almafuerte (T 02227/430090; 4), which has large rooms, an all-hours café and includes a buffet breakfast. The best of the many **campsites** around the lake is the *Club de Pesca* (T 02227/494089; 1), where you can rent boats or fish from the jetty. For eating, there are many *parrillas* on the road by the lake, or try resto/bar *La Esquina* at the corner of Perón and Balcarce. The town has a surprisingly lively nightlife – one good bar is *La Porteña*, at Salgado and Junín – and there are regular *peñas* (folklore shows); ask at the tourist office for a schedule.

Estancias around Lobos

Upmarket accommodation is provided by nearby **estancias**, most notably the famous **La Candelaria**, RN-205 at Km114, 10km southwest of Lobos (T 02227/424404, W www.estanciacandelaria.com; 8). Distinguished by the extravagant turrets and towers of its **casco** – hence its local name, El Castillo – it features a garden laid out by Charles Thays (see box, p.130). The rooms – either inside El Castillo itself or in bungalows or a converted mill on the estate – are fairly simple although comfortable, and the meals – four are included – are served in the *casco*'s sumptuous dining room. The price also covers activities such as riding, tennis and swimming, and there's an on-site polo club that gives lessons.

Santa Rita (T 02227/495026, W www.santa-rita.com.ar; 8), just beyond the tiny village of Carboni, is more low-key, but its faded-pink *casco* has been renovated with great taste and aplomb by its new owners. The rooms are gorgeous – choose between fresh, clean Caribbean decor or darker Old World antique elegance; all have views over the estate. You can arrive at the estancia by train from Buenos Aires (Constitución); the train tracks run right past it and, with prior notice, you can arrange to get off in Carboni, from where the estancia's friendly, English-speaking owners will pick you up.

Azul and around

In the centre of Buenos Aires Province, 300km south of the capital, **AZUL** is useful mainly as a transport hub, with around one hundred buses a day connecting the town with the rest of the interior and the coast. There's little to detain you in the town itself, but excursions can be made to some gently rolling sierras 50km to the south, where there are a number of unusual sights, including Latin America's first **Trappist monastery**.

Plaza San Martín, Azul's main square, is noteworthy for its distinctive black and white Art Deco paving, which gives the rather unnerving impression of walking on an undulating surface. It is surrounded by an eclectic mixture of buildings, including the Neoclassical Palacio Municipal and the Neo-Gothic Catedral Nuestra Señora del Rosario. At Bartolomé Ronco 654, the Museo y Archivo Histórico E. Squirru (Tues–Sun 3–7pm; free) holds a good selection of Mapuche silverware, *mate* gourds and rifles. It also features examples of the traditional crafts that are currently being revived in Azul, including a pampas poncho, distinguished from other Argentine ponchos by its geometric design, predominantly black and white interspersed with a little red.

Practicalities

Azul's **train station** is on Cáneva, about twelve blocks east of Plaza San Martín, and its **bus terminal** at Mitre 1000. Azul's exceptionally helpful **tourist office** (Mon–Fri 7.30am–7.30pm, Sat & Sun 9am–1pm & 4.30–7.30pm; Ⓣ02281/431796, Ⓦwww.azul.gov.ar) is at Av 25 de Mayo 619. There are plenty of **accommodation** options in town. It's nicest to stay near the plaza – try the *Roma*, Bolívar 543 (Ⓣ02281/425286, Ⓔhotelroma1@speedy.com.ar; ❹), whose spotlessly clean rooms have fans and cable TV, or the smarter three-star *Gran Hotel Azul* on Plaza San Martín (Ⓣ02281/422011, Ⓔgranhotelazul@ciudad.com.ar; ❺). The municipal **campsite** (Ⓣ02281/434801), on the banks of the Arroyo del Azul just beyond the *balneario municipal*, is cheap and pleasant.

Azul's most enjoyable restaurant is the stylish *La Fonda*, San Martín 875. Terrific value for money, *La Fonda* has a daily changing menu; around six home-made dishes are offered, including excellent pasta, but best of all are the abundant and delicious *picadas*, which are served free of charge before the meal. *Dime*, Perón 490, is another good choice for reasonably priced and well-cooked Argentine standards.

Monasterio de Nuestra Señora de los Angeles and Pablo Acosta

Some 50km south of Azul, along RP-80, the **MONASTERIO DE NUESTRA SEÑORA DE LOS ANGELES** (Ⓣ02281/498005, Ⓦwww.trapenses.com.ar) – Latin America's first Trappist monastery – lies in the region known as Boca de las Sierras, a gentle pass through Azul's low, undulating sierras. The monastery's Sunday Masses (10am) are popular with visitors as well as inhabitants of the surrounding area and the monks also accept guests (men and married couples only) for spiritual retreats. The retreats run from Tuesday to Friday, and from Friday to Tuesday; reservations should be made by phone. Women can stay with nuns at a separate site in nearby Hinojo (Ⓣ02284/491083).

About 5km further along the same road, the tiny village of **PABLO ACOSTA** has a charming *almacén*, a traditional country store and bar. In the other direction, 50km north of Azul along RP-51 and RP-50, there is an unusually well-preserved and attractive *pulpería*, **San Gervasio** (Ⓣ02283/420630). Painted the traditional pink, and with a post outside for guests to tie up their horses, *San Gervasio* – despite being well off the beaten track – opens every day from around 3pm and serves *picadas.*

It is possible to go walking and horse-riding in the sierras but there are no marked trails and exploring the area entails scrambling over rocks and pushing your way through shoulder-high pampas grass. In addition, the military has an explosives range just to the north of the monastery. Exploring the area unsupervised is therefore not recommended – ask at Azul's tourist office or at travel agency La Veleta Viajes, Moreno 659 (Ⓣ02281/429200, Ⓦwww.laveletaviajes.com.ar) to see if accompanied visits are possible, or to arrange an excursion to the Monastery, Pablo Acosta or San Gervasio; there is no public transport service.

Tandil and around

TANDIL, 70km southeast of Azul, is set among the central section of the range of hills known as the **Sistema de Tandilia**. The range begins around 150km northwest of Tandil, running across the province to Mar del Plata, on the coast, and only rarely rising above 200m. Around Tandil, however, there are peaks of

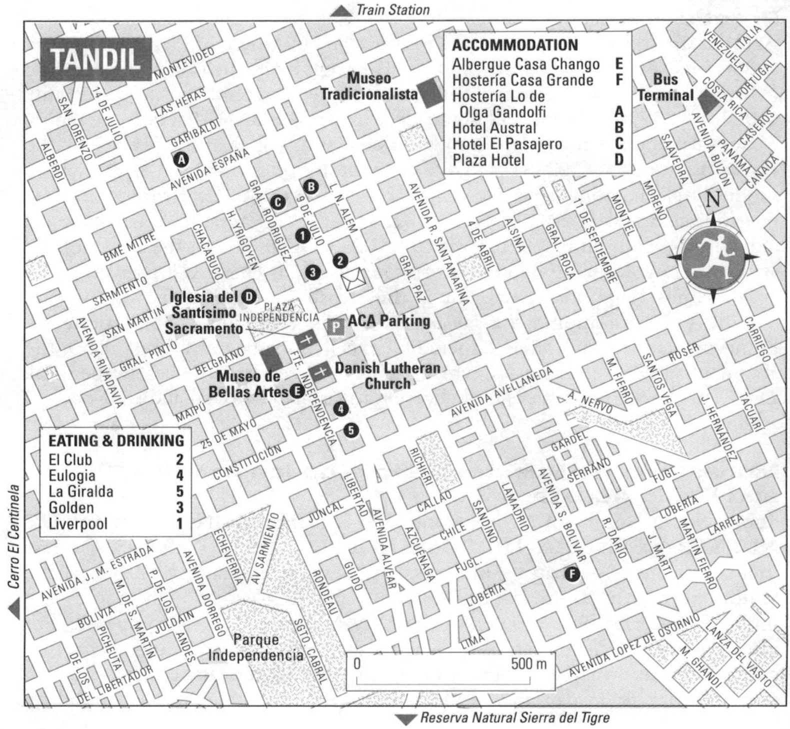

up to 500m. This is not wild trekking country, but Tandil's hills – somewhat reminiscent of the landscape of Wales or Ireland – are good for **horse-riding** and **mountain-biking**. The town itself is well geared for the holidaymakers that come all year on weekend breaks, with some very good delicatessens and restaurants and a lively, bustling feel in the evening. Tandil is particularly popular at Easter, the time of the **Vía Crucis** (Stations of the Cross) procession, which ends at Monte Calvario, a small hillock topped by a giant cross to the east of the town centre.

Arrival and information

Tandil's **bus terminal** (ⓣ02293/432092) is around fifteen blocks east of the main square, at Buzón 650; there are usually plenty of taxis (ⓣ02293/422466) waiting at the terminal to take you into town, or you could take local bus #503. The **train station** is at Avenida Machado and Colón, around twenty blocks northeast of the main square – trains leave weekly from Buenos Aires on Fridays and return on Sundays (ⓣ0800/2228736; 7hr). The main **tourist office** is east of the city centre, on the main route in at Av Espora 1120 (Mon–Sat 8am–8pm, Sun 9am–1pm; ⓣ02293/432073, ⓦwww.tandil.gov.ar), but there are also smaller, helpful offices at the bus terminal and on the Plaza Independencia.

Accommodation

Popular for short breaks throughout the year, Tandil is absolutely inundated in January and even more so at Easter, when most **hotels** substantially increase their prices and are often fully booked up to a month beforehand; otherwise, there is generally a good choice of mid-range accommodation. There are also numerous **cabañas** on the outskirts of the town (the tourist office has plenty of leaflets), although you'll need your own transport to reach most of them. Tandil also has a number of **campsites**: *Camping Chacra El Centinela* lies 4km west of town along Avenida Estrada (ⓣ02293/433475, ⓦwww.chacraelcentinela.com.ar); it's a quiet and attractive wooded site with hot water round the clock and firepits on the road out towards Cerro El Centinela. Log cabins are also available.

Albergue Casa Chango 25 de Mayo 451 ⓣ02293/422260, ⓦwww.casa-chango.com.ar. Youth hostel in a large, attractive house, colourfully decorated with an artistic touch. Decent dormitories ($20 per person) or double rooms (3). Scattered throughout the house are a series of pretty patios perfect for playing chess or chatting with one of the many Argentine students who make up the bulk of the guests.

Hostería Casa Grande Bolívar 557 ⓣ02293/431719, ⓦwww.hosteriacasagrande.com.ar. Very comfortable *hostería* in a one-storey stone building, with its own decent-sized pool. There's a recreation area with a bar, pool table and even a darts board. 7

Hostería Lo de Olga Gandolfi Chacabuco 977 ⓣ02293/440258, ⓦwww.lodeolgagandolfi.com.ar. A lovely rambling old building with a garden and *parrilla*. The furniture's a bit old and creaky, but the rooms are still good value; there's only a few of them and the place is particularly popular with families, so try to reserve in advance. 5

Hotel Austral 9 de Julio 725 ⓣ02293/425606, ⓦwww.hotel-torino.com.ar. A very friendly hotel in a modern building. The en-suite rooms are equipped with TV and telephone; the hotel does not offer breakfast but there is an adjoining *confitería*. 5

Hotel El Pasajero Rodriguez 783 ⓣ02293/443400, ⓦwww.cybertandil.com.ar/elpasajero. This central hotel's fresh, spacious rooms are relatively new and a particularly good deal. Breakfast and parking are included. 4

Plaza Hotel Gral Pinto 438 ⓣ02293/427160, ⓦwww.plazahoteltandil.com.ar. A three-star hotel with slightly sterile but comfortable a/c rooms and restaurant; rooms at the front overlook the plaza. 6

The Town

Many of the streets in Tandil's attractive town centre are cobbled with stones quarried from the surrounding sierra. Its central square, **Plaza Independencia**, on the site of the old fort, is overlooked by the rather grand municipalidad and the **Iglesia del Santísimo Sacramento**. Neo-Romanesque in style, it was inspired by Paris's Sacré Coeur – hence the unusual elongated domes which top the three towers. The streets surrounding the plaza, especially 9 de Julio, have a pleasant bustling feel, particularly in the evenings, when they are filled with people out for a stroll, or sitting outside the cafés and ice-cream parlours.

Northwest of the plaza, on the corner of San Martín and 14 de Julio, is one of Tandil's oldest buildings, a simple, white construction which originally functioned as a staging post and which now houses the *Epoca de Quesos* (daily 9am–dusk, www.epocadequesos.com) – a delicatessen and bar where you can buy local specialities, including every conceivable kind of salami, delicious garlic and herb cheeses, strong whisky cheddar, berry conserves and artisan dark stout. The house behind the deli has been as beautifully preserved as the jams and you can wander its tiny, antique rooms, with their homely little hearths straight out of a Hans Christian Andersen tale.

To the south, Tandil's streets slope down towards **Parque Independencia**. The park's entrance, on Avenida Avellaneda, is marked by the twin towers of a mock-Venetian palazzo, while its central wooded hill is topped by a kitsch Moorish castle. A road snakes around to the summit of the hill, from where there's a clear view over the city and an equally kitschy Moorish bar and restaurant, the *Morisco*, complete with belly dancers.

North of the town centre, at 4 de Abril 845, the **Museo Tradicionalista** (Tues–Sun 2–6pm; $3), is in a handsome old building and consists of a staggeringly large collection of artefacts donated by locals. Slightly disorganized, the museum is still a pleasant place to wander and boasts some interesting curiosities, including photos of the enormous **Piedra La Movediza** (literally "the moving stone"), which rested at an inconceivably steep angle on one of the town's many rocky outcrops, before finally smashing to the valley floor eighty years ago. The stone is so nationally famous that many Argentines are disappointed to arrive and find that it's no longer there; local authorities are hoping they will now be placated by the positioning in May 2007 of a cement replica in the place where the original once hovered. Outdoors in the museum's warehouses there are many valuable examples of the huge carts, or *chatas*, used to transport cereals around Argentina; the enormous wheels in the courtyard, the largest in the country, come from a *chata* that needed fifteen horses to pull it. Look out also for the *materas* – huge country hearths – where the gaucho and his clan would take their *mate*, roast their *asado*, stay warm, wash their clothes and just about everything else in between.

Eating, drinking and nightlife

There are plenty of good **restaurants** in Tandil, most of them within a few blocks of Plaza Independencia. *La Giralda* and *Eulogia*, on opposite sides of the intersection of Constitución and General Rodríguez, are attractive, old-fashioned places that both do classic, well-priced *parrilladas*, while *El Club*, Pinto 636, has a quietly elegant interior and serves up dishes with an emphasis on fish, such as salmon stuffed with spinach. On warm evenings, you'll find plenty of people sitting outside **bars** such as *Golden*, on the corner of 9 de Julio and Pinto, or *Liverpool*, on 9 de Julio and San Martín; the latter's Anglo-inspired interior comes complete with a red phone box and photos of England. Most **nightclubs** in Tandil are out towards the lake, on Avenida Alvear, since licensing laws prohibit clubs in the centre of town; an established favourite is the *Macoco Disco* at España 741.

The sierras

Opportunities for independent trekking in **Tandil's sierras** are somewhat limited, as much of the area is privately owned. The highest peak here is the **Sierra Las Animas** (504m), southeast of the town centre, not far from the end of Avenida Brasil. It's a two-hour scramble over rocks to the top, but the peak lies on private land and to access it you must go with a guide – the tourist office has a list. Much more visited, and more accessible, is **Cerro El Centinela**, a small peak in the sierras topped by **El Centinela**, an upright seven-metre rock balanced on an unfeasibly tiny base. Head southwest along Avenida J.M. Estrada, the continuation of Avenida Avellaneda. The signposted track to the Cerro lies to the left, about 5km out of town. The Cerro has been turned into a *complejo* (complex) with all kinds of attractions, and consequently is perhaps a bit too developed for some tastes. The road now stops just a few metres short of El Centinela, and – should all that driving make you hungry – there's a *parrilla* here, too. Nearby is the base of the *aerosilla*, or chairlift (noon–dusk; $10 return), a fifteen-minute ride over the pines of the valley to another, higher peak from where you can enjoy views over the hills as well as waffles and milkshakes at the *Salon de Cumbre*, a *confitería*. Short walks are possible in the vicinity of the chairlift.

Perhaps the best way to explore the region is with the growing number of companies offering **adventure tourism** opportunities, embracing a range of activities including trekking, abseiling, canoeing and mountain-biking, such as Nido de Condores, Necochea 166 (ⓣ02293/426519, ⓦwww.nidodecondores.com.ar). If you fancy getting to know the sierras on horseback, contact Gabriel Barletta, Avellaneda 673 (ⓣ02293/427725, ⓔcabalgatasbarletta@yahoo.com.ar), who organizes adventurous half-day rides, and regularly takes groups swimming. Mountain bikes can be rented at Perón 1361 (ⓣ02293/436320).

Several blocks south of town, on the corner of Don Bosco and Suiza, the **Reserva Natural Sierra del Tigre** (daily 10am–6pm; $3) is a privately run stretch of sierra of some 1.5 square kilometres where you can see indigenous species such as guanacos as well as exotic deer and antelope. The sierra is also home to the tiny *marí marí* frog, barely the size of a thumbnail and only found here and in Córdoba. The reserve's highest point is **Cerro Venado** (389m), an easy walk along the unsealed road that winds to the top, from where there are good views over the surrounding sierra. Near the entrance to the reserve there is a small zoo housing pumas, grey foxes and ñandús.

The Western Pampas

Moving west across the province, you'll cross an unbroken stretch of pampas with little except farmland, homesteads and the odd market town for several hundred kilometres. Around the border area between Buenos Aires Province and La Pampa Province, however, things get more interesting, with several nature-based attractions. The area is off the beaten track for most foreign tourists, and you won't find the grand scale of Patagonia or the Andes here, but you will find a friendly welcome and some fun day-trips.

Increasingly popular with domestic visitors, the mountains of the **Sierra de la Ventana** range offer good trekking near two pretty villages – Sierra de la Ventana and Villa Ventana – and their many well-equipped *cabañas*, perfect to use as a base for exploring the area. La Pampa Province itself is not the country's most exciting, but the sunny capital **Santa Rosa** is a decent enough place to break a journey. There are two parks in the province, **Parque Provincial Luro** and **Parque Nacional Lihué Calel**, as well as a sprinkling of working estancias, where you can help out at harvest and learn to lasso.

Sierra de la Ventana and around

The rugged **Sierra de la Ventana** mountain range, 550km southwest of Buenos Aires, is the principal attraction of southern Buenos Aires Province. Running from northeast to southwest for 100km or so, the sierras' craggy spine forms an unlikely backdrop to the serene pampas and provides the best opportunities in the province for walking and climbing. The range is named after one of its highest points, the **Cerro de la Ventana**, a 1134-metre peak pierced by a small "window", or *ventana*; it's located within the **Parque Provincial Ernesto Tornquist**, bisected by RP-76, the main highway through the sierras. There are plenty of options for accommodation in the area: as well as a base camp within the park, there are two villages within striking distance of the range, with **Sierra de la Ventana** being the best set-up for visitors, around 30km southeast of the park entrance. **Villa Ventana** is a quiet wooded village south of the park, just 5km from the park entrance; it has a more laid-back atmosphere than Sierra village.

Compared to the older and gentler Tandilia range to the northeast, these are proper mountains, with peaks tall enough to be shrouded with dark grey clouds in bad weather and to dominate the horizon for some distance. Formed principally from sedimentary rock during the Paleozoic period, the range is

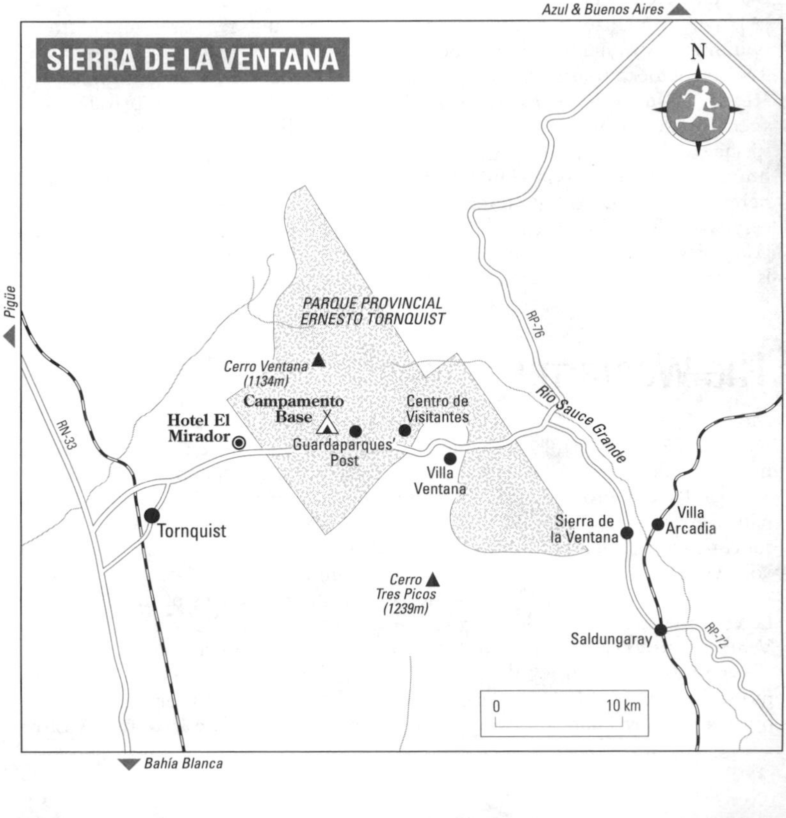

notable for its intensely folded appearance and for its subtle grey-blue and pink hues – thrown into relief in late summer against the yellowing cultivated fields that surround the sierras. Though the harsh, somewhat threatening, peaks may appear rather barren, the area also supports a surprising range of **wildlife**, including pumas, foxes, guanaco, armadillos, vizcachas and the copper iguana, which is named for its distinctive colour and is one of over forty species endemic to the region. The area around the foot of the sierras is also notable for being one of the last remaining tracts of original pampas grassland, roamed by herds of wild horses.

The province's highest peak, **Cerro Tres Picos** (1239m), sits on private land 6km south of Villa Ventana. It is less dramatic looking than Cerro de la Ventana, but its height, combined with its distance from the nearest base, makes it a more substantial hike. It is usually done as a two-day trek, overnighting in a cave on the way up. The route passes through the **Estancia Funke** and you must go with a guide provided by them. The estancia has an on-site campsite and *albergue*; rooms in the nineteenth-century homestead are reserved for German-speakers only, in keeping with the estancia's Germanic origins. Rock-climbing and mountain-biking are also possible. For all the above, contact Monica Silva at the estancia (Ⓣ0291/494-0058, Ⓦwww.cerrotrespicos.com).

The easiest way of **getting around** the sierras is with your own transport; if you're relying on public transport you'll need to plan carefully: local services by La Estrella and tour agency Sergio Rodriguez (see p.255) run along RP-76, stopping more or less everywhere along the route, including both park entrances, the turn-off to Villa Ventana and Sierra de la Ventana. Buses go two or three times a day in either direction. Alternatively, you could take a taxi – try Radio Taxi San Bernardo (Ⓣ0291/491-5031), based in Sierra de la Ventana.

Parque Provincial Ernesto Tornquist

The majority of walking and climbing activities take place within a relatively small stretch of the sierras, mostly contained within the **Parque Provincial Ernesto Tornquist**, which covers about 67 square kilometres. There are two **entrances** to the park (summer 8am–6pm, winter 9am–4pm), both just off RP-76. The main entrance is around 22km from Sierra de la Ventana village, signposted "Acceso Reserva Nacional". This is where you'll find the **Centro de Visitantes**, with a good display of photos of the region's flora and fauna and a useful 3D topographical map. From the Centro de Visitantes you can also visit the **Reserva Natural Integral**, a strictly controlled sector of the park where herds of wild horses can be seen, and caves, including one with ancient paintings, can be explored. Visits to the reserve are in your own vehicle accompanied by a guide ($5) and generally take place twice a day in high season and weekends only in low season – enquire at the Centro. If you don't have your own vehicle, you may be able to join a Sergio Rodriguez Turismo excursion (see p.255). Two **treks** also start here: the moderately difficult walk to the top of nearby peak **Cerro Blanco** (2.5hr return trip), with great views of the surrounding area; and the easy **Claro Oscuro** trek (2hr), which is a guided visit to two ecosystems – one introduced, one endemic.

The rest of the park's treks are in the **Monumento Natural**, an area of the park that includes the national monument of Cerro Ventana; the entrance is around 5km west of the main entrance. There is a helpful *guardaparques*' post (Ⓣ0291/491-0039) here, which can usually provide you with a sketchy map of the main attractions, as well as indications of distance, direction and estimated duration of the walks. A well-marked trail to the summit of 1134-metre **Cerro Ventana** leads northeast from the *guardaparques*' post. The peak is pierced by a hole that measures eight by four metres that was formed by the collapse of a cave. On clear days, the hole is visible from the road – although from this distance it appears a rather insignificant opening. You'll get a much more rewarding view from the summit, where the phenomenon lives up to its name (*ventana* meaning window in Spanish), its jagged edges framing a wonderful view of the surrounding sierras and pampas. Though the climb to the summit (5hr return trip; access 8am–noon; $4) is not difficult, you need to be basically fit. Follow the park keepers' guidelines, and be aware that conditions can change dramatically. There are a couple of short walks around the same area that are worth trying: to the **Piletones**, or rock pools, to the northwest of the *guardaparques*' post (2hr; $2); and to the **Garganta Olvidada**, a small waterfall enclosed on three sides by jagged shelves of pinkish-grey rock, which lies to the northeast (2hr; $2). More dramatic is the **Garganta del Diablo**, a gorge reached on a five-hour guided trek (9am daily if there's enough interest – enquire at the *guardaparques'* post; $4). Along the way, you can swim in natural rock pools.

Campamento Base (Ⓣ0291/491-0067, Ⓔrhperrando@uol.com.ar), a few minutes' walk west of the *guardaparques*' post, and recognizable from the road by its iron gate, is the best **place to stay** if you want to start out early for the park; as well as a shady campsite, the site provides dormitory accommodation (❶) and some cabins with wood-burning stoves for up to six people. You'll need to bring sleeping bags for all accommodation options. Cooking facilities and hot showers are provided and there is a small shop with a few basics. For more luxurious accommodation, head for *Hotel El Mirador* (Ⓣ0291/494-1338, Ⓦwww.complejoelmirador.com.ar; ❻ with breakfast; half- and full board also available), just outside the park; it has some pleasant rooms overlooking the sierras as well as attractive and well-equipped wooden cabins that hold from four to eight people (❽ with breakfast). The hotel also has a good restaurant and swimming pool. A few kilometres west along RP-76 good home cooking is on offer at the *Ich-Hutu* **restaurant** whose specialities include pasta, and rabbit with peppers and onions in *escabeche*, a delicious sour-sweet vinaigrette.

Sierra de la Ventana village

Away from its rather drab main street, Avenida San Martín, **SIERRA DE LA VENTANA** is a pretty, quiet little village with sandy lanes encircled by streams. The colourful train station, with its green iron roof and turquoise shutters, gives a happy, holiday feel to the place, while, tucked away down leafy lanes, there are some quaint old-fashioned buildings that lend a more rustic air. Divided into several barrios and dissected by both a railway line and the Río Sauce Grande, the village has a rather disjointed layout. Its centre is really **Villa Tivoli**, which lies west of the railway tracks; here you'll find most shops and restaurants. By following San Martín east over the rail tracks, you'll come first to **Barrio Parque Golf**, a mostly residential area of curving streets and chalet-style buildings. More appealing is quiet **Villa Arcadia** to the north, separated from Barrio Parque Golf by a bridge over the Río Sauce Grande (note that, technically, Villa Arcadia is in a different district, so the tourist office has no information on it). There are various swimming spots throughout the village, mostly to the north of Avenida San Martín, along the banks of the Río Sauce Grande.

Practicalities

Buses from Buenos Aires, La Plata and Bahía Blanca drop you at the small bus terminal on Av San Martín. For return journeys to the capital, it's best to buy tickets in advance. The **train station**, also with services from Buenos Aires and Bahía Blanca, is at the intersection of Avenida Roca and San Martín. At

Av Roca 15, you'll find the busy **tourist office** (daily 8am–2pm & 5–10pm, although hours may vary slightly according to the season; ⓣ0291/491-5303, ⓦwww.sierradelaventana.org.ar), with maps, accommodation lists and transport details for the area.

There's a good range of **accommodation** in and around Sierra de la Ventana village. One option is the enormous and attractive *Pillahuincó Parque Hotel*, Av Raíces 161, Villa Arcadia (ⓣ0291/491-5423, ⓦwww.hotelpillahuinco.com.ar), which is set in beautiful grounds with a swimming pool (❺, half-board ❻). It organizes trekking and biking excursions in the area and also has a campsite. There are many other **campsites** around the village, including some free ones near the municipal pool, which lies north along Diego Meyer, the last road on your left before you reach the rail tracks in Villa Tivoli. However, the most popular form of accommodation on both sides of the river is the area's **cabañas**, which can represent good value for money, especially if there's two or more of you. They range in price from $100 to $300 for two people (around double that for six), are usually quite cosy and come fully equipped with kitchen, bathroom, beds and living area; if you are on your own, you will generally have to pay the two-person price. The tourist office has a complete list, or you could try the friendly *Balcón del Golf* (ⓣ0291/491-5222, ⓦwww.balcondelgolf.com; ❻), which has comfortable cabins with all mod cons as well as a sauna and pool. To get there head over the bridge into Villa Arcadia and follow the road straight for about 500m.

There are few **restaurants** in the village, although there's one very good *parrilla*, the *Rali-Hue*, at San Martín 307, which does an excellent *parrillada* for two people. Other than this, it's mostly typical pizza and empanada joints. A good alternative, especially if you're staying in a *cabaña*, is to visit the popular deli *La Rueda*, San Martín 250, and arm your own *picada* from its range of delicious salamis and cheeses; you can also get a bottle of wine here.

Sergio Rodriguez Turismo, sometimes referred to by its old name, Geotur, Av San Martín 193 (ⓣ0291/491-5355), organizes a number of **excursions** in the area, including to the nearby Estancia El Pantanoso, where aromatic plants and herbs such as lavender and thyme are cultivated, and to the Reserva Natural. They also do horse-riding and bike trips.

Villa Ventana

About 18km northwest of Sierra de la Ventana village, and just off RP-76, lies **VILLA VENTANA**. The village is squeezed between two streams, the Arroyo de Las Piedras and the Arroyo Belisario, and its chief appeal lies in its dense forestation and rambling lanes. Although it is growing fast, it's still a laid-back place that makes a relaxing base for exploring the area. The village has an elongated shape, making a fair bit of walking inevitable. Orienting yourself, however, is fairly straightforward: the main thoroughfare, Avenida Cruz del Sur, runs north–south through the village from the access road. The local museum, **Sendero de los Recuerdos** (Thurs–Sun 3–8pm; $3), 1km behind the village out along Las Piedras, has lots of info on the local area, including the story of the nearby **ex-Club Hotel**, which was built in 1911, before Villa Ventana existed. Initially, the hotel was a grand enterprise, filled with expensive European furniture and visited by the Argentine and foreign upper classes, who arrived by the purpose-built railway to gamble in the country's first casino. In 1917, gambling was banned and the hotel closed soon after, remaining shuttered until 1940, when 350 German soldiers were given safe haven. There, they saw out the war – playing tennis, doing up the rooms, giving Wagner concerts to the community and charming the local girls. After they left, the building gradually fell into disrepair and a plan in the 1980s to rebuild it was cut short after a suspicious fire gutted what was left. There are regular **guided visits** to the ruins, 2km to the west of the village – ask at the tourist office.

Practicalities

Villa Ventana has a useful **tourist office** (daily 9am–2pm & 4–8pm; ⓣ0291/491-0095) in a cabin at the village's main entrance. Accommodation is all in **cabañas**. *Aventura*, Gorrión and De Las Piedras (ⓣ0291/491-0062, ⓦwww.aventuralodge.com.ar; ❺), offers compact but cute log cabins which sleep two to eight people; all come with TV and kitchen. They also do excursions into the sierras in jeeps or on horseback. You could also try *Piuquelom* on the corner of Cruz del Sur and Chingolo (ⓣ0291/491-0079, ⓦwww.piuquelom.com.ar; ❺), which has fully kitted-out wooden bungalows that come with real fires to warm your feet in winter.

There are a number of **teahouses** in the village, including the lovely *Heidi* (ⓣ0291/491-0155), whose scrumptious home-made cakes and fairy-tale garden are well worth the trek to the southern end of Calle Curumalal. For something a bit more substantial, there's good Italian food at *Da Roberto*, on Cruz del Sur and Carpintero. At Cruz del Sur and Canario, near the village entrance, there's a small arcade that offers pizza and Internet access, with a *locutorio* just across the way.

Santa Rosa and around

SANTA ROSA promotes itself as the gateway to Patagonia, and indeed the only real reasons to visit La Pampa Province's capital, at the southwestern end of RN-5, are to break a long journey to or from Patagonia, or to use it as a base from which to visit the **Parque Nacional Lihué Calel**, the province's major attraction. **Parque Luro**, 35km south, is much less wild than the national park but offers a few gentle walks and opportunities for bird-watching. Santa Rosa is well connected to Buenos Aires, Neuquén, Bahía Blanca and Bariloche by public transport – but connections to the rest of the province from the town are less frequent and require planning. As you head south and west, the condition of roads in general also starts to deteriorate.

As elsewhere in the country, declining agricultural fortunes are prodding ever-increasing numbers of **estancias** to open their gates to visitors. Although the grander, more luxurious ones tend to be closer to Buenos Aires, there are quite a few smaller, less-visited places in La Pampa Province, including working estancias where you can muck in with jobs around the farm.

In a rather different mode, plans are afoot to build a casino town at Casa de Piedra, 400km southwest of Santa Rosa, next to an artificial lake. The tourist board hopes that one day this will be Argentina's answer to Las Vegas, but for now it's nothing more than desert dust and dreams.

Arrival and information

Santa Rosa's **airport**, with flights to Buenos Aires three times a week, is out on RN-35, a few kilometres north of the town centre. The **bus terminal** is at Av Luro 365, where a not terribly helpful 24-hour information office (ⓣ02954/422952) may be able to provide you with maps and accommodation lists. Across the road is the provincial **tourist office**, Av Luro 400 (daily summer 7am–10pm, winter 7am–8pm; ⓣ02954/425060, ⓦwww.turismolapampa.gov.ar), whose patient and helpful staff can provide information on the province's lesser-known regions and assist you in working out transport routes.

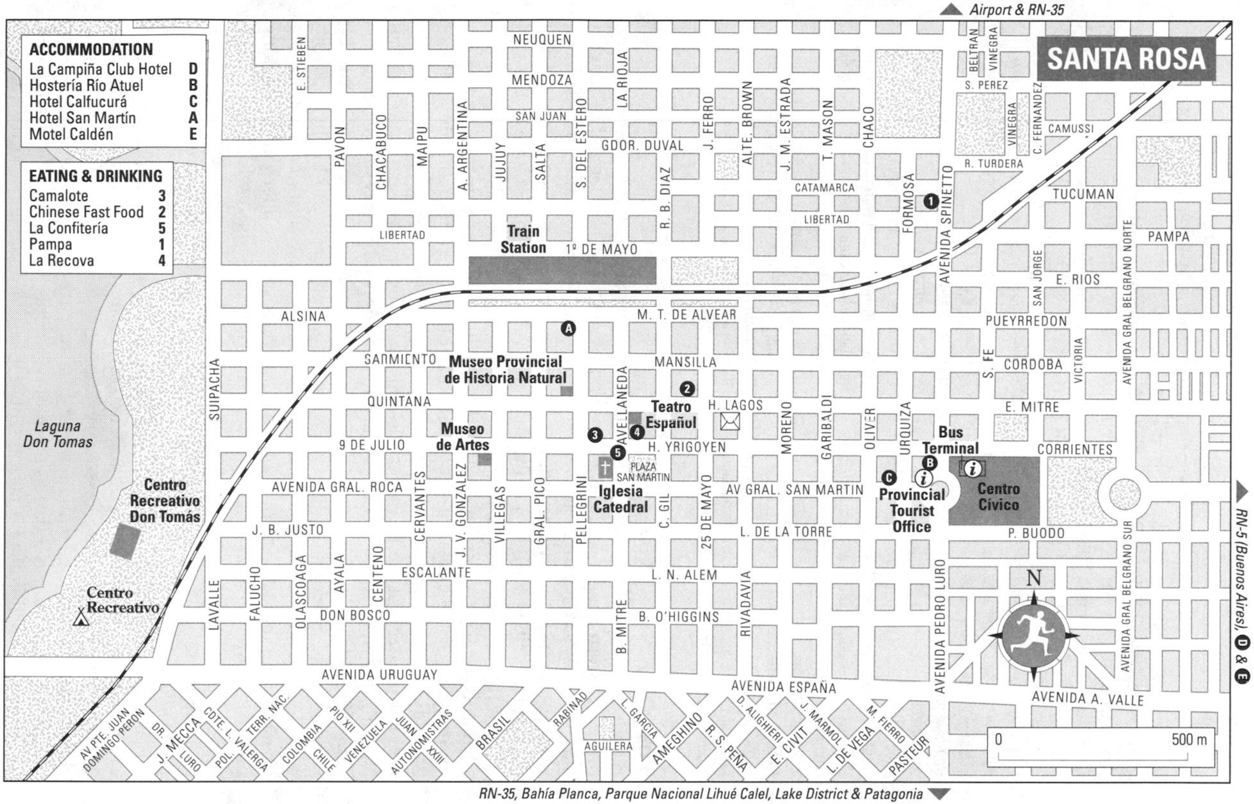
SANTA ROSA
ACCOMMODATION
La Campiña Club Hotel D
Hostería Río Atuel B
Hotel Calfucurá C
Hotel San Martín A
Motel Caldén E
EATING & DRINKING
Camalote 3
Chinese Fast Food 2
La Confitería 5
Pampa 1
La Recova 4
Airport & RN-35
RN-5 (Buenos Aires), D & E
RN-35, Bahía Planca, Parque Nacional Lihué Calel, Lake District & Patagonia
Train Station
Museo Provincial de Historia Natural
Museo de Artes
Teatro Español
Iglesia Catedral
PLAZA SAN MARTIN
Bus Terminal
Provincial Tourist Office
Centro Cívico
Centro Recreativo Don Tomás
Centro Recreativo
Laguna Don Tomas
AVENIDA SPINETTO
1º DE MAYO
M. T. DE ALVEAR
AVENIDA GRAL. ROCA
AV GRAL. SAN MARTIN
AVENIDA URUGUAY
AVENIDA ESPAÑA
AVENIDA PEDRO LURO
AVENIDA GRAL BELGRANO NORTE
AVENIDA GRAL BELGRANO SUR
AVENIDA A. VALLE
N
0 500 m

Accommodation

In general, Santa Rosa's places to stay are pretty nondescript. Most **hotels** are within a few blocks of the bus terminal, with some reasonable motels on the main roads in and out of the city – but these are only really accessible if you have your own transport. The *Centro Recreativo*, a spacious if rather dreary-looking park on the banks of the Laguna Don Tomás, hosts the municipal **campsite** (ⓣ02954/455358) – though it's mostly used for picnicking by day-trippers. The park, which redeems itself somewhat thanks to its sporting facilities, including a large swimming pool, is ten blocks west of Plaza San Martín along avenidas Uruguay or Roca.

La Campiña Club Hotel RN-5 Km604 ⓣ02954/456800 ⓦwww.lacampina.com. The most luxurious place to stay in Santa Rosa, *La Campiña* has a country-club feel to it, with very comfortable rooms and a good, popular swimming pool. It's 6km out of town on RN-5. ❻

Hostería Río Atuel Av Luro 356 ⓣ02954/422597. The best of the budget bunch, with modern, airy rooms that have TVs and private bathrooms; price includes breakfast. ❸

Hotel Calfucurá San Martín 695 ⓣ02954/423612, ⓦwww.hotelcalfucura.com. This four-star place has comfortable modern rooms and a swimming pool. The concrete monolith of a building is easily recognizable by a nine-storey mural of the eponymous indigenous chief painted on its side. ❻

Hotel San Martín Alsina and Pellegrini ⓣ02954/422549, ⓦwww.hsanmartin.com.ar. Opposite the defunct train station, *San Martín* is a classic mid-range hotel with large, modern rooms; facilities include laundry service and parking. ❺

Motel Caldén Av Perón and Farinatti ⓣ02954/424311, ⓦwww.hotelescalden.com.ar. Typical Santa Rosa motel, 3km north of the bus terminal on RN-5. The rooms have a/c and TV, and there is a sizeable swimming pool. ❺

The City

A rather squat modern city of around 100,000 inhabitants, Santa Rosa is sited on the western fringes of the wet pampa. Its predominantly flat and somewhat exposed position means that it receives the full brunt of the pampas' harsh winters and its bakingly hot summers. It's primarily a business and administrative centre – albeit with a friendly, small-town feel – and offers little in the way of conventional sightseeing.

Santa Rosa has two centres, which lie about eight blocks apart. The **centro cívico**, site of the province's governmental offices, lies immediately south of Santa Rosa's busy bus terminal; the surrounding streets are also where you'll find the majority of the town's hotels. On the corner of avenidas Luro and San Martín, and well worth a visit, you'll find the **Mercado Artesanal** (Mon–Fri 7am–1pm & 4–8pm, Sat 8am–noon & 5–9pm), a regional crafts outlet run by the provincial government. The market sells leather goods and kitchen utensils carved from the reddish-brown caldén tree, whose distinctive spreading branches can be seen throughout the province. The outlet's most striking products, however, are the hand-woven pampas textiles dyed with vivid aniline dyes. More subtle hues are obtained from natural substances extracted from indigenous shrubs. One of the plants, piquillín, is also used to make syrup (*arrope de piquillín*).

Following Avenida Roca eight blocks west will bring you to Santa Rosa's other centre, a more relaxed and social area. Its main square is the **Plaza San Martín**. The plaza has the customary leaping equestrian statue at its heart; a slightly more unexpected sight is the bizarre **cathedral** on its western side. Regarded, no doubt, as a daring piece of Modernism when it was inaugurated, the honeycombed concrete facade sadly looks more like a contorted piece of novelty pasta. The plaza's most appealing feature is probably its pavement cafés on its northwest corner.

Santa Rosa's extremely modest museums are not worth going out of your way for, but if you're really stuck for something to do, the old-fashioned **Museo Provincial de Historia Natural** at Pellegrini 180 (Mon–Fri 8am–noon & 2–6pm, Sun 6–9pm; closed Jan; free), one block northwest of Plaza San Martín, bears visiting, if only to see what elusive species like the mara or the Patagonian hare actually look like. The museum also has a small collection of Indian artefacts as well as dinosaur fossils, discovered when the town centre was redeveloped in 1994.

Eating, drinking and nightlife

Eating options in Santa Rosa are limited, a situation made worse by the fact that most of the best places are *parrillas* on the main roads in and out of the city, such as *Restaurante Calden*, at a Caldén motel found by following Avenida Spinetto out to Km330 on RN-35, whose menu includes local specialities such as *jabalí* (boar) and vizcacha. In the centro cívico, your best bet is the decent restaurant in *Hotel Calfucurá*, which serves a variety of chicken and fish dishes. Otherwise, at H. Lagos 245 there's a cheap *tenedor libre*, the not particularly Chinese *Chinese Fast Food*, while long-running *Pampa*, Catamarca 15, does large portions of home-made pasta.

The majority of Santa Rosa's **confiterías** are concentrated around Plaza San Martín, which has a lively atmosphere on summer evenings as groups assemble around tables set on the pavement around *La Recova* and *La Confitería*, both on the corner of Avellaneda and H.Yrigoyen. Santa Rosa's best **bar** is *Camalote*, 9 de Julio 48, which has outdoor tables from where you can watch Santa Rosa in full swing. There are a handful of **nightclubs**, mostly catering to a very young crowd, around this same area at Yrigoyen and 9 de Julio. It's also worth checking to see if there's anything on at the pretty Teatro Español, at H. Lagos 44 (ⓣ02954/455325), which is notable for its rather Baroque interior and often puts on tango or folklore shows.

Listings

Airlines Aerolíneas Argentinas, Moreno 197 ⓣ02954/433076.
Exchange There are several banks and ATMs in the streets surrounding Plaza San Martín; there's also the useful Banco de la Pampa ATM next to the tourist office on Av Luro. You may be able to change travellers' cheques at one of the town's travel agents.
Hospital Av Circunvalación and Raúl B. Díaz ⓣ02954/455000.
Internet access *Locutorio* at 9 de Julio 49.
Laundry H. Yrigoyen, between Oliver and Garibaldi.
Post office Corner of H. Lagos and Rivadavia.
Taxis Radio Taxi Centro ⓣ02954/428682.
Travel agents Great Travels, T. Mason 26 ⓣ02954/454300, has excursions to Lihué Calel and other towns in La Pampa.

Estancias around Santa Rosa

There are a number of **estancias** in the vicinity of Santa Rosa that offer a different perspective on La Pampa life. They can be difficult to access, but the owners will generally arrange for someone to come and pick you up from Santa Rosa; prices usually include this transfer, plus all meals and activities. The closest to the provincial capital and with perhaps the most creature comforts is **Estancia Villaverde** (ⓣ02954/438764, ⓦwww.estanciavillaverde.com.ar; ❽), a fully functioning estancia that has some pleasant, if rather floral, rooms for guests. As well as joining in at sowing and harvest time, you can do horseback and carriage excursions around the grounds and further afield. A little wilder and further out, life at **Estancia La Mercedes** (ⓣ02954/454375,

Ⓔ estancia_lamercedes@hotmail.com; ⑥), 40km from the city, revolves around horses – pureblood racehorses are bred here. If you're an experienced rider, you can enjoy galloping around, practising the sport of pato and getting involved with tasks such as lassoing bulls; if not, riding lessons will be given. The tourist office in Santa Rosa has a complete list of the province's estancias.

Reserva Provincial Parque Luro

A gently rolling park of grassland and open forest, the **Reserva Provincial Parque Luro** (March–Nov Tues–Sun 9am–7pm, Dec–Feb same days 8am–8pm; $1; Ⓣ02954/499000) lies 35km south of Santa Rosa. Originally created as a preserve for hunting game, the park was bought by the province in 1965 and is now a haven for wildlife in a region where hunting is still widespread. Its seven and a half square kilometres are home to native pumas and ñandús, but you're actually much more likely to catch sight of red deer, imported from Europe for hunting at the beginning of the twentieth century. The park's other exotic inhabitant is the wild boar, although this surprisingly shy creature is harder to see. Though both species are now protected within the park, escapees have multiplied throughout the rest of the province, where they once again face the business end of a rifle.

Over fifty species of **birds** visit the reserve, and on a quiet day you have a good chance of seeing many of them, including the White-browed Blackbird, with its startling bright red breast; the brilliant White Monjita and the Fork-tailed Flycatcher. Look out, too, for large flocks of the *loro barranquero*, a brightly coloured parrot, and noisy budgerigars, common in Argentina though often regarded as a nuisance for their ear-piercing squawk. Flocks of flamingoes also gather around the park's lake, the Laguna del Potrillo Oscuro; less welcome are the vicious mosquitoes that also hang out here.

On sunny weekends, the park is often dominated by picnicking day-trippers; if you fancy doing something a little more strenuous than eating, follow one of the three short signposted **walks**. None of them takes more than half an hour or so and each visits a different kind of environment – lake (*laguna*), woods (*bosque*) and dunes (*médanos*). At the centre of the park lies a clunky white mansion, whose permanently closed green shutters lend it a rather spectral air. Known as **El Castillo**, the mansion was built by Pedro Luro, son of one of the founders of Mar del Plata and the park's creator. The mansion's still-furnished interior can be visited on regular guided tours ($2); ask at the park's **Centro de Interpretación**, which also features good photos of the reserve's wildlife. Past the information centre, a road leads round to a picnic area, where there is also a restaurant and a privately run and not particularly welcoming **campsite**, which also has en-suite *cabañas* (Ⓣ02954/420071).

A **bus** service from Santa Rosa stops at the park entrance several times a day.

Parque Nacional Lihué Calel

A rather austere park, **Parque Nacional Lihué Calel** is dominated by the softly contoured granite sierras that run east to west across its hundred square kilometres. Formed through volcanic activity 200 million years ago, the sierras emerge from a tract of wild open scrub, typical of the south of the province. Their slippery layers of ignimbrite rock retain hints of a violent origin in the cavities formed by the burst bubbles that pockmark their surface. The sierras help to retain water from the region's scarce rainfall and, it is claimed, to moderate La Pampa's fierce summer temperatures. As a result, the park harbours a richer variety of vegetation than is found in the surrounding area. This microclimate was more succinctly described by the region's indigenous inhabitants when they called the place Lihué Calel – Araucanian for "Sierra of Life".

Despite its modest topography, Lihué Calel can be a stunning place: enhanced by the low light of sunrise or sunset, the intense reddish hues of the sierras glow against the surrounding countryside. In dull or rainy weather, however, scrub and rock merge gloomily with the threatening sky and the park can seem bleak indeed. A couple of days should suffice to see Lihué Calel: much of the park is off-limits to visitors, although the part that has been made accessible contains its most scenic areas, including the highest peak, the **Cerro Alto** (590m).

△ Vulture, Parque Nacional Lihué Calel

The region's first inhabitants, hunter-gatherers, have left behind paintings in the park's **Valle de las Pinturas**. The meaning of these delicate 2000-year-old geometric designs is still unclear – indeed they may have been purely decorative. Though protected from the elements by overhanging rock formations, they have been damaged by vandalism and a barrier has been put up to stop you getting too close. In the nineteenth century, Lihué Calel was the last base of Namuncará, a famous Araucanian chief, who finally surrendered to Argentine forces in 1884, after various bloody battles.

As well as caldén trees and jarilla bushes, common throughout the rest of the province, the park harbours an unusual mixture of **vegetation**, which includes both humidity-loving ferns and cacti and the endemic delicate yellow flower of the margarita pampeana. The star of Lihué Calel's varied **fauna** is undoubtedly the puma. Sadly, though, you've a very slim chance of actually seeing one of these shy and beautiful cats – pumas appear to be in decline in the park and are only rarely seen these days. It seems likely that this is partly due to a shortage of their favourite meal, the vizcacha, a member of the chinchilla family. Slightly easier to see are grey foxes – who are occasionally found lurking around the campsite – and herds of guanaco, although picking out their well-camouflaged forms against the sierra requires a keen eye. Other species found in the park include ñandús, armadillos and wild cats, while red deer and wild boar, unwelcome exotic migrants from Parque Luro, have also found their way into the park. Both the highly venomous and aggressive yarará and the similarly toxic, less aggressive coral snake also inhabit the park. There are also around 150 species of birds found here, including various types of vultures, buzzards, falcons, hummingbirds, the exquisitely coloured Tanager, the Yellow Cardinal and the Rufous-bellied Thrush.

Practicalities

Lihué Calel is 226km south of Santa Rosa on RN-152, between General Acha (120km north) and Puelches (35km south). **Buses** to Puelches from Santa Rosa – several a day – will drop you at the entrance. There is a free **campsite** in the park itself, with showers and toilets. Bring your own food – the nearest stop for provisions is at Puelches – and a torch. For general information on the park, contact Lihué Calel's *guardaparques*, who maintain a small **visitors' centre** (Ⓣ02952/436595).

Travel details

Buses

Azul to: Buenos Aires (hourly; 4–5hr); Mar del Plata (7 daily; 4hr).
Bahía Blanca to: Bariloche (5 daily; 12–14hr); Buenos Aires (hourly; 9hr); Neuquén (5 daily; 7hr); Sierra de la Ventana (1 daily; 2hr 30min); Tornquist (1 daily; 1hr); Viedma (2 daily; 3–4hr).
Claromecó to: Buenos Aires (2 daily; 9hr); Tres Arroyos (2 daily; 1hr).
La Plata to: Buenos Aires (every 30min; 1hr).
Lobos to: Buenos Aires (every 30min; 2hr).
Mar del Plata to: Bahía Blanca (5 daily; 6hr); Bariloche (1 daily; 20hr); Buenos Aires (hourly; 7hr); Córdoba (3 daily; 18hr); Neuquén (1 daily; 12hr); Santa Rosa (4 daily; 11hr).
Miramar to: Buenos Aires (7 daily; 8hr); Mar del Plata (every 30min; 1hr); Necochea (2 daily; 2hr).
Necochea to: Bahía Blanca (5 daily; 4hr); Bariloche (2 daily; 18hr); Buenos Aires (hourly; 9hr); Mar del Plata (hourly; 3hr); Neuquén (2 daily; 10hr); Tandil (4 daily; 3hr); Tres Arroyos (5 daily; 3hr).
Pinamar to: Buenos Aires (10 daily; 5hr); Mar del Plata (hourly; 2hr).
San Clemente to: Buenos Aires (10 daily; 5hr).
San Miguel del Monte to: Buenos Aires (hourly; 2hr); Tandil (3 daily; 3hr).
Santa Rosa to: Bariloche (2 daily; 13hr); Buenos Aires (hourly; 8–10hr); Neuquén (8 daily; 7–8hr).

Sierra de la Ventana to: Azul (Mon–Fri & Sun 1 daily; 4hr); Bahía Blanca (2 daily; 2hr 30min); Buenos Aires (Mon–Fri & Sun 1 daily; 8hr).
Tandil to: Azul (6 daily; 2hr); Bahía Blanca (3 daily; 6hr); Buenos Aires (hourly; 5hr); Mar del Plata (hourly; 3hr); Necochea (4 daily; 3hr); San Miguel del Monte (3 daily; 3hr); Santa Rosa (2 daily; 9hr).
Villa Gesell to: Buenos Aires (hourly; 6hr); Bariloche (1 daily; 22hr); Córdoba (1 daily; 17hr); Mar del Plata (5 daily; 2hr).

Trains

Azul to: Buenos Aires (1 daily; 7hr).
Bahía Blanca to: Buenos Aires (1 daily; 13hr); Sierra de la Ventana (5 weekly; 2hr 30min).
La Plata to: Buenos Aires (every 30min; 1hr 15min).
Lobos to: Buenos Aires (every 2hr; 2hr 30min).
Mar del Plata to: Buenos Aires (3 daily; 6hr).
Pinamar to: Buenos Aires (3 weekly; 5hr 15min).
Sierra de la Ventana to: Bahía Blanca (5 weekly; 2hr 30min); Buenos Aires (5 weekly; 9hr 45min).
Tandil to: Buenos Aires (1 weekly; 8hr).

Flights

Bahía Blanca to: Buenos Aires (1 daily; 1hr).
Mar del Plata to: Buenos Aires (2 daily; 1hr 15min).
Santa Rosa to: Buenos Aires (3 weekly; 1hr 30min); Viedma (3 weekly, 1hr 15min).
Villa Gesell to: Buenos Aires (4 daily, summer only; 1hr).

3

Córdoba and the Central Sierras

CHAPTER 3

Highlights

* **Córdoba city** Argentina's second city is home to important colonial architecture and one of South America's oldest universities. See p.270
* **Jesuit architecture** Beautifully preserved estancia museums offer an insight into early colonial Argentina. See p.284
* **Cerro Colorado** Fascinating pre-Columbian pictures etched onto the side of a cliff. See p.287
* **Hang-gliding** The region's rugged sierras and professional infrastructure make it a great place for adventure sports. See p.292
* **Estancias** Ride on handsome horses, swim or just relax and enjoy breathtaking views in the unspoilt countryside. See p.294
* **Las Quijadas** San Luis Province's only national park is a dinosaur-freak's paradise. See p.312

△ Hang-gliding, La Cumbre

3

Córdoba and the Central Sierras

The **Central Sierras**, also known as the Sierras Pampeanas, are the highest **mountain ranges** in Argentina away from the Andean cordillera. Their pinkish-grey ridges and jagged outcrops alternate with fertile valleys, wooded with native carob trees, and barren moorlands, fringed with pampas grass – a patchwork that's one of Argentina's most varied landscapes. Formed more than four hundred million years before the Andes and gently sculpted by the wind and rain, the sierras stretch across some 100,000 square kilometres, peaking at **Cerro Champaquí**, its 2884-metre summit often encircled by cloud. Irrigated by countless rivers and brooks, and refreshingly cool in the summer when the surrounding plains become torrid and parched, the highlands straddle the provinces of Córdoba and San Luis, each of which shares its name with its historic capital. The cities of **Córdoba** and **San Luis**, separated by the tallest peaks, the Sierra Grande and Sierra de Comechingones, are totally unlike each other: the former is a teeming metropolis, battling it out with Rosario for the title of Argentina's second city, while modest San Luis struggles to shake off its sleepy backwater image.

Colonized at the end of the sixteenth century by settlers heading south and east from Tucumán and Mendoza, **Córdoba** was the region's first city. The Society of Jesus and its missionaries played a pivotal part in its foundation, establishing it at a strategic point along the Camino Real ("Royal Way"), the Spanish route from Alto Peru to the Crown's emerging Atlantic trading-posts on the Río de la Plata. From that point on, the Jesuits dominated every aspect of life in the city and its hinterland, until King Carlos III of Spain had them kicked out of the colonies in 1767. You can still see their handsome temple in the city centre, among other examples of **colonial architecture**. Further vestiges of the Jesuits' heyday, **Santa Catalina** and **Jesús María** are two of Argentina's best-preserved **Jesuit estancias**, located between Córdoba city and the province's northern border, just off the Camino Real, promoted locally as the **Camino de la Historia**. Slightly north of Santa Catalina is one of the country's most beguiling archeological sites, **Cerro Colorado**, where hundreds of pre-Columbian petroglyphs decorate open-air galleries of red sandstone at the foot of cave-riddled mountains.

Northwest from Córdoba city is the picturesque **Punilla Valley**, along which are threaded some of the oldest, most traditional holiday resorts in the country,

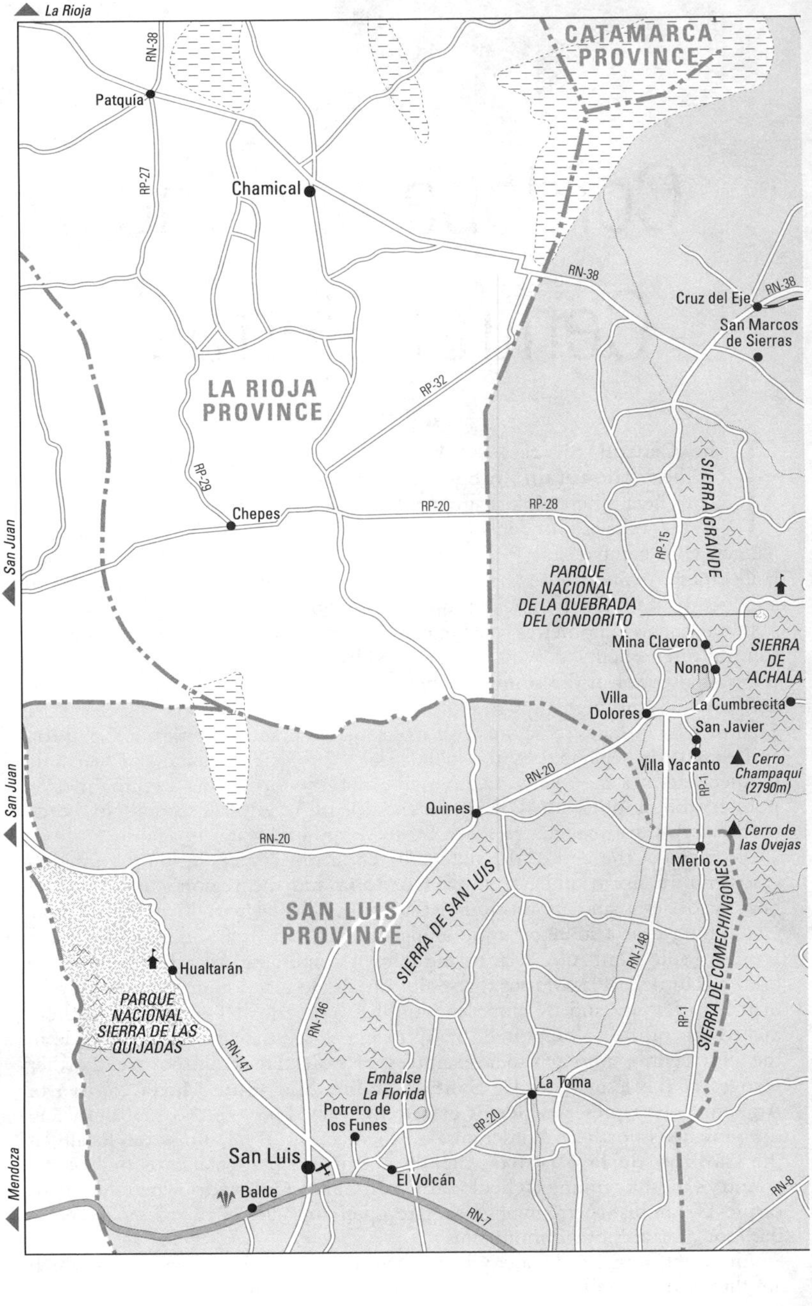

La Rioja
CATAMARCA PROVINCE
RN-38
Patquía
RP-27
Chamical
RN-38
Cruz del Eje
RN-38
San Marcos de Sierras
LA RIOJA PROVINCE
RP-32
RP-29
Chepes
RP-20
RP-28
SIERRA GRANDE
RP-15
San Juan
PARQUE NACIONAL DE LA QUEBRADA DEL CONDORITO
Mina Clavero
Nono
SIERRA DE ACHALA
Villa Dolores
La Cumbrecita
San Javier
Villa Yacanto
Cerro Champaquí (2790m)
San Juan
RN-20
RP-1
Quines
Cerro de las Ovejas
RN-20
Merlo
SAN LUIS PROVINCE
SIERRA DE SAN LUIS
SIERRA DE COMECHINGONES
RN-148
Hualtarán
PARQUE NACIONAL SIERRA DE LAS QUIJADAS
RN-146
RP-1
RN-147
Embalse La Florida
La Toma
Potrero de los Funes
RP-20
San Luis
El Volcán
Mendoza
Balde
RN-7
RN-8

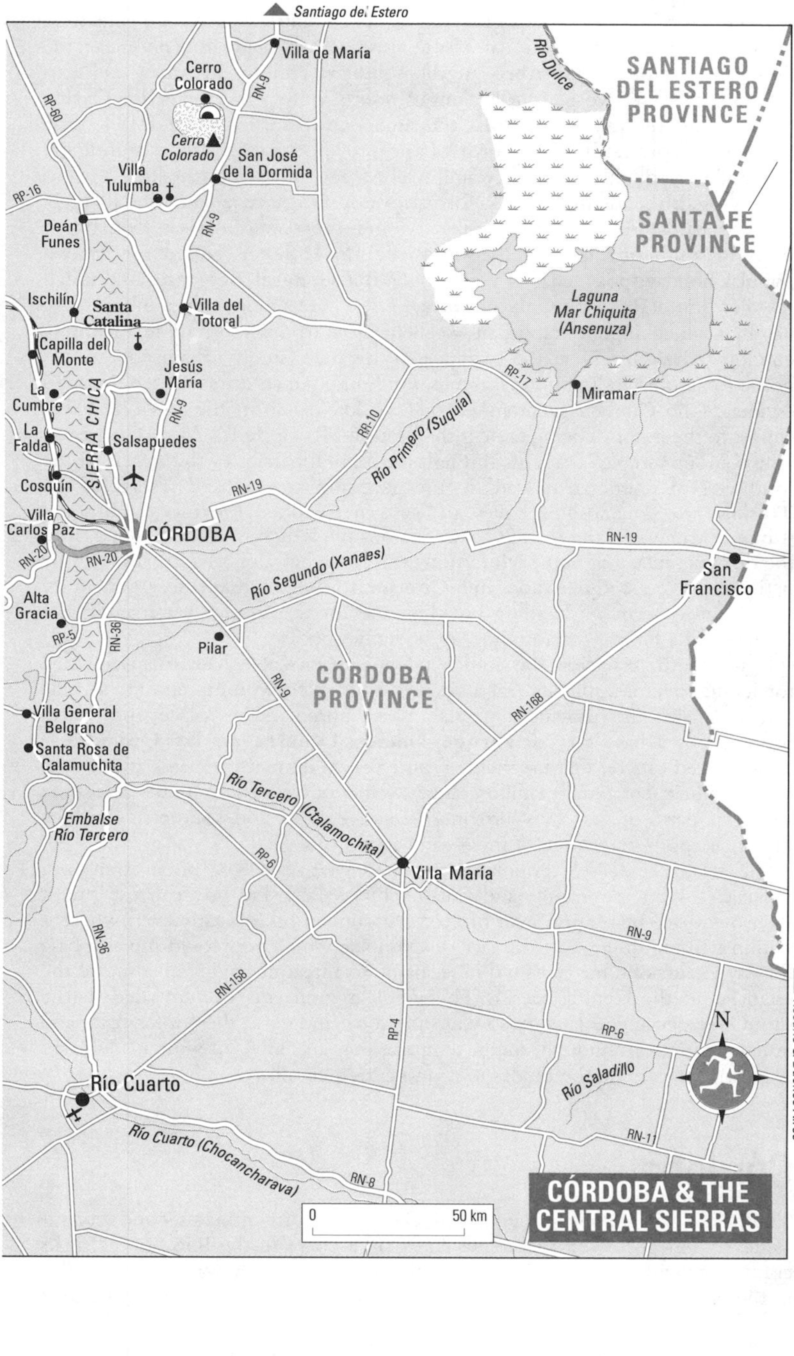
Santiago del Estero
CÓRDOBA & THE CENTRAL SIERRAS
SANTIAGO DEL ESTERO PROVINCE
SANTA FE PROVINCE
CÓRDOBA PROVINCE
Villa de María
Cerro Colorado
San José de la Dormida
Villa Tulumba
Deán Funes
Ischilín
Santa Catalina
Villa del Totoral
Capilla del Monte
La Cumbre
Jesús María
La Falda
Salsapuedes
Cosquín
SIERRA CHICA
Villa Carlos Paz
CÓRDOBA
Alta Gracia
Pilar
Villa General Belgrano
Santa Rosa de Calamuchita
Embalse Río Tercero
Villa María
Río Cuarto
Miramar
Laguna Mar Chiquita (Ansenuza)
San Francisco
Río Dulce
Río Primero (Suquía)
Río Segundo (Xanaes)
Río Tercero (Ctalamochita)
Río Cuarto (Chocancharava)
Río Saladillo
RP-60
RN-9
RP-16
RN-19
RP-17
RR-10
RN-20
RP-5
RN-36
RN-168
RP-6
RN-158
RP-4
RN-11
RN-8
Santa Fe
Rosario & Buenos Aires
N
0
50 km

such as **La Falda** and **Capilla del Monte**, sedate towns with exclusive golf courses and genteel hotels. Many of the activities here are targeted at families with children but you can also indulge in demanding adventure pursuits such as hang-gliding – international championships are held annually near the Punilla resort of **La Cumbre**. At the southern end of the valley, close to Córdoba city, are two nationally famous resorts: noisy, crowded **Villa Carlos Paz** and slightly quieter **Cosquín**, the latter known for its annual folk festival. By way of contrast, the far north of the province, particularly a stunningly unspoilt area roughly between Capilla del Monte and Santa Catalina, remains little visited: the dramatic rock formations at **Ongamira** and the lovingly restored hamlet of **Ischilín** are just two of the secret marvels hereabouts. Directly south of Córdoba, the **Calamuchita Valley** is famed for its two popular holiday spots, sedately Germanic **Villa General Belgrano** and much rowdier **Santa Rosa de Calamuchita**, from where alpine trails climb into the nearby Comechingones range, an excellent place to observe birdlife, including condors. **Alta Gracia**, at the entrance to this increasingly urbanized valley, is home to an outstanding historical museum housed in an immaculately restored estancia; Che Guevara spent much of his adolescence in the town. Peaceful almost to the point of being eerie is the beautiful **Ruta de las Altas Cumbres**, a high mountain pass that cuts through the natural barrier of the sierras to the southwest of Córdoba. It leads to the generally more placid resorts of the **Traslasierra**, a handsome valley in western Córdoba Province, and some stunning scenery in the lee of Cerro Champaquí, which is easily climbed from the thriving village of **San Javier**. Along this route lies Córdoba Province's only national park, the **Quebrada del Condorito**, whose dramatic, often misty ravines provide an outstanding breeding site for the sinister yet magnificent condor and a habitat for a number of endemic species.

To the south, just across the border in San Luis Province, **Merlo** is renowned for its microclimate, but its real attraction is its splendid mountainside setting. San Luis city, the provincial capital, is an unremarkable place and serves primarily as a base for the **Parque Nacional Sierra de las Quijadas**, a dramatic red canyon that has yielded some prized dinosaur remains and is now home to guanacos and armadillos. Huge swathes of flat pasture stretch across the southern parts of San Luis Province – and eastern and southern Córdoba Province, too – with none of the sierras' attractions.

This relatively densely populated region is well served by public transport, especially along the Punilla and Calamuchita valleys, but you can explore at your own pace by renting a car or even a mountain bike. Nearly everywhere is within striking distance of the city of Córdoba, which you could use as a base for day excursions, but it would be a shame to miss out staying at some of the estancias in the Central Sierras. The whole region gets overcrowded in the summer, especially in January, so you should try and go in the cooler, drier and quieter months; although night temperatures are low in winter (June to August), the days can be mild, sunny and extremely pleasant.

Córdoba

The bustling, modern metropolis of **CÓRDOBA**, Argentina's second city, sits some 700km northwest of Buenos Aires, on a curve in the Río Suquía, at its confluence with the tamed La Cañada brook, sprawling idly across a wide valley in the far northwestern corner of the pampas. The jagged silhouettes visible at the western end of its broad avenues announce that the cool heights of the **sierras** are not far away, and it's in these, or in the lower hills nearer the city centre, that many of the one-and-a-quarter million Cordobeses take refuge from the valley's sweltering heat.

Córdoba is reputed nationwide for its hospitable, elegant population of predominantly Italian descent, and its caustically ironic sense of humour, which sometimes borders on the insolent, and is enhanced by the lilting drawl of the distinctive regional accent. These days Córdoba lacks the dynamism and style of Rosario, its Santa Fe rival for the title of Argentina's second city (see p.372), and many people spend only an hour or two here before sprinting off to the nearby resorts. But as the capital of one of the country's largest and most populous provinces, Córdoba has a wide range of services on offer, and its plentiful, cheap accommodation and location make it an ideal base for exploring the area, while the colonial architecture at its heart remains an attraction in its own right.

Some history

On July 6, 1573, **Jerónimo Luis de Cabrera**, Governor of Tucumán, declared a new city founded at the fork in the main routes from Chile and Alto Peru to Buenos Aires, calling it Córdoba la Llana de la Nueva Andalucía, after the city of his Spanish ancestors. Mission accomplished, Cabrera went east to oversee trade on the Río Paraná, leaving the city's new settlers to their own devices. The Monólito de la Fundación, on the north bank of the Río Suquía nearly a kilometre northeast of the Plaza San Martín, supposedly marks the precise spot where the city was founded and commands panoramic views. The first steps taken by the colonizers, mostly Andalucians like Cabrera, were to shorten the settlement's name to Córdoba de Tucumán and to move it to a better site, less prone to flooding, on the other side of the river. They prosaically rebaptized the river Río Primero ("first river") – the name Río Suquía was officially reinstated in the 1990s, as part of a general policy in the province to restore the pre-Hispanic names of rivers and lakes.

Almost from the outset the **Society of Jesus** played a crucial role in Córdoba's development (see box, p.285), and King Carlos III of Spain's order to expel the Jesuits from the Spanish empire in 1767 inevitably dealt Córdoba a serious body blow. That, plus the decision in 1776 to make Buenos Aires the headquarters of the newly created Viceroyalty of the Río de la Plata, might well have condemned the city to terminal decline had it not then been made the administrative centre of a huge *Intendencia*, or viceregal province, stretching all the way to Mendoza and La Rioja. By another stroke of luck, a forward-looking governor, **Rafael de Sobremonte**, was appointed by Viceroy Vértiz in 1784. This aristocratic visionary from Seville expanded Córdoba to the west of La Cañada, which, among other things, provided the growing city with secure water supplies. Sobremonte lived in a suitably patrician house, the oldest residential building still standing in the city and now the Museo Histórico Provincial. In the nineteenth century, Córdoba was involved in the country's battle for independence from imperial Spain via the key revolutionary figure of **Gregorio Funes**, better known under his religious title of Deán. Like so many Argentine cities, Córdoba benefited from the arrival of the railways in 1870, its station acting as a hub for its expanding eastern districts. A period of prosperity followed, still visible in some of the city's lavishly decorated banks and theatres. By the close of the nineteenth century, Córdoba had begun to spread south, with European-influenced urban planning on a huge scale, including the **Parque Sarmiento**, designed by Argentina's favourite landscape artist, Charles Thays (see box, p.130). This all coincided with a huge influx of immigrants from

Europe and the Middle East, enticed by jobs in the city's flourishing economy, based largely on food-processing and textiles industries.

The strong leadership of a series of progressive mayors in the first half of the twentieth century helped Córdoba emerge as one of the country's main manufacturing centres, dominated by the automobile and aviation industries. The **Cordobazo**, a protest movement masterminded by students and trade unions in 1969 and partly inspired by Europe's May 1968 uprisings, brought considerable pressure to bear on the military junta and helped trigger political change at the national level. The city has always vehemently opposed the country's dictatorships, including the 1976–83 military regime, with mass demonstrations and civil disobedience, and was a hive of anti-Menemism. Today it is still common to see graffiti by Peronist youth brigades on the university walls proclaiming "Peronismo o muerte!" ("Peronism or death!"). Sadly, the post-crisis economic boom that has occurred in other parts of the country does not seem to have reached Córdoba, and the industries that once ruled here are now shadows of their former selves. Whether these entrenched political attitudes have been a factor in this slowdown is debatable – certainly, an unresponsive local government hasn't helped – but there's little doubt that the city has become sluggish in recent years, with many places boarded up or looking in need of a lick of paint.

Arrival, information and city transport

Córdoba's **Aeropuerto Internacional Taravella** is at Pajas Blancas, 13km north of the city centre. A **tourist information office** operates in the main concourse (daily 8am–8pm; ⓣ0351/434-8390), and a regular **minibus** service privately run by Transfer Express (ⓣ0351/475-9201) takes passengers to the city centre and a selection of hotels for $8. A **taxi** or *remise* ride to the microcentro will set you back at least $20.

The long-distance **bus station** (ⓣ0351/423-4199 or 423-0532) is at Blvd Perón 380 (the boulevard is usually referred to by locals as Avenida Reconquista). Its impressive array of **facilities** includes banks and ATMs, a pharmacy, travel agency, telephones, restaurants, showers and dozens of shops. Tickets for destinations throughout the region and rest of the country are sold in the basement – advance booking is advisable. The terminal is several blocks east of the city centre, so you might need to take a bus or a taxi to get to and fro, especially if laden with luggage; stops for city buses and taxi ranks are close to the exit. In the future, it should be possible to get a **train** from Buenos Aires to Córdoba via Rosario – a high-speed link was announced in 2006. Local buses serving some provincial destinations such as Santa Rosa de Calamuchita, Jesús María and Cerro Colorado leave from the cramped **Terminal de Minibuses** behind the Mercado Sur market on Boulevard Arturo Illia, between calles Buenos Aires and Ituzaingó.

The city's main **tourist office** is in the Cabildo on Independencia, just off Plaza San Martín (daily 8am–8pm; ⓣ0351/434-1200, ⓦwww.cordobaturismo.gov.ar). Though not the most helpful of offices, the staff nonetheless have piles of maps and flyers and there are useful weekly events and walking-tour lists pinned on a board. The staff at the **information centre** (ⓣ0351/433-1982) in the bus station tend to be more helpful, with stacks of maps and leaflets plus travel information and online accommodation details, though they cannot book rooms.

Informative, guided **walking tours** of selected downtown sights, lasting two hours, start from the city tourist office (daily summer 9.30am & 4.30pm, winter 10am & 4pm, in English upon request; ⓣ0351/434-1227). Privately run City

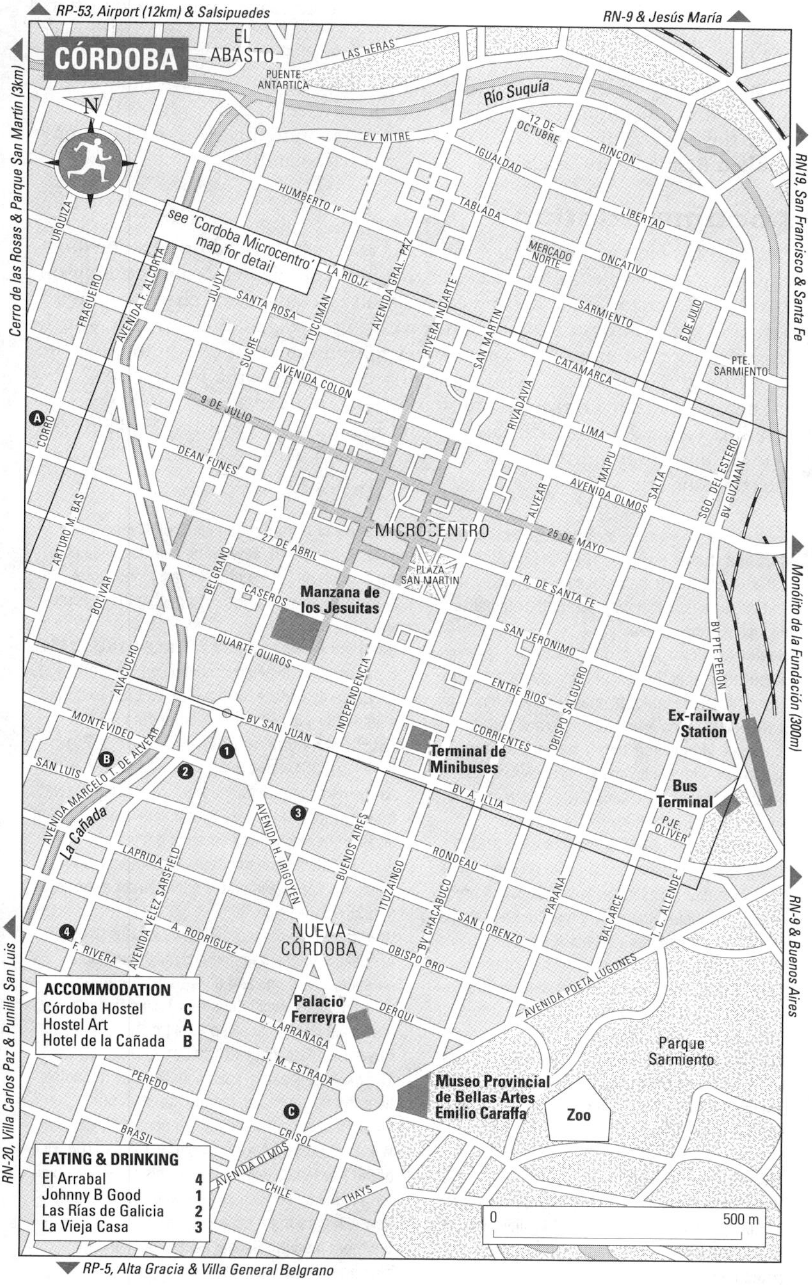
CÓRDOBA
RP-53, Airport (12km) & Salsipuedes
RN-9 & Jesús María
Cerro de las Rosas & Parque San Martín (3km)
RN19, San Francisco & Santa Fe
Monólito de la Fundación (300m)
RN-9 & Buenos Aires
RN-20, Villa Carlos Paz & Punilla San Luis
RP-5, Alta Gracia & Villa General Belgrano
N
EL ABASTO
PUENTE ANTARTICA
Río Suquía
see 'Cordoba Microcentro' map for detail
MERCADO NORTE
PTE. SARMIENTO
MICROCENTRO
PLAZA SAN MARTIN
Manzana de los Jesuitas
Terminal de Minibuses
Ex-railway Station
Bus Terminal
La Cañada
NUEVA CÓRDOBA
Palacio Ferreyra
Museo Provincial de Bellas Artes Emilio Caraffa
Zoo
Parque Sarmiento
LAS HERAS
EV MITRE
12 DE OCTUBRE
IGUALDAD
RINCON
HUMBERTO I°
TABLADA
LIBERTAD
ONCATIVO
SARMIENTO
LA RIOJA
SANTA ROSA
AVENIDA COLON
CATAMARCA
9 DE JULIO
LIMA
DEAN FUNES
AVENIDA OLMOS
27 DE ABRIL
25 DE MAYO
R. DE SANTA FE
CASEROS
SAN JERONIMO
DUARTE QUIROS
ENTRE RIOS
BV SAN JUAN
CORRIENTES
MONTEVIDEO
SAN LUIS
BV A. ILLIA
PJE. OLIVER
RONDEAU
LAPRIDA
SAN LORENZO
A. RODRIGUEZ
F. RIVERA
OBISPO ORO
AVENIDA POETA LUGONES
DERQUI
D. LARRAÑAGA
J. M. ESTRADA
PEREDO
BRASIL
CRISOL
AVENIDA OLMOS
CHILE
THAYS
URQUIZA
FRAGUEIRO
AVENIDA F. ALCORTA
JUJUY
SUCRE
TUCUMAN
AVENIDA GRAL. PAZ
RIVERA INDARTE
SAN MARTIN
RIVADAVIA
6 DE JULIO
CORRO
ARTURO M. BAS
BOLIVAR
BELGRANO
AVACUCHO
AVENIDA MARCELO T. DE ALVEAR
AVENIDA H. IRIGOYEN
INDEPENDENCIA
BUENOS AIRES
ITUZAINGO
BV CHACABUCO
AVENIDA VELEZ SARSFIELD
ALVEAR
MAIPU
SALTA
SGO. DEL ESTERO
BV GUZMAN
BV PTE PERÓN
OBISPO SALGUERO
PARANA
BALCARCE
T. C. ALLENDE
ACCOMMODATION
Córdoba Hostel C
Hostel Art A
Hotel de la Cañada B
EATING & DRINKING
El Arrabal 4
Johnny B Good 1
Las Rías de Galicia 2
La Vieja Casa 3
0 500 m

Tour (Mon 3pm & 5pm, Tues 5pm, Fri 10am, 3pm & 5pm, Thurs, Sat & Sun 10am & 5pm; $18; ⓣ0351/424-6605, ⓦwww.cordobacitytour.com.ar) offers sightseeing in a red double-decker bus, starting from the Plaza San Martín near the cathedral.

The majority of the city sights are within easy reach of each other, in the microcentro; to venture further afield you are advised to take a taxi rather than brave the city's terrible **buses**. If you do take a bus, note that you must first buy a **token** (*cospel*; $1.20), available at kiosks and newsstands.

Accommodation

Córdoba has plenty of centrally located and reasonably priced **hotels**. The more expensive establishments tend to cater to a business clientele, concentrating on facilities such as fax machines and cable TV and lacking much charm or finesse. Demand at the **budget** end of the market is improving, with a few new **youth hostels** cropping up to join a sometimes squalid bunch of cheap hotels at the eastern end of calles Entre Ríos and Corrientes, towards the bus station.

There's a passable **campsite**, offering free parking and a range of facilities, at Avenida General San Martín, behind the Fair Complex, on the banks of the Río Suquía 10km northwest of the city centre. The #E1 bus from Plaza San Martín runs there.

Hostels and residenciales

Córdoba Hostel Ituzaingó 1070 ⓣ0351/468-7359, ⓦwww.cordobahostel.com.ar. Friendly, lively and spotless hostel in the heart of the student district. $18 per person.

Hostel Art Corro 112 ⓣ0351/423-0071, ⓦwww.hostelart.com.ar. The slightly scratty rooms at this hostel are made up for by the warm welcome from owners and tattoo artists Christian and Nellida. The ambience in the large, comfy common area is bohemian, with the hostel favoured by visiting artists and musicians. Beds $18 per person, and some double rooms (❸).

Palenque Hostel General Paz 371 ⓣ0351/423-7588, ⓦwww.palenquehostel.com.ar. The pick of Córdoba's new hostels, the *Palenque* is in a prettily converted nineteenth-century townhouse that has retained such features as a black- and white-tiled floor, stained-glass windows and wrought-iron banisters. The elegant wood-panelled common areas are great for meeting both local and foreign backpackers. Dorm beds $20.

Pensión Entre Ríos Entre Ríos 567 ⓣ0351/423-0311. A simple, family-run B&B in the vicinity of the bus station; safe, clean and quiet with plenty of hot water. ❸

Hotels

Dorá Entre Ríos 70 ⓣ0351/421-2031. In a central location, offering a wide range of facilities including a swimming pool and garage, and big, smart bedrooms. ❻

Hotel de la Cañada Marcelo T. de Alvear 580 ⓣ0351/421-4649, ⓦwww.hoteldelacaniada.com.ar. Comfortable, if slightly old-fashioned, hotel in a modern tower with swimming pool, garage, sauna and gym. ❻

Hotel del Boulevard Blvd A. Illia 184 ⓣ0351/424-3718, ⓦwww.delboulevardhotel.com.ar. Modern Art Deco-style place, with rooms that are clean but a little tatty, plus lots of cooling marble. ❺

NH Panorama Marcelo T. de Alvear 251 ⓣ0351/410-3900, ⓦwww.nh-hotels.com. As the name suggests, the hotel enjoys fine views from its rooms, roof garden and small pool; pleasant bedrooms and en-suite bathrooms. Another establishment of the stylish Spanish NH chain, the *Urbano*, is on the same street at no. 363 (ⓣ0351/410-3960). ❼

Quetzal San Jerónimo 579 ⓣ0351/422-9106. Appealing, bright, summery decor throughout, en-suite bathrooms and ultra-friendly, English-speaking staff. Avoid the street-facing bedrooms and you'll be able to sleep at night. ❹

Royal Blvd Reconquista 180 ⓣ0351/422-7155. The freshest-looking, least squalid of all the hotels near the bus terminal. Rooms are plain but comfortable and breakfasts are generous. ❸

Windsor Buenos Aires 214 ⓣ0351/422-9164. One of the few hotels with charm in this category, going for a resolutely British style. Rooms in the classy new wing are more expensive, and the bathrooms are more modern. Sauna, heated pool and gym, plus pretentious restaurant. ❼

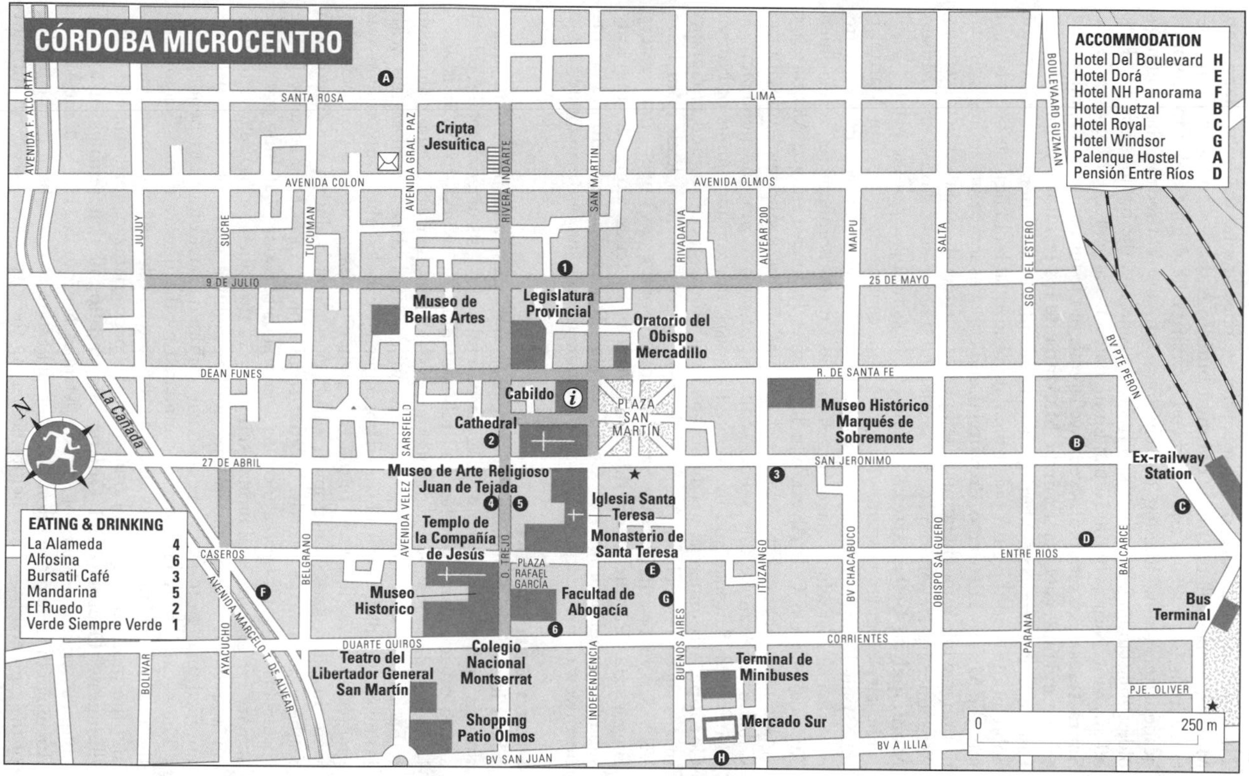
CÓRDOBA MICROCENTRO
ACCOMMODATION
Hotel Del Boulevard H
Hotel Dorá E
Hotel NH Panorama F
Hotel Quetzal B
Hotel Royal C
Hotel Windsor G
Palenque Hostel A
Pensión Entre Ríos D
EATING & DRINKING
La Alameda 4
Alfosina 6
Bursatil Café 3
Mandarina 5
El Ruedo 2
Verde Siempre Verde 1
Cripta Jesuítica
Museo de Bellas Artes
Legislatura Provincial
Oratorio del Obispo Mercadillo
Cabildo
Cathedral
PLAZA SAN MARTÍN
Museo Histórico Marqués de Sobremonte
Museo de Arte Religioso Juan de Tejada
Templo de la Compañía de Jesús
Iglesia Santa Teresa
Monasterio de Santa Teresa
PLAZA RAFAEL GARCÍA
Facultad de Abogacía
Museo Historico
Colegio Nacional Montserrat
Teatro del Libertador General San Martín
Shopping Patio Olmos
Terminal de Minibuses
Mercado Sur
Ex-railway Station
Bus Terminal
La Cañada
SANTA ROSA
LIMA
AVENIDA COLON
AVENIDA OLMOS
9 DE JULIO
25 DE MAYO
DEAN FUNES
R. DE SANTA FE
27 DE ABRIL
SAN JERONIMO
CASEROS
ENTRE RIOS
DUARTE QUIROS
CORRIENTES
BV SAN JUAN
BV A ILLIA
PJE. OLIVER
AVENIDA F. ALCORTA
JUJUY
SUCRE
TUCUMAN
AVENIDA GRAL. PAZ
RIVERA INDARTE
SAN MARTIN
RIVADAVIA
ALVEAR 200
MAIPU
SALTA
SGO. DEL ESTERO
BOULEVAARD GUZMAN
BV PTE PERON
BOLIVAR
AYACUCHO
AVENIDA MARCELO T. DE ALVEAR
BELGRANO
AVENIDA VELEZ
SARSFIELD
O. TREJO
INDEPENDENCIA
BUENOS AIRES
ITUZAINGO
BV CHACABUCO
OBISPO SALGUERO
PARANA
BALCARCE
0
250 m
N

The City

You can see most of the sights in Córdoba's compact centre in a couple of days. The city's **historic core**, or microcentro, wrapped around the leafy **Plaza San Martín**, contains all the major **colonial buildings** that sealed the city's importance in the seventeenth and eighteenth centuries. Its elegant **Cabildo** (colonial headquarters), now housing the city museum, and **cathedral**, the country's oldest still standing, are conveniently side by side, and the obvious place to kick off any visit. Nearby, beyond a handsome Baroque convent, the **Monasterio de Santa Teresa**, is a group of several well-preserved Jesuit buildings, including the temple and university, that form the **Manzana de los Jesuitas** ("Jesuits' Block"). East of the Plaza San Martín, the eighteenth-century home of Governor Sobremonte (and the city's oldest standing residential building) has been turned into the **Museo Histórico Provincial**, and contains some outstanding colonial paintings, while some interesting examples of nineteenth- and twentieth-century Argentine art are on display in a splendid French-style house, the **Museo Municipal de Bellas Artes**, a couple of blocks northwest of the plaza.

The city's regular Hispano-American grid, centred on Plaza San Martín, is upset only by the winding **La Cañada** brook a few blocks west of the centre, on either side of which snakes one of the city's main thoroughfares, acacia-lined Avenida Marcelo T. de Alvear, which becomes Avenida Figueroa Alcorta after crossing Deán Funes. Street names change and numbering begins level with the Cabildo: for example, this is where San Martín morphs into Independencia.

Boulevards San Juan and Presidente Illia mark the northern limits of **Nueva Córdoba**, a commercial neighbourhood with some good bars and restaurants that is sliced through by Avenida Hipólito Yrigoyen, which leads from Plaza Vélez Sarsfield to the **Parque Sarmiento**, one of the city's open, green spaces. Bigger still, **Parque General San Martín** stretches alongside the leafy suburban neighbourhood of **Cerro de las Rosas**, on high ground to the northwest of the centre; head here to sample the restaurants or nightlife.

Plaza San Martín

The **Plaza San Martín** has always been the city's focal point. The square throngs with people, some striding purposefully along its diagonal paths, others sitting on its quaint benches and idly watching the world go by. It is at its liveliest and most enjoyable during the *paseo* hour in the early evening, although it becomes a less appealing place to wander after dark, when it fills with homeless people. Originally used for military parades, the shady square was granted its recreational role in the 1870s when the Italianate cast-iron fountains were installed and semi-tropical shrubberies planted: lush palm-fronds and feathery acacias, the prickly, bulging trunks of the *palo borracho* and, in the spring, blazing pink *lapacho* and purple jacaranda blossoms. Watching over all the activity is a monumental bronze **sculpture** of the Liberator himself, victorious on a splendid mount and borne aloft on a huge stone plinth, which was unveiled in 1916 to mark the centenary of the declaration of independence.

The square's southern edge is dominated by the dowdy Banco Nación and the Teatro Real; more banks sit along the eastern edge. Wedged between shops and the modern municipal offices on the pedestrianized northern side is the diminutive **Oratorio del Obispo Mercadillo**, all that remains of a huge colonial residence built for Bishop Manuel Mercadillo. He had the seat of Tucumán diocese moved from Santiago del Estero to Córdoba at the beginning of the eighteenth century, before becoming the city's first bishop. An intricate and rather flimsy-looking wrought-iron balcony protrudes over the busy pavement from the upper-floor former chapel. At ground level, the **Museo**

Gregorio Funes (daily 9am–1pm & 4–7pm; free) sporadically hosts temporary exhibitions of icons, altarpieces and other religious artefacts, or local artwork of a profane nature.

The Cabildo

On the traffic-free western side of the square is the **Cabildo**, or colonial headquarters, a sleekly elegant two-storey building whose immaculate white **facade** dates to the late eighteenth century. Fifteen harmoniously plain arches, enhanced at night by lighting, alleviate the otherwise sober exterior. Old-fashioned lamps hang in the **Recova**, a fan-vaulted colonnade held up by slender pillars, in front of a row of wooden doors alternating with windows protected by iron grilles. On the pavement in front of the Cabildo, as elsewhere in the historic centre, a clever *trompe-l'oeil* device of mock shadows has been incorporated into the flagstones.

△ Cabildo and cathedral, Córdoba city

The original Cabildo was built on the same spot at the end of the sixteenth century, but the present facade was added when the Marqués de Sobremonte became governor-mayor in 1784. Put to many different uses throughout its long history – law court, prison, provincial parliament, government offices and police headquarters – nowadays the building and its inner courtyards are mainly used for exhibitions, official receptions, the occasional concert and regular summer tango evenings (at the Patio de Tango; Fri midnight, following lessons at 9pm; $7; in cold or wet weather, the musicians and dancers take refuge in the Cripta Jesuítica – see p.282). The Recova, meanwhile, hosts the **Paseo de la Artes** (Mon–Sat 9am–2pm & 4–9.30pm), where you can find good-value artisan products such as ponchos and *mates* in unusual designs, as well as Córdoban souvenirs; these also form the core of a larger, excellent evening craft fair that takes place in Nueva Córdoba, at Belgrano and Achaval Rodriguez, every Saturday and Sunday from 6pm.

The cathedral

Immediately south of the Cabildo, and completing the plaza's western flank, is Córdoba's eighteenth-century **cathedral**. Argentina's oldest if not its most beautiful cathedral, it is part Baroque, part Neoclassical – its most imposing external feature, the immense **cupola**, was inspired by Salamanca cathedral's, and is surrounded by stern Romanesque turrets that contrast pleasingly with its Baroque curves. However, the building's highly porous, cream-coloured stone has suffered badly from ambient pollution and, scrubbed clean only a few years back, is already a sooty black colour again. The cathedral's **clock towers** are decorated at each corner with angelic trumpeters dressed in skirts of exotic plumes, like those worn by the Guaraní craftsmen who carved them. You enter the cathedral first through majestic filigreed wrought-iron gates, past Deán Funes' solemn black mausoleum to the left, and then through finely carved **wooden doors** transferred here from the Jesuit temple at the end of the eighteenth century. The first thing you notice is the almost tangible gloom of the interior: scant daylight filters through small stained-glass windows onto an ornate but subdued **floor** of Valencian tiles, and the nave is separated from the aisles by hefty square columns designed to support the cathedral in the event of an earthquake (rare hereabouts), compounding the effect of almost oppressive melancholy. The ornate Rococo **pulpit**, in the left-hand aisle, momentarily lifts the atmosphere, as does the decoration of the **ceiling** and **chancel**. This was inspired by the Italian Baroque and Tiepolo's frescoes in particular, but executed in the early twentieth century by local artists of Italian origin, supervised by Emilio Caraffa, whose pictures are displayed at the Museo de Bellas Artes Dr Genaro Pérez (see p.281).

The cathedral's main **altar** is a dull early nineteenth-century piece, which replaced a Baroque work of art moved to Villa Tulumba, a tiny hamlet in the north of the province (see p.286). To the left, a minor altar is redeemed by a finely worked silver **tabernacle**, also dating from the early nineteenth century, although some of its features are clumsily executed – the Lamb of God looks as if it's made of whipped cream, while the Sacred Heart somewhat resembles a beetroot.

Monasterio de Santa Teresa

Immediately southwest of Plaza San Martín, across Calle 27 de Abril from the cathedral, lies the lavish pink and cream-coloured **Monasterio de las Carmelitas Descalzadas de Santa Teresa de Jesús**, part of a set of buildings dedicated to St Teresa. As it is a working nunnery, only the soberly decorated **Iglesia Santa Teresa**, built in 1717, is open to the public (Matins daily 7.30am) – the entrance is at Independencia 146. Founded by local dignitary Juan de Tejeda, great-nephew of St Teresa of Ávila, the monastery was built out of gratitude for the miraculous recovery of one of his daughters from a fatal disease; after Tejeda's death, his widow and two daughters became nuns and never left the convent. It was designed by Portuguese architects brought over from Brazil, whose influence can be seen in the ornate cross and gabled shape of the church's two-dimensional bell tower.

Housed in the northern side of the complex, in a part no longer used by the holy order, the impressive **Museo de Arte Religioso Juan de Tejeda**, Independencia 122 (Wed–Sat 9.30am–12.30pm; $5), is entered through an intricate, cream-coloured Baroque doorway, typical of Portuguese craftsmanship, which contrasts with the pink outer walls. Informative guides, some of whom speak English, will show you around the partly restored **courtyards**, the garden of hydrangeas, orange trees, jasmine and pomegranates and the rooms and cells of the former nuns' quarters. On display alongside all manner of religious artefacts and sacred relics, mainly of St Teresa and St Ignacio de Loyola, the founder of the Jesuits, are a very fine polychrome wooden statue of St Peter, a lavish silver-embroidered banner made for Emperor Charles V and some striking paintings from **Cusco**. Also from Alto Peru is a seat with carved armrests in the shape of jaguars, a symbol of power in pre-Columbian Peru; the original Spanish shield on the seat back was later removed and replaced with the Argentine one. The nuns' devout asceticism and utter isolation is evident in their bare **cells**, lit only by ground-level vents, blocked off by forbidding grilles. Apart from these vents, the austere confessionals positioned against so-called communicating walls were the sisters' only means of contact with the outside world. Life for members of the Carmelite Order, still in residence next door, has barely changed.

Manzana de los Jesuitas

Two blocks west and south of Plaza San Martín is the **Manzana de los Jesuitas**, a whole block, or *manzana*, apportioned to the Society of Jesus a decade after Córdoba was founded. At Obispo Trejo 242, the main offices of the **Universidad Nacional de Córdoba (UNC)** also serve as the entrance for the **Museo Histórico de la Universidad Nacional de Córdoba Manzana Jesuitica** (Tues–Sun 9am–1pm & 4–8pm; $5; free guided tours of university and Templo de la Compañía de Jesús 10am, 11am, 5pm & 6pm). Now attended by more than 80,000 students, the university here is the oldest in the country and the second oldest on the continent, dating from 1621. Venture beyond its harmonious cream- and biscuit-coloured facade and take a look around its shady patios, ablaze with bougainvilleas for much of the year. The **libraries** contain a priceless collection of maps, religious works and late fifteenth-century incunabula, while a ceiling fresco in the **Salon de Grados** shows naked students reaching out to the Muses. Fittingly, this was where applicants for doctorates were quizzed for eight hours a day for three days by their seniors – one wrong answer and they were out.

To the north is Argentina's oldest surviving Jesuit temple, the **Templo de la Compañía de Jesús**, built by Felipe de Lamer in 1640. The almost rustic simplicity of its restored facade, punctuated only by niches used by nesting pigeons, is a foretaste of the severe, single-naved interior, with its roof of Paraguayan cedar in the shape of an upturned ship – Lamer began his career as a shipbuilder in Antwerp. Fifty painted canvas panels huddled around the ceiling and darkened by time, depict the figures and legends of the Society of Jesus – at ten metres above ground level they're hard to make out without the aid of binoculars. Even more striking is the handsome **Cusqueño altarpiece** and the floridly decorated pulpit. The chapel to the side is dedicated to Our Lady of Lourdes and is known as the Capilla de los Naturales: it was a roofless structure where indigenous churchgoers were graciously allowed to come and pray until the nineteenth century, when it was covered and lined with ornate marble. Priests perform ablutions in a seventeenth-century soapstone sculpture that features a beautifully sensual polychrome wood Mary Magdalen.

Around the corner on Calle Caseros is the **Capilla Doméstica**, the residents' private chapel and "gateway to heaven" – at least according to the inscription over the doorway. Its intimate dimensions, finely painted altarpiece and remarkable ceiling are in total contrast with the grandiose austerity of the main temple. The ceiling is a primitive wooden canopy, held together with bamboo canes and decorated with rawhide panels which have been painted with natural vegetable pigments. While the main temple is easily accessible, you have to ask the concierge to let you into the chapel.

South of the UNC, and rounding off the trio of Jesuit buildings, is the prestigious **Colegio Nacional de Nuestra Señora de Montserrat**, founded at a nearby location in the city in 1687 but transferred to its present site in 1782, shortly after the Jesuits' expulsion; the building had been their living quarters, arranged around quadrangles. This all-male bastion of privilege finally went co-ed in 1998 despite fierce opposition. The building's studiously Neocolonial appearance – beige-pink facades, a highly ornate doorway, grilled windows and a pseudo-Baroque clock tower looming at the corner with Calle Duarte Quirós – dates from remodelling in the 1920s. Through the embellished doors and the entrance hall with its vivid Spanish majolica floor tiles are the original, seventeenth-century Jesuit cloisters.

Teatro del Libertador General San Martín

The austere building a block southwest of the Colegio Nacional Montserrat, at Av Vélez Sarsfield 317, is the Neoclassical **Teatro del Libertador General San Martín** (Ⓣ0351/433-2319). Of world-class calibre, with outstanding acoustics and an elegant, understated interior, it was built in 1887 and inaugurated four years later, making it the oldest of its kind in the country. Its creaking wooden floor, normally steeply tilted for performances, can be lowered to a horizontal position and the seats removed for dances and other social events.

Museo Histórico Provincial Marqués de Sobremonte

East of Plaza San Martín, at Rosario de Santa Fe 218, the **Museo Histórico Provincial Marqués de Sobremonte** (Tues–Fri 10am–3pm, Sat 9am–2pm; $2; Ⓣ0351/423-7687) is a well-preserved and carefully restored showpiece residence and the city's last private colonial house. Built at the beginning of the eighteenth century, it was the home of Rafael, Marqués de Sobremonte, between 1784 and 1796. As governor of Córdoba he was responsible for modernizing the city, securing its water supplies and extending it westwards beyond La Cañada.

The building's unassuming exterior, sturdily functional with thickset walls, is embellished by a wrought-iron balcony resting on finely carved wooden brackets, while delicate whitewashed fan-vaulting decorates the simple archway of the entrance. Guarding the door are two monstrous creatures, apparently meant to be lions, made of *piedra de sapo*, a relatively soft stone quarried in the nearby sierras. The leafy **patio** is shaded by a pomegranate tree, supposedly planted when Sobremonte lived here.

Although only a few of the exhibits belonged to the Marqués himself, most date from the period when he lived here. Downstairs, the first rooms to the right house collections of silver and arms, while the rest have been arranged to reflect a nineteenth-century interior; each has an information sheet in English narrating how a typical day there may have passed. Best of all is the museum's outstanding set of paintings of the **Cusco School**, scattered throughout the house. Some of them, such as the *Feast of King David* and *Santa Rita de Cascia*, both downstairs, have been recently and very successfully restored, but some others are still in dire need of attention. The portrait of Bishop Salguero de Cabrera displayed in the chapel, dated 1767 and painted at Arequipa, Peru, is a minor masterpiece, while upstairs there is a fantastic *Descent from the Cross*, featuring a wonderfully contrite Mary Magdalen. Also upstairs, the relentless religious imagery is given a more secular counterpoint by a huge map of South America from 1770 that gives an idea of perceptions of regional geography in the era, and a surprisingly irreverent, scarlet four-poster bed in the "female" bedroom.

Legislatura Provincial and around

One block west of the Cabildo, the **Legislatura Provincial** (guided tours on request Mon–Fri 9.30am–noon; free) squats at the corner of calles Deán Funes and Rivera Indarte. Designed by Austro-Hungarian architect Johan Kronfuss, it's an extremely austere Neoclassical structure, but it's typical of the grandiose buildings that went up in Córdoba in the early twentieth century, when the city prospered – and wanted to look European. Built to house the provincial parliament, which later moved to a modern headquarters in the west of the city, it's now used for civic ceremonies. The *belle époque* interior is lavishly decorated with imperious portraits of city dignitaries and paintings depicting the city's pivotal role in Argentina's independence. The half-hour guided tours, in Spanish only, are highly informative if rather automated.

The monumental Legislatura looks somewhat out of place among the colourful maze of shopping arcades, boutiques, cafés, fast-food joints and miscellaneous emporia, animated by a hubbub of shoppers, hawkers and the odd street-entertainer that surrounds it. This lively **commercial area**, stretching along the pedestrianized streets to the northwest of Plaza San Martín, is shaded by an elaborate system of pergolas, draped with bright bougainvilleas and vines. Over the past decade it has gradually lost out to the swish new shopping malls, such as Shopping Patio Olmos to the south on Plaza Vélez Sarsfield, or Nuevocentro Shopping at Duarte Quiros 1500, a dozen blocks west of the Manzana de los Jesuitas.

Museo de Bellas Artes Dr Genaro Pérez

To take in Argentine art from the nineteenth and twentieth centuries, head for the **Museo de Bellas Artes Dr Genaro Pérez**, a block west of the Legislatura Provincial at Av General Paz 33 (Tues–Sat 10am–8pm; free). The municipal art gallery is housed in a handsome late nineteenth-century building, designed in a French style for the wealthy Dr Tomás Garzón, who bequeathed it to the city in his will. Impeccably restored in the late 1990s, and with fine iron and glass details including an intricate **lift**, the museum is worth a visit for its interior alone, an insight into how the city's prosperous bourgeoisie lived a century ago. Most of the paintings on permanent display belong to the **Escuela Cordobesa**, a movement whose leading master was **Genaro Pérez** – after whom the museum is named – mostly brooding portraits and local landscapes, some imitating the French Impressionists. Other names to watch out for are those of the so-called **1880s Generation** such as Fidel Pelliza, Andrés Piñero and Emilio Caraffa, the last famous for his supervision of the paintings inside Córdoba Cathedral. The **1920s Generation**, markedly influenced by their

European contemporaries including Matisse, Picasso and de Chirico, is represented by Francisco Vidal, Antonio Pedone and José Aguilera. Temporary exhibitions, usually of local artists, are also held from time to time.

Cripta Jesuítica

One block east and one north of the Museo de Bellas Artes, where pedestrianized Calle Rivera Indarte intercepts noisy, traffic-infested Avenida Colón, steps lead down into one of the city's previously hidden treasures. Beneath the hectic street lies the peaceful and mysterious **Cripta Jesuítica** (Mon–Fri 10am–4pm; free), all that remains of an early eighteenth-century Jesuit noviciate razed to the ground during mid-nineteenth-century expansion of the city, and rediscovered by accident in 1989 when telephone cables were being laid under the avenue. The rough-hewn **rock walls** of its three naves, partly lined with bare brick, are a refreshing counterpoint to the cloying decoration of some of the city's other churches, and the space is used to good effect for exhibitions, plays, concerts and, in inclement weather, the Friday-night Patio de Tango usually held at the Cabildo (see p.278).

Nueva Córdoba and Parque Sarmiento

South of the historic centre and sliced diagonally by Avenida Hipólito Yrigoyen, **Nueva Córdoba** was laid out in the late nineteenth century. It was designed as an exclusive residential district, but many of Nueva Córdoba's villas and mansions were taken over by bars, cafés, restaurants and offices after the prosperous middle classes moved to the northwestern suburb of Cerro de las Rosas in the 1940s and 1950s. Architectural styles here are eclectic, to say the least: Neo-Gothic churches, mock-Tudor houses, Georgian facades and Second Empire mini-palaces. René Sergent, the architect of Buenos Aires' Museo de Arte Decorativo, never set foot in Argentina (see p.144), but still managed to design one of Nueva Córdoba's finest buildings, the **Palacio Ferreyra**. Set in a large garden at the southern end of Avenida Hipólito Yrigoyen, it was built in 1913 in an opulent Neo-Bourbon style, complete with Art Nouveau windows and doors. On the eastern side of the busy Plaza España roundabout is the **Museo Provincial de Bellas Artes Emilio Caraffa** (Tues–Sun 11am–7pm; free), a ponderous Neoclassical pile inaugurated in 1916. It was designed by Johan Kronfuss, architect of the Legislatura Provincial (see p.281), and is named for the influential 1880s Generation artist who oversaw the decoration of the cathedral interior. Its airy galleries and shady gardens are used for temporary exhibitions, mostly featuring local artists.

Due east of the Plaza España stretches **Parque Sarmiento**, the city's breathing space. The centre of the park occupies high ground, affording it panoramic views of otherwise flat Nueva Córdoba and the surrounding city. French landscape architect **Charles Thays** (see box, p.130) was called in to design this park for Córdoba, with the support of the 1880s Generation of painters. Work was completed by 1900, and included the boating lake, complete with two islands, and the planting of several thousand native and European trees. This huge open area, crisscrossed by avenues of plane trees, is where the city's main **sports facilities** are located, including tennis courts, jogging routes and an Olympic-sized swimming pool.

Cerro de las Rosas and Chateau Carreras

The fashionable and prosperous northwestern suburbs of **Cerro de las Rosas** and **Chateau Carreras**, some 3km from the microcentro, are home to many of Córdoba's best dining options and trendiest nightclubs. Avenida Figueroa

Alcorta leads out of the El Abasto barrio, on the northern bank of the Río Suquía, becomes Avenida Castro Barros and eventually turns into **Avenida Rafael Núñez**, the wide, main street of Cerro de las Rosas, lined with shops, cafés and restaurants. Otherwise, it's a mainly residential area of shaded streets and large villas, built on the relatively cool heights of a wooded hill – the city's most desirable barrio since low-lying Nueva Córdoba lost its cachet in the 1940s and 1950s.

From the northern end of Avenida Rafael Núñez another avenue, Laplace, swings southwest and crosses a loop in the Río Suquía. On the peninsula formed by the river is the leafy district known as Chateau Carreras, named after a Neo-Palladian mansion built in 1890 for the influential Carreras family. This picturesque building, painted the colour of Parma violets, save for a row of slender white Ionic columns along the front portico, houses the **Centro de Arte Contemporáneo** (Tues–Fri 11am–7pm, Sat & Sun 3–7pm; free), which stages uneven temporary exhibitions of contemporary paintings and photographs. The mansion is tucked away in the landscaped woods of **Parque San Martín**, another of the city's green spaces, which, like Parque Sarmiento, was designed by Charles Thays. Incidentally, the area immediately around the museum is regarded as unsafe and it's best not to linger here alone or after dusk. Just to the north of the park is the city's **Fair Complex**, while just across Avenida Ramón J. Cárcano, to the east, is Córdoba's massive football stadium, built for the 1978 World Cup finals. Along the avenue, just south of here, are clustered a number of the city's most popular nightclubs (see p.284).

Eating, drinking and nightlife

Interesting **restaurants** and cafés are disappointingly thin on the ground in Córdoba, although the city cranks up a gear during university term time. With a couple of notable exceptions, the city centre has little to offer in the evenings, even becoming rather seedy. Nueva Córdoba and the cooler heights of the Cerro de las Rosas feel safer and have a number of eating places, but they can also be rather colourless. Most of the nightlife has moved to two outlying areas: El Abasto, a revitalized former warehouse district close to the centre on the northern banks of the Río Suquía that buzzes with **bars**, **discos** and **live music venues**, many stretched along Boulevard Las Heras; and the even trendier Chateau Carreras area, just south of Cerro de las Rosas, which has a number of more upmarket **nightclubs** to choose from. One of Argentina's best **theatres**, the Teatro del Libertador General San Martín, puts on excellent dance and music shows, while the city's many **cinemas** screen a variety of films; try Ⓦwww.undercba.com.ar for listings. The locals are split by allegiance to two of the nation's leading **football** clubs, Belgrano and Talleres, and the local derby is a highlight of the sporting calendar.

Restaurants and cafés

Alfosina Duarte Quirós 66. Lively, colourfully decorated café that offers a wide range of typical Argentine fare including *minutas*, pizzas and *locro*, along with the chance to sip *mate* and listen to the occasional live folklore performance.

El Arrabal Belgrano 899, at Fructuoso Rivera Ⓣ0351/460-2990, Ⓦwww.elarrabal.com.ar. Good-value meals – featuring excellent steaks – but the main reason to come is for the brilliant tango shows, different each night of the week; a three-course meal and the show will cost far less than in Buenos Aires.

Bursatil Café Ituzaingo and San Jeronimo. In Córdoba's small financial district, this lunch-time café takes its name from the Spanish for "stock exchange", and names its main dishes for international exchanges – possibilities include the "Noquis Merval", the "Entrecot Bovespa" or the "Trucha Dow Jones". Breakfasts, however, are free from global financial overtones.

Mandarina Obispo Trejo 175. Along with *La Alameda* directly opposite (see below), this coolly decorated restaurant is one of the few decent places to eat out in the city centre. The menu has plenty of meat, fish and vegetarian dishes, including *rabas a la marinera*, gnocchi, *cazuela de calamar* and *fugazzas*.

Las Rías de Galicia Montevideo 271 ⓣ0351/428-1333. You can choose from top-quality, Spanish-influenced seafood, fish and meat dishes at this swish restaurant; the weekday lunch-time *menú ejecutivo* is great value.

Verde Siempre Verde 9 de Julio 36. Appetizing pizzas, quiches, soya burgers and fresh salads are served by weight in cool surroundings here at Córdoba's best vegetarian restaurant.

Victorino Piazza Av Rafael Núñez 4005, Cerro de las Rosas. A rusty locomotive and an old British telephone box on the forecourt serve as landmarks for this café/bar, which prepares hearty meals and huge cocktails.

La Vieja Casa Independencia 512. Attractive decor and a small patio help create an inviting ambience at this friendly *parrilla* offering juicy *milanesas* and other traditional fare; the *budín de pan* is especially memorable.

Bars and nightclubs

La Alameda Obispo Trejo 170. With a great bohemian ambience, *Alameda* serves reasonably priced food including empanadas and *humitas* alongside its beers. Patrons leave scribbled notes and minor works of art pinned to the wall.

Carreras Av Piamonte s/n, Chateau Carreras. Large disco with "beach" decor plus an eclectic music selection that ranges from country to golden oldies via the latest hits, salsa and Argentine rock. Fri–Sun.

El Infierno ⓦwww.infiernocordoba.com. Av del Piamonte and Carcano, Chateau Carreras. Large, popular, commercial dance venue, featuring a slightly odd mix of cutting-edge house and fashion parades. Sat only.

Johnny B Good Av Hipólito Yrigoyen 320, Nueva Córdoba, and Av Rafael Núñez 4791, Cerro de la Rosas. These identical twins are trendy cocktail bars-cum-restaurants and popular meeting-places, with live rock music most weekends.

Peekaboo Life Project Tillard 125, El Abasto. The hip club of the moment, *Peekaboo* boasts regular appearances by the country's best DJs, as well as the occasional set spun by international stars.

El Ruedo Obispo Trejo and 27 de Abril. Lively café/bar with music and a mixed clientele, serving fast-food snacks; day-time and early evening hours only.

Voodoo Lounge Av Hipólito Yrigoyen and San Lorenzo, Nueva Córdoba. One of the few discos left in the downtown area, mostly frequented by under-25s. Fri–Sun.

Xero Av Las Heras 124, El Abasto. Nightclub playing mostly Latin rhythms. Fri–Sun.

Listings

Airlines Aerolíneas Argentinas, Av Colón 520 ⓣ0351/410-7676; LAN Chile, Figueroa Alcorta ⓣ0351/425-3030.

Banks and exchange The best for exchanging money are: Citibank, Rivadavia 104, and Banco Mayo, 9 de Julio 137. ATMs are everywhere, especially around Plaza San Martín.

Car rental Avis, Blvd San Juan 137 ⓣ0351/424-6185; Localiza, Av Rafael Nuñez 3448 ⓣ0351/482-7777.

Consulates Bolivia, Blvd San Juan 639 3A ⓣ0351/481-2016; Chile, Crisol 280 ⓣ0351/469-2010; Germany, Elíseo Canton 1870 ⓣ0351/489-0826; Paraguay, General Paz 73 ⓣ0351/423-7043; Uruguay, San Jeromino 167 7A ⓣ0351/424-1028.

Internet access CyberUNO, Duarte Quiros 201.

Laundry Laveraps at Chacabuco 301, Belgrano 76 and R. Indarte 289.

Post office Av General Paz 201.

Taxis Tala Car Remis ⓣ0351/494-7000; Taxi-Com ⓣ0351/464-4444.

Telephones Telecom, General Paz 36 and 27 de Abril 27, and *locutorios* everywhere.

Tour operators Nativo Viajes, 27 de Abril 11 ⓣ0351/424-5341, ⓦwww.cordobanativoviajes.com.ar.

Travel agents Asatej, Shopping Patio Olmos ⓣ0351/426-2005.

The Camino de la Historia

The first 150km stretch of **RN-9** that runs north from Córdoba city towards Santiago del Estero is promoted by the provincial tourist authority as the

Camino de la Historia ("Historical Route"), as it coincides with part of the colonial Camino Real ("Royal Way"), the Spanish road from Lima and Potosí to present-day Argentina. This was the route taken, albeit in the opposite direction, by the region's first European settlers – the founders of Córdoba city – and the **Jesuit missionaries** who quickly dominated the local economy and culture. Eastwards from the road stretch some of Argentina's most fertile cattle ranches; to the west the unbroken ridge of the Sierra Chica runs parallel to the highway. One of the country's finest Jesuit estancias, now host to the well-presented **Museo Jesuítico Nacional**, can be visited at **Jesús María**, while beautiful **Santa Catalina**, lying off the main road to the north in a bucolic hillside setting, is still inhabited by direct descendants of the family who moved here at the end of the eighteenth century. Further north, in **Villa Tulumba**, a timeless little place well off the beaten track, the utterly nondescript parish church houses a masterpiece of Jesuit art, the altarpiece that once adorned the Jesuits' temple and, later, Córdoba Cathedral, until it was moved up here in the early nineteenth century. As they developed their intensive agriculture, the Jesuits all but wiped out the region's pre-Hispanic civilizations, but some precious vestiges of their culture, namely intriguing rock paintings, can be seen in the far north of the province, just off RN-9 at **Cerro Colorado**, one of Argentina's finest pre-Columbian sites.

Jesús María

Lying just off busy RN-9 50km north of Córdoba, **JESÚS MARÍA** is a sleepy little town that comes to life for the annual Festival Nacional de la Doma y el

The Jesuits in Córdoba Province

Even today the city of **Córdoba** owes its importance largely to the **Jesuits** who founded a college here in 1613. It would later become South America's second university, the Universidad San Carlos, in 1621, making Córdoba the de facto capital of the Americas south of Lima. In 1640, the Jesuits built a temple (see p.279) at the heart of the city, and for the next 120 years the Society of Jesus dominated life there. Their emphasis on education earned the city the nickname *La Docta* ("the Learned"), and even today Córdoba is still regarded as an erudite kind of place – albeit politically radical.

But while the Jesuits and other missionaries turned Córdoba into the cultural capital of this part of the empire, their presence elsewhere resulted in the decline in numbers of the native population. The indigenous Sanavirones, Comechingones and Abipones resolutely defended themselves from the invaders. Finally conquered, they thwarted attempts by the Spanish to "civilize" them under the system of *encomiendas*. Nonetheless, devastated by influenza and other imported ailments, the indigenous population dwindled from several thousand in the late sixteenth century to only a few hundred a century later. Apart from a few archeological finds, such as rock paintings, the only signs of their former presence are the names of villages, rivers and the mountain range to the south of the city, and discernible indigenous features in the *serranos*, or rural inhabitants of the sierras.

Despite their profound effect on the area's original inhabitants, the Jesuits were relatively enlightened by colonial standards, educating their workforce and treating them comparatively humanely. In addition to various monuments in the city itself, you can still visit their estancias, whose produce sustained communities and boosted trade in the whole empire. The Jesuit buildings in Córdoba and four of the remaining estancias around the province – including **Santa Catalina** (see p.286), **Alta Gracia** (see p.297), **Jesús María** (see above) and **Caroya**, near Jesús María – have all been declared UNESCO World Heritage Sites.

△ Museo Jesuítico Nacional, Jesús María

Folklore, a gaucho fiesta with lively entertainment held every evening during the first fortnight of January. Unfortunately, in recent years it has seen a fall in quality and fairly rowdy crowds. On the town's northern outskirts, near the amphitheatre where the festival takes place, is the **Museo Jesuítico Nacional** (April–Sept Mon–Fri 8am–7pm, Sat & Sun 2–6pm, Oct–March Mon–Fri same hours, Sat & Sun 3–7pm; $2), housed in the former residence and the bodega, or wineries, of a well-restored **Jesuit estancia**. Next to the missionaries' living quarters and the adjoining eighteenth-century church are a colonial *tajamar*, or reservoir, and apple and peach orchards – all that remain of the estancia's once extensive territory, which in the seventeenth and eighteenth centuries covered more than a hundred square kilometres. In contrast to the bare, rough-hewn granite of the outside walls of the complex, a whitewashed courtyard lies beyond a gateway to the right of the church. Its two storeys of simple arches on three sides set off the bright red roofs, which are capped with the original ceramic tiles, or *musleros*. These slightly convex tiles, taking their name from *muslo*, or thigh, because the tile-makers shaped the clay on their legs, are common to all the Jesuit estancias. The U-shaped *residencia* contains the former missionaries' cells, storehouses and communal rooms, now used for temporary exhibits and various permanent displays of archeological finds, colonial furniture, sacred relics and religious artwork from the seventeenth and eighteenth centuries, along with farming and wine-making equipment. The local wine, Lagrimilla, is claimed to be the first colonial wine served in the Spanish court – Argentina's earliest vineyards were planted here at the end of the sixteenth century. Much newer vintages accompany first-rate *parrillas* at the excellent *El Faro* **restaurant**, on RN-9 at Juan Bautista Alberdi 245 (Ⓣ03525/466258) in neighbouring Colonia Caroya, effectively a suburb of Jesús María; try the succulent goat.

Santa Catalina and Villa Tulumba

West of Jesús María, RN-156 leads to Ascochinga, from where an easily passable trail heads north through thick forest to **SANTA CATALINA**, 20km to the northwest. Almost completely hidden among the hills, Santa Catalina is the biggest, and undoubtedly the finest, Jesuit **estancia** (summer Tues–Sun 10am–1pm & 3–7pm, winter Tues–Sun 10am–1pm & 2–6pm; $1) in the region, an outstanding example of colonial architecture in the Spanish Americas. A sprawling yet harmonious set of early eighteenth-century buildings, it is dominated by its church, whose elegant silhouette and symmetrical towers suddenly and unexpectedly appear as you emerge from the woods. Whitewashed to protect the porous stone from the elements, the brightness of the building almost dazzles you when you approach. The **church** is dedicated to St Catherine of Alexandria, whose feast day is celebrated with pomp every November 25; the sternly imposing facade is reminiscent of the Baroque churches of southern Germany and Austria. Inside, the austere single nave, whitewashed like the exterior, is decorated with a gilded wooden **retable** that houses an image of St Catherine, and a fine carob-wood pulpit. The peaceful inner courtyards of the estancia's *casco*, or living quarters, are furnished with graceful wicker, leather and calfskin chairs, shaded by magnolias and bougainvilleas and cooled by Italianate fountains. On the right-hand flank of the church is an overgrown little cemetery, whose outer wall bears a plaque commemorating the Italian composer and organist Domenico Zípoli, who died here in 1726.

Accessible through a narrow passageway to the right of the church is the stylish *La Ranchería*, a small restaurant/*confitería*, plus a shop selling high-quality local crafts; someone should be on hand to serve you some delicious home-cured ham, a platter of cheese or cooked meals before showing you around the estancia. The charm of this place is that it looks and feels so lived-in: it's still the residence of direct descendants of Antonio Díaz, a mayor of Córdoba who acquired it in the 1770s, following the Jesuits' expulsion from the Spanish empire. Although you can't stay at the estancia itself, **accommodation** in the area can be found at the modern *Posada Camino Real* (Ⓣ0351/6134287, Ⓦwww.posadacaminoreal.com.ar; ⑥), 10km north from Santa Catalina; the rooms are extremely comfortable, riding and other activities in the unspoilt countryside are laid on and a swimming pool and massages provide welcome relaxation.

The winding track that leads to Santa Catalina continues northeast for some 20km, to where RN-60 forks left from RN-9. Another 50km north along RN-9, at San José de la Dormida, a signposted road heads west to **VILLA TULUMBA**, 22km beyond, a tiny hamlet that's home to a Baroque masterpiece: a subtly crafted seventeenth-century **tabernacle**, complete with polychrome wooden cherubs and saints, and decorated with just a hint of gold, inside the otherwise nasty parish church. Soon after Argentina's independence, Bishop Moscoso, a modernizing anti-Jesuit bishop of Córdoba, decided that the city's cathedral should have a brand new altarpiece, and asked all the parishes in his diocese to collect funds for it. The citizens of Villa Tulumba were the most generous, and were rewarded with this tabernacle, which had been transferred to the cathedral from the city's Jesuit temple after the Society of Jesus was expelled from the Spanish empire by King Carlos III in 1767.

Cerro Colorado

Nearly 120km north of Jesús María, at the far northern end of the Camino de la Historia, is the **Parque Arqueológico y Natural Cerro Colorado** (daily 9am–1pm & 2–6pm; $1), home to some fascinating vestiges of pre-Columbian culture. It's located next to **Cerro Colorado village**, 10km down a meandering dirt track off RN-9 to the west of Santa Elena. Drivers beware: there's a deep ford lurking round a bend, 1km before you enter the village, followed by another in the village itself.

CERRO COLORADO village, no more than a few houses dotted along a riverbank, nestles in a deep, picturesque valley, surrounded by three looming peaks, the Cerro Colorado (830m), Cerro Veladero (810m) and Cerro Inti Huasi (772m), all of which are easily explored on foot and afford fine views of the countryside. The main attraction, though, is one of the country's finest collections of **petroglyphs**, several thousand drawings that were scraped and painted by the indigenous inhabitants onto the pink rock face at the base of the mountains and in caves higher up between 1000 and 1600 AD; compulsory **guided tours** leave four times daily from the *guardería* at the entrance to the village. Nearby is the diminutive **Museo Arqueológico** (daily 8.30am–6pm; free), with some photographs of the petroglyphs and native flora, though it is made slightly redundant by the guide who takes you round the petroglyphs, pointing out the many plant varieties along the way. Some of the glyphs depict horses, cattle and European figures as well as native llamas, guanacos, condors, pumas and snakes, but few of the abstract figures have been satisfactorily or conclusively interpreted – though your guide will offer convincing theories. The deep depressions, or *morteros*, in the horizontal rock nearby were caused over the centuries by the grinding and mixing of paints. Of the different **pigments** used – chalk, ochre, charcoal, oils and vegetable extracts – the white and black stand out more than the rest, but climatic changes, especially increased humidity, are taking their toll, and many of the rock paintings are badly faded. Some of them have disappeared altogether: one drawing, representing the Sun God, was removed to the British Museum; all that remains is a gaping hole in the rock, high up on the Cerro. The petroglyphs are best viewed very early in the morning or before dusk, when the rock takes on blazing red hues and the pigments' contrasts are at their strongest.

Several **buses** a day run from Córdoba to Santa Elena, 11km from Cerro Colorado village; the only practical way to get to Cerro Colorado from here is by *remise*, costing around $20. There are **camping** facilities with river bathing in the village, and two simple **hotels** – the modern but spartan *Descanso del Indio* (Ⓣ0351/156466778; ❷), and the basic *La Italiana* (Ⓣ0351/4246598; ❷). Of the **places to eat**, the best is *Purinqui Huasi*, near the ford and stepping stones across the river, and serving reasonably priced grilled meats and sandwiches.

The Punilla Valley

Squeezed between the continuous ridge of the Sierra Chica to the east, and the higher peaks of the Sierra Grande to the west, the peaceful **Punilla Valley** is Argentina's longest-established inland tourist area, drawing a steady stream of visitors with its idyllic mountain scenery and fresh air, family-friendly resorts and numerous top-class outdoor pursuits. The valley, whose name means "little *puna*" (*puna* in turn meaning "highland plain" in Quichoa), has for many years served as a home for Anglo-Argentines and artists from North America.

The RN-38 to La Rioja bisects the valley, which stretches northwards for about a hundred kilometres from horrendously noisy **Villa Carlos Paz**, the self-styled "Gateway to the Punilla", some 35km along RN-20 west of Córdoba. Tens of thousands of Cordobeses and Porteños migrate to this brash inland beach resort every summer in an insatiable quest for sun, sand and socializing – the town is renowned for its mega-discos and crowded bars. A short distance north and overlooked by a sugar-loaf hill, El Pan de Azúcar, is **Cosquín**, a slightly calmer place famed for its once-prestigious annual folk festival. The further north you go, the more tranquil the resorts become: **La Falda**, **La Cumbre** and **Capilla del Monte** have all retained their slightly old-fashioned charm while offering a mixture of high-quality services and a propensity for New Age pursuits. Relatively less crowded, they make for better bases from which to explore the mountains on foot, on horseback or in a vehicle, or to try out some of the adventurous sports on offer. Anyone looking for remote locales to explore should head for the dirt roads between Capilla del Monte and Santa Catalina, where from **Ongamira** and **Ischilín** you can discover some of the region's most remarkable landscapes, while **San Marcos Sierras** has been a magnet for those of a counterculture persuasion since the 1960s.

Buses between Córdoba and Villa Carlos Paz are fast and frequent, running around the clock; many of them continue up the valley towards La Rioja and San Juan, stopping at all the main resorts along the way. Naturally, the hinterland is best visited with your own locomotion.

Villa Carlos Paz and Cosquín

The abysmal resort of **VILLA CARLOS PAZ** lies at the southern end of the Punilla Valley, on the southwestern banks of a large, dirty reservoir, the Lago San Roque. It sits at a major junction, that of the RN-20, which heads south to Mina Clavero and on to San Luis and San Juan, and the RN-38 toll-road, which goes north through the valley towards Cruz del Eje and La Rioja. Nationally famous, but now totally spoilt by chaotic construction, pollution and overcrowding, the resort is frequently compared with Mar del Plata (see p.218), only without the ocean. It started out in the 1930s as a holiday centre for well-off Cordobeses, with sandy beaches created along the lakeside. Nowadays people whiz around the lake in catamarans and motor-boats, or on water skis. In the town centre, dozens of tacky amusement arcades and entertainment theme parks blare music, while most of the bars and *confiterías* show video clips or offer karaoke. The town sprawls in a dis-orderly way around the lake – the western districts are generally greener, airier and more attractive. The local population of 60,000 more than doubles at the height of summer, when the staggering four hundred or so hotels and *hosterías* are all booked up and the dozen campsites are crammed full. There's absolutely nothing to detain you here.

Some 25km north of Villa Carlos Paz, and barely more appealing, the small but bustling town of **COSQUÍN** nestles in a sweep of the river of the same name and in the lee of the 1260-metre **Pan de Azúcar**. It's one of the region's oldest settlements – dating from colonial times – and has been a holiday resort since the end of the nineteenth century. The summit of the sugar-loaf mountain, which affords panoramic views of the valley and mountains beyond, can be reached by a chairlift, or *aerosilla* (daily 10am–7.30pm; $12 return), from the well-signposted Complejo Aerosilla, which sits about 6km north of town and also houses a bronze monument to **Carlos Gardel**, the legendary tango singer, as well as the inevitable *confitería*. Alternatively, you can skip the chairlift and use your legs – from the Complejo Aerosilla it's about half an hour up a steep path. Cosquín has always been associated nationwide with the **Festival Nacional de Folklore** (Ⓦwww.aquicosquin.org), held every year in the second half of January and attended by folk artists, ballet troupes and classical musicians from across the country, although it has declined in quality in recent years. The festival takes place in the so-called Plaza Nacional del Folklore (actually the Plaza Próspero Molina) just off RN-38, which threads through the centre of town.

Practicalities

With services to dozens of local, regional and national destinations, including Buenos Aires and Córdoba, Villa Carlos Paz's busy and cramped **bus terminal** is on Avenida San Martín, between calles Belgrano and Maipú. Right in front of it, the main **tourist information office**, Av San Martín 400 (Dec–March 7am–11pm, rest of year 8am–8pm; Ⓣ03541/421624), will help you find a bed for the night. During peak periods finding a **place to stay** can be difficult, even though there are many hotels, but residents often stand by the road advertising rooms for rent. There are dozens of **places to eat**, mostly pizzerias, but the best is a Spanish-style *tasca, La Albufera*, at Km743 on RN-20. In the centre, many restaurants are clustered around Avenida General Paz.

Cosquín's **bus station**, with half-hourly services to and from Córdoba and other Punilla resorts, lies one block west of Plaza San Martín at Presidente Perón s/n. The poor **tourist information office** is at San Martín 560 (Mon–Fri 8am–9pm, Sat & Sun 9am–6pm; Ⓣ03541/454644, Ⓦwww.cosquinturismo.com.ar), five blocks north opposite Plaza Próspero Molina. You can eat very well at two **restaurants** in particular: *Saint Jeans parrilla* at Avenida San Martín and Soberanía Nacional, or *San Marino*, Av San Martín 715, which serves excellent seafood.

La Falda and around

Twenty kilometres north of Cosquín and a little more peaceful still, **LA FALDA** is today just another Punilla town, a base from which to explore the nearby mountains – just a taste of the far finer scenery to come some way up the valley. In the early twentieth century, however, La Falda was an exclusive resort, served by the newly built railway and luring the great and the good from as far afield as Europe. A major advertising campaign was conducted here by a German-run luxury hotel, **Hotel Edén**, now a dilapidated and unusual tourist attraction (guided visits Dec–March & July daily 10am–noon & 3–6pm, rest of year same hours Fri–Sun only; $6; Ⓦwww.hoteledenlafalda.com). At the far eastern end of Avenida Edén, the magnificent holiday palace was built in the 1890s. Nearly all of Argentine high society stayed here in the 1920s and 1930s, as well as such famous international guests as the Prince of Wales and Albert Einstein, and some say even Adolf Hitler. The state confiscated it from its German owners in the 1940s, after which it fell into decline, but its grandiose design and opulent decor are still discernible, especially in the newly renovated lobby, wine cellar and *confitería*. The guided tours take you around the faded rooms; night tours, which are good, creepy fun, are also run during the summer (10pm), though you'll need decent Spanish if you want to understand the ghost stories.

The RN-38 winds through the western side of the town as Avenida Presidente Kennedy; from it, Avenida Edén heads straight towards the mountainside to the east. For exhilarating views of the valley, head for nearby **Cerro Banderita**; go to the far end of Avenida Edén and then, just past the dull railway museum, take Calle Austria as far as El Chorrito, a small waterfall among lush vegetation. This is the starting-point of the steep one-hour climb to the peak, which many people do on horseback, before riding along the mountaintop. Of the longer routes, one of the most impressive takes you east over the Sierra Chica towards **Río Ceballos**; the views into the Punilla Valley from the peak at **Cerro Cuadrado**, 20km from La Falda, are stunning. To the west, past the Dique La Falda reservoir, a dirt track leads across the windswept but hauntingly beautiful **Pampa de Oláen**, where several well-preserved colonial chapels dot the

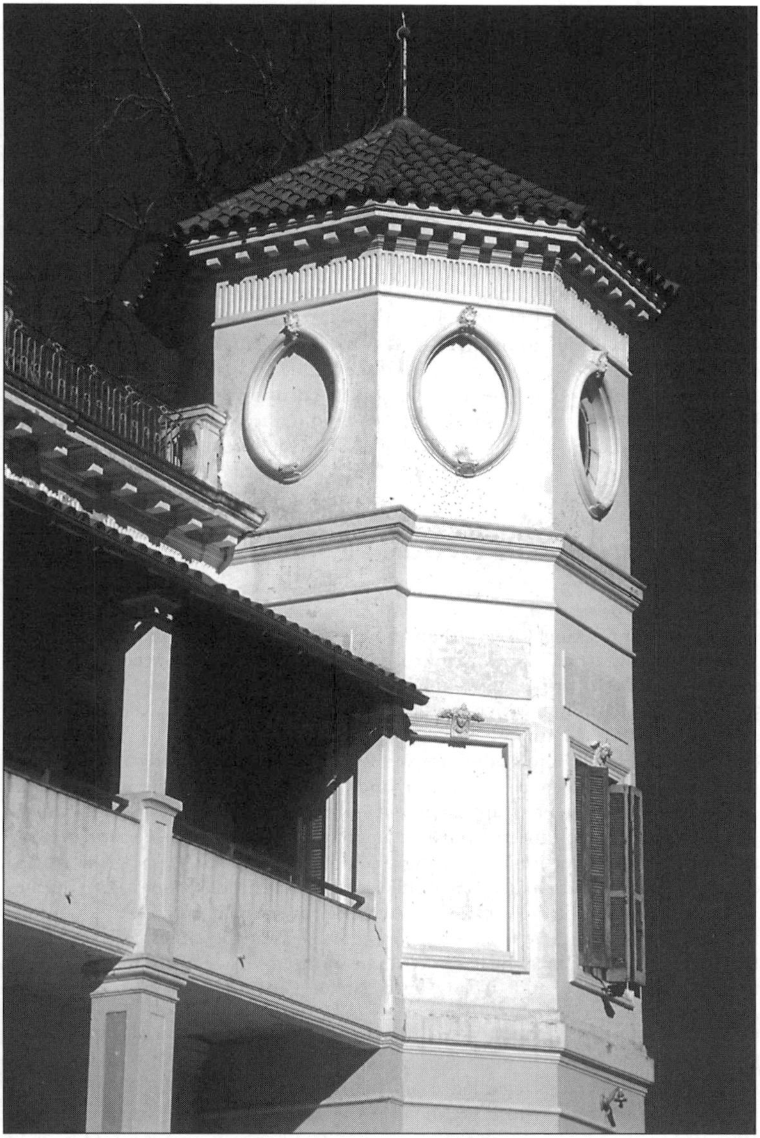

△ Ex-Hotel Edén

moor-like landscape. The finest is the eighteenth-century **Capilla Santa Barbara** (erratic opening hours) near Oláen, its simple, curvaceous white silhouette framed by gnarled trees; inside is equally stark, apart from some fine polychrome statues decorating the altarpiece. Note that it is often impossible to drive along this track, especially after heavy rain, even in a 4WD vehicle.

Practicalities

La Falda's **bus station** (Ⓣ03548/423186) is on Avenida Buenos Aires just north of the intersection of avenidas Presidente Kennedy and Edén; all buses from Córdoba and Carlos Paz to San Juan and La Rioja stop here. Next door at España 50, the **tourist office** (daily 8am–9pm; Ⓣ03548/423462) has stacks of information on accommodation and services, including where to hire horses or rent motorbikes or mountain bikes. There are a number of agencies running **tours** in the surrounding area, including Carlitur at Diagonal San Martín 38 (Ⓣ03548/423448). **Accommodation** ranges from the old-fashioned but roomy *Hotel Nor Tomarza*, Av Edén 1063 (Ⓣ03548/425531, Ⓔnortomarza@arnet.com.ar; ❺), to the very comfortable *Hotel Ollantay*, La Plata 236 (Ⓣ03548/422341, Ⓔhtlollantay@punillanet.com.ar; ❺), to the inexpensive but pleasant *Hostería Ana Clara*, Av Argentina 239 (Ⓣ03548/422450, Ⓔelhostaldeanaclara@hotmail.com; ❸). *Hostal L'Hirondelle*, Av Edén 861 (Ⓣ03548/422825, Ⓦwww.lhirondellehostal.com; ❹), has bright rooms, clean bathrooms and a pool. The best-equipped **campsite** is the *Siete Cascadas* (Ⓣ03548/423869), on the banks of the reservoir, due west of the bus terminal. Places to **eat** include *La Parrilla de Raúl*, Calle Buenos Aires 111, and its twin establishment at Av Edén 1002, while simple vegetarian fare can be found at *Pachamama*, Av Edén 127.

La Cumbre and around

LA CUMBRE, a small, leafy town just east of RN-38, 13km north of La Falda, is a great spot for fishing, exploring the mountains, participating in adventure pursuits or just relaxing. Over 1100m above sea level, it enjoys mild summers and cool winters, and has been known to be blanketed in snow. Several trout-rich streams rush down the steep mountains and gurgle through town, among them the Río San Gerónimo, which runs past the central Plaza 25 de Mayo. A British community was established here when the railways were built in the nineteenth century, and La Cumbre's prestigious golf club, its predominantly mock-Tudor villas and manicured lawns testify to a long-standing Anglo-Saxon presence. But despite the resort's genteel appearance it has become synonymous with **hang-gliding**; every March international competitions are held here. Cerro Mirador, the cliff-top launching-point for hang-gliding and parasailing, is near the ruined colonial estancia and chapel of **Cuchi Corral**, 10km due west of La Cumbre and worth visiting for the views alone, whether or not you join in the lemming-like activities. Anyone with a literary bent will enjoy the small museum at **El Paraíso**, in Cruz Chica, over 2km to the north of La Cumbre as you head towards Los Cocos (guided daily visits Jan & Feb 10.30am–1pm & 4–8pm, April–Sept 2–6pm, March & Oct–Dec 3–7pm; $5). The handsome Spanish-style house, built in 1915 and with an exquisite garden designed by Charles Thays (see box, p.130), was home to hedonistic writer Manuel "Manucho" Mujica Laínez, whose novel *Bomarzo* is regarded as an Argentine classic. Written in 1962, it was turned into an opera whose premiere at the Teatro Colón in Buenos Aires in 1967 was banned by the military dictatorship. The house, where it is said he held frequent orgies – he and his wife kept separate lovers, his mostly men – contains a delightful collection of his personal effects, including 15,000 books, paintings, photographs and all manner of objects. Look out in particular for the "Gate to Heaven", an ornate iron door decorated with erotic figures; a small gallery in the basement hosts exhibitions of mostly local artists.

Running roughly parallel to RN-38 as it heads south to Villa Giardino is the winding **Camino de los Artesanos**, along which you'll find over two dozen establishments selling all manner of crafts – silver- and pewterware, macramé, ceramics, woollens – along with breweries, shops serving *dulce de leche* and home-made cakes and even places offering yoga and massages.

One of the province's most spectacular scenic routes, ideal for mountain bikes and strong calf muscles, takes you east along the **Camino del Pungo**. Beyond **Estancia El Rosario** (daily 8.30am–6.30pm), a farmhouse selling its own jams, *dulce de leche*, *alfajores* and other goods to delight a sweet tooth, signposted from La Cumbre golf course to the southeast of La Cumbre's town centre, it climbs the mountainside and plunges into dense pine forest, before fording the Río Tiu Mayu. It then passes through luxuriant forest – eucalyptus, cacti, palms, firs and osiers – and crosses the summit of the Sierra Grande, before reaching Ascochinga, 41km away, and Santa Catalina (see p.286). A right-hand fork immediately before the Río Tiu Mayu takes you south along a roughly surfaced but spectacular road. At the end of the road, some 45km from La Cumbre, is the old **Estancia Santa Gertrudis** (Tues–Fri 10am–6pm, Sat & Sun 10am–8pm; Ⓣ0351/155294778, Ⓦwww.candonga.com.ar), whose most interesting feature is the splendid eighteenth-century Jesuit chapel of **Candonga**, with its pristine walls, ochre-tiled roof and rough-hewn stone steps. The majestic curve of its porch, the delicate bell tower and lantern-like cupola fit snugly into the bucolic valley setting, set off by a fast-flowing brook that sweeps through the pampas fields nearby. The estancia serves lunch and tea at the remodelled *casco* (farmhouse), with many of the ingredients coming from the estancia's own orchards.

Practicalities

La Cumbre's **tourist office** (daily 8am–10pm; Ⓣ03548/452966, Ⓦwww.lacumbre.gov.ar) is in the former train station where Avenida San Martín intersects Avenida Caraffa, 300m southwest of the central square. Immediately to the south, the **bus station** is at Caraffa and General Paz; services to and from Córdoba and Capilla del Monte (see below) are half-hourly. La Cumbre has a good choice of upmarket **accommodation**, including the *Posada San Andrés*, at Benitz and Monteagudo (Ⓣ03548/451165, Ⓦwww.posadasanandres.com; ❺), which has excellent breakfasts and a swimming pool; the very comfortable *Posada Los Cedros*, Argentina 837 (Ⓣ03548/451028, Ⓔposadaloscedros@arnet.com.ar; ❻); and the *Gran Hotel La Cumbre*, near the golf course at Posadas s/n (Ⓣ03548/451550, Ⓦwww.granhotellacumbre.com; ❺) – a rather old-fashioned but cosy place, with great views. There's less choice at the budget end – *Posada de la Montaña*, 9 de Julio 753 (Ⓣ03548/451867, Ⓦwww.posadadelamontania.com.ar; ❸), is probably your best bet. La Cumbre's top **campsite** is the *El Paso*, up near the Cristo Redentor statue at Monseñor Pablo Cabrera s/n (Ⓣ03548/452545). The finest **restaurant** for trout and other regional specialities is *La Casona del Toboso*, Belgrano 349. Delicious cakes are on offer at *Dani Cheff*, opposite the tourist office at Avenida Caraffa and Belgrano.

Should you be tempted by the prospect of something a bit adventurous, try Escuela de Montaña George Mallory (Ⓣ03548/492271) for **rock-climbing**, or Aero Club La Cumbre (Ⓣ03548/452544) for **hang-gliding**. **Horses** can be hired from El Rosendo at Juan XXIII s/n (Ⓣ03548/451688).

Capilla del Monte and around

Lively **CAPILLA DEL MONTE**, 16km north of La Cumbre, sits at the confluence of the rivers Calabalumba and Dolores against the bare-sloped Cerro Uritorco, at 1979m the highest peak of the Sierra Chica. It was a resort for Argentina's bourgeoisie at the end of the nineteenth century, as testified by

Estancias around the Sierra Chica

Although the Jesuit **estancias** in the Sierra Chica themselves do not generally allow the opportunity to stay the night, there are a number of estancias around Santa Catalina and in the Punilla Valley that have opened their doors to visitors. These places can make excellent spots to laze away a few days in the countryside, horse-riding and swimming; they can also be used as a base for visiting the area's other attractions.

Near La Cumbre, *Estancia Los Potreros* (ⓣ011/48782692 or 03548/452121, ⓦwww.estancialospotreros.com) is an authentic working estancia that has been owned by the same Anglo-Argentine family for four generations. This is the place to come if you want to do some horse-riding – the friendly owners will take you on trips around the area, organize polo lessons and tournaments and even allow you to observe or help with farm activities. The animals are so well looked after and trained that even reluctant riders usually end up happily on horseback. Accommodation is in the attractive adobe *casco*, and you dine with the family; the price of US$340 per person per night includes all activities and facilities, transport from Córdoba and delicious food and drink. Three- or seven-day **trail rides**, staying at local homesteads, also take place throughout the year, but must be arranged in advance.

A different kind of stay can be had at *Estancia La Paz* (ⓣ03525/492073, ⓦwww.estancialapaz.com), near Santa Catalina. In the nineteenth century, this was the beloved homestead of President Roca (see Contexts, p.792) where he entertained many of the powerful men of his day. In many ways resembling a country hotel, with a spa, putting green, rowing lake and large, comfortable rooms, it's the place to head for if you'd rather feel like a pampered politician than a pioneer. Meals are served on a tiled verandah that offers great views over the estancia's extensive, manicured grounds, landscaped by the omnipresent Charles Thays. Day visits possible (US$80); otherwise, half-board stays are US$145 per person per night, excluding drinks and transfers.

the many luxurious villas, some of them slightly or very dilapidated. These days it attracts more alternative vacationers, as you can tell from the number of hotels and restaurants calling themselves *naturista*, or back-to-nature. The town has little to offer in the way of sights, but it serves as an appealing base along the valley for treks into the mountains or for trying out hang-gliding and other pursuits. Central Plaza San Martín lies only a couple of blocks east of RN-38, which runs through the west of the town, parallel to the Río de Dolores. From the plaza, Diagonal Buenos Aires, the busy commercial pedestrian mall, runs southeast to the quaint former train station on Calle Pueyrredón; it's claimed to be South America's only roofed street, an assertion nowhere else has rushed to contend. A number of safe bathing areas, or *balnearios*, can be found along the Río Calabalumba, including *Balneario Calabalumba*, at the northern end of General Paz, and *Balneario La Toma*, at the eastern end of Avenida Sabattini.

In addition to the fresh air, unspoilt countryside and splendid opportunities for sports pursuits, such as trekking and fishing, many visitors are also drawn to the area by claims of **UFO sightings**, "energy centres" and numerous local **legends**. One such legend asserts that when Calabalumba, the young daughter of a witch-doctor, eloped with Uritorco, the latter was turned into a mountain while she was condemned to eternal sorrow, her tears forming the river that flows from the mountainside. Incidentally, the **Cerro Uritorco**, the focus for Capillo del Monte's supposed paranormal activity, is well worth the climb (about 3hr to the top; $6; register with tourist office) for the grandiose views across the valley to the Sierra de Cuniputo to the west. The steep clamber up a well-trodden path starts near the *Balneario Calabalumba*, northeast of Plaza San Martín, and cuts through private property. Only part of the climb is shaded, so take water with you. You must set off between 8 and 11am and be back by 5pm, which rather rules out opportunities for UFO-hunting.

A short drive out of Capilla del Monte is the entrance to **LOS TERRONES** (Ⓦwww.losterrones.com; daily 9am–dusk; $8), an amazing formation of multi-coloured rocks on either side of a five-kilometre dirt track. You can drive through the privately owned park quickly enough, but it's far better to walk along the signposted path that winds in between the rocks (a 1.5hr circuit), to more clearly admire the strange shapes, all gnarled and twisted, some of them resembling animals or human forms. To get here head 8km north of town, along RN-38, then turn east along RP-17, which climbs into the heights of the northern Sierra Chica; the entrance to the site is 5km past the turn-off.

Practicalities

Capilla del Monte's **bus station** is at the corner of Corrientes and Rivadavia, 200m south of Plaza San Martín; there are regular bus services down the valley to Córdoba and up to the transport hub of Cruz del Eje. The station building houses the dynamic **tourist information centre** (daily 8am–8pm; Ⓣ03546/481903, Ⓦwww.capilladelmonte.gov.ar), whose eager staff have the details of dozens of guides and operators offering treks, horse-riding, and hang-gliding in the nearby mountains. The town's **hotel** options include the very pleasant *Hotel Principado* with its own beach along the Río Calabalumba and a large park, at 9 de Julio 550 (Ⓣ03546/481043, Ⓔprincipado_hotelspa@yahoo.com.ar; ❻); the clean and smart *Hotel Petit Sierras*, Pueyrredón 622 and Salta (Ⓣ03546/481667, Ⓔpetitsierras@acapilladelmonte.com.ar; ❺); and the plain but tidy *Hostería Las Gemelas*, L.N. Além 967 (Ⓣ03546/481186, Ⓔhosterialasgemelas@yahoo.com.ar; ❸), with its own health-food restaurant. *Hostería Tercero Milenio*, Corrientes 471 (Ⓣ03546/481958, Ⓔhosteriatercermilenio@hotmail.com; ❸), is one of many *naturista* places to stay, and its excellent health-food restaurant is open to non-guests. The town's best **campsite** is the *Calabalumba*, on the riverbank, near the bridge at the end of General Paz (Ⓣ03546/489601, Ⓔturismocapilla@arnet.com.ar). Most of the **cafés and restaurants** are strung along Diagonal Buenos Aires: *Maracaibo*, Buenos Aires 182, does a vegetarian set lunch, while *Valpisa*, Buenos Aires 102, specializes in pizzas and pasta.

Ongamira and Ischilín

The winding cliffside RP-17 takes you across the impressive **Quebrada de la Luna**, a deep valley spiked with palm trees, until you reach **ONGAMIRA**, some 25km northeast of Capilla del Monte. At 1400m above sea level, it is a remote hamlet, though it is famed for its **Grutas**, strange caves amid rock formations sculpted by wind and rain in the reddish sandstone, and painted with black, yellow and white pigments by indigenous tribes some six hundred years ago. The drawings depict animals, human figures and abstract geometric patterns, and must be surveyed from a special viewpoint (daily 9am–dusk; $3), as the extremely fragile stone is gradually crumbling away and many of the paintings have already been lost. Nearby is the **Parque Natural Ongamira** (daily 9am–dusk; $2), a private park affording breathtaking views of the cerros Pajarillo, Áspero and Colchiquí; you can see condors and go on horseback rides. The road, with magnificent panoramas all the way, eventually leads on to Santa Catalina and Cerro Colorado (see p.287).

A dirt road immediately west of Ongamira snakes through mesmerizing rocky landscapes and past an unexpected polo ground to the once-abandoned village of **ISCHILÍN**, some 20km further north. A couple of kilometres before you reach the village is the signposted **Casa Museo Fernando Fader** (Tues 9am–3pm, Wed–Sat 9am–7pm, Sun 1–7pm; free), a brick house built by the painter **Fernando Fader**, an adoptive Argentine born of German parents who settled here in the vain hope of curing his chronic tuberculosis. His paintings, well-executed if strongly influenced by Van Gogh and at times Monet, are best seen at the provincial fine-arts museum near Mendoza (see p.527). Only one is on show at this museum, alongside various personal effects and furniture, but the mock-Italianate garden is worth a visit. In the village itself, the charming *Hostería La Rosada* (ⓣ03521/423057, ⓦwww.ischilinposada.com.ar; $95 per person, full-board) is run by the artist's grandson and family; you can **stay the night** or just enjoy the fine food and swimming pool. Don't miss the chance of being taken around the village, devotedly renovated by Carlos Fader himself, including the ancient school, now in use once more, the recreation of a traditional *pulpería* and the old police station. Ischilín's spectacular **Plaza de Armas**, not unlike an English village green, is dominated by a venerable algarrobo tree, its gigantic gnarled trunk host to epiphytic cacti and skeins of moss, and by the early eighteenth-century Jesuit church, **Nuestra Señora del Rosario**, its facade painted a gaudy but not unattractive mustard yellow. Ask around for the key to visit the delightfully primitive interior, with its rickety choir balcony made of algarrobo wood, bearing a pithy Latin inscription.

San Marcos Sierras

Some 43km northwest of Capilla del Monte along RN-38, the village of **SAN MARCOS SIERRAS** has been around since the 1730s – a history attested to by the small, lemon-coloured church on the main plaza – but since the 1960s has been chiefly known for being a counterculture community. Proudly proclaiming its local rules on organic-only agricultural production, the village is largely self-sufficient, exporting mainly honey to the wider world. The community is constantly fed by an influx of bohemians from Argentina and further afield – if you fancy hanging out for a month or two, it is easy to **rent** houses or *cabañas*; the **tourist kiosk** (ⓣ03549/15432281, ⓦwww.sanmarcossierras.com) on the main square, Plaza Cacique Tulían, has a list. *Hostería Cielo y Tierra* (ⓣ03549/496135, ⓔcieloytierra_ar@yahoo.com.ar; ④) provides overnight accommodation with reiki, vegetarian food and a solarium alongside the more usual horse rides and pool. **Buses** to San Marcos run directly from Córdoba a couple of times a day, with more frequent services from Cruz del Eje; tours are also possible from the nearby resorts. As you might expect, most cafés and **restaurants** are of the *naturista* kind – even *Los Olivos*, a *parrilla* by the river on San Martín and Siete Colores, has a veggie menu – while the *heladería* on the plaza does ice creams in exotic flavours such as cactus pear and *chañar* (a local herb).

The Calamuchita Valley

Long established as one of Córdoba Province's major holiday destinations, and where many cityfolk have weekend or summer homes, the green **Calamuchita Valley** begins 30km south of Córdoba city at the Jesuit estancia town of **Alta Gracia** – a popular day-trip destination from Córdoba – and stretches due south for over 100km, between the undulating Sierra Chica to the east and the steep Sierra de Comechingones to the west. The fertile valley gets its name from the Camiare indigenous language, and the Río Ctalamochita, which flows down from the Comechingones peaks – *ktala* and *muchi* are locally abundant native shrubs known as *tala* and *molle* in Argentine Spanish. Colonizers later prosaically baptized the river Río Tercero ("Third River"). The varied vegetation that covers the valley's sides provides a perfect habitat for hundreds of species of birds and other fauna. Two large and very clean reservoirs, Embalse Los Molinos in the north and Embalse Río Tercero in the south, both dammed in the first half of the twentieth century for water supplies, electricity and recreational angling, give the valley its alternative name, sometimes used by the local tourist authority: **Valle Azul de los Grandes Lagos** ("Blue Valley of the Great Lakes"). It's believed that the area's **climate** has been altered by their creation, with noticeably wetter summers than in the past.

The valley's two main towns could not be more different: **Villa General Belgrano** is a chocolate-box resort with a predominantly Germanic population, whereas **Santa Rosa de Calamuchita**, the valley's rather brash capital, is youthful and dynamic but far less picturesque. Both, however, are good bases for exploring the beautiful Comechingones mountains, whose Camiare name means "mountains and many villages". One of these villages, the quiet hamlet of **La Cumbrecita**, would not look out of place in the Swiss Alps, and is the starting-point for some fine highland walks. All the villages offer a wide range of accommodation and high-quality places to eat, making them ideal for anyone wanting to avoid big cities like Córdoba. Frequent **buses** and *trafics* run along the arterial RP-5 between Córdoba and Santa Rosa de Calamuchita, some stopping at Alta Gracia en route.

Alta Gracia

Less than 40km south of Córdoba and 3km west of busy RP-5, historic **ALTA GRACIA** lies at the northern entrance of the Calamuchita Valley. It is now rather nondescript, but in the 1920s and 1930s its location between the city and the mountains made it popular with the wealthy bourgeoisie of Buenos Aires and Córdoba, who built holiday homes in the town – Che Guevara, surprisingly, spent some of his youth here, and revolutionary composer Manuel de Falla fled here from the Spanish Civil War. The original colonial settlement dates from the late sixteenth century, but in 1643 it was chosen as the site for a **Jesuit estancia** around which the town grew up – most of the other estancias in the province, like Santa Catalina and Jesús María, remained in open countryside. After the Jesuits' expulsion in 1767, the estancia fell into ruin but was inhabited for a short time in 1810 by Viceroy Liniers, forced to leave Córdoba following the Argentine declaration of independence. The **Museo Casa del Virrey Liniers** is housed in the Residencia, the Jesuits' original living quarters and workshops (Dec–Easter Tues–Fri 9am–8pm, Sat & Sun 9.30am–8pm; Easter–Nov Tues–Fri 9am–1pm & 3–7pm, Sat & Sun 9.30am–12.30pm & 3.30–6.30pm; $2; guided tours in English upon request; Ⓦwww.museoliniers.org.ar). Entered through an ornate Baroque doorway on **Plaza Manuel Solares**, the town's main square, the beautifully restored Residencia, with its colonnaded upper storey, forms two sides of a cloistered courtyard. Exhibits consist mainly of furniture and art dating from the early nineteenth century, but there are also some magnificent examples of colonial religious paintings and sculptures, many of them executed by indigenous artists. Perhaps the most interesting sections of the museum are the painstakingly recreated **kitchen** and the coyly named *áreas comunes*, or toilets, from which human waste was channelled into a cistern used to irrigate and fertilize the estancia's crops. The church adjoining the Residencia, though in pitifully poor repair, is used regularly for Mass; it lies immediately to the south.

Directly north of the estancia are the peaceful waters of the **Tajamar**, or estancia reservoir, one of Argentina's earliest hydraulic projects, dating from 1659; it both supplied water for the community and served as a mill-pond. In its mirror-like surface is reflected the town's emblematic **clock tower**, erected in 1938 to mark 350 years of colonization in the area. The tower is decorated at each corner by a stone figure portraying the four major cultures of Córdoba Province: native, conquistador, Jesuit missionary and gaucho. Avenida Sarmiento leads up a slope from the western bank of the Tajamar into **Villa Carlos Pellegrini**, an interesting residential district of quaint timber and wrought-iron dwellings, dating from when rich Porteños built summer houses here in the fashionable so-called *estilo inglés*, a local interpretation of mock-Tudor. Many of them are sadly dilapidated, but one, Villa Beatriz, at Avellaneda 501, was for several years in the 1930s home to the family of **Che Guevara**. His doctor recommended the dry continental climate of the sierras, and his family rented various houses in Alta Gracia during his adolescence in the vain hope of curing his debilitating asthma. Homage is paid to the young revolutionary-to-be here in the **Museo Casa de Ernesto "Che" Guevara** (daily 9.30am–7pm; $3), where photographs, correspondence and all manner of memorabilia are lovingly displayed.

Another villa, Los Espinillos, nearby at Av Carlos Pellegrini 1011, was Spanish composer **Manuel de Falla's home** for seven years until his death in 1946; like Che Guevara, he came to the sierras for health reasons, in his case because he suffered from chronic tuberculosis. Now the **Museo Manuel de Falla** (daily 9.30am–7pm; $2), exhibiting his piano and other personal effects, the well-preserved house affords fine views of the nearby mountains. Piano and other music recitals are given, normally on Saturday evenings, in the small concert hall in the garden.

Regular **buses** from Córdoba use the terminal at Plaza de las Américas, ten blocks west of the Tajamar, while the **tourist office** is in the landmark clock tower at the corner of Avenida del Tajamar and Calle del Molino (Dec–Easter daily 7am–10pm, Easter–Nov 9am–5pm; ⓣ03547/428128, ⓦwww.altagracia.gov.ar). Of the town's several, mostly uninspiring **restaurants**, you are best off

△ Museo Casa de Ernesto "Che" Guevara

Che Guevara

Despite being one of Argentina's most famous sons, **Ernesto "Che" Guevara** is little celebrated in his homeland, with nothing like the number of monuments and museums and the amount of fanfare you might expect for such as international icon. This is no doubt at least in part due to Che fighting his battles elsewhere – primarily, of course, in Cuba, where he is idolized, but also in places like Bolivia, where he finally met his end. It is hard to know whether Argentine authorities ignore his legacy because he was, well, anti-authoritarian, or whether they feel offended that he had the cheek to go and instigate revolution outside of *la gran Argentina*. Whatever his claims to supra-nationality may be, though, Che was certainly Argentine – a fact reflected even in his nickname ("che" being a common interjection, more or less meaning "hey", and very characteristic of the River Plate region). He was born to a middle-class family in **Rosario** (see p.372) in 1928, and moved to **Alta Gracia** with his family at the age 5, going to school in Deán Funes before moving on to the Universidad de Buenos Aires to study medicine. Three years later, he set off on his famous **motorbike trip** around South America, during which he was exposed to the continent's poverty and inequalities, as well as the cultural similarities that led him to believe in the need to foster a sense of regional rather than national identity. He did return to Buenos Aires to finish his studies, but a month after graduating he was back on the road, this time heading to Guatemala and a meeting with local radicals which eventually led him to Fidel Castro, Cuba and his status as one of the great revolutionary figures of the twentieth century.

at *Morena*, occupying a fine Neocolonial house at Sarmiento 417, heading towards the Manuel de Falla museum; the rabbit, trout, pasta and pizza are all excellent, as is the service.

Villa General Belgrano

Fifty kilometres south of Alta Gracia, reached along attractive corniches skirting the blue waters of the **Embalse Los Molinos**, and less than a couple of kilometres west of RP-5, is the demure resort of **VILLA GENERAL BELGRANO**. The unspoiled alpine scenery of its back country, the folksy architecture and decor and the Teutonic traditions of the local population all give the place a distinctly alpine feel. Many of the townspeople are of German, Swiss or Austrian origin, some of them descended from escapees from the *Graf Spee*, the pocket battleship scuttled by its captain off the Uruguayan coast on December 13, 1939 after it was surrounded by Allied cruisers during World War II's landmark Battle of the River Plate. The older generations still converse in German, maintain a Lutheran outlook and read the local German-language newspaper, while souvenir shops sell cuckoo clocks, tapes of oompah music and other such curios. Whether or not the place's kitsch Gemütlichkeit holds appeal, Villa General Belgrano is an excellent base for the region if you'd rather avoid Córdoba itself, with plentiful and varied accommodation choices. However, if adventure sports or discoing are what you're after, you're better off heading for Santa Rosa de Calamuchita, a short way to the south (see p.301).

Essentially a sedate place favoured by families and older visitors attracted by its creature comforts and hearty food – especially welcome during winter snow – Villa General Belgrano suddenly shifts up a gear or two during one of its many festivals. While the Feria Navideña, or Christmas festival, the Fiesta de Chocolate Alpino, in July, and the Fiesta de la Masa Vienesa, a Holy Week binge of apple strudel and pastries, are all eagerly awaited, the annual climax, during the second week of October, is the nationally famous **Oktoberfest**, Villa General Belgrano's answer to Munich's world-renowned beer festival. Stein after stein of foaming Pilsener is knocked back, after which merry revellers stagger down Villa Belgrano's normally genteel streets to their hotels, while elderly ladies barricade themselves in their favourite tearooms and consume blackberry pie until the whole thing is over.

Two streams, Arroyo del Molle and Arroyo La Toma, trickle through the town before joining Arroyo del Sauce, 1km to the south. **Avenida Julio Roca**, the town's main drag, is lined with shops, cafés, restaurants, hotels and other amenities, many of them located in replicas of Swiss chalets or German beer-houses, and runs south from oval Plaza José Hernández, where the Oktoberfest takes place. On the plaza stands a 1989 bronze memorial to the Battle of the River Plate. Frankly, the town's three museums – one containing some vintage carriages, another housing a jumble of pre-Hispanic ceramics and the third with an exhibit about UFOs, supposedly a common phenomenon hereabouts – are not worth your time. The real attraction of Villa General Belgrano is its proximity to the great Sierra de Comechingones, looming to the west.

Practicalities

Regular services from Buenos Aires, Córdoba and Santa Rosa de Calamuchita arrive at the small **bus terminal** on Avenida Vélez Sarsfield, five minutes northwest of Plaza José Hernández. Pájaro Blanco runs a shuttle minibus service several times a day to and from La Cumbrecita and Córdoba; its bus stop is on Avenida San Martín, 100m north of Plaza José Hernández. The **tourist office**, in the German town hall at Av Julio A. Roca 168 (daily 8.30am–8.30pm; ⓣ03546/461215, ⓦwww.elsitiodelavilla.com), has been doing its best in recent years to give the town a younger, more modern image. Banks and **ATMs** can be found along Avenida Julio A. Roca.

You're spoilt for choice when it comes to accommodation, although if you're planning to attend the popular Oktoberfest you should book well ahead and be prepared for steeper prices. Most of the **hotels** are on the expensive side, but they're nearly all of a high standard, spotlessly clean and comfortable. Try the twee but fun *Hotel Baviera*, El Quebracho 21 (ⓣ03546/461476, ⓦwww.bavierahotel.com; ❺), a motel-style place with an attractive pool and garden; or the bright *Posada Nehuen*, San Martín 17 (ⓣ03546/461412, ⓦwww.elsitiodelavilla.com/nehuen; ❺). The laid-back **youth hostel** *El Rincón*, Calle Alexander Fleming s/n, fifteen minutes' walk northwest of the bus station (ⓣ03546/461323, ⓦwww.calamuchitanet.com.ar/elrincon), has dorms ($20), rooms with private bath (❶) and a place to pitch your tent ($10). There are a number of **campsites** out along RP-5 a short way out of the town centre: the best is eco-friendly *Rincón de Mirlos* (ⓣ03546/420850, ⓦwww.rincondemirlos.com.ar), signposted 7km west of the centre on the road towards La Cumbrecita; from there it is another 2km through handsome farmland and woods to the bucolic riverside setting, where there are clean dorms (❶), isolated tent-pitching sites among the trees, a bar and restaurant and long stretches of sandy beach.

Not surprisingly, many of the town's plentiful **places to eat** offer German and Central European dishes such as goulash, sauerkraut, sausages and tortes. *Ciervo Rojo*, Av Julio A. Roca 210, serves schnitzels and wurst, washed down with tankards of home-brewed beer, while *Café Rissen*, Av Julio A. Roca 36, is the place to go for Black Forest gâteau, strudel and fruit crumbles, served on floral tablecloths. *Rissen*'s excellent ice-cream parlour stands opposite.

Santa Rosa de Calamuchita and around

In 1700, a community of Dominicans built an estancia and a chapel dedicated to the patron saint of the Americas, Santa Rosa of Lima, after which nothing much else happened in **SANTA ROSA DE CALAMUCHITA**, 11km south of Villa General Belgrano, until the end of the nineteenth century. Then, thanks to its mountainside, riverbank location and its mild climate, the place suddenly took off as a holiday resort, an alternative to its more traditional neighbour to the north. Now it's a highly popular destination, swamped by thousands of visitors from many parts of the country in the high season, and makes an excellent base for exploring the relatively unspoilt **mountains** nearby. The main attraction of Santa Rosa de Calamuchita is the way that it's geared to all kinds of **outdoor activities**, from diving and kayaking to jet-skiing and flying. Noticeably less sedate than Villa General Belgrano but more bearable than Villa Carlos Paz, from Christmas until Easter it throbs with disco music blaring from convertibles packed with holidaymakers from Córdoba and Buenos Aires, or through loudspeakers atop vans advertising nightclubs. The town's compact centre is built in a curve of the Río Santa Rosa, just south of where the Arroyo del Sauce flows into it. There's no main plaza, but a number of busy streets run off the main Calle Libertad. You can take refuge from the hullabaloo at the northern end of Libertad in the beautifully restored **Capilla Vieja** – the ruined estancia was demolished at the beginning of the twentieth century. It houses the **Museo de Arte Religioso** (Wed–Sun 6–8pm; free), where you can see a superb late seventeenth-century wooden Christ, crafted by local Jesuit artisans, and other works of colonial religious art.

Practicalities

Regular **bus** services from Buenos Aires, Córdoba and Villa General Belgrano drop and pick up passengers at stops along Libertad. The staff at the **tourist information office**, Güemes 13 (daily 8am–11pm; ⓣ03546/429654, ⓦwww.starosacalamuchita.com.ar) – a side street off Libertad two blocks south of the sacred art museum – dish out brochures on accommodation, activities and tour operators.

Accommodation tends to be less expensive here than in Villa General Belgrano, and includes the stylish 1930s *Hotel Yporá*, 1km outside town on RP-5 (ⓣ03546/421233, ⓦwww.hotelypora.com; ❻); the charming, family-oriented *Hotel Santa Rosa*, at Entre Ríos and Córdoba (ⓣ03546/420186; ❺); and the *Hospedaje Aurora*, Libertad 600 (ⓣ03546/421414; ❸), which has small, plain but pleasant rooms. The best **campsite** is *Miami* (ⓣ03546/499613, ⓦwww.campingmiami.com.ar; ❶), on the road up to Yacanto. The town's best **restaurants** are the upmarket, Basque-influenced *Azkaine*, Córdoba 560, the reliable *parrilla La Pulpería de los Ferreyra*, Libertad 578, and *El Gringo*, an inexpensive pizzeria at Libertad 270.

Half- or full-day **treks** and 4WD **safaris** into the Comechingones range are arranged by Naturaleza y Aventura (ⓣ03546/464144, ⓦwww.elsitiodelavilla.com/naturaleza). **Motorcycles** and **buggies** can be rented all along Playa de Santa Rita, and it is also possible to hire **horses** or **mountain bikes** in town.

Yacanto de Calamuchita

Just over 30km to the west of Santa Rosa de Calamuchita by a paved road is **YACANTO DE CALAMUCHITA**, a straggly village from where a mostly driveable road leads almost to the summit of the region's tallest peak, **Cerro Champaquí** (2884m), which can also be reached on foot from Villa Alpina (see p.303). Unless you have a 4WD the final stretch cannot be done in a vehicle, so

Nature's medicine in the Central Sierras

A bewildering variety of vegetation grows on the mountainsides of the Central Sierras and is representative of three of the country's principal phytogeographic zones – the Andes, the Pampas and the Chaco. Many of these plant species are not only pleasing to the eye – and a precious habitat for a variety of wildlife, especially birds – but they are also reputed to possess remarkable **medicinal properties**. Perhaps best known is the *peperina*, of which there are two varieties: *Mintostachys verticillata* and *Satureja parvifolia* (the latter often known as *peperina de la sierra)*. Both are highly aromatic and extremely digestive but, in men, diminish sexual potency. The *yerba del pollo* (*Alternanthera pungens*), on the other hand, is a natural cure for flatulence, while ephedrine, a tonic for heart ailments, is extracted industrially from *tramontana* (*Ephedra triandra*), a broom-like bush found all over the highlands at altitudes of 800–1300 metres. Anyone suffering from problems of the gall bladder might do well to drink an infusion of *poleo* (*Lippia turbinata*), a large shrub with silvery foliage and an unmistakable aroma. Appropriately enough, since Santa Lucia is the patron saint of the blind, the *flor de Santa Lucia* (*Commelina erecta*), whose intense blue or lilac blooms carpet the ground to astonishing effect, exudes a sticky substance that can be used as effective eye drops. The *cola de caballo* (*Equisetum giganteum*) – or "horsetail" – is used to control arterial pressure thanks to its diuretic powers; its ribbed, rush-like stems grow alongside streams and are crowned with hairy filaments that give it its popular name. Whatever you do, however, steer clear of *revienta caballos* (*Solanum eleagnifolium* or *S. sisymbrifolium*), a distant relative of the deadly nightshade. Its pretty violet flowers give way to deceptively attractive yellow berries, but the whole plant is highly toxic.

Obviously, you should **seek expert advice** before putting natural cures to the test, and they should not be used instead of conventional medicine for the severest of complaints. Pharmaceutical herbs, known as *yuyos*, are sold (usually in dried form) in pharmacies and in stores selling dietetic products throughout the region. The staff at such outlets can always be of help if you need advice.

you'll have to leave your car and walk for three hours, but the panoramic views are stunning, especially early or late in the day, when the hike will be less exacting. Pájaro Blanco runs a bus service here six times daily from Santa Rosa (30min). The **tourist office** at the entrance to the village (Mon–Fri 8am–6pm; ⓣ03546/485001, ⓦwww.villayacanto.gov.ar) can advise you on somewhere to stay, mostly in reasonably priced **cabañas**. *Comedor Doña Custodia*, in the village "centre", serves a variety of local **food** specialities.

La Cumbrecita and around

Around 35km northwest of Villa Belgrano along a winding scenic track, **LA CUMBRECITA** is a small, peaceful alpine-style village in the foothills of the Comechingones range. Benefiting from a mild microclimate and enjoying views of wild countryside, it has developed as a relatively select holiday resort ever since it was built in the 1930s by Swiss and Austrian immigrants. From Villa Belgrano, take Avenida San Martín, which leads north from Plaza José Hernández, and keep going until you reach the edge of town; from here the dirt road swings in a westerly direction and climbs through hills that open to sweeping views of the Río Segundo Valley.

Two paths wind their way through the village, parallel to the Río del Medio that cuts a deep ravine below. **Paseo Bajo**, the lower of the two, passes several cafés and hotels and the mock-medieval Castillo, on the way to the Río Almbach, which flows into the Río del Medio north of the village; the upper trail climbs the hill to the west of the village, cutting through a well-tended cemetery from where you can enjoy wonderful views of the Lago Esmeralda and the fir-wooded mountains behind. Private motor vehicles are banned from the whole village during the day (9am–7pm), but many people rent electric buggies to get around – distances are walkable, however, and visitors are allowed to drive to their hotel's car park.

To cool off in hot weather, head for one of the **balnearios** along the clean Río Almbach, such as *Forellensee* or *Grottensee* – the former named for the plentiful trout in the stream and the latter named for its caves – both with bucolic settings and views up the craggy mountaintops. La Cumbrecita is also a perfect base for some of the region's most rewarding mountain walks, including some well-trodden but uncrowded trails going up to 2000m or more. Signposted treks lasting between one and four hours each way head off to the eyrie-like *miradores* at Casas Viejas, Meierei and Cerro Cristal, while one of the most popular trails climbs from El Castillo, past *Balneario La Olla*, with its very deep pools of crystal-clear water created by the gushing waterfalls, to the 1715-metre-summit of Cerro Wank. From here, and from **Yatán**, a wild gorge three hours away on foot up a steep trail, impressive views of the valley are guaranteed and sightings of condors are frequent.

Much less visited but set in idyllic countryside to the south, **Villa Alpina**, as its name suggests, is another Swiss-style hamlet, though far less twee than La Cumbrecita. It can be reached from there by a four-hour trek, but also by bumpy roads from both Villa Belgrano and Santa Rosa de Calamuchita. It's the eastern base camp for treks to the top of **Cerro Champaquí**. This involves a long haul – at least a couple of days of gentle climbing – but it's not especially difficult and you can spend the night in the basic mountain **refuge** (❶) at Puesto Dominguez, halfway up. Although this climb is by no means dangerous, it isn't well signposted and is therefore best done with a local guide – ask at *Albergue Piedras Blancas* (see below) about the possibility of hiring horses and guides, or try Alto Rumbo, a local guide collective that charges $700 for two people (Ⓣ0351/155649556, Ⓦwww.altorumbo.com.ar).

Practicalities

Pájaro Blanco runs a shuttle **bus** service five times daily to La Cumbrecita from Villa General Belgrano, and twice daily on Mondays, Wednesdays, Saturdays and Sundays to Villa Alpina. La Cumbrecita has a **tourist office** across the bridge over the Río del Medio (daily 9am–9pm; Ⓣ03546/481088, Ⓦwww.lacumbrecita.gov.ar).

The **accommodation** in La Cumbrecita is pretty much all faux-alpine and includes the grand but rather old-fashioned *Hotel La Cumbrecita* (Ⓣ03546/481052, Ⓦwww.hotelcumbrecita.com.ar; ❺ half-board), and the more modest but equally comfortable *Hotel Las Verbenas* (Ⓣ03546/481008, Ⓦwww.lasverbenashotel.com.ar; ❸ half-board), both with swimming pools and great sunrise views. In Villa Alpina there are a handful of *cabaña* outfits plus the *Albergue Piedras Blancas* (Ⓣ03547/155-95163; ❶), right at the entrance to the village, which has a very decent restaurant and organizes **treks** into the Comechingones, especially to Cerro Champaquí.

The string of generally excellent *confiterías* and **restaurants** along La Cumbrecita's Paseo Bajo mostly offer fondues, strudels and other Central European specialities, plus the odd steak. For meals, *Bar Suizo*, near the river end of the village, leads the way, serving a hearty range of Germanic pork-dominated dishes and tarts, while the village's best cakes and pastries are at *Conditorei Liesbeth* (*Almbachklause*), in a quaint little cabin with a garden right at the far end of the Paseo Bajo, across the Arroyo Almbach.

The Traslasierra: from Córdoba to Merlo

By far the most rewarding route from Córdoba to San Luis, the other provincial capital, is by the RN-20 beyond Villa Carlos Paz, continuing along RP-1 via Merlo. The winding **Nueva Ruta de las Altas Cumbres** climbs past the **Parque Nacional de la Quebrada del Condorito**, a deep ravine where condors nest in cliffside niches, and over a high mountain-pass before winding back down a series of hairpin bends. The serene, sunny valleys to the west of the high Sierra Grande and Sierra de Achala, crisscrossed by gushing streams and dotted with oases of bushy palm trees, are known collectively as the **Traslasierra**, literally "across the mountains". The self-appointed capital of the subregion, **Mina Clavero**, is a popular little riverside resort and minor transport hub, but not the best place to stay, owing to the hordes of holidaymakers who spend the summer here. Several **buses** a day run between Córdoba and Mina Clavero, and may drop you at the ranger station of the national park.

Near **Nono**, a tiny village at the foot of the northern Comechingones, a short distance down RN-20 to the south of Mina Clavero, is the oddball **Museo Rocsen**, an eclectic jumble of artefacts, archeological finds and endless miscellanea. Not far from here, RP-148 forks off towards the bustling resort of **Merlo**, just over the border into San Luis Province, while RN-20 continues southwest towards San Luis city, across uninteresting countryside, via Quines. Forever vaunting its apocryphal microclimate, Merlo is above all a relaxing place from which to explore the nearby mountain trails or try out some adventurous pursuits. Along RP-148/RP-1 to Merlo, in a long valley parallel to the Sierra de Comechingones, are the picturesque villages of **Yacanto** and **San Javier**, from where you can climb the highest summit in the Central Sierras, the majestic **Cerro Champaquí**. And from Merlo you can continue to **San Luis**, either south along scenic RP-1 and west by RP-20, or west along RP-5 and south by RN-148; buses tend to take the latter option, and the two routes converge at La Toma.

Parque Nacional de la Quebrada del Condorito

About 60km from Villa Carlos Paz, just to the south of RN-20, is the **PARQUE NACIONAL DE LA QUEBRADA DEL CONDORITO** (daily 9am–6pm; ⓣ03541/433371, ⓦwww.quebradacondorito.com.ar), which takes its name from the Quebrada de los Condoritos, a misty canyon eroded into the mountains that, in turn, gets its name from the baby condors reared in its deep ravines; it's the condor's most easterly breeding site.

Get here via the splendid **Nueva Ruta de las Altas Cumbres**, the section of RN-20 that sweeps across the **Pampa de Achala**, an eerily desolate landscape, ideal for solitary treks or horse rides. For the first 15km or so, this road, which starts just 12km southwest of crowded Villa Carlos Paz, is quite narrow, but several viewpoints have been built at the roadside. From them, you have unobscured vistas of the Icho Cruz and Malambo valleys to the northwest, the distant peak of **Cerro Los Gigantes**, at 2370m the highest mountain in the Sierra Grande, to the north, and the **Sierra de Achala** to the south; the views are framed by nodding pinkish *cortaderas*, or pampas grass. Some 20km further on, the bleak granite moorlands of the Pampa de Achala, reaching just over 2000m above sea level, are barren save for thorny scrub and a few tufty alpines. An even narrower mid-nineteenth-century mule-trail, the Camino de las Altas Cumbres, now RP-14, still winds along ledge-like roads almost parallel to RN-20, which superseded it in the 1960s, and makes for an even more pleasurable alternative route to the Quebrada, should you have your own vehicle and time to spare. Condors, some with wingspans exceeding three metres, can be seen circling majestically overhead.

Just before the derelict *Hotel Cóndor*, you reach an interpretation centre run by the **Fundación Cóndor** (daily 9am–6pm; ⓣ0351/464-6537), which looks after the park. There's a small exhibition of striking photos of the park's flora and fauna – mostly condors and their young, of course. The *guardaparques* can give you information about the park and its rich wildlife, indicate the trails, supply important weather details – hazards include fog and thunderstorms – and they may even be available to accompany you. The various **hikes** take between one and twelve hours; the longer ones are physically demanding as they take you down steep, sometimes slippery paths into the bottom of the canyon. All kinds of trees, shrubs and ferns can be spotted, even some endemic species such as rare white gentians, while the plentiful fauna includes various wild cats, a number of indigenous rodents, foxes and hares and several snake varieties, including three never observed anywhere else. Birdlife is prolific but the stars are the condors themselves, especially their young; if you're lucky you might see condors and their chicks bathing in the water at the bottom of the gorge.

About 5km further along RN-20 from the Fundación, a signposted track to the right leads to the appealing **hotel** *La Posta del Qenti* (ⓣ03544/472532, ⓦwww.qenti.com; $199 full board per person per day, including one trek), a tastefully converted nineteenth-century post-house where salt convoys on the way to Córdoba used to stop for a change of horses. Its remote location on the barren pampas lends it an almost eerie atmosphere, offset by the designer-magazine interior, snug rooms, fully equipped gym and good food. **Horses** can be hired to explore the surrounding countryside, dominated by unbeatable views of Cerro Champaquí, and a whole range of other activities are available, including trekking, mountain-biking and rock-climbing.

Mina Clavero and around

Some 15km west of the Quebrada de los Condoritos, RN-20 begins to snake along narrow corniche roads, which offer stunning views of the Traslasierra valley and a cluster of extinct volcanic cones in the distance; the sheer cliffs and fissured crags look as if they might crumble into the wide plains below. Just 3km up RP-15, north of the junction with the RN-20, is **MINA CLAVERO**, wedged between the Sierra Grande and the much lower Sierra de Pocho, to the west. A transport hub for routes between Córdoba, San Luis, Merlo and Cruz del Eje, at the northern end of the Punilla Valley, it's also a boisterous riverside resort. The place is noteworthy for little else, though, other than its attractive black ceramics, made at various workshops in and around the town; the metallic glaze on the vases, pots and animal figures, with a bluish sheen, is made from cow dung.

Mina Clavero can become quite lively during the holiday season, especially in January and February, when people come to relax at the many *balnearios* along the three rivers – Los Sauces, Mina Clavero and Panaholma – that snake through the small town. Of all the bathing areas, the cleanest is the Nido de Aguila, set among beautiful rocks on the Río Mina Clavero 1km east of the centre, along Calle Corrientes. The nearby mountains lend themselves to a number of pursuits, such as mountain-biking, horse-riding, trekking and climbing, while trout-fishing is possible in the many brooks.

A compact place, it's not difficult to find your way around; the two main streets are Avenida San Martín and Avenida Mitre, which forks off it at the southern end of the village. From the town's central plaza take Jorge Raúl Recalde street and follow the signs to the **Camino de los Artesanos**, a stretch of road about 18km along that is lined with excellent **ceramics workshops**, with little stalls set up on the roadside; the pick of the lot belongs to Atilio López, whose clearly signposted house is set among a lush garden some 5km east of town.

Practicalities

Mina Clavero's **bus terminal** is along Avenida Mitre, next to the municipalidad; there are regular services from Córdoba, Merlo, San Luis, Mendoza and Buenos Aires. Seven blocks south, in the cleft of the fork with Avenida San Martín, is the **tourist information centre** (daily Dec–Easter 7am–midnight, Easter–Nov 8am–10pm; ⓣ03544/470171, ⓦwww.minaclavero.gov.ar); as well as helping you with accommodation, the staff can provide information on local activities. Owing to its popularity and despite its diminutive size, Mina Clavero has a wide choice of **hotels**; out of season, prices can be half the cost of the high summer season ones quoted below. Options include the comfortable and recently renovated *Panaholma Sierras*, Av San Martín 1840 (ⓣ03544/472181, ⓦwww.traslasierra.com/panaholmasierras; ❻); the French-run *Du Soleil* motel, with a good restaurant and smart rooms with modern bathrooms, Avenida Mitre and La Piedad (ⓣ03544/470066, ⓦwww.dusoleil.com.ar; ❻); and the bright and airy *España*, Av San Martín 1687 (ⓣ03544/470123; ❺). There are a dozen or so **campsites** in and around Mina Clavero, with the best ones at Villa Cura Brochero, 2km to the north: *Los Serranitos*, Av Cura Gaucho 350 (ⓣ03544/470817, ⓦwww.losseranitos.com.ar), offers pitches (❶) or simple cabins (❸). Restaurants selling the usual Argentine trio of pasta, pizza and *parrilla* line avenidas San Martín and Mitre; the pick is *Lo de Jorge*, Poeta Lugones 1417, a *parrilla* known for its excellent meat.

Nono and Museo Rocsen

From the junction with RP-15, RN-20 heads due south through rolling countryside, in the lee of rippling mountains, whose eroded crags change colour from a mellow grey to deepest red, depending on the time of day. Their imposing peak, Cerro Champaquí, lurks to the southeast at the northern end of the Comechingones range, sometimes crowned by cloud. Some 10km south of Mina Clavero you reach the sleepy village of **NONO**, a huddle of picturesque brick buildings around a little plaza. Its name is a corruption of the Quichoa *ñuñu*, meaning breasts, an allusion to the bosom-shaped hills poking above the horizon. For good, reasonably priced food, snacks or a drink with a fabulous valley vista, head to *La Terraza*, on the main road next to the YPF service station.

Some 5km from the village centre, a well-maintained dirt road leads eastwards to one of the country's weirdest museums, the hallucinatory **Museo Rocsen** (daily 9am–sunset; ⓣ03544/498218, ⓦwww.museorocsen.org; $5). Its imposing pink sandstone facade is embellished with a row of 49 statues – from Christ to Mother Teresa and Buddha to Che Guevara – representing key figures who, according to the museum's owner and curator, Juan Santiago Bouchon, have changed the course of history. After many years as cultural attaché at the French embassy in Buenos Aires, Bouchon opened his museum in 1969, with the intention of offering "something for everybody". The result is an eclectic collection of more than ten thousand exhibits, from fossils and mummies to a two-headed cow, clocks and cars – even the proverbial kitchen sink, a nineteenth-century curio. You're well advised to select what interests you from the useful plan available at the entrance, rather than to try and see everything.

Another 3km towards the mountains along a signposted track is the French-run *Estancia La Lejanía* (☎03544/498960, Ⓦwww.lalejania.com; $200 per person full board), an outstanding **hotel** with comfortable rooms and all amenities in a secluded, pastoral setting with a private riverside beach and delicious French cuisine on offer, accompanied by select Argentine champagnes and wines from the cellar. The hotel also conducts treks and horse riding in the nearby mountains. Also signposted off the road to the museum, *Hostería La Manantial* (☎03544/498179, Ⓦwww.hosteriamanantial.com.ar; $210 per person, full- and half-board options available) provides a very acceptable alternative in terms of accommodation. Its huge grounds stretch across to another river beach, while a swimming pool and delicious food are further bonuses.

San Javier and Yacanto

Some 35km south of Mina Clavero, RP-148 branches off RN-20 and heads due south towards **SAN JAVIER**, another 12km away, and Yacanto, just 2km further along. The tree-lined road, which takes you through some of the province's most attractive scenery and traditional settlements, offers outstanding views of the northern Comechingones mountains to the east. If you're driving, though, watch out for the often treacherous *badenes*; these are very deep fords that suddenly flood after storms, and even when dry their sudden drop and rough surface can damage a car's undercarriage or tyres.

San Javier and Yacanto are both pretty little places, set amid peach orchards, and serve as bases for climbing to the 2884-metre summit of **Cerro Champaquí**, directly to the east. San Javier, in particular, has developed swiftly as an exclusive tourist centre in recent years, offering a variety of services including massages, reiki and even solar shamanism. Ask at the municipalidad on the main square with its oddball church (☎03544/482077, Ⓦwww.sanjavieronline.com.ar) for information about **guides** to accompany you on the seven-hour hike to the top of Champaquí; also try Sierras y Aventura (☎03544/482149, Ⓔsierrasyaventura@vdolores.com.ar). For **accommodation**, San Javier offers the secluded *Hostería San Javier* (☎03544/482006, Ⓦwww.sanjavier-cordoba.com.ar; ❻), set among pastoral grounds and blessed with the inexpensive French restaurant *L'Hibou*. It's 3km up the bumpy dirt road towards the mountain peak, leading up from the main square past a number of interesting **crafts workshops**. Another 4km beyond is the superb *Estancia-Hostería La Constancia* (☎03544/482826, Ⓦwww.laconstancia.net; ❽ full board), a designer-built hotel set in stunning environs. The quaint *Posada del Cerro* (☎03544/482038, Ⓦwww.laposadadelcerro.com.ar; ❻), down near the main plaza, has less expensive accommodation in a fabulous renovated inn built of adobe dating from around 1800. A couple of blocks from the main square *Amelie* is a charming teahouse and restaurant, serving an unusual combination of Asian and local cuisine to lift jaded tastebuds. Along the road in **YACANTO**, by far the best accommodation is at the charming *Posada El Pucará* (☎03544/482849, Ⓦwww.posadaelpucara.com.ar; ❼ half-board). Its immaculate grounds afford marvellous sierra views while the spacious rooms combine agreeable comfort with rustic simplicity.

Merlo

MERLO, just over the border into San Luis Province, some 95km south of Mina Clavero and 280km southwest of Córdoba, is a charming resort whose main claim to fame is its **microclimate** – the whole thing's rather exaggerated in the tourist literature, though Merlo does enjoy a superbly sunny yet cool location, at around 1000m above sea level. It lies amid dense woodland at the foot of the green-sloped Comechingones range and is overlooked by San Luis Province's highest peak, the **Cerro de las Ovejas** (2207m). The settlement was founded in 1797 by the governor of Córdoba, Rafael de Sobremonte, who named it after the viceroy of the River Plate, Don Pedro Melo de Portugal – Melo gradually became Merlo. Sobremonte, meanwhile, gave his name to the town's shady main square, at the northeast corner of which stand the remains of an attractive Jesuit-built church, with a rickety *quebracho* roof; sadly the bell tower collapsed in 2003, causing terrible damage, and a new church is being built right behind it to replace it. Don't waste your time on the terrible museums or the "main sight", a thousand-year-old **carob tree** known as *algarrobo abuelo*, 5km out of town. Instead, make the most of the nearby mountains: adventurous pursuits such as hang-gliding, paragliding, horse-riding, rock-climbing, trekking and rambling are all possible here. A newly paved scenic road winds up the mountains to join a dirt track that drops into the **Calamuchita Valley** on the Córdoba side, just to the south of Santa Rosa (see p.301); it can be a useful and extremely beautiful shortcut, but ask around to see if it is usable without a 4WD.

Practicalities

Buses from Buenos Aires, Córdoba, Mendoza and San Luis drop passengers at Merlo's busy **bus station**, at the corner of calles Pringles and Los Almendros, one block south and east of Plaza Sobremonte. Merlo's tiny **airport**, a couple of kilometres south on the road to San Luis, receives flights a couple of times a week from Buenos Aires. The main **tourist office** (daily 8am–10pm; Ⓣ02656/476078, Ⓦwww.weboficialdemerlo.com.ar) at Coronel Mercau 605 on the plaza has plenty of leaflets and brochures plus a comprehensive list of places to stay. For information on the various sporting pursuits and activities, contact **tour operators** such as Los Tabaquillos, Av de los Césares 2100 (Ⓣ02656/474010, Ⓔguiasbaqueanos@merlo-sl.com.ar).

In high season the place is inundated with visitors – during the summer, at Easter and in July you should definitely book your **accommodation** in advance; outside of these times, discounts of well over fifty percent are common. There are plenty of central options, but for peace and quiet, mountain views and quick access to surrounding countryside, stay at *Hotel Piedra Blanca*, Av de los Incas 3000 (Ⓣ02656/479661, Ⓦwww.hotelpiedrablanca.com.ar; ⑤), in Piedra Blanca, 3km north, or family-run *Hotel Altos del Rincón*, Av de los Césares 2977 (Ⓣ02656/476333, Ⓦwww.hotelaltosdelrincon.com.ar; ⑤), in Rincón del Este, 5km east. In Merlo itself, *Hotel Algarrobo*, Av del Sol 1120 (Ⓣ02656/475208, Ⓦwww.hotelalgarrobo.com; ⑤), is typical of the small, quiet hotels on offer. *Hotel Villa de Merlo*, at Av del Sol and Pedernera (Ⓣ02656/475335; Ⓦwww.hotelvillademerlo.com.ar; ⑦), a short way southeast of the centre, is a beautiful brick-and-timber construction with charming rooms overlooking a large, well-cared-for garden, and a rustic dining room. All of the **campsites** have excellent facilities and are located in attractive settings in the sierra foothills: *Cerro de Oro*, at Cerro de Oro, 3km southeast of Merlo (Ⓣ02656/477496, Ⓦwww.campingmerlo.com.ar) has an inviting swimming pool. Nearer to the town centre is *Las Violetas*, at Chumamaya s/n (Ⓣ02656/475730, Ⓦwww.campinglasvioletas.com.ar), also with a pool.

There are dozens of **eating** options to choose from in Merlo, offering everything from roast kid to staples like pasta and pizza. The extensive menu at reasonably priced *El Establo*, arguably the town's best restaurant, in a thatched hut at Av del Sol 540, includes trout and frog, plus excellent *chivito* (roast goat), while the speciality at *Cirano*, Av del Sol 280, is kid in white wine sauce. There are several **cafés** dotted around the main square, but the best are the laid-back *Comechingones*, Coronel Mercau 651, and its rival, *Cunto*, next door at Coronel

Mercau 625, which has delicious ice cream. *La Cervecería*, at RP-1 and San Isidro, just beyond the tourist office, makes its own lager, pale ale and stout, served with pizzas, steaks and *picadas*.

San Luis and around

SAN LUIS has always been a stopover on the colonial route between Santiago de Chile and Buenos Aires. Some 467km southwest of Córdoba, it is known as the *Puerta del Cuyo*, or "Gateway to the Cuyo", the region centred on Mendoza, 280km to the west. The city's location at the southernmost point (*punto*) of the crinkly Sierra de San Luis, a dramatic backdrop of forever-changing colour that slopes down to the flat, sandy pampas, earns its inhabitants, the Sanluisinos, their nickname of "puntanos". Running past the city to the south, the Río Chorrillos, no more than a trickle except in the spring, gives its name to the bracing *chorrillero*, the prevailing southerly wind that almost constantly sweeps the city clean. A friendly, cheerful little place, it's essentially a base for visiting one or two nearby attractions, exploring the sierras and soaking up the easy-going atmosphere. The microcentro is very compact, and the city has a villagey feel to it; high-rises are mercifully rare, with most people living in small houses and bungalows, lovingly tending their gardens and patios – cool havens perfumed with jasmine and garlanded with bougainvillea. If you stop over, at least you'll eat well; the eastern suburbs are favourite weekend haunts for their traditional *parrillas*.

San Luis was founded in 1594 by **Luis Jufré de Loaysa y Meneses**, an Andalucian grandee, officially as a tribute to King Louis of France; founding cities evidently ran in the family, as his father Juan had established San Juan. Until the *malones*, or Indian uprisings, were brutally crushed in the 1830s by **Juan Manuel de Rosas**, San Luis never managed to control all of its hinterland, and, whereas Córdoba was a flourishing Jesuit capital by the seventeenth century, San Luis did not come into its own until the very end of the nineteenth century, after the arrival of the railways.

While in the San Luis area, you could relax at the spa resort of **Balde**, only 30km west, or take a longer trip to San Luis Province's leading attraction, the **Parque Nacional Sierra de las Quijadas**. The highlight of the park's beautiful scenery is a huge canyon of orange-pink rock that turns cochineal red at sunset. Between San Luis and Merlo, to the northeast, stretch the **Sierras de San Luis**, mountains rich in metals, minerals and precious stones such as **onyx**, and the scene of a gold rush and intensive mining in the nineteenth century; today they're quiet and seldom visited, being less dramatic than the ranges to the north and east.

Arrival and information

San Luis's tiny **airport** is 4km northwest of Plaza Pringles; the only way to reach the centre is by **taxi**. Regular buses from Buenos Aires, Córdoba, Merlo, Mendoza and San Rafael arrive at the very basic **bus terminal**, six blocks north of Plaza Pringles. The excellent provincial **tourist information centre** (daily 8am–8pm; ⓣ02652/423479, ⓦwww.sanluis.gov.ar) is wedged in the fork of avenidas Presidente Arturo Illia and San Martín, close to Plaza Pringles, and supplies accommodation lists and all manner of leaflets, plus first-rate maps; top-quality crafts are also on sale. Most of the banks around the main square have **ATMs**.

Accommodation

There's not much in the way of **accommodation** in San Luis: options range from hotels primarily aimed at commercial travellers – functional and pricey but cheaper at weekends – to downmarket *pensiones* and *residenciales*. The city's most reputable hotel is the smart *Hotel Quintana*, Av Presidente Illia 546 (ⓣ02652/438400; ❻); slightly less luxurious but far better value with its airy rooms and a fine swimming pool and terrace is *Hotel Aiello*, Av Presidente Illia 431, opposite (ⓣ02652/431142, ⓦwww.hotelaiello.com.ar; ❺). The best budget options are *Hotel Inca*, Bolívar 943 (ⓣ02652/424923; ❹), where you get a copious breakfast as well as cheerily decorated en-suite rooms, and *Residencial Los Andes*, Ejército de los Andes 1180 (ⓣ02652/422033, ⓔsergioproperzi@yahoo.com.ar; ❸), much more basic but clean and comfortable. If you want to **camp** you should head out to the nearby villages of Potrero de los Funes, El Volcán or Trapiche.

The City

Plaza Pringles – dominated by a statue of the eponymous colonel, a local hero who fought alongside San Martín in the Campaign of the Andes – is the nerve centre of the city, complete with cafés, ice-cream parlours and shops, as well as a miniature park shaded by giant palm trees and subtropical shrubs. In the southeast corner of the square stands the Italianate **cathedral** (daily 8am–1pm & 5–10pm), built between 1880 and 1940. A fairly nondescript church, it is of note only for its unusual onyx fonts, one green, one grey, both extracted from quarries up in the Sierra de San Luis. The delightfully kitsch **electronic crib** is accessible through a door to the left of the main entrance. Built by a local engineer, it is beautifully modelled and painted, and performs for five minutes by lighting up, while the various figures, apart from Jesus in his manger, whiz up and down, and different hymns and carols blare out from loudspeakers.

Three blocks south of Plaza Pringles, down busy, commercial Calle San Martín, is the city's other central square, **Plaza Independencia**. Here, you'll find the early eighteenth-century **Convento San Domingo** and its eye-catching white **church** (daily 8am–1pm & 5–10pm), complete with handsome **Mozarabic facade** – an elegant, brick-edged horseshoe arch surrounded by intricate Moorish stucco, a style often found in Spain but seldom in Latin America. The convent is the oldest building in the city; founded by the Dominican Order, the first religious community to settle in San Luis, in its early years it frequently doubled up as a refuge for the city's population during the repeated attacks by natives.

Way up at the northern end of the city, seven blocks from Plaza Pringles, is the tiny **Museo de Historia Natural de la Universidad Nacional de San Luis**, housed in a tin hut on the university campus at Italia and Ejército de los Andes (Tues–Sun 9am–1pm; Ⓦhttp://museo.unsl.edu.ar; $1). This interpretation centre is a useful prelude to a visit to the Parque Nacional Sierra de las Quijadas, over 120km from San Luis (see p.312). It houses a small but fascinating collection of geological and archeological finds, mostly fossils, like those of strange tiny flying dinosaurs, unique to this region, and a model of a huge prehistoric spider, whose original is stored in Córdoba.

Eating and drinking

While you're in San Luis be sure to try the local speciality, *chivito con chanfaina*, or roast goat with gravy. The best **places to eat** lie along RP-20 to the east, mostly in the leafy suburbs of Visitadores Médicos and Juana Koslay; the pick of a large bunch are *La Porteña* and *Raquel*, opposite each other on RP-20, just past the junction with RN-147; the former has a downtown branch at Junín and Gral Paz. Otherwise, apart from the *Hotel Quintana*'s expensive, chic restaurant the only downtown place worth trying is *La Pulpería del Arriero*, 9 de Julio 753, where regional specialities are served in handsome surroundings. The most colourful **café** is *Aranjuez*, at Pringles and Rivadavia, a traditional café-cum-snack-bar with wooden panelling, laying on live music – rock, folk or jazz – after midnight at weekends.

Listings

Banks On Rivadavia no. 600–800.
Car rental Budget, Belgrano 1140, ⓣ02652/440288.
Hospital Clínica Privada Italia, Av Italia and Martín de Loyola, ⓣ02652/421241.
Laundry Rini, Av E.D.L. Andes 1408.
Post office Correo Central, Presidente Illia and San Martín.

Balde

Until 1999, the **hot springs** at the small village of **BALDE**, 4km off RN-7 30km west of San Luis, were a basic affair, just mineral water at 44°C bubbling into a pool. But then some enterprising locals gave the place a face-lift, and **Los Tamarindos** (Tues–Sun 9.30am–9.30pm; ⓣ02652/442220,

Ⓦ www.paginasdoradas.com/lostamarindos), named after the nearby feathery tamarind grove, is now a pleasant **spa** where you can soak in spotlessly clean pools of crystalline hot and warm water, in tasteful surroundings with an understated Roman baths theme. Professional **massages**, mud therapy and beauty treatments are also available. There is a decent **restaurant**, a café/bar and comfortable **rooms** (④).

Parque Nacional Sierra de las Quijadas

Along RN-147 towards San Juan (see p.550), some 125km northwest of San Luis, a left fork along a dirt road leads from the tiny village of Hualtarán to the entrance to the **PARQUE NACIONAL SIERRA DE LAS QUIJADAS** (daily 8am–9pm or dusk; $6; Ⓣ 02652/490182, Ⓔ sierradelasquijadas@apn.gov.ar). Covering an enormous area of the mountain range of the same name – *quijadas* means jaw-bones – it's San Luis Province's only national park, operational since 1995. The centrepiece of its outstandingly beautiful scenery is the much-photographed **Potrero de la Aguada**: a majestic canyon 8km long, 6km wide and up to 300m deep, its giant red sandstone walls folded like curtains, castellated like medieval fortresses and eroded into strange shapes by millions of years of rain and wind. The canyon is best enjoyed at sunset, when the ochre cliffs and rock battlements turn the colour of blood oranges, and should be avoided between 11am and 2pm when the strong sun makes walking unbearable, the scenery is bleached by the light and spotting wildlife is difficult.

The park is extremely rich in flora and fauna – guanacos and peccaries are plentiful and condor sightings frequent. It's also home to the *pichiciego*, a rare diminutive armadillo, and several endangered species of birds and reptiles such as the hawk-like crowned eagle and striking yellow cardinal, the boa *de las vizcacheras* and a species of land turtle; among gnarled *quebrachos* and carobs you can find the leafless chica shrub, unique to the region and now rare, and an endemic gorse-like plant, *Gomphrena colocasana*.

Over the past decade or two, geologists and palaeontologists have giddily unearthed numerous fossils here from the Cretaceous era, most of which are on display at the Museo de Historia Natural de la Universidad Nacional de San Luis. Nonetheless, Sierra de las Quijadas is still a treasure trove of the fossilized remains of dinosaurs, including those of a unique kind of pterosaurus, the pterodaustrus, a flying dinosaur the size of a sparrow that lived here 120 million years ago. The **Loma del Pterodaustro** fossil field, a thirty-minute hike from the entrance, is particularly rich in pterosaurus and pterodactyl remains still *in situ*. From Mirador Elda, the first of two vantage points you come to, with views towards the sierras, you have a choice of two trails: a physically demanding two-hour hike to see fossilized dinosaur footprints or a much easier path to the upper vantage point, or *mirador*, with its exhilarating views across the crenellated Potrero de la Aguada.

Park practicalities

Most **buses** from San Luis to San Juan will drop you at Hualtarán. The *guardaparques* have a hut (daily 8am–9pm) at the northern edge of the tiny village, where the dirt track turns off the main road, which deserves a visit before heading into the park. The rangers will give you the **information** you need to get around, guide you or put you in touch with a guide – a wise precaution as the trails are not signposted and it's easy to get lost in the 150 square kilometres of reserve; circuits include Miradores (viewpoints; 1hr),

Huellas de los Dinosaurios (tracks of the dinosaurs; 2hr), and Farallones (5hr). Most of the park destinations are also accessible by vehicle along dirt tracks. Alternatively, you could go on an **organized tour**. Tour operators in San Luis and Merlo run trips here, but the best is the one organized by David Rivarola, an English-speaking geologist at San Luis University (Ⓣ02652/155-43629, Ⓔrivarola@unsl.edu.ar). His regular weekend excursions kick off at his university lab with an informal talk, followed by a quick visit to the university museum and then a hike around the park's main sites with a lively commentary, aiming to be at the Potrero de la Aguada in time for sunset. Right by the vantage point over the Potrero is a flat area where you're allowed to **camp** wild, but there's no other accommodation nearer than San Luis. Next to the camping area is a basic canteen-cum-store.

Travel details

Buses

Córdoba to: Alta Gracia (every 15min; 1hr); Buenos Aires (hourly; 11hr); Capilla del Monte (every 30min; 2hr); Catamarca (4 daily; 6hr); Cerro Colorado (2 daily; 3hr 30min); Chilecito (2 daily; 7hr); Jesús María (5 daily; 1hr 30min); La Rioja (5 daily; 6hr); Mendoza (7 daily; 9hr); Merlo (3 daily; 5hr); Mina Clavero (5 daily; 3hr); Rosario (6 daily; 6hr); Salta (4 daily; 12hr); San Juan (5 daily; 8hr); San Luis (8 daily; 7hr); Santa Rosa de Calamuchita (every 15min; 2hr 20min); Santiago del Estero (5 daily; 6hr); Villa General Belgrano (every 15min; 2hr).

Merlo to: Buenos Aires (6 daily; 12hr); Córdoba (3 daily; 5hr); San Luis (4 daily; 3hr).

San Luis to: Buenos Aires (9 daily; 12hr); Córdoba (8 daily; 7hr); Mendoza (hourly; 3hr); Merlo (4 daily; 3hr); San Juan (3hr 30min); San Rafael (2 daily; 3hr).

Flights

Córdoba to: Buenos Aires (8 daily; 1hr 15min).

Merlo to: Buenos Aires (2 weekly; 1hr 30min).

4

The Litoral and the Gran Chaco

CHAPTER 4

Highlights

* **Colón** This picturesque riverside resort has it all: sandy beaches, hot springs, a golf course – even a winery. See p.327

* **Esteros del Iberá** Glide in a boat across a mirror-like lagoon where capybaras splash, deer trampoline on spongy islets and thousands of birds fly overhead. See p.335

* **Estancia Santa Inés** A splendid colonial-style mansion, near its own *yerba mate* plantation, offering hospitality, relaxation, delicious food – and a monkey colony. See p.346

* **San Ignacio Miní** The best preserved of all the Jesuit settlements is set among impeccably mown lawns worthy of a cricket pitch. See p.354

* **Garganta del Diablo** Of the 250 waterfalls at Iguazú, the "Devil's Throat" is the most powerful, most dramatic – and wettest. See p.364

* **Fogón de los Arrieros** Visited over the years by leading artists and artistes, Resistencia's top culture club offers tango, folk and poetry recitals. See p.407

△ The ruins, San Ignacio Miní

4

The Litoral and the Gran Chaco

The defining feature of northeastern Argentina is water. Dominated by two of the continent's longest rivers, plus several of the country's other major waterways, it's a land of powerful cascades and gushing streams, blue-mirrored lagoons and rippling reservoirs, vast marshes and fertile wetlands. In addition, there are whole series of relaxing thermal springs and rowdier fishing-cum-hunting resorts. The riverine landscapes of the **Litoral** (meaning "Shore" or "Coastline") – a term generally used to refer to the four provinces of **Entre Ríos**, **Corrientes**, **Misiones** and **Santa Fe** – range from the caramel-coloured maze of the Paraná Delta, just north of Buenos Aires, via the gentle sandy banks of the Río Uruguay and the jungle-edged Río Iguazú to the wide translucent curves of the upper Río Paraná. All of them exude a seductive subtropical beauty enhanced by the unhurried lifestyle of the locals and a warm, humid climate. To Argentines, however, the Litoral above all means two things: **mate** and **chamamé**. Litoraleños, as the inhabitants are called, are fanatical consumers of Argentina's national drink (see box, pp.392–393), and their passion for the tea-like infusion makes the rest of their countrymen look like amateurs. Chamamé, infectiously lively dance music popular throughout the region, is most reliably heard in the highly traditional province of Corrientes.

The **Iguazú Falls**, shared with Brazil, in the far north of Misiones Province, are the region's major attraction by a long chalk: Iguazú's claim to the title of the world's most spectacular waterfalls has few serious contenders. Promoted as a tourist destination as early as the beginning of the twentieth century and described by a steady stream of superlative – but never quite adequate – adjectives ever since, the Falls, or Cataratas (rapids, as they are called in both Spanish and Portuguese), are the kind of natural phenomenon that some countries build entire tourist industries around – and, in fact, both Argentina and Brazil rightly promote the waterfalls as a world-class destination.

Running a remote second, in terms of the number of visitors, **San Ignacio Miní** is one of the best-preserved ruins in the huge Jesuit Mission region, which spills from Paraguay across Argentina into southern Brazil – though some may find picking their way through nearby gothically overgrown **Loreto** and **Santa Ana** a more magical experience. Iguazú and San Ignacio aside, however, this region is surprisingly little exploited in terms of tourism, and as

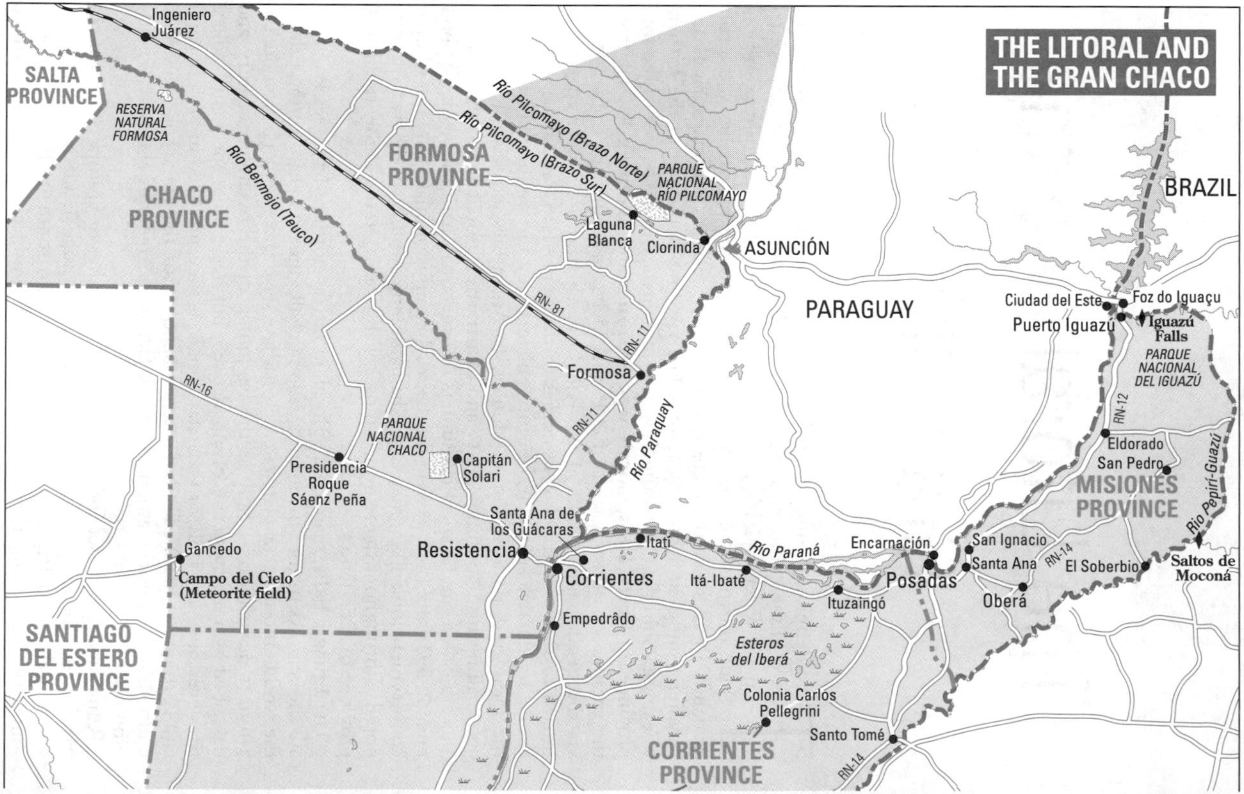
THE LITORAL AND THE GRAN CHACO
BRAZIL
PARAGUAY
ASUNCIÓN
SALTA PROVINCE
FORMOSA PROVINCE
CHACO PROVINCE
SANTIAGO DEL ESTERO PROVINCE
CORRIENTES PROVINCE
MISIONES PROVINCE
Ingeniero Juárez
RESERVA NATURAL FORMOSA
Río Bermejo (Teuco)
Río Pilcomayo (Brazo Norte)
Río Pilcomayo (Brazo Sur)
PARQUE NACIONAL RÍO PILCOMAYO
Laguna Blanca
Clorinda
RN-81
RN-11
Formosa
RN-16
PARQUE NACIONAL CHACO
Capitán Solari
Presidencia Roque Sáenz Peña
Río Paraguay
Santa Ana de los Guácaras
Resistencia
Gancedo
Campo del Cielo (Meteorite field)
Corrientes
Itatí
Itá-Ibaté
Empedrâdo
Río Paraná
Ituzaingó
Esteros del Iberá
Colonia Carlos Pellegrini
Santo Tomé
RN-14
Encarnación
Posadas
San Ignacio
Santa Ana
Oberá
El Soberbio
Saltos de Moconá
Río Pepirí-Guazú
Eldorado
San Pedro
RN-12
PARQUE NACIONAL DEL IGUAZÚ
Ciudad del Este
Foz do Iguaçu
Puerto Iguazú
Iguazú Falls

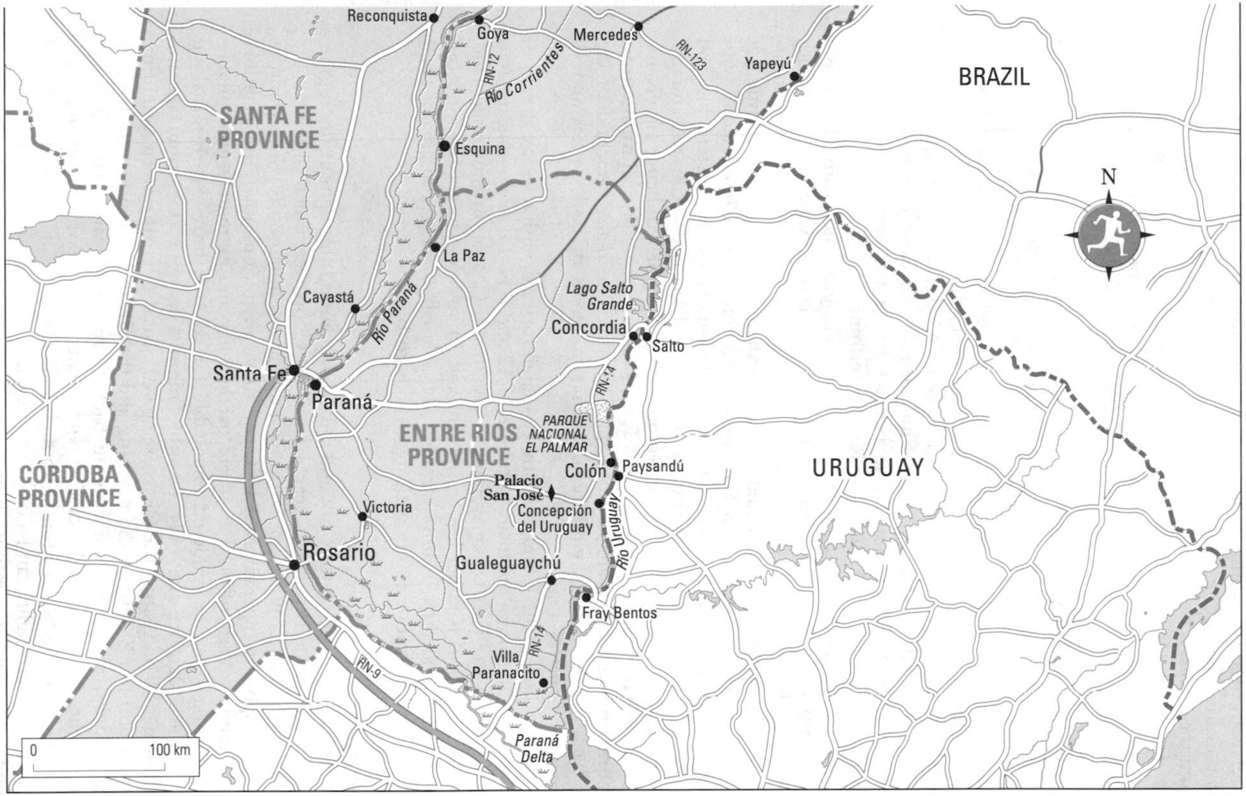
BRAZIL
URUGUAY
SANTA FE PROVINCE
ENTRE RIOS PROVINCE
CÓRDOBA PROVINCE
N
Reconquista
Goya
Mercedes
RN-123
Yapeyú
RN-12
Río Corrientes
Esquina
La Paz
Cayastá
Río Paraná
Lago Salto Grande
Concordia
Salto
Santa Fe
Paraná
RN-14
PARQUE NACIONAL EL PALMAR
Colón
Paysandú
Palacio San José
Concepción del Uruguay
Río Uruguay
Victoria
Rosario
Gualeguaychú
Fray Bentos
RN-9
Villa Paranacito
Paraná Delta
0
100 km

yet few travellers make the very worthwhile detours to two of Argentina's most unusual attractions: the strange and wonderful – but capricious – **Saltos del Moconá**, the world's most extensive longitudinal waterfalls, that tumble for nearly 3km along the middle of a gorge dividing Argentina and Brazil; and the **Esteros del Iberá**, a vast wetland reserve stretching across the centre of Corrientes Province. Away from these dramatic interludes, the landscape is marked by gradual shifts in terrain or vegetation rather than major topographical incidents, though the verdant sierras of Misiones Province are an area of outstanding beauty.

On the face of it, the dullest province in the Litoral region is Santa Fe, a huge oblong of farmland west of the Río Paraná, without a single national park or tourist resort to its name. The city of **Santa Fe**, the old-fashioned provincial capital, is not exactly exciting either. However, urbanites will definitely enjoy **Rosario**, the region's biggest city, and Argentina's third in size. It is home to a vibrant cultural life, including its own laid-back version of **tango**, fabulous restaurants and some exquisite late nineteenth- and early twentieth-century architecture. Moreover, some fine beaches fringe the various islands lying within easy reach of the city's handsome riverfront.

Bordering the Litoral and, to the northwest, Paraguay, the **Gran Chaco** is a vast, little-visited area of flatlands forming the central watershed of South America, lying partly in eastern Bolivia and southwestern Brazil, but predominantly in western Paraguay and the far north of Argentina. In Argentina, it encompasses the provinces of **Formosa** and (confusingly) **Chaco**, along with northern Santiago del Estero and Santa Fe provinces and the eastern lowland slice of Salta Province. Varying from brutally desiccated scrub to saturated marshes and boggy lagoons, the region is thinly populated, being largely inhospitable to humans, though some of Argentina's most traditional **indigenous communities** live there (see box, pp.402–403). The main attraction of the Chaco, however, is its **wildlife**, including hundreds of bird species and all manner of native animals.

Travel around the Litoral is relatively straightforward, with a steady stream of buses heading along the main arteries, RN-12 and RN-14, shadowing the Río Paraná and the Río Uruguay respectively; in the Chaco, on the other hand, public transport is rather less convenient and, in any case, to get the most out of a visit a guided excursion is strongly advisable. All of the region's major cities also have an airport, mostly with flights only to Buenos Aires.

When to go

Summers can be torridly hot and unbearably humid throughout the region, with temperatures regularly reaching 35–40°C, or even much higher in the far north. Las Lomitas, in Formosa Province, is infamously the country's hottest spot – temperatures of 45°C and above are not unknown in December and January. Parts of the Chaco are parched dry and extremely inhospitable, while roads can be rendered impassable for days by heavy storms, making April to October the only plausible months to visit (for more specific information on visiting the Chaco, see p.401). In all of northeastern Argentina, most business is done in the morning and the **siesta** is a serious and lengthy affair, with the streets not coming back to life until early evening. Insect repellent, sunscreen, light clothes and plenty of drinking water are vital, especially in the hotter months, though something warmer will be necessary in the winter (nights can be chilly) and even in the summer, when cold snaps and cooling storms are not unknown.

Mesopotamia

Mesopotamia (literally, "land between rivers") was the name the ancient Greeks gave to the region between the rivers Tigris and Euphrates, or modern-day Iraq. Argentina's **MESOPOTAMIA** offers quite a different landscape, but it too lies between two great waterways, the **Río Paraná** and **Río Uruguay**. The former, which has its source in deepest Brazil, measures just over 4700km – making it the longest river in South America outside Amazonia and the fourteenth longest in the world – and forms much of Argentina's frontier with Paraguay; the latter, less mighty but impressive nonetheless, divides Argentina from its tiny eastern neighbour, Uruguay, and further upstream, from Brazil. The closest of the Litoral's provinces to Buenos Aires is **Entre Ríos**, or "Between Rivers": also one of the country's smallest provinces, it offers a soothing verdant landscape characterized by low hills – mostly little more than ripples – known locally as *cuchillas*. The province's most impressive attraction is the **Parque Nacional El Palmar**, an enormous protected grove of dramatically tall *yatay* palms towering over the surrounding plains. North of Entre Ríos is the largely flat province of **Corrientes**; a short distance across the provincial border, just off RN-14, the quaint little town of **Yapeyú** is most famous for being the birthplace of national hero **General San Martín** (see box, p.789) and is a semi-obligatory patriotic stopover for Argentines making the long road journey from Buenos Aires to Iguazú. However, the subregion's main highlights for the traveller are **Colón** and a string of other slow-paced riverside resorts running up the Río Uruguay along the eastern border of Entre Ríos; and the countless lagoons and wildlife treasures of **Iberá** in central Corrientes Province. Furthermore, one of Argentina's liveliest **carnivals**, heavily influenced by Brazilian customs, is held in this region, with major celebrations in **Gualeguaychú** and elsewhere throughout the austral summer months.

Along the Río Uruguay

The first leg of the much-used but well-maintained RN-14 toll-road, which begins at Ceibas, 160km northwest of Buenos Aires, and heads towards Iguazú, ending up at the Brazilian border, is lined by a string of towns on the banks of the Río Uruguay. Languid and picturesque **Colón** is by far the most attractive of these, and has the most developed tourist infrastructure, including good hotels and numerous campsites right by its sandy beaches. It is also the most convenient base for making a trip to nearby **Parque Nacional El Palmar**. The **Palacio de San José**, once General Urquiza's luxurious residence, lies closer to the depressingly drab town of Concepción del Uruguay (best given a wide berth), while **Concordia**, further north, is home to a spectacular palace of its own. Both Concordia and Colón have road links to Uruguay, as does **Gualeguaychú** – home of Argentina's most renowned carnival festivities – the most southerly of these resorts.

Gualeguaychú

Apart from having a name that sounds like a tongue-twister followed by a sneeze, **SAN JOSÉ DE GUALEGUAYCHÚ**, or just plain Gualeguaychú (its name is possibly derived from the Guaraní words for "tranquil waters"), is most notable for its **Carnival**, generally regarded as Argentina's most important; during the months of January and February, the town is mobbed with people, particularly at weekends. Gualeguaychú's passion for processions is given further vent in October, when local high-school students take part in the **desfile de carrozas**, in which elaborate floats, constructed by the students themselves, are paraded around the streets. During the rest of the year – with the exception of long weekends, when it still attracts holidaymakers from Buenos Aires – Gualeguaychú is a tranquil town with some handsome old buildings and a pleasant *costanera* (riverfront) and park, plus decent accommodation and numerous campsites. Just over 230km from Buenos Aires by RN-9 and RN-14, it's a mere 33km from the southernmost **road crossing from Argentina to Uruguay**, the General San Martín International Bridge, which connects the city with Fray Bentos via Puerto Unzué. Note that in recent years the bridge has often been blocked by demonstrators protesting against the construction of gigantic paper-pulp plants on the Uruguayan side of the river (see box, pp.324–325).

Arrival and information

Gualeguaychú's **bus terminal** (Ⓣ03446/427987) is at the corner of Bulevard Pedro Jurado and Avenida General Artigas, 2km from the centre – taxis cost about $3. There is a local **car-rental** office at Urquiza 1267 (Ⓣ03446/155-73336), and **bicycles** can be rented at the corner of the Costanera and D. Jurado. Tourist information is available at the terminal (daily 8am–8pm; Ⓣ03446/440706), but the main **tourist office** (daily winter 8am–8pm, summer 8am–10pm; Ⓣ03446/423668, Ⓦwww.gualeguaychuturismo.com) is on the Plazoleta de los Artesanos, Paseo del Puerto, down by the port; it's useful if you're having trouble finding accommodation, maintaining a list of families renting rooms, plus an up-to-date price list of cabins and bungalows in the area. The staff can also offer information on excursions on the Río Gualeguaychú and on the *jineteadas*, or rodeo events, held in the vicinity throughout the year.

△ Carnival, Gualeguaychú

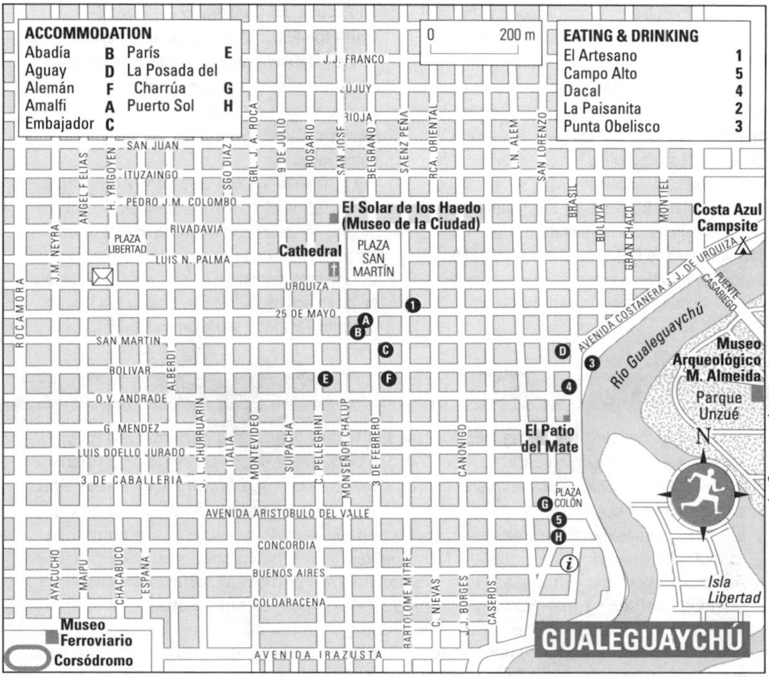

Accommodation

Gualeguaychú has one of the best selections of reasonably priced and attractive **accommodation** of all the towns along the Río Uruguay. You'll need to make reservations in advance if you plan to stay during Carnival, and probably on long weekends, too, when most places also raise their prices. At these times, the situation is alleviated by the number of impromptu notices that spring up offering rooms to rent: look around in the vicinity of the Costanera, particularly along San Lorenzo. There are numerous **campsites** in Gualeguaychú and the surrounding area; most are along the banks of the Río Gualeguaychú, or out towards the Río Uruguay. The most centrally located is *Costa Azúl* (☎03446/433130; $5 per person), just north of Puente Casariego, the bridge to the Parque Unzué. Far better, albeit far pricier, *Ñandubaysal* (☎03446/423298; $16 per tent plus $1.50 per person) is on the banks of the Río Uruguay, 15km east of the town. It's an extensive site forested with *ñandubay*, a thorny plant typical of the region and whose fruit is a favourite of the ñandú (rhea) – hence the name.

Abadía San Martín 588 ☎03446/427675, ⓔhotelabadia@yahoo.com.ar. An attractive old building with pleasant rooms done out in pastel shades. No discounts for singles. ❹

Aguay Av Costanera 130 ☎03446/422099, ⓦwww.hotelaguay.com.ar. Smart, modern hotel with top-floor swimming pool and *confitería* overlooking the river, and a reliable ground-floor restaurant, *Di Tulia*, that specializes in fish dishes. Spacious, bright rooms all have river-view balconies. Copious buffet breakfasts. ❻

Alemán Bolívar 535 ☎03446/426153. Professionally run and centrally located hotel with well-equipped rooms. Rates include breakfast and parking. ❸

Amalfi 25 de Mayo 571 ☎03446/426818, ⓔamalfihotel@yahoo.com.ar. One of the best of the budget hotels, with some particularly spacious – though slightly dark – rooms at the front and a cheery, laid-back young owner. Cable TV. ❸

Embajador 3 de Febrero and San Martín ⓣ03446/424414, ⓦwww.hotel-embajador-com.ar. Prestigious, but old-fashioned, establishment whose rooms are comfortable enough. Unless you make use of all the extras – free entrance to the tennis courts and swimming pool, some distance from the hotel – it's not really much better value than less expensive accommodation. ❻

París Bolívar and Pellegrini ⓣ03446/423850. Elegant hotel with various categories of rooms, most of them are spacious, with TV, fan and breakfast. ❸

La Posada del Charrúa Av del Valle 250 ⓣ03446/426099. A rustic name somewhat belied by the hotel's appearance, which is bland and modern. It is spick and span, though, and well located by the Costanera, and with parking. A little expensive, nonetheless, particularly as breakfast is not included. ❸

Puerto Sol San Lorenzo 477 ⓣ03446/434017, ⓦwww.puerto-sol.com.ar. The immaculate and friendly *Puerto Sol* has attractively decorated, comfortable rooms, some looking onto the hotel's interior patio. You can also be taken across the river by boat to Isla Libertad opposite, for quiet relaxation and a drink. ❺

Argentina v Uruguay: the paper plant conflict

The global demand for **paper** has rocketed in recent years, and continues to grow at a remarkable pace. In an effort to meet this demand, major paper-producing companies in the northern hemisphere have already devastated huge swathes of forest and contaminated countless rivers and lakes. As a result, international authorities are enforcing ever-stricter environmental protection regulations, obliging these companies to look elsewhere for raw materials. Many have now set their sights on southern South America, where the climate, soil and plentiful freshwater provide perfect conditions for planting and felling fast-growing non-native trees, such as **eucalyptus** – which can harm the soil and lower the water-table – and for producing low-added-value paper chips and pulp for export. Though the long-term **environmental impact** in the region is difficult to predict, independent analysts are already sounding alarm bells.

The main problem, though, is that the region's governments appear to see each other as rivals and, instead of encouraging environmental protection, they have been falling over themselves to chalk up juicy contracts, with an eye on immediate financial gain (minimal) and fatter export figures (a fallacy). Foreign companies, meanwhile, have taken advantage of this situation and have seized an unmissable opportunity to transfer production away from North America and Europe, where it is distinctly unpopular.

Ence and Botnia

A dozen or so paper and pulp mills (*papeleras* or *pasteras*), mostly run or financed by foreign companies, have been functioning in Argentina for several years. Dotted all over the country, the largest of these lie along the **Río Paraná** and in the provinces of Buenos Aires, Tucumán and Jujuy, away from international borders and in areas with little alternative employment.

In the early years of the twenty-first century, **Ence** (a Spanish paper manufacturer with an appalling environmental record back home) and Oy Metsä-Botnia Ab, commonly known as **Botnia** (a massive concern with only a marginally better record in its native Finland), both announced plans to build large paper mills near **Fray Bentos**, on the Uruguayan side of the Río Uruguay. The Argentine communities across the river protested loudly and publicly. The Uruguayans said it was sour grapes, because the plants would not benefit the Argentine economy, but on the face of it the complaint was on environmental grounds. The people of **Gualeguaychú**, the large Argentine town on the opposite bank, heavily dependent on tourism for its income, led the protest – the plants would be a blot on the landscape, would pollute

The Town

Gualeguaychú's two focal points are the streets surrounding its main square, **Plaza San Martín**, where the majority of hotels and shops are, and – particularly in the summer – the **Costanera**. On the northwestern corner of Plaza San Martín, you will find **El Solar de los Haedo** (Jan & Feb Wed–Sat 9–11.45am, Fri & Sat 5–7.45pm, April–Dec Wed–Sat 9–11.45am, Fri & Sat 4–6.45pm; free), officially Gualeguaychú's oldest building – it dates from around 1800 – and housing a small museum, the **Museo de la Ciudad**. Built in a primitive colonial style, the simple whitewashed building opens onto a garden of grapevines and orchids. Inside, the wood-floored rooms are filled with original furniture and objects belonging to the Haedos, one of Gualeguaychú's early patrician families. Among other exhibits, there's a beautiful Spanish representation of the Virgen del Carmen, made of silver and real hair; a number of fine

the river and would subject them to nasty smells and dust, owing to prevailing winds. Uruguay and the two companies disagreed. With government support, an impressive popular movement in Argentina blocked the major bridge crossings between the two countries, and apparently influenced Ence's decision in 2006 to move its plant downriver, along the banks of the Río de la Plata, 30km upstream from **Colonia del Sacramento**.

Botnia, now public enemy number one in Argentina, has already completed much of its gigantic plant, undeniably an eyesore, and timber, ready for processing, has begun to pile up. Requests by Argentine authorities for a screen of trees to be planted on the riverfront to reduce the visual impact have fallen on deaf ears.

The International Court of Justice

Argentina, believing the plants near Fray Bentos to be in violation of the Statute of the River Uruguay, a bilateral agreement to protect the river from environmental and industrial damage signed by the two countries in 1975, took its case to the International Court in **The Hague**. In July 2006, Argentina lost its initial request for provisional measures to halt the construction of the mills by a massive margin. The road blockades continued, and on several occasions demonstrators even tried to stop ferries crossing the River Plate from Buenos Aires to Colonia and Montevideo. Occasional scuffles between angry locals and Argentine tourists were reported in Uruguayan resorts. In response, Uruguay went to The Hague, complaining that the protests were in breach of international law and harming the country's economy. Since then presidents Néstor Kirchner and Tabaré Vásquez have not been on speaking terms, especially since Uruguay signed trade agreements with the US, to the detriment of Mercosur. The International Court ruled on January 21, 2007, again almost unanimously, that Uruguay had *not* proven such a breach, to the joy of the *asambleistas*, as the Argentine demonstrators are known. The Casa Rosada could not conceal its delight at what was announced as a historic victory. The Court has yet to rule on the more fundamental issue of whether the construction breaches the statute.

Whatever the merits of the case, visitors should know that for the time being all fixed **crossings** between Argentina and Uruguay are subject to delays or total blockades, and that river traffic may be disrupted. All hopes are pinned on the official negotiations being overseen by King Juan Carlos of Spain. Meanwhile, construction of the paper plant continues and the dispute drags on.

pieces of French porcelain; and a collection of the satirical magazine *Caras y Caretas*, whose founder, José Alvarez, better known as Fray Mocho, was born in Gualeguaychú in 1858. El Solar de los Haedo is also notable for having been occupied by Italian hero Giuseppe Garibaldi in 1845, when he ransacked Gualeguaychú for funds and provisions to assist General Oribe, who was under siege in Montevideo.

Gualeguaychú's most original retailing experience is provided by **El Patio del Mate** (open daily until late), on Gervasio Méndez down by the Costanera: a shrine to Litoraleños' most pervasive habit, it sells *mates* carved out of every material imaginable – from simple and functional calabazas or gourds (generally regarded as the best material for *mates*) to elaborate combinations of hoof and hide, best described as gaucho kitsch.

The **Costanera J.J. de Urquiza**, quiet during the day and out of season, heaves with life on summer evenings, when locals and holidaymakers indulge in an obligatory evening stroll or simply while away the hours on a bench, sipping on an equally obligatory *mate*. The southern end of the Costanera leads to the **old port** and if you head down this way just before the October *desfile de carrozas* you will come across scenes of frenetic activity as students – many of whom barely sleep for the last few days – put the finishing touches to their floats, which are assembled in huge riverside warehouses. The port was the termination point for the old railway tracks, which reached Gualeguaychú in 1873. If you follow the tracks round along Avenida Irazusta, you will come to the old train station, now the open-air **Museo Ferroviario**, or railway museum, where an old steam locomotive is displayed along with other relics; access is unrestricted. Just next door is the **Corsódromo**, where up to 30,000 spectators pile in to watch Gualeguaychú's *comparsas*, or processions, during Carnival.

At the intersection of Luis N. Palma and the Costanera, the Puente M. Casariego leads to the **Parque Unzué**, bisected by the road leading to the *Ñandubaysal* campground and the crossing to Uruguay. The park is the new location for the **Museo Arqueológico Prof. Manuel Almeida** (Mon–Fri 7–9pm; free), containing a small collection of weapons – predominantly *bolas de piedra*, the stone balls favoured for hunting by Argentina's indigenous inhabitants – adornments and locally found fragments of pottery made by the Chana and Guaraní peoples.

Eating, drinking and nightlife

Most of Gualeguaychú's best **restaurants** and **bars** are down by the Costanera. The consistently good *Dacal*, on the corner of Andrade and the Costanera, sports a wide-ranging menu that includes river fish and a popular *parrilla*. Another excellent *parrilla*, specializing more in meat than fish, is *Campo Alto*, which has seating in a roomy *quincho*-style building or outside in a secluded garden-terrace. Sample good pizza at *El Artesano*, on the corner of 25 de Mayo and Mitre, while down-to-earth *La Paisanita*, 25 de Mayo 1176, is popular with locals for *parrilla* and pasta. Opposite the *Hotel Aguay*, overlooking the river is *Punta Obelisco*, one of the trendiest places for a beer or coffee – you can't miss it, thanks to the obelisk-flanked entrance.

During the summer, **nightlife** also focuses on the area around the Costanera, where the city's youth congregate to chat and drink *mate* while deciding where to go and dance. The town centre is somewhat lacking in enticing bars or even *confiterías*. Gualeguaychú's most popular nightclub is *Garage*, on Rocamora and Bolívar, which plays a standard mix of dance music and *cumbia*.

Colón and around

Thanks to its setting, variety of activities and attractive hotels and restaurants, **COLÓN**, 120km or so north of Concepción, is easily the most appealing of Entre Ríos' resorts. It also makes a good base for visiting the wonderfully exotic-looking **Parque Nacional El Palmar**, just 50km north, or the European-style splendour of **Palacio San José**, about 40km southwest. Moreover, Colón is linked to the major Uruguayan city of Paysandú, 15km southeast, via the Puente Internacional General Artigas. Closer by, you can take memorable boat trips on the enticing **Río Uruguay**, swim at a riverine **beach**, hunt for semi-precious stones, taste wine at the region's only commercial **vineyard** (see box, p.330) or tour the abandoned **Liebig meat-processing plant**, a vestige of the area's once-thriving beef export industry. A day's exploration is well rewarded with a soak in the city's thermal springs, or with a visit to the **Termas Villa Elisa**, only a short distance north. Every February Colón hosts an important craft fair, the **Fiesta Nacional de la Artesanía**, with over five hundred exhibitors from Argentina, the rest of Latin America and Europe, as well as various musical events.

Arrival and information

Colón's **bus terminal** (ⓣ03447/421716) lies fifteen blocks or so northwest of Plaza San Martín, on the corner of Paysandú and 9 de Julio. The busy and mostly helpful **tourist office** (Mon–Fri 6am–10pm, Sat 7am–10pm, Sun 8am–10pm; ⓣ03447/421233, ⓦwww.colon.gov.ar) is in an attractive mansion down in the port area, two blocks north of the plaza, on the corner of Avenida Costanera and Gouchón, and is a useful place to get accommodation information; the staff also have details of the sights in Colón's environs and of ways of exploring the river.

Accommodation

Colón's **accommodation** ranges from decent *residenciales* to fairly swish hotels, plus one remarkable boutique hotel, *Hostería del Puerto*, and the fine *cabañas* at the Vulliez Sermet winery (see box, p.330). It is worth noting that the town's accommodation is severely overstretched at summer weekends, and bookings should be made weeks ahead. For budget travellers there is one of the most agreeable **youth hostels** in the country: *Sophie Hostel*, at Laprida 128 (ⓣ03447/424136, ⓔsophiehostel@yahoo.com.ar). It offers spotless accommodation in dorms ($26) and double rooms (❺) as wells as a large kitchen area, a garden and a library, and lays on fishing and other excursions. It also fixes up bookings at other hostels in the country and organizes onward travel. There are also plenty of **campsites**, spread out along the length of Colón's waterfront. At the northern end, on the beach at the foot of Calle Paysandú, is simple *Camping Municipal Playa Norte* (ⓣ03447/421917; $5 per person), with showers, electric light and barbecue facilities. Along the southern section of the Costanera there is a long chain of campsites starting with the organized – and sometimes noisy – *Piedras Coloradas* (ⓣ03447/421451; $10 per two-person tent), reached via the southern end of Calle General Belgrano; it has volleyball and basketball courts plus the usual facilities. Beyond this site, the campsites have a slightly more rustic feel. The last of them, *Camping Agreste* (ⓣ03447/424108; $5 per person), is an attractive wooded site popular for fishing.

Cabañas del Urú Mauricio Viollaz 330 ⓣ03447/424029, ⓦwww.cabanasdeluru.com.ar. Six-bed thatched *cabañas* in a small garden with an equally small swimming pool; well-appointed "rustic chic" and in quiet away-from-it-all location, but a shame they are crammed into a tiny plot. ❺

Hostería del Puerto Gouchón and Alejo Peyret 158 ⓣ03447/422698,

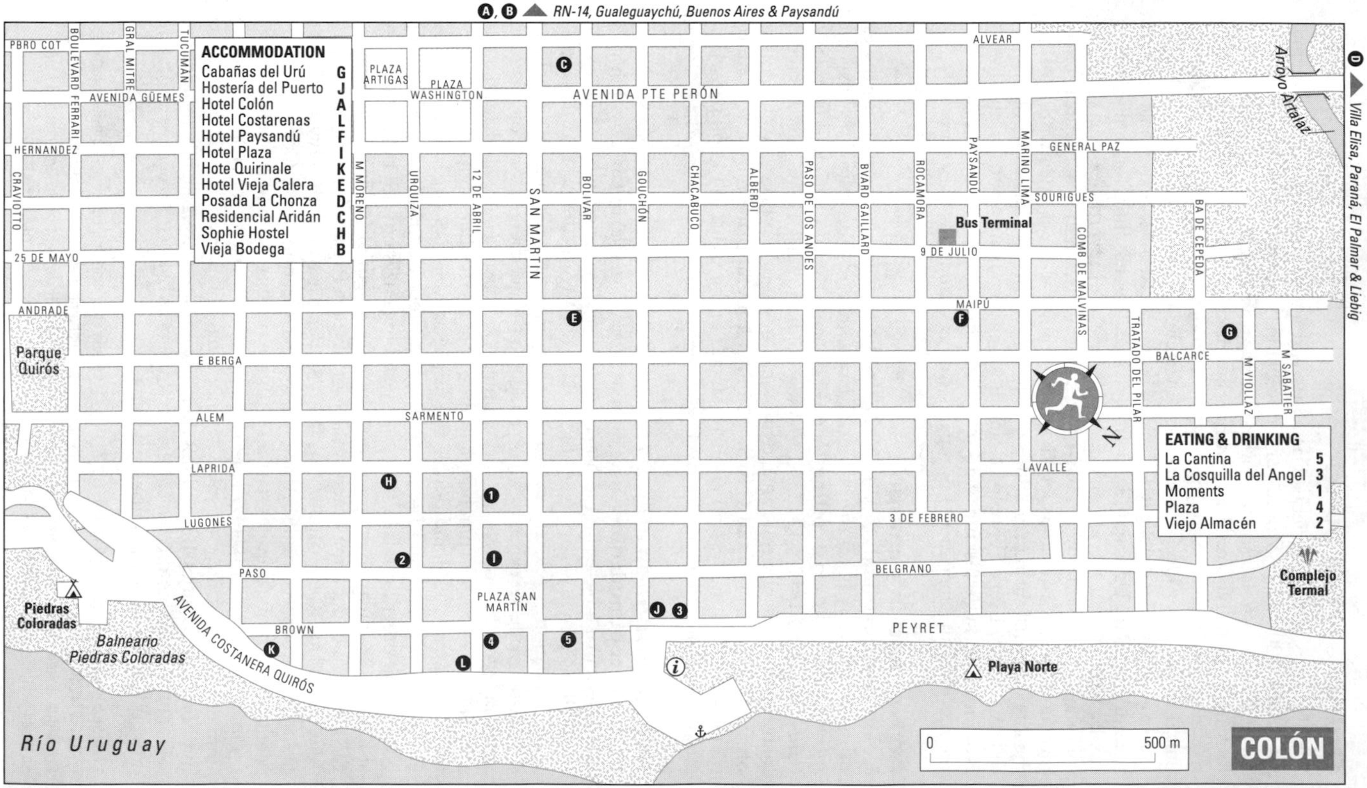
A, B RN-14, Gualeguaychú, Buenos Aires & Paysandú
D Villa Elisa, Paraná, El Palmar & Liebig
COLÓN
ACCOMMODATION
Cabañas del Urú G
Hostería del Puerto J
Hotel Colón A
Hotel Costarenas L
Hotel Paysandú F
Hotel Plaza I
Hote Quirinale K
Hotel Vieja Calera E
Posada La Chonza D
Residencial Aridán C
Sophie Hostel H
Vieja Bodega B
EATING & DRINKING
La Cantina 5
La Cosquilla del Angel 3
Moments 1
Plaza 4
Viejo Almacén 2
PBRO COT
BOULEVARD FERRARI
GRAL MITRE
TUCUMÁN
AVENIDA GÜEMES
HERNANDEZ
CRAVIOTTO
25 DE MAYO
ANDRADE
Parque Quirós
PLAZA ARTIGAS
PLAZA WASHINGTON
AVENIDA PTE PERÓN
ALVEAR
M MORENO
URQUIZA
12 DE ABRIL
SAN MARTIN
BOLIVAR
GOUCHÓN
CHACABUCO
ALBERDI
PASO DE LOS ANDES
BVARD GAILLARD
ROCAMORA
PAYSANDÚ
MARINO LIMA
GENERAL PAZ
SOURIGUES
Bus Terminal
9 DE JULIO
COMB DE MALVINAS
BA DE CEPEDA
Arroyo Artalaz
MAIPÚ
TRATADO DEL PILAR
BALCARCE
M VIOLLAZ
M SABATIER
E BERGA
ALEM
SARMENTO
LAPRIDA
LUGONES
PASO
BROWN
LAVALLE
3 DE FEBRERO
BELGRANO
PEYRET
PLAZA SAN MARTÍN
AVENIDA COSTANERA QUIRÓS
Piedras Coloradas
Balneario Piedras Coloradas
Playa Norte
Complejo Termal
Río Uruguay
0
500 m
N

ⓦwww.hosteriadecolon.com.ar. By far the best option in town, and remarkably good value, this boutique hotel, housed in a pink colonial building just one block from the port, has a refreshing swimming pool in a secluded garden. The mostly large, attractively decorated rooms are around a central courtyard with an unusual well; some rooms enjoy a view over the river, but you are better off avoiding noisy street-side bedrooms. A delicious breakfast is included and there is a twenty percent discount during the week. ⑤

Hotel Colón RN-14 and Acceso ⓣ03447/422144. Roadside hotel at the turn-off to Colón on RN-14, with swimming pool and bungalow-style accommodation – the rooms sleep up to four people. On the outmoded side, but a reliable overflow in case of unavailability in town. ⑥

Hotel Costaneras Av Quirós and 12 de Abril ⓣ03447/425050, ⓦwww.hotelcostaneras.com.ar. Undoubtedly Colón's most luxurious hotel, enjoying a prime location overlooking the river. The spa is enticing, the indoor pool a mini-oasis, the gym functional and the restaurant bright and efficient. The rooms are spacious, comfortable and decorated tastefully with a native element. However, it is so shiny and new it still lacks character. ⑦

Hotel Paysandú Maipú and Paysandú ⓣ03447/421140, ⓦwww.hotelpaysandu.com.ar. A good option near the bus terminal, this spruce modern place has clean and comfortable rooms, parking and very friendly owners; breakfast is included. ⑤

Hotel Plaza Belgrano and 12 de Abril ⓣ03447/421043, ⓦwww.hotel-plaza.com.ar. In addition to a good location on Plaza San Martín, the *Plaza* has a sauna and swimming pool. It's popular with groups in summer. Good breakfasts. ⑤–⑥

Hotel Quirinale Av Quirós s/n ⓣ03447/421133, ⓔhquirinale@ciudad.com.ar. This bunker of a hotel is an eyesore when seen from the river, but it is nonetheless the best bet if you want a comfortable place but haven't booked for busy periods. Decent rooms and attentive service. ⑦

Hotel Vieja Calera Bolívar 350, at Maipú ⓣ03447/423761, ⓔviejacalera@ar.inter.net. A passable option, its rooms are well equipped with TV, a/c and private bathrooms, though all are slightly gloomy. Prices go up by two-thirds on busy weekends. ③

Posada La Chozna Arroyo Caraballo, RN-14 Km169.1 ⓣ03447/421912, ⓦwww.posadalachozna.com.ar. Extremely welcoming and beautifully decorated posada in an English-style estancia building 29km north of town, with a fine swimming pool set among trimmed lawns. Features barbecues and hearty breakfasts and makes a good base for visiting the Parque Nacional El Palmar. ⑧

Residencial Aridán General Alvear 57 ⓣ03447/421830. Pleasant place where the rooms all have TV, fan and private bathroom. ⑤

The Town

Colón spreads along the Río Uruguay, with a narrow strip of beach running for several kilometres alongside its alluring riverside avenue, the **Costanera Gobernador Quirós**. The town's central square, **Plaza Washington**, where you will find the municipalidad, covers four blocks and lies ten blocks inland; far more elegant, however, is smaller **Plaza San Martín**, east of Plaza Washington along Colón's main commercial street, Avenida 12 de Abril – named for the town's foundation date in 1863. The most distinctive district is the sleepy **port area**, a small but charming cobbled quarter lined with a clutch of handsome colonial-style buildings which slopes down to the riverbank, immediately to the north of Plaza San Martín; if you are driving, watch out for the huge toads that often hop across the street here.

A few hundred metres from Colón's "coast", in the middle of the Río Uruguay, there are some lush **islands** flanked with dense vegetation and pristine sandbanks, both of which offer opportunities for observing local flora and fauna, especially birdlife. Excursions to the islands in motorized dinghies (2–5 times daily; 45min–2hr 30min; $15–60 per person; take sunscreen, bathing clothes, insect repellent and a sweater on cool evenings) can be made with Ita-i-Corá (ⓣ&ⓕ03447/423360, ⓦwww.itaicora.com), a wonderfully dynamic outfit whose co-owner, Charlie Adamson, speaks excellent English. Their office is at San Martín 97, on the corner of Plaza San Martín, but they also have an information stand on the corner of the Costanera and General Noailles, three blocks south. The same operator runs land-based trips (2–3hr; $20–30 per person) to see petrified tree trunks, a display of locally discovered semi-precious stones and the sadly disused **Pueblo Liebig** (open to public every afternoon), a former meat-packing plant 12km north of town, where beef extract was invented. The surprisingly interesting stones are on display at the **Reservorio de Piedras Semipreciosas** (daily 9am–8pm; $1), RP-130 Km3.5; Selva, queen of the agates, is always delighted to show visitors the collection.

Although there's a thermal spa complex right in the middle of town, the best place hereabouts for a relaxing, therapeutic soak is at **Villa Elisa** (daily 8am–10pm; ⓣ03447/480687, ⓦwww.termasvillaelisa.com; $14), about 30km northwest, 15km off the fork of RN-14 and RN-130. This huge, spacious, state-of-the-art **thermal complex** has seven pools with mineral waters especially good for sufferers from rheumatism, with massages and refreshments available; the restaurant is decent. You can also stay on site at the comfortable, modern *Hotel Vertientes* (ⓦwww.hotelvertientes.com.ar; ❹), or you can **camp** ($6 per tent).

Eating, drinking and nightlife

There are some very good **restaurants** in Colón, most of which are within a few blocks of Plaza San Martín. The best place is the enticingly decorated *La Cosquilla del Angel*, Peyret 186, down at the old port, (ⓣ03447/423711); fish, meat and delicious salads are on the menu, prices are moderate and the wine list is commendable. On the corner of calles 12 de Abril and Alejo Peyret, the *Plaza* is a lively pizzeria and *parrilla* and is also a good place for a drink – sit in its popular courtyard area or on the pavement tables overlooking the plaza. Another excellent choice is the *Viejo Almacén* (ⓣ03447/422216), on the corner of calles Urquiza and J.J. Paso, one block southeast of the plaza, a stylishly old-fashioned place that does excellent river fish – try the grilled *surubí* or *pacú*. There is good, reasonably priced pasta at the long-established and homely *La Cantina*, on Alejo Peyret 79, which also does decent freshwater fish and has tables outside on a quiet street.

Colón's unique winery

In defiance of Colón's subtropical climate, usually regarded as totally hostile to wine grapes, in 1857 a Swiss immigrant named **Joseph Favre** planted a few **vines** from his homeland just outside the city. Seventeen years later, with his vines not only succeeding, but thriving, he added a handsome **bodega** (winery) in the Piedmontese style – an Italianate villa with ochre walls that would not look out of place in the countryside around Turin. In 1936, the national government banned the commercial production of wine anywhere outside the Cuyo and the Andean Northwest, but Favre's descendents continued making wine for their own consumption. When the law was finally repealed in 1998, Jesús Vulliez, a local descendant of other Swiss immigrants, bought the nineteenth-century bodega and began producing wine for commercial distribution under the label **Vulliez Sermet**, planting five hectares with chardonnay, malbec, merlot, cabernet sauvignon, tannat, syrah and sangiovese vines. If you call ahead, you can visit the beautiful bodega, with its impeccably restored interior and cool cellars, and taste the fine red and white wines, along with a selection of cheeses and cold cuts. In the attractive grounds nearby – there is a large swimming pool – three luxurious **cabañas** sleeping up to six are also available as accommodation ($230–320 for two nights), under the name of *Vieja Bodega* (ⓣ03447/421890 or 156-45925, ⓔinfo@vulliezsermet.com.ar). To reach the whole complex from RN-14, take the RP-135 Colón–Paysandú road and stay on it for another 200m after the turn-off to Colón.

As far as **bars** go, the main hub of activity is Avenida 12 de Abril, an obligatory stop for locals on their evening stroll. Nicest of the slew of bars along here is the modern and lively *Moments*, between Lavalle and 3 de Febrero. Colón's main **nightclub** is *Mediterráneo*, housed in a distinctive white building along Alejo Peyret between Alberdi and Chacabuco. Just about all of Colón ends up here at weekends.

Palacio San José

When it was built in the middle of the nineteenth century for General Justo José de Urquiza, the **Palacio San José** (Mon–Fri 8am–6.45pm, Sat & Sun 9am–5.45pm; Jan & Feb also Fri 8.30pm–midnight; 1hr guided visits, in Spanish, at 10am, 11am, 3pm & 4pm, plus noon at weekends, and Jan & Feb 8.30pm, 8.40pm, 8.50pm and 9pm; $3; Ⓦwww.palaciosanjose.com.ar), 40km southwest of Colón and a short way off RP-39, was Argentina's most luxurious private residence. *Caudillo* of Entre Ríos Province in the early nineteenth century and its governor from 1841, Urquiza was also the province's largest and wealthiest landowner, possessing a huge *saladero* (meat-salting plant). Restrictions imposed by Buenos Aires on the provinces' freedom to trade led Urquiza to revolt against dictator General Rosas, finally defeating him at the Battle of Caseros, outside Buenos Aires, in 1853. The lavishness of the palace seems clearly intended as a challenge to the Buenos Aires elite's idea of provincial backwardness – it had running water before any building in the capital. The architect was Pedro Fosatti – who also designed the Italian hospitals in Buenos Aires and Montevideo – and, despite the colonial watchtowers that dominate its facade, it shows a strong Italian influence in its elegant Tuscan arches.

The entrance to the palace is at the back of the building, now painted the deep pink of national monuments; to your right as you enter stands a tiny **chapel** lined with spectacular frescoes by nineteenth-century Uruguayan academic painter Juan Manuel Blanes and an imposing three-metre high baptismal font, entirely carved from Carrara marble, a gift from Pope Pius IX (who kept a copy in the Vatican). The palace's 38 rooms are laid out around two vast courtyards. The first of these, the **Patio del Parral**, is named for its grapevines, many of which were brought for Urquiza from France by naturalist Eduardo Holmberg. A long, rectangular courtyard, flanked by a wrought-iron pergola, the Patio del Parral was essentially the service section of the palace; to its right lies a large kitchen, and the rooms here were used by family members, officials and Urquiza's least important guests. There is a room dedicated to the Battle of Caseros to your left as you enter the patio. The rooms in the second courtyard, the **Patio de Honor**, were occupied by Urquiza's most immediate family and by important guests such as General (later President) Bartolomé Mitre and President Domingo Sarmiento. The arches reflect those of the facade and are tiled with Italian marble slabs. The most significant room within the Patio de Honor is the dramatically named **Sala de la Tragedia** (Room of Tragedy), Urquiza's bedroom and the place where, on April 11, 1870, he was assassinated by followers of rival *caudillo* López Jordán. It was turned into a shrine by Urquiza's widow, and traces of blood can still be seen on the door, along with bullets embedded in the wall. Beyond the Patio de Honor extends a small French-style **garden**, from where the Palacio's harmonious facade appears to best advantage.

During the high season (January, February and Easter), various **tour** companies offer trips from Colón (see p.329). Otherwise, a *remise* will charge you around $60 for the trip, plus an hour or so wait, or you can take a bus from Concepción del Uruguay (just south of Colón) to Caseros or Paraná and ask to be let off at the turn-off to the Palacio San José, from where it's a three-kilometre walk.

Parque Nacional El Palmar

As you head north from Colón along RN-14, the first sign that you are approaching **PARQUE NACIONAL EL PALMAR** is a sprinkling of tremendously tall palm trees towering above the flat lands that border the highway. This 85-square-kilometre park was set up in 1966 to conserve examples of the **yatay palm**, which once covered large areas of Entre Ríos Province, Uruguay and southern Brazil. Intensive cultivation of the region almost wiped out the palm, and the national park is now the largest remaining reserve of the *yatay*; it is also one of the southernmost palm groves in the world. Though the terrain itself is nondescript rolling grassland, the sheer proliferation of the majestic *yatay* – with many examples over 300 years old and up to eighteen metres in height – makes for a wonderfully exotic-looking landscape. Bordering the Río Uruguay along its eastern fringe, the park is composed of **gallery forest**, dense pockets of subtropical vegetation formed when seeds and sediment are borne downstream from Brazil and Misiones. It is best appreciated on an overnight stay – the extensive acres of palm forest are absolutely stunning in the late afternoon light, when their exotic forms sing out against the deepening blue sky and reddish gold of the earth; sunsets are also spectacular. There are a number of well-signposted trails in the park, taking you both along the streams and through palm forests; the longer of these are designed for vehicles, though if you don't mind trekking along several kilometres of gravel road, there's nothing to stop you from doing them on foot. There are great views from **La Glorieta**, a gentle bluff from where you can take in the surrounding sea of palms. Wildlife in the park includes ñandús, armadillos, foxes and capybaras and, particularly around the campsite, vizcachas and monitor lizards. **Guided walks** take place in the park, organized by Jorge Díaz (Ⓣ03447/493031); best are the night-time excursions, which involve a fairly adventurous scramble through the gallery forest that flanks the river.

The **entrance** to the park lies just 50km north of Colón, along RN-14. There is a *guardaparques*' post at the entrance where you pay a $12 entrance fee and can pick up a map and information leaflet. It's a hefty ten-kilometre or so walk from the entrance to the visitors' centre and campsite, though at all but the quietest times it should be possible to get a lift with someone else entering the park. The only place to stay within the park is *Los Loros* **campground** (Ⓣ03447/493031; $4 per tent, plus $5 per person), a spacious and shady site with showers and a provisions store; the best pitches have a great view over the Río Uruguay. There is also a decent restaurant in the park, next door to the visitors' centre.

You can stay near the park, though, at the ecology-minded *Aurora del Palmar* complex (Ⓣ03447/421549, Ⓦwww.auroradelpalmar.com.ar; ⑤), set well back from RN-14 at Km202, on the opposite side to the park entrance. The 1.5 square kilometres of preserved land host a grove of *yatay* palms, plus a set of disused train carriages that have been converted into **accommodation**; there are also more spacious rooms in a colonial-style building nearby, overlooking citrus orchards and a large swimming pool. You can eat in the main building whether you are a guest or not (mostly well-prepared sandwiches, *minutas* and other snacks), go on a horse ride, take a canoe trip along a creek inhabited by capybaras, otters and a large quantity of birdlife or do a one-and-a-half-hour 4WD bird-watching safari or trek into the Palmar; all trips cost $20. Even as you have lunch on the terrace you are treated to a bucolic scene and effortless sightings of several bird species. **Camping** is also allowed, for $5 per person.

Concordia

Just over 120km north of Colón, **CONCORDIA** is known nationally as the Capital de la Citricultura, lying at the heart of Argentina's orange-growing region. It's a sprawling, somewhat nondescript place – albeit with a handful of handsome late nineteenth- and early twentieth-century buildings – and only really of interest as a stopover either on your way north to Corrientes and Misiones, or as a **border crossing** into Uruguay: Concordia is linked with the Uruguayan town of Salto via the Puente Internacional Salto Grande. With around 150,000 inhabitants, it is the largest town along the Río Uruguay and the second city of Entre Ríos after the capital, Paraná.

Arrival and information

Concordia's **bus terminal** (with left-luggage facilities) is fourteen blocks north of Plaza 25 de Mayo, on Juan B. Justo and H. Yrigoyen (Ⓣ0345/421-7235). Local bus #1 will take you from the terminal to the plaza – catch it on Avenida Juan B. Justo. The chaotic **tourist office** is next to the cathedral, on the eastern side of Plaza 25 de Mayo, at Urquiza 636 (Mon–Fri 7am–9pm, Sat & Sun 8am–8pm; Ⓣ0345/421-2137, Ⓦwww.concordiaturistica.com.ar). If you are bringing your own car, enquire about the *tarjeta de turista*, a special permit that enables tourists to park free of charge in the city centre. The **post office** on the main square also has reliable **Internet** access.

Accommodation

Accommodation is reasonably abundant, with a spread to suit all budgets within a few blocks of the centre. *Hotel Salto Grande*, Urquiza 581 (Ⓣ&Ⓕ0345/421-0034, Ⓔhotelsg@arnet.com.ar; ➎–➏), is a smart modern block, with views from the higher floors over the plaza and the riverside. There are various categories of rooms ranging from basic but comfortable *turista* to more luxurious *especial*, all with TV and a/c; buffet breakfast and parking are included and there's also an outdoor pool. A couple of blocks away, *Hotel Federico I*, 1 de Mayo 248 (Ⓣ0345/421-3323; ➍), has a quiet location and pleasant rooms, some with balconies. Some way from the centre, near Playa Nébel, *Hotel Betania*, on Coldaroli y Remedios de Escalada de San Martín (Ⓣ0345/431-0456; ➋), is a family-style hotel with lovely sunny rooms around a garden with a swimming pool. There are a couple of uninspiring **campsites** along Concordia's Costanera, including the free site *Los Sauces*, right by Playa Los Sauces, and the *Centro de Empleados de Comercio*, on the corner of the Costanera and Colón (Ⓣ0345/422-0080). If you have your own transport, try the lovely wooded site on the shores of the Lago Salto Grande, some way to the north.

The Town

Concordia is centred on **Plaza 25 de Mayo**, a shady square with the obligatory monumental equestrian statue of San Martín along with a particularly impressive example of the almost comically swollen *palo borracho* tree. To the east lies Concordia's main commercial district, whose main street is **Calle Entre Ríos**, pedestrianized for three blocks between Bernardo de Irigoyen and Catamarca. By following Entre Ríos seven blocks north you'll come to the town's most unusual building, the extravagant **Palacio Arruabarrena**, on the corner of calles Entre Ríos and 3 de Febrero. Though both the exterior and interior have suffered severe deterioration over the years, it's still a fabulously exotic and decorative construction. Built in 1919 by a local land-owning family, the Arruabarrenas, its four storeys show a strong French influence, especially in the steeply pitched mansard roof punctuated with elliptical windows. A sweeping marble staircase leads up to the grand loggia-style porch and marble statues – a buxom caryatid and very camp telamon – flank the entrance, supporting a heavy pediment over the arched windows of the first floor. Inside you'll find the **Museo Regional de Concordia** (Mon–Fri 9am–noon & 4–8pm; free), with a patchy collection of local exhibits plus occasional shows featuring work by area photographers.

Concordia's **riverside area**, Avenida Costanera, is twelve blocks southeast of Plaza 25 de Mayo. There's a sandy beach here, the **Playa Los Sauces**, named for the willow trees that flank it. Rather desolate out of season, it hums with life on summer evenings as locals patrol the avenue by car and on foot. From the old port, at the eastern end of Calle Sáenz Peña, boats ferry passengers to and from **Salto** in Uruguay (Mon–Fri 9am, noon, 3pm & 6.30pm, Sat 8am, noon, 3pm & 6.30pm; $5.50) – the journey takes only fifteen minutes, making it a quicker way to cross the border than via the road bridge. The ticket office on the quay opens fifteen minutes before departure.

A couple of kilometres north of the town centre lies **Parque San Carlos** (aka Rivadavia). It's a pleasantly hilly, if sometimes slightly unkempt park, whose most unusual feature is a huge and rather gory wooden sculpture of Christ on the cross. At the eastern end of the park, overlooking the river, stand the ruins of the **Castillo San Carlos**, a grand residence built in 1888 by a French magnate, Édouard de Machy, who spent only three years in the expensive house before inexplicably returning to France with his family in 1891. During the 1920s, French aviator and writer **Antoine de St-Exupéry** made an emergency landing nearby and befriended the family then inhabiting it – an anecdote included in his collection of short stories *Terre des Hommes* (published in English as *Wind, Sand and Stars*). Fire and general neglect have taken their toll and now there's little to see apart from some fine views of the river and a wild expanse of gallery forest. Close to the entrance, there's a sculpture of *The Little Prince*, in homage to St-Exupéry. At the northern end of the park, there's a **botanical garden** (Mon–Fri 8am–6pm, Sat & Sun 8am–noon & 2–6pm; free) dedicated to conserving indigenous plants and trees; look out for the *yatay* palm entwined by a strangler fig. Local bus #2 from Calle Pellegrini drops you a block from the park entrance.

Just over 12km north of the town centre, along Avenida Monseñor Rosch (bus #7 from Calle Pellegrini), are Concordia's **thermal baths** (daily 7–1am; $12; ⓣ0345/425-1963, ⓦwww.termasconcordia.com.ar), a pleasant enough complex of six artificial pools with temperatures ranging from 33°C to 42°C.

Eating and drinking

Eating and drinking options in Concordia are few and far between. Next to the *Hotel Salto Grande*, on the central square, is the *Restaurante de la Plaza*, which serves some unusual versions of usual dishes – fish, *parrillas* – garnished with fruit sauces and in a trendy setting. One of the best deals in town is friendly *Yantar*, Pellegrini 570, with good, fresh, standard Argentine food and a takeaway next door. On the corner of Urquiza and Alberdi, *La Glorieta* is a popular, reasonably priced *parrilla*. Down on the Costanera there are a number of lively *parrillas*, busiest on summer evenings; one of the best is spacious *Parrilla Ferrari*, on the corner of the Costanera and Calle Bolivia. Several popular *confiterías* cluster around Plaza 25 de Mayo, including glitzy air-conditioned *Cristóbal* with outside tables and live music at weekends.

Yapeyú

As you head north of Concordia towards Misiones and the Iguazú Falls, RN-14 offers little of interest. Two hundred fifty kilometres north, and across the border in Corrientes Province, you pass by Paso de los Libres, but this dull frontier town is best avoided, owing to its alarming crime rate; there is, however, a river crossing here, a bridge leading to the Brazilian city of Uruguaiana. Another 60km on is one of the route's few appealing stopovers, the sleepy riverside village of **YAPEYÚ**. Once an important Jesuit *reducción* (see box, pp.352–353), it was largely destroyed in the early nineteenth century by the Portuguese army, who left little more than the blocks of stone used to build the village. Nowadays, everyone in Argentina has heard of Yapeyú, as national liberator **General San Martín** was born here.

Yapeyú's unassuming buildings – many of them painted in the traditional colonial colours of mustard and white with green doors – sit on a grid of streets with the large **Plaza San Martín** at the centre. The centrepiece is a huge truncated arch, a monument to soldiers who died in the Falklands/Malvinas conflict: the arch will be completed if ever the islands are regained by Argentina. At the eastern end of the square, the mock-colonial **Templete Histórico Sanmartiniano** (daily 8am–6pm; free) is built around the foundations of San Martín's birthplace; his mausoleum is in Buenos Aires' cathedral but there is an urn containing the remains of San Martín's parents, moved here from their original resting place in Recoleta Cemetery. Slightly more interesting is the modest **Museo Sanmartiniano** (daily 7am–11pm; free), at the far southern end of the village, displaying a collection of documents, uniforms and items belonging to the San Martín family. There's a reconstruction of San Martín's bedroom in the house in Boulogne-sur-Mer, France, where he died, and a couple of relics from the Jesuit mission, including a sturdy baptismal font. More Jesuit pieces can be seen at the **Museo Jesuítico Guillermo Furlong** (Tues–Sun 8am–noon & 4–7pm; free), on the south side of the plaza. The museum is laid out in the form of an *oga* (a Guaraní term for a collection of small huts) and contains various pieces of stonework from the missions, including a sundial. There are also highly informative panels on the region's history.

Accommodation is limited but agreeable: the *Hotel San Martín*, on the south side of the plaza (Ⓣ03772/493120; ❸), is a cosy little place in an old-fashioned building, with decent en-suite rooms. Down towards the riverfront, northeast of the plaza, the *Hostería Yapeyú*, on the corner of Juan de San Martín and Paso de los Andes (Ⓣ03772/493053; ❸), offers more attractive self-contained *cabaña*-style accommodation. There's a pleasant grassy **campsite** at the southern end of town, again by the river ($5 per tent), offering hot showers and barbecue facilities. On the southern side of the square, there's a simple but friendly **restaurant**, the *Comedor El Paraíso*, where you can sit at tables outside.

Central Corrientes: the Esteros del Iberá

Covering nearly 13,000 square kilometres (one sixth of Corrientes Province), the delicate ecosystem of the **ESTEROS DEL IBERÁ** is a magical landscape that offers some of the best opportunities in the country for close-up observation of wildlife. A large stretch of these lands is protected within the **Reserva Natural del Iberá**, where birds and other fauna are so used to a benign human presence that viewing and photographing them is a piece of cake. An elongated sliver of land running through the centre of Corrientes Province, the *esteros* (marshes) are bordered to the north by RN-12, to the east by tributaries of the Aguaypey and Miriñay rivers and to the west by tributaries of the Paraná. The southern tip touches RN-123, which runs east–west from the border town of

Paso de los Libres, joining RN-12 150km south of Corrientes city. In addition to the *esteros* that give the area its name, you will see a good many lakes, ponds, streams and wonderful floating islands, formed by a build-up of soil on top of intertwined waterlilies.

For many years this was one of Argentina's wildest and least-known regions – a local legend even had it that a tribe of pygmies lived on the islands – harbouring an isolated community who made their living from hunting and fishing the area's wildlife. Since the Reserva was created in 1983, hunting in the area has been prohibited and many locals have been employed as highly specialized guides, or *baqueanos*, and park rangers, thus helping to preserve the unique environment. The ban on hunting has led to an upsurge in the region's abundant bird and animal population – there is an amazingly diverse range of species (see box, pp.340–341).

In the heart of the reserve, beside the ecosystem's second largest lake, the Laguna del Iberá, is the spread-out village of **Colonia Carlos Pellegrini** ("Pellegrini"). The main gateway to the *esteros*, though is **Mercedes**, a picturesque traditional town 120km southwest of Pellegrini. Buses go there from Buenos Aires, and there is a handful of good places to stay. If **driving**, note that the road linking Pellegrini to Posadas in a northeasterly direction is not always viable, especially after rain (in any case, best in a 4WD); whatever you do, enquire about its current state before attempting it.

Mercedes

Nearly 250km north of Concordia via RN-14 and RP-119, and approximately 200km southeast of the city of Corrientes (also reachable via the well-maintained RN-123 from Paso de los Libres, around 100km southeast), **MERCEDES** is unlikely to impress at first sight. Set among the flatlands of central Corrientes Province, it appears as a sprawling modern settlement with little to tempt you into staying. Head into the centre, though, and you'll find an appealing agricultural town given a distinctive flavour by a mix of old-fashioned adobe and galleried-roof buildings plus some elegant nineteenth-century architecture. The town is a real hub of country life, too: horses and carts are a common sight on its streets and on Saturdays gauchos come to town, traditionally dressed Corrientes-style, with shallow, wide-brimmed hats, ornate belts and wide *bombachas* (trousers) and accompanied by their wives, who wear frilly, old-fashioned dresses. Around 9km west of town, along RN-123, there is a roadside shrine to a popular local hero, **Gauchito Gil** (see box opposite).

The town, built on a regular grid pattern, is centred on **Plaza 25 de Mayo**, a densely planted square with little fountains. At its southern end stands the town's rather unusual church, the **Iglesia Nuestra Señora de las Mercedes**, a lofty, late nineteenth-century red-brick construction whose towers are topped with Moorish domes. Along the southern side of the square runs Juan Pujol, an attractive street lined with some fine buildings and a number of good bars and restaurants.

Three blocks east of the square, on the corner of San Martín and Batalla de Salta, there's a beautifully preserved example of the local building style: a low whitewashed adobe-walled construction with a gently sloping red-tiled roof which overhangs the pavement, supported on simple wooden posts. This building houses the **Fundación Manos Correntinas**, a nonprofit enterprise that functions as an outlet for locally produced crafts. The small but superior collection of goods includes basketwork, simple gourd *mates*, heavy woollens and hand-turned bone and horn buttons. The friendly manager is as happy for visitors to wander around the building as to purchase goods – so long as you sign her visitors' book. There are various other craft outlets throughout town: try the shops along San Martín and Juan Pujol selling belts, gaucho knives, *mates* and the like – all with a sturdy utilitarian feel and far less gimmicky than the pieces on sale in more touristy towns.

Practicalities

Mercedes' **bus terminal** is six blocks west of Plaza San Martín, on the corner of Avenida San Martín and El Ceibo; you can leave luggage at the terminal bar. The **tourist office** (daily 8am–noon & 4–8pm; ⓣ03773/420100), inconveniently located in an isolated building at the western entrance to town, can provide useful information and a map. **Internet** access is available at the photography shop on the corner of Belgrano and Juan Pujol. There's an **ATM** at the Banco de Corrientes, on the corner of Pedro Ferre, three blocks west of Plaza San Martín; note that there are no banking facilities or decent stores in Pellegrini, the settlement in the heart of the *esteros*.

Accommodation options in Mercedes are surprisingly good for a small provincial town, though there aren't that many beds available. The best place is

Gauchito Gil

Along roadsides throughout Argentina you'll see mysterious **shrines** of varying sizes, smothered in red flags, red candles, empty bottles and other miscellaneous bits and pieces. These are erected in homage to the semi-mythical **Gauchito Gil**, a kind of nineteenth-century gaucho Robin Hood – one of those folkloric figures whose story has some basis in reality yet has undoubtedly been embellished over the years.

Born – perhaps – in 1847 in Corrientes, Antonio Gil refused to fight in that province's civil war and fled to the mountains, robbing from the rich, helping the poor and healing with his hands. Captured by the police, he claimed that he had deserted from the army as he had been told in a dream by a Guaraní god that brothers shouldn't fight. An unimpressed sergeant took him out to a spot near Mercedes and decided to execute him, even though a pardon was likely forthcoming. Gil told the sergeant that when he returned to town he would find that his son was seriously ill, but as Gil's blood was innocent it could perform miracles, so the sergeant must pray for his intervention. Unmoved, the sergeant cut Gil's throat. When he returned to town, he found that the situation was indeed as the gaucho had described, but – after fervent prayer – his son made a miraculous recovery.

The sergeant put up the first shrine to thank him, and Gauchito Gil has since been credited with numerous **miracles** and honoured with many **shrines**, all bedecked in the distinctive **red flags** – which may represent his neck scarf soaked in blood – making the shrine look like the aftermath of a left-wing political demonstration after all the protesters have gone home. The shrine erected near **Mercedes**, on the place where he was killed, presumably began life as a simple affair, but such is the popularity of **Gauchito Gil** that the site has mushroomed over time into a vast complex of restaurants, campsites and souvenir shops; there is even a kind of museum exhibiting the offerings made to the Gauchito – including football shirts, wedding dresses and children's bicycles, along with more conventional rosaries. Simpler offerings, often made by passing motorists and bus passengers to ensure a safe journey, are ribbons and candles. January 8 sees Gauchito Gil pilgrims flock to the main shrine from the whole country. There is a close, pagan-like parallel with the shrines to the Difunta Correa, whose main pilgrimage site lies near San Juan (see p.557) but also is honoured by smaller versions nationwide.

★ *La Casa de China* (☎03773/156-27269; ⑤), a fabulous B&B at Fray Luis Beltrán 599 and Mitre; the tastefully furnished, quiet, patrician villa has a limited capacity of four double rooms. There's a private botanical garden behind, and China herself will prepare delicious meals if given notice. You could always fall back on the quaint *Hotel Sol*, San Martín 519, a few blocks east of the plaza (☎03773/420283; ⑤); it is in a lovely old building with spotless if dingy rooms – all of them en suite with TV and fans – set around an attractive flower-filled courtyard. *Hotel Recova*, a newcomer ambitiously calling itself a boutique hotel, at Fray Luis Beltrán 1110 (☎03773/420400, Ⓦwww.corrientes.com.ar/hotelrecova; ⑥), is rather disappointing – the cramped rooms are in a modern block, with poor sound-proofing, slack service and skimpy breakfasts – but it might bail you out if all else is booked. The best budget option is the *Hostel Delicias del Iberá*, Pujol 1162 (☎03773/422508, Ⓔdeliciasdelibera@yahoo.com.ar; $23 per person); the rooms are a little small but the ambience is ultra-friendly and the bus terminal only nine blocks away. The hostel's breakfast room also acts as a **café** serving fresh juices, good espresso, sandwiches, cocktails and delicious home-made *alfajores*. For more substantial dishes, the best **restaurant** is *El Quincho*, housed in the Club Social, on the corner of Juan Pujol and Ferré, with low-priced standards such as *milanesas*, pastas, steaks and chicken. Otherwise try the *Café de la Plaza*, on the plaza, for passable pizzas.

Colonia Carlos Pellegrini and the esteros

COLONIA CARLOS PELLEGRINI lies at the heart of the Reserva Natural del Iberá, 120km northeast of Mercedes, and is mainly accessed via unsealed but well-maintained RP-40 (allow 2hr if driving). The journey there takes you through flat, unremarkable land, reminiscent of the African savannah, but with little to prepare you for the wonderfully wild, watery environment of the *esteros* themselves. The village sits on a peninsula on the edges of the Laguna del Iberá, a 53 square-kilometre expanse of water. The banks of the sparkling lake (*iberá* means "shining" in Guaraní) are spread with acres of waterlilies, most notably the striking lilac-bloomed *camalotes* and yellow *aguapés*, and dotted with bouncy floating islands formed of matted reeds and grass, known as *embalsados*.

△ Capybaras, Esteros del Iberá

If you come from Mercedes by bus or via your own transport, access to the village is over a temporary-looking – and sounding – narrow bridge constructed of earth and rock. There's a small **visitors' centre** (open daily during daylight hours) immediately to the left just before you cross the bridge, where you can see a small photographic display on the *esteros* and their wildlife. Short trails on either side of the road lead through a small forested area south of the visitors' centre; the densely packed mix of palms, jacarandas, *lapachos* and willows here is a good place to spot and hear black howler monkeys who typically slouch in a ball shape among the branches or swing from tree to tree on lianas. Easiest to see are the yellowish young, often ferried from tree to tree on the backs of their mothers. As the monkeys mature the females' fur turns brown while the males' turns black. Birds and butterflies abound, while capybaras often graze on the grass.

The village itself is composed of a small grid of sandy streets, centred on grassy **Plaza San Martín**. There's a hospital, a school and a handful of rather limited grocery stores but otherwise few services: there's only one public phone, used by the whole village to receive calls, and nothing in the way of banking facilities, so make sure you bring enough cash with you for your stay (nobody takes credit cards).

Accommodation

The best **accommodation** in the village is provided by various posadas that offer full board (there are no good eateries in town), with at least one **boat trip** to the lagoon included and other activities laid on. A little over 30km from Pellegrini, to the south via the road to Mercedes, an old estancia has been transformed into a luxury **hotel**. There are also a couple of extremely basic **hospedajes** in the village, only one of which is recommended. A municipal **campsite** is immediately to the left as you enter the village from the bridge; it's a pleasant riverside site with showers but is almost entirely bereft of shade.

Estancia Rincón del Socorro ⓣ03782/497073, ⓦwww.rincondelsocorro.com. Five kilometres from the main road, 90km north of Mercedes, this recently converted working estancia is efficiently run by the hospitable Cook family. The traditional main building and luxurious rooms are all decorated with handsome furnishings and splendid photos of Iberá flora and fauna. Food includes home-grown, organic fruit, vegetables and herbs. A small plane can take you to a sister estancia, *San Alonso*, on the shores of Laguna Paraná, bang in the middle of the *esteros*, where it is also possible to spend the night. ⑨

Hospedaje San Cayetano ⓣ03773/156-27060. The only commendable budget accommodation in the village, this *hospedaje* offers simple but just about acceptable rooms with a shared bathroom. ③

Irupé Lodge ⓣ03773/154-402193, ⓦwww.irupelodge.com.ar. Handsome wooden *hostería* with five down-to-earth, brightly decorated rooms overlooking the lagoon, as well as its own jetty and launch. $278 per person.

Posada Aguapé ⓣ03773/499412, ⓦwww.iberaesteros.com.ar. Another traditional building set in spacious grounds with twelve appealing en-suite rooms overlooking the lake. There's also a swimming pool and a cosy bar area. $355 per person.

Posada de la Laguna ⓣ03773/499413 or 156-29827, ⓦwww.posadadelalaguna.com. Particularly well situated in a quiet lakeside spot at the eastern edge of the village, this pioneering posada offers pared-down luxury with a rustic feel. The elegant and spacious but simple en-suite rooms are in a galleried building whose verandah provides a good vantage point for observing the birds that gather around the lake; food and service are top-notch and the swimming pool is another great vantage-point for some very laid-back bird-watching. From $560 per person; two-night minimum.

Posada Ñandé Retá ⓣ03773/499411, ⓦwww.nandereta.com. Located towards the western end of town, this modern wood and stone construction, more Swiss than Correntino, looks rather out of place, but is hidden away within wooded grounds, with a sun terrace and bright en-suite rooms. The posada doesn't overlook the lake, but the owners have a separate stretch of lakeside land where they have installed a watchtower from which you can take in commanding views of the area. $330 per person.

Posada Rancho de los Esteros ⓣ03773/154-93041, ⓦwww.ranchodelosesteros.com.ar. Just two handsomely decorated suites in a wonderful

Wildlife in the Esteros del Iberá

Home to well over three hundred species of **birds** and a mindblowing variety of **reptiles** and **mammals**, the Esteros del Iberá are a paradise for any visitor who takes a delight in seeing all manner of animal life. Armed with binoculars and a guidebook to South American species, you stand an excellent chance of observing and putting a name to dozens of different varieties in just an hour or two; a good guide will help, too.

A common sight and sound around the Laguna del Iberá are *chajás* (**Southern Screamers**), large grey birds with a patch of red around the eyes and a look of bashful nervousness. They frequently perch on the trees on the lakeside, nonchalantly chanting "aha-aha" but occasionally emitting a piercing yelp (hence the English name) not dissimilar to the sound a dog makes when trodden on. Other large birds include sleek, black **Olivaceous Cormorants**; **Maguari Storks**, with striking black and white plumage, and a tendency to soar on the thermals above the lake; and **Striated Herons**, characterized by a black crown and a lazy disposition. A particularly impressive sight during the spring nesting period is that of the *garzales*, where hundreds of normally solitary herons unite in a spectacular mass gathering. Another magical, if rarer sight, is the elegant *jabirú*, a long-legged relative of the stork with a white body, bright crimson collar and a black head and beak. Different species of **kingfisher** also put on a show of aviation prowess, swooping across the water or diving into it. **Wattled Jacanas**, on the other hand, prefer to scuttle over waterlilies and floating weeds, seldom showing off their lemon-tipped wings. Another strange-moving bird is the **Giant Wood-Rail**, or *ipacaá*, whose Guaraní name is onomatopoeic; it croaks plaintively as it tip-toes around near houses, grabbing any food left out for it and scampering off to peck away at it.

Among the smaller, non-aquatic birds that flit around the lake, look out for the **Scarlet-headed Blackbird**, which has a jet-coloured body and a head and neck that look as if they have been dipped in dark orange paint. Aptly named **White** and **Black-and-white Monjitas** ("little nuns") love to pose on branches. Three varieties of flycatcher, descriptively known as "tyrants" – owing to their bossy nature and habit of picking fights with larger birds (and, at times, unsuspecting humans) – flutter all over the place. The common **Forked-tailed Flycatcher**, or **tijereta**, is ubiquitous, whereas much fewer and farther between are the **Streamer-tailed Tyrant** and the **Strange-tailed Tyrant**, proof if nothing else that bird-namers sometimes find it difficult to think up new monikers. Veritable punk-rockers of the avian world, **Red-crested Cardinals** – white and grey,

ranch with a traditional gallery. This newcomer is a welcome addition to the typical Pellegrini posadas. $310 per person.

Posada Ypa Sapukai ⓣ03773/420155, ⓦwww.ypasapukai.com.ar. The name of this posada means "cry of the lagoon" in Guaraní. *Ypa Sapukai* is rather more modest than the other posadas in Pellegrini but each of the five rooms has an en-suite bath. Similar facilities and activities as are offered elsewhere. $490 per person; three-night package.

The esteros

Wildlife-spotting excursions are organized through the posadas, which take visitors out in their small motorboats, with the boatmen acting as guides. After speeding across the centre of the lake, the boats dip under the causeway-bridge, calling in at the visitors' centre to register, before cutting their engines to drift through the narrow streams that thread between the islands on the other side of the Laguna. This silent approach allows you an incredibly privileged view of the *esteros*' wildlife (see box above); turning a corner you suddenly find yourself among a wonderful landscape of water lilies and verdant floating islands, the whole of it teeming with bird and animal life. Sometimes guides will take you onto the floating islands themselves; it's a particularly bizarre experience to feel the ground vibrating beneath your feet with a defiant scarlet quaff – are very easy to see, even with the naked eye, but their **yellow** cousins, looking a bit like a crested budgerigar, are an endangered species and spotting one is a real privilege. Several varieties of **woodpeckers** can be seen – and heard – in the areas of woodland such as the one near the visitors' centre. That is also a likely spot to view one of the most beautiful birds of all, the **Plush-crested Jay**. These splendid birds, with black, blue, yellow, violet and cream plumage, sport a velvety dark pom-pom at the back of their heads.

Birds are not the only wonders around the *esteros*. Among the reedbeds at the edges of the lake you may catch sight of large **snakes**, such as the handsome **yellow anaconda**, its golden skin dotted with black patches; they can reach up to three metres in length. As you approach the edges of the floating islands, in particular, charcoal-grey **caymans**, or *yacarés*, freeze, often with their ferocious-looking jaws stuck open, or else they suddenly slither into the water, where they observe you with only their eyes peeking above the surface. Another startling spectacle is provided by creepily large **spiders**, which lurk in huge webs among bushes and reeds, waiting for their helpless insect prey. Some guides delight in making it look as though the boat is heading straight for them, so arachnophobes be warned. Rather more appealing are the hundreds of **butterflies**, in every colour imaginable, an enchanting sight you will see all over the region.

Mammals are well represented, too. **Howler monkeys** – which really growl rather than howl – are much easier to hear than to see, but you might be lucky, if you are patient, to observe their antics near the visitors' centre or in other tall trees in the area. Listen, too, for the sudden splash of a **capybara**, or *carpincho*, diving into the water. On land, this guinea pig-like mammal, the world's largest rodent, looks almost ungainly, but they are incredibly graceful as they glide through the water. The floating islands are where the capybaras go to sleep and graze. There, and on the marshy lands and pastures around the more isolated extremes of the lake, you may also spot the rare **marsh deer**, South America's largest, equally at home in the water and on dry land. If you approach them gently, these astonishingly beautiful animals seem to accept your presence and continue grazing lazily on aquatic plants. Rarest of all of the *esteros*' wildlife, and certainly the hardest to spot, is the endangered *aguara-guazú*, or **maned wolf**, a reddish long-legged creature that awkwardly lopes through the vegetation, moving first its two left legs and then the two right ones – or so they say.

as you move. Another trip takes you along the Río Miriñay, home to slightly different varieties of flora and fauna to the lake. Enquire also about **horse rides** in the nearby marshes, another excellent way to see birds and the like, especially in the morning.

Misiones Province

The proboscis-shaped territory of **Misiones**, in the extreme northeast of the country, is one of Argentina's smallest, poorest but most beautiful provinces. **Posadas**, the relaxed capital, is usually bypassed by most travellers, but the province has a lot more to offer than the juggernaut that is **Iguazú Falls**, the only place most travellers ever see, zipping in and out by plane. What looks odd on the map makes perfect sense on the ground: Misiones' borders are almost completely defined by the wide Paraná and Uruguay rivers and one can even imagine that the province's sierras have been formed through the land being compressed by neighbouring Brazil and Paraguay. Even the province's distinctive iron-rich **red earth** ends abruptly just over the border with Corrientes, while the torrent of water that hurtles over the waterfalls at Iguazú must surely mark one of world's most dramatic and decisive frontiers.

The territory was named for the Jesuit settlements that flourished in the region – also across the present-day borders in Paraguay and Brazil – in the seventeenth and eighteenth centuries; the most impressive mission on Argentine soil is the much photographed ruins of **San Ignacio Miní**. Along the Brazilian frontier, formed by the upper reaches of the Río Uruguay, you can see one of the world's most unusual, if not most powerful, sets of cascades, the **Saltos del Moconá**, weather conditions permitting. The province's wildlife-filled **jungle** and its emerald fields and orchards – pale tobacco, vivid lime trees, darker manioc and neatly clipped tea plantations, painting the landscape endless shades of green – are further attractions that make wandering off the beaten tracks that are RN-12 and RN-14 infinitely rewarding. Misiones was also the centre of considerable immigration in the early twentieth century: the hilly town of **Oberá** boasts of having over a dozen national communities, including Ukrainians, Swedes, Japanese and Germans. A Guaraní influence is also obvious, with small native communities scattered throughout the province. This cross-cultural phenomenon is echoed in the speech of inhabitants in the more rural areas, where a mix of Guaraní and Spanish can be heard; throughout the Litoral, Guaraní words are a common feature of speech: you may hear a child referred to as a "gurí" or a woman as a "guaina". Although away from Iguazú tourist facilities are few and far between, a number of **estancias** and **lodges** (see box, pp.346–347) make for some of the country's most enjoyable accommodation experiences.

Posadas and around

If you arrive in **Posadas** expecting your first taste of the jungle, you'll be sorely disappointed: the provincial capital sits on a rather bare patch of land bordering the Río Paraná, which – bar the red earth – has more in common with northern Corrientes than with the luscious emerald sierras of central and northern Misiones Province. Thanks to the construction of a road to Paraguay via the **Puente Roque González de Santa Cruz** in 1980, and the town's proximity to the massive Yacyretá Dam, Posadas' population has dramatically swollen and some local people lament the increase in crime, though it remains relatively safe. In addition to the road crossing here, Posadas is also one of the few places you can get across to Paraguay via the river (see box, p.350).

With over 300,000 inhabitants, Posadas is Misiones' most important city and is indeed an important urban centre for a large hinterland of neighbouring Paraguay and Corrientes Province. Not exactly postcard-worthy, it is primarily a **stopover city** and appears to do little to reap any benefit from the modest but nonetheless steady stream of tourists who pass through. While there's a handful of mildly interesting **museums** here, there is little – bar the odd craft shop – specifically aimed at the holidaymaker. Nonetheless, Posadas is a pleasant and prosperous place with a lively feel. Some attractive buildings are tucked away among the centre's mostly modern constructions, though the only part of town that can lay a claim to being seriously picturesque is the old road to the port, known as the **Bajada Vieja**. Posadas has revamped its **Costanera**, or riverside esplanade, a sign that the city is starting to exploit its location, but if you really want to make the most of the river, you'd be better off heading up the road to San Ignacio, where you can pitch your tent with unbeatable views of the Paraná and the Paraguayan side of the river. The town hosts a lively provincial festival, known as the **Estudiantina**, which runs over three weekends in September. During the festival local schools prepare and perform dance routines – all with a strong Brazilian influence.

Some history

The first recorded settlement in the vicinity of modern-day Posadas was the **Jesuit Mission Nuestra Señora de Itapuá**, founded by Roque González de Santa Cruz in 1615. Disease soon forced the mission to transfer to the Paraguayan side of the Río Paraná and, for the next couple of centuries, the settlement progressed little until its strategic position was exploited during the War of the Triple Alliance when, under the name Trinchera San José, the town served as a supply post for Brazilian troops. In 1879, the fledgling city was renamed after **José Gervasio de Posadas**, who, in 1814, had become the first Supreme Director of the Provincias Unidas del Río de la Plata – a title that

rather outdid his reign, which lasted only until January of the following year. On the creation of the new territory of Misiones in 1881, Posadas was left behind in Corrientes, but in 1884 the neighbouring province and the national government were persuaded to redraw the boundaries and Posadas, by far the most important settlement in the region, became Misiones' provincial capital. Since then it has largely been a quiet backwater, a status reflected in its languid ambience and lack of much to do.

Arrival and information

The quiet **airport** is around 7km southwest of the centre; bus #8 will take you right into town from here, or you could take a taxi (around $20). Posadas' **bus terminal** (ⓣ03752/454887 or 454888) is about 4km south of the centre at the intersection of Avenida Santa Catalina and RN-12. It's a modern building with good facilities, though no ATM machine. From the terminal there are numerous local buses (including #24, #25 and #21) heading into the centre; the taxi ride will cost about $7.

Posadas' well-stocked **tourist office**, Colón 1985 (daily 7am–8pm, sometimes closing 1–2pm; ⓣ03752/447539, ⓦwww.misiones.gov.ar), has fairly decent maps of both the town and the province, though it doesn't have an awful lot of information on anything beyond the well-worn Posadas/San Ignacio/Iguazú groove. Posadas' streets were renumbered in the 1990s but, confusingly, both systems are still in use. You will generally find that the address will be written as the new number, with the old number in brackets, while either may be used on the building itself – where necessary, we have followed this custom.

Accommodation

The majority of people seeking **accommodation** in Posadas are businessmen and, as you would therefore expect, the majority of hotels are expensive and fairly bland, with a couple of worthy exceptions. There's also a very pleasant **cabin and camping complex**, *La Aventura*, on the riverbank towards the outskirts of town. Note that Posadas can be extremely hot and sticky during the summer, so you'll need to plan on spending more than your normal budget in order to get air-conditioning. You might well consider staying at one of the two excellent **estancias** nearby (see box, pp.346–347) as an alternative to staying in the city, but for that your own transport will be useful.

La Aventura Av Urquiza and Av Zapiola ⓣ03752/465555, ⓔaventuraclub@hotmail.com.ar. Swish camping and cabin complex on the outskirts of town, complete with good recreational facilities – including tennis courts. The swimming pool is popular with locals during the summer. Buses #3 and #13 go from the corner of San Lorenzo and Sarmiento. ⑤

Hotel Posadas Bolívar 1949 (ex 272) ⓣ03752/440888, ⓦwww.hotelposadas.com.ar. Rated as one of Posadas' best hotels, this centrally located place comes with all mod cons, though the rooms are rather cramped and uninspiring for the price. ⑤

Julio César Entre Ríos 1951 ⓣ03752/427930, ⓔhoteljuliocesar@arnet.com.ar. Posadas' most upmarket hotel – four-star comfort including a swimming pool and gym for only a little more than you pay at the *Hotel Posadas*. ⑥

Le Petit Santiago del Estero 1630 ⓣ03752/436031, ⓔlepetithotel@ciudad.com.ar. On a quiet, tree-lined street away from the centre and by far the nicest hotel in its price range, this small, prettily decorated place has light and spacious rooms. Facilities include TV, telephone and a/c, and breakfast is provided. The friendly owner is also a good source of tourist information. Reservations advisable. ③

Residencial Colón Colón 2169 (ex 485) ⓣ03752/425085. The *Colón*'s rooms are rather strangely located around the hotel's garage. However, it's central, well kept and perfectly adequate for the price, which includes parking. ③

Residencial El Colonial Barrufaldi 2419 ☎03752/436149. One of Posadas' better hotels; a little off the beaten track in the vicinity of the old bus terminal, but worth making the trek – particularly as there are few comparably priced decent hotels in the centre itself. Includes breakfast, fan, TV and parking. Popular with travelling salesmen, so reservations are advisable. ❸

Residencial Misiones Félix de Azara 1960 (ex 382) ☎03752/430133. This is just about the cheapest recommendable place in the centre of town: an old-fashioned hotel with rooms around a central patio. The whole family mucks in with the running of the hotel and there's a friendly atmosphere, although some of the rooms are in serious need of an overhaul. ❷

The City

The centre of Posadas is demarcated by four main avenues – Sáenz Peña, Guacurarí, Corrientes and B. Mitre, the last of which leads towards the international bridge. Within this area you will find the majority of hotels and points of interest. Just beyond Guacurarí, Calle Fleming, more commonly known as the **Bajada Vieja**, leads down to the port, from where boats take passengers over to Paraguay. The

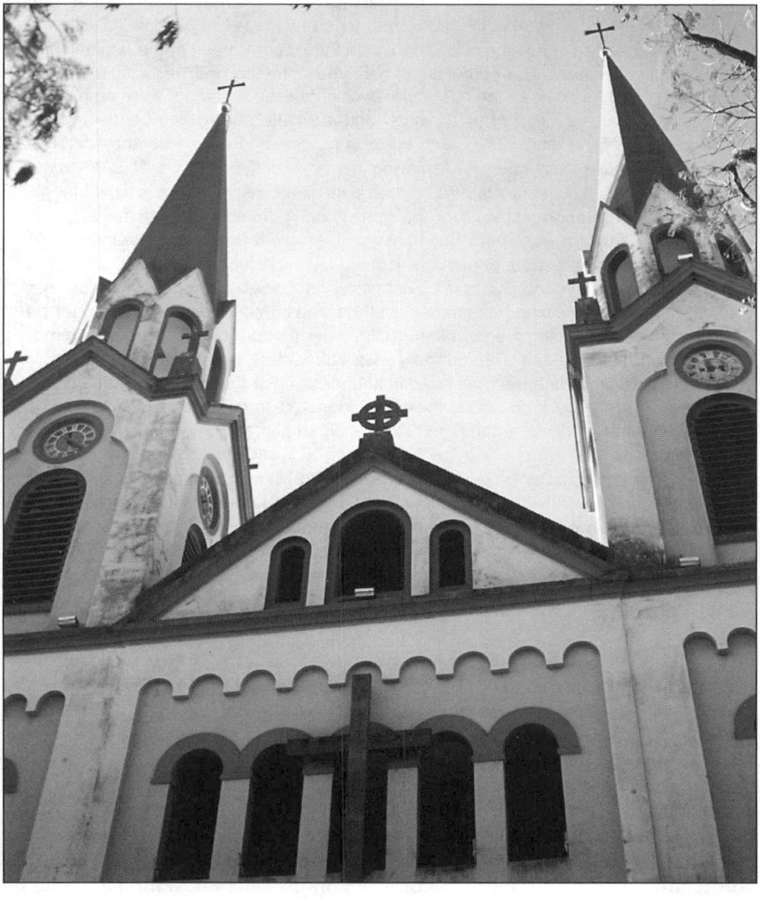

△ Iglesia Catedral, Posadas

Estancias and lodges in Misiones Province

The hotel infrastructure in Misiones Province is not the finest in the country – many small-town hotels are bland at best, while most of the better establishments in Iguazú, for example, are not good value for money. Fortunately there is a widespread network of distinguished **estancias** – many of them noble houses in glorious surroundings – and, more recently, ecofriendly **lodges**, where you can spend a relaxing night or two, lapping up understated luxury, getting to know locals and enjoying the province's flora and fauna. There are two estancias outside **Posadas** that make excellent alternatives to lodging in that city, and another within reach of **Iguazú**. In northern Misiones three lodges enjoy fabulous jungle settings, but are a bit too far from the Falls to serve as bases for visiting them. Another three outstanding places in the **Selva Misionera** are detailed in a separate box, on p.369. It is vital to book ahead at all these establishments for both day-time visits and overnight accommodation.

Near Posadas

The *Estancia Santa Inés* (T03752/156-39670 or 155-01941, Enannymisiones@hotmail.com), 20km southeast of Posadas, just off RN-105 (Km8.5) towards San José, is run by descendants of Pedro Núñez, a partner in the Núñez y Gibaja shipping company, one of the pioneers of navigation on the Upper Paraná at the beginning of the twentieth century. The outbuildings near the entrance and majestic tree-lined drive testify to the scale of the operation: over a thousand workers were employed, primarily in the cultivation of *yerba mate*, and a private railway line connected the estancia's extensive lands. The *casco* appears modest on the outside, though it has a lovely, old-fashioned interior, displaying a marvellous collection of silver *mate* paraphernalia, but the estancia's trump card is its exotic setting: there is a mini-jungle of luxuriant vegetation just outside the front door. A small pool near the house is partly shaded by araucaria trees but, 5km away along dirt tracks (best negotiated on horseback), a huge outdoor pool made of stone blocks is fed by a natural spring. You can also wander among the *mate* plantations on horseback, or visit the family's private chapel, containing handsome Jesuit carvings. Prices range from $60 for an afternoon visit, including tea (or *mate*), to $270 per person for full-board accommodation, activities included. The four daily meals (breakfast, lunch, tea and dinner) are absolutely delicious and the wine flows in abundance. For those without wheels, bus #30 from Posadas will leave you at the well-signposted entrance, 2km from the *casco* – you can arrange for someone from the estancia to pick you up from here.

Sitting on a bluff overlooking the Río Paraná at Candelaria, 30km northeast of Posadas, *Estancia Santa Cecilia* (T03752/493018, Wwww.santacecilia.com.ar; 9 full board), built in 1908, has horses for rides along the riverbanks, puts on impressive displays of gaucho horsemanship and horse-related crafts and serves traditional regional cuisine in a patrician house. The six rooms are delightful and full of colonial charm, and the whole place is refined but not snobbish. The grounds are subtly

main reason for heading further northeast is to visit the **Parque Paraguayo**, where there is a crafts market and the Museo Regional Aníbal Cambas, and the **Costanera**, a popular hangout for local youth during the evening.

Plaza 9 de Julio and around

Posadas' central plaza, the **Plaza 9 de Julio**, is flanked to the north by the early twentieth-century **Iglesia Catedral**, a work by super-prolific Alejandro Bustillo, who designed Buenos Aires' Banco Nación, among many other buildings. The plaza's best-looking building, however, is the **Casa de Gobierno**, a sugar-pink Rococo construction on Félix de Azara. The building sits perfectly alongside the manicured splendour of the square, where there's a landscaped, containing a variety of native and non-native trees, but the general feeling is one of open space – the swimming pool is fabulous.

Near Iguazú

Another wonderful estancia further north is *Las Mercedes* (03751/431497 or 431092, www.estancialasmercedes.com.ar; 6 B&B, 9 full board), a 1920s property founded as a ranch by a family of British origin and now both a working farm and an ecotourism resort. Just outside El Dorado, barely 100km south of Iguazú, *Las Mercedes* is also an interesting and not too distant stay-over option from the Falls. The five charming rooms, delicious food (you can call ahead for just lunch or tea) and beautiful swimming pool, set among immaculate lawns, make this a superb spot for a few days' relaxation. You can also go on a horse ride or even canoeing on the nearby river. Ask the delightful family who run the place for details about the fascinating story behind the foundation of the farm; it's a gripping tale of love and dentistry.

Accurately calling itself an ecolodge – *Yacutinga* (www.yacutinga.com; US$350 per person, full board; three-day/two-night minimum) lies just 60km east of Iguazú airport via a dirt road that runs parallel to the Río Iguazú, and is another great way to stay near the Falls. Part of Argentina's Wildlife Foundation's Private Nature Reserve Programme, the lodge is tucked away amid one of the last remaining patches of unspoilt jungle. The main building is beautifully designed, while the rooms are in twenty well-camouflaged cabins. Expert multilingual guides take you on walks, pointing out all kinds of wildlife, including an astounding array of birds and butterflies. All meals are served in the airy restaurant, with emphasis on local produce. One of the highlights is a nocturnal ramble into the bush, to see creatures that are active after dusk; another is the boat ride on the nearby creek and river. You must arrange in advance to be picked up from Puesto Tigre, the junction by the police control, where the Andresito road forks off the main road from Puerto Iguazú to the airport. Trying to negotiate the muddy track under your own steam is not advisable; read the information in the website carefully so you know what to take with you, and note that young children are not allowed.

A mere 50km from Puerto Iguazú, in the same direction as *Yacutinga*, *Panambí Lodge* (03757/497418, www.panambilodge.com.ar; $280 per person, full board) lies within the National Park, also on the jungle-clad banks of the Río Iguazú. The rugged stone-and-timber lodge has five large rooms with huge picture windows and all mod cons, and offers bird-watching and fishing opportunities along with rides in a horse-drawn carriage.

Finally, there is *La Alegría Lodge* (03751/421442, www.laalegrialodge.com.ar; 9), 180km southeast of Iguazú on RP-17, north of San Pedro. Set amid three hundred square kilometres of lush rainforest, it offers horse rides, abseiling, hikes, 4WD trips, bird-watching and a driving range among its invigorating activities. The two eight-person *cabañas* are harmoniously designed and furnished, with all mod cons.

healthy selection of local vegetation, including *pindó* palms and *lapacho*, neatly displayed in densely packed flowerbeds that are like little urban squares of jungle. Throughout the town you will find examples of the bright red and yellow *chivato* tree, originally imported from Madagascar, together with ficus or rubber trees, whose enormous leaves provide welcome shade.

The city's **commercial centre** is concentrated on the streets west of the plaza, with Calle Bolívar in particular forming the hub of the clothes shops that make up much of the town's retail activity. There's usually a huddle of street traders, too, though for a real market atmosphere, you should head for the **Mercado Paraguayo** (daily 8am–6pm), towards the port on the intersection of San Martín and Avenida Presidente Roque Sáenz Peña. Known locally as

"La Placita", it sells a vast range of electronic goods, toys, clothes and shoes, all imported from Paraguay.

A few blocks southwest of Plaza 9 de Julio, at San Luis 384, you will find the **Museo de Ciencias Naturales e Históricas** (July daily 8am–noon & 3–7pm, rest of year Tues–Fri 7.30am–noon & 2–8pm, Sat & Sun 9am–noon; free), which houses an interesting enough hotchpotch of local history, from the Jesuits and the Guaraní, the region's original inhabitants, to the colonization of the province in the late nineteenth and early twentieth centuries. There are also displays on natural history and ecology, with special reference to locally endangered species such as the *yaguaraté*, of which only a handful remain in the Parque Uruguai provincial reserve. You'll find a tiny **zoo** in the patio, inhabited chiefly by some very inquisitive monkeys, while snake fans might check out the **serpentarium**: in addition to live snakes (principally *yararás*, the most common cause of snake bites in the province), there are pickled snakes, stuffed spiders and a very lifeless-looking human finger amputated with a machete after a snake bite. The serpentarium is not all cheap thrills, though – there's also an informative section showing you how to deal with bites and, during July, a demonstration of **snake venom extraction** (Tues–Sun 10am).

Parque Paraguayo and the Museo Regional Aníbal Cambas

Ten blocks northwest of the Plaza 9 de Julio, the small Parque Paraguayo hosts a **crafts market** (daily 8am–noon & 2.30–6.30pm), where you can see examples of Guaraní basketwork made from local wild cane and carved wooden animals, among other items. The far end of the park leads to the Anfiteatro Municipal Antonio Ramírez and, below, to the Costanera, while at the other end, at Alberdi 600, you will find the **Museo Regional Aníbal Cambas** (Tues–Fri 7.30am–noon & 3–7pm, Sat 9am–noon & 4–7pm, Sun 4–7pm; free) housed in a handsome century-old brick building and loyally maintained by its friendly staff in the face of a fairly obvious shortage of funds. The museum's particularly unhealthy-looking collection of stuffed and pickled animals is not worth much of your time but there are some interesting and well-labelled exhibits in the **historical and ethnographical collection**, such as objects culled from the ruins of Jesuit missions and artefacts produced by the region's indigenous populations: the Guayaquí, the Chiripá, the Mbyá and the Guaraní. The last are particularly strongly represented, with a large collection of clay funerary urns, known as *yapepo*, meaning "handmade" in Guaraní. There are also a number of musical instruments, notably the *mimby*, a kind of wooden flute used by men and the *mimby reta*, similar but much smaller and used by women. The importance of music to the Guaraní is documented as far back as Alvar Núñez Cabeza de Vaca's first incursion into the Paraná region, when he noted that the Indians "received them covered in many-coloured feathers with instruments of war and music". You can reach the museum on local buses, including #4 and #14 from Colón and Catamarca.

Eating, drinking and nightlife

Although the Costanera is lively at night there still aren't that many interesting places to **eat** or **drink** down here, though a couple of places do great things with the fish from the river. Posadas has a thriving **nightlife**, however, which from Thursday to Saturday goes on till around 7am. As usual in Argentina, it's not worth going near a club until the early hours: most places don't open their doors until 1.30am. In addition to home-grown rock and *cumbia*, the musical mix usually includes a bit of *marcha* (commercial dance) and Brazilian music, very popular in the region.

Regional food specialities

The food you find around Argentina is remarkably homogeneous for such a huge country. However, there are **regional variations** that reflect the culinary influence of neighbouring nations more than most Argentines realize or care to admit. The most notable of these cross-border gastronomic influences can be found in the northern reaches bordering **Paraguay**. In the Chaco, northern Corrientes and much of Misiones you will find dishes that are part of the staple diet in Asunción and the rest of Paraguay. **Chipas** – savoury cheese-flavoured lumps of manioc-flour dough – are extremely popular snacks sold on the street, served in restaurants instead of bread and cooked in people's homes. **Sopa paraguaya** is actually not a soup at all, but a hearty maize and cheese dish, said to have been invented during the War of the Triple Alliance, when the beleaguered Paraguayan soldiers needed more sustenance than was provided by their traditional chicken broth, so army cooks thickened it with corn flour. **Borí borí**, on the other hand, *is* a soup, made from chicken, with little balls of maize and cheese floating in it. Last but not least, **tereré**, or cold *mate*, is hugely popular in Paraguay, but can also be tasted in the borderlands of northeast Argentina.

Bahía Bar Bolívar 1911. Centrally located café/bar, good for reasonably priced snacks such as hamburgers and *lomos*.

Dileto Bolívar 1929. Sophisticated à la carte restaurant specializing in fish – try the delicious grilled *surubí* and the reasonably priced pasta and steaks. Occasional live music. Closed Mon.

Fellini Bolívar 1979 and San Lorenzo. Unlikely though it may seem, Posadas' most refined cuisine is on offer inside a shiny shopping mall; on the upper floor, this café/restaurant paying homage to Italian cinema serves up delicious fare, has an excellent wine list and the best espresso in town.

El Mensú Coronel Reguera and Fleming ☎03752/434826. Regarded by some locals as the best restaurant in Posadas, *El Mensú* specializes in excellent home-made pasta and seafood and has a very good wine list – plus the bonus of being on the corner of Posadas' prettiest street. Open every evening and also midday at weekends.

La Querencia Bolívar 322. A bustling and stylish place that's a surprisingly good deal, particularly as you can easily share some of the dishes. Try their juicy *bife de chorizo* – shipped in from Buenos Aires Province, as local beef is of poorer quality – and accompany it with fried manioc for a local touch, or go for the excellent *galetos*, a kind of chicken and vegetable kebab. Closed Sun eve.

La Rueda Costanera. This two-storey wooden building, decorated with facsimiles of historic photos of the city, does a mean, moderately priced *parrilla* and delicious river fish. There are great views of the Río Paraná across to Paraguay from the upstairs dining room.

Saint Thomas San Martín 1788, on the corner of Félix de Azara. Standard *tenedor libre* offering all you can eat for a small price and catering for vegetarians, carnivores and pasta fans.

Sociedad Española Córdoba between Colón and Félix de Azara. Very popular lunch-time spot – not surprising, as the basic two-course menu, which goes for next to nothing, could possibly feed a small family. There are also more Spanish – and more expensive – dishes available à la carte.

Listings

Airlines Aerolíneas Argentinas/Austral in the city (☎03752/435031), and at the airport (☎03752/451104).

Banks and exchange There are plenty of banks along calles Bolívar, Félix de Azara and around Plaza 9 de Julio, most of which will change money at good rates, without commission.

Books There are some excellent local publications – good for information on Misiones' nature reserves and the like – at the Librería Montoya on the corner of Ayacucho and La Rioja.

Car rental Express Car, Colón 1909, and at the airport ☎03752/435484; Localiza, Colón 1933, and at the airport ☎03752/430901, or central reservations ☎0800/999-2999. Localiza is currently the only firm in Posadas to offer 4WDs.

Internet access There are *locutorios* spread around the city, with several around central Plaza 9 de Julio.

Post office Bolívar and Ayacucho.

Travel agencies and tour operators Abra Tours, Entre Ríos 1896 (ex 309) (☎03752/422221,

River crossings to Paraguay and Brazil

In addition to the major road crossings at Posadas, Puerto Iguazú and Bernardo de Irigoyen, various small **ferries** take foot passengers and cars from towns and villages in Misiones Province across to Brazil and Paraguay. Crossings to Brazil can get very busy in summer months, when tourists on both sides rush to visit their neighbours. Most ferries now run every day of the week (8am–5pm, Sat also 9–11am & 3–5pm), with reduced services sometimes on Sundays; times and availability may change, so it's as well to check before setting out. A contact telephone number on the Argentine side – in some cases, the customs post – is given where available.

To Paraguay

Puerto Rico to Puerto Triunfo (Ⓣ03743/420044)

Puerto Maní to Bella Vista

Posadas to Encarnación (Customs Ⓣ03752/425044)

To Brazil

Alba Posse to Porto Mauá (Ⓣ03755/482014)

San Javier to Porto Xavier (Ⓣ03754/482000)

El Soberbio to Porto Soberbio (Ⓣ03755/495077)

Panambí to Veracruz

Ⓔabra@misiones.org.ar), does standard San Ignacio and Iguazú tours plus more unusual ones to Moconá or fishing on the Paraná. Guayrá Turismo Alternativo, San Lorenzo 2208 (Ⓣ03752/433415, Ⓦwww.guayra.com.ar), is run by an enthusiastic young couple who specialize in more alternative tourism, including trips to the Esteros del Iberá.

The Jesuit missions

After Iguazú Falls, the province's major tourist attractions are the **Jesuit missions**, north of Posadas. The largest, **San Ignacio Miní**, is also the best preserved in the whole of the missions region, which extended beyond the Paraguay and Uruguay rivers to Paraguay and Brazil, and also into Corrientes Province. Far less well preserved – and much less visited – are the ruins of **Santa Ana** and **Loreto**, south of San Ignacio; these crumbling monuments, set among thick jungle vegetation, are less dramatic but are appealing if only because they do attract fewer visitors. All three missions can be visited on a day-trip from Posadas, though it's well worth spending more than a day in San Ignacio, visiting the ruins in the morning light and seeing them again at night. In addition to the attractive village, there's a stunning area of forest and beaches to the southwest with a good campsite and perhaps the finest stretch of river scenery in the whole region. Accommodation is available in San Ignacio (and, if you don't mind roughing it, in Loreto, too), or you could base yourself at one of the local estancias (see box, pp.346–347). Note that foreigners must pay $12 for a **ticket** that is valid at all the Argentine missions for two weeks from the date of issue.

Santa Ana and Loreto

Heading northeast from Posadas along RN-12, the first mission site you come to, after approximately 40km, is **Santa Ana** (daily 7am–6pm). Originally founded in the Tapé region (see box, p.352) in 1633, Santa Ana was refounded, with a population of two thousand Guaraní, on its present site after the *bandeirante* attacks of 1660. At the entrance, accessed via a signposted, unsealed road just south of the village of Santa Ana, there's a small display detailing the restoration work currently being undertaken at the site, with assistance from the Italian government. Like all the *reducciones*, Santa Ana is centred on a large square, to the south of which stand the crumbling walls of what was once one of the finest of all Jesuit churches, built by the Italian architect Brazanelli, whose body was buried underneath the high altar. A lot of work has been carried out on the site, yet the roots and branches of trees are still entangled in the reddish sandstone of the buildings around the plaza, offering a glimpse of the way the ruins must have appeared when they were rediscovered in the late nineteenth century. North of the church, on the site of the original orchard, you can still make out the channels from the *reducción*'s sophisticated irrigation system.

Around 12km north of Santa Ana, the ruins of **Loreto** (daily 7am–6pm) are even wilder than those of Santa Ana. This site, founded in 1632, was one of the most important of all the Jesuit missions, housing six thousand Guaraní by 1733 and noted not only for its production of cloth and *yerba mate* but also for having the missions' first printing press. Like Santa Ana, Loreto has a small visitors' centre at its entrance, reached via a six-kilometre stretch of unsealed road (impassable after heavy rain), which branches off RN-12. Restoration work is being carried out with the assistance of the Spanish government. When you head out from the visitors' centre to the *reducción* itself, it's actually difficult at first to work out where the buildings are. After a while, though, you begin to see the walls and foundations of the settlement, heavily camouflaged by vegetation and lichen, upon which tall palms have managed, fantastically, to root themselves. If you fancy staying the night in Loreto, try one of the three-bed **dormitories**, with bathroom and kitchen facilities, available in the building opposite the visitors' centre ($12 per person).

San Ignacio and around

Considering it's home to such a major attraction, the grand Jesuit ruins of San Ignacio Miní, **SAN IGNACIO**, 60km northeast of Posadas via RN-12, is a remarkably low-key place – away from the restaurants and souvenir stands around the ruins themselves, the town has little in the way of tourist facilities. There are, however, a few worthwhile attractions southwest of the village.

San Ignacio is laid out on the usual grid pattern; it's rather long and thin, dissected east–west by broad Avenida Sarmiento and north–south by Bolívar. The western extremity is bounded by Avenida Horacio Quiroga. Heading south along this avenue for a kilometre or so, you'll come to the **Casa de Horacio Quiroga** (daily 8am–7pm; $4; ⓣ03752/470130), a museum to the Uruguayan writer, who made his home here in the early twentieth century. Quiroga, famed for his rather Gothic short stories – one of the best collections is *Cuentos de Amor, de Locura y de Muerte*, filled with morbid but entertaining tales of blood-sucking beasts hidden in pillows and demented, murderous children – first visited the region in 1903, taking some of the earliest pictures of the then little-known ruins. Adopting Argentine nationality, Quiroga moved to San Ignacio in 1910, where the tropical setting further fired his imagination, inspiring stories of sunstroke and giant snakes. The museum is composed of two houses – a replica of the first wooden house built by the writer, containing many of his possessions, and a later stone construction also built by him. Though the buildings are pleasant to wander around, much of the museum's charm is derived from its wonderful setting, amidst thick vegetation. At the back of the wooden house there's a small swimming pool built by the writer

The Jesuits and their missions

The first Jesuit **missions** in Argentina were established in 1609, three decades after the order founded by San Ignacio de Loyola first arrived in the region. Known in Spanish as **reducciones**, these missions were largely self-sufficient settlements of Guaraní Indians who lived and worked under the tutelage of a small number of Jesuit priests. Missions were initially established in three separate zones: the **Guayrá**, corresponding to the modern Brazilian state of Paraná, bordered to the west by the Paraná and Iguazú rivers, to the south by the Iguazú and to the east by the sierras, which run down Brazil's Atlantic coast; the **Tapé**, corresponding to the southern Brazilian state of Río Grande do Sul, present-day Misiones Province and part of Corrientes Province; and the **Itatín**, least successful of the regions, lying between the Upper Paraná and the sierras to the north of the modern Paraguayan city of Concepción.

If the Jesuits were essentially engaged in the imperialist project of "civilizing" the natives, they did at least have a particularly enlightened approach to their task – a marked contrast to the harsh methods of procuring native labour practised elsewhere in Latin America. Work was organized on a co-operative basis, with those who could not work provided for by the rest of the community. Common land was known as *tupambaé*, while each family was also provided with a small parcel of land, or *abambaé*, on which they cultivated crops for their own personal use. **Education** and culture also played an important part in mission life, with Guaraní taught to read and write not only in Spanish but also in Latin and Guaraní, and music and artisanship actively encouraged.

The early growth of the missions was impressive, but in 1628 *bandeirantes*, slave traders from São Paulo, attacked, destroying many of the missions, and carrying off their inhabitants, leading the Jesuits to seek more sheltered areas to the west, away from the Guayrá region in particular. The mission population soon recouped – and then surpassed – its former numbers, and also developed a strong standing **army**, making it one of the most powerful military forces in the region. By 1650 there were 22 *reducciones* in the Upper Paraná region, and thirty by 1700, with a combined population of around 50,000 Guaraní. The early *reducciones* mostly operated on a subsistence basis; however, in 1648, the Crown removed the order's previous exemption from taxes, and the missions began to develop **trade** with the rest of their territory. Their most important crop proved to be *yerba mate*, which had previously

for his second wife (the first committed suicide, as would Quiroga himself in 1937, and his children after his death). She later left him, at which point Quiroga filled the pool with snakes.

Continuing south past the museum, the unsealed road winds down for another 2km or so to the stunning **Puerto Nuevo**, where there's a lovely strip of sandy beach and, best of all, a fantastic view across the curves of the Paraná to the Paraguayan side of the river – all rolling wooded slopes tumbling down to the water. Many Paraguayans cross to San Ignacio on Wednesdays and Fridays to sell produce at the town's market, and towards the end of the day you may see them heading back home in small rowing boats. Camping facilities are available at the beach (see p.354).

The **Parque Provincial Teyú Cuaré**, 10km south of the village via a good unsealed road, is accessed from the southern end of Bolívar. It's a small but stunning park of less than a square kilometre, notable for its golden-hued rocky formations, which jut out over the Paraná, and dense vegetation. The name Teyú-Cuaré, meaning "the lizard's cave", refers to a local legend that tells of a giant reptile that inhabited the region, attacking passing boats. In the river been gathered from the wild but was now grown on plantations for export as far as Chile and Peru; other products sold by the missions included cattle and their hides, sugar, cotton, tobacco, textiles, ceramics and timber. They also exported musical instruments, notably harps and organs from the Reducción de Trinidad in Paraguay.

By the end of the seventeenth century, the *reducciones* were among the most populous and successful areas of Argentina, and in the 1680s the Jesuits paid the Portuguese back for the earlier *bandeirante* attacks by sending three thousand Guaraní soldiers to join forces with Buenos Aires in their attack on the Portuguese city of Colónia do Sacramento on the Río de la Plata's eastern bank. By the 1730s, the larger missions such as Loreto (see p.351) and Yapeyú (see p.334) had over six thousand inhabitants – second only to Buenos Aires. Nonetheless, the mission enterprise was beginning to show cracks: a rising number of epidemics was depleting the population, and the Jesuits were becoming the subject of **political resentment**. Settlers in Paraguay and Corrientes were increasingly bitter at the Jesuit hold over the "supply" of Guaraní labour and also at the Jesuits' domination of the market with Buenos Aires for *yerba mate* and tobacco. These tensions led to the **Comunero Revolt** of the 1720s and 1730s, which culminated in a mass military invasion of the missions, followed by famine and kidnappings. Simultaneously, the previous climate of Crown tolerance towards the missions' almost complete autonomy also began to change. With the accession of Ferdinand VI to the Spanish throne in 1746 secular absolutism became the order of the day, and the Jesuits' power and loyalty began to be questioned. Local enemies of the missions took advantage of this, claiming that the Jesuits were hiding valuable silver mines within the *reducciones* and that foreign Jesuit priests were agents of Spain's enemies. In 1750, an exchange treaty between Spain and Portugal was proposed, according to which Spain would give up its most easterly mission in return for Colónia. The Jesuits and Guaraní put up considerable military resistance and the treaty was eventually abandoned in 1759, with the accession of Carlos III. The Jesuit victory proved a double-edged sword, however; the success of their resistance against the Crown only reinforced their image as dangerous rebels and, following earlier expulsions in France, Portugal and Brazil, the Jesuits were **expelled from Argentina** in 1767. Their magnificent buildings fell into disuse – lumps of stone were used for other constructions and the jungle did the rest – resulting in the ruins that can be visited today.

nearby lie a number of tiny islands, notably the Isla del Barco Hundido, whose name means "the island of the sunken boat". The park's most publicized feature is its high rocky cliff, the **Peñón Reina Victoria**, named for its supposed similarity to the profile of the British monarch. There is a wild **campsite** within the park.

En route to the park, a small **private reserve**, the **Osununú** ($1; ⓣ03752/156-44937), is a wonderful wild patch of forest managed by a friendly local, Porota, with some fantastic views over the river and islands and to the Parque Provincial. The reserve can be visited on a day-trip, when horse riding can be arranged. The two-hour or so walk to Osununú should be avoided at midday as there's no shade en route; a *remise* from San Ignacio will cost around $10.

Practicalities

Buses to San Ignacio all arrive at the western end of Avenida Sarmiento. It's not a terminal as such, but there's a kiosk whose friendly owner may agree to look after left luggage for a few hours. The **tourist office** (daily 7am–7pm) is at the main entrance road, the turn-off from RN-12.

Accommodation options in the town are limited but agreeable enough. The largest hotel is the *San Ignacio* (ⓣ03752/470047, ⓔhotelsanignacio@arnet.com.ar; ❸), on the corner of San Martín and Sarmiento 823. It's a slick modern place with comfortable en-suite rooms, all with a/c. There's also an adjoining restaurant. Several kilometres south, signposted from the centre, is *Club de Río* (ⓣ03755/404184, ⓦwww.clubderio.com; ❺), with comfortable *cabañas* set around a huge swimming pool, at a quiet location. Eternally popular with foreign travellers on a budget is *Hospedaje Salpeterer*, on Avenida Horacio Quiroga 50m west of the bus terminal (ⓣ03752/470362; ❷ with shared bathroom). It's a pleasant family house with basic but attractive rooms and access to kitchen facilities; tents can also be pitched for $5 per day. Towards the outskirts of the village, *Hospedaje El Descanso*, Pellegrini 270, around ten blocks south of the bus stop (ⓣ03752/470207; ❸), offers smart little *cabañas* with private bathrooms. The best **campsite** in town is at the *Club de Pesca y Deportes Acuáticos*, down at Puerto Nuevo (ⓣ03752/156-83411); tents can be pitched here on a bluff with a great view over the river to Paraguay. On Puerto Nuevo's beach, Playa del Sol, tents can be pitched behind the *cantina*.

Eating and drinking options are even more limited than accommodation; in addition to the passable restaurant in the *San Ignacio* there's a clutch of very similar large restaurants geared up for day-trippers around the entrance to the ruins. All of them serve snacks plus some more substantial dishes such as *parrilla*. One of the most popular is *Carpa Azul*, with a swimming pool and shower facilities, at Rivadavia 1295.

San Ignacio Miní

The most famous of all the *reducciones*, **San Ignacio Miní** (daily 7am–7.30pm or sunset if earlier) was originally founded in 1610 in the Guayrá region (see box, pp.352–353), in what is now Brazil. After the *bandeirantes* attacked the mission in 1631, the Jesuits moved thousands of miles southwards through the jungle, stopping several times en route at various temporary settlements before finally re-establishing the *reducción* at its present site in 1696.

The ruins occupy six blocks at the northeastern end of the village of San Ignacio: from the bus stop head east along Avenida Sarmiento for two blocks and turn left onto Rivadavia. Follow Rivadavia, which skirts around the ruins, for six blocks and then turn right onto Alberdi, where you'll find the entrance to the site. At the entrance, there's an excellent **Centro de Interpretación Regional** (ⓣ03752/470186) with a series of themed rooms depicting various aspects of Guaraní and mission life, plus a detailed maquette of the entire *reducción*. A separate smaller museum contains many pieces garnered from the ruins, including bits of walls, ceramic vessels and mortars.

Upon entering the settlement itself, you'll come first to rows of simple *viviendas*, or living quarters, a series of six to ten adjoining one-roomed structures, each of which housed a Guaraní family. Like all the mission settlements, these are constructed in a mixture of basaltic rock and sandstone. Passing between the *viviendas*, you arrive at the spacious Plaza de Armas, whose emerald grass provides a stunning contrast with the rich red hues of the sandstone. At the southern end of the plaza, and dominating the entire site, stands the magnificent facade of San Ignacio's **church**, designed, like Santa Ana's, by the Italian architect Brazanelli. The roof and much of the interior have long since crumbled away, but two large chunks of wall on either side of the entrance remain, rising out of the ruins like two great Baroque wings. Though somewhat eroded, many fine details can still be made out: two columns flank either side of the doorway and much of the walls' surface is covered with decorative bas-relief sculpture executed by Guaraní craftsmen; most striking are the pair of angels that face each other high up on either side of the entrance, while a more austere touch is added by the prominent insignia of the Jesuit order on the right-hand side of the entrance. Sadly, though, the visual impact of this imposing architectural relic has been somewhat diminished by the addition of wooden supports and crude scaffold steps between the two remaining sections.

To the left of the main entrance, you can wander around the **cloisters** and **priests' quarters**, where a number of other fine doorways and carvings remain. Particularly striking is the doorway connecting the cloisters with the church baptistry, flanked by ribbed columns with heavily moulded bases and still retaining a triangular pediment over the arched doorway. Look out too for a curiosity, the "*arbol corazón de piedra*", towards the exit – it's a tree whose trunk grew around a stone pillar, part of the ruins, completely enclosing the column at its core.

Note that the best light for photographing the church is in the morning, when the low light enhances its deep reddish hue. There are also **sound and light shows** – ask at the tourist office for details.

Iguazú Falls and around

Poor Niagara!

Eleanor Roosevelt

Composed of over 250 separate cascades, and straddling the border between Argentina and Brazil, the **Iguazú Falls** (or "Cataratas", as they are known locally) are quite simply the world's most dramatic waterfalls. Set among the exotic-looking subtropical forests of **Parque Nacional Iguazú** in Argentina, and **Parque Nacional do Iguaçu** in Brazil, the Falls tumble for a couple of kilometres over a complex set of cliffs from the Río Iguazú Superior to the Río Iguazú Inferior below. At their heart is the dizzying **Garganta del Diablo**, a powerhouse display of natural forces in which 1800 cubic metres of water per second hurtle over a three-kilometre semicircle of rock into the boiling river canyon 70m below.

The first Europeans to encounter the Falls, in 1542, were members of a Spanish expedition led by Cabeza de Vaca, who named them the Saltos de Santa María. Cabeza de Vaca had disembarked in Santa Catalina (Brazil) to investigate possible land and river links with the recently founded city of Asunción. For nearly five hundred years, however, the Falls remained practically forgotten in this remote corner of Argentina. It wasn't until the early twentieth century that tourism began to arrive, encouraged by the then governor of Misiones, Juan J. Lanusse. The first hotel was constructed in 1922, right by the Falls, and by the mid-twentieth century Iguazú was firmly on the tourist map. Today, the Falls are one of Latin America's major tourist attractions, with around 500,000 visitors a year entering the Argentine park and around twice that number entering on the Brazilian side.

The Falls are not the only attraction in the parks, though. The surrounding subtropical **forest** is packed with animals, birds and insects, and opportunities for spotting at least some of them are good. Even on the busy catwalks and paths that skirt the edges of the Falls you've a good chance of seeing gorgeously hued bright blue butterflies as big as your hand (just one of over 250 varieties that live around the Falls) and – especially on the Brazilian side – you will undoubtedly be pestered for food by greedy coatis (a raccoon relative). For a real close-up encounter with the parks' varied wildlife, though, head for the superb **Sendero Macuco**, a tranquil nature trail that winds through the forest on the Argentine side. Commonly spotted species along here include various species of toucans and shy capuchin monkeys.

The Falls are well worth seeing at any time of year, but the cooler months between March and November are regarded as the **best time to visit** the park – although the steamy heat, intense blue skies and sparkling spray in summer have undeniable appeal too. The rainy season runs from May to July, so you've a good chance of getting wet then, though the Falls are at their most spectacular after heavy rain, even if the water is often stained a rusty colour by the region's red soil. Easter and July are best avoided, since thousands of visitors arrive every day. Only twice in recent history have the Falls been known to disappoint. First in 1978 – when the *Sheraton Hotel* was opened within the park to coincide with Argentina's staging of the World Cup and visitors from all over the world were to be treated to a sight of the cascades – Iguazú chose to dry up completely, following a severe drought in Brazil. The same happened in mid-2006, when for several months the Falls were little more than a trickle. Whenever you visit, you should allow yourself a couple of days' leeway to be sure of seeing the Falls at their best.

Unless you stay within the national parks (both Brazil and Argentina have one luxury hotel each in their respective parks), and discounting the nasty Paraguayan city of Ciudad del Este, there are two towns at which you can base yourself. In Argentina, **Puerto Iguazú** lies approximately 18km northwest of

the park entrance and has a slightly sleepy, villagey feel, while on the Brazilian side the city of **Foz do Iguaçu**, much larger and with a modern, urban feel, is a good 20km northwest of the access to the park. There are pros and cons to staying in both places. If you've been travelling for a while in Argentina then the novelty factor of staying in Brazil might win out: Foz is neither the most beautiful nor most exotic of Brazilian cities, but it'll still give you the chance to hear another language, try some different food and sample some lively nightlife. On the negative side, Foz definitely feels less secure – something much exaggerated by Argentines, who warn you not to use Brazilian taxis, but nonetheless you should be on your guard in the city. Puerto Iguazú, on the other hand, is so low-key as to verge on dull, but with a tranquil and largely secure atmosphere that belies both its proximity to such a major tourist attraction and its location in an area rife with corruption. Puerto Iguazú is depressingly poor, however, apparently scarcely benefiting from tourist revenue and suffering from social problems such as begging and alcoholism. In fact most visitors never set foot in either town, taking refuge instead in one of the many comfortable hotels and complexes (all of which have their own restaurants) located on the roads out to each park and airport.

Puerto Iguazú and around

PUERTO IGUAZÚ, just under 300km northeast of Posadas, is a strange place. Its tropical vegetation and quiet streets seem more in keeping with the region than the high-rise concrete of the Brazilian city of Foz, but while the town's tranquillity provides a restful contrast to the goings-on just over the border, it also really lacks anything that would make you want to stay here for longer than necessary. Consequently, few tourists seem to do anything more than move between hotel, restaurant and bus terminal, and the town wears a slightly resigned air, to say the least – be prepared for an alarming number of barefoot street kids trying to persuade you to spare them a peso or two. That said, it has a certain simple charm that can grow on you, and of the three border towns (the commercial settlement of Ciudad del Este in Paraguay, notoriously unsavoury and unsafe, is definitely best avoided) Puerto Iguazú is the only one to have a really secure and accessible riverfront area from which you can take in the surrounding panorama.

Arrival and information

Puerto Iguazú's international **airport** lies around 20km southeast of the town, along RN-12 just past the entrance to the park. Aristóbulo del Valle (ⓣ03757/421996) runs a shuttle between the airport and the recently modernized **bus terminal**, on the corner of avenidas Córdoba and Misiones. There's no official tourist information kiosk here, though there are plenty of private companies who tout for your custom as you get off the bus. The most helpful of the numerous kiosks offering **information** is probably friendly Agencia Noelia (ⓣ03757/422722), which also sells the tickets for the bus to the national park. There's a restaurant in the terminal, a *locutorio* and a **left-luggage** service.

Puerto Iguazú's **tourist office** is at Av Aguirre 311 (daily 8am–9pm; ⓣ03757/420800). They have very little printed matter, though, other than a rather schematic map, so it's not a very useful port of call: most answers to practical transport and accommodation queries can be answered by the kiosks in the bus terminal. For more detailed information on the national park, its development and wildlife, there's a good library, the NEA, at Avenida Tres Fronteras (Mon–Fri 8am–4pm).

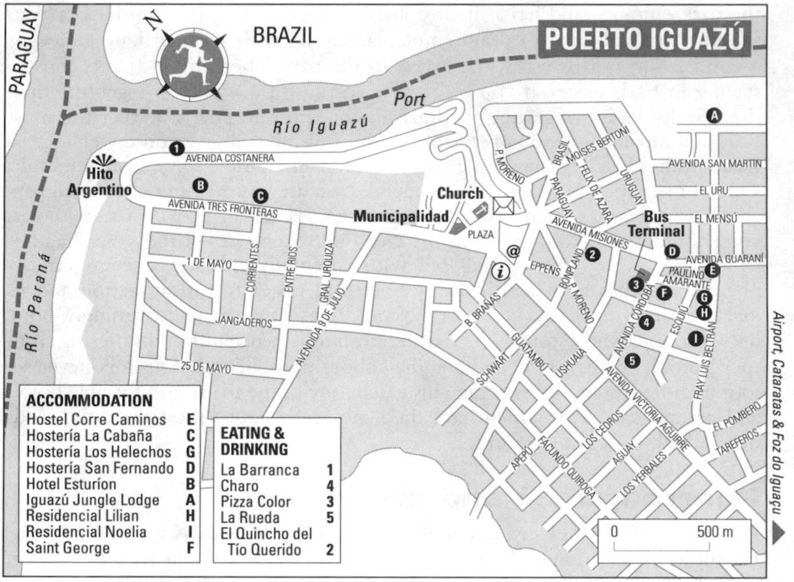

Accommodation

Puerto Iguazú has a decent range of fairly priced **accommodation**, with some particularly good deals at the budget end. The greatest concentration of inexpensive places is around the bus terminal, certainly the most convenient area to stay; there are also a few restaurants around here. Puerto Iguazú now has a few **youth hostels**: the best is *Hostel Inn* (ⓣ03757/421823, ⓦwww.hostel-inn.com; dorms $27–33 per person; ❺), a large, well-run place with different sized dorms, doubles and triples, in enormous grounds with a large swimming pool, at Km5 on RN-12. An honourable second place goes to the far more central but less well-appointed *Corre Caminos*, P. Amarante 48 (ⓣ03757/420967, ⓦwww.correcaminos.com.ar; dorms $20 per person; ❸), a friendly hostel with decent kitchens and sanitation, plus hammocks in a cool yard, just a stone's throw from the bus terminal. While a couple of good options are downtown, most of the more luxurious hotels are on the road towards the national park, and the airport. Reservations are a good idea at any time of year if you want to be sure of getting your first choice – during July and at Easter they're a must. Note that you may get a better deal at some of the more expensive hotels by booking a package, with flight, from a travel agency in Buenos Aires. The best-organized **campsite** is large and well-equipped *Camping Viejo Americano* (ⓣ03757/420190), about 5km out of town along RN-12 towards the national park, with showers, store, telephone and swimming pool. The campsite can be reached on the Cataratas bus or by taxi (around $5 from terminal). You are not allowed to camp inside the park.

Hostería La Cabaña Av Tres Fronteras 434 ⓣ03757/420564, ⓔlacabana@hostels.org.ar. Quiet, motel-style place affiliated to Hostelling International and with comfortable if slightly musty rooms. ❺

Hostería Los Helechos Paulino Amarante 76 ⓣ03757/420338, ⓦwww.hosterialoshelechos.com.ar. Slick and well-maintained hotel on a quiet street near the bus terminal. Small but attractive rooms with TV and a/c. There's an excellent buffet breakfast with tropical fruit, and a small swimming pool. ③

Hostería San Fernando Av Córdoba and Guaraní ⓣ03757/421429. Friendly hotel opposite the bus terminal. Simple, pleasant rooms all with fan, much improved following renovation. Breakfast included. ④

Hotel Cataratas RN-12, 4km from Puerto Iguazú ⓣ03757/421100, ⓦwww.hotelcataratas.com. Spacious and quietly luxurious hotel on the way to the *cataratas*. Large outdoor swimming pool and small gym. Attractive rooms with big comfortable beds. ⑧

Hotel Esturión Av Tres Fronteras 650 ⓣ03757/421429, ⓦwww.hotelesturion.com. With fine river views, a large swimming pool, spacious, cool rooms and decks and gardens brimming with native flora, this extremely professional hotel has a definite tropical feel to it. ⑧–⑨

Hotel Saint George Av Córdoba 148 ⓣ03757/420633, ⓦwww.hotelsaintgeorge.com. The best of Iguazú's mid-range hotels, the *Saint George* is a recently revamped and courteous hotel with some exceptionally light and attractive first-floor rooms with balconies overlooking the swimming pool. Good restaurant downstairs and buffet breakfast with fresh fruit included in room rate. ⑦

Iguazú Grand Hotel RN-12 Km1640 ⓣ03757/498050, ⓦwww.iguazugrandhotel.com. This is the place to stay for film-star glamour – a fabulously luxurious hotel with enormous suites supplied with everything from CD players to glossy picture books on Misiones. Landscaped outdoor pool and two very good restaurants. Weekends are reserved for high-rolling gamblers whom the hotel flies in from São Paulo and Buenos Aires to play at the adjoining casino. Rates start at US$360.

Iguazú Jungle Lodge Hipólito Irigoyen and San Lorenzo ⓣ03757/420600, ⓦwww.iguazujunglelodge.com. Simply fabulous *cabañas* sleeping up to seven – plus a couple of doubles – in a landscaped plot overlooking the jungle at the edge of the village. Extremely well equipped and tastefully appointed, they are really luxurious houses, with ample verandahs, a huge kitchen and barbecue facilities. Large swimming pool and decent breakfasts served either poolside or in the *cabañas*. ⑦–⑧

Residencial Lilian Fray Luis Beltrán 183 ⓣ03757/420968. Spotless, light and airy rooms with good fans and modern bathrooms. ⑤

Residencial Noelia Fray Luis Beltrán 119 ⓣ03757/420729. The best deal in Iguazú, this friendly, family-run place largely caters to backpackers. Scrupulously maintained three- and four-bed rooms with fans and private bathroom and breakfast of toast, fruit and coffee brought to your room or the shady patio. ②

Sheraton International Iguazú Parque Nacional Iguazú ⓣ03757/491800, ⓦwww.iguazufalls.com. Big, ugly modern hotel inside the national park. The crime of its construction during the last dictatorship is compounded by the fact that you only get a decent view of the Falls from a few of its rooms (for which you pay more), but it has to be admitted it is well located from the guests' viewpoint. Rates start at US$225.

The Town

A small town of around 30,000 inhabitants, Puerto Iguazú sits high above the meeting of the Paraná and Iguazú rivers, at the most northern extremity of Misiones Province. The town is bisected diagonally by **Avenida Victoria Aguirre**, which runs from Puerto Iguazú's modest **port** out towards RN-12 and the national park. You wouldn't exactly call Iguazú's **town centre** bustling, but most of what goes on goes on around the intersection of Avenida Aguirre, Calle Brasil and Calle Ingeniero Gustavo Eppens. From here the Avenida Tres Fronteras runs west for 1.5km to the **Hito Argentino de las Tres Fronteras**, a vantage point over the rivers with views over to Brazil and Paraguay that is marked by an obelisk painted in the colours of the Argentine flag; similar markers across the rivers in the neighbouring countries are painted in their national colours, too. An alternative route to the Hito is via Avenida Aguirre, which forks right just before the town's triangular grassy plaza. From here, Avenida Aguirre snakes down through a thickly wooded area of town to the port area; you can then follow the pleasant Avenida Costanera, popular with joggers and cyclists, left uphill towards the Hito.

There is an unusual attraction on the outskirts of town: 4km along RN-12 towards the national park, rustic signposts direct you to **La Aripuca**

(8am–sunset; ⓣ03757/423488; $5, children free). An *aripuca* is an indigenous wooden trap used in the region to catch birds; La Aripuca is a giant replica of the trap, standing over 10m high and constructed out of 29 species of trees native to Misiones Province (all obtained through unavoidable felling or from victims of thunderstorms). Above all, La Aripuca is a kind of eco-symbol: the friendly German- and English-speaking family who constructed the strange monument hope to change visitors' conscience about the environment through tours designed to explain the value and significance of these trees.

Eating, drinking and nightlife

Puerto Iguazú doesn't have a particularly exciting range of **restaurants**, with most of them seemingly fond of regaling customers with either television or live music – possibly to drown out the lack of atmosphere. Most of the better places to eat are grouped near the bus terminal. Iguazú's not the best place in Argentina for meat but there's a *parrillada* with reasonable prices, *Charo*, at Av Córdoba 106. *La Rueda*, a short walk along the same avenue towards its junction with Avenida V. Aguirre, and *El Quincho del Tío Querido*, next door to the *Libertador* hotel on Calle Bompland, both also offer grilled river fish – the former in especially congenial surroundings, all rustic wood and old photos. There's a decent restaurant inside the *Hotel Saint George*, offering a reasonably priced *menú turístico*. The bright and modern *Pizza Color*, Av Córdoba 135, does excellent *pizza a la piedra* and good salads.

For **drinking** and **nightlife**, the choice is even more limited – indeed many locals head over to Brazil for a good night out. There's a handful of bars-cum-nightclubs on Calle Brasil just before the junction with Aguirre. There's an older, more relaxed crowd at *La Barranca* pub along the Avenida Río Iguazú, just east of the Hito Tres Fronteras, a welcoming bar with good views over the river to Brazil and Paraguay and live music on Friday and Saturday nights – usually folk or Brazilian music.

Listings

Airlines Aerolíneas Argentinas/Austral, Av Aguirre and B. Brañas ⓣ03757/420168 and at the airport ⓣ03757/420915.
Banks and exchange There are now several ATMs in Puerto Iguazú. The only place to change travellers' cheques is Argecam, Av Aguirre 562 ⓣ03757/420273 (daily 7am–6.30pm).
Car rental Ansa International Rent a Car, *Hotel Esturión*, Av Tres Fronteras 650 ⓣ03757/420100; Localiza, Av Aguirre 271 ⓣ03757/422744; VIP Rent a Car, Av Aguirre 211 ⓣ03757/420289.
Consulates Brazil, Córdoba 264 ⓣ03757/421348 (Mon–Fri 8am–1pm).
Internet access Telecentro at the corner of Av Victoria Aguirre and Brasil.
Laundry Lava Rap Ljuba, corner of Misiones and Bompland.
Post office Puerto Iguazú's main post office is at Av San Martín 780, though there's a more convenient branch inside the Telecabinas on the corner of Av Aguirre and Brasil.
Taxis Remises Centro, Gustavo Eppens 210 ⓣ03757/420907; Agencia Remise La Estrella, Av Córdoba 42 ⓣ03757/423500.
Telephones Telecentro at the corner of Av Aguirre and Brasil.
Travel agents and tour operators Aguas Grandes, Mariano Moreno 58 ⓣ03757/421140, ⓔaguasgrandes@interiguazu.com.ar, with French-, English- and Italian-speaking guides; Caracol, Av Victoria Aguirre 653 ⓣ03757/420064, ⓔcaracol.turismo@foznet.com.br; Cuenca del Plata, Paulino Amarante 76 ⓣ03757/421062, ⓔcuencadelplata@cuencadelplata.com; Sol Iguazú Turismo, Av Aguirre 316 ⓣ03757/421147, ⓔsoliguazu@soliguazu.com; Turismo Dick, Av Aguirre 226 ⓣ03757/420778, ⓔturismodick@interiguazu.com.ar.

Foz do Iguaçu (Brazil)

The modern city of **FOZ DO IGUAÇU** faces its Argentine counterpart, Puerto Iguazú, across the Río Iguazú and is separated from the unappealing Paraguayan city of Ciudad del Este, 7km northwest across the Río Paraná, by the Ponte da Amizade/Puente de la Amistad. Until the 1970s, Foz had only around 30,000 inhabitants, but its population soared with the construction of the titanic Itaipú Dam. Today, the city has over 400,000 residents and though the dam is still an important source of employment, the vast majority of the them are involved in the tourism industry. In addition to servicing the hundreds of thousands of tourists who pass through every year on their way to the Falls, Foz gains a lot of business as a retail outlet for Argentines and Brazilians in search of bargain clothes and shoes. The town's growth is evident around its sprawling outskirts and in its scattering of high-rise buildings, but the city centre remains a fairly modest and compact area.

Foz is laid out on a fairly regular grid, with the main access route from Argentina being via the **Avenida das Cataratas**, which heads into town from the southeast, joining up with Avenida Jorge Schimmelpfeng, off which the town's main drag, Avenida Juscelino Kubitschek (often referred to as Avenida JK – *jota ka*) runs north towards Paraguay. The main shopping centre, where you'll also find plenty of banks, is Avenida Brasil, which runs parallel to Avenida Juscelino Kubitschek, one block east.

You'll hear a lot about the supposed dangers of Foz on the Argentine side, but the central area around the local bus terminal and shops is normally safe during the day, and the vast majority of people are welcoming and friendly in a way that belies the volume of tourists they are accustomed to seeing. You should, however, avoid heading down to the river below the bus terminal, where there is a shantytown whose inhabitants may be less hospitable.

Practicalities

Foz's local **bus terminal**, the arrival point for buses from Argentina, is at the intersection of avenidas Juscelino Kubitschek and República Argentina. From here, Transbalan buses leave approximately every 20–30 minutes for the airport and Falls (7am–6pm). The city centre is easy to walk around, though a taxi isn't a bad idea at night if you feel at all cautious. Be warned, though, that taxis are relatively expensive here. Foz's **tourist information** service is vastly superior to that of Puerto Iguazú, with excellent maps, transport information and accommodation listings doled out by friendly and helpful staff. There are various offices throughout the town but the best is on the corner of Avenida Jorge Schimmelpfeng and Rua Benjamin Constant (daily 7am–11pm; Ⓣ(0055)45/574-2196, Ⓦwww.fozdoiguacu.pr.gov.br).

Accommodation, ranging from campsites and youth hostels to five-star hotels, is abundant in Foz but, if the Brazilian real (R$) maintains its exchange rate (around two to the US dollar), not very good value, unless you negotiate a promotion or book through an agent. Close to the terminal, decent *Hotel del Rey*, Rua Tarobá 1020 (Ⓣ(0055)45/523-2027, Ⓦwww.hoteldelreyfoz.com.br; ❺), offers clean, uncluttered en-suite rooms with good a/c and a tiny outdoor swimming pool; an excellent buffet breakfast is included. Favoured by backpackers, *Pousada da Laura*, Rua Naipi 629 (Ⓣ(0055)45/574-3628; R$20 per person; ❹), offers a friendly family atmosphere and simple rooms on a quiet street a few blocks southwest of the terminal. There's a good youth hostel, *Paudimar Campestre*, at Rua Rui Barbosa 634 (Ⓣ(0055)45/574-5503, Ⓦwww.paudimar.com.br; R$20 per person with breakfast), near the local bus terminal; it's a secure and very friendly place with hotel-style bedrooms, a kitchen and

Internet facilities. Modern *Foz Presidente*, Rua Xavier da Silva 1000 (ⓣ(0055)45/572-4450, ⓦwww.fozpresidentehoteis.com.br; ❻) has spacious rooms with big comfortable beds and an attractive outdoor swimming pool and sunbathing area. The fabulous *Hotel Tropical das Cataratas* (ⓣ(0055)45/521-7000, ⓦwww.tropicalhotel.com.br; rates from US$100), inside the national park itself, just metres from the Falls, is a charming old building, with cool tiled floors and elegantly decorated rooms, packing in all the style that the *Sheraton* on the Argentine side lacks. There's a great outdoor swimming pool and an excellent restaurant. The best place to camp is at *Camping Club do Brasil* (ⓣ(0055)45/574-1310; R$10 per person) has a swimming pool, restaurant and laundry area, all set in attractive forested grounds.

There are plenty of inexpensive buffet-style **restaurants** along central Rua Marechal Deodoro, while the route out to the Cataratas is lined with *churrascarias*, Brazil's version of the *parrilla*, specializing in *espeto corrido*, in which hunks of meat are carved onto your plate by waiters who pass from table to table. If you've been travelling in Argentina, though, you're less likely to be impressed by the meat, much of it from the zebu – a kind of humped ox, originally from India, and far less appetizing than Argentina's beef – than by the buffet accompaniment of fresh salads, rice, beans and plantain: a typical example is *Rafain*, on Avenida das Cataratas, Km6.5. The one real gastronomic highpoint in Foz is provided by *Tempero da Bahia*, Av Paraná 1419 (evenings only), which specializes in the exquisite cuisine of northeastern Brazil, with dishes such as *moqueca de peixe*, a delicious fish stew flavoured with palm oil and coconut milk, and spicy *acarajé*, a fried bean mix with shrimp and hot pepper. There's outdoor seating overlooking a quiet street and excellent live Brazilian guitar music every night.

The Falls and the two national parks

The vast majority of the **Iguazú Falls** themselves lie on the Argentine side of the border, within the Parque Nacional Iguazú. This side offers the most extensive experience of the Cataratas, thanks to its well-thought-out system of trails and catwalks taking you both below and above them – most notably to the Garganta del Diablo. The surrounding forest also offers excellent opportunities to discover the region's wildlife. To complete your trip to Iguazú, however, you should also try and visit the Brazilian side. Though it offers a more passive experience, the view is more panoramic and the photography opportunities are amazing.

The Argentine side

The **Parque Nacional Iguazú** lies 18km southeast of Puerto Iguazú, along RN-12. A bus runs to the park every hour from the bus terminal in town, with the first one leaving at 7.30am and the last one returning at 8pm. The bus stops at the entrance to the park, where you have to get off and pay an entrance fee of $30 (for foreigners; keep your ticket and its stamp, which will entitle you to a 50 percent discount the following day), before it leaves you at the visitors' centre.

As you get off the bus within the park, you're greeted by the sound of rushing water from the Falls, the first of which lies just a few hundred metres away. There's a **visitors' centre** to the left of the bus stop, where you can pick up maps and information leaflets. There's also a small but interesting museum here with photographs and stuffed examples of the park's wildlife. Various operators, such as Iguazú Jungle Explorer (ⓣ03757/421600,

△ Iguazú Falls

Ⓦwww.iguazujungleexplorer.com), will accost you and tempt you with different trips and tours, involving trucks, boats and walks, ranging from $20 to $90, depending on their length and the transport involved. Take time to let them explain – most of the young staff speak English and other languages in addition to Spanish – and to decide how best to use your time and money. All boat rides are definitely worth it, for the exhilarating experience of coming so close up to the gush of the Falls.

From the visitors' centre, the so-called *Sendero Verde* ("Green Path") or the *Tren de la selva* ("Jungle Train") both lead to the Estación Cataratas, from where two well-signposted trails, formed by a series of catwalks and paths, take you past the Falls. A recommended approach is probably to tackle the **Paseo Superior** first, along a short trail through the forest above the first few waterfalls. For more drama, segue into the **Paseo Inferior**, which winds down through the forest before bringing you within metres of some of the smaller but still spectacular waterfalls – notably **Saltos Ramírez** and **Bossetti** – which run along the western side of the river. Around the waterfalls, look out for the swallow-like *vencejo*, a remarkable small bird that, seemingly impossibly, makes its nest behind the gushing torrents. As you descend the path, gaps in the vegetation offer great views across the Falls: photo opportunities are so numerous that you might want to remind yourself every now and then to put your camera down and just enjoy the experience of looking and listening. Even better, plan two days at the Falls and spend just one of them looking round, then return to record the experience on film. Note that new catwalks have made **wheelchair access** to all of the Paseo Superior and much of the Paseo Inferior possible, although there is little room to turn round in many sections.

Another signposted trail leads down to the jetty from where a regular free boat service leaves for **Isla San Martín**, a gorgeous high rocky island in the middle of the river. More trails circumnavigate the island, through thick vegetation and past emerald green pools. There's a small sandy beach at the northern end of the island, though bathing is allowed only in summer. From the departure point to Isla San Martín, river conditions permitting, you can also go on short **boat trips** ($40) on which you get really close up to the Falls, while the crew delight in treating you to a thorough soaking – for some this is the best fun to be had (provided they left behind their expensive cameras, in safe keeping) but others find this impromptu shower is not quite compensation for the rather cursory nature of the excursion. The same company, which maintains an information post near the visitors' centre, also organizes longer, better-value excursions combining jeep trips through the forest with boat trips along the rapids north of the Falls.

To visit the **Garganta del Diablo** ("Devil's Throat"), you must return to the Estación Cataratas and take the train to the Estación Garganta del Diablo, 3km southeast. From here a catwalk with a small viewing platform takes you to within just a few metres of the staggering, sheer drop of water formed by the union of several immensely powerful waterfalls around a kind of horseshoe. As the water crashes over the edge, it plunges into a dazzling opaque whiteness in which it is impossible to distinguish mist from water. The *vencejos* often swirl around the waterfall in all directions, forming giant swarms that sometimes swoop up towards you and performing miraculous acrobatic twists and turns – quite a sight. If you're bringing your camera, make sure you've an airtight bag to stash it in, as the platform is invariably showered with a fine spray.

Heading west from the visitors' centre, a well-marked trail leads to the start of the **Sendero Macuco**, a four-kilometre nature trail down to the lower banks of the Río Iguazú, past a waterfall, the **Salto Arrechea**, where there is a lovely secluded bathing spot. The majority of the trail is along level ground, through a dense wood. Despite appearances, this is not virgin forest. In fact, it is in a process of recuperation: advances in the navigation of the Upper Paraná – the section of the river that runs along the northern border of Corrientes and Misiones – in the early twentieth century allowed access to these previously impenetrable lands and economic exploitation of their valuable timber began. In the 1920s, the region was totally exploited and stripped of its best species and traversed by roads. Only since the creation of the park in 1943 has the forest been protected.

Today, the forest is composed of several layers of vegetation. Towering above the forest floor is the rare and imposing *palo rosa*, which can grow to 40m and is identifiable by its pale straight trunk that divides into twisting branches higher up, topped by bushy foliage. At a lower level, various species of palm flourish, notably the *pindó* palm and the palmito, much coveted for its edible core, which often grows in the shade of the *palo rosa*. Epiphytes, which use the taller trees for support but are not parasitic, also abound as does the *guaypoy*, aptly known as the strangler fig, since it eventually asphyxiates the trees around which it grows. You will also see lianas, which hang from the trees in incredibly regular plaits and have apt popular names such as *escalera de mono*, or "monkey's ladder". Closer still to the ground there is a stratum of shrubs, some of them with edible fruit, such as the pitanga. Ground cover is dominated by various fern species.

The best time to spot wildlife is either early evening or late afternoon, when there are fewer visitors and the jungle's numerous birds and mammals are at their most active: at times the screech of birds and monkeys can be almost cacophonic. At all times, you have the best chance of seeing wildlife by treading as silently as possible, and by scanning the surrounding trees for signs of movement. Your most likely reward will be groups of agile capuchin monkeys, with a distinctive black "cowl", like that of the monks they are named after. Larger, lumbering black howler monkeys make for a rarer sight, though their deep growl can be heard for some distance. Along the ground, look out for the tiny corzuela deer. Unfortunately, you've little chance of seeing the park's most dramatic wildlife, large cats such as the puma and the jaguar or the tapir, a large-hoofed mammal with a short, flexible snout. Toucans, however, are commonly spotted; other birds that can be seen in the forest include the solitary Black Cacique, which makes its nest in the *pindó* palm; various species of woodpecker and the striking Crested Yacutinga. Of the forest's many butterflies, the most striking are those of the *Morphidae* family, whose large wings are a dazzling metallic blue.

The Brazilian side

You'll only need a few hours on the **Brazilian side**, but it's worth crossing in order to take photos of the Falls – particularly in the morning – as it provides you with a superb panorama of the points you will have visited close-up in Argentina.

You will need to cross to Brazil via the Ponte Presidente Tancredo Neves, the bridge that crosses the Río Iguazú between the two towns. There are international buses (companies Pluma, El Práctico, Itaipú and Nuestra Señora de Asunción) every 45min from Puerto Iguazú to Foz do Iguaçu between about 6.20am and 7pm. Immigration formalities take place on the Brazilian side of the bridge, where you are given first an exit stamp for Argentina and are then stamped into Brazil. Standard "wisdom" among many travellers is that it's unnecessary to get either exit and entry stamps or visas when travelling between Argentina and Brazil for the day. However, the official line is that everyone, apart from Argentines, Brazilians and Paraguayans, must acquire the necessary stamps and visas, even if crossing the border for only a few hours. In practice you may well get away without these formalities, but you're also setting yourself up for possible problems and it's worth taking the trouble to get stamped in and out. If you do cross several times between the two countries, make sure that you are given enough days when returning to Argentina to continue your journey, as passport control often gives only thirty days here – though you can ask for the normal ninety.

Once in Brazil, you can join the Brazilian Cataratas bus by getting off just east of immigration on the Brazilian side on Avenida das Cataras, the access road to the Falls, but it's more straightforward (if slightly more time-consuming) to head into Foz itself and get on the bus there (see p.361). You'll need a small supply of the Brazilian currency, the real, both for the bus and for entrance to the park itself. Change can be obtained from the Micki kiosk in Puerto Iguazú's bus terminal or from various kiosks at Foz's terminal. There's also a change facility and an ATM just before the Brazilian entrance to the park. Note that between November and February Brazil is one hour ahead of Argentina – this time difference could be vital for making sure you catch the last bus back into town. The Parque Nacional do Iguazú lies around 20km southeast of Foz. Buses stop at the entrance to the park, where an entrance fee of R$20.15 is payable, before dropping you just outside the *Hotel Tropical das Cataratas* (see p.362). From here a walkway takes you high along the side of the river; it is punctuated by various viewing platforms from where you can take in most of the Argentine Falls, the river canyon and Isla San Martín. Along the path, stripe-tailed coatis accost visitors, begging for food – ignore them, but don't let them run off with your belongings. The one-and-a-half-kilometre path culminates in a spectacular walkway offering fantastic views of the Garganta del Diablo and of the Brazilian Santo Salto Maria, beneath the viewing platform and surrounded by an almost continuous rainbow created by myriad water droplets. Watch out for spray here and carry a plastic bag to protect your camera. At the end of the walkway you can take an elevator to the top of a cliff for more good views.

From a point opposite the hotel, helicopter flights are offered over the Falls. The view from the helicopters is of course superb, but they're a noisy and intrusive presence in the surrounding area and seriously disruptive to local wildlife: Argentina has banned them from flying over its side. A less controversial excursion is offered by Macuco Safari de Barco (Ⓣ(0055)45/574-4244), which maintains an information post inside the park, 3km north of the Falls area. The hour-and-a-half excursion combines a jeep trip through the forest, followed by a short walk and a boat trip onto the rapids of the lower river area.

If you've not been lucky enough to see some of Iguazú's exotic birds at the Falls themselves, head for the **Parque Das Aves**, 300m north of the park entrance (daily 8.30am–6.30pm; Ⓣ(0055)45/523-1007, Ⓦwww.parquedasaves.com.br), where walk-through aviaries allow for close encounters with some of the most stunning of them. The first of these is populated with various smaller species such as the noisy Bare-throated Bellbird, with a weird resonant call, the bright blue Sugar Bird and the Blue-black Grosbeak. For most people, though, the highlight is a sighting of the bold toucans – almost comically keen to have their photo taken.

Oberá and the Saltos del Moconá

Just over 100km east of Posadas via RN-12 and RP-103, the town of **Oberá** acts as the hub of central Misiones and can be a useful stopover for anyone crossing the province from east to west, since RP-103 is one of the main links between RN-12 and more scenic RN-14, which currently peters out in the north of the province near San Pedro. Over 180km northeast, the quiet village of **El Soberbio** lies in one of the province's most striking areas, with some of the finest scenery in the whole region; at this border Brazil and Argentina sit like plumped-up cushions on either side of the curvaceous Río Uruguay. El Soberbio is also the point of access for the **Saltos de Moconá**, an unusual but decidedly uncooperative set of waterfalls.

Oberá

OBERÁ, Misiones' second city, is an orderly modern settlement sitting amidst the province's gentle central sierras. The town was first settled in the early twentieth century by Swedish and then Swiss immigrants who had come to Brazil but stayed there for less than a generation. Others from other countries followed, and today Oberá boasts of having fourteen different ethnic communities among its population of 40,000, including Ukrainians, Russians, French and Japanese.

Despite a smattering of Russian Orthodox and Ukrainian churches – and Latin America's only Swedish cemetery – you probably wouldn't actually be that aware of Oberá's cosmopolitan mix on a brief visit. During the second week of September, however, the city runs an enjoyable **Fiesta Nacional del Inmigrante**, with a week-long programme of international dances, music and food. It takes place in the Parque de las Naciones, a large park on the eastern side of town mainly notable for its collection of houses representing each of the communities. These come to life at the weekend, when many of them open as restaurants, serving national dishes.

It's easy to find your way around town: the bus terminal lies just one block west of wide Avenida Sarmiento, which runs through the centre of town roughly north–south. Running diagonally east from Avenida Sarmiento, Avenida Libertad heads out towards RN-14. At the intersection of Avenida Sarmiento and Avenida Libertad stands the very austere modern Gothic **Iglesia San Antonio**, a pristine white church whose rather curious electronic chime is an insistent presence in the town centre. Two blocks southeast of the terminal, Oberá's central square, the quiet and grassy **Plaza San Martín** is unusually bereft of either a municipalidad (it's on the corner of Jujuy and Avenida Sarmiento) or a church. In the evening, there's more life around Plazoleta Güemes, which lies in front of the Iglesia San Antonio.

Practicalities

Oberá's **bus terminal** is right in the centre of town on the corner of José Ingenieros and G. Barreiro. There are toilets, left-luggage facilities and a rather dingy waiting room. For a really offbeat way to kill time between buses, there's also the **Museo de Ciencias Naturales** (Mon–Fri 6.30am–noon & 1–7pm, Sat 7am–noon; free) with a particularly gruesome collection of stuffed and pickled animals including a two-headed cow from Santa Fe. The moth-eaten and insalubrious birds in particular make the "do not touch" signs somewhat superfluous. The **tourist office** is on the corner of Avenida Libertad and Entre Ríos, a couple of blocks east of the terminal (Mon–Sat 8am–9pm; ⓣ03755/421808, ⓔmuniobera@arnet.com.ar).

Accommodation in Oberá is adequate but – with a couple of exceptions – a little on the drab side. Many commercial travellers pass through the town, meaning that places are more likely to be booked up during the week than at weekends. The most upmarket place in Oberá is *Cabañas del Parque*, out in the Parque de las Naciones, on the corner of Ucrania and Tronador (ⓣ03755/426000; ❺–❻). Looking more like suburban villas than typical *cabañas*, the *Cabañas del Parque* make up for their rather dreary exteriors with rustic but comfortable interiors equipped with such luxuries as mini-bars, a/c, cable TV and telephone; there's also a large swimming pool. The handful of mid-range hotels around the town centre are very similar in style, with

The Green Corridor

Apart from the famous red of its laterite soil, the dominant colour in Misiones is green: *mate*, tobacco, tea, citrus groves and some of the country's densest jungle offer every possible shade of the colour. By getting off the beaten tracks that are RN-12 and RN-14 – which means having your own transport – you can see some of the province's lushest, least spoilt landscapes along what is promoted as the **Corredor Verde**, or Green Corridor. The name does not refer to any single route but to the last remaining swathe of **Selva Misionera**: a hilly sliver of thick native forest, dotted with small settlements, squeezed between the province's two main trunk highways, and offered a certain level of state protection – it covers over three thousand square kilometres in all. Several roads criss-cross this beautiful countryside: RP-5 (for Oberá), RP-6, RP-16 and RP-17, but the most rewarding in terms of scenery are the newly paved RP-11, which joins El Alcázar with Dos de Mayo – before leading to San Vicente and El Soberbio – and the even more spectacular RP-7, which starts at Jardín América, on RN-12, and takes you over a rocky pass offering wonderful panoramas of the jungle canopy, and down into the strange town of Aristóbulo del Valle, on RN-14, where all of the inhabitants' energy seems to have gone into decorating the main avenue with contemporary sculptures.

modern, slightly box-like rooms, all with private bathrooms: try basic *Hotel Vito I*, Corrientes 56 (ⓣ03755/421892; ❷); *Cuatro Pinos*, Av Sarmiento 853 (ⓣ03755/425102; ❷), which does not offer breakfast; or optimistically named *Premier*, 9 de Julio 1164 (ⓣ03755/406171; ❸). If you have your own transport, it might be worth heading down to **Leandro N. Alem**, only 32km south, where the excellent *Hotel Portal de Alem* (ⓣ03754/420600, ⓦwww.portadealem.com.ar; ❺–❻) sits along RN-14; set among manicured lawns, this attractive place offers smart rooms, friendly service, mod cons and a beautiful swimming pool. There's also an exceptionally well-maintained but pleasingly natural **campsite**, one of the best in Misiones, at Salto Berrondo, 6km west of town towards Posadas along RP-103 ($2 entrance, plus $3 per tent; sometimes free during quiet periods). The campsite's chief attraction is a gorgeous **waterfall**, the Salto Berrondo, which tumbles down into a lovely, shady bathing pool. There's also an artificial swimming pool, a barbecue area and plenty of room to pitch your tent. Local **buses** marked "Guaraní" or "Cementerio" go to Salto Berrondo, as do long-distance buses towards Posadas.

As far as eating goes, you can try *yacaré* and other well-prepared dishes at *Engüete*, in a rather unappealing part of town at A. Nuñez Cabeza de Vaca 340, eight blocks east of the intersection of avenidas Sarmiento and Libertad. There's also an exceptionally good buffet restaurant, the *Moscow*, near the corner of Avenida Sarmiento and Salta, with a cool, spotless interior and plenty of fresh salads, along with meat, fish and pasta dishes prepared *à la minute*. On the corner of Entre Ríos and 9 de Julio, *Juan Alfredo* offers good steaks, pastas and *milanesas* while the best *parrillada* is *Los Troncos*, on RN-14, which does a very good-value *tenedor libre*.

El Soberbio and the Saltos del Moconá

One of Argentina's strangest sights, the **Saltos del Moconá** are made up of nearly 3km of immensely powerful waterfalls which spill down the middle of the Río Uruguay, tumbling from a raised riverbed in Argentina into a 90-metre river canyon in Brazil. The split-level waterfalls – the longest of their kind in the world – are formed by the meeting of the Uruguay and Pepirí-Guazú rivers just upstream of a dramatic gorge. As the waters encounter this geological quirk, they "split" once again, with one branch flowing downstream along the western side of the gorge and the other plunging down into it. This phenomenon is visible only under certain conditions: if water levels are low, all the water is diverted into the gorge, while if water levels are high the river evens itself out. At a critical point in between, however, the Saltos magically emerge, as water from the higher level cascades down into the gorge running alongside, creating a curtain of rushing water between three and thirteen metres high. The incredible force of the water as it hurtles over the edge of the gorge before continuing downstream explains its Guaraní name – *moconá* means "he who swallows everything".

El Soberbio

EL SOBERBIO, the main gateway to the Saltos del Moconá, is perched on the banks of the Río Uruguay, 170km east of Oberá, via RN-14 to San Vicente and then RP-212. The village's charm is derived not so much from its buildings, which are unassuming modern constructions, but from its gorgeous riverside setting, amidst lush undulating sierras. There's also an intriguing **mix of cultures** – sunburnt, blond-haired Polish and German immigrants rub shoulders with Argentines of Spanish and Italian descent, all with a hefty dose of Brazilian culture thrown in. Locals have a refreshingly cavalier attitude to the idea of national boundaries, popping over to Brazil for Saturday-night dances and listening to Brazilian country music on the radio; Portuguese is often the main language at home.

El Soberbio's **layout** is simple: Avenida Rivadavia runs into the village from the northwest, ending at the small **ferry terminal** (for departures to Brazil see box, p.350) down on the riverfront. In the centre of the village, a few blocks back from the river, Avenida San Martín crosses Avenida Rivadavia and leads north towards the Saltos. A large grassy **plaza** lies at the intersection of these two streets.

El Soberbio's modest **bus terminal** is right in the village centre at the intersection of Avenida San Martín and Avenida Rivadavia. There's a sporadically open **tourist information** kiosk on Avenida Rivadavia as you head into the centre (ⓣ03755/495133). You're best off staying at one of the posadas and lodges deep in the nearby jungle (see box below); otherwise, the least offensive of the poor **accommodation** in the village itself is the run-down and grossly overpriced *Hostería Puesto del Sol*, sited high above the village at the southern end of Calle Suipacha (ⓣ03755/495161, ⓦwww.hostpuestadelsol.com.ar; ⑥). The rustic rooms with very noisy a/c have French windows opening onto a verandah from where there are great views over the valley and the river, its only saving grace. There's also an outdoor pool with an unusual crazy-paved lining and a bar/restaurant; breakfast, for what it is worth, is included in the price.

Posadas and lodges in the Selva Misionera

Most **accommodation** in the vicinity of the Saltos del Moconá is no great shakes, to say the least – but there are three truly wonderful options tucked away in the dense jungle of the Selva Misionera. To experience the awe-inspiring beauty of this remote, virgin jungle at its best, it is worth treating yourself to a couple of days being pampered at one – or all three – of them. Access is difficult even in a 4WD, so you're advised to fork out the extra for a transfer to and from your accommodation; if you have a vehicle they will arrange for its safekeeping while you are away. All offer full-board packages that usually include other activities, such as walking, climbing, riding, boating or swimming.

Posada La Misión (ⓣ011/154-9278343 or 03755/155-20783, ⓦwww.posadalamision.com.ar; ⑦) at Ruta Costera 2, Km40, Puerto Paraíso, 45km north of El Soberbio on the banks of the Río Uruguay, is extremely convenient for visits to the falls; you can use their mountain bikes or kayaks, or go fishing. The six *cabañas* are handsome cedar and stone constructions, the food is good, the welcome warm and the views of the river and jungle are fantastic.

Posada La Bonita (ⓣ011/154-4908386 or 03755/156-80380, ⓦwww.posadalabonita.com.ar; ⑦), 30km north of El Soberbio, is a fabulous construction smack in the middle of the jungle. Built from stone and timber, and furnished with rustic pieces made of dead wood, it sets the trend for the other lodges in the region. The three isolated units stand apart from the main house and have their own little verandahs.

Don Enrique Lodge (ⓣ011/4723-7020 or 011/155-9326262, ⓦwww.donenriquelodge.com.ar; ⑦), just beyond *La Bonita* on the aptly named Río Paraíso, took up the concept of its neighbour and perfected it. Hospitable hostess Bachi and her family run this place with dedication and affection, offering fabulous service, delicious meals and, above all, peace and quiet. The individual wooden lodges, each with a balcony and sundeck, are furnished with impeccable taste, and you are provided with environmentally friendly toiletries (don't use your own). You can explore the jungle with a guide – on one side of the river up to a lookout, on the other to a waterfall to admire tree-ferns and all manner of flora and fauna.

Bring a torch – the road down to the village is unlit at night. At Av San Martín 800, on the way to the Saltos, you'll find the *Cabañas Saltos del Moconá* (☎03755/495179; ❷), offering fairly plain but comfortable *cabañas* for up to four people. There's a good municipal **campsite**, *La Plata*, around 3km northwest of the village off RP-13 towards San Vicente. In a lovely riverside spot, the low-priced site has toilets, electricity and barbecue facilities. Forty kilometres out along the road to the Saltos, for a $2 fee you can pitch your tent alongside the waterfall Salto El Paraíso; there are as yet no facilities, so bring all provisions. The Salto can be reached via local Empresa Juan bus on Tuesdays and Thursdays or on the daily bus to Puerto Paraíso from where it's an eight-kilometre walk. **Eating** options in El Soberbio are painfully limited – friendly *Don Enrique* by the central crossroads does a decent *milanesa*.

There is only one **bank** in El Soberbio, a sub-branch of the Banco Macro Misiones, but it has very restricted opening hours (Tues & Thurs 4–6pm) and no ATM, so bring enough money to cover all your expenses.

The waterfalls

The **Saltos del Moconá** themselves lie just over 80km northeast of El Soberbio, via a partly paved road, and can be seen from both Argentina and Brazil (where the waterfalls are known as Yucumã), the latter only by taking a boat trip from El Soberbio (unless you make arrangements on the Brazilian side directly). As with Iguazú, the better view is from Brazil, while the Argentine side wins out in the adventure stakes.

The first 40km of the road north takes you through tobacco plantations and communities of Polish and German immigrants clustered around numerous simple wooden Lutheran, Adventist and Evangelical churches. Like many of Misiones' immigrants, the Poles and Germans of this region arrived in Argentina via Brazil and many of them use Portuguese as their first language. Despite the incredible lushness of the landscape, this is a region afflicted by considerable poverty, and local small farmers carry out much of their work using old-fashioned narrow wooden carts, pulled by oxen. Various side-trips can be made en route, including to the **Salto El Paraíso**, 40km from El Soberbio, a gentle waterfall with swimming spots and camping facilities, and to the simple **perfume distilleries** (*alambiques*) where locals extract essential oils from native plants. If you are taking a **boat trip**, your guide will drive you down to the river and you will complete the journey by water – a fabulous experience in itself. Having surveyed the waterfalls from the spectacular Brazilian side, you will be transferred to land on the Argentine side, where you can look across the apparently "normal" river from the shore, swim in the shallows and admire the butterflies, and, if possible, wade over to view the waterfalls from above.

Forty kilometres from El Soberbio the road strikes into the heart of an area of secondary forest, the last stretch of which is protected as the **Parque Provincial Moconá**. A small park of just ten square kilometres, it was created in 1988. As yet, little work has been done on registering the park's flora and fauna; sighted species of birds include the condor and the peculiarly noisy Bare-throated Bellbird. It is thought (despite no recent sightings) that the park is one of the last refuges in Argentina of the rare *yaguareté*, or jaguar, whose presence has been registered on the Brazilian side. The Brazilian park is far older (created in 1947) and larger (its total area is approximately seventeen square kilometres) and the degree of protection is higher – surveys of its wildlife have confirmed the presence not only of the *yaguaraté*, but also the capuchin monkey, the tapir and over two hundred species of birds, including various toucans. After another 40km or so, you arrive at the *guardaparques'* post, from where there are a number of short trails through the forest. A trail of just over a kilometre leads to the edge of the Río Uruguay, from where – compulsorily accompanied by a *guardaparque* or local guide, and conditions permitting – you can embark on an adventurous wade across 300m of knee-high water to reach the edge of the waterfalls.

Practicalities

Before setting out for the Saltos, you should check the state of the river with the police, who maintain a post nearby (☎03755/441001), and with locals in El Soberbio as to the condition of the road and for precise directions – the Saltos are not signposted. Though the road is negotiable in good weather in an ordinary car, a 4WD is certainly preferable and the only option for periods when sections of the road are flooded. If you are prepared to hang around in El Soberbio for a few days, it may be possible to catch a lift to the waterfalls; vehicles do travel regularly to and from the site, taking provisions and sometimes school parties. The easiest – if most expensive – option is to travel with an **organized tour**: a growing number of companies in Posadas and Puerto Iguazú offer packages to the waterfalls, though the pioneer in this field is Ruli Cabral, of the *Hostería Puesto del Sol* in El Soberbio (see p.369). Ruli organizes trips to both sides of the waterfalls, taking the best part of a day and costing over $200 per group (regardless of the number in the group, whose maximum is determined by the boat capacity); he has an office at Avenida Rivadavia 619 (☎03755/495010 or 156-53211). Also in El Soberbio, Miguel Taszi (☎03755/495266 or 156-52853) offers 4WD and boat tours to the waterfalls at similar prices, along with transfers to some of the lodges in the Selva Misionera (see box, p.369), to be arranged through the lodges themselves.

Up the Río Paraná: Rosario to Corrientes

The mighty **Río Paraná** is an attraction in itself, with its lush islands, delicious fish and relaxing aquatic landscapes. Anyone looking for urban pleasures should head for **Rosario**, the country's third largest city, whose famously handsome people, active cultural life and fascinating architecture make it one of most attractive cities in Argentina. Nearby **Santa Fe**, the much-overshadowed provincial capital, is at first sight less enticing, but its faded grandeur and monuments to the colonial era merit a stopover. Opposite, the dynamic city of **Paraná** shares not only its name with the river, but also its slow pace and a certain subtropical beauty. To the south, since it was linked to Rosario by a splendid bridge, the traditional town of **Victoria**, famous for its monastery, has been opening itself up to tourism. Some way to the north, past the spa resort of **La Paz** and the angling mecca of **Esquina**, is the provincial capital of

Corrientes, named for the strong currents in a sweeping loop of the Paraná. One of the region's oldest and most dynamic cities, it is also the gateway to the Gran Chaco (see p.400).

Rosario and around

Rosario, vital and crude, tough and tender: the true city of Argentina.

Waldo Frank

Confident and stylish, with a vibrant cultural scene and a lively nightlife, **ROSARIO** dominates the whole region. With a little over one million inhabitants, it is Argentina's third biggest city – Córdoba just beats it for second place. However, Rosario likes to see itself as a worthy rival to Buenos Aires, 300km southeast – in some ways it is a far smaller version of the capital, but without the hordes of foreign visitors or the political clout. Geographically the comparison certainly holds: Rosario is a flattish riverside city and major **port**, lying at the heart of a vital agricultural region. Its cobbled streets lined with handsome buildings and leafy trees – both with a tendency to flake – manage to be decadent and dynamic at the same time. Unlike Buenos Aires, however, whose back has until recently been firmly to the water, Rosario has always enjoyed a close relationship with the **Río Paraná**; the attractive riverfront area runs for 20km along the city's eastern edge, flanked by parks, bars and restaurants and, to the north, popular beaches. One of its main attractions is the splendidly unspoilt series of so-called **"delta islands"** with wide sandy beaches, just minutes away from the city by boat. Packed with locals during the sweltering summers that afflict the region, they give Rosario the feel of a resort town, despite the city's little-developed tourist industry.

Rosario may not have any of the impressive ecclesiastical and colonial architecture of, say, Salta or Córdoba. However, as the legacy of its late nineteenth-century wealth, it does boast some particularly handsome examples of rather more worldly constructions. You can see some of Argentina's finest turn-of-the-century **architecture** here, with an eclectic spread of styles ranging from English chalets to Catalan Modernism – a decorative early twentieth-century style incorporating elements of Moorish and Gothic architecture – plus some of the finest examples of Art Deco in Latin America. The French-, Spanish- and British-style mansions and old department stores make it a rewarding city to simply wander around. The last decades of the twentieth century saw the city stagnate somewhat, with buildings falling down or being demolished and nothing noteworthy replacing them, but the new millennium has already seen a rash of architectural projects, including the municipal headquarters in the southern sector of the city, designed by world-class architect Álvaro Siza. Another sign of a budding renaissance in the city's fortunes can be detected in the series of cultural centres that have recently sprung up, led by the **Museo de Arte Contemporáneo**, housed in a conspicuously converted grain silo on the riverside. In terms of traditional sightseeing, Rosario has a handful of conventional museums and galleries, notably the excellent **Museo de Bellas Artes J.B. Castagnino** and the **Museo Histórico Provincial**, both in the city's major green space, the **Parque de la Independencia**. Its most famous sight, nationally at least, is the monolithic **Monumento a la Bandera**, a 70-metre marble paean to the Argentine flag.

Che Guevara, one of the twentieth-century's most powerful icons, was born in an apartment block on the corner of Santa Fe and Urquiza; the city seems slightly embarrassed by this fact, however, and apart from a plaque marking the spot virtually nothing has been done to commemorate him. Other **Rosarino celebrities** include leading artists Antonio Berni and Lucio Fontana, three of Argentina's most popular singers – Fito Páez, Juan Carlos Baglietto and Litto Nebbia – and cartoonist Roberto Fontanarrosa, whose most famous creation, the luckless gaucho Inodoro Pereyra, is a staple of the back pages of the national newspaper, *Clarín*. Rosario's other key cultural icons are sporting: allegiances to two major teams – **Rosario Central** and **Newell's Old Boys** – divide the city with a fervour possibly greater than that provoked in the capital by River Plate and Boca Juniors.

Some history

Unusually for a Hispano-American city, Rosario lacks an official founding date. Having slowly grown up around a simple chapel, built in the grounds of an estancia in the late seventeenth century and dedicated to the **Virgen del Rosario**, the original settlement became known as La Capilla del Rosario. Despite its strategic location as a port for goods from Córdoba and Santa Fe provinces, early growth was slow: as in the whole region, Rosario's progress was hindered by Buenos Aires' stranglehold on the movement of trade between the interior and foreign markets through blockades of the Río Paraná. With General Urquiza's freeing-up of the rivers following the Battle of Caseros in 1852, Rosario was finally set on course for expansion and the city's population ballooned from 3000 in 1850 to 23,000 in 1869.

A further spur to the city's growth occurred in 1870 when the **Central Argentine Railway**, owned and largely financed by the British, was completed, providing a link between Rosario and Córdoba. By 1895, Rosario was Argentina's second city, with 91,000 inhabitants – many of them immigrants attracted by the promise of the by now flourishing port, giving the city its other soubriquet, **"Hija de los Barcos"** (Daughter of the Ships). By the early twentieth century, the city had an important banking district populated by representatives from the world's major financial institutions, and a growing number of industries. Like Buenos Aires, Rosario also had its sleazy side, one that won it another nickname, the "Chicago of the South": during the late nineteenth and early twentieth centuries, the city was claimed to be a centre of white slave traffic with a notorious zone of **prostitution** known as the Barrio de Pichincha.

As in the rest of the country, the latter half of the twentieth century saw a periods of intense political conflict and a steady decline in Rosario's fortunes – notably in May 1969 during the uprising known as the *Rosariazo*, provoked by the police shooting and killing a student in Corrientes during a protest at an unprecedented rise in prices at the university canteen. Towards the end of the century the city suffered one of the country's highest jobless rates, but the municipality's social policies, based on decentralized power, and the post-crisis turnaround, have helped to mitigate its potentially dangerous effects. The first few years of the new millennium have seen Rosario once again become a vital link between its hinterland's rejuvenated farmland (producing beef, dairy goods, soya, wheat and maize) and the outside world. To the casual visitor, at least, the city looks like a boomtown.

Arrival and information

Rosario's **airport** lies around 10km northwest of the city centre, along RN-9 (ⓣ0341/451-3220). There is no bus service to the centre from the airport – the

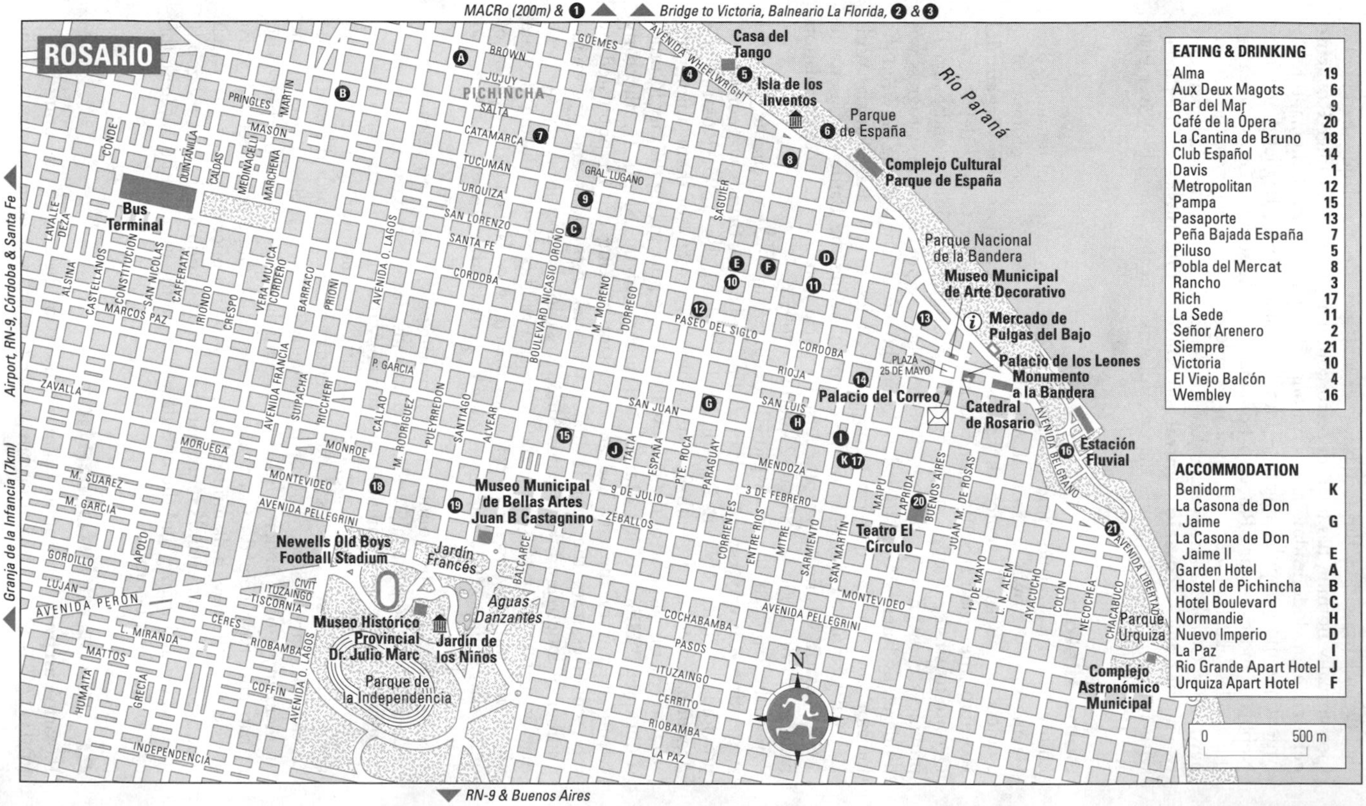
ROSARIO
MACRo (200m) & 1
Bridge to Victoria, Balneario La Florida, 2 & 3
Airport, RN-9, Córdoba & Santa Fe
Granja de la Infancia (7km)
RN-9 & Buenos Aires
Río Paraná
Casa del Tango
Isla de los Inventos
Parque de España
Complejo Cultural Parque de España
Parque Nacional de la Bandera
Museo Municipal de Arte Decorativo
Mercado de Pulgas del Bajo
Palacio de los Leones
Monumento a la Bandera
Catedral de Rosario
Palacio del Correo
PLAZA 25 DE MAYO
Estación Fluvial
Teatro El Círculo
Parque Urquiza
Complejo Astronómico Municipal
PICHINCHA
Bus Terminal
Museo Municipal de Bellas Artes Juan B Castagnino
Newells Old Boys Football Stadium
Jardín Francés
Aguas Danzantes
Museo Histórico Provincial Dr. Julio Marc
Jardín de los Niños
Parque de la Independencia
AVENIDA WHEELWRIGHT
AVENIDA BELGRANO
AVENIDA LIBERTAD
AVENIDA PELLEGRINI
AVENIDA FRANCIA
AVENIDA O. LAGOS
AVENIDA PERÓN
BOULEVARD NICASIO OROÑO
PASEO DEL SIGLO
GÜEMES
BROWN
JUJUY
SALTA
CATAMARCA
TUCUMÁN
URQUIZA
SAN LORENZO
SANTA FE
CÓRDOBA
RIOJA
SAN LUIS
SAN JUAN
MENDOZA
3 DE FEBRERO
9 DE JULIO
ZEBALLOS
MONTEVIDEO
COCHABAMBA
PASOS
ITUZAINGO
CERRITO
RIOBAMBA
LA PAZ
GRAL. LUGANO
SAGUIER
M. MORENO
DORREGO
ITALIA
ESPAÑA
PTE. ROCA
PARAGUAY
CORRIENTES
ENTRE RIOS
MITRE
SARMIENTO
SAN MARTÍN
MAIPU
LAPRIDA
BUENOS AIRES
JUAN M. DE ROSAS
1º DE MAYO
L. N. ALEM
AYACUCHO
COLÓN
NECOCHEA
CHACABUCO
BALCARCE
ALVEAR
SANTIAGO
PUEYRREDON
M. RODRIGUEZ
CALLAO
RICCHERI
SUIPACHA
P. GARCIA
MONROE
MORUEGA
PRIONI
BARRACO
CORDERO
VERA MUJICA
CRESPO
IRIONDO
CAFFERATA
SAN NICOLAS
CONSTITUCIÓN
MARCOS PAZ
CASTELLANOS
ALSINA
DEZA
LAVALLE
CONDE
QUINTANILLA
CALDAS
MEDINACELLI
MARCHENA
MASON
PRINGLES
MARTIN
ZAVALLA
M. SUAREZ
M. GARCIA
GORDILLO
LUJAN
APOLO
CIVIT
ITUZAINGO
TISCORNIA
CERES
L. MIRANDA
MATTOS
RIOBAMBA
COFFIN
HUMAITA
GRECIA
INDEPENDENCIA
N
0 500 m
EATING & DRINKING
Alma 19
Aux Deux Magots 6
Bar del Mar 9
Café de la Ópera 20
La Cantina de Bruno 18
Club Español 14
Davis 1
Metropolitan 12
Pampa 15
Pasaporte 13
Peña Bajada España 7
Piluso 5
Pobla del Mercat 8
Rancho 3
Rich 17
La Sede 11
Señor Arenero 2
Siempre 21
Victoria 10
El Viejo Balcón 4
Wembley 16
ACCOMMODATION
Benidorm K
La Casona de Don Jaime G
La Casona de Don Jaime II E
Garden Hotel A
Hostel de Pichincha B
Hotel Boulevard C
Normandie H
Nuevo Imperio D
La Paz I
Rio Grande Apart Hotel J
Urquiza Apart Hotel F

half-hour taxi ride will cost around $20. Note that it is often quicker to reach Rosario by bus from Buenos Aires than to come by air.

Long-distance buses arrive at Rosario's clean and user-friendly **Terminal de Omnibus Mariano Moreno**, twenty blocks west of the city centre, at Santa Fe and Cafferata (ⓣ0341/437-3030). An information kiosk there (erratic hours) can provide you with a list of hotels and a map. At the terminal you can buy a magnetic card (*tarjeta magnética*) used instead of cash on the city's local buses – walk one block north along Cafferata to catch buses #116 or #107 to the centre from the corner with San Lorenzo. Plenty of taxis pull up outside the front entrance, however, and will set you back only $5 to the city centre.

There's a good **tourist information office** (ETUR) down by the riverfront, on the corner of Avenida Belgrano and Calle Buenos Aires (daily 9am–7pm; ⓣ0341/480-2230, ⓦwww.rosarioturismo.com). They produce an informative map covering most of the city, together with accommodation and restaurant lists.

Accommodation

The main drawback to Rosario is **accommodation**. The more expensive places are on the characterless side, including chain hotels such as Holiday Inn and Howard Johnson, but there are one or two pleasant and reasonably priced *apart-hotels* (hotels whose rooms include small kitchens and dining areas, suitable for self-catering), in small, modern blocks. There is also a good B&B and some other good-value lodgings, and discounts are often available at weekends as it's a commercial city. Furthermore, there are now several **youth hostels** in the city, including two centrally located in well-restored townhouses – *La Casona de Don Jaime*, Presidente Roca 105 (ⓣ0341/527-9964, ⓦwww.youthhostelrosario.com.ar; $22 per person; ❷), and *La Casona de Don Jaime II*, San Lorenzo 1530 (ⓣ0341/530-2020, ⓦwww.youthhostelrosario.com.ar; $25 per person; ❸). Both are modern, friendly and efficient; the second is a little more spacious. Or try ★ *Hostel de Pichincha*, Avenida Francia 241 (ⓣ0341/439-6798, ⓦwww.pichinchahostel.com.ar; $25 per person; ❷), with bright, airy rooms and dorms, regular *asados* and bike tours.

Benidorm San Juan 1049 ⓣ0341/421-9368, ⓔhotelbenidorm@hotmail.com. Airy, clean and modern rooms, all with external windows, a/c and TV. Rates include breakfast and parking. ❺

★ **Boulevard** San Lorenzo 2194 ⓣ0341/440-4164, ⓦwww.hotelboulevard.com.ar. Great B&B in a converted 1920s villa on the majestic Bulevar Oroño. Rooms share a bathroom, except for the matrimonial suite, which has its own. ❸–❹

Garden Callao 45 ⓣ0341/437-0025, ⓔreserva@hotelgardensa.com. An attractive modern hotel in a quiet area of town. Rooms have large, comfortable beds, a/c and cable TV, and rates include breakfast and parking. Spacious bar area. ❸

Normandie Mitre 1030 ⓣ0341/421-2694, ⓔhotelnormandie@ciudad.com. Basic, slightly gloomy rooms with TV and private bathroom around a central courtyard. Friendly staff, though, and good central location. ❸

Nuevo Imperio Urquiza 1264 ⓣ0341/448-0091, ⓦwww.hotelimperio.com.ar. A bland 1970s construction grafted on to a venerable old hotel (part of the stunning but dilapidated Moorish interior survives but is not in use). A spotless, if slightly overpriced, place with decent rooms (facilities include cable TV and a/c), a bar and restaurant. ❺

La Paz Cda Barón de Mahuá 36 ⓣ0341/421-0905, ⓔlapashotel@hotmail.com. Plain but adequate rooms with TV and private bathroom, some with balconies. Prices include breakfast. ❸

★ **Río Grande Apart Hotel** Dorrego 1261 ⓣ0341/424-1144, ⓦwww.rosario.com/riograndeapart. The best of the *apart-hotels*, with bright, roomy suites in a smart, renovated building in a fairly quiet part of the city. Outstanding buffet breakfasts, reliable Internet and a safe garage. ❻

Urquiza Apart Hotel Urquiza 1491 ⓣ0341/449-4900, ⓦwww.apart-urquiza.com.ar. Spacious apartments with kitchenettes, comfortable bedrooms, cool sitting rooms – but avoid the street side. Decent buffet breakfast. ❻

The City

Though Rosario is a large city, stretching for over 20km along the Río Paraná, most points of interest lie within a fairly compact area and – with the exception of excursions to the city's popular *balneario*, **La Florida**, to the north, and to the island beaches, to the south – there is seldom any need to take public transport. It's an easy city to find your way around, too, with streets following an exceptionally regular grid pattern, and the river itself making a useful reference point. Rosario's main square is the quiet **Plaza 25 de Mayo**, where you'll find the post office, the cathedral and the **Museo Municipal de Arte Decorativo Firma y Odilo Estévez**. One block east lies the **Monumento a la Bandera**, which faces the city's main riverside avenue, Avenida Belgrano. The southern end of Avenida Belgrano leads to **Parque Urquiza**, popular with joggers and walkers in the evening and home to the city's astronomical observatory.

South and west of Plaza 25 de Mayo lies Rosario's main commercial and shopping district, centred on the pedestrianized streets of San Martín and Córdoba. Beyond Calle Corrientes, Córdoba is known as the **Paseo del Siglo**, a stretch of street that is home both to some of Rosario's best-preserved architecture and to the city's most upmarket shops and bars. The Paseo del Siglo ends at **Bulevar Oroño**, an elegant boulevard fringed with palms and plane trees, dissected by a cycle path and lined with seigniorial French-style villas, mostly now converted into clinics and offices; it runs south towards Rosario's oasis of a main park, the **Parque de la Independencia** where you will find some of the city's main **museums**.

Plaza 25 de Mayo and around

Built on the site of the first modest chapel built to venerate the Virgen del Rosario, **Plaza 25 de Mayo** sits on the edge of the city before it slopes down to Avenida Belgrano and the river. The plaza itself is a pleasantly shady space laid out very formally around its central marble monument, the **Monumento a la Independencia**. Around the square lie a number of grand public buildings, including the imposing **Palacio del Correo** on the corner of Córdoba and Buenos Aires and, on the northeast corner, the terracotta-coloured Municipal Palace, also known as the **Palacio de los Leones**, in reference to the majestic sculptured lions that flank the main entrance.

South of the Palacio lies the **Catedral de Rosario** (Mon–Sat 7.30am–12.30pm & 4.30–8.30pm, Sun 8–1pm & 5–9.30pm), a late nineteenth-century construction in which domes, towers, columns and pediments are mixed to particularly eclectic effect. Inside, there's a fine Italianate altar carved from Carrara marble and, in the crypt, the colonial wood-carved image of the Virgin of Rosario, brought from Cádiz in 1773.

At Santa Fe 748 you'll find the **Museo Municipal de Arte Decorativo Firma y Odilo Estévez** (Thurs–Sun Jan to mid-March 9am–2pm, mid-March to Dec 3–8pm; free). Housed in a fantastically ornate mansion, whose facade reflects the early twentieth-century fashion for heavily ornamental moulding, the museum exhibits the collection of the building's former occupants, the Estévez family, Galician immigrants who made their fortune by growing *mate*. It's a stunning display – every inch of the interior is furnished and ornamented with objects seemingly chosen to exemplify the wealth and taste of the owners, from Egyptian glassware and tiny Greek sculptures to Flemish tapestry and Limoges porcelain, via pre-Columbian ceramics and Spanish ivory figures. There's a small but impressive **painting collection**, too, including *Portrait of a Gentleman* by French Neoclassicist Jacques Louis David and a Goya portrait of *Doña Maria Teresa Ruiz de Apodaca de Sesma* with strikingly piercing black eyes.

Monumento a la Bandera

Your first sight of the **Monumento a la Bandera** (aside from its picture on the ten-peso note) is likely to be through the gap between the cathedral and the Palacio de los Leones, from where the Pasaje Juramento, lined with marble figures by the great sculptress Lola Mora (see box, p.843), leads down to the monument itself. Finished in 1957 under the direction of architect Ángel Guido, the Monumento a la Bandera is basically a huge allegorical sculpture based on the idea of a ship (representing Argentina) sailing towards a glorious future. General Manuel Belgrano "created" the flag in the city in 1812, and Rosario enjoys the official title of "Cuna de la Bandera" (Cradle of the Flag). The country's major Flag Day celebrations are held at the monument on June 20 each year; for the fiftieth anniversary in 2007 a strong contender for the world's longest official flag – thirteen kilometres of blue and white cloth – was unfurled in the presence of President Kirchner.

Physically, it is divided into three sections: the so-called **Propileo**, a kind of temple-like structure within which burns an eternal flame commemorating Argentines who have died for their country; the **Patio Cívico**, a long, shallow rectangular flight of stairs leading away from the Propileo; and, looming above everything, the **central tower** – a massive 70-metre block of unpolished marble whose coarse lines seem particularly inappropriate in a city otherwise distinguished for its graceful architecture – though you might say they are in keeping with Waldo Frank's description of Rosario as "vital and crude, tough and tender". It's worth taking the lift to the top of the tower (Mon 2–7pm, Tues–Sun 9am–7pm; $1), from where there's a commanding **view** of the river and the city. Over the years the tower has been a magnet for patriotic suicide victims, and the lift operators need little encouragement to recount the gory effects of falling onto the road below. The erection of a barrier – after a depressed Falklands/Malvinas veteran threw himself off in the 1990s – should prove a serious obstacle to any future attempts.

Below the tower, there's a **crypt** dedicated to the creator of the flag, General Belgrano, and, below the Propileo, there's the rather pointless and pompous **sala de banderas**, in which flags of all the American countries are exhibited, together with the national flower, the national anthem, the national shield and a sample of earth.

The Costanera

Stretching over 20km from north to south, Rosario's **Costanera**, or riverfront, is one of the city's most appealing features, offering numerous green spaces and views over the Río Paraná. You'll find this area's most central park, the **Parque Nacional de la Bandera**, a narrow wedge of grass lining the river, just to the east of the Monumento a la Bandera. At the southern end of the park lies the **Estación Fluvial** (Ⓣ0341/448-3737), from where regular boat services run to various islands. On weekends you can **cruise** the river on the sightseeing boat, *Ciudad de Rosario* (Sat & Sun 2.30 & 5pm; $9; Ⓣ0341/449-8688). Every Saturday and Sunday evening around Av Belgrano 500, which runs past the western edge of the park, there is a flea market, the **Mercado de Pulgas del Bajo**, where you can browse through a selection of crafts, antiques and books. The park merges to the north with the **Parque de España**, where a cultural and exhibition centre, the **Complejo Cultural Parque de España**, has been imaginatively installed above some old nineteenth-century tunnels. The park is also the setting – in good weather – for a popular *milonga* on Sunday evenings.

Fifteen blocks south of the Parque Nacional de la Bandera – follow Avenida de la Libertad, which climbs the bluff just south of the Monumento – lies

Parque Urquiza, a small park most notable for being the spot to go for an evening jog or stroll, ending up in the nearby *Siempre*, a local institution (see "Eating and drinking", p.381). The park is also home to Rosario's astronomical observatory, the **Complejo Astronómico Municipal** (ⓣ0341/480-2533), which consists of the observatory itself (when skies are clear Wed–Sun 8.30–10pm; free), a planetarium (Sat & Sun at 5pm & 6pm; $2) and an experimental science museum (Sat & Sun 5.30–8.30pm; $2).

Around 8km north of the centre, Rosario's most popular mainland beach, **Balneario La Florida** (bus #101 from Rioja) is packed on summer weekends, and has bars, restaurants and shower facilities. At the southern end of the *balneario* you'll find the **Rambla Catalunya** and Avenida Carrasco, lined with glitzy bars, smart restaurants and see-and-be-seen nightclubs the summertime focus of Rosario's famed *movida*.

Parque de la Independencia and its museums

Dissected by various avenues and containing several museums, a football stadium – Newell's Old Boys, known affectionately as "El Coloso" – and a racetrack, the **Parque de la Independencia** feels like a neighbourhood in itself. The park was inaugurated in 1902 and is an attractively landscaped space with shady walkways and beautifully laid-out gardens such as the formal **Jardín Francés**, just west of the main entrance on Bulevar Oroño. Just south of the entrance there is a large lake which is the setting for a rather kitsch but not unattractive spectacle every evening known as the **Aguas Danzantes** (literally the "dancing waters"), a synchronized fountain display complete with coloured lights and music (Thurs & Sun 7.30–10pm, Fri & Sat 4.30–11pm).

At Avenida Pellegrini 2202, which runs through the park, you'll find the **Museo Municipal de Bellas Artes Juan B. Castagnino** (Mon & Wed–Sat 2–8pm, Sun 1–7pm; $1), regarded as the country's most important fine arts museum after the Museo de Bellas Artes in Buenos Aires. The museum has two permanent collections: European painting from the fifteenth to the twentieth

△ Parque de la Independencia, Rosario

Kids' Rosario

Rosario's city government has a justified reputation for progressiveness, and one of its most positive achievements is the existence of not one but three different cultural venues specially devised for **young visitors**, a rarity in Argentina. The **Isla de los Inventos** (Sat & Sun 4–8pm; $2, $1 for children) is housed in the stunning former central train station at Corrientes and Wheelwright. Literally the "Island of Inventions", it features a series of hands-on or interactive exhibits based on Rosario and its history – such as a contraption representing fluvial navigation on the Río Paraná – plus workshops where visitors can help assemble toys. It is open during the week, in term time, for schoolchildren, but visitors are always welcome. Adults will enjoy some of the more abstract sections, such as one dedicated to infinity, and may need to hold toddlers' hands when they enter the magical dark chamber that comes to life to explain the history of the universe since the Big Bang. All locomotive fans will enjoy the only remaining train engine still on the rails, in the part of the museum that is due to be developed further – the station proper.

Inside the **Parque de la Independencia** (see opposite), the former zoo has been metamorphosed into another kids' attraction, the **Jardín de los Niños** (Children's Garden) mostly aimed at youngsters aged 4 and above (Wed–Fri 8.30am–noon & 2–5.30pm, Sat & Sun 1.30–6pm; $1, free for children). An ingenious theme park whose only (strictly non-commercial) theme is enabling young people to discover everyday phenomena such as sound, mystery, flight and balance, it is adventurous but extremely safe and great fun and bound to be a success.

Completing the trio is the **Granja de la Infancia** – "Youngsters' Farm" – some way out of the centre at Avenida Perón 8100 (Tues–Fri 10am–5pm, Sat & Sun 10am–6pm; $0.50). Aimed at urban youth who think chickens are born oven-ready and have never seen a real-life goat or capybara, it is so well designed that even the most field-wise kids get something out of it and, like all the other child-targeted venues, it will keep grown-ups entertained for a while too.

centuries, with works by Goya, Sisley and Daubigny, among others, and Argentine painting with examples from major artists such as Spilimbergo and Quinquela Martín, plus Antonio Berni and Lucio Fontana, both born in Rosario. The museum, arranged on two floors with large and well-lit rooms, also puts on some excellent temporary exhibitions – it's well worth looking out for exhibitions featuring local artists, who are producing some of Argentina's most interesting contemporary work.

West of the lake sits the **Museo Histórico Provincial Dr Julio Marc** (Thurs & Sat 3–6pm, Sun 10am–1pm; free), a large and well-organized museum containing a vast collection of exhibits spanning the whole of Latin America. Among its most notable collections are those dedicated to **Latin American religious art**, with a stunning eighteenth-century silver altar from Alto Peru, which was used for the Mass given by Pope John Paul II when he visited the city in 1987, and some fine examples of polychrome works in wood, wax and bone, representing the famed Quiteña School (named after the capital of Ecuador). In the room dedicated to San Martín, look out for the strange navigational instrument known as an **astronomical ring**, used by San Martín during his historic crossing of the Andes: the piece's curiosity value lies in the fact that it was already somewhat archaic in San Martín's time. There's also an important collection of **indigenous American ceramics**, including some valuable musical pieces known as whistling glasses (*vasos silbadores*) from the Chimú culture of northern Peru and some stunningly well-preserved and delicate textiles. Parque de la Independencia can easily be reached on foot from the centre – it's a particularly attractive walk along the Paseo del Siglo and the Bulevar Oroño, or you can take buses #129 and #123 from Rioja.

Museo de Arte Contemporáneo de Rosario (MACRo)

West of the northern reaches of the elegant Bulevar Oroño lies the former red-light district, the Pichincha. This barrio has undergone earnest gentrification in recent years and is now home to trendy bars, fashionable restaurants and, above all, antique shops, the latter mostly clustered along Avenida Rivadavia. At the far end of the boulevard, on the waterfront, set among the verdant Parque Sunchales, is an unmissable hulk of a building, looking like a row of upturned giant liquorice allsorts. Once a grain silo belonging to the Davis family, it has been turned into one of the country's most promising museums of contemporary art, the **Museo de Arte Contemporáneo de Rosario**, or **MACRo** (Mon, Tues & Thurs–Sun: winter 2–8pm, summer 4–10pm; $2; Ⓦwww.macromuseo.org.ar). The most striking aspects of the museum are its exterior, especially the huge silo cylinders painted in vibrant pink, purple and azure shades, and its riverside location – both the top-floor viewpoint and the Perspex lift-shaft leading to it offer fine views of the majestic Paraná. The exhibitions, mostly dedicated to up-and-coming local and national artists, have thus far been rather disappointing, drawing parallels with similar daring projects such as the Bilbao Guggenheim, but the museum is worth a visit alone for the building, location and excellent café/restaurant, *Davis* (see opposite), where you can enjoy watching boats, barges and bits of vegetation float past.

The Alto Delta islands

Known as the **Alto Delta**, the low-lying **islands** off Rosario's "coast" in fact fall under the jurisdiction of the neighbouring province, Entre Ríos. Like the islands of the Tigre Delta, in Buenos Aires (see p.183), they host subtropical vegetation fed by sediment from the Upper Paraná River. The Alto Delta is far less developed than Tigre, however. With the exception of the more remote island of **Charigüé**, where there is a small settlement that has its own school, police station and a handful of restaurants, it is largely uninhabited. If you can afford it, the best way of seeing the Delta is on an **excursion**; try Rosario-based Carlos Vaccarezza (Ⓣ0341/156-156066) or El Holandés (Ⓣ0341/156-415880). Alternatively, there are various islands offering camping facilities, accommodation and restaurants which you can reach by one of the regular passenger services from the Estación Fluvial (see p.377), or by arranging to be picked up by the owners.

Isla Buenaventura (Ⓣ0341/155-425607), a resort on the island of the same name due east of Rosario, offers **accommodation** in well-equipped bungalows holding up to four people (④) with kitchen, private bathroom and fans. The friendly and ecologically minded young owners also offer canoeing trips along the Riacho Los Marinos and beyond plus guided walks into the island's wild interior. You can also camp in the interior (no facilities). Some provisions can be supplied on the island, including fresh fish from local fishermen, but you should bring extra with you if you're planning on staying for a while. In addition to the regular passenger service, you can arrange to be picked up by the island's owners ($40 return trip for up to four people). Just next door to *Isla Buenaventura* there's an excellent **restaurant**, *La Aldea* (Ⓣ0341/156-177402), where extremely fresh fish is cooked to order and can be eaten at one of the outside tables on the riverbank. Another option is the *Cabañas del Francés* (Ⓣ0341/155-473045; ⑤ for five to seven people; 20 percent discount for two people or single), where there are attractive rustic-style *cabañas* and a bar. There is no regular boat service to the *cabañas*, but the owner will pick up a party of up to five people from the mainland.

If you fancy just spending a day swimming or sunbathing, head for **Vladimir**, just south of the Estación Fluvial, where there are good beaches and a couple of snack bars; be warned, though, that the sun can be very fierce and there is little or no shade – take a high-factor sun cream and sunshade. Not far north of the city, there is another good bar and restaurant, *Puerto Pirata* (daily 10am–10pm; ⓣ0341/156-174596) with great views over the river from its terrace and a long strip of beach; to get there, take a bus to Granadero Baigorria, where you can ring the owners to come and pick you up.

From November to March, from 9am to dusk, there are **regular boat services** from the Estación Fluvial to the various islands of Rosario's Alto Delta. Boats to nearby bathing spots leave every 15 minutes ($7 return), while departures for Charigüé are at 9am, 11am and 5pm; out of season, services are less frequent.

Eating and drinking

In recent years Rosario's food scene has undergone a sea change, and some of its restaurants are dazzlingly adventurous, easily rivalling the best places in the capital. Rosario has plenty of **restaurants** to suit all budgets, though, both in the city centre and along the Costanera. In addition to pasta, pizza and *parrillada*, there are a number of excellent fish restaurants specializing in *boga*, *dorado* and *surubí*. What the city has always excelled in, however, is a **bar culture** – there are so many stylishly revamped bars around the city centre that you're spoilt for choice when it comes to drinking. The best spots for bar-hopping are just north of the centre, roughly between Santa Fe and Avenida Belgrano, and to the west, in the Pichincha, centred on an oblong formed by calles Ricchieri, Suipacha, Salta and Güemes.

Restaurants

Alma Montevideo 2394 ⓣ0341/449-2397. Quiet, toned-down place in a charming corner house, all done in soothing lime-green and pastel shades, with mellow music, laid-back service and interesting fusion fare – try the rabbit stuffed with bacon or the sucking-lamb tajine. Relatively expensive.

La Cantina de Bruno Ovidio Lagos 1599. Long-established, family-run Italian restaurant serving excellent home-made pasta. Closed Mon.

Club Español Rioja 1052. Friendly restaurant housed in a beautiful old building with stunning decorative glass ceilings and an astonishingly elaborate facade. Simple daily menu includes a main course, dessert and wine and soda. Sun lunch times are popular for Spanish specialities such as paella and tortilla.

Davis Blv Oroño s/n. Named for the silo that was converted into the fabulous MACRo museum, this waterside restaurant is open every day, noon and night, even when the museum is closed. The location is incredible, the food adventurous – sweetbread pasta in a tomato and raisin sauce – and the ambience lively.

Metropolitan Córdoba 1680. Lots of wannabes, including the handpicked waiters, watching silly things on giant screens in this modern loft-like space, but the food is actually excellent and includes the likes of *surubí* in a herb, lime and ginger, garnished with prawns and rösti.

Pampa Moreno 1206. Elegant tables in a trendy restaurant with a consciously industrial look, bare brickwork and all. Food is more conventional, though some dishes have a twist, such as the tomato, mozzarella and basil empanadas.

Peña Bajada España Av Illia and España. Friendly and unpretentious fish restaurant on the Costanera specializing in river fish.

Pobla del Mercat Salta 1424 ⓣ0341/447-1240. A wine club and gourmet grocery that happens to have a smart restaurant attached. Attentive service, an impressive wine list and all manner of culinary wonders – from the fish carpaccio to the peach tart – make this one of the top restaurants in the city. The decor is in keeping, plastic wall vases now being "in".

Rich San Juan 1031 ⓣ0341/440-8657. Rosario's most venerable restaurant, a lovely old-fashioned place with a vast, moderately priced, mouthwatering menu that mixes traditional dishes such as *puchero* with more elaborate creations such as sea bass with champagne sauce or sirloin steak with shallots, mushrooms, bacon and red wine. Vegetarians can choose from dishes such as pasta with tomato pesto, cream and mushrooms, and asparagus omelette. Closed Mon.

Señor Arenero Av Carrasco 2568. Big glitzy restaurant specializing in fish, in the popular Rambla Catalunya area; prices are above average.

Victoria San Lorenzo and Pte Roca. Old-fashioned corner café/bar and restaurant with a sober wooden interior and tables on the pavement. Good-value *menú ejecutivo* with a main dish such as pork chops, a dessert and drink. Closed Sun lunch.

El Viejo Balcón Wheelwright and Italia. One of the city's best *parrillas*, serving up all the usual cuts at an attractive riverside location. Moderate prices.

Wembley Av Belgrano 2012 ⓣ0341/481-1090. Busy upmarket restaurant opposite the port. Daily specials such as salmon with capers though the most successful dishes are the more simply executed grilled river fish or *parrillada*.

Cafés and bars

Aux Deux Magots Entre Ríos 2. Spacious café/bar serving excellent coffee overlooking the river – a lovely spot for a leisurely Sun breakfast.

Bar del Mar Balcarce and Tucumán. Cool bar with aquatically inspired blue walls. Good selection of laid-back music and a trendy but friendly crowd.

Café de la Ópera Laprida and Mendoza 787 ⓣ0341/421-9402156-422024. Beautiful old-fashioned café adjoining the Teatro El Círculo, serving specials like tarragon chicken, along with pasta, omelettes and salads, and putting on lively musical or cabaret events on Fri and Sat from 10pm. Or just have a coffee and a slice of date tart.

Pasaporte Maipú and Urquiza. Stylish bar with outside tables on a pleasant corner down near the riverfront. Coffee, alcoholic drinks and a large selection of filled crepes. Board games available.

Piluso Alvear and Catamarca. Pleasing wood-panelled bar on an attractive corner in Pichincha. Good range of beers and also fruity non-alcoholic drinks.

Rancho Av Carrasco 2765. Popular summer bar along the Rambla Catalunya and a good place to pick up free invites for one of the area's clubs. Vast outside seating area and a range of beers, cocktails and fast food.

La Sede San Lorenzo and Entre Ríos. Elegant and rather literary bar in a fabulous Art Nouveau building – a favourite meeting-place for Rosario's artistic celebrities. Theatrical/cabaret evenings.

Siempre Av de la Libertad 10. This large café and *cervecería* on the southern Costanera is an almost obligatory early-evening pit-stop for Rosarinos on their way back from a walk around Parque Urquiza – try the excellent draught lager. The outside tables are good for a spot of people-watching.

Nightlife and entertainment

Rosario is noted for its nightlife, **la movida**, but its **clubs** can be a little disappointing and in summer, when all the action moves to the Rambla Catalunya, a beachfront avenue at the northern end of town, you're limited to one or two very popular but faceless mega-discos. You'll be far better off if you check out one of the city's popular *milongas*, a far more authentic experience; Rosario has a hard core of **tango** enthusiasts and most nights of the week there is something going on – one of the most popular events in good weather is a regular Sunday evening *milonga* in the Parque España. Tango fans might be interested to know that Rosarinos are said to dance a slightly showier version of the tango than Porteños.

Berlín Pje Zabala 1128, between the 300 block of Mitre and Sarmiento. Regular cabaret and musical events from Thurs to Sun at this popular bar.

Catalinas Av Colombres 2600. *The* club in the summer – a big, mainstream disco along the Rambla Catalunya with outside bar area and a young, lively crowd.

Centro Asturiano San Luis 644. Setting for popular *milonga* on Sat from 11pm – also tango classes at 10pm and salsa classes at 9pm.

Las Chirusas Av Rivadavia 2455. Tango classes for beginners and above every Tues at this popular *milonga*.

Gotika City Club Mitre 1739. A loft, three bars and a garden are all features at the city's main gay disco, with regular shows and events.

Peña La Amistad Maipú 1121 ⓣ0341/447-1037. A good spot to listen to folk music, especially chamamé and other regional styles. Snacks such as empanadas and tamales are served. Fri and Sat from 11pm.

Teatro El Círculo Laprida 1235 ⓣ0341/448-3784. In addition to theatrical and musical events, Rosario's most famous theatre hosts a popular Wed night *milonga*.

Timotea Av Colombres 1340, just before Rambla Catalunya. Similar atmosphere to *Catalinas*; a swish mainstream disco attracting the tanned hordes of summer.

Vudú Patio de la Madera, Av Santa Fe. Located next to the bus terminal, this big techno club attracts a trendy crowd. Closed during the summer season.

Listings

Airlines Aerolíneas Argentinas/Austral, Santa Fe 1410 ⓣ0341/424-9332 and at the airport ⓣ0341/451-1470; Southern Winds, Mitre 737 ⓣ0341/425-3808 and at the airport ⓣ0341/451-6708.

Car rental Avis, San Nicolás 620 ⓣ0341/435-2299; Dollar, Paraguay 892 ⓣ0341/426-1700; Olé, Gorriti 751 ⓣ0341/437-6517.

Bike tours Sebastián ⓣ0341/155-713812 or ⓦwww.bikerosario.com.ar.

Internet access and telephones There are dozens of *locutorios* in the centre, including Telefónica with Internet access at Urquiza 1275 (8am–midnight).

Laundry Both Tintorería Rosario, San Lorenzo 1485 (ⓣ0341/425-3620), and Lavandería VIP, Maipú 654 (ⓣ0341/426-1237), will deliver to your hotel free of charge.

Post office Correo Central at Buenos Aires and Córdoba, on Plaza 25 de Mayo.

Travel agent ASATEJ, Corrientes 653 ⓣ0341/425-3798.

Victoria

Since a stunning road **bridge** ($9 toll for cars, valid both ways, so keep the ticket) across the Río Paraná was inaugurated in 2003, the somnolent little market town of **VICTORIA**, 122km southeast of Paraná, has been cajoled into life. Founded by immigrants from northern Italy and the Basque country, it has been brought physically much closer to Rosario, 58km

△ Rosario–Victoria bridge over the Río Paraná

southwest – and seems to relish its prospects as an up-and-coming holiday resort. The RN-11 Paraná-to-Gualeguaychú road bypasses the town to the north, while Avenida Costanera Dr Pedro Radio skirts round the southern edge, following the contours of the riverbanks, where summer tourists flock to bathe along the sandy beaches. Centred on an alluring main square, its mostly unpaved streets, forming a regular grid, are lined with a number of fine neocolonial buildings in varying states of repair that reward aimless wanderings. Look out for a local architectural feature, the highly ornate late nineteenth-century **wrought-iron grilles** (*rejas*) that adorn many of the town's doors and windows. On the square itself you should focus on the **cathedral**, or **Templo Parroquial** – an Italianate nineteenth-century pile that looks dreadful outside but conceals some fabulously delicate frescoes, especially those depicting the four Evangelists, with their pronounced Pre-Raphaelite style – and the adjacent wedding cake of a **municipalidad**, whose exotic eccentricity marries well with the palm fronds and other subtropical vegetation in the plaza, where you'll find the usual collection of statues, benches and a bandstand, plus stalls selling handicrafts.

Victoria's main tourist attraction is the **Abadía del Niño Dios** (daily 8am–noon & 3–6.30pm; guided visits on request), home to Latin America's oldest Benedictine foundation, dating from 1899. The modern monastery and cheerfully designed church are certainly worth a visit – on Sundays the latter may be closed to non-worshippers, though do try and sneak in to hear the monks singing *a capella* – but the highlight for most visitors is the excellent shop selling delicious, and mostly healthy, products, true to the Benedictine tradition, ranging from unusual jams and bee products to liqueurs and cheeses. The abbey sits alongside the main RN-11 artery, between the turn-off to the Rosario bridge and the town proper.

Practicalities

Victoria's little **bus terminal** is halfway between the main northern entrance and the central plaza, just four blocks north of the latter, at Junín and L.N. Alem. The helpful little **tourist office** (daily 9am–7pm; ⓣ03436/421885, ⓦwww.turismovictoria.com.ar) is conveniently situated at the northern access, on the corner of main drag 25 de Mayo and Bulevar Sarmiento. **Accommodation** possibilities are getting better. The best option is the smart new *Hotel Sol* (ⓣ03436/424040, ⓦwww.hotelsolvictoria.com.ar; ❼–❾), which is also a casino – the spacious, well-appointed rooms are extremely comfortable, and there is a fine dining room and swimming pool, all with views down to the river. Otherwise *Hotel Casablanca* (ⓣ03436/424131, ⓔcasablan01@hotmail.com; ❹), a hospitable medium-sized establishment at Bulevar Moreno s/n, in the southern neighbourhood of Barrio Quinto Cuartel, with large, slightly kitsch rooms, a beautiful garden and swimming pool, plus ample parking space. Lower down the budget scale is *Residencial Ponte Via* (ⓣ03436/423374; ❸), on RN-11 near the abbey; it also has a pool and pleasant rooms with river views. You can **camp** down in the busy port area at the fairly basic *Camping Brassesco*. Otherwise ask at the tourist office for details of estancias in the nearby countryside offering *ecoturismo* rooms.

Places **to eat** are also improving, especially down on the riverfront, where *Fontanarrosa* is a smart *parrilla*. Or else you might head for the *Jockey Club*, L.N. Alem 91, one block north of the central square, for simple fish or pasta; to popular *Parrilla Del Bajo*, down at the portside; or easiest of all, to *Plaza Bar*, at the corner of San Martín and Sarmiento, where decent pizzas are on offer along with drinks and snacks.

Santa Fe

Capital of its namesake province and an important commercial centre for the surrounding agricultural region, **SANTA FE** lies 475km north of Buenos Aires, along the banks of the Río Paraná. A sizeable city of about 400,000 inhabitants, Santa Fe is of interest mainly as a stopover – although even on those terms the city loses out to the nearby and more appealing cities of Rosario and Paraná. Apart from a particularly hot and humid climate in summer, owing to its low-lying riverside location, Santa Fe's main handicap is a rather sprawling and disjointed layout that makes getting to and from the city's modest attractions a bit of a slog.

Though Santa Fe is one of Argentina's oldest settlements – it was founded in 1573 by Juan de Garay in **Cayastá**, 80km north, and then moved to its current site in 1660 after repeated Indian attacks – careless development has made for a rather scruffy city in which unremarkable modern buildings largely overshadow the few remnants of a fine architectural heritage. What is left is largely grouped around the city's **centro histórico**, where there are a handful of sights worth visiting, notably the seventeenth-century **Iglesia y Convento de San Francisco** and the well-organized **Museo Etnográfico y Colonial Juan de Garay**.

Santa Fe is linked to Entre Ríos' provincial capital, Paraná (see p.389), by the **Túnel Subfluvial Uranga-Sylvestre Begnis**, better known as "Hernandarias", which runs for nearly 3km under the Río Paraná.

Arrival and information

Santa Fe's **airport**, with flights to Buenos Aires, is at Sauce Viejo, 7km south of the city along RN-11 (Ⓣ0342/475-0386). The local bus marked "L" or "aeropuerto" runs between the airport and Calle San Luis in the city centre (45min). The **bus terminal** is on the corner of Avenida Belgrano and Hipólito Yrigoyen (Ⓣ0342/455-3908), just northeast of the town centre and within walking distance of most accommodation.

The main **tourist office** (daily 7am–1pm & 3–9pm; Ⓣ0342/457-4123, Ⓦwww.santafe.gov.ar) is in the bus terminal. The staff can provide you with a map and accommodation lists, and may agree to look after left luggage. There are other, smaller offices at Boca del Tigre, on the corner of Dr Zavalia and J.J. Paso (Ⓣ0342/457-1862) at the southern entrance to the town, and at Paseo del Restaurador, on the corner of Boulevard Gálvez and Rivadavia (Ⓣ0342/457-1881), north of the town centre. The city's sprawling layout means you'll probably need to take the odd **bus** in Santa Fe: the standard fare is $0.75 within the centre, which is bordered by Gálvez, Rivadavia, Freyre and López.

Accommodation

Santa Fe's **hotels** are uninspiring, with some horrid budget options in the immediate vicinity of the bus terminal – best avoided. With a couple of exceptions, accommodation is business-oriented and overpriced. The *Río Grande*, San Jerónimo 2586 (Ⓣ0342/450-0700, Ⓦwww.rio-grande.com.ar; ❻), is the best of Santa Fe's more expensive hotels. It's been refurbished with spotless, comfortable rooms – some large suites with rather kitsch decor – with cable TV, safe, mini-bar and a/c; you are given a good buffet breakfast and the staff are courteous. A close second comes the new *Holiday Inn*, San Jerónimo 2779 (Ⓣ0342/410-1212, Ⓦwww.holidaystafe.com.ar; ❺–❻), which rises above the usual blandness of the chain, though it still lacks real character – that said, the rooms are faultless, the service impeccable and everything works, including the sauna, gym and pool. Although *Castelar*, 25 de Mayo and Falucho (Ⓣ&Ⓕ0342/456-0999, Ⓔcastelarhotel@arnet.com.ar; ❺), is a pleasant, old-fashioned hotel, its exterior and lobby promise rather more than the slightly dreary rooms deliver; while parking and breakfast are included, it is still overpriced. Sadly run-down *Emperatriz Hotel*, Irigoyen Freyre 2440 (Ⓣ&Ⓕ0342/453-0061; ❷), is potentially the best in its price range and is the only accommodation in Santa Fe with any character: it's an unusual 1920s, Mudéjar construction – combining Moorish and Gothic features – with arched wooden doors and a tiled interior; all rooms come with private bathroom, but some may find the hotel lacking in terms of cleanliness.

The City

Santa Fe doesn't actually sit on the Río Paraná, but at the western extremity of a series of delta islands, which separate it from the city of Paraná. Ships enter Santa Fe's important **port**, the most westerly along the Paraná, via an access channel. The Río Santa Fe borders the southern end of the city, running north to feed into the **Laguna Setúbal**, a large lake east of the city, and bordered by the city's lively Costanera, which runs for 5km or so from north to south. At the far northern end there is a *balneario*, while at the southern end lies the road bridge over the lake to Paraná, plus the remnants of the old suspension bridge, ripped apart by floods in 1983.

Santa Fe's mostly modern **downtown** area is centred on busy Calle 25 de Mayo, pedestrianized between Tucumán and Juan de Garay and lined with shops and *confiterías*. The quieter **centro histórico**, where you will find the majority of Santa Fe's older buildings, lies ten blocks south of Tucumán and is centred on **Plaza 25 de Mayo**. This is the most interesting area to explore on foot and you could while away an afternoon moving between its museums and churches, including the **Iglesia y Convento de San Francisco** and the **Museo Etnográfico y Colonial Juan de Garay**.

Plaza 25 de Mayo and around

Like the rest of the city, Santa Fe's main square, the **Plaza 25 de Mayo**, is an architecturally disjointed kind of place, with the styles of its surrounding buildings leaping from colonial through French Second Empire to nondescript modern. The square is somewhat unusual in having two churches. On the north side stands the rather stark white **Catedral Metropolitana** (daily 8am–8pm), originally built in the mid-eighteenth century but subsequently modified to give it a simple Neoclassical facade crowned with domed and majolica-tiled bell towers. Little remains of the original building except the massive studded wooden entrance doors. On the east side of the square is the **Iglesia de Nuestra Señora de los Milagros**, its pleasingly simple and typically colonial facade looking rather overwhelmed by the more modern constructions around it. Built between 1667 and 1700, it is the oldest church in the province; look inside to see the fine carvings produced by Guaraní in the Jesuit Missions – most notably the impressive Altar Mayor, produced in Loreto.

On the southeastern corner of the square you'll find the **Museo Histórico Provincial Brigadier General Estanislao López** (March, April, Oct & Nov Tues–Fri 8.30am–noon & 3–7pm, Sat & Sun 4–7pm; May–Sept Tues–Fri 8.30am–noon & 2.30–6.30pm, Sat & Sun 3–6pm; Dec–Feb Tues–Fri 9am–noon & 5–8pm, Sat & Sun 5.30–8.30pm; free). Housed in a cool late-colonial family house, the museum's collection comprises furniture, paintings, silverwork, religious icons and everyday items from the seventeenth century. There is a room dedicated to the famous *caudillo* of Santa Fe, Estanislao López, and a room of religious imagery with some notable carvings from the missions and paintings from the Cusco School.

Three blocks east, at 4 de Enero 1510, is the **Museo Provincial de Bellas Artes Rosa Galisteo de Rodríguez** (Tues–Fri 9am–noon & 4–8pm, Sat & Sun 4–8pm; free), an imposing Neoclassical building with a large collection of Argentine painting and sculpture from the likes of Spilimbergo, Petorutti and Fontana, along with a smaller selection of European painting with works from Delacroix and Rodin; temporary exhibitions of local artists' works are held from time to time.

Museo Etnográfico y Colonial Juan de Garay

One block east of the main plaza, at 25 de Mayo 1470, is the **Museo Etnográfico y Colonial Juan de Garay** (Jan & Feb Tues–Fri 8.30am–noon & 5–8pm, Sat & Sun 5–8pm; March & April Tues–Fri 8.30am–noon & 3.30–7pm, Sat & Sun 4–7pm; May–Sept Tues–Fri 8.30am–noon, Sat & Sun 3.30–6.30pm; Oct–Dec Tues–Fri 8.30am–noon & 3.30–7pm, Sat & Sun 4–7pm; free; ⓣ0342/459-5857). The bulk of the museum's well-organized and coherently displayed collection comprises pieces recovered from the site of **Santa Fe La Vieja** at Cayastá. The most commonly recovered pieces were *tinajas*, large ceramic urns – many of them in a surprisingly complete state considering they spent around 300 years underground – and delicate amulets in the form of shells or the *higa*, a clenched fist symbol, used to ward off the evil eye. There's also a fine collection of **indigenous ceramics** with typical zoomorphic forms ranging from birds – especially parrots – and bats, to capybaras, cats and snakes. Particularly amusing are the pieces in which the animal forms are moulded in such a way as to form a spout or handle. The arrival of the Spaniards had a significant impact on the pieces produced, both in the form (new shapes, such as jugs, began to appear) and in the design, with more floral and organic touches being introduced to the previously strongly geometric designs. At the centre of the museum there's a maquette showing the layout of Santa Fe La Vieja.

Iglesia y Convento de San Francisco

One block south of Plaza 25 de Mayo, at Amenábar 2557, lies the **Iglesia y Convento de San Francisco** (March–Nov Mon–Sat 8am–noon & 3–6.30pm, Sun 3.30–6pm; Dec–Feb Mon–Sat 8am–noon & 4–7pm, Sun 9.30am–noon & 4.30–7pm). Built in 1676, the church is notable for its incredible solid but rustic construction: the walls are nearly two metres thick and made of adobe, while the stunning and cleverly assembled interior **ceiling** was constructed using solid wooden beams of Paraguayan cedar, *lapacho*, *algarrobo* and *quebracho colorado* held together not with nails but with wooden pegs. The intricate dome at the centre of the church is a particularly impressive example of the application of this technique and also has a rather light-hearted touch: at the centre a beautifully carved pinecone is suspended. To your left when you are facing the altar is an ornate **Baroque pulpit** laminated in gold, which came from the original church at Cayastá. Of the various icons around the church the most notable is that of **Jesús Nazareno**, immediately to your left as you enter. The beautifully detailed image was produced by one of Spain's most famous *imagineros*, or religious image makers, Alonso Cano, in 1650. It was presented to the church by the Queen of Spain, Doña María Ana de Austria, wife of Felipe IV, when the city was moved from Cayastá, to show sympathy for the repeated Indian attacks.

One of the strangest relics in the church is found in the sacristy, a simple table scored by claw marks and known as the *mesa del tigre* ("the tiger's table"). According to a gory tale, in 1825 a jaguar – the word "*tigre*" often means a jaguar in Latin America – was washed up by a flood and found itself in the convent orchard. From there the animal sought refuge in the sacristy where it encountered its first victim, Brother Miguel Magallanes. Once the monk's body was discovered, a chase ensued with local bigwigs, monks and tracking dogs pursuing the jaguar. It was eventually shot in a small room off the convent cloisters, but not before it had attacked and killed two more monks and severely wounded another of the party of hunters.

Eating, drinking and nightlife

There are plenty of **restaurants** in Santa Fe, mostly within a few blocks of San Martín, though few really stand out. Stylish *El Brigadier*, San Martín 1670, is housed in an old colonial building and has a fine selection of well-prepared fish (both fresh- and saltwater) and meat; there is also a good-value *menú promocional*, consisting of a starter, main course of pasta or chicken and dessert. *Baviera*, San Martín 2941, does basic, well-prepared standards and is good for snacks at any time of the day. *Mi Casa*, San Martín 2777, is a popular *tenedor libre parrilla*.

Santa Fe's most famed gastronomic delights are the sweet snack *alfajores merengo* – a particularly tempting version of Argentina's favourite cake, coated in a crispy, white sugar frosting and produced in the city for more than a century and a half; they can be bought from the *Alfajorería* at General López 2634. **Beer** is particularly good in Santa Fe, and locals ask for a *liso* – a draught lager served in a straight glass. A good place to try one is in *Las Delicias*, on the corner of San Martín and Hipólito Yrigoyen, a traditional *confitería* serving good sandwiches and cakes. Santa Fe's liveliest **bars** are found around the intersection of San Martín and Santiago del Estero, all with tables on the pavement and a fun atmosphere on summer evenings: try *Triferto*, San Martín 3301, or *Mostaza*, San Martín 3299. For a totally different kind of atmosphere, head for the splendidly old-fashioned *Bar Tokio* (Mon–Sat 8am–10pm), on Plaza España, with snooker, pool and billiard tables and run by friendly Amelia, whose Japanese immigrant family have had the place for over sixty years.

Paraná

Lying just 30km southeast of Santa Fe, to which it is linked by the **Túnel Subfluvial Uranga-Sylvestre Begnis**, better known as "Hernandarias", **PARANÁ** is a far more appealing city than its cross-river neighbour. Favoured by a gentle hilly terrain and a handsome, pedestrian-friendly riverfront area, the city is a fine place to chill out for a day or two. In addition to some fine sandy **beaches**, the city has a particularly attractive park, the **Parque Urquiza**, whose shady walkways and thick vegetation provide welcome respite in the summer. Paraná's most famous landmark is its imposing, heavily Neoclassical **cathedral**, which dominates the city's main square. On another fine square, the Plaza Alvear, the **Museo Histórico Martiniano Leguizamón** has a well-presented section on the history of the region and a more than usually interesting

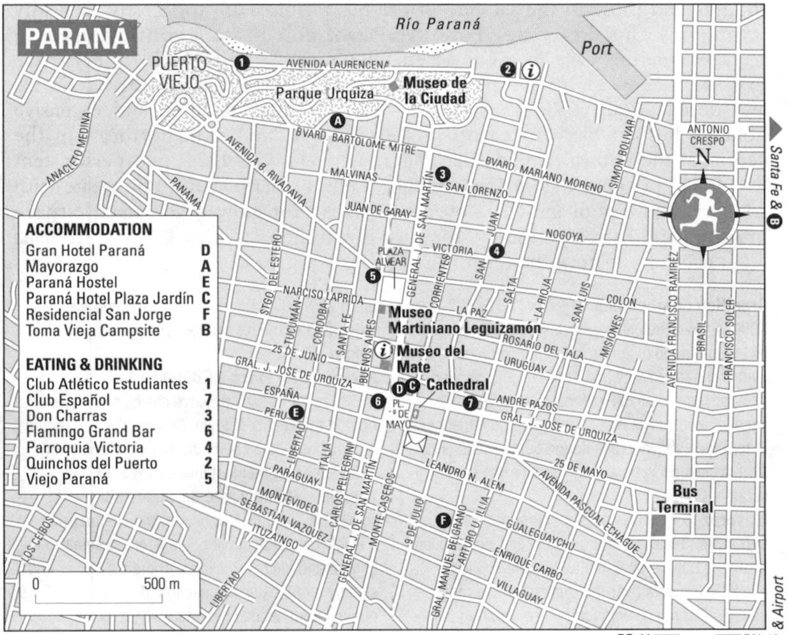

collection of *criollo* silverwork, while the **Museo de la Ciudad** is a friendly and accessible museum taking a more light-hearted look at the everyday life of the city; a comprehensive collection of *mate* paraphernalia from Argentina and, surprisingly, many other countries around the world is on display at the unmissable **Museo del Mate**.

Like Rosario, Paraná lacks a true **foundation** date: the area was simply settled by inhabitants from Santa Fe, who regarded the higher ground of the eastern banks of the Paraná as providing better protection from Indian attack. The city was declared provincial capital in 1822 and leapt to prominence as capital of General Urquiza's short-lived Confederación Argentina between 1854 and 1861, when the city's major public buildings were constructed. Like most of Argentina, Paraná had its most significant period of growth in the late nineteenth century when the city received thousands of European immigrants. Today, Paraná's population of around 250,000 makes it the largest city in Entre Ríos Province.

Arrival and information

Paraná's small **airport**, with daily flights to Buenos Aires, is around 5km southeast of the city, along RN-12 (ⓣ0343/424-3320). Paraná's confusing **Terminal de Omnibus** is at Av Ramírez 2550, around nine blocks east of central Plaza 1 de Mayo (ⓣ0343/431-5053); in the middle of it, a helpful bus-information-cum-tourist-office (daily 8am–2pm & 4–8pm) offers accommodation lists and maps. The central **tourist office** is at Buenos Aires 132 (daily 8am–8pm; ⓣ0343/423-0183).

Accommodation

Paraná's **hotels** tend to be far more appealing than Santa Fe's, and they include a couple of really attractive places. Budget places are thin on the ground, though, and those in the vicinity of the bus terminal are too costly to justify staying in such a dreary area. However, Paraná now boasts a **youth hostel** – a truly wonderful place in a converted townhouse: *Paraná Hostel*, Perú 342 (ⓣ0343/422-8233, ⓦwww.paranahostel.com.ar; $20 per person; ❷), has dorms and doubles with TV, plus a laundry, fully equipped kitchen and extensive library. The best place to **camp** is *Toma Vieja*, around 4km northeast of the centre, at the end of Avenida Blas Parera (ⓣ0343/433-1721; two-person tent $6, plus $1 per person; four-person tent $8, plus $2 per person), a huge site with a large outdoor pool and views over the Paraná. Hot showers and electricity are provided and there's a grocery store just down the road. Bus #5 goes to *Toma Vieja* every hour from the terminal.

Gran Hotel Paraná Urquiza 976 ⓣ0343/422-3900, ⓦwww.hotelesparana.com.ar. Smart modern block on the main square with its own restaurant, gym and parking facilities. Three slightly varying categories of room, all with a/c and cable TV. Its snooty French-style restaurant, *La Fourchette*, goes in for much showy presentation but the food is not all it is claimed to be and the service not up to scratch. ❹–❻

Mayorazgo Av Etchevere and Miranda ⓣ0343/423-0333. Paraná's most self-consciously luxurious hotel – an ostentatious and soulless block that towers over the Costanera: the rather blandly decorated rooms are more inspiring for the great views over the river than anything else. Large and attractive outdoor swimming pool, though. ❻

Paraná Hotel Plaza Jardín 9 de Julio 60 ⓣ0343/423-1700. Attractive old-fashioned hotel right in the centre of town. Comfortable a/c rooms grouped around a courtyard. Cable TV and 24hr room service. Breakfast included. ❸–❹

Residencial San Jorge Belgrano 368 ⓣ0343/422-1685. The best of the cheaper places: a lovely old building with tiled floors, a small garden and kitchen facilities. There's a newer and slightly more expensive section at the back but the original front section has more style. ❸

The City

While Paraná is a pleasant place to wander round – though at night the poor street lighting can be a hazard – there aren't any major sights, and the city is probably best treated as a place to take a bit of a break. The main square is the **Plaza 1° de Mayo**, ten blocks inland. The single most outstanding building here is the **cathedral**, built in 1887. It's a superficially handsome if somehow rather awkward Neoclassical edifice distinguished by an intense blue brick-tiled central dome and rather exotic, almost Byzantine bell towers.

Pedestrianized Calle San Martín leads to Plaza Alvear, three blocks north, on the southwestern corner of which, at Buenos Aires 285, you'll find the mostly well-organized **Museo Histórico de Entre Ríos Martiniano Leguizamón** (Tues–Fri 8am–noon, Thurs & Fri also 3.30–7.30pm, Sat 9am–noon; $1; ⓣ0343/431-2735). The upper floor is devoted to the history of Entre Ríos Province from pre-Columbian times to the present day. The informative panels are sometimes more interesting than the objects themselves, which are often notable mainly for their illustrious owners – they include such highlights as a 1976 Julio Iglesias LP and a wheelbarrow used by builders of the railways. Downstairs, however, there's an excellent collection of *criollo* silverwork. Among the more interesting pieces are vicious-looking spurs known as *lloronas* – *llorar* means "to cry", and it's debated whether they were thus called for the sound they made when the horse was moving or for the fact that they made the animal "cry blood". There's also a fine collection of gaucho *facas*, or knives, with inscriptions such as "do not enter without cause nor leave without honour". Look out, too, for the beautifully crafted *yesqueros*, elaborate precursors of the cigarette lighter formed by a stone and chain contraption – the last two creating a spark to light the tinder – made out of materials as diverse as silver and the tail of an armadillo.

At the corner of Buenos Aires and Cervantes, the modest but fun **Museo de la Ciudad** (daily 8am–noon & 4–8pm, free; ⓣ0343/420-1838) provides information on the founding of the city, including a maquette of the early settlement,

△ Swimmers before a race, Paraná beach

Mate: more than just a drink

The herby leaves used in making **mate**, Argentina's national beverage, come from an evergreen tree, *Ilex paraguayensis*, a member of the holly family that grows wild or in plantations in northeastern Argentina, especially in Misiones Province, southern Brazil and Paraguay. Its spring flowers are white and insignificant – it's the young leaves and buds that are of interest. They're harvested with machetes in the dry southern winter (June–Aug) and used to make the *yerba* or *mate* herb. The **preparation** process for good *yerba* is complex and subtle: first comes the *zapecado*, literally "opening of the eyes", when the *mate* leaves are dry-roasted over a fire, to prevent fermentation and keep the leaves green. The leaves are then coarsely ground – the *cancheo*, bagged and left to mature in dry sheds called *noques* for nine months to a year, though this is sometimes artificially accelerated to two months or even less. A milling process then results in either coarse *caá-guazú*, or "big herb", or the more refined *caá-mini*. *Yerba* is sometimes combined with other herbs (*yerba compuesta* or *con palo*), in a mountain blend using *hierbas serranas*, or mountain herbs, or flavoured with lemon essence, spearmint or cinnamon, though all such practices are frowned upon by serious *materos*.

The **vessel** you drink it out of is also called a *mate*, or *matecito*, originally a hollowed-out gourd of the climbing species *Lagenaria vulgaris*, native to the same region. It's dried, hollowed out and "cured" by macerating *yerba mate* inside it overnight. These gourds are still used to this day and come in two basic **shapes**: the pear-shaped *poro*, traditionally used for sweet *mate* – some people always add a little sugar, but most cognoscenti disapprove of such heresy – and the squat, satsuma-shaped *galleta*, meant for *cimarrón*, literally "untamed", one of the names for unsweetened *mate*. Many *mates* are **works of art**, sometimes intricately carved or painted, and often made of wood, clay or metal – again, connoisseurs claim gourds impart extra flavour to the brew. *Mates* or *matecitos* make great souvenirs from all over the country, but especially the northeast. The *bombilla* – originally a reed or stick of bamboo – is the other vital piece of equipment. Most are now straw-shaped tubes of silver, aluminium or tin, flattened at the end on which you suck, and with a bulbous or spoon-shaped protruberance at the other; this is perforated to strain the *mate* as you drink it. Optional extras include the *pava hornillo*, a special kettle that keeps the water at the right temperature. A thermos-flask is the latter-day substitute for this kettle, lovingly clutched by dedicated *materos* and replenished along the way at

but its more interesting pieces are the quirkier bits of paraphernalia donated by local businesses and individuals: there's a display of objects from old pharmacies including a gruesome dummy with nails stuck in its head used to advertise Geniol aspirins and a special pair of glasses apparently used by a local dentist to hypnotize patients instead of using anaesthetic.

The best museum in the city, however, is the **Museo del Mate** (daily 7–11am & 4–7pm; $2), at 25 de Junio 72. This new municipal institution presents a breathtakingly obsessive private collection of over a thousand objects related to Argentina's national beverage (see box above), ranging from kettles and posters to the world's biggest and smallest *matecitos*. Of particular interest are the porcelain *mates* used in Syria, now one of the main consumers of the herb, thanks to returnee immigrants, plus receptacles made in Japan, France, Australia and Central Europe.

Flanking Paraná's riverside, the **Parque Urquiza** is a 44-hectare park created on land donated by General Urquiza's widow. It is on a fairly narrow but hilly stretch of ground which slopes up from Avenida Laurencena, Paraná's Costanera, to the higher ground of the city. Designed, like so many of Argentina's parks, by shops and cafés; "hot water available" signs are a common sight all over Argentina but especially in the Litoral, and even more so across the border in Uruguay; a token sum is usually charged for the service.

Mateine is a gentler **stimulant** than the closely related caffeine, helping to release muscular energy, pace the heartbeat and aid respiration without any of the nasty side-effects of coffee. In the 1830s it even met with the approval of a wary Charles Darwin, who wrote that it helped him sleep. It's a tonic and a **digestive agent**, and by dulling the appetite can help you lose weight. Although its laxative, diuretic and sweat-making properties can be inconvenient when they take effect at the wrong time, *mate* is very effective at purging toxins and fat, perfect after excessive *asado* binges.

If ever you do find yourself in a **group** drinking *mate*, it's just as well to know how to avoid gaffes. The *cebador* – from *cebar* "to feed" – is the person who makes the *mate*. After half-filling the *matecito* with *yerba*, the *cebador* thrusts the *bombilla* into the *yerba* and trickles very hot – but not boiling – water down the side of the *bombilla*, to wet the *yerba* from below, which requires a knack. If asked "*¿Como lo tomás?*" answer "*amargo*" for without sugar, or "*dulce*" for sweetened; the latter's a safer bet if it's your first *mate* session, even if you don't have a sweet tooth. The *cebador* always tries the *mate* first – the "fool's *mate*" – before refilling and handing it round to each person present, in turn – always with the right hand and clockwise. Each drinker must drain the *mate* through the *bombilla*, without jiggling it around, sipping gently but not lingering, or sucking too hard (it's not milkshake), before handing it back to the *cebador*. Sucking out of the corner of the mouth is also frowned upon. A little more *yerba* may be added from time to time but there comes a moment when the *yerba* loses most of its flavour (it is said to be *lavado*) and no longer produces a healthy froth. The *matecito* is then emptied and the process started afresh. When the *cebador* has had enough, he or she "hangs the *mate* up". Saying "*gracias*" means you've had enough, and the *mate* will be passed to someone else when your turn comes round. The greatest honour comes when it's your turn to be *cebador*.

In addition to the standard hot brew, typically drunk in the Litoral region without sugar from a wide-mouthed gourd, a refreshing cold version, *tereré*, drunk from metal cups and sometimes mixed with fruit juice, is very popular in summer and anyone not used to *mate* might find they prefer it.

landscape gardener Charles Thays, it's particularly attractive and verdant, traversed by serpentine walkways and with great views over the river, but the area is best avoided at night. At its western end, there's a picturesque little neighbourhood called the **Puerto Viejo**, distinguished by its winding cobbled streets and handsome old-fashioned residences.

The real hub of Paraná life on summer evenings, the Costanera itself, is lined with a handful of bars and restaurants and some good public **beaches**; you can also become a member for the day of various clubs, giving you access to the smartest beaches and facilities such as swimming pools and showers – one of the most reasonable is the *Paraná Rowing Club* (Ⓣ0343/431-2048), where day membership is a possibility.

Eating, drinking and nightlife

There are enough decent **places to eat** to keep you happy for a day or two in Paraná. In the centre try the venerable *Club Español*, Urquiza 722, for good-value Spanish dishes. There are a couple of excellent fish restaurants and *parrillas* down by the river, notably *Club Atlético Estudiantes*, at the western end of the

Avenida Costanera (Ⓣ0343/421-8699), and highly rated if relatively expensive *Quinchos del Puerto*, in a rustic thatched construction at the corner of Avenida Laurencena and Santander (reservations advised at summer weekends; Ⓣ0343/423-2045). For a traditional *parrilla* you can try *Don Charras*, at Avenida Uranga 1127 – the meat is excellent but they also throw fish on the barbecue too. Several kilometres west of the Puerto Viejo, at a splendid riverside location at Avenida Estrada 3582, *Cangrejo* is the place to be seen in Paraná, specializing in fusion cuisine, fish, pasta and cocktails; its tropical decor and large terraces fill up with the city's young and beautiful from Thursday to Sunday throughout the summer.

For **drinks and snacks** in the city centre try the welcoming and classic *Viejo Paraná* with pavement tables on the corner of Buenos Aires and Rivadavia, or the very upmarket *Flamingo Grand Bar* on the corner of San Martín and Urquiza. A few blocks northeast of the town centre, on the corner of San Juan and Victoria, the beautifully restored *Parroquia Victoria* bar is an old-fashioned wood-panelled building with an outside patio and a lively clientele (open until the small hours).

La Paz and Esquina

LA PAZ and **ESQUINA**, respectively 185km and 250km north of Paraná, could both best be described as worthy stopovers rather than destinations in their own right, but their appealing riverside locations and a couple of fun activities – taking the waters at La Paz and fly-fishing at Esquina – make them more than just a place to bed down for the night. The former is tucked in the far northwest corner of Entre Ríos Province, while the latter is just a hop over the border into Corrientes, and both act as excellent alternatives to Paraná – smaller, quieter – for overnighting if you are headed for northern Corrientes or the Chaco. With more time on your hands and a yearning to experience traditional rural life, you might consider spending a day or two at one of the wonderful estancias near Esquina (see box opposite). Further north two more small towns on the mighty river's banks – **Goya** and **Empedrado** – have a venerable history as fishing resorts, especially the latter, which is known nostalgically as the "Pearl of the Paraná", but they are too run-down and have too little in the way of attractions or decent accommodation to serve as workable options. Forge on to Corrientes city, if you have gone that far.

La Paz

The small resort of **La Paz** is named for the Virgin to whom its early twentieth-century French-style Neo-Gothic church is dedicated – but its name could also refer to the peaceful atmosphere that it enjoys for most of the year – broken only by the odd festival devoted to fishing and folk singing. The main reason to visit is to soak in the modern thermal baths right down by the Río Paraná, a short way south of the town itself. The best accommodation by far is *Costa Dorada Resort* (Ⓣ03437/425164, Ⓦwww.costadoradaresort.com; ❻), right next to the *termas*, where eleven pools of highly mineralized waters are maintained at around 42°C. The rooms at the resort are modern, bright and tastefully decorated, with large windows and small terraces for river views, particularly attractive at sunset. The complex includes the elegant restaurant, *Terramillán*, serving national and international specialities, including fish from the Paraná.

Esquina

Strategically wedged in the angle formed by the Corrientes and Paraná rivers – hence its name, "corner" in Spanish – **Esquina**'s main claim to fame is that football hero Diego Maradona's family originated from here – the municipality even began proceedings against the ailing sportsman in 2007 for not paying local taxes. However, most people visit this sleepy market town to try and catch huge river fish such as *boga*, *surubí* and *dorado*, while every March Esquina hosts the National Pacú Festival – *pacú* being another native species much appreciated by anglers and fish-eaters alike. Plaza 25 de Mayo, the town's hub, has retained

The estancias of western and northern Corrientes Province

Accommodation in the western and northern reaches of Corrientes Province tends not to be that great, much of it being aimed at fishing fanatics more interested in the size of their catch than the comfort of their rooms. However, a few outstanding **estancias** take in guests – often regaling them with horse rides or hands-on experiences of genuine ranch life. Don't forget that you cannot just turn up on spec but must book ahead; sometimes they will arrange for you to be picked up at the nearest town, airport or bus terminal, even if you have your own car – often the lengthy approach roads are impassable other than by 4WD.

West of the province

South of Esquina, *Estancia La Rosita* (T011/4804-0416, Wwww.estancialarosita.com.ar; 7 full board), lies some way from the river among huge pastures, which are dotted with ever-changing lakes and marshes, and is very much a working estancia, with lots of cattle and horses – galloping is a definite option. The house is an agreeable low-rise farmstead, with shady galleries and a noble dining room, while the guest rooms are simple and homely. Alicia Cometta de Landgraf runs the place with her sons, who are avid polo players – take a look at the impressive pitch even if you never get to see or participate in a game. An Australian tank swimming pool and barbecue facilities are added attractions; the food is authentic *criollo*.

Estancia Buena Vista (T011/4342-6290, Wwww.estanciabuenavista.com.ar; 7 full board), several kilometres north of Esquina off the road to Corrientes, is another traditional working estancia, with large numbers of cattle and sheep but specializing in game, which can be sampled in the fine menus on offer. Run by a Swiss Argentine, Sara Röhner, and her German-born husband, Klaus Liebig, the estancia combines a high level of comfort with old-fashioned *correntino* hospitality. The German-style teas are memorable.

North of the province

Just visible from RN-12, near the turn-off to Berón de Astrada, 120km east of Corrientes city, is handsome *Estancia Atalaya* (T03783/433269, Emmoncada@arnet.com.ar; 6), which has six rooms and organizes wildlife safaris, horse rides, canoe trips, surrey carriage rides and rodeo shows.

More isolated and more dramatic, *Estancia San Juan Poriahú* (T03781/497045, Esanjuanporiahu@latinmail.com; 7) lies near the picturesque little village of Loreto, 30km down RN-118 from its junction with RN-12. Concealed among 150 square kilometres of pasture and forest, it is on the northernmost edge of the Esteros del Iberá – caymans, or *yacarés*, lurk in the lagoon by the entrance to the seventeenth-century *casco*. The attractive main buildings house six rooms, with wonderful old-fashioned but perfectly functional bathrooms. There is a fine swimming pool and the flamboyant owner will take you on horse rides or onto the lagoon in a leaky (but safe) tub of a boat.

its colonial feel – locals laze on warm days in the shade of its many plane trees, *lapachos* and magnolias.

Alternatives to staying at the nearby estancias – highly recommended (see box, p.395) – include three **accommodation** options: *Posada Casablanca* at Quinta IV Bis (ⓣ03777/460967, ⓦwwwposadacasablanca.com.ar; ❹), a smart white building with several rooms, of two categories, many of which have fabulous river views; and *Posada Hambaré* (ⓣ03777/460270, ⓦwww.posadahambare.com.ar; ❽ full board) with some very classy rooms in the original thatched house, plus very decently appointed, all en-suite rooms, in the modern extension. Both are at the northern edge of the town and cater very much to fishers and dove hunters. *La Casona de Cotota* (ⓣ03777/460169, ⓦwww.lacasonadecatota.com.ar; ❹), the historic family home of Sara Röhner, the owner of *Estancia Buena Vista* (see box, p.395), now run as a charming B&B by her son Klausi is in the centre of town, at Bartolomé Mitre 691, and has a fine dining room, five comfortable rooms and fishing trips on offer.

Corrientes

Sensual, sultry, subtropical and sitting on a bend in the Río Paraná, **CORRIENTES** is one of the region's oldest and most attractive cities, founded in 1588 as an intermediary port along the river route between Buenos Aires and Asunción. Its charm is derived largely from the number of traditional *correntino* buildings in its crumbling – but very handsome – centre, based around the **Plaza 25 de Mayo**. These Neocolonial edifices, with overhanging roofs supported on wooden posts, are interspersed with more elaborate late nineteenth-century Italianate architecture. Corrientes' modest museums, most notably the original **Museo de Artesanía**, where you can see fine examples of the province's distinctive crafts, are given added appeal by being housed in these traditional buildings, and its central streets make it a pleasant place to just wander around for a day or two. If you visit from November to February, though, be aware that both temperatures and humidity can be very high. As a result, locals take the siesta very seriously, not emerging from indoors until dusk on the hottest days: if you must hit the streets on a summer afternoon, head for Corrientes' attractive **Costanera**, curving for 2.5km around the northwest of the city centre where native *lapacho* trees, with exquisite pink blossom in spring, provide a welcome bit of shade – though mosquitoes like it here, too.

Corrientes is linked to Resistencia, the capital of Chaco Province, 20km to the west, via the Puente General M. Belgrano, a suspension bridge across the Río Paraná. Like many other cities in the region, Corrientes has an important **carnival**, held throughout January and February until Mardi Gras in the Corsódromo – a kind of open-air stadium specially constructed for the festival. A more locally authentic affair, though, is the **Festival del Chamamé**, a celebration of the region's most popular folk music with plenty of live music and dancing, held on the second weekend in December.

Arrival and information

Corrientes' **Aeropuerto Fernando Piragine Niveyro** (ⓣ03783/458340), lies 10km northeast of the city, along RN-12. Aerolíneas Argentinas has its office at Junín 1301 (ⓣ03783/428678). The city's **bus terminal** (ⓣ03783/442149) is around 4km southeast of Plaza 25 de Mayo, along one of the city's main access

roads, the Avenida Maipú. Various local buses, including the #103, run between the terminal and the centre. A taxi from the terminal to the centre will cost around $10. Local buses from Resistencia arrive at a smaller bus terminal on the Costanera, opposite the northern end of La Rioja, within walking distance of most accommodation. Corrientes' rather basic **tourist office** (daily 7am–1pm & 3–8pm) is down on the Costanera, where it meets Pellegrini.

Accommodation

Corrientes' **hotels** are particularly oriented towards businessmen, and while there are some good upmarket places, simple, pleasant budget accommodation is thin on the ground. There are some cheaper hotels around the bus terminal but – unless you are literally just spending a night in transit – this area is too far away from anything. The city's particularly hot and humid summers make air-conditioning almost a necessity – though a shady room with a good fan can be acceptable. There's a good **campsite**, with showers, electricity and barbecue facilities around 10km northeast of town at Laguna Soto, on the way to Santa Ana (see p.350). Local bus #109 from the terminal goes there every ten minutes or so, taking about 45 minutes.

Gran Hotel Guaraní Mendoza 970
☎ 03783/433800, ⓔ hguarani@espacio.com.ar.
The doyen of Corrientes' hotels, this is a business-oriented establishment in a modern glass-fronted

building, with an inviting pool and bar area. There are several categories of rooms ranging from standard to VIP and two categories of suites; all have a/c and cable TV. ❺

Hospedaje San Lorenzo San Lorenzo 1136 (no phone). The best of the cheaper places to stay, friendly *San Lorenzo* offers basic, well-kept rooms on a quiet central street. Fans and private bathrooms. ❷

Hostal del Río Plácido Martínez 1098 ⓣ03783/436100. Modern block facing the river with slightly bland but spacious rooms, featuring cable TV and good a/c. The hotel has a small outdoor swimming pool, and the very efficient staff speak some English. ❸

Hotel de Turismo Entre Ríos 650 ⓣ03783/429112. A quaintly old-fashioned place (Graham Greene stayed here in the 1960s) at a good location down by the Costanera. Cool tiled floors and wooden furniture – though some of the rooms are showing their age a bit as is the very noisy a/c. There's a great outdoor pool. Rates include breakfast. ❸

Hotel Orly San Juan 867 ⓣ03783/427248. Well located, this comfortable small hotel in a 1970s-style block has pleasant rooms and a smart ground-floor *confitería*. ❹

Plaza Hotel Junín 1549 ⓣ03783/466500, ⓦwww.corrienteshotel.com.ar. The best hotel in town – which is no accolade – the *Plaza* overlooks the animated Plaza Cabral and is a shiny modern block blessed with a refreshing pool and bright rooms but noisy a/c. ❻

The City

Corrientes is reasonably compact: all the major points of interest lie within the streets north of Avenida 3 de Abril, which runs east–west through the city towards Puente General Belgrano. The whole of this approximately triangular area is bordered to the northwest by the **Avenida Costanera General San Martín**. There are two centres: the centro histórico, with **Plaza 25 de Mayo** at its heart, lies to the north and is where you'll find most of Corrientes' historic buildings and museums, including the **Museo de Artesanía** and the **Museo Histórico**, while the less interesting Centro Comercial is focused on Plaza Cabral, ten blocks southeast of Plaza 25 de Mayo and Corriente's main pedestrianized shopping street, Calle Junín.

Plaza 25 de Mayo and around

An old-fashioned leafy square surrounded by some of Corrientes' most striking buildings, **Plaza 25 de Mayo** encapsulates the city's sleepy subtropical ambience. The square lies one block south of the Costanera, to which it is linked by the narrow streets of Buenos Aires and Salta, the former in particular lined with fine examples of late nineteenth-century architecture. One of the most striking buildings on the square itself, the pink **Casa de Gobierno**, on the eastern side, was constructed in 1886 in the ornate Italianate style that replaced many of the older, colonial buildings at the end of the nineteenth century. Particularly attractive are the delicate filigree window grilles, best admired on the building's northern wall, along Fray José de la Quintana.

Opposite, on the corner of Fray José de la Quintana and Salta, you'll find the **Museo de Artesanía** (Mon–Fri 7am–noon & 4–7pm; free) and the craft workshops, or *talleres*. The museum is housed within a typical colonial Corrientes building; a low, whitewashed residence constructed around a central patio flanked by a gallery, providing shade from the fierce summer sun. Inside you'll find a selection of local crafts, including fine examples of leather, ceramics and basketwork. Perhaps the most intriguing pieces, sold by craftsmen working in the workshops within, are the carvings of San La Muerte (literally "Saint Death"). These solemn little skeletons, carved of wood, gold or bone are carried around – or, in the case of the smallest figures, inserted under the skin – to ensure the bearer a painless death; they're a typical example of the popular cults, many of them inherited from the Guaraní, which coexist in Corrientes with profound Catholic beliefs. At the southern end of the square, the nineteenth-century **Iglesia de Nuestra Señora de la Merced** (daily 7am–noon & 4–8pm) houses a handsome hand-carved wooden retable, or altar screen, with twisted wooden pillars and rich golden inlay work.

Five blocks southeast of the Plaza, at 9 de Julio 1052, the **Museo Histórico** (Mon–Sat 8am–noon & 4–8pm; free) is in an attractively renovated old family house, dating from the nineteenth century. It's a fairly eclectic and not particularly well-organized collection covering various aspects of provincial history, though there is a fine collection of religious artefacts, including some Jesuit wood-carvings.

Heading directly south from the square you'll come, after seven blocks, to the **Iglesia Santísima Cruz de los Milagros** (open by appointment only; ⓣ03783/427073), at the southern end of the Plaza de la Cruz. Both the square and the church – an austere Italianate construction dating from 1897 – are named after Corrientes' first cross, brought by the Spaniards on the city's founding in 1588. The cross gained its epithet, the "Cross of Miracles", when, according to legend, it proved impervious to native attempts to destroy it with fire. A piece of the original cross is preserved as part of the altar within the church, while a replica of it can be seen in the Museo Histórico (see above).

The Costanera

Corrientes' attractively maintained riverside avenue, the **Avenida Costanera General San Martín**, runs from the small **Parque Mitre**, at the northern end of the city, as far as the Puente General Belgrano. Lined with fine examples of native trees, it's a lovely spot on summer evenings, when the heat dissipates a little and locals leave the cool refuge of their homes to pack its promenades for a jog or a stroll, or simply sit sipping *mate* or *tereré* on stone benches – but be prepared to share the experience with persistent mosquitoes. Just to the west of Parque Mitre, where there is a small beach, restaurants and a children's playground, you'll find the port buildings and the **Mercado Paraguayo** – a standard fixture in northern Argentine cities – selling all manner of cheap imported Paraguayan goods, from shoes to stereos. Buses to Resistencia also leave from here and unofficial taxis also tout for business along this section of the avenue. Beyond here, the wide avenue sweeps southeast, with various panoramic points jutting out over the river, from where there are views to the flat Resistencia "coast". A number of small beaches dot the Costanera – they're fine for sunbathing, but you should avoid swimming here unless there is a lifeguard on duty (summer only; check with tourist office for details): the unexpectedly strong currents here gave rise to Corrientes' full name, San Juan de Vera de Las Siete Corrientes, "San Juan de Vera of the Seven Currents".

Eating, drinking and nightlife

There are a handful of good places to **eat** and **drink**, mostly along the Costanera. One of these, at the junction with Junín, is the excellent buffet-style restaurant, *El Solar*, serving plenty of appetizing fresh salads, fruit juices and a variety of hot dishes. Along the southern end of the Costanera, between San Martín and Bolívar, you'll find a number of good *parrillas* with outside seating, including the glitzy ★ *Las Brasas*. By far the best food and most stylish ambience in Corrientes are to be had at ★ *La Princesa*, an attractively converted

Neocolonial house, at Buenos Aires 628. It's not in line for a gastronomic award but the cuisine is relatively innovative for these parts, including dishes such as fish with an Asian-style sauce or meat with fresh fruit, and is well prepared, at moderate prices, and late at night you can dance to jazz and bossa nova. Snacks and coffees are on offer at a wonderfully kitsch and extremely popular *confitería*, *Martha de Bianchetti*, at Mendoza and 9 de Julio. For a more traditional café/bar atmosphere, head for *El Café del Sol*, at Rioja 708. Several fast-food joints are strung along Junín, and hamburger stalls and pizzerias can be found along the Costanera.

A popular **nightlife** option is a chamamé show held at various restaurants; chamamé is perhaps Argentina's most infectious folk music, a lively danceable rhythm punctuated by a rather bloodcurdling cry, known as the *sapucay*. *Parrilla El Quincho*, on Av Juan Pujol and Pellegrini, and *La Peña Puente Pesoa*, at the intersection of RN-12 with Avenida P. Ferrer (the continuation of Avenida 3 de Abril), both do a very reasonable *tenedor libre parrilla* and live chamamé shows on Fridays and Saturdays from about 10pm.

The Gran Chaco

One of Argentina's forgotten corners and poorest regions, the **GRAN CHACO** is a land of seemingly unending alluvial plains, with areas of arid thornscrub in the dry west, and subtropical vegetation and palm savannah in the humid east. It has little in the way of dramatic scenery, no impressive historical monuments and few services for the visitor, but if you have a special interest in **wildlife** you will find it rewarding, provided you avoid the blistering heat of summer. In the sizeable sectors not yet cleared for agriculture, it harbours an exceptional diversity of **flora and fauna** (see box opposite), making it worth your while to break your journey for a day or two as you cross the region. Bird-watchers fare best: more than three hundred bird species have been recorded in the dry Chaco; and anglers come from all over the world in search of fish such as the *dorado*.

Wet Chaco scenery is mostly found near the **river systems** of the **Río Paraguay** and the **Río Paraná**, where the rainfall can be as high as 1200mm a year, causing heavy flooding at times. It is characterized by palm savannahs, patches of jungle and plantations of sugar cane, soya and fruit. Narrow strips border the main rivers that cross the region from west to east: the Río Pilcomayo, which forms the border with Paraguay for most of its course; and the less erratic Río Bermejo (or Teuco), which separates Formosa and Chaco provinces. These rivers, after a fairly energetic start in the Bolivian highlands, grow weary with the heavy load of sediment they carry by the time they reach the Chaco plains. They meander tortuously, frequently change course, and sometimes lose their way entirely. In some places they dissipate into swamps called *esteros* or *bañados*, or **lagoons** that can become saline in certain areas owing to high evaporation. Rainfall diminishes the further west you travel from the Paraná and Paraguay rivers and the habitat gradually alters into dry Chaco scenery, typified by dense **thornscrub** that is used to graze zebu-crossbreed cattle, but cleared in those areas where irrigation has made it possible to cultivate crops such as cotton. This zone was known to the conquistadors as **El Impenetrable**, less because of the thornscrub than for the lack of water, which only indigenous groups seemed to know how to overcome.

The Gran Chaco records some of the highest **temperatures** anywhere in the continent from December to February, often reaching 45°C or more. At these times, the siesta becomes even more sacred and people take to drinking chilled *tereré*. The best times to see wildlife are in the early morning or late afternoon and the best time of year to visit is from June to September: although night frosts are not unknown in June and July, daytime temperatures generally hover in the agreeable 20–25°C bracket. Moreover, the deciduous trees lose their leaves, so you've more chance of seeing wildlife. The **rainy season** generally lasts from October to May but violent downpours are possible throughout the year. For outdoor activities arm yourself with insect repellent, sunscreen and a hat, especially in summer; and make sure you have plentiful drinking water supplies.

Wildlife viewing in the Chaco

The main reason for visiting the Chaco is to see its varied and fascinating **wildlife**. Despite the vast lists of elusive, endangered mammals given in the region's tourist literature, though, only the very luckiest or most patient observers will see a **jaguar**, maned wolf, giant armadillo or *mirikiná* (nocturnal monkey). The surest bet for seeing any animals is to hire the services of one of the region's few but excellent **tour operators**; recommendations are listed in a separate box on p.409.

In the northeast corner of Santiago del Estero Province, the **Parque Nacional Copo** is the best remaining chunk of prime dry Chaco left in the country and the only area of protected land in the Argentine Chaco big enough to provide a sustainable habitat for some of the region's most threatened wildlife, including the elusive **Wagner's peccary**. Giant and honey anteaters also inhabit the park, as do the threatened Crowned Eagle, the Greater Rhea and the King Vulture. Frequently parched, it's a huge expanse of approximately 1140 square kilometres, with 550 square kilometres of provincial reserve attached to the west.

The edges of the woodland patches of the **Parque Nacional Río Pilcomayo**, to the north of Formosa city, can be great for glimpsing the larger mammals, including giant anteaters, honey anteaters, peccaries, deer, three types of monkey and pumas. Capybara, the two species of cayman, and even tapir live in the wetter regions of the park. Jaguars are believed to be extinct here, but the maned wolf can, very occasionally, be found – indeed, this park offers one of your best chances of seeing one. Almost three hundred species of **birds** have been recorded here, including the **Bare-faced Curassow** and **Thrush-like Wren**, both highly endangered in Argentina.

The **Complejo Ecológico Zoo** (daily dawn–dusk; $1), on RN-95 near **Presidente Roque Sáenz Peña**, however, is really the best place for guaranteed viewing of the endangered beasts of the Chaco, including the maned wolf, jaguar, puma, tapir, honey anteater, bare-faced curassow, giant anteater and giant armadillo. This zoo fulfils an important educational role in an area where ecological consciousness is sometimes acutely lacking. Poorly funded, it nonetheless does an excellent job at rescuing, releasing or housing wounded or impounded specimens that are the victims of road traffic accidents, fires, illegal hunting and unscrupulous animal trading. A surprising side to its activities, given the distance from the Andes, is its captive breeding programme for condors; Chaco-reared birds have even been sent to Venezuela, where they had died out.

An ethnographic history of the Gran Chaco

For some seven thousand years, the **Gran Chaco** was a melting pot of indigenous cultures from across the continent: Arawak peoples from the north, Andean groups from the west, nomadic tribes from the south. "Chaco" is believed to mean "place of hunting", derived from the Quichoa *chacú*, a traditional system of hunting employed by the indigenous groups in the area. This co-operative method involved encircling a vast area on foot, and driving all animals therein to a central point, where pregnant females and very young animals would be let free and a quota of the rest killed.

European settlement

In colonial times, the Spanish soon discovered that conquest here was not an attractive proposition: no precious metals, and indigenous groups as hostile as the climate. Barring several short-lived incursions by the Jesuits in the seventeenth and eighteenth centuries, the only serious attempt at settlement was the colony of **Concepción de la Buena Esperanza del Bermejo**, founded in 1585 by Alfonso de Vera y Aragón. The Spanish tried to introduce the **mita system** of forced labour to produce cotton, a crop native to the area and used as money in the pre-Columbian era. The attempt backfired: press-ganged Abipone warriors revolted in 1632, destroying the colony. After this, the Spanish opted for a policy of containment of the region, with some limited contacts through trade. The inhospitable nature of the terrain meant that this was the last area to be incorporated into the nation-state of Argentina, at the end of the nineteenth century.

After the **War of the Triple Alliance** with Paraguay (1865–70) and the fixing of the frontier – in 1879, after the arbitration of the United States – the Argentine authorities sought to formalize control over its sensitive northern border area by subjugating its indigenous inhabitants and opening it up to white settlement. However, it was only after the conclusion of the Campaign of the Desert in Patagonia that President Roca could focus military attention on the region. During the 1880s, a series of short campaigns conducted from a chain of military forts brought most organized indigenous resistance in the region to an end, although **Chaco campaigns** continued into the early twentieth century. Some of these were bloodless: when faced by the prospect of a pitched battle, the indigenous tribes tended to scatter and withdraw to Bolivia or Paraguay. The end result was the same: territory was ceded, and the indigenous groups became second-class citizens in their own land. The last indigenous uprising on Argentine territory occurred here: in 1919, a group of Pilagá destroyed Fortín Yunká, near the Paraguayan border, northwest of today's Parque Nacional Pilcomayo.

European settlers began to arrive in the region in the late nineteenth century, attracted by government grants and the prospect of exploiting the natural resources, especially its virgin tracts of *quebracho* forests: the tree is prized among other things for its resistant, rot-proof timber. So began a period of dramatic environmental change, hastened by the **construction of railways** into the interior, as millions of trees were felled by companies such as the British-owned La Forestal to provide sleepers for the world's railways, charcoal for Argentina's trains, posts to fence off the estancias of the south and tannin for the world's leather tanneries. Land clearance paved the way for a **cotton boom in the 1940s and 1950s**, and cattle were introduced in the thousands to graze the scrub. In recent decades, the region has suffered from severe economic recession. Forestry resources have been massively depleted; the tannin industry is in crisis, since the introduction of artificial substitutes; and soil exhaustion, floods and competition from other areas of the world have hit the profitability of crops like cotton. Sustainable economic development still seems a long way off.

The Gran Chaco's indigenous tribes today

Formosa and Chaco provinces still have one of the most numerous and diverse indigenous populations in the country, although the casual visitor is unlikely to have much contact with the major ethnic groups in the region.

The **Komlek** (or **Toba**) are members of the Guaraní group and, with a population of about 50,000, they are one of the most numerous of the area's indigenous groups, living mainly in the central eastern band of Chaco Province, but also in Formosa Province, northern Santa Fe Province, plus small communities in Salta and Buenos Aires provinces. They took to the horse after contact with the Spanish, and became known for their fierce fighting ways, repelling Spanish attempts at conquest and expanding their range at the expense of other indigenous groups in the interior of the Chaco. Many of their communities are in rural areas and others in town barrios such as the one found in Resistencia, where people make a living from manual labour and crafts: basket-weaving, pottery, wood-carving and weaving. The Komlek have a rich musical tradition, playing instruments such as the *nvike*, a type of fiddle.

The **Wichí** are the second most numerous group after the Komlek, with a population of 20,000 or so, spread across western Formosa, northeastern Salta Province and along the Río Bermejo in the far northwest of Chaco Province. They still rely on hunter-gathering for their economic and cultural life. Hunting these days is often with guns, when they can afford to buy them, but other more ancestral forms are still practised, such as fishing with different types of net: the use of the scissor net (*red de tijera*) involves remarkable skill, as fishermen dive into silty rivers, fishing blind underwater by sensing movement around them. The Wichí are also collectors of wild honey, gathering it from twenty species of bee. Much of their diet comes from seeds of trees such as the *algarrobo* and *chañar* – the latter has fruits somewhat like small dates. In addition, families cultivate small plots of beans, watermelons and maize and raise small herds of goats. A limited interaction with the market economy involves seasonal labour and the sale of fish and beautiful handicrafts. The Wichí are especially famous for the beautifully woven *yica* bags made of a sisal-like fibre, prepared laboriously from the *chaguar*, a type of ground-growing bromeliad resembling a yucca. These are dyed with natural colours, some of them startlingly rich, obtained from a variety of plants. However, a constant problem for all the indigenous groups is finding markets for their produce, though some of it is on sale as far away as Tarragona, Catalonia.

The **Mocoví** people live principally in the central south of Chaco Province and parts of Santa Fe, in communities around Villa Angela and Charata. Much less numerous than the Komlek, their population numbers around 7000, but only about half the population speak their native language, a tongue that belongs to the Guaycurú group, like that of the Komlek. The Mocoví are noted for their pottery, and families buy what they can't grow by working in domestic service or forestry or as seasonal farm-labourers.

The **Pilagá**, numbering approximately 5000, live in central Formosa Province. They make their living by a combination of settled agriculture and hunter-gathering, including fishing with home-made spears, known as *fijas*. In addition, some work as labourers on cotton plantations and in forestry. The Pilagá have no written language, although committees are currently trying to formulate a standardized alphabet. If you see members of their community, in the Bañado La Estrella, for example, remember that they are generally reluctant to be photographed, especially without permission.

Chaco Province

The **easternmost strip of Chaco Province**, along the Paraná and Paraguay rivers, is the heartland of the wet Chaco. Most of the original forests and swamps have fallen victim to agricultural developments, dedicated to the production of beef cattle and crops such as fruit, soya and sugar cane. The main highway through this region is **RN-11**, which connects Santa Fe with **Resistencia**, the starting point for trips along RN-16 to **Parque Nacional Chaco** (see p.408) and the interior of the province.

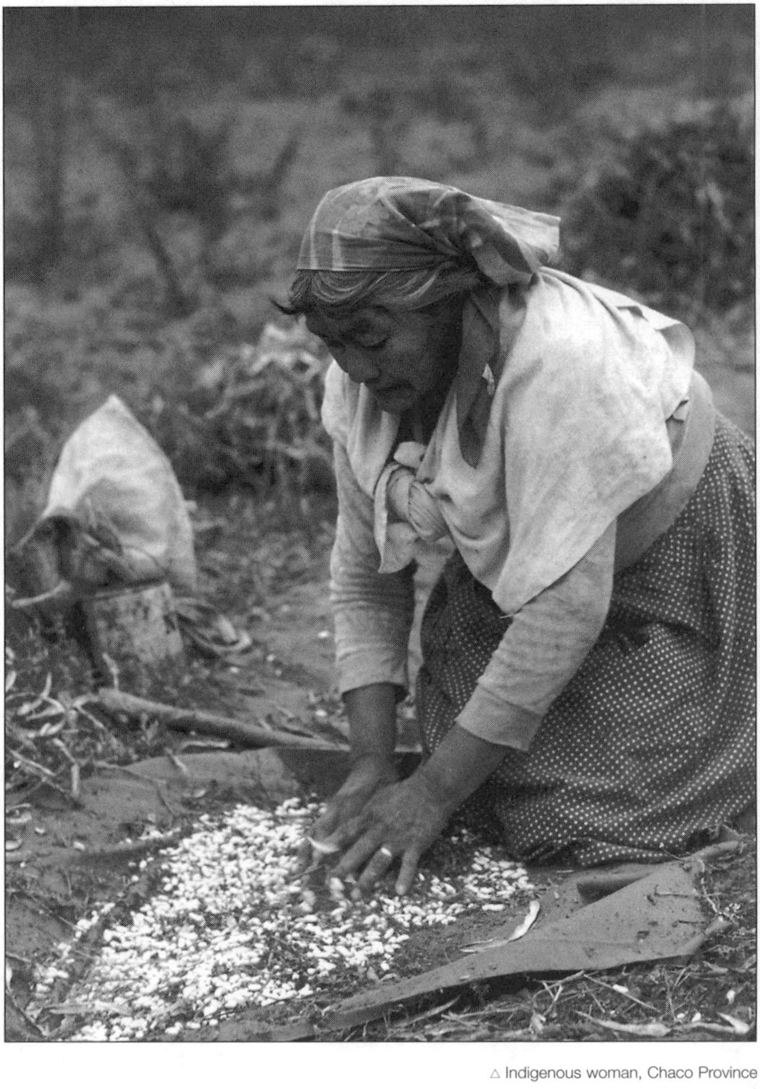

△ Indigenous woman, Chaco Province

Resistencia

RESISTENCIA is Chaco Province's sprawling administrative capital, with nearly half a million inhabitants, and the principal gateway to the Gran Chaco. Despite its commercial importance and lack of colonial architecture, the city is a pleasant enough place; it has a feeling of spaciousness about it and is known for the outstanding friendliness of its inhabitants. The city's nickname is "Ciudad de las Esculturas" ("City of Sculptures"), owing to the outdoor statues throughout town; they also inspired the main attraction, the remarkable cultural centre called the **Fogón de los Arrieros**. In the same vein, plans are being laid to open a special building, the Domo del Centenario (Centenary Dome) to house the Bienal de Escultura, at which sculptors would demonstrate and display their works every two years; the Dome is being built near the Parque 2 de Febrero, and may be worth checking out.

Arrival and information

The city's modern **airport** is 6km west of town; there are daily flights to Buenos Aires. A taxi to downtown will cost you $10–12; major international car-rental firms have stands in the terminal. The **bus terminal** (ⓣ03722/461098) is at the junction of avenidas Malvinas Argentinas and MacLean, 4km southwest of Plaza 25 de Mayo. Bus #3 connects the two, leaving from the kiosk opposite the terminal (every 20–30min). A *remise* from here to the centre costs around $8. To reach Corrientes, you might want to consider a *remise colectivo* as an alternative to the bus: these leave from the south side of Plaza 25 de Mayo at Alberdi ($1.50).

The rudimentary municipal **tourist office** (Mon–Fri 8am–8pm, Sat 8am–1pm; ⓣ03722/458289) is in a bandstand-like booth on the Plaza 25 de Mayo. Slightly better is the provincial tourist office at Santa Fe 178 (Mon–Fri 7.30am–8pm, Sat & Sun 8am–noon & 5–8pm), though oddly they have little information about the rest of the province.

Accommodation

Most of the town's **accommodation** is well located, within four blocks of the main square; the larger hotels usually offer a ten percent discount for cash payment, but ask first; those in the lower categories tend to charge extra for air-conditioning. The nearest **campsite** is *Camping 2 de Febrero*, Av Avalos 1100 (ⓣ03722/458323), 1.5km north. Set in the attractive park of the same name, near the Río Negro, due northwest of the Plaza 25 de Mayo, the site has full services and a pool; take bus #9 from the plaza ($0.70).

Gran Hotel Royal Obligado 211 ⓣ03722/443666. A reasonable mid-range option, it is neither grand nor especially regal but it has spruce, somewhat bland rooms, and its facilities do include a squash court. 3

Hospedaje Santa Rita Alberdi 311 ⓣ03722/459719. A family-run establishment offering some large rooms, but with fans rather than a/c. 2

Hotel Bariloche Obligado 239 ⓣ03722/421412, ⓔjag@cpsarg.com. Really more of a guesthouse with an institutional feel, this modest hotel offers good-value rooms, some without external windows, for up to four people; popular with local salesmen it's at its busiest on weekdays. 2

Hotel Casino Gala (Amerian) J.D. Perón 330 ⓣ03722/452400, ⓦwww.hotelcasinogala.com.ar. This welcome new addition to the region's hotels knocks spots off the competition. In a converted Neoclassical building, it houses the city casino and convention rooms, but the rooms are comfortable and enormous (all effectively are suites), the swimming pool is glorious and the efficient spa offers massages and foot-rubs that will be a delight after a day looking for maned wolves. *Valentino*, the restaurant, could best be described as ambitious, but the breakfasts are plentiful and it is fine if you don't want to go out to eat, or the city restaurants are closed, as often occurs in January. Check for good-value weekend deals. 7

Hotel Colón Santa María de Oro 143 ⓣ&ⓕ 03722/422861. This decent place has pleasant if poorly lit rooms for up to five people; breakfast is included, for what it's worth. ❸

Hotel Covadonga Güemes 200 ⓣ 03722/444444, ⓔ hotelcovadonga@infovia.com.ar. A well-run, albeit old-fashioned establishment with smart rooms and comfy beds; facilities include a pool, gym and sauna. ❺

The City

The vast main square, **Plaza 25 de Mayo**, is dotted with *caranday* palms and native trees; a neatly laid-out place occupying four whole blocks, the square is dominated by a statue of San Martín and hosts a small artisans' market. A couple of blocks southeast, the **Museo del Hombre Chaqueño** (daily 8am–noon & 5–9pm; free) has a modest but clearly presented collection detailing provincial history, with information on the province's pre-Columbian cultures (see box, pp.402–403); models of figures from Guaraní mythology; beautiful nineteenth-century silver *mate* gourds; and a small section on the War of the Triple Alliance. A more extensive archeolo-gical and ethnographical collection is housed in the **Museo de Antropología**, further southeast at Las Heras 727 (Mon–Fri 9am–noon & 4–8pm; free); it displays objects recovered from the ruins of the failed sixteenth-century Spanish settlement of Concepción del Bermejo. North of the centre, natural history is covered by the **Museo de Ciencias Naturales** at Pellegrini and Lavalle (Mon–Fri 8.30am–12.30pm & Mon–Wed 1.30–8pm; Sat & Sun 5–8.30pm; free); it's housed in the clean-cut nineteenth-century Estación Francesa train station.

The best place in the Chaco to purchase indigenous crafts is the **Fundación Chaco Artesanal**, Pellegrini 272 (Mon–Fri 8am–1pm & 4–8pm, Sat & Sun 9am–noon & 5–8pm; ⓣ03722/459372, ⓕ423954), a smart, nonprofit outlet which sells items such as smooth earthenware Mocoví Nativity figures, rougher Wichí pottery, Komlek basketware and graceful *palo santo* crucifixes.

Fogón de los Arrieros

Resistencia's **Fogón de los Arrieros**, Brown 350 (ⓣ03722/426418), is a cultural foundation where a tongue-in-cheek bohemianism mixes quite naturally with a more serious artistic agenda, a testament to the vision of its founding members – led by Aldo Boglietti, who set the ball rolling in 1943, and the sculptor, Juan de Dios Mena. Its name means "The Drovers' Campfire", and was intended to evoke a sense of transitoriness: like drovers who would meet up around the campfire to relate a story or sing a song before moving on the next day, artists would come to this meeting-place, share their particular art form and then continue their journey.

As the centre's fame spread, especially in the 1960s and 1970s, it attracted an impressive list of major national and international artistic figures. Not everyone came to sing, and the walls are plastered by less transitory legacies. **Paintings** include the intense, energetic *Cuarteto de Cuerda* (*String Quartet*) by Julio Vanzo, along with works by Chagall and Raúl Soldi (who painted the cupola in the Teatro Colón). Demetrio Urruchua, Argentina's most famous **muralist**, left *Crisol de Razas* (*Crucible of the Races*) in 1954, intending to promote a pluralist spirit. Look out, too, for Dios Mena's appealing *criollo* **statues**, carved in *curupí*, a very light wood, and very much in the mould of Molina Campos caricatures. Eclectic curiosities range from a prisoner's shirt from Ushuaia to a Jíbaro shrunken head from Ecuador.

The idea for Resistencia's statues also started with Aldo Boglietti: for him art had a vital role to play in the region and he felt that it should not just be confined to museums. The concept of art as a tool for engendering civic pride has been amply demonstrated: Resistencia's citizens are very proud of their city's two hundred-plus statues and graffiti are almost unheard of.

You can pay the Fogón a visit in the morning (Mon–Sat 8am–noon; $5), but it's perhaps more fun in the evening (Mon–Fri 9–11pm; $5), when you will be able to have a drink at its cosy bar, while food such as empanadas is often available. Best of all, try to catch one of the **events** – concerts, poetry recitals and the like – staged once or twice a week in the main salon or, weather permitting, the patio (most reliably Sat 10pm). Further attractions include academic conferences and tango lessons (Tue & Wed 9–11pm).

Eating, drinking and nightlife

Resistencia has a very poor choice of **restaurants**, with only a couple of exceptions. One is *Charly*, Güemes 213 (closed Sun eve and most of Jan), which serves delicious *mollejas al champán*, pastas and *surubí* dishes at reasonable prices, complemented by a wide selection of wines; it's a shame about the atrocious floral decor. It also runs the *rotisería* for takeway dishes round the corner at Brown 71. Nearby ★ *Kebon*, at Güemes and Don Bosco (closed most of Jan), has a more tasteful ambience and offers well-cooked classics and tasty river fish at slightly higher prices.

For **nightlife**, the bar at *El Fogón* is excellent for a friendly conversation or one of its first-rate events; or catch a folklore show at the *Peña Nativa Martín Fierro*, 9 de Julio and Hernández (ⓣ03722/423167; Fri from 9pm), where they also serve empanadas and *parrilla* meals. *Don Angelo*, Güemes 183, is a café-cum-bar, with a varied choice of beers, whose sedate ambience is ideal for chatting (open round the clock at weekends). Less restrained is *El Viejo Café*, Yrigoyen and Pellegrini, a café during the day and a bar late at night, popular with the younger crowd. The city's best coffee and cakes by far are on offer at *La Imprenta*, Av Alberdi 254, inside one of the few branches of Yenny bookstores to be located outside Buenos Aires.

Parque Nacional Chaco

Paved **RN-16** shears straight through Chaco Province, northwest from Resistencia, clipping the northeastern corner of Santiago del Estero Province, before reaching Salta Province; it's the route taken by all trans-Chaco buses. Much of the land has been cleared to plant bananas, while *caranday* palms grow in the drier land between streams and reed- and lily-beds. Dedicated naturalists can spend a few days trying to track down the region's fauna in the **PARQUE NACIONAL CHACO** in the province's humid east. Within easy striking distance of Resistencia, the park conserves a mix of threatened wet- and semi-dry Chaco habitat around the banks of the Río Negro. In quick succession,

"El Chaco" and the Campo del Cielo meteors

An estimated five thousand years ago an asteroid shattered on impact with the earth's upper atmosphere, sending huge chips of matter plummeting earthwards, where they fell on a fifteen-kilometre band of the Chaco. This cataclysmic spectacle and the subsequent fires that would have been triggered must have terrified the locals. When the Spanish arrived in South America, the Komlek called the area *Pigüen Nonraltá* – or Field of the Heavens – Campo del Cielo in Spanish. They venerated the "stones from the sky", whose surface, when polished, reflected the sun. Mysterious legends reached Spanish ears, arousing an insatiable curiosity for anything that smacked of precious metal, and even sparking illusions of the fabled City of the Caesars, a variant of the El Dorado myth. In 1576, Hernán Mexía de Miraval struggled out here hoping to find gold but, instead, he found iron. The biggest expedition of all came in 1783, when the Spanish geologist and scientist, Miguel Rubín de Celis, led an expedition of two hundred men to find out if the **Mesón de Fierro** – a 3.5m long curiosity and the most famous of the **meteors** – was in fact just the tip of a vast mountain of pure iron. When they dug below, they found only dusty earth. The latitude was recorded, but since there was no way of determining its co-ordinate of longitude, the Mesón de Fierro was subsequently lost – it's probable that the indigenous inhabitants reburied their "sunstone".

The largest of the meteorites you can see today, **"El Chaco"**, has been reliably estimated to weigh 33,700kg, a strong contender for the second biggest in the world (the biggest, almost twice the size, is in Namibia). It, too, has aroused the avarice of speculators. In 1990, a local policeman foiled the plot of US citizen, Robert Haag, to steal El Chaco and sell it on to a private collector – or, according to some far-fetched rumours, to NASA. Haag was released on $20,000 bail but fled the country. Back home in the States, he became known as "Meteorman". Since 1997, El Chaco has been protected by a provincial law but that hasn't stopped local pranksters debasing it with graffiti; at least the perpetrators were thoughtful enough to spray it a suitably cosmic neon green.

you can pass from riverine forest to open woodland, palm savannah and wetlands. Its 150 square kilometres are too restricted a space to provide a viable habitat for the largest Chaco predator, the jaguar, but plenty of mammals still inhabit the park, even if your chances of seeing them are slight. Birdlife, however, is plentiful and easy to spot.

Practicalities

The turn-off to the park ($5 entrance fee) is 56km west of Resistencia along RN-16, from where paved RP-9 heads 40km north to Capitán Solari, 6km from the park headquarters. If coming from Resistencia under your own steam, take the twice-daily Marito Tours **minibus** to Solari, from Vedia 334 (ⓣ03722/422000). You can also take the regular **bus** from the terminal in Resistencia to the second stop in the village; there are three buses a day back to the city. Getting the remaining 6km to the park is not difficult but it can be a haphazard affair: the municipality may help arrange a lift; or ask around for a *remise* (arrange the price first, as it can range from nothing to $15 or more per trip). If you have to walk to or from the park in rainy weather, it's easier to squelch along barefoot, owing to the heavy clay soil. There's no **food** to buy in the park, and little in Solari, so bring supplies.

A board by the park headquarters displays the trails, which are also marked on a pamphlet available from the *guardaparques*. A good introduction to the park is the well-shaded, nature-trail loop that leads from a suspension bridge behind the park headquarters (1.5km). But the most popular walk is the one to the lookouts at the ox-bow lagoons of **Laguna Carpincho** and **Laguna Yacaré**, with a deviation to see an enormous *quebracho*, El Abuelo, which is an estimated 500 years old. From the base camp at park headquarters, it's 6km direct to Laguna Yacaré, to which you must add half an hour if you make the detour to see El Abuelo, signposted to the left approximately half an hour from camp. With prior permission from the *guardaparques*, you may continue 4km northwards from Laguna Yacaré to the **Tranquera Norte** (North Gate) that marks the park boundary.

A longer walk (9km) is to **Laguna Panza de Cabra**, a swamp choked with lilac-bloomed *camalote* waterlilies and offering excellent bird-watching opportunities. Leave the campsite along the Laguna Yacaré trail to find the trail's start, signposted fifteen minutes' walk away. Turn left here, before taking the left-hand peel-off immediately after the signpost. Soon you come to a sharp right-hand bend at a wire fence, and thereafter you enter open *quebracho*

Tours in the Gran Chaco

The logistics of **visiting the parks and reserves** in the Gran Chaco region, and Formosa Province in particular, are complicated to say the least. Argentina's hottest climate, poorest roads and most inaccessible terrain are likely to frustrate even the most adventurous of travellers. Signposts are erratic and wildlife lurks where you least expect it. You will certainly need a helping hand if you are to get the most out of the Chaco and you will be best off going on an **organized tour**.

Chaco Aventuras (ⓣ03722/425493, ⓦwww.northargentinaoverland.com). Based in Resistencia, Néstor Guarnieri and Jorge Sánchez organize alternative tours of the Chaco and the whole Litoral region.

Aventura Formosa, Paraguay 520, Formosa (ⓣ03717/156-83934, ⓔfiznardo@hotmail.com). Extremely reliable tours run by an experienced local guide with a tremendous in-depth knowledge of the region, its geography, wildlife and culture.

woodland. Follow the path around to the right as you leave the woodland to reach the Laguna.

Formosa Province

Formosa Province is dominated by its eponymous **capital city**, at its eastern end and second in importance to Resistencia in the Argentine Chaco; it's really a base for visiting the province's wildlife – but not in the height of summer. To the north are the nasty border town of Clorinda, best avoided unless curiosity really gets the better of you; the internationally significant wetland site of **Parque Nacional Río Pilcomayo**, on the border with Paraguay; and the Paraguayan capital, Asunción, effectively the historical and spiritual nerve centre of the whole Gran Chaco. For those really set on seeing deepest Argentina, the aptly named **El Impenetrable** poses a real challenge – the weather, bad roads and virtually non-existent infrastructure being the main obstacles. The **Bañado La Estrella** is a remote wetland that rewards the most intrepid and determined with fine birdlife, but go on an organized tour to make it worthwhile.

Formosa city

The city of **FORMOSA**, the provincial capital, seems as though it has been pressed flat by the heat: few buildings rise above a single storey and many exhibit the grey mouldy stains of subtropical decay. Situated on a great loop in the Río Paraguay, it acts as a **port** for the entire province. Not a particularly attractive place, despite its name (an archaic form of *hermosa*, "beautiful"), it's given a pink facelift when the *lapacho* trees flower in September, the best time to see it. Graham Greene, in *Travels With My Aunt*, wrote that "there was a pervading smell of orange petals, but it was the only sweet thing about Formosa", for him "an ignoble little town" – but then he wasn't that impressed by Buenos Aires either. The main commercial district is concentrated within a block or two either side of the **Avenida 25 de Mayo** east of the Plaza San Martín. This boulevard leads down to Calle San Martín by the port, where, for three days over a November weekend, the **Fiesta Nacional del Río** is held – a modest event, with chamamé folk-music concerts, watersports and parades. Inexpensive merchandise – knick-knacks, clothes, *mate* gourds, fishing gear and electronics – is sold at the **Mercado Paraguayo**, along the three blocks of Calle San Martín running south from the port; but of more interest is the **Casa de la Artesanía**, a nonprofit organization based at San Martín and 25 de Mayo (Mon–Sat 8am–12.30pm & 4.30–8pm; free), the best outlet for the province's indigenous crafts. It stocks a good selection of Wichí *yica* bags, Pilagá woollen carpets, tightly woven Komlek *carandillo* and *tortora* basketwork, plus *palo santo* carvings and *algarrobo* seed jewellery. A block inland from here, on the corner of 25 de Mayo and Belgrano, is the pink, hacienda-style **Museo Histórico** (Mon–Fri 8am–7.30pm; free), housed in the former residence (built 1885) of General Ignacio Fotheringham, the Southampton-born first governor of what was then Formosa Territory. It is an eclectic and poorly organized collection, and exhibits include a stuffed Swiss bear and Komlek artefacts, plus information on early exploration of the region.

Arrival and information

The city's **airport**, El Pucú (Ⓣ03717/426349), lies just off RN-11, 6km southwest of the town centre. Buses #4, #9, and #11 run between the two.

Arriving in Formosa from the southwest, you'll be welcomed by **La Cruz del Norte**, a white Meccano-style cross that's a common reference point. The **bus terminal** is to the east of here on Avenida Gutnisky, a multi-laned thoroughfare that changes its name to Avenida 25 de Mayo before it reaches the Plaza San Martín, the start of the town centre and nearly 2km from the terminal. Buses #4, #9, and #11 head into the centre of town: upon reaching the large Plaza San Martín, they take Uriburu, which runs one block to the south of Avenida 25 de Mayo on its way down to the port, and return along Calle España, one block the other side of the main drag. A *remise* into the centre costs about $6.

There's a small **tourist office** on Plaza San Martín, at Uriburu 820 (Mon–Fri 8am–noon & 4–8pm; ⓣ03717/420442 or 425192), where you can hunt down an accommodation list for the entire province, including a handful of tourism estancias. Avenida 25 de Mayo is where you'll find **banks**, airline offices, car-rental offices and most other utilities.

Accommodation

Accommodation is a bit of a problem, with only three places that can be recommended; the budget lodgings, including a couple of *residenciales* near the bus terminal, are dire. One of the trio of comfortable, modern places is *Colón*, Belgrano 1068 (ⓣ&ⓕ03717/420719, ⓔamstelturismo@infovia.com.ar; ❸ with breakfast), whose prices include free use of a sports complex and pool, 5km away (free shuttle bus). *Casa Grande*, González Lelong 185 (ⓣ&ⓕ03717/431612 or 431406, ⓔmabelmaglietti@arnet.com.ar; ❺) is a more attractive little complex whose well-equipped rooms have kitchenettes, and whose facilities include a pool and garden, massages and a gym, plus one of the best restaurants for miles. Best of all, however, is the new *Asterión* (ⓣ03717/452999, ⓦwww.asterionhotel.com.ar; ❻), on RN-11 just before you reach the Cruz del Norte roundabout when arriving from Resistencia; the hotel's name comes from a Borges short story about the Minotaur, and you will find a small collection of Borges memorabilia, including several of his works, on display in the lobby. As for the rooms, they are bright, spacious and appealingly decorated, with an ethnic touch, and all the facilities are impeccable, from the safe garage to the shady swimming pool. **For campers**, *Camping Banco Provincia de Formosa* (ⓣ03717/429877; $5 per person), off RN-11 two blocks west of La Cruz del Norte as you head out of town, has an Olympic-sized swimming pool.

Eating, drinking and nightlife

El Copetín "Yayita", Belgrano 926 and Uriburu, is the best place in town for a keenly priced feed: delicious *licuados* and low-priced lunch-time menus, often featuring Paraguayan specialities (see box, p.349), are particularly good value. *El Fortín*, at Mitre and Saavedra (ⓣ03717/439955), serves good fish and wines; try the *milanesa de surubí* – breaded river-fish fillet. *Raices*, 25 de Mayo 65 (closed Sun eve), is a popular place serving good portions of *surubí* and pastas, while *Il Viale*, 25 de Mayo 287, is open until late for burgers and snacks. The best fare of all is to be had at *Mirita*, the airy upstairs restaurant at the *Casa Grande apart-hotel*; open daily, it specializes in delicious fish dishes and has a very decent wine list. The town's **casino**, at San Martín y España, is open 24 hours and puts on **folklore shows**.

Parque Nacional Río Pilcomayo

The 519-square-kilometre **PARQUE NACIONAL RÍO PILCOMAYO** was created in the 1950s to protect some of the best remaining subtropical wet Chaco habitat. Extensive areas are subject to spring and summer flooding, whereas in the winter months it is prone to droughts. The park is protected under the international Ramsar Convention – designed to protect the planet's key wetland ecosystems – and its biological diversity was safeguarded by a concerted and largely successful campaign in the 1990s to get rid of most of the semi-wild cattle left by former settlers. In addition to swampy wetlands, it conserves some remnant gallery forest along the Río Pilcomayo, and large swathes of savannah studded with copses of mixed woodland.

The park has **two entrances** – to the Estero Poí and Laguna Blanca sectors – both within striking distance of **Laguna Blanca**, a village 52km west of Clorinda. The **national park administration office** (Mon–Fri 7am–4pm; Ⓣ&Ⓕ03718/470045), for information, is on RN-86 at the entrance to the village (opposite the YPF fuel station). This is where you gain permission to explore the interior of the park on horseback or by 4WD. Arriving from Clorinda, *remises colectivos* drop you where you ask, while buses often do a loop of town, stopping at several points before getting to their main office. *Remises colectivos* can be flagged down along San Martín or the main RN-86.

Park practicalities

The best times to **visit the park** are sunset and dawn, when it's cooler and you stand a better chance of seeing the wildlife. To get the most out of Estero Poí Sector you really need your own transport, be it a 4WD or horse –otherwise head to the more compact Laguna Blanca Sector.

The turn-off to **Estero Poí** lies 2km from Laguna Blanca village in the direction of Clorinda, from where it's 9km of dirt road to the *guardaparques*' house. An interpretation trail runs from the campsite through the adjacent scrub, and within easy walking distance is a pair of swamps, dominated by the attractive *pehuajó* reed with its banana-palm leaves, along with bulrushes, horsetails and the mauve-flowered waterlilies. Further into the park lie swathes of savannah grassland and the gallery forest of the Río Pilcomayo – good for spotting wildlife.

At Naick Neck, 12km east of Laguna Blanca village and 40km west of Clorinda, a dirt track leads to the **Laguna Blanca Sector**. Walking the 5km from RN-86 to the *guardaparques*' post takes an hour and a half, longer if the rain has turned the road to sticky clay. If coming by *remise colectivo*, it's worth paying the extra fare to get dropped at the entrance, not the turn-off. Next to the *guardaparques*' dwelling is a pleasant free **campsite**, shaded by *algarrobos* and palms, with drinking water and showers; bring all your own food supplies. Along a 300-metre **nature trail** from behind the toilet block you have a good chance of seeing howler monkeys, while an excellent boardwalk from the campsite takes you 500m through reedbed marshland to lookout points and a ten-metre **tower** on the shore of the shallow lagoon itself. If you swim here, wear shoes so the piranhas don't snack on your toes. There are excellent opportunities for **bird-watching** here, especially at dawn.

El Impenetrable

The straight RN-81 runs northwest of Formosa through an area so difficult to enter it has been dubbed El Impenetrable. For those with a specialist interest in wildlife – especially birdlife – the route gives access to the **Bañado La Estrella**, a fascinating wetland near Las Lomitas, 300km from Formosa. Otherwise, avoid it: if you wanted to cross the Chaco region, take the much faster RN-16 from Resistencia.

Buses pass regularly in both directions (north to Tartagal and Pocitos; south to Embarcación, Jujuy and Salta) and can be flagged down. **Driving times** on unsealed roads in this area of the world are dependent on rainfall. Many vehicles can't negotiate the mud, and the ones that do often take far longer than they would in good conditions (if in doubt, call the Vialidad Provincial in Formosa; ⓣ03717/426040 or 426041). Rainfall causes major problems, however, only when it is sustained, after which roads are closed for 48 hours: the intense heat or winds soon dry the roads otherwise.

Bañado La Estrella

As you head west, the scenery becomes drier scrub with some virulently green wetland. The land is mainly used for grazing cattle and goats, but charcoal is also produced – witness the roadside ovens. About 45km north of the village of Las Lomitas, on unsealed RP-28, is the **Bañado La Estrella**, a huge swathe of wetland swamp in the central northern part of the province, fed by the waters of the Río Pilcomayo, a river that dissipates into numerous meandering channels.

The RP-28 crosses the Bañado by means of a long causeway (*pedraplén*), usually just beneath the water line. The scenery looks like a Dalí painting: tree skeletons (known as *champales*) swaddled in vines, as if the floodwaters had once covered them and then receded, leaving them snagged with weed; beneath their branches shines the mirror-smooth blue water, dotted with rafts of lilac-flowered *camalote* waterlilies. It's a **bird-watcher's paradise**, but unless you go on an organized tour, you'll have to content yourself with viewing from the road, as there's no infrastructure. If you are lucky you might even get to see members of the **Pilagá community** (see box, pp.402–403) fishing for *sábalo* with spears.

Travel details

Buses

Colón to: Buenos Aires (hourly; 5hr 30min); Concordia (9 daily; 2hr 15min); Corrientes (2 daily; 10hr); Gualeguaychú (8 daily; 2hr); Paraná (9 daily; 5hr); Santa Fe (6 daily; 6hr).
Concordia to: Buenos Aires (30 daily; 6hr); Corrientes (5 daily; 8hr); Paraná (15 daily; 4hr); Puerto Iguazú (1 daily; 11hr).
Corrientes to: Buenos Aires (6 daily; 12hr); Concordia (1 daily; 8hr); Córdoba (1 daily; 14hr); Goya (6 daily; 3hr); Itatí (10 daily; 2hr); Posadas (9 daily; 5hr); Puerto Iguazú (1 daily; 10hr); Rosario (3 daily; 10hr).
El Soberbio to: Posadas (7 daily; 4hr 30min).
Formosa to: Buenos Aires (7 daily; 14–15hr); Corrientes (10 daily; 2hr 45min); Jujuy (1 daily; 13–14hr); Posadas (1 daily; 6hr); Puerto Iguazú (1 daily; 10hr); Resistencia (15 daily; 2hr 15min); Salta (1 daily; 14hr); Santa Fe (5 daily; 10hr).
Gualeguaychú to: Buenos Aires (21 daily; 3hr 30min); Colón (8 daily; 2hr); Concordia (6 daily; 4hr); Corrientes (3 daily; 12hr); Paraná (7 daily; 5hr); Rosario (4–5 daily; 8hr); Santa Fe (5 daily; 6hr).
Mercedes to: Buenos Aires (10 daily; 10hr); Colonia Carlos Pellegrini (1 daily; 4hr); Corrientes (14 daily; 3hr); Posadas (3 daily; 4hr); Resistencia (6 daily; 3hr 30min).
Oberá to: Buenos Aires (3 daily; 14–16hr); El Soberbio (3 daily; 4hr); Posadas (2 hourly; 1hr 30min); Puerto Iguazú (2 daily; 5–8hr); Resistencia (1 daily; 6hr 20min).
Paraná to: Buenos Aires (30 daily; 7hr); Concordia (hourly; 4hr); Corrientes (3 daily; 8hr); Posadas (7 daily; 10hr); Puerto Iguazú (3 daily; 14hr); Rosario (2 hourly; 3hr); Santa Fe (every 20min; 50min).
Posadas to: Buenos Aires (hourly; 12hr 30min–14hr); Córdoba (5 daily; 16–18hr); Corrientes (2 daily; 5hr); El Soberbio (7 daily; 4hr 30min); Formosa (1 daily; 7hr); Goya (1 daily; 6hr 30min); Oberá (15 daily; 1hr 30min); Puerto Iguazú (1–2 hourly; 6hr); Resistencia (hourly; 5hr 30min); Rosario (5 daily; 14hr); San Ignacio (9 daily; 1hr).
Puerto Iguazú to: Buenos Aires (7 daily; 14hr 30min–19hr); Córdoba (2 daily; 22hr); Corrientes (1 daily; 10hr); Posadas (1–2 hourly; 6hr); Rosario (2 weekly; 18hr); San Ignacio (hourly; 5hr); Tucumán (1 daily; 24hr).

Resistencia to: Buenos Aires (hourly; 12hr 30min–14hr); Corrientes (hourly; 30min); Formosa (hourly; 2hr 15min); Posadas (hourly; 5hr); Puerto Iguazú (1 daily; 10hr); Santiago del Estero (3 daily; 10–11hr).
Rosario to: Buenos Aires (2–3 hourly; 4hr); Concordia (3 daily; 7hr 30min); Córdoba (40 daily; 6hr); Corrientes (7 daily; 10–12hr); Resistencia (17 daily; 8–10hr); Posadas (5 daily; 15hr); Puerto Iguazú (1 daily; 18hr); Salta (9 daily; 16hr); Tucumán (hourly; 12hr); Victoria (5 daily; 1hr 20min).
Santa Fe to: Buenos Aires (1–2 hourly; 6hr); Concordia (9 daily; 4hr 30min); Córdoba (hourly; 5hr); Posadas (8 daily; 14hr); Puerto Iguazú (2 daily; 20hr); Resistencia (hourly; 7hr); Rosario (1–2 hourly; 2hr 20min).

Flights

Corrientes to: Buenos Aires (1–2 daily; 1hr 30min).
Formosa to: Buenos Aires (1 daily; 1hr 50min).
Paraná to: Buenos Aires (1 daily; 1hr).
Posadas to: Buenos Aires (1 daily; 1hr 30min).
Puerto Iguazú to: Buenos Aires (4 daily; 2hr).
Resistencia to: Buenos Aires (1daily; 1hr 40min).
Rosario to: Buenos Aires (2 daily; 45min).
Santa Fe to: Buenos Aires (1 daily; 1hr).

5

The Northwest

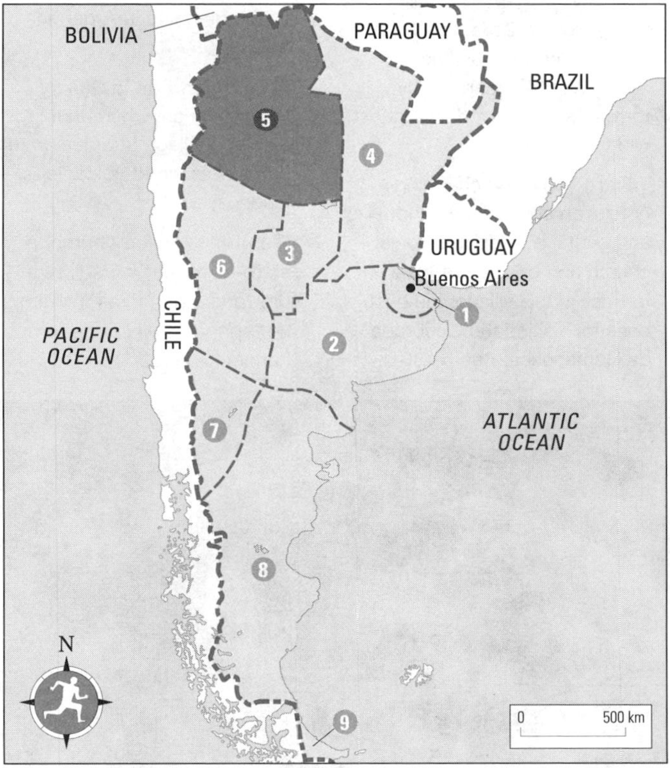

CHAPTER 5

Highlights

* **Peñas of Salta** Listen to the drums and guitars or haunting voices at the city's traditional music venues. See p.434
* **Cuesta del Obispo** Spiral up (or down) a mind-boggling mountain road, zigzagging from sultry plains to the rarefied air of the Valles Calchaquíes. See p.444
* **Vineyards of Cafayate** Try fruity cabernet sauvignons, earthy malbecs and heady torrontés at the world's highest wineries. See p.447
* **Tilcara** You'll find charming hotels, an abundance of arts and crafts, a massive colonial church and even a pre-Incan fortress in this village, the best base for visiting the Quebrada de Humahuaca. See p.460
* **Parque Nacional Calilegua** Follow author Gerald Durrell's footsteps in the most accessible of the region's cloudforest reserves, looking out for tapirs, peccaries and all manner of birds. See p.470
* **Ruins of Shinkal** Play archeologist as you explore arguably the best pre-Columbian site in Argentina. See p.496
* **Antofagasta de la Sierra** Miles from anywhere, this altiplano village huddles among out-of-this world volcanic landscapes. See p.498
* **Fiambalá** A bijou church, a state-of-the-art winery, two pre-Incan mummies and limpid hot springs – all in one remote hamlet. See p.501

△ Nuestra Señora del Rosario, Tilcara

5

The Northwest

Argentina's **Northwest** (El Noroeste Argentino, El NOA or just plain El Norte) is a region of infinite variety: ochre deserts where flocks of llamas roam, charcoal-grey lava flows devoid of any life form, blindingly white salt-flats and sooty-black volcanic cones, pristine limewashed colonial chapels set against striped mountainsides, lush citrus groves and emerald-green sugar plantations, impenetrable jungles populated by peccaries and parakeets. Today regarded as a marvellously secluded, far-flung corner of the country, this region is in fact the birthplace of Argentina – a Spanish colony thrived here when Buenos Aires was still an unsteady trading post on the Atlantic coast. One of these colonial cities, enticing and youthful **Salta**, is indisputably the region's tourism capital, with some of the country's best hotels, finest architecture and a well-earned reputation for hospitality. Northwest of Salta you can meander up the harsh yet enchanting **Quebrada del Toro** on a safari or, if you're feeling slightly less adventurous, on the poetically named **Tren a las Nubes**, or Train to the Clouds, one of the world's highest railways, which runs to a much photographed metal viaduct called Polvorilla. Alternatively, you can head due east or north across the subtropical lowlands, where jungle-clad **cloudforests**, or *yungas*, poke out of flat, fertile plains into the raincloud that gives them their name. Three of these *yungas* – **El Rey**, **Calilegua** and **Baritú** – are protected by national park status.

By far the most accessible of the three cloudforest parks, Calilegua is in Jujuy Province, one of the federation's poorest and remotest, shoved up into the far northwestern corner of the country against Chile and Bolivia, where in the space of a few kilometres humid valleys and soothingly green jungles give way to the austere, parched altiplano (known in northwestern Argentina as *puna*, its name in Quichoa, the language of the Inca), home to flocks of flamingoes, herds of llamas and very few people. **San Salvador de Jujuy**, the slightly oddball provincial capital, cannot rival Salta for its amenities or architectural splendours, but it's the best starting-point for exploring one of the country's most photogenic features, the many-coloured **Quebrada de Humahuaca**. Lying off RN-9, which swerves up this gorge and clambers ever higher to the Bolivian border at La Quiaca, are time-stood-still hamlets such as **Iruya**, **Cochinoca** and **Yavi**.

Further south, snaking mountain roads scale the verdant **Cuesta del Obispo** and the stark but vividly coloured **Quebrada de Cafayate** from Salta to the **Valles Calchaquíes**, dry, sunny valleys along which high-altitude vineyards somehow thrive, particularly around the airy regional capital of **Cafayate**. At the southern end of the valleys, one of the region's most thoroughly restored pre-Columbian sites, **Quilmes**, enjoys a fabulous mountainside location, while nearby **Tafí del Valle**, almost Alpine in feel, is the favourite weekend and

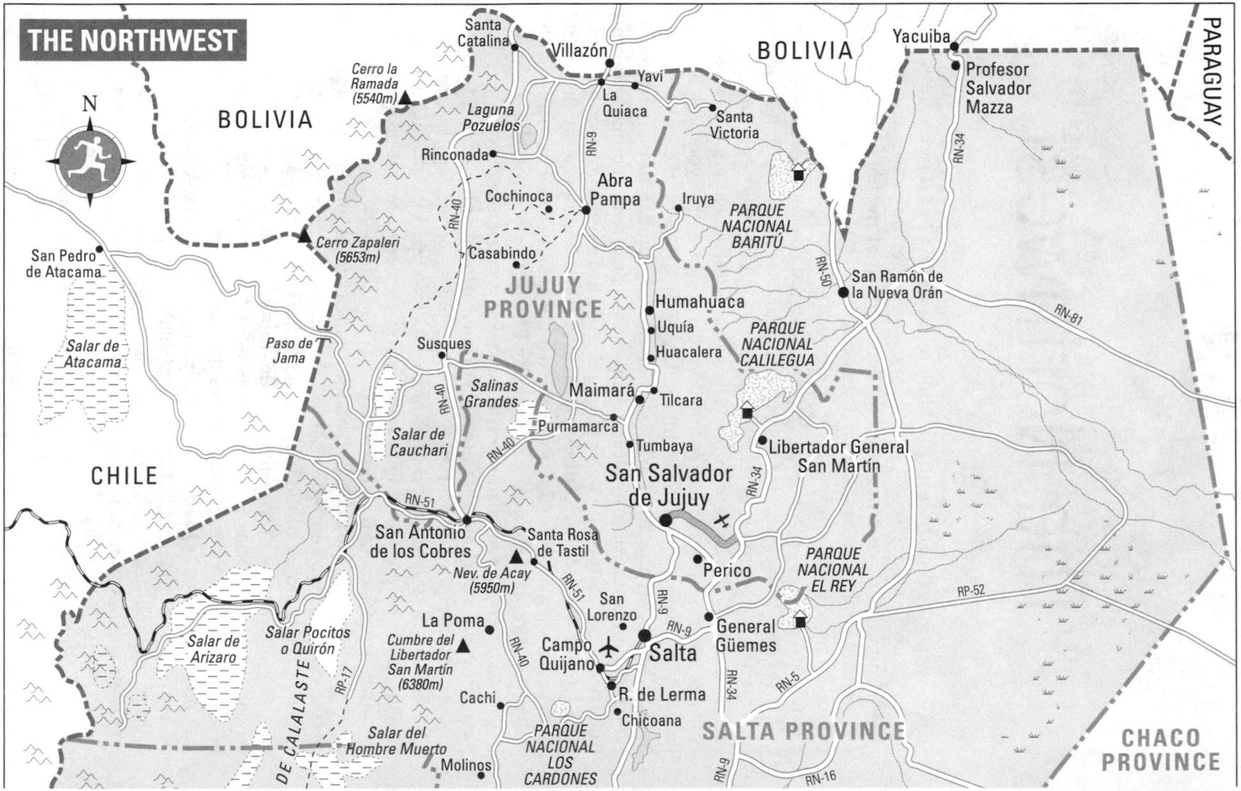
THE NORTHWEST
N
BOLIVIA
BOLIVIA
PARAGUAY
CHILE
JUJUY PROVINCE
SALTA PROVINCE
CHACO PROVINCE
Santa Catalina
Villazón
Yaví
La Quiaca
Santa Victoria
Yacuiba
Profesor Salvador Mazza
Cerro la Ramada (5540m)
Laguna Pozuelos
Rinconada
Abra Pampa
Cochinoca
Iruya
PARQUE NACIONAL BARITÚ
Cerro Zapaleri (5653m)
Casabindo
San Pedro de Atacama
Salar de Atacama
Paso de Jama
Susques
Humahuaca
Uquía
Huacalera
PARQUE NACIONAL CALILEGUA
San Ramón de la Nueva Orán
Salinas Grandes
Maimará
Tilcara
Purmamarca
Tumbaya
Salar de Cauchari
Libertador General San Martín
San Salvador de Jujuy
San Antonio de los Cobres
Santa Rosa de Tastil
Nev. de Acay (5950m)
Perico
PARQUE NACIONAL EL REY
San Lorenzo
General Güemes
La Poma
Cumbre del Libertador San Martín (6380m)
Campo Quijano
Salta
Salar de Arizaro
Salar Pocitos o Quirón
R. de Lerma
Chicoana
Cachi
Salar del Hombre Muerto
Molinos
PARQUE NACIONAL LOS CARDONES
DE CALALASTE
RN-9
RN-34
RN-40
RN-50
RN-81
RN-51
RN-5
RN-16
RP-52
RP-17

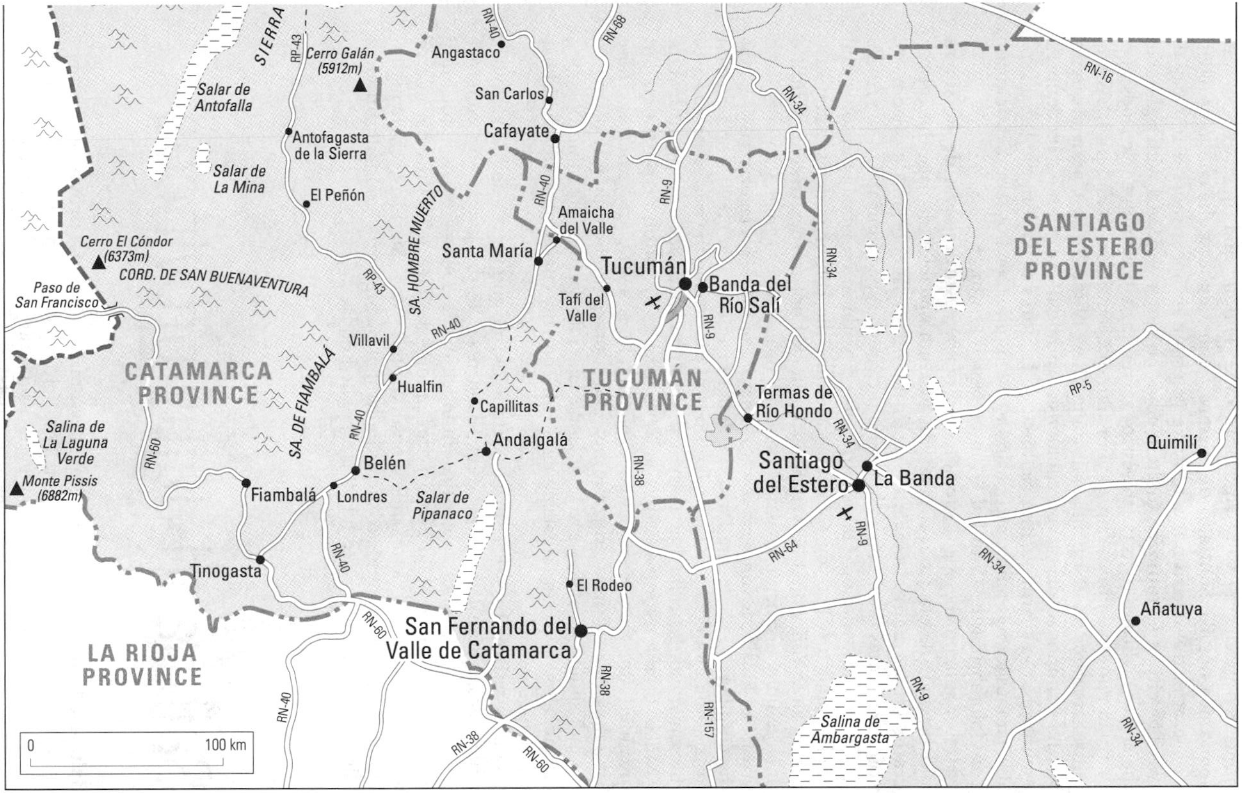
SANTIAGO DEL ESTERO PROVINCE
TUCUMÁN PROVINCE
CATAMARCA PROVINCE
LA RIOJA PROVINCE
Tucumán
Banda del Río Salí
Santiago del Estero
La Banda
San Fernando del Valle de Catamarca
Termas de Río Hondo
Tafí del Valle
Amaicha del Valle
Santa María
Cafayate
San Carlos
Angastaco
Antofagasta de la Sierra
El Peñón
Villavil
Hualfin
Capillitas
Andalgalá
Belén
Londres
Fiambalá
Tinogasta
El Rodeo
Quimilí
Añatuya
Salar de Antofalla
Salar de La Mina
Salar de Pipanaco
Salina de La Laguna Verde
Salina de Ambargasta
Cerro Galán (5912m)
Cerro El Cóndor (6373m)
Monte Pissis (6882m)
Paso de San Francisco
CORD. DE SAN BUENAVENTURA
SA. HOMBRE MUERTO
SA. DE FIAMBALÁ
SIERRA
RN-9
RN-16
RN-34
RN-38
RN-40
RN-60
RN-64
RN-68
RN-157
RP-5
RP-43
0
100 km

summer retreat for the people of nearby **Tucumán**. Tucumán is the region's biggest metropolis by far and its commercial powerhouse; it sprawls across a brilliantly green valley where sugar cane, lemons and quinces grow in abundance, but like **Santiago del Estero** to the southeast, the country's oldest city, its attractions are too few to make you want to linger more than a day or two. The city of **Catamarca** to the south is no better endowed with sights, but the empty highlands to its northwest are staggeringly beautiful: noble landscapes that will tempt you to use up all your film or even sit down and paint. As you journey towards the sharp altiplanic atmosphere of the **Puna Catamarqueña**, via the transitional valleys, you could visit **Andalgalá**, surrounded by dramatic mountains, the charming, historic town of **Londres** or **Belén**, the last justifiably famous for its textiles, particularly its handsome ponchos. Another dramatic pre-Columbian site – **Shinkal** – can be visited nearby.

Higher still, on the way to remote and rarefied **Antofagasta de la Sierra** and beyond, desolate tracks take you past inhospitable salt-flats, the biggest **crater** on the Earth's surface and eternally frozen lagoons, in the shadow of **volcanic cones** the colour of tar, with the snowcapped ramparts of the Andes as a beguiling backdrop. This is a part of the world so remarkably unspoilt and thinly populated that you sometimes feel like the last, or better still the first, person alive. You would be very unlucky indeed not to spy **Andean wildlife** in large numbers: flamingoes and condors, alpacas and vicuñas, grey foxes and vizcachas. Finally, as you head towards one of the most spectacular passes across the cordillera to Chile, the **Paso de San Francisco**, you could stop over and relax at the mountainside thermal springs of **Fiambalá**, the perfect antidote to the sometimes gruelling but always exhilarating experience of the Northwest.

Much of the Northwest region is accessible by **public transport**, but organized tours or, even better, exploring in a 4WD, are generally more rewarding ways of discovering the area, and at times are the only way of getting around. Should you choose to go it alone, take into account the mind-boggling distances involved, the challenging road, climatic conditions and the sheer remoteness of it all.

The best **time to go** is spring (Sept–Nov) or autumn (March and April), which, apart from busy Holy Week, happen to be the low season. Summer (Dec–Feb) can be a lot cooler than in much of the country, but is notoriously wet, too, and January and February are among the busiest months, because of school holidays, local fiestas and carnival. Winters (May–Aug) have chilly nights, but daytime temperatures are surprisingly high owing to the constant sunshine; July is a busy month, since July 9 is a public holiday.

Salta and Jujuy provinces

Salta and **Jujuy** are the country's quintessentially **northern provinces**, the ones most Argentine and foreign visitors head for, a trend that has resulted in a well-developed but not yet asphyxiating tourist industry. Slotted into each other like a couple of misshapen jigsaw pieces, the two provinces have much to offer those who venture this far north. The city of **Salta** is undoubtedly one of the country's

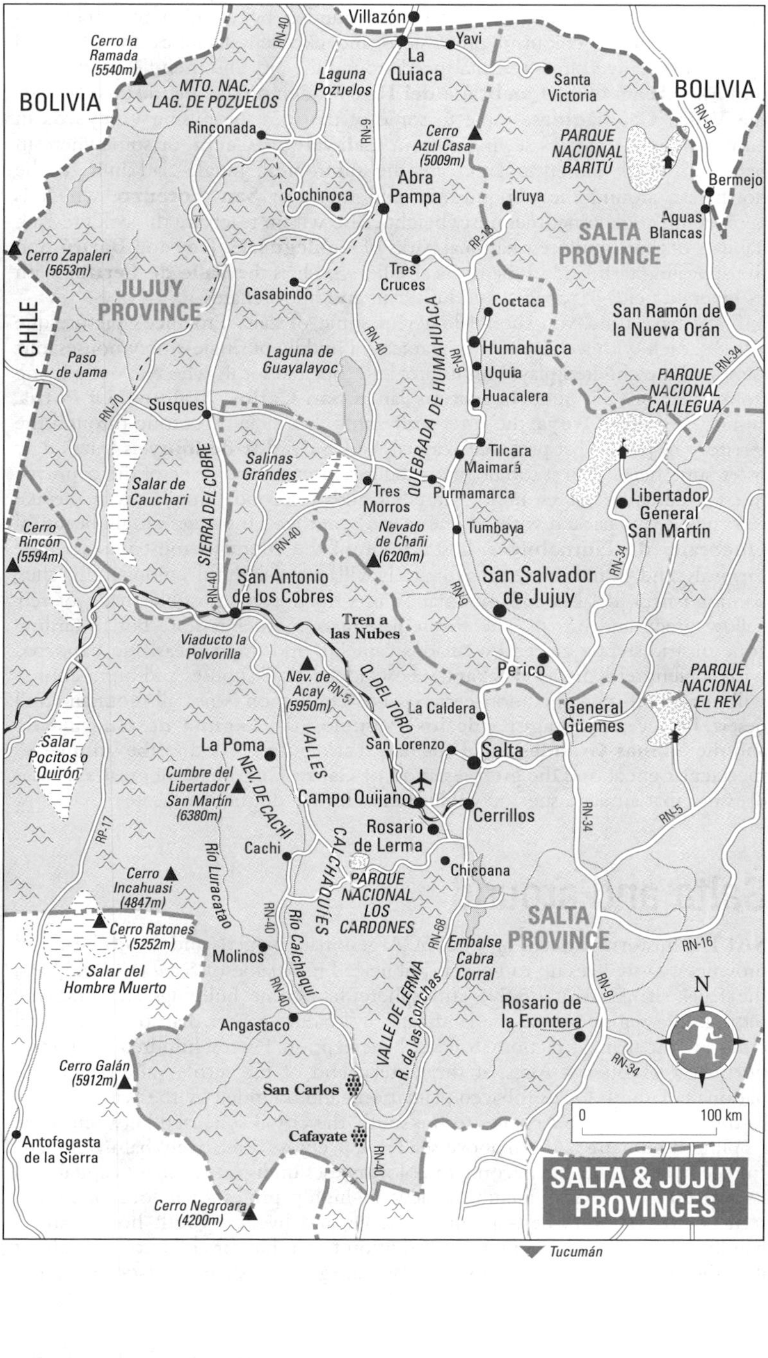
SALTA & JUJUY PROVINCES
BOLIVIA
CHILE
JUJUY PROVINCE
SALTA PROVINCE
Villazón
La Quiaca
Yavi
Santa Victoria
Cerro la Ramada (5540m)
MTO. NAC. LAG. DE POZUELOS
Laguna Pozuelos
Rinconada
Cerro Azul Casa (5009m)
PARQUE NACIONAL BARITÚ
Bermejo
Aguas Blancas
Abra Pampa
Cochinoca
Iruya
Cerro Zapaleri (5653m)
Tres Cruces
Casabindo
Coctaca
San Ramón de la Nueva Orán
Humahuaca
Uquía
Huacalera
QUEBRADA DE HUMAHUACA
Laguna de Guayalayoc
Paso de Jama
Susques
PARQUE NACIONAL CALILEGUA
Tilcara
Maimará
Salinas Grandes
Salar de Cauchari
SIERRA DEL COBRE
Tres Morros
Purmamarca
Libertador General San Martín
Cerro Rincón (5594m)
Nevado de Chañi (6200m)
Tumbaya
San Antonio de los Cobres
San Salvador de Jujuy
Tren a las Nubes
Viaducto la Polvorilla
Nev. de Acay (5950m)
Q. DEL TORO
Perico
PARQUE NACIONAL EL REY
La Caldera
General Güemes
Salar Pocitos o Quirón
La Poma
NEV. DE CACHI
VALLES
San Lorenzo
Salta
Cumbre del Libertador San Martín (6380m)
Campo Quijano
Cerrillos
Rosario de Lerma
Cachi
CALCHAQUÍES
Río Luracatao
Chicoana
Cerro Incahuasi (4847m)
PARQUE NACIONAL LOS CARDONES
Cerro Ratones (5252m)
Río Calchaquí
Molinos
Embalse Cabra Corral
Salar del Hombre Muerto
VALLE DE LERMA
R. de las Conchas
Rosario de la Frontera
Angastaco
Cerro Galán (5912m)
San Carlos
Cafayate
Antofagasta de la Sierra
Cerro Negroara (4200m)
Tucumán
RN-40
RN-9
RP-13
RN-50
RN-34
RN-70
RN-51
RP-17
RN-68
RN-16
RN-5
N
0
100 km

most traditional, most hospitable and best preserved, with an architectural harmony and aesthetic beauty lacking in many other urban centres in Argentina. Fabulously set in a cool, high valley surrounded by wooded mountains, its enchanting music, colourful processions and excellent facilities are all added attractions. Many visitors to Salta speed around the city and then head off to the multi-hued cliffs of the **Quebrada del Toro** – often on the *Tren a las Nubes* – or the **Valles Calchaquíes**, home to some of the most promising **vineyards** in South America, perhaps staying over in **Cafayate** or **Cachi**, or somewhere in between. Much closer to hand are the subtropical, jungle-clad hills to the northwest, around the tranquil weekend resort of **San Lorenzo**, which is perched on cool, sometimes misty heights. Also within reach are the wildlife-rich habitats of the cloudforest national parks of **Calilegua**, **El Rey** and **Baritú**, and the appealing farmland in the tropical valleys, such as the **Valle de Lerma**, with its emerald fields of tobacco and lush fruit and nut orchards.

If you have time, you should linger in some of Salta Province's picturesque villages, each with a chapel nestling among a huddle of single-storey houses, dirt streets where children play with improvised toys and locals who eke out a living from maize or their quota of goats or llamas: **San Carlos**, **Molinos**, **La Poma**, and steep-streeted **Iruya**, the latter really only accessible by cutting through the territory of Jujuy. That province's capital, **San Salvador de Jujuy**, is Salta's ugly sister, superficially, but it too boasts a fabulous location and some of the country's finest colonial treasures in its cathedral and a second church. Its namesake province is jam-packed with natural marvels, not least the staggeringly beautiful **Quebrada de Humahuaca**, host to one of the country's most idiosyncratic carnivals, and home to a string of lively villages, delightful colonial churches, flamingo-flecked lakes and mountainsides striped every possible shade of red, yellow, green and brown. The **Puna Jujeña** is another remote but rewarding zone of arid steppe grazed by curious camelids and timid rheas, and peppered with ancient settlements like **Yavi**, whose adobe-brick houses and bijou church will move you with an almost eerie beauty. The region is not all mountain and desert, however: the **Laguna de los Pozuelos**, the **Laguna de Guayalayoc** and the **Salinas Grandes**, huge salt-flats that regularly flood in the summer to spectacular effect, and the great reservoir of **Cabra Corral** are all great expanses of water that attract a specific wildlife and create a distinct landscape.

Salta and around

SALTA, historic capital of one of Argentina's biggest and most beautiful provinces, easily lives up to its well-publicized nickname of *Salta la Linda* (Salta the Fair), thanks to its festive atmosphere, handsome buildings and dramatic setting. In a region where the landscape and nature, rather than the towns and cities, are the main attractions, Salta is the exception. Fifteen hundred kilometres northwest of Buenos Aires, at the eastern end of the fertile Valle de Lerma, nationally famous for its tobacco plantations, and bounded by the Río Vaqueros to the north and Río Arenales to the south, the city is squeezed between steep, rippling mountains; 1190m above sea level, it enjoys a relatively balmy climate. In recent years, Salta has become the Northwest's undisputed tourist capital, and its top-quality services include a slew of highly professional tour operators, some of the region's best-appointed hotels and liveliest youth hostels and a handful of very good restaurants. In addition to a cable car and a tourist railway, its sights include the marvellous Neoclassical **Iglesia San Francisco**, and a raft of excellent **museums** dedicated to subjects as varied as pre-Columbian culture, anthropology, local history and modern art. A generous sprinkling of well-preserved or well-restored **colonial architecture** has survived, giving the place a pleasant homogeneity and certain charm.

San Lorenzo, a self-contained suburb of Salta only fifteen minutes west, enjoys a slightly cooler mountain climate and is awash with lush vegetation,

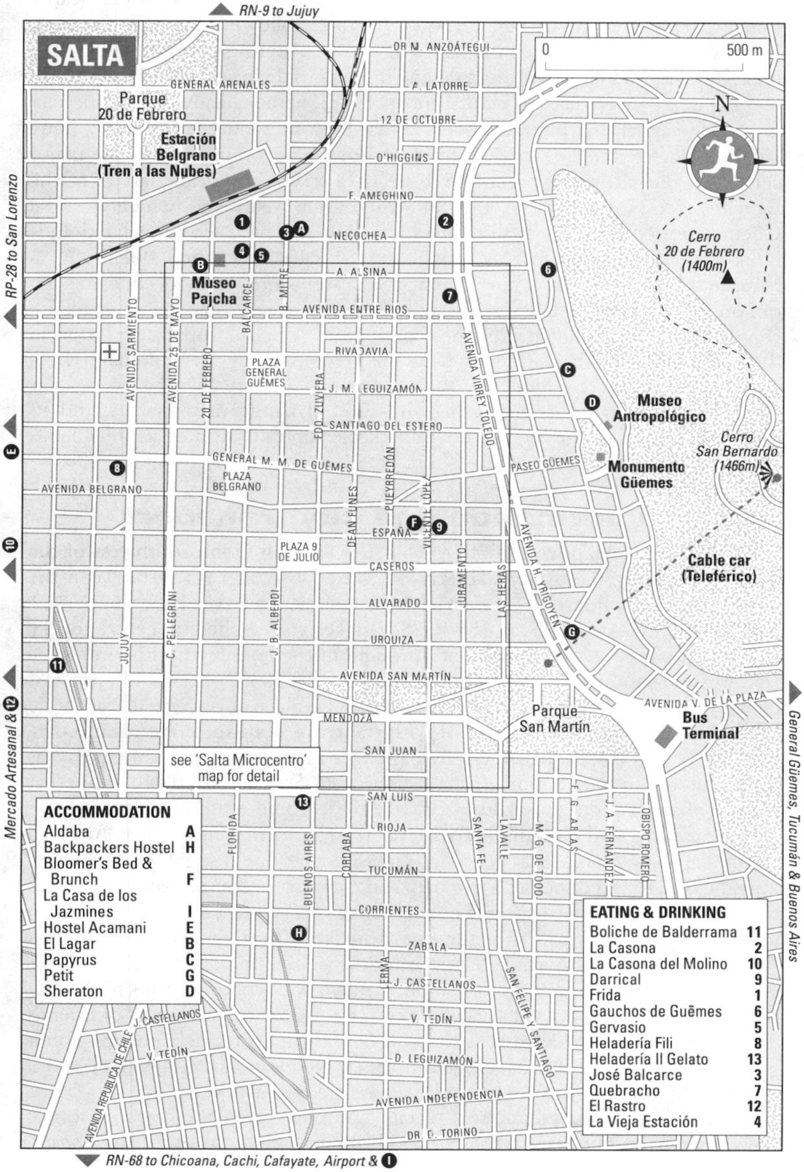

making it alluring for both visitors and locals who want to escape from the big city, especially in the summer. The tobacco fields and traditional villages along the **Valle de Lerma**, to the south, form an appealing landscape, but there is little there to detain visitors on the way to the Valles Calchaquíes, via Cerrillos and Chicoana.

Some history

Governor Hernando de Lerma of Tucumán, who gave his name to the nearby valley, founded the city of Salta on April 16, 1582, following the instructions of Viceroy Toledo, to guarantee the safety of anyone entering or leaving Tucumán itself. The site was chosen for its strategic mountainside location, and the streams flowing nearby were used as natural moats. In 1776, the already flourishing city was made capital of a huge intendencia that took in Santiago del Estero, Jujuy and even the southern reaches of modern Bolivia, becoming one of the major centres in the viceroyalty. From 1810 to 1814 it was the headquarters of the Ejércitos del Norte and for the following seven years was where General Güemes posted his anti-royalist forces, creating the now traditional red-and-black-poncho uniform for his gaucho militia. However, once Buenos Aires became the capital of the young country, Salta went into steady decline, missing out on the rest of the country's mass immigration of the mid- and late nineteenth century; the railway didn't arrive here until 1890. A belated urban explosion in the 1920s and 1930s has left its mark on the predominantly Neocolonial style of architecture in the city. Since the turn of the millennium, Salta has joined the ranks of Argentina's fastest growing and most dynamic metropolises, and its increased wealth can be seen in the remarkable sophistication of its inhabitants and the services they share with visitors.

Arrival, information and city transport

Salta's **El Aybal Airport** (ⓣ0387/424-2904) is about 10km southwest of the city centre, along motorway-like RN-51. Buses #8A and 6 run between the airport and central Avenida San Martín; a taxi will set you back about $22. AirBus (ⓣ0387/431-5327 or 156-832897) takes you to the city centre for $8. Buses from all across the region and throughout the country use the modernized **bus terminal** at Avenida Hipólito Yrigoyen (ⓣ0387/401-1143), just east of the Parque San Martín, five blocks south and eight east of central Plaza 9 de Julio. Bus #5 links the bus terminal with the **train station**, at Ameghino 690, via Plaza 9 de Julio, though the only passenger train serving Salta these days is the privately run tourist train, *Tren a las Nubes/del Sol* (see box, p.440); note that at time of writing the train and track were undergoing refurbishment.

The excellent and dynamic **provincial tourist office** at Buenos Aires 93 (Mon–Fri 8am–9pm, Sat & Sun 9am–8pm; ⓣ0387/431-0950, ⓦwww.turismosalta.gov.ar) dispenses a free map and extensive accommodation information; some staff members speak English. Rather less impressive, but awash with useful brochures and leaflets, is the **city tourist office** further down Buenos Aires at the corner of Avenida San Martín (daily 8am–9pm; ⓣ0387/437-3341). Another excellent source of information, mainly about cultural events in the city, is La Gauchita (ⓦwww.revistalagauchita.com.ar), a kiosk on the corner of Buenos Aires and Avenida San Martín; while you buy a drink or snack, enquire about *peñas*, or ask owner Eduardo Ceballos – poet, broadcaster, commentator and a colourful local personality – about his website, poems or novella.

You're unlikely to need any sort of city transport, given the compactness of downtown Salta, but **taxis** (with red and black livery) are plentiful and cheap.

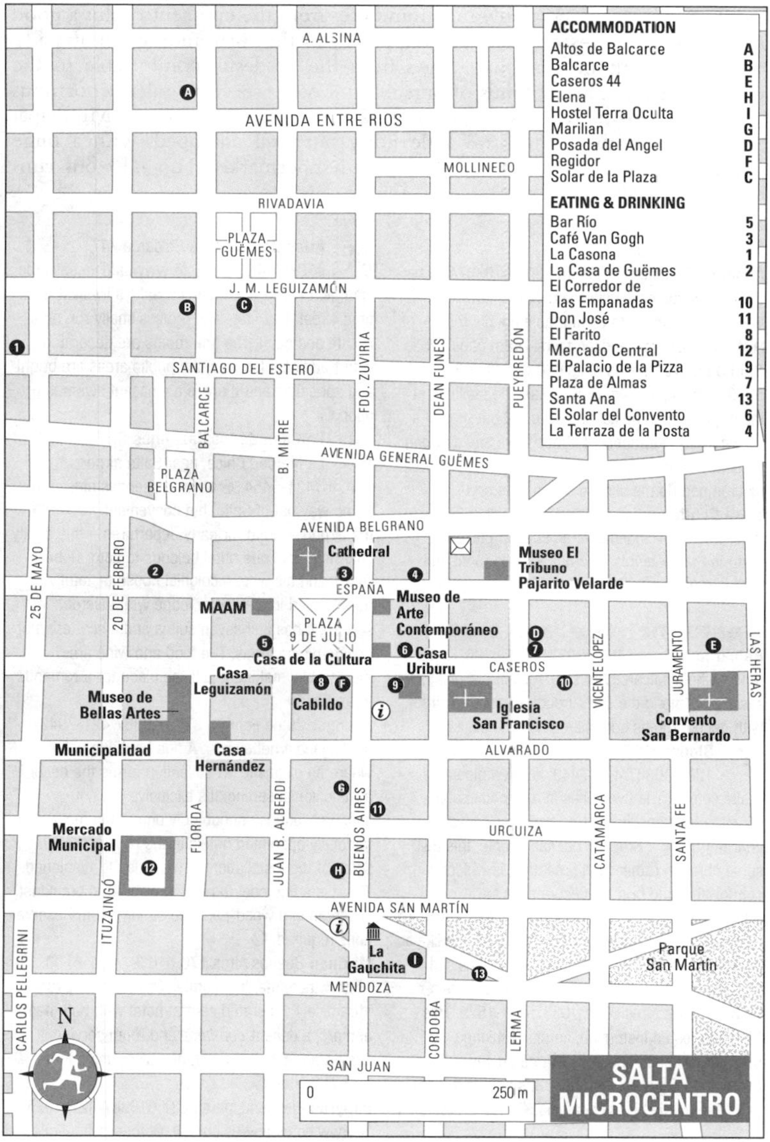

Accommodation

As you might expect of such a regional hub, Salta has a wide variety of **places to stay**, everything from five-star international hotels to a handful of exquisite boutique hotels to several lively youth hostels, plus plenty of decent middle-range hotels and good-value *residenciales* in between. If you'd rather avoid the city, you'll also find a number of excellent accommodation options in nearby

San Lorenzo (see p.436), only fifteen minutes from the city centre, plus a good many **fincas** and **estancias** (see box, p.438) in the surrounding countryside, offering accommodation that ranges from the modestly comfortable to the plain luxurious, plus all kinds of pursuits and other services. Salta's enormous municipal **campsite**, *Casino* (ⓣ0387/423-1341), in the Parque Municipal 3km south of the centre, is a little noisy but well equipped, with a huge swimming pool, hot showers, *balneario* and supermarket. The #13 bus runs there from Calle Jujuy.

Hostels

Acamani Santiago del Estero 2302 ⓣ0387/421-6156, ⓦwww.residencialacamani.com.ar. Welcoming place with comfortable double rooms (3). Organizes well-priced tours. Dorm beds $25.

Backpackers Buenos Aires 930 ⓣ0387/423-5910, ⓔbackpack@hostels.org.ar. The facilities at the city's veteran hostel are not great but there's a very friendly, international atmosphere and a strong tendency to have fiestas. Double rooms (3) as well as cramped dorms costing $28 per person.

Terra Oculta Córdoba 361 ⓣ0387/421-8769, ⓔterraoculta@ciudad.com.ar. Popular place featuring table-tennis, Internet, a video room and double rooms (2). Dorm beds $20.

Residenciales and B&Bs

Balcarce Balcarce 460 ⓣ0387/431-8135, ⓦwww.hotelbalcarce.8m.com. A plain but pleasant *residencial* along the city's trendiest nightlife street, with decent rooms and shared bathrooms. (2)

Bloomer's Bed and Brunch Vicente López 129 ⓣ0387/422-7449, ⓦwww.bloomers-salta.com.ar. The five suites in a colonial patio – all with mod cons like flat-screen TVs – ooze charm. Run by a British–Peruvian couple, this B&B serves brunch rather than breakfast, is welcoming, comfortable and brightly decorated. (6)

Caseros 44 Caseros 44 ⓣ0387/421-6761, ⓦwww.caseros44bandb.com.ar. Homely little B&B just like a private house. All the rooms have ceiling fans and en-suite bathrooms, and there's Internet access. (5)

Elena Buenos Aires 256 ⓣ0387/421-1529. This tried and tested institution, an old-fashioned Spanish-run guesthouse, has large dowdy bedrooms with en-suite bathrooms around a leafy patio like a little bit of Andalucia. (3)

Hotels

Aldaba Mitre 910 ⓣ0387/421-9455, ⓦwww.aldabahotel.com. A wonderful boutique hotel with six rooms, each with its own decor and style, though there's lots of crisp white linen, antique furniture and attention to detail in each. The owners, golf fans, will arrange for guests to visit Salta's course. (5)

Altos de Balcarce Balcarce 747 ⓣ0387/431-5454, ⓦwww.altosdebalcarce.com.ar. Despite a location on Salta's liveliest night-time street, this first-rate, professionally run hotel is safe and quiet. The fine rooms are decorated with traditional touches, the public areas are bright and appealing and there is a pleasant swimming pool. (6)

La Casa de los Jazmines RN-51 Km11, La Merced Chica, near Salta airport ⓣ0387/431-5454, ⓦwww.houseofjasmins.com. Some way out of Salta, but conveniently close to the airport – great for early departures – this totally charming boutique hotel belongs to actor Robert Duvall and his wife. A colonial house tastefully transformed into a luxury lodge with discreet service, it has just seven suites and a scattering of private dining areas. The food and wine are memorable, making it just the place for a romantic treat. (8)–(9)

El Lagar 20 de Febrero 877 ⓣ0387/421-7943, ⓔellagar@arnet.com.ar. A fine boutique hotel where an exquisite art collection forms the decor in a Neocolonial setting. It's exclusive but not snobbish, and is undoubtedly one of the most tastefully appointed hotels in the region, though some of the installations are a little old-fashioned. There is a fine pool to relax in or by, and breakfast is served in a wood-panelled dining room. Reservations required. (7)

Marilian Buenos Aires 176 ⓣ0387/421-6700, ⓦwww.hotelmarilian.com.ar. Professionally run, attractively decorated central hotel with both heat and a/c, a decent *confitería* and room service. It has an *apart-hotel* branch and also runs a low-budget hostel. (6)

Papyrus Pje Luis Linares 237 ⓣ0387/422-4075, ⓦwww.hotelpapyrus.com.ar. Gorgeous boutique hotel in a quiet, residential district; the dozen rooms, including spacious suites, are named after plants. There's a pool with Jacuzzi, and exquisite fusion food concocted by an expert chef is served in the elegant dining room (7)–(8)

Petit Hipólito Yrigoyen 225 ⓣ0387/421-3012, ⓔpetit_hotel@ciudad.com.ar. Good service and plush rooms. From the swimming pool, café terrace and the rooms at the back you get wonderful mountain views. 5

Posada del Angel Pueyrredón 25 ⓣ0387/431-8223, ⓦwww.hotelposadadelangel.com.ar. Delightful colonial-style modern hotel in a great location. The rooms, some of them suites, are quaint, with rather old-fashioned bedsteads. 6

Regidor Buenos Aires 10 ⓣ0387/431-1305, ⓦwww.hotelregidor.com.ar. Charming place with character, a rustic *confitería* and very pleasant rooms. Rooms overlooking the square tend to be noisy. 5

Sheraton Avenida Ejercito del Norte 330 ⓣ0387/432-3000, ⓦwww.sheraton.com/salta. Although part of the international chain, this impeccably run hotel, shoved up against the hillside in a slightly awkward location, has real personality – the decor is unmistakably north-western, based on Andean rugs and indigenous masks. There's a handsome pool, a fine restaurant and a decent gym. 8–9

Solar de la Plaza Leguizamón 669 ⓣ0387/431-5111, ⓦwww.solardelaplaza.com.ar. Definitely one of the classiest acts in the city, *Solar* is housed in a converted Neocolonial mansion with beautifully furnished, large rooms, rooftop pool, professional service and outstanding buffet breakfast featuring delicious local products. 8–9

The City

Salta's central square, **Plaza 9 de Julio**, is one of the country's most harmonious, especially since it was spruced up in the early years of the new millennium. Surrounded on all four sides by graceful, shady *recovas*, or arcades, under which several café terraces lend themselves to idle people-watching, it's a great place to while away an hour or two. The well-manicured central part of the square is a collection of palms and tipas, fountains and benches, plus a quaint late nineteenth-century bandstand. Around it stand the city's Neoclassical **cathedral**, the snow-white **Cabildo**, a number of popular cafés and two of the city's newest and best **museums**. A couple of blocks west huddle some well-preserved eighteenth- and nineteenth-century houses, including the immaculately white-washed Casa Arías Rengel, now home to the **Museo Provincial de Bellas Artes**. Two of the most striking sights in the city are the **Iglesia San Francisco**, an extravagant piece of Neocolonial architecture, and the more subdued but equally imposing **Convento de San Bernardo**. All of these places of interest are concentrated in the square kilometre or so of the microcentro and can comfortably be seen in a couple of days. The liveliest and trendiest part of the city, however, is the area around **Calle Balcarce**, especially north of Avenida Entre Ríos, near the Estación Belgrano; arts and crafts are on sale in the evenings and on weekends, and this is also where you'll find the largest number of restaurants, bars, discos and folk-music venues.

Heavy traffic and the related noise and exhaust pollution are something of a growing problem in Salta but getting around on foot is not difficult and it's hard to get lost, since the grid system is almost perfect in the microcentro; north–south streets change name at Calle Caseros; east–west streets on either side of avenidas Virrey Toledo and Hipólito Yrigoyen.

The cathedral

Towering over the northern side of the Plaza 9 de Julio at España 537, and mirrored in the innocuous plate-glass building next door, the brightly painted **cathedral** dates from 1882, the city's third centenary year. It's an Italianate Neoclassical pile of the kind found all over the region, with some well-executed interior frescoes – the one of the Four Apostles around the cupola is particularly fine. Inside, and immediately to the left of the entrance, is the grandiose Panteón de los Héroes del Norte, where local liberator General Güemes is buried. The Capilla del Señor del Milagro and Capilla de la Virgen del Milagro, at the far end of the left and right aisles respectively, house the sacred images that are the centrepieces of major celebrations every September (see box, p.429).

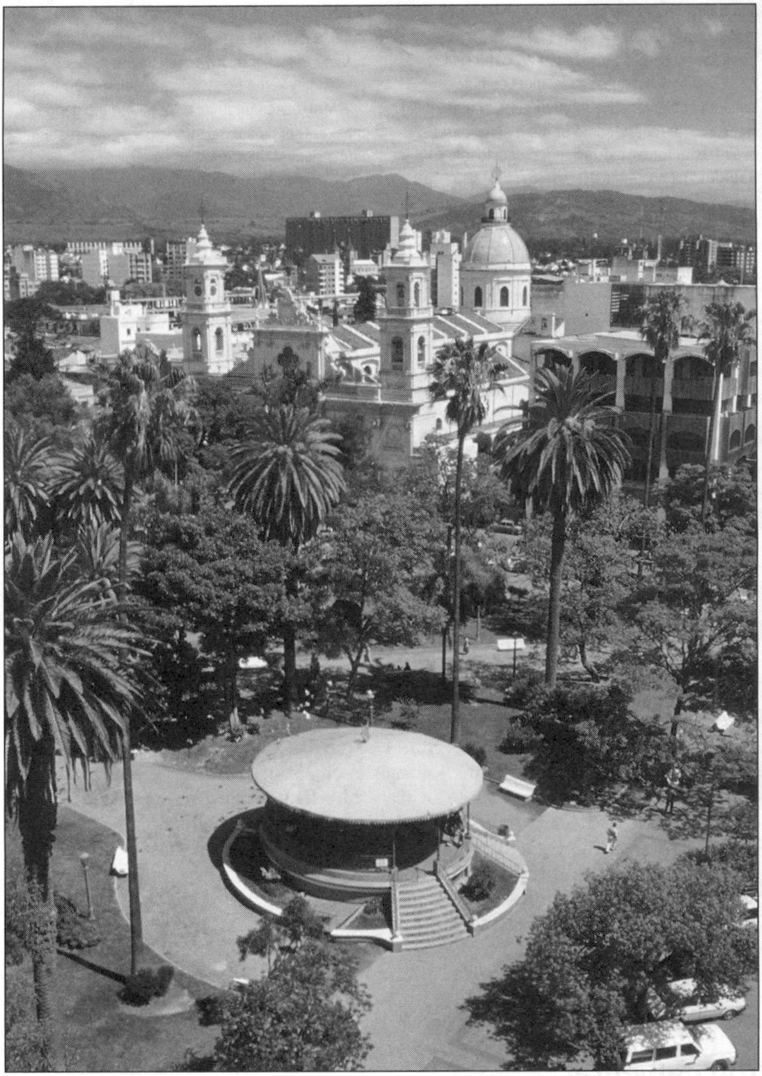

△ Plaza 9 de Julio

Museo de Arte Contemporanea (MAC)

Housed on the first floor of a handsomely renovated Neocolonial building on the northeast corner of Plaza 9 de Julio, the outstanding **Museo de Arte Contemporanea** (MAC; Tues–Fri 9am–1pm & 4.30–8.30pm, Sat & Sun 10.30am–1pm & 5–8.30pm; $2) – all sleek white walls and dark parquets – puts on exhibitions of mainly local artists, from up-and-coming wannabes straight out of art school to more established local names, who are often given shows of their own. Painting dominates but video and photography are not unknown.

Earthquakes and the Fiesta del Milagro

No earthquake as destructive as those that flattened the cities of Mendoza in 1861 and San Juan in 1944 has struck the Northwest region of Argentina within recent history, but this part of the country lies along the same fault line that was responsible for that seismic activity and is prone to occasional tremors, some of them violent. The **Nazca plate**, beneath the eastern Pacific, and the **South American plate**, comprising the whole continent, are constantly colliding – a continuation of the tectonic activity that formed the Andean cordillera. To make matters worse, the Nazca plate is subducting – nudging its way beneath the landmass – an action that accounts for the abundance of **volcanoes** along the range; some of them are extinct, others lie dormant, but none in the Northwest is very active. Nonetheless, a number of **earthquakes** of varying strength have rocked Northwest Argentina since the Europeans arrived, accounting for the repeated displacement of many settlements and the absence of colonial architecture in some of the oldest cities, such as Santiago del Estero.

Salta still thanks its lucky stars for **El Milagro**, the legend according to which two sacred images have spared the city the kind of destruction caused by seismic disasters. An image of **Christ** and another of the **Virgin Mary** were found floating in a box off the coast of Peru in 1592, exactly a century after the Americas were discovered by Columbus, and somehow ended up in Salta. Precisely one century later, on September 13, 1692, a series of tremors began to shake the city, damaging some public buildings and houses. During that night, a priest named José Carrión dreamed that if the images of Christ and Mary were paraded through the streets for nine days the earthquakes would stop and Salta would be spared forever. Apparently it worked and, ever since, the **Fiesta del Milagro** has been a major event in the city's calendar. Festivities and religious ceremonies starting on September 6 reach a climax on September 15, when the now-famous images, which are kept in the cathedral, are paraded through the city's streets in a massive, solemn but colourful procession.

Museo El Tribuno Pajarito Velarde

Two blocks east of the MAC, at Pueyrredón 106 and España, the curious **Museo El Tribuno Pajarito Velarde** (Mon–Sat 9am–6pm; $2) was the home of a colourful local personality, Guillermo Velarde Mors (born 1895), who died in his magnificent wooden bed here in 1965. Mors was nicknamed "Pajarito" ("little bird"), apparently because of his tendency to peck away at his food and to whistle in public. A controversial bohemian born into a wealthy, influential family, he worked in turn as a lawyer, journalist and banker, but retired from his last job, at the Banco Provincial de Salta, at the age of 37 to create a kind of arts club. While promoting artists, writers and musicians, especially local folk singers and groups, at a time when they lacked social kudos, he also went out of his way to cause scandals – he particularly liked provoking the nuns who ran the girls' school opposite his house. Respected as a great patron of the arts, he was also marginalized by local society, owing to his outlandish lifestyle – he never married, had lots of affairs and his music sessions often degenerated into drunken orgies. Crammed full of his fascinating belongings – including a hat donated by an admiring Carlos Gardel (two tangos were composed in Pajarito's honour) – this humble adobe house is a fitting tribute to both an original local character and the history of Salta's socio-cultural life in the twentieth century. The mischievous curator, Carol, delights in shocking visitors with some of Pajarito's prize trinkets, several of which are in dubious taste, but unfortunately her lively explanations are in Spanish only.

Museo de Arqueología de Alta Montaña (MAAM)

In an attractive Neo-Gothic building on the western side of the plaza, at Mitre 77, the **Museo de Arqueología de Alta Montaña** (MAAM; Tues–Sun 9am–1pm & 4–9pm; $10, free on weekdays for the first hour; ⓦwww.maam.org.ar) is the one museum in Salta that you should not miss. It was specially created to present to the public the discovery of the so-called **Llullaillaco Children**, one of the most important archeological finds ever made in Argentina. Three naturally mummified Inca children were uncovered in 1999 atop **Volcán Llullaillaco**, due west of Salta on the Chilean border and over 6700m above sea level, by an expedition of mountaineers and scientists. They were a 6-year-old girl, visibly struck by lightning some time after her burial, her hair arranged in two small braids and with a metal plaque as an adornment (which attracted the lightning); a teenage girl whose face was painted with a red pigment and who had small fragments of coca leaves above her upper lip; and a 7-year-old boy wearing a white feather ornament tied around his head. Their incredibly well-preserved corpses – all three lived around 1490 AD – have since been kept in a university laboratory in the city as tests on their tissue and other remains have been completed.

The jury is still out as to whether it would be sacrilegious to display the bodies in a public museum, so for the time being you must make do with vivid photos that can be seen by pressing a switch. Even these are quite creepy, as you can see expressions of fear on their young faces – the children were sacrificed to the Inca deities, possibly in a fertility ceremony or as an offering to the gods of the sun and moon. They were probably knocked out with a blunt weapon (so their bodies were not rendered imperfect by wounds) and then left to die of the lack of oxygen and the extreme cold.

Over a hundred **artefacts**, part of the remarkably intact treasure trove buried with the children at the end of the fifteenth century, are on display in the museum's rooms, where the temperature and humidity are kept artificially low – bring something warm to wear. The exhibit is both scientific and didactic, including a video about the expedition, displays of textiles and the like, but it is no musty old-fashioned museum. The ground-floor bookshop is prime hunting ground for souvenirs, mostly of very high quality, while the marvellous **cafeteria**, decorated in keeping with the museum and offering local specialities, is open daily from 9am to 10pm.

Cabildo (Museo Histórico del Norte)

Opposite the cathedral, on the southern side of the plaza at Caseros 549, stands the white-facaded **Cabildo**. Originally built in the early seventeenth century, it took on its current appearance in the late eighteenth, when the city became capital of the intendencia. It underwent a facelift that left its slightly lopsided structure – the two rows of graceful arches don't quite tally – essentially intact in the middle of the twentieth century, over a hundred years after it ceased to be the colonial headquarters. It now houses the highly eclectic **Museo Histórico del Norte** (Tues–Fri 9.30am–1.30pm & 3.30–8.30pm, Sat 9.30am–1.30pm & 4.30–8pm, Sun 9.30am–1pm & 4.30–8pm; $2), whose collections range from coins and eighteenth-century paintings to wooden saints and archeological finds to wonderful horse-drawn carriages parked in the cobbled courtyards, amongst them an elegant nineteenth-century hearse. Of the religious art in the first two rooms, the moving *San Pedro de Alcántara*, by eighteenth-century Altoperuvian artist Melchor Pérez de Holguín, stands out. Excellent temporary exhibitions, usually of regional art, are staged in the beautifully restored building, but the superb views across the plaza from the upper-storey verandah alone make a visit worthwhile.

Museo Provincial de Bellas Artes Arías Rengel and around

More colonial and Neocolonial buildings are clustered in the few blocks to the west of Plaza 9 de Julio. Just 100m west of the Cabildo, at La Florida 20, is the **Museo Provincial de Bellas Artes Arías Rengel** (Mon–Sat 8.30am–1pm & 4–8pm; $1). The pedestrianized street allows you an unrestricted view of its brilliant white facade, with its elaborate arched doorway and handsome green door. Erected towards the end of the eighteenth century, and virtually intact, albeit well restored, it's the finest viceregal building left in the city. The home of Sergeant-Major Félix Arías Rengel, who conquered the Argentine Chaco and had the house built, it has splendid patios, full of lush trees and plants, while the fine interior details include verandahs, banisters and rafters of red *quebracho* timber.

Occasionally putting on regional or national art exhibitions, the museum houses the city's rich fine art collection, ranging from paintings from Cusco to twentieth-century sculpture. Highlights are a *St Matthew* of the **Cusqueña School** (see p.132), an eighteenth-century polychrome *Asunción de la Virgen* from the Jesuit missions, a large painting of *The City of Salta*, painted in 1854 by Giorgio Penutti, and some fine engravings by nineteenth-century artists Basaldúa, Spilimbergo and Quinquela Martín.

Contrasting effectively with the pristine museum building is the **Casa Leguizamón** next door, at Caseros and La Florida. Constructed at the beginning of the nineteenth century for a rich merchant, it's painted a deep raspberry pink, and its plain two storeys are set off by fine detailing, a delicate wrought-iron balcony and zinc gargoyles. A few steps south is the **Municipalidad**, whose unusual twelve-columned oval patio is worth investigating, while opposite, at La Florida 97, is the **Casa de Hernández**, a typical Neocolonial corner house with a chamfered angle. Built around 1870, with a delightful patio at its heart, it now houses the **Museo de la Ciudad** (Mon–Fri 9am–1pm & 4–8.30pm, Sat 9am–1pm; free), a collection of artefacts and documents tracing the city's history.

Casa Uriburu and Casa de Cultura

Calle Caseros, a busy thoroughfare leading east from the southern side of Plaza 9 de Julio, takes you past a number of striking Neocolonial buildings and a fine late eighteenth-century house built to a simple design and with one of the most charming patios in the city: the **Casa Uriburu**, at Caseros 417. Now containing a museum of period furniture and Uriburu memorabilia (Tues–Fri 9.30am–1.30pm & 3.30–8.30pm, Sat 9.30am–1.30pm & 4.30–8pm, Sun 9.30am–1pm & 4.30–8pm; $1), it was once home to the influential Uriburu family, who produced two presidents of Argentina. The most impressive room is undoubtedly the reconstructed kitchen, with its polished copper and earthenware pots.

At the modern **Casa de la Cultura**, opposite at Caseros 460, you can see local art on display but, more importantly, you can hear the city's pride and joy, the Orquesta Sinfónica, in concert throughout much of the year. Considered to be up to international standards, the orchestra consistently plays to a packed house; tickets cost only a couple of pesos. Occasionally major artists, such as Martha Argerich, play here too, but expect to pay considerably more for the privilege of hearing them. Tango and folklore complete the programme.

Iglesia San Francisco and Convento San Bernardo

Further east still, at the corner of Caseros and Córdoba, and taking up a whole block, stands a city landmark and one of the most beautiful religious buildings in the country, the **Iglesia y Convento San Francisco**. An extravaganza of Italianate Neocolonial exuberance by architect **Luigi Giorgi**, it displays a textbook compliance with architectural principles combined with clever idiosyncrasies. The first thing that strikes you is the colour: pure ivory-white columns stand out from the vibrant ox-blood walls, while the profuse detailing of Latin inscriptions, symbols and Neoclassical patterns is picked out in braid-like golden yellow. Seen against a deep blue sky – virtually perennial hereabouts – the whole effect is stunning. While the main building and the adjoining convent were built in the middle of the eighteenth century, the facade and atrium were later additions, in keeping with the mid-nineteenth-century obsession with Neoclassicism. The church's most imposing feature is the slender **campanile**, towering over the low-rise Neocolonial houses of downtown Salta and tapering off to a slender spire. Following the convention of three progressively smaller storeys on a plain base, each level is ornamented according to the classic Jesuit order of four styles of column: Tuscan, Ionic, Corinthian and Composite. The highly elaborate **facade** of the church itself, behind a suitably austere statue of St Francis in the middle of the courtyard, is lavishly decorated with balusters and scrolls, curlicues and pinnacles, Franciscan inscriptions and the order's shield, but the most original features are the organza-like **stucco curtains** that billow down from each of the three archways, nearly touching the elegant wrought-iron gates below. Inside, the decoration is subdued, almost plain in comparison, but the most eye-catching elements are the three eighteenth-century Portuguese-style jacaranda-wood **armchairs** behind the altar. The **cloisters** of the convent sometimes shelter exhibitions of local arts and crafts. If you can, do go on a **guided tour** ($2; Spanish only), which will also get you into the fascinating Museo de Arte Sacro (Mon–Sat 9.30am–1pm & 3–7pm) – where the surprising archeological section features a perfect terracotta Etruscan head dating from the fourth century BC.

Three blocks further east along Caseros, on a large, open square, stands another convent, the **Convento San Bernardo**, and its relatively dull church. Still a Carmelite nunnery and closed to the public, this sixteenth-century convent building is one of the oldest still standing in Salta, albeit heavily altered and restored over the centuries. The convent's sturdy limewashed facade, punctuated by the tiniest of windows and a couple of dainty lamps on simple iron brackets, contrasts pleasingly with the backdrop of chocolate-brown mountains, the stark plaza in front and two heavily ornate **Rococo-style doors**. The first, to the left, is the former entrance to the early nineteenth-century Bethlemite Hospital, now blocked off: framed by four Tuscan columns, it comprises an oval ox-eye and a curvaceous fan-shaped lintel, dripping with Baroque mouldings. A large Argentine flag flutters over the other convent entrance, further to the right, knocked through the wall in the middle of the nineteenth century. Its decoration is a carbon copy of the first, except it has spiralling columns on either side and, instead of a blind window, its centrepiece is a lavishly carved **cedar door**, dating from 1762 and transferred from a patrician house elsewhere in the city. A smaller door, for daily use, has been cut into the enormous portal, which is opened only for special processions.

Museo Antropológico Juan Martín Leguizamón and Cerro San Bernardo

Starting three blocks north of the Convento San Bernardo, and two east, across Avenida Hipólito Yrigoyen, tree-lined **Paseo Güemes** is the main thoroughfare of a leafy, well-to-do barrio crammed with later Neocolonial houses; it climbs up towards a bombastic **monument** of General Güemes, Salta's local hero. Surrounded by a grove of eucalyptus, the bronze equestrian statue, dating from 1931, is decorated with bas-reliefs depicting the army that defended newly independent Argentina from several last-ditch invasions by the Spanish. Immediately behind it, where the streets begin to slope up the lower flanks of the mountain, is the modern **Museo Antropológico Juan Martín Leguizamón** at Ejército del Norte and Ricardo Sola (Mon–Fri 8am–7pm, Sat & Sun 9am–1pm & 3-6pm; $1). The varied collection could be better presented, and most of the explanations in Spanish are sketchy and inaccurate, but many of the items on display are worth seeing. One highlight is another well-preserved **mummy** found on **Volcán Llullaillaco** (see p.443), also bearing signs that it may have been a human sacrifice, while the centrepiece of the extensive ceramics collection is a set of finds from Tastil (see p.441), along with a petroglyph known as the **Bailarina de Tastil**, a delightful dancing figure painted onto rock, removed from the *pukará*, or pre-Columbian fortress, to the safety of a glass case. A well-executed reconstruction of a pre-Columbian burial urn shows how the local climate preserved textiles and wood in perfect condition for centuries. Finally, the section on festivals and **carnival** includes photographs of celebrations in Iruya (see p.465) and displays examples of the so-called *máscaras de viejo*, the old-man **masks** worn during the ceremonies there, along with the distinctive Chané masks, animal and bird heads made of *palo borracho* wood and the grotesque carnival masks from Oruro in Bolivia.

Immediately behind the museum a steep path zigzags up the overgrown flanks of **Cerro San Bernardo** (1458m), but you might prefer to take the **teleférico**, or cable car, from the base-station on Avenida Hipólito Yrigoyen, between Urquiza and Avenida San Martín, at the eastern end of Parque San Martín (daily 10am–7.30pm; $12 each way, $4 for children). The smooth cable-car gondolas take you to the summit in less than ten minutes, and from them and the small garden at the top you can admire panoramic **views** of the city and the snowcapped mountain range to the west. A **café** with a terrace serves drinks and simple meals.

Museo de Arte Étnico Americano Pajcha

Proof that the lively Balcarce district is not all about eating and drinking, the new **Museo de Arte Étnico Americano Pajcha**, 20 de Febrero 838 (Mon–Sat 9am–7pm, closed Mon but open Sun during Holy Week, the whole of July and Sept; $5; Ⓦwww.museodearteetnico.com.ar), is a strong contender for the best museum of American ethnic art in the whole country, the result of the lifelong work of Liliana Madrid de Zito Fontán, a local ethnologist. Her magnificent collection is arranged thematically and geographically in seven rooms, each with its own music. Native Argentine art and handicrafts loom large, but there are many outstanding items from all over South America, along with some beautiful photographs. Painting, textiles, religious objects (Christian and pre-Columbian) and wooden articles represent all the main ethnic groups; the silver jewellery crafted by the Mapuche of Chile and Andean ceramics are undoubtedly the highlights. There is also a fine example of a *pajcha*, an Inca offering tray with several compartments, looking not unlike an ancient muffin-mould. A selection of contemporary crafts is on sale at the reception, and there's also an excellent café on site.

Eating, drinking and entertainment

Salta has plenty of **eating** places to suit all pockets, ranging from simple **snack bars** where you can savour the city's famous **empanadas** to a growing number of classy **restaurants** where people dress smartly for dinner. The most traditional **cafés** huddle together around the Plaza 9 de Julio, while the city's many lively **peñas**, informal folk-music clubs mainly found in the Northwest, also serve food and drink. Calle Balcarce and the surrounding area towards the train station are firmly established as the hub of Salta's nightlife, focused on a row of bars, *peñas* and restaurants along Balcarce itself. People go to see and be seen – and have a good time in the process.

Restaurants

Darrical Vicente López 146 ☎0387/431-4848. Housed in the *Hotel Almeria*, this bright, quiet restaurant with mellow music is home to an up-and-coming chef by the name of Gonzalo Doxandabarat who serves up the likes of fillet steak stuffed with goat's cheese on a bed of courgettes and carrots. Top-rate wines and amazing desserts, such as fondant chocolate cake with cream and a glass of port.

Don José Urquiza 484. Cheap and cheerful restaurant serving up home cooking in a laid-back atmosphere; the paintings on the walls are Don José's too.

Frida Balcarce 935. Stylish restaurant serving Argentine and other Latin American dishes, though the links with Ms Kahlo and her native Mexico are more than tenuous.

Gervasio Balcarce 892. Rustic restaurant serving regional specialities and a variety of fish and meat dishes – with good local wine.

José Balcarce Mitre and Necochea. José López presides over the kitchen at this charming Neo-colonial corner restaurant and uses regional products like quinoa and grain amaranth (another Andean cereal) to accompany llama; also try the llama carpaccio or, for the less adventurous, the steak and roast potatoes.

Plaza de Almas Pueyrredón 6. Lively, happening joint open all day – mainly to sell crafts and clothes – and until very late to feed and make merry. Salads, kebabs and stir-fries to tempt all palates, plus live music in the patio, weather permitting.

Quebracho Virrey Toledo 702. One of the best restaurants in the city, with reliable if predictable food, plus fish – unusual for Salta – all at reasonable prices.

Santa Ana Mendoza 208. An elegant establishment serving international cooking, which makes a change from the usual *locro* and *humitas*.

El Solar del Convento Caseros 444 ☎0387/421-5124. Elegant surroundings, classical music and a free glass of champagne set the tone for this high-class restaurant, serving juicy steaks and with an excellent wine list.

La Terraza de la Posta España 476. A family *parrilla*, ideal for children, with no-nonsense traditional food, such as *locro* and *humitas*, as well as tender steaks and the usual desserts.

Cafés and bars

Bar Río Plaza 9 de Julio. An institutional bar, with fewer tourists than most around the square, despite the inexpensive drinks.

La Casona Virrey Toledo 1017, and at 25 de Mayo and Santiago del Estero. Both branches, open round the clock, churn out a never-ending supply of empanadas, including the best cheese pasties in town.

El Corredor de las Empanadas Caseros 117. Pleasant decor and a large patio are the settings for outstanding empanadas, *humitas*, tamales and other Northwestern dishes.

El Farito Caseros 509, Plaza 9 de Julio. Tiny empanada joint, dishing out delicious piping-hot cheese and meat pasties all day long.

Heladeria Fili Av Güemes 1009. In a handsome Art Deco building, one of the two best ice-cream places in town.

Heladería Il Gelato Buenos Aires 606. The other of the two excellent ice-cream parlours in Salta.

Mercado Central La Florida and San Martín. A number of small stalls serving all the local fare at very low prices; great for a lunch-time snack.

El Palacio de la Pizza Caseros 427. It lives up to its name, with the best pizzas in Salta by far. Also good empanadas.

Van Gogh Plaza 9 de Julio. The best coffee in town, excellent cakes, quick meals, appetizing snacks and the local glitterati are the attractions, plus live music late at weekends.

Peñas

Boliche de Balderrama San Martín 1126 ☎0387/421-1542. One of the most popular *peñas*; well known as a bohemian hangout in the 1950s, nowadays it's a more conventional place, attracting tourists and local folk singers alike. Some nights an additional charge is added to the bill for the music.

La Casa de Güemes España 720. A mellow atmosphere combines with decent food and spontaneous music-making starting at midnight at the earliest.

La Casona del Molino Luis Burela and Caseros 2500 ☎0387/434-2835. Empanadas, *locro*, *guaschilocro*, tamales, *humitas*, sangria and improvised live music much later on, all in a handsomely restored Neocolonial mansion.

Gauchos de Güemes Av Uruguay 750 ⓣ0387/421-0820. One of the more touristy *peñas*, but it's still worth a try. Delicious food but be prepared for a music charge on top.

El Rastro San Martín 2555. One of the least known and therefore most authentic of all the *peñas salteñas*, with spurts of spontaneous guitar in between large helpings of *locro*.

La Vieja Estación Balcarce 885 ⓣ0387/421-7727. Modern *peña* in one of the city's trendiest streets, dishing out food, draught beer and music shows nightly.

Tours from Salta

A number of outfits offering a wide variety of highly professional **tours**, **expeditions** and other **activities** in the Northwest region are based in and around Salta city. The following is a selection of the best.

Clark Expediciones Caseros 121 ⓣ0387/421-5390, ⓦwww.clarkexpediciones.com. Specializes in bird-watching trips to Calilegua and El Rey national parks, to the Laguna de los Pozuelos and further afield (Chile, Bolivia, Paraguay and Brazil, plus other parts of Argentina).

Marina Turismo Caseros 489 ⓣ0387/431-2097, ⓦwww.marina-semisa.com.ar. One of the most professional outfits in the region, Marina's friendly and dynamic team will bend over backwards to get you a vehicle (and driver-guide, should you need one), find you a guided excursion, book your hotel, change your flight or even just give you useful tips about where to eat, sleep or drink. English spoken.

MoviTrack Buenos Aires 28 ⓣ0387/431-6749, ⓦwww.movitrack.com.ar. Offers the "Safari a los Nubes", a fun and adventurous way of discovering the Quebrada del Toro; there's an optional extension via the Quebrada de Humahuaca, in a special vehicle giving all passengers panoramic views. In addition to safaris to Cachi, Quilmes and Cafayate, and day-trips to Molinos and Tilcara, they also arrange an outing to Iruya and a five-day expedition to San Pedro de Atacama, Chile.

Norte Trekking Los Juncos 173 ⓣ0387/436-1844 or 156-832543, ⓔfede@nortetrekking.com. Federico Norte and his experienced team can take you on a safari into the *puna*, on a two-day trip to the Valles Calchaquíes or to the Parque El Rey. Norte Trekking also organizes longer tours to the Atacama Desert, Chile.

Salta Rafting Buenos Aires 88, local 13 ⓣ0387/401-0301, ⓦwww.saltarafting.com. Highly professional, youthful team of operators specializing in rafting on the Río Juramento, southeast of the city, plus kayaking, horse riding and mountain-biking.

Siempre Viajeros Caseros 121 ⓣ0387/421-5390, ⓦwww.clarkexpediciones.com. Natural history excursions and longer journeys to various locations in the region. Operating out of the same office as Clark Expediciones, they also do excellent city tours in Salta itself, can put you in touch with people running bike tours, help you with local accommodation and show you around the Reserva del Huaico in San Lorenzo (see p.437).

Tastil Caseros 468 ⓣ0387/431-0031, ⓦwww.turismotastil.com.ar. Professionally run but mostly routine trips to the Salinas Grandes, Humahuaca, Cafayate, the cloud-forest national parks, Laguna de Pozuelos and even as far as Chile. Expect to waste lots of time collecting and dropping off passengers and not much English in the commentary.

Tailored Expeditions ⓦwww.tailoredexpeditions.com.ar. Internet-based tour company specializing in tailor-made tours – with native English-speakers as guides – of the Argentine Northwest for very small groups with emphasis on culture, leisure and luxury.

Uriburu – Father and Son J.M. Leguizamón 446 ⓣ0387/431-0605, ⓔhru@salta-server.com.ar. Unforgettable horseback, bike and trekking excursions to Molinos, La Poma and other less-visited routes around the province, all run by the prophet-like Hernán – a highly experienced guide and real character – and his son Marco.

Listings

Airlines Aerolíneas Argentinas at the airport ☎0387/424-1185, and at Caseros 475 ☎0387/431-1331; Andes, España 478 ☎0387/437-3514-19; LAN ☎0810-9999526; Lloyd Aéreo Boliviano, at the airport ☎0387/424-1181, and at Caseros 529 ☎0387/431-0320.
Banks and exchanges Banco de la Nación, Mitre 151; Masventas, España 610. There's nowhere reliable to change travellers' cheques, but there are plenty of ATMs.
Car rental Marina Turismo, Caseros 489 ☎0387/431-2097, Ⓦwww.semisa-marina.com.ar.
Consulates Bolivia, Mariano Boedo 32 ☎0387/422-3377; Paraguay, Mariano Boedo 38.
Internet access There are *locutorios* all around the city offering reasonably priced Internet and phone services.
Laundry Tía Maria, Av Belgrano 236; Laverap, Santiago del Estero, 363.
Post office Deán Funes 170.
Taxis Remises Sol ☎0387/431-7317, or Balcarce ☎0387/421-3535 or 431-5142.
Tour operators See box, p.435.

San Lorenzo

Just 11km northwest of Salta along RP-28, little **SAN LORENZO** is part dormitory town, part retreat for many Salteños, appreciated for its spotlessly clean ceibo-lined avenues and patrician villas. Plentiful walking and riding opportunities, a private nature reserve, an excellent range of **accommodation** and a couple of very good restaurants all make it an ideal alternative to staying in downtown Salta.

Turismo San Lorenzo on Juan Carlos Dávalos (ⓣ0387/492-1757, ⓦwww.turismosanlorenzo.com) offers a variety of tours of the region on horseback, on foot or by bike, ranging from $40 for a trek through the Quebrada de San Lorenzo to $350 for overnight trips to Iruya and the Quebrada de Humahuaca. You could also go for a walk at your own pace up the **Quebrada de San Lorenzo**, a rocky gorge down which a stream flows, sometimes forming falls and pools; the walk takes you through unspoilt woodland to the foot of the hulking mountains that form a natural barrier behind the village. Another enticing stroll can be taken through the newly created **Reserva del Huaico** (daily 8am–6pm, by prior appointment only; ⓣ0387/497-1024 or 154-449521, ⓔhuaico1790@gmail.com), a nature reserve set up to protect the native forest and its endogenous flora and fauna (especially its birds); the exploration of its trails culminates at a viewpoint from where you can take in the whole valley to Salta city and beyond.

Buses run at regular intervals from central Salta to the Camino de la Quebrada, just before the gorge, stopping along Avenida San Martín and Juan Carlos Dávalos.

Accommodation

Even if you don't have your own transport, it's worthwhile bedding down for the night in the calm fresh air of San Lorenzo, where the range of accommodation goes from the basic and rustic to the positively luxurious. Some of these lodgings are located outside the village itself, but the staff at these places can arrange transport to and from the city and/or the airport for those who need it.

Cabañas del Sol RP-28 Km11.5 ⓣ0387/492-2072, ⓦwww.saltacabanasdelsol.com.ar. Wonderful complex of *cabañas*, some of them right down by the riverside, in a fabulous rural setting some way out of San Lorenzo; ideal for anyone who wants to have self-catering accommodation. ❻

Casa de Campo Arnaga Aniceto la Torre, on the road to Lesser ⓣ0387/492-1478, ⓔarnaga@arnet.com.ar. This wonderfully located handsome Basque-style patrician home drips with old-world charm and Salta's new-world colonial tradition. The slightly old-fashioned rooms are comfortable and the mountain views breathtaking. ❼

Eaton Place Av San Martín 2457 ⓣ0387/492-1347, ⓦwww.eatonplace.todowebsalta.com.ar. As the name hints, this exquisite hotel – whose English-speaking owner has a collection of antiques that reflect his impeccable taste – is inspired by London mansions, though what townhouse in Belgravia boasts a palm-lined driveway? The plush rooms, classy service, dreamy swimming pool, toothsome food and marvellous grounds make this a plum choice. ❻–❼

Hostería Los Ceibos 9 de Julio and España ⓣ0387/492-1675 or 492-1621, ⓦwww.hlosceibos.com.ar. This relatively modest *hostería* in an attractive Neocolonial building has clean if uninspiring rooms, a swimming pool and other sports facilities. ❸–❹

Hotel Cerros de San Lorenzo Joaquín V. Gonzales s/n, Loteo los Berros ⓣ0387/492-2500, ⓦwww.cerrosdesanlorenzo.com.ar. A new hotel built in a fabulous Neocolonial style around a shady patio; the rooms are commodious and most attractive, and the bathrooms modish. The high location makes for breathtaking views. ❼

Posada Don Numas Pompilio Guzmán 1470 ⓣ0387/492-1918, ⓦwww.donnumas.com.ar. This home-from-home posada boasts twelve spacious rooms with modern bathrooms, ultra-friendly service, two swimming pools, a fully equipped spa (saunas, massages, gym) and a prime setting affording mountain views. The breakfast, complete with home-made cakes and pies, will keep you going all day, but other simple meals or *asados* are offered on request. ❻–❼

Eating and drinking

San Lorenzo's best **restaurant** by far is *Lo de Andrés*, in a shocking pink galleried building with a large terrace, at Juan Carlos Dávalos and Gorriti (ⓣ0387/492-1600); the extensive menu includes unforgettable empanadas,

Estancias and fincas in Salta and Jujuy provinces

Salta and, to a lesser degree Jujuy, are provinces with a very long colonial history, which among other things has left behind many **estancias** (traditional ranches), known locally as *fincas*, some of which now offer rooms to guests. Estancia stays are a wonderful way of combining rest – and sometimes even luxury – with a chance to get to know locals, tune in to nature and experience *criollo* customs and farming activities.

Remote *Finca Puerta del Cielo* (ⓣ0387/156-840400 or 0387/492-1757; ❼ full board) is up in the Andean foothills not far from the city of Salta. Reachable only on horseback, though, it's a difficult place to get to, but rewarding once you are there. It's famous for its round-the-bonfire *asados*. You need to book your stay (1–3 nights) through a tour operator, such as Turismo San Lorenzo in San Lorenzo (see p.437).

Finca Santa Anita (ⓣ0387/490-5050 or 431-3858, ⓦwww.santanaita.com.ar; ❻), is in the Valle de Lerma, 75km south of Salta by RN-68, near Coronel Moldes, on the west bank of the huge Embalse Cabra Corral reservoir. Between swimming in the pool and organized horse rides, you can see tobacco being processed. There is even a tobacco museum on the premises.

Between Chicoana and Rosario de Lerma, along RP-33, is the oddly named *Finca Los Los* (ⓣ0387/431-7258; ❻), where the food's excellent and the welcome very friendly, but make sure you book ahead if you want to stay. Otherwise, you can enjoy a *día de campo* (day of farm activities, horse rides, lunch and tea) for $130 per person. The *finca* sits among superb parkland and the rooms are charming, and there is a small collection of archeological finds as an added attraction.

Another historic tobacco farm, *El Bordo de las Lanzas* (ⓦwww.estanciaelbordo.com; US$150 per person full board), at Rivadavia s/n near General Güemes, 80km northeast of Salta, can be reached via the RN-9 to Jujuy and then a side road that heads north from the village of Cobos; it is an early seventeenth-century house and maintains its colonial structures but with all modern conveniences added – the furniture and artefacts come from Jesuit missions in the Northwest, Peru and Bolivia.

Commanding stunning mountain views through a huge picture window just outside the mountain village of Cachi (see p.445) is luxurious *Finca El Molino* (ⓣ03868/491094 or 0387/421-9368; ❽). The very comfortable rooms are mostly located in a purpose-built annexe but the delicious meals are served in an aristocratic dining room. The small vineyards now produce remarkable high-altitude wines, made in the state-of-the-art bodega.

Just over 20km from Molinos along RP-53, off RN-40 between Cachi and Cafayate, is the outstanding luxury lodge of *Colomé* (ⓣ03868/494044, ⓦwww.bodegacolome.com; from US$240 per night). Spanish settlers set up a winery here in early colonial times, and it was revived in the nineteenth century. Then Swiss wine magnate Donald Hess – who owns vineyards in his home country, plus California, South Africa and Australia – bought the land a few years ago, began making fine wines under the Colomé brand and created an eco-resort. A handful of spacious, modern rooms with huge bathrooms, are set around a handsome colonial-style patio, where a fountain gurgles. The rooms look out across cactus gardens and a turquoise pool at breathtaking mountain scenery. In addition to touring the estate, you can go on horse rides into the highland surroundings or taste malbec and cabernet sauvignons made *in situ*. The food is of good quality, too.

Finca Los Lapachos (ⓣ0388/491-1291, ⓔlapachos@jujuytel.com.ar; ❼ full board) sits along RP-42 near the village of Perico, fairly close to Jujuy airport. It's definitely the place if you're looking for charm, luxury, peace and quiet and an authentic *finca* experience, with horse riding and a beautiful swimming pool. The Leach family, who call this place home, are related to the British settlers who set up the regional sugar industry. Extremely hospitable, they nonetheless prefer you to book ahead.

delicious *locro*, home-style *cazuela de cabrito*, fresh trout (best simply grilled, rather than smothered in sauce) and excellent pasta, with friendly service to boot. Just along the road, at Juan Carlos Dávalos 1450, is *Confitería Don Sanca*, a charming place serving delicious food, including a very good stab at tea. Further uphill, at the entrance to the Quebrada, *El Duende de la Quebrada*, Juan Carlos Dávalos 2309, is an attractive rustic construction, with seemingly endless wooden balconies overlooking the stream; it serves very decent fare, with emphasis on local specialities, plus cakes, teas, coffees, juices and the like.

Valle de Lerma

South of Salta, paved RN-68 runs along the fertile **Valle de Lerma** before climbing up the course of the Río de las Conchas to Cafayate, 180km away (see p.446). This is an area of prosperous *fincas*, or ranches, some of which are great places to stay, amid green tobacco fields and cattle pastures (see box opposite). Throughout the densely populated valley, typical buildings include open-sided, barn-like *secaderos*, or tobacco-drying sheds, *estufas*, or brick tobacco-kilns, and tiled-roofed *casas de galería*, long, low houses with colonnades along one side, some with straight pillars, others decorated with a row of mock-Gothic ogival arches.

The first small towns you come to, such as Cerrillos and El Carril, hold no attractions apart from the first examples of *casas de galería*. **Chicoana**, 50km south and 5km west, at the gateway to the RP-33 Cuesta del Obispo route to the Valles Calchaquíes (see p.443), is a quaint gaucho settlement easily reached by bus from Salta. Two colourful festivities, the **Encuentro Nacional de Doma** and the **Festival del Tamal** coincide here in mid-July. For several days Argentina's best horsemen show off their talents, risking life and limb to entertain an audience whose task it also is to judge the best tamale, traditional corn-meal parcels filled with chopped meat. Later on, in early August, the **Fiesta del Tabaco** is another excuse for festivities and the downing of large quantities of *Fernet con coca*, the gaucho's favourite tipple – a combination of Fernet Branca, a dark, herb-based liqueur, with Coca-Cola.

Chicoana's harmonious main square is surrounded by Italianate buildings – many of them ornamented with slender iron pillars – a fine, well-restored colonial church and the *Hostería de Chicoana*, at España 45, which has a lovely courtyard inhabited by free-roaming cats, dogs, an owl and other birds; the excellent **restaurant** serves local specialities, including goat stew and empanadas. The owner, Martín Pekarek, speaks perfect English and runs 4WD **tours**, horse rides, photo safaris and rafting trips in the area.

Quebrada del Toro

Whether you travel up the magnificent gorge called the **Quebrada del Toro** by train – along one of the highest railways in the world (see box, p.440) – in a tour operator's jeep, in a rented car or, as the pioneers did centuries ago, on horseback, the experience will be unforgettable, thanks to the constantly changing dramatic mountain scenery and multicoloured rocks. The gorge is named after the **Río El Toro**, normally a meandering trickle, but occasionally a raging torrent and as bullish as its name suggests, especially in the spring. It swerves up from the tobacco fields of the Valle de Lerma, 30km southwest of Salta, through dense thickets of **ceibo**, Argentina's national tree, ablaze in October and November with their fuchsia-red spring blossom, past **Santa Rosa de Tastil** and the pre-Inca site of

Tastil, to the desiccated highlands of the Puna Salteña, Salta's altiplano, focused on the ghostly mining village of **San Antonio de los Cobres**. Between this highest point and **Campo Quijano**, in the valley bottom, RN-51 and the railway wind, loop and zigzag side by side for over 100km, joining two distinct worlds: the fertile, moist lowlands of Salta's populous central valleys, and the waterless highland wastes at an altitude of over 3000m.

Many tour operators in Salta (see box, p.435) offer alternative, more adventurous **tours by road**, many of which ironically follow the train for much of the way, offering passengers the chance to photograph the handsome locomotive and wave at it frantically, expecting passengers to reciprocate. Clark Expediciones (see box, p.435) can meet you at the train when it stops at Polvorilla Viaduct, and guide you around the altiplano in a jeep; although you miss out on the return train journey and the folk show, you get the best of both worlds: the train ride plus a chance to explore the area more independently. MoviTrak runs the most popular jeep safari excursions up the Quebrada del Toro, often combined with a return leg down the Quebrada de Humahuaca (see box, p.435).

The Train to the Clouds – and to the Sun

Travelling through the Quebrada del Toro gorge on the Tren a las Nubes, or **Train to the Clouds** – when it is operational – is an unashamedly touristic experience. At the time of writing, however, the train had been out of service for several months while undergoing repairs – you should refer to the local tourist offices for the most up-to-date information.

Clambering from the station in Salta to the magnificent Meccano-like **La Polvorilla Viaduct**, high in the altiplano, the smart train – with a leather-upholstered interior, shiny wooden fittings, spacious seats, a dining car, a post office and even altitude-sickness remedies – was originally built to service the borax mines in the salt-flats of Pocitos and Arizaro, 300km beyond La Polvorilla. The viaduct lies 219km from Salta, and on the way the train crosses **29 bridges** and **twelve viaducts**, threads through **21 tunnels**, swoops round two gigantic **360° loops** and chugs up **two switchbacks**. La Polvorilla, seen on many posters and in all tour operators' brochures, is 224m long, 64m high and weighs over 1600 tonnes; built in Italy, it was assembled here in 1930. The highest point of the whole line, just 13km west of the viaduct, is at Abra Chorrillos (4475m). Brief stopovers near La Polvorilla, where the train doubles back, and in San Antonio de los Cobres, allow you to stretch your legs and meet some locals, keen on selling you llama-wool scarves and posing for photos (for a fee). Folk groups and solo artists interspersed with people selling arts, crafts, cheese, honey and souvenirs galore help while the time away on the way down, when it's dark for the most part.

When running, the train leaves (and returns to) Salta's Ferrocarril Belgrano station several times a week in July and August, with a less frequent service from April to June and from September to November. In January and February, and on a few days in April, May and June, a shorter trip leaves Salta at 7am and returns at 8pm; known as the Tren del Sol, or **Sun Train**, it goes only as far as the Estación Diego de Almagro, 3503m above sea level. Ironically, you are likelier to see clouds from the rainy-season Sun train – trips on the Train to the Clouds normally take place under a blazing winter sun without a cumulo-nimbus in sight.

Tickets for either route should be reserved in advance; once up and running again the train will no doubt have its own website – ask at the tourist office in Salta for more information. The Ferrocarril Belgrano station in Salta is at Ameghino 690, ten blocks north of the central Plaza 9 de Julio, and can be reached by buses #5 and #13 from downtown, the bus terminal and the campsite.

Santa Rosa de Tastil and Tastil

The middle section of the Quebrada del Toro is a narrow valley where tall, cliff-like mountains loom, revealing strata of reds, purples, ochres and yellows that look their best in the early light. Along them run great walls of grey rock, like long battlements, and the whole landscape is spiked with tall **cardón cacti**. Intermittent stretches sport gigantic flint-arrowhead stone formations jutting out of the bedrock. Tiny settlements of adobe houses, with their adjoining corrals of goats, perch on the bare mountainsides, and RN-51 and the railway, both clinging to the cliffside, crisscross the riverbed several times, occasionally running alongside each other. Picturesque *chacras* (farmhouses) are niched in the cliffs, and photogenic walled cemeteries, dotted with gaudy paper flowers, pepper the slopes beneath the stark Cerro Bayo (4250m). After parting ways temporarily with the rail track, RN-51 – now a good dirt road – continues to climb and, 75km from Campo Quijano and 3000m above sea level, you reach minute **SANTA ROSA DE TASTIL**, with its tiny **Museo del Sitio** (Tues–Fri 10am–6pm, Sat & Sun 10am–2pm; $1), set beneath cactus-clad rocks. It contains a fine pre-Inca mummy and miscellaneous finds from nearby excavations, including arrowheads, plus some fine paintings of the region. A short distance away is the newer **Museo Regional Moisés Zerpa** (same times and entrance fee), furnished and decorated like a traditional local house, complete with cooking utensils, ceramics and textiles. If you're lucky, the curator of both museums might also take you around the pre-Inca site, signposted 3km west, at **TASTIL** proper. The well-restored remains of one of the region's largest pre-Inca towns, it was inhabited by some three thousand people in the fourteenth century AD. The **mirador**, on once-fortified heights commanding fabulous valley and mountain views, overlooks the clearly terraced farmland from which the people of Tastil eked out a living. Nearly 35km beyond here the road runs above the railway before slipping through the narrow **Abra de Muñano** gorge and emerging into open, mountain-edge altiplano, entering the final run into San Antonio, after the junction with RN-40, south to La Poma (see p.443) at over 4000m.

San Antonio de los Cobres and around

A major regional crossroads, just over 130km northwest of Salta by RN-51 – halfway to the Chilean border – and a dizzying 3775m above sea level, **SAN ANTONIO DE LOS COBRES** is the small, windswept "capital" of an immense but mostly empty portion of the altiplano, rich in minerals, as its name ("of the coppers") suggests, and little else, except some breathtaking **scenery**. The **Salinas Grandes**, to the north of San Antonio de los Cobres, are among the continent's biggest salt-flats, a huge glistening expanse surrounded by brown mountains, snow-peaked volcanoes and sparse pasture. To the west a little-used road heads across to Chile by **Paso de Sico**, reached via the ultra-remote hamlet of Cauchari, while to the south, along an alternative route to the marvellous Valles Calchaquíes, is **La Poma**, a typical altiplano settlement that's far more picturesque than San Antonio.

Most people only ever see San Antonio de los Cobres from its train station – the Tren a las Nubes (when it is up and running) makes a short stop here on its way back down to the plains, during which the blue and white Argentine flag is hoisted and the national anthem played. You won't be missing much if you don't hop off: the town's low houses (many of them built by the borax and lithium mining firms for their workforce in a highly utilitarian style), dusty streets and lack of vegetation make for a rather forlorn little town, not especially inviting and displaying few signs of the wealth generated by the valuable metals running in rich veins through the nearby mountains. **Overnight stays** can be accommodated at the *Hostería de las Nubes*, Caseros 441 (ⓣ0387/490-9059; ⑤); it's fairly basic but the plumbing and central heating work and **meals** are fine. Otherwise, there are a number of places that cannot really be recommended. There's nothing in the way of tourist information here, but the police next to the train station can give you news about the state of the road and any weather hazards.

El Quebracho runs a twice-daily **bus service** between Salta and San Antonio; there are also services onwards to the Paso de Jama (see p.459).

North to the Salinas Grandes

Northwards from San Antonio de los Cobres, re-routed RN-40 starts its final, partly surfaced, run towards the northernmost reaches of Argentina, and the border settlement of Ciénaga, more than 200km away. The RP-75 branches off 21km from San Antonio, eventually leading to Abra Pampa via Casabindo (see p.467) – 130km north – over very difficult terrain but through eerily dramatic altiplano scenery, well worth exploring if you have plenty of time (and fuel supplies), while the main RN-40 route veers northwest to Susques (see p.459). Where it crosses into Jujuy Province, 60km further on, you're treated to wonderful views of the snow-peaked Nevado de Chañi (6200m), an extinct volcanic cone poking above the brown slopes of the stark range where the Río El Toro has its thaw-fed source, in the east. To the north stretches the glistening expanse of the aptly named **Salinas Grandes** (also accessible from Purmamarca, Jujuy Province, via the fabulous Cuesta de Lipán; see p.459) one of the country's biggest salt-flats and certainly the most impressive, ringed by mountains on all sides and beneath almost perennial blue skies. This huge rink of snow-white crystals, forming irregular octagons, each surrounded by crunchy ridges, crackling like frozen snow under foot, acts as a huge mirror. The salt, shimmering in the nearly perpetual blazing sunshine, often creates cruel water mirages, though there are in fact some isolated pools of brine where small groups of flamingoes and ducks gather. This is a likely place for spotting vicuñas and llamas, too, flocks of which often leap across the road to reach their scrawny, yellow pastureland, or *tola*, on either side of RN-40. Way over to the north you can make out the dark bulk of Cerro Negro, a hill sticking out from the plain.

Some 13km before joining the RN-52 Purmamarca to Susques road (see p.459), you pass the tiny hamlet of **Tres Morros**, with its simple but beautiful church – a typical altiplano design with a plain facade and a single sturdy tower, all built in solid adobe that will resist all but the strongest earthquakes. The village also has a curious, walled graveyard, built on the gently sloping hill, or *morro* – one of the three that gives the village its name – only a fraction full of graves, as if patiently waiting for dozens of future generations to die. No public transport comes along here so you'll either need your own transport or to come on a tour from Salta (see box, p.435).

West to Chile via the Paso de Sico

West of San Antonio de los Cobres, RN-51 crosses both the railway and the provincial border between Salta and Jujuy provinces several times as it climbs steeply towards **Cauchari**, 68km away. About halfway there, it heaves itself over the Abra de Chorrillos pass, at an altitude of 4650m, marked by a sign and a traditional *apacheta*, or cairn. From it you are treated to exhilarating views in all directions of the snowy Chañi, Acay and Cachi mountains, the plains around San Antonio and the lichen-yellow pastures of Campo Amarillo, grazed by sizeable flocks of camouflaged **vicuña**. Cauchari itself is a one-llama town at just below 4000m, comprising a quaint single-towered church, a house and a police station, the last before the border. To the north is the seemingly never-ending salt-flat, **Salar de Cauchari**, and the road continues to the frontier via the picturesque hamlet of **Catúa**, surrounded by spongy *bofedales*, bog-like pastures where alpacas and llamas munch nonchalantly on slimy grass. The **Chilean border** at the **Paso de Sico** (4080m), marked by a terse sign, runs through some out-of-this-world scenery: splashes of dazzling salt-flat sit among dusky **volcanoes**, whose perfect cones frequently surpass 5000m, with views across to the majestic **Volcán Llullaillaco** (6739m) way across to the southwest; this is where the mummified children, for whom the MAAM museum in Salta (see p.430) was created, were found.

There's no public transport across the pass, so you'll need your own vehicle, preferably a 4WD, to do this fabulous trip.

South to La Poma via the Abra de Acay

From its junction with RN-51, just southeast of San Antonio de los Cobres, unsealed and often poorly maintained RN-40 snakes its difficult way over the **Abra de Acay**, at 5061m one of the world's highest mountain passes. It's frequently blocked by snowdrifts in the winter and rock falls in the summer – check with locals before attempting it. Only 90km but sometimes several hours away, **LA POMA**, lying 5km off RN-40 near the Río Calchaquí, is a modern but pleasant village of adobe houses, built near the phantom-like ruins of La Poma Vieja, which was razed to the ground by a severe earthquake in 1930. La Poma lies in the shadow of the mighty **Cumbre del Libertador General San Martín**, whose 6380-metre summit is never without at least a tip of snow. Although it's far from luxurious, the comfortable *Hostería La Poma* (☎03868/491003; ④), on the main street, offering basic meals, will come in very useful if you've had a difficult trip down the pass or are contemplating crossing it. Fifty kilometres south, along one of the finest scenic routes in the region, with massive and imposing mountain peaks on either side, is Cachi (see p.445), the gateway into the Valles Calchaquíes proper.

Valles Calchaquíes

Named after the Río Calchaquí, which has its source in the Nevado de Acay (at over 5000m) near San Antonio de los Cobres, in the north of Salta Province, and joins the Río de las Conchas, near Salta's border with Tucumán, the **Valles Calchaquíes** are a series of beautiful highland valleys that enjoy over three hundred days of sunshine a year, a dry climate and much cooler summers than the lowland plains around Salta. The fertile land, irrigated with canals and ditches that capture the plentiful snowmelt from the high mountains to the west, is mostly given over to vineyards – among the world's highest – that produce the characteristic torrontés grape. The scenery is extremely varied and of an awesome beauty, constantly changing as you make your way along winding mountainside roads. Organized tours from Salta squeeze a visit into one day, stopping at the valleys' main settlement, the airy village of **Cafayate**, for lunch. However, by far the most rewarding way to see the Valles Calchaquíes is under your own steam, by climbing the amazing **Cuesta del Obispo** (go in the morning before clouds hide the views), through the **Parque Nacional Los Cardones**, a protected forest of gigantic cardón cacti, to the picturesque village of **Cachi**; then follow the valley south through some memorable scenery via **Molinos** and **San Carlos**, on to **Cafayate**, where plentiful accommodation facilitates a stopover. The scenic road back down to Salta, sometimes known as the **Quebrada de Cafayate** but more accurately called the Cuesta de las Conchas – a name avoided only because of its unfortunate linguistic connotations – snakes past some incredible rock formations, optimally seen in the late afternoon or early evening light. All along the valleys, you'll see typical *casas de galería*: long, single-storey houses similar to those in the Valle de Lerma (see p.439), some with a colonnade of rounded arches, others decorated with pointed ogival arches or straight pillars.

Regular **public transport** to Salta and Tucumán makes travelling around the valleys straightforward even without your own vehicle, though it is less frequent in the northern reaches around Cachi. **Organized tours** from Salta are your best bet if you have no transport of your own and don't have time to wait for buses. Apacheta Viajes, Buenos Aires 33 (Ⓣ0387/431-1622 or 421-2333; Ⓔapacheta@salnet.com.ar); Hernán Uriburu, J.M. Leguizamón 446 (Ⓣ0387/431-0605, Ⓔhru@salta-server.com.ar); MoviTrack, Buenos Aires 68 (Ⓣ0387/431-6749, Ⓕ431-5301, Ⓦwww.movitrack.com.ar); and Siempre Viajeros, Caseros 121 (Ⓣ0387/421-5390, Ⓦwww.clarkexpediciones.com), all run a variety of tours to the valleys.

Up to Cachi

The northern Calchaquí settlement of Cachi sits 170km southwest of Salta, via Chicoana, in the Valle de Lerma (see p.439). To get there you go along partly sealed RP-33, a scenic road that squeezes through the dank Quebrada de Escoipe, before climbing the dramatic mountain road known as the **Cuesta del Obispo**, 20km of hairpin bends, offering views of the rippling Sierra del Obispo. These fabulously beautiful mountains, blanketed in olive-green vegetation and heavily eroded by countless brooks, are at their best in the morning light. A good place to stop before negotiating the steep, meandering climb is the rudimentary *Hostería El Maray*, where you can have a delicious snack, tea or coffee. About 60km from Chicoana, just before you reach the top of the *cuesta*, a signposted track leads south down to the **Valle Encantado**, 4km away; this is a fertile little valley, set around a marshy lagoon, that becomes a riot of colour in September and October, when millions of wild flowers burst into bloom, but it makes for a rewarding detour all year round; its cool temperatures and delightfully pastoral scenery make it a good place for a short rest, especially if you're driving. Foxes, vizcachas and other small animals are often spotted here. Back on the main road, 1km further on, is the **Abra Piedra del Molino**, a narrow mountain pass at 3347m, marked by the mysterious "mill-stone" that gives the pass its name; nobody knows how this perfectly circular stone got here, but the idea that it is a discarded mill-stone is probably apocryphal.

Some 20km west of the Abra Piedra del Molino, where the road forks to the left – an uninteresting shortcut to Seclantás and RN-40 – RP-33 continues straight northwards, cutting through the **Parque Nacional Los Cardones**, an official reserve recently set up to protect the forest of *cardón* cacti that covers the dusty valley and creeps up the arid mountainside, mingled with the parasol-like *churquis* and other spiny trees typical of desert regions; there's no *guardería* and you can wander as you like among the gigantic cacti, many of them more than five metres tall. *Cardones* grow painfully slowly, less than a couple of millimetres a year, and their wood has been excessively exploited for making furniture and crafts and for firewood; it's now protected, so don't remove any specimens. Part of this road, known as the **Recta Tin-Tin**, 10km of straight-as-a-die roller-coaster track, is well known for its optical illusion – the lie of the valley makes it look as though you're climbing when in fact you're going down (heading in this direction that is). At the tiny village of **Payogasta**, where RP-33 joins RN-40, you have a choice of roads. You can either head north to explore the furthest reaches of the Valles Calchaquíes, with dramatic high mountains on either side and beguiling desert-like scenery accompanying you all along the rough track to La Poma, 40km north (see p.443); or, especially if time is short or night is drawing in, you can head straight south for **Cachi**.

The picturesque village of **CACHI**, 2280m above sea level, is overshadowed by the permanently snowcapped **Nevado del Cachi** (6380m), whose peak looms only 15km to the west. The village is centred around the delightful Plaza Mayor, shaded by palms and orange trees. On the north side of the plaza stands the much-restored **Iglesia San José**, with its plain white facade, fine wooden floor and unusual cactus-wood altar, pews and confessionals. On the east side, in a Neocolonial house around an attractive whitewashed patio, is the **Museo Arqueológico Pío Pablo Díaz** (Mon–Sat 8.30am–6.30pm, Sun 10am–1pm; $2), displaying a run-of-the-mill collection of locally excavated items. Apart from that, there's little in the way of sights in Cachi; it's simply a place to wander, investigating the various local crafts, including ponchos and ceramics, or climbing to the **cemetery** for wonderful mountain views and a panorama of the pea-green valley, every arable patch of which is filled with vines, maize and capsicum plantations. Further afield, the scenic tracks to **Cachi Adentro** and **La Aguada**, each 6km west of the village, lead from the end of Calle Benjamín Zorrilla and take you through fertile farmland where, in late summer (March–May), the fields are carpeted with drying paprika peppers, a dazzling display of bright red that features in many postcards on sale in the region.

Practicalities

Buses from Salta (and local buses from various villages) arrive very close to the main plaza, where there is a helpful **information office** in the municipalidad (Mon–Fri 8am–9pm, Sat & Sun 9am–3pm & 5–9pm; ⓣ03868/491053, ⓦwww.cachionline.com.ar); the staff should be able to find you guides to take you up into the surrounding mountains.

Hill-top *Hostería ACA Sol del Valle*, Av del Automóvil Club Argentino s/n (ⓣ03868/491105, ⓦwww.soldelvalle.com.ar; ❻), is a leading contender for the title of the village's most comfortable **accommodation**, especially since a much-needed refurbishment, and has a swimming pool with a view and a very passable restaurant. Nearby *Hostal El Cortijo* (ⓣ03868/491034, ⓦwww.elcortijo.com.ar; ❼), in a colonial house at the bottom of the hill, is more expensive but still incredibly good value, with its unusual "native" decor combined with sophisticated Neocolonial furnishings and very attentive service. Welcoming *Hotel Llaqta Mawka* (ⓣ03868/491016, ⓔhostal_llaqta_mawka@hotmail.com; ❺), at Ruíz de los Lanos s/n, has made a concerted effort to respect local building and decoration customs and techniques and offers interesting tours of the immediate region. *Hospedaje Nevado de Cachi*, also on Ruíz de los Llanos (ⓣ03868/491004; ❸), is a good budget place to stay, with basic rooms and curious cactus-wood furniture but erratic hot water. A reliable **place to eat**, other than at one of the hotels, is basic *El Jagüel*, on Avenida General Güemes (ⓣ03868/491135), which serves memorable *locro* and empanadas. *Luna Cautiva* in Pasaje Borja, at the corner of Suárez, and the

Confitería del Sol, on the main square at Ruíz de los Llanos s/n, are more upmarket, have more atmosphere and serve a range of classic Argentine dishes and local specialities such as goat. For real espresso coffee and all manner of snacks, charming little *Oliver*, on the main square just along from the *Confitería del Sol*, has no rivals.

From Cachi to Cafayate

The mostly unsealed RN-40 from Cachi to Cafayate takes you along some stupendous corniche roads that wind alongside the Río Calchaquí itself, offering views on either side of sheer mountainsides and snowcapped peaks. It's only 180km from one town to the other, but allow plenty of time as the narrow track slows your progress and you'll want to stop to admire the views, take photographs and visit the picturesque valley settlements en route, oases of greenery in an otherwise stark landscape. **Molinos**, 60km south of Cachi, lies a couple of kilometres west of the main road, in a bend of the Río Molinos, and is worth the side-trip for a peek at its lovely adobe houses and the eighteenth-century **Iglesia de San Pedro Nolasco**, currently undergoing restoration; the expansive facade, topped with two sturdy turrets, is shored up with props. Opposite, in Finca Isasmendi, the eighteenth-century residence of Nicolás Severo de Isasmendi, the last royalist governor of Salta, is the beautiful *Hostal Provincial de Molinos* (a quaint rural inn, currently closed for refurbishment). The justly famed *Estancia Colomé* (see box, p.438) lies some 20km away, towards the cordillera.

At **Angastaco**, 40km away in the direction of Cafayate and 2km down a side road heading south, you'll find modest but clean and attractive **accommodation** in the *Hostería de Angastaco*, on Libertad (Ⓣ03868/156-39016; ❸). Just beyond Angastaco, the already impressive scenery becomes even more spectacular: after 10km you enter the surreal **Quebrada de las Flechas**, where the red sandstone cliffs form a backdrop for the flinty arrowhead-like formations on either side of the road that give the gorge its name. For 10km, weird rocks like desert roses dot the landscape and, beyond the natural stone walls of **El Cañón**, over 20m high, the road squeezes through **El Ventisquero**, the "wind-tunnel".

The oldest settlement in the valley, dating from 1551, is picturesque **San Carlos**, 35km further, straddling RN-40; it's a wine-growing village and the several bodegas welcome visitors at all times, but do not provide proper guided visits. The nineteenth-century **Iglesia San Carlos Borromeo** has interior walls decorated with naive **frescoes** depicting the life of St Charles Borromeo himself. The last stretch of the road to Cafayate threads its way through extensive **vineyards**, affording views of the staggeringly high mountains – many of them over 4000m – to the west and east.

Cafayate

The sprawling village of **CAFAYATE** is nearly 190km south of Salta, via RN-68 at its junction with RN-40; the latter is called Avenida Güemes within the village limits, the Río Chuschas in the north and the Río Loro Huasi in the south. The self-appointed capital of the Valles Calchaquíes and the main settlement hereabouts, it's also the centre of the province's wine industry and the main tourist base for the valleys, thanks to its plentiful (and now often high-quality) accommodation, and convenient location at a crossroads between Salta, Cachi and Amaicha (see p.482). Though not that big, it's nonetheless a lively, modern place, originally founded by Franciscan missionaries who set up

The Cafayate vineyards

While Mendoza and, increasingly, San Juan are the names most associated with wines from Argentina, supermarkets and wine shops around the world are selling more and more bottles with the name **Cafayate** on their labels. These **vineyards**, which are some of the highest in the world, at around 1700m, are planted with the malbec and cabernet varieties for which Mendoza is justly famous, but the local speciality is a grape thought to have been brought across from Galicia: the torrontés. The delicate, flowery white wine it produces, with a slight acidity, is the perfect accompaniment for the regional cuisine, but also goes well with fish and seafood. You can try some excellent samples and see how the wine is made at one of the many bodegas in and around Cafayate, where tastings and wine sales round off each tour (Spanish only). Bodegas Domingo Hermanos, Etchart, La Banda, Don David and Finca Las Nubes open their doors every weekday and sometimes at weekends too (daily usually 9am–1pm & 3–7pm).

encomiendas, or Indian reservations with farms attached, in the region. However, apart from exploring the surroundings on foot, by bike or on horseback, or tasting wine at the bodegas (see box above), there's not actually a lot to do here. The late nineteenth-century **Iglesia Catedral de Nuestra Señora del Rosario** dominates the main plaza but is disappointingly nondescript inside, while the **Museo de Arqueología Calchaquí**, one block southwest, at Calchaquí and Colón (Mon–Fri 11am–9pm; $1), comprises one room piled with **ceramics** of the Candelaria and Santamaría cultures, including some massive urns, followed by another room cluttered with *criollo* antiques and curios. Two blocks south of the plaza, at avenidas Güemes and Chacabuco, is the feeble **Museo de la Vid y del Vino** (Mon–Fri 8am–8pm, Sat & Sun 8am–1pm & 2–8pm; $1), a motley collection of wine-related relics and photographs, in a defunct winery. About 2km south, on RN-40 to Santa María, you'll find the workshop and salesroom of one of the region's finest artisans, Oscar Hipaucha.

△ Vineyard, Cafayate

He sells wonderfully intricate wood and metal boxes, made of *quebracho*, *algarrobo* and copper, at justifiably high prices. Way up to the north of the town, the Cristofani ceramic workshop makes elegant urns but most tend to be too big to make practical souvenirs.

Arrival and information

Frequent **buses** from Salta and less frequent ones from Cachi, via Molinos, plus daily services from Tucumán via Amaicha (see p.482) arrive at the cramped terminus just along Belgrano, half a block east of the plaza, or sometimes deposit passengers wherever they want to get off in the village. A kiosk (daily 8am–9pm) on the plaza dispenses **information** about where to stay, what to do and where to rent bikes or hire horses.

Accommodation

You'll have little trouble finding a room except during the popular, but not very exciting, **folk festival**, the Serenata Cafayateña, held on the first weekend of Lent. The range extends from the humblest *residencial* to a couple of truly memorable establishments. Be warned that there have been reports of theft and other unpleasant experiences at a number of places in the village – to our knowledge there have been none concerning our recommendations.

Casa de la Bodega RN-68 Km18.5 03868/421555, www.casadelabodega.com.ar. Off the road to San Carlos that branches off the Quebrada road (RN-68), but only 15min from Cafayate, this sumptuous wine boutique hotel has only eight rooms, some of which are giant suites; the decor, comfort, service and, of course, the wine are all top-notch. 8–9

El Hospedaje Camila Quintana de Niño and Salta 03868/421680, elhospedaje@nortevirtual.com. Great little *hospedaje* that boasts a swimming pool in its grounds – a charming Neocolonial house, with comfortable rooms. If you are looking for somewhere even less costly, ask about their *Colonial* annexe where a dorm bed costs $12. 3

Hospedaje El Portal de las Viñas Nuestra Señora del Rosario 165 03868/421098. Traditional *hospedaje* just off the main square – large rooms sleeping up to four, with en-suite bathrooms. 3

Hostal del Valle San Martín 243 03868/421039, hostaldelvalle@nortevirtual.com. Wonderful family-run B&B in an impeccably clean house. Rooms are comfortable but the highlight is a top-floor conservatory set aside for reading, listening to music and admiring the all-round views. Home-made jams served at breakfast. 3

Hostel Ruta 40 Av Güemes 178 03868/421689, hostel_ruta40@hotmail.com. Look for the handsome yellow front just a block south of the main plaza. This is the best hostel in Cafayate, without a doubt – dorm beds go for just $15 and there are some decent doubles (2) too.

Hotel Asturias Av Güemes 154 03868/421328, asturias@infonoa.com.ar. This centrally located hotel with a northern Spanish facade has a swimming pool, a reliable restaurant and tasteful rooms decorated with beautiful photographs of the region. 6

Hotel Killa Colón 47 03868/422254, www.killacafayate.com.ar. Only a block from the central plaza, this splendid hotel is charming, comfortable and incredibly classy – it successfully combines Neocolonial elegance with rustic cosiness; some of the upstairs rooms have dream-like views of the surrounding mountains. 6–7

Hotel Los Patios de Cafayate RN-40 and RN-68 03868/421747, www.starwoodhotels.com/luxury/property/overview/index.html?propertyID=1702. Handwoven carpets, chandeliers, colonial tapestries, native textiles and local arts and crafts all give this beautiful Sheraton-group hotel a feeling of luxury. This is enhanced by the beautiful swimming pool and the fabulous spa, housed in a modern annexe and offering wine and grape massages. The rooms will make you feel like a local aristocrat for a day. 8

Hotel Portal del Santo Silverio Chavarría 250 03868/422500, www.portaldelsanto.com.ar. New hotel built in a Neocolonial style – note the arched galleries. The handsome rooms are well equipped, with mini-bars and cable TV, while breakfasts are delicious and generous, using home-made products. There's a swimming pool with Jacuzzi. 6

Hotel Los Sauces Calchaquí 62 03868/421158, lossauces@arnet.com.ar. A pleasant, modern hotel, only a couple of blocks from the central plaza, with attractively decorated rooms looking onto a garden – avoid those facing the noisy street – and a bright *confitería* where a copious breakfast is served. ⑤

Hotel Villa Vicuña Belgrano 76 ⓣ03868/422145, ⓦwww.villavicuna.com.ar. Picturesque, slightly quirky hotel in a mustard-yellow Neocolonial house right next to the bus terminal. The rooms are delightful, as is the central patio where you can have breakfast or tea, weather permitting. ⑦–⑧

Eating and drinking

The choice of **eating** establishments is more limited than for lodging. Reliable – and popular, so grab tables while you can – *El Rancho*, at Güemes and Toscano, on the southern flank of the main plaza, specializes in regional cooking, as does the much frequented and well-priced *Carreta de Don Olegario* on the east side. *Baco* at Avenida Güemes (N), at the corner of Rivadavia, is a pleasant bistro-style joint serving good traditional food. The ice creams at *Heladería Miranda*, on Avenida Güemes half a block north of the plaza, are outstanding: try the wine sorbets, both the cabernet and torrontés.

Quebrada de Cafayate

The RN-68 forks off RN-40 only 2km north of Cafayate, north of the Río Chuschas, before heading across fertile land, some of it given over to vineyards. It soon begins its winding descent, following the Río de las Conchas through the **QUEBRADA DE CAFAYATE** north to the Valle de Lerma and onwards to Salta. The gorge is seen at its best on the way down, in the mellow late afternoon or early evening light; organized tours aim to take you down this way and you should follow suit if travelling under your own steam. Leave plenty of time, as once in the gorge you'll be tempted to make several stops, to admire the views and take pictures. At the northernmost part of the gorge you enter an invariably windy stretch, where you're better off inside your vehicle unless you want to be sandblasted. One positive result of frequent sandstorms, though, is the formation of wonderful sand dunes, **Los Médanos**, like gigantic piles of sawdust by the road. This is where the canyon proper begins, and the road snakes its way down alongside the river-bed. The majestic Sierras de Carahuasi – the northernmost range of the Cumbres Calchaquíes – loom behind as a magnificent backdrop, while in the foreground rock formations have been eroded and blasted by wind and rain to form buttresses, known as **Los Castillos**, or "the castles", and a huge monolith dubbed **El Obelisco**. The reds, ochres and pinks of the sandstone make it all look staggeringly beautiful. Further on, **La Yesera**, or "chalk quarry", is actually a strange group of eerily grey and yellow rocks exposed by millions of years of erosion, while a monk-like figure, skulking in the cliff-side, has earned the name **El Fraile**. Just off the road, about 50km from Cafayate, two semicircular ravines carved in the mountainside are called **La Garganta del Diablo** (Devil's Throat) and **El Anfiteatro**, while the animal-like figure nearby is **El Sapo** (Toad). Still passing through delightful scenery, you leave the stupendous canyon, spiked with cacti, behind you to enter the forested valley bottom. Halfway between Cafayate and Salta, a convenient stop-off is provided by the excellent *Posta de Las Cabras*, where in addition to the goat's cheese implicit in its name, you can sample all kinds of local delicacies, buy fine crafts, or just have a cup of coffee. From La Viña, 100km northeast of Cafayate and just south of Embalse Cabra Corral, the enormous reservoir serving Salta, it's another 90km or so to the city, along relatively busy RN-68.

San Salvador de Jujuy

Just over 90km north of Salta by the direct and scenic but rather slow RN-9, **SAN SALVADOR DE JUJUY** – Jujuy for short – is a tranquil place and, at 1260m above sea level, enjoys an enviably temperate climate. It is the capital of the federation's most remote mainland province, a small but intensely beautiful patch of land, ostensibly having more in common with next-door Chile and Bolivia than with the rest of Argentina, and little with Buenos Aires, nearly 1600km away. Dramatically situated, Jujuy lies in a fertile natural bowl, with the spectacular multicoloured gorge of the **Quebrada de Humahuaca** (see p.455), a major reason for heading in this direction, immediately north. The Cerro de Claros (1704m) and Cerro Chuquina (1987m) loom just to the southeast and southwest, and the city is wedged between two rivers, the Río Grande and Río Chico or Xibi Xibi, both bone-dry for most of the year. In *The Old Patagonian Express* (1978), Paul Theroux wrote that Jujuy "looked peaceful and damp; just high enough to be pleasant without giving one a case of the bends; it was green, a town buried, so it seemed, in lush depthless spinach". The river beds, overgrown with lush vegetation though certainly not spinach, only add to the rather abandoned appearance, while the city's outskirts spill along the riversides, sometimes in the form of shantytowns. Despite, or perhaps because of, its location, Jujuy lacks the buzz of Salta and Tucumán, and good hotels are few and far between. Scratch the lacklustre surface, though, and you'll unearth some real treasures, among them one of the finest pieces of sacred art to be seen in Argentina, the **pulpit** in the **cathedral** – and the interior of **Iglesia San Francisco** is almost as impressive. A day or two in this slightly strange "world's end" kind of place will probably suffice; you'll soon want to start exploring the rich hinterland, its polychrome gorges and typical altiplano villages of adobe houses. Jujuy is also the ideal springboard for visiting the most accessible of the three cloudforest national parks, **Calilegua** (see p.470), as well as the less accessible and utterly remote **Baritú** (see p.472).

Some history

Jujuy was founded, after a couple of early false starts thwarted by attacks by indigenous peoples, on April 19, 1593. Earthquakes, the plague and further sackings, culminating in the Calchaquí Wars (see box, p.498), all conspired to hamper the city's growth during the seventeenth and eighteenth centuries and have deprived it of any of its original buildings. Even after the famous **Jujuy Exodus** ordered by General Belgrano at the height of the Wars of Independence – on August 23, 1812, he ordered the whole of the city's population to evacuate the city, which was then razed to the ground to prevent its capture by the royalist commander – Jujuy continued to bear the brunt of conflict, sacked by the royalists in 1814 and 1818. It then remained a forgotten backwater throughout the nineteenth century, and the railway did not reach it until 1903. Since the 1930s, its outskirts have spilt across both rivers and begun to creep up the hillsides, and it now has a sizeable immigrant population, mostly from across the Bolivian border to the north. The province – and therefore the city, which lives off the province's agricultural production – have traditionally grown rich on sugar and tobacco, with a little copper and lead mining thrown in, but earnings from all these products have declined in recent years and forced farmers to diversify into other crops, including fruit and vegetables. Tourism may be the solution for the city's economic woes but so far has been exploited only half-heartedly, with very little state assistance.

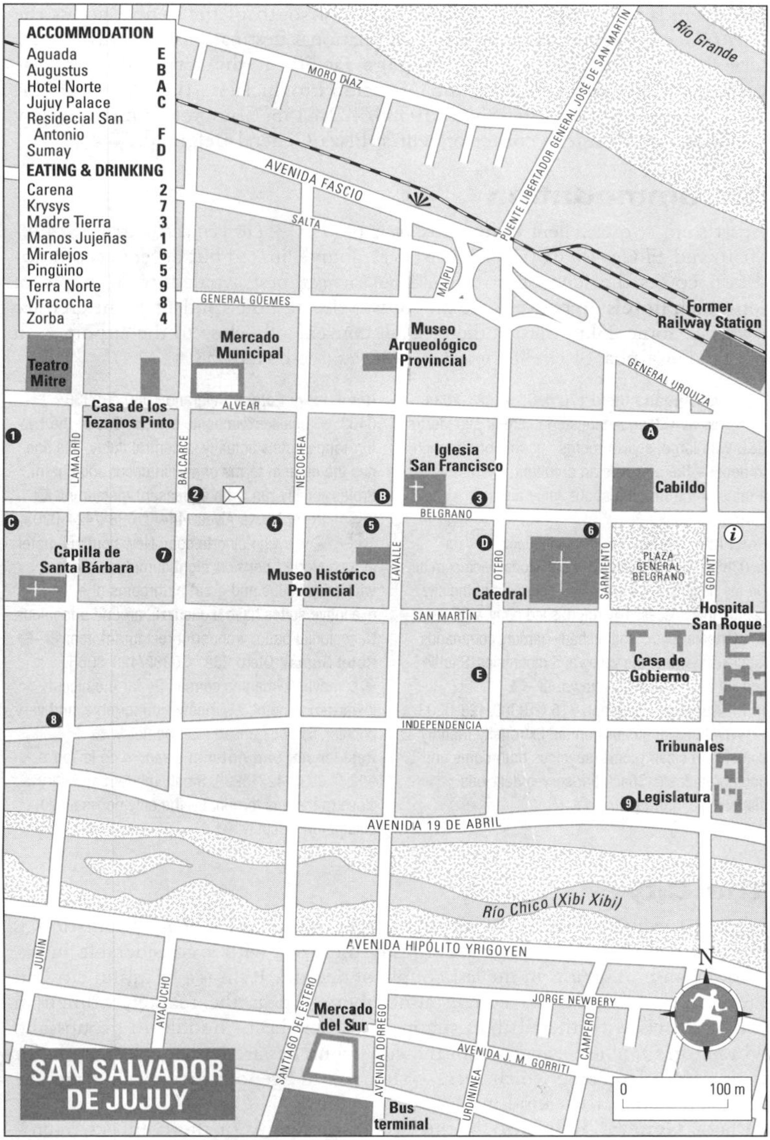

Arrival and information

Jujuy's **airport**, Dr Horacio Guzmán (ⓣ0388/491-1109), is over 30km southeast of the city, along RN-66 near Perico. TEA Turismo (ⓣ0388/423-6270 or 156-857913) runs a shuttle service to and from the city centre for $10, while the **taxi** fare is around $35. The rudimentary **bus terminal**, at Iguazú and Avenida Dorrego (T 0388/422-6299), just south of the centre, across the Río Chico, serves all local, regional and national destinations, and also runs a service to Chile. There's a **left-luggage** facility at the terminal. For basic **tourist information**, head for the Dirección Provincial de Turismo (Mon–Fri 7am–9pm, Sat & Sun 8am–8pm; T 0388/422-8153, W www.turismo.jujuy.gov.ar), at the northeastern corner of central Plaza General Belgrano.

Accommodation

Apart from two excellent **campsites** near the city – *Los Vertientes* (T 0388/498-0030) and *El Carmen* (T 0388/493-3117) – Jujuy's limited but decent accommodation covers the range from squalid *residenciales*, best avoided, to a couple of top-notch **hotels**. In between are one or two decent hotels and a few inexpensive *pensiones*. Some 25km outside the city, but conveniently close to the airport, is an outstanding **finca**, or ranch, *Finca Los Lapachos* (see box, p.438).

La Aguada Otero 170 T 0388/423-2034, W www.laaguadahosteria.com.ar. Wonderful B&B with large, stylish rooms and lots of attention to detail – the owner is an architect. The family is a mine of information about Jujuy and its surroundings. 5

Hotel Altos de la Viña Pasquini López, La Viña T 0388/426-1666, W www.hotelaltodelavina.com.ar. On the heights of La Viña, 4km northeast of the city centre, this successfully refurbished hotel, with large, comfortable rooms and a shady garden, commands fabulous views of the valley and mountains. Shuttle service to and from downtown. 6–7

Hotel Augustus Belgrano 715 T 0388/423-0203, W www.hotel-augustus.com.ar. Extremely friendly place, with clean rooms, spacious bathrooms and good breakfasts. Snack bar serves delicious sandwiches and *lomitos*. 5

Hotel Jujuy Palace Belgrano 1060 T 0388/423-0433, E jupalace@imagine.com.ar. One of the two top-range hotels actually in central Jujuy, this one has the edge in terms of stylish decor and charm. Professionally run, with a pleasant restaurant. 6

Hotel Norte Alvear 444 T 0388/424-0903, W www.hotelnorte.com. New boutique hotel in a converted *pension*: eight sumptuous rooms, with crisp linens and great bathrooms (the executive suites have a Jacuzzi), around a fabulous Neocolonial patio; wonderful restaurant, too. 6–7

Hotel Sumay Otero 232 T 0388/423-5065, E sumayha@imagine.com.ar. By far the nicest lower-range hotel, it's roomy, comfortable, and very popular, so book ahead. Can be noisy. 3

Residencial San Antonio Lisandro de la Torre 993 T 0388/422-5998. Small, modern and very close to the bus terminal – the only non-squalid place in the vicinity. 2

The City

Jujuy is the most Andean of all Argentina's cities: much of its population is descended from indigenous stock, mostly mestizos, with a considerable influx of Bolivian immigrants in the last couple of decades. It's not a beautiful city, but the central streets have a certain atmosphere – near the market, women in bright shawls with their babies strapped to their backs huddle in groups and whisper in Quichoa – and two of the city's churches are remarkable, mainly for their colonial pulpits, which were crafted by indigenous artisans and are the most splendid of their kind in the whole country.

Plaza General Belgrano, at the eastern extremity of the compact microcentro, was the colonial settlement's central square, Plaza Mayor, and is still the city's hub, partly occupied by craftsmen, mainly potters, displaying their wares. Planted with orange trees, it is dominated to the south by the French-style Neoclassical **Casa de Gobierno** (Mon–Fri 9am–noon & 4–8pm; free) with its slate mansard roof, where the national flag donated to the city by General Belgrano, as a tribute to the Exodus, is proudly guarded. In the grounds of the government house, dotted around the building, there stand five large **statues** by renowned sculptress **Lola Mora** (see box, p.843). Representing Peace, Progress,

Justice, Freedom and Labour, the set was originally designed for the Congreso Nacional in Buenos Aires, inaugurated in 1906, but the reactionary federal government vetoed the project and had the statues dumped in a store room. Luckily Jujuy's government at that time was less intransigent and in 1915 it appointed Lola Mora as the city's director of parks and squares, in order to erect the statues in their present position.

On the west side of the plaza stands Jujuy's late eighteenth-century **cathedral** (Mon–Fri 7.30am–1pm & 5–9pm, Sat & Sun 8am–noon & 5–9pm), topped by

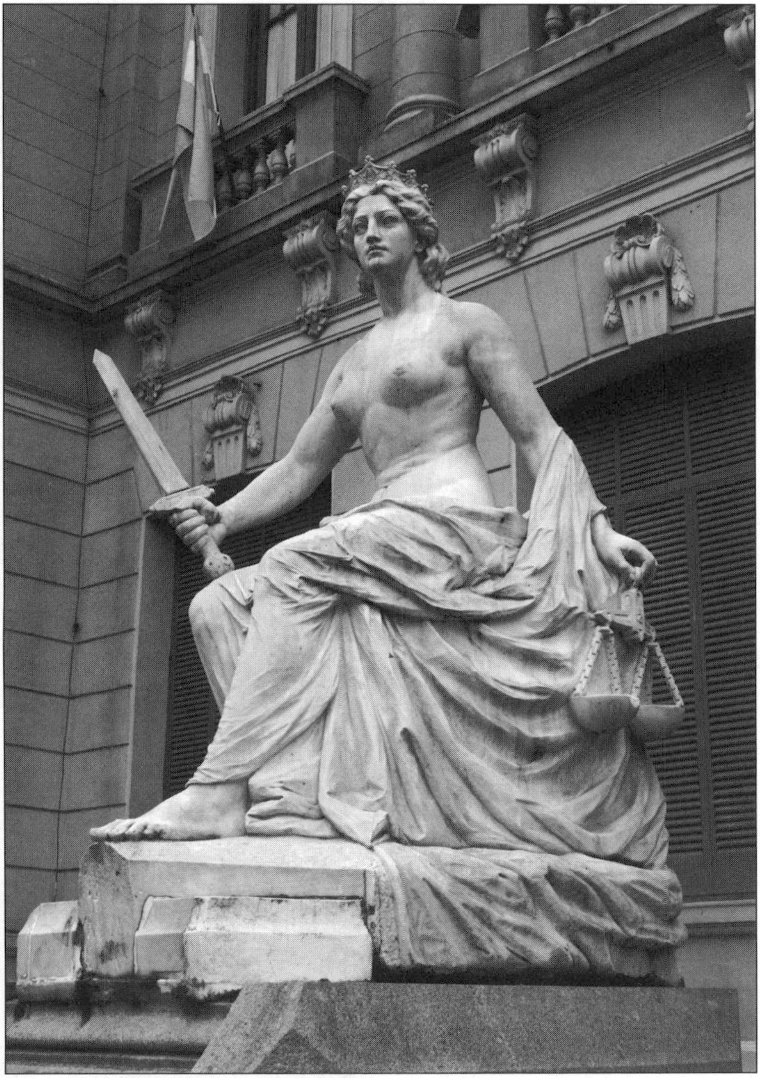

△ Lola Mora statue, Jujuy

an early twentieth-century tower and extended by an even later Neoclassical atrium. The exterior, painted a pale biscuit colour, is unremarkable, but the interior, a layer of painted Bakelite concealing the original timber structure, is impressively naive: a realistic mock-fresco of sky and clouds soars over the altar, while above the nave is a primitive depiction of the ceremony in which Belgrano awarded the Argentine flag to the people of Jujuy. Two original doors and two confessionals, Baroque masterpieces from the eighteenth century, immediately catch the eye, thanks to their vivid red and sienna paint, picked out with gilt, but the undisputed highlight – and the main attraction of the whole city – is the magnificent **pulpit**. Decorated in the eighteenth century by local artists, it easily rivals those of **Cusco** (see p.132), its apparent inspiration, with its harmonious compositions, elegant floral and vegetable motifs and the finesse of its carvings. Its various tableaux in gilded, carved wood, gleaming with an age-old patina, depict subjects such as Jacob's ladder and St Augustine along with biblical genealogies from Adam to Abraham and David to Solomon. One of the curiosity is the error in the symbols of the four **apostles**: Matthew and John are correctly represented by a human figure and an eagle respectively, but Mark, symbolized by a bull, and Luke, by a lion, are the wrong way round.

Not of quite the same calibre as the cathedral's, but very striking nonetheless, is the Spanish Baroque **pulpit** in **Iglesia San Francisco**, two blocks west of the plaza at Belgrano and Lavalle; also inspired by the pulpits of Cusco and almost certainly carved by craftsmen in eighteenth-century Bolivia, it drips with detail, with a profusion of little Franciscan monks peeking out from row upon row of tiny columns, all delicately gilded. Although the church and separate campanile are built to the traditional colonial Franciscan design, in a Neo-Baroque style, the church was built as recently as the 1930s.

Museums are not Jujuy's forte but the two that are worth a passing visit are conveniently located nearby. One block north of the church, at Lavalle 434, is the **Museo Arqueológico Provincial** (daily 9am–noon & 3–8pm; $1), with its diorama representing life in the region around 7000 BC and a small collection of locally unearthed mummies. One block south, in the Casa de Lavalle, Lavalle 256, is the **Museo Histórico Provincial** (Mon–Fri 7am–1pm & 4–8pm, Sat 8am–noon; $1), housing an eclectic collection representing the city's more recent history, noteworthy for two seventeenth-century Cusco oil paintings and a pre-Inca silver crown discovered at the *pukará*, or pre-Inca fortress, at Abra Pampa (see p.467), and famous for the perforated door through which the bullet that killed the hero of the War of Independence, General Lavalle, on October 9, 1841, supposedly passed.

Three blocks west of the Casa de Lavalle at San Martín and La Madrid is the stark, whitewashed **Capilla de Santa Bárbara**, built in the late eighteenth century. Its style – despite much restoration – is similar to that of the typical Quebrada chapels that you find throughout the rest of the province: a plain thick-walled nave and a single squat tower. This chapel's extra tower was added in the nineteenth century. Inside is an outstanding set of religious paintings from **Cusco**, including a *St Barbara*, a *St Stanislas* and the *Lives of the Virgin and Jesus*. It's not always open, so attending Mass (Sun 8am & 10am) is the surest way of gaining access.

Eating, drinking and nightlife

Jujuy is no gastronomic paradise but its **restaurants** will give you more than enough variety between local specialities and *parrilladas*. Apart from a couple of snazzy **bars**, sometimes hosting musicians, the nightlife is confined to a couple of out-of-town **discos** and the beautiful Italian-style theatre and opera house, **Teatro Mitre**, at Alvear 1009 (☎0388/442-2782). Its gleaming white exterior and plush interior are the result of recent refurbishment; plays and classical concerts are regularly staged here, and are often of a high standard.

La Candelaria Alvear 1346. This very stylish *parrilla*, ten blocks or so out to the west of the city, offers you mountains of meat until you burst. Heavenly desserts, too.
Carena Balcarce and Belgrano. Mellow *confitería*, serving snacks and acting as a community centre – concerts, seminars and group meetings are held here.
Krysys Balcarce 272. Trout is the speciality on an otherwise not very inventive meat-dominated menu, but the service is impeccable.
Madre Tierra Belgrano 619. Delightful, airy vegetarian lunch-only spot with an unbeatably low-priced menu. Even if you're not a vegetarian, though, you'll find the fresh salads, meatless empanadas and delicious fruit juices a great change from the meat overdose, and you can stock up on all manner of goodies for a picnic. Closed Sun.
Manos Jujeñas Senador Pérez 379. Absolutely fabulous Northwestern food, including memorable *locro* and delicious empanadas, accompanied by jugs of honest wine and, from time to time, by live folk music. Incredibly friendly service, too. Closed Sun lunch & Mon eve.
Miralejos Sarmiento 268. Classic Northwestern gastronomy at its best in this popular place, with a few tables out on the plaza.
Pingüino Belgrano 718. This is Jujuy's finest *heladería*, scooping out delicious ice cream by the bucketful; every flavour imaginable.
Terra Norte 19 de Abril 475. Specializing in trout from nearby Yala – considered the best in the region – this smart restaurant also acts as a *confitería*; try the trout ravioli.
Viracocha Independencia and Lamadrid. Unusual dishes like llama in dark beer sauce, or smoked llama ravioli, plus delicious classic Andean fare – lots of quinoa and native potatoes – make this one of the top eateries in Jujuy.
Zorba Belgrano and Necochea. Greek food – feta salads, moussaka, *pastitsio* and stuffed vine leaves – along with Argentine favourites and delicious sandwiches in a bright, modern venue with a real buzz that would not look out of place in Kolonaki.

Listings

Airlines Aerolíneas Argentinas, at the airport ☎0388/422-1373, and at Belgrano 1053 ☎0388/422-2575; LAB, Güemes 779 ☎0388/423-0699.
Banks and exchanges Quilmes, Belgrano 902; for exchange and traveller's cheques: Masventas, Balcarce 223 (Mon–Fri 8am–1.30pm & 5–8pm). Several ATMs dotted around.
Consulate Bolivia (the most helpful in the Northwest), Av Senador Pérez and Independencia.
Internet access Telecentro, Güemes and La Madrid.
Laundry Laverap, Belgrano 1214.
Post office Belgrano, between Necochea and Balcarce.
Telephones Telecom, Belgrano and Lavalle.
Tour operators TEA, Belgrano 775 ☎0388/423-6270. Well-run tours into Quebrada de Humahuaca and Puna Jujeña, plus smaller circuits near the city.

Quebrada de Humahuaca

Although the intense beauty of the **Quebrada de Humahuaca** gorge features so often in tourist literature, posters and coffee-table books that some of the surprise element is taken away, a trip along it is nonetheless an unforgettable and moving experience. Stunning, varied scenery is on display all the way up from the valley bottom, just northwest of San Salvador de Jujuy, to the namesake town of **Humahuaca**, 125km north of the provincial capital. Here, in addition to some decent accommodation and a monument or two, you will also find an outstanding cultural centre that includes a surprisingly good cinema. While most day-trips along the gorge from Jujuy (and Salta) take you up and down by the same route, RN-9, you're actually treated to two spectacles: you'll have your attention fixed on the western side in the morning, and on the eastern flank in the afternoon, when the sun lights up each side respectively and picks out the amazing geological features: polychrome strata, buttes and mesas, pinnacles and eroded crags. What's more, the two sides are quite different, the western mountains rising steeply, often striped with vivid colours, while the slightly lower, rounded range to the east is for the most part gentler, more mellow, but just as colourful.

Most (day) tours organized out of Jujuy and Salta only go as far as Humahuaca and then head back, but this still gets you two tracking-shot views of multicoloured mountains, the highlight of which is the photogenic **Cerro de los Siete Colores**, overhanging the picturesque village of **Purmamarca**. From Purmamarca a dramatic side road leads across splendid altiplano landscapes, via pretty little **Susques**, to the Chilean border at the Paso de Jama, high in the Andes. Purmamarca has enough accommodation options to make it a possible stopover, especially if you are forging on towards Chile, but most of the lodgings are on the expensive side. Further up the gorge, just outside the village of **Maimará** and overlooked by oyster-shaped rock formations in the mountainside, is one of the region's most photographed cemeteries. Two-thirds of the way to Humahuaca, the small town of

A calendar of festivals in the Northwest

Owing to its attachment to tradition and its high proportion of ethnic communities, the Northwest has maintained or revived more **pre-Hispanic festivals** than any other Argentine region – nearly every village seems to have one. There are also many religious and secular celebrations observed here that are a blend of indigenous and imported customs, so subtly melded that the elements are indistinguishable. Carnival, Holy Week and saints' days predominate among the latter.

January & February

The **first fortnight of the year** sees pre-Carnival revelry all along the Quebrada de Humahuaca, where Carnival itself is a big holiday. **January 6** is the date of processions in Belén (see p.494) in honour of the Virgin Mary. In the **second half of January**, Tilcara (see p.460) holds its annual bean-feast, followed by Humahuaca's (see p.464) tribute to the Virgen de Candelaria on **February 2**. Pachamama, the Mother Earth deity dear to the indigenous peoples, is feted on **February 6** in Purmamarca (see p.458) and Amaicha (see p.482), where festivities last a whole week. Cheese fans should head for Tafí del Valle (see p.480), where the **Fiesta Nacional del Queso** takes place in early February.

Carnival is a boisterous time in Santiago del Estero (see p.484) and Salta (see p.422). The **Serenata Cafayateña** is a folk jamboree held on the weekend following Shrove Tuesday in Cafayate (see p.446). Londres (see p.495) hosts a lively walnut festival in early February, while Fiambalá's (see p.501) **Festival del Camino Hacia el Nuevo Sol** takes place on **February 18** and **19**. The third Wednesday of the month sees the **Fiesta Nacional del Aguardiente** in Valle Viejo, and the third Thursday the hangover.

March & April

In **March**, the **Feria Artesanal y Ganadera de la Puna** transforms normally quiet Antofagasta de la Sierra (see p.498). **March 19**, St Joseph's Day, is a red-letter day in Cachi (see p.445), while a major pilgrimage, with night vigils and processions, converges on the tiny village of Puerta de San José, near Belén, on **March 18** and **19**.

Sports and outdoor activities

Few countries are as scenically blessed as Argentina. Its vast expanse incorporates mighty peaks, humid jungles and windswept steppe, making it the perfect destination for outdoor enthusiasts. Trekking is an obvious joy, but there are also rivers to be rafted, lakes to be fished and slopes to be skied. Few countries, too, are as addicted to sport. The equestrian games of polo and pato are both interesting in their own right, but everything pales in comparison to football – a truly national obsession.

▲ Trekking in Santa Cruz Province

Trekking and climbing

Argentina's superb national parks form the backdrop to some of the continent's most diverse **trekking**; from the sandstone canyons of Talampaya in La Rioja to the granite peaks of the mighty Patagonian parks, there is something for everyone.

Most visitors head to the Andes, to tackle the trails crisscrossing the northern sector of **Parque Nacional Los Glaciares**, often combining it with a trip to Chile's **Parque Nacional Torres del Paine**. Argentines, however, tend to prefer the more developed infrastructure of **Parque Nacional Nahuel Huapi**, the country's first national park, centred around the town of Bariloche.

Within Huapi's borders are also **Cerro Catedral** and **Monte Tronador**, both fine **climbing** peaks, although there are even higher summits to crack: straddling the border with Chile, **Ojos del Salado**, the highest active volcano in the world, is challenging for even experienced mountaineers, while **Aconcagua** – at 6962m the highest peak in South America – can be conquered by anyone with reasonable fitness and a mule.

Top treks

- **Sendero La Junta** Parque Nacional Calilegua, Jujuy. This trek through jungle canopy is the longest trail in Calilegua, a cloudforest park that's home to abundant birdlife, as well as (supposedly) jaguars. See p.470.
- **Pampa Linda–Lago Frías** Parque Nacional Nahuel Huapi, Neuquén & Río Negro. One of a multitude of great hikes in Nahuel Huapi, this scenic two-day walk takes in the best of the Lake District's sublime scenery. See p.613.
- **Monte Fitz Roy–Cerro Torre Loop** Parque Nacional Los Glaciares, Santa Cruz. A combination of several trails that weave around the Fitz Roy massif, this three-day jaunt is done in the shadow of two of the world's most beautiful mountains. See p.708.
- **The "W"** Parque Nacional Torres del Paine, Chile. The most popular of the park's trails, the "W", named after the route it traces on a map, gives hikers panoramas of some of Patagonia's most recognizable peaks. See p.740.

River deep, mountain high

▲ Fly-fishing in Neuquén Province

Fringed by some 4725km of coastline and home to South America's second-longest river (the Río Paraná) and second-largest lake (Lago Buenos Aires), it should come as no surprise that Argentina has some of the continent's best fishing. **Sport-fishing** is popular in the north, but it's **fly-fishing** where Argentina truly excels: anglers flock to southern Patagonia, where the waters of the Río Grande, in Tierra del Fuego, are home to some of the world's largest sea-running brown trout.

With the mighty Andes running down the country's western flank, there are also plenty of opportunities to hit the **ski** slopes, whether it's schussing down black runs at Las Leñas or Cerro Catedral or cross-country skiing in the Sierra de Alvear. The latest kid on the (ice) block is Cerro Castor in Ushuaia, where the novelty of skiing at the end of the world is enhanced by the piste's spectacular views of the Beagle Channel.

Polo and pato

▼ Pato

Despite their physical similarities, Argentina's two horseback sports couldn't be more different. **Polo** has been thrilling the capital's elite since the 1880s, when the Buenos Aires Hurlingham Club was established. Argentine polo is considered among the best in the world: Argentina won gold at the 1936 Olympics, the last time it was an Olympic sport, and has won more World Championships than any other nation.

Less glamorous but more intriguing is **pato**, played by gauchos since the early 1600s and declared the country's national sport in 1953 by Juan Perón. Named after the trussed duck that once served as the "ball" – a leather version with six handles is now used – pato is won and lost over the *cinchada*, the moment when opposing players stand up in their stirrups and fight for possession of the ball, attempting to hurl it through a basket at either end of the pitch.

▲ Football match at La Bombonera

Futból: the people's game

Ever since two teams of British merchants lined up against each other at the Buenos Aires Cricket Club for a kick-about in 1867, **futból** (football, or soccer) has been an integral part of Argentine identity. Wander through the streets of La Boca – home of Boca Juniors, the capital's traditionally working-class side and the most popular team in Argentina – and you'll see young boys playing with a battered leather ball while *mate*-sipping old men discuss upcoming matches.

There are twenty teams in the **Primera División**, the country's top flight, including the "Big Five": River Plate, Boca Juniors, Independiente, San Lorenzo and Racing Club. Watching any of them in action is a thrill (see p.50 for details of attending a game), but if you can catch the **superclásico**, the Buenos Aires derby between Boca and River Plate, then you're in for a real treat. To be crammed inside La Bombonera, Boca's compact stadium, with 55,000 fans all twirling their blue-and-yellow scarves, is an unforgettable experience.

El Diego

Few people have captured the imagination of the Argentine public as much as **Diego Armando Maradona**. The diminutive no. 10 was the finest footballer of his generation, and arguably of all time – a bull of a player with exceptional close control, balance and on-field vision.

Born in a poor neighbourhood on the outskirts of Buenos Aires, Maradona's playing career (1976–97) was peerless. He made his first-team debut for **Argentinos Juniors** in the *Primera División* in 1976, when he was just 15 years old. He wore the colours of seven clubs in total, including **Boca Juniors**, **Barcelona** and **Napoli**, and led Argentina to World Cup glory in 1986.

Like many geniuses, though, Maradona was flawed – in his case, by the excesses of alcohol and, particularly, drugs. He was suspended in 1991 for testing positive for cocaine, and then again for the banned substance ephedrine during the 1994 World Cup. He never played for his country after that, and continues to battle alcohol and cocaine addiction. But while each rising superstar of Argentine football is hailed as the "next Maradona", there will only ever be one El Diego.

Tilcara is worth lingering in, if only for its beautiful pre-Inca fortress, or *pukará*; Tilcara boasts the best range of lodgings and eateries in the whole area, plus an interesting archeological museum. Between Tilcara and Humahuaca, in the little village of **Uquía** is one of the finest churches along the gorge; in these parts the typical chapel design is utterly simple, a plain whitewashed facade, sometimes embellished with an arch, and a single squat tower, usually acting as a campanile; many retain their straw roofs.

Beyond Humahuaca, RN-9 crosses bleak but stunningly beautiful altiplano landscapes all the way up to La Quiaca on the Bolivian border, nearly 2000m higher yet only 150km further on. A side road off RN-9 climbs to the incredibly isolated and highly picturesque hamlet of **Iruya**, if you really want to get off the beaten track. The whole of RN-9 and some of the side roads are accessible by regular **buses** from Jujuy, many of them also serving Salta.

The gateway to the Quebrada: Yala and the Termas de Reyes

Just a few kilometres northwest of Jujuy is the dormitory town of **YALA**, Jujuy's answer to Salta's San Lorenzo, with its cool climate and dense forest. There are no attractions as such here, but there are two excellent accommodation choices

Holy Week is a serious affair throughout the region but the highlights are Maundy Thursday at Yavi (see p.469), the pilgrimage to El Señor de la Peña at Aimogasta, in northern La Rioja Province, and the procession of the Virgen de Punta Corral, from Punta Corral to Tumbaya (see p.458). A week after Easter sees a minor performance of the momentous rituals in honour of the Virgen del Valle, in Catamarca (see p.487).

May–August

May kicks off with Santa Cruz celebrations at Uquía (see p.463), on **May 4**, while **May 25** is celebrated in El Rodeo, in Catamarca Province, by a *destreza criolla* – or rodeo – and St John's Day, **June 24**, is a major feast throughout the region.

Late July is when Catamarca (see p.487) stages one of the country's biggest folk and crafts festivals, the **Festival Nacional del Poncho**. St James' Day, **July 25**, is a major holiday in Santiago del Estero but also in Humahuaca. Argentina's only **bullfight**, an unusually bloodless tradition, is the main event at Assumption celebrations held at Casabindo (see p.467) on **August 15**. Santa Rosa de Lima is honoured at Purmamarca (see p.458) on **August 30**.

September–December

Salta's (see p.422) big feast thanks God for the Virgin of the Miracle during the nine days leading up to **September 15** while Iruya (see p.465) holds a highly photogenic feast for **Our Lady of the Rosary** on the first Sunday in October. In early October, it's Cafayate's (see p.446) turn to honour the Virgin. Two Sundays later (usually around October 20), La Quiaca (see p.467) holds its Fiesta de la Ollas, or "Manca Fiesta".

All Souls' Day and the Day of the Dead, **November 1** and **2**, are important feasts all along the Quebrada de Humahuaca and especially in Antofagasta de la Sierra (see p.498). The city of Catamarca (see p.487) attracts thousands of pilgrims for processions involving the Virgen del Valle, on **December 8**. Angastaco (see p.446) hosts a gaucho festival in honour of the Virgin around the same time. Nativity plays and other Yuletide activities are popular throughout the Northwest but **Christmas** itself isn't associated with any special customs.

that make nice alternatives to staying in Jujuy. In the village itself, set among huge landscaped grounds at Pedro Ortiz de Zárate s/n, is welcoming *La Casona del Camino Real* (T 0388/490-9263, W www.lacasoncr.com.ar; 6), a marvellous hotel with spacious, attractive rooms, a swimming pool and an excellent restaurant where you can sample local trout. Up RP-4 at Km19, the *Hotel Termas de Reyes* (T 0388/492-2522, W www.termasdereyes.com; 7) is a spa hotel, with a beautiful outdoor thermal pool, indoor water-therapy facilities, saunas and massages, in a style reminiscent of the great central European bathing resorts, including a rather stiff atmosphere and luxurious appointment.

Tumbaya and the lower Quebrada

As you climb the first stretch of the Quebrada, you soon leave the subtropical forest around Yala behind and enter an arid, narrow valley, gouged out by the Río Grande. The tiny village of Volcán, 40km from Jujuy, scarred by huge lime quarries, stands at 2000m; its name refers not to volcanic eruptions but to the frequent rock slides that sometimes block the whole length of the road after storms, referred to as *volcanes*, as they can be violent. Only 7km further, you come to **TUMBAYA**, a tiny village with a handsome colonial church, the first of many along the Quebrada; the **Iglesia de Nuestra Señora de los Dolores y Nuestra Señora de la Candelaria** houses some fine colonial art, including a painting of *Nuestra Señora La Aparecida*, another of *El Cristo de los Temblores*, and a *Jesús en el Huerto*. Originally built at the end of the eighteenth century, it was partially rebuilt after two earthquakes in the nineteenth century and restored in the 1940s; its design is typical of the Quebrada, a solid structure clearly influenced by the Mudéjar churches of Andalucia. The domed campanile is particularly elegant.

Purmamarca

About 13km north of Tumbaya RN-52, the region's main trans-Andean route, forks off to the left, heading northwest towards Susques and the Chilean border. Lying just off RN-52, 4km to the west, the tiny, picturesque village of **PURMAMARCA**, at the base of the gorge of the same name, has had its peace and quiet disrupted of late, owing to an increase in traffic resulting from stronger trading links with Chile. The main square is still a haven of tranquillity, though, flanked to the south by a pretty seventeenth-century church, the **Iglesia Santa Rosa de Lima**, built to the typically plain, single-towered design of the Quebrada, and a huge *algarrobo* tree that is claimed to be a thousand years old. At the northeast corner of the plaza, the four graceful arches of the **Cabildo** (daily 10am–noon & 5–7pm; free) embellish its otherwise simple white facade. The real attraction, though, is the famous **Cerro de los Siete Colores**, a dramatic bluff of rock overlooking the village. The mountain's candy stripes range from pastel beiges and pinks to orangey ochres and dark purples, though you may not be able to make out all seven of the reputed shades. A signposted route marked "Los Colorados", following an irrigation canal, takes you round the back of the village for the best views of the polychrome mountainside. There is a helpful little **tourist information office** (daily 8am–8pm) on the main plaza. Frequent **buses** to Tilcara, Humahuaca and Jujuy leave from a block east of the main square.

Accommodation

Purmamarca now has some excellent **accommodation** options, mostly at the upper end of the budget range.

Casa de Adobe RN-52 Km4 ⓣ0388/490-8003, ⓦwww.casadeadobe.com.ar. A small set of hyper-luxurious *cabañas*, affording magnificent mountain views and with a terrific display of good taste and technological progress. Gorgeous materials and textiles, plus plasma-screen TVs with international satellite channels. ❼

Hospedaje El Viejo Algarrobo Salta s/n ⓣ0388/490-8286, ⓔelviejoalgarrobo@hotmail.com. A cosy *hospedaje* under its namesake *algarrobo* tree behind the church, with small but very adequate rooms. ❸

Hostal La Posta de Purmamarca Pantaleón Cruz s/n ⓣ0388/490-8029, ⓦwww.postadepurmamarca.com.ar. Sturdy wooden beds in a white room – not exactly luxury but good value and in a great central location. ❺

Hostería del Amauta Salta s/n ⓣ0388/490-8043, ⓦwww.hosteriadelamauta.com.ar. Oozing with charm, this well-designed *hostería* has a selection of rooms impeccably decorated with soft linens, local timber and wrought-iron detailing. Breakfasts are delicious, healthy and copious. ❻–❼

Hotel La Comarca RN-52 Km3.8 ⓣ0388/490-8001, ⓦwww.lacomarcahotel.com.ar. In a stunning setting with unbeatable views of the coloured mountains, this stylish adobe-and-stone complex has twelve huge rooms, four *cabañas* sleeping four, two houses (for four to six persons) and a presidential suite, plus a beautiful heated pool, a mini-spa and a gourmet restaurant with a cellar worth visiting alone. ❼

Hotel Manantial del Silencio RN-52 Km3.5 ⓣ0388/490-8080, ⓦwww.hotelmanantial.com.ar. This delightful, convent-like Neocolonial building in a large parkland a short distance out of the village houses small but comfortable rooms. The restaurant varies in quality, the swimming pool is unheated and the service leaves a lot to be desired, but as the pioneer boutique hotel in the area it has its merits. ❼

Residencial Bebo Vilte Salta s/n and Rivadavia ⓣ0388/490-8038. A classic B&B that still offers some of the best inexpensive rooms in the village. ❹

Residencial Zulma Salta s/n ⓣ0388/490-8023. This cosy, basic little *residencial* is the nicest of the lowest-budget options. ❸

Eating and drinking

You can find various places to eat or have a drink or a coffee around or near the central plaza. Next to the Cabildo, *La Posta* serves simple meals, snacks and drinks, and sells local crafts, in a rich red-ochre walled building. A short way from the church is the area's best **restaurant** by far, *Los Morteros*, at Salta s/n (closed Mon); the gourmet food, using the region's excellent natural produce, including goat's cheese empanadas and chicken fricassee with broad beans and quinoa, is served in a classy decor, adorned with traditional textiles and other crafts. You could also try *Sabor a Tierra* at Lavalle and Sarmiento, which serves snacks, pasta and regional dishes.

Susques and the road to the Paso de Jama border crossing

Leading west from Purmamarca, RN-52 follows the Río Purmamarca, quickly climbing up the remarkable zigzags of the **Cuesta de Lipán**, one of the most dramatic roads in the region. This is the road towards the Chilean border at Paso de Jama, but is worth exploring if you have the time, as it crosses some of the country's most startling landscapes – barren steppe alternating with crinkly mountains, often snow-peaked even in the summer. Some 30km west of Purmamarca, just after the Abra de Potrerillos pass, you reach the road's highest point, at nearly 4200m, and enter majestic altiplanic landscapes: ahead you have open views to gleaming salt-flats and to the north, beyond the valley of the Río Colorado, the shallow, mirror-like **Laguna de Guayatayoc** glistens in the sun. Beyond the junction with RN-40, which runs north–south from San Antonio de los Cobres (see p.441) to Abra Pampa (see p.467), the pastures on either side of the road are home to considerable communities of vicuña. Where the road snakes between the **Cerro Negro** and the valley of the Río de las Burras, through the **Quebrada del Mal Paso**, it crosses the Tropic of Capricorn several times, before reaching **SUSQUES**, some 180km from Purmamarca. A minute but wonderfully picturesque village, formerly belonging to Chile, it's now where the Argentine customs point is located; expect lengthy clearance procedures, especially if coming from Chile. While waiting, take a look at the sumptuous church, with its delicate thatched roof and rough adobe walls, like those of all the houses in the village, and the naive frescoes on the inside.

Accommodation in Susques really boils down to three options: the very basic but clean *Hostería Las Vicuñitas* (Ⓣ03887/490207; ❷), serving simple food and located close to the village centre; *Hostería El Unquillar* (Ⓣ03887/490210 or 0388/425-5252, Ⓦwww.elunquillar.com.ar; ❹), a gorgeous adobe house, blending into the environment, with a cosy sitting room, comfortable rooms and excellent cuisine, a couple of kilometres out on RN-52 towards Chile; or slightly further out of the village towards the Paso de Jama, well-run *Hostal Pastos Chicos* (Ⓣ0388/423-5387, Ⓦwww.pastoschicos.com.ar; ❹). Conveniently next to the strategic fuel station, its rooms are perfectly adequate and the restaurant is cosy.

From Susques, it's another 100km to the border crossing at the **Paso de Jama**, where only a road sign tells you that you're leaving Argentine territory. This last stretch is trying and, given the altitude at well over 3500m, may give you *puna* symptoms (see p.66), as you first climb the **Cordón de Taire** – offering sweeping vistas back into the valley, from its peak at 4070m, and forward into the white expanses of the Salares de Olaroz and Cauchari – before descending into the plains, still at 3800m, following RP-70 southwards for 40km, and then negotiating the final ascent to the pass itself. The landscapes are fabulous, though: harsh desert-like plains relieved by unearthly volcanic cones and snowy Andean peaks at well over 5000m. On the other side of the border, a good sealed road swings down to the **customs post** at San Pedro de Atacama, 170km away.

Pullman (Ⓣ0388/422-1366) runs **buses** from Salta, via Jujuy, Purmamarca and Susques, to San Pedro de Atacama and on to Antofagasta, Iquique and Arica, in Chile, twice a week, leaving Salta at 7am and arriving at San Pedro in the evening. Another company, Géminis, runs a less reliable service.

Maimará

From Purmamarca, RN-9 continues north, climbing through the Quebrada de Humahuaca past coloured mountainsides, ornamented with rock formations like organ-pipes or elephants' feet with painted toes. One highly photogenic sight, conveniently visible from the main road, is the extraordinary cemetery at **MAIMARÁ**, 75km from Jujuy; a honeycombed mountain of a graveyard, surrounded by rough-hewn walls and covered with a jumble of centuries-old tombs of all shapes and sizes, crowned with bouquets of artificial flowers and rickety crosses, it appears even bigger than the village it serves. Behind it, the rock formations at the base of the mountain resemble multicoloured oyster-shells. The multiple shades of creams and reds, yellows and browns have earned the rocks the name La Paleta del Pintor ("the artist's palette"). Maimará isn't the most happening place in the Quebrada, but if you choose to stay your best bet is *Hostal Posta del Sol* (Ⓣ0388/423-5387, Ⓦwww.pastoschicos.com.ar; ❹), at Rodríguez and San Martín, which has a number of very smart, simply decorated rooms.

Tilcara

Only 5km further along RN-9 you are treated to your first glimpse of the great pre-Inca *pukará*, or fortress, of **TILCARA**. Just beyond it is the side road off to the village itself. At an altitude of just under 3000m and yet still dominated by the dramatic mountains that surround it, this is one of the biggest settlements along the Quebrada and the only one on the east bank; it lies just off the main road, where the Río Huasomayo runs into the Río Grande. The pleasant, easy-going village is always very lively, but even more so during **Carnival**; like the rest of the Quebrada, it also celebrates **El Enero Tilcareño**, a religious and popular procession and feast held during the latter half of January (good to avoid if you dislike crowds and have not booked accommodation well ahead), as well as **Holy Week**, and **Pachamama**, or the Mother Earth festival, in August, with remarkable festivities, wild games, all manner of music, noisy processions and frenzied partying. Frequent **buses** from Humahuaca and Jujuy stop at the terminal along Avenida Alvear.

Accommodation

Thanks to a number of recent additions, mostly of a luxurious nature, Tilcara is not short of **places to stay**, including a couple of the region's best **youth**

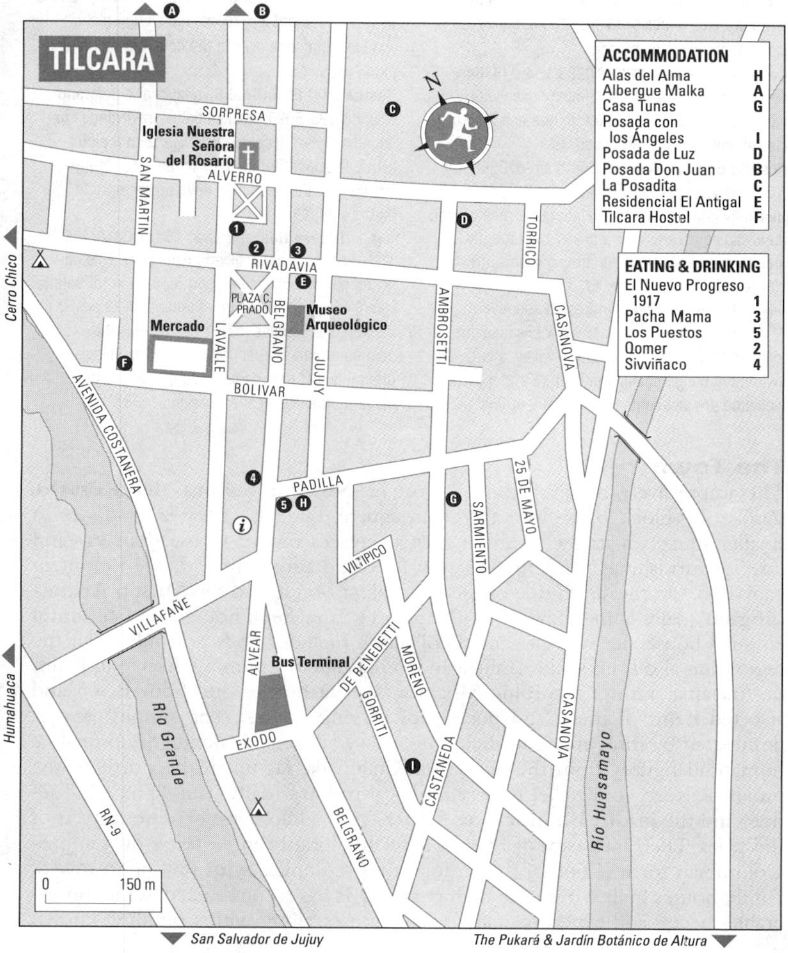

hostels, though prices tend to reflect the area's growing popularity. *El Jardín* (ⓣ0388/495-5128) is Tilcara's main **campsite**, well run and in an attractive riverside location 1km northwest of the village.

Alas del Alma Padilla 437 ⓣ0388/495-5572, ⓦwww.alasdelalma.com. Extremely comfortable adobe-and-stone *cabañas* sleeping two or four, done out in an appealing traditional style with local textiles and ceramics, conveniently located at the entrance to the village. ❻

Albergue Malka San Martín s/n ⓣ0388/495-5197, ⓦwww.malkahostel.com.ar. An outstanding, rather upmarket youth hostel, 400m up a steep hill, east of Plaza Alvarez Prado, commands sweeping views, is extremely comfortable and serves excellent breakfasts. The friendly owner runs treks and 4WD tours in the area. A dorm bed costs $35 including breakfast; there are also doubles (❹–❺) and *cabañas* sleeping three to ten persons.

Casa Tunas Padilla 765 ⓣ0388/154-045784, ⓦwww.casatunas.com.ar. Simple house with whitewashed walls, antique furniture and a lot of charm; half-board is an option. ❸

Posada con los Ángeles Gorriti s/n ⓣ0388/495-5153, ⓦwww.posadaconlosangeles.com.ar. Heavenly hotel, as the name intimates, built around an idyllic courtyard, with a quirky but attractive architectural style decor, charming rooms, great views and tip-top service. ❺–❻

Posada de Luz Ambrosetti and Alverro ⓣ0388/495-5017, ⓦwww.posadadeluz.com.ar. Panoramic views up the valley, a large swimming pool, original architecture and a friendly welcome are just some of the assets of this wonderful posada, where each tastefully furnished and decorated room has its own cachet. Book well ahead as knowledge of the posada is no longer the secret it once was. ❻

Posada Don Juan Lavalle s/n ⓣ0388/495-5422, ⓦwww.posadadonjuan.com.ar. Wonderful semi-detached units, each with a small terrace, spaced evenly around a fine park affording marvellous views of Tilcara and its surroundings. Simple, tasteful decor, excellent breakfasts and professional staff. ❺

La Posadita La Sorpresa s/n ⓣ0388/154-4729997, ⓦwww.laposadita.com.ar. A marvellous newcomer in a similar style to its "mother", *Posada de Luz*; the bright airy rooms have huge picture-windows that look over to the coloured mountains to the west. ❹

Residencial El Antigal Rivadavia and Belgrano ⓣ0388/495-5020, ⓔelantigaltilcara@yahoo.com.ar. A basic but decent *residencial* with a picturesque tearoom that doubles up as a bar in the evening; all the beds now have proper sprung mattresses. ❹

Tilcara Hostel Bolívar 166 ⓣ0388/495-5105, ⓦwww.tilcarahostel.com. This new hostel has established a good reputation for safety, cleanliness and comfort in its dorms ($23 per person) and doubles (❷). It has a pleasant common room, barbecue facilities (the village market is just next door, for supplies) and the owners organize local excursions.

The Town

The impressively massive colonial church, **Nuestra Señora del Rosario**, stands one block back from the main square, Plaza C. Alvarez Prado, on a smaller square of its own; cardón cactus replaces timber in the doorway and interior furnishings, while the beige walls blend agreeably with the mountain backdrop. On the south side of the main plaza, you'll find the **Museo Arqueológico** (daily 9am–12.30pm & 2–6pm; $2, Tues free); housed in a beautiful colonial house, the well-presented collection includes finds not only from the region but also from Chile, Bolivia and Peru, such as a mummy from San Pedro de Atacama, anthropomorphic Mochica vases, a bronze disc from Belén and assorted items of metal and pottery, of varying interest. The simple patio is dominated by three menhirs, including a very tall one, depicting Simpson-like humanoid figures, from the *pukará* of Rinconada, far up in the north of the province. Keep your ticket to visit the local **pukará** (daily 9am–6pm; $2, Tues free) and the **Jardín Botánico de Altura**, both a kilometre or so southwest of the plaza. The University of Buenos Aires has long been working on the pre-Columbian fortress, one of the region's most complex, with row upon row of family houses built within the high ramparts. It has reconstructed, with considerable success and expertise, many of the houses, along with a building known as La Iglesia or "church", thought to have been a ceremonial edifice, no doubt used for sacrifices. The whole magnificent fortress is spiked with a grove of cacti and, with the backdrop of imposing mountains on all sides, it affords marvellous panoramic views in all directions. The garden, in the lee of the *pukará*, is an attractively landscaped collection of local **flora**, mostly cacti, including the hairy *cabeza del viejo* ("old man's head") and equally hirsute "lamb's tail" varieties. There are fabulous views of the *pukará* from its stone paths.

Eating and drinking

Apart from facilities provided by the hotels, there are a number of different possibilities for **meals** or a **drink** in Tilcara. *Pacha Mama*, Belgrano 590, prepares reliable regional fare, as does *Sivviñaco*, an ultra trendy joint that puts on live music most nights, at Belgrano and Padilla. An excellent place for a coffee, a snack or a more elaborate meal, such as a hearty *locro* – plus top-rate breakfasts – is *Qomer*, right on the central plaza at Rivadavia 225. Another ideal place for good food and some excellent folk music is the appealing *El Nuevo Progreso 1917*, on the smaller plaza opposite the church at Lavalle 351. For a special meal, in exceptionally beautiful surroundings, with handsome photos on the walls, *Los Puestos*, at the corner of Belgrano and Padilla, rules supreme: the varied menu features tender grilled llama, mouthwatering empanadas, juicy *humitas* and succulent pasta.

Uquía

After a short, steep climb beyond the side road from Tilcara, RN-9 levels off and crosses the Tropic of Capricorn – marked by a giant sundial monument built in the 1980s and meant to align with the noon shadow at the solstice, but curiously installed at the wrong angle by mistake – one kilometre south of **Huacalera**, a tiny hamlet dominated by its seventeenth-century chapel. The road then climbs past Cerro Yacoraite, a polychrome meseta to the west, streaked with bright reds and yellows, to picturesque **UQUÍA**, just over 100km north of Jujuy. Also set against a vivid backdrop of brick-red mountains and surrounded by lush *quebrachos*, behind a delightful square, is the seventeenth-century **Iglesia de San Francisco de Paula**, with its separate tower integrated in the churchyard wall, all painted pristine white, except the smart green door. Inside, the simple nave directs your gaze to the fine **retable**, the original, with its little inset painted canvases. Nine beautiful and unusual **paintings**, also from the seventeenth century, line the walls: these are unique to Collao, Alto Peru, and depict warrior-like *ángeles militares*, or angels in armour, holding arquebuses and other weapons. Formerly they numbered ten, but one went missing while they were being exhibited in Buenos Aires, where the remaining nine were restored, excessively to some tastes – they seem to have lost their centuries' old patina. If the church is closed – which is likely – ask around for the old lady who keeps the key, apparently the 300-year-old original.

There are two **places to stay**: in the village, at Belgrano and Lozano, is the delightful *Hostal de Uquía* (Ⓣ03887/490508, Ⓦwww.hostaldeuquia.com.ar; ❹), with a big homely sitting room, done out in colonial pink, and fine dining room. *Hosteria Huasadurazno* (Ⓣ0388/154-398457; ❷–❸) is set back slightly from RN-9, about 1km north of the village; its bright rooms, some with bath, are arranged along a traditional galleried house, and delicious meals, using home-grown vegetables, are served to order. After Uquía, along the final stretch before Humahuaca, you have views to the east of some very high mountains: Cerro Zucho (4995m), Cerro Santa Bárbara (4215m) and Cerro Punta Corral (4815m).

Humahuaca

The main town in the area, **HUMAHUACA**, 125km north of Jujuy, spills across the Río Grande from its picturesque centre on the west bank. Its enticing cobbled streets, lined with colonial-style or rustic adobe houses, lend themselves to gentle ambling – necessarily leisurely at this altitude, a touch below 3000m. Most organized tours arrive here for lunch and then double back to Jujuy or Salta, but you may like to stay over, and venture at least as far as the secluded village of **Iruya**; Humahuaca is also an excellent springboard for trips up into the desolate but hauntingly beautiful landscapes of the altiplano or **Puna Jujeña**.

Most tours to and around the town aim to deliver you at the beautifully lush main square at midday on the dot, in time to see a kitsch **statue of San Francisco Solano** emerge from a niche in the equally kitsch tower of the whitewashed **Municipalidad**, give a sign of blessing, and then disappear behind his door. A crowd gathers, invariably serenaded by groups of folk musicians; the saint repeats his trick at midnight to a smaller audience. On the western side of the square, and far more impressive, is the **cathedral**, the Iglesia de Nuestra Señora de la Candelaria y San Antonio, built in the seventeenth century and much restored since. Within its immaculate white walls is a late seventeenth-century retable, and another on the north wall by Cosmo Duarte, dated 1790, depicting the Crucifixion. The remaining artworks include a set of exuberantly Mannerist paintings of the *Twelve Prophets*, signed by leading Cusqueño artist Marcos Sapaca and dated 1764. Looming over the church and the whole town is the controversial **Monumento a la Independencia**, a bombastic concoction of stone and bronze, built in the 1940s by local artist Ernesto Soto Avendaño. Triumphal steps lead up to it from the plaza, but the best thing about it is the view across the town and valley to the mountainside to the east. The twenty-metre high monument is topped by a bronze statue of an Indian in a ferociously warrior-like pose. Behind it, and far more appealing, framed by two giant cacti, is an adobe tower decorated with a bronze plaque, all that remains of the Iglesia Santa Bárbara, whose ruins were destroyed to make way for the monument.

Buses from Jujuy, Salta, La Quiaca and Iruya arrive at the small bus terminal a couple of blocks southeast of the main square, at Belgrano and Entre Ríos. If you're travelling by car, be prepared for the local boys who will approach you at the RN-9 turn-off and offer to guide you. They'll show you around for a small tip, but speak only Spanish.

Accommodation

The range of **accommodation** in Humahuaca is not so extensive and is less upmarket than in Tilcara, but the variety is certainly greater than in Purmamarca. Many people tend to prefer staying in Tilcara, as it is at considerably lower altitude, but Humahuaca is still lower down than, say, La Quiaca or Iruya. A couple of the best options are some way from the village centre, across the Río Grande, in the Barrio Medalla Milagrosa, but if you call ahead they will come and collect you from the bus terminal.

Albergue El Portillo Tucumán 69 ⓣ03887/421288, ⓦwww.elportillohumahuaca@yahoo.com.ar. This simple, cheery inn has both shared bathrooms and en suite, and a fairly decent canteen-style restaurant. ❸

Hospedaje Kuntur Wasi Santa Fe 520 ⓣ03887/421337, ⓔkunturwasi@argentina.com. The rustic stone exterior is matched by a rustic stone interior, but the rooms are comfortable, albeit a little offbeat in design. The excellent restaurant is open only to patrons. ❹

Hostal Azul Barrio Medalla Milagrosa ⓣ03887/421596, ⓦwww.hostalazulhumahuaca.com.ar. The excellent-value rooms are a little cramped but exquisitely decorated and built around a tranquil patio (only the facade is blue), according to traditional techniques. The bread and jams served at breakfast are homemade. ④

Hostal Humahuaca Buenos Aires 447 ⓣ03887/421064. A decent enough little place, it acts as an unofficial youth hostel, charging $30 per person in shared rooms; it also has some rooms with baths (④).

Hostal Inti Sayana La Rioja 83 ⓣ03887/154-099806, ⓦwww.intisayanahostal.com.ar. Lively, clean little hostel that organizes all kinds of cultural events – mostly music and dance. Some of the larger rooms ($135) sleep up to five persons. ③

Hostería Camino del Inca Ejército del Norte s/n ⓣ03887/421136, ⓔhosteriainca@imagine.com.ar. Near the market, this luxurious *hostería* offers a relaxing atmosphere, soothing decor and a handsome Neocolonial design. ⑤

Hostería Solar de la Quebrada Santa Fe 450 ⓣ03887/421986, ⓦwww.solardelaquebrada.com.ar. Gorgeous new *hostería* with fabulous views, six stylishly appointed rooms with excellent mattresses on the beds and appealing, bright decor. ⑥

Posada El Sol Barrio Medalla Milagrosa ⓣ03887/421466, ⓔelsolposada@imagine.com.ar. Fun little posada that doubles up as a youth hostel charging $25 for a dorm bunk; otherwise there are neat doubles (③) and larger rooms, too. The house is built of adobe brick with a straw roof, and the atmosphere is young, with lots of guitar-centred evenings.

Residencial Colonial Entre Ríos 110 ⓣ03887/421007. Decent, clean place, with reliable hot water and some en-suite rooms. ③

Residencial Humahuaca Córdoba 401 and Corrientes ⓣ03887/421141. Conveniently located right next to the bus terminal, this homely *residencial* has very reasonable doubles, triples, quadruples and even quintuples. Breakfast is served in the *confitería* and there is a sunny patio. ②

Eating and drinking

Regional **food** is delicious, plentiful and accompanied by live folk music, albeit aimed at tour groups, at the *Peña de Fortunato Ramos*, at San Luis and Jujuy. You can have a more authentic experience – and delicious fare based on llama and quinoa – at *K'allapurca*, Buenos Aires 175. The *Bar del Tantanakuy*, up at Salta 370, serves regional dishes, wines and real espresso coffee and holds literary, artistic and musical events, and in its marvellous little projection room it screens non-blockbuster films by the likes of Orson Welles and Wong Kar Wai. For a decent coffee, proper tea made in a pot, scrumptious cakes and, occasionally, live music, try the more central *Hebras Andinas*, a stone's throw from the central plaza at Jujuy 393.

Iruya

Just 25km due north of Humahuaca along RN-9, RP-13 forks off to the northeast, crosses a couple of oases and stony riverbeds before winding up a stunningly beautiful narrow valley, and then down again to **Iruya** via a dramatic corniche road along which you wonder how two buses can pass each other – yet they somehow manage. The point where you cross the border into Salta Province is the Abra del Cóndor pass, at a giddying and often gale-blown 3900m. Iruya seems loath to share its beautiful little church with the outside world. The Andean hamlet fits snugly into the side of the valley of the Río Iruya, in the far northern corner of Salta Province, and its fortified walls, steep cobbled streets, whitewashed houses and timeless atmosphere, accentuated by the rarefied air – at an altitude of 2780m – alone make it worth a visit. You certainly feel a long way from the hectic streets of Jujuy or Salta – especially since the whole place is reminiscent of certain Greek island villages, transposed to an Andean landscape. On the first Sunday of October, its **Iglesia de Nuestra Señora del Rosario y San Roque** – a typical Quebrada chapel built to the by-now familiar Mudéjar design – is the focal point for a wonderfully picturesque festival, half-Catholic, half-pre-Columbian, culminating in a solemn procession of weirdly masked figures, some representing demons. Of all the Northwest's festivals, and there are many (see box, pp.456–457), this is the most fascinating and mysterious. The only really decent **place to stay**, should you want to soak up this otherworldly atmosphere, is the comfortable but overpriced *Hostería de Iruya* (☎03887/156-29152; ❻–❼), where the food is agreeable. You can also ask around for rooms for rent, though comfort is minimal and many houses suffer from damp. Two or three Empresa Mendoza **buses** (☎03887/421016 or 156-829078) a day make the at least three-hour trip from Humahuaca.

Up to the Puna Jujeña

Due north of Humahuaca and the turn-off to tiny Iruya, RN-9 begins its long winding haul up into the remote **altiplano** of northern Jujuy, known as the **Puna Jujeña**; this is a fabulously wild highland area of salt-flats, **lagoons** speckled pink with flamingoes and tiny hamlets built of mud-bricks around surprisingly big Quebrada-style chapels. Some 30km north of Humahuaca, RN-9 enters the **Cuesta de Azul Pampa**, a dramatic mountain pass peaking at 3730m and offering unobstructed views across to the huge peaks to the east. Past the bottleneck of the Abra de Azul Pampa, where fords along the road sometimes freeze, causing extra hazards, the road winds along to the bleak little mining town of **Tres Cruces**, where there's a major *gendarmería* post – personal and vehicle papers are usually checked. Nearby, but out of sight, are some of the continent's biggest

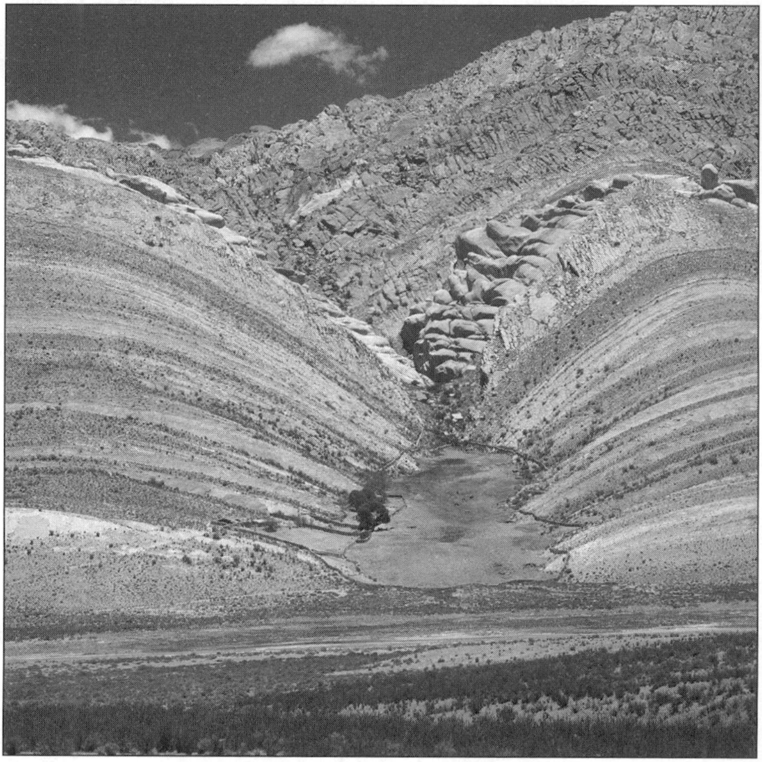

△ Espina del Diablo

deposits of lead and zinc, along with silver mines, while overlooking the village is one of the strangest rock formations in the region, the so-called **Espina del Diablo**, or "Devil's Backbone", a series of intriguingly beautiful stone burrows, clearly the result of violent tectonic activity millions of years ago, ridged like giant vertebrae. This road continues all the way to the Bolivian border at **La Quiaca** – an ideal base for visiting the remote corners of the province, such as **Yavi**, and its superb colonial church, and **Laguna de los Pozuelos**, with its sizeable wildfowl colony. On the way you pass through the crossroads village of **Abra Pampa**, from where you can branch off to visit the picturesque villages of **Cochinoca** and **Casabindo**, with their fine churches and colonial art treasures.

Abra Pampa and around

ABRA PAMPA, a forlorn village of llama herdsmen living in adobe houses amid the windswept steppe, 80km north of Humahuaca, lives up to its former name of Siberia Argentina. This really isn't a place that you'd choose to spend the night, but should you need to, pick from one of the rather spartan **residenciales**: *Cesarito*, Senador Pérez 200 (Ⓣ03887/491001; ❷), the better of the two, and *La Coyita*, Fascio 123 (Ⓣ03887/491052; ❷). Due southwest, the rough surfaced RP-11 follows the Río Miraflores to **Casabindo**, nearly 60km away, a tiny unspoilt village dwarfed by its huge church. Nicknamed La Catedral de la Puna, the **Iglesia de la Asunción** houses a collection of Altoperuvian paintings of *ángeles militares*, or angels in armour, similar to those in Uquía (see p.463). The church itself was built in the late eighteenth century to a Hispano-Mexican design and its several chapels are the theatre of major celebrations on August 15, the **Feast of the Assumption**, when plume-hatted angels and a bull-headed demon lead a procession around the village, accompanied by drummers. The climax of the festival is a bloodless *corrida*, a colonial custom known as the **Toreo de la Vincha**. The bull, representing the Devil, has a rosette hung with coins stuck on his horns and the Virgin's "defenders" have to try and remove it. Coca leaves and fermented maize are buried in another ceremony on the same day, as an offering to Pachamama, the Earth Mother, in a fusion of pre-Christian and Christian rituals; these are among the most fascinating and colourful of all the Northwest's festivals and well worth catching if you're here at the right time. The only **place to stay** in Casabindo is the very rudimentary *Albergue Casabindo* (Ⓣ03887/491126; ❶). **Cochinoca** is another unspoilt village, 22km along a numberless dirt track heading in a westerly direction from Abra Pampa. Its nineteenth-century church, **Iglesia de Nuestra Señora de la Candelaria**, shelters some fine colonial paintings and a magnificent retable. The alabaster windows were rescued from the colonial church destroyed in a major earthquake in the mid-nineteenth century, as was the *Lienzo de la Virgen de la Almudena*, an oil painting depicting the construction of the original building, put up on the same site in the late seventeenth century. Both Casabindo and Cochinoca are very hard to reach – there's no public transport – but are great destinations if you're looking to get well off the beaten track.

La Quiaca and around

LA QUIACA, the largest settlement in the Puna Jujeña, almost 165km north of Humahuaca, is a border town that has seen better days. Immediately to the north, the river of the same name, gushing through a deep gorge, forms the natural frontier with Bolivia; on the other side of it the twin town of Villazón thrives on cross-border trade, while La Quiaca stagnates because its shops are losing trade to cheaper stores in Bolivia. Although there's simply nothing to do here, except get used to the altitude – 3445m – and perhaps plan your trip into Bolivia, its accommodation makes it a possible base for exploring this furthest corner of Argentina, with side-trips easily made to nearby **Yavi**, with its unusual church, **Tafna**, also dominated by a chapel, and the **Laguna de los Pozuelos**. **Buses** from Jujuy and Yavi stop at the corner of Calle Belgrano and Avenida España; the latter is the final stretch of RN-9, which comes to an abrupt end at the town's surprisingly grandiose football stadium, where Argentina's national team occasionally train before games in Bolivia, to build up their stamina at high altitude. La Quiaca livens up a little on the third and fourth Sundays of October, when the **Manca Fiesta**, also known as the Fiesta de la Olla, or cooking-pot festival, is staged; ceramists and other artisans show off their wares, while folk musicians put on concerts. The best **place to stay** is the well-run *Hostería Munay Tierra de Colores*, Belgrano 51 (Ⓣ03885/423924, Ⓦwww.munayhotel.jujuy.com; ③), which has pleasant rooms in a modern building and a safe garage. This is followed at a distance by the simple but clean *Hotel de Turismo*, two blocks southeast of the bus terminal at Siria and San Martín (Ⓣ03885/422243, Ⓔhotelmun@laquiaca.com.ar; ③), while *Residencial Cristal*, Sarmiento 539 (Ⓣ03885/422255; ②), has very basic rooms leading off a stark courtyard, and serves decent food at very low prices. A new **restaurant** worth trying is the *Casola* at the southwestern corner of the Plaza Independencia, specializing in pasta and *parrillas*.

Tafna and Laguna de los Pozuelos

Heading west from La Quiaca on RP-5 takes you along parallel to the Bolivian border, past the northern tip of the steeply scarped Cordón de Escaya, to **TAFNA**, 20km away. This tiny settlement consists of three adobe houses and an enormous **colonial chapel**, whose ochre walls and towers, unusually two in number, and straw roof blend into the beige landscape; huge flocks of sheep and goats overrun the nearby colonial cemetery. Immediately west of Tafna, beyond the **Cuesta del Toquero**, a narrow pass lined with curious cobweb-like rock formations, you reach the crossroads and police checkpoint of Cieneguillas, from where you can continue another 30km along corrugated dirt track, to the tiny mountain village of Santa Catalina, just to say you've been to the northernmost settlement in Argentina. Otherwise head south for 50km, through parched pastureland, dotted with farmsteads and corrals, to the entrance to the **Monumento Natural Laguna de los Pozuelos**, 150 square kilometres of protected land in a basin between the rippling Sierra de Cochinoca and Sierra de Rinconada. Access to the reserve is unlimited, but call in at the **guardería**, south of the lake, just off the road to Rinconada, if only for a friendly chat with the *guardaparques*; they'll let you camp in the forecourt, if you need somewhere to stay. The lagoon itself, a couple of kilometres to the north, has shrunk in recent years, after a series of dry summers, but is still a considerable stretch of water covering seventy square kilometres, home to large flocks of Andean flamingoes and over thirty other varieties of wildfowl, including teals, avocets and ducks. Don't try and drive over the soft, spongy lakeside; the lake edge is a quagmire and the shy flamingoes take off in great clouds long before you get anywhere near them, forming long pink skeins streaked against the backdrop of dark brown mountains. Instead, walk from the reserve entrance, where a sign explains what fauna you'll see. You're also likely to see ñandús (lesser rheas) scuttling away to find cover as you approach. **Buses** come out here every morning from Abra Pampa, 50km southeast, on their way to Rinconada, and return in the afternoon, just giving you time – three hours or so – to get to the lagoon and back.

Yavi

The RP-5 also leads east from La Quiaca, ostensibly to an airport that has yet to materialize. Across the rolling Siete Hermanos mountain range, 17km away along this road, sits the charming altiplanic village of **YAVI**, with sloping cobbled streets, adobe houses and a splendid working flour mill. From a mirador at the top of main drag Avenida Senador Pérez, to the north of the village, you have a panoramic view, taking in the dilapidated but attractive eighteenth-century **Casa del Marqués de Tojo**, the erstwhile family home of the region's ruling marqués, the only holder of that rank in colonial Argentina; the house, on the Plaza Mayor, is a museum of sorts with erratic opening hours (in theory daily 9am–1pm & 2–6pm; $2). A motley collection of artefacts and junk, such as the bedstead used by the last marqués, is arranged in various rooms around a fabulous patio shaded by a willow and an elm. Next to it is the village's seventeenth-century church, **Iglesia de Nuestra Señora del Rosario y San Francisco** (Mon 3–6pm, Tues–Fri 9am–noon & 3–6pm, Sat & Sun 9am–noon). Behind its harmonious white facade – ask around for the lady who keeps the key, she won't always be there at the hours posted at the entrance – is one of the region's best-preserved colonial interiors, lit a ghostly lemon-yellow by the unique wafer-thin onyx-paned windows. Some of the church's treasures were stolen during the border conflict with Chile – when *gendarmes* left the village to guard Argentine territory – and were recently traced to a private collection in the US. The ornate Baroque pulpit, three retables decorated with coloured wooden statuettes of saints and a fine sixteenth-century Flemish oil painting that must have been brought here by early colonizers, look wonderful in the simple white nave. Apart from a couple of grimly basic *hospedajes*, there are two recommendable **places to stay**, both offering half-board, which is just as well, as there are no restaurants to speak of. The better of the two is *Hostería Pachama* right at the entrance to the village, Senador Pérez s/n (Ⓣ03887/490508; ③), though the ultra-simple, plain rooms come as a disappointment after the appealing decor of the main building; they can concoct a basic but tasty meal if required, served in an attractive dining room. If it is full then you'll have to stay at the far less interesting *Hostería de Yavi*, Güemes 222 (Ⓣ03887/423235, Ⓦwww.pachamahosteria.com; ③), run by the owners of the *hostería* in Uquía, who'll book ahead for you; the rooms are OK but not especially attractive, and the service can be shoddy. You can also **camp** across the *acequia* (irrigation channel) from the church, but the site has no facilities. Guides – ask at the *Hostería de Yavi* – can take you to local attractions, such as pre-Columbian petroglyphs and cave-paintings in the nearby mountains; the petroglyphs are nothing special but the walk there, through stunning countryside, is worthwhile. La Quiaqueña runs frequent **buses** from La Quiaca, or you could try and hitch a lift from the market.

The cloudforest national parks: El Rey, Calilegua and Baritú

A trio of the Northwest's cloudforests, or *yungas* – areas of dense jungle draped over high crags that thrust out of the flat, green plains of lowlands on either side of the Tropic of Capricorn – are protected by national park status. The biggest of the three, the **Parque Nacional Calilegua**, is also the most accessible and best developed – it's the pride and joy of Jujuy Province – and within easy reach of San Salvador de Jujuy, though it might be better to stay in nearby **Libertador General San Martín**. **Parque Nacional El Rey**, in Salta Province, much closer to the provincial capital, is often made difficult to visit owing to impassable roads after the heavy seasonal rains. Slightly smaller than Calilegua, **Parque Nacional Baritú**, away to the north in a far-flung corner of Salta Province, is the hardest to get to, and therefore even less spoilt, than either of the other two national parks; the small town of **San Ramón de la Nueva Orán** can act as a springboard for getting there. The microclimates of all three *yungas* are characterized by clearly distinct dry and wet seasons, winter and summer, but relatively high year-round precipitation. The peaks are often shrouded in cloud and mist, keeping most of the varied plant life lush even in the drier, cooler months. They are worth a visit for the dramatic scenery alone, though the incredibly varied fauna that lives amid the dense vegetation is perhaps the main attraction.

Parque Nacional El Rey

PARQUE NACIONAL EL REY straddles the borders of Salta and Jujuy provinces, nearly 200km by road from the city of Salta, from where it can be quickly reached, though heavy rains can sometimes make the route impassable. Covering 400 square kilometres of land once belonging to Finca El Rey near the provincial border with Jujuy, the national park (9am–dusk; free) perches at an average of 900m above sea level and nestles in a natural horseshoe-shaped amphitheatre, hemmed in by the curving **Crestón del Gallo** ridge to the northwest, and the higher crest of the **Serranía del Piquete**, to the east, peaking at around 1700m. A fan-shaped network of crystal-clear brooks, all brimming with fish, drains into the Río Popayán. The handsome **toucan** (*Ramphastos toco*) is the park's striking and easily recognizable mascot, but other birdlife abounds, totalling over 150 species. Despite this, it is not that easy to see birds here; however, the park is the best place in the region for spotting tapirs, peccaries and wild cats.

Public transport to the park is non-existent and through-traffic very slight, so visiting the park without your own transport is quite difficult. If you have no vehicle – and even if you do – an organized trip is the best option. Norte Trekking (see box, p.435) can take you on an informative and enjoyable safari to the park; equally professional Clark Expediciones (see box, p.435) specializes in natural history and bird-watching trips here. If you do plan to come under your own steam, make sure you have a 4WD. The park's only access road is RP-20, branching left from RP-5, which in turn leads eastwards from RN-9/34, near the village of Lumbrera halfway between Metán and Güemes. **Guardaparques** at the entrance can advise you on how to get around in your vehicle. The only **accommodation** option is to pitch your tent in the clearing in the middle of the park. A road of sorts follows the **Río La Sala**, while more marked trails through the park are currently being planned to add to the two-hour climb from the rangers' station to **Pozo Verde**, a lakelet coloured green by lettuce-like *lentejas de água*, and a nearby pond where birds come to drink.

Parque Nacional Calilegua

Spread over 760 square kilometres, just south of the Tropic of Capricorn, in a province better known for its arid mountains, multicoloured valleys and parched altiplanic landscapes, the **PARQUE NACIONAL CALILEGUA** sticks up above rich fertile land that is home to some of the country's biggest sugar farms. It's the setting for amusing anecdotes in Gerald Durrell's book *The Whispering*

Land; his tales of roads cut off by flooding rivers can still ring true but his quest for native animals to take back to his private zoo cannot be imitated – the park's rich flora and fauna (see Contexts, p.816) are now strictly protected by law. The land once belonged to the Leach brothers, local sugar barons of British origin, whose family donated it to the state to turn it into a national park in the 1970s. This was a shrewd business move: sugar plantations need a lot of clean water and the only way to keep the reliable supplies which run through the park free of pollution, uncontrolled logging and the general destruction of the fragile ecosystem was through the state regulations that come with national park status.

The park **entrance** (daily 9am–6pm; free) is at Aguas Negras, 120km from Jujuy city via RN-34. At **Libertador General San Martín** take RP-83, which climbs to **Valle Colorado**, and is paved as far as Aguas Negras. Libertador General San Martín is an uninviting little town, dominated by the huge Ledesma industrial complex – the world's biggest sugar refinery – and usually referred to as Libertador or LGSM on signs, but is a possible stopover base for visiting the park. Cars can make it along the main road, punctuated by numerous viewpoints, some offering splendid panoramas, as far as the **Mesada de la Colmenas**, near the other rangers' headquarters, but a 4WD will be required beyond here – the road continues its climb to the highest point, at 1700m, marked by the **Abra de las Cañas** monolith. You should certainly walk off the beaten track, well away from noisy trucks, if you want to have the slightest chance of spotting any of the wildlife. Trekking around Calilegua takes time and it's a very good idea to spend a night or two in the park. Morning and late afternoon are the best times to see animals and birds by streams and rivers. Seven trails of varying length and difficulty have been hacked through the dense vegetation, and it's worth asking the rangers for guidance – there aren't any maps.

The summits of the **Serranía de Calilegua**, marking the park's northwestern boundary, reach heights of over 3300m, beyond which lies grassland and rocky terrain. The trek to the summit of Cerro Amarillo (3320m) takes three days from the park entrance; the nearby shepherds' hamlet, **Alto Calilegua**, is certainly worth a visit. From the tiny settlement of San Francisco within the park it's even possible to link up with **Tilcara** (see p.460), a four-day trek; some of the organized trips arranged in Salta and Tilcara itself, including horse rides, offer this amazing chance to witness the stark contrast between the verdant jungle and the desiccated uplands.

Practicalities

At the park entrance, you'll find the ranger's house (the intendencia is in the town of **Libertador General San Martín**; see p.472), definitely worth a visit before you head in, for maps and extra information about the park; general **tourist information** about the area can be obtained at Confianza Turismo, Av Libertad 350 in Libertador (Ⓣ03886/424527, Ⓔconfianza@cooplib.com.ar). **Accommodation outside the park** is also in Libertador. Offering top-notch service and excursion possibilities is the plush *Posada del Sol* (Ⓣ03886/424900, Ⓦwww.posadadelsoljujuy.com.ar; ❺), with inviting rooms arranged around an attractive courtyard and swimming pool, hidden away at Los Ceibos and Pukará. A little cheaper and rather less appealing, but clean enough, is the *Hotel Los Lapachos*, Entre Ríos 400 (Ⓣ03886/423790; ❸). Alternative accommodation is available at the *Complejo Termal Aguas Calientes* spa resort (Ⓣ0388/156-50699; ❸), 30km northeast of Libertador along RP-1, which turns eastwards off RN-34 past the straggly village of Caimancito. Near the banks of the Río San Francisco in a bucolic setting, it offers excellent meals and clean rooms, camping or the opportunity to splash around in the various curative mineral pools for the day. Barring the mosquitoes (bring repellent), this is an excellent place to rest, conveniently near Calilegua in an area rich in trails and scenery. Alternatively, try the *Portal de Piedra* at nearby Villa Monte (ⓣ0388/156-820564; ❹), across the eastern border of Salta Province – gaucho traditions, fine countryside walks and excellent wildlife-spotting are the attractions, with the emphasis firmly on ecotourism. The best **places to eat** in the area are in Libertador: *Del Valle*, Entre Ríos 793, is a restaurant serving plain but well-cooked meals at reasonable prices, while *La Yapa*, Victoria 698 is an excellent *parrilla*.

Buses from Salta stop at Libertador's terminal on Avenida Antartida Argentina, 200m east of RN-34. Buses for Valle Grande pass through the park, leaving the terminal early in the morning, returning late at night – times vary – but you could also contact the intendencia (ⓣ03886/422046, ⓔpncalilegua@cooperlib.com.ar) to find out whether any timber trucks are going towards the park at a time convenient for you; there's no problem hitching a lift if there are. Buses from Salta to San Ramón de la Nueva Orán sometimes stop at the *Club Social San Lorenzo*, near the park entrance, but otherwise hitching might well be the only way to get that far; RN-34 is a busy route. Announce yourself to the rangers at the park entrance, 8km from RN-34; nearby a camouflaged **campsite**, with basic facilities, has been cleared ($3 per person). For the time being, it's the only practical way of being **on site** early enough in the morning or late enough at dusk to be assured of spotting wildlife – though the voracious insects may deter you. If you get as far as **Valle Grande**, you could stay at either of the village's extremely basic **accommodation** options: *Albergue San Francisco* (no phone; ❷) or *Albergue Valle Grande* (ⓣ03886/461000; ❷).

Like the other two parks, Calilegua should be visited in **spring** or **autumn**, as the summer months – December to March or April – can see sudden cloudbursts cut off access roads and make paths much too slippery for comfort. At all times bring **insect repellent** since mosquitoes and other nasty bugs are also plentiful and virulent, especially in the warmer months and in particular around Aguas Negras. You may wish to visit the park on an **organized tour**; TEA (see p.451) can get you here and fix up accommodation, while Clark Expediciones (see box, p.435) regularly runs expert bird-watching safaris to the park.

Parque Nacional Baritú and San Ramón de la Nueva Orán

Located in an isolated corner of northeastern Salta Province, the all but inaccessible **Parque Nacional Baritú** is one of the country's least visited national parks. Baritú's mascot is the red **yunga squirrel** (*ardilla roja*), but you will find most of the cloudforest animal life here, enjoying the relative seclusion. In addition to the typical flora (see p.816), the virgin vegetation includes large numbers of the impressive **tree-fern**, a dinosaur of a plant surviving from the Palaeozoic era, whose scaly trunk and parasol of fronds can reach five or six metres in height; they are hard to see, however, preferring the densest parts of the forest for their habitat. Less pleasant is the *maroma*, a parasite that ungratefully strangles its host tree to death.

A poor road, usually cut off in the rainy season, runs for 30km west from the customs post at Aguas Blancas on the Bolivian border, 50km north of **SAN RAMÓN DE LA NUEVA ORÁN**, a rather grandiose name for an insignificant little town (it's usually shortened to Orán), and enters the park at the rangers' post known as **Sendero Angosto**, on the Río Pescado. Though of little interest in itself, Orán is the ideal base for visiting Baritú. **Accommodation** ranges from the fairly luxurious *Hotel Alto Verde*, Pellegrini 671 (ⓣ03878/421214, ⓔhotelaltoverde@arnet.ar; ❹–❺), boasting a/c in all rooms and a fair-sized swimming pool, to the *Crillon*, 25 de Mayo 225 (ⓣ03878/421101; ❷), and *Colonial*, on Pizarry Colón (ⓣ03878/421103; ❷). Both are basic but have clean bathrooms and decent rooms. The alternative, even more adventurous, route means going into Bolivia, following the Río Bermejo in a northwesterly direction as far as Nogalitos, crossing the river and border at La Mamora and entering the park at Los Pozos – this is really only for anyone who likes making life difficult. It may be more convenient to stay at **Los Toldos**, on the way into the park, where you will find the ranger's house and maybe some *cabañas* to rent.

Covering 720 square kilometres, the park has a geography that is complicated by a maze of *arroyos* and largely impervious high mountains: the steep Las Pavas and Porongal ranges both exceed 2000m while the park's southern reaches are dominated by the **Cerro Cinco Picachos**, at nearly 2000m. The lack of public transport, lack of on-the-spot facilities and the challenging terrain all but rule out individual travel and hardly any tour operators based in nearby towns seem interested in taking you there. Contact Hugo Luna, at 9 de Julio 430 in Orán, or see if an operator in Jujuy or Salta will take you there: try TEA, in Jujuy (see p.451), or Clark Expediciones, in Salta (see box, p.435).

Tucumán, Santiago del Estero and Catamarca provinces

Whereas Salta and Jujuy have an established international tourist industry, the three more southern provinces of the Northwest remain virtually unknown. Domestically they are dismissed as poor, dull backwaters with more than their fair share of political, social and economic woes, and there is more than a little truth in that analysis, especially in the case of Santiago. Yet some of Argentina's most mind-blowing landscapes are hidden away in **Catamarca Province**; the city of **Tucumán** – the region's biggest urban centre by far – has an addictively lively atmosphere; and **Santiago del Estero** has a much-deserved nationwide reputation for the quality of its **musicians**. Tucumán may be one of Argentina's smallest provinces, but it does contain some real treasures, including the impressive pre-Inca ruins at **Quilmes** and the dramatic mountain scenery around **Tafí del Valle**. Equally impressive are the eternally snowy peaks that give their name to the Nevados del Aconquija, the natural border with neighbouring Catamarca Province, where a plethora of picturesque villages, each more isolated than the previous, reward patient visitors with rural hospitality, wondrous natural settings and some fabulous handmade crafts: **Andalgalá**, **Belén** and **Londres** stand out. Even more awe-inspiring than Quilmes, the less-publicized pre-Columbian

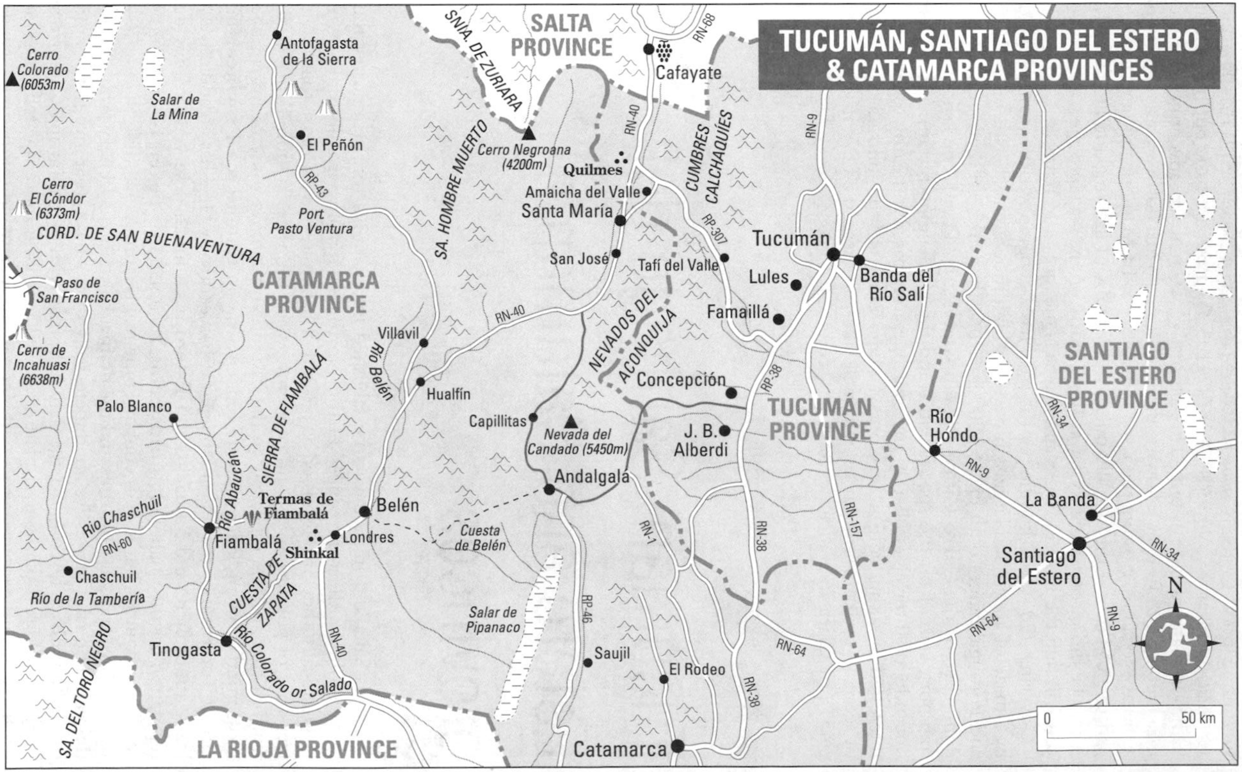
TUCUMÁN, SANTIAGO DEL ESTERO & CATAMARCA PROVINCES
SALTA PROVINCE
CATAMARCA PROVINCE
TUCUMÁN PROVINCE
SANTIAGO DEL ESTERO PROVINCE
LA RIOJA PROVINCE
Cerro Colorado (6053m)
Salar de La Mina
Antofagasta de la Sierra
El Peñón
RP-43
Cerro El Cóndor (6373m)
Port Pasto Ventura
CORD. DE SAN BUENAVENTURA
Paso de San Francisco
Cerro de Incahuasi (6638m)
Palo Blanco
SNIA. DE ZURIARA
SA. HOMBRE MUERTO
Cerro Negroana (4200m)
Quilmes
Cafayate
RN-68
RN-40
CUMBRES CALCHAQUÍES
Amaicha del Valle
Santa María
San José
Tafí del Valle
RP-307
Tucumán
RN-9
Banda del Río Salí
Lules
Famaillá
NEVADOS DEL ACONQUIJA
Concepción
RP-38
J. B. Alberdi
Villavil
Río Belén
Hualfín
Capillitas
Nevada del Candado (5450m)
Andalgalá
SIERRA DE FIAMBALÁ
Río Abaucán
Termas de Fiambalá
Belén
Río Chaschuil
Fiambalá
Shinkal
Londres
Cuesta de Belén
RN-60
Chaschuil
Río de la Tambería
CUESTA DE ZAPATA
Tinogasta
Río Colorado or Salado
SA. DEL TORO NEGRO
Salar de Pipanaco
RP-46
Saujil
El Rodeo
Catamarca
RN-1
RN-38
RN-157
Río Hondo
RN-34
La Banda
Santiago del Estero
RN-64
N
0
50 km

remains at **Shinkal**, near Londres, look almost more Maya than Inca, with their mercifully well-preserved pyramids and symbolic temples, whose real purposes have so far defied the archeologists. Try and make it all the way to **Fiambalá**, for its delicious wine, irresistible fabrics and healthy thermal springs, or even to **Antofagasta de la Sierra**, an amazingly out-of-the-way market town set among rock and lava formations and reached via some of the emptiest roads in the country. Other stretches of track not to be missed, if you have time on your side, include the giddying passes leading to Andalgalá, the **Cuesta de Belén**, and the international route into Chile via the breathtaking **Paso de San Francisco**. Beware that summers can be steamy in the valleys, making large cities like Tucumán unbearable, whereas in July and August night-time **temperatures** up around Antofagasta are bitterly low, so your first purchase there will be an alpaca-wool poncho.

San Miguel de Tucumán

In the humid valley of the Río Salí, in the eastern lee of the high Sierra de Aconquija, **SAN MIGUEL DE TUCUMÁN** (or simply **Tucumán**) is Argentina's fourth largest city, 1190km northwest of Buenos Aires and nearly 300km south of Salta by RN-9. It hasn't changed much, it seems, since Paul Theroux was here in 1978 and wrote, in *The Old Patagonian Express*, that it "was thoroughly European in a rather old-fashioned way, from the pin-striped suits and black moustaches of the old men idling in the cafés or having their shoes shined in the plaza, to the baggy, shapeless school uniforms of the girls stopping on their way to the convent school to squeeze – it was an expression of piety – the knee of Christ on the cathedral crucifix"; it still looks a bit like a European city caught in a time-warp.

The capital of a tiny but heavily populated sugar-rich province, Tucumán is by far the biggest metropolis in the Northwest, the region's undisputed **commercial capital** and one of the liveliest urban centres in the country, with a thriving business centre, bustling, traffic-choked downtown streets, a youthful population and even a slightly violent undercurrent, by Argentine standards. Tucumán certainly has a boisterous image, perhaps partly since it's Argentina's rugby capital, but its confidence has been trimmed over the past two or three decades by municipal political and economic crises – and the city seems to have taken longer than the rest of the country to recover from the turmoil of 2001. Tucumanos themselves admit – they're known for their self-derision – that the city's people have a knack of "finding other people's property before it's lost", but you're unlikely to find Tucumán any more dangerous than any other large city. Despite a heavy-duty nightlife that quietens down only on Mondays, it's not a place you're likely to spend long in, as attractions are in very short supply.

Some history

Originally founded in 1565 by Diego de Villarroel, Tucumán's first home was near the town of Monteros, 50km southwest of the present city, but mosquitoes proved an intolerable nuisance, and the settlement was moved to its current drier spot in 1685. The etymology of the name Tucumán is something of a mystery – it is probably a corruption of the Quichoa (see box, p.477) for "place where things finish", a reference to the abrupt mountains that loom above the fertile plains, but may have been derived from the Kana word *yukuman* meaning "welling springs". For a while, the city flourished and its name was applied to

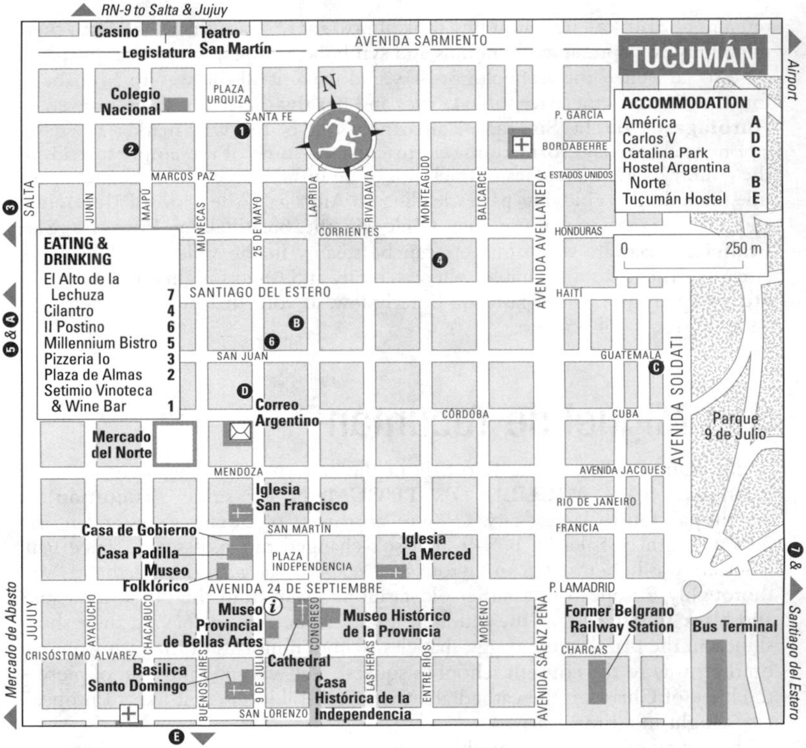

a whole region of Spanish America corresponding to southern Bolivia and the northwestern quarter of today's Argentina. Soon, though, the city was eclipsed by Salta and Córdoba, whose climates were found to be more bearable. Then came its moment of glory, on July 9, 1816, when the city hosted a historic Congress of Unitarist politicians at which Argentina's independence from Spain was declared. In the late nineteenth century, after the arrival of the railways and sizeable influxes of immigrants, from Italy mainly, along with thousands of Jews from Central Europe, the city underwent the expansion that turned it into today's metropolis. British investment and climatic conditions favoured Tucumán's sugar industry, and most of the city's wealth, built up around the end of the nineteenth century, accrued from this "white gold". A slump in international sugar prices and shortsighted over-farming have now forced local sugar-growers to branch out into alternative money-earners, such as tobacco and citrus fruit. Tucumán has become the world's biggest lemon-producing area, but also grows mandarins, grapefruit and kumquats. With a climate similar to that around Santa Cruz de la Sierra in Bolivia, much of the area has also been given over to growing blueberries and strawberries – with large numbers of Bolivian workers helping local farmers at harvest time.

Arrival, information and city transport

Tucumán's international **airport**, Aeropuerto Benjamín Matienzo (☎0381/426-0121), is 9km east of the centre of town; a **taxi** will cost about

Quichoa: the language of the Inca

Of all the country's regions, the Northwest now has the biggest concentration of people of native origin, the largest single group being the 150,000-strong Kolla mostly in Jujuy Province, many of whom have kept their customs alive despite decades of "Europeanization". Other ethnic groups in the Northwest include the Toba, Wichí, Chané, Chorote, Tapiete, Chulupi and Zuritas. Until the Inca empire swallowed up the region only a century or so before the European invasion, the different groups – and even their distinct *ayllúes* or clans – spoke quite separate **languages**, that were often mutually incomprehensible, but just as the Romans imposed Latin, so the Inca made **Quichoa** the *lingua franca* of their vast realms. Uninterrupted cross-border contacts helped to keep the Quichoa language alive in Northwestern Argentina, and academic interest in this ancient heritage has recently been growing. Quichoa is now even being taught in some local schools. As a result, albeit artificially, Quichoa is undergoing a revival; by contrast, other non-European tongues such as Kana have died out without trace, although fragments seem to have survived in some local place names.

Quichoa (or **Quechua** as it is often called – in fact the language only has three vowels: a, i and o) was subdivided into numerous dialects, and spoken throughout Northwest Argentina, to the north and west of present-day **Santiago del Estero Province** – the only province where speakers are still found to this day. An oral language without a written form, as we know it, it was adapted to the Roman alphabet by the colonizers, so its spelling roughly corresponds to the phonetic system of Castilian Spanish (ch is pronounced like the Spanish – and English – sound). Obviously totally unrelated to any Indo-European languages, Quichoa nonetheless follows most of the familiar rules of grammar, especially syntax and morphology, though it ignores any concept of gender or articles; its grammar is fairly regular and not too hard to learn. Although inevitably Quichoa-speakers now sprinkle their speech with many Spanish words, over the years Quichoa has managed to infiltrate Spanish: most famously, *cancha* – one word always on all Argentines' lips – meaning a sports field or stadium (especially for football), comes from the Quichoa word for "field". Other familiar Quichoa words mostly relate to flora and fauna: llama, alpaca, cóndor, vicuña, guanaco, vizcacha, *mate*, tuna, chañar and palta, plus the all-important term *puna*, referring both to the altiplano and the altitude sickness you might suffer from up there. Otherwise topology is the main treasure-house of the indigenous peoples' tongues: Tucumán, Purmamarca, Amaicha, Catamarca and Cafayate all have names rooted in the pre-Hispanic past.

$15. Tucumán is quite fog-prone and flights are sometimes inconveniently re-routed as far away as Santiago del Estero. Tucumanos are justifiably proud of their modern and efficient **bus terminal** (Ⓣ0381/422-2221), at Brígido Terán 350, six blocks east and two south of Plaza Independencia. It has sixty wide-berthed platforms, a shopping centre ("Shopping del Jardín") and supermarket, restaurants, bars, post office, telephone centres, left-luggage and even a hairdresser – but no working ATMs: try the supermarket for cash withdrawals. Most **city buses** run between the centre and the bus terminal, and you'll need a token for each trip, on sale at all kiosks. Trains still run to and from Buenos Aires via Santiago del Estero from the **train station** (Ⓣ0381/431-0725) at Catamarca and Corrientes, but perhaps not for much longer. **Tourist information** is available at the provincial office at 24 de Septiembre 484 (Mon–Fri 7am–1pm & 5–9pm, Sat & Sun 9am–1pm & 5pm–9pm), on Plaza Independencia. The branch at the **bus station** (same hours) can sometimes scrape a map together.

Accommodation

Rather than stay in the city, especially in the unbearable summer heat (Nov–March), you may well prefer to do as the locals do and **stay** in the cooler heights of Tafí del Valle (see p.480) or near the archeological site of Quilmes (see p.483). Tucumán has a wide selection of **hotels**, but the quality is poor. Many mid-range hotels are conveniently clustered around the central Plaza Independencia, but even they are shoddily run and overpriced. At the budget end, you can choose from a number of decent **residenciales** and a couple of excellent **youth hostels**.

Catalina Park Hotel Av Soldati 380 ⓣ0381/450-2250, ⓦwww.grandhotel.com.ar. It is rather bland and aimed mainly at the conference and business market, but is nonetheless worth trying for its fine location overlooking Parque 9 de Julio, large rooftop pool, saunas and all mod cons; rates are cut at weekends. ❼

Hostel Argentina Norte Laprida 456 ⓣ0381/430-2716, ⓔhostel@argentinanorte.com. Excellent hostel situated in a beautiful Neocolonial townhouse. Dorm beds $22, and some double rooms (❷).

Hotel América Santiago del Estero 1064 ⓣ0381/430-0810. Hotel well known for its bar, but it also has smart rooms, with bright bathrooms. ❸

Hotel Carlos V 25 de Mayo 330 ⓣ0381/431-1666, ⓦwww.hotelcarlosv.com.ar. Extremely well run, with a friendly reception and comfortable, classy rooms with reproduction furniture and a decent restaurant. ❹

Tucumán Hostel Buenos Aires 669 ⓣ0381/420-1584, ⓦwww.tucumanhostel.com. Another exceptional hostel with kitchen-use, bar, Internet access and local tours. Breakfast included. Dorm beds $22, and some double rooms (❸).

The City

Despite its narrow, traffic-clogged streets and the slightly down-at-heel pedestrianized shopping area northwest of the centre, Tucumán lends itself to a gentle stroll and you could easily spend a full day visiting its few sights, including a couple of decent museums. As usual, orientation is simplified by the regular grid system; streets change name on either side of Avenida 24 de Septiembre, the street running past the cathedral, and change name twice as they go from west to east, first at avenidas Mitre and Além, and again at avenidas Avellaneda and Sáenz Peña.

Plaza Independencia is the city's focal point; a grove of native trees jostle with orange trees in the central area of the main plaza, each helpfully labelled, while a large pool with a fountain, a statue to Liberty and a monolith marking the spot where Avellaneda's head was spiked, after his opponent Rosas had him executed in 1841, take up the rest. In the southeast corner of the square is the mid-nineteenth-century Neoclassical **cathedral**, its slender towers topped with blue-and-white tiled domes. On the western side of the square is the imposing, early twentieth-century **Casa de Gobierno**, pleasingly harmonious with its two rows of porticoes along the facade, topped with an elegant slate mansard roof, and Art Nouveau detailing.

Much more interesting is the **Museo Folklórico**, around the corner at Avenida 24 de Septiembre (daily 9am–12.30pm & 5.30–8.30pm; $1). Its quaintly eclectic collection is housed in a beautiful Neocolonial house, around an overgrown patio, and ranges from *mate* ware and textiles, including the typical local lace, known as "randas", to an exquisite set of traditional musical instruments, including the little banjos or *charangos* made of mulita shell – a small species of armadillo – and *bombo* drums made of cardón cactus wood.

Two blocks south of the cathedral, at Congreso 151, is the **Casa Histórica de la Independencia** (Mon–Fri 10am–6pm, Sat & Sun 1–7pm; $3; free guided tours in the morning). Behind the gleaming white facade, between two grilled windows and mock-Baroque spiralling columns, the mighty *quebracho* doors lead into a series of large patios, draped with bougainvillea, jasmine and tropical creepers. This house, originally built for Francisca Bazán de Laguna, a leading Tucumán noblewoman, at the end of the eighteenth century, was where Argentina declared its independence from Spain and its first Congress was held. Most of it was demolished in the late nineteenth century, however – this replica was completed in the 1940s. Now a national monument, it houses a fine collection, spanning three centuries, of armour, furniture, paintings, silverware and porcelain, while a rather kitsch but nonetheless interesting sound-and-light show in Spanish (daily 8pm; closed Thurs; $4; tickets from the tourist information office on Plaza Independencia) re-enacts the story of how the country gained its independence.

To the north of Plaza Independencia, Calle 25 de Mayo leads to the leafy, well-heeled barrio around Plaza Urquiza, past trendy boutiques and cafés, to a set of three Neoclassical landmarks, the **Casino**, **Legislatura** and **Teatro San Martín**. On the way, at the corner of Córdoba, you pass one of Argentina's most impressive **post offices**, built in the 1930s to a curious design that recalls the civic buildings of Renaissance Tuscany, complete with a castellated tower.

Eating, drinking and nightlife

There are plenty of places to **eat**, some trendy bars and cafés in downtown, especially up Calle 25 de Mayo, and a number of **nightspots** mostly located in the chic neighbourhood of **Yerba Buena**, three or four kilometres west of the centre, on slightly higher ground. **Discos** change name and location at the drop of a hat, so ask around.

El Alto de la Lechuza 24 de Septiembre 1199. One of the oldest *peñas*, or traditional music venues, in the country – there's great improvised music in an ancient building where the empanadas are particularly succulent. It's busy till late every day Wed–Sun.

Cilantro Monteagudo 541. Fusion food and an excellent wine list at this highly regarded – and very fashionable – restaurant. Leave room for dessert and one of the delicious liqueurs on offer. Closed Sun dinner.

Il Postino Córdoba 501 and 25 de Mayo. A reliable pizzeria, also serving good pasta, in a laid-back atmosphere.

Millennium Bistró Av Aconquija 1702, Yerba Buena. A popular, trendy pre-disco restaurant, bar and tearoom all rolled into one, with fashionable decor, in the cool heights of suburban Yerba Buena.

Pizzeria lo Salta 602. Vying for the best pizza award, this place bakes its pizzas in a wood oven and shows more than usual imagination with the toppings.

Plaza de Almas Maipú 791. Popular place where locals flock to see the latest art exhibition, or just have a drink among friends. It also serves sandwiches, pizzas and other simple dishes.

Setimio Vinoteca & Wine Bar Santa Fe 512. As the full name suggests, this is a place that takes it wine seriously – either sample it by the glassful with a hearty *picada* or enjoy the braised lamb and other fine dishes with a bottle of top-quality malbec or syrah.

Listings

Airlines Aerolíneas Argentinas, 9 de Julio 110 ⓣ0381/431-1030.

Exchange Noroeste Cambios, San Martín 771.

Internet access *Locutorios* all around the city offer Internet services.

Laundry Lavadero 25, 25 de Mayo 950.

Post office 9 de Julio and Córdoba.

Tafí del Valle, Amaicha and Quilmes

Some of the Northwest's finest scenery is within easy reach of Tucumán. Nothing can provide a more startling contrast than the steep ascent from the steamy lowlands, through the tangled mossy jungle of the Selva Tucumana, up to **Tafí del Valle** amid the bare mountains of the Sierra del Aconquija. An unusual museum, at **Amaicha**, and a restored pre-Inca fortress, at **Quilmes**, are the attractions in the far west of Tucumán Province, at the southern end of the Valles Calchaquíes (see p.443), on the other side of the sierra. While these are included in classic day-trips from Tucumán, you may wish to stay over in Tafí or Quilmes.

Tafí de Valle

TAFÍ DEL VALLE, 128km west of Tucumán by RP-307 – which turns off RN-38 at Acheral, 42km southwest of the provincial capital – makes an ideal alternative stopover to Tucumán itself, especially in the summer when the city swelters, or a cool day-trip. The dramatic journey lifts you out of the moist lowlands of eastern Tucumán Province, emerald-green sugar plantations as far as the eye can see, up through the tangled mass of **Selva Tucumana** – ablaze with blossom from September to December – to the dry steppe of the highland valley that gives Tafí its name. As RP-307 snakes up steep jungle-clad cliffs, it offers fewer and fewer glimpses of the subtropical plains way below, where the sugar fields look increasingly like paddyfields and the individual trees of the citrus orchards resemble the dots of a pointillist painting. At 2000m, the road levels off and skirts the eastern bank of **Dique la Angostura**, a large reservoir; the often-snowy peak of extinct volcano **Cerro Pelao**, 2680m, is mirrored in the lake's still surface. If you head in a westerly direction towards Potrerillo along RP-355, a signposted turning to El Mollar brings you to the **Parque de los Menhires**, where a number of engraved **monoliths**, deceptively Celtic-looking in appearance – but in fact the work of the Tafí tribes who farmed the area around two thousand years ago – have been planted haphazardly in a field. They used to be scattered decoratively on an exposed hill overlooking the lake at La Angostura, but weathering and graffiti led the authorities to move the historic standing stones to a safer, but not aesthetically pleasing, location.

From the turn-off to Potrerillo, RP-307 continues north to reach Tafí del Valle itself, a sprawling village in the western lee of the Sierra del Aconquija, and sandwiched between the Rio del Chusquí and the Río Blanquita, both of which flow into the Río Tafí and then into the reservoir. Although blue and sunny skies are virtually guaranteed year-round, occasionally thick fog descends into the valley in the winter, making its alpine setting feel bleak and inhospitable. While Tafí is a favourite weekend and summer retreat for Tucumanos – the average temperature is 12°C lower than in the city – there's very little to do here except explore the surrounding mountains and riverbanks, but the trekking is very rewarding. Popular trails go up **Cerro El Matadero** (3050m; 5hr), **Cerro Pabellón** (3770m; 4hr), **Cerro Muñoz** (4437m; one day) and **Mala-Mala** (3500m; 8hr); go with a guide, as the weather is unpredictable. The town's main streets, lime-tree-lined Avenida San Martín, and avenidas Gobernador Critto and Diego de Rojas (Av Perón on some maps), converge on the semicircular plaza, around which most of the hotels, restaurants, cafés and shops are concentrated. Across the Río Tafí, 1km from the Plaza, the **Capilla Jesuítica de la Banda** (Mon–Fri 10am–6pm, Sat & Sun 9am–noon; $1; guided tours), is a late eighteenth-century Jesuit building now housing archeological finds, mostly ceramic urns, from nearby digs, plus some items of furniture and modest paintings from the colonial period. Famous for its delicious cow's and goat's cheese, available at small farms and stalls all around the town, Tafí holds a lively **Fiesta Nacional del Queso**, with folk music and dancing and rock bands, in early February.

Arrival and information

Buses from Tucumán, Santa María and Cafayate arrive at the terminal on the corner of avenidas San Martín and Gobernador Campero (Ⓣ03867/421025). Information can just about be gleaned from the **tourist office** on the south-eastern edge of the main square (Ⓣ03867/421020, Ⓦwww.tafidelvalle.com), though you are better off heading for *La Cumbre* hostel (see below).

Accommodation

Accommodation in Tafí is plentiful, and often very good, ranging from a very comfortable hostel to luxurious lodgings offering haute cuisine. Rooms can get booked up at weekends in the summer, and during the cheese festival (early Feb) will be like gold dust. There is a campsite, *Los Sauzales* (Ⓣ03867/421084), at Los Palenques on the banks of Río El Churqui.

Estancia Las Carreras RP-325 Km13 Ⓣ03867/4214732, Ⓦwww.estancialascarreras.com. Rather a way from the village centre, this traditional Jesuit estancia is very much a family-oriented place. Guests have contact with farm animals, dogs and horses; there's a cheese dairy on the premises; and rooms are large and beautifully decorated, with lots of locally produced textiles. ❻

Estancia Los Cuartos Juan Calchaquí Ⓣ03867/421444, Ⓦwww.estancialoscuartos.com. A truly *criollo* estancia experience – you can even visit for the day (including lunch and horse ride, for $120) – at this traditional family home conveniently located right next to the bus terminal. There are seven charming rooms in the long galleried *casco* or in a more recent extension. ❺

Hospedaje Celia Correa Belgrano 443 Ⓣ03867/421170. The pick of the budget options, it has basic but en-suite rooms. ❷

Hostel La Cumbre Av Presidente Perón 120 Ⓣ03867/421768, Ⓦwww.lacumbretafidelvalle.com. Tafí's hostel – highly recommended – is in a Neocolonial house built on two floors around a bright patio, all painted yellow; it doubles up as a de facto information office, a million times better than the official one, plus an adventure travel tour company, Yungas. ❷

Hostería ACA Sol del Valle San Martín and Gobernador Campero Ⓣ03867/421027, Ⓔtafi@soldelvalle.com.ar. This well-refurbished institution is excellent value, and the bright, clean and comfortable rooms have been jazzed up into life. Also a very good restaurant on the premises. ❻

Hostería Castillo de Piedra La Banda s/n Ⓣ03867/421199. This fabulously professional place is a quaint stone mock castle on the outside, but has designer-magazine rooms on the inside, with exquisite furnishings, great views, a swimming pool, a sauna and, above all, a gourmet restaurant – call ahead if you are not staying at the *hostería* but want to come for a meal. ❽

Hostería Huayra Puca Los Menhires 71 Ⓣ03867/421190, Ⓦwww.huayrapuca.com.ar. Unpretentious place with characterful, spacious, centrally heated rooms, soothing decor, unobjectionable artwork and a fine bar/*confitería*. ❻

Eating and drinking

The best **places to eat**, apart from the wonderful restaurant at the *Castillo de Piedra* (call ahead to book; Ⓣ03867/421199), are *El Portal de Tafí*, on Avenida Diego de Rojas; *La Rueda*, on Avenida Gobernador Critto; and *Rancho de Félix*, at avenidas Diego de Rojas and Belgrano, south of the plaza; they all serve local dishes plus *parrilladas* in a cosy alpine atmosphere. *El Parador Tafinista*, on the corner of avenidas Gobernador Critto and Diego de Rojas, dishes up hefty portions of pasta and grilled meat. For scrumptious coffees, teas, cakes, scones and, above all, *alfajores*, head for *El Blanquito*, a fabulous tearoom with outside tables on the road towards Amaicha.

Amaicha

To get to the village of **AMAICHA**, take RP-307, which zigzags northwards from Tafí, offering views of the *embalse* and the mountains – but be warned that low cloud often persists here, so you might be penetrating a blanket of thick fog instead – and heaves you over the windswept pass at Abra del Infiernillo (3042m). From here, the road steeply winds back down, along the banks of the

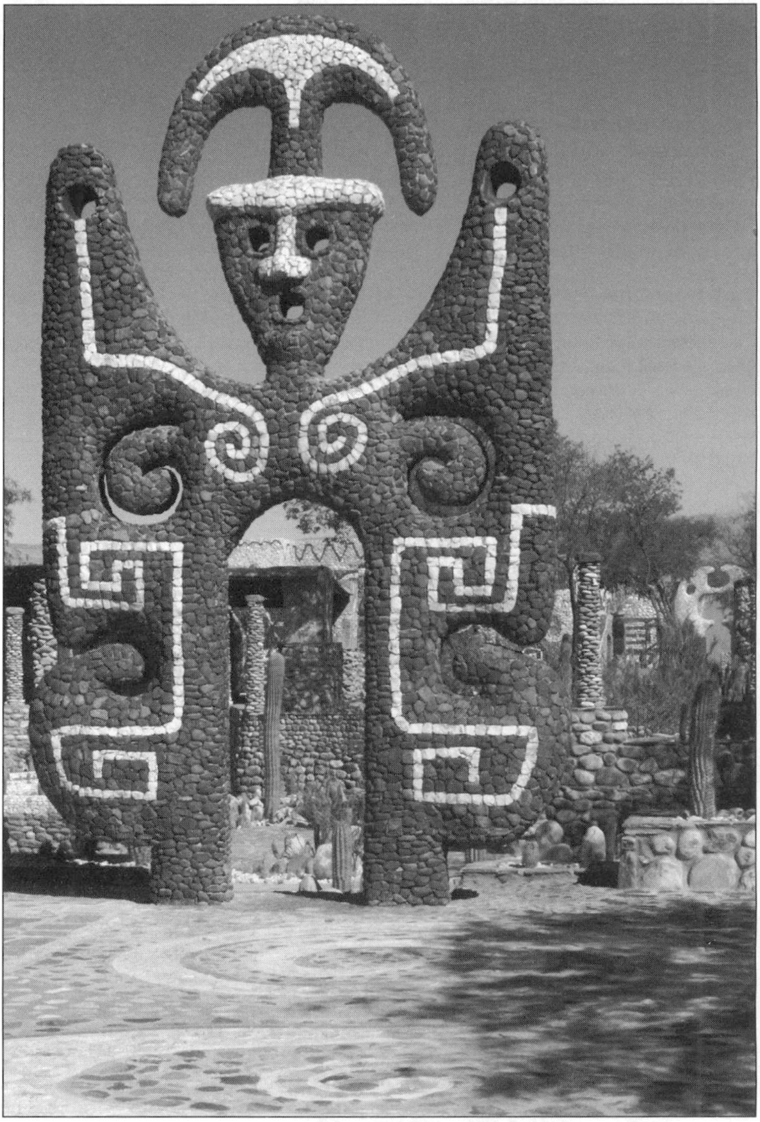

△ Museo Pachamama, Amaicha

Río de Amaicha. It takes you through arid but impressive landscapes thickly covered with a forest of cardón cacti, with the Cumbres Calchaquíes to the east and the Sierra de Quilmes ahead of you, until you reach Amaicha itself. The peaceful, nondescript little place livens up during the **Fiesta de la Pachamama** in carnival week, when dancers and musicians lay on shows, while locals enact, in a kind of pre-Columbian Passion Play, the roles of the different pagan deities: Pachamama herself – Mother Earth, confused rather incongruously in the animist-Christian fusion with the Virgin Mary; as well as Ñusta, the goddess of fertility; Yastay, the god of hunting; and Pujllay, a faun-like sprite representing joyful festivity. Little stalls spring up along the main streets, selling food, drink and crafts. Along with a number of small eateries serving delicious *locro*, is the *Casa de Piedra*, offers something to eat year-round; it also sells local crafts.

Just 200m along the road from the village centre, near the junction with RP-357, is the splendid **Museo Pachamama** (daily 8.30am–1pm & 2–6pm; $6). The brainchild of local artist Héctor Cruz, it's actually several museums rolled into one, and it's worth a look to see the structure itself, built around fabulous cactus gardens and incorporating eye-catching stone mosaics, depicting llamas, pre-Hispanic symbols and geometric patterns. Each large room in turn displays an impressive array of local archeological finds, the well-executed reconstruction of a mine along with impressive samples of various precious and semi-precious ores and minerals extracted in the area, plus paintings, tapestries and ceramics from Cruz's own workshops, to modern designs inspired by pre-Columbian artistic traditions.

Beyond Amaicha, RP-307 veers westwards before running south to Santa María, in Catamarca Province, from where you can travel down to Belén (see p.494) and Andalgalá (see p.493), whereas RP-357, a straight well-surfaced road, takes you northwest for 15km to RN-40, which heads north along the west bank of the Río Calchaquí towards Quilmes (see below) and Cafayate (see p.446). The regular **buses** from Tafí to Quilmes and Cafayate will drop you off by Amaicha's museum.

Quilmes

Just 3km north of the RP-357/RN-40 junction, 15km north of Amaicha, is the westward turn-off to the major pre-Inca **archeological site** of **Quilmes**, one of the most extensively restored in the country. **Buses** to Cafayate running along RN-40 will drop you at the junction, leaving you with the 5km trek along the dusty side road to the site (daily 9am–dusk; $5). Inhabited since the ninth century AD, the settlement of Quilmes had a population of over 3000 at its peak in the seventeenth century, but the whole Quilmes tribe was punished mercilessly by the Spanish colonizers for resisting evangelization and enslavement. Walls and many buildings in this terraced **pukará**, or pre-Columbian fortress, have been thoroughly, if not always expertly, excavated and reconstructed, and the overall effect is extremely impressive, especially in the morning light, when the mountains behind it are illuminated from the east and turn bright orange. The entrance fee also entitles you to visit the site **museum**, which contains some items found here, such as ceramics and stone tools, and displays more expensive modern crafts by Héctor Cruz, who now owns the site and the luxurious *Hotel Ruinas de Quilmes* (Ⓣ03892/421075; ❻), on the same grounds as the site – it offers llama rides, a decent *confitería* and very comfortable, spacious rooms, giving wonderful views of the site, affording you the opportunity to see it at its early-morning best; unfortunately, the otherwise enticing swimming pool is very prone to wasps.

Santiago del Estero

SANTIAGO DEL ESTERO – 150km southeast of San Miguel de Tucumán, in the transition between the Central Sierras and the Northwest – is the easy-going capital of the dreary, flat and impoverished province of the same name. For many people it's the entrance to the Northwest region and, although you won't be tempted to linger for long, it has one good museum, reputedly the best folk music in the country and some lively evening entertainment.

Francisco de Aguirre founded "the Noble and Royal City of Santiago del Estero" – Argentina's oldest – on St James' Day 1553, after various false starts due to earthquakes, attacks by the indigenous inhabitants, repeated floods and petty administrative squabbles with officials in Chile. Aguirre's city was located at a relatively safe distance from the capricious Río Dulce and, in 1577, was made capital of the region of Tucumán, a home base for founding the other major cities in Northwest Argentina. Over the years, it surrendered its religious and secular privileges in turn to San Miguel de Tucumán, Córdoba and, later, Buenos Aires and, despite the nineteenth-century advent of the railway and large influxes of immigrants, it never got its act together. Later floods and other natural disasters account for the paucity of colonial architecture in the modern city while poor planning, a series of criminally negligent *caudillo* governments (dominated by provincial strongmen more interested in nepotism than democracy) and acute administrative inefficiency have compounded Santiago's failure to hit upon an agricultural or industrial answer to its economic woes. Since the last *caudillos* were removed by President Kirchner in 2005, things have started to improve. Cotton remains the province's main crop, grown in nearby *bañados* or seasonally flooded plantations, painfully dependent on efficient

irrigation, and on commodity prices. Santiago remains a scruffy place, though, many of its streets becoming quagmires when it rains, while the rest are riddled with potholes. Given the city's hot and sticky subtropical summers, the siesta is sacrosanct here, and even in the cooler winters life is lived at a slow, gentle pace. Of little interest to foreign tourists, for Argentines the main attraction of the city is a rare authenticated **copy of the Turin Shroud**, on display at the Iglesia San Domingo and visited by thousands of pilgrims every year.

Arrival and information

The **airport**, Mal Paso, is 6km northwest of the central Plaza Libertad, on Av Madre de Ciudades (Ⓣ0385/422-2386). To get to the centre either take a **taxi** or the #19 bus. It is planned that the abysmally run-down **bus terminal** (Ⓣ0385/434-0337) at Pedro León Gallo 480, two blocks south and five west of Plaza Libertad, should be replaced by a super modern terminal out of town in 2008. Buses run to most regional destinations and some further afield. Unless you are staying in a nearby hotel or *residencial*, hop into one of the many taxis – they're very inexpensive. Within the city you are unlikely to need transport other than to reach the campsite in the Parque Aguirre – any bus going along Avenida Libertad and marked with the park's name will get you there. For basic **information** – maps, accommodation details but not much else – the city and provincial tourist offices (Mon–Fri 7am–1pm & 3–9pm, Sat & Sun 10am–1pm & 6–9pm; Ⓣ0385/422-6777, Ⓦwww.sde.gov.ar/turismo) are conveniently in the same fine Art Nouveau house next to the Jefatura de Policía, on the north side of Plaza Libertad.

Accommodation

There's a dearth of decent **accommodation** in town; the better hotels cater mainly for a business clientele, very expensive for what they are and often booked up during the week, while some of the more modest ones double up as *albergues transitorios*. The nicest hotel in town is *Hotel Carlos V* (Ⓣ0385/424-0303, Ⓦwww.carlosvhotel.com; ❼), at Independencia, centrally located at the corner of the central plaza; the covered swimming pool is a boon, when they bother to look after it, while the rooms are quite elegant in a provincial way, especially the suites that cost upwards of $500. However, breakfast is disappointing and service is poor. *Hotel Centro*, 9 de Julio 131–137 (Ⓣ0385/421-9502, Ⓦwww.hotelcentro.com.ar; ❺), is more keenly priced but its dour concrete exterior is not greatly outshone by its bland interior – clean and comfortable are the kindest words to describe it. The best value is to be found at *Hotel Savoy* (Ⓣ0385/421-1234; ❸), which has more charm than the other two put together, with neat if rather cramped rooms, and is in a fine Neoclassical building at the beginning of pedestrianized Calle Tucumán, at no. 39. A bunch of *residenciales* are handily located near the bus station, but none of them is outstanding and some are downright squalid; the most commendable is the spruce *Santa Rita*, Santa Fe 273 (Ⓣ0385/422-0625; ❷). It's no great shakes, but is fine for a night if you don't mind the garish yellow decor. Campers are well catered for, however, in the (mosquito-friendly) Parque Aguirre: campsite *Las Casuarinas* has good facilities in a green location on the banks of the Río Dulce.

The City

Santiago's **grid system** is a slightly irregular one and not all of its thoroughfares run straight, starting with the dog-legged main drag, Avenida Belgrano, the city's north–south axis, divided into Avenida Belgrano Norte (N) and Sur (S); the main east–west street is Avenida Libertad. Being flat and compact, the city centre is easy to find your way around, however: leafy **Plaza Libertad** is the city's commercial and social hub. Some pleasant **cafés** line the square's south and east flanks, while the luxuriant trees and shrubs provide shade, especially welcome in December and January. The **cathedral**, on the west side of the square, was inaugurated in 1877, and is the fifth to be built on the site of Argentina's very first cathedral. Its biscuit-coloured facade, in a rather self-consciously Neo-classical style, is instantly forgettable and the twin towers look out of proportion. Far more attractive is the **Jefatura de Policía**, usually erroneously referred to as the Cabildo, because its white facade resembles the colonial cabildos of Buenos Aires and Córdoba, and easily the most striking building on the whole square: the lower storey is decorated by a series of elegant arches and the upper floor by a row of Ionic columns. The **Mercado Armonia**, one block north on Pellegrini, lies at the city's commercial hub, along pedestrianized Avenida Hipólito Yrigoyen. Housed in an impressive building dating from the 1930s, the market stalls are heaped with bright fruit and vegetables, herbs and spices, local sweetmeats and other exotic produce, making it one of the city's highlights.

Two blocks east of Plaza Libertad, along Calle Avellaneda immediately before the corner with Calle 25 de Mayo, stands the bombastic Neoclassical edifice housing not only the **Teatro 25 de Mayo**, but also, in the left wing, the **Legislatura Provincial**. In the same building, at Avellaneda 355, unscathed but in need of some updating, is the fascinating and potentially fabulous **Museo Arqueológico Emilio y Duncan Wagner** (Mon–Fri 8am–noon & 2–8pm; \$2; free guided visits). This is the collection of a French diplomat and his sons, whose main interests were the archeology, paleontology, ethnography and folklore of the Santiago region, especially its rich pre-Columbian and post-colonial history. Really more an anthropological museum, it contains exhibits of local textiles and crafts as well as archeological finds. Ceramics are the mainstay, mostly vases, urns and figurines, tracing the artistic development of the Tonocote and Juríes tribes, from the primitive Mercedes period (300–700 AD) – mostly rather squat, unadorned pots – through the vividly coloured Suchituyoj period (800–1400 AD), with a predominance of zoomorphic figures such as snakes and owls representing the elements, to the more sophisticated designs, more elegant forms, very subtle colours and richer glaze of the Averías period (1100–1500 AD).

Eating, drinking and nightlife

There's not much in the way of choice when it comes to **restaurants** and **cafés**, but you're unlikely to be spending very long here, after all. The best food in town is at *Nicomedes*, at Roca (S) 570, where polite waiters serve well-prepared gourmet fare in interior-design magazine surroundings; the caramelized pork is particularly good. *Mia Mamma*, 24 de Septiembre 15, is a reliable plaza-side *parrilla*, also serving pasta, as the name suggests, and fresh salads. *Heladeria Cerecet*, at Avenida Libertad and Córdoba, is one of several Italian-style ice-cream parlours, serving fantastic flavours in no-nonsense surroundings. On the east side of Plaza Libertad, the *Jockey Club* is one of the more sedate cafés on the main square, with beautiful wooden tables and a clubbish atmosphere.

At weekends, young Santiagueños like to let their hair down at their favourite **nightclub**, and Santiago has a long folk tradition that has spawned a couple of lively joints, surprisingly full even on week-nights. The *Peña Casa del Folklorista*, Av Vargas s/n, puts on folk-music shows at weekends, aimed at locals and tourists alike, but retains an authentic atmosphere. Dedicated folk fans should head out to the *Peña Siete Algarrobos* at Bolivia 785 and Aguirre – definitely not catering for foreigners. Better still, time your visit for a Sunday, when one of the region's top folk venues comes into its own. *El Patio del Indio Froilán* (Ⓦwww.indiofroilan.desantiago.net.ar), several kilometres out to the north of the city, past the hippodrome and the Boca del Tigre campsite, opens its doors around lunch time but really gets going in the late afternoon and evening, when live music and dancing accompany much eating and drinking, all presided over by El Indio himself, widely regarded as the greatest maker of the *bombo* – traditional drum – in the country.

Listings

Airlines Aerolíneas Argentinas, 24 de Septiembre 547 ⓣ03833/422-4335.
Banks and exchange Various banks around the main square.
Internet access At *locutorios* in the centre.
Laundry Lavadero Laveya, Av Belgrano Sur 888.
Post office 9 de Julio and Buenos Aires.

San Fernando del Valle de Catamarca

The wedge-shaped province of Catamarca, immediately west of Tucumán and Santiago del Estero, is one of the country's poorest and most thinly populated. Nearly half of its population of a quarter of a million live in the quiet capital, **SAN FERNANDO DEL VALLE DE CATAMARCA**, often just called Catamarca, the smallest of all the Northwest's provincial capitals and the youngest, founded in 1683. A little over 230km south of Tucumán along RN-38, and slightly less from Santiago del Estero along RN-64, the city lies at the end of a long, flat valley that gives it its name, loomed over by high mountains on all sides. The majestic, green-sloped Sierra de Graciana to the north climbs steeply to over 1500m; to the east, the Sierra de Anacasti, or Sierra del Alto, is higher still, while the stark, honey-brown Sierra de Ambato forms an all but impenetrable barrier to the northwest, peaking at Cerro El Manchao (4351m). With few sights of its own, Catamarca is the ideal base for exploring the province's undeservedly ignored **hinterland**, mostly deserted altiplano, with some of the most hauntingly dramatic scenery in the whole of Argentina. In the second half of July, the city hosts one of Argentina's major folk festivals, the **Festival Nacional del Poncho**, which is also a gathering for the region's outstanding artisans, along with some of the country's most popular folk musicians; it takes place every year in the third week of the month. But the main reason for stopping over in Catamarca is to get your bearings before heading for the transitional valleys around Andalgalá, Belén and Londres, to the west. From there you can climb up to the almost disturbingly remote and staggeringly authentic altiplano settlement of Antofagasta de la Sierra (see p.498), and its stark surroundings, or to the fabulous Paso de San Francisco, via the charming spa village of Fiambalá (see p.501).

Some history

The valleys of present-day Catamarca Province have been inhabited for some 10,000 years, though the earliest known settlements date back only two millennia. The Calchaquí tribes of the **Diaguita** people, whose territory stretched north as far as San Antonio de los Cobres in Salta Province, built their villages and fortresses in the area around Belén and Pomán, and lived peacefully until they were dominated by the Inca in the late fifteenth century. Considerably weakened, they still managed to harass the Spanish colonizers enough to prevent them from establishing any major town in the area until after the Guerras Calchaquíes (see box, p.498), a drawn-out rebellion that kept the invaders on their toes until the late seventeenth century. Only on July 5, 1683, did the governor of Tucumán, Fernando Mate de Luna, found the city of San Fernando, to be capital of the new province of Catamarca, established only four years earlier. When Buenos Aires became the national capital, Catamarca felt the pinch more than most provinces, and the government's decision to shelve a project to link it by rail to Chile dealt it a severe blow. Cotton and wool have

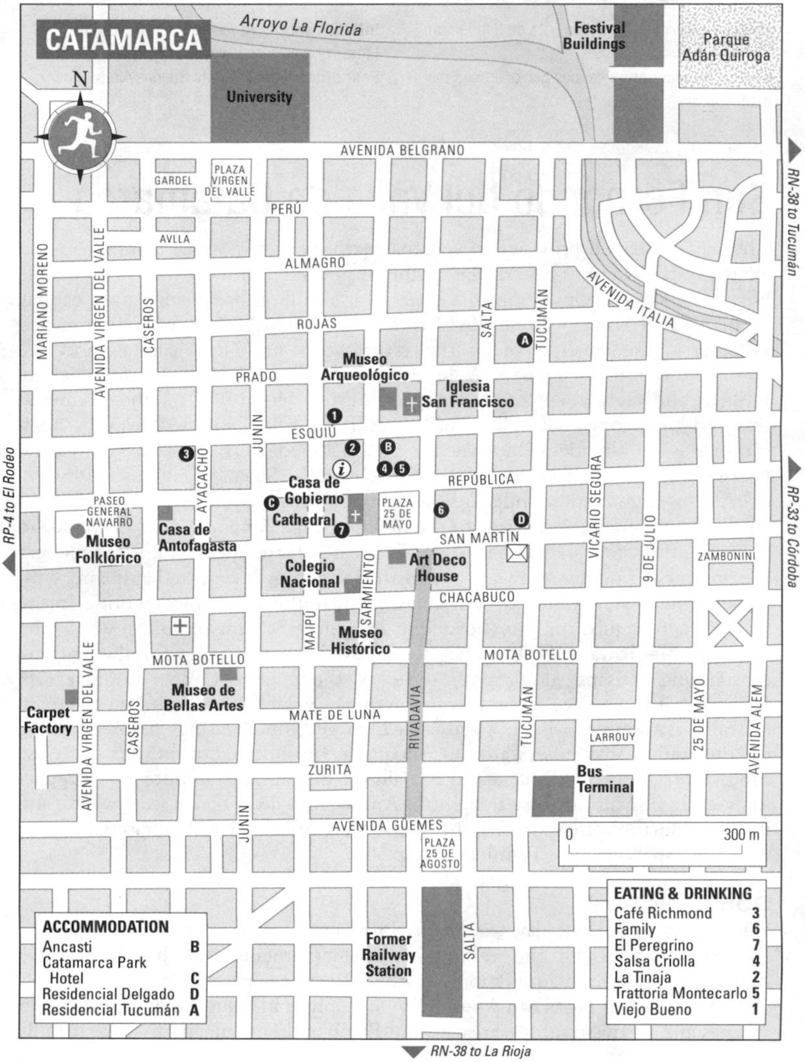

earned it a meagre income over the past three centuries while agriculture in the fertile valley is mostly aimed at local self-sufficiency in staple products such as oil, meat and cereals. Sizeable gold, silver, copper and bauxite deposits are exploited by multinationals.

Arrival and information

Catamarca's location in a narrow valley meant that its **airport**, Aeropuerto Felipe Varela (Ⓣ03833/430080), had to be built 22km south, on a service road off RP-33, in the direction of San Martín. A **taxi** will charge around $25 to $30. Catamarca has a modern **bus terminal** (Ⓣ03833/437577), six blocks south and three east of central **Plaza 25 de Mayo**, at Avenida Güemes and Tucumán. In addition to a *locutorio*, restaurant and left-luggage office, it boasts shops selling everything from children's clothes to cactus-wood lampshades. Plenty of taxis wait outside.

Staff at the provincial **tourist office** (daily 8am–9pm; Ⓣ03833/437593, Ⓦwww.turismocatamarca.gov.ar), on Calle República, half a block west of Plaza 25 de Mayo, do their best despite the lack of resources and can supply a map of sorts and an accommodation list. If you plan to visit Antofagasta de la Sierra (see p.498) you would do well to visit the extremely enthusiastic **Casa de Antofagasta** at República 119 (Ⓣ03833/422300).

Accommodation

Accommodation in Catamarca is thin on the ground, mostly aimed at the business traveller and especially limited at the lower end of the market, though a couple of the cheaper *residenciales* are all right for a night or two. Usually you'll have no trouble finding a room, but for the Poncho Festival (late July) and the two pilgrimages to the Virgen del Valle, the week after Easter and, more so, from December 8 to 16, when over 30,000 people converge on Catamarca, hotels are booked up well in advance.

The nearest **campsite** to the city is the municipal one at *La Quebrada*, 5km out along RP-4, the road to El Rodeo. It's well located, with a *balneario* on the banks of the Río El Tala, but can get extremely busy and in the hotter, wetter months, from December to March, mosquitoes are also a problem; facilities include a *confitería*. The #101 bus from the bus terminal, via the Convento San Francisco, runs here.

Catamarca Park Hotel República 347 Ⓣ03833/425444, Ⓦwww.amerian.com. Smart, sleek and modern, with bright public areas, commodious rooms and a swimming pool. ⑦

Hotel Ancasti Sarmiento 520 Ⓣ03833/431464. Venerable hotel that has been tastefully renovated and boasts a stylish café/restaurant, spacious bedrooms and is very central. ⑤

Residencial Delgado San Martín 788 Ⓣ03833/426109. Basic rooms with private bathrooms. Much more appealing inside than out. ②

Residencial Tucumán Tucumán 1040 Ⓣ03833/422209. Nothing much to report about this tidy, clean, well-run *residencial* apart from the startlingly bright red bedcovers. ②

The City

Orientation in mostly flat Catamarca, with its typical grid plan, poses no problems: the compact microcentro is bounded by avenidas Além to the east, Güemes to the south, Belgrano to the north and Virgen del Valle to the west. In the long summer months, you'll soon get into the swing of taking a siesta to survive the blistering afternoon heat, which is why the shady vegetation of the city's epicentre, **Plaza 25 de Mayo**, is so welcome. A creation of Argentina's favourite landscape architect, Charles Thays (see box, p.130), the square is slovenly kept but its palms, orange trees, acacia-like tipas and pot-bellied *palos borrachos* are luxuriant. At the western end of the square stands the late nineteenth-century **cathedral**, housing one of the most venerated images in the whole of Argentina. Hovering between brick-red and rich terracotta, depending on the light, the colour is the best thing about its unoriginal Neoclassical facade, but the blue-tiled cupolas are also striking. To the left of the cathedral is a passage leading to the **Camarín** (daily 7am–noon & 5–8pm; free), a specially built chamber where a hideously kitsch statue of the **Virgen del Valle** is kept, crowned by a priceless diamond-studded diadem. This Virgin appeared before locals in the nineteenth century, rather like the miracle of Lourdes, and ever since has been the subject of mass pilgrimages and devotion. The extravagant construction of white marble, gold and stained glass is served by a double staircase, to cope with the huge crowds who file past the Virgin on her feast day on December 16. The other three sides of Plaza San Martín are lined with shops, cafés and restaurants, mostly built in a nondescript style, but on the southern side, at San Martín 543, you'll see a beautifully proportioned **Art Deco house**, and next to it a harmonious Neo-Renaissance building, built in the style very much in vogue in Argentina at the end of the nineteenth century.

At Sarmiento 450, two blocks north of the cathedral, the **Museo Arqueológico Adán Quiroga** (Mon–Fri 8am–2pm & 3.30–8pm, Sat & Sun 10am–7pm; $1) is potentially superb, but its musty and dull presentation lets it down. The museum actually comprises six sections, of which the archeological display is by far the best. It includes some exquisite black ceramics from the Aguada people, with some very fine abstract geometric detailing inscribed in paler pigments, typical of the so-called Middle Period (600–900 AD), which would look fabulous if properly exhibited. The intriguing ceramics of the earlier but by no means primitive Cóndor-Huasi, Ciénaga and Alamito cultures (500 BC–500 AD) are also represented here, including animal and human figurines, urns, vases and pots, and intricate statues, along with ancient mummies kept in antique fridges and some very fine carved stone. The other five sections – colonial history, natural history, iconography, philately and numismatology – respectively consist of little more than all-too-familiar jumbles of leather trunks and spurs, stuffed birds, mediocre statues of saints, dreary stamps and coins and Esquiú memorabilia.

One of the country's most curious religious relics is the shrivelled heart of local hero **Fray Mamerto Esquiú** (the rest of his corpse is in Córdoba cathedral) – a revolutionary cleric and fiery orator famous for speeches in favour of the country's new constitution in the mid-nineteenth century – kept in a delicate glass case in the right-hand aisle of **Iglesia San Franscisco**, one block east of the museum at Esquiú and Rivadavia. The church was designed by Luigi Giorgi, the Italian architect of Salta's sumptuous Franciscan church. Far less exuberant in design and colour than Salta's, Catamarca's church nonetheless has a handsome late Baroque facade, painted pale salmon and off-white, and despite its anti-seismic robustness – the previous church collapsed, along with many other buildings in the city, during a powerful earthquake in 1873 – manages to convey an airy elegance, contrasted with the fierce puce of the over-elaborate interior.

Way over to the west of the microcentro, at the far end of Calle Mota Botello, the **Feria Artesanal** (daily 8am–9pm; free) displays and sells some of the province's finest traditional products, from delicious sugared walnuts and grape jelly to some of the finest ponchos in Argentina (see box opposite) together with expensive jewellery made of rhodochrosite (see box, p.493) and musical instruments. You can also see attractive traditional rugs being woven on the looms in the showroom at the Fábrica de Alfambras, half a block south. Three blocks north, on the Paseo General Navarro, a mini-park at the western end of Avenida República, the curious **Museo Folklórico Juan Alfonso Carrizo** (Mon–Fri 8am–1pm & 3–8pm, Sat & Sun 9am–noon & 4–8pm; free) is easily spotted thanks to the ostentatiously outsized replica of the Virgen del Valle's diamond-studded crown above it. The extensive display of traditional Catamarcan objects includes some fine pottery, fascinating musical instruments (including *bombos*, or large drums, and *sikus*, or reed-flutes), weaving-looms and brandy-stills.

Eating and drinking

Catamarca is not gastronomically exciting, but it does have a few **restaurants** worth trying. You'll find some fast-food joints along pedestrianized Calle Rivadavia, while the **cafés** are grouped around Plaza 25 de Mayo. *Café Richmond*, República 534, is a slightly old-fashioned but popular plaza café, serving excellent coffee and decent breakfasts. *El Peregrino*, San Martín 446, churns out traditional empanadas, tasty pasta and simple dishes, while *Family*, Rivadavia 640, is Catamarca's best pizzeria – it will never win prizes for originality, but the food tastes good and is cheap. At *La Tinaja*, Sarmiento 533, live music at weekends sometimes adds to the otherwise calm ambience at this reasonably priced *parrilla*, the finest restaurant in the city, if only for its juicy meat. *Salsa Criolla*, República 542 (closed Mon), dishes up traditional Argentine *criollo* food, as the name suggests, with an excellent-value *menú ejecutivo*. *Viejo*

Catamarca's handicrafts

Catamarca's National Poncho Festival draws not only Argentina's major folk musicians but also the country's leading craftspeople. The Catamarcan town of Belén is the country's self-styled **Poncho Capital** and some of its textiles, mostly made of llama, alpaca and sheep's wool, are works of art – and don't come cheap. While Salta produces its distinctive red ponchos and Jujuy has a preference for deep blue, the weavers of Catamarca go for natural tones, using the wool's blacks, greys, browns and whites, occasionally dying the yarn using vegetable pigments, with ochre, yellow and maroon being the most frequent colourings. The best ponchos sell for at least $500–800. Catamarca's weavers, many of whose workshops you can visit – in Belén, Andalgalá, Fiambalá and elsewhere – also make rugs, blankets, bedspreads, shirts, jackets, sweaters, caftans and bags, while bonnets, hats, gloves, mittens and scarves are often knitted from the much-prized silky fleece of the elegant vicuña.

The ancient art of **ceramics** is also undergoing a revival throughout the Northwest, and some of the best can be found in and around Catamarca. Many indigenous artists have resuscitated ancient pre-Columbian designs, often using museum exhibits as their models, with a preference for geometric patterns, while other potters have taken inspiration from their ancestors to produce original art. Souvenir-hunters might also consider the high-quality leatherware, especially items related to horse riding, finely woven basketware, all manner of items made of *cardón*, the giant cactus, *Trychocereus pasacana*, that flourishes at altitudes of 2000–3500m throughout the region, and musical instruments. **Instrument-makers** in Catamarca, as well as in Jujuy, Purmamarca and elsewhere, still use ancient methods to fashion flutes and pipes out of native canes and twigs, to make animal-skin drums and to turn armadillo shells into the typical little ukuleles called *chorongos*. Tubes of *cardón* cactus filled with beans to make rain-sticks, or whole mate gourds, dried with their seeds inside and embellished with ornate, abstract patterns or naive etchings of llamas, pumas and other indigenous animals, make for unusual, easily transported mementoes.

Bueno, Esquiú 480, is a dowdy but reasonably priced restaurant serving excellent river fish, including delicious trout with Roquefort. *Trattoria Montecarlo*, República 548, prepares Italian-style food, with lots of fresh pasta, best followed by the fresh fruit salad.

Listings

Airlines Aerolíneas Argentinas, Sarmiento 589 ⓣ03833/424460.
Internet access At the *locutorios* in the centre.
Laundry Marva, Prado 482.
Post office San Martín and Tucumán.

Andalgalá, Belén and Londres

Mysteriously overlooked by most visitors – no doubt because of its relative inaccessibility by public transport – Catamarca Province becomes utterly spectacular as you leave behind the populated eastern valleys and climb towards the lonely **altiplano**. Across the barrier of the Sierra de Ambato from Catamarca city lies a transitional zone of dazzling **salt-flats**, rugged highland scenery and small hamlets whose inhabitants harvest walnuts, distil fabulously grapey *aguardiente* or weave rugs and ponchos for a living. Three historic villages, **Andalgalá**, **Belén** and **Londres**, serve as useful halts and are worth a longer stop if you're venturing further into this dramatic outback; the first two have the area's only accommodation to speak of.

Up to Andalgalá

Much of the joy of Andalgalá is in the getting there, and you have a choice of three spectacular approach routes. From Catamarca, it is most easily reached by travelling southwest along RP-38 for 70km, branching northwest along the winding **Cuesta La Sébila**, part of RN-60 that cuts through the southernmost tip of the mighty Sierra del Ambato, to El Empalme, 48km away. From here RP-46 heads due north, with open views to the west across the huge **Salar de Pipanaco**, a sugary-white salt-lake stretching for nearly 60km. It's worth branching off RP-46 onto RP-25, a good dirt road that edges you closer to the crinkled western flanks of the Ambato range, taking you through farming villages such as Pomán and Rincón, where olives, oranges, vines and walnuts flourish thanks to a sophisticated network of irrigation channels, dating from pre-Columbian times. This is the route taken by the regular but infrequent buses from Catamarca to Andalgalá.

The other approaches to Andalgalá, from Tucumán and Amaicha, take you along nail-bitingly dramatic *cuestas*, or narrow mountain passes, with dozens of hairpin bends. Negotiating these narrow roller-coaster roads, with only the odd passing place shored up by stone walls that look more decorative than protective, requires absolute concentration and plenty of horn-blowing, but the views for passengers are unforgettable. The route from Tucumán, along the **Cuesta de las Chilcas**, is a continuation of RP-365 that forks off RP-38 in a westerly direction at Concepción, over 60km south of Tucumán. After skirting the northernmost point of the Sierra de la Canela you enter the mountain pass, and climb through forests of tall cacti to 1950m, with amazing views of the Salar de Pipanaco to the south, and the valley of Andalgalá to the northwest, before descending and entering Andalgalá from the east.

Rhodochrosite

Rhodochrosite is a semi-precious stone, similar to onyx but unique to Argentina. It is mined only from a generous seam in the Capillitas mine, to the north of Andalgalá. Known popularly as the Rosa del Inca – and believed by the indigenous people to be the solidified blood of their ancestors – rhodochrosite is reminiscent of Florentine paper, with its slightly blurred, marble-like veins of ruby red and deep salmon-pink, layered and rippled with paler shades of rose-pink and white. Its rarity has made it Argentina's unofficial **national stone**. Some of it is sold in luscious blocks, suitable as paperweights or book-ends, while much of it is worked into fine jewellery, none of it cheap, or into animal and bird figures, many of them kitsch. If you're searching for rhodochrosite as an unusual keepsake, your best bet is in either Andalgalá or Catamarca city, where a number of artisans specialize in fashioning it.

From the north, the **Cuesta de Capillitas** also slaloms among cacti, reaching an altitude of 3100m, in the western lee of the majestic Nevado de Candado (5450m). It's the final stage of RP-47, an initially decent track branching off RN-40, 62km south of Amaicha (see p.482), running alongside the stupendous crags of the Nevados de Aconquija and the Cerro Negro, before deteriorating into a trail as it takes you past the **rhodochrosite mines** at Capillitas, nearly 70km north of Andalgalá. Obstacles along the way include deep fords and dry riverbeds, making a 4WD preferable, and since the area is prone to sudden blizzards from May to October, this route must be attempted only after a weather-check or asking at a police checkpoint along the way.

Andalgalá

After the journey there, the next best thing about the village of **ANDALGALÁ**, 250km northwest of Catamarca by the shortest route, is its setting: dominated to the north by the hulking **El Candado** (5450m), nearly always crested with snow, by the Sierra del Ambato to the east and the Sierra de Belén to the west, it lies at a strategic crossroads, on the east bank of the Arroyo El Huaco. Middle Eastern in feel, with its many immigrants from Syria and Lebanon, laid-back cafés, busy streets and markets and mountain setting, it makes a living from cotton, potatoes, olives, fruit and spices, such as aniseed and cumin, and from the **rhodochrosite mines** (see box above) at nearby Capillitas. The local *pukará*, or fortress, and other pre-Inca sites have yielded up sufficient material for two museums, the better of which is the small **Museo Arqueológico** (Mon–Fri 8am–1pm & 5–9pm, Sat 9am–1pm; $1), at Belgrano and Mercado, a block south of the main plaza, with its shady plane and orange trees and cafés. Created with money from the Paul Getty Foundation, the museum comprises a fascinating collection of well-preserved ceramics from the Belén, Santa María and Aguada cultures, including an unusual egg-shaped funerary urn.

Buses from Catamarca stop on San Martín one block north of the main square. Three blocks to the south, just before the market, is a fledgling **tourist information office** (daily 9am–1pm & 4–8pm). Ask here about visits to the rhodochrosite mines at Capillitas. The Club Andino at San Martín 41 (Ⓣ03835/156-95716) offers trekking in the nearby mountains. **Accommodation** is a choice between overpriced but comfortable *Hotel del Turismo* (Ⓣ03835/422210; ④), with its decent restaurant, half a kilometre east of the centre on Avenida Sarmiento, and the much more basic *Residencial Galileo*,

Núñez del Prado 757 (☎03835/422268; ❷). The **campsite**, *La Aguada*, is just across the river to the west.

Belén

Just 85km west of Andalgalá, along mostly unsealed RP-46 (it can get almost impassable at times; enquire first) whose dullness is alleviated only by the Cuesta de Belén pass, the region's main settlement of **BELÉN** is squeezed between the Sierra de Belén and the river of the same name. Olive groves and plantations of capsicum – paprika-producing peppers (*pimentones*) – stretch across the fertile valley to the south. A convenient stopover, Belén offers the area's best accommodation and a couple of restaurants, and it's also a base for **adventure tourism**, including trekking and horse riding. And since Belén promotes itself as the **Capital del Poncho** you might like to visit the many excellent *teleras*, or textile workshops, dotted around the town; they also turn out beautiful blankets and sweaters made of llama, vicuña and sheep's wool, mostly in natural colours. The wool is sometimes blended with walnut bark, to give the local cloth, known as *belichas* or *belenistos*, its typical rough texture. As for **festivals**, every January 6 a pilgrimage procession clambers to a huge statue of the Virgen de Belén, overlooking the town from its high vantage point to the west, the Cerro de la Virgen.

On the western flank of its main square, **Plaza Presbítero Olmos de Aguilera**, shaded by whitewashed orange trees and bushy palms and ringed by cafés and ice-cream parlours, stands the Italianate **Iglesia Nuestra Señora de Belén**, clearly inspired by the cathedral in Catamarca and designed and built by Italian immigrants at the beginning of the twentieth century. Its brickwork is bare, without plaster or decoration, lending it a rough-hewn but not displeasing look. Housed on the first floor of a rather grim commercial arcade, at San Martín and Belgrano, half a block from the main square, the **Museo Provincial Cóndor Huasi** (Tues–Sat 8am–noon & 4–8pm; $1) has one of the country's most important collections of **Diaguita** artefacts, but is poorly laid out. The huge number of ceramics, and some bronze and silver items, trace the Diaguita culture through all four archeological "periods": the Initial Period, 300 BC–300 AD, is represented by simple but by no means primitive pieces, often in the shape of squashes or maize-cobs; in the Early Period (Cóndor Huasi and Ciénaga; 300–550 AD), anthropomorphic and zoomorphic ceramics dominate, including naive representations of llamas and pumas; the Middle or Aguada Period, 650–950 AD, produced some of the museum's most prized pieces, such as a ceramic jaguar of astonishing finesse; and the Late Period, from 1000 AD onwards, includes the so-called Santa María culture, when craftsmen produced large urns, vases and amphoras decorated with complex, mostly abstract geometric patterns, with depictions of snakes, rheas and toads. There are a few Inca artefacts, too.

Practicalities

Regular but infrequent **buses** from Catamarca, Salta and Santa María arrive at the corner of Sarmiento and Rivadavia, near the museum. For **tourist information** ask at the municipalidad, one block to the east. The best **place to stay** in the whole region is relative newcomer *Hotel Belén* (☎03835/461501, Ⓦwww.belencat.com.ar; ❸), part of a large complex that includes a convention centre and a games room-cum-cybercafé at Belgrano and Cubas – rooms are divided into Sullka (small) and Suma (large), but both are decorated in pristine white, with dark wood furnishings and amusing ethnic bathrooms, with lots of stone and ceramic tiling; there is also a clean hostel-style dorm ($10 per person without breakfast, $13 with breakfast). *Hotel Samai*, Urquiza 349, one block east and south of the main square (Ⓣ03835/461320, Ⓦwww.samaihotel.com.ar; ❸) is clean, and warm in winter (fans cool it enough in the summer), but certainly not luxurious. In the unlikely event that it's full, you can try the very basic *Hotel Gómez*, Calchaquí 213 (Ⓣ03835/461388; ❷). Most of the **restaurants** cluster around the main square. A classic favourite is *Parrillada El Único*, housed in a rustic hut at Sarmiento and General Roca, one block north of the church. It serves excellent empanadas and does a great *locro*. However, it is now outdone by the fabulous *1900*, Belgrano 390, a couple of blocks away towards the *Hotel Belén*); smart waiters serve up lovingly prepared lunches and dinners in a cheery brightly coloured decor – try the huge *bife de chorizo* with cheese and a potato tortilla plus the earthy house wine.

Londres

Fifteen kilometres west of Belén and even more charming, with partly crumbling adobe houses and pretty orchards, **LONDRES** lies 2km off RN-40 along a winding road that joins its upper and lower towns, on either side of the Río Hondo, a usually dry river that peters out in the Salar de Pipanaco. Known as the Cuna de la Nuez, or Walnut Heartland, the town celebrates the **Fiesta de la Nuez** with folklore and crafts displays during the first few days of February. Londres de Abajo, the lower town, is centred on Plaza José Eusebio Colombres, where you'll find the simple, whitewashed eighteenth-century **Iglesia de San Juan Bautista**, in front of which the walnut festival is held. The focal point for the rest of the year is Londres de Arriba's **Plaza Hipólito Yrigoyen**, overlooked by the quaint **Iglesia de la Inmaculada Concepción**, a once lovely church in a pitiful state of repair but noteworthy for a harmonious colonnade and its fine bells, said to be the country's oldest. As yet, there's no accommodation in the town, but ask around, just in case someone has a room to let.

△ Shinkal ruins

Londres' humble present-day aspect belies a long and prestigious history, including the fact that it's Argentina's second oldest "city" (*ciudad*), founded in 1558, only five years after Santiago del Estero. **Diego de Almagro** and his expedition from Cusco began scouring the area in the 1530s and founded a settlement which was named in honour of the marriage between Philip, heir to the Spanish throne, and Mary Tudor: hence the tribute to the English capital in the village's name. Alongside the municipalidad, on the wall of which is a quaint fresco testifying to the town's glorious past, is the small but interesting **Museo Arqueológico** (Mon–Fri 8am–1pm; $1), displaying ceramics and other finds from the impressive **Shinkal ruins**. The ruins themselves lie 5km west (daily Dec–April 9am–1pm & 4–7pm, May–Nov 10am–5pm; $2); just follow the well-signposted scenic road, next to the Iglesia de la Inmaculada Concepción. Amazingly intact, though parts of it are over-restored in a zealous attempt to reconstruct the fortress, it was the site of a decisive battle in the **Great Calchaquí Uprising** (see box, p.498). After Chief Chelemín cut off the water supplies to Londres and set fire to the town, forcing its inhabitants to flee to La Rioja, he was captured and had his body ripped apart by four horses. Shinkal gives you an insight into what Diaguita settlements in the region must have looked like: splendid steps lead to the top of high **ceremonial mounds**, with great views of the oasis and Sierra de Zapata.

The Puna Catamarqueña

The altiplano of northwestern Catamarca Province, known as the **Puna Catamarqueña** (*puna* is the Quichoa word for altiplano, a word of Spanish coinage), stretches to the Chilean border and is one of the remotest and most deserted, but most outstandingly beautiful parts of the country. **Antofagasta de la Sierra**, a ghostly town of adobe-brick miners' houses and whispering womenfolk, is far flung even from Catamarca city in this sparsely populated region, but the tiny **archeological museum** is worth seeing for its fantastic mummified infant. Dotted with majestic ebony volcanoes and scarred by recent lava-flows, with the Andean cordillera as a magnificent backdrop, the huge expanses of altiplano and their desiccated vegetation are grazed by hardy yet delicate-looking **vicuñas** while **flamingoes** valiantly survive on frozen lakes. This is staggeringly unspoilt country, with out-of-this-world landscapes, and a constantly surreal atmosphere, accentuated by the sheer remoteness and emptiness of it all; the trip out here is really more rewarding than the destination, **Antofagasta**, which is primarily a place to spend the night before forging on northwards, to San Antonio de los Cobres in Salta Province (see p.441), or doubling back down to Belén. As you travel, watch out for *apachetas*, little cairns of stones piled up at the roadside as an offering to the Mother Goddess, Pachamama, and the only visible signs of any human presence. Although a **bus** shuttles back and forth between Catamarca and Antofagasta twice a week, the surest way to get around is by 4WD, along RP-43, one of the quietest roads in Argentina; it's quite possible not to pass another vehicle all day. Take all the necessary precautions including plenty of fuel, and don't forget warm clothing as the temperature can plummet several degrees below freezing at night in July.

In **Hualfín**, a tiny village where RP-43 branches northwestwards from RN-40, 60km north of Belén, you can find rooms for rent, if you need **accommodation**, but most people use Hualfín as their last **fuel stop** before the long haul to Antofagasta de la Sierra; provisions can also be bought here. The village itself is famous for its paprika, often sprinkled on the delicious local goat's cheeses, and a fine **colonial church**, dedicated to Nuestra Señora del Rosario and built in 1770; ask for the key at the municipalidad to see the pristine interior adorned with delicate frescoes. Hualfin was also the birthplace and stronghold of Chelemín, the Calchaquí leader who spearheaded the Great Uprising in the 1630s (see box, p.498). **Thermal springs** with rudimentary facilities, and slightly better ones 14km north at **Villavil**, are open from January to April only.

Up to Antofagasta de la Sierra

Between **Corral Quemado** and **Villavil**, the first stretch of RP-43 to Antofagasta de la Sierra, all of 200km from Hualfin to the northwest, takes you through some cheery if understated countryside, planted with vines and maize, with feathery acacias and tall poplars acting as windbreaks, and dotted with humble mud-brick farmhouses. Potentially treacherous fords at Villavil and, more likely, at **El Bolsón**, 10km further on, are sometimes too deep to cross even in a 4WD, especially after spring thaws or summer rains; you'll either have to wait a couple of hours for the rivers to subside or turn back. Just over 70km from the junction at Hualfin, the road twists and climbs through the dramatic **Cuesta de Randolfo**, hemmed in by rocky pinnacles and reaching an altitude of 4800m before corkscrewing back down to the transitional plains.

Along this flat section, you're treated to immense open views towards the dramatic crags of the Sierra del Cajón, to the south, and the spiky rocks of the Sierra Laguna Blanca, to the north. Impressive white **sand dunes**, gleaming like fresh snow against the dark mountainsides, make an interesting pretext for a halt. Down in the plain, the immense **salt-lakes** stretch for miles and this is where you'll probably spy your first **vicuñas** – the shy, smaller cousins of the llamas with much silkier wool – protected by the **Reserva Natural Laguna Blanca**. All along this road, with photogenic ochre mountains as backdrops, whole flocks of vicuñas graze off scrawny grasses, less timid than usual, perhaps because the flocks are so big and they feel the safety of numbers. You'll also see nonchalant llamas and shaggy alpacas and, if you're very fortunate, the ostrich-like suris or ñandús, before they scurry away nervously. You could make a short detour to visit the shores of **Laguna Blanca** itself, a shallow, mirror-like lake fed by the Río Río and home to thousands of teals, ducks and **flamingoes**; it's clearly signposted along a track off to the north. A few kilometres on, the road then climbs steadily again up the often snow-streaked Sierra Laguna Blanca to reach the pass at **Portezuelo Pasto Ventura** (4000m), marked by a sign: this is the entrance to the altiplano, or *puna* proper. From here you have magnificent panoramas of the Andes, to the west, and of the great volcanoes of northwestern Catamarca, plus your first glimpse of wide-rimmed **Volcán Galan** (5912m), whose name means "bare mountain" in Quichoa. It's an incredible geological feature: some 2,500,000 years ago, in a cataclysmic eruption, blasting over 1000 cubic kilometres of material into the air, its top was blown away, leaving a hole measuring over 45km by 25km, the largest known crater on the Earth's surface, or in the solar system as locals like to boast.

Delightful **El Peñón**, 135km from Hualfin, is the first altiplano settlement you reach along RP-43: just a few gingerbread-coloured adobe houses, some proud poplar trees and an apple orchard, surprising given the altitude. The village nestles in the **Carachipampa Valley**, which extends all the way to the Cordillera de San Buenaventura, to the southwest, and its striking summit **Cerro El Cóndor** (6000m), clearly visible from here in the searingly clear atmosphere. Soon the chestnut-brown volcanic cones of **Los Negros de la**

The Calchaquí wars

After the European invasions of this region in the late sixteenth and early seventeenth centuries, the indigenous tribes who lived along the **Valles Calchaquíes**, stretching from Salta Province in the north, down to central Catamarca Province, steadfastly refused to be evangelized by the Spanish invaders and generally to behave as their aggressors wanted; the region around Belén and Londres proved especially difficult to colonize. Even the Jesuits, usually so effective at bringing the "natives" under control, conceded defeat. The colonizers made do with a few *encomiendas*, and more often *pueblos*, reservations where the Indians were forced to live, leaving the colonizers to farm their "own" land in peace. After a number of skirmishes, things came to a head in 1630, when the so-called **Great Calchaquí Uprising** began. For two years, under the leadership of **Juan Chelemín**, the fierce cacique of Hualfín, natives waged a war of attrition against the invaders, sacking towns and burning crops, provoking ever more brutal reactions from the ambitious new governor of Tucumán, Francisco de Nieva y Castilla. Eventually Chelemín was caught, drawn and quartered, and various parts of his body were put on display in different villages to "teach the Calchaquíes a lesson", but it took until 1643 for all resistance to be stamped out, and only after a network of fortresses was built in Andalgalá, Londres and elsewhere.

War broke out once more in 1657, when the Spanish decided to arrest "El Inca Falso", also known as Pedro Chamijo, an impostor of European descent who claimed to be Hualpa Inca – or Inca emperor – under the nom de guerre of **Bohórquez**. Elected chief at an impressive ceremony attended by the new governor of Tucumán, Alonso Mercado y Villacorta, amid great pomp and circumstance, in Pomán, he soon led the Calchaquíes into battle, and Mercado y Villacorta, joined by his ruthless predecessor, Francisco de Nieva y Castilla, set about what today would be called ethnic cleansing. Bohórquez was captured, taken to Lima and eventually garrotted in 1667, and whole tribes fell victim to genocide: their only remains are the ruins of Batungasta, Hualfín and Shinkal, near Londres. Some tribes like the **Quilmes**, whose settlement is now an archeological site near Amaicha (see p.482), were uprooted and forced to march to Buenos Aires. Out of seven thousand Quilmes who survived a long and distressing siege in their *pukará*, or fortress, despite having their food and water supplies cut off, before being led in chains to Buenos Aires, where they were employed as slaves, only a few hundred were left to face a smallpox epidemic at the end of the eighteenth century, which successfully wiped out these few survivors.

Laguna come into view, a sign that you're in the final approaches to Antofagasta. One of twin peaks, **La Alumbrera**, deposited enormous lava flows when it last erupted, only a few hundred years ago. The huge piles of visibly fresh **black pumice** that it tossed out, all pocked and twisted, reach heights of ten metres or more. Like giant chunks of licorice or the broken-up tyres of an outsize vehicle, they contrast starkly with the smooth volcanic mounds on the horizon and the serene white salt-lakes all around. Just before Antofagasta, the road swings round **Laguna Colorada**, a small lake often frozen solid and shaded pink with a massive flock of altiplanic flamingoes which somehow survive up here.

Antofagasta de la Sierra and around

Perched 3440m above sea level, 260km north of Belén, **ANTOFAGASTA DE LA SIERRA** lies at the northern end of a vast, arid plain hemmed in by volcanoes to the east and south, and by the cordillera, which soars to peaks of over 6000m, a mere 100km over to the west. With a population of under a thousand it exudes a feeling of utter remoteness, while still managing to exert a disarming fascination. It's a bleak yet restful place, an oasis of tamarinds and green alfalfa fields in the middle of the *meseta altiplánica* – a harsh steppe that looms above the surrounding altiplano. Two rivers, Punilla and Las Paitas, meet just to the south, near the strange volcanic plug called **El Torreón**, adopted as the town's symbol. Named after the Chilean port-city, this is a tough town with a harsh climate, where night temperatures in midwinter drop well below freezing, accompanied by biting winds and a relentless sun during the day: its name means "home of the Sun" in the language of the Diaguita. Salt, borax and various minerals and metals have been mined in the area for centuries and Antofagasta has the hardy feel of a mining town, but most of its people are now subsistence farmers and herdsmen, scraping a living from maize, potatoes, onions and beans or rearing llamas and alpacas, whose wool is made into textiles. The people here are introverted and placid, hospitable but seemingly indifferent to the outside world.

The best views of the immediate surroundings can be enjoyed from the top of the Cerro Amarillo and Cerro de la Cruz, two unsightly mounds of earth that look like part of a huge building-site and dominate the town's humble streets of small mud-brick houses. The **Cerro de la Cruz** is the destination of processions held to honour Antofagasta's patron saints, St Joseph and the Virgin of Loreto, from December 8 to 10. In another sombre ceremony, the town's dead are remembered on November 1 and 2, when villagers file to and from the cemetery before a feast, talking in whispers so as not to disturb the spirits. And every March the town comes to life, for the **Feria Artesanal y Ganadera de la Puna**, a colourful event attended by craftspeople and herdsmen from all over the province. The only tourist attraction in the town is the beautifully presented **Museo Arqueológico** (Mon–Fri 8am–6pm; $1), recently created primarily to house a perfectly preserved, naturally mummified baby, found in the mountains nearby and believed to be nearly 2000 years old; surrounded with jewels and other signs of wealth, suggesting the child belonged to a ruling dynasty, it exerts a morbid fascination. The museum's other exhibits, few in number but of extraordinary value, include an immaculately preserved pre-Hispanic basket, the pigment colouring and fine weave still intact.

The **bus** from Catamarca will drop you in the main street. Apart from rooms in private houses, the only **accommodation** is near the municipalidad, at the basic but scrupulously clean and much improved *Hostería de Antofagasta* (Ⓣ03835/471001; ❸), where you can also **eat**. **Fuel** can be bought at inflated prices from the pump opposite the municipalidad, so it's better to fill up before making this trip. Antofagasta has no tourist office as such; for visiting the immediate and farther-flung surroundings ask at the municipalidad for the town's most experienced guides, Catalino Soriano, Antolín Ramos and Jesús Vásquez.

Around Antofagasta de la Sierra

Unless it's cut off by winter snows or rocks brought down by the summer rains, an alternative route to and from Antofagasta is the mostly unsealed and sometimes very bumpy RP-43 (in Catamarca Province, becoming RP-17 in Salta Province), leading north to **San Antonio de los Cobres** (see p.441), 330km away via Cauchari. Antofagasta could therefore be visited as part of a gigantic loop, taking in vast, lonely yet dramatically memorable tracts of Salta and Catamarca provinces, but allow plenty of time and take far more provisions and fuel supplies than you think you'll need – in other words reckon on two or three days' food and several jerry-cans of petrol in reserve. The same road leads to the desolate, disorientingly mirage-like landscapes of the great **Salar del Hombre Muerto salt-flats**, 75km to the north of Antofagasta and best explored using the services of a *baqueano*, or guide. **Cerro Ratones** (5252m) and Cerro Incahuasi (4847m) form a breathtaking backdrop to the bright whiteness of the flats.

Within easy excursion distance of Antofagasta are a number of archeological and historical sites, such as the ruins at **Campo Alumbreras**, 5km south, and **Coyparcito**, 3km further away. The pre-Columbian **pukará**, or fortress,on the flanks of the Alumbrera volcano, a few kilometres south of Antofagasta, and nearby **petroglyphs** (mostly depicting llamas and human figures) are also worth a visit; you'll definitely need the services of a guide to find them, and for the necessary explanations to make a visit worthwhile, but they are all open to the public at all times and no entrance fee is charged. Ask at Antofagasta's museum for archeological information and guided visits. The abandoned onyx, mica and gold **mines** in the region are another interesting attraction, while long treks on mule-back are the only way of seeing **Volcán Sufre** (5706m) on the Chilean border. If you want quieter recreation than climbing mountains or scrambling through disused mines you might care for a day's **trout fishing** at **Paicuquí**, 20km north of Antofagasta. In the crystal-clear streams you can catch delicious rainbow trout – apparently the streams used to swarm with fish but stocks are still at safe levels, albeit less plentiful than a few years ago. The **Río de los Patos**, another 70km north, is said to be a more reliable source of trout.

Up to the Paso San Francisco

The mostly sealed RN-60, which starts way down in Córdoba, crosses RN-40 in Catamarca Province at Alpasinche, 90km south of Belén. At **Tinogasta**, a rather nondescript little market town with little to detain you at the southern extremity of the province, overlooked by the imposing Sierra de Copacabana, RN-60 begins its gradual ascent towards the Chilean border. What Tinogasta does have is one of the best **places to stay** in this part of the province: the *Hostal de Adobe – Casagrande* ⓣ0387/421140, ⓦwww.casagrandetour.com; ⑤-⑥), a converted Necolonial house just a couple of blocks from the main plaza, at Moreno 801; its seven charming rooms, some built in adobe, are a combination of rustic quaintness and modern comfort, the meals are hearty and there's a fine swimming pool, plus a small meditation-room-cum-spa. The enthusiastic young Porteño couple who run it also arrange excursions in the area.

From Tinogasta, El Cordillerano's buses ⓣ0387/420636 or 420314) go over the **Paso San Francisco** to Copiapó in Chile's Norte Chico about once a week, sometimes more often in the summer (Dec–March), and this is undoubtedly one of the most dramatic ways of entering Chile. The ruins of the Calchaquí *pukará*, or pre-Inca fortress, of Batungasta, a strategic Diaguita stronghold during the Calchaquí wars (see box, p.498), lie just off RN-60, 10km west of Tinogasta, in a beautiful gorge. The road to **Fiambalá**, the last settlement to speak of before the frontier, passes through lovely oasis countryside, with small, picturesque villages of adobe farmhouses such as San José, El Puesto and Anillaco – the last not to be confused with Anillaco, La Rioja Province, the birthplace of former president Menem. The nearby **Termas de Fiambalá** are among the country's best located thermal springs, and are fabulous at night when the warm waters contrast with the fresh air and you can gaze up at the starry desert skies. From Fiambalá, RN-60 leads ever higher into the cordillera to the border; if driving make sure you fill up the tank and any jerry-cans you have, in either Tinogasta or Fiambalá, as there are no service stations after the latter. Be prepared for bad weather, too, and take passports, plus Chilean visas if necessary, your driving licence and all vehicle papers. The **pass**, at 4800m, is seldom cut off, but heavy snow can occasionally block the road in midwinter – though rarely for more than a couple of days. The journey takes you through the Cuesta de Loro-Huasi, with its weirdly beautiful sandstone formations, and the narrow gorge of Las Angosturas, past different species of cactus and extensive guanaco pastures. The sights on the other side of the frontier are even more spectacular: the turquoise waters of Laguna Verde, Cerro Ojos del Salado (6893m), the world's highest active volcano, the Cuesta Colorada, Parque Nacional Nevado de Tres Cruces and the Salar de Maricunga.

Fiambalá

Aptly meaning "deep in the mountains" in the native Kakano language, **FIAMBALÁ**, 50km north of Tinogasta, is near the olive groves of the fertile Abaucán Valley, an area reminiscent of North Africa or the Middle East. It's a quiet oasis town of crumbling adobe houses, set among extensive vineyards, whose fruit is eaten fresh, dried as raisins or fermented into very drinkable wine. Some of the locals are excellent **artisans**, specializing in weaving, and you can buy their work at various workshops around the village, including a crafts market just off the main square. In the town, on Calle Abaucán, just north of the Plaza Mayor, is the new, small **Museo del Hombre** (daily 9am–1pm & 4–8pm; $1) with an intriguing little collection, including two particularly well-preserved mummies and some striking stone sculptures. Two kilometres to the south, aside RN-60 from Tinogasta, stands the well-restored silhouette of **Iglesia San Pedro**, a colonial chapel built in 1702, set amid shady trees. During renovation, part of the reed roofing was left bare of plaster to reveal the construction. Chocolate-brown streaks from the mud and straw roof have attractively trickled down the curvaceous, impeccably whitewashed walls. A family living nearby has the key to the church, whose handsomely plain interior, decorated with **paintings of the Cusqueña school** (see p.132) of the Virgin, Infant Jesus and saints, is well worth seeing. Together with the splendid building next door – the mid-eighteenth-century **Comandancia de Armas**, ambitiously earmarked for the Museo Histórico Colonial and the Museo del Sitio, whose motley exhibits so far amount to little more than odds and ends – the church is part of what the provincial authorities are currently promoting as the **Ruta del Adobe**, a tourist circuit taking in other churches and historic buildings en route between Tinogasta and Fiambalá itself. Close to the church is the fabulous new state-of-the-art winery, **Finca Don Diego**, open for tastings in its superb cool cellar (Mon–Fri 9am–1pm & 3–6.30pm; ⓦwww.fincadondiego.com.ar). It produces some of the region's most promising wines, especially using the syrah grape.

The town's other claim to fame is as a spa, and the **thermal baths** (daily 9am–10pm; $2) are perched in a beautiful mountain setting 15km to the east, at an altitude of over 2000m. The mineral spring gushes out at over 70°C but, by the time the water trickles down into the cascade of attractive stone pools, it cools to 30°C or so, very pleasant when the outdoor temperatures plummet well below freezing; in fact the baths are especially fun to relax in at night, when you can look up at the stars, wallow in the warm waters and listen to the campers singing fireside songs. You can **camp** by the pools, and there are spartan shared *cabañas* (❷) to rent; the only way to get here is by taxi ($35 return fare, including waiting time). Some 200m downhill is a *hostería* (☎03837/496095; ❷) with an outdoor pool and decent **rooms**.

Buses from Catamarca and Tinogasta, or to Chile, use the stop on Plaza Mayor. Some **tourist information** can be obtained at the municipalidad, 100m to the west (daily 9am–12.30pm & 5–9pm; ☎03837/496250), including for places to **stay** (private houses), such as the recommended *Doña Pocha* at Islas Malvinas s/n (☎03837/496137; ❷); otherwise you can always overnight at the clean but extremely basic *Hosteria Municipal*, right next door at Diego de Almagro s/n (☎03837/496291; ❷), whose rooms have their own bath; you're advised to book ahead. Excellent pizzas and other Italian-style **food** are on offer at the friendly *Pizzeria Roma*, calles Abaucán and Padre Arch, a couple of blocks north of the main square, should you want a change from the snacks and basic fare served at the *hostería*. You'd be far better off, however, staying in Tinogasta.

Travel details

Buses

Catamarca to: Andalgalá (3 daily; 6hr); Antofagasta de la Sierra (2 weekly; 13hr); Belén (2 daily; 5hr); Buenos Aires (10 daily; 15hr); Fiambalá (2 daily; 6hr); La Rioja (6 daily; 2hr 30min); Salta (6 daily; 7hr); Tinogasta (hourly; 5hr); Tucumán (5 daily; 3hr).
Jujuy to: Buenos Aires (hourly; 20hr); Córdoba (10 daily; 13hr); Humahuaca (hourly; 3hr); La Quiaca (hourly; 7hr); Purmamarca (hourly; 1hr 15min); Resistencia (1 daily; 14hr); Salta (hourly; 1hr 30min); Tilcara (hourly; 2hr); Tucumán(10 daily; 5hr 30min).
Salta to: Buenos Aires (hourly; 18hr); Cachi (2 daily; 5hr); Cafayate (7 daily; 3hr); Córdoba (10 daily; 12hr); Jujuy (hourly ; 1hr 30min); Resistencia (1 daily; 13hr); Santiago del Estero (10 daily; 5hr); Tucumán (10 daily; 4hr).
Santiago del Estero to: Cafayate (3 daily; 7hr). Córdoba (6 daily; 6hr); Tucumán (10 daily; 2hr 30min);
Tucumán to: Buenos Aires (10 daily; 15hr); Catamarca (5 daily; 3hr); Córdoba (6 daily; 8hr); Jujuy (10 daily; 5hr 30min); Salta (10 daily; 4hr); Santiago del Estero (10 daily; 2hr 30min); Tafí del Valle (6 daily; 3hr).

Trains

Tucumán to: Buenos Aires (3 weekly; 23hr).
Santiago del Estero to: Buenos Aires (3 weekly; 19hr).

Flights

Catamarca to: Buenos Aires (1 daily; 2hr 30min); La Rioja (1 daily; 30min).
Jujuy to: Buenos Aires (3 daily; 2hr 10min); Salta (1 daily; 20min).
Salta to: Buenos Aires (6 daily; 2hr); Jujuy (1 daily; 20min).
Santiago del Estero to: Buenos Aires (1 daily; 1hr 40min).
Tucumán to: Buenos Aires (6 daily; 1hr 50min).

6

Mendoza, San Juan and La Rioja

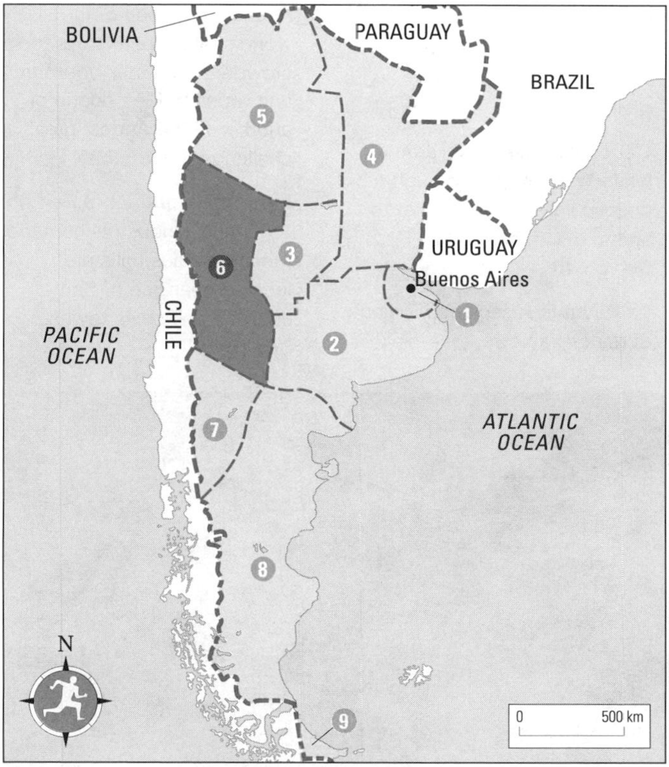

CHAPTER 6

Highlights

* **Mendoza city** Argentina's wine capital has a lot to offer, from top-class dining to a vibrant nightlife. See p.509

* **Bodega Salentein** Who said the Dutch can't make wine? This "Wine Cathedral" is one of the most impressive wineries in South America. See p.525

* **Laguna Diamante** This ultramarine lake with a perfectly symmetrical volcano for a backdrop is a great picnic spot. See p.536

* **Cañon del Atuel** Exhilarating white-water rafting through a bucolic valley – how better to spend a summer's day? See p.540

* **La Payunia** A secluded region of dark lava flows, rose-pink mountains, mysterious caves, curvaceous volcanoes and photogenic guanacos. See p.547

* **Ischigualasto and Talampaya** The pride and joy of La Rioja and San Juan provinces – gigantic red cliffs and an eerie moonscape. See p.559 & p.561

* **Mountain climbing** If Aconcagua – one of the world's tallest peaks – is too crowded, then take your tent and ropes to Mercedario or another of the Andes' great challenges. See p.565

* **Flour mills of Jáchal** Part of Argentina's industrial heritage, these fabulous mills are located near one of San Juan's many oasis towns. See p.569

△ Trekking Aconcagua

6

Mendoza, San Juan and La Rioja

Argentina's midwestern provinces of **Mendoza**, **San Juan** and **La Rioja** stretch all the way from the chocolate-brown pampas of **La Payunia**, on the northern borders of Patagonia, to the remote highland steppes of the **Reserva Las Vicuñas**, on the edge of the altiplano, more than a thousand kilometres to the north. Extending across vast, thinly populated territories of bone-dry desert, they are dotted with vibrant oases of farmland and the region's famous **vineyards**: the sophisticated metropolis of **Mendoza**, one of Argentina's biggest cities, is the epicentre of the country's blossoming wine – and wine tourism – industry, while the two smaller provincial capitals, **San Juan** and **La Rioja**, continue to be quiet backwaters by comparison.

More than towns and cities, though, the area's dynamics are about its highly varied **landscapes** and **wildlife**. In the west of the provinces loom the world's loftiest peaks outside the Himalayas, culminating in the defiant **Aconcagua**, whose summit is only a shade under 7000 metres. Ranging from these snowy Andean heights to totally flat pampas in the east, from green, fertile valleys to barren volcanoes – the world's second highest cone, extinct **Monte Pissis** (6882m), is in the far north of La Rioja Province – the scenery also includes two of the country's most photographed national parks: the sheer red sandstone cliffs of **Talampaya** and the moonscapes of **Ischigualasto**. All this provides a backdrop for some of Argentina's best **sporting** opportunities – from **skiing** in exclusive **Las Leñas**, to rock-climbing, white-water rafting and even, if you're tempted by more demanding challenges, the ascent of Aconcagua or the **Mercedario** and **Tupungato** peaks.

European settlers have wrought changes to the environment, bringing the grape vine, the Lombardy poplar and all kinds of fruit trees with them, but the thousands of kilometres of irrigation channels that water the region existed long before Columbus "discovered" America. Pumas and vicuñas, condors and ñandús, plus hundreds of colourful bird species inhabit the thoroughly unspoilt wildernesses of the region, where some of the biggest known dinosaurs prowled millions of years ago. Countless flowering **cactus** and the dazzling yellow *brea*, a broom-like shrub, add colour to the browns and greys of the desert in the spring.

MENDOZA, SAN JUAN & LA RIOJA
0 100 km
Monte Pissis (6882m)
Cerro Bonete (6759m)
RESERVA PROVINCIAL LAS VICUÑAS
CATAMARCA PROVINCE
SANTIAGO DEL ESTERO PROVINCE
PARQUE NACIONAL SAN GUILLERMO
Famatina
Chilecito
RN-40
Villa Unión
La Rioja
RN-74
LA RIOJA PROVINCE
RESERVA PROVINCIAL SAN GUILLERMO
PARQUE NACIONAL TALAMPAYA
Angualasto
Huaco
RN-150
Patquía
Chamical
Rodeo
Jáchal
PARQUE PROVINCIAL ISCHIGUALASTO (VALLE DE LA LUNA)
Iglesia
RN-150
SAN JUAN PROVINCE
RP-412
RP-510
Valle Fértil
RN-141
Talacasto
CÓRDODBA PROVINCE
Calingasta
Chepes
CHILE
San Juan
Barreal
RN-141
Cerro Mercedario (6770m)
RP-39
RN-20
Cerro Aconcagua (6959m)
PARQUE PROVINCIAL ACONCAGUA
RN-40
Río Mendoza
RN-7
MENDOZA
SAN LUIS PROVINCE
PARQUE PROVINCIAL VOLCÁN TUPUNGATO
RN-7
Tupungato
SANTIAGO DE CHILE
Cerro Tupungato (6570m)
Tunuyán
MENDOZA PROVINCE
Volcán Maipo (5323m)
RN-146
N
RN-143
Laguna Diamante
San Rafael
Río Diamante
RN-40
General Alvear
RN-188
Las Leñas
RESERVA PROVINCIAL LAGUNA DE LLANCANELO
Río Atuel
RN-143
Malargüe
RESERVA PROVINCIAL LA PAYUNIA
LA PAMPA PROVINCE
RN-151
RN-40
Río Colorado
NEUQUÉN PROVINCE

El Cuyo

Mendoza, San Juan and San Luis provinces are sometimes still referred to as **El Cuyo** and, more recently, with La Rioja thrown in, as El Nuevo Cuyo, a political entity set up to look after the region's commercial interests and international relations. Although it's often dubbed *La Puerta del Cuyo*, or "gateway to the Cuyo", San Luis has closer geographical ties with Córdoba and is therefore covered with that province in Chapter 3. The etymological origins of the word *cuyo* are not entirely clear, but it probably comes from the native Huarpe word *xuyu*, meaning riverbed. The first recorded use of the term to describe the area dates back to 1564, when the colonial Spanish authorities gave the name to an administrative region in Chile. In 1776, this region was detached from Chile and incorporated into the fledgling Viceroyalty of the River Plate, and in 1820 it finally fell apart, with the provinces of Mendoza, San Luis and San Juan in newly independent Argentina going their separate ways. The Nuevo Cuyo came into being under a treaty signed by the four provincial governors – including La Rioja's – in 1988. You will often see the words *Cuyo* and *Cuyano* used by transport companies and other businesses, suggesting that a strong regional identity still lies behind this enigmatic name.

Mendoza Province

The southern half of El Nuevo Cuyo (see box above) is taken up by **Mendoza Province**, the self-styled Tierra del Sol y del Buen Vino, the "land of sunshine and good wine". Within its borders are enough attractions to occupy a whole holiday, including some of the country's most dramatic mountain **landscapes**, where you can try a host of adventure pursuits, from kayaking to hang-gliding. The charms of its lively capital, the city of **Mendoza**, can satisfy yearnings for creature comforts after muscle-aching treks, tough climbs into the Andes or an afternoon of white-water rafting. Although Mendoza Province shares many things with San Juan and La Rioja, to the north – bleak wildernesses backed by snow-peaked mountains, remarkably varied flora and fauna, an incredibly sunny climate prone to sudden temperature changes and pockets of rich farmland mainly used to produce beefy red wines – it differs in the way it exploits all these assets. At the national, not just regional, level Mendoza leads the way in **tourism** just as it does in the **wine industry**, combining professionalism with enthusiasm plus a taste for the alternative or avant-garde. The two industries come together for Mendoza city's nationally famous **Fiesta de la Vendimia**, or Wine Harvest Festival, held in early March, a slightly kitsch but exuberant bacchanalia at which a carnival queen is elected from candidates representing every town in the province.

For travelling purposes Mendoza Province can be divided into three sections, each with its own base. The north, around the capital, has the country's biggest concentration of vineyards and top-class **wineries**, clustered around **Maipú** and **Luján de Cuyo**, while the scenic **Alta Montaña** route races up in a westerly direction towards the high Chilean border, passing the mighty **Cerro Aconcagua**, an increasingly popular destination for mountaineers from around the globe. Not far to the southwest are the much more challenging **Cerro Tupungato** (6570m) and the remote **Laguna Diamante**, a choppy altiplanic lagoon in the shadow of

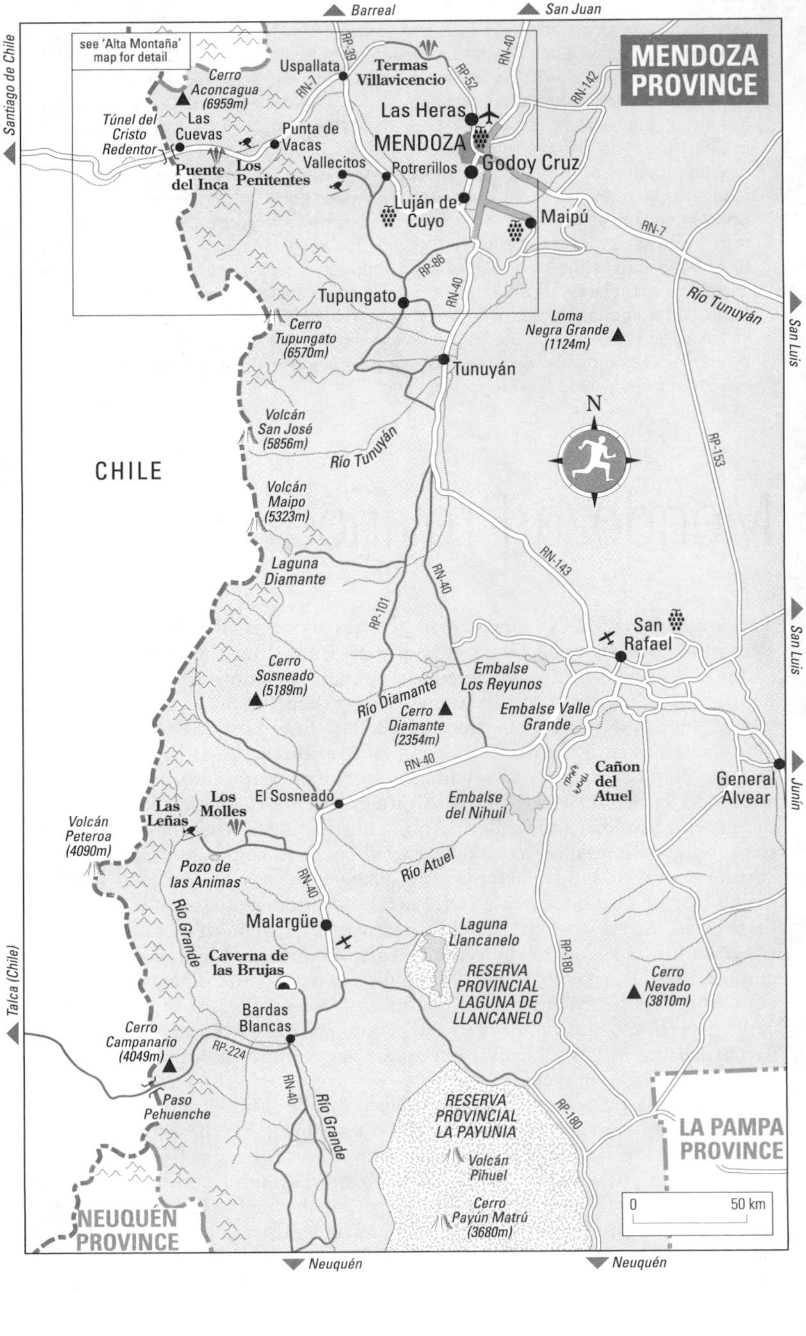
MENDOZA PROVINCE
see 'Alta Montaña' map for detail
Barreal
San Juan
Santiago de Chile
San Luis
San Luis
Junín
Talca (Chile)
Neuquén
Neuquén
Cerro Aconcagua (6959m)
Uspallata
Termas Villavicencio
Las Heras
MENDOZA
Godoy Cruz
Túnel del Cristo Redentor
Las Cuevas
Punta de Vacas
Puente del Inca
Los Penitentes
Vallecitos
Potrerillos
Luján de Cuyo
Maipú
Tupungato
Cerro Tupungato (6570m)
Tunuyán
Loma Negra Grande (1124m)
Río Tunuyán
Volcán San José (5856m)
Río Tunuyán
CHILE
N
Volcán Maipo (5323m)
Laguna Diamante
San Rafael
Cerro Sosneado (5189m)
Río Diamante
Cerro Diamante (2354m)
Embalse Los Reyunos
Embalse Valle Grande
Cañon del Atuel
General Alvear
El Sosneado
Los Molles
Las Leñas
Volcán Peteroa (4090m)
Embalse del Nihuil
Pozo de las Animas
Río Atuel
Río Grande
Malargüe
Laguna Llancanelo
Caverna de las Brujas
RESERVA PROVINCIAL LAGUNA DE LLANCANELO
Cerro Nevado (3810m)
Bardas Blancas
Cerro Campanario (4049m)
Paso Pehuenche
RESERVA PROVINCIAL LA PAYUNIA
Volcán Pihuel
Cerro Payún Matrú (3680m)
Río Grande
LA PAMPA PROVINCE
NEUQUÉN PROVINCE
0 50 km
RP-39
RN-7
RP-52
RN-40
RN-142
RN-7
RP-86
RN-40
RP-153
RN-143
RN-40
RP-101
RN-40
RN-40
RP-180
RP-224
RN-40
RP-180

the perfectly shaped **Volcán Maipo**, which can only be visited from December to March. Central Mendoza is focused on the laid-back town of **San Rafael**, where you can taste more wine, and from where several tour operators offer excursions along the nearby **Cañon del Atuel**, usually taking in a beginner's-level session of white-water rafting. If skiing or snowboarding in July is your fantasy, try the winter-sports complex at **Las Leñas**, where you'll be sharing pistes with South America's jet-set and northern-hemisphere giant-slalom champions. The third, least-visited section of the province wraps around the southern outpost of **Malargüe**, a final-frontier kind of place promoting itself as a centre for nature, scientific discovery and adventure. Within easy reach are the mirror-like **Laguna de Llancanelo**, home to an enormous community of **flamingoes**, the charcoal-grey and rust-red lava deserts of **La Payunia** and a speleologists' delight, the karstic caves of **Caverna de las Brujas**. The province's dull eastern fringe bordering San Luis Province can be missed.

Tourism is so well developed in the province it's possible to visit virtually all of these places by **public transport** or on organized tours from Mendoza and other towns. However, to see them at your own pace and have many of them to yourself, consider renting a vehicle, preferably a 4WD, since many of the roads are, at best, only partly sealed.

Mendoza and around

MENDOZA is a mostly low-rise city, spread across the wide valley of the Río Mendoza, over 1000km west of Buenos Aires and less than 100km east of the highest section of the Andean cordillera – whose perennially snowcapped peaks are clearly visible from downtown. Its airy microcentro is less compact than that of most comparable cities, partly because the streets, squares and avenues were deliberately made wide when the city was rebuilt in the late nineteenth century (see p.511), to allow for evacuation in the event of another major earthquake. Another striking feature is that every street is lined by bushy sycamore and plane trees – providing vital shade in the scorching summer months, they are watered by over 500km of *acequias*, or irrigation ditches, which form a natural, outdoor air-cooling system. Watch out, though, when you cross the city's streets, as the narrow gutters are up to a metre deep and often full of gushing water, especially in the spring when the upland snows melt.

The city has an attractive park and one or two museums that are worth taking a visit, but most people come to Mendoza principally to do a **wine-tasting tour** at the many **bodegas** in or near the city (see box, pp.524–525). Mendoza's leading restaurants serve seafood from the Pacific coast and delicious local produce, all accompanied by the outstanding local wines – another reason to make the city your base for exploring the region's spectacular countryside. Within easy reach to the south of the city are two small satellite towns, **Luján de Cuyo** and **Maipú**, where, in addition to the majority of the region's wineries, you'll find a few more interesting museums, one displaying the paintings of Fernando Fader – a kind of Argentine Van Gogh – and the other focusing on the wine industry. And, in a very different vein, the city also acts as a base for some of the world's most thrilling **mountain-climbing** opportunities.

Some history

Mendoza started out as part of the **Spanish colony of Chile**, even though Santiago de Chile lies across a snowy mountain pass nearly 4000m above sea

Argentine wine

While Argentina's earliest recorded vineyard is the late sixteenth-century one at Jesús María in Córdoba Province (see p.285), and the wines of Cafayate in Salta Province (see p.447) are deservedly becoming better known nationally and internationally, the heart of the country's wine industry has always been **Mendoza**. The provinces of **La Rioja**, whose wineries are concentrated around Chilecito and Anillaco (where former President Menem's family built their wealth on wine), and **San Juan** also produce great vintages, as do isolated wineries as far south as **Río Negro**. Nonetheless, Mendoza steadfastly remains Argentina's answer to Bordeaux – an apt comparison, since its producers still look to France for inspiration for names, such as **Comte de Valmont**, **Pont l'Evêque** or **Carcassonne**, and for vinification methods – such as imitations of sauternes, beaujolais and champagne. Three-quarters of the country's total production comes from the province's vines, mostly concentrated in the oases that spread across the valley south of the city, focused on Maipú and Luján de Cuyo. **San Rafael**, at the heart of the province, is another major wine-growing centre (see p.540).

Mendoza's vines were originally planted by **colonizers from Chile**, theoretically for producing Communion wine. Chile was the first South American country to have its wines recognized internationally, and early on prosperous Chilean wine-growers bought up many of the vineyards in the Mendoza area. However, Argentina's wines have caught up fast and the country is now the world's fifth largest producer (after France, Italy, Spain and the US). Although most wine experts would still purchase Chile's first, many think the days are fast approaching when Argentina's vintages will outstrip those of its western neighbour in terms of quality, reflecting the sunnier climate, cleaner air and richer soil.

Other than the lure of exports, the main reason for the improvement in Argentina's wines is that the domestic market has become much more discerning, with the market share taken up by superior *vinos finos* and *reservas* rocketing in the past decade or two. **Table wines** still dominate, often sold in huge *dama-joanas* – demijohn flagons – that people drag along to vintners for a refill. These are sometimes marketed under usurped names such as *borgoña*, or burgundy, and chablis. Younger Argentines often prefer fizzy drinks or beer with their daily meals, however, only drinking wine on special occasions, plumping for lighter **New Wave** wines such as Chandon's **Nuevo Mundo**.

Although the most attractive wineries to visit are the old-fashioned ones, with musty cellars crammed with ancient oak barrels, some of the finest vintages are now produced by growers who've invested in the latest equipment, including mammoth stainless-steel vats, hygienic storage tanks lined with epoxy resin and computerized temperature controls. They tend to concentrate on making varietal wines, the main grape varieties being riesling, chenin blanc and chardonnay, for whites, and pinot noir, cabernet sauvignon and malbec, for reds – the reds tend to be better than whites. Malbec is often regarded as the Argentine grape par excellence, giving rich fruity wines, with overtones of black currant and prune that are the perfect partner for a juicy steak. The latest trend is for a balanced combination of two grapes rather than just the one: for example, mixing malbec for its fruitiness and cabernet for its body, while toning down the sometimes excessive oakiness that characterized Argentine wines in the 1980s. Growers have also been experimenting with previously less popular varieties such as tempranillo, san gervase, gewurztraminer, syrah and merlot. Very convincing sparkling wines are being made locally by the *méthode champenoise*, including those produced by Chandon and Mumm, the French champagne-makers. For info on visiting bodegas around Mendoza, see the box on pp.524–525.

Unlike Chile, where most of the best wine is exported, Argentina consumes a lot of its premium wines. Many upmarket restaurants offer extensive wine lists including older, more subtle vintages – but beware of exorbitant corkage charges. Commonly found bodega names to look for include **Chandon, Graffigna, Navarro Correas, Salentein, Finca Flichmann** and **Weinert**.

level – the only way over the Andes until the Cristo Redentor tunnel opened in 1980. Despite the obstacles, in 1561 García Hurtado de Mendoza, captain-general of Chile, sent over an expedition led by Pedro del Castillo to establish a colony from which to civilize the indigenous Huarpe, who had for centuries eked out a living by farming maize, beans and potatoes, herding llamas and hunting guanacos; Castillo named the town he founded after his boss. Soon flourishing, Mendoza continued to be ruled from across the Andes, though its isolation enabled it to live a life of its own. The extensive network of pre-Hispanic **irrigation canals** was exploited by the colonizers, who planted **vineyards** that soon became South America's most productive. By 1700, the city's merchants were selling wine to Santiago, Córdoba and Buenos Aires. After the Viceroyalty of the River Plate was created in 1777, Mendoza was incorporated into the huge **Córdoba Intendencia**. Mendocinos are still proud of the fact that San Martín's Army of the Andes was trained in their city before thrashing the Spanish royalist troops at the Battle of Maipú, Chile, in 1818.

Once Argentina gained its independence, however, Mendoza began to suffer from its relative isolation within the new state, stagnating by the mid-nineteenth century. Worse was to come, though: as night fell on March 20, 1861 – Holy Week – three hundred years after the city's founding, an earthquake smashed every building in Mendoza to rubble, and some four thousand people, a third of the population, lost their lives. Although it's believed to have been less powerful than the earthquake that hit nearby San Juan in 1944, this was probably one of the worst ever to have hit South America, an estimated 7.8 on the Richter scale. Seismologists now believe that the epicentre lay right in the middle of the city, just beneath the surface, explaining why the damage was so terrible and yet restricted in radius. Pandemonium ensued, God-fearing Mendocinos seeing the timing – the city's anniversary and Eastertide – as double proof of divine retribution. Thousands of refugees relied on charity from the rest of the nation, Europe and especially Chile. Remarkably, a new city was quickly built, overseen by the French urban planner **Ballofet**, who created wide streets, open squares and low buildings for the new-look Mendoza. The city's isolation ended soon afterwards, with the arrival of the railway in 1884. Another tremor in 1985 left some people in the suburbs homeless and claimed a dozen lives, and the earth continues to shake noticeably at frequent intervals, but all construction in modern Mendoza is designed to be earthquake resistant.

Gran Mendoza (or "Greater Mendoza"), with a population of close to one million, includes the city centre – home to around 150,000 people – plus leafy suburbs such as **Chacras de Coria** and **Las Heras**, and industrial districts, such as Godoy Cruz. Wine, petrochemicals, a thriving university and, more recently, **tourism** have been the mainstays of the city economy. The effects of Chile's fast-growing economy have spilled over onto Mendoza's prosperity, and the long-neglected cultural, political and commercial ties between the city and Santiago, dating back to colonial times, have been revived over the past twenty years.

Arrival, information and city transport

Officially called Aeropuerto Internacional Ing. Francisco J. Gabrielli, but known popularly as "Plumerillo" after the suburb where it's located, Mendoza's modern and efficient **airport** (☎0261/430-7837, 430-6484 or 448-7128) is only 7km north of the city centre, just off RN-40. The terminal features some shops, a bank and a cafeteria. There are regular domestic flights, including several daily to and from Buenos Aires, as well as a couple of flights a day to and from Santiago

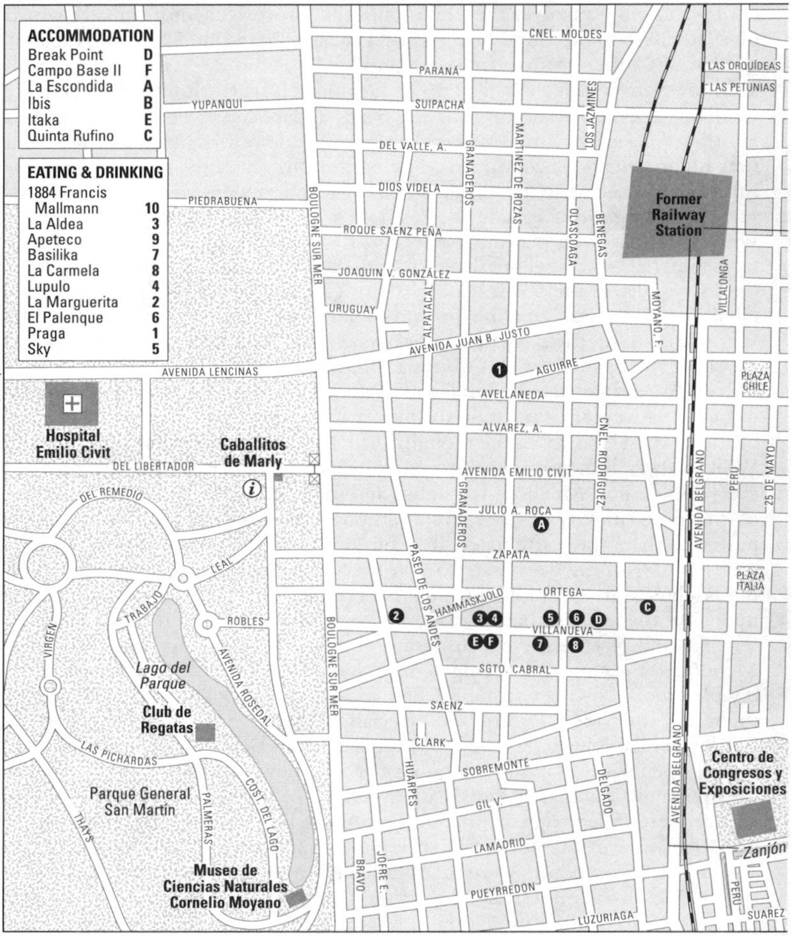

de Chile. **Taxis** and *remises* are in plentiful supply, or **buses** #6/63 or #3/115 can also take you downtown; heading back to the airport, be sure to catch a bus that has an "Aeropuerto" sign in the windscreen. There is an airport **tourist information office** (☏0261/520-6000), but it is open only sporadically.

Mendoza's modern, efficient and very busy **bus station** (☏0261/431-5000) is slightly drab, but has plenty of facilities: a small **tourist information office** (7am–11pm), bank and ATM, cafeteria and snack bars, toilets and showers, several shops – including a supermarket – and a post office. There are buses to and from just about everywhere in the country, plus Santiago de Chile, Lima, Montevideo and a number of Bolivian cities. It's due east of the microcentro, on the edge of the suburb of Guaymallén, at the corner of avenidas Gobernador Videla and Acceso Este (RN-7); this is less than 1km from the city centre but if the fifteen-minute walk is too much, the "Villa Nueva" trolley-bus ($0.90) is a cheaper alternative to a taxi.

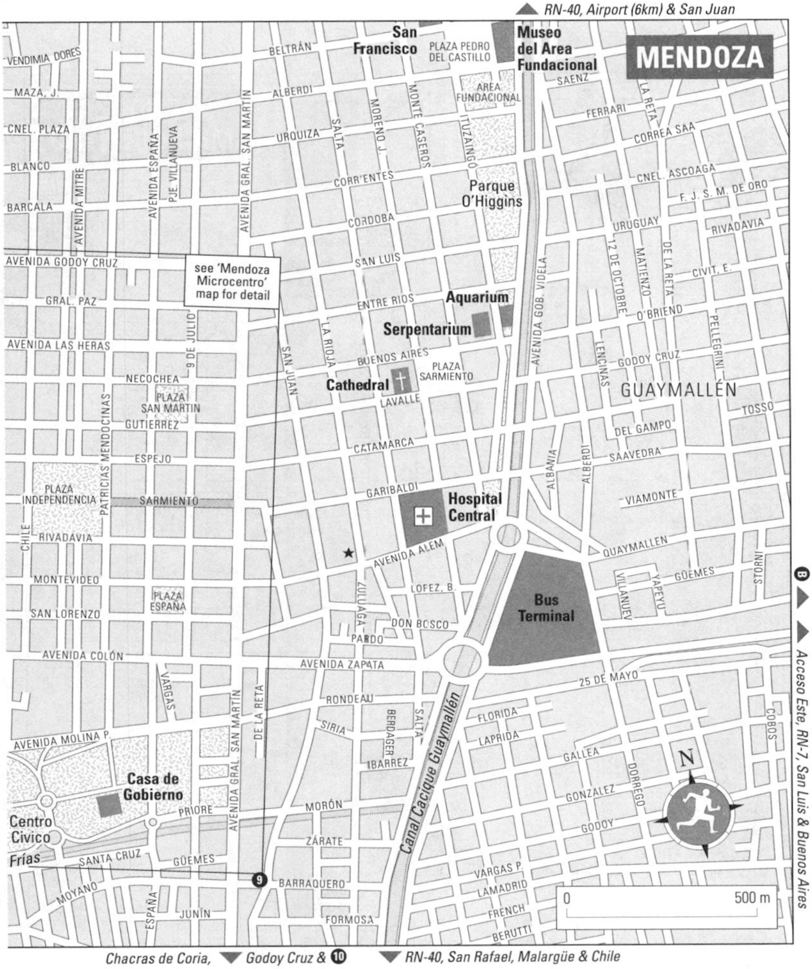

The main **tourist office** (daily 8am–9pm; ⓣ0261/420-2656, 420-2357 or 420-2800, ⓦwww.turismo.mendoza.gov.ar), with information on both the city and the province, is at San Martín 1143, a building that was previously the aristocratic Jockey Club; this is also the place to obtain Aconcagua climbing permits. There are two smaller city **tourist information centres** at Edificio Municipal, 9 de Julio 500 (Mon–Fri 9am–1pm; ⓣ0261/449-5185) and San Martín and Garibaldi (daily 9am–9pm; ⓣ0261/420-1333), as well as one in the satellite town of Luján de Cuyo (see p.527) at Sáenz Peña 1000 (Mon–Fri 8.30am–6pm, Sat & Sun 10am–4pm; ⓣ0261/498-1912). You'll get an especially warm welcome at **Pro Malargüe**, España 1075 (Mon–Fri 9am–1pm & 5–8pm, Sat 9am–1pm; ⓣ0261/429-2515), which, as the name indicates, is a regional tourist office with information on Malargüe. Just inside the main gates of the Parque General San Martín is another tourist office (daily 9am–8pm), mainly dispensing information about the park.

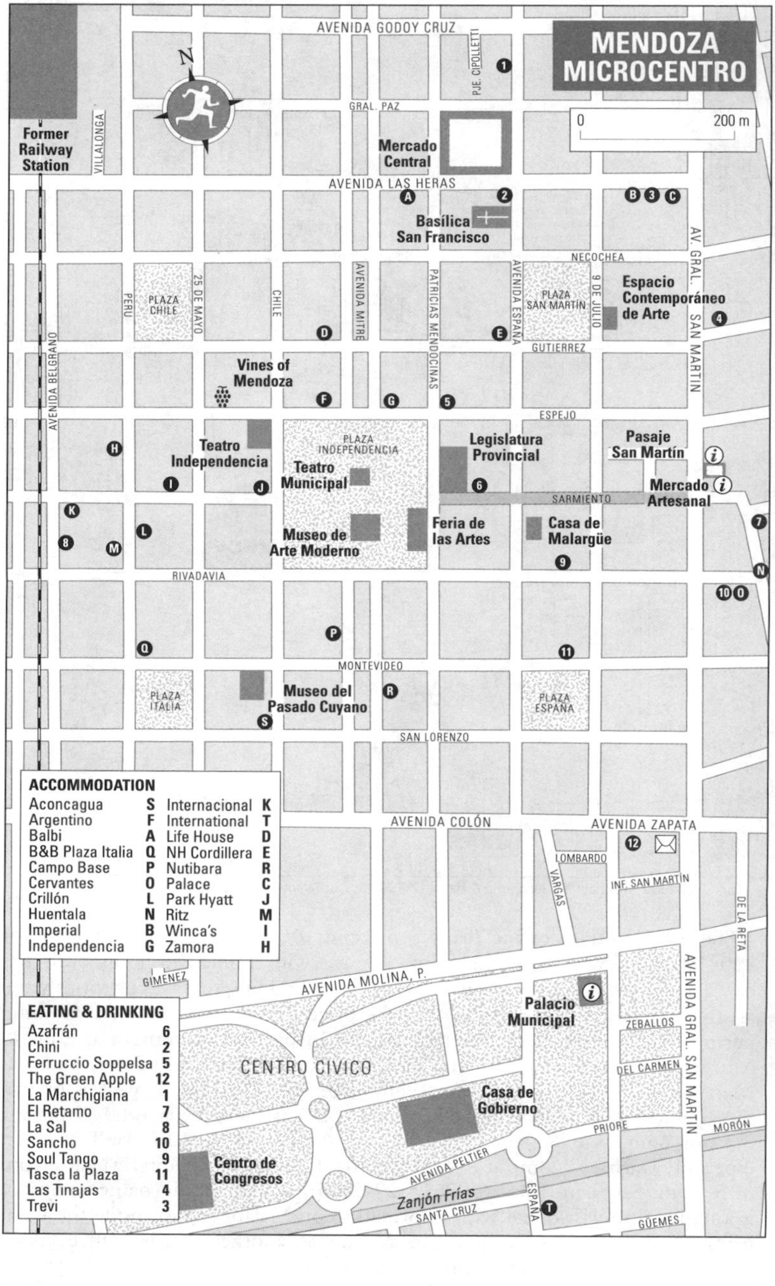
MENDOZA MICROCENTRO
0
200 m
N
AVENIDA GODOY CRUZ
PJE. CIPOLLETTI
GRAL. PAZ
Former Railway Station
VILLALONGA
Mercado Central
AVENIDA LAS HERAS
Basílica San Francisco
NECOCHEA
PERU
PLAZA CHILE
25 DE MAYO
CHILE
AVENIDA MITRE
PATRICIAS MENDOCINAS
AVENIDA ESPAÑA
PLAZA SAN MARTÍN
9 DE JULIO
Espacio Contemporáneo de Arte
AV. GRAL. SAN MARTIN
GUTIERREZ
AVENIDA BELGRANO
Vines of Mendoza
ESPEJO
Teatro Independencia
PLAZA INDEPENDENCIA
Teatro Municipal
Legislatura Provincial
Pasaje San Martín
Mercado Artesanal
SARMIENTO
Museo de Arte Moderno
Feria de las Artes
Casa de Malargüe
RIVADAVIA
MONTEVIDEO
PLAZA ITALIA
Museo del Pasado Cuyano
PLAZA ESPAÑA
SAN LORENZO
AVENIDA COLÓN
AVENIDA ZAPATA
LOMBARDO
VARGAS
INF. SAN MARTÍN
DE LA RETA
GIMENEZ
AVENIDA MOLINA, P.
Palacio Municipal
AVENIDA GRAL. SAN MARTIN
ZEBALLOS
CENTRO CIVICO
DEL CARMEN
Casa de Gobierno
PRIORE
MORÓN
Centro de Congresos
AVENIDA PELTIER
ESPAÑA
Zanjón Frías
SANTA CRUZ
GÜEMES
ACCOMMODATION
Aconcagua S
Argentino F
Balbi A
B&B Plaza Italia Q
Campo Base P
Cervantes O
Crillón L
Huentala N
Imperial B
Independencia G
Internacional K
International T
Life House D
NH Cordillera E
Nutibara R
Palace C
Park Hyatt J
Ritz M
Winca's I
Zamora H
EATING & DRINKING
Azafrán 6
Chini 2
Ferruccio Soppelsa 5
The Green Apple 12
La Marchigiana 1
El Retamo 7
La Sal 8
Sancho 10
Soul Tango 9
Tasca la Plaza 11
Las Tinajas 4
Trevi 3

A number of tour operators run half-day **city tours** (see "Listings", p.526), or you could give the municipal Trolley Turistico Cultural (Tues–Fri 11am, Sat 11am & 4pm; $5) a whirl: the seventy-minute trip departs from Plaza San Martín and visits the main sites, with onboard actors giving a colourful rendition of the city's history. The tourist office also runs guided walks with themes such as history or religion – ask for the latest timetable. For finding your own way around, there are plenty of **buses** and **trolley-buses** – the latter mostly serving the inner suburbs plus the bus station. The two have a complex numbering system, with a logic that escapes most people; study the map displayed at each stop. You pay a flat $0.90 fare for both – no change given – except for much longer distances such as the airport.

Accommodation

Compared with many Argentine cities, Mendoza is very well-off for places to stay: it has more than enough beds for its needs, except during the Fiesta de la Vendimia in early March. It boasts several luxurious **hotels**, including branches of top-class international chains, while **budget** lodgings tend to be less squalid than elsewhere and are also relatively easy to come by – most are close to the bus terminal. Mendoza now has over a dozen **youth hostels** (average dorm price $25), plus a couple of **B&Bs**. In the middle range are countless nondescript but very decent smaller hotels. At the higher end, particularly interesting options are **bodega hotels or posadas**, many of which are in the swish suburbs of Chacras de Coria and Maipú (see box, p.517). If you haven't got anything booked, the best street to head for is Aristides Villanueva (usually referred to as Aristides), three blocks south and four blocks west of the Plaza Independencia – it's packed with both hostels and more upmarket options. You can also ask at the tourist office for their list of rooms to rent in private houses. Campers should make for the heights of El Challao, 6km northwest, where **campsite** *El Suizo* (ⓣ0261/444-1991, ⓦwww.campingsuizo.com.ar) sits among shady woods on Avenida Champagnat. It has a swimming pool, a small restaurant and even an open-air cinema; tent pitches and *cabañas* (both ❶) are available. **Bus** #110 runs out to El Challao from the corner of Salta and Avenida Além.

Hostels

Break Point Av Arístides Villanueva 241 ⓣ0261/423-9514, ⓦhttp://breakpointhostel.com.ar. At the heart of the city's *movida* zone, this hostel offers free Internet, all kinds of tours, a large TV lounge and a small pool. An added bonus is the excellent-value *parrilla*. The private rooms (❸) are particularly good value for solo travellers.

Campo Base Mitre 946 ⓣ0261/429-0707, ⓦwww.campo-base.com.ar. The youth hostel traditionally preferred by Aconcagua climbers, as the owners organize their own treks. Clean, friendly and very laid-back, with lots of barbecues, parties and general fun, though some of the dorms are slightly cramped. If it's full, try its sister, *Campo Base II*, at Arístides Villanueva 470 (ⓣ0261/420-2486).

Independencia Mitre 1237 ⓣ0261/423-1806, ⓦwww.hostelindependencia.com.ar. Nicely located in an attractive lemon-coloured townhouse on the plaza of the same name, this has a fully equipped kitchen, a games room, a patio and doubles (❸) and triples in addition to pleasant dorms. The staff organize bodega tours and treks and offer free *mate*.

International España 343 ⓣ0261/424-0018, ⓦwww.hostelmendoza.net. The best-established of all the hostels, with a bright patio, stimulating ambience, small dorms with private bathroom and an excellent kitchen; the staff can also fix you up with tours and sports activities in the whole region. Its *El Carajo* bar is a popular meeting-place, and there's an *asado* cook-out most Fri. Private rooms available (❸).

Itaka Av Arístides Villanueva 480 ⓣ0261/4239793, ⓦwww.itakahouse.com. Fun and friendly newcomer with attractive patio and garden, above-average kitchen facilities and a small pool. Dorms and doubles (❹).

Life House Gutiérrez 565 ⓣ0261/420-4294, ⓦwww.lifehouse.com.ar. Two-, four- and six-bed rooms with their own bath, pleasant kitchen, barbecue area and swimming pool, at this professionally run hostel. Doubles also available (3).

Winca's Sarmiento 717 ⓣ0261/425-3804, ⓦwww.wincashostel.com.ar. Smart, clean and attractive, this central hostel has dorms plus some double rooms (3) with private bath and offers complimentary breakfast and a small pool. The decor – the name means "traveller" in the Huarpe indigenous tongue – has a decidedly pre-Columbian flavour.

B&Bs and hospedajes

Bed and Breakfast Plaza Italia Montevideo 685 ⓣ0261/423-4219, ⓦwww.plazaitalia.net. Genuine B&B in a comfortable family house with en-suite rooms, a/c and a delicious breakfast; parking available. 6

La Escondida Julio A. Roca 344 ⓣ0261/425-5202, ⓦwww.laescondidabb.com. Wonderfully welcoming B&B in a quiet residential part of the city, with a superb swimming pool at the end of a long garden; rooms are extremely comfortable. 5

Quinta Rufino Rufino Ortega 142 ⓣ0261/420-4696, ⓦwww.quintarufinohostel.com.ar. A converted house in a peaceful neighbourhood, with pleasant en-suite rooms and friendly staff. 4

Zamora Perú 1156 ⓣ0261/425-7537. A Neocolonial villa with clean rooms around a leafy patio; ask for the room with a roof terrace. Larger rooms, with four or five beds, and group discounts available. Very popular with Aconcagua climbers. 5

Hotels

Aconcagua San Lorenzo 545 ⓣ0261/520-0500, ⓦwww.hotelaconcagua.com. Professionally run modern hotel, with small but comfortable rooms with TV and mini-bar; it's worth paying an extra $20 for a room with a glorious mountain view. A swimming pool and sauna are welcome facilities. 7

Argentino Espejo 455 ⓣ0261/405-6300, ⓦwww.argentino-hotel.com. Shiny place on the Plaza Independencia aimed squarely at the foreign tourist dollar, with ultra-stylish rooms, a gym, swimming pool and attentive service. 7

Balbi Av Las Heras 340 ⓣ0261/423-3500, ⓦwww.hotelbalbi.com.ar. Superior three-star place with a lavish reception space, huge dining area and spacious rooms with fresh decor. Swimming pool and terrace. 6

Cervantes Amigorena 65 ⓣ0261/520-0400, ⓦwww.hotelcervantesmza.com.ar. Traditional-style, comfortable hotel, with pleasant rooms. Has one of the best hotel restaurants in town, the *Sancho* (see p.523). 6

Crillón Perú 1065 ⓣ0261/429-8494, ⓦwww.hcrillon.com.ar. An above-average three-star hotel, the *Crillón* has well-kept bathrooms and efficient service. 6

Huentala Primitivo de la Reta 1007 ⓣ0261/4200766, ⓦwww.huentala.com. Trendy new four-star boutique hotel with stylish lobby and rooms, pool and a French restaurant, *Chimpay Bistro*. 8

Ibis Acceso Este 4241, Villa Nueva, Guaymallén ⓣ0261/426-4600, ⓔh2161@accor.com. This chain hotel is rather anonymous but good value for money, with smart, modern rooms and up-to-date facilities including Internet access and cable TV. 5

Imperial Av Las Heras 88 ⓣ0261/425-3992, ⓔhotel_imperial@hotmail.com. An old-fashioned but reliable hotel, with professional service and quiet, comfortable rooms. 4

Internacional Sarmiento 720 ⓣ0261/425-5606, ⓦwww.hinternacional.com.ar. The best in this class in Mendoza, this hotel has understated, tasteful furnishings in spacious a/c rooms. A swimming pool and an enormous garage are two further assets. 7

NH Cordillera España and Gutiérrez ⓣ0261/441-6464, ⓦwww.nh-hotels.com. Jazzy hotel, one of the nicest of the Spanish chain in Argentina, with professional reception service, sleek rooms, agreeable bathrooms and a swimming pool. 8

Nutibara Av Mitre 867 ⓣ0261/429-5428, ⓦwww.nutibara.com.ar. Rather dated but comfortable hotel, with large rooms, a/c, cable TV and efficient room service, plus a swimming pool. 6

Palace Av Las Heras 70 ⓣ0261/423-4200, ⓔhpalace@infovia.com.ar. Chintz-upholstered furniture and comfortable rooms, with decent bathrooms, so ignore the gloomy reception. Downstairs there's a very reasonable Italian restaurant, the *Trevi*. 5

Park Hyatt Chile 1124 ⓣ0261/441-1234, ⓦwww.mendoza.park.hyatt.com. Easily the top hotel in the city, this modern block is located on the site of the famous *Plaza Hotel* where Perón and Eva stayed soon after they first met. Apart from the much vaunted casino, facilities include a luxurious spa, where Thai massages are on offer, a large outdoor pool, the stylish *Uvas* cocktail bar and *Bistro M*, one of the classiest restaurants in the city. Rooms are spacious and the bathrooms made for lingering over ablutions. 9

Ritz Perú 1008 ⓣ0261/423-5115, ⓦwww.ritzhotelmendoza.com.ar. This place tries very hard to look British, and partly succeeds with its chintz furnishings and plush fitted carpets. Reliable plumbing and a/c. 6

Bodega accommodation

Many bodegas in and around Mendoza (see box, pp.524–525) have begun offering **accommodation** in addition to tours and tastings. The quiet, suburban location of these bodega hotels – which are generally at the higher end of the price range – is one of their selling points, although it does mean that unless you have your own car you may be more or less limited to the delights the bodega has to offer. However, this is not at all a bad proposition for a day or two, especially as most places offer full board as well as all kinds of extra activities – many of them wine-related, of course. Always book bodega accommodation ahead, and let them know if you don't have your own transport, as they will usually pick you up from Mendoza city or airport.

Cavas Wine Lodge Costa Flores s/n, Alto Agrelo ⓣ0261/4106927, ⓦwww.cavaswinelodge.com. Impeccably designed luxury lodge out in the countryside near Luján de Cuyo. Each of the fourteen rooms is individually decorated and comes with its own wooden deck, pool and circular terrace with an unobstructed view of the cordillera. The final Bacchanalian touch is a red-wine spa bath in an ancient tub; this and other wine-based spa treatments, such as a crushed malbec scrub, can be booked by non-guests, too. US$420 for a double room; US$30 for just the bath.

Club Tapiz Pedro Molina s/n, Maipú ⓣ0261/4964815, ⓦwww.tapiz.com.ar. Affiliated with Bodega Tapiz in Maipú, *Club Tapiz* has seven tastefully appointed rooms in a renovated villa dating from 1890, as well as a spa, pool, gaucho-style *pulpería* bar and its own gourmet restaurant, *Terruño*, surrounded by a vineyard. US$150 per person per night, breakfast included.

Finca Adalgisa Pueyrredón 2222, Chacras de Coria ⓣ0261/4960713, ⓦwww.fincaadalgisa.com.ar. Small *finca* (ranch) now geared more towards tourism than wine production, though still with its own vineyard. The attractive rooms are in an annexe with a jasmine-covered verandah running alongside, there's a swimming pool among the vines, and visitors have the chance to eat meals with the family in the original ranch house and sample wines and cheese under the nogal tree at dusk. From US$100 per person per night.

Posada Salentein RP-89 and E. Videla, Tunuyán ⓣ02622/423550, ⓦwww.salenteintourism.com. A posada belonging to the Salentein winery, which can also be visited on a tour (see p.525). Regional cooking and horse-riding are part of the package. US$100 per person per night.

The City

Mendoza's sights are few and far between – much of its interest lies in its wide avenues, lively plazas and green parks. The centre of the urban layout is the **Plaza Independencia**, the size of four blocks. Near its corners lie four orbital squares, **plazas Chile**, **San Martín**, **España** and **Italia**, each with its own distinctive character. Museums are not Mendoza's forte, but the **Museo del Pasado Cuyano**, which offers an insight into late nineteenth-century life for the city's richer families, is worth a visit, as is the **Museo de Ciencias Naturales y Antropológicas**, a wide-ranging natural history museum. The latter sits in the handsomely landscaped **Parque General San Martín**, which slopes up a hill to the west of the microcentro and commands views of the city and its surroundings. One of the country's finest green spaces, with avenues of planes and palms, a boating lake, a manicured rose garden and a zoo, it's also the venue for the city's major annual event, the **Fiesta de la Vendimia**, held every March. The ruins of colonial Mendoza's nucleus, where it was founded between the Guaymallén and Tajamar canals to the northeast of the present-day centre, have been preserved as the **Área Fundacional**, where there's another small museum. The most impressive sight in the whole city, however, is the historic **Bodega Escorihuela** (see p.524), the beautiful **winery** in Godoy Cruz, a southern suburb.

Mendoza has the most complicated **street-name system** of any city in Argentina. Streets that run north–south keep the same name from end to end, but those that run west–east have up to four names within the city limits alone. From west to east, names change at Avenida Belgrano, Avenida San Martín and Avenida Gobernador R. Videla, the latter running along the Guaymallén canal, the city's eastern boundary. Beyond it lies the residential town of Guaymallén, part of Greater Mendoza, itself divided into several districts, where you'll find the bus terminal, a cluster of budget accommodation, a number of restaurants and a couple of wineries. On all street signs is a useful number telling you how many blocks you are from the city's point zero, at San Martín and Sarmiento; 100 (O) means one block west, 500 (N) five blocks north. Paseo Sarmiento, a busy pedestrian precinct lined with loads of shops and cafés with terraces, joins Plaza Independencia, the city's centre-point, to Avenida San Martín.

For an overview of the city, to get your bearings and to enjoy unobstructed views towards the Andes, preferably in the morning when the mountains are lit by the rising sun, you can take a lift up to the **Terraza Mirador**, on the roof of the **Palacio Municipal**, 9 de Julio 500 (Mon, Wed & Fri 8.30am–1pm, Tues, Thurs & Sat 8.30am–1pm & 4–7pm; free).

Plaza Independencia

Four blocks in size, **Plaza Independencia** lies at the nerve-centre of the post-earthquake city and at the crossroads of two of Mendoza's main streets, east–west Avenida Sarmiento and north–south Avenida Mitre. Originally intended as the city's administrative headquarters – which were built instead in the centro cívico, four blocks south – it's modern Mendoza's recreational and cultural focus, planted with shady acacias, magnolias, sycamores and other trees. It is also the setting for festivals, concerts and outdoor cinema-screenings, and bustles with life both during the day and on summer evenings. During remodelling in 1995, monumental fountains, backed by a mosaic mural depicting the story of Argentina's independence, were installed, and beneath them is a late nineteenth-century bunker originally designed as an emergency hospital to deal with quake victims. It now houses the **Museo Municipal de Arte Moderno** (Mon 4–8pm, Tues–Sat 9am–1pm & 4–8pm, Sun 4–8pm; free), where local contemporary art is on display. The building also hosts a patio café and a new theatre, the Teatro Julio Quintanilla, that specializes in plays for children. Along the eastern edge of the plaza, a crafts fair is held at weekends. Just west of the central fountains stands a seventeen-metre-high steel structure, dating from 1942, on which a mass of coloured lights form the national coat-of-arms at night.

Beyond it, along Calle Chile, are a number of prestigious buildings, including, between Avenida Sarmiento and Rivadavia, the **Colégio Nacional Agustín Alvarez**, housed in a fine Art Nouveau quake-resistant edifice of reinforced concrete. Just north of it, on the corner of Sarmiento, is the site of the illustrious 1920s **Plaza Hotel**, famous because the Peróns stayed here soon after first meeting in San Juan; the building was abandoned for many years but finally refurbished to become the Hyatt's five-star luxury establishment (see "Accommodation", p.516). Next door is the Neoclassical facade of the **Teatro Independencia**, one of the city's more traditional playhouses, while, over on the eastern side of the plaza, is the **Legislatura Provincial**, built in 1889 but remodelled to take on its present grim appearance in 1918.

Plaza España

The small plaza that lies a block east and a block south of Independencia's southeast corner, called Plaza Montevideo until 1949, is now known as **Plaza**

△ Plaza España, Mendoza

España. It's the most beautiful of all Mendoza's plazas – its benches are decorated with brightly coloured Andalucian ceramic tiles, and the paths are lined with luxuriant trees and shrubs. Although Mendoza's population is of overwhelmingly Italian origin, the city's old, traditional families came from Spain, and they had the square built in the late 1940s. The mellow terracotta flagstones, picked out with smaller blue and white tiles, and the lily ponds and fountains set off the slightly uncanny monument to the Spanish discovery of South America, standing at the southern end of the plaza. It comprises a *zócalo* or brightly tiled pedestal, decorated with scenes from *Don Quixote* and the Argentine gaucho epic *Martín Fierro*, along with Columbus's "discovery" and depictions of missionary work. At the centre of the plinth stand two female statues: one is a Spanish noblewoman clasping a book, the other a mestiza (part Spanish, part native American) woman, a Mendocina, holding a bunch of grapes. Dancing and folk music take place here on October 12, the **Día de la Raza**, which in Latin America is a celebration of mestizo culture.

Plaza Italia and Museo del Pasado Cuyano

Four blocks west of Plaza España's northwest corner along Calle Montevideo – an attractive street lined with plane trees and picturesque Neocolonial houses with brightly coloured facades – is **Plaza Italia**, called Plaza Lima until 1900, but renamed when its Italian community built two monuments to their country of origin here. A monument on the south side of the square is a bronze statue of the mythical Roman wolf feeding Romulus and Remus, next to a marble Roman pillar. The main monument in stone and bronze, to its west, represents La Patria, flanked by a statue of an Indian and a Roman philosopher. A frieze running around the monument, showing scenes of building, ploughing and harvesting, is a tribute to the Italian immigrants whose labour helped build the country. In November, the park blazes with the bright red flowers of its tipas, and in March, during the week leading up to the Fiesta de la Vendimia, the plaza hosts the **Festa in Piazza**, a big party at which stalls representing every Italian region serve their local culinary specialities. The climax is an extravagant fashion parade.

Half a block east of the plaza is the **Museo del Pasado Cuyano** (Mon–Fri 9am–12.30pm; $2), at Montevideo 544. It's the city's history museum, housed in part of an aristocratic late nineteenth-century mansion, the Quinta de los Civit. The adobe house, built to resist earthquakes, belonged to the family of Francisco Civit, governor of Mendoza, and his son Emilio, who was a senator at the start of the twentieth century and was responsible for many of Mendoza's civic works, including the great park. It contains a large amount of San Martín memorabilia and eighteenth-century furniture, artworks and weapons, all rescued from the earthquake rubble. The most valuable exhibit is a fifteenth-century polychrome **wooden altarpiece**, with a liberal dose of rosy cherubim, that somehow turned up here from Sant Andreu de Socarrats in Catalonia and is now housed in the mansion's chapel.

Plaza San Martín and Plaza Chile

The square to the northeast of Plaza Independencia is the relatively nondescript **Plaza San Martín**; it's dominated by an early twentieth-century statue of General San Martín on a horse, looking towards the Andes, which he crossed with his army to defeat the Spanish. This square was previously called Plaza Cobo in honour of another local hero, the entrepreneur who introduced the Lombardy poplar to the region – the tree not only acts as a windbreak, but its lightweight wood is also perfect for making fruit crates. Near the plaza's northwest corner is the city's only church of note, the **Basílica de San Francisco**, one of the first buildings to go up after the 1861 quake. Its Belgian architect modelled it on Paris's Église de la Trinité, but the pink- and cream-painted stucco make it look Neocolonial rather than Neoclassical. This isn't the complete picture, either, as part of the structure had to be demolished after another earthquake in 1927, leaving the church looking a bit truncated. Despite its architectural shortcomings, it's locally venerated, since some members of San Martín's family are buried in simple tombs inside. A special chamber up the stairs next to the altar (Mon–Sat 9am–noon; free) contains a revered image of Our Lady of Carmen, the patron saint of the Army of the Andes, along with San Martín's stylish rosewood staff, with a topaz hilt and a silver tip – it, too, has the status of a religious relic among the people of Mendoza. It's also a fine piece of craftsmanship.

The surrounding district is Mendoza's **"City"**, or financial district, whose opulent banks and insurance-company offices, most built in a "British" style, are among the city's most impressive buildings. Both the Banco de Galicia and the Banco de la Nación were built in the 1920s and 1930s, the city's heyday, as was the ex-Banco de Mendoza, lying on the eastern side of Plaza San Martín, diagonally opposite the basilica. The latter now houses the **Espacio Contemporáneo de Arte** (Mon–Sat 9am–1pm & 4–9pm, Sun 4–9pm; free), worth a look for both its contemporary art exhibitions and its eight-sided lobby crowned with a huge stained-glass cupola.

Four blocks west of Plaza San Martín is the least interesting of the four orbital plazas, **Plaza Chile**. It was named in recognition of Chile's assistance after the 1861 quake, and its centrepiece is a monument to the heroes of the two countries' independence, José de San Martín and Bernardo O'Higgins, seldom seen together in a sculpture – this is a 1947 piece by a Chilean artist. The plaza is shaded by an enormous *aguaribay* tree.

Área Fundacional

The **Museo del Área Fundacional**, at Alberdi and Videla Castillo (Tues–Sat 8am–7pm, Sun 3–8pm; $2), is built on the Plaza Mayor, where the city was originally founded, 1km northeast of Plaza Independencia. The modern building houses an exhibition of domestic and artistic items retrieved from the rubble after the mammoth earthquake of 1861. It's built over part of the excavated colonial city foundations, which you can peer at through a glass floor. The exhibition relates the story of Mendoza's foundation and development before and after the great disaster. Nearby, across landscaped Plaza Pedro del Castillo, named for the city's founder, are the eerie ruins of the colonial city's Jesuit temple, popularly but erroneously known as the Ruinas de San Francisco. Immediately south extends a rather straggly park, the Parque Bernardo O'Higgins. At its southern end, you'll find a corner of the city best for visiting if you have children to entertain. As well as a playground, there's a decent-sized **aquarium** (daily 9am–8pm; $2), the country's first, and home to fresh- and saltwater fish of various stripes as well as caymans and turtles, and the **Serpentario Anaconda** (daily 9am–1pm & 3–7.30pm; $3), a kind of large greenhouse with a varied and impressive collection of snakes, poisonous toads and spiders – some of them, disturbingly, native to the region.

Parque General San Martín

Just over 1km due west of Plaza Independencia by Avenida Sarmiento, on a slope that turns into a steep hill overlooking the city, **Parque General San Martín** is one of the most beautiful parks in the country. As well as large areas of open land, used for impromptu football matches and picnics, its four square kilometres are home to the main football stadium, the amphitheatre where the finale of the Fiesta de la Vendimia is staged, a meteorological observatory, a monument to the Army of the Andes, a rowing lake, a tennis club, a hospital, the university campus, the riding club, an agricultural research centre, several restaurants, Mendoza's best jogging routes, a rose garden and an anthropological museum – in short, a city within the city.

First created in 1897 by **Charles Thays** (see box, p.130), it was extensively remodelled in 1940 by local architect Daniel Ramos Correas. It contains over fifty thousand trees of 750 varieties, planted, among other reasons, to stop landslides from the Andean foothills. The aristocratic Avenida de los Plátanos and Avenida de las Palmeras, lined with tall plane trees and Canary Island palms, and the romantic Rose Garden, with its five hundred rose varieties and arbours of wisteria, are popular walks.

The main entrance is through magnificent bronze and wrought-iron gates, topped with a rampant condor, at the western end of Avenida Emilio Civit. They were not, as a popular legend would have it, ordered for Ottoman Sultan Hamid II, who couldn't pay the bill; the crescent motif in their fine lace-like design, which lead to the apocryphal anecdote, was simply a fashionable pattern at the time. The gates were actually ordered by city authorities in 1910 to celebrate the country's centenary, and were made by the McFarlane ironworks in Glasgow. A road open to traffic runs westwards from here, skirting the northern edge of the park after going round the Caballitos de Marly, an exact reproduction in Carrara marble of the monumental horses in the middle of Paris's Place de la Concorde. From here you can rent a bike, take a horse and cart or catch a bus to the park's furthest points. A short walk southwest of the entrance, near the northern shores of the rowing lake, the recently restored **Fuente de los Continentes** is a dramatic set of sculptures meant to represent the diversity of humankind, and is a favoured backdrop for wedding photographs.

A good 2km west of the entrance you'll find the city's **zoo** (Tues–Sun 9am–5pm; $4; ⓣ0261/425-0130), one of the best in the country for its variety of animals and, more to the point, for the conditions in which they are kept. It's a landscaped forest of eucalyptus, *aguaribay* and fir trees, built into the lower slopes of the Cerro de la Gloria, from which also you get sweeping views of the city.

Another popular destination is the top of the Cerro de la Gloria, where there's an imposing 1914 monument to the Army of the Andes, the **Monumento al Ejército Libertador**. All cast in bronze, a buxom, winged *Liberty*, waving broken chains, leads General San Martín and his victorious troops across the cordillera. Around the granite plinth are bronze friezes depicting more picturesque scenes: the anti-royalist monk Luis Beltrán busy making weapons for the army, and the genteel ladies of Mendoza donating their jewellery for the good cause – these "Patricias Mendocinas", after whom a city street is named, were rumoured to have been particularly excited by the presence of so many soldiers billeted in the city; babies and infants sadly watch their valiant fathers head off to battle.

At the southern tip of the park's one-kilometre-long, serpentine rowing lake, in its southeastern corner, is the **Museo de Ciencias Naturales y Antropológicas** (Tues–Fri 8am–1pm & 2–7pm, Sat & Sun 3–7pm; $2; ⓣ0261/428-7666). Built in the 1930s to imitate the shape of a ship's bridge by local architects who introduced German Rationalism to Argentina, the museum is a series of mostly private collections of stuffed animals, ancient fossils, indigenous artefacts and mummies. The most interesting exhibits are a female mummy discovered at over 5000m in the Andes – along with a brightly coloured shawl – shrunken heads from Ecuador and fossils or skeletons of dinosaurs unearthed near Malargüe in southern Mendoza. Sometimes temporary exhibitions about pre-Columbian civilizations or paleontological subjects are staged here.

Eating, drinking and nightlife

Mendoza is the prosperous capital of Argentina's western region, and the produce grown in the nearby oases is tip-top; as a result, the city's many, varied and often highly sophisticated **restaurants** and **wine bars** are usually full, and

Fiesta de la Vendimia

Mendoza's main festival is the giant **Fiesta de la Vendimia**, or Wine Harvest Festival, which reaches its climax during the first weekend of March every year. Wine takes over the city – bottles even decorate clothing boutique windows – and the tourist trade shifts into high gear. On the Sunday before the carnival proper (the last Sun in Feb), the *Bendición de los Frutos*, or Blessing of the Grapes, takes place, in a ceremony involving the bishop of Mendoza. During the week leading up to the grand finale, events range from folklore concerts in the centro cívico to Italian food and entertainment in the Plaza Italia. On Friday evening is the **Vía Blanca**, a parade of illuminated floats through the central streets, while on Saturday it's the *Carrusel*, when a carnival parade winds along the same route, each department in the province sending a float from which a previously elected beauty queen and her entourage of runners-up fling local produce, ranging from grapes and flowers to watermelons and packets of pasta, into the cheering crowds lining the road. On Saturday evening, the *Acto Central* is held in an amphitheatre in the Parque San Martín; it's a gala performance of song, dance and general kitsch-o-rama, hosted by local TV celebs, eventually leading up to a drawn-out vote – by political leaders representing each department in the province – to elect the queen of the festival. The same show is re-run, minus the election, and therefore less tedium, on Sunday evening. The spectacle costs millions of pesos and is a huge investment by the local wine-growers, but as it's attended by some 25,000 people it seems to be financially viable. The organizers boast that it's the biggest such festival in South America and one of the most lavish wine-related celebrations in the world. For more information contact the city's tourist office (see p.513).

serve some of the best food and drink in the country. Its **bars** are lively and it has a well-developed café-terrace culture, with Avenida Arístides Villanueva, to the west of the centre, a hotspot; **nightlife** is also vibrant, and is mostly concentrated in outlying places such as El Challao, to the northwest, and, especially, fashionable Chacras de Coria to the south.

Restaurants

1884 Francis Mallmann Belgrano 1188, Godoy Cruz ⓣ0261/424-2698 & 424-3336. This ultra-chic wine bar and award-winning restaurant with fashion-model staff, swish decor and crystal wine-glasses – rare in Argentina – is considered one of the country's finest. It is next to the sumptuous Bodega Escorihuela, and serves the bodega's fine wines with a balanced menu that includes Patagonian lamb, trout from Malargüe and plums from General Alvear.

Azafrán Sarmiento 765 ⓣ0261/429-4200. A deli-cum-restaurant with an excellent cellar, lively decor and delicious food – specialities include smoked venison ravioli – plus home-brewed beer; portions are a bit on the miserly side, though.

Basilika Av Arístides Villanueva 332. One of the best pizzerias in the city, dishing up an array of toppings on delicious crusts until the early hours. There's also a giant screen showing football matches on Sun. Closed Mon & Tues.

La Carmela Av Arístides Villanueva 298. Great, no-fuss Argentine cooking with a menu that changes daily, speedy service and an attractive outdoor seating area from which to watch the lively Arístides streetlife.

Don Mario 25 de Mayo 1324, Guaymallén. An institutional *parrilla* in the neighbourhood of Guaymallén (east of the city centre), frequented by Mendocino families in search of comforting decor and an old-fashioned *parrillada*.

The Green Apple Colón 458. This agreeable vegetarian restaurant serves breakfast, lunch and dinner, with natural fruit juices; the *tenedor libre* is especially good value.

La Marchigiana Av España 1619 ⓣ0261/423-0751. This is *the* Italian restaurant in the city, run by the same family for decades. For a reasonable price you can eat fresh *caprese* salad, have delicious cannelloni and finish with one of the best tiramisus in the country.

La Margeurita Av Arístides Villanueva 687. Succulent pizzas and fresh pasta in a bright modern setting, with good music and friendly staff.

El Patio de Jesús María Viamonte 4961, Chacras de Coria. Well-known and respected classic *parrilla* out in Chacras. There are also other branches in the city suburbs.

Praga L. Aguirre 413 ⓣ0261/425-9585. Top-quality culinary venue, with understated decor, delicately prepared fish and seafood, a fitting wine list and impeccable service. Book ahead.

El Retamo Garibaldi 93. Vegetarian and health-food restaurant serving run-of-the-mill, but totally fresh and appetizing, food.

La Sal Belgrano 1069 ⓣ0261/420 4322. Striking surroundings, great music – including jazz – and impeccable service are all pluses at this outstanding downtown restaurant where the rotating menu is an experience in itself – save room for the desserts. Everything is accompanied by amazing wines as recommended by the staff. Prices range from moderate to expensive.

Sancho Amigorena 65. Conventional meals such as *milanesas* and steaks, together with pasta and fish dishes, are on offer at this smart institutional establishment with an attractive patio seating area.

Tasca la Plaza Montevideo 117. Intimate little bistro, or *tasca*, conveniently located on the Plaza España and serving appropriately Hispanic fare, including tapas, along with sangría and good wines; charming service.

Las Tinajas Lavalle 38. Good-value *tenedor libre* in the city centre. The food quality is a cut above the usual all-you-can-eat establishments – there's an excellent *asado* and heaving salad bar.

Trevi Las Heras 70. You could be in Bologna or Genoa in this home-style northern Italian restaurant with old-fashioned, discreet service, dowdy decor and delicious food.

Bars and cafés

La Aldea Av Arístides Villanueva 495. A lively pub-style bar that does great sandwiches and *lomitos*.

Apeteco San Juan and Barraquero. A city institution, this pre-club bar used to be called *El Rancho*, and still hosts "El Rancho" nights on Wed – an essential stop on a Wed night out.

Chini Av España and Las Heras. One of the best ice-creameries in the city, doing dozens of flavours – the best are the range of *dulce de leche*-based ones.

Ferruccio Soppelsa Belgrano and Emilio Civit, and branches at Espejo 299 and Paseo Sarmiento 45. This chain of *heladerías*, run for years by the same Italian family, is guaranteed to give you enough calories to last you to the top of Aconcagua.

Bodegas in and around Mendoza

There are dozens of **wineries** in the **Mendoza area** that are open to visitors. The easiest way to visit bodegas is on a **tour** organized by one of the many agencies operating out of Mendoza (see "Listings", p.526). A typical half-day trip visits two or three bodegas, while a full day visits five or six and includes lunch; full-day trips are better value if you have the time. Most agencies dictate the bodegas you will visit, though if you don't mind paying for the privilege you can usually tailor your own tour. Wine enthusiasts and those willing to splurge should contact Grapevine (ⓣ0261/429-7522, ⓦwww.thegrapevine-argentina.com), which does a range of small group "premium" tours led by native English speakers who are also expert tasters; lunch is included. For something a bit different, the slightly alarmingly named Bikes and Wines, at Urquiza 1606 in the satellite town of Maipú (ⓣ0261/410-6686, ⓦwww.bikesandwines.com), will provide you with bikes, maps and reservations so you can make a bodega tour at your own pace.

Though most people choose to use a tour agency, **public transport** is also an option, or you can rent a car and **drive** yourself; if you are planning to go under you own steam, be sure to ask at a tourist office or call ahead to check times, to book a visit and to ask for an English-speaking guide, if you need one. The bodegas tend to be concentrated in the eastern suburb of **Guaymallén**, in **Maipú** (see p.528) and in another satellite town, **Luján de Cuyo** (see p.527), which is about 12km south of the city. For transport to Maipú and central Luján de Cuyo, see the respective town accounts; buses referred to in the listings in this box stop at the bus terminal or along Avenida San Martín.

Most visits and tastings are **free** (where there is a cost it is stated), but you're pointedly steered to a sales area at the end (have cash, not plastic, to hand if you want to take advantage of this) and there's a surcharge if you want to taste the best tipples. Try and see different kinds of wineries, ranging from the old-fashioned, traditional bodegas to the highly mechanized, ultra-modern producers; at the former you're more likely to receive personal attention and get a chance to taste finer wines. Some wineries have a **restaurant** on the premises, as Argentines wisely prefer to eat when they drink, and some have also started offering on-site **accommodation**, generally a luxurious (and expensive) option – see the box on p.517 for more information.

Bodega tours

Chandón Agrelo 5507, Luján de Cuyo ⓣ0261/490-9966, ⓔvisitorcenter@chandon.com.ar. Tours Feb–Mar & July Mon–Fri 9.30am, 11am, 12.30pm, 2.30pm & 4.30pm, Sat 9.30am, 11am & 12.30pm; rest of year Mon–Fri 10.30am, noon, 2.30pm & 4pm. A modern bodega, somewhat lacking in character but impressive all the same, with excellent wine-tasting. The tours start with a video and end up at the salesroom. English or premium-tasting tours should be requested ahead. Bus #380.

Domaine St Diego Franklin Villanueva 3821, Maipú ⓣ0261/499-0414, ⓔjuanmendoza@sinectis.com.ar. Tours (limited to six people) Mon–Fri 9am–5pm, Sat 9am–2pm; reserve 24hr ahead. Small producer, specializing in cabernet sauvignon. One of the more intimate wineries in the region, giving visitors the chance to try good-quality wines after an hour in the vineyards and an hour in the bodega.

Escorihuela Belgrano 1188 and Presidente Alvear, Godoy Cruz ⓣ0261/424-2744. Tours Mon–Fri 9.30am, 10.30am, 11.30am, 12.30pm, 2.30pm & 3.30pm. Just 2km south of Mendoza's city centre in Godoy Cruz, this historic bodega, founded in 1884, is famous for its fantastic and enormous barrel from Nancy, France, a work of art in itself, housed in a cathedral-like cellar. The sumptuous buildings include an art gallery, huge vaulted storage rooms stacked with aromatic casks and a gourmet restaurant, *1884 Francis Mallmann* (see p.523 for review).

Giol ("La Colina de Oro") Ozamis 1040, Maipú ⓣ0261/497-2592. Tours Mon–Sat 9am–6.30pm, Sun & public holidays

11am–2pm. A wonderfully old-fashioned place, with its fair share of antique barrels – including one of the biggest in South America – alongside the Museo Nacional del Vino y la Vendimia. Bus #160.

El Lagar Carmelo Patti San Martín 2614, Luján de Cuyo ⓣ0261-4981379. Known as "El maestro del vino" (the wine master), local personality Carmelo has been working in the wine trade since 1971. Now with his own bodega, his enthusiasm and knowledge make him one of the best guides to wine in the area and its production (though request a translator if you don't speak Spanish). Visits are informal, but call ahead to arrange a mutually convenient time.

Lagarde San Martín 1745, Luján de Cuyo ⓣ0261/498-0011, ⓦwww.lagarde.com.ar. Tours Mon–Fri 10am, 11am, noon, 2.30pm & 3.30pm. Lagarde is a major producer, and the site is enormous, but well worth seeing. There's also an impressive vintage car exhibition.

Luigi Bosca San Martín 2044, Luján de Cuyo ⓣ0261/498-1974, ⓦwww.luigibosca.com.ar. Tours Mon–Fri 10.30am, 3.30pm & 5pm, Sat noon. One of the best-known wine brands in Argentina, Luigi Bosca appears on many of the agency-run bodega trips. The professional guides are keen to emphasize the family credentials of the winery, but it all feels a bit too neat and commercial. There's an interesting art exhibition, though, which focuses on the parallels between the Stations of the Cross and wine production.

Nieto Senetiner Ruta Panamericana, Chacras de Coria ⓣ0261/498-0315, ⓦwww.nietosentiner.com.ar. Tours Mon–Fri 10am, 11am, 12.30pm & 4pm. Some of Argentina's finest wines are produced by this traditional winery. The 12.30pm tour is followed by a delicious lunch, which must be reserved in advance.

Norton RP-15, Perdriel, Luján de Cuyo ⓣ0261/488-0480, ⓔturismo@norton.com.ar. Tours Mon–Fri 9am, 10.30am, noon, 1.30pm, 3pm & 4.30pm. A prize-winning producer, making top-class if slightly old-fashioned wines, but well worth the visit. Tours must be reserved in advance. Bus #380.

Salentein RP-89 and E. Videla, Tunuyán ⓣ02622/423550, ⓦwww.bodegasalentein.com. Tours daily 11am, 1pm, 3pm (English); $10. One of the few bodegas to charge for tours, but also one of the most beautiful wineries in the country. Known as the "Cathedral to Wine", this magnificent state-of-the-art building, constructed using sumptuous stone, makes for a memorable experience; the wines themselves are also outstanding.

San Felipe ("La Rural") Montecaseros s/n, Coquimbito, Maipú ⓣ0261/497-2013. Tours (bilingual) Mon–Sat 9am, 1pm, 2pm & 5.30pm, Sun 10am & 1pm. This magnificent traditional bodega stands among its own vineyards and has its own small museum. An interesting contrast with some of the more urban wineries. Bus #170.

Santa Ana Roca and Urquiza, Villa Nueva, Guaymallén ⓣ0261/421-1000, ⓔavivas@bodegas-santa-ana.com.ar. Tours Mon–Fri 9.30am, 10.45am, noon, 2.30pm, 3.45pm & 5pm. One of the closest worthwhile bodegas, near the city centre, with an enchanting mix of old-style and ultra-modern. The tours are especially friendly, and English is spoken. Bus #20.

Viña El Cerno Moreno 631, Coquimbito, Maipú ⓣ0261/ 481-1567, ⓔelcerno@lanet.com.ar. Tours Mon–Fri 10am–5pm, weekend tours (Spanish only) can be arranged if you call; US$5 per person, including bottle to take away. One of the most satisfying boutique wineries, in a small traditional country house with a tiny vineyard. The malbec and chardonnay are delicious and the tour highly personalized and enthusiastic. Tapas evenings can be arranged for groups.

Weinert San Martín 5923, Chacras de Coria ⓣ0261/4960409, ⓦwww.bodegaweinert.com. Tours Mon–Sat 10am–4.30pm. One of Argentina's top wine producers, Weinert is also one of the country's oldest, with an enormous antique barrel still in use, a fabulous cellar and mud and cane buildings – characteristic of the area's indigenous population – used to provide the perfect temperature for fermentation. Tasting tours are family-friendly, with grape juice on hand so kids can feel included.

Lupulo Av Arístides Villanueva 471. Small bar with a tiny patio serving locally brewed beer and a warm welcome.
El Palenque Av Arístides Villanueva 287. A *pulpería*-style bar with bags of old-fashioned pampas atmosphere and a range of empanadas and wines; popular with the city's youth.
Sky Av Arístides Villanueva and Coronel Olascoaga. Funky decor, good music, enormous cocktails and chunky sandwiches at this fun bar.
Soul Tango Rivadavia and 9 de Julio. Fun little café that plays both soul and tango music, as the name suggests, and hosts occasional tango classes and live bands.
Vines of Mendoza Espejo 567 ⓦwww.vinesofmendoza.com. Not a bar as such, but rather a sophisticated wine-tasting room in the city centre. The friendly and knowledgeable staff can recommend wines to try and bodegas to visit, and also make the necessary reservations – it's an ideal starting point for anyone thinking of heading off on the viniculture trail.

Nightclubs

Aloha Ruta Panamericana s/n, Chacras de Coria. Extremely fashionable disco playing Argentine music, frequented by a thirties crowd. Best on Sat, but also open Fri and Sun.
Alquimia Ruta Panamericana s/n, Chacras de Coria. Restaurant/bar/club with disco on one floor, varied electronica on another and patios at which to eat throughout. One of the most popular places to dance the night away on Fri and Sat.
Carilo Av Champagnat s/n, El Challao. The über-fashionable club during the summer season (Sept–March), spinning house and techno.
Estación Miró Ejército de los Andes 656, Dorrego, Guaymallén. The city's main gay nightclub, open every weekend night, although Sun is the best night to go. Cocktails, shows and even an alternative Fiesta de la Vendimia in March.
Omero Av Champagnat s/n, El Challao. Great atmosphere, eminently danceable music and a young crowd.

Listings

Airlines Aerolíneas Argentina and Austral, Paseo Sarmiento 82 ⓣ0261/ 420-4101, and at the airport ⓣ0261/448-7065; LAN Chile, Rivadavia 135 ⓣ0261/425-7900; United, Espejo 183 1st floor ⓣ0261/423-4683.
Banks and exchange Boston, Necochea 165; Banex, Río San Martín 898; Citibank, Sarmiento 20; Banco Mendoza, Av San Martín and Gutiérrez. ATMs everywhere.
Bike rental Espejo 65, in the basement ⓣ0261/4290002.
Car rental Alamo, Primitivo de la Reta 928 ⓣ0261/429-3111; Automendoza, Montevideo 245 ⓣ0261/4200022; Avis, Primitivo de la Reta 914 ⓣ0261/429-6403; Budget, Primitivo de la Reta 923 ⓣ0261/425-3114; Localiza, Primitivo de la Reta 936 ⓣ0261/429-6800.
Consulates Bolivia, Garibaldi 380 ⓣ0261/429-2458; Brazil, Pedro Molina 497 ⓣ0261/438-0038; Chile, Belgrano and Liniers ⓣ0261/425-5024; Ecuador, Francisco Moyano 1597 ⓣ0261/423-3197; France, Houssay 790 ⓣ0261/429-8339; Germany, Montevideo 127 ⓣ0261/429-6539; Peru, Granaderos 998 ⓣ0261/429-9831; Spain, Agustín Alvarez 455 ⓣ0261/425-3947; UK/Netherlands, Emilio Civit 778 ⓣ0261/498-3504.
Internet access WH at Sarmiento 219, Colón 136 and Las Heras 61.
Laundry 5a Sec, Las Heras 345 and Av Arístides Villanueva 376; Laverap, Colón 547 and Mitre 1623; Lavandería Necochea, 25 de Mayo 1357.
Post office San Martín and Colón.
Taxis Mendocar ⓣ0261/423-6666; Radiotaxi ⓣ0261/430-3300; Radiomóvil ⓣ0261/445-5855; Veloz del Este ⓣ0261/4239090.
Telephones Fonobar, Paseo Sarmiento 23 ⓣ0261/429-2957; Teléfonos Mendoza, San Martín and Rivadavia ⓣ0261/438-1291; Sertel, San Martín and Las Heras ⓣ0261/438-0219.
Tour operators Other than bodegas, popular tours from Mendoza include Alta Montaña and Villavicencio. Many operators also offer longer trips to La Payunia, Cañon del Atuel, Talampaya and Ischigualasto, but Malargüe, San Rafael, San Juan and La Rioja are closer bases for these. Mountain-bike tours in the foothills and white-water rafting on the Río Mendoza are also possible. Try Aymará, 9 de Julio 1023 (ⓣ0261/420-4304, ⓔaymara@satlink.com); Campo Base Adventures and Expeditions, Av Mitre 946 (ⓣ0261/429-0707, ⓦwww.campo-base.com.ar); Cata, Las Heras 601 (ⓣ0261/4251750); El Cristo, Espejo 228 (ⓣ0261/429-1911, ⓕ429-6911); Mendoza Viajes, Sarmiento 129 (ⓣ0261/438-0480, ⓦwww.mdzviajes.com.ar); and Sepean, Primitivo de la Reta 1088 (ⓣ0261/420-4162). Argentina Mountain, Lavalle 606, San Jose, Guaymallén (ⓣ0261/4318356, ⓦwww.lagunadeldiamante.com), offers trips to Laguna Diamante and Tupungato.

Luján de Cuyo

Immediately south of Mendoza are two satellite towns, the first of which, sitting where the Guaymallén Canal meets the Río Mendoza, is **LUJÁN DE CUYO**. Lying just west of the Ruta Panamericana, or RN-40, it's part residential, part industrial, with a huge brewery and some of the city's major **wineries**. The northern district, known as **Carrodilla**, 7km south of downtown Mendoza, is an oasis of the colonial city that survived the 1861 earthquake. Here you'll find the **Iglesia de la Carrodilla** (Mon–Fri 10am–noon & 4–8pm; free), usually included in the city's wine tours. Built in 1778, it's now a museum of seventeenth- and eighteenth-century religious art as well as the parish church. The naive frescoes depict scenes of grape harvesting, and the church's main relic is an oakwood statue of the Virgin and Child, which is the star of the religious processions that precede Mendoza's Fiesta de la Vendimia. Artistically, the finest exhibit is the moving *Cristo de los Huarpes*, an exceptional piece of mestizo art carved out of *quebracho* wood in 1670 by local Indians.

The western district of Luján de Cuyo is called **Chacras de Coria**, a leafy suburb of European-style villas, golf courses, more bodegas and several new, upmarket hotels. It's also full of outdoor *parrillas*, bars and nightclubs, frequented at weekends and in the summer by affluent Mendocinos. On its eastern edge, in a rural area called Mayor Drummond, at San Martín 3251, is Mendoza's **Museo Provincial de Bellas Artes Emiliano Guiñazú**, also known as the **Casa de Fader** after Fernando Fader (see p.296), the artist who decorated the interior (Tues–Fri 8am–1pm & 2.30–6pm, Sat & Sun 2–6.30pm; $1). It's housed in a grandiose red sandstone villa, which was built at the end of the nineteenth century for Emiliano Guiñazú, an influential landowner and socialite, in a style influenced by Art Nouveau, and is set off by a luxuriant garden of cacti, cypresses, magnolias and roses, among which Neoclassical marble statues lurk. Having heard that Fader had been to art school in France, Guiñazú commissioned him to decorate the

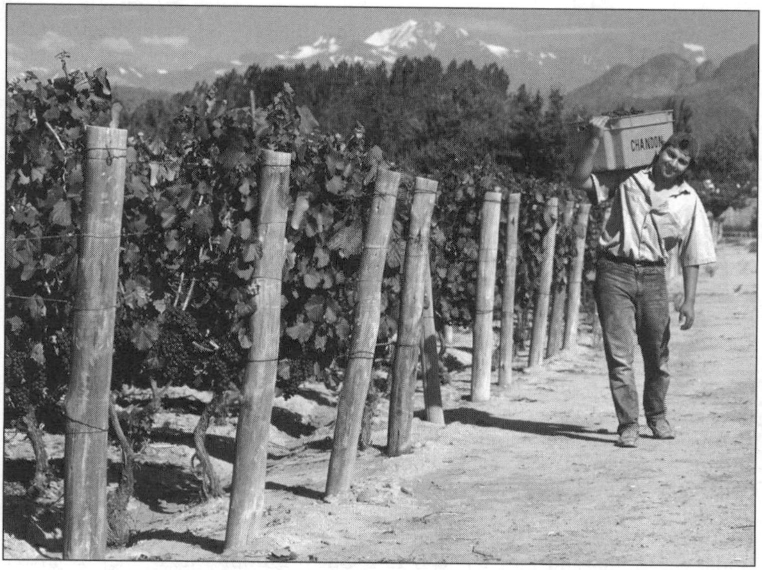

△ Vineyard, Luján de Cuyo

house interior. Fader's **Impressionistic murals** – especially appealing are the frescoes of tropical vegetation painted on the walls of the bathroom, alongside Art Nouveau tiles – are the main attraction here. His paintings also dominate the museum's collection of nineteenth- and early twentieth-century Argentine art. Temporary exhibits are staged from time to time. Bus #200 from downtown Mendoza or the bus terminal runs to Luján de Cuyo.

Maipú

The self-styled "Cuna de la Viña", or birthplace of the grapevine, **MAIPÚ**, lying some 15km southeast of Mendoza via RN-7, is the city's other small satellite town. Founded in 1861 by the Mercedarian monks Fray Manuel Apolinario Vásquez and Don José Alberto de Ozamis as a new site for the earthquake-levelled Mendoza, it quickly became the centre of wine-making in the region, and is where many of the city's **wineries** are located today (see box, pp.524–525). The wine-growing district, to the north of the town's centre, is called Coquimbito, where green vineyards alternate with dusky olive groves. The large Bodega La Rural at Montecaseros is where you'll find Mendoza's **Museo del Vino** (Mon–Sat 9am–5pm, Sun 10am–2pm; free; ⓣ0261/497-2013), a summary explanation of the region's wine industry housed in a fabulous Art Nouveau villa, with elegant fittings and detailing, including some delicate stained glass – the venue far outstrips the contents. **Buses** #150, #151, #170, #172, #173 and #180 all go to Maipú, taking slightly different routes from downtown Mendoza; once there, you can rent bikes for exploring the area at Urquiza 2288 (ⓣ0261/4974067).

Alta Montaña

The Andean cordillera, including some of the world's tallest mountains, loom a short distance west of Mendoza, and its snow-tipped peaks are visible from the city centre almost all year round, beyond the picturesque vineyards and fruit orchards. Even if you've come to the region for the wine, you'll want to head up into the hills before long: the scenery is fabulous, and skiing, trekking and highland walks are all possible, or you can simply enjoy the views on an organized excursion.The so-called **Alta Montaña Route** – RN-7 – is also the international highway to Santiago de Chile, via the upmarket Chilean ski resort of Portillo, and one of the major border crossings between the two countries, blocked by snow only on rare occasions in July and August. If you're in a hurry to get to or from Santiago, try to travel by day, as much of the stunning scenery in the area can be seen from this road. However, if you've more time to explore, there are several possible stop-offs along RN-7, including the spa town of **Cacheuta**, the pretty village of **Potrerillos** and **Vallecitos**, a tiny ski resort that caters for a younger crowd than exclusive Las Leñas (see p.541). As the road climbs further up into the mountains it passes another village, **Uspallata**, and then a variety of colourful rock formations – look for the pinnacle-like **Los Penitentes**, near another small ski resort. Closer to the border, **Puente del Inca** is a popular place to pause, both for its sulphurous thermal spring and its location – near the trailhead, base camp and muleteer-post for those brave enough to contemplate the ascent of mighty **Aconcagua**, just north and the continent's tallest peak. The last settlement before you travel through a tunnel under the Andes and into Chile is **Las Cuevas**, from where there is an old mountain pass that can be ascended, weather permitting, to see the **Cristo**

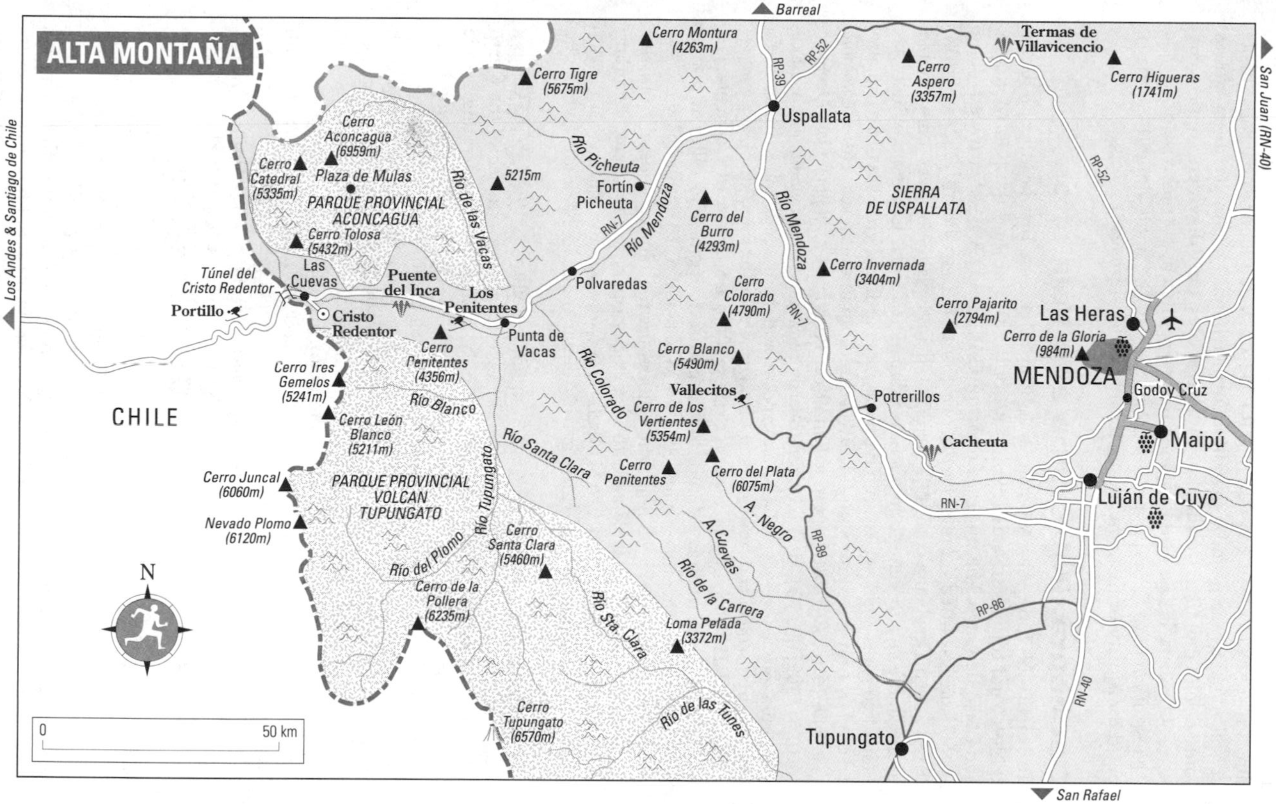

ALTA MONTAÑA
Barreal
San Juan (RN-40)
San Rafael
Los Andes & Santiago de Chile
Cerro Montura (4263m)
Termas de Villavicencio
Cerro Higueras (1741m)
Cerro Tigre (5675m)
Cerro Aspero (3357m)
Uspallata
RP-39
RP-52
Cerro Aconcagua (6959m)
Cerro Catedral (5335m)
Plaza de Mulas
PARQUE PROVINCIAL ACONCAGUA
Cerro Tolosa (5432m)
Río de las Vacas
5215m
Río Picheuta
Fortín Picheuta
RN-7
Río Mendoza
SIERRA DE USPALLATA
Cerro del Burro (4293m)
Cerro Invernada (3404m)
Túnel del Cristo Redentor
Las Cuevas
Puente del Inca
Los Penitentes
Polvaredas
Cerro Colorado (4790m)
Cerro Pajarito (2794m)
Las Heras
Cerro de la Gloria (984m)
MENDOZA
Godoy Cruz
Maipú
Luján de Cuyo
Portillo
Cristo Redentor
Cerro Penitentes (4356m)
Punta de Vacas
Río Colorado
Cerro Blanco (5490m)
Vallecitos
Potrerillos
Cacheuta
Cerro Ires Gemelos (5241m)
Río Blanco
Cerro de los Vertientes (5354m)
CHILE
Cerro León Blanco (5211m)
Río Santa Clara
Cerro Penitentes
Cerro del Plata (6075m)
Cerro Juncal (6060m)
PARQUE PROVINCIAL VOLCAN TUPUNGATO
Río Tupungato
A. Negro
A. Cuevas
RP-89
Nevado Plomo (6120m)
Cerro Santa Clara (5460m)
Río del Plomo
Río de la Carrera
N
Cerro de la Pollera (6235m)
Río Sta. Clara
Loma Pelada (3372m)
RP-86
RN-40
Cerro Tupungato (6570m)
Río de las Tunes
Tupungato
0
50 km

Redentor, a huge statue of Christ, erected as a sign of peace between the old rivals, and for the fantastic mountain views. As an alternative to driving RN-7 direct to Uspallata, you can take the RP-52 via **Villavicencio**, famous for its crystal mineral waters and a grandiose former hotel. This longer route crosses some deadly dull desert plains, but the **Caracoles de Villavicencio**, between it and Uspallata, is one of the region's most magnificent corniche roads.

Most of Mendoza's travel operators offer tours of the sights along these roads, but the majority of them are also accessible by local **buses**.

Cacheuta, Potrerillos and Vallecitos

To reach RN-7, the Alta Montaña road from Mendoza, first head south along RN-40, and turn westwards 15km south of the city, beyond the Río Mendoza and Luján de Cuyo. The small spa resort of **CACHEUTA** lies 27km west along RN-7 and is centred on the *Hotel & Spa Termas de Cacheuta* (Ⓣ0262/4490153, Ⓦwww.termascacheuta.com; ❾). Here you'll find plain but very comfortable rooms and a health centre, the Centro Climático Termal Cacheuta, which has individual baths and large swimming pools in an artificial grotto – these can also be used by non-guests for a small fee. You can camp in the area, at either *Camping Cacheuta* (Ⓣ02624/490154; ❶) at Km39 on RN-7, or *Camping Don Domingo* (Ⓣ0261/4225695; ❶), at Km44. The nearby restaurant *Mi Montaña*, just west of Cacheuta proper, serves delicious roast kid and ham sandwiches made with home-cured *serrano* and home-baked bread, as well as teas and drinks.

POTRERILLOS, in a picturesque valley 10km northwest of Cacheuta, is a village that styles itself as a centre for adventure tourism. The valley is dotted with poplar trees that turn vivid yellow in March and April, while the views up to the precordillera are fabulous: the colours form a blurred mosaic from this distance. A number of adventure-tour agencies operate from here, including Argentina Expediciones (Ⓣ02624/482037, Ⓦwww.argentinarafting.com), who run exciting **white-water rafting** trips down the Río Mendoza when the weather allows.

Some 25km west of Potrerillos, via an unnumbered track, **VALLECITOS** is a relatively inexpensive resort nestling in the Valle del Plata, in the lee of the Cerro Blanco, at an altitude of around 3000m. Popular with students and young people in general, it functions as a small ski resort – with twelve pistes of varying levels of difficulty – in winter and as a base for climbing and treks into the Cordón del Plata, as well as acclimatization for Aconcagua, in summer. The ski centre itself (Ⓣ0261/4236569 in Mendoza, Ⓣ02622/488810 in Vallecitos) is open daily from July to September, snow permitting. Vallecitos can be reached easily from Mendoza, 80km away, but there is basic **accommodation** if you want to stay over. This includes pleasant *Hostería La Canaleta* (Ⓣ0261/431-2779; ❷), with bunk-beds and private bath, more functional *Hostería Cerro Nevado* (no phone; ❷), which also has a restaurant and bar, and *Refugio San Antonio* (no phone; ❶), with shared baths and a canteen – you can also rent equipment and find instructors here. During the ski season there are **buses** to and from Mendoza.

Uspallata

The **Sierra de Uspallata**, which blocks Mendoza's view of Aconcagua, was described in the 1830s by Charles Darwin in the *Voyage of the Beagle*: "Red, purple, green and quite white sedimentary rocks, alternating with black lavas broken up and thrown into all kinds of disorder, by masses of porphyry, of every shade, from dark brown to the brightest lilac. It really resembled those pretty sections which geologists make of the inside of the earth."

USPALLATA itself, a village 54km north of Potrerillos by RN-7, has been an important crossroads between Mendoza, San Juan and Chile for centuries. It lies in the valley of the Río Uspallata, a fertile strip of potato, maize and pea fields, vineyards, pastures and patches of farmland where flocks of domesticated geese are kept. The village's cool climate, plentiful accommodation and stressless ambience make it an ideal place for a few days' relaxation; otherwise there's really not much to do here. You could visit the unusual **Bóvedas de Uspallata** (☎02624/420045; Tues–Sun 10am–7pm; $1), late eighteenth-century furnaces used for smelting iron mined in the nearby mountainside, a short way north of the village. Famously, the ovens were used by the patriotic monk Fray Luis Beltrán to make cannons and other arms for San Martín's army. The base is an adobe rectangle, but the whitewashed domed cupolas of the ovens make the building look like a North African mosque.

The centre of Uspallata is the junction of RN-7 and Las Heras, where frequent **buses** arrive from Mendoza and head towards Puenta del Inca and into Chile. A hut serves as a rudimentary **tourist office** (daily 8am–10pm). For **somewhere to stay**, nearby at Las Heras s/n is *Hotel Viena* (☎02624/420046; ④), with simple rooms, private bath and cable TV. Closer to the junction, with nicer rooms – albeit with hard beds – enormous modern bathrooms and a *confitería*, is *Hostal Los Cóndores* (☎02624/420002; ⑤); the buffet breakfast is excellent, and they also offer horse-riding and treks into the nearby mountains. Some way south, lying just off RN-7, is the more luxurious *Hotel Valle Andino* (☎02624/420033, Ⓦwww.hotelvalleandino.com; ⑥), which has spacious rooms, tennis courts and a pleasant sitting room, and has a full-board option for $30 more. *Café Tibet*, near the junction, serves good coffee in a very imaginatively stylized Tibetan temple (in homage to the movie *Seven Years in Tibet*, some of which was shot here). The best **place to eat** is *Lo de Pato*, 1km south of the junction; it's a popular stop-off for coach trips and buses to and from Chile, but despite the frequent crowds the food is tasty, especially the trout.

Up to Los Penitentes

From Uspallata, RN-7 swings round to the west and rejoins the Río Mendoza, whose valley it shares with the now-disused rail line all the way to its source at Punta de Vacas. Along here you are following an ancient Inca trail; several mummified corpses have been found in the mountains to the south and are displayed in Mendoza at the Museo de Ciencias Naturales y Antropológicas (see p.522). The scenery is simply fantastic: you pass through narrow canyons, close by the Cerro del Burro (4293m) and the Cerro División (4603m) to the south, with the rugged ridges of the Cerros del Chacay culminating in the Cerro Tigre (5700m) to the north. Stripes of different coloured rock – reds, greens and yellows caused by the presence of iron, copper and sulphur – decorate the steep walls of the cordillera peaks, while the vegetation is limited to tough highland grass and *jarilla*, a scruffy, gorse-like shrub gathered for firewood. The road climbs a gentle slope, slips through a series of tunnels, takes you through the abandoned hamlet of Polvaredas and past the police station at Punta de Vacas, at 2325m above sea level; the public customs post is further on at Los Horcones.

Some 65km from Uspallata is the small ski resort of **LOS PENITENTES**, or more properly Villa Los Penitentes – the "penitents" in question are a series of strange pinnacles of rock, high up on the ridge atop Cerro Penitentes (4356m), towering over the small village of typical, brightly coloured ski resort buildings to the south. The pointed rocks are thought to look like cowled monks, of the kind that traditionally parade during Holy Week in places such as Seville – hence the name. The resort's 21 pistes vary from nursery slopes to the black "Las Paredes", with most of the runs classified as difficult and the biggest total drop being 700m. The modern ski lifts also run at weekends in the summer, so you can enjoy the fabulous mountain and valley views from the top of Cerro San Antonio (3200m); the fissured peak looming over it all is the massive Cerro Leña (4992m).

As well as a ski school, a rental shop, a supermarket and a hospital, the resort (Ⓣ02624/420110) offers several types of **accommodation** during the ski season. In addition to a number of *apart-hotels* run by the resort, there's also the extremely comfortable *Hostería Los Penitentes* (Ⓣ0261/427-1641; ❻), usually booked by the week, or the simple *Hostería Ayelén* (Ⓣ0261/427-1123, Ⓦwww.ayelen.net; ❶), which can be booked by the night. A modest but still pleasant alternative is the *cabañas* run by Gregorio Yapurai (Ⓣ0261/430-5118; $20 per person) at the *Hostel Yapur* in nearby Puente del Inca (see below). The horseshoe-shaped La Herradura building houses both a pleasant *confitería* and a disco for après-ski.

Puente del Inca

Just 6km west of Los Penitentes is **PUENTE DEL INCA**, a compulsory stop for anyone heading along the Alta Montaña route and also near the track that leads north towards the Aconcagua base camp (see opposite). At just over 2700m, this natural **stone bridge** is an impressive sight, featuring on many a postcard. Formed by the Río de las Cuevas, it nestles in an arid valley, overlooked by majestic mountains; just beneath the bridge are the remains of a once sophisticated spa resort, built in the 1940s but swept away by a flood. The ruins, the bridge itself and the surrounding rocks are all stained a nicotine-yellow by the very high sulphur content of the warm waters that gurgle up nearby. Stalls sell souvenirs here, including all kinds of objects that have been left to petrify and yellow in the mineral springs: shoes, bottles, hats, books, ashtrays and statues of the Virgin Mary have all been treated to this embellishment, and are of dubious taste, but the displays make for an unusual photograph. Only 4km west of Puente del Inca is the dirt track that heads into the Parque Nacional Aconcagua.

There are only a couple of possibilities for **accommodation**, both popular with Aconcagua climbers: the relatively luxurious *Hostería Puente del Inca* (Ⓣ02624/420266; ❸), which also has some cheap dormitory-style rooms; and the *Refugio La Vieja Estación* (no phone; ❶), which has basic bunk-beds and shared bath.

Aconcagua

At 6959m, **CERRO ACONCAGUA** is the highest peak in both the western and southern hemispheres, or outside the Himalayas. Its glacier-garlanded summit dominates the Parque Provincial Aconcagua, even though it is encircled by several other mountains that exceed 5000m: cerros Almacenes, Catedral, Cuerno, Cúpula, Ameghino, Güssfeldt, Dedos, México, Mirador, Fitzgerald, La Mano, Santa María and Tolosa, some of which are easier to climb than others, and many of which obscure views of the great summit from most points around. The five glaciers that hang around its faces like icy veils are Horcones Superior, Horcones Inferior, Güssfeldt, Las Vacas and Los Polacos. For many mountain purists, Aconcagua may be the highest Andean mountain, but it lacks the morphological beauty of Cerro Mercedario to the north or Volcán Tupungato to the south; it's also not as difficult a climb to the summit as some of the other Andean peaks. Nevertheless, ever since it was conquered by the Italian-Swiss mountaineer Mathias Zurbriggen in 1897 – after it had been identified by German climber Paul Güssfeldt in 1883 – Aconcagua has been one of the top destinations in the world for expeditions or solo climbs. In 1934, a Polish team of climbers made it to the top via the glacier now named after them; in 1953, the southwest ridge was the route successfully taken by a local group of mountaineers; and in 1954, a French team who had successfully conquered Cerro Fitz Roy made the first ascent of Aconcagua up the south face, the most challenging of all – Plaza Francia, one of the main base camps, is named after them. In recent years, Aconcagua has become a major attraction for less experienced mountaineers, and a couple of thousand visitors reach the top every season (Dec to early March).

Although **climbing** Aconcagua is technically less demanding than many lower-altitude peaks, it is still a challenge to be taken seriously. Fitness, patience and acclimatization are key, and, unless you're fairly experienced at tough high-altitude treks, you shouldn't even consider going up; despite what the agencies may tell you, both independent climbers and people climbing as part of organized treks often end up turning back. The two biggest obstacles are coping with the altitude and the cold – temperatures can plummet to -40°C at night even in the summer – and fickle weather is also a major threat. Expeditions always descend when they see milky-white clouds shaped like the lenses of eyeglasses, known as *el viento blanco*, which announce violent storms. Over a hundred people have died climbing Aconcagua, and in 1999 the perfectly preserved body of a 1960s climber from Norway was lifted from a glacier. Frostbite and altitude sickness (see p.66) are the main health hazards, but proper precautions can prevent both. Allow at least a fortnight for an expedition, since you should acclimatize at each level, and take it easy throughout the climb; many of the people who don't make it to the top fail because they try to rush. Given the huge amount of supplies needed to make the ascent most people invest in a mule.

Of the three **approaches** – south, west or east – the western route from the Plaza de Mulas (4230m) is the most accessible and most used, and is known as the Ruta Normal. Very experienced climbers take either the Glaciar de los Polacos route, with its base camp at Plaza Argentina, reached via a long track that starts near Punta de Vacas, or the very demanding south face, whose Plaza Francia base camp is reached from Los Horcones, branching off from the Plaza de Mulas trail at a spot called Confluencia (3368m). For more details of the different routes, advice on what to take with you and how to acclimatize, consult the Aconcagua website (Ⓦwww.aconcagua.com.ar) or the excellent *Bradt Trekking Guide to Chile and Argentina*. For more specialist information, especially for serious climbers who are considering one of the harder routes, the best publication is R.J. Secor's *Aconcagua, A Climbing Guide* (1994).

The origins of the name Aconcagua are not entirely clear, although it probably comes either from the Huarpe words *Akon-Kahuak* ("stone sentinel") or from the Mapuche *Akonhue* ("from the beyond"). That it was a holy site for these and/or other native peoples is evidenced by the discovery in 1985 of an Inca mummy – now in the Museo del Área Fundacional, Mendoza (see p.520) – on the southwest face. Found at an altitude of 5300m, the presence of the mummy implies that ceremonies, including burials and perhaps sacrifices, took place at these incredible heights.

Practicalities

Unless you are having everything arranged by a tour operator, the first place you need to go to is the **Dirección de Recursos Naturales Renovables**

(Mon–Fri 9am–6pm, Sat & Sun 9am–1pm; Ⓦwww.aconcagua.mendoza.gov.ar), whose offices are in the basement of Mendoza's main tourist office at Av San Martín 1143; this is where you must apply for the compulsory permits to climb Aconcagua. For foreign trekkers these cost up to $1000, depending on the time of year and whether you just want park access or a climbing permit, too; January is the most popular month, and therefore most expensive, as it coincides with Argentine summer holidays and is when the weather is usually most settled. Don't be surprised if you hear that Argentine nationals have paid much less – they are officially charged a lower fee.

To get to either Los Horcones or Punta de Vacas, you can take the twice-daily **buses** from Mendoza, or hop off a through bus headed to Santiago de Chile. It's definitely preferable, though, whether trekking or climbing, to go on an **organized trip**, if only because of the treacherous weather – local guides know the whims of the mountain and its sudden storms. Several outfits in Mendoza specialize in tours, which cost around US$2000 per person, including Aconcagua Xperience, Av Mitre 1237 (Ⓣ0261/423-1806, Ⓦwww.aconcagua-xperience.com.ar); Campo Base Adventures and Expeditions, Pt Sarmiento 229 (Ⓣ0261/429-0707; Ⓦwww.campobase.com.ar); Aymará Viajes, 9 de Julio 983 (Ⓣ0261/420-0607); and Fernando Grajales, José Moreno 898 (Ⓣ0261/428-3157, Ⓦwww.grajales.net), where you can also hire mules if climbing independently. The only possible **places to stay** near the base camps are at Puente del Inca (see p.532) or at Las Cuevas (see below).

Las Cuevas and Cristo Redentor

It's just 15km from Puente del Inca, via the customs post at Los Horcones, to **LAS CUEVAS**, the final settlement along the Alta Montaña road before the **Túnel Cristo Redentor** – a toll-paying tunnel under the Andes into Chile (open 24hr; passport and vehicle documents required; no perishable foods or plant material allowed into Chile). At 3112m, Las Cuevas is a bit of a ghost town, a feeling enhanced by the rather grim Nordic-style stone houses, one of which houses a *confitería, Nido de Cóndores*, which serves decent hot food and snacks. The *Hostel Refugio Paco Ibañez* is popular with Aconcagua climbers (Ⓣ0261/429-0707; $10 per person), as is the smarter *Arco de la Cuevas* (Ⓣ0261/4265273, Ⓦwww.arcodelascuevas.com.ar; $30 per person) hostel and restaurant, housed in an attractive stone building arching over RN-7. From January to March, but usually not for the rest of the year because of snowfalls or frost, you can drive up the several hairpin bends to the **Monumento al Cristo Redentor**, an eight-metre-high, six-tonne statue of Christ as the redeemer. It was put here in 1904 to celebrate the so-called May 1902 Pacts, signed between Argentina and Chile, under the auspices of British King Edward VII, to determine once and for all the Andean boundary between the two countries. Designed by Argentine sculptor Mateo Alonso, the statue was made from melted-down cannons and other weapons, in a reversal of Fray Luis Beltrán's project a hundred years before (see p.531). Nearby is a disused Chilean customs post – the Paso de la Cumbre, also nearby, is no longer used by international traffic. The views towards Cerro Tolosa (5432m), immediately to the north, along the cordillera and down into several valleys, are quite staggering; make sure you have something warm to wear, though, as the howling winds up here are bitterly cold. When the road is open, most Alta Montaña tours bring you up here as the grand finale to the excursion; would-be Aconcagua conquerors often train and acclimatize by clambering to the top on foot.

Villavicencio

You often see **VILLAVICENCIO**, a spa resort 50km northwest of Mendoza, without actually going there – the ubiquitous bottles of mineral water from its springs, which you'll find in the region's supermarkets and restaurants, carry an excellent likeness on their labels. To get there, take sealed RP-52 from Mendoza, crossing some flat, dusty plains before climbing over 1000m to the tiny settlement, 1800m above sea level. Its curative springs were exploited by the indigenous peoples and not rediscovered until 1902. When Darwin stopped here in 1835 he dismissed it as a "solitary hovel bearing the imposing name of Villa Vicencio, mentioned by every traveller who has crossed the Andes", but admitted there was "a nice little rivulet". The *Gran Hotel*, long since abandoned, but certainly no hovel, was frequented by the wealthy of Mendoza and Buenos Aires in the 1940s and 1950s when Villavicencio became a smart spa resort. The hotel owners have announced several refurbishment plans over the years, though it remains closed; you can look around the grounds and eat at the nearby **confitería**. Beyond it, a good dirt road covers the 38km to Uspallata, offering stunning views of the Mendoza valley and its oasis, from viewpoints such as El Balcón, 10km west of Villavicencio. The road has what seem like endless hairpin turns, earning it the somewhat exaggerated local nickname *Ruta del Año*, or "one-year road" (in reference to the 365 bends it's said to have; in reality there are only about 20). It's also known as the "Caracoles de Villavicencio", literally "snails of Villavicencio", referring to the tightly spiralling bends of the pass. Just before Uspallata, RP-39 turns off to the north, towards San Juan Province. Although **buses** link Villavicencio and Mendoza several times a week, the circuit is usually visited on a tour organized from Mendoza.

South of Mendoza

The cordillera south of Mendoza city contains two remote and little visited but stunning provincial parks – the fabulous **Parque Provincial Tupungato**, 80km southwest from Mendoza and dominated by the soaring volcano of the same name, and the **Reserva Provincial Laguna Diamante**, with a turquoise altiplanic lake, the **Laguna Diamante**, at its heart. The latter is a further 140km southwest of Tupungato and only open during the summer; both are well worth the effort it takes to reach them.

Tupungato and Parque Provincial Tupungato

Now that Aconcagua has become almost a victim of its own success, anyone looking for a challenging mountain trek with fewer people crowding the trails and paths should head for the better-kept secret of Cerro Tupungato, an extinct volcano peaking at 6570m. Its Matterhorn-like summit dominates the **PARQUE PROVINCIAL TUPUNGATO**, which stretches along the Chilean border to the south of RN-7 at Puente del Inca, but is most accessible from the town of **TUPUNGATO**, reached from Mendoza via RN-40 and RP-86, a journey totalling nearly 80km. There's nothing to see in the small market town, apart from some attractive Italian-style single-storey houses from the end of the nineteenth century, but this is where you can contract guides to take you to the top of the mighty volcano; ask at the *Hotel Turismo* (see p.536), which also acts as the town's tourist information centre. You'll need plenty of time as the treks last between three and fifteen days, depending on how long you're given to acclimatize at each level – the longer the better. The virgin countryside within the park is utterly breathtaking, completely unspoilt and unremittingly stark. Apart from the companies recommended for Aconcagua, which also arrange tours to Tupungato (see p.534), you might also check out Rómulo Nieto at the *Hostería Don Rómulo*, at Almirante Brown 1200 (ⓣ02622/489020, ⓦwww.donromulo.com.ar; ❸). Not only does he arrange reasonably priced tours, but you can stay here in the small, plain but comfortable rooms. Alternatively, you could **stay** at the *Hotel Turismo*, Av Belgrano 1066 (ⓣ02622/488007; ❸), which is a little more spacious, with more modern bathrooms and a full-board option. There's also a very decent **campsite** on Calle La Costa, with barbecue facilities and clean toilets and showers. The best **place to eat** is *Pizzeria Ilo*, at Av Belgrano and Sargento Cabral, which serves up an excellent margarita and delicious home-made pasta. **Buses** run fairly regularly from Mendoza, arriving at Plaza General San Martín.

Reserva Provincial Laguna Diamante

Some 220km southwest of Mendoza, **LAGUNA DIAMANTE**, set amid its own provincial reserve of guanaco pasture and misty valleys, is the destination of one of the least-known but most unforgettable excursions in the area. The source of the Río Diamante, which flows through San Rafael, the lake is so called because the choppy surface of its crystalline waters suggests a rough diamond. One reason for its relative obscurity is that weather conditions make it possible to reach Laguna Diamante only from mid-December to the end of March, with blizzards often blocking the road for the rest of the year. At Pareditas, 125km south of Mendoza by RN-40, take the RP-101, which forks off to the southwest; the drive down is one marvellous long panoramic view of the Andean precordillera. The RP-101 is a reliable unsealed road that follows Arroyo Yaucha through fields of gorse-like *jarilla* and gnarled *chañares*, affording views of the rounded summits of the frontal cordillera, before entering the Cañón del Gateado, through which the salmon-rich Arroyo Rosario flows past dangling willows. At another fork in the road, 20km on, the track to the left eventually leads to El Sosneado, while the right fork heads for the Refugio Militar General Alvarado, the entrance to the **Reserva Provincial Laguna Diamante**. As the road twists and climbs across the Pampa de los Avestruces you'll catch your first sight of **Cerro Maipo** (5323m), the permanently snowcapped volcano that straddles the international frontier. The spongy plateau averages 4000m above sea level, so you might start noticing some *puna* symptoms (see p.66). Nestling beneath the Cordón del Eje, a majestic range of dark ochre rock, and towered over by the snow-streaked Maipo opposite – a perfect cone worthy of a Japanese woodcut – this ultramarine lake is constantly buffeted into white horses by strong breezes and its waves noisily lap the springy, mossy banks. The silence is broken only by the howl of the wind or the occasional plop of a *puna*-free trout. An off-the-track site along the banks of the brook makes a wonderful picnic spot, protected from howling gales by the moraine, with an unbeatable backdrop. Rangers at the **guardería**, which you pass on the final approach to the lagoon, can offer some information on the reserve and its wildlife, and appreciate the offer of a cigarette or the chance to share a *mate*.

The place is so remote that there's no public transport out here – you need a 4WD – and few tour agencies offer the trip; try Argentina Mountain, at

Lavalle 606, San Jose, in Guaymallén, Mendoza (Ⓣ0261/4318356, Ⓦwww.lagunadeldiamante.com), which offers day-trips from Mendoza as well as longer horse treks and climbs up Maipo and Tupungato. You may also be able to pick up a tour from San Rafael, which is closer in distance. Since it's in an area under military control, near a strategic point on the Chilean border, take your passport.

San Rafael and around

The small city of **SAN RAFAEL** is the de facto capital of central Mendoza Province; around 230km south of Mendoza via RN-40 and RN-143, it's a kind of mini-Mendoza, complete with wide avenues, irrigation channels along the gutters and scrupulously clean public areas. The town was founded in 1805 on the banks of the Río Diamante on behalf of Rafael, Marques de Sobremonte – hence the name – by militia leader Miguel Telles Meneses. Large numbers of Italian and Spanish immigrants flocked here at the end of the nineteenth century, but the so-called Colonia Francesa expanded further when the railway arrived in 1903. Favoured by French immigrants during the nineteenth century, San Rafael built its prosperity on vineyards, olives and tree-fruit, grown in the province's second biggest oasis, and its industry has always been agriculture-based: fruit preserves, olive oil and fine wines. In all, there are nearly eighty **bodegas** in San Rafael department, most of them tiny, family-run businesses, some of which welcome visitors. Tourism has been a big money-spinner over the past couple of decades, especially since adventure tourism has taken off. The **Cañon del Atuel**, a short way to the southwest, is one of the best places in the country to try out white-water rafting. Accommodation is one of San Rafael's fortes, and you could use the town as a base for exploring the southern parts of the province, centred on Malargüe, where good places to stay are harder to come by.

Arrival and information

San Rafael's small **airport**, with daily flights to Buenos Aires, is 5km west of the town centre, along RN-143 towards Mendoza. There are no buses, but taxi rides into town won't break the bank. The **bus terminal** – buses arrive here from Mendoza, Malargüe, San Juan and places further afield – is central, wedged in between calles Almafuerte and Avellaneda, at Coronel Suárez. It's surrounded by shops and cafés and has its own tourist information kiosk (Mon–Fri 8am–2pm). The city's main **tourist information office** is at the corner of avenidas Hipólito Yrigoyen and Balloffet (daily 8am–9pm; Ⓣ02627/424217, Ⓦwww.sanrafael-tour.com.ar) and can give information about tour operators, provide you with a map and fix you up with somewhere to stay.

Accommodation

San Rafael has no shortage of **places to stay**, ranging from basic refuges to luxurious *apart-hotels*, while one of the country's best youth hostels lies in very attractive grounds just outside town. The best **campsite** hereabouts is *Camping El Parador* (Ⓣ02627/420492; tents ❶, *cabañas* ❸), on the Isla Río Diamante, 6km south of the centre; it has excellent facilities and is in a beautiful wooded location.

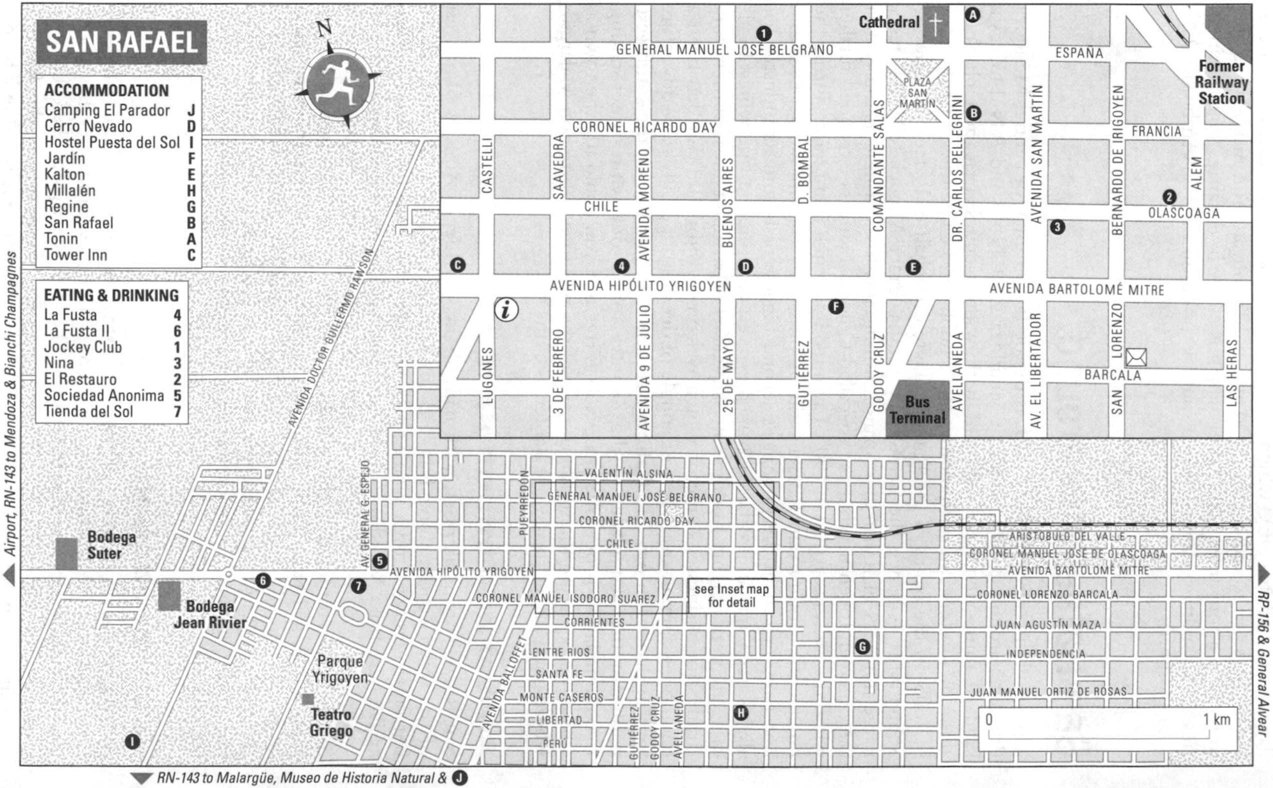
SAN RAFAEL
ACCOMMODATION
Camping El Parador J
Cerro Nevado D
Hostel Puesta del Sol I
Jardín F
Kalton E
Millalén H
Regine G
San Rafael B
Tonin A
Tower Inn C
EATING & DRINKING
La Fusta 4
La Fusta II 6
Jockey Club 1
Nina 3
El Restauro 2
Sociedad Anonima 5
Tienda del Sol 7
N
Cathedral
Former Railway Station
Bus Terminal
PLAZA SAN MARTÍN
GENERAL MANUEL JOSÉ BELGRANO
CORONEL RICARDO DAY
CHILE
AVENIDA HIPÓLITO YRIGOYEN
AVENIDA BARTOLOMÉ MITRE
ESPAÑA
FRANCIA
OLASCOAGA
BARCALA
CASTELLI
SAAVEDRA
AVENIDA MORENO
BUENOS AIRES
D. BOMBAL
COMANDANTE SALAS
DR. CARLOS PELLEGRINI
AVENIDA SAN MARTÍN
BERNARDO DE IRIGOYEN
ALEM
LUGONES
3 DE FEBRERO
AVENIDA 9 DE JULIO
25 DE MAYO
GUTIÉRREZ
GODOY CRUZ
AVELLANEDA
AV. EL LIBERTADOR
SAN LORENZO
LAS HERAS
AVENIDA DOCTOR GUILLERMO RAWSON
AV. GENERAL G. ESPEJO
PUEYRREDÓN
VALENTÍN ALSINA
CORONEL MANUEL ISODORO SUAREZ
CORRIENTES
ENTRE RIOS
SANTA FE
MONTE CASEROS
LIBERTAD
PERÚ
AVENIDA BALLOFFET
ARISTOBULO DEL VALLE
CORONEL MANUEL JOSÉ DE OLASCOAGA
CORONEL LORENZO BARCALA
JUAN AGUSTÍN MAZA
INDEPENDENCIA
JUAN MANUEL ORTIZ DE ROSAS
see Inset map for detail
Bodega Suter
Bodega Jean Rivier
Parque Yrigoyen
Teatro Griego
0 1 km
Airport, RN-143 to Mendoza & Bianchi Champagnes
RN-143 to Malargüe, Museo de Historia Natural & J
RP-156 & General Alvear

Cerro Nevado Hipólito Yrigoyen 376 ⓣ02627/428209, ⓦwww.cerronevadohotel.com.ar. This spotless place has a pleasant restaurant, but avoid streetside rooms, as they can be noisy. ④

Hostel Puesta del Sol Deán Funes 998 ⓣ02627/434881, ⓔpuestadelsol@infovia.com.ar. One of the most beautiful hostels in the country, with modern facilities, a huge swimming pool amid landscaped grounds, and a lively atmosphere. $15 per person; double room ③

Jardín Hipólito Yrigoyen 259 ⓣ02627/434621. Very comfy rooms, all en suite, arranged around a lush patio shaded by an impressive palm tree. ⑤

Kalton Hipólito Yrigoyen 120 ⓣ02627/430047, ⓦwww.kaltonhotel.com. Typical mid-range town hotel near the bus station, with well-kept, albeit unremarkable, rooms. ⑤

Millalén Ortíz de Rosas 198 ⓣ02627/422776, ⓔricardoloparco@yahoo.com.ar. Modern hotel with pleasantly understated rooms, sparkling bathrooms and unfussy decor. ⑤

Regine Independencia 623 and Colón ⓣ02627/421470, ⓦwww.hotelregine.com.ar. All the rooms are well-furnished and charming, while the rustic dining room serves reliably good food; there's also a beautiful garden dominated by a ceibo tree, and a small pool. ⑤

San Rafael Coronel Day 30 ⓣ02627/430125, ⓦwww.hotelsanrafael.com.ar. Another of San Rafael's comfortable mid-range hotels; this one has a bar, reception with log fire and cable TV in the rooms. ⑤

Tonin Pellegrini 330 ⓣ02627/422499, ⓦwww.sanrafael-tour.com/tonin. Very pleasant, good-value rooms with modish stainless-steel washbasins in gleaming bathrooms. ③

Tower Inn Hipólito Yrigoyen 774 ⓣ02627/427190, ⓦwww.towersanrafael.com. This sandy-hued tower of stone and plate-glass may be a bit of an eyesore, but the interior is comfortable, pleasant and well run, and a large swimming pool and patio bar make it San Rafael's no. 1 hotel. ⑦

The City

San Rafael has a flat, compact centre that lends itself to a gentle stroll, but otherwise there aren't any sights to speak of – the town is essentially a base for visiting the surrounding area. The main drag, with most of the shops and cafés and many of the hotels, is a continuation of RN-143 from Mendoza, called **Avenida Hipólito Yrigoyen** west of north–south axis **Avenida General San Martín** and **Avenida Bartolomé Mitre** to the east. Streets change name either side of both axes and, while they follow a strict gridiron pattern across the city, whole sections are at an oblique angle, such as Avenida Balloffet, which leads south towards the Río Diamante, a wide river that marks the town's southern boundary. Two blocks north of Avenida Hipólito Yrigoyen and one west of Avenida San Martín is the town's main square, leafy and peaceful **Plaza San Martín**, dominated by the modern cathedral.

To fill an hour or so with something cultural, take a taxi or a bus marked "Isla Diamante" from Avenida Hipólito Yrigoyen. Isla Diamante is a large island 6km south of the town centre, in the middle of the river of the same name, and is home to the **Museo de Historia Natural** (Mon–Fri 8am–1pm & 3–8pm, Sat & Sun 8am–8pm; $1), a working museum with research labs. Among masses of bedraggled stuffed birds, moth-eaten foxes and lumps of rock, you'll find some fabulous pre-Columbian ceramics, the best of which are statues from Ecuador; there's also a small collection of crafts from Easter Island and some particularly fine ceramics from northwestern Argentina. You'll also see a mummified child dating from 40 AD and a gorgeous multicoloured leather bag decorated with striking, very modern-looking geometric designs, found in the Gruta del Indio in the Cañon del Atuel.

Eating, drinking and nightlife

Good **restaurants** and **bars** are fewer and further between than good hotels in San Rafael, but one or two stand out. In addition, there are a couple of atmospheric bars and fun **discos** some way out of town towards the west.

Bodegas in and around San Rafael

Mendoza is undeniably Argentina's wine capital, but **San Rafael** is also a major **wine centre** that doesn't always get much of a look-in. Its wineries are among the finest in the country, and several of them open their doors willingly to visitors, although tours are more informal than in Mendoza – they do not run at set times, and you can usually just turn up during the listed opening hours; do not be surprised to find no one speaks English. The following is a selection of the best.

Champañera Bianchi Hipólito Yrigoyen s/n ⓣ02627/435353. An interesting contrast with the old downtown bodega, this ultra-modern sparkling wine-production unit, housed in a postmodern steel and glass building, is 4km west of the town centre. Excellent sparkling wines made according to the *méthode champenoise.* Twenty-minute tours possible Mon–Sat 9am–noon & 2–5pm. English spoken.

Jean Rivier Hipólito Yrigoyen 2385 ⓣ02627/432675, ⓦwww.jeanrivier.com. Friendly small winery, founded by Swiss winemakers; their tip-top wines include an unusual cabernet sauvignon–fer blend. Delicious chardonnays, too. Mon–Fri 8–11am & 3–6.30pm, Sat 8–11am.

Simonassi Lyon 5km south of San Rafael by RN-143, at Rama Caida ⓣ02627/430963, ⓦwww.bodegasimonassi.com. Family-run, prize-winning winery, housed in an attractive farmhouse. Guided visits Mon–Fri 8am–5pm.

Suter Hipólito Yrigoyen 2850 ⓣ02627/421076, ⓔturismo@sutersa.com.ar. Slightly mechanical guided visits every half-hour, but you're given a half-bottle of decent wine as a gift. Traditional-style winery. Mon–Sat 9am–5pm.

Daikiri Disco Hipólito Yrigoyen 3177. New, large club that's the place to go out in the city on Fri night, with a sizeable garden area and outside bars.

La Fusta Hipólito Yrigoyen 538. By far the town's best *parrilla*, serving succulent steaks, full *parrilladas* and local wines at very reasonable rates.

La Fusta II Hipólito Yrigoyen and Beato Marcelino Champagnat. Sister restaurant to the above, in ultra-modern surroundings with fine decor and a large terrace.

Jockey Club Belgrano 330. Good old-fashioned service and hearty food, with a good-value *menú turista* at lunch time.

Nina San Martín and Olascoaga. Very smart cocktail bar doubling as a café and tearoom.

El Restauro Chile and Salas. Friendly service and creative, interesting but inexpensive cuisine at this new, ample restaurant.

Sociedad Anonima Hipólito Yrigoyen 1530. Upper crust for San Rafael, this bar is a place to be seen – and a great place to people-watch.

Tienda del Sol Hipólito Yrigoyen 1663. Trendy, postmodern resto-bar, serving seafood and pasta dishes alongside cocktails and other drinks, at slightly inflated prices.

La Zona Deán Funes 1000. Hip dance club, popular on Sat nights.

Listings

Banks Most major banks on Av Hipólito Yrigoyen, nos. 0–200.

Bike rental Bicipartes, Chile 445 ⓣ02627/430260.

Car rental Localiza, Day and Castelli ⓣ02627/420995; Rent A Car, Alvarez 670 ⓣ02627/423145.

Internet access Locutorio Tavares, Sarmiento y Gutiérrez.

Laundry Laverap, Las Heras 180.

Taxis El Nihuil, Av Libertador 999.

Tour operators Kintum, Lencinas 617 ⓣ02627/429653; Risco Viajes, Av Hipólito Yrigoyen 284 ⓣ02627/436439, ⓦwww.riscoviajes.com. Many more in Valle Grande (see opposite).

Cañon del Atuel

The **CAÑON DEL ATUEL** is San Rafael's main attraction, a beautifully wild canyon linking two man-made lakes along the Río Atuel, to the southwest of the town. Visits begin at the reservoir furthest away, the **Embalse del Nihuil**, reached along winding RP-144 towards Malargüe, up the Cuesta de los Terneros to the 1300-metre summit, which offers stunning views of the fertile valley below; and then via RP-180, which forks off to the south. The lake, one hundred windsurfers – boards can be rented at the Club de Pescadores, just off the road on the north-eastern banks of the *embalse* – lies 92km southwest of San Rafael. Partly sealed RP-173 then squeezes in a northeasterly direction through a narrow gorge whose cliffs and rocks are striped red, white and yellow, contrasting with the beige of the dust-dry mountainsides. Wind and water have eroded the rocks into weird and often rather suggestive shapes that stimulate the imagination: tour guides are fond of attaching names like "the Nun" or "the Toad" to the strange formations. The road then passes a couple of dams, attached to power stations, before swinging round the other reservoir, the **Embalse Valle Grande**. Sticking out of these blue-green waters are more strange rock formations, one of which does indeed look like the submarine its nickname suggests. From the high corniche roads that skirt the lakeside you are treated to some staggering views of the waters, dotted with kayaks and other boats, and the mountains beyond.

At the northern end of the reservoir you'll find two *confiterías*, which serve decent snacks and drinks. Near here starts the stretch of the Río Atuel used for **white-water rafting**. Raffeish, at RP-173 Km35, Valle Grande (Ⓣ02627/436996, Ⓦwww.raffeish.com.ar), is the most reliable and ecology-conscious operator, and has an office here. Trips last an hour, along an easy stretch for beginners, or a couple of hours or more, taking in a tougher section of the river, for more experienced rafters; take swimwear, as you get soaked. The scenery along the way is charmingly pastoral along the more open parts and staggeringly beautiful in the narrower gorges. Further downstream, Hunuc Huar is a wonderful crafts workshop (daily 9.30–1pm & 4–9pm) run by an indigenous family, specializing in very fine ceramics, set in an idyllic garden. There's also a restaurant here, *Arytuca*, where you can dine on classy food and admire the local arts and crafts on display.

San Rafael is only 25km away from the canyon by RP-173, but unless you have your own transport, you'll have to get here on an **organized tour**; the best operator in San Rafael is Risco Viajes (see "Listings", opposite). If you want to **stay** nearby, there is the upmarket *Hotel Valle Grande* (Ⓣ02627/155-80660, Ⓦwww.hotelvallegrande.com; ❹), with all kinds of sports facilities and a fine swimming pool, though it can get very crowded during the summer months; the hotel also has *cabañas* for rent (❸) that can sleep up to four.

Las Leñas

To Argentines, **LAS LEÑAS** means chic: this is where the Porteño jet-set come to show off their winter fashions, to get photographed for society magazines and to have a good time. **Skiing** and **snowboarding** are only part of the fun – as in the most exclusive Swiss and American winter resorts, the *après-ski* is just as important as the snow conditions. More seriously, many ski champions from the northern hemisphere head down here during the June to October season, when there's not a lot of snow in the US or Europe; the Argentine, Brazilian and South American skiing championships are all held here in August, while other events include snow-polo matches, snow-rugby, snow-volleyball and fashion shows. But even though Las Leñas is a playground for the rich and famous, it's possible to visit without breaking the bank; you could stay in the least expensive accommodation, or overnight elsewhere nearby, such as in El Sosneado or Malargüe (see p.544). Las Leñas is also trying to branch out into **summertime adventure travel**, making the most of its splendid upland setting and pleasant daytime temperatures.

The road to Las Leñas heads due west from the Mendoza to Malargüe section of RN-40, 28km south of the crossroads settlement of El Sosneado. It climbs past the ramshackle spa resort of Los Molles, and the peculiar **Pozo de las Animas**, a set of two huge well-like depressions that make for a diverting photo stop. Caused by underground water erosion, each is several hundred metres in diameter, with a pool of turquoise water in the bottom. The sand-like cliffs surrounding each lake have been corrugated and castellated by the elements, like some medieval fortress, and the ridge dividing the two looks in danger of collapse at any minute. The resort lies 50km from RN-40, a total of nearly 200km southwest of San Rafael. If you are booked at the resort, you might get a transfer from Mendoza or San Rafael, and during the ski season you can take the daily **bus** run by TAC from Mendoza, a seven-hour journey (US$20 one way). Otherwise you need your own transport.

The resort

Though no Gstaad or St Moritz, Las Leñas is an aesthetically pleasing **resort** with excellent **skiing** and **snowboarding** – when there is enough snow – and a breathtaking backdrop of craggy mountain-tops, of which Cerro Las Leñas is the highest (4351m) and Cerro Torrecillas (3771m) the most daintily pinnacled. The whole area covers more than 33 square kilometres, with 28 pistes, ranging from several gentle nursery slopes to a couple of sheer black runs; cross-country and off-piste skiing are also possible.

△ Skiing at Las Leñas

Experienced skiers will want to head direct for **El Marte** lift, the only one which accesses the harder runs, but be aware that this is often closed due to the resort's characteristic high winds, which can be a source of some frustration. Nature is, of course, unpredictable, but **early September** is probably your best bet for serious powder, as well as for lower winds (and prices) and thinner crowds. For the less experienced, **instruction** in skiing and snowboarding is given in several languages, including English. The equipment-rental service (next to the *Hotel Acuario*) is pricey, as are the lifts – day passes cost around $100–150, depending on the season – although many hotels offer discounts on these as part of their package. An early start to the day definitely pays off – the slopes are relatively empty, since most people need much of the morning to recover from all-night discoing.

Skiing isn't completely off the agenda even in the **summer** – a two-hundred-metre-long slope, called "Iris", at 3500m above sea level, has snow year-round, helped a little by an artificial snow machine. Iris is a ninety-minute trip from the resort by 4WD and can be visited as a half-day tour, equipment provided; ask at any of the resort hotels. Other, more seasonally apt possibilities include mountain-biking, rafting and horse-riding. Note that the resort is completely **closed** down, however, in April, May, October and November.

Practicalities

All **accommodation** booking in Las Leñas is organized centrally through Las Leñas resort, whose office is in Buenos Aires at Cerrito 1186, 8th floor (Ⓣ011/4819-6000, Ⓦwww.laslenas.com). Usually booked as weekend, five- or seven-day packages, sometimes with ski lifts and half- or full-board meals included, all the hotels are within tramping distance of the slopes. The following cost around $500 per person per night in the peak weeks of July and August, though prices tend to drop by about fifty percent at either end of the season. The *Hotel Piscis* has a beautiful swimming pool, plus Jacuzzis, saunas, comfortable rooms with piste views and its own equipment for rent, including special boot-warmers. Much further away from the central village, and therefore rather quieter, is the *Hotel Aries*, which has a modern gym, comfortable rooms, a lobby bar and impeccable service. The *Hotel Acuario* is very comfortable and has a *parrilla* restaurant, while the new *Virgo Hotel* has a heated pool and a restaurant with panoramic views of the slopes, a spa and large, elegant rooms. The *Club de la Nieve*, in an Alpine-style chalet, has its own reasonable restaurant and spacious, functional rooms and is a tad cheaper than some of the other options. Alternatively, and more economical, particularly if you're in a group, are the "dormy houses", *Laquir*, *Lihuén*, *Milla* and *Payén*, chalets grouped at the edge of the village that can sleep up to five and have simple kitchens and bedrooms; they cost around $450 a night per house in high season. Budget accommodation is also available at *Hostería El Sosneado* (Ⓣ02627/154-00523; ❸ half-board), nearly 80km away; it has very clean, no-fuss rooms or *cabañas*, central heating and a small restaurant. Excursions, including horse rides, are arranged in the summer.

For **eating** at the ski village, there's the *confitería* and popular meeting-place *Innsbruck*, which serves beer and expensive snacks on its terrace with piste views. *Santa Fe* is an on-piste snack bar with Tex-Mex food, while *Olimpos* serves lunch and is accessible by the Minerva chairlift. *La Cima* is a pizzeria by day and a more chic restaurant by night, and the *Hotel Piscis*' luxury restaurant, *Cuatro Estaciones*, is the place to be seen for dinner; a strict dress code applies. Rather more informal, if still expensive, and serving delicious, huge-portioned fondues and raclettes with the best Argentine white wines, is *El Refugio*, in the central Pirámide building. Apart from Hotel Piscis' casino, for until-dawn **nightlife** – which does tend to be dominated by under-25s – you have a choice between *Ufo Point* and *Budweiser Club.*

Malargüe and around

MALARGÜE is a laid-back town 186km south of San Rafael by RP-144 and RN-40. The biggest settlement in the far southern portion of Mendoza Province, it serves as a possible alternative base to San Rafael for exploring this region. At 1400m above sea level, the town enjoys warm summers and cool winters, and snow is not unknown. Like San Rafael, its most important asset is its location, useful for visiting some of the least known, but most spectacular landscapes in Argentina, let alone Mendoza Province; accommodation is the weak link in the chain, though, with less variety and inferior quality than in San Rafael.

The town is within day-trip distance of the black and red pampas of **La Payunia**, a nature reserve where flocks of guanacos and ñandús roam over lava flows. Far nearer – and doable as half-day outings – are some remarkable underground caves, the **Cueva de la Brujas**, and **Laguna Llancanelo**, a shining lagoon flecked pink with flamingoes and crammed with other aquatic birdlife. You could also consider staying here in order to go skiing at the exclusive winter sports resort of **Las Leñas**, 77km away (see p.541).

Arrival and information

Buses from Mendoza and San Rafael go all the way to the bus terminal at Esquibel Aldao and Av General Roca, six blocks south and two west of central Plaza San Martín, but will also drop off and collect passengers at the plaza en route. Malargüe's excellent **tourist office** (daily 8am–9pm; ⓣ02627/471659, ⓦwww.malargue.gov.ar), in a fine rustic building on RN-40 by the Parque de Ayer, four blocks north of the plaza, has loads of information on what to see and do, and on places to stay, tour operators and fishing in nearby rivers. There's

Reliving Alive

In 1972, a group of young **rugby players** from **Uruguay** caught the attention of the world after they survived an **air crash** and over two months of brutal subzero temperatures in the Andes, at a place on the Argentine-Chilean border in the mountains west of the Cerro Sosneado and Río Atuel, now called the **Glaciar de la Lágrimas** (glacier of tears). The students survived by consuming snow and their colleagues' corpses and fashioning sleeping bags from the insulation in the plane's tail, before two of them finally made it west over the mountains and alerted the Chilean authorities, who had long since given them up for dead. Their incredible story was told in the 1993 movie *Alive* and the documentary *Alive: 20 Years Later*. It is now possible to **visit the site** of the crash, where parts of the plane are still scattered, though getting there is naturally enough no walk in the park – count on at least three days of trekking and horse-riding through the snow, although you'll also get to take a unique hot bath in the warm blue waters bubbling up out of the ground at the ruins of the old *Hotel Sosneado*. Tours are run by Risco Viajes in San Rafael (see p.540) or with guides from Malargüe – ask at Malargüe's tourist office (see above).

also a good info centre about all things Malargüe in the city of Mendoza (see p.513). **Internet** access is available at Rucanet Cyber, Av San Martín 845.

The town's **tour operators**, which offer excursions to places like La Payunia and Caverna de las Brujas, are of a high standard. Check out Karen Travel, Av San Martín 1056 (Ⓣ02627/470342); Huarpes del Sol, Av San Martín 85 (Ⓣ02627/155-84842); Receptivo Malargüe, Batallón Nueva Creación 234 (Ⓣ02627/471524, Ⓦwww.receptivomalargue.com.ar); and Choique, Prolongación Constitución Nacional s/n, Finca 65 (Ⓣ02627/154-02439), all of which can also fix you up with a vehicle (4WD is best). Prices range from $50 for a transfer to Las Leñas to over $300 for an all-inclusive, two-day trip to La Payunia. Ski-wear and other equipment can be hired from Aires de Libertad, Av San Martín 129, which also organizes transfers to Las Leñas.

Accommodation

Accommodation in Malargüe is relatively limited, and not as good value as in San Rafael. Additionally, twice a year (in March and Nov), what there is gets packed out with physicists, who come for an international convention on the Pierre Auger experiment (see p.546). You do, however, get a fifty percent discount on Las Leñas ski lifts if you stay at least two nights in Malargüe during the season. At the northern extremity of town is the *Hotel Río Grande* (Ⓣ02627/471589, Ⓔhotelriogrande@infovia.com.ar; ⑤), with a choice between decent but very plain rooms and more spacious, tastefully decorated ones in a British style. The owners are very friendly, and the restaurant serves delicious food. *Hotel Cisne* (Ⓣ02627/471350; ⑤), at Civit and Villegas, is one of Malargüe's better mid-range options, or try the smart *Hotel Rioma*, Fray Inalicán 68 (Ⓣ02627/471065, Ⓔhotelrioma@rucared.com.ar; ⑤). Budget accommodation is available at *Hostel Andysol*, Av Rufino Ortega 158 (Ⓣ02627/471151; ③), which has attractive double and triple bedrooms, and a decent Alpine-style, pine-clad bar-cum-*confitería*. Alternatively, there is the youth hostel *Internacional Malargüe* at Prolongación Constitución Nacional s/n, Finca 65 (Ⓣ02627/154-02439, Ⓦwww.hostelmalargue.net; $23 per person), which benefits from an attractive setting; and a branch of Mendoza's successful *Campo Base* hostel called – logically enough – *Campo Base Malargüe* (Ⓣ02627/471534, Ⓦwww.malarguehostel.com; $18 per person), at Telles Meneses 897, which is popular with young skiers. Otherwise you could **camp** at *Camping Polideportivo*, at Capdeval and Esquibal Aldao (Ⓣ02627/470691), or in a wonderful setting at Castillos de Pincheira, 27km southwest of town.

The Town

The core of the town lies on either side of RN-40, called Avenida San Martín within the town's boundaries, a wide, rather soulless avenue along which many of the hotels are located, as well as a couple of cafés, the bank and telephone centres. **Plaza General San Martín** is the focal point, with its benches shaded by pines and native trees, but it's nothing to get excited about. Being totally flat and compact, however, the town is extremely easy to find your way around, and in any case, its handful of attractions are clustered together at the northern reaches, beyond the built-up area. Conveniently close to the tourist office, the beautiful landscaped **Parque del Ayer**, or "Park of Yesteryear", is planted with pines, cypresses, willows, acacias, dog-roses, pyracanthus and native *retamos*. Various sculptures and items such as old hay-carts are dotted among the vegetation. Malargüe's pride and joy, though, is the splendid **Centro de Convenciones y Exposiciones Thesaurus** (daily

10am–8pm; free; ⓣ02627/471659), subtly plunged underground in the middle of the garden. Its beautiful post-modern design, incorporating some fine workmanship, including superb stained glass, is certainly impressive, as is the wonderful auditorium with its perfect acoustics. The centre also houses an art gallery with small exhibition rooms linked by corridors, intended to echo a cave's labyrinth. The centre complements the **Observatorio Pierre Auger** (guided visits Mon–Sat 5pm; free; ⓦwww.auger.org.ar), opposite at San Martín Norte 304, part of an astrophysics project to measure the mysterious ultra-high-energy cosmic rays that bombard Earth from space. When the project is complete, 1600 cream-coloured water tanks that serve as particle detectors will be scattered over the pampas, 1.5km apart – look out for them as you drive into town.

Completely down to earth by comparison, just along from the park, three blocks north of Plaza San Martín, is the **Molino de Rufino Ortega**, a handsome adobe flour mill not currently open to visitors. Next to the mill, in a fine, impeccably refurbished colonial building, is the **Museo Regional** (Tues–Sun 9am–12.30pm & 4–7.30pm; free). The beautifully displayed collection includes objects as varied as ammonites, guanaco leather, clay pipes for religious ceremonies, a mummified corpse, jewellery, dinosaur remains and even a set of vehicle registration plates dating from the early 1950s, when the town was temporarily renamed Villa Juan Domingo Perón. A new annexe to the museum houses Mi Viejo Almacén, a store selling local artisan goods.

Eating

Quinto Viejo, at Av San Martín 355, is the town's main meeting-place, offering breakfasts, coffee and evening drinks. Apart from the *Hotel Río Grande*, the top place **to eat** in town is *La Posta*, Av Roca 374, an excellent *parrilla* serving goat and trout. For the best trout, though, head out of town to El Dique, 8km west of Malargüe, where at the *Cuyam-Co* trout farm (ⓣ02627/15661917) you can even catch your own fish. It is then perfectly cooked and served with an excellent local rosé; book ahead and note that the kitchen closes around 10pm. If you're too full to move after dinner, you can also pitch your tent at the nearby shady campsite.

Reserva Faunística Laguna de Llancanelo

Spring is by far the best time to make the easy half-day trip from Malargüe to the **RESERVA FAUNÍSTICA LAGUNA DE LLANCANELO**, since that's when you're likely to see the largest numbers of waterfowl, as many species come here to nest. Throughout the year, though, the shallow saline lagoon's mirror-still waters in the middle of a huge dried-up lakebed make for a fantastic sight. You'd be very unlucky not to spot flocks of flamingoes, at times so huge that whole areas of the lake's surface are turned uniformly pink. Other species of birds frequenting this special habitat include Black-necked Swans, several kinds of duck, grebe and teal, gulls, terns and curlews. Parts of the reserve are out of bounds all year, and access to others is restricted to non-critical seasons. The park is patrolled by *guardaparques*, and it is best to go on an organized tour from Malargüe, as you'll get more out of visiting the lagoon with someone who knows the terrain and the fauna. Preferably come very early in the morning or in the late afternoon and evening, when the light is fabulous and the wildfowl more easily spotted. Access to the reserve is via RP-186, which branches east off RN-40 some 20km south of Malargüe; it's then another 20km to the reserve entrance, near the shallow cavern known as the Cueva del Tigre.

Caverna de las Brujas

The **CAVERNA DE LAS BRUJAS** is a marvellous cave that plunges deep into the earth at an altitude of just under 2000m, just 73km southwest of Malargüe, 8km off RN-40 along a marked track. The road climbs over the scenic **Cuesta del Chihuido**, which affords fantastic views of the Sierra de Palauco to the east, in a region of outstanding beauty enhanced by sparse but attractive vegetation. This area is covered by a thick layer of marine sedimentary rock, through which water has seeped, creating underground cave systems, such as the Caverna de las Brujas. The name, literally "witches' cave", is thought to be linked to local legends that it was used as a meeting-place for sorcerers. Las Brujas is a karstic cave, filled with amazing rock formations, including some impressive **stalactites and stalagmites**; typically they have been given imaginative names such as "the Virgin's Chamber", "the Pulpit", "the Flowers" and "the Crystals". Water continues to seep inside, making the walls slippery, as if they were awash with soapsuds. Although the tourist circuit is only 260m long and never descends more than 6m below the surface, the experience is memorable.

The *caverna* lies within a provincial park, and a small *guardería*, manned by a couple of *guardaparques*, stands nearby; they have the key to the padlocked gates that protect the grotto. It's compulsory to enter with a guide, and again the best option is to go on an organized tour from Malargüe. Wear good walking shoes and take a sweater – the difference in temperature between inside and out can be as much as 20°C – and a pocket torch, though miners' helmets are also supplied; a highlight inside the cave is experiencing the total darkness by turning out all lights and getting used to the spooky atmosphere.

Just 5km west of the side road to the caves is the turn-off to the **Paso Pehuenche**, a mountain pass across the cordillera into Chile some 80km away. At 2500m, this pass is hardly ever blocked by snow and is becoming a major route between the two countries.

La Payunia

The highlight of any trip to southernmost Mendoza Province, yet overlooked by most visitors because of its relative inaccessibility, **LA PAYUNIA**, protected by the Reserva Provincial La Payunia, is a fabulously wild area of staggering beauty, sometimes referred to as the Patagonia Mendocina. Dominated by Volcán Payún Matru (3690m), and its slightly lower inactive neighbour Volcán Payún Liso, it is utterly unspoilt apart from some remnants of old fluorite and manganese mines plus some petrol-drilling derricks, whose nodding-head pump-structures are locally nicknamed "guanacos", after the member of the llama family they vaguely resemble in shape. Occasionally, you will spot real guanacos, sometimes in large flocks, standing out against the black volcanic backdrop of the so-called **Pampa Negra**. This huge expanse of lava in the middle of the reserve was caused by relatively recent volcanic eruptions, dating back hundreds or thousands of years rather than millions, as is the case of most such phenomena in the region. "Fresh" trails of lava debris can be seen at various points throughout the park, and enormous boulders of igneous rock are scattered over these dark plains, also ejected during the violent volcanic activity. The only vegetation is flaxen grass, whose golden colour stands out against the treacle-coloured hillsides. Another section of the reserve is the aptly named **Pampa Roja**, where reddish oxides in the lava give the ground a henna-like tint. The threatening hulk of Volcán Pihuel looms at the western extremity of the reserve – its top was blown off by a particularly violent explosion that occurred when the mountain was beneath the sea.

The approach to the park from Malargüe is past the Caverna de las Brujas, along RN-40. After crossing the Río Grande at Bardas Blancas, you travel another 100km or so, following the river valley and the golden expanse of the Pampa de Palauco. The road crosses the river again at a narrow gorge, called La Pasarela, or the footbridge, where the waters quickly cooled a lava flow thousands of years ago and created a rock formation that looks as brittle as charcoal. The park's volcanic cones soon loom into view, and the entrance to the reserve is via a side turning to the east, at a place called El Zampal.

To visit the park, take one of the excellent day-trips run by Karen Travel in Malargüe (see p.545). If you plan to drive there independently, note that you must also take a guide with you – ask in the travel agencies or tourist office in Malargüe. You can also stay at the lovely eco-conscious **accommodation**, *Kiñe* (Ⓣ02627/155-88635 or 02627/471344, Ⓦwww.kinie.com.ar; from $222 per person for two days full board, with trips included), in a basic but comfortable little farmstead at the remote hamlet of La Agüita, on RP-186 in the northeast corner of the reserve. In addition to simple but tasty meals the friendly family of goatherds also lays on treks in the mountains and horse rides across plains full of guanacos. There is no public transport to *Kiñe* but the owners will pick you up in Malargüe.

San Juan and La Rioja

San Juan and **La Rioja** provinces share some memorable countryside, with range after range of lofty mountains alternating with green valleys of olive groves, onion fields and vineyards. Forming the northern half of Argentina's midwestern region, they're often regarded as the poorer cousins, in every sense, of Mendoza Province, and certainly neither of their capitals could be called sophisticated; rather, they give the impression of being resigned to backwater status, even though La Rioja was Carlos Menem's power base. The provinces' **bodegas**, for example, continue to take a back seat to those of Mendoza and San Rafael, even though their wine can be just as good. One advantage of this relative seclusion is that you have more space to yourself and are usually treated with more spontaneous hospitality than is sometimes the case further south. **Tourism** has not quite got off the ground here, though, a fact that may present some drawbacks – transport and other facilities are sometimes below par, when not lacking entirely. But as long as you see this as a challenge rather than an obstacle, you can still enjoy the breathtaking scenery. The small southeastern corner of the region should be bypassed or given short shrift, however: it's a horrendous, flat area of dusty gorse and drab salt-flats.

To say that both provinces are sparsely inhabited is a gross understatement: outside the capital, La Rioja's population density barely reaches one inhabitant per square kilometre, while San Juan, where the equivalent ratio is around three, is on average half as densely populated as Mendoza Province. If these statistics seem too abstract, you'll soon understand what they mean in practice – leaving the cities behind to scout around the outback, you'll experience a real sense of setting off into uncharted territory, a sensation heightened by the often-challenging terrain.

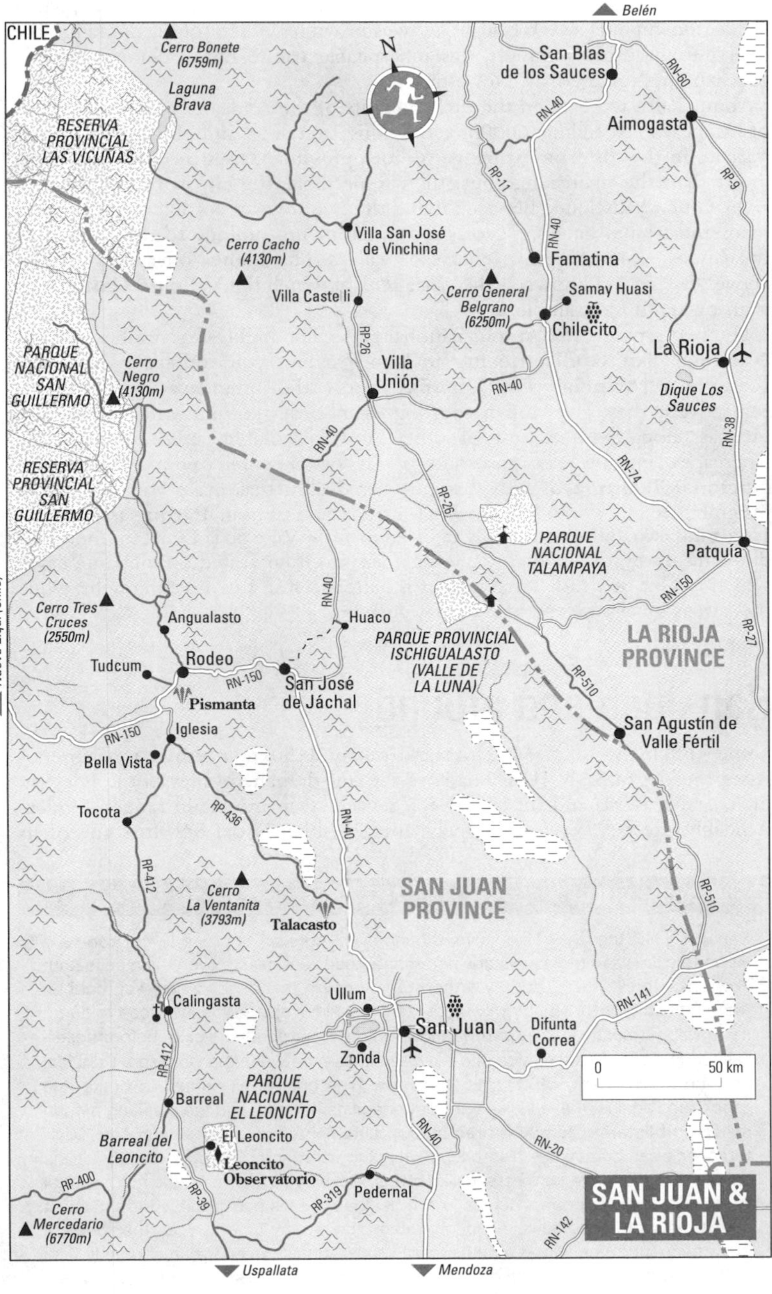
CHILE
Cerro Bonete (6759m)
Laguna Brava
RESERVA PROVINCIAL LAS VICUÑAS
Belén
San Blas de los Sauces
RN-60
RN-40
Aimogasta
RP-11
RP-9
Villa San José de Vinchina
Cerro Cacho (4130m)
Famatina
Villa Castelli
Cerro General Belgrano (6250m)
Samay Huasi
Chilecito
RP-26
La Rioja
Catamarca
PARQUE NACIONAL SAN GUILLERMO
Cerro Negro (4130m)
Villa Unión
RN-40
Dique Los Sauces
RN-38
RN-74
RESERVA PROVINCIAL SAN GUILLERMO
RP-26
PARQUE NACIONAL TALAMPAYA
Patquía
RN-150
Nueva Elqui (Chile)
Cerro Tres Cruces (2550m)
Angualasto
Huaco
RP-27
PARQUE PROVINCIAL ISCHIGUALASTO (VALLE DE LA LUNA)
LA RIOJA PROVINCE
Tudcum
Rodeo
RN-150
San José de Jáchal
Pismanta
RP-510
RN-150
Iglesia
San Agustín de Valle Fértil
Bella Vista
RP-436
Tocota
RP-412
Cerro La Ventanita (3793m)
Talacasto
SAN JUAN PROVINCE
RP-510
Chepes
Calingasta
Ullum
San Juan
Difunta Correa
RN-141
Zonda
0
50 km
PARQUE NACIONAL EL LEONCITO
Barreal
El Leoncito
Barreal del Leoncito
Leoncito Observatorio
RN-20
RP-400
RP-39
Pedernal
RP-319
Cerro Mercedario (6770m)
RN-142
SAN JUAN & LA RIOJA
Uspallata
Mendoza

Mostly unpaved roads frequently peter out into tracks barely passable in the hardiest jeep, and the weather conditions are equally inclement in summer, when sudden downpours sweep bridges away, as in winter, when squalls unpredictably turn into blizzards. However, this inhospitable nature does offer up fantastic opportunities for alternative tourism.

About halfway between the dizzy heights of the Andean cordillera – many of its peaks exceeding 6000m along this stretch – and the tediously flat *travesías* in the easternmost fringe of both provinces, rises the **precordillera**, lower than the main range but still a respectable 4000m or more above sea level. Club-sandwiched between it and the two rows of cordillera – known as main and frontal ranges, a geological phenomenon unique to this section of the Andes – are successive chains of valleys. The higher ones over 1500m above sea level are known as the *valles altos*, of which the **Valle de Calingasta** is an outstanding example.

The two provinces boast four national parks. The highly inaccessible **Parque Nacional San Guillermo** in San Juan Province pairs off neatly with the **Reserva Provincial Las Vicuñas** across the boundary in La Rioja; respectively, they give you a sporting chance of spotting wild pumas and vicuñas, along with a host of other Andean wildlife, amid unforgettable landscapes. Further east is a duo of far better publicized parks: **Parque Nacional Talampaya**, with vertiginous red cliffs that make you feel totally insignificant and – only 70km south – its unidentical twin, **Parque Provincial Ischigualasto**, more commonly referred to as the Valle de la Luna, an important dinosaur graveyard in a highly photogenic site. Often visited on the same day – which is a bit of a rush – the former is better seen in the morning light, while the latter's lunarscapes are dazzling at dusk.

San Juan and around

Some 165km north of Mendoza and nearly 1150km northwest of Buenos Aires, the city of **SAN JUAN** basks in the sun-drenched valley of the Río San Juan, which twists and turns between several steep mountain ranges. Understandably, the city revels in its pet name, Residencia del Sol. In some of its

The zonda effect

San Juan, like the rest of the Cuyo, though even more so, is prone to the **zonda**, a legendary dry wind that blows down from the Andes and blasts everything in its path like a blowtorch. It's caused by a **thermal inversion** that arises when wet, cold air from the Pacific is thrust abruptly up over the cordillera and suddenly forced to dump its moisture, mostly in the form of snow, onto the skyscraper peaks before helter-skeltering down the other side into the deep chasm between the Cordillera Principal and the precordillera, which acts like a very high brick wall. Forced to brake, the *zonda* rubs against the land like tyre-rubber against tarmac, and the resulting friction results in **blistering temperatures** and an atmosphere you can almost see. Mini-tornadoes can sometimes also occur, whipping sand and dust up in clearly visible spirals all along the region's desert-like plains. The Cuyo's answer to the *föhn*, mistral or sirocco, ripping people's nerves to shreds, the *zonda* is one of the world's nastiest meteorological phenomena. Although it can blow at any time of year, the *zonda* is most frequent in the winter months, particularly August, when it can suddenly hike the temperature by ten to fifteen degrees in a matter of hours.

barrios it has rained only a couple of times over the past decade, and the provincial average is less than 100mm a year. When it does rain, it's usually in the form of violent storms, as savage as the *zonda* wind that occasionally stings the city and shortens people's tempers (see box opposite). All this sunshine – more than nine hours a day on average – and the generally mild climate quickly ripen the sweetest imaginable grapes, melons and plums, irrigated by pre-Columbian canals and ditches, that have helped the city and its mainly Spanish and Middle Eastern immigrant population to prosper over the years. But nature is also a foe: periodic tremors, some of them alarmingly high on the Richter scale, remind Sanjuaninos that they live along one of the world's most slippery seismic faults; the Big One is dreaded as much here as in California but, as they do there, people just live their lives, trusting the special techniques used in the construction of the city's newer buildings.

Modern but attractive – one of South America's strongest ever recorded earthquakes flattened the city in 1944 and as a result the city has hardly any buildings more than half a century old – San Juan is also quite conservative and, compared with its much bigger rival Mendoza, seems to drag its feet somewhat. Around a third of a million people live in Greater San Juan, but in the compact microcentro, rebuilt according to the model implemented in Mendoza after its own catastrophic quake, everyone seems to know everyone else. Broad pavements, grand avenues and long boulevards shaded by rows of flaky-trunked plane trees lend the city a feeling of spaciousness and openness. Although none of the sights amounts to much, San Juan is a comfortable starting-point for touring some of the country's finest scenery. Destinations close to the city include the man-made **Dique de Ullum** and oasis landscapes to the west, an **archeological museum** in the southern suburbs and the mind-bogglingly grotesque pilgrim site of **Difunta Correa**, 60km to the east.

Some history

The city was founded by the Spanish aristocrat Juan Jufré as San Juan de la Frontera on June 13, 1562 during an expedition from Santiago de Chile, and since then it has had a persistently troubled history. In 1594, the settlement was washed away by floods, and in 1632 it was again destroyed, this time in attacks by natives. The following year an uprising by the indigenous inhabitants was brutally put down; seventeen were hanged on the Plaza Mayor as an example. In the middle of the nineteenth century, San Juan found itself at the heart of the country's civil war when its progressive leader, Dr Antonino Aberastain, was assassinated by federalist troops. In 1885, though, the arrival of the railways heralded something of an end to San Juan's backwater status, as Basque, Galician and Andalucian immigrants began arriving.

Like Mendoza, the city has had terrible luck with seismic shocks: several violent earthquakes struck the city in the 1940s, but the strongest of all, attaining around 8.5 on the Richter scale, hit San Juan on January 15, 1944. It flattened the city and killed more than ten thousand people; during a gala held in Buenos Aires to raise funds for the victims shortly afterwards, a relatively unknown army officer, Juan Domingo Perón, met an equally obscure actress, Eva Duarte. Quakes have continued to trouble the city regularly since then, the most severe being the 7.4 tremor with its epicentre on nearby Caucete on November 23, 1977, which left 65 dead and hundreds injured.

Arrival and information

Las Chacritas **airport**, small but functional, is 12km east of the city, just off RN-141 (☎0264/425-4133); there are plenty of taxis and *remises* to the centre.

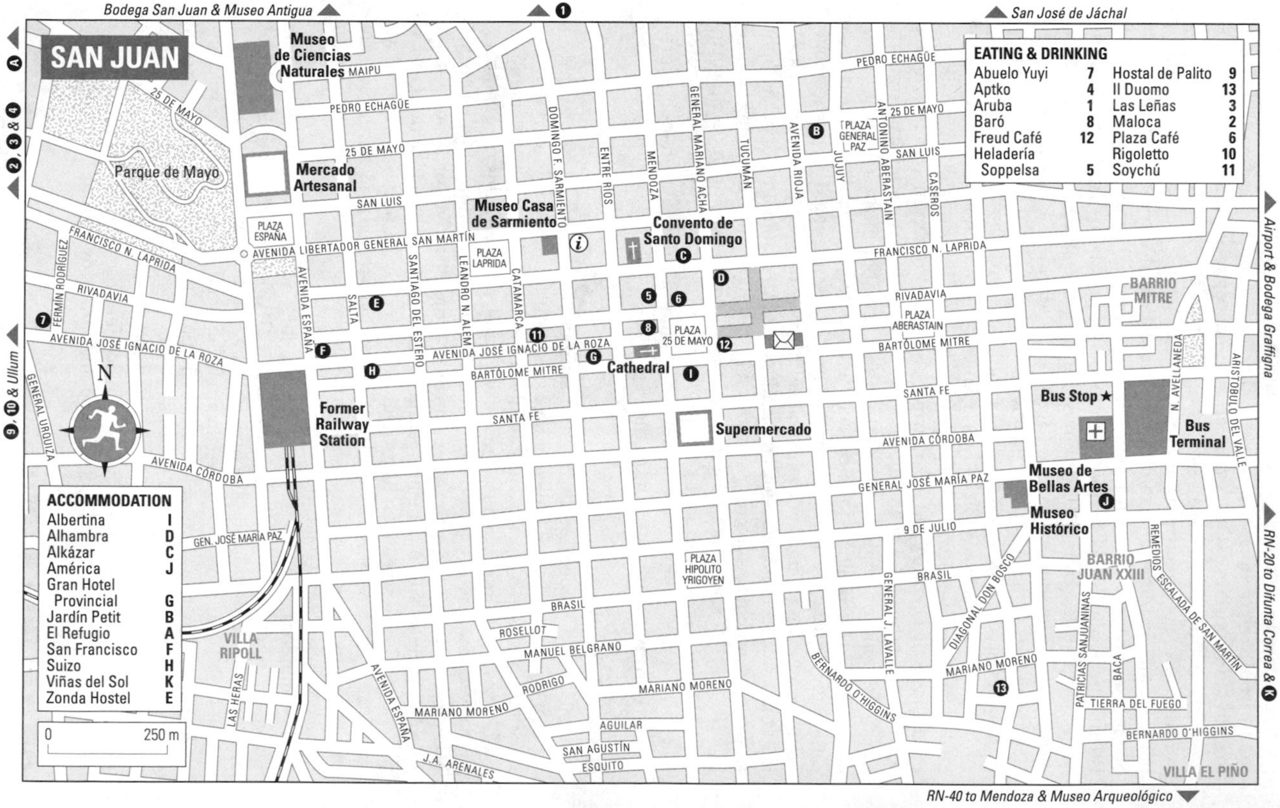
SAN JUAN
Bodega San Juan & Museo Antigua
1
San José de Jáchal
Airport & Bodega Graffigna
RN-20 to Difunta Correa & K
RN-40 to Mendoza & Museo Arqueológico
9, 10 & Ullum
A
2, 3 & 4
EATING & DRINKING
Abuelo Yuyi 7
Aptko 4
Aruba 1
Baró 8
Freud Café 12
Heladería Soppelsa 5
Hostal de Palito 9
Il Duomo 13
Las Leñas 3
Maloca 2
Plaza Café 6
Rigoletto 10
Soychú 11
ACCOMMODATION
Albertina I
Alhambra D
Alkázar C
América J
Gran Hotel Provincial G
Jardín Petit B
El Refugio A
San Francisco F
Suizo H
Viñas del Sol K
Zonda Hostel E
0 250 m
N
Museo de Ciencias Naturales
Mercado Artesanal
Parque de Mayo
Museo Casa de Sarmiento
Convento de Santo Domingo
Cathedral
Supermercado
Former Railway Station
Bus Stop
Bus Terminal
Museo de Bellas Artes
Museo Histórico
BARRIO MITRE
BARRIO JUAN XXIII
VILLA RIPOLL
VILLA EL PIÑO
PLAZA ESPAÑA
PLAZA LAPRIDA
PLAZA 25 DE MAYO
PLAZA ABERASTAIN
PLAZA GENERAL PAZ
PLAZA HIPOLITO YRIGOYEN
MAIPU
PEDRO ECHAGÜE
25 DE MAYO
SAN LUIS
AVENIDA LIBERTADOR GENERAL SAN MARTÍN
FRANCISCO N. LAPRIDA
RIVADAVIA
BARTÓLOME MITRE
AVENIDA JOSÉ IGNACIO DE LA ROZA
SANTA FE
AVENIDA CÓRDOBA
GENERAL JOSÉ MARÍA PAZ
GEN. JOSÉ MARÍA PAZ
9 DE JULIO
BRASIL
ROSELLOT
MANUEL BELGRANO
RODRIGO
MARIANO MORENO
AGUILAR
SAN AGUSTÍN
ESQUITO
J.A. ARENALES
AVENIDA ESPAÑA
SALTA
SANTIAGO DEL ESTERO
LEANDRO N. ALEM
CATAMARCA
DOMINGO F. SARMIENTO
ENTRE RÍOS
MENDOZA
GENERAL MARIANO ACHA
TUCUMÁN
AVENIDA RIOJA
JUJUY
ANTONINO ABERASTAIN
CASEROS
GENERAL J. LAVALLE
BERNARDO O'HIGGINS
DIAGONAL DON BOSCO
PATRICIAS SANJUANINAS
BACA
TIERRA DEL FUEGO
REMEDIOS ESCALADA DE SAN MARTÍN
N. AVELLANEDA
ARISTOBULO DEL VALLE
FERMÍN RODRÍGUEZ
GENERAL URQUIZA
LAS HERAS

The city's user-friendly, spacious **bus station**, with regular services all over the province, region and country, is eight blocks east of the central Plaza 25 de Mayo, at Estados Unidos 492 sur (☎0264/422-5147). En-Pro-Tur, the **provincial tourist office**, is at Sarmiento 24 (Mon–Fri 7am–9pm, Sat & Sun 9am–9pm; ☎0264/421-0004, Ⓦwww.turismo.sanjuan.gov.ar), next to a mighty 200-year-old carob tree. The staff are extremely helpful and can propose excursions to major sights, such as Ischigualasto (see p.559). You won't be needing city transport, but all **buses** to nearby destinations such as Zonda or La Laja leave from stops alongside the bus station.

Accommodation

San Juan has a whole crop of middling **hotels**, nothing special but pleasant enough, which should meet your needs for the short time you're probably going to stay in the city. If you're on a tighter budget, there are also a handful of generally clean **hostels** and *residenciales*, or if you do want some creature comforts, there's one snazzy five-star establishment with all mod cons. Campers should head west to either Zonda's campsite, *Camping Municipal Rivadavia* (❶), on RP-12 opposite the racetrack, with a swimming pool and very decent facilities, or Ullum's *Camping El Pinar* (❶) within the grounds of the Parque Sarmiento, along RP-14 just before the Dique Nivelador. Set amidst a refreshing wood of pines, cypresses and eucalyptus, it has a bathing area, a canteen and well-kept facilities.

Hostels & hotels

Albertina Mitre 31 este ☎0264/421-4222 or 422-5442. The reception is strangely located in the basement, but the rooms are comfortable, albeit slightly dated. ❺

Alhambra General Acha 180 sur ☎0264/421-4780. Medium-sized rooms, each with bath, in this well-run establishment with friendly staff. ❺

Alkázar Laprida 84 este ☎0264/421-4965/8, Ⓦwww.alkazarhotel.com.ar. San Juan's only luxury hotel to date; although on the impersonal side, it does have extremely smart, well-kept rooms, with ultra-modern bathrooms and sweeping views across the city, and a swimming pool in the grounds. ❻

América 9 de Julio 1052 este ☎0264/421-4514, Ⓦwww.hotel-america.com.ar. Pleasant, traditional, small hotel popular with foreign visitors, so call ahead to reserve. All rooms have an en-suite bathroom. ❹

Gran Hotel Provincial Av J.I. de la Roza 132 ☎0264/422-7501, Ⓦwww.granhotelprovincial.com. An old-fashioned hotel with old-fashioned polite service, right at the centre of San Juan, a few steps from the Plaza 25 de Mayo. ❻

Jardín Petit 25 de Mayo 345 este ☎0264/421-1825, Ⓦwww.jardinpetithotel.com.ar. Small, functional rooms with bath, and a bright patio overlooked by the breakfast room. ❷

El Refugio Ramón y Cajal 97 and San Luis ☎0264/421-3087, Ⓔelrefugio@inserv.com.ar. Attractive, professionally run *apart-hotel*, with car park, a refreshing little pool, and tastefully decorated duplex apartment-like rooms, with kitchenettes, bright bathrooms and breakfast served in the room or sitting outside. ❺

San Francisco Av España 284 sur ☎0264/422-3760. Extremely reliable place, with smart, pleasant rooms, new bathrooms and friendly service. ❸

Suizo Salta 272 sur ☎0264/422-4293. An odd mixture, with a rather chaotic entrance and twee bedrooms, in an unsurprisingly Swiss style; good value, though. ❸

Viñas del Sol RN-20 and General Roca ☎0264/425-3922, Ⓦwww.viniasdelsol.com.ar. Very comfortable hotel, one of San Juan's newest, between the city and the airport. There's a nice swimming pool. ❺

Zonda Hostel Laprida 572 oeste ☎0264/4201009, Ⓦwww.zondahostel.com.ar. In a mustard-coloured building a few blocks west of the city centre, San Juan's new youth hostel offers clean dorm rooms ($20 per person) and a small garden, with breakfast included – whenever you want it.

The City

The total area of San Juan city, girdled by the Circunvalación, the city ring road, is extensive but easy to find your way around, as the grid is fairly regular and the streets don't change name. In all directions from the point zero, the intersection of Calle Mendoza and Avenida San Martín, the cardinal directions are added to the street name; for example, Avenida Córdoba oeste (west) or este (east), or Calle Tucumán norte (north) or sur (south). **Plaza 25 de Mayo** is the city centre, surrounded by terraced cafés and shops. The controversial **cathedral**, too modern for many tastes, on the northwest edge of the plaza, has a fifty-metre brick campanile that takes its inspiration from the tower of St Mark's in Venice. It was built in the 1970s and its practical purpose is to provide a viewpoint over the city. You can climb almost to the top of the **bell tower** (daily 9am–1pm & 5–9.30pm; $2) – which plays a Big Ben chime, and the Argentine national anthem for special occasions – for panoramas of the city and surrounding countryside.

Two blocks west and one north, opposite the tourist office, is the city's sole museum of any interest, the **Museo Casa de Sarmiento** (Tues–Fri 8am–1pm & 3–8pm, Mon & Sat 8am–1pm; $1; guided tours every 30min, in Spanish only) at Sarmiento 21 sur. The house where Sarmiento, Argentine president and Renaissance man, was born on February 15, 1811, was only slightly damaged in the 1944 earthquake, thanks to its sturdy adobe walls and sandy foundations, and has since been restored several times, to attain its present gleaming state – for the Sarmiento centenary in 1911 it was declared a national historic monument, Argentina's first. It's a beautiful, simple whitewashed house built around a large patio, with a huge rubber tree. The rooms contain an exhibition of Sarmiento relics and personal effects, plenty of portraits and signs of sycophancy, echoed by the gushing commentary of the guides who steer you round.

Of San Juan's several other museums, only three have any potential whatsoever. The **Museo de Bellas Artes Franklin Rawson** and **Museo Histórico Provincial Agustín Gnecco**, both in the same building at General Paz 737 este (both Mon–Fri 8am–noon; both free), contain rather motley collections of paintings and antiquities, respectively. The art collection, named after the unimaginative nineteenth-century painter Franklin Rawson, includes work by him as well as some more interesting pictures, including a portrait of a chillingly tight-lipped widow by Prilidiano Pueyrredón. Major Argentine artists Berni, Spilimbergo, Petorutti and Raquel Forner (see Contexts, p.843) are all represented here, though not at their best. Among the thrown-together exhibits at the Museo Histórico is a set of coins, lots of nineteenth-century furniture and some *criollo* artwork, including spurs, stirrups and *mate* vessels. The **Museo de Ciencias Naturales** (daily 9am–1pm; free), meanwhile, housed in the former train station at avenidas España and Maipú, contains an exhibition focusing on the remarkable **dinosaur skeletons** unearthed at Parque Provincial Ischigualasto (see p.559), and features both the actual fossil remains and models showing how the dinosaurs may have looked. You can see the scientific workshop where the finds are examined and analysed, while the collections of semi-precious stones extracted from the province's mines are for once imaginatively displayed, using modern techniques.

If you have time to kill or a penchant for the nooks and crannies of Argentine history, the cell where General San Martín stayed in 1815, part of a well-restored seventeenth-century Dominican convent, **Convento de Santo Domingo**, at Laprida 57 oeste (Mon–Sat 8.30am–12.30pm; $1), may be of interest. The cloisters were wrecked by the 1944 quake, but the cell was almost intact, taken as a sign of the Libertador's sainthood. The stark cell contains some of the hero's belongings, but that's all.

You could round off your exploration of the city with a visit to one of its bodegas. Although generally not as well organized as those in Mendoza Province, there are a few alluring exceptions, most notably the monumental **Bodega Graffigna**, now incorporating a wine museum – the **Museo Santiago Graffigna**, at Colón 1342 norte (Tues–Fri 9am–1pm, Sat 9am–8pm, Sun 10am–2pm; free; ⓣ0264/421-4227). Housed in a beautiful brick reconstruction of the pre-quake winery, it still produces red and white wines, among the best in the province. The displays use audio-visual techniques to give a guided tour (English included), and are a tribute to the Graffigna family, who went on producing wine despite major setbacks, not least the 1944 quake. There is also a scintillating wine bar, open on Friday and Saturday evenings until late. Alternatively, the newly opened **Museo Antigua Bodega San Juan**, in an attractive salmon-coloured building at Salta 782 norte (Mon–Sat 8.30am–12.30pm & 4–8pm; free) that once housed one of the city's oldest, eponymous bodegas, has preserved the original wine-making equipment, but with little in the way of information – this one is really for enthusiasts only.

Eating, drinking and nightlife

San Juan has a wide range of **places to eat**, including one of the region's best vegetarian restaurants, as well as plenty of Italian eateries and the usual pizzerias, *parrillas* and *tenedor libre* joints. Most of the best places are in the western, residential part of the city, near the Parque de Mayo. **Café** life is all part of the *paseo* tradition, imported lock, stock and barrel from Spain, but later in the evening most Sanjuaninos seem to entertain themselves in their gardens, round a family *asado*. There's also a wine bar at Bodega Graffigna, and a couple of decent **discos**, mostly in the outskirts.

Restaurants

Abuelo Yuyi Av José Ignacio de la Roza and Urquiza. The most popular pizzeria in town, offering delicious thick-crust pies with a variety of toppings.

Baró Rivadavia 55 oeste. San Juan's fashionable restaurant of the moment, serving tasty Italian food.

Hostal de Palito Av Circunvalación 284 sur. This is one of the best *parrillas* in town, with a delightful garden terrace.

Il Duomo Av San Martín 1802 oeste. Open all day for lunch and dinner, this classic Italian-style restaurant is popular with locals for its reliable pasta and meat dishes.

Las Leñas Av San Martín 1670 oeste. Cavernous dining room often packed with large parties; delicious meat.

Maloca Del Bono 321. Off-beat place with psychedelic decor, Latino music and an unusual range of Mexican tacos, Colombian *arepas* and Cuban rice dishes, plus tropical cocktails.

Rigoletto Paula A. de Sarmiento 418 sur. Cosy atmosphere and friendly service, as well as delicious pizzas and pasta.

Soychú Av José Ignacio de la Roza 223 oeste. Delightful vegetarian restaurant serving fabulous dishes, in a bright, airy space; office workers flock here to take food away, so come early.

Bars, cafés and nightclubs

Aptko Av San Martín 1369 oeste. Not terribly aesthetically appealing, but still the city's trendiest night spot, where San Juan's affluent youth come to be seen, chat and dance the night away to a mixed soundtrack, dominated by house.

Aruba Rioja and Maipú. Disco with a bar and *confitería* attached, playing mostly salsa and other Latin rhythms.

Freud Café Plaza 25 de Mayo. An establishment on the eastern side of the main square; coffee, drinks, lots of gossip and football chat.

Heladería Soppelsa Av José Ignacio de la Roza 639 oeste and Mendoza 163 sur. Undoubtedly the best ice cream in the city.

Plaza Café Plaza 25 de Mayo. Another institutional café on the central plaza; snacks and small meals, while you watch the world go by.

Listings

Airlines Aerolíneas Argentinas, San Martín 215 oeste ⓣ0264/442-0205.
Banks and exchange Cambio Santiago, General Acha 52 sur, for traveller's cheques and exchange. Stacks of ATMs all over town, especially around Plaza 25 de Mayo.
Car rental Avis, San Martín 163 oeste ⓣ0264/422-4622; Renta Auto, San Martín 1593 oeste ⓣ0264/423-3620.
Laundry Fast, Sarmiento and 9 de Julio; Laverap, Rivadavia 498 oeste.
Post office Av José Ignacio de la Roza 259 este ⓣ0264/422-4430.
Internet access There are *locutorios* all over, including several clustered around Plaza 25 de Mayo.
Tour operators San Juan has plenty of tour agencies that run day-trips to Talampaya and other local points of interest – three of the best established are Valley of the Moon, Rivadavia 414 oeste (ⓣ0264/421-4868, ⓦwww.valleymoon.com); Leonardo Galvez, Mendoza sur 122 (ⓣ0264/421-4200); and Triassic Tour, Hipólito Yrigoyen 294 sur (ⓣ0264/423-0358).

Around San Juan

Around San Juan you'll find wildly different sights that can be visited either on a short trip from the city, or on your way to somewhere else. In an otherwise dull industrial park to the south there is an incongruous but fabulous **archeological museum** whose prize exhibit is a magnificent Inca mummy; to the west you can go wine-tasting at **Zonda** or windsurfing on the **Dique de Ullum**, in a bone-dry valley dotted with oases; to the east the shrine to the **Difunta Correa** is the most concrete example of how Amerindian legends and Roman Catholic fanaticism have melded together into one belief.

Museo Arqueológico Profesor Mariano Gambier

Some 6km south of San Juan centre, the **Museo Arqueológico Profesor Mariano Gambier**, on RN-40 between Progreso and Calle 5 in the neighbourhood of Rawson (Mon–Fri 8am–8pm, Sat & Sun 9am–1pm & 5–9pm; $2; ⓣ0264/4241424), is worth the trek. Don't be put off by its (possibly temporary) location in an industrial park warehouse – inside, the highly academic presentation, run by San Juan University, takes you through the pre-history and history of the provinces' cultures, from the so-called Cultura de la Fortuna (10,000–6000 BC), of which we just have a few tools as evidence, to the Ullum-Zonda civilization of the Huarpe people, whose land was invaded first by the Inca in the fifteenth century and then by colonizers from Chile in the sixteenth. A number of digs near the city of San Juan have uncovered a treasure of ceramics and domestic items from the latter, well displayed here in glass cases. The museum's highlight, though, is a set of mummified bodies dating from the first century BC through to the fifteenth century AD, with the most impressive of all discovered in 1964 at over 4500m in the cordillera, in northern San Juan Province. Kept in an antiquated fridge is **La Momia del Cerro el Toro**, probably the victim of an Inca sacrifice; the body is incredibly well preserved, down to her eye lashes and leather sandals. Other items worth a mention are a 2000-year-old carob-wood **mask**, some fine **basketwork** coloured with natural pigments and ancient ponchos with geometric patterns. All the exhibits are labelled in both Spanish and English, and if you press the red button in each of the rooms you're treated to a rather monotone Spanish audio commentary. The only way to get out to the museum is by car – take a taxi if you don't have your own transport.

Zonda and the Dique de Ullum

In Quichoa, **Zonda** means "high sky", and, true to its moniker, the valley of that name to the west of San Juan, reached along RP-12, seems to enjoy blue skies nearly every day of the year. Vineyards and olive groves alternate with lush fields of camomile that become snow-white in the spring – all watered almost entirely with irrigation channels that distribute the ice-melt from the Andes; the only blot on the landscape is the huge cement works which belches clouds of dust high into the atmosphere. The air around here is so dry it tingles. Leaving San Juan city, the road soon enters a narrow gorge, formed by the crinkly Serranía de Marquesado; partly landscaped with native and European trees, the open Parque de Zonda, which nestles in the gorge by the roadside, includes a **Jardín de los Poetas**, where verses of Argentine poetry are inscribed on the rock-face. The most noteworthy piece of graffiti is a quotation by Sarmiento, who passed through in 1840, on the way to his Chilean exile imposed by his arch-enemy Rosas – his words, "Ideas cannot be killed", were written in French so that Rosas' followers wouldn't understand them. Near the El Zonda racing track, 15km from the city, you'll see a sign for the **Cavas de Zonda** (Mon–Fri 10am–5pm, Sat & Sun 11am–5pm; ⓣ0264/494-5144). It claims to be South America's only wine cellar housed in a natural cave; in the cool tunnel drilled into the cliff-side the temperature hovers around 17°C, much lower than outside and ideal for storing some of Argentina's finest ciders and sparkling wines, the latter marketed here as champagne (*champaña*); you're taken on a tour of the cellars before tasting a selection of the wines, which includes a rich malbec. **Bus** #23 from San Juan's bus terminal runs to Zonda on a regular basis.

Just north of Zonda, but reached directly from San Juan by RP-113 and RP-14, the **Dique de Ullum**, a large reservoir, is the city's vital water source, but its perennially ultramarine waters are also used for non-polluting watersports such as windsurfing, fishing and swimming – when the *zonda* blows, windsurfers race along at incredible speeds and the conditions can even be quite dangerous, especially for the inexperienced. Several clubs and associations on the east bank

Difunta Correa

As legend would have it, during the Civil War in the 1840s, a local man named Baudilio Correa was captured, taken to La Rioja and killed; his widow Deolinda decided to walk to La Rioja with their baby boy to recover Baudilio's corpse. Unable to find water she dropped dead by the roadside, where a passerby found her, the baby still sucking from her breast. Her grave soon became a holy place and lost travellers began to invoke her protection, claiming miraculous escapes from death on the road. The story of the widow Correa is believed to be Amerindian in origin but has been mingled with Catholic hagiography in a country where the borderline between religion and superstition can often be very faint. The **Difunta Correa** – *difunta* meaning deceased – is now the unofficial saint of all travellers, but especially bus- and truck-drivers, and thousands of people visit the shrine every year, over 100,000 of them during Holy Week alone, many of them covering part of the journey on their knees; national truck-drivers' day in early November also sees huge crowds arriving here. Some people visit the shrine itself – where a hideous statue of the Difunta, complete with sucking infant, lies among melted candles, prayers on pieces of paper and votive offerings including people's driving licences, the remains of tyres and photographs of mangled cars from which the occupants miraculously got out alive – while others just deposit a bottle of mineral water on the huge collection that is creeping along like a small-scale replica of the Perito Moreno glacier (see p.723).

of the reservoir rent out boards and other equipment and give instruction. The surrounding mountains are excellent for rock-climbing and hiking; if you decide to give either of these activities a go, take lots of water, as the hottest part of the day can be brutal. **Bus** #29 comes out here from the city.

El Santuario de la Difunta Correa

Some 65km east of San Juan, **EL SANTUARIO DE LA DIFUNTA CORREA** (see box, p.557; Ⓦwww.visitedifuntacorrea.com.ar) is both a repellent and an intriguing place. All around Argentina you'll come across mini-Difunta shrines, sometimes little more than a few bottles of mineral water heaped at the roadside – and easily mistaken for a particularly bad bout of environmental pollution. But the original shrine is here, in San Juan Province. To get there, go past the airport, beyond which a couple of rather dreary satellite towns, including Caucete, badly damaged in the 1977 earthquake, are strung along RN-141 towards Chepes and La Rioja. The landscape then turns into desert-like plains, complete with sand dunes, though the most impressive aren't visible from the main road; to the north the reddish Sierra Pie de Palo ripples in the distance, relieving the monotony. Suddenly, in the middle of nowhere, amid its own grim complex of hotels, *confiterías* and souvenir shops and on top of a small hill, is Argentina's answer to Lourdes. There are regular Vallecitos **buses** out here, but unless you're really curious, it's only worth the short stop you get on the bus route from San Juan to La Rioja.

Parque Provincial Ischigualasto and Parque Nacional Talampaya

San Juan and La Rioja provinces boast two of the most photographed protected areas in the country, both of which have been declared UNESCO World Heritage Sites. In San Juan, the **Parque Provincial Ischigualasto** is better known as Valle de la Luna – Moon Valley – because of its eerily out-of-this-world landscapes and apocryphal legends. The province has jealously resisted repeated attempts to turn it into a national park, and this is probably a godsend, since the provincial authorities are doing an admirable job of providing easy access and looking after the fragile environment. President Menem, on the other hand, made sure that his native province of La Rioja got its first national park while he was in office: **Parque Nacional Talampaya**, another vulnerable biotope. Home to several rare varieties of flora and fauna, including condors, it's best known for its giant red sandstone cliffs, which are guaranteed to impress even the most jaded traveller. While the latter is closer to the La Rioja town of Villa Unión (see p.569), both parks are within reach of the delightful little town of **San Agustín de Valle Fértil**, high in the mountains of eastern San Juan Province. Most visitors take in both parks in the same day, though each merits a longer visit; in any case, it is wise to go to Talampaya in the morning, when the sun lights up the coloured rocks and illuminates the canyon, whereas Ischigualasto is far more impressive in the late afternoon and at sunset in particular. You can then make it back to San Agustín de Valle Fértil before nightfall. Another possibility is a gruelling but rewarding day-trip from San Juan, or even La Rioja. Public transport can get you to these destinations, but it is erratic and your own vehicle is preferable; it's advisable to either go as part of an organized trip or rent a 4WD, as the remote roads are both deserted and difficult to drive on.

San Agustín de Valle Fértil

Set among enticing mountainside landscapes some 250km northeast of San Juan by RN-141 and mostly unpaved RP-510, and about 80km south of the entrance to Ischigualasto, the oasis town of **SAN AGUSTÍN DE VALLE FÉRTIL** is the best place to spend the night in eastern San Juan Province. It's built around a mirror-like reservoir, the Dique San Agustín – cacti and gorse grow on its banks, and a small peninsula juts artistically into the waters. The town prospered in the nineteenth century thanks to the gold, iron and quartz mines and marble quarries in the mountains nearby, but it has now turned to tourism as its source of income, to supplement meagre farm earnings. The fertile valley that gives it its name – sometimes it's referred to simply as "Valle Fértil" – is a patchwork of maize fields, olive groves and pasture for goats and sheep – and the local cheese and roast kid are locally renowned. Valle Fértil's *raison d'être* for the traveller is as a base for visiting the twin parks of Talampaya and Ischigualasto, as an alternative to the less attractive Villa Unión.

Practicalities

Buses from San Juan and La Rioja arrive at Mitre and Entre Ríos. The **tourist office** (daily 7am–10pm; ⓣ02646/420104) at Plaza San Agustín is extremely helpful and can fix you up with guides and transport both to Ischigualasto and to other less dramatic sites in the nearby mountains, including pre-Hispanic petroglyphs.

The best **place to stay** is the comfortable *Hostería Valle Fértil*, on a hilltop overlooking the reservoir, at Rivadavia (ⓣ02646/420015, ⓦwww.alkazarhotel.com.ar/vallefertil; ❺). Run by the *Hotel Alkázar* in San Juan, it has a decent restaurant, specializing in casseroled kid, and good, if cramped, rooms – the more expensive ones with lake views – but the bathrooms are small. You'll find a number of cheap *pensiones* downtown, and two hostels charging around $20 per person – *Posada Los Olivos* (ⓣ02646/420115, ⓦwww.posadalosolivos.alojar.com.ar), at Santa Fe s/n, with an attractive wood-beamed patio restaurant area, and the *Campo Base Valle de la Luna* youth hostel at Tucumán and San Luis (ⓣ02646/420063, ⓦwww.hostelvalledelaluna.com.ar), which can help organize tours in the area. The best campsite is the well-kept *Camping Valle Fértil*, at the lower end of the road leading up to the *Hostería Valle Fértil* and ran by the *hostería*.

Parque Provincial Ischigualasto

Just under 100km north of Valle Fértil, the **PARQUE PROVINCIAL ISCHIGUALASTO**, also known as the Valle de la Luna, or Moon Valley, is San Juan's most famous feature by far, yet even in the high season it is big enough not to be swamped by visitors. Covering nearly 150 square kilometres of astonishingly varied terrain, it can be visited only in a vehicle, whether your own or that of a tour operator. For paleontologists, Ischigualasto's importance is primarily as a rich burial ground of some of the earth's most enigmatic inhabitants – the dinosaurs – models of which litter the park. The park is also unique for geologists, as all stages of the 45-million-year Triassic era are represented in its rocks. Most visitors, however, come simply to admire the spectacular lunar landscapes that give the park its popular nickname, and the much publicized and alarmingly fragile rock formations – some have already disappeared, the victims of erosion and the occasional flash floods that seem to strike with increasing frequency. **Cerro El Morado** (1700m), a barrow-like mountain that according to local lore is shaped like an

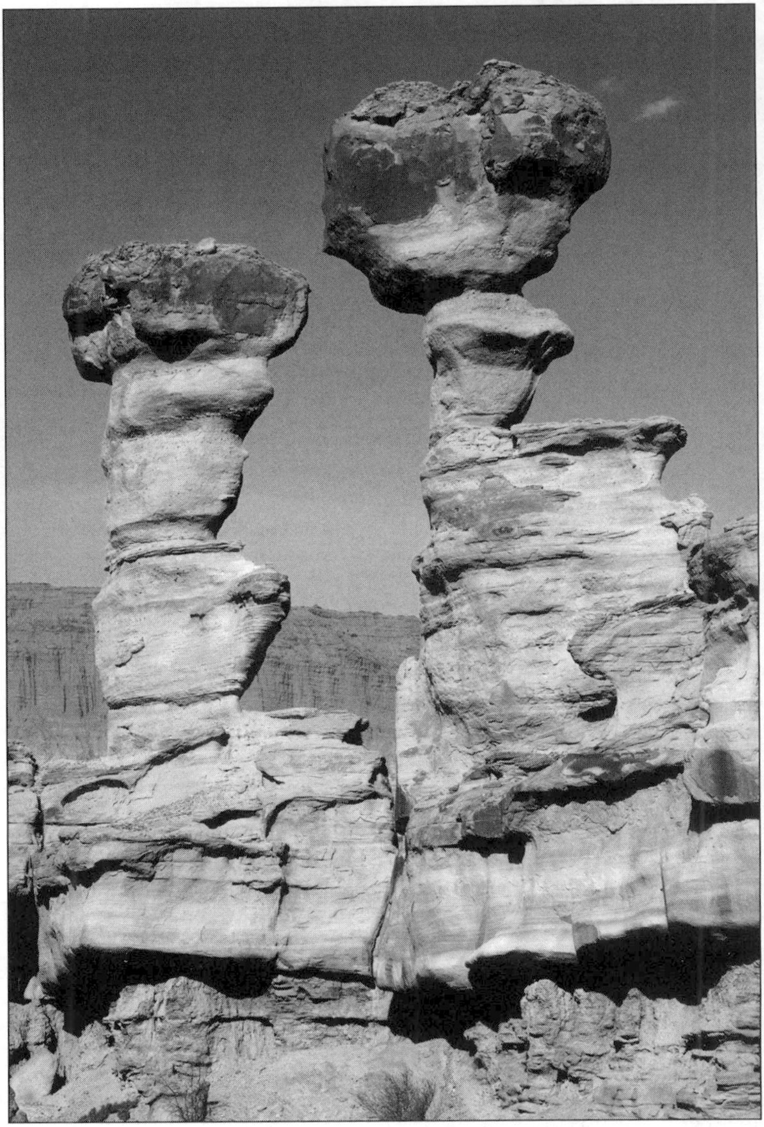

△ Parque Provincial Ischigualasto

Indian lying on his back, dominates the park to the east. A segmented row of rocks is known as El Gusano (the Worm); a huge set of vessel-like boulders, including one resembling a funnel, is known as El Submarino; a sandy field dotted with cannon-ball-shaped stones is dubbed the Cancha de Bolas (the Ball-court). One famous formation, painfully fragile on its slender stalk, is El Hongo (the Mushroom), beautifully set off against the orange sandstone cliffs behind.

The park is in a desert valley between two ranges of high mountains, the Sierra Los Rastros to the west and Cerros Colorados to the east. As witnessed by the mollusc and coral fossils found in the cliffsides, for a long time the whole area was under water. Over the course of millions of years the terrain has been eroded by wind and water, and sections built of volcanic ash have taken on a ghostly greyish-white hue. A set of red sandstone mountains to the north acts as a perfect backdrop to the paler stone formations and clay blocks, all of which are impressively illuminated in the late evening. The landscapes have often been compared with national parks in the Southwest US, such as Bryce Canyon.

Another of the park's attractions is its wealth of flora and fauna. The main plant varieties are the native broom-like *brea*, three varieties of the scrawny *jarilla*, both black and white species of *algarrobo*, the *chañar*, *retamo* and *molle* shrubs and four varieties of cactus. Animals that you are likely to spot here include criollo hares, Patagonian hares, the vizcacha, the red fox, armadillos and small rodents, plus several species of bat, frog, toad, lizard and snake. Condors and ñandús are often seen, too, while guanaco may be spotted standing like sentinels atop the rocks, before scampering off.

Tours follow set **circuits**, beginning in the more lunar landscapes to the south. Panoramic outlook points afford stunning views of ghoulish, empty landscapes of oceans of hillocks. These are the typical moonscapes, but they look uncannily like the famous landscapes of Cappadocia, with their Gaudiesque pinnacles and curvaceous mounds. Then you head north, where sugary white fields are scattered with petrified tree-trunks and weird and wonderful rocks. This whole tour needs at least a couple of hours to be done at all comfortably; be warned that sudden summer storms can cut off the tracks for a day or two, in which case you may not be able to see all the park.

Park practicalities

The **guardería** (entrance allowed daily 8am–4pm, you must leave by dusk; $15), manned by *guardaparques* who will accompany every group, lies at the entrance to the park, along a well-signposted lateral road off RP-510 at Los Baldecitos. There is no camping or accommodation and most people stay at either Villa Unión or, preferably, Valle Fértil (see p.559). You could also come on an **organized tour** from San Juan (see "Listings", p.556). The optimal time of day for visiting the park is in the mid- to late afternoon, when the light is the most flattering. That way you also catch the mind-boggling sunsets that illuminate the park, turning the pinkish orange rock a glowing crimson, which contrasts with the ghostly greyish white of the lunarscapes all around. If you want to see both Ischigualasto and Talampaya in the same day, go to the latter first.

Parque Nacional Talampaya

The entrance to **PARQUE NACIONAL TALAMPAYA**, known as the Puerta de Talampaya, is 55km down RP-26 from Villa Unión, and then 12km along a signposted track to the east. Coming from the south, it's 93km north of Ischigualasto and 190km from Valle Fértil. The park's main feature is a wide-bottomed canyon flanked by 180-metre-high, rust-coloured sandstone cliffs, so smooth and sheer that they look as if they were sliced through by a giant cheese-wire. Another section of the canyon is made up of rock formations that seem to have been created as part of a surreal Gothic cathedral. Added attractions are the presence of several bird species, including condors and eagles, as well as rich flora and some pre-Columbian petroglyphs. The park's name comes from the indigenous people's words *ktala* – the locally abundant *tala* bush – and *ampaya*, meaning dry riverbed.

Talampaya's cliffs appear so frequently on national tourism promotion posters and in coffee-table books, you think you know what you're getting before you arrive. But no photograph really prepares you for the belittling feeling you have when standing at the foot of a massive rock wall, where the silence is broken only by the derisive caw of a pair of condors. Even the classic shots of orange-red precipices looming over what looks like a toy jeep, included for scale, don't really convey the astonishment. The national park, covering 215 square kilometres, was created in 1997 to protect the canyon and all its treasures. Geologically it's part of the Sierra Los Colorados, whose rippling mass you can see in the distance to the east, along with the giant snowcapped range of the Sierra de Famatina to the north. These mountains were all formed over 250 million years ago, during the Permian Period, and have gradually been eroded by torrential rain and various rivers that have exploited geological faults in the rock, the reason why the cliffs are so sheer.

Just south of the entrance to the canyon, huge sand dunes have been swept up by the strong winds that frequently howl across the Campo de Talampaya to the south. The higgledy-piggledy rocks at the foot of the cliffs host a gallery of white, red and black **rock paintings**, made by the Ciénaga and Aguada peoples who inhabited the area around a thousand years ago. The pictures include animals such as llamas, suris and pumas, a stepped pyramid, huntsmen and phallic symbols, and the nearby ink-well depressions in the rock are formed by decades of grinding and mixing pigments. There is a huge *tacu*, or carob tree, here, thought to be more than 1000 years old. Inside the canyon proper, the so-called **jardín botánico**, or more accurately the *bosquecillo* – thicket – is a natural grove of twenty or so different native cacti, shrubs and trees. They include *algarrobos*, *retamos*, *pencas*, *jarillas* and *chañares*, all labelled; occasionally grey foxes and small armadillos lurk in the undergrowth and brightly coloured songbirds flit from branch to branch. Nearby, and clearly signposted, is the **Chimenea** (chimney), also known as the Cueva (cave) or the Canaleta (drainpipe), a rounded vertical groove stretching all the way up the cliff-side; guides revel in demonstrating its extraordinary echo, which sends condors flapping.

Rock formations in the canyon have been given imaginative names, mostly with a religious slant, but many of them do fit. **El Pesebre** (Crib) is a set of rocks supposed to resemble a Nativity scene, and appropriately nearby are **Los Reyes Magos**, the Three Kings, one of them on camel-back. A cluster of enormous needles and pinnacles is known as **La Catedral** – the intricate patterns chiselled and carved by thousands of years of erosion have been compared variously with Albi cathedral or the facade of Strasbourg cathedral, both built of a similar red sandstone. A set of massive rock formations is known as **El Tablero de Ajedrez**, or the Chessboard, complete with rooks, bishops and pawns, while a 53-metre-high monolith, resembling a cowled human figure is El Cura, the priest, or El Fraile, the monk, depending on whom you ask. **El Pizarrón**, or the Blackboard, is fifteen metres of flat rock-face of darker stone etched with more suris, pumas, guanacos and even a seahorse – more pre-Columbian petroglyphs showing that the peoples who lived here a thousand years ago had some kind of contact with the ocean.

Park practicalities

The **guardería**, located at the end of the trail off RP-26, at the Puerta de Talampaya (daily May–Sept 8.30am–5.30pm, Oct–April 8am–6pm; $12; no phone), is staffed throughout the year. Most visitors come here on an **organized tour** from La Rioja (p.570) or San Juan (p.550), but if you want to get here via public transport you can be dropped off on the main road by the buses from Villa Unión to La Rioja and Valle Fértil, or take the regular bus from Villa Unión to the village of **Pagancillo**, 27km north of the park entrance. There is a basic **campsite** (☎03825/470397) here where you can pitch a tent, but bear in mind that it's often windy and can get extremely cold at night. There's also a *confitería* serving simple, reasonably priced snacks and small meals.

Private vehicles are not allowed to tour the park, so if you arrive here under your own steam you must choose between two guided **circuits** with Rolling Travel (☎0351/5709909), which operates inside Talampaya. Both circuits visit the main points of interest – the shorter is 2.5 hours and the longer 4.5 hours. The Cooperativa de Transporte Talampaya (☎03825/15662086) is the other concessionary, providing a three-hour tour as well as transfers from Villa Unión. Bike tours may also be possible – enquire at the entrance or contact the park guides' association (Ⓔsergiolei_guiatur@hotmail.com). Avoid the midwinter, when it can be bitterly cold; the middle of the day in the height of summer, when it can be unbearably hot; and the day after a storm, when the park closes because of floods. The best time of day by far to visit is soon after opening, when the dawn light deepens the red of the sandstone; in the afternoon and evening the canyon is shaded and the colours are less intense.

Valle de Calingasta

The marvellous, fertile **VALLE DE CALINGASTA** is a bright green strip of land around 100km west of San Juan, on the other side of the Sierra del Tontal range. Its major settlement of interest is **Barreal**, a pleasant little town set amid fields of alfalfa, onions and maize, with a stupendous backdrop of the sierra, snowcapped for most of the year. Barreal's environs are home to the **Complejo Astronómico El Leoncito**, one of the continent's most important space observatories, and the sand-flats of the **Barreal del Leoncito**, used for wind-car championships. To the east of town is a series of mountains, red, orange and deep pink in colour, known aptly as the **Serranías de las Piedras Pintadas**. To the southwest of Barreal, RP-400 leads to the tiny hamlet of Las Hornillas, the point of departure for adventurous treks and climbs to the summit of **Cerro Mercedario** (6770m), said by many mountaineers to be the most satisfying climb in the cordillera. In the sedate town of **Calingasta** itself, north of Barreal, the main sight is a fine seventeenth-century **chapel**.

The most straightforward route to the valley from San Juan is breathtaking RP-12, although it is subject to **traffic controls**: you can drive up towards Calingasta daily from 7am until noon and drive down Monday to Friday from 3.30pm until 8pm and weekends from 8pm until dawn. Otherwise, the main alternative route is to drive south along RN-40 from San Juan to Villa Media Agua, nearly 50km away; from here RP-319 heads west across a dusty plain, through Pedernal, and up over a difficult mountain pass before joining RP-412 south of Barreal.

Barreal and around

The small oasis town of **BARREAL**, set alongside the Río de los Patos, 1650m above sea level, at the southern extreme of the Valle de Calingasta, enjoys a pleasant climate. As the only settlement in the valley with any infrastructure, it has become the default tourist base for visiting the immediate environs. The views to the west, of the cordillera peaks, including the majestic Mercedario,

El Polaco, La Ramada and Los Siete Picos de Ansilta, seen across a beautiful plain, shimmering with onion and maize fields, are superb. To the east you can climb up into the coloured mountains, or up to the **Cima del Tontal**, which affords panoramas across to San Juan city. Just south is the **Barreal del Leoncito**, a great plain in the middle of which is a strange sand-flat whose windswept expanse lends itself to the exhilarating sport of wind-car racing. Up on nearby hills are two space **observatories**, among the most important in the world because of the outstanding meteorological conditions hereabouts – more than 320 clear nights a year on average. Barreal also makes a good base if you want to conquer one of the Andes' most challenging yet climbable mountains, the **Cerro Mercedario**.

Barreal town has no monuments or museums, but is pleasant enough to wander around. The central square, **Plaza San Martín**, is the focal point, at the crossroads of Avenida Presidente Roca and General Las Heras. **Buses** from Mendoza and San Juan stop here. For **trips** in the surrounding area try Fortuna Viajes (ⓣ0264/4040913, ⓦwww.fortunaviajes.com.ar), next door to *Cabañas Doña Pipa* at Mariano Moreno s/n, which also rents out cabins (❺ for up to five people) in pleasant grounds and has a simple new hotel annexe (❸). Another good **place to stay** is *Cabañas Kummel*, Presidente Roca s/n (ⓣ0264/8441206, ⓔcabaniaskummel@infovia.com.ar; ❹ for up to five people), whose friendly owners are very knowledgeable about the area and can also help arrange trips. The plain but comfortable *Hotel de Turismo Barreal*, Av San Martín s/n (ⓣ0264/8441090; ❷), has its own restaurant and a swimming pool, decent rooms and can organize fishing and other activities. The top accommodation award, though, goes to the appealingly designed *Posada de Campo La Querencia* (ⓣ0264/154-364699, ⓦwww.laquerenciaposada.com.ar; ❻), whose charming rooms all have fabulous views of open country. Breakfasts are irreproachable, as is the friendliness of the welcome; follow the signs when you enter the village. Another fine option is the *Posada San Eduardo,* set in delightful grounds at Av San Martín s/n (ⓣ0264/8441046; ❺), with plain but charming rooms around an old colonial-style patio and a restaurant serving well-cooked, if a little unimaginative, food. The best place to eat by far is *El Alemán*, Belgrano s/n (ⓣ0264/8441193), where huge servings of sauerkraut, smoked hams and slabs of pork are served with well-prepared vegetables and German-style beer in a bucolic setting – follow signs from the *Posada San Eduardo*.

Around Barreal

Immediately south of Barreal along the western side of RP-412 is a huge flat expanse of hardened sand, the remains of an ancient lake, known as the **Barreal del Leoncito**, the Pampa del Leoncito, or simply the Barreal Blanco. Measuring 14km by 5km, this natural arena, with a marvellous stretch of the cordillera as a background, is used for **wind-car** championships (*caravelismo* in Spanish) – the little cars with yacht-like sails have reached speeds of over 130km per hour here; ask around in Barreal if you want to have a go.

Some 15km or so further south along this road is a turn-off eastwards up into the **Reserva Astronómica El Leoncito**, which enjoys national park status, and is symbolized by the suri, or Andean rhea. About 12km up this track is the entrance (daily 10am–noon & 3–6pm; $5) where you must announce your presence to the *guardeparques*. You then go up a narrow canyon, past a colonial estancia building, to the Complejo Astronómico, where two observatories, both located at 2500m and affording fabulous views of the valley and the cordillera, are open to the public. The **Observatorio Félix Aguilar** (guided visits at 10.15am, 11.15am, 12.15pm, 2.15pm, 3.15pm, 4.15pm & 5.15pm; free) is recognizable from afar, with its huge white dome sticking out from the brown mountainside. Inaugurated in 1986, this observatory uses Brazilian technology, Argentine know-how and Swiss funds, with some input by the Vatican. It was built to resist earthquakes registering 10 or higher on the Richter scale, an absolute necessity in this area of violent seismic activity. The main telescope weighs nearly 50 tonnes and its 2.13-metre diameter mirror has to be replaced every two years. The guided tour, led by enthusiastic staff members (English spoken), takes you through the whole process; take warm clothing as the inside is kept cold. You can also visit the more modest-looking **Estación Astronómica Dr Carlos U. Cesco** (daily Jan–Feb and holidays 10am–6pm, rest of year 10am–noon & 4–6pm; $2; ⓣ02648/441087, ⓔcentrohugomira@yahoo.com.ar), where the staff will also be only too happy to show you the visitors' centre and explain the observatory's work. Contact them to check about the possibility of night visits, which cost $10 and take place most evenings from 9pm to midnight – these are more interesting, as you actually get to use telescopes; take a torch and warm clothing.

Scenic RP-400 strikes out in a southwesterly direction from Barreal to **Las Hornillas**, over 50km away. This tiny hamlet is inhabited mostly by herdsmen and their families amid pastureland and gorse scrub and is effectively the base camp for the mighty **Mercedario**, which looms nearby. If you want to climb this difficult but not impossible mountain, regarded by many as the most noble of all Argentina's Andean peaks, contact Fortuna Viajes in Barreal (see opposite). The nearby rivers are excellent for fishing for trout; also ask in Barreal.

The mountainsides to the immediate east of Barreal, accessible by clear tracks, are a mosaic of pink, red, brown, ochre and purple rocks, and the so-called **Cerros Pintados**, or "Painted Mountains", live up to their name. Among the rocky crags, tiny cacti poke out from the cracks, and in the spring they sprout huge wax-like flowers, in translucent shades of white, pink and yellow, among golden splashes of broom-like *brea* shrubs. About 8km north of Barreal, another track heads eastwards from the main road, climbing for 40km past some idyllic countryside inhabited only by the odd goatherd or farming family, to the outlook atop the **Cima del Tontal**, at just over 4000m. To the east there are amazing views down into the San Juan valley, with the Dique de Ullum glinting in the distance, or west and south to the cordillera, where the peak of Aconcagua and the majestic summit of the Mercedario are clearly visible.

Calingasta

The small village that gives the valley its name is 37km north of Barreal, along RP-412. On the eastern side you are treated to more painted mountainsides, striped red like toothpaste. A marked side road, at the locality called Tamberías, halfway between Calingasta and Barreal, leads to an unusual rock formation of pale sandstone, called the **Alcázar**, because it looks just like a Moorish castle, with towers and solid curtain-walls. **CALINGASTA** itself is a peaceful place, where the Río Calingasta flows into the Río de los Patos; its only attraction apart from its idyllic location is the seventeenth-century **Capilla de Nuestra Señora del Carmen**, a simple whitewashed adobe building, with an arched doorway and a long gallery punctuated by frail-looking slender pillars. The bells are among the oldest in the country – they are visible in the bell tower – and the iron and wooden ladder leading onto the roof is a work of art, too. **Accommodation** in town consists of a choice between two basic but clean places in the centre: *Hotel Calingasta* (ⓣ02648/421220; ❷) and *Hospedaje Nora* (ⓣ02648/421027, ⓔcalingasta22@hotmail.com; ❸), which charges a few pesos more as it has cable TV and car parking. From Calingasta it's almost 150km along RP-412 north to

Iglesia, along a dry valley, through the occasional ford, with the Sierra del Tigre to the east and the Cordón de Olivares providing stupendous views to the west.

Valle de Iglesia

The **VALLE DE IGLESIA**, named after its main settlement, **Iglesia**, a sleepy village of Italianate adobe houses, is a fertile valley separated from the Valle de Calingasta by the dramatic Cordón de Olivares range of mountains. You can get there directly from San Juan via RN-40, which forks off to the northwest at Talacasto, some 50km north of the provincial capital. From there a mountain road, RP-436, snakes round the Sierra de la Invernada, before descending in free fall into the valley. Alongside the highest section of the road, the Pampa de Gualilán is covered with tufts of glaucous vegetation that forms a glacier-like landscape on the mountainside. The cliffs are riddled with the tunnels of disused goldmines. Portezuelo del Colorado, 130km from San Juan, is a pass at nearly 2900m, affording panoramic views of Iglesia, 40km to the northwest, and beyond. Iglesia lies nearly 150km north of Calingasta via RP-406 and RP-412. Several villages succeed each other along the valley, including the thermal spa resort of **Pismanta**, the small market town of **Rodeo** and the idyllic village of **Angualasto**, along the dirt track that leads to one of the country's most recent national parks, **San Guillermo**, the place in Argentina where you are most likely to spot pumas in the wild.

Iglesia and around

IGLESIA is a tiny village at the southern end of its eponymous valley, watered by various streams, or *arroyos*. To the southwest, just 2km away, is the aptly named Bella Vista, a picturesque "suburb" of Iglesia made up of crumbling mud-brick houses. Here you will find the area's best **campsite**, *Camping Bella Vista* (ⓣ02647/496036; ❶), in a beautifully landscaped location with basic but clean facilities. **Buses** drop you wherever you want in the village, but you'll have to make your own way to the campsite. Some 14km north is the farming village of **Las Flores**, amidst fields of alfalfa, lettuce, potatoes and beans; ask around for the delicious goat's cheeses and also for traditional weavers' workshops, which produce beautiful ponchos. About 6km northeast is the **Capilla de Achango**, an early eighteenth-century Jesuit chapel with a very simple whitewashed facade, a tiled roof and a wonderfully rickety bell tower. Inside, it is almost painfully simple, adorned only by a couple of ancient statues of saints. Also 6km from Las Flores, but northwest, is the spa resort of **Pismanta**, where the *Hotel Nogaró Termas de Pismanta* (ⓣ02647/497091, ⓦwww.pismantaspa.com.ar; ❻ full board), affords you the opportunity to soak in mineral waters that spurt out of the earth at 45°C in an outdoor pool with a spectacular view. The hotel is typically Peronist in appearance but the rooms are pleasant enough, and certainly the best to be had in the whole area; plus you'll eat well at the **restaurant**. At Pismanta, RP-412 joins RN-150, which heads west to Chile across the Paso del Agua Negra at 4779m. The Chilean town of Vicuña lies over 260km away; the customs post is just 3km west of Pismanta.

Rodeo and around

The RN-150 arches round the pleasant, easy-going market town of **RODEO**, 19km east of Pismanta, bypassing it completely. If you want to see the town, you must turn off onto its main street, Santo Domingo, which leads past the Plaza Mayor and the municipalidad to the **Finca El Martillo** (daily 9am–6pm; ⓣ02647/493019, ⓔelmartillo@impsat1.com.ar), at the northernmost end. You can buy all kinds of wonderful local produce here, including herbs, fresh and preserved fruit and excellent jam and honey. Ask about the eight-bed *cabaña* the people at the *finca* rent out nearby (❸), the only decent **accommodation** hereabouts. Rodeo hosts one of the region's major folk festivals in the first half of March, the **Fiesta de la Manzana y la Semilla**, when you can try local specialities, such as empanadas and *humitas*, and watch dancing and musical groups in the lakeside Anfiteatro, just off Santo Domingo at the heart of the town.

North of Rodeo, you can head off towards Angualasto and the Reserva San Guillermo (see below), while to the east RN-150 takes you past the turquoise waters of the **Embalse Cuesta del Viento**, favoured by windsurfers (ask at Finca El Martillo for access; you'll need your own equipment). The **Quebrada del Viento** is an impressive gorge, followed by a winding cliff-side road, carved out by the Río Blanco.

Angualasto and Parque Nacional San Guillermo

From Rodeo, RP-407 heads north, cutting through a ridge of rock and sloping down into the valley of the Río Blanco. The little village of **ANGUALASTO**, which has preserved a delightful rural feel, seemingly detached from the modern world, is set among rows of poplars, fruit orchards and small plots of maize, beans and other vegetables. It is proud of its little **Museo Arqueológico Luis Benedetti** (Tues–Sun 9am–12.30pm & 4–6.30pm; $1), though you may have to ask around in the village to find someone with the key. The museum's tiny collection of mostly pre-Columbian finds includes a remarkable 400-year-old mummified corpse, found in a *tumbería*, or burial mound, nearby. To the north the road follows the beautiful Río Blanco valley, fording it once – often impossible after spring or summer rains or heavy thaws – to the incredibly remote hamlets of Malimán and **El Chinguillo**, where the Solar family's delightful farmhouse (no phone; ❶) provides the only **accommodation** in the area, as well as delicious empanadas and roast lamb. This is the entrance to San Guillermo, in a beautiful valley surrounded by huge dunes of sand and mountains scarred red and yellow with mineral deposits.

Part of the Reserva Provincial San Guillermo, in the far northern reaches of San Juan Province, has enjoyed national park status since 1999, with investment and loans by the World Bank and the Interamerican Bank for Reconstruction and Development. The **PARQUE NACIONAL SAN GUILLERMO**, on great heights to the west of the Río Blanco valley, is home to a huge variety of wildlife. Guanacos and vicuñas abound, along with suris or ñandús, eagles, condors, several different kinds of lizards, foxes and all kinds of waterfowl, including flamingoes, which match the seams of jagged pink rock that run along the mountainsides like a garish zip-fastener. Above all, this is a part of Argentina where you are almost guaranteed a rare spotting of a puma; for some reason the pumas living here are less shy of humans than elsewhere and often approach vehicles; extreme caution is recommended, as these powerful machines of feline muscle are effective mankillers. The highest peaks, at well over 4000m, are permanently snowcapped, and the weather is capricious. There is no *guardería* as such, and no entrance fee as yet, but *guardeparques* patrol the territory, mostly to prevent hunting. Visiting requires some preparation – you must obtain a permit, and you will also require a 4WD and, ideally, a guide, as negotiating the fords can be dangerous if you don't know the terrain. Ask at the **park office** in Rodeo (ⓣ02647/493214, ⓔsanguillermo@apn.gov.ar), located in the same building as the post office, which can fix you up with all of the above, or enquire at the national parks office in Buenos Aires before you depart (see p.56).

RN-40 from San José de Jáchal to Villa Unión

The section of **RN-40**, Argentina's longest road, that stretches for 145km northeast from the sleepy little town of **San José de Jáchal**, in San Juan Province, to **Villa Unión**, in La Rioja Province, passes through outstanding countryside, including the lush farmland immediately north of the town, where you can see some beautiful early nineteenth-century flour mills amid a landscape rather like that of North Africa or the Middle East. You then squeeze through the Cuesta de Huaco, a narrow mountain road that affords magnificent views of the virgin wastes and dust-dry valleys to the north. The little village of **Huaco** also boasts a delightful old mill. From there the road runs through a wide river valley, that of the Río Bermejo, bone dry for most of the time but suddenly and treacherously flooding after storms. Beware of the many deep *badenes*, or fords, along the road; if they are full of water, you should wait for the level to drop before attempting to cross and, even when dry, they can rip tyres or damage undercarriages if taken too fast. The dull town of Villa Unión is your destination, though it is no more than a dormitory for visiting the amazing Parque Nacional Talampaya (see p.561), or for going to see wildlife in the **Reserva Provincial Las Vicuñas**, in the far north of this region, in the middle of which is the beautiful **Laguna Brava**, an altiplanic lake of the sharpest blue. From Villa Unión you can get to Chilecito (see p.575) via RN-40 and the staggeringly beautiful Cuesta Miranda, or to the provincial capital of La Rioja (see p.570) via RP-26, past Talampaya, RN-150 and RN-38, a total journey of over 250km.

San José de Jáchal

The small town of **SAN JOSÉ DE JÁCHAL** lies in the fertile valley of the Río Jáchal, 155km due north of San Juan by RN-40; it's also 65km due east of Rodeo via scenic RN-150 (see p.566). The town was founded in the seventeenth century on the site of a pre-Columbian village. Destroyed in a severe earthquake in 1894, the town was rebuilt using mud-bricks in an Italianate style, with arched facades and galleried patios, focused on the Plaza Mayor. San José itself isn't much to write home about, but it makes for a convenient stopover, if you need a bed for the night or want to have lunch. If you have a moment to spare, you could visit the astonishingly eclectic **Museo Arqueológico Prieto** (ⓣ02647/420298 to arrange visit), at 25 de Mayo 788 oeste, signposted along RN-150. It is a motley collection of all manner of odds and ends, but among the curios are some fine pre-Columbian artefacts, painstakingly collected and displayed by a local who handed it all over to the town's police force. During the first fortnight in November every year, the town stages the **Fiesta de la Tradición**, a festival of folklore, feasts and music.

Buses from San Juan stop at the terminal four blocks east of the main plaza. A few **accommodation** possibilities exist, but the only one that can be recommended is the *Plaza Hotel*, San Juan 545 (☎02647/420256; ❷), which offers pleasant rooms with or without bath. The best place to eat is *El Chatito Flores*, at San Juan and Juan de Echegaray, which offers hearty, inexpensive food in very unexceptional surroundings.

North of San José, RN-40 suddenly swerves to the east and the road continuing straight ahead, RP-456, cuts through San José's rural northern suburbs amid bucolic farmland, used to grow wheat, maize, alfalfa and fruit. With the stark mountain backdrop of the Sierra Negra to the east, Sierra de la Batea to the north and Cerro Alto (2095m) to the west, this dazzlingly green valley, dotted with adobe farmhouses, some of them with splendid sun-faded wooden doors, looks like the parts of Morocco in the lee of the Atlas. Canals and little ditches water the fields, using snow melt from the cordillera and precordillera, as rain is rare here. At the beginning of the nineteenth century, a number of **flour mills** were built here, and they are now rightly historic monuments. Their pinkish-beige walls, wonderfully antiquated machinery and enthusiastic owners make for a memorable visit. El Molino, the Molino de Pérez and the Molino de Reyes, all within a few hundred metres of each other on either side of the road, are open to visitors, but the most rewarding is the extremely well-preserved **Molino de Sardiña** at the corner of calles Maturrango and Mesias. The charming owner will be delighted to show you around, but always appreciates a tip. Try to be here in the early evening when the warm light adds to the magically timeless atmosphere.

Huaco

Back on RN-40, the road hugs the Sierra Negra, before skirting the eerie little reservoir called Dique Los Cauquenes. Then you enter the Cuesta de Huaco, a narrow mountain road accurately described as a place "where the reddish dawn lingers on the even redder clay of the mountainside". Those words were sung by deep-voiced crooner **Buenaventura Luna**, real name Eusebio de Jesús Dójorti Roco, who was a highly popular star in the 1940s and 1950s, and is buried in nearby **HUACO**. This small village, lying just off the main road, shaded by *algarrobos* and eucalyptus, is no more than a cluster of picturesque mud-brick houses around a small square, but just before you get to the village you pass a splendid adobe **flour mill**, similar to those north of San José. Built at the beginning of the nineteenth century, it belonged to the Docherty family, Irishmen who fought in the British army that invaded Buenos Aires, were captured and decided to settle in Argentina; Buenaventura Luna, poet and folksinger, was one of their descendants.

Villa Unión

The only thing to say about the small town of **VILLA UNIÓN**, in the parched Valle de Vinchina, 120km northeast of Huaco, is that it has a couple of places to stay and eat, so you can overnight here before visiting the amazing canyon and rock formations of the Parque Nacional Talampaya (see p.561), 70km south. It's also a possible springboard for heading up to the staggeringly desolate Reserva Provincial Las Vicuñas, wrapped around the beautiful Laguna Brava (see p.570) and over 150km northwest. The town, formerly called Hornillos, received its name in the nineteenth century in recognition of the hospitality of its people towards peasants thrown off a nearby estancia by the ruthless *estancieros*. Today's town is utterly charmless, has no sights and offers no entertainments, but at least an **ATM** has been installed at the bank on the featureless main square, Plaza Mayor. A couple of blocks east is the tiny **bus station**, serving La Rioja, Chilecito and Valle Fértil. The **park office** for Talampaya (daily 7am–2pm; ⓣ03825/4703567, ⓦwww.talampaya.gov.ar) is at San Martín s/n, half a block from the plaza, while Coop Transporte Talampaya (ⓣ03825/15662086) runs transfers to the park, as well as a couple of circuits within it. For **accommodation**, the best place, albeit overpriced, is the modern *Hotel Pircas Negras* (ⓣ03825/470611, ⓦwww.hotelpircasnegras.com; ❻), a large, rambling affair a couple of kilometres south of town near the RN-40 junction. It has smart rooms, parking facilities and a passable restaurant, although service is sloppy. In town you have a choice of several less expensive places: one block east of the main plaza, *Hotel Noryanepat*, Joaquín V. González s/n (ⓣ03825/470133; ❹), has just about acceptable rooms with cramped bathrooms; *Hospedaje Doña Gringa*, with tiny but very clean rooms, a leafy patio and a laid-back atmosphere, is a few blocks north of the plaza, at Nicolás Dávila 103 (ⓣ03825/470528; ❷). The only place worth trying for something to **eat** is the *Pizzería La Rosa*, on the northwest corner of the plaza.

Reserva Provincial Las Vicuñas

Much easier to access than the Parque Nacional San Guillermo, just south, the **RESERVA PROVINCIAL LAS VICUÑAS** is nearly 150km northwest of Villa Unión, via RP-26 and then a numberless track that twists and turns to the park's central feature, the volcanic **Laguna Brava**. The main attractions are fabulous altiplanic scenery – most of the terrain is at over 4000m – the mountainous backdrop and the abundant wildlife, mainly vicuñas, as the name suggests. Large flocks of this smaller cousin of the llama graze on the reserve's *bofedales*, the typical spongy marshes watered by trickles of run-off that freeze nightly. The best time to visit is in spring and autumn, since summer storms and winter blizzards cut off roads and generally impede travel. On the way to the reserve you pass through **Villa San José De Vinchina**, 65km north of Villa Unión, a nondescript village near which are six mysterious circular mounds, nearly 30m in diameter. Made of a mosaic of pink, white and purple stones, these **Estrellas de Vinchina** form star-shapes and are thought to have had a ceremonial purpose, perhaps serving as altars. Otherwise head on through the Quebrada de la Troya, a magnificent striped canyon, into the fertile Valle Caguay, dominated by the majestic cone of Volcán Los Bonetes. From here the road is best negotiated in a 4WD – in any case it is wise to visit the reserve on an organized tour from San Juan (see p.550). The track heads to the southern banks of the Laguna Brava, a deep blue lake 17km by 10km, whose high potassium-chloride levels make it undrinkable. When there is no wind the mirror-like waters reflect the mountains behind; when it's blowing a gale, huge waves can be whipped up. Other lakes in the reserve are the smaller Laguna Verde – a green lake as its name suggests – and the Laguna Mulas Muertas, often covered with pink flamingoes, Andean geese and other wildfowl. There's no public transport, no *guardería* and nowhere to stay: just you and the wilds.

La Rioja and around

LA RIOJA – or Todos los Santos de la Nueva Rioxa, as it was baptized at the end of the sixteenth century – is an indolent kind of town, built in a flat-bottomed valley, watered by the Río Tajamar, and nearly 1200km northwest of Buenos Aires and 517km northeast of San Juan. In the spring the city is perfumed by the famous orange trees that have earned it the much-bandied sobriquet "Ciudad de los Naranjos". In spite of the plentiful shade of this luxuriant vegetation, the blistering summer heat is refracted off the brutally arid mountains looming to the west and turns the city, notoriously one of the country's hottest, virtually into a no-go zone even for its hardy inhabitants. At all times the place has a rough and ready, Wild West edge to it, and the heat seems to make people tetchy even when they've had their institutional siesta – everything shuts down from 1pm to 5pm. Yet La Rioja is not without its fashionable boutiques and cafés, and the city's chic business people in sharp suits love to strut along the tree-lined streets, clutching mobile phones that chirp in competition with the omnipresent and vociferous cicadas. The spick-and-span buildings, some of them showcases for contemporary architecture, are fronted by well-manicured gardens and radiate an impression of relative prosperity.

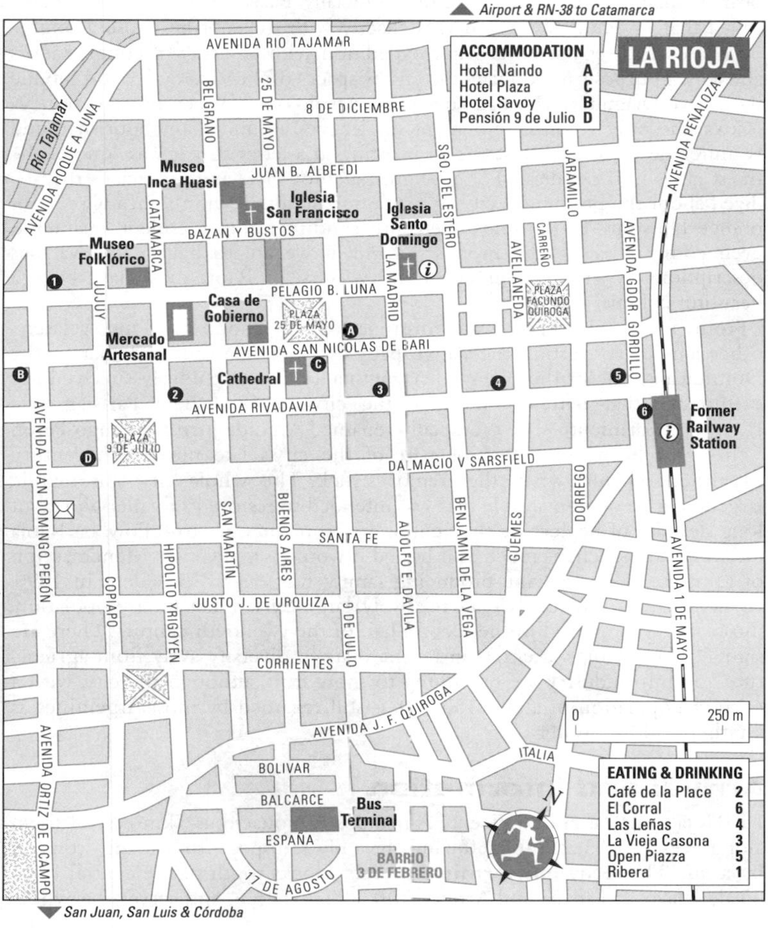

La Rioja is not a sightseers' city, but it is a good base for exploring the region, and you'll certainly find enough to occupy a full day, not forgetting to do as the Riojanos do and take a full-length nap in the afternoon. Among the highlights are two of the country's best **museums** of indigenous art, one archeological and the other with a folkloric slant. Nearby, the **Quebrada de los Sauces**, named for the shady willows trailing in the **Dique de los Sauces**, a man-made lake that is the city's reservoir, offers refreshing bathing and sports activities, acting as a vital safety valve during the most relentless heatwaves. Unquestionably, the best time to come to La Rioja is when the orange blossoms are out and the jacarandas ablaze, from October to November, but whatever you do, avoid the midsummer, when temperatures have been known to approach 50°C.

Some history

La Rioja came into being on May 20, 1591 when the governor of Tucumán, Juan Ramírez de Velasco, a native of La Rioja in Castile, founded the city in its strategic valley location – in the lee of the mountain range that would later bear his name. Today's Plaza Mayor – officially Plaza 25 de Mayo but never called that by Riojanos – coincides exactly with the spot he chose. Ramírez de Velasco had set out on a major expedition with an army of conquistadors and a dual purpose: to populate the empty spaces of the Viceroyalty and subdue the native Diaguitas, who had farmed the fertile oasis for centuries. La Nueva Rioxa, the only colonial settlement for leagues around, soon flourished and Ramírez de Velasco felt justified in boasting in a letter that it was "one of the finest cities in the Indies". For a long time chroniclers and politicians rhapsodized about the prosperous city, its fertile surroundings and the heady scent of orange blossoms. In the mid-nineteenth century, future president Sarmiento even compared it to the Promised Land; if we are to believe the various descriptions by visiting dignitaries and writers, La Rioja must have been a beautiful colonial city.

From it, mainly Franciscan missionaries set about fulfilling Velasco's other aim of converting the native peoples. Their convent and that of the Dominicans, one of the oldest in Argentina, both miraculously survived the earthquake that flattened most of the city in 1894. The Parisian-style Boulevard Sarmiento – now officially renamed Avenida Juan Domingo Perón – had just been completed, as part of the city's late nineteenth-century expansion scheme, when the tremor struck. The whole city was rebuilt, largely in a Neocolonial style that was intended to restore its former glory, but long decades of neglect by the central government were to follow. La Rioja did not even benefit as much as it hoped it would when Carlos Menem, scion of a major La Rioja wine-producing family was elected president in 1990. Menem came from La Rioja's relatively large Syrian/Lebanese population, most of whom arrived in the second half of the twentieth century. There are signs that La Rioja's attempts in recent years to diversify away from agriculture and into industry are beginning to show fruit, although the city, with a current population of about 150,000, is still regarded by most Argentines as a rather arid backwater.

Arrival and information

La Rioja's small **airport**, Vicente Almandos Almonacid, is 7km east of town along RP-5 (Ⓣ03822/462160), and the only transport from it into town is by *remise*. The seedy **bus terminal** is eight blocks south of the central Plaza 25 de Mayo, at España and Artigas (Ⓣ03822/425453), and serves the whole province, including Chilecito and more distant destinations such as Mendoza, Córdoba, Catamarca, Salta and Resistencia. Nearby are some Formica-and-neon cafés and a souvenir shop or two. The city's **tourist office**, called DiMuTur, is on Avenida Gobernador Gordillo, in the former railway station (daily 8am–1pm & 5–8pm; ⓣ03822/4341227, ⓦwww.larioja.gov.ar); in addition to a list of hotels and *residenciales*, staff can provide a list of rooms to rent, plus a map of the city. At Pelagio B. Luna 345, the **Agencia Provincial Turistico** (daily 8am–9pm; ⓣ03822/426384) has glossy leaflets and some rudimentary information about the rest of the province. For tours to Talampaya, Ischigualasto and other local sites of interest, try Juan Molina (ⓣ03822/422786) or Jaris Travel, J.J. de Urquiza 731 (ⓣ03822/428998). Most services, such as **banks**, *locutorios* and **Internet access**, can be found grouped around Plaza 25 de Mayo.

Accommodation

You're unlikely to want to stay long in La Rioja, but it's good to know that it's not badly off for **accommodation**, covering the whole range with a few reliable options. If you're looking for five-star luxury, there's the sparkling new Casa Rosada-coloured *Hotel Naindo*, at San Nicolás de Bari and Joaquin Victor Gonzalez (ⓣ03822/470700, ⓦwww.naindoparkhotel.com; ❼), with comfortable if characterless rooms and its own restaurant, decent-sized pool and bar. *Hotel Plaza*, at San Nicolás de Bari and 9 de Julio (ⓣ03822/425215, ⓦwww.plazahotel-larioja.com.ar; ❺), has a well-located *confitería* that is one of the places to be seen in La Rioja; everything is squeaky clean, almost clinically so, but the rooms are smart and the roof-top pool and terrace enjoy views of the cathedral and mountains beyond. Middle-range *Hotel Savoy*, at San Nicolás de Bari and Avenida Roque A. Luna (ⓣ03822/426894; ❸), has an unimaginative neutral decor, but is friendly and the rooms are quite spacious, with decent bathrooms. The only really budget establishment that can be recommended is basic *Pensión 9 de Julio*, Copiapó 197 (ⓣ03822/426955; ❶), where the resident cat and leafy patio give some atmosphere and the rooms are cramped but acceptably clean. Enquire about B&B-style **casas de familia** (❶–❸), the best bet at the budget end, at the municipal tourist office.

The City

La Rioja's microcentro really is small and all the places of interest are grouped around the two main squares, Plaza 25 de Mayo, and, two blocks west and one south, Plaza 9 de Julio. On the west side of the former is the striking white Casa de Gobierno, built in a Neocolonial style with a strong Andalucian influence, which contrasts with the **Catedral San Nicolás de Bari** (daily 8am–9pm) on the south of the plaza. This Neoclassical hulk of a church, built at the beginning of the twentieth century in beige stone, with a huge Italianate cupola, Neo-Gothic campaniles and Byzantine elements in the facade, is primarily the sanctuary for a locally revered relic: a seventeenth-century walnut-wood image of St Nicholas of Bari, carved in Peru. It's the centrepiece of two major processions, the first of which is the saint's day in July; the other is on December 31, when the statue is the joint star of the **Tinkunaku** – meaning "casual meeting" in Quichoa – joined in the procession by an image of the Christ Child – the "Niño Alcalde", idolized as La Rioja's eternal guardian and mayor and kept at the Iglesia San Francisco. The ceremony represents St Francisco Solano's role in pacifying the indigenous inhabitants of the region in the late sixteenth century. The statue of St Nicholas is kept in a special *camarín*, or side room, abutting the cathedral building and kept locked; to see it ask around for the key in the cathedral.

One block north of Plaza 25 de Mayo, at 25 de Mayo and Bazán y Bustos, is the **Iglesia San Francisco** (daily 9am–noon & 5–9pm) itself, an uninspiring Neoclassical building visited by St Francisco Solano when he was travelling around South America. The stark cell where he stayed, containing only a fine statue of the saint and a dead orange tree, said to have been planted by him, is treated as a holy place by Riojanos. Another block north is the **Museo Arqueológico Inca Huasi** (Tues–Sat 9am–noon; $1), set up in the 1920s by a Franciscan monk who was interested in the Diaguita culture – rather ironic, considering that the Franciscan missionaries did all they could in the seventeenth century to annihilate it. One of the pieces of art on display is a quite hideous seventeenth-century painting of the conversion of the Diaguita people by St Francisco Solano, but the rest of the exhibition is a fabulous collection of **Diaguita ceramics** and other pre-Columbian art. The dragon-shaped vase near the entrance is around 1200 years old; another later piece, inside one of the dusty cases, is a pot with an armadillo climbing it, while fat-bellied vases painted with, among other things, phalluses and toads – symbols of fertility and rain – line the shelves. Sadly, the display techniques do not do justice to the quality of the items on display.

Far more impressive is the **Museo Folklórico**, at Pelagio B. Luna 811 (Tues–Sun 9am–noon & 5–9pm; $1). It contains a reconstruction of a nineteenth-century Riojano house, complete with furnishings, a bodega, gaucho paraphernalia and a kitchen. In the display on local mythology, a set of beautiful terracotta statuettes representing the various figures brings to life the whole pantheon, such as Pachamama, or Mother Earth, and Zapam-Zucum, the goddess of children and the carob tree – she has incredibly elongated breasts the shape of carob-pods. Zupay is the equivalent of the Devil, while a series of characters called Huaira personify different types of wind. Opposite, on the corner of Pelagio B. Luna and Catamarca, is one of the region's best **crafts markets** (Tues–Fri 8am–noon & 4–8pm, Sat & Sun 9am–noon); the *artesanía*, all of it local, is of very high quality, especially the regionally famous *mantas*, or blankets.

One block east of Plaza 25 de Mayo, the **Iglesia Santo Domingo** (daily 9am–noon & 5–9pm), at Pelagio B. Luna and La Madrid, is the only building of interest to have survived the 1894 earthquake; it's one of the oldest buildings in Argentina, dating from 1623. The extremely long, narrow and very white nave is utterly stark, apart from a fine altar decorated with seventeenth-century statuary, as is the simple whitewashed facade – but the carob-wood doors, carved by Indian craftsmen in the late seventeenth century, are one of the finest pieces of **mestizo art** in the whole country.

Eating and drinking

Not as hard up as it sometimes likes to make out, La Rioja has a gaggle of sophisticated **places to eat**, most of which are clustered along Avenida Rivadavia towards the old train station – though the best of the rest are mostly pizzerias and simple *confiterías*. During heatwaves a lot of locals go and cool down at the Dique Los Sauces (see opposite), where you can also have a meal or a snack on the refreshing banks of the reservoir; better still, take a picnic. Two pizzerias stand out: *Ribera*, on the corner of Avenida Perón and Pelagio B. Luna, with decades of tradition but a polished, fresh setting with attractive wooden tables; and glitzier *Open Piazza*, a sophisticated pub/bar at the corner of Rivadavia and F. Quiroga, with a summer terrace, men-in-black waiters and decent music – plus a good range of toppings. *La Vieja Casona*, Rivadavia 427, is probably La Rioja's best *parrilla*, serving outstanding meat and delicious home-made pasta, with a wine list from local bodegas. It has serious competition from a newer, trendier rival, *El Corral*, right next to the train station, and large, top-quality *Las Leñas*, Av Rivadavia 245. *Café de la Place*, at Rivadavia and Hipólito Yrigoyen, is one of the most strategically located places to have a **drink** or snack – the service is a bit nonchalant, but the decor is resolutely late 1990s, all brushed metal and diffused lighting.

Dique Los Sauces

Avenida San Francisco heads westwards out of the city and, as RN-75, eventually leads to Aimogasta, in the north of La Rioja Province. Along a narrow valley formed by the Sierra de Velasco, with its violet, red and ochre rocks, is the Quebrada de los Sauces, in which a reservoir, **Dique Los Sauces**, was built at the end of the nineteenth century. Slightly higher than the city and cooled by the water and the willows that surround it – *sauce* means willow – its banks have become the Riojanos' weekend and summer resort, only 16km away from the city. You can picnic here, eat and drink at the lakeside bar or have a meal at the nearby *Club Sírio-Libanés*, where you can get delicious *mezze* and kebabs. Near the dam a signpost shows the way to El Morro, or **Cerro de la Cruz** (1680m), up a steep twelve-kilometre road best tackled in a 4WD or, if on foot, during the coolest part of the day. The views from here of the mountains, valley and city are amazing; nearby is a launching-pad for hang-gliding and paragliding, used for international competitions because the weather conditions are so reliable. If you're tempted, contact the Asociación Riojana de Vuelo Libre, at San Nicolás de Bari 1 (Ⓣ03822/422139).

Buses to Sañogasta stop at Los Sauces, but whatever you do don't catch any marked "Los Sauces" – confusingly, this refers to San Blas de los Sauces, a God-forsaken village at the northern tip of La Rioja Province.

Chilecito and around

La Rioja Province's second city, **CHILECITO** is an old mining town in a beautiful mountainside setting, some 205km by road from La Rioja city – but less than 70km west as the crow flies. It was founded in the early eighteenth century as Santa Rita de Casca, but the present name derives from the fact that most of the miners who worked in the gold mines in the early nineteenth century came from across the border. In the middle of that century, La Rioja's government moved here because of harassment from Facundo Quiroga, Rosas' right-hand man – Sarmiento, one of Rosas' fiercest opponents is still something of a local hero for taking part in Rosas' overthrow. One of Chilecito's two self-styled names, the Cuna del Torrontés, or birthplace of the torrontés, refers to the **wineries** based here, one of which can be visited, though the torrontés grape produces more subtle wines further north in Salta Province; the other, La Perla del Oeste, literally the "pearl of the west", is harder to justify, though the city is the only settlement in the province with any charm, despite its scruffiness. The city's **museum** contains a collection of archeological and other items spanning the area's history since the Stone Age, and the early twentieth-century

mine installations just outside the town are also intriguing. But best of all is the cultural centre in an early nineteenth-century *finca* at **Samay-Huasi**, a short way east, which also makes for an idyllic place to stay. A longer trip, for which you need your own transport – though buses to Villa Unión can take you there – is along the fabulous **Cuesta de Miranda**, a sinuous, parapet-like mountain pass across the Sierra de Famatina that reaches 2025m above sea level, some 50km west of Chilecito, on RN-40 towards Villa Unión. The Río Miranda snakes through a deep gorge, hemmed in on both sides by multi-coloured cliffs and peaks, striped red, green, blue and yellow with oxidized minerals and strata of volcanic rock.

To get to Chilecito from La Rioja, head south down RN-38, and then switch back in a northwesterly direction, taking RN-74, followed by RN-40. To the west stretch the Sierras de los Colorados, Sierra de Vilgo, Sierra de Paganzo and Sierra de Sañogasta, reddish and purplish cliffs and crags that form a dramatic backdrop for the fertile valley, with its olive groves, walnut groves and vineyards. To the east is the impenetrable barrier of the Sierra de Velasco – which is why it's such a long detour to get from La Rioja to the central valleys of La Rioja Province. To the northwest stretches another wall of mountains, the majestic Sierra de Famatina, which peaks at Cerro General Manuel Belgrano (6250m), permanently snowcapped; this is the highest outcrop of the Andean precordillera. Several **buses** a day also take this route between La Rioja and Chilecito.

The Town

Built on the southern banks of the often bone-dry Río Sarmiento, Chilecito itself is centred on Plaza Domingo Faustino Sarmiento, built in the mid-nineteenth century as the heart of the new Villa Argentina; its enormous plane trees, Judas trees, ash trees and palms provide welcome shade when the summer sun is at its strongest. All around are huddled most of the town's restaurants, cafés, hotels and a service station. Few of the buildings – least of all the dreadful concrete Iglesia Sagrado Corazón de Jesús, built in the 1960s, on the southern side of the square – are of any interest. Instead, head west four blocks to the Molino San Francisco, J. Ocampo 63, which houses the **Museo de Chilecito** (Nov–April Tues–Sun 8am–noon & 3–7pm, May–Oct Tues–Sun 8am–noon & 2–4pm; $1 voluntary contribution), a motley but interesting assemblage ranging from mineral samples from the nearby mines to all kinds of arts and crafts, indigenous, colonial and contemporary. The attractive building itself, an eighteenth-century flour mill, is a partly whitewashed, robust stone building, surrounded by huge cart wheels. One block north and west, at La Plata 646, is the **Cooperativa Vitivinifrutícola Riojana** (tours at 8am, 10am & 12.30pm; free; ⓣ03825/423150), where you can visit the wineries and fruit-drying sheds and taste the produce, including the refreshingly flowery torrontés wine and succulent walnuts and raisins.

About 2km southeast of the centre, past the abattoir along RN-40, is the Cable Carril La Mexicana, where you'll find the **Museo del Cablecarril** (daily 8am–8pm; free), housed in the disused cable-car station dating from 1903. The display about mining isn't exactly scintillating, but the German-built installations – a bit like a nineteenth-century pier stranded in the middle of South America – are impressive; a massive crane made of spruce timber and old ore-wagons still sits next to the station, which is built on dainty stilts. The cable car, which was in use until 1929, was the second longest in the world; the route stretched nearly 40km up to the huge mine in the Sierra de Famatina, at an altitude of nearly 4500m above sea level. **Chirau Mita** is a botanical garden dedicated to the study and preservation of cacti, not only from Argentina but also countries as far flung as Namibia, Guatemala, Mexico and the Canary Islands (call for visits: ⓣ03825/422139) – it is on a hillside along RP-12 en route towards La Puntilla.

Practicalities

Buses, several times daily from La Rioja, less frequently from Córdoba, Villa Unión and Buenos Aires, arrive at the tiny **bus station** one block north and west of Plaza Sarmiento, at La Plata and 19 de Febrero. Chilecito's rudimentary **tourist information office** is half a block north of the plaza, at Castro y Bazán (Mon–Fri 7am–1pm & 3–9pm, Sat, Sun & public holidays 8am–9pm; ⓣ03825/422688). The best **place to stay** hereabouts is at Samay-Huasi (see below), or you could try ACA-owned *Hotel Chilecito* three blocks east of the centre at Timoteo Gordillo 101 (ⓣ03825/422201; ④), with plain, clean rooms, an airy *confitería* and views of the foothills. For **places to eat** the best reputation is enjoyed by *La Posta*, a traditional *parrilla* at the corner of 19 de Febrero and Roque de Lanús that also serves an excellent *locro* and sells a wide range of delicious wines and preserves, including giant olives and garlic. *Café Keops* on the southeast corner of Plaza Sarmiento has reasonably priced coffee, drinks and snacks.

Samay-Huasi

Just 3km east of Chilecito is the British-built ★ *finca* – or estancia – of **Samay-Huasi**, now belonging to the University of Plata and housing the **Museo Samay-Huasi** (daily 9am–1pm & 3–7pm; $1; ⓣ03825/422629). At the beginning of the twentieth century this was the rural retreat of an eminent Riojano jurist, poet and mystic, Joaquín V. González, who founded the University of La Plata and was particularly interested in Argentina's pre-Columbian history. The Quichoa name means "house of rest", and the mock-Etruscan doorway to the estate bears a Latin inscription which translates as "nothing and nobody shall disturb my peace". It's still a tranquil place, amid a luxuriant oasis-like garden and surrounded by steep rocky outcrops. The main rooms of the Neocolonial house, draped in bougainvillea, remain as they were when González lived here, complete with his furniture, paintings and personal effects. The adjoining bodega has been converted into a museum, with portraits and landscape oil-paintings by Argentine artists on the ground floor – some good, some excellent – and a varied collection of insects, stuffed birds, local crafts and bits of minerals in the cellar. This is a great (and good-value) place **to stay**; the outbuildings have been converted into simple rooms, with shared baths – but book ahead as it often fills with university groups, especially during the vacations (ⓣ03825/422629; ③ full board).

Travel details

Buses

Chilecito to: Buenos Aires (3 daily; 20hr); Córdoba (2 daily; 7hr); La Rioja (4 daily; 3hr).
La Rioja to: Buenos Aires (3 daily; 17hr); Catamarca (7 daily; 2hr); Chilecito (4 daily; 3hr); Córdoba (hourly; 5hr); Salta (7 daily; 11hr); San Juan (7 daily; 6hr); Valle Fértil (2 weekly; 4hr); Villa Unión (2 daily; 5hr).
Malargüe to: Mendoza (3 daily; 4–5hr); San Rafael (2 daily; 2hr 30min).
Mendoza to: Buenos Aires (hourly; 17hr); Córdoba (7 daily; 9hr); General Alvear (3 daily; 4hr 30min);

La Rioja (7 daily; 8hr 30min); Las Leñas (June–Sept 2 daily; 4hr 30min); Los Penitentes (6 daily; 4hr); Malargüe (3 daily; 4–5hr); Neuquén (2 daily; 12hr); Río Gallegos (1 daily; 40hr); Salta (7 daily; 19hr); San Rafael (hourly; 3hr 15min); San Juan (hourly; 2hr 20min); San Luis (hourly; 3hr 40min); Santiago de Chile (4 daily; 7hr); Uspallata (6 daily; 1hr 40min); Valparaíso, Chile (4 daily; 8hr 30min).
San Juan to: Barreal (2 daily; 5hr); Buenos Aires (10 daily; 16hr); Córdoba (5 daily; 8hr); La Rioja (7 daily; 6hr); Mendoza (hourly; 2hr 20min); San José de Jáchal (5 daily; 3hr 30min); San Rafael (2 daily; 5hr 30min); Valle Fértil (3 daily; 4hr).
San Rafael to: Buenos Aires (4 daily; 13hr); General Alvear (3 daily; 1hr 20min); Las Leñas (June–Sept 3 daily; 2hr 40min); Malargüe (2 daily; 2hr 30min); Mendoza (hourly; 3hr 15min); Neuquén (2 daily; 12hr); San Juan (2 daily; 5hr 30min); San Luis (2 daily; 3hr).

Flights

La Rioja to: Buenos Aires (daily; 2hr); Catamarca (daily; 30min).
Mendoza to: Buenos Aires (4 daily; 1hr 50min); Córdoba (3 daily; 1hr 20min); Neuquén (3 daily; 1hr 30min).
San Juan to: Buenos Aires (daily; 1hr 50min); Córdoba (daily; 30min); Mendoza (daily; 30min).
San Rafael to: Buenos Aires (daily; 1hr 50min).

7

Neuquén and the Lake District

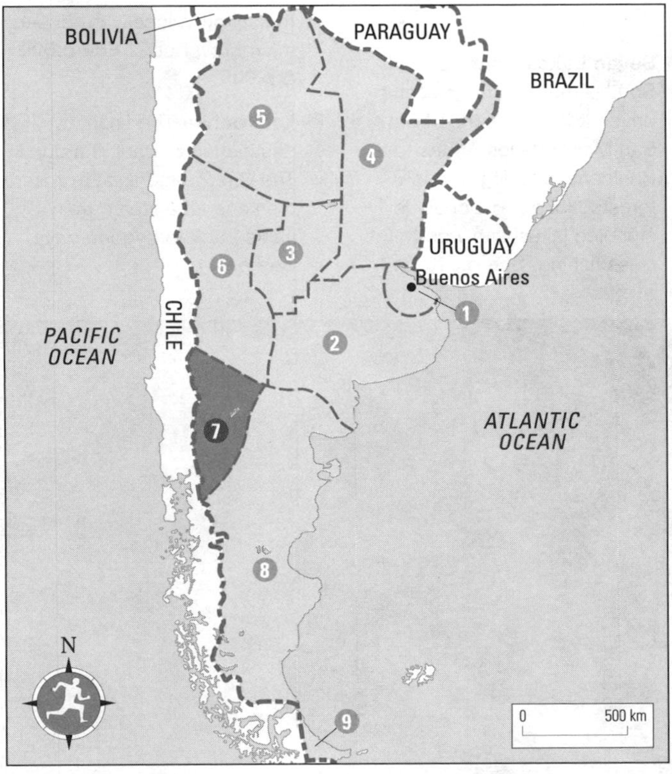

CHAPTER 7

Highlights

* **Dinosaurs** Gape upwards at Neuquén Province's fossils of some of the biggest dinosaurs known to mankind. See p.588

* **Volcán Lanín** The eminently photogenic volcano reigns over a vast swathe of Parque Nacional Lanín and offers spectacular climbing opportunities on its slopes. See p.607

* **Seven Lakes Route** One of South America's most scenic drives, the route winds from San Martín de los Andes to Bariloche, passing through forested hills and alongside stunning lakes with world-class fishing. See p.616–617

* **Bariloche** A perennial favourite with the Argentine student population, but with magnificent trekking in the nearby Parque Nacional Nahuel Huapi it is much more than just a party town. See p.622

* **Local beer** El Bolsón Brewery in El Bolsón and Blest Brewery near Bariloche are among the best places to sample the savoury, locally produced microbrew beers. See p.629 & p.635

* **La Trochita** The final destination of Paul Theroux in *The Old Patagonian Express*, the venerable steam train harks back to bygone days. See p.641

△ La Trochita

7

Neuquén and the Lake District

Covering an area larger than Portugal and with the distinction of being Argentina's only palindromic province, **Neuquén** marks Patagonia's northern limits. The arid, desert-like conditions that dominate much of the region give way in its southwestern sector to the **Lake District**, an area defined by immense glacial lakes, thick forests, jagged peaks and extinct volcanoes, which was controlled, until a little over a century ago, by the Mapuche. Also comprising western Río Negro and the northwestern corner of Chubut, this dramatic landscape is famous for its network of easily accessible national parks strung along the cordillera, making it one of Argentina's most popular holiday destinations.

Characterized by expanses of parched steppe and *meseta*, central and eastern Neuquén hides abundant deposits of fossils and fossil fuels and, as a result, is of great paleontological interest – it's known locally as "**Dinosaur Paradise**". You can see this legacy firsthand in the museum at **Villa El Chocón** or at a handful of other sites around **Neuquén**, the province's namesake capital. Centred on sleepy **Chos Malal**, the little-visited mountainous north is a zone of transition, much more akin in scenery to Mendoza and the Cuyo than to Patagonia. At this latitude, the mountains are harsh and barren, typified by the spiky Cordillera del Viento around the mining region of **Andacollo** and the hump-backed **Volcán Domuyo**. The great Patagonian Andean forests that are so magnificently represented in **Parque Nacional Lanín** in the south of the province are little in evidence here, although the most northerly vestiges of the Patagonian *Nothofagus* forests can be found at the beautiful **Lagunas de Epulafquen**.

South of Andacollo, at the mountain resort village of **Caviahue**, you find the first significant groves of araucaria, or monkey puzzle tree, growing on the harsh basalt soils of Volcán Copahue. The area from Paso Pino Hachado down into the north of Parque Nacional Lanín abounds with some phenomenal opportunities for trekking, horse-riding and mountain-biking. Check out the **Pehuenia Circuit** around lagos Aluminé, Moquehue and Ñorquinco, or explore Quillén or the Aigo **Mapuche** community of **Rucachoroi** in the northern sector of Parque Nacional Lanín, a wild area popular with fishermen but otherwise much less disturbed than the rest of the vast park system in the Lake District.

Both **Junín de los Andes** and the scenic resort of **San Martín de los Andes** provide good bases for exploring the better-known central and southern sectors

NEUQUÉN & THE LAKE DISTRICT
Santiago
Mendoza
Buenos Aires, Bahia Blanca (428km) & Carmen de Patagones (450km)
0
100 km
MENDOZA PROVINCE
LA PAMPA PROVINCE
NEUQUÉN PROVINCE
RÍO NEGRO PROVINCE
CHILE
Chillán
Concepción
Los Angeles
Temuco
Villarica
Pucón
Valdivia
Volcán Domuyo (4709m)
Varvarco
Las Ovejas
Lagunas de Epulafquen
Andacollo
Chos Malal
Rincón de los Sauces
Catriél
PARQUE NACIONAL LAGUNA DEL LAJA
Copahue
Caviahue
Volcán Copahue (2969m)
Loncopué
RN-40
RP-21
Río Neuquén
RP-7
Embalse Cerros Colorados
RP-51
Las Lajas
P.N. CONGUILLIÓ
Volcán Llaima
Paso de Icalma
Paso Pino Hachado
Lago Moquehue
Lago Aluminé
Lago Ñorquinco
Lago Rucachoroi
Aluminé
Zapala
Cutral-Có
RP-17
RN-22
Plaza Huincul
NEUQUÉN
Cipolletti
General Roca
Río Negro
Villa Regina
SIERRA DE CATAN LIL
PARQUE NACIONAL LAGUNA BLANCA
Villa El Chocón
Embalse Ezequiel Ramos Mexía
Picún Leufú
Lago Quillén
Paso Mamuil Malal
Volcán Villarica
Volcán Lanín
PARQUE NACIONAL LANÍN
Río Aluminé
Paso Carirriñe
Lago Huechulafquen
Río Limay
Lago Pirehueico
Junín de los Andes
Paso Hua-Hum
Lago Lolog
Piedra del Aguila
Lago Lácar
San Martín de los Andes

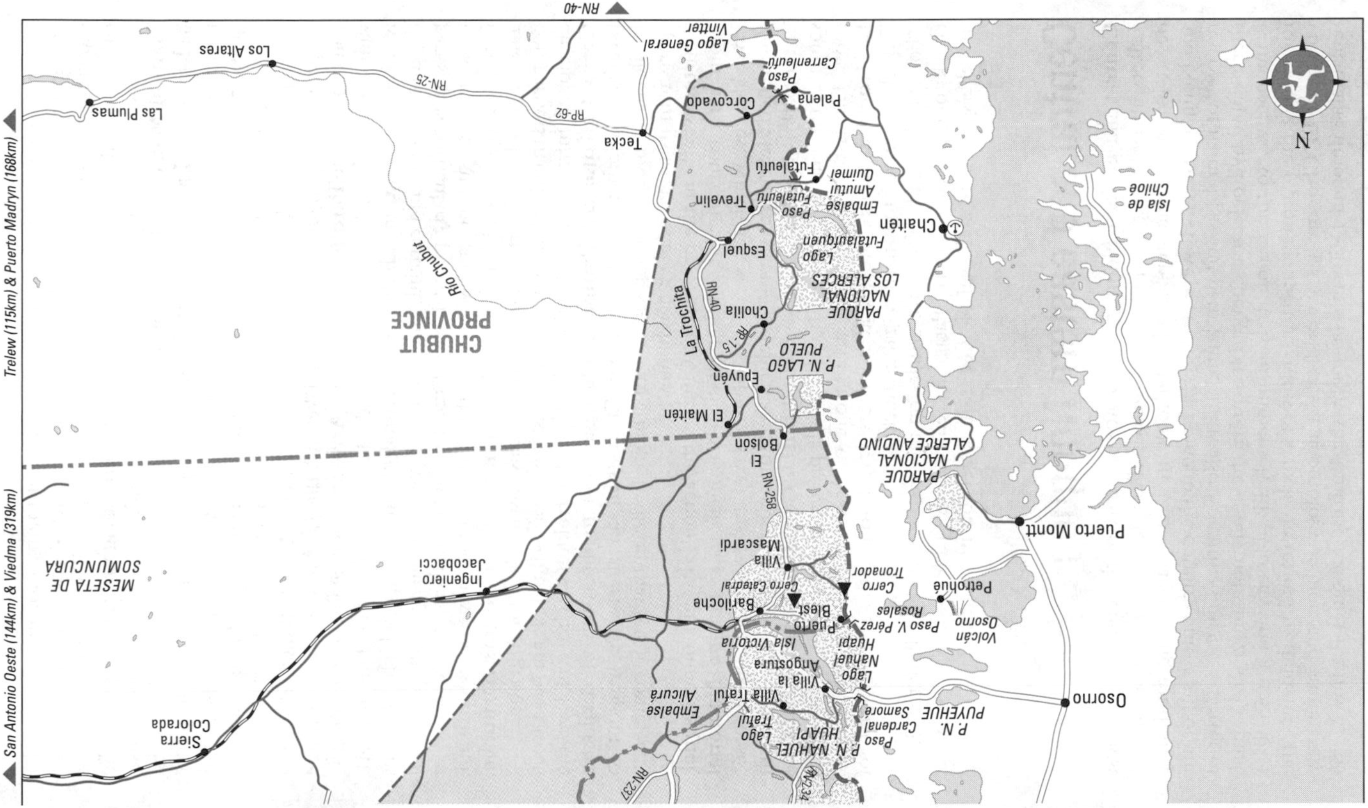
San Antonio Oeste (144km) & Viedma (319km)
Trelew (115km) & Puerto Madryn (168km)
RN-40
MESETA DE SOMUNCURÁ
Sierra Colorada
Ingeniero Jacobacci
CHUBUT PROVINCE
Río Chubut
Las Plumas
Los Altares
RN-25
RP-62
Tecka
Lago General Vintter
Paso Carrenleufú
Palena
Corcovado
Futaleufú
Trevelin
Esquel
La Trochita
RN-40
RP-15
Cholila
Epuyén
El Maitén
El Bolsón
RN-258
P. N. LAGO PUELO
PARQUE NACIONAL LOS ALERCES
Lago Futalaufquen
Paso Futaleufú
Embalse Amutui Quimei
Chaitén
PARQUE NACIONAL ALERCE ANDINO
Puerto Montt
Isla de Chiloé
Villa Mascardi
Cerro Catedral
Bariloche
Puerto Blest
Cerro Tronador
Paso V. Pérez Rosales
Petrohué
Volcán Osorno
Isla Victoria
Villa la Angostura
Lago Nahuel Huapi
Villa Traful
Embalse Alicurá
Lago Traful
P. N. NAHUEL HUAPI
Paso Cardenal Samoré
P. N. PUYEHUE
Osorno
RN-237
RN-234
N

of Parque Lanín. Junín is the more convenient of the two for investigating the area around the park's remarkable centrepiece, extinct **Volcán Lanín**, a fairytale snowcapped cone of 3776m and a mecca for climbers. The easiest route to its rim – physically challenging but technically fairly straightforward – is from the northeast: head with your gear for one of the Andes' most scenic passes, **Paso Mamuil Malal** near **Lago Tromen**; the classic views of the volcano are to be had from the **Lago Huechulafquen** and **Lago Paimún** area to the south, however. The region's volcanic undertones can be witnessed at a series of hot spring resorts: the **Termas de Epulafquen**, and the ones near **Lago Queñi** at the western end of San Martín's wonderful **Lago Lácar**.

San Martín is at the northern end of the scenic **Seven Lakes Route**, a gorgeous drive past forested mountain lakes to **Villa La Angostura**, from where you can visit the **Parque Nacional Los Arrayanes**, formed to protect a captivating wood of myrtle trees at the end of the Peninsula Quetrihué. This tiny park is enveloped by the goliath **Parque Nacional Nahuel Huapi**, which is perhaps the most famous, and certainly one of the most visited, of all Argentina's national parks. It is particularly popular with Argentine holidaymakers, who descend in packs in both summer and winter for the many outdoor adventures on hand, filling towns such as the archetypal Patagonian resort, Río Negro's **Bariloche**. They're also lured by the alpine flavour of this "Switzerland of Argentina" – a comparison that does, in some places at least, bear out. Nahuel Huapi has a well-developed infrastructure of trails and refuges for **trekkers**, who will love the **Cerro Catedral** and **Pampa Linda** region just to the south of Bariloche. Nearby is another base for trekking, **El Bolsón**, an alternative hangout to Bariloche in more than one sense, with a hippy tradition that sets it completely apart from its larger, brasher neighbour.

Further south, in the province of Chubut, the action is based around **Esquel**. From here, you can visit another classic Patagonian park, **Parque Nacional Los Alerces**, which has some exceptional lakes and is the best place to see threatened **alerce trees**, some of which are thousands of years old. To the north of the park is **Cholila**, where you'll find **Butch Cassidy's cabin**, while to the south is the engaging **Trevelin**, which still preserves something of its Welsh roots. The last highlight of the area is one of Argentina's two timeless trains: **La Trochita**, which rattles and hoots its way through the steppe north of Esquel on a precarious narrow-gauge track.

For excellent and informative articles on the area written by fellow travellers, check out Traveller's Guru Patagonia edition, available online at Ⓦwww.travellersguru.com and available free from larger tourist offices.

Central and eastern Neuquén

Central and **eastern Neuquén Province** is a part of the country that most visitors hurry through on journeys to the cordillera or the coast. It is an area of desert-like *meseta* and steppe, cultivated only in a few places along the Limay and Neuquén rivers. However, the area is home to the country's most important reserves of natural gas and petroleum, and is also Argentina's major exporter of thermal and hydroelectric energy. **Neuquén**, the eponymous provincial capital, is the gateway to the region. It is an immensely likeable city and a good base for visiting the region's attractions, most of which are related to dinosaurs: the village of **El Chocón** has a world-class paleontology exhibit and some truly remarkable dinosaur footprints *in situ* by the Embalse Ezequiel Ramos Mexía reservoir, while in **Plaza Huincul** you can see bones from the largest dinosaur ever discovered, the *Argentinosaurus huinculensis*, and further north at **Lago Barreales** you can watch paleontologists in action. At **Rincón de los Sauces**, in the extreme north of the province, the world's first fossilized dinosaur eggs were unearthed.

Unfortunately for wildlife lovers, **Parque Nacional Laguna Blanca** no longer boasts the flocks of fowl that it once did, but anyone heading for the southern lakes will find that passing through the town of **Zapala**, near the park, is almost inevitable, and there is little else to see in the area.

Neuquén

The bustling provincial capital of **NEUQUÉN** sits at the confluence of the rivers Neuquén and Limay, whose waters unite to become the Río Negro. With a population of 215,000, this plains metropolis functions as the commercial, industrial and financial centre of the surrounding fruit- and oil-producing region. It's a surprisingly attractive and friendly place to pass a few days, the local government having worked hard in recent years to change the city's industrial image: there are now a cluster of museums as good as anywhere else in the region, and a beach resort on the banks of the Río Limay that is an excellent place to relax after a hard day on the road.

Arrival, information and city transport

Neuquén is the gateway to northern Patagonia and is a major transport nexus. Its new **bus terminal** is 3.5km east of the city centre on RN-22, and styled

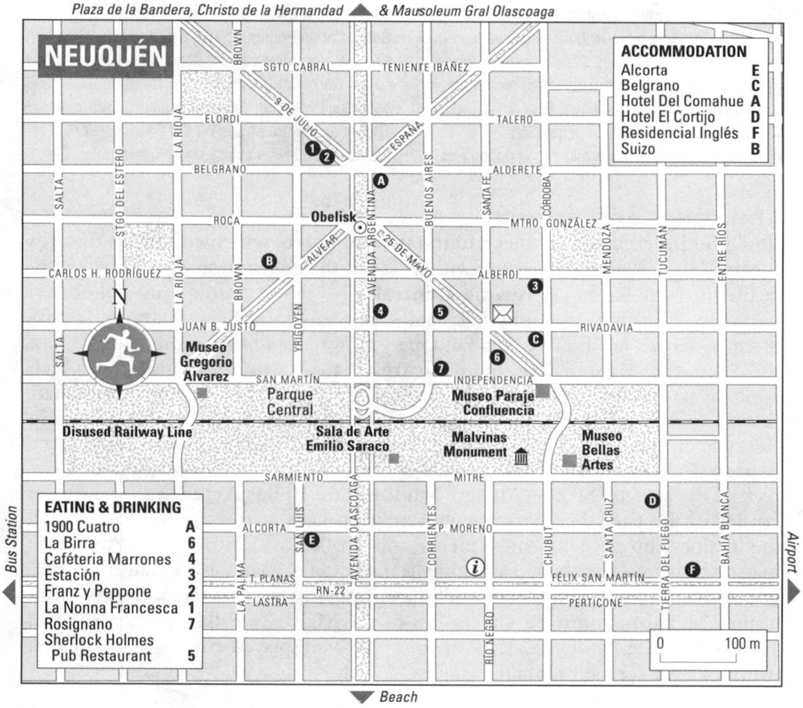

along airport lines (bags come through on a conveyor belt and passengers have to check in to platforms). El Ko-Ko runs a bus service to the centre every fifteen minutes; buy tickets from Kiosk 39 before boarding. You can also take a **taxi**. Neuquén's **airport** (☎0299/444-0448) is 5km west of town off RN-22. Indalo runs a bus to the city centre; it departs from the main road in front of the airport every twenty minutes (pay on the bus). To use Neuquén's other city buses, you must buy a ticket in advance from marked kiosks scattered throughout the city.

There are tourist information booths at both the airport and the bus terminal, but the main **tourist office** (daily 7am–11pm; ☎0299/442-4089, www.neuquentur.gov.ar) is at Félix San Martín 182, two blocks east of Avenida Olascoaga. It is a mine of information on the whole province.

Accommodation

Hotels in Neuquén are busy even during the week, so it's well worth booking in advance. Several unspectacular though centrally located mid-range places are clustered around avenidas Olascoaga and Argentina – a simple breakfast is generally included in the price. The nearest **campsite** is *Camping Las Araucarias*, 13km from the centre along RN-22 towards Plotier ($12 per person); take a *remise* from the centre.

Alcorta Alcorta 84 ☎0299/442-2541. Clean and comfortable hotel, with bright, if slightly cramped, rooms. Conveniently located for museums. ❸

Belgrano Rivadavia 283 ☎0299/448-0612. This agreeable hotel with wooden chalet exterior is probably the best value for money at the lower end of the price range. ❸

Hotel Del Comahue Av Argentina 377 ☎0299/443-2040, www.hoteldelcomahue.com. Popular with businessmen, *Del Comahue* is the most expensive hotel in town, though rooms are functional rather than luxurious. ❽

Hotel El Cortijo Tierra del Fuego 255 ☎0299/442-1795. Decent mid-range option just off the Parque Central. Heated rooms are clean and well maintained, if a little plain, and are arranged around small sunny courtyards. ❺

Residencial Inglés Félix San Martín 534 ☎0299/442-2252. A fallback budget choice, with clean but dated and slightly tatty rooms. Marginally the cheapest in town, and the garden with a vine is quite pleasant. ❸

Suizo Carlos Rodríguez 167 ☎0299/442-2602, www.hotelsuizo.com.ar. Good value higher-end option with bright, stylish rooms for up to four people, all with mini-bar and spacious bathroom. The reception area plays on the Swiss-chalet theme, but this is a classy and modern hotel. ❻

The town and around

You'll find everything you need in the **microcentro**, which comprises the area north of RN-22, three blocks on either side of the central boulevard. The centre of life in town is the vast **Parque Central**, bisected by an old railway line and home to four free museums (all Mon–Fri 8am–9pm, Sat–Sun 6pm–10pm), three of which are housed in abandoned railway buildings. From west to east these are: the **Museo Gregorio Alvarez**, San Martín and Misiones, which contains several works by the local sculptor for whom the museum was named, as well as a small display on Patagonian history; the **Sala de Arte Emilio Saraco**, an old cargo shed featuring temporary exhibitions by local artists; the **Museo Paraje Confluencia**, which specializes in the city's history; and, the pick of the bunch, the new **Museo Nacional de Bellas Artes**, at the southeast corner of the park. The permanent exhibition here features examples from all the major European art movements and works by all the great Argentine masters. The most valuable painting is *La Ultima Copla*, by Joaquín Sorolla, which has been valued at 3.5 million euros. Adjacent to the museum is an impressive **monument to the fallen** of the Malvinas/Falklands campaign of 1982 – the names of the dead are poignantly displayed on a glass wall that overlooks the serene fountain.

Tree-lined Avenida Argentina heads north from the Parque Central, its central reservation consisting of a series of commemorative plazas that includes an **obelisk** marking the founding of the city. At the far north of the avenue are a cluster of impressive monuments: the **Plaza de las Bandera**, featuring a huge flag flying high over the city; **El Christo de la Hermandad**, an enormous figure of Christ crucified on a red iron cross; and the **mausoleum of General Olascoaga**, who gave his name to one of the city's other major thoroughfares.

Heading south from the Parque Central, Avenida Argentina becomes the aforementioned Avenida Olascoaga. At the road's southernmost point a delightful, artificial **river beach** has been created along the wooded banks of the Río Limay. Hugely popular with families on warm afternoons, it's lined with bars and has safe swimming. Sitting here, it's easy to forget that you are over 600km from the real seaside.

Eating and drinking

Neuquén's best places to **eat** and **drink** are scattered around Avenida Argentina between San Martín and Roca, where there are a number of pool bars and pizzerias in addition to more upmarket restaurants.

1900 Cuatro on the first floor of the *Hotel Del Comahue*, Av Argentina 377 ⓣ0299/443-2040. Serves eclectic and imaginative foreign dishes and appetizing meals, though overall ambience is somewhat formal and staid and prices are predictably high.

La Birra Santa Fe and Independencia ⓣ0299/443-4344. Housed in a beautiful warehouse-style building with Hollywood-themed interior, this restaurant serves an international menu and the food is superb.

Caféteria Marrones Av Argentina 125 ⓣ0299/442-5489. Despite the plush interior and bow-tied waiters, this café/bar/restaurant is surprisingly affordable. Ten different varieties of coffee will keep the caffeine junkie happy.

Estación J.B. Alberdi and Córdoba. Sports bar with requisite TVs and simple eats. Outdoor tables in summer, if you fancy a drink in the sun.

Franz y Peppone 9 de Julio and Belgrano ⓣ0299/448-2299. Next door to *La Nonna Francesca* and on a similar theme, though aimed more squarely at those on a backpacker's budget.

La Nonna Francesca 9 de Julio 56 ⓣ0299/430-0930. Pizza, pasta and all things Italian in this atmospheric if slightly pricey trattoria. Large portions mean you won't go hungry.

Rosignano Independencia and Buenos Aires. Hugely popular deli and takeout joint (there's no room for eating in) packed with office workers at lunch time. Varied and inventive menu includes fish, vegetarian offerings and grilled meats.

Sherlock Holmes Pub Restaurant Buenos Aires 133 ⓣ0299/442-5520. British-style pub lunches and all night drinking. With a menu of over a hundred cocktails, there is enough choice to keep even serious drinkers occupied for several nights.

Listings

Airlines Aerolíneas Argentinas, Santa Fe 52 ⓣ0299/447-2656.

Arts and crafts Artesanías Neuquinas, San Martín 57 (Mon–Fri 8.30am–8.30pm, Sat 9.30am–2pm), a nonprofit organization. There's also a branch at the airport.

Banks and exchanges Among the many banks with ATMs, Banco de la Provincia, Av Argentina 13 (April–Nov 8am–1pm, Dec–March 7am–1pm), changes traveller's cheques. There's also Cambio Pullman, Alcorta 144 ⓣ0299/442-8304.

Car rental Avis (ⓣ0299/444-1297) and Europcar (ⓣ0299/444-0146) both have offices at the airport, the latter with an unlimited mileage package. Centrally, Alamo, Perticone 465 (ⓣ0299/443-5700) and Neuquén, José Rosa and Perticone (ⓣ0299/448-1666) are reliable.

Consulate Chile, La Rioja 241 ⓣ0299/442-2727.

Hospitals Hospital Regional Neuquén, Buenos Aires 421 ⓣ0299/449-0800; Hospital Bouquet Roldán, Tte. Planas 1555 ⓣ0299/443-1328. Polyclínico ADOS, Av Argentina 1000 (ⓣ0299/442-4110), is a private clinic with some English-speaking doctors.

Internet access Abundant, including at Av Olascoaga 331 (open 24hr).

Laundry RapiLav, Independencia 326 on Parque Central.
Pharmacy Farmacia del Pueblo, San Martín 99 (ⓣ0299/442-4032), is open 24hr.
Police Jefatura, Richieri 775 ⓣ0299/442-4100; ⓣ101 for emergencies.
Post office Correo, Rivadavia and Santa Fe (Mon–Sat 8am–2pm & 4–8pm).
Travel agents Sebastian & Co, Santa Fe 64 ⓣ0299/442-3592.

The dinosaur sites around Neuquén

Since 1988, the area around Neuquén has become a hotbed of activity, with paleontologists here uncovering **fossils** of both the largest herbivorous sauropod and the largest carnivorous dinosaur ever found. As you head west out of Neuquén towards the sites of discovery it is easy to imagine dinosaurs roaming the stunted plains and pterodactyls launching themselves into the air from the imposing cliff-faces.

Seventy-nine kilometres southwest from Neuquén along RN-237, on the banks of the picturesque Embalse Ezequiel Ramos Mexía hydroelectric reservoir, is the little oasis of **Villa El Chocón**. Small and trim, the town is a purpose-built company settlement originally intended to house the workers on the vast neighbouring dam, whose turbines supply up to thirty percent of the country's electricity. It's the **Museo Municipal Ernesto Bachmann** (daily 8am–9pm; $1) here that holds the town's showpiece attraction – a virtually complete, 100-million-year-old skeleton of *Giganotosaurus cardinii*, discovered 18km away in 1993. This fearsome creature puts even *Tyrannosaurus rex* in the shade: it measured a colossal 13m long (its skull alone accounting for 1.8m), stood 4.7m tall and weighed an estimated eight tonnes. Cono Sur run buses to El Chocón from the Neuquén bus terminal, but getting there and back in one day can be difficult, as departure and return times are inconvenient. If you find yourself stranded, the **tourist office** (ⓣ0299/490-1230; 8am–7pm) at the entrance to town can help you find family **accommodation** if necessary. On the hill opposite the tourist office is a dinosaur dig, which you can visit with a guide in summer ($25).

Three kilometres further south along RN-237, a left turn-off leads another 2km down to the shores of Embalse Ezequiel Ramos Mexía. Here, at the northwest corner of the lake, is the **Parque Cretácico**, where you'll find some huge, astonishingly well-preserved **dinosaur footprints**. Not realizing what they were, fishermen once used these as barbecue pits. The footprints resemble those of a giant rhea, but were probably left by an iguanadon – a ten-metre-long herbivore – or some kind of bipedal carnivore. Other kidney-shaped prints are of four-footed sauropods, and smaller prints were probably left by three-metre long theropods. Should you decide to linger, there's a pleasant **campsite** at *Club Chocón Lauquén* (ⓣ0299/156-304909; $10 per tent plus $4 per person) with tennis courts and a swimming pool (open Dec–March). The only hotel in town is the *Posada del Dinosaurio* (ⓣ0299/490-1200, ⓦwww.posadadinosaurio.com.ar; ❼), which has large, airy rooms and a decent restaurant.

Plaza Huincul, just over 110km west of Neuquén along RN-22, is where the region's petroleum reserves were discovered in 1918. Memorabilia from those pioneering days is displayed at the **Museo Carmen Funes** on the main street (Mon–Fri 9am–7.30pm, Sat & Sun 9am–8.30pm; $1), though you'll find it impossible to concentrate on petroleum with the full-size reconstruction of *Argentinosaurus huinculensis* looming in the hangar next door. Walking between the legs of this beast – 40m long, 18m high and weighing 100 tonnes – is a bit like walking under a jumbo jet. The only fossils of this giant beast that have been found are the pelvis, tibia, sacrum and some vertebrae – the reconstruction of the rest of the animal is based on educated guesswork. María del Carmen Gravino, who was responsible for the reproduction, also worked on dinosaur models for the film *Jurassic Park*. Gravino lives at Perito Moreno 155 (☎0299/496-2116), and he usually has smaller, equally realistic pieces for sale at his museum. From Neuquén, the easiest way to Plaza Huincul is on the Zapala bus from the terminal (Centenario, El Petróleo or Cono Sur hourly). Though you won't want to linger in town, if necessary there's **accommodation** at *Hotel Tunquelén*, Alberdi 1553 (☎0299/496-3423; ❸); the **tourist office** on the main street (daily 8am–8pm) can also help you find family lodging.

Heading northwest from Neuquén approximately 90km along RP-51 or RP-7 brings you to the shores of **Embalse Cerros Colorados**, where you can watch paleontologists at work on the **"Dino Project"** at Lago Barreales (☎0299/154-048614, Ⓦwww.proyectodino.com.ar). Considered a "complete ecosystem of the Mesozoic era", the project, overseen by the University of Comahue, gives you the chance to help with the excavation. The most important finds are displayed at the on-site museum.

Further afield, 250km northwest of Neuquén along RP-8, is the isolated town of **Rincón de los Sauces**, home to the **Museo Argentino Urquiza** (Mon–Fri 8am–6pm; ☎0299/488-6643). The collection features the only known fossils of a titanosaurus, including an almost complete specimen, but what makes the trip worthwhile are the fossilized set of titanosaur eggs from nearby Auca Mahuida. The first set of **dinosaur eggs** ever to be found, they are approximately 14cm in diameter and have thin, porous shells through which the embryonic dinosaurs are thought to have breathed. **Accommodation** in town is limited and pricey, but a decent option is *Hotel Express* (☎0299/488-6870, Ⓦwww.ehotelexpress.com; ❼), at Gregorio Alvarez y San Martin.

Zapala and the Parque Nacional Laguna Blanca

ZAPALA, 150km west of Neuquén, sits at the confluence of two *ruta nacionales* (22 and 40) and two *ruta provinciales* (13 and 46), all four of which converge on the **Plazoleta Central**, marked by its scale monument of an immigrant family with an ox-cart. It is a depressingly grey and lifeless town that serves mainly as a transport hub for northern Neuquén and as a base for visiting **PARQUE NACIONAL LAGUNA BLANCA**. The park was originally set up to protect breeding colonies of Black-necked Swans, but the human introduction of a voracious species of native perch to the lake have all but wiped out the huge flocks of waterfowl that once inhabited it. Smaller numbers of swans and flamingoes can still be seen on the perch-free smaller satellite lakes off the northern site of the main laguna, but it's a considerable and often very windy hike to get there and you should consult with park guards before attempting it.

Practicalities

Buses arrive at Zapala's **bus terminal**, at the corner of Etcheluz and Ejército Argentino. The **tourist information** office is well outside town on RN-22 at Km1389 (summer daily 7am–10pm, winter Sat & Sun 7am–11pm; ☎02942/424296, Ⓦwww.zapala.ar), while the park's **information office** is at Ejército Argentino 260 (Mon–Fri 8.30am–2.30pm; ☎02942/431982). In a futile effort to control the perch, an open-fishing season has been declared, with permits available from the park office and no catch limit. Radio Taxi Lihuén (☎02942/430300), opposite the bus terminal, will run you to the park.

Otherwise, buses headed for Aluminé pass the laguna, though getting back to Zapala is more difficult, as they follow a circuitous one-way route.

It's all too easy to get stuck in Zapala, and **accommodation** can be hard to find. The best budget option is at *CIRSE*, six blocks northeast of the terminal, at Italia 139 (Ⓣ&Ⓕ02942/431891; ❷); this is a police officers' hotel with clean rooms for up to four people. Two blocks east of the terminal are the *Coligueo*, Etcheluz 155 (Ⓣ02942/421308; ❸ including breakfast), with dreary, run-down rooms, and the much better *Pehuén*, Etcheluz and Elena de la Vega (Ⓣ&Ⓕ02942/423135; ❸ including breakfast), which is clean, quiet and hospitable. *Hue Melén*, Almirante Brown 929 (Ⓣ02942/422407, Ⓦwww.interpatagonia.com/huemelen/index.html; ❺) is Zapala's largest hotel, and includes breakfast in its rates.

Northern Neuquén

Northern Neuquén is a remote and fiercely traditional region that rewards tourists who make the considerable effort required to visit. The most popular destination here is the area around **Volcán Copahue**, with its twin resorts of **Caviahue** and **Copahue**. Further north, the scenery around the market town of **Chos Malal** becomes more reminiscent of Mendoza than Patagonia.

The Mapuche

Knowing themselves as the people (*che*) of the earth (*Mapu*), the **Mapuche** were, before the arrival of the Spanish in the sixteenth century, a loose confederation of tribal groups who lived exclusively on the Chilean side of the cordillera. The aspiring conquistadors knew them as Araucanos, and so feared their reputation as indomitable and resourceful warriors that they abandoned attempts to subjugate them and opted instead for a policy of containment. Encroachments into Araucania sparked a series of Mapuche migrations eastwards into territory that is now Argentina, and they soon became the dominant force in northern Patagonia east of the Andes, their cultural and linguistic influence spreading far beyond their territories.

By the eighteenth century, four major Mapuche tribes had established territories in Argentina: the **Picunche**, or "the people of the north", who lived near the arid cordillera in the far north of Neuquén; the **Pehuenche**, or "the people of the monkey puzzle trees", dominant in the central cordillera; the **Huilliche**, or "the people of the south" (also called Manzaneros; see p.623), of the southern cordillera region based around Lago Nahuel Huapi; and the **Puelche**, or "the people of the east", who inhabited the river valleys of the steppe. These groups spoke different dialects of **Mapudungun**, a tongue that belongs to the Arawak group of languages. Lifestyles were based around a combination, in varying proportions, of nomadic hunter-gathering, rearing livestock and the cultivation of small plots around settlements of *rucas* (family homes that were thatched usually with reeds). Communities were headed by a *lonco*, or cacique, but the "medicine-men", or *machis*, also played an influential role.

The arrival of the Spanish influenced Mapuche culture most significantly with the introduction of **horses and cattle**. Horses enabled tribes to be vastly more mobile, and hunting techniques changed, with the Mapuche adopting their trademark lances in lieu of the bow and arrow. As importantly, the herds of wild horses and cattle that spread across the Argentine pampas became a vital trading commodity.

Relations between the Mapuche and the Hispanic *criollos* in both Chile and Argentina varied: periods of warfare and indigenous raids on white settlements were

Exploring the mountainous area around **Andacollo** is not easy, even if you have your own transport (4WD is recommended) – roads are very dusty, and livestock wander freely, particularly the ubiquitous **angora goats**.

Chos Malal

Strategically situated near the confluence of the rivers Neuquén and Curi Leuvú, **CHOS MALAL** – which means Yellow Corral in Mapuche (see box below) – is the oldest surviving white settlement in Neuquén. It served as the provincial capital from its founding in 1887 – when General Uriburu stationed the Fourth Division of Roca's troops here during the Campaign of the Desert – to 1904. You'll need to pass through here if heading to the Andacollo region, but there's little to see. The main attraction lies northwest of town, overlooking the Plaza San Martín – here, on a landscaped rocky outcrop, stands the original **fort**, a protected historical monument. It comprises the surprisingly informative little **Museo Olascoaga** (Tues–Fri 7am–2pm; free), with a fine analysis of the Campaign of the Desert, and the **Torreón**, a whitewashed tower and lookout point with views of the Río Curi Leuvú valley. An interesting day-trip 31km along RN-43 and RN-41 is the archeological site of **Caepe Malal**. Discovered in 1984, it is an extensive aboriginal burial ground dating back to the eighteenth century in which a number of important artefacts relating to the Pehuenche group (see box below) have been found.

interspersed with times of relatively peaceful coexistence. By the end of the eighteenth century, the relationship had matured into a surprisingly symbiotic one, with the two groups meeting at joint *parlamentos* where grievances would be aired and terms of trade regulated. Tensions increased after Argentina gained its independence from Spain, and the Mapuche resisted a military campaign organized against them by the dictator Rosas in the early 1830s, but they were finally crushed by Roca's Campaign of the Desert in 1879. The military humiliation of the Argentine Mapuche nation was completed with the surrender, in 1885, of Valentín Sayhueque, dynastic head of the Manzaneros. Following that, Mapuche communities were split up, forcibly relocated and "reduced" onto reservations, often on some of the most marginal lands available.

Nevertheless, today the Mapuche remain one of Argentina's **principal indigenous peoples**, with a population of some forty thousand divided among communities dotted around the provinces of Buenos Aires, La Pampa, Chubut, Río Negro and, above all, Neuquén. Most families still earn their livelihood from mixed animal farming, but increasingly, Mapuche communities are embarking on tourist-related ventures. These include opening campsites; establishing points of sale for home-made cheese or *artesanía* such as their fine woven goods, distinctive silver jewellery, ceramics and wood-carvings; offering guided excursions; or receiving small tour groups.

Today Mapuche culture is not as visibly distinct in Argentina as it is in Chile – you will not find elderly women dressed day-to-day in old-style traditional outfits in Argentina. Political organization is also less developed; nevertheless, the Mapuche are one of Argentina's best-organized indigenous groups. The **Nguillatún** – a religious ritual which aimed to root out evil and ensure good harvests – is still practised in some Argentine Mapuche communities. After decades of being in steep decline, there is some evidence too that there may be a reawakening of interest in such ceremonies. The *rehue* (Mapuche altar) at Ñorquinco (see p.600), for example, stood neglected between 1947 and 2000, when the first Nguillatún in fifty years was held, attended by Mapuche delegations from both sides of the border.

Practicalities

The **bus terminal** is southeast of town; to get to the centre from the terminal, head one block southwest along Calle Neuquén and turn right onto Sarmiento. Ten blocks along from here you get to the Plaza San Martín, where there's a **tourist office**, 25 de Mayo 89 (daily 8am–10pm; ⓣ02948/421425). **Accommodation** is cheap. Two and a half blocks southeast of the plaza is the comfortably equipped *Hostería Anlu*, Lavalle 60 (ⓣ02948/421109; ④), with a/c and free covered parking. More economical is *Residencial Baalback*, 25 de Mayo 920 (ⓣ02948/421495; ③). The municipal **campsite** is three blocks northeast of the main plaza on the route to Andacollo ($8 per pitch), by the bridge over the Río Curi Leuvú. *El Viejo Caicallén*, General Paz 345 (ⓣ02948/421373), serves a filling *parrilla* and home-made pasta. During early November the **Fiesta del Chivito** (Kid Festival) gives you the chance to sample the area's fabulous roast goat.

Andacollo and around

ANDACOLLO is a dusty mining town on the shores of the silty Río Neuquén, in a rugged bowl of infertile beige mountains. It serves as a base for adventures into the cordillera to the north and west, though you'll need your own transport to explore these areas. Its sister town of **Huingancó** is 6km away, in a fold of the mountains at the foot of the dramatic **Cordillera del Viento**, a range that is both higher at this point (almost 3000m) and older than the parallel Andes. Huingancó is characterized by its plantations of pines, so it's perhaps not surprising to find a tiny museum dedicated to trees, the **Museo del Arbol y de la Madera** (Mon–Fri 1–5pm, Sat & Sun 3–6pm; ⓣ02948/499059). The museum's collection of cross-slices of different regional trees includes one from a cypress felled by wind in nearby Cañada Molina that was more than 1200 years old.

The **bus** from Chos Malal drops you by the YPF fuel station in Andacollo at Valvarco and Nahueve, outside *Hostería La Secuoya* (ⓣ&ⓕ02948/494007; ④), which has good, airy rooms but is usually full. In fact, there's very little **accommodation** in Andacollo, so if you're planning on staying here it's best to book well in advance. The municipal **campsite** (ⓣ02948/494205; $10 per person; no services April–Nov) has a swimming pool and a shop and is 1km past the village, just after the bridge over the Río Neuquén (the bus heading from Chos Malal to Las Ovejas will drop you here). There's a **tourist office** in the Municipalidad at Nahueve 194 (Mon–Fri 8am–2pm; ⓣ02948/494205). For **food**, try *El Torreón* (ⓣ02948/494002), the restaurant at the *Hosteria Andacollo*.

Lagunas de Epulafquen and Volcán Domuyo

The most interesting trip from Andacollo is to the **LAGUNAS DE EPULAFQUEN**, a pair of Andean lakes 70km to the northwest that have been made into a protected nature reserve. Lago Superior is particularly beautiful, with a cinematic backdrop: a deeply notched cliff-face, a series of shelving platforms of tousled low Andean woodland and a small waterfall; the lake's startling turquoise colour is best seen in the morning. The area was the site of the 1832 battle in which the last Spanish royalists were defeated, finally liberating the continent from Spanish rule. **Camping** along the lakeshore is free, but you'll need to bring all your own supplies.

A second excursion takes you to **thermal springs** on the bald slopes of hump-backed **VOLCÁN DOMUYO** – at 4702m, officially the highest peak in Patagonia. This trip is more rewarding for the spectacular views of the bleak and barren scenery than for the springs themselves. En route, you pass through the village of **Las Ovejas**, and, 25km further on, the hamlet of **Vavarco**, where the beige Río Vavarco splices dramatically with the turquoise Río Neuquén. The centrally located **tourist office** (☎02948/421329) has a list of guides for climbs up the volcano. Continuing on is the **Cajón del Atreuco** and **Los Bolillos** – bizarrely eroded formations of volcanic tufa stone. You arrive at the hot springs, 36km from Vavarco, at the isolated **Termas Domuyo** complex, which rents **cabins** with kitchens and cooking utensils, though no electricity (☎0299/449-6388; closed April–Nov; ❺ for up to eight people); bring sleeping bags and non-perishable food. **Camping** and drinking water are free.

It's a three-day excursion for **climbers** heading for the summit of **Domuyo** (altitude sickness is a real possibility; see p.66). You can hire guides in Vavarco to organize horses for the full-day journey from near the complex to base camp, where most people rest a day to acclimatize. From base camp, you can climb to the summit and get back down again in a day.

Loncopué, Caviahue and Copahue

Heading northwest from Zapala along RN-40 you reach the uninteresting junction town of Las Lajas after 55km. Here you have a choice: 160km to the northeast lies Chos Malal (see p.591), or you can continue a further 68km in a northwesterly direction along RP-21 to the village of **LONCOPUÉ**, a farming town with a fiercely traditional indigenous population. The crafts fair held here on weekends is locally famous for the quality of the workmanship, seen especially in the *telares verticales*, wall-cloths that retain a pre-Hispanic style.

From here it is a 52-kilometre drive and 800-metre ascent along RP-21 before you reach **CAVIAHUE**. A small, sprawling town of tin-roofed houses, it lies in a bowl of low hills, on the shores of **Lago Caviahue**, also known as Lago Agrio ("Bitter Lake") due to its sulphurous waters. The peeled aridity of the slopes here is broken by groups of araucaria, which are reflected picturesquely in the lake whenever the sky assumes its usual clear diaphanous blue. A series of exquisite **waterfalls** in the surroundings make for pleasant day-trips, though you will need your own transport to get to most of them. The most worthwhile is the **Siete Cascadas** route along the Arroyo Agrio, with its entrancing scenes of cascades plunging over columned basalt rock. The initial section of the route (approximately 45min) is well marked, and takes you past four or five falls, including the stunning Cabellera de la Virgen (25m) and up to the Cascada del Gigante (8m), set by a clump of *ñire* trees. To see all seven falls, it's best to go by horse or mountain bike, which can be rented locally. Northeast of Caviahue, 16km away and signposted 2km to the left of RP-27, is the **Salto del Agrio**, an impressive 70m waterfall that plunges off a basalt terrace. Caviahue has some **skiing** in winter, but it's better for scenic cross-country options (16km of trails) than downhill (5km of pistes).

Tiny **COPAHUE**, whose name means "place of sulphur" or "place where you collect water" in Mapudungun, is 19km north of Caviahue, further up the slopes of Volcán Copahue and above the tree line. The Mapuche have long praised and sampled the health-giving qualities of its **thermal springs** and mineral mud baths, hyped in tourist brochures as being "the best in the world". In reality, it's a dated assemblage of overpriced hotels, though the swirling clouds of steam rising from its pools and the amphitheatre setting gives the place some atmosphere. A $12-million investment in thermal under-street heating (the only system of its kind in the world) means the resort can remain open year-round. The central feature is the **Complejo Termal** (mid-Nov to Semana Santa daily 8am–9pm; Ⓦwww.termasdecopahue.com), where you can indulge in a multitude of saunas, hydro-massage tanks, swimming baths and mud baths. Laguna Verde is cold but free, while Laguna del Chancho represents decent value.

The area around the resorts of Caviahue and Copahue is a provincial reserve, established principally to protect the country's northernmost stands of **araucaria** woodland. These grow largely on the slopes of the domed shield volcano, **Volcán Copahue** (2953m), the summit of which marks the border with Chile. Between January and March, you can **climb** Volcán Copahue from either Copahue or Caviahue (6hr). The crater makes for a rewarding and unusual sight, as glacial ice often reaches right up to the crater lake, despite the water being thermally heated to between 20°C and 70°C. Ask at the tourist office in Caviahue for guides.

Practicalities

In Caviahue, Centenario **buses** stop in front of *Hotel Instituto*, on the RP-21 through town. Buses continue to Copahue, or you can take a *remise*. On entering the village, you'll pass the **tourist office** (daily 8am–9pm; ⓣ02948/495036, ⓦwww.caviahue-copahue.com.ar). There's also a small office of Club Andino at Las Lengas (ⓣ02948/495081) that can help with trekking arrangements.

As for **accommodation**, half- or full board is offered in many places in high season. In Caviahue, the most luxurious place is the large *Apart Hotel Lago Caviahue* fronting the lake (ⓣ&ⓕ02948/495110, ⓦwww.hotellagocaviahue.com; ❻), with optional full board in high season. *Hotel Caviahue*, 8 de Abril s/n (ⓣ&ⓕ02948/449638; ❻), imports thermal waters for its bathing rooms and offers discounts from Easter to December. Somewhat cheaper is the log cabin *Refugio de Caniche*, Mapuche s/n (ⓣ02942/15579260; ❸), owned by local guide Vargas Ruben, nicknamed "Caniche". *Camping Hueney* ($8 per person; closed April–Nov) has fairly basic services – just a *confitería* and some toilets – but a pleasant site, 3km out of town on the route to Copahue. In Copahue, the least expensive options are *Bravo Departamentos*, Doucloux s/n (ⓣ02948/495028; closed March–Oct; ❺ for four-person self-catering apartments); *Hostería Pino Azul*, Olascoaga and Doucloux (ⓣ&ⓕ02948/495071; closed Easter–Nov; ❻ with half- and full-board options); and the friendly but rudimentary *Hotel S.U.P.E*, Doucloux s/n (ⓣ02948/495092; ❺ including breakfast). Comfortable

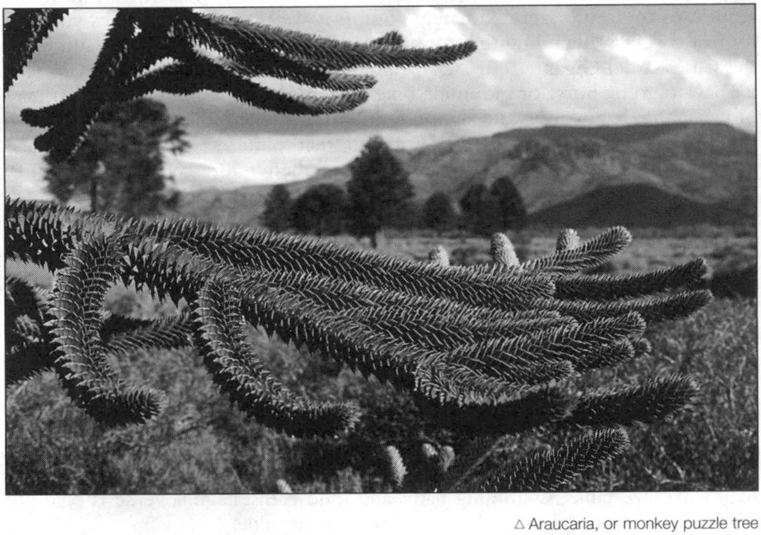

△ Araucaria, or monkey puzzle tree

Valle del Volcán, Doucloux 120 (Ⓣ&Ⓕ02948/495048, Ⓔcopahueclub@sinectis.com.ar; closed May–Oct; ⑥ per person), is one of the few modern places, with satellite TV in the rooms. You can **camp** at *Pino Azul* (Ⓣ02948/495071; closed Easter–Nov; $8 per person).

Parque Nacional Lanín

The most northerly of Patagonia's superb national parks, **PARQUE NACIONAL LANÍN** (Ⓦwww.parquenacionallanin.gov.ar) was formed in 1937 and protects 42,000 hectares of Andean and sub-Andean habitat that ranges from barren, semi-arid steppe in the east to patches of temperate Valdivian rainforest pressed up against the Chilean border. To the south, it adjoins its sister park, the even more colossal Nahuel Huapi, while it also shares a boundary with Parque Nacional Villarrica in Chile.

The great appeal of Parque Lanín lies in its three most characteristic features. The first is the presence of **Mapuche communities** in and around the park (see box, pp.590–591). The second is its geographical centrepiece – the cone of **Volcán Lanín**, which rises to 3776m and dominates the scenery around. This volcano, and the central sector of the park around lakes Huechulafquen, Paimún and Tromen, is best reached from **Junín de los Andes** (see p.602). The park's other trump card is the **araucaria**, or monkey puzzle tree (see box below), which grows as far south as Lago Curruhue Grande, but is especially prevalent in the northern sector of the park, an area known as the **Pehuenia region**. It's not the easiest area of the park to get around, but this makes for fewer visitors and there are some excellent day-treks, some of which can be linked to make a fantastic, if tough, multi-day hike. Most people access this region via Zapala (see p.589).

The araucaria, or monkey puzzle tree

The distinctive and beautiful **araucaria** (*Araucaria araucana*), more commonly known as the **monkey puzzle tree**, is one of the world's most enduring species of trees. It grows naturally only in the cordillera of Neuquén Province and at similar latitudes in Chile, where it favours impoverished volcanic soils at altitudes between 600m and 1800m. This prehistoric survivor has been around for more than one hundred million years.

Araucarias grow incredibly slowly, though they can live for over **1000 years**. Young trees grow in a pyramid shape, but after about a hundred years they start to lose their lower branches and assume their trademark umbrella appearance – mature specimens can reach 45m in height. Their straight trunks are covered by panels of thick bark that provide resistance against fire. The female trees produce huge, head-size cones filled with up to 200 fawn-coloured pinenuts called *piñones*, some 5cm long, and rich in proteins and carbohydrates.

Known to the Mapuche as the *pehuén*, the tree was worshipped as the daughter of the moon. Legend has it that there was a time when the Mapuche, though they adored the *pehuén*, never ate its *piñones*, believing them to be poisonous. This changed, however, during a terrible famine, when their god, Ngüenechén, saved them from starvation by sending a messenger to teach them both the best way of preparing these nutritious seeds (roasting them in embers or boiling), and of storing them (burying them in the earth or snow). *Piñones* became the staple diet of tribes in the area (principally the Pehuenche, named for their dependence on the tree), and have been revered by the Mapuche ever since.

Parque Lanín's lakes, located in the southern sector of the park, drain eastwards, with the exception of Lago Lácar, which drains into the Pacific. This area, along with the famous **Seven Lakes Route** through the north of Nahuel Huapi towards Villa La Angostura and Bariloche, is covered under **San Martín de los Andes** (see p.608). San Martín is by far the more scenic of the two principal towns for accessing the park, but is more expensive than its low-key rival, Junín.

As well as the araucaria, other tree species endemic to the park are the *roble pellí* and the *raulí*, both types of deciduous *Nothofagus* southern beech. Parque Lanín also protects notable forests of *coihue* and, in the drier areas, cypress. Flowers such as the *arvejilla* purple sweet pea and the introduced lupin abound in spring, as does the flame-red *notro* bush. Fuchsia bushes grow in some of the wetter regions.

As for **fauna**, the park is home to a population of *huemules*, a shy and rare deer (see box, p.633). *Pudú*, the tiny native deer, is present but rarely seen. Pumas are also present, but you're more likely to see a coypu, a grey fox or two species introduced for hunting a century ago: the wild boar and the red deer, which roam the semi-arid steppes and hills of the east of the park. Bird-watchers will want to keep an eye out for the active White-throated Treerunner, a bizarre bird with an upturned bill adapted for removing beech nuts, while the acrobatic Thorn-tailed Rayadito is another regional speciality.

The whole park can be covered in snow from May to October, and it can snow in the higher mountain regions at almost any time of year. The **best time to visit** is in spring (especially Oct–Nov) or autumn (March to mid-May), when the deciduous trees adopt a spectacular palette, particularly in the Pehuenia area. Trekking is possible between late October and early May, although the season for some of the higher treks is shorter, usually from December to March. January and February see an influx of Argentine holiday-makers, but in general it is less crowded than Nahuel Huapi even in high season. If you want to hike and can read Spanish, the *Guía Sendas & Bosques de Lanín y Nahuel Huapi* is very useful. Two reasonably reliable maps (1:200,000) accompany the guide.

The Pehuenia Circuit and northern Lanín

The **northern** sector of Parque Nacional Lanín and the adjoining Pehuenia region is one of the least developed and most beautiful areas of the Argentine Lake District. This "forgotten corner" of Mapuche communities, wonderful mountain lakes, basalt cliffs and araucaria forests has largely escaped the commercial pressures found further south in the park system, although locals and recent settlers are fast waking up to its potential and tourists are arriving in ever-increasing numbers. However, infrastructure links are still fairly rudimentary, and having your own transport is a boon – otherwise, you'll need to take a taxi, as there is almost nothing in the way of public transport. Roads branch off RP-23 to the lakes at Quillén (RP-46), Rucachoroi (RP-18) and Ñorquinco (RP-11). One of the most popular routes is the **Pehuenia Circuit**, which links **Villa Pehuenia** on the northern bank of Lago Aluminé with tiny **Moquehue**, at the southwest tip of the lake of the same name, and passes along **Lago Ñorquinco**, the northernmost boundary of the park. Most people finish or start the circuit in **Aluminé**, the region's most important settlement.

The lack of convenient road routes acts as an encouragement to **trek**: there is great potential in the area around Quillén, Moquehue, Ñorquinco and Rucachoroi, but local politics and unreliable weather mean you should carefully discuss your plans and route with local *guardaparques* or, even better, take a guide

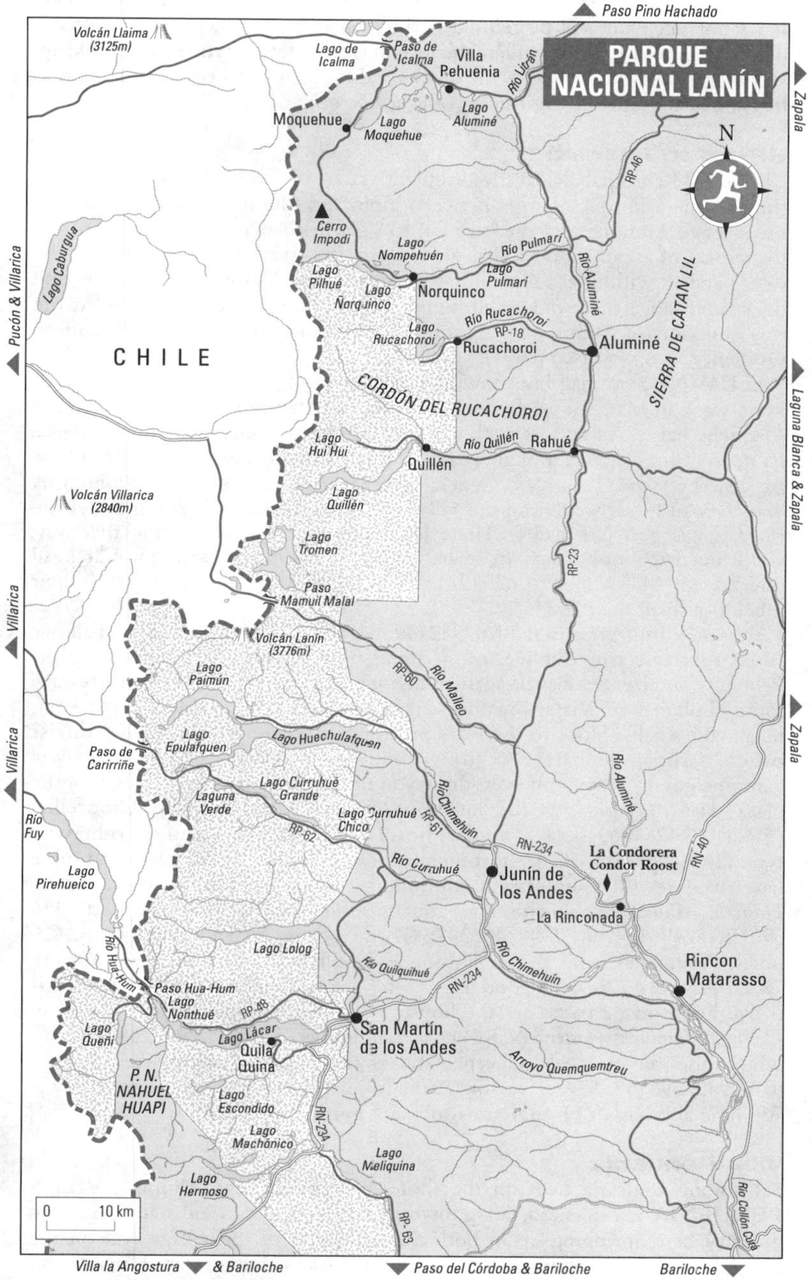
PARQUE NACIONAL LANÍN
N
Paso Pino Hachado
Zapala
Laguna Blanca & Zapala
Zapala
Pucón & Villarica
Villarica
Villarica
Villa la Angostura & Bariloche
Paso del Córdoba & Bariloche
Bariloche
Volcán Llaima (3125m)
Lago de Icalma
Paso de Icalma
Villa Pehuenia
Río Litrán
Lago Aluminé
Moquehue
Lago Moquehue
RP-46
Cerro Impodi
Lago Caburgua
Lago Nompehuén
Río Pulmarí
Lago Pulmarí
Lago Pilhué
Lago Ñorquinco
Ñorquinco
Río Aluminé
SIERRA DE CATAN LIL
Lago Rucachoroi
Río Rucachoroi
RP-18
Rucachoroi
Aluminé
CHILE
CORDÓN DEL RUCACHOROI
Lago Hui Hui
Quillén
Río Quillén
Rahué
Volcán Villarica (2840m)
Lago Quillén
Lago Tromen
RP-23
Paso Mamuil Malal
Volcán Lanín (3776m)
Lago Paimún
RP-60
Río Malleo
Lago Epulafquen
Lago Huechulafquen
Paso de Carirriñe
Lago Curruhué Grande
Laguna Verde
Río Chimehuín
Río Aluminé
Río Fuy
Lago Curruhué Chico
RP-61
RP-62
RN-234
La Condorera Condor Roost
RN-40
Río Curruhué
Junín de los Andes
Lago Pirehueico
La Rinconada
Río Hua-Hum
Lago Lolog
Río Quilquihué
Río Chimehuín
Rincon Matarasso
Paso Hua-Hum
Lago Nonthué
RN-234
RP-48
Lago Queñi
Lago Lácar
San Martín de los Andes
Quila Quina
Arroyo Quemquemtreu
P. N. NAHUEL HUAPI
Lago Escondido
RN-234
Lago Machónico
Lago Meliquina
Lago Hermoso
0 10 km
RP-63
Río Collón Curá

who knows the area. Remember that it is obligatory to register your departure with a *guardaparque* before setting out and clock in your arrival at the other end. If it's not safe, you will be refused permission to trek. Except for the stretch linking Rucachoroi and Quillén, the terrain is also ideal for **mountain-biking**, and there's tremendous scope for other outdoor activities here as well, such as **horse-riding** and **rafting** through the scenic gorge of the Río Aluminé.

RP-23 to Aluminé

The **RP-23** runs parallel to the turbulent waters of the Río Aluminé, carving through the arid rocky gorges between Junín and Aluminé, before continuing on to Lago Aluminé and the turn-off to Villa Pehuenia, and passing through the groves of araucaria trees that grow along the river's upper reaches. To the east, parallel with the valley, lies the **Sierra de Catan Lil**, a harsh and desiccated range that's older and higher than the neighbouring Andes. At the tiny junction of **Rahue**, 16km south of Aluminé, RP-46 branches off to Quillén, 25km west (see p.601).

ALUMINÉ is a small but growing riverside town with a gentle pace of life. For a week in March it celebrates the **Fiesta del Pehuén** to coincide with the Mapuche harvest of *piñones*, with displays of horsemanship, music and *artesanía*. Its main claim to fame, though, is as a summer **rafting centre**: organized trips are run by *Servicio Amuyén*, General Villegas 348 (ⓣ&ⓕ02942/496368). A branch road heads west from the village to Rucachoroi and (28km away) the *guardaparque* post (see p.601). There is no public transport heading that way; you'll need to book a taxi (ⓣ02942/496397 or 496200) or inquire at local travel agent Mali Viajes (ⓣ02942/15-662984) about group transport – their office is just off the plaza.

Aluminé's **bus terminal** (ⓣ02942/496041) is on Avenida 4 de Caballería. Albus runs two daily services on a circuit from Zapala, via Aluminé to Villa Pehuenia, and back to Zapala again. Only one overnight service runs the reverse route, though Mali Viajes organize day-trips to Villa Pehuenia. From the bus terminal it's half a block to the Plaza San Martín, where you'll find the **tourist office**, Cristian Joubert 326 (daily 8am–10pm; ⓣ02942/496001, ⓦwww.alumine.gov.ar). Just about everything you need is within a block or two of the plaza. *Hotel Pehuenia*, at the junction of RP-23 and Capitán Crouzeilles (ⓣ&ⓕ02942/496340; ❻), is a resort **hotel** a little out of place in the otherwise typically Patagonian village. Its rooms are comfortable, if a little twee, and some have river views. The hotel rents out mountain bikes and arranges horse-riding. *Hostería Aluminé*, opposite the tourist office at Cristian Joubert 336 (ⓣ02942/496174, ⓕ02942/496347; ❺), is a clean, straightforward ex-ACA hotel, though it's a bit pricey for single travellers. The adjacent **restaurant**, *La Posteria del Rey*, is a good place to try a sort of *piñones* paté, while imaginative home-made pastas are the house speciality. Basic but better value than *Hostería Aluminé* is *Hostería Nid-Car*, Cristian Joubert 559 (ⓣ02942/496131; ❹), which also serves meals. Cheaper still is the pleasant **campsite**, *La Anita* (ⓣ02942/496158; $7 per person), 2km from the southern entrance to town. Aluminé also has a YPF **fuel station** and a **bank** with ATM.

Villa Pehuenia

Set among araucaria trees on the shores of pristine Lago Aluminé, **VILLA PEHUENIA** is a splendid, fast-growing holiday village. *Cabañas* are the boom industry here, springing up in both the main part of the village and on the lumpy, tree-covered peninsula that juts into the lake's chilly waters. High-season prices start around $250 for up to eight people. To the north is **Volcán Batea**

Mahuida, a mountain that has a minuscule Mapuche-run ski resort and a picturesque crater lake.

The well-informed **tourist office** (summer 9am–9pm, winter 10am–6pm; ⓣ02942/498011; ⓦwww.villapehuenia.gov.ar) is at Km11 on the main road to Aluminé. From here it is 700m to the commercial centre – a cluster of buildings that sell food and other provisions. If you're walking around town, note that there are no street names and that the map provided by the tourist office lacks distinguishing features. You can also take a taxi; try *Remise Pehuenia* (ⓣ02942/498033).

Camping Lagrimitas (ⓣ02942/498003; $10 per person plus $2 per tent; ❻ for apartments for five or six people) has some fantastic, tranquil pitches beneath araucarias by the lakeshore. The higher-end **accommodation** is on the peninsula, a picturesque twenty-minute walk from the main village. The best lodging is at the luxurious *Posada La Escondida* (ⓣ02942/156-91166, ⓦwww.posadalaescondida.com.ar; ❾), on the west coast of the peninsula. The suite-like rooms all have their own sun-decks. *Cabañas Caren* (ⓣ02942/155-801227, ⓦwww.cabanascaren.com.ar) rents well-designed luxury cabins with fully equipped kitchen for up to five people (❽), though there is a minimum stay of five nights. Nearby is the excellent *Hostería La Serena* (ⓣ02942/156-65068, ⓦwww.complejolaserena.com.ar; open Dec–April only), a well-designed, rustic hotel with wonderful views and *cabañas* for up to eight people (❼–❽).

Following the road that runs by the side of the tourist office and then branches left at the lake brings you to a cluster of **eating options** – besides the hotel restaurants there is little else on the peninsula. Try *Anhedonia* (ⓣ02942/156-69846) for fondue, or *Iñaki* (ⓣ02942/498047), which has more of a pub-type atmosphere.

Moquehue and around

Villa Pehuenia is connected to the pioneer village of **MOQUEHUE** by an unsurfaced road (15km) that runs around the northwestern shores of **Lago Moquehue**, Lago Aluminé's sibling. The two lakes are joined at La Angostura by a twenty-metre-wide, five-hundred-metre-long channel of captivating turquoise waters. Just west of La Angostura, a turn-off leads 4km to the **Paso de Icalma** (1303m), the pass closest to Temuco in Chile. A mere 30km past the border, you can access the Parque Nacional Conguillío, centred on imposing **Volcán Llaima** (3125m). There is no public transport to Moquehue – you'll need to have your own car or organize a taxi from Villa Pehuenia.

A loose conglomeration of farmsteads set in a broad pastoral valley at the southwestern end of its lake, Moquehue is overlooked on both sides by splendid ranks of rugged, forested ranges and **Cerro Bella Durmiente**, so named because the summit supposedly looks like the profile of a sleeping beauty. As yet, there's none of the contrived feel that comes from an excess of holidaymakers, and most residents have deep roots here. There is also no electricity in the village, though some places have generators. The *Hostería Bella Durmiente* (ⓣ02942/496172; closed June–Aug, reserve in advance in Jan; ❹) is a wonderfully authentic, wood-built guesthouse with a camping option and commanding vistas of the scenery. There is another **campsite**, *Camping Trenel* (ⓣ02942/156-64720; $8 per person), at the southeast corner of the lake on a slightly raised area with glorious views. Owner Fernando López is a well-known hiking guide in the area.

Unguided **hiking** around Moquehue has created local political problems, with landowners complaining that hikers ignore private-property signs and are causing damage to the countryside. While the effects of hiking are probably exaggerated, the depth of feeling is not, and the tourist office strongly recommends that any hiking in the area be accompanied by an authorized guide. Guides are available through LM Aventura (☎02942/156-64705). Other outdoor activities (lake excursions, mountain-biking, trekking, etc) can be arranged through Mundo Creativo (☎02942/156-66654).

There are some excellent walks nearby: one short leg-stretch (35min one way) leads to an attractive **waterfall** in mystical mixed araucaria woodland; longer options include a hike up **Cerro Bandera** (2hr one way), with excellent views to Volcán Llaima. One of the best day-hikes takes you around the southeastern shores of **Lago Moquehue**, through land belonging to the **Puel Mapuche** community (you must be accompanied by a guide for this hike). The trail leads past several Puel farmsteads as well as diminutive, secluded lakes, including Cari Laufquén, and beautiful woodland of *ñire*, *radal*, *notro*, araucaria and *coihue*.

Lago Ñorquinco

From Moquehue, a wide dirt road runs 31km to **LAGO ÑORQUINCO**, the northern border of Parque Nacional Lanín and 1060m above sea level. There's no public transport along this route, and little other traffic. On the way there are good views of peaks along the Chilean border and mountainsides half-clad in araucaria. **Cerro Impodi** (2100m) is an impressive silvery-grey massif of bare rock halfway along the route. South of Impodi, a waterfall gushes on the eastern side of the road and further on there are some stunning, sheer **basalt cliffs** topped by araucaria, at the foot of which runs the Arroyo Remeco. Much of this region formed the focus for a heated dispute in the 1990s, when Mapuche groups tried, unsuccessfully, to reclaim land that had been ceded to the private Pulmarí Corporation and which passed into government hands during the Perón administration.

At the west end of Lago Ñorquinco is a signposted turn-off to a free national park **campsite** (no services), from where a track runs around the south of the lake to the *guardaparque* post. Alternatively, stay on the main road and pass small **Lago Nompehuén**, which is good for fishing, to get to *Eco Camping* (☎02942/496155; $8 per person; closed mid-April to mid-Nov), a beautiful lakeside site run on commendably rigorous environmental lines that outclasses almost anything else in the country. They sell fishing permits, and guided hikes and horse rides are also available in peak season. There are two lakeside cabins (3), and the restaurant offers excellent home-made meals.

The *guardaparque* will inform you of walks in the area, including a one-hour route that visits three waterfalls, and one to see the only surviving **rehue**, or Mapuche altar, *in situ* in Argentina. A cypress post crudely carved into the shape of a man, and badly weathered, the *rehue* stood unused from 1947 until 2000, when the first Nguillatún prayer ceremony in fifty years was held here (see box, p.591).

Trekking to Lago Rucachoroi

There's a beautiful full-day **trek** from Lago Ñorquinco to **LAGO RUCACHOROI**, taking you past some of the best araucaria forests you can access. A day or two before starting out ask at the Ñorquinco *guardaparque* post for advice and a guide – you should not attempt this walk without one. The trails are little-used and frequently overgrown and no up-to-date maps are currently available for the route, which involves traversing a high pass between **Cerro Liuco** (1964m) to the west, and **Cerro Clucnú Chumpirú** (2192m) to the east, before continuing alongside the **Río Coloco** and passing a spectacular thirty-metre **waterfall**. Snow can be expected as late as December. It's best to start the walk early (preferably by 7am), so you're not climbing the pass in the midday heat. The walk eventually brings you to the *Seccional Rucachoroi* **guardaparque** post.

Rucachoroi

RUCACHOROI, a farming settlement strung out for several kilometres on either side of RP-18, is the heart of the Aigo Mapuche community, with a population of around seven hundred. There's no real centre, and not much of a definite beginning or end – the westernmost farmsteads lie within Parque Nacional Lanín's boundaries. Bordering the region to the south is the **Cordón Rucachoroi**, with peaks over 2100m. A trail leads from behind the *guardaparque* post here to Quillén (see below), but it's not advisable to try it without a guide. Consult the *guardaparque* about conditions and guiding possibilities.

Rucachoroi's only **shop** lies 5km east of the *guardaparque* post and offers succulent home-made chorizos that are ideal for barbecuing. Nearby, an outlet sells **artesanía** made by the locals. There is no accommodation in town, but you can camp for free near the lake. To get there, other than on foot, you'll need to catch a **taxi** from Aluminé (☎02942/496397 or 496200).

Quillén

The tiny settlement of **QUILLÉN**, near the eastern tip of **Lago Quillén**, has the atmosphere of a very scenic ghost town. No more than a handful of estancia buildings, it once depended on the sawmill that operated here, but it is now a private fishing lodge. The name derives from the Mapuche word *quellén* – their name for the wild strawberries that grow in the region. It has no shops or facilities other than a **public phone** (no international calls) where you can call for a taxi to take you into Aluminé (☎02942/496397 or 496200); there's no public transport.

Some 3km beyond the fishing lodge along the northern bank of the Río Quillén are the buildings of the **guardaparque** post. For information, knock on the door of the main building (8am–10pm), and if no one is in, try one of the neighbouring houses. You must register here for the walk to Rucachoroi (see p.602) and it is also a good place to ask about a guide.

The **lake** itself, shaped like an arm bent at the elbow, is bordered by some of the park's very finest Andean-Patagonian forests and is one of the most beautiful in the region. A deep green when still, its colour darkens in the afternoon, when it often gets very windy. A distinctive phallic rock sticks up at the sky at the top of a high ridge on the southern shore: tastefully called Ponom on maps, its real spelling is *ponan*, the Mapuche word for penis. In the distance, the summit ofVolcán Lanín can be seen poking above an intervening mountain range. There are great views of this from the lovely lakeshore **campsite** *Camping Quillén* (with showers and shop; $6 per person), less than 1km west of the *guardaparque*'s house. A tranquil free site, *Camping Pudú Pudú* (no facilities), is some 5km further down the track.

Apart from the Rucachoroi trek (see p.602), there are two principal **trails**, both of which take the road that forks inland from near the *Pudú Pudú* campsite (4WD preferable), heading for **Lago Hui Hui**, a wild lake hemmed in by an amphitheatre of forest-clad hills and dotted with a couple of small islands. The first option is the walk through to the lake (6km from *Pudú Pudú*; 4hr return). At the low pass, you come to flat pampas and a long line of old tree trunks laid end-to-end which used to act as a corral for oxen. Up above is the **Cerro de la Víbora** (1720m), a mountain whose rocky summit resembles the broad head of a snub-nosed viper. The lake is just past an old disused *guardaparque*'s hut, over a wooden bridge.

The second trail makes for a two-day return hike (10hr each way; return along same route) to the **Añihueraqui** *gendarmería* post, at the far western end of Lago Quillén, by the Chilean border. You'll need prior permission from the *guardaparque* and, if you're planning to continue into Chile, the Quillén *gendarmería* post. A guide is also strongly recommended, as the trail can be overgrown and difficult to find in parts. You'll need to camp at Añihueraqui – one of the wettest regions of the park, with annual rainfall in excess of 4000mm – and on the way you pass through superlative wet temperate forest. This hike is best done late in the summer (Jan–March), as you need to ford a fine fishing stream, the **Arroyo Hui Hui**, which can be more than waist-high outside these months. The local indigenous community offers guided horseback excursions along many of these routes and also fishing trips – ask at *Camping Quillén*. It is not possible to walk right around the lake unless you have prior permission from both the *guardaparque* and the fishing estancia that controls the land on the southern shore.

Quillén to Rucachoroi trek

The trek from Quillén to Rucachoroi (9–10hr) crosses the **Cordón Rucachoroi**, whose highest summit, **Cerro Rucachoroi**, is 2296m above sea level. It gives excellent views of mountains such as **Cerro de la Víbora** and **Cerro Mesa** to the northwest, as well as the unmistakable cone of **Volcán Lanín** to the southwest. Passing through patches of araucaria woodland, the trail is generally well signed with yellow paint blotches on rock, trees and stakes, but you should verify the current state with the *guardaparque*. The hike should only be tackled in summer (Dec–March), as snowfall can obscure parts of the trail in winter, and you should leave as early as possible (the *guardaparque* will insist you depart before 9am) to avoid having to climb to the pass at midday. Bring plenty of water. Ideally, you should ask the *guardaparque* to recommend a guide. There are currently no detailed maps of the route, about the best being the IGM map #3972-23 "Lago Ñorquinco" (1:100,000) – which does not figure the trail (see p.70 for details of IGM maps).

Junín de los Andes and around

Set in a dry, hilly area of the steppe at the foot of the Andes, **JUNÍN DE LOS ANDES** is aptly named – Junín means "grassland" in the Aymara language. It's a relaxed town popular with fishermen, largely due to the rivers in the region

Lanín: a political balancing act

The area forming **Parque Nacional Lanín** was once the heartland of the **Mapuche** and served as the centre of the Pehuenche and their forebears. Lanín, more than any other Argentine park, is where the authorities must engage in a highly complex trade-off between the right of the area's indigenous inhabitants to continue their traditional **lifestyle** and the need to protect a **sensitive ecosystem**. Since 2001, park authorities have operated a joint-management system, called **Co-Manejo**, with the five main Mapuche communities: Aigo, around Lago Rucachoroi; Cayun and Curruhuinca, near Lago Lácar; and the Cañicul and Raquithue communities near Lago Huechulafquen. In practice, it means things such as opening and closing sections or trails are done in consultation with local communities and on some treks a Mapuche guide is obligatory. Many campsites and shops in the park are also Mapuche-run.

that teem with trout. Though not as aesthetically attractive as its bigger neighbour, San Martín de los Andes (see p.608), Junín is immensely likeable, lacking the trappings of a tourist town and the high prices that generally accompany them. It is also better placed for making trips to the central sector of Parque Nacional Lanín (see p.604), especially if you plan to climb Volcán Lanín itself, or to explore the **Lago Huechulafquen** area.

A good time to visit is mid-February, when the **Fiesta del Puestero**, with gaucho events, folklore music in the evenings, *artesanía* and *asados*, takes place. In winter, Junín is also a good alternative base for skiing at **Chapelco**.

Arrival and information

Chapelco **airport** (Ⓣ02972/427636) lies halfway between Junín and San Martín and is shared by the two towns. There are no facilities for arrivals, though a small tourist office does open to meet incoming flights. You'll need to take a *remise* into town; try El Rapido (Ⓣ02972/491666). The RN-234, called Boulevard J.M. Rosas for the stretch through Junín, cuts across the western side of town. All you'll need is to the east of this, including the **bus terminal** (Ⓣ02972/492038), one block over at Olavarría and F.S. Martín. Continue east along Olavarría for two blocks and turn right (south) for one block along Calle San Martín to reach the main square, Plaza San Martín, the hub of the town's activity. Diagonally opposite, at Padre Milanesio and Coronel Suárez, is the **tourist office** (daily 8am–9pm; Ⓣ02972/491160, Ⓦwww.junindelosandes.gov.ar). Almost next door on the Paseo Artesanal is Parque Nacional Lanín's **information office** (Mon–Fri 8am–9pm summer, 8–5pm winter; Ⓣ02972/492748).

Banco de la Provincia, at San Martín and Lamadrid, has an **ATM** and changes Amex traveller's cheques, and there are a couple of **telephone** offices that also provide **Internet** on the main square. The **post office** is at Don Bosco and Coronel Suárez (Mon–Fri 8.30am–1pm & 4–7pm, Sat 9am–1pm). Alquimia, Milanesio 840 (Ⓣ02972/491355; Ⓦwww.alquimiaturismo.com.ar), is a helpful **travel agency** that sells flights and organizes professional day-tours in the region, including one to lakes Huechulafquen and Paimún with a visit to a Mapuche community. They specialize in adventure tourism, such as climbing Lanín (see box, p.607) and rafting on the Río Aluminé, and rent climbing equipment.

Accommodation

Junín's **hotel** tariffs rise slightly in summer, when it's worth reserving a little in advance. There are a couple of good places on the *ruta* a block from the bus terminal; otherwise, head for the streets east of the plaza. A pair of decent **campsites** on an island in the Río Chimehuín are accessed from the eastern extreme of Ginés Ponte, a few blocks from the centre. Both offer similar, shady pitches: the larger and cheaper of the two is *La Isla* (Ⓣ02972/492029; $8 per person). The other, *Camping Laura Vicuña* (Ⓣ02972/491149; $10 per person), also has small apartments for four to seven people (❸–❺). In the summer the town opens a municipal campsite on the Costanera between Olavarria and Lamadrid ($5) that lacks shade and feels a bit like a compound, though there is access to an indoor *parrilla* and dining room.

Albergue de la Casa de Marita y Aldo 25 de Mayo 371 Ⓣ02972/491149. Rustic dormitory-style accommodation in a traditional fishing lodge down by the river ($15 per person). Also basic four-bed apartments with kitchen ($25 per room). The owner is a fishing guide (US$200 per day per boat load), and smokes his own trout and cheese at the on-site *ahumado*.

Aparthotel Alina Gines Ponte 80 and Felíx San Martín Ⓣ02972/492636. Close to the bus terminal and ideal for small groups, with rooms and cabins for four to six people, but no double rooms. Tours can be arranged, and yoga and massages are also on offer. $150 for five people.

Hostería Chimehuín Coronel Suárez and 25 de Mayo ⓣ02972/491132, ⓦwww.interpatagonia.com/hosteriachimehuin. A rare gem, the *Chimehuín* combines excellent value with a cottage-like setting among well-tended gardens, and engenders great loyalty from its regular guests, especially fishing aficionados. A fine home-made breakfast is included in the price. Book at least two weeks in advance in summer. ❺

Residencial El Cedro Lamadrid 409 ⓣ&ⓕ02972/492044. One of the most comfortable options, with a good breakfast included in the rates and colour TVs in all rooms. Evening meals also served. ❻

Residencial Marisa J.M. Rosas 360 ⓣ&ⓕ02972/491175. The best of the budget options and just around the corner from the bus terminal, the *Marisa* is a neat, amiable place, and not too noisy, despite having some rooms that face the main road. ❹

The Town

The few sites of interest in Junín are all within a couple of blocks of **Plaza San Martín**, and can be seen in an hour or two. The **Paseo Artesanal** on the east side of the square is a cluster of boutiques selling a selection of crafts, among which Mapuche weavings figure heavily. More Mapuche artefacts and some dinosaur bones can be seen at the tiny **Museo Mapuche**, Ginés Ponte 541 (Mon–Fri 9am–1pm & 2.30–7pm; free), while opposite stands the imposing, alpine-style tower of the **Santuario de la Beata Laura Vicuña**, also called by its old name of the Iglesia Nuestra Señora de las Nieves. Splendid in its simplicity, it is dedicated to the beatified Laura Vicuña, and rates as the most original and refreshing church in Argentine Patagonia. Its airy, sky-blue interior is suffused with light, and its clean-cut lines are tastefully complemented by the bold use of panels of high-quality Mapuche weavings, with strong geometric designs and natural colours. Laura Vicuña, famed for her gentleness, was born in Santiago de Chile in 1891. She studied in Junín with the Salesian sisters for four years, and died here, aged just 13, in 1904. Rather macabrely, one of her vertebrae resides in an urn at the entrance to the sanctuary.

A block north along Don Bosco is the **Paseo Parque Centenario**, a pleasant commemorative garden built to mark the site of the fort that established the settlement of Junín in 1883. If the Santuario isn't enough to quench your thirst for religious imagery, **El Via Christi** at the western end of Avenida Antártida on Cerro de la Cruz, will be. Here 21 statues in an eight-hectare conifer forest depict major scenes from the life of Jesus Christ.

Trout-fishing is a popular pastime along the river, a short walk of six blocks east from the terminal along Olavarría. A humpbacked bridge crosses the fast-flowing waters here to a pleasant **park**, enjoyed by picnicking families in summer.

Eating and drinking

There are a cluster of *parrillas* and other **eateries** on the plaza. The largest of these is *Ruca Hueney* (ⓣ02972/491113), which has trout as its speciality but also offers some Arabic dishes and takeout options. *El Preferido de Junín* (ⓣ02972/491322), a block north of the square at Lamadrid 260, is an attractive wood-panelled *parrilla* with some outdoor tables. *Roble Bar*, Ginés Ponte 331, is the town's most happening **pub**, and serves a *menú del día* at lunch and burgers, etc, in the evenings. *La Morocha*, in Costanera, is a **disco** worth trying out in high season (Fri & Sat from 1am; $5 entrance).

Lago Huechulafquen and around

The RP-61 branches west off RN-234 just north of Junín, entering Parque Nacional Lanín and skirting the shores of **LAGO HUECHULAFQUEN**. On the first stretch of this road are a couple of sights that are easily visited in a few hours with your own vehicle. Just 4km from the junction is the **Centro de Ecologia Aplicada de Neuquén** (Mon–Fri 9am–1pm), which undertakes studies of regional fauna and has a trout farm that raises fish for restocking the area's rivers. A few kilometres further on is the **Escuela Granja San Ignacio** (Sept–May Mon–Fri 8am–2pm), a charming initiative where pupils take you on a guided tour of the school and offer you jams and honey that they produce themselves.

When you arrive at the park gate, you will be charged $12 entrance and have to fill in a *registro de trekking*. The park's largest lake, Huechulafquen is an enormous finger of deep blue water extending into the steppe, its northern shores black with volcanic sand. The mouth of the Río Chimehuín, at the lake's eastern end, is a notable fly-fishing spot, and on the north shore, between Km47 and Km60, there are plenty of places to **camp**, with no fewer than fifteen sites with varying facilities run by the Raquithué and Cañicul Mapuche communities. *Bahía Cañicul* ($10 per person) is about halfway along the lake at Km54, and has good, secluded pitches on top of the peninsula but basic toilets. As you get further into the park the sites become gradually busier.

At the western end of the lake is the settlement and jetty of **Puerto Canoa**, where you can look up at the fantastic, crevassed **south face** of Volcán Lanín. From Puerto Canoa, a fun **boat trip** plies a circuit that includes lakes Huechulafquen, Paimún and Epulafquen, where you'll see the solidified lava river of Volcán Achen Ñiyeu. At Puerto Canoa, there is **accommodation** at *Hostería Huechulafquen* (Ⓣ&Ⓕ02972/427598; ❻), a snug fishing lodge in full view of Lanín. Its **restaurant** is open to the public. Just beyond is more expensive *Hostería Paimún* (Ⓣ02972/491211, Ⓦwww.interpatagonia.com/hosteriapaimun/index.html; ❽) in another delightful spot on the shore of Lago Paimún. In summer Co-op Litran (Ⓣ02972/492038) operates four daily bus services between Lago Huechulafquen and Junín de los Andes, or you can take a taxi to Puerto Canoa.

South of Junín, RP-62 also heads into the park, taking you 70km to the **Termas de Epulafquen** (also called Termas de Lahuen-Có): a collection of small circular thermal and mud pools up to 2m in diameter, southeast of Lago Epulafquen. The hottest pool, Pozo Central, can reach temperatures of 65°C. Agencies in Junín run day-trips; you could also make your own way here and pitch a **tent** at *Camping Nires*, on the shores of Laguna Verde. The laguna is the starting point for a thirty-kilometre hike south that links up with the valley of Río Auquineo, which flows into **Lago Lolog**, and from where there is a bus (summer only) to San Martín de los Andes. From the *termas*, RP-62 continues 8km west to **Paso Internacional Carirriñe**, a Chilean border crossing (open summer only).

Hiking in Parque Nacional Lanín

Before planning **hikes** in the Lanín area you should discuss your plans thoroughly with park officials in Junín or San Martín. Make sure your map is new – this is an area of active volcanoes, and trails and refuges change constantly. Do not attempt to climb Volcán Lanin without a guide (see box, p.607), especially if you are not an experienced mountaineer. Before trekking, remember that it is obligatory to fill out a *registro de trekking*, which must be presented at the *guardaparque* post before departure and on your return.

On entering Parque Nacional Lanín, the first of many trekking possibilities is the four-hour hike to **Cerro del Chivo**, which starts opposite *Camping Bahía Cañicul*. It's a steep climb and you'll need to concentrate not to lose the trail

△ Volcan Lanín

above the tree-line, but the views are spectacular. From the *guardaparque* in Puerto Canoa there's another good, if somewhat arduous, day-hike to the **base of Lanín**. The last forty minutes are steep and there's no water source for the final hour. You can take a short detour to the waterfall at Cascada El Saltillo from *Camping Piedra Mala* at Km64, where there's space to pitch a tent. Beyond is the Río Paimún, which is currently the furthest point you can hike before you'll have to back-track to Puerto Canoa.

An excellent two-day option for losing the crowds is to cross the narrows linking the two lakes at La Unión near Puerto Canoa (there's normally a rowing-boat service) and head along the south shore of Lago Paimún. Initially, you strike inland skirting round the southern slopes of Cerro Huemules (1841m) before reaching the lake again mid-way along its length at **Don Aila**, where you can camp. From here it's a straightforward hike out to RP-62 near the Termas de Epulafquen, where you can soothe any aching muscles (see p.605).

East to Rincon Matarasso

The RP-234 heads east from Junín and after about 20km passes a **condor roost** on the left-hand side. All the Andean Condors that forage in the surroundings come here to pass the night on a high cliff, the white guano stains on the rocks revealing their favoured roosting places. The condors leave in the early morning and begin to arrive in late afternoon, with the number present depending on the number feeding that day in the local area. As many as thirty may roost here on some evenings, though you will need binoculars to see them properly. Strike a deal with a local taxi firm to bring you out here and wait for an hour or so.

Further east, RP-40 splits right at La Rinconada, following the course of the Rio Aluminé. At **Rincon Matarasso**, 26km from the turn-off, large numbers of waterbirds gather, including several species of duck and the beautiful Ashy-headed Goose (*cauquén real*).

Climbing Lanín

Volcán Lanín (3776m) – meaning "choked himself to death" in Mapudungun – is now believed to be extinct. It is a good mountain to climb: easy to access, it also retains the balance between being possible for non-expert climbers to ascend while still representing a real physical challenge. The most straightforward route is from Lago Tromen; the heavily glaciated south face is a much fiercer option that's suitable only for experienced climbers. For more information, consult the national park office in Junín (see p.603).

The route **from Lago Tromen** takes two to three days in good weather. There is a slight danger of altitude sickness towards the top (see p.66) and you must have a fairly good level of fitness to attempt the climb, especially if you go for the two-day option, which involves a very tiring second day that includes the summit push and a complete descent. Group climbing through an agency is possible: a good one to book with is Alquimia in Junín (see p.603), or else the park offices (© lanin@apn.gov.ar) can email you a list of authorized guides. They also rent all the essential mountaineering gear: good boots, waterproof clothing, helmet, ice-axe, crampons, torch (or, better still, a miner's headlamp) and cooker. UV sunglasses, high-factor sunblock, matches and an alarm clock are likewise essential. Optional items are gaiters (especially in late summer when you have to negotiate volcanic scree), black bin liners (for melting snow in sunny weather), candles, a two-way radio and emergency whistle. You are unlikely to need a compass or climbing rope, but an incense stick will help to counter pungent refuge odours. *La Guía Verde* (on sale locally) comes with a reasonable map and an aerial photo with the climbing route superimposed.

You'll need to register for the climb at the Lago Tromen **guardaparque's office** (8am–6pm), and the *guardaparque* will check that you have all the equipment listed above. If permission is granted you'll need to start the climb by 1pm at the latest. It will be necessary to acclimatize for a night in one of the three refuges on the mountain. The *guardaparque* will assign one to you, and will try to accommodate your preference. In high season, get to Tromen early, as all refuges might otherwise be full (about fifty people in total). The first refuge that you reach following the main trail is, **Refugio RIM**, which sleeps fifteen to twenty people, though it is not the lowest altitudinally. Its big advantage is that it has meltwater close by (Jan & Feb; if climbing outside high summer, you'll need to melt snow for water anyway). You may prefer to try for the **CAJA**, further up the slope, especially if you plan to make the final ascent and total descent in one day, as this saves you half an hour's climb in the early morning. CAJA sleeps six comfortably and up to ten at a squeeze. The **BIM** refuge, down from RIM via a second path, has pleasant tables and chairs, but is the lowest down the slope. It's also the largest of the three, sleeping up to thirty people.

West to Chile: Paso Mamuil Malal

One of the most scenic border crossings anywhere in the continent, the **Paso Mamuil Malal** (also called **Paso Tromen**; 1253m; open 9am–9pm year-round) lies at the northeastern foot of **Volcán Lanín** and connects Junín de los Andes with the Chilean resort town of **Pucón**, a favourite backpackers' haunt 72km from the frontier.

North of Junín, turn off RP-23 onto RP-60, a superb panoramic route through the valley of the Río Malleo. After crossing the national park boundary, you pass through a fine grove of araucaria and come to the Argentine immigration post and *guardaparque*'s house. You can pitch a **tent** here or continue the remaining 2km to the Argentine customs post. A further 16km beyond this is the Chilean counterpart.

San Martín de los Andes and around

Nestled between mountains on the eastern shores of Lago Lácar, **San Martín de los Andes** is an excellent base for exploring the southern and central sectors of Parque Nacional Lanín (see p.695 for general information on the park). San Martín is the northern terminus of the famous **Ruta de los Siete Lagos** (see box, pp.616–617) and is just a stone's throw from **Chapelco** ski resort, one of the country's best. Unsurprisingly, San Martín is Neuquén's most-visited destination and it gets pretty busy during high season.

San Martín de los Andes

One of the most beautiful of all Patagonian towns, **SAN MARTÍN DE LOS ANDES** is a resort of chalets and generally low-key architecture set in a sheltered valley at the eastern end of **Lago Lácar**. There's a sandy, if often windy, beach here, and in spring, the introduced broom (*retama*) daubs the scenery on the approach roads a sunny yellow. Expansion has been rapid, but – with the exception of the hideous derelict *Hotel Sol de Los Andes* that overlooks town – by no means as uncontrolled as in its much larger rival resort, Bariloche, and, whereas Bariloche caters to the young party crowd, San Martín

has deliberately set itself up for a more sedate type of small-town tourism, pitching for families rather than students. **El Trabún** (meaning the "Union of the Peoples") is the main annual **festival**, held in early December in the Plaza San Martín. Local and Chilean musicians hold concerts (predominantly folklore), and big bonfires are lit at the corners of the square to prepare *asados* of lamb and goat.

Arrival and information

Chapelco Airport (Ⓣ02972/427636) lies 25km away in the direction of Junín de los Andes. Caleuche minibuses connect the airport with the town (Ⓣ02972/422115 or 425850 for hotel pick-up), or you can take a *remise*. The **bus terminal** is scenically located in the southwest of town, across the road from Lago Lácar and the **pier**. Pretty much everything you need is found along avenidas Roca and San Martín, or the parallel Villegas.

On the Plaza San Martín, the **tourist office** (daily 8am–10pm; Ⓣ02972/427347, Ⓦwww.smandes.gov.ar) will lend a hand if you can't find a room in high season. The **Intendencia of Parque Nacional Lanín** (Mon–Fri 8am–3pm; Ⓣ02972/429106, Ⓔlanin@apn.gov.ar) is on the opposite side of the plaza – it should be your first stop if you are planning on trekking. They also sell fishing permits, as do all the fishing shops in town. Aquaterra, at Villegas 795, rents camping equipment.

Accommodation

During the peak summer and skiing seasons you should **reserve rooms** as far in advance as possible. If you haven't, the tourist office keeps a daily list of vacancies, though you may find these choices limited. Some hotels have three or four price brackets, with the ski season often more expensive than summer. Out of season, room prices can be as much as halved.

There are three **hostels** in the northwest of town. The most established are the small, well-scrubbed and modern *Puma*, Fosbery 535 (Ⓣ02972/422443, Ⓔpuma@smandes.com.ar; $30 per person), with a couple of double rooms (❺), kitchen and washing facilities, and *Rukalhue*, Juez de Valle 682 (Ⓣ02972/427085, Ⓦwww.rukalhue.com.ar; US$20 per person) – a drab ex-YPF workers' building with a barrack feel, it has four-bed dorms and four doubles (❹). Better is the new *Secuoya*, Rivadavia 411 (Ⓣ02972/424485, Ⓦwww.hostelsecuoya.com.ar; $50 per person), which has some double rooms (❺) and is modern, safe and friendly. For **camping**, there's a choice of three sites, though none offers facilities in winter: the *ACA* site, Av Koessler 2175 (Ⓣ&Ⓕ02972/429430; $15 per person), is popular with families; *Amigos de la Naturaleza* (Ⓣ02972/426351; $13 per person), is about 7km out on the road to Junín; *Camping Lolen* ($12 per person) is a lakeside site with superb views, run by the Curruhuinca Mapuche community – it's 4km southwest of town, 1km off RN-234 at Km78 and down a very steep track to Playa Catritre.

Aparthotel Cascadas Obeid 859 Ⓣ02972/420133, Ⓦwww.apartcascadas.com.ar. Great value, aesthetically pleasing six-person *cabañas* (❽) on a quiet street with superb facilities for the price. Includes a heated pool, hydromassage and PC with Internet connection in every cabin. Double rooms (❼) also available.

Hostería Ayelén Pasaje Arrayanes, Casilla de Correo 21 Ⓣ02972/425660, Ⓦwww.hosteriaayelen.com.ar. High above town near Mirador Arrayán, this splendidly homely house serves an excellent breakfast and boasts four rooms that command some of the finest hotel views in Patagonia. Organizes fishing trips and arranges horse riding and trekking. ❼

Hostería Hueney Ruca Obeid and Coronel Pérez Ⓣ02972/421499, Ⓦwww.hueneyrucahosteria.com.ar. Spacious and airy with attractive minimalist decor and modern bathrooms. Some rooms accommodate up to five people and breakfast is included in the price. ❻

Hostería Italia Coronel Pérez 977 T 02972/427590. Clean accommodation in white, wooden-clad building covered with geraniums. ⑤

Hostería Laura Mascardi 632 T 02972/427271. Simple but pleasant with airy rooms. Among the cheaper places in town in summer. ④

Hostería Las Lucarnas Coronel Pérez 632 T 02972/427085, E laslucarnas@smandes.com.ar. The best of the cheaper spots, *Las Lucarnas* boasts excellent, spacious rooms in a family-run, central but tranquil place. ⑤

Hostería La Posta del Cazador San Martín 175 T 02972/427501, W www.postadelcazador.com.ar. Close to the bus terminal, this place is kitted out in the style of a Tyrolean hunting lodge with a huge set of antlers on the front. Serves large breakfasts and provides babysitting services ($7/hr). ⑥

Hostería y Cabañas del Chapelco Av Brown and Costanera T 02972/427610, W www.interpatagonia.com/hcchapelco. With an excellent lakeshore location, large, chalet-style seasonal accommodation (July–Aug & Jan–Feb only; ⑤) and six-person cabins that are open year-round (US$70).

Hotel Caupolicán San Martín 969 T 02972/427658, W www.interpatagonia.com/caupolican. Fancy three-star hotel in the centre of town with a range of facilities, including a sauna and a living room with log fire. ⑦

Hotel Intermonti Villegas 717 T 02972/427454, W www.hotelintermonti.com.ar. Functional, comfortable, well-lit rooms in an excellent location a block from the main plaza and surrounded by eating options. ⑥

Hotel Turismo Mascardi 517 T 02972/427592, W www.interpatagonia.com/hotelturismo. Another excellent budget option with large, simply decorated but comfortable rooms and ample bathrooms. There´s a bar with pool table and a TV room with a selection of DVDs to while away rainy days. ⑤

Patagonia Plaza Hotel San Martín and Rivadavia T 02972/422280, W www.hotelpatagoniaplaza.com.ar. Plush, four-star hotel with shiny wood floors, as well as an indoor pool, gym and Internet access. ⑨

The Town

There is little to do in town itself apart from bar-hopping, sunning yourself on the small beach by the lake or popping into the tiny **Museo de los Primeros Pobladores** (Mon–Fri 10.30am–1.30pm & 5.30–8.30pm, Sat 10am–1pm; free) on the main square. It has an interesting Spanish guided tour of its exhibits on the Mapuche and skiing.

If you can muster the energy, drag yourself away from the bars to visit the two compelling *miradores*, both within easy walking distance of the centre. Mirador Bandurrias is 3km along the northeast shore of Lago Lácar and has marvellous views along its length. Take the bridge across Arroyo Pocahullo (meaning "place of seagulls" in Mapuche) on Calle Juez del Valle and head left past the water treatment plant. The path divides and subdivides through cypress and oak woods, but keep heading more or less northwest until you reach the lookout. Alternatively, Mirador Arrayán is 3km in the other direction and overlooks the town, with good mountain views. From the lakeshore, the road forks, with RN-234 heading right towards Bariloche while a smaller left fork climbs above the town. Follow this road past *Hotel Sol de los Andes*, after which it becomes a dirt track. There's another fork, right this time following the signs, leading to the *mirador*. If you can't face the climbing, the town's tour bus – an old red London double-decker – leaves from Plaza San Martín and goes as far as the *Hotel Sol de los Andes*.

A historical curiosity is **La Pastera por el Camino de Che**, at the corner of Sarmiento and General Roca. Hidden behind a whitewashed wall is the shack where Che Guevara spent the night on January 31, 1952 during his first trip across South America – later immortalized in *The Motorcycle Diaries*. Overseen by Parques Nacionales, it is being developed as a community and cultural centre with regular poetry recitals and music performances.

Eating, drinking and nightlife

There's a good selection of places to **eat** in town, most staying open past midnight but closing between 3pm and 7.30pm. There's little in the way of **nightlife**, however. Options include *Casino Magic*, at Villegas and Elordi (2pm–4am), which has a dated, 1970s feel but is good for cheap eats late at night, and *Experience*, at Elordi 950 (1.30–6am; $20 cover) – a nightclub open daily in season and playing a wide mix of music.

Avataras Teniente Ramayón 765 ⓣ02972/427104. Offers an exquisite, if expensive, menu with a select choice of gourmet foods from around the world, including Thai, Moroccan and Indian dishes. Closed Sun.

La Barra Brown and Costanera ⓣ02972/425459. A superb wood-cabin restaurant with a lakeside location. Patagonian specialities are the order of the day and the wine list is extensive. Artisanal pasta and stone-baked pizza will appeal to those who have had enough of trout and lamb.

Confitería Deli Costanera and Villegas. Snacks and beers at this deli with a lakeside view.

La Costa del Pueblo Costanera at Villegas ⓣ02972/429289. With good, if slightly obscured lake views, *La Costa del Pueblo* is an excellent place to grab a snack while waiting for a bus. The food is abundant and cheap.

Kawen Villegas 624 ⓣ02972/429242. Arab restaurant and *parrilla*. It's not cheap but portions are large, the food is different and the desserts are particularly tasty.

Ku San Martín 1053 ⓣ02972/427039. This restaurant offers a varied menu that includes *parrillas* and pastas as well as regional trout, venison and wild boar dishes in a rustic setting decorated with wine barrels and bottles.

Pulgarcito San Martín 461 ⓣ02972/427081. Inexpensive home-made pasta a couple of blocks from Plaza San Martín.

El Quincho Rivadavia 815 and San Martín ⓣ02972/422564. Classy wood-cabin restaurant offering traditional Argentine and Patagonian dishes, including the inevitable *parrilla*. The walls are adorned with gaucho artefacts.

Taco's San Martín 1100 ⓣ02972/429444. Another place for budget travellers to head for good, cheap and filling pizzas and pasta.

Listings

Airlines Southern Winds, in Pucara travel agency, San Martín 943 ⓣ02972/427218.

Banks and exchange Andina Internacional, Capitán Drury 876 ⓣ02972/428392; Banco de la Nación, San Martín 687; Banco de la Provincia, Belgrano and Obeid; Banco Francés, San Martín and Sarmiento.

Bike rental H.G. Rodados, San Martín 1061 ⓣ02972/427345.

Books Patalibro, San Martín 866, has an English book section, mostly secondhand.

Car rental Concentrated along Villegas and San Martín. Avis, San Martín 998 ⓣ02972/427704; Sur, Villegas 830 ⓣ02972/429028.

Hospital Hospital Ramón Carrillo, San Martín and Coronel Rohde ⓣ02972/427211. Private clinic at Centro Médico del Sur, Sarmiento 489 ⓣ02972/427148.

Internet access Ciberpatagonia, San Martín 866, local 10 ⓣ02972/421319.

Laundry Laverap, San Martín 1109. Su Lavadero, San Martín 490, delivers to your hotel.

Pharmacy San Jorge, San Martín 405 ⓣ02972/428842.

Police Gendarmería, Gral. Roca 965 ⓣ02972/427339. Emergency ⓣ134.

Post office Roca 690, on Plaza San Martín (Mon–Fri 8.30am–1pm & 4–7pm, Sat 9am–1pm).

Taxis Del Sol, Roca and Rohde ⓣ02972/425005. There's also a nameless kiosk at Belgrano and San Martín (ⓣ02972/427730).

Telephone PST Locutorio San Martín 747 & 836.

Travel agents Many agencies offer trips to Los Siete Lagos (see box, pp.616–617), including 7 Lagos Turismo, Gral Roca 826 (ⓣ02972/427877), and Chapelco Turismo, San Martín 876 (ⓣ02972/427550). Bird-watching tours are available with AvesPatagonia (ⓣ02972/422022, ⓦwww.avespatagonia.com.ar), and fishing with Fly-fishing 3x (ⓣ02972/422216).

Lago Lácar and around

Southwest of San Martín, **LAGO LÁCAR** ("lake of the sunken city") is best explored by combining boat or road trips with the odd hike. Unsurfaced RP-48 runs for 46km along the northern shore of Lácar and the adjoining **Lago Nonthué** to **Hua-Hum**, at the far western end of Nonthué. On the way, 13km from San Martín, is the trailhead for an excellent two-hour hike up **Cerro Colorado** (1774m). You'll go towards a broad V-shaped valley, then along the banks of a stream – a steep climb with views of the valley and lake below.

Three kilometres on from Hua-Hum is the **Paso Hua-Hum**, one of the most enjoyable of the Andean routes through to Chile, open all year round and leading towards the town of Villarrica. Following the Río Hua-Hum northwest brings you to the slender, gorgeous Lago Pirehueico, which can be crossed only by **car ferry** (timetable changes frequently; check Ⓦwww.sietelagos.cl or call Ⓣ0056/63 1971585). A bus service run by Lofit (Ⓣ02972/422800) connects San Martín with the ferry three times a week (2hr) and there are various campsites along the route. Alternatively, Chapelco Turismo in San Martín (see "Listings", p.611) offers twelve-hour day-trips crossing Lago Pirehueico into Chile, looping north past Termas de Liquiñe, Pucón or Huilo Huilo and returning to San Martín.

To the southeast of Hua-Hum, 12km by dirt track, is the *guardaparque*'s post at **Lago Queñi**. The area around this lake is one of the wettest places in Parque Nacional Lanín, and is covered with Valdivian temperate rainforest and dense thickets of *caña colihue*. The star attraction here is the enchanting **Termas de Queñi** – unadorned hot springs, set in lush forest near the southern tip of the lake. Late September to early May is generally the best time to visit the springs: register with the *guardaparque*, and you can **camp** just past the post, on the other side of Arroyo Queñi. You can walk to the springs on an easy route from the campsite (1hr).

From San Martín's pier you can take a **boat excursion** to Hua-Hum and back (leaves 12.30pm, returns 8pm; some English-speaking guides). Hourly ferries also leave the pier on the hour (last boat 7pm) for the beautiful, sheltered bay at **Quila Quina**, an incongruous mix of agricultural smallholdings of the Curruhuinca Mapuche community and holiday homes on the southern shore of Lago Lácar. You can also reach the settlement by signposted dirt road off RN-234. There's a beach and walks in the area, including a two-day trek to the western end of Lago Lácar at **Pucará**.

Cerro Chapelco

One of Argentina's prime resorts and particularly attractive to adventurous skiers, **CERRO CHAPELCO** is in the Cordón del Chapelco, an offshoot range of the Andes. It has 29 ski runs that descend 750 vertical metres from a maximum height of 1980m and take in views of Volcán Lanín, as well as a snowboard park and floodlit night-time skiing.

In summer, the area is especially appealing for those with young families, with a range of activities including archery, horse-riding and mountain-biking. There's also a lift you could take to the top of Cerro Teta (Mount Teat), which at 1970m offers excellent views of Lago Lácar and Volcán Lanín, and an enjoyable walk down its slope.

Practicalities

Cerro Chapelco is 21km south of San Martín, 5km along a spur road off RN-234. There are El Ko-Ko **buses** (Ⓣ02972/427422) connecting the resort with San Martín which, given that there is no accommodation at Chapelco itself, is where most skiers base themselves. The **ski season** runs from June to September, peaking in late July, when a daily ski pass costs nearly double the low-season rate. The 29 pistes are served by a cable car and eight chair- or drag-lifts. There's a good range of slopes, from beginners' green runs to double blacks for experts.

You can **rent ski equipment** at the resort, though there's more choice in San Martín. The Nieves del Chapelco organization now controls access to the *cerro* and sells ski passes. At the time of writing, they were relocating to new offices at Rivadavia 880, but details are available on their website, Ⓦwww.cerrochapelco.com.

Parque Nacional Nahuel Huapi

The mother of the Argentine national park system, **PARQUE NACIONAL NAHUEL HUAPI** protects a glorious chunk of the northern Patagonian cordillera and its neighbouring steppe. Its origins lie in a grant of 7000 hectares of land made by Dr Francisco P. Moreno to the national government in 1903 on the condition that it be safeguarded for the enjoyment of future generations. What started as the Parque Nacional del Sur has since grown to embrace its current colossal 710,000 hectares.

Most of the park falls within the watershed of the immense **Lago Nahuel Huapi**, an impressive expanse of water that can seem benign one moment and a froth of seething whitecaps the next. Of glacial origin, it's 557 square kilometres in area, and, with its peninsulas, islands and attenuated, fjord-like tentacles that sweep down from the thickly forested border region, forms the centrepiece of the park. The lake's name comes from the Mapudungun for Isle (*huapi*) of the Tiger (*nahuel*) and refers to the jaguars that once inhabited regions even this far south. Rainfall is heaviest by the border with Chile, especially in places such as Puerto Blest and Lago Frías – the nucleus of the land donated by Moreno – where over 3000mm fall annually. This permits the growth of Valdivian temperate rainforest and individual species such as the *alerce*, found here at the northernmost extent of its range in Argentina. Other species typical of the sub-antarctic Patagonian forests also flourish: giant *coihues*, *lengas* and *ñire* among others.

A second important habitat is the high alpine environment above the tree line (upwards of 1600m), including some summits that retain snow all year. The

△ Lago Nahuel Huapi

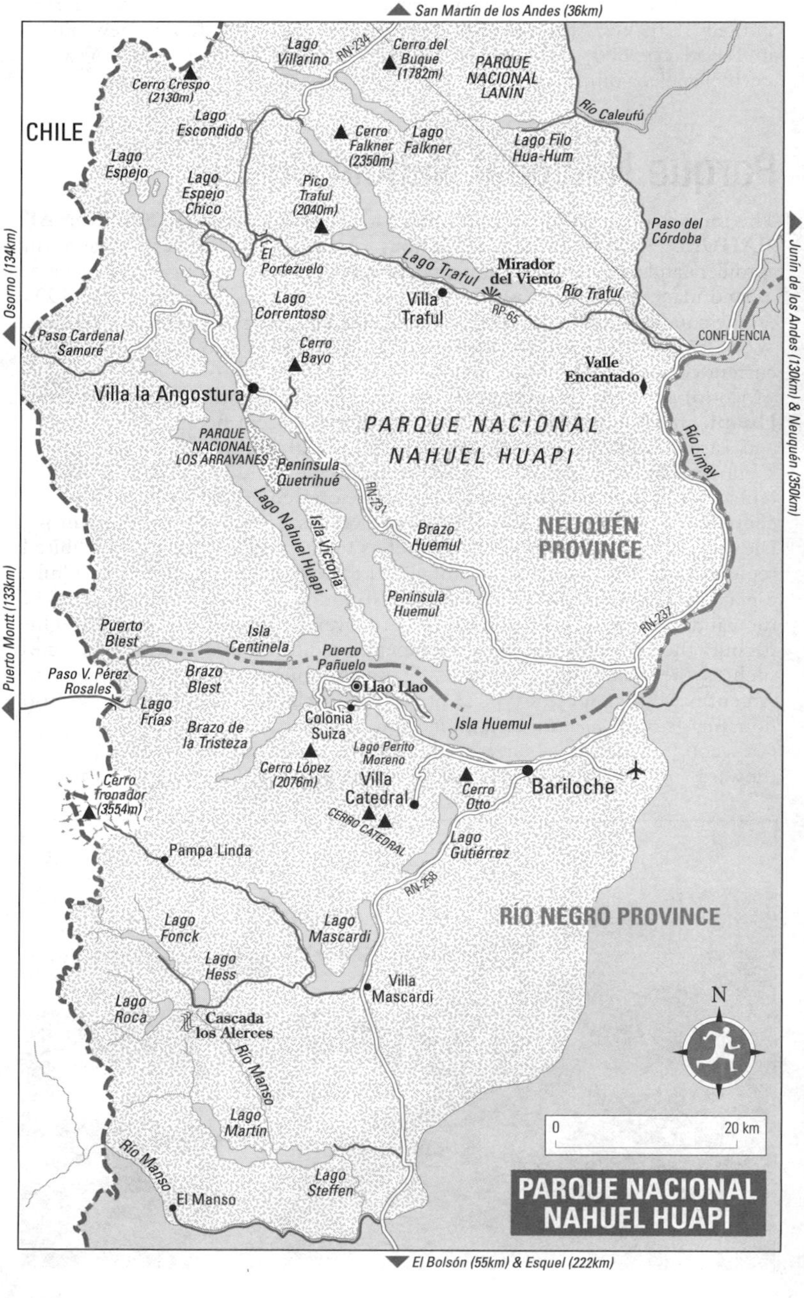
San Martín de los Andes (36km)
Osorno (134km)
Puerto Montt (133km)
Junín de los Andes (130km) & Neuquén (350km)
El Bolsón (55km) & Esquel (222km)
CHILE
Cerro Crespo (2130m)
Lago Villarino
RN-234
Cerro del Buque (1782m)
PARQUE NACIONAL LANÍN
Río Caleufú
Lago Escondido
Cerro Falkner (2350m)
Lago Falkner
Lago Filo Hua-Hum
Lago Espejo
Lago Espejo Chico
Pico Traful (2040m)
Paso del Córdoba
El Portezuelo
Lago Traful
Mirador del Viento
Río Traful
Villa Traful
RP-65
Lago Correntoso
Paso Cardenal Samoré
Cerro Bayo
CONFLUENCIA
Valle Encantado
Villa la Angostura
PARQUE NACIONAL NAHUEL HUAPI
PARQUE NACIONAL LOS ARRAYANES
Península Quetrihué
Río Limay
RN-231
Lago Nahuel Huapi
Isla Victoria
Brazo Huemul
NEUQUÉN PROVINCE
Península Huemul
Puerto Blest
Isla Centinela
Puerto Pañuelo
RN-237
Paso V. Pérez Rosales
Brazo Blest
Llao Llao
Lago Frías
Colonia Suiza
Brazo de la Tristeza
Isla Huemul
Lago Perito Moreno
Cerro López (2076m)
Villa Catedral
Cerro Otto
Bariloche
Cerro Tronador (3554m)
CERRO CATEDRAL
Lago Gutiérrez
Pampa Linda
RN-258
RÍO NEGRO PROVINCE
Lago Fonck
Lago Mascardi
Lago Hess
Villa Mascardi
Lago Roca
Cascada los Alerces
Río Manso
N
Lago Martín
0
20 km
Río Manso
Lago Steffen
El Manso
PARQUE NACIONAL NAHUEL HUAPI

dominant massif of the park is an extinct volcano, **Cerro Tronador**, whose three peaks (Argentino at 3410m; Internacional at 3554m; and Chileno at 3478m) straddle the Argentine-Chilean border in the south. Glaciers slide off its heights in all directions, though all are in a state of rapid recession. The "thundering" referred to in its Spanish name is not volcanic, but rather the echoing roar heard when vast chunks of ice break off its hanging glaciers and plunge down to the slopes below. Rainfall decreases sharply as you move eastwards from the border. Cypress woodland typifies the transitional semi-montane zone, and at the eastern side of the park you find areas of arid, rolling steppe. Snow can fall as late as December and as early as March at higher altitudes: it's not advisable to hike certain trails outside the high season. Average temperatures are 18°C in summer and 2°C in winter. The strongest winds blow in spring, which is otherwise a good time to visit, as is the calmer autumn, when the deciduous trees wear their spectacular late-season colours.

The park has abundant **birdlife**, with species such as the Magellanic Woodpecker, the Green-backed Firecrown, the ground-dwelling Chucao Tapaculo and the Austral Parakeet. You'll hear mention of rare **fauna** such as the *huemul* (see box, p.633) and the *pudú*, though you have only a slightly greater chance of seeing them than you do of spying Nahuelito, Patagonia's version of the Loch Ness monster. Animals that make their home in the steppe regions of the park (guanaco, rheas and foxes) are more easily seen. Of the non-native species, the most conspicuous are the **red deer** (*ciervo colorado*) and the **wild boar** (*jabalí*), which were introduced by hunt-loving settlers. In an effort to cull numbers of these, the authorities issue shooting permits, which continue to serve as a source of revenue for the park.

Orientation

North to south, the park is divided into three zones. The **zone to the north** of Lago Nahuel Huapi centres around **Lago Traful**, but tends to be visited more for the Seven Lakes Route (see box, pp.616–617). *Guardaparques* stationed at points along the route are helpful when it comes to recommending day-treks in their particular sectors. In the far south of this zone is the main overland pass through to Chile – **Paso Cardenal Samoré** (formerly called Paso Puyehue; Argentine immigration open 9am–9pm). The **central zone** is the one centred on Lago Nahuel Huapi itself, and embraces the "park within a park", **Parque Nacional Los Arrayanes**, on the Península Quetrihué (see p.622). It is umbilically attached to **Villa La Angostura** (see p.619), which has experienced meteoric growth in the past decade and caters mostly to upper-end tourists. Apart from visiting the peninsula from Villa La Angostura, exploring this central zone is largely dependent on boat trips from **Bariloche** (see p.622), the park's biggest town and one of Argentina's most visited destinations. One of these trips heads to **Isla Victoria**, the elongated, thickly forested island to the northwest.

At the western end of Brazo Blest is the outpost of **Puerto Blest**, surrounded by some of the park's most impressive forest. A short and scenic trail connects this with the north side of the bay, where a stepped walkway leads up past the **Cascada Los Cántaros**, a series of cascades in the forest. A dirt road runs south for 3km to Puerto Alegre at the northern end of tiny Lago Frías, and a launch crosses the lake daily to Puerto Frías, from where you can cross to Chile or hike south across the Paso de las Nubes towards the **southern zone**. It is in the south where you'll find most of the longer and more mountainous treks, either around Cerro Catedral or Pampa Linda. If you want to hike and can read Spanish, the *Guía Sendas & Bosques de Lanín y Nahuel Huapi* is very useful. Two reasonably reliable maps (1:200,000) accompany the guide.

Ruta de los Siete Lagos

The **Ruta de los Siete Lagos**, or "Seven Lakes Route", one of Argentina's classic scenic drives, cuts right through Parque Nacional Nahuel Huapi, connecting **San Martín de los Andes** to **Villa La Angostura**, and continuing on to **Bariloche** (see p.622) in spectacular fashion. Along the way, the route goes through forested valleys and gives access to many more than seven wild lakes. You'll pass several fishing spots – buy permits before setting off (from tourist offices, YPF stations or campsites). The route is mostly paved, but the remaining unsealed section – between Lago Villarino and Lago Espejo – can get extremely dusty, especially in summer. El Ko-Ko and Albus conveniently run daily services along the route between San Martín and Villa La Angostura.

The seven principal lakes dotting the roadside are, from north to south: Machónico, Falkner, Villarino, Escondido, Correntoso, Espejo and Nahuel Huapi. The route straddles Parque Nacional Lanín and Nahuel Huapi, though only Lago Machónico lies in Lanín. Leaving San Martín, you climb up into the mountains on winding RN-234, passing through *ñire* and *coihue* woods – stop at the Mirador de Pil Pil to look back at the superb panorama of Lago Lácar. About twenty kilometres from San Martín, and just before the RN-63 junction, you pass *Cabañas Rio Hermoso* (no phone, Ⓔcab_riohermoso@yahoo.com.ar) with four excellent cabins (❺). Worth a stop just to taste the owner's home-made liqueurs, *Río Hermoso* also arranges horse-riding. Further on, you skirt the eastern shore of **Lago Machónico**, and, soon after, a detour west leads to Lago Hermoso, where you'll find the *Lago Hermoso* campsite (mid-Dec to Feb; $6 per person), which sells provisions and has showers. A few metres further on is the basic *Refugio Winka Mawida* (no phone, Ⓦhttp://winkamawida.tripod.com/id2.html; summer only) with one twelve-bed dorm ($25 per person) and a three-person *cabaña* (❺). Back on the main road opposite the Lago Hermoso junction is the excellent *Refugio Lago Hermoso* (Ⓣ02972/425290 or 02944/155-69176, Ⓦwww.refugiolagohermoso.com; open Nov–Easter), offering half-board and full-board stays in a charming rustic lodge ($60 per person) as well as horse-riding, canoeing and fishing.

South of Lago Hermoso, you leave the boundaries of Lanín and enter Nahuel Huapi, where, just to the north of **Lago Falkner**, you pass Cascada Vulliñanco, a twenty-metre waterfall to the west of the road. Lago Falkner, a perennial favourite of fishermen, sits at the foot of **Cerro Falkner** (2350m) to the south. The beautiful lakeside *Camping Lago Falkner* has a small shop, toilets and showers ($6 per person, plus $3 per vehicle). Just beyond, at Km50, is *Hostería Lago Villarino* (Ⓣ02972/427483, Ⓦwww.hosteriavillarino.com.ar; closed April–Oct; ❼). It's a 1940s lodge with character-filled rooms and cosy fireplaces, and bungalows for four to six people. There are excellent horse-riding opportunities in the vicinity, and it's possible to rent mountain bikes and fishing boats. A four-hour trail to the summit of

Lago Traful

LAGO TRAFUL is a pure, intense blue, like a pool of liquid Roman glass. It is a popular destination for fishermen trying to hook trout and the rare landlocked salmon, and is best accessed along RP-65, which follows its entire southern shore. The most beautiful approach is from the Ruta de los Siete Lagos (see box above), crossing the pass of El Portezuelo and heading through the **Valle de los Machis** (with its majestic *coihue* trees), beneath the heights of Pico Traful (2040m). The road levels out in mixed woodland of cypress, *radal*, *retamo*, *maitén* and *espina negra*. If coming from the east, the steppe scenery loses its harshness the closer you come to the cordillera.

Cerro Falkner, which has views of Volcán Lanín and Chile's Volcán Villarrica, starts about 150m from the *hostería*. Opposite Lago Falkner is **Lago Villarino**, another popular place for fishing, with Cerro Crespo (2130m) as a picturesque backdrop. There's also a free lakeside campground here.

Four kilometres further south is pint-sized **Lago Escondido**, the most enchanting of all the lakes, hiding its emerald-green charms demurely in the forest. After crossing the limpid waters of Río Pichi Traful, you enter Seccional Villarino (8am–8pm), where the *guardaparque* will give you information on recommended walks, such as the trek up Cerro Falkner. Some 2km east of here, down a bumpy track, is a pleasant fisherman's campsite on the Brazo Norte of Lago Traful. Back on the main road you pass through a magnificent valley with sheer cliffs towering over 600m. It's worth stopping at the signposted track to a series of five waterfalls known collectively as Cascadas Ñivinco. Reaching them involves an easy two-kilometre walk through *ñire* and *caña colihue* forest but you'll have to get your feet (and possibly knees) wet when you ford the river. South of here is the RP-65 turn-off to Lago Traful (see below).

Beyond here you trace the northern shores of **Lago Correntoso** – magical at dawn – and pass the excellent *Hostería Siete Lagos* (no phone, reservations on ⓣ02944/494218; $28 per person). The cabin is the home of one of the area's original indigenous families who, apart from lodging, offer *tortas fritas*, meals and provisions, and run the lakeshore campground ($6). About 6km further on you pass another detour to **Lago Espejo Chico**, which lies 2.5km northwest of RN-234, down a rutted dirt road. Here you'll find *Camping Lago Espejo Chico* ($6 per person), which has a shop and showers and is popular with Argentine adolescents. You can register here for the four-hour trek to Cerro La Mona; the trailhead is 500m before the campground. Six kilometres down RN-234 you reach **Lago Espejo**, the warmest lake in the park. Alongside the Seccional Espejo *guardaparque* post is a free campsite, by a beach that's good for swimming. Opposite is an easy forest trail (30min) through the woods to an isolated part of Lago Correntoso. Shortly after the *guardaparque*'s house is another campground ($6) with spacious pitches and beach. Beside it is tidy, cosy *Hostería Lago Espejo* (ⓣ02944/494583; mid-Dec to Easter; ⑧), with well-appointed rooms and fantastic views. Its beach bar and restaurant are open to non-residents. The RN-234 ends at a T-junction a couple of kilometres further south. Here you can turn southeast along the paved RN-231 to Villa La Angostura, 12km away; (see p.619), where you'll get your first views of **Lago Nahuel Huapi**, the seventh and largest lake on the route. Before reaching Villa La Angostura, the road crosses Río Correntoso, a famous fishing spot and, at barely 250m long, one of the planet's shortest rivers. Turning west along RN-231 takes you to Paso Cardenal Samoré (formerly called Puyehue), which is the region's most important year-round border crossing into Chile, heading to Osorno (8am–8pm, 9pm in summer).

Midway along the lake on RP-65 is **Villa Traful**, a loose assemblage of houses spread out along several kilometres of the shoreline. There are a number of interesting hikes in the vicinity and one particularly impressive lookout point: the **Mirador Pared del Viento** (or Mirador del Traful). Five kilometres east of the village on RP-65, this is a precipitous rock-face that survived the onslaught of the glaciers and presents superb views down its sheer seventy-metre face into the Mediterranean-blue waters below.

Set back from the village's main jetty is a **guardaparque post** (daily 9am–8pm; ⓣ02944/479033), where they can provide you with information on local hikes – you should register before setting out. Some of the trekking options include hikes to various waterfalls, climbing **Cerro Negro** behind the village (1999m; 7–9hr)

Trekking in Parque Nacional Nahuel Huapi

To say **Parque Nacional Nahuel Huapi** is an ideal destination for **trekking** would be a sizeable understatement. Myriad spectacular trails lace the park, though its principal trekking region is the sector southwest of Bariloche (see p.630), where the two foremost points of interest are **Cerro Catedral** and the **Pampa Linda** area, southeast of Cerro Tronador. An impressive network of well-run **refuges** ($20–30 per person) makes trekking that much more appealing: you'll need a sleeping bag, but can buy **meals** and basic supplies en route and thus cut down on the weight you need to lug around. In high season, refuges and trails in the more popular areas can get very busy, so carry a tent with you. There are authorized **camping sites**, but you need to get a camping **permit** from the intendencia or any *guardaparque* in order to use them; the park has suffered a series of devastating **fires** in recent years, so restrictions have tightened up as regards free camping and you must now carry your own stove for cooking. Before departure it is obligatory to fill out a *registro de trekking* at the *guardaparque* station on entering the park and to check out again before leaving.

The **trekking season** is between December and March, but you should always heed weather conditions (Ⓦwww.accuweather.com has forecasts) and come prepared for unseasonal snowfalls. Check in advance with the *guardaparques* to find out which refuges are open. As a rule, trails or *sendas* to refuges are well marked; the high-mountain trails (*sendas de alta montaña*) are not always clearly marked, though, while the less-frequented paths (*picadas*) are not maintained on a regular basis, and close up with vegetation from time to time. Before you set out, you should also visit the Club Andino Bariloche, at 20 de Febrero 30 in Bariloche. Their information office and shop is in the wooden hut alongside the main building (Jan & Feb daily 9am–1pm & 4–8.30pm, rest of year weekdays only; Ⓣ02944/527966, Ⓦwww.clubandino.org or Ⓦwww.activepatagonia.com.ar). They sell a series of trekking **maps**: the standard one is the *Carta de Refugios, Sendas y Picadas* (1:100,000), which has been expanded into three larger-scale (1:50,000) maps. These are useful and include stage times, but the route descriptions are in Spanish only, and not all topographical details are accurate. A newer *Infotrekking* map, compiled from satellite images, is better but may not have all the trails marked. CAB also sells a slim volume, *Infotrekking de la*

or making a trip to **Laguna Las Mellizas** on the northern side of the lake to see indigenous rock paintings. You'll need to contract someone with a boat for the fifteen-minute crossing, preferably someone who will also guide you through the multiple animal paths to the paintings (5hr return); try at *Hostería Villa Traful* (see below). To the east of the village, near the YPF **fuel station**, is the **tourist office** (daily 9am–9pm; Ⓣ02944/479099). As well as advising on accommodation, they sell fishing permits and have information on fishing guides.

The village's only **hotel** as such is homely *Hostería Villa Traful* (Ⓣ&Ⓕ02944/479005; ❹ with breakfast; closed Easter to mid-Nov), which rents cabins all year (❻ for up to four people). *La Vulcanche* (Ⓣ02944/494015, Ⓦwww.vulcanche.com) is a pleasant budget **hostel** with dorm rooms ($25 per person) and a **campsite** ($10) in addition to double rooms (❹) and good-value cabins ($120 for four people). English is spoken and they can arrange excursions. *Camping Costa Traful*, near the tourist office (Ⓣ02944/479049, Ⓦwww.interpatagonia.com/costatraful/; $10), also has cabins (❺). More scenic is the free *Paloma Araucana* site (no facilities), by the foot of the Mirador Pared del Viento. Ten kilometres out of town to the west is another lakeshore campsite: *Cataratas* has only basic services ($8 per person; closed Feb to mid-Nov) but is near a beautiful waterfall.

Patagonia by Diego Cannestraci, which has good route descriptions for those who can read Spanish.

In the **Cerro Catedral** area, popular day- or two-day hikes include ones to **Refugio Frey,** which can be reached by a gentle ascent up the valley or by taking the ski lift to Refugio Lynch and then a rocky traverse (medium difficulty). Follow the ridge heading southwest picking up the red paint blotches on the rocks – after an hour or more the trail forks left on a steep descent to Refugio Frey, while the right fork leads to Refugio San Martín. From here the standard descent is to the northeast, along the course of the Casa de Piedra stream.

In the **Pampa Linda** sector there are a number of day-treks and longer possibilities. Very popular is the hike to **Refugio Otto Meiling**, above even the summer snowline and with spectacular views of Cerro Tronador, where you can stay or camp. Much less frequented is the trek to **Refugio Tronador**, also with mountain vistas. You'll need a permit from both the Pampa Linda *guardaparque* and the nearby *gendarmaría*, since the trek takes you into Chile before doubling back into Argentina. There are no services at Refugio Tronador and many prefer to overnight near the Chilean *carabineros* and make a day-hike to Refugio Tronador, returning to Pampa Linda the third day.

At Pampa Linda there's **accommodation** at *Hostería Pampa Linda* (Ⓣ02944/490517, Ⓦwww.hosteriapampalinda.com.ar; closed May and June; ⑦–⑧) which offers half- and full-board options, or the *refugio* next door. Nearby there's also upmarket *Hotel Tronador*, at the northwestern end of Lago Mascardi (Ⓣ02944/441062, Ⓦwww.hoteltronador.com; Nov–April; $70 per person full board). **Campsites** are at all major destinations: *Lago Roca* near the Cascada Los Alerces ($15 per person); *Los Rápidos* (Ⓣ02944/461861; $15 per person) and *La Querencia* (Ⓣ02944/520665; $15 per person) at Lago Mascardi; and *Pampa Linda* ($15 per person) or the camping *libre* site opposite. Check with the intendencia in Bariloche as to the current status of other authorized sites.

A useful Transportes RM **bus** connects Bariloche to Pampa Linda, leaving from outside the Club Andino Bariloche (summer daily 8.30am, returning 5pm; reserve in advance). A Vía Bariloche bus goes to Paraje El Manso at the extreme southwest corner of the park, by the park boundary (buy tickets from company office at Mitre 321).

In Villa Traful a popular tearoom and **restaurant**, *Ñancú Lahuen* (Ⓣ02944/479017), serves high-quality chocolates and cakes, as well as pasta and trout. Turismo Traful (no phone) runs half-day trips to the Valle Encantado (see p.631), boat excursions and horse-riding. The latter can also be done with Eco Traful (Ⓣ02944/479139, Ⓔecotraful@yahoo.com.ar). Mountain bikes can be rented at Del Montaña, signposted off the main road.

Villa La Angostura

Spread along the lakeshore of Nahuel Huapi, **VILLA LA ANGOSTURA** has grown enormously in the past decade, capitalizing on the Lake District's surging popularity, to become the second largest holiday destination in Neuquén. The settlement originally swelled due to its proximity to the trout-fishing at Río Correntoso, one of the world's shortest rivers, but today caters mostly to upper-end tourists, with whole new areas of wooded hills giving way to luxury hotels, cabins and spas. The ubiquitous and somewhat forced log-cabin architecture gives the town a clichéd feel, almost like a mountain village theme park, and may not be to everyone's taste.

For those not into fly-fishing, the main reason for visiting Villa La Angostura is that it provides the only land access to **Parque Nacional Los Arrayanes** (see p.622). The park is reached by crossing the isthmus at **La Villa**, a 3km-long peninsula west of the centre – the old harbour. In winter, there's skiing on the slopes of **Cerro Bayo**, 10km east from the centre, while in summer you can get good views from the summit; you can hike up but you'll need a guide – ask at the tourist office. Another good local hike (or short drive) is to **Mirador Belvedere** and Cascada Inacayal, a delightful waterfall, both along the southeast shore of Lago Correntoso.

Arrival, orientation and information

The town sprawls along the lakeside and is split into six barrios; the two most northerly – Villa Correntoso and Epulaufquen – overlook Lago Correntoso. You pass through the two southerly barrios, Las Balsas and Puerto Manzano, on the approach from Bariloche. The town centre is known as **El Cruce** and west of here is **La Villa**, which provides access to the park. The RN-231 is known as Avenida Arrayanes as it transects the town; everything you are likely to need during your stay is concentrated in a 200m stretch between Boulevard Nahuel Huapi and Cerro Bayo. The **bus station** (Ⓣ02944/494961) is just off Avenida Arrayanes at Avenida Siete Lagos. Opposite is the **tourist office** (daily summer 8am–10pm, winter 9am–8.30pm; Ⓣ02944/494124, Ⓦwww.villalaangostura.gov.ar), which can help you find accommodation if you haven't made reservations in advance. Empresa 15 de Mayo (Ⓣ02944/495104) runs seven daily buses between La Villa and El Cruce (last return 8.45pm).

Accommodation

The most affordable **accommodation** tends to be in El Cruce, with more upmarket choices in the northern and southern suburbs – prices increase as the lake view improves. There are a few decent **hostels**, the best and most central of which is the modern and tastefully designed *Hostel La Angostura*, two blocks from the bus station at Barbagelata 157 (Ⓣ02944/494834, Ⓦwww.hostellaangostura.com.ar; $30 per person), which has four- to six-bed dorms, two double rooms (❺) and a pleasant communal area. The most convenient **campsite** is *Camping Unquehué* (Ⓣ02944/494103; $15 per person), 500m west of the bus terminal at Av Siete Lagos 727. *Camping Cullunche* (Ⓣ02944/494160; $13 per person) is closest to the **port**, 2km down Boulevard Quetrihue, a signposted northwest turn-off from Boulevard Nahuel Huapi in Barrio La Villa.

Epulafquen and Correntoso

Las Cumbres Confluencia 944 Ⓣ02944/494945, Ⓦwww.hosterialascumbres.com. This welcoming lodge offers good views that are somewhat diminished by its proximity to the main road, though the light, wood-panelled rooms are good value in high season. ❻

Hostel del Francés Lolog 2057 Ⓣ02944/155-64063, Ⓦwww.lodelfrances.com.ar. A beautiful cabin with lake views and double rooms with wooden bathrooms 4km from the tourist office. ❺–❻

Hostería Pichi Rincón Blvd Quetrihue 86 Ⓣ02944/494186, Ⓦwww.pichirincon.com.ar. This stone and wood building boasts views of Lago Nahuel Huapi and decent-sized rooms. Half-price in low season. ❻

Hotel Correntoso Av Siete Lagos 4505 Ⓣ02944/156-19728, Ⓦwww.correntoso.com. Overlooking Río Correntoso, the settlement's original fishing lodge, dating from 1917, was closed for fourteen years and completely renovated before reopening in Nov 2003. Making the most of its spectacular setting, the *Correntoso*'s historic charm, created by abundant natural light and highly tasteful decor, mixes well with its modern services, which include a herbal spa and gourmet restaurant. ❾

Puerto Manzano

Patagonia Paraiso Los Pinos 367 Ⓣ02944/475429, Ⓦwww.patagoniaparaiso.com. Luxury amid a forest of *coihue* trees, and glorious views over the lake from your balcony. There is a private volcanic-sand beach here, too. ❽–❾

El Cruce and La Villa

Cabañas Los Ñires Arrayanes 675 ⓣ02944/494021, ⓦwww.laangostura.com/losnires/default.htm. Though the views aren't exactly great (apart from the highway), these well-built cabins are among the cheaper options in high season. ⑤

Cabañas Rincón del Bosque Caciqué 363 ⓣ02944/494647, ⓦwww.rincondelbosque.com. Charming, peaceful forest setting with cabins for up to seven people. ⑥

Don Pedro Los Maquis and Cerro Belvedere ⓣ02944/494269. Another decent budget option in a central location. Pleasant, heated wood-panelled rooms and a rather droopy stuffed condor in the dining room. Rates include breakfast. ⑤

Hotel Angostura Blvd Nahuel Huapi 1911, La Villa ⓣ02944/494224, ⓦwww.hotelangostura.com. There's a quality old-lodge feel (up to the creaking floorboards) to this charismatic place, which has wonderful lake views. Its restaurant, open to guests and non-guests alike, serves home-made regional food, and there are also three bungalows for rent. ⑥–⑨

Rio Bonito Tora Topa 260 ⓣ02944/494110, ⓔriobonito@ciudad.com.ar. This spotlessly clean and pleasant *residencial* offers airy rooms, among the cheapest in town. ⑤

Verena's Haus Los Taiques 268 ⓣ02944/494467, ⓦwww.verenashaus.com.ar. White, wooden-clad and homely establishment run with tender loving care. The breakfasts are excellent, with a selection of home-made breads, cakes and jams. Children under 12 not permitted. ⑥

Eating and drinking

Most of Villa La Angostura's **restaurants** are located along a two-hundred-metre stretch of RN-231 in El Cruce. Prices are high and the gentrification can be a bit over the top, but the quality of food is generally good.

Asador Loncomilla Arrayanes 176 ⓣ02944/155-59442. With high wooden ceilings hung with Spanish-style hams, this is an excellent place for a meat feast, particularly Patagonian lamb.

La Encantada Belvedere 69 ⓣ02944/495436. Great home-brewed beer and wood-fired artisanal pizzas served in a well-appointed cabin. Popular with locals.

Estancia La Esperanza Av Siete Lagos next to bus station ⓣ02944/488281. Excellent *parrilla* with meat brought fresh from the estancia of the same name. Also a good cheap *menú del día*.

Hub Arrayanes 256 ⓣ02944/495700. Trendy bar/restaurant with imaginative variations on a typically Patagonian theme. Live music some nights.

Lado Sur "Los Amigos" Los Taiques 55. The tables here have views over the restaurant's beautiful garden. Dishes include reasonably priced wild boar and venison.

La Macarena Arrayanes 44 ⓣ02944/494248. Set in an attractive "gingerbread house" building, *La Macarena* serves an evocatively named set of dishes such as "Sublime Bambi" and "Pasión por Ella".

Listings

Arts and crafts Paseo de Productores y Artesanos, behind the bus station between Fucsia and Av Arrayanes.

Banks and exchange Banco Francés, Cerro Belvedere and Av Arrayanes (Mon–Fri 8am–1pm). Andina International Exchange, Av Arrayanes 256.

Car rental Hertz, Av Arrayanes 310 ⓣ02944/494297; Techuelche, Av Arrayanes 21 ⓣ02944/495860.

Hospital Dr. Oscar Arraiz, Blvd Amancaray, on the road to La Villa ⓣ02944/107494170.

Internet access Drugstore.com, Av Arrayanes 256; Clip, Av Arrayanes 167.

Laundry At Los Notros 120.

Pharmacy Marten, Av Arrayanes and Cerro Belvedere (Mon–Sat 9am–1.30pm & 4–9pm).

Police Av Arrayanes 242 ⓣ02944/101494121.

Post office Fucsia, behind the bus station (Mon–Fri 8.30am–1pm & 4–7pm, Sat 9am–1pm).

Taxi Angostura Remises ⓣ02944/494218.

Travel agents and tour operators City Tour, from bus terminal daily 2.30pm (ⓣ02944/495251). Kayaks and bike hire from Aventura Maxima at port building on Playa Mansa (ⓣ02944/495545). Fishing through Bananafly, Av Arrayanes 282 (ⓣ02944/494634). Horse-riding with Cabalgatas Correntoso, Cacique Antriao (ⓣ02944/15510559).

Parque Nacional Los Arrayanes

A park within a park, **PARQUE NACIONAL LOS ARRAYANES** was created to protect the world's best stand of myrtle woodland, the **Bosque de los Arrayanes**, which is found at the far tip of the Península Quetrihué, the narrow-necked peninsula jutting out from Barrio La Villa. Quetrihué, in Mapudungun, means "place of the *arrayanes*", and the peninsula is a legacy from the glaciation of the Pleistocene era, as its rock proved more resilient to erosion than that which surrounded it. It is now covered with forests of *coihue*, *radal* and uncommon species such as *palo santo* (different from the species found in the Chaco), which sports rich, glossy foliage and an ashy grey bark. These forests provide cover for native fauna such as Des Mur's Wiretail.

The **arrayán**, a member of the myrtle family, is a slow-growing tree characterized by flaky, cinnamon-coloured, paper-like bark and amazing trunks, which look rather like barley-sugar church columns. It can reach heights of up to 15m and live for 300 years (although some specimens here may be as much as 600 years old), and it only grows close to cool water. The canopy of the *arrayán* is made up of delicate glossy clusters of foliage, and in late summer, it flowers in dainty white blossoms, with the edible blue-black berries maturing in autumn.

The Bosque can be reached by hiking or cycling from La Villa (12km one way), or by boat from La Villa or Bariloche. Last entry into the park is at 2pm if arriving by land or 4.30pm if arriving by boat. Boulevard Nahuel Huapi terminates in La Villa with the stretch that connects the two bays on either side of the peninsula's narrow neck: **Bahía Mansa** ("Peaceful Bay"), on the eastern side, is where you'll find the **Intendencia** (daily 8am–8pm; ⓣ02944/494152) of the park and the Puerto Angostura **jetty** for boats to the Bosque; and **Bahía Brava** ("Wild Bay") on the western side, which is used only by fishing boats. The park **entrance** ($12) is halfway between the two.

If you're **hiking**, count on a five- to six-hour return trip. Start early (the park opens at 8am) to enjoy the wildlife of the peninsula and avoid most of the crowds. The first twenty minutes, when you climb steeply to the lookout, is by far the hardest part. If you go by mountain bike (3–4hr return trip), you'll have to push it up this initial section but you should be able to get to the myrtle forest before the first boat arrives. Greenleaf (ⓣ02944/494004) runs three daily **catamaran excursions** year-round (10.30am, 2pm and 5pm). In January and February they get very busy, so book in advance. The Bosque is open till 7pm and there's a *guardaparque* post and a *cafetería* here.

When seen from the lake, the Bosque doesn't look much different from the surrounding forest – it's when you're underneath the canopy that its magic envelops you. The rumour that Walt Disney took his inspiration for the forest scenes in *Bambi* from this enchanted woodland is not true (he actually took it from photographs of birch forests in Maine), but that doesn't much matter, as it certainly feels that way: walk around the 600-metre **boardwalk** at your leisure whilst the contorted corkscrew trunks creak against each other in the breeze and the light plays like a French Impressionist's dream, and you'll see why.

Bariloche and around

Approaching from the north, you can take in the enviable mountainous backdrop of the holiday capital of Argentine Patagonia, **SAN CARLOS DE BARILOCHE**. Bariloche, as most people call it, rests up against the slopes of

Cerro Otto, behind which rear the spiky crests of the Cerro Catedral massif, and is spread along the dry southeastern shore of Lago Nahuel Huapi. Everything in Bariloche faces the lake but something went massively wrong with the town planning – the main road artery was built along the shore, severing the settlement's centre from its best feature.

The town's lifeblood is tourism, with 700,000 visitors arriving annually. This is a place of pilgrimage for the nation's students, who flood here in January and February on their summer breaks. They don't necessarily come in search of the mountain experience, but often end up having one, pushed out of town by the inflated high-season prices of hotels and clubs. The area's main attraction, **Parque Nacional Nahuel Huapi**, surrounds the town, although in winter, it's specifically the **ski resort** of Cerro Catedral nearby.

At peak times of year the excesses of commercialization and crowds of tourists may spoil elements of your visit. Nevertheless, the place does work well in giving remarkably painless access to many beautiful, and some genuinely wild, areas of the cordillera and, out of season, the town is still big enough to retain some life.

Some history

Before the incursions of either Mapuche or white settlers, the Nahuel Huapi area was the domain of the Poya, the Vuriloche, the Pehuelche and the Puelche, whose livelihood largely depended on the lake. These groups used the region's mountain passes to conduct trade with their western, Mapuche counterparts. The discovery of these routes became an obsession of early Spanish explorers in Chile, many of whom were desperate to hunt down the wealth of the City of the Caesars, rumoured to exist in these parts. Early expeditions were frustrated, and knowledge of the passes' whereabouts were a closely guarded indigenous secret until the late seventeenth century.

The history of the white presence in the region really begins with the Jesuit **Nicolás Mascardi**, who was dispatched by the viceroy of Perú and Chile to found a **mission** in the area in 1672. The job proved too tough even for the Jesuits: the indigenous tribes put paid to Mascardi and several of his successors and, in 1717, the mission was abandoned once and for all. Past experience of Spanish slaving expeditions probably had much to do with this hostile attitude. Fearing the image of the Virgin, they wrapped it in horsehide and hid it in the forest nearby, from where it was recovered by another Jesuit father and taken to Chiloé and then Concepción, before disappearing in the mid-nineteenth century. The local indigenous groups took one seventeenth-century Jesuit introduction more to their hearts than the Virgin: the humble apple, or *manzana*. Used for brewing *chicha*, wild apples became so popular that the region's Mapuche tribes became known as **Manzaneros**.

After the defeat of the indigenous groups during the Conquest of the Desert (see p.792), permanent white settlement became a possibility. Modern Bariloche has its roots in the arrival of German settlers from southern Chile around the starts of the twentieth century, but was a small town of only a few thousand until the creation of the national park in 1937. Since then, in many ways, it has become a liability for the park, forcing it to cede the area to the west to development. In recent decades, the population has skyrocketed, and the town is now a major urban centre, though lack of planning restrictions has meant that the homogeneity of its original alpine-style architecture has been swamped by a messy conglomerate of high-rise apartment blocks, a fact bemoaned by its long-term residents.

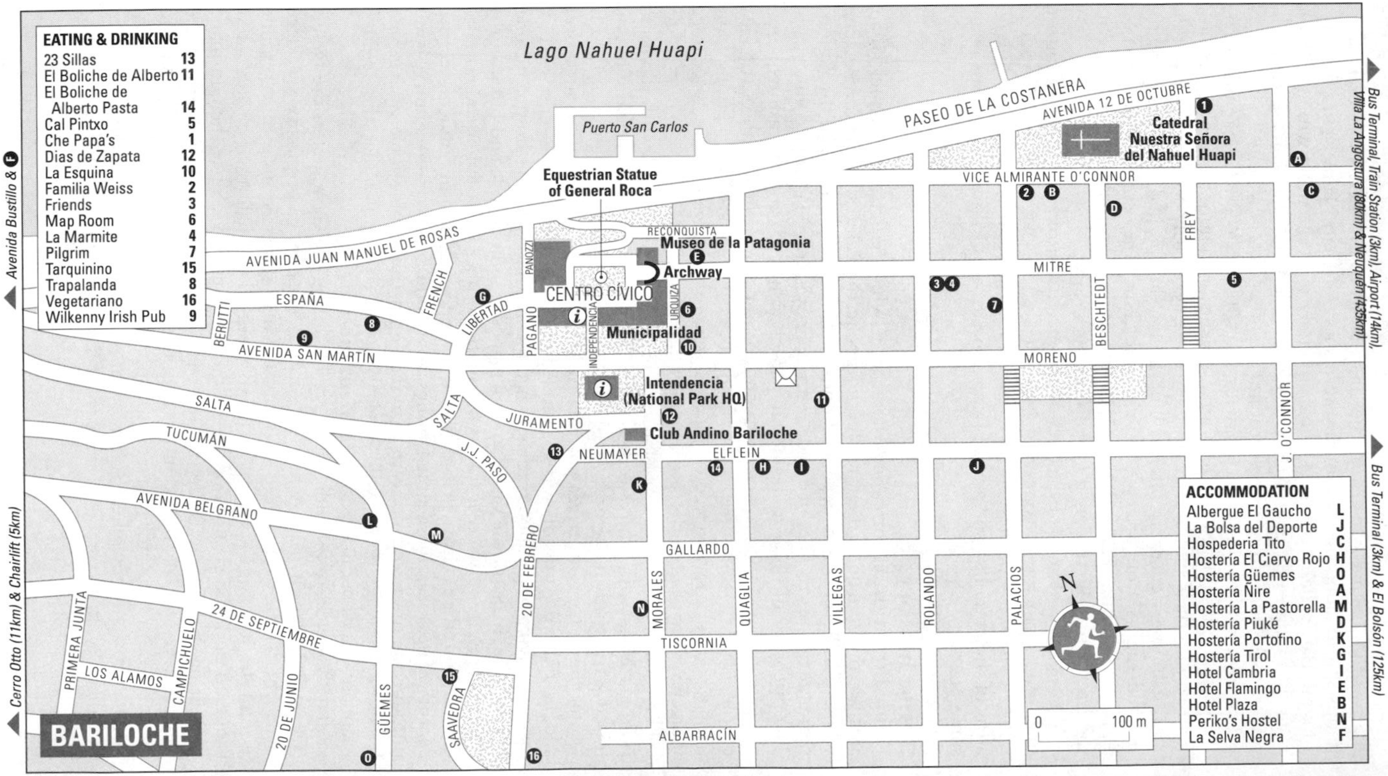
BARILOCHE
EATING & DRINKING
23 Sillas 13
El Boliche de Alberto 11
El Boliche de Alberto Pasta 14
Cal Pintxo 5
Che Papa's 1
Dias de Zapata 12
La Esquina 10
Familia Weiss 2
Friends 3
Map Room 6
La Marmite 4
Pilgrim 7
Tarquinino 15
Trapalanda 8
Vegetariano 16
Wilkenny Irish Pub 9
ACCOMMODATION
Albergue El Gaucho L
La Bolsa del Deporte J
Hospederia Tito C
Hostería El Ciervo Rojo H
Hostería Güemes O
Hostería Ñire A
Hostería La Pastorella M
Hostería Piuké D
Hostería Portofino K
Hostería Tirol G
Hotel Cambria I
Hotel Flamingo E
Hotel Plaza B
Periko's Hostel N
La Selva Negra F
Lago Nahuel Huapi
Puerto San Carlos
Equestrian Statue of General Roca
Catedral Nuestra Señora del Nahuel Huapi
Museo de la Patagonia
Archway
Centro Cívico
Municipalidad
Intendencia (National Park HQ)
Club Andino Bariloche
Paseo de la Costanera
Avenida 12 de Octubre
Avenida Juan Manuel de Rosas
Avenida San Martín
Avenida Belgrano
Vice Almirante O'Connor
Mitre
Moreno
Elflein
Neumayer
Gallardo
Tiscornia
Albarracín
Reconquista
Panozzi
Pagano
Independencia
Urquiza
Beschtedt
Frey
J. O'Connor
Palacios
Rolando
Villegas
Quaglia
Morales
20 de Febrero
Juramento
Salta
Tucumán
J.J. Paso
Libertad
French
España
Berutti
24 de Septiembre
20 de Junio
Güemes
Saavedra
Campichuelo
Los Alamos
Primera Junta
Bus Terminal, Train Station (3km), Airport (14km), Villa La Angostura (80km) & Neuquén (435km)
Bus Terminal (3km) & El Bolsón (125km)
Avenida Bustillo & F
Cerro Otto (11km) & Chairlift (5km)
N
0 100 m

Arrival and information

Bariloche's **airport** (Ⓣ02944/426162) is 14km east of town. A shuttle bus run by Del Lago Turismo meets most flights and ferries passengers to outside the company's central office at Villegas 222 (Ⓣ02944/430056). There are always *remises* hanging around, or you can take local bus #72, which runs every two hours (7.10am–10pm). The main **bus terminal** is next door to the **train station**, 3km east of the city centre along RN-237, here known as Avenida 12 de Octubre. The best local buses for the centre are #10, #20 or any bus marked "Catedral" (every 15–20min; 10min; $1). In town, buses to the terminal leave from Elflein and Quaglia.

The **tourist office**, in the centro cívico, operates a queuing system in summer (daily 9am–9pm; Ⓣ02944/429850, Ⓦwww.barilochepatagonia.info or Ⓦwww.bariloche.com). It keeps a list of available accommodation if you haven't reserved in advance, including *casas de familia*. A few blocks south is the **Intendencia of the Parque Nacional Nahuel Huapi**, Av San Martín 24 (summer Mon–Fri 8am–8pm, Sat–Sun 9am–8pm, winter daily 9am–3pm; Ⓣ02944/423111), which should be your first point of call if you are planning a visit to the park. A block behind is the **Club Andino Bariloche**, 20 de Febrero 30 (Jan & Feb daily 9am–1pm & 4–8.30pm, rest of year weekdays only same hours; Ⓣ02944/527966, Ⓦwww.clubandino.org), which can offer more detailed information on trekking routes.

Most of what you'll need in town can be found in the commercial area east of the **centro cívico** – sandwiched between the lake and Calle Elflein. Avenida 12 de Octubre from the terminal runs along the lake front, past the cathedral and the elevated centro cívico, where its name changes to Avenida Juan Manuel de Rosas. Further west this becomes **Avenida Bustillo**, which runs through the western suburbs and is the start of the Circuito Chico (see p.630). The main tourist street is **Calle Mitre**, which leads directly to the centro cívico.

A complicated **parking** scheme operates in the heart of the city (restrictions apply basically from Elflein and Avenida San Martín to the lake). After the first day in town, you must purchase an "ALTEC" sticker from any kiosk, which works in conjunction with tickets for the time you need ($4 per day). Fix them in the back windscreen of your vehicle on both sides. You can move your car as often as you like within the time allotted.

Accommodation

Accommodation in Bariloche is plentiful but pricey, and you should reserve in advance throughout the year to avoid missing out on the cheaper options, which fill rapidly. There is one **campsite** within easy reach of town: *La Selva Negra*, Av Bustillo Km2.95 (Ⓣ02944/441013; $15 per person), which has all the usual facilities.

In the town centre

Hotels

Hospedería Tito Vice Almirante O'Connor 745 Ⓣ02944/435241. The decor is unintentionally retro, but *Tito* is clean and pleasant with a good location just east of the action. One of the better budget hotels in town. ❹

Hostería El Ciervo Rojo Elflein 115 Ⓣ02944/435241, Ⓦwww.elciervorojo.com. More pink than *rojo*, but nevertheless a tastefully remodelled and centrally located townhouse which successfully fuses modest old-style charm with modern comforts. Continental breakfast is included in the price and discounts are offered for stays of more than one night. ❻

Hostería Güemes Güemes 715 Ⓣ02944/424785, Ⓕ435616. One of the best budget options in town sits on a tranquil side street with a prize-winning garden. The owner was a tourist guide for 45 years and has an in-depth knowledge of the surroundings. A spacious living room with a central coal fire makes for cosy winter evenings. ⑤

Hostería Ñire John O'Connor 44 ⓣ02944/423041, ⓦwww.elnire.com.ar. Another faux chalet with a cosy interior, which compensates for the slightly cold service. Neat and comfortable rooms with TV and en-suite bathroom. ⑤

Hostería La Pastorella Av Belgrano 127 ⓣ02944/424656, ⓦwww.lapastorella.com. Tasteful French decor gives this place a homely feel. Rooms are tidy and spacious but lack the charm of the rest of the hotel. There's a small tranquil garden and a sauna for relaxing. ⑥

Hostería Piuké Beschtedt 136 ⓣ02944/423044. Despite having a name that could easily be mispronounced, this is an attractive chalet-style hotel with flowery gardens just a block from the cathedral. Rooms are simple but comfortable and breakfast is included. ⑤

Hostería Portofino Morales 435 ⓣ02944/422795. All rooms have private bathroom in this family-run place; the one drawback is the poor lighting. ⑤

Hostería Tirol Libertad 175 ⓣ02944/426152, ⓦwww.hosteriatirol.com.ar. Ideally located a block from the centro cívico, this is a modern but tastefully decorated hotel. Rates include breakfast served in a dining room with stunning lake views – the huge glass windows will shield you from any cold wind blowing from the lake. ⑥

Hotel Cambria Elflein 183 ⓣ&ⓕ02944/430400. A modern, business-oriented, mid-range hotel, though the bathrooms are on the small side. ⑤

Hotel Flamingo Mitre 24 ⓣ02944/434868. Lake views and a handy location on the main street. Ask for rooms at the back if you are affected by noise. ⑤

Hotel Plaza Vice Almirante O'Connor 431 ⓣ02944/424100, ⓦwww.hotelplazabariloche.com.ar. Nothing flashy, but good value for its lakeside location and a simple breakfast is included in the price – served in the dining room with panoramic views over the lake and cathedral. Popular with students, particularly in the winter. ⑤

Hostels

Albergue El Gaucho Belgrano 209 ⓣ02944/522464, ⓦwww.hostelgaucho.com. Slightly rickety backpacker stronghold, this is a basic but essentially good option for budget travellers. Dorms ($28 per person) and double rooms (④) are available, as is excellent information on local excursions.

La Bolsa del Deporte Palacios 405 ⓣ02944/423529, ⓦwww.labolsadeldeporte.com.ar. Excellent wooden cabin-style hostel with thirty beds and good attention to detail (eg bunk-bed reading lights). Kitchen facilities and Internet access available. Reservations one day ahead only. ④

Periko's Hostel Morales 555 ⓣ02944/522326, ⓦwww.perikos.com. Best of the youth-hostel-type accommodation, this excellent, well-built and well-run place is loaded with information about trips. Its travel agency arm, Overland Patagonia, is next door. Reserve well in advance. Bunks $28 per person, double rooms ④

Along Avenida Bustillo

Avenida Bustillo runs for 25km along the lakeshore to Puerto Pañuelo and is packed, at least for the first dozen kilometres, with bungalows and cabins, some of which have sensational lake views, though most of which have been gentrified in the worst possible taste.

Alaska Hostel Lilinquen 328 ⓣ02944/461564, ⓦwww.alaska-hostel.com. A wooden cabin hidden among trees approximately 400m off the main road, this homely hostel offers kitchen use, laundry, bike rental and a great Jacuzzi. To get here, take bus #10, #20 or #21 to Av Bustillo Km7.5, then walk down the side road Palo Santo to Calle Laura, which leads to Lilinquen. Dorm beds $25 per person; one double room (④) and bungalows ③–⑤.

Arelauquen Lodge Ruta 82, 8km from junction with Av Bustillo ⓣ02944/467626, ⓦwww.arelauquen.com. Set among parkland and a golf course near the shores of Lago Gutiérrez, this Belgian-owned hotel is an exceptional upmarket option. Fine mountain views with tasteful and original decoration and an excellent restaurant. ⑧

La Cebra Av Bustillo Km7 ⓣ02944/461390, ⓦwww.lacebrabungalows.com. One of the first bungalows to be built along Av Bustillo and still among the best, with its own beach and sensational scenic views. ⑦

Hostería Lonquimay Lonquimay 3672, Barrio Melipal ⓣ02944/443450. Nicely appointed chalet-style hotel with an intimate feel not far from the Cerro Otto chairlift. Take bus #10 to Av Bustillo Km3.8. ④

Llao Llao Av Bustillo Km28 ⓣ02944/448530, ⓦwww.llaollao.com. One of Argentina's most famous hotels, designed and built (twice) by Alejandro Bustillo along the lines of an enormous Canadian cabin. Excellent views and services, including indoor and outdoor pools, a golf course and even a presidential suite. More details in Circuito Chico coverage, p.630. ⑨

Las Marías del Nahuel Av Bustillo Km7 ⓣ02944/462327, ⓦwww.lasmarias-bariloche.com. Next to *La Cebra*, with classy wooden bungalows set in beautifully manicured gardens. On-site Jacuzzi and private beach. ⑦

Mont Blanc Av Bustillo Km6.1 ⓣ02944/441360, ⓦwww.mont-blanc.com.ar. Well-run, friendly and refreshingly simple, Swiss-style stone chalets for four to seven people – though on the wrong side of the road for a lake view. ⑥

The Town

The **centro cívico**, an ensemble of buildings constructed out of timber and local greenish-grey stone that resolutely face the lake, is Bariloche's focal point. Dating from 1939, it's a noble architectural statement of permanence designed

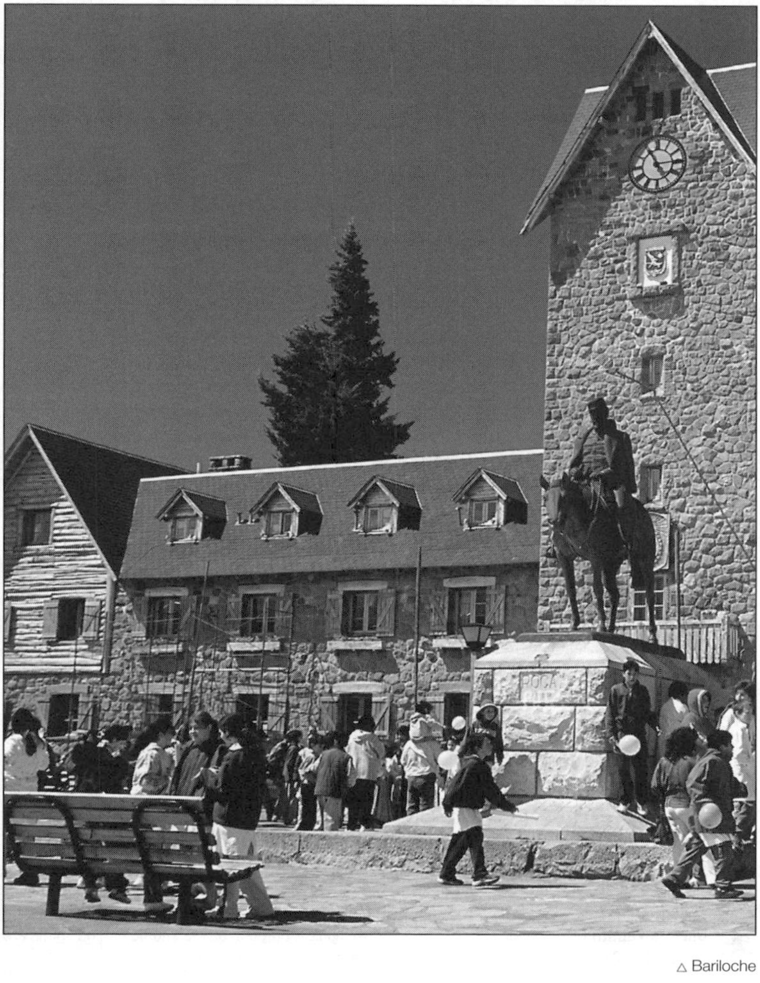

△ Bariloche

by Ernesto de Estrada, who collaborated with Argentina's most famous architect, Alejandro Bustillo, in the development of an alpine style that has come to represent the region. In the centre of the main plaza, around which these buildings are grouped, stands a graffiti-strewn equestrian **statue** of General Roca, whose horse looks suitably hang-dog after the trying Campaign of the Desert. Of the plaza's attractions, the most interesting is the **Museo de la Patagonia** (Mon & Sat 10am–1pm, Tues–Fri 10am–12.30pm & 2–7pm, closed Sun; $2.50), which also rates as one of Patagonia's very best museums. Look out for the caricature of Perito Moreno as a wet nurse guiding the infant Theodore Roosevelt on his trip through the Lake District in 1913. Superb, too, are the engraved Tehuelche tablet stones that experts speculate may have been protective amulets, Aónik'enk painted horse hides and playing cards made of guanaco skin, one of the Mapuche's famous lances and Roca's own uniform. Informative booklets are on sale, but only the one on the Campaign of the Desert is translated into English – ask about guided tours.

On the lakeshore to the east of the museum is the Bustillo-designed **Catedral Nuestra Señora del Nahuel Huapi**, whose attractive stained-glass windows illustrate Patagonian themes such, as the first Mass held by Magellan – the oppression of the indigenous peoples is clearly evident.

The town's **beach** is narrow but pleasant enough and the views are predictably spectacular, but the water is cold even in summer. If you want to swim there is a wonderful **outdoor pool** nearby at the Albergue Deportivo Municipal (Mon–Sat noon–8pm, Sun 1–8pm; $1) which offers the same experience without the chill.

For five days in August, Bariloche celebrates the **Fiesta Nacional de la Nieve**, with ski races, parades and a torch-lit evening descent on skis to open the season officially, as well as the election of the Reina Nacional de la Nieve, or Snow Queen.

Eating

Bariloche has a large and excellent selection of places to **eat**, ranging from cheap diners to gourmet and expensive restaurants. Most are within walking distance of the centre. Calle Mitre is also lined with stores selling local specialities such as chocolate – think chocolate sculptures – smoked trout, ice cream and *alfajores*.

23 Sillas 20 de Febrero 40 no phone. This is one of the few places where vegetarians can eat without fear. Whole-grain sandwiches, fresh fruit juices and other dishes (including some with meat) will tempt anybody looking to detox.

El Boliche de Alberto Villegas 347 ⓣ02944/431433 and Av Bustillo 8800 ⓣ02944/462285. The juiciest and largest *parrillas* in town: prepare to gorge yourself. Also runs a pasta restaurant under the same name at Elflein 49 for when your arteries need relief.

Cal Pintxo Mitre 633 ⓣ02944/456888. Spanish-style tapas bar with a good selection of seafood dishes at reasonable prices. Beer on tap is cheap by Bariloche standards, and there is live music at weekends.

Dias de Zapata Morales 362 ⓣ02944/423128. Mexican-run Mexican restaurant, so you are guaranteed the real deal. Portions are large and of high quality, and you can even choose your spice level from mild to mind-blowingly hot.

La Esquina Urquiza and Perito Moreno. Corner by name and corner café by nature, this popular local haunt is a good place to have a drink and while away the time with a newspaper or book at outdoor tables sheltered from the summer sun.

Familia Weiss Palacios and O'Connor ⓣ02944/435789. A perennial hit with visitors, especially for its *ciervo a la cazadora* (venison in a creamy mushroom sauce) or *picada* selection of smoked specialities. Open 8–3am.

Friends Mitre and Rolando. Open 24hr in summer, *Friends* is well suited for night owls with the munchies. Burgers, pizzas and beers and spirits are served, all at good prices.

La Marmite Mitre 329 ⓣ02944/423685. Not a bargain by any means, the intimate, old-fashioned *Marmite* is nonetheless worthwhile for its regional and Swiss specialities, especially its fondues. Closed Sun lunch.

Tarquinino 24 de Septiembre and Saavedra. In a tasteful lodge with trees growing through its roof, this *parrilla*, with succulent 5cm-thick *bife de lomo*, is a popular local haunt.

Vegetariano 20 de Febrero 730 ⓣ02944/421820. If you've had your fill of *parrillas* this excellent veggie restaurant will provide relief. Vegans beware though – most dishes contain egg and dairy products, and there are also fish dishes on the menu.

Drinking and nightlife

With the constant influx of Argentine students mixing with an onslaught of thirsty backpackers, Bariloche has a lively *movida*. **Bars** are scattered around town but the majority of the action is in the area between Elflein and the waterfront. However, drinking can be expensive – plan on spending about thirty percent more than elsewhere in Argentina in the trendiest bars, while discos charge $50 entry fee for non-Argentines. The two most famous **discos** in town are *Roket*, a futuristic dance club, and *Grisu* for Latin and pop music. Both are at the western end of J.M. de Rosas.

Blest Microcervecería Av Bustillo Km11.6 ⓣ02944/461026. This microbrewery has an excellent selection of very good home-made brews – their potent strawberry beer is especially worth sampling. It also serves meals. Open noon–1am daily.

Che Papa's John O'Connor 33. A relaxed, bohemian hangout, this is a cosy and friendly little bar that will be a hit with Che Guevara-philes.

Map Room Urquiza 248. Run by a US and Argentine couple of ex-backpacker origin, this restaurant/bar is packed with memorabilia from their extensive travels. The food is good too, and very reasonably priced. Closed Sun.

Pilgrim Palacios 167 ⓣ02944/421686. Owned by the same folk as *Blest*, the *Pilgrim* has an equally fine selection of beer, serves burgers and more and boasts a good atmosphere to boot.

Trapalanda España 322. One of the few bars in Bariloche with a terrace and beer garden, this bar is rapidly turning into a traveller's hangout. Fresh fruit cocktails are delicious.

Wilkenny Irish Pub San Martín 435 ⓣ02944/424444. Standard wannabe Irish bar with happy hour on selected drinks each night 7–9pm. This is the most famous party pub in Patagonia – drinks are not cheap.

Listings

Airlines Aerolíneas Argentinas, Mitre 185 ⓣ02944/423234 or 422144 at airport; American Falcon, Mitre 159 ⓣ02944/425200; LADE, Villegas 480 ⓣ02944/423562; Southern Wings, Quaglia 262 ⓣ02944/423704 or 430002 at airport.

Arts and crafts Available at the Paseo de los Artesanos, at Moreno and Villegas.

Banks and exchange Bank hours vary depending on season: April–Nov 9am–2pm; Dec–March 8am–1pm. Banco de la Nación, Mitre 178; Banco Francés, San Martín 336; Banco de Galicia, Moreno 77. Cambio Sudamericana, Mitre 63.

Books Some English titles at La Barca, Quaglia 247, and Cultura Librería, Elflein 74.

Car rental Bariloche, Moreno 115 ⓣ02944/427638; Budget, Mitre 106 ⓣ02944/429999; Avis, Av San Martín 162 ⓣ02944/431648.

Consulate Chile, J.M. de Rosas 180 ⓣ02944/423050.

Hospital Perito Moreno 601 ⓣ02944/426100.

Internet access At very many places along Mitre, from $2/hr.

Laundry Patagonia, Palacios 191.

Pharmacies Del Centro, Rolando 699; De Miguel, Mitre 130.

Police Centro cívico ⓣ02944/422772 or 423434.

Post office Moreno 175 (Mon–Fri 8.30am–1pm & 4–7pm, Sat 9am–1pm).

Spanish school ECELA, Pasaje Gutiérrez 843 ⓦwww.ecela.com.

Taxis Usually some hanging around the centro cívico. Dina Huapi ⓣ02944/468136; Patagonia Remise ⓣ02944/443700.

Telephone Several along Mitre, including Telecom, Mitre and Quaglia (8.30am–midnight).

Travel agencies and tour operators Most of the following offer a variety of excursions, including rafting, fishing and boat trips: Alternativa Patagonia, Quaglia 262 (ⓣ02944/430845,

Ⓔanorana@bariloche.com.ar); Del Lago Turismo, Villegas 222 (Ⓣ02944/430056); Turisur, Mitre 219 (Ⓣ02944/426630); Catedral Turismo, Palacios 263 (Ⓣ02944/423918, Ⓔtransita@bariloche.com.ar). Mountain-bike rental is available from Dirty Bikes, Vice Almirante O'Connor 681 (Ⓣ02944/425616). For steam-train trips from Bariloche to Perito Moreno see Ⓦwww.trenhistoricovapor.com.ar. Kayaking through Senzalimiti (Ⓦwww.slimiti.com). For Rafting Aguas Blancas (Ⓦwww.aguasblancas.com.ar) book through local travel agents.

Around Bariloche

The numerous **excursions** possible from Bariloche comprise a wide range of adventures and can be divided into two categories: land and lake. The town's travel agents offer more or less identical packages and prices, though in some cases you may prefer to do it at your own pace on public transport or by private car. Apart from those listed below, see also the "Trekking in Parque Nahuel Huapi" box, pp.618–619.

Circuito Chico

Bariloche's most popular, if not the most exciting, excursion is along the **Circuito Chico**, a 65-kilometre road course that follows Avenida Bustillo. You could join one of the organized tours (4hr; see "Listings", p.629) or visit the highlights on public transport. **Buses** leave from the terminal and from Moreno and Rolando: #20 for Puerto Pañuelo and *Llao Llao* (hourly 8am–9pm) and #10 or #11 for Colonia Suiza (every 20min 4.10am–11pm).

The first ten or so kilometres of the circuit are disappointing. Although the lake views are great, they are accompanied by a steady stream of twee boutiques, hotels, restaurants, workshops and factory outlets for cottage industries. It's good for buying regional produce – you can get everything from woollen sweaters to preserves, smoked trout and meats, ceramics, chocolates and wood-carvings – but for very little else.

The circuit's best sights lie at its westernmost end. Before you reach **Puerto Pañuelo** – where boats depart for excursions to the Isla Victoria, the Bosque de los Arrayanes and Puerto Blest (see p.632) – you pass a tiny neat chapel, the **Capilla San Eduardo**, on the left-hand side. Built with cypress and tiled with *alerce* shingles, it was designed by Estrada under the supervision of Bustillo. Across from the chapel is the imposing **Llao Llao**, one of Argentina's most famous hotels (Ⓣ02944/448530; see p.626). From below it looks like a carbuncle set on top of a verdant knoll, though Alejandro Bustillo's alpine design strangely improves the closer you get. The original building burnt down in 1939, less than a year after completion, in a closed-season blaze caused by an inattentive housekeeper. The forests were plundered again, and the hotel reopened in 1940. State-owned until 1991, it is now owned by a private company and can be visited as part of a **guided tour** (booking essential; free). The sensational views are worth a hike up alone, but for guests, facilities include an indoor pool, gym, tennis courts and a fine restaurant – *Los Césares* – with superbly cooked regional cuisine. The restaurant is open in the evenings to non-guests – reservations are a must.

The wildest scenery of the circuit is found along the road that runs through the forested stretch beyond *Llao Llao*. Four kilometres beyond the hotel a track heads north to **Villa Tacul**, where you'll find a pretty sandy beach. There are also a couple of short forest walks, one around Cerro Llao Llao, the other between *Llao Llao* and **Lago Escondido**. The latter walk brings you to **Mirador López**, which overlooks the deep blue waters of Nahuel Huapi and has excellent views of **Cerro Capilla** (2167m). At nearby Bahía López you'll find the *Alun Nehuen* hotel, Av Bustillo Km32 (Ⓣ02944/448005, Ⓦwww.alunnehuen.com.ar; ❻–❼), a lakeside hotel with spectacular views that offers forty percent off prices in the low season. The last point of call on the circuit is **Colonia Suiza**, originally settled by Swiss immigrants. There's nothing particular to see here, but it's a good place for gorging yourself on Sunday lunch. The local speciality is a mixed meat-fest called *curanto*, traditionally prepared with hot stones: try *Curanto Emilio Goye* (Wed & Sun lunch only; reservations on Ⓣ02944/448250), with lamb, sausages, pork, sweetcorn, potatoes, *matambre*, pumpkin and chicken.

Circuito Grande

The **Circuito Grande** is a 240km loop that leads east out of Bariloche on RN-237 past the incredible rock formations of the **Valle Encantado** ("Enchanted Valley"). Here you'll see pine forests lining the steep valley outcrops and stone fingers pointing skywards while the blue waters of the Río Limay flow below. The Río Traful joins the Río Limay at Confluencia, 70km from Bariloche. Here RN-237 continues on towards Neuquén while RP-65 turns north towards Villa Traful. At the junction is a service station and, from a good vantage point above the other shore, *Hostería Gruta de las Vírgenes* (Ⓣ02944/426138, Ⓦwww.glvpatagonia.com.ar; ❺), which can put you in contact with fishing guides. Take RP-65 north towards Mirador del Traful and Villa Traful (see p.617), soon after which the circuit joins the latter part of the Ruta de los Siete Lagos (see box, pp.616–617) near Lagos Correntoso and Espejo, and then returns to Bariloche via Villa La Angostura (see p.619). Alternatively, you could turn right when you meet the Ruta de los Siete Lagos and head to San Martín de los Andes, a good stopover point. Returning to Bariloche you can take either the Paso Córdoba (a return trip of 360km) or the paved route via Junín and La Rinconada (460km).

Renting a car (see "Listings", p.629) is the ideal way in which to embark on the Circuito Grande, though you could also take the full-day guided tour – ask at the tourist office. Alternatively, you could arrange an itinerary with a taxi.

Cerro Catedral

Some 20km south of Bariloche is **Cerro Catedral**, named after the Gothic spires of rock that make up its craggy summits (2405m). In summer, the village of **Villa Catedral**, at the foot of the bowl, is the starting-point for a couple of fantastic treks up and around Cerro Catedral, though you could just take a cable car and then a chairlift to reach Refugio Lynch near the summit (1870m; 10am–5.30pm). Views from here and from the ridge above are superb, and you just might catch a glimpse of condors. Experienced hikers can follow the ridge southwest; it later forks either to Refugio San Martín or to Refugio Frey. From here an easy descent leads back to Villa Catedral (see box, pp.618–619).

In winter, the village is the main **ski resort** (Ⓦwww.catedralaltapatagonia.com) that competes with Cerro Chapelco (see p.612), near San Martín de los Andes. While Chapelco tends to attract more hard-core skiers, Cerro Catedral has comfortable lifts and excellent access to the *après-ski* in Bariloche. July is the busiest month. There are 67km of runs in all, some with descents of up to 4km in length. Buses (marked "Catedral") leave from Moreno 470 in Bariloche to Villa Catedral; alternatively, you could take a half-day organized trip to the village (4hr 30min).

Cerro Tronador

The RN-258 heads south from Bariloche past Lago Gutiérrez to the southernmost point on Lago Mascardi, where a dirt road strikes west around the lakeshore and you must pay a $12 park entrance fee. Further along, at Los Rápidos (where there's an organized campground), the road forks, and you can go west along the southern Río Manso to Lago Hess and Cascada de los Alerces or north towards Pampa Linda. The latter route has terrific views of the glaciers on **Cerro Tronador**. Both roads here become single-track, necessitating a timetable for travelling in each direction. To Cascada de los Alerces, you can drive east to west 8–10.15am, returning 11.15am–1pm. After 2pm the road is open to traffic in both directions. For Cerro Tronador, you can enter 10.30am–2pm and return 4–6pm, after which the road reverts to double direction. Tours increasingly miss out the Cascada de los Alerces fork and waterfall – a twenty-metre plunge of white water that resembles to some extent the shape of a seated Victorian woman with her dress spread out.

Organized trips take you past Pampa Linda as far as the Ventisquero Negro lookout, a moraine-encrusted glacier and offshoot of Glaciar del Manso on the upper slopes of Cerro Tronador. You may also have time for the short walks to the fifty-metre-high Saltillo de las Nalcas or Garganta del Diablo and there are plenty of hiking options from Pampa Linda (see box, pp.618–619). Day-tours are run by several travel agents, with some also offering the possibility of a boat trip on Lago Mascardi, though you should consult about availability at the tourist office in advance.

Isla Victoria and Puerto Blest

A very popular boat trip from Bariloche heads to **Isla Victoria** from Puerto Pañuelo (see p.630; 10.30am–5.30pm or 2–7pm; remember to add costs of transfer and park entrance to tour quotes), where there are rock paintings, beaches and a chairlift to Cerro Bella Vista with the requisite stunning views. The boat continues north to the Parque Nacional de los Arrayanes on the Peninsula Quetrihué (see p.622).

Equally worthwhile, and much less crowded, is the excursion to **Puerto Blest** in the western fringes of the Parque Nacional Huapi, which takes in lake vistas along the way and starts with a 75-minute boat trip from Puerto Pañuelo. A minibus continues the trip to the shores of Lago Frías, with its peppermint-coloured waters. During the early morning and late afternoon you can see condors gathering at their nearby roost. Returning to Puerto Blest, the boat crosses the channel to dock on the north shore after which there is a forty-minute stroll to the stepped Cascada Los Cántaros waterfall.

Three Lakes Crossing

The **Cruce Internacional de los Lagos**, or "Three Lakes Crossing" (Mon–Sat only), via the Paso Pérez Rosales to **Puerto Montt** in Chile, is one of the classic border crossings of the continent, and also the priciest. The joy of this one- or two-day crossing is the scenery: if the weather turns sour or if you need to get to Chile fast, you'd be better off taking the standard bus route via Paso Cardenal Samoré (see p.617). Also, in high season, the sheer volume of tourists can detract from the trip's charm. The highlights are, of course, the lake cruises: Puerto Pañuelo to Puerto Blest on Lago Nahuel Huapi; across **Lago Frías**; and across enchanting **Lago Todos Los Santos**, with wonderful views of **Volcán Osorno**, one of the cordillera's most shapely cones. On the two-day version (from May–Aug only) you will be able to make the short climb to see the Cascada Los Cántaros (see above). On the Chilean side, the Saltos de Petrohué waterfalls near the foot of Osorno are very beautiful, as are the views of Tronador from Peulla. Minibuses cover the land stages, including the 30km between Lago Frías and Peulla.

The huemul (Hippocamelus bisculus)

If you spend any time in the Patagonian Lake District it won't be long before you hear talk of the almost legendary **huemul**. Bizarrely, this little deer, which stands 1m at the shoulder, was declared a "National Monument" in 1996 in response to an alarming decline in population. A secretive denizen of high Patagonian forests, it once played an important role in the livelihood of indigenous groups who relied on it for food and often depicted it in cave-paintings. The arrival of the Europeans and their firearms had disastrous consequences for the remarkably tame species, and there are even tales about them being killed with knives after having been approached to a few metres. Coupled with increasing destruction of their forest habitat, their numbers declined rapidly and today only an estimated six hundred remain in Argentina. Your best chance of glimpsing one is in winter, when harsh weather may drive them down to lower altitudes and more open areas in search of food.

The *huemul* shows a series of adaptations to its tough environment, possessing a thick, dense coat to protect against the cold and short strong legs that help it gain a foothold on rocky slopes. They are also remarkably good swimmers, and can cross lakes and rivers with ease. Male *huemul* are identifiable by their antlers and the dark "Y" shape that appears on the snout and between the eyes.

Crossings can be booked through Catedral Turismo, Palacios 263 (Ⓣ02944/425444, Ⓦwww.crucedelagos.cl). From September to April, the entire trip to Puerto Montt can be made in one or two days, with an optional overnight stop in **Peulla**. The catch is there is only one (expensive) place to stay, the *Hotel Puella* (Ⓣ00562/1964182, Ⓦwww.hotelpeulla.cl; ⑧), and camping is not permitted. If you do the one-day tour, you'll leave Bariloche at 7am, and should arrive in Puerto Montt by 8pm.

El Bolsón and around

El Bolsón, to the south of Parque Nacional Nahuel Huapi, is a growing tourist centre with numerous trekking opportunities nearby. It also acts as the staging-point for attractions just across the provincial border in Chubut: the small **Parque Nacional Lago Puelo**, and two minor settlements close to the mountains – **Epuyén** and **Cholila**, the latter once home to Butch Cassidy. The 123-kilometre drive along RN-258 from Bariloche to El Bolsón should be done during the day for its excellent mountain and lake views.

El Bolsón

Set in the bowl of a wide, fertile valley and hemmed in by parallel ranges of mountains, straggly **EL BOLSÓN** was Latin America's first non-nuclear town and the first to declare itself an "ecological municipality". The claim that the jagged peak of the nearby **Cerro Piltriquitrón** is one of the earth's "energy centres" led to it become a popular hippy hangout in the 1960s, and while it's a bit more commercial these days, the laid-back atmosphere persists. In summer it's particularly popular with young Argentine backpackers, since it's far easier on the wallet than nearby Bariloche. Spiritual life in El Bolsón is cosmopolitan, and you'll find Buddhist temples as well as a variety of practitioners of alternative paths. Unsurprisingly, UFOs and spirits (*duendes*) are also said to stop off regularly, being guaranteed an especially sympathetic reception on the last

Saturday of February, when the town's main party, the **Fiesta del Lúpulo** (Hops Festival) is held. It celebrates the harvest of an important local crop, with music in the main square and an enjoyable, well-lubricated atmosphere. The **Olimpiadas Agrarias** (Farm Olympics) is another offbeat festival worth checking out, occurring over four days in mid-February, with ox races and other oddities. More refined, the town's **Jazz Festival** (Ⓦwww.elbolsonjazz.com.ar) is held over a long weekend in early December. Also worth visiting is the **crafts market** (Tues, Thurs & Sat) on the **Plaza Pagano**, famous throughout the Lake District for the quality of its merchandise, including locally brewed beers. A small **ornithological museum** (daily 8am–3pm; $3; Ⓦwww.avespatagonicas.com.ar) two blocks east of the plaza, on Saavedra and Feliciano, features over one hundred exhibits of stuffed Patagonian birds.

East of town, on the wooded slopes of **Cerro Piltriquitrón** (2260m), is another unconventional and interesting site – the **Bosque Tallado** (Sculpted Forest) – 31 tree stumps carved by local craftsmen into a variety of fascinating and often grotesque figures. You'll need to take a taxi to the base of the Cerro, but there is a forty-minute uphill walk before you get there. If dairy products float your boat, head to Humas (Mon–Fri 9am–1pm & 3–9pm, Sat 9am–1pm) on Camino los Nagales, signposted from Avenida San Martín north of the plaza. Here you can learn all about the making of organic yogurt, cheese and ice cream on one of the two daily guided tours (10am & 12.30pm)

Arrival and information

Arriving from the north, RN-258 is called Avenida Sarmiento; from Esquel in the south it's called Avenida Belgrano. These two converge on the ACA fuel station that lies in the centre of town on **Avenida San Martín**, the avenue that forms the backbone of the town. Local **buses** drop you off at their respective offices, most of which are on or just off Avenida Sarmiento. On the north side of the plaza, at the corner of San Martín and Roca, is the useful **tourist office**, bursting with promotional material (Mon–Sat 8am–11pm, Sun 9am–11pm; Ⓣ02944/492604, Ⓦwww.bolsonturistico.com.ar), opposite is the **post office** (Mon–Fri 8.30am–1pm). If you come in a car it's worth filling your tank – fuel is half-price in El Bolsón. **Taxis** can be hard to find and should be booked in advance: try Remises Patagonia (Ⓣ02944/493907). Fran's Remises (Ⓣ02944/493041) offers return services to local attractions such as Cascada Escondida and Bosque Tallado.

Accommodation

El Bolsón has no shortage of **accommodation** choices, particularly the more inexpensive variety, many of which are within walking distance of Plaza Pagano. Leafy *La Chacra* **campsite**, Belgrano 1128 (Ⓣ02944/492111; $12 per person), is close to the centre, less than fifteen minutes' walk down RN-258 towards Esquel. Alternatively, if you like a drink you can camp in the garden of El Bolsón Brewery (see "Eating, drinking and nightlife", opposite; Ⓣ02944/492595).

Albergue Gaia 7km north of the centre Ⓣ02944/492143, Ⓦwww.bolsonturistico.com.ar/gaia/. A stellar hostel, the airy, ecologically minded *Gaia* boasts laundry facilities, a swimming pool and a kitchen. Take a Transporte Urbano bus to Km118 on RN-258. ❶

Albergue El Pueblito Ⓣ02944/493560, Ⓦwww.elpueblitohostel.com.ar. The well-run, HI-affiliated *El Pueblito* is 4km north of the centre. Take a Transporte Urbano bus or a taxi to get there. ❶

Cabañas Paraiso at access to Cerro Piltriquitrón Ⓣ02944/492766, Ⓦwww.cabaniaparaiso.com.ar. Ideally located for the Bosque Tallado. Well-equipped cabins for up to six people. The staff can organize rafting, trekking and horse-riding excursions. ❺

Hospedaje Salinas Roca 641 Ⓣ02944/492396. Though this *hospedaje*'s rooms with shared bathrooms are a bit dull, it does offer a convenient location near Plaza Pagano, friendly service and use of the kitchen. ❷

Hostería del Campo Ruta 258 ⓣ02944/492297, ⓦwww.cabaniasdelcampo.com.ar. On the northern outskirts of town, this *hostería* is styled along the lines of an American motel and all rooms come with phone and TV. There are also cabins (❻ for five people) and it has the added bonus of being next to the El Bolsón Brewery. ❺

Hosteria Valle Nuevo 25 de May and Berutti ⓣ02944/492087. Small but clean, bright rooms with stunning mountain views. Well maintained with excellent customer care – there are even fire escapes. ❹

La Posada de Hamelín Granollers 2179 ⓣ02944/492030, ⓦwww.posadadehamelin.com.ar. In town, *La Posada de Hamelín* is in a lovely brick building with hops growing up the walls and adobe interiors to some rooms. ❺

Eating, drinking and nightlife

El Bolsón is one of the few towns in Argentina where finding vegetarian **food** is not a problem. The valleys around are chock-a-block with smallholdings that produce organic vegetables, and fruits and berries for jams or desserts. Local honey and cheeses are also good. *Calabaza*, San Martín 2518, offers some appetizing vegetarian dishes, including cheese *milanesas*, and maintains a pioneering feel. Next door, at *Cerro Lindo*, you'll find an imaginative menu that includes rabbit and wild boar. For the less adventurous, *Boulevard*, at the corner of San Martín and Hube, has a relaxed atmosphere and does superb pizza. Next to the tourist office, *Jauja* (ⓣ02944/492448) is a Patagonian restaurant, ice-cream parlour and artisanal chocolate shop all in one.

The in-crowd tend to hang out at *Dos Ruedas* on San Martín, while those preferring a quieter **drink** go across the road to more chilled *Boulevard* or the scattering of open-air, summer-only bars around the plaza. There are a couple of discos – *Barr* and *Insomnia* – on Dorrego a block north of Plaza Pagano. El Bolsón Brewery (Mon–Sat 9am–midnight, Sun 10am–10pm; ⓦwww.cervezaselbolson.com) is outside town at Km124 on the main road north. Here the aficionado owner serves up a variety of beers, including fruity brews. Free guided tours of the brewing process are given on Tuesday, Thursday and Saturday afternoons.

Trekking and other outdoor activities

The Club Andino Piltriquitrón (CAP; daily 9am–9pm mid-Dec to Easter ⓣ02944/492600), at Roca and Sarmiento, can guide you through **trekking** possibilities in the area, most of which consist of considerable ascents – they will also mind your bags for you for a small fee. Among the most popular is the **Cerro Hielo Azul Circuit** (4–6hr), which brings you high enough to present glacier vistas. Further north you can make side treks to less visited areas of **Cerro Dedo Gordo** (4–5hr) and **Los Laguitos** (6–8hr). To the south, the hike to *Refugio Cerro Lindo* (5–7hr) takes in the lake of the same name with beautiful blue waters encased by sheer cliffs. Another interesting, relatively gentle hike to **Cajón Azul** (4–5hr) starts from the same point as Dedo Gordo and passes an excellent *refugio* that serves hot food. The Cajón itself is an opening one metre wide and forty metres deep; the Río Azul roars through the bottom. CAP sells a Spanish guidebook, *Ingreso a los Refugios*, which details local hikes.

Local tour operators offer a variety of excursions and day-trips, most incorporating a mix of horse-riding, trekking, rafting and boating. Particularly good is Grado 42, Av Belgrano 404 (ⓣ02944/493124, ⓦwww.grado42.com), which offers tours to the Bosque Tallado and Butch Cassidy's cabin at Cholila. The Aeroclub El Bolsón, San Martín and Pueyrredón (ⓣ02944/491125), gives flights in four-seater planes. Year-round trout-fishing is available at the Criadero de Truchas at Km117.3 on RN-258.

Parque Nacional Lago Puelo

In the northwest corner of Chubut Province, 19km south of El Bolsón, the relatively small **PARQUE NACIONAL LAGO PUELO** (meaning "waters of the east") protects an area of rugged mountains, forests and pasture that surrounds the windswept, turquoise lake of the same name. In recent years, several fires in the region have damaged swathes of the native forest, but it still offers some excellent trekking possibilities. A few endangered *huemules* (see box, p.633) inhabit the remoter border areas of the park, and some 116 species of birds have been recorded here, including the resident Chilean Pigeon (*paloma araucana*), a species that came close to extinction due to disease but whose numbers are now recovering.

There are incursions here of several tree species usually found only in Chile, such as the *avellano*, the *olivillo* and the *ulmo*, which flowers in late summer with large white blossoms reminiscent of magnolia blooms. The park also protects *alerces* (see box, p.645) and groves of the water-loving *patagua* (or *pitra*), a species related to the *arrayán*.

The park can be accessed via two routes. The most common way is from El Bolsón, passing through **Lago Puelo Village**, 3.5km north of the lake and outside the park boundary. Certain scheduled **bus** services (hourly; 40min) from Bariloche and El Bolsón only go as far as the village (especially in the winter), so check first. There's a small, understocked information office at the first junction on entering town, but you're better off staying on the bus and waiting until you reach the park. Should you get off, it's a short trip by *remise* (Ⓣ02944/499125) from the village to the park headquarters and pier. A plethora of places in the area rent out **cabins**, of which *Puelo Ranch*, near the YPF fuel station (Ⓣ02944/499234; ❺) is the most upmarket. Try also *Cabañas La Osa* (Ⓣ02944/499208, Ⓦwww.cabanialaosa.com.ar), at Km3.5 on RN-40, which has cabins for up to eight people (❽) and some doubles (❺), or *Cabañas Nosotros* (Ⓣ02944/492586, Ⓦwww.cabaniasnosotros.com.ar; ❻), which boasts a pool and home-grown vegetables. They also have *cabañas* for six people (❼) and often cut prices by half in the low season.

You'll be charged $6 to enter the park at the **intendencia** (Ⓣ02944/499232, Ⓕ02944/499064) and given a basic map of trails in the park. Where the road ends at the north end of the lake, you have a choice of **campsites**, the better of which is *Camping Lago Puelo* (Ⓣ02944/499183; $15 per person), to the left of the pier. Further round the shore from the *autocamping* is a beach popular with locals in the summer. A walk along the lake's forested north shore leads to the Chilean border, 9km away. Before setting out, check on the trail's status at the intendencia, and ask for information on where to cross the Río Azul if water levels are high. A **boat** service crosses the lake south to **El Turbio** (18km away), a glorious base for treks in the park, though few people bother to make the effort to get here

The second park access (no charge) is via a minor road, 13km long, from El Hoyo de Epuyén, just south of El Bolsón. It reaches the lake at the mouth of the Río Epuyén, where there is a campsite ($15 per person). From here you can hike 18km south to El Turbio where there's a park ranger's post and campsite, but you'll have to take all provisions with you. It's possible to make an expedition hike through to Cholila (see below), passing the spectacular ramparts of **Cerro Tres Picos**, or Three Peak Mountain (2492m), beyond the park's southern boundary.

Epuyén and Cholila

Just west of the main El Bolsón to Esquel road is the strung-out settlement of **EPUYÉN**, most of which is just by the turn-off. The more interesting section is some 6km away on the shores of **Lago Epuyén**. Parts of the picturesque mountain area around here were badly hit by forest fires in 1999 and have yet to recover fully, but it still makes a good base for trekking, especially if you're seeking to avoid the better-known and busier centres.

On the shores of Lago Epuyén, at the base of Cerro Pirque, you'll find *El Refugio del Lago* (Ⓣ&Ⓕ02945/499025; ❸), a rustic **guesthouse** and campground (❶) run by a multilingual French couple who organize fishing, trekking, canoeing and horse-riding expeditions in the area and prepare wholesome organic meals. Or you can camp at *El Faro* (Ⓣ02944/471719; ❶), though access is easier from the El Hoyo turn-off, continuing on through the village of Puerto Patriada. It's just 600m from the beach on the lakeshore.

Sitting amidst prairie grasslands, 3km east of the junction of RP-71 and RP-15, the hamlet of **CHOLILA**, with its spectacular backdrop of savage peaks, seems to belong in the American West. The area's main tourist attraction lies 12km north of the village itself along RP-71 towards Leleque. When you reach the police commissionaire's white house (with Argentine flag flying) at El Blanco, turn left down the track towards *La Casa de Piedra* teahouse. Fifty metres down this lane, there's a basic sign for Cabañas Butch Cassidy (with a confusing arrow); jump the fence and head parallel to RP-71. After 200m you'll see a cluster of three buildings among trees ahead. This is the site of the **cabin** of **Butch Cassidy**, who fled incognito to this isolated area at the start of the twentieth century with his partner, the **Sundance Kid**. The Sundance Kid and his beautiful gangster moll, **Etta Place**, also lived here for a short while. The group of buildings, which were already in a lamentable state of repair when Bruce Chatwin visited in the 1970s, are falling to pieces, but are of undoubted interest for Wild West fans.

Cholila's **bus terminal** is on the main square (Ⓣ02945/498173). Comfortable, roomy **lodging** is available at tranquil *Hostería El Trebol*, 2.7km from the terminal along RP-15 (Ⓣ02945/498055, Ⓦwww.interpatagonia/hosteriatrebol/; ❹–❺), which offers a half-board option. From Cholila, you can continue southwest

△ Cholila

Butch Cassidy and the Sundance Kid

Butch Cassidy, Etta Place and the **Sundance Kid** were fugitives together in the Argentine frontier town of Cholila between the years 1901 and 1906, as attested by both the Pinkerton Agency and provincial records of the time. Butch and Sundance had begun to grow weary of years of relentless pursuit, and had heard rumours that Argentina had become the new land of opportunity, offering the type of wide-open ranching country they loved, and where they could live free from the ceaseless hounding of Pinkerton agents.

It appears that, at first, the *bandidos* tried to go straight, even living under their real names – Butch as "George Parker" (an old alias derived from his name at birth, Robert Leroy Parker), and Etta and Sundance as Mr and Mrs Harry Longabaugh – and in this they succeeded, for a while at least. They were always slightly distant from the community and were evidently viewed as somewhat eccentric, yet decent, individuals. Certainly no one ever suspected they had a criminal past.

Various theories are mooted as to why the threesome sold their ranch in such a rush in 1907, but it seems as though the arrival of a Wild Bunch associate, the murderous Harvey "Kid Curry" Logan, following his escape from a Tennessee jail, had something to do with it. The robbery of a bank in Río Gallegos in early 1905 certainly had the hallmarks of a carefully planned Cassidy job, and a spate of robberies along the cordillera in the ensuing years have, with varying degrees of evidence, been attributed to the *bandidos norteamericanos*.

What happened to Cholila's outlaws next is a matter of conjecture. Etta returned to the US, putatively because she needed an operation for acute appendicitis, but equally possibly because she was pregnant, as a result of a dalliance with a young Anglo-Irish rancher. The violent deaths of Butch and Sundance were reported in Uruguay, and in several sites across Argentina and Bolivia. The least likely scenario is the one depicted by Paul Newman and Robert Redford in the famous 1969 Oscar-winning film. Bruce Chatwin in his classic *In Patagonia* proposes that the Sundance Kid was shot by frontier police in Río Pico, south of Esquel (see opposite).

Countless books have been written on the trio, including *In Search of Butch Cassidy*, by Larry Pointer, and most recently, *Digging Up Butch and Sundance*, by Anne Meadows.

through a glorious lush valley hemmed in by snow-capped mountains towards the northern gate of Parque Nacional Los Alerces (see p.643). Before the park entrance at Villa Lago Rivadavia, 16km from Cholila, there are a number of good-quality, good-value cabins for rent including *Cabañas Carrileufú* (Ⓣ02944/527851, Ⓦwww.cabcarrileufu.com; ❺) and *Cabañas Wanalen* (Ⓣ02945/1549986293, Ⓦwww.friosur.com.ar/wanalen/; ❸).

Esquel and around

Beyond Epuyén you'll notice a distinct change in the scenery, as the pine forests are abruptly replaced by stunted *meseta*-style vegetation. **Esquel**, the main town in the area, is a starting-point for visits to **Parque Nacional Los Alerces**, as well as a scattering of Welsh villages of which **Trevelin** is the most appealing. This is also the stage through which the steam train **La Trochita**, one of the region's most enduring attractions, plies its trade.

Esquel

For a place so close to exuberant Andean forests, **ESQUEL**, 180km south of El Bolsón, can surprise you on arrival for the aridity of its setting. Enclosed in a bowl of dusty ochre mountains, it is a stark contrast to Bariloche and El Bolsón. The town itself is pretty drab and uninteresting – most people make the trip to access the nearby **Parque Nacional Los Alerces** (see p.643), with the trip on *La Trochita* (see box, p.641) as the next biggest attraction. If you're looking to kill some time in town, the **Museo de Arte Naif**, next to the post office on Avenida Alvear, hosts a display of pictures by local artists, charmingly child-like in their simplicity.

Some 13km northeast of Esquel is the **skiing** centre of **La Hoya** (Ⓦwww.interpatagonia.com/lahoya/index.html), which often has snow lasting into mid-October. It has nine lifts, is good for powder and is promoted as a low-key family centre with moderately challenging pistes.

Arrival and information

The town's **airport** (Ⓣ02945/451676) is 21km east of the centre; you can take a *remise* to town or the Gales al Sur – who have a kiosk at the bus terminal (Ⓣ02945/455757) – and Patagonia Verde (Ⓣ02945/454396) minibus services. The stylish **bus terminal** (Ⓣ02945/451566) is on the main boulevard, **Avenida Alvear**, at no. 1871, about 1km from the town centre, while the *La Trochita* **train station** (see box, p.641) is at Roggero and Brun, nine blocks northeast of the terminal. The **tourist office**, just past the post office, at Alvear and Sarmiento

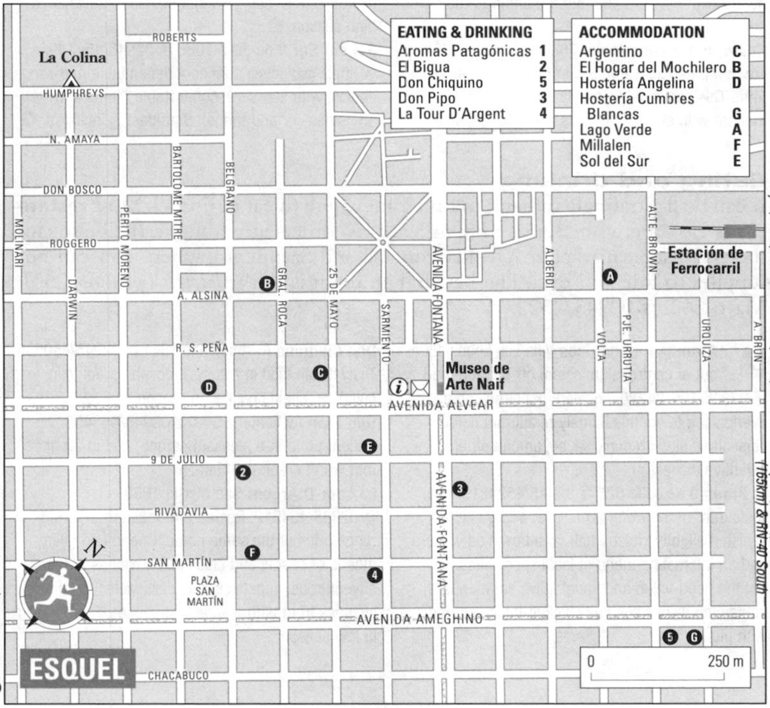

(daily Jan–Feb 7am–11pm, March–Dec 8am–8pm; ⓣ02945/451927, ⓦwww.esquel.gov.ar), operates a number system; get one as soon as you walk in. They can help you find accommodation if you haven't reserved.

Accommodation

There's a wide range of **accommodation** in town. Outside January and February you'll find huge discounts (up to two-thirds off), though most cabins are two or three kilometres outside the centre. There are a number of **campsites** within easy reach of town: *La Rural* (ⓣ02945/15684062) on RN-259, 1km southwest of town (❶), is spacious and, well, rural; *Millalen*, Av Ameghino 2063 (ⓣ02945/456164), has cabins and a small camping area with individual pitches.

Argentino 25 de Mayo 862 ⓣ02945/452237. You could be forgiven for thinking you had stepped into a time machine when you walk into this old traveller's inn. The adjacent bar is laden with rusting old museum pieces, and the sparsely furnished rooms are clean and comfortable, though they might have looked the same a century ago. It's a basic budget hotel popular with a young party crowd – expect noisy weekends at the bar. ❷

El Hogar del Mochilero Roca 1028 ⓣ02945/452166. Cheap but cheerful, and particularly popular with Argentine backpackers, *El Hogar* is much as you would expect from a hostel with dorm rooms and a camping area adjacent. ❶

Hostería Angelina Alvear 758 ⓣ02945/452763, ⓦwww.patagoniaexpress.com/hosteriaangelina.htm. This comfortable, family-run *hostería* is modern with stone-clad walls and a fountain out back. Ask for a room at the back, as the front can be a bit noisy. ❻

Hostería Cumbres Blancas Av Ameghino 1683 ⓣ02945/455100, ⓦwww.cumbresblancas.com.ar. A classy motel feel pervades this upmarket establishment. Large airy rooms come with free Internet connection and safe, and there's a sauna and "Scottish shower" (lateral water jets) for guests. ❽

Lago Verde Volta 1081 ⓣ02945/452251, ⓦwww.patagonia-verde.com.ar. Peaceful and welcoming guesthouse (its family also runs the Patagonia Verde travel agency) with clean rooms overlooking a rose garden. Reserve in advance in high season. ❸

Sol del Sur 9 de Julio 1086 ⓣ02945/452189, ⓦhttp://hsoldelsur.com.ar. A dependable mid-range choice, with standard, comfortable rooms and amenities (TV and fridge). Breakfast is included. ❻

Eating and drinking

It can be frustratingly difficult to find somewhere to eat in Esquel. Most **restaurants** close between 3pm and 8pm, with last orders at midnight. If all else fails, there is a supermarket at Avenida Fontana and Sarmiento, where you can buy supplies to tide you over. The best **bar** in town is in the *Hotel Argentino*, 25 de Mayo 862 (ⓣ02945/452237).

Aromas Patagónicos Villa Los Lobos, 2km out of centre (signposted) off Trevelin road ⓣ02945/156-84220. Located in a large cabin overlooking town, this homely restaurant serves venison steak with berry sauce, among other inventive dishes.

El Bigua 9 de Julio 825 ⓣ02945/452421. The restaurant of the *Hotel Tehuelche*, *El Bigua* is a stylish if slightly kitsch affair with bow-tied waiters and an interesting menu of local specialities. Try out the good-value and imaginative set menus containing dishes such as chicken thighs stuffed with plums.

Don Chiquino Av Ameghino 1641 ⓣ02945/450035. Tasty Italian food in a cosy atmosphere. You can count on it being packed in season.

Don Pipo Av Fontana 649 ⓣ02945/453458. Decent pizza in a pleasant setting, and at a price that won't break the bank.

La Tour D'Argent San Martín 1063 ⓣ02945/454612. Restaurant attached to a mid-range hotel of the same name. Cheap and filling menus of pastas and chicken, as well as a more adventurous, appetizing à la carte selection that includes trout with a variety of sauces. Closed Tues in low season.

Listings

Airlines Aerolíneas Argentinas, Av Fontana 408 ☎02945/453413; LADE, Alvear 1085 ☎02945/452124.
Banks Banco del Chubut, Alvear 1147; Banco de la Nación, Alvear and Roca; and Bansud, 25 de Mayo 752. All have ATMs.
Bike rental Coyote Bikes, Rivadavia 887 and Roca (☎02945/455505), or Carlos Barria, Don Bosco 259 (☎02945/454443).
Car rental Los Alerces, Sarmiento 763 ☎02945/456008; Avis, Av Fontana 331 ☎02945/15690580.
Hospital 25 de Mayo 150 ☎02945/451074 or 451224.
Internet Many places, including Cyberclub, Alvear 961, which has a fast connection.
Laundry Laverap, Roca and 9 de Julio (8.30am–9pm); Marva, San Martín 941.
Pharmacies Dra. Bonetto, San Martín 1018; Pasteur, 9 de Julio and Belgrano.
Police Rivadavia and Mitre ☎02945/450789 or 450001.
Post office Alvear 1192 (Mon–Fri 8.30am–1pm & 4pm–7pm; Sat 9am–1pm).
Swimming pool Natatorio, Alvear 2300.
Taxis Alvear and Fontana ☎02945/452233; Remises, 9 de Julio 875 ☎02945/451222.
Telephone At the bus terminal; Su Central, 25 de Mayo 415.
Travel agencies Patagonia Verde, 9 de Julio 926 ☎02945/454396, Ⓦwww.patagonia-verde.com.ar. Gales al Sur (☎02945/455757, Ⓦwww.galesalsur.com.ar) has a kiosk at the bus terminal.

Trevelin and around

The most Welsh of the cordillera towns, **TREVELIN** is a small, easy-going settlement that retains a pioneering feel, with several low brick buildings characteristic of that era. Lying 24km south of Esquel, it has beautiful views across the grassy valley to the peaks in the south of Parque Nacional Los Alerces.

La Trochita: The Old Patagonian Express

A trip on the **Old Patagonian Express** rates as one of South America's classic journeys. The steam train puffs, judders and lurches across the arid, rolling steppe of northern Chubut, like a drunk on the well-worn route home, running on a track with a gauge of a mere 75cm. Don't let Paul Theroux's disparaging book *The Old Patagonian Express* put you off: travelling aboard it has an authentic Casey Jones aura and is definitely not something that appeals only to train-spotters. Along the way you'll see guanacos, rheas, maras and, if you are lucky, condors, as you traverse the estate of Estancia Leleque, owned by Italian clothes magnate Benetton, Argentina's biggest landowner.

Referred to lovingly in Spanish as **La Trochita**, from the Spanish for "narrow gauge", or *El Trencito*, the route has had an erratic history. It was conceived as a branch line to link Esquel with the main line joining Bariloche to Carmen de Patagones on the Atlantic coast. Construction began in Ingeniero Jacobacci in Río Negro Province in 1922, but it took 23 years to complete the 402km to Esquel. Originally, it was used as a mixed passenger and freight service, carrying consignments of wool, livestock, lumber and fruit from the cordillera region. The locomotives had to contend with snowdrifts in winter, and five derailments occurred between 1945 and 1993, caused by high winds or stray cows on the track. Proving unprofitable, the line was eventually closed in 1993. The Province of Chubut took over the running of the 165km section between Esquel and El Maitén soon afterwards, and *La Trochita* has matured into a major tourist attraction.

For most people, a ride on *La Trochita* means the half-day trip north from Esquel to Nahuel Pan, 22km away (see Ⓦwww.latrochita.org.ar/cronograma_servicios.html for latest timetables or call ☎02945/451403). There is an occasional sporadic service running the 165km to El Maitén and returning the following day.

The town was founded by Welsh settlers from the Chubut Valley following a series of expeditions to this region that began in 1885 with a group led by Colonel Fontana of the Argentine army and John Evans. Its Welsh name means "village of the mill", and the vital **flour mill**, a stalwart brick structure dating from 1918, now forms the main museum in town, the **Museo Regional Molino Andes** or **El Viejo Molino** (daily 10am–9pm; $4). Well worth a visit, it displays clothing of the original colonists and even a combine harvester from circa 1900. By the entrance is a fascinating group photo of the 1902 plebiscite when the whole colony had to vote on whether it wanted to be Chilean or Argentine: those who want to know more should read *Down Where the Moon Is Small* by Richard Llewellyn, which is evocative in its recreation of the early years of the Welsh community here.

Another worthwhile attraction is **La Tumba de Malacara**, 200m northeast of the plaza (daily 10am–noon & 2.30–9pm; $8). Clery Evans, granddaughter of the village's founder John Evans, will relate the origins of the settlement (knowing Spanish helps). In the garden is the **grave** of her granddad's faithful horse, El Malacara – who leapt heroically down a steep scarp to save his master from the same grisly fate that befell his companions – butchery by enraged Mapuche warriors who, in the wake of an atrocity committed against their tribe during the Campaign of the Desert, were bent on reprisals against any whites. The house attracts a steady stream of Bruce Chatwin pilgrims, as the story features in his classic travelogue, *In Patagonia* (see p.834 for book review).

The town's Welsh heritage is evoked in the celebration of a minor **Eisteddfod** (two days in the second week of October), and two **casas de té**, the best of which is *Nain Maggie*, at Perito Moreno 179 (3–10.30pm; ⓣ02945/480232). Nain Maggie was the grandmother of teashop owner Lucia Underwood, who was born in Trelew, came to Trevelin in 1891 and died in the town ninety years later at the age of 103.

If you have time, you won't be disappointed by the day-trip to **Nant y Fall** (Welsh for "stream of waterfalls"; 8am–8pm; $15), 19km from Trevelin, off RN-259 to Futaleufú. Here a series of sparkling **cascades** tumble over rock ledges in the midst of hillside *coihue* and cypress forests. There are fine views across the valley to the mountains of Parque Nacional Los Alerces from here, and in a couple of hours you can wander around the circuit and have time to bathe in the pools.

Practicalities

The RN-259 from Esquel arrives at the octagonal Plaza Coronel Fontana at the north end of town, where you'll find the **tourist office** (daily 8am–10pm; ⓣ02945/480120, ⓦwww.trevelin.org). Gales Al Sur, Av Patagonia 186 (ⓣ02945/480427, ⓦwww.galesalsur.com.ar), runs excursions to Los Alerces national park, horse-riding trips and a full-day white-water rafting trip on Río Corcovado. **Internet** access and public **telephones** are available at the same address.

Although cabins are springing up on the outskirts there's not a lot of **accommodation** in town. Among the best is snug *Hostal Casaverde* (ⓣ02945/480091, ⓦwww.casaverdehostel.com.ar; ❸), HI-affiliated and with laundry and kitchen facilities and a privileged view from its little hilltop up Los Alerces; it's off Avenida Fontana, five to ten minutes' walk from the plaza. *Ruca Ñancú*, John Daniel Evans and San Martín (ⓣ02945/480427; ❹), is family-run, clean and spacious. Owner Alec Byrne is also a tour operator. *Hotel Estefania*, Perito Moreno s/n next to *Nain Maggie* (ⓣ02945/480148; ❸; closed Sept & Oct), has inexpensive rooms for up to five and also serves meals. *Oregón*, on San Martín eight blocks south of the plaza (Ⓣ02945/480408, Ⓦwww.oregon.alojar.com.ar; ❺), has good *cabañas* with a kitchen in an orchard. For those with **tents**, *Camping El Chacay* (Ⓣ02945/15681827; $10 per person) near the south end of San Martín – turn left one block beyond *Oregón* restaurant (see opposite) – with showers and a shop, has a rural feel and a decent view of the hills. Contact Gales Al Sur travel agency to take you to Refugio Wilson, in the countryside 7km away. This funky, open-plan, cabin-style **refuge** has bunk-beds (with your own sleeping bag; ❶), or you can camp, as well as helpful advice on interesting hikes in the valley's foothills. Concerts and shows are held here on weekends.

Restaurant choices are limited but if it's a slap-up *parrilla* you want, head to *Oregón*, near the southern exit of the village at San Martín and Laprida. Another worthwhile option is *Patagonia Célta*, Molino Viejo and 25 de Mayo (Ⓣ02945/156-87243), which serves meat and fish in a classy atmosphere. For a drink, *Zweli*, at Fontana and Perito Moreno, offers cold beers and an authentic taste of local life.

Crossing to Chile

Just south of Trevelin, two border crossings lead to Chile's beautiful Carretera Austral, the last leg of the Panamerican Highway. They're useful for travelling through to the port of Chaitén, from where you can catch a ferry to the rustic island of Chiloé. Buses run several times a week from Esquel, passing through Trevelin. Adjacent to the national park's southern boundary is **Paso Futaleufú** (Argentine immigration open daily 9am–9pm). Some 10km from the border is the first Chilean settlement, the appealing wood-built **Futaleufú**. This is a base for some of Patagonia's most spectacular **white-water rafting**, on the turquoise river of the same name.

The hamlet of **Carrenleufú** is 26km west of the pleasant, little-visited village of Corcovado, and its nearby pass connects through to the Chilean settlement of Palena, 8km past the border. The Río Corcovado (called the Río Palena on the Chilean side) is noted for its Pacific salmon, and it also offers medium-grade rafting. To the south of Corcovado lies the wild scenery of Lago Vintter (also called Lago Winter).

Parque Nacional Los Alerces

Established in 1937, and part of the Pacific watershed, the 2630-square-kilometre **PARQUE NACIONAL LOS ALERCES** protects some of the most biologically important habitats and scenic landscapes of the central Patagonian cordillera. Its lakes are superb, famous for both their rich colours and their fishing, while most have a backdrop of sumptuous forests that quilt the surrounding mountain slopes. In the northeast of the park these lakes form a network centred on **lakes Rivadavia**, **Menéndez** and **Futalaufquen**, whose waters drain south to the dammed reservoir of **Embalse Amutui Quimei**, and from here into the Río Futaleufú (also called Río Grande).

Los Alerces doesn't have any mountain peaks of the calibre or altitude of Volcán Lanín or Cerro Tronador in Nahuel Huapi. Nevertheless, some of the two-thousand-metre ranges that divide the park are spectacular, with dramatic rock colorations and cracked and craggy summits such as those that can be seen in the **Cordón Situación** in the southeast, whose peaks rise to 2300m. **Cerro Torrecillas** (2253m), in the north of the park, has the only glacier you'll see, but patches of snow can last on the upper peaks into mid-summer.

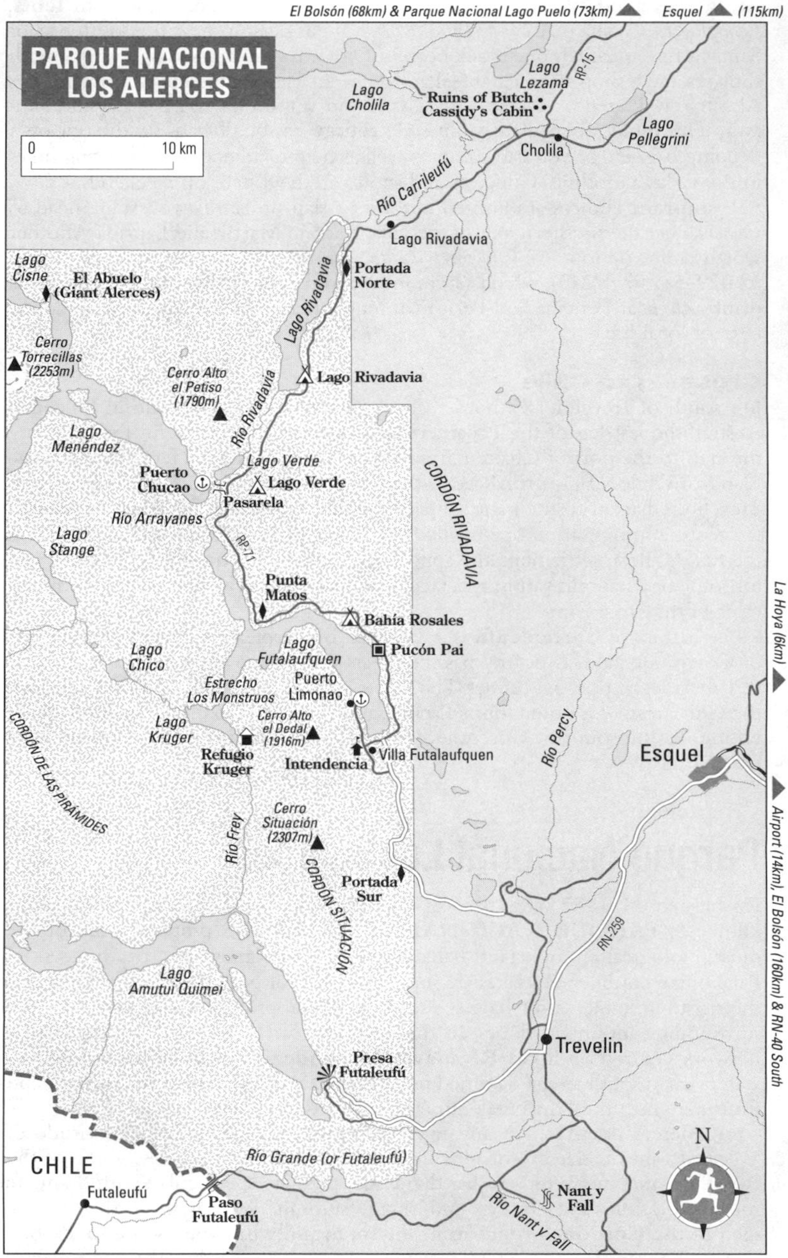
El Bolsón (68km) & Parque Nacional Lago Puelo (73km)
Esquel (115km)
PARQUE NACIONAL LOS ALERCES
0 10 km
Lago Cholila
Ruins of Butch Cassidy's Cabin
Lago Lezama
RP-15
Cholila
Lago Pellegrini
Río Carrileufú
Lago Rivadavia
Portada Norte
Lago Cisne
El Abuelo (Giant Alerces)
Lago Rivadavia
Cerro Torrecillas (2253m)
Cerro Alto el Petiso (1790m)
Lago Rivadavia
Río Rivadavia
Lago Menéndez
Lago Verde
Puerto Chucao
Lago Verde
Pasarela
Río Arrayanes
CORDÓN RIVADAVIA
Lago Stange
RP-71
Punta Matos
Bahía Rosales
Lago Futalaufquen
Pucón Pai
Lago Chico
Estrecho Los Monstruos
Puerto Limonao
Lago Kruger
Cerro Alto el Dedal (1916m)
Refugio Kruger
Intendencia
Villa Futalaufquen
Río Percy
Esquel
CORDÓN DE LAS PIRÁMIDES
Río Frey
Cerro Situación (2307m)
CORDÓN SITUACIÓN
Portada Sur
La Hoya (6km)
Airport (14km), El Bolsón (160km) & RN-40 South
RN-259
Lago Amutui Quimei
Trevelin
Presa Futaleufú
N
CHILE
Río Grande (or Futaleufú)
Futaleufú
Paso Futaleufú
Nant y Fall
Río Nant y Fall
Chaitén (154km)
Corcovado (46km) & Paso Carrenleufú (72km)
Lago Rosario (6km)

The peaks also seem to act as regular moorings for some remarkable high-altitude cloud formations.

As in other parks in this region, the vegetation changes considerably as you move east from the Chilean border into the area affected by the rain shadow cast by the cordillera. Up against the border, rainfall exceeds 3000mm a year, enough to support the growth of dense **Valdivian temperate rainforest** (*selva Valdiviana*), and most interestingly, the species for which the park is named: the **alerce**. The ground is dominated by bamboo-like *caña colihue*, while two species of flower are everywhere: the orange or white-and-violet *mutisias*, with delicate spatula-like petals, and the *amancay*, a golden-yellow lily growing on stems 50cm to 1m high. In contrast, the eastern margin of the park is much drier, receiving 300mm to 800mm of rainfall annually. Cypress woodland and *ñire* scrub mark the transitional zone here between the wet forests and the arid steppe near Esquel.

The western two-thirds of the park are off-limits, being designated a strict scientific reserve. This is the haunt of the endangered *huemul* (see box, p.633); and the shy *pudú*, a tiny deer just 40cm tall. The non-native mink (*visón*), an escapee from a fur farm in Cholila, has wreaked havoc amongst the wildlife, eating birds' eggs and small mammals.

You'll need patience to see the Chilean Pigeon (*paloma araucana*), now making a comeback from the verge of extinction, and the Des Mur's Wiretail (*colilarga*), which hides itself in clumps of *caña colihue*. More accommodating are the chattering Austral Parakeet (*cachaña*), the dull-grey Giant Hummingbird (*picaflor gigante*), and its wee relative, the Green-backed Firecrown (*picaflor chico*). At the other end of the scale, you may glimpse a majestic Andean Condor. In mature woodland, listen out for the double-drum of the Magellanic Woodpecker (*carpintero negro*), a powerful bird with a torpedo-shaped black body, white dorsal patch, and a scarlet flame of a crest on the male. **Anglers** try to hook introduced species – landlocked salmon, plus brook, rainbow and brown trout – but not the protected native species, such as the *puyén grande* and the *perca criolla*. If caught, these should be returned, preferably without removing them from the water.

The alerce (Fitzroya cupressoides)

Similar in appearance to the Californian redwood, the **alerce**, or Patagonian cypress, can reach heights of 57m and is one of the four oldest species of tree in the world. To the Mapuche it is *lahuán*, meaning "long-lived" or "grandfather", and the oldest specimens are an estimated 4000 years old. They grow in a relatively narrow band of the central Patagonian cordillera, on acidic soils by lakes and only in places where the annual rainfall exceeds 3000mm, so are more common on the wetter Chilean side of the Andes than in Argentina. Growth is extremely slow (0.8–1.2mm a year), and it takes a decade for a tree's girth to gain 1cm in diameter – though the trunk may eventually reach 3m across.

From the late nineteenth century onwards, the *alerce* was almost totally logged out by pioneers: the reddish timber is not eaten by insects and does not rot, so was highly valued for building, especially for roof shingles. Other uses included musical instruments, barrels, furniture, telegraph poles and boats. In Argentina, the only trees to survive the forester's axe were the most inaccessible ones, or those like El Abuelo, a titanic millennial specimen whose wood was bad in parts. In Argentina, a few stands exist north of Los Alerces, in Parque Nacional Lago Puelo and the Lago Frías area of Nahuel Huapi, and the trees that remain are generally well protected.

The **northeastern section** of the park is the most interesting for the visitor, especially around the area of the beautiful but small **Lago Verde**. Sandwiched between the three giants of Lago Rivadavia to the northeast, Menéndez to the west and Futalaufquen to the south, it is a useful base for camping and trekking. The transcendental **Río Arrayanes** drains Lago Verde and a **pasarela** or suspension bridge, 34km from the intendencia, gives access to a delightful hour-long loop walk that takes you along the riverbank to Puerto Chucao. For most visitors the highlight is the trip from Puerto Chucao across Menéndez to see **El Abuelo**, the ancient *alerce*. The savage Lago Rivadavia area is the least visited of those accessed by the park's principal road, **RP-71**.

The south of the park is a subsidiary destination. The **Futaleufú hydroelectric complex** 18km from Trevelin was a controversial project from the 1970s, designed to provide power for the aluminium smelting plant at Puerto Madryn. Ironically, submerged in the depths of the expansive reservoir are *Cuide Los Bosques* signs, telling you to look after the forests.

Arrival and information

Los Alerces is becoming more popular as holidaymakers begin to explore further afield from saturated Bariloche. Over 110,000 people a year visit, most from late November to late March or Easter, and the park gets extremely busy in January and February. Campsites at this time of year can be overcrowded and noisy, not the kind of "national park experience" many are looking for. Visit the park off-peak, if possible. **Autumn** months are perhaps the best, as the deciduous trees put on a blaze of colour; but spring is also very beautiful, if subject to some fierce winds. Year-round access is possible, although RP-71, can, on rare occasions, be cut off by snow for a day or so. If you come in winter, remember that many places close outside the fishing season (mid-Nov to Easter), so you'll have to be more self-sufficient.

Entrance to the park costs $12, and you have three points of access. Most people come from Esquel via the **Portada Sur** (Southern Gate; 33km from Esquel and 12km before Villa Futalaufquen), which misleadingly serves the central sector of the park. This route is the most practical as it heads to the park headquarters and the useful information centre (see below). The RP-71 continues unpaved through the northeast corner of the park and exits it beyond the **Portada Norte**, by the headwaters of Lago Rivadavia near to Cholila (see p.636). Arriving along this route from the north is the most scenic way of entering the park, but it's a long way (55km) to the information centre. The third gate, **Portada Futaleufú**, is in the southeast corner of the park, 14km from Trevelin and 12km before the dam.

Those who don't have their own transport can get around the park with Transportes Esquel (Ⓣ02945/453429), which has a twice-daily service along RP-71 in summer from Esquel to Cholila. Plans to pave RP-71 from the Futalaufquen lakehead to Rivadavia have been thwarted up to now by budgetary and environmental concerns.

Set on manicured lawns alongside the bus stop in **Villa Futalaufquen** is the intendencia (daily 8am–2pm; Ⓣ02945/471020); the **visitors' centre** here (daily 8am–9pm; Ⓣ02945/471015) is staffed by volunteers who give information on hikes and fishing, and sell fishing permits. Ask them about lodging opportunities. There is a good range of services in the village – including a fuel station, post office and general stores – but it's much cheaper to pick up everything you need in Esquel. *El Abuelo Monje* on Calle Los Retamos (Ⓣ02945/471029; closed Easter to mid-Nov) serves the best **meals** in town, and is especially recommended for its roast lamb (*cordero*). Alternatively, try *El Lugar del Lago* on Calle Corcolen, a tearoom that serves trout meals and sells home-made bread, jam and cheese.

Accommodation

In season, you have a wide choice of **accommodation** in the park, especially along Lago Futalaufquen's eastern shore, though most establishments close outside the fishing season. Those who don't want to camp must splash out heavily on private **hotels** or rent a **cabin**, though these are geared towards groups of fishermen or whole families. Reserve in advance, especially in high season. Just over 4km north of the intendencia, 400m beyond Puerto Limonao, is the *Hostería Futalaufquen* (ⓣ02945/471008, ⓕ471009; ❾; closed Easter–Nov), a solid, four-star granite-block and log lodge designed by Alejandro Bustillo. It's in an attractive setting by the lake, but the atmosphere is spoilt somewhat by the "ambient" piped music; the restaurant has a limited choice and is extremely overpriced.

Heading up the eastern shore of Futalaufquen from the intendencia, the first place you come to is the expensive *Hostería Quimei Quipan* (ⓣ02945/454134; ❼). Further on is *Pucón Pai* (ⓣ02945/471010, ⓦwww.issys.gov.ar/puconpai.html; ❸–❺), at Km10, which has camping with full facilities as well as accommodation in rather regimented, barrack-style buildings; the *Tejas Negras* tearoom, which rents attractive cabins all year (ⓣ02945/471046; ❼ for four); and the pretty white house of the *Hostería Cume Hue* (ⓣ02945/453639, ⓦwww.hosteriacumehue.com.ar; ❻ per person full board), which is popular with fishermen. Just north of the park in Villa Lago Rivadavia, on the road to Cholila, are a number of cabins at much more attractive prices and in a beautiful setting (see p.638).

Los Maitenes (ⓣ02945/451006; $10 per person; closed Easter to mid-Nov) is the closest **campsite** to Villa Futalaufquen (400m from the intendencia) and is generally good, although packed. On the other side of the road before the Río Desaguadero is *Rahue-Calel*, a quieter place, but one that doesn't front the lake ($8 per person). As for free sites, avoid *Las Lechuzas* and head for lakeside *Las Rocas* (about 2km from the intendencia), which is cleaner, quieter and smaller, though more exposed. Roughly 14km from the intendencia is *Complejo Bahía Rosales* – with a shop and hot water ($12 per person); it rents bikes, kayaks and horses and is the starting point of the boat trip to Lago Kruger. It also has twelve cabins with kitchen facilities (ⓣ02945/471044, ⓦwww.bahiarosales.alojar.com.ar; ❺ for four people). At Km21 is *Punta Matos*, a small free site with excellent views and fine swimming, while *Playa El Francés* is also free and has a good beach. There are several sites in the Lago Verde region, but the cheaper ones can get crowded. A two-day maximum stay applies in *camping libre Río Arrayanes*, 2km before the *pasarela* footbridge. Just north of the *pasarela* are popular paying sites (one *agreste* and one *organizado*) at Lago Verde. Lago Rivadavia has organized and free sites at both northern and southern ends. *Bahía Solís* ($8 per person) is recommended, and has fine fishing. Lago Krugger has a fishing *hostería* (ⓣ011 46651014; ❽), which offers full board as well as a campsite.

El Abuelo

The most popular excursion in the park is the Safari Lacustre to the far end of Lago Menéndez's northern channel to see **El Abuelo** ("The Grandfather", also named *El Alerzal*), a gigantic *alerce* 2.2m in diameter, and 57m tall. This magnificent tree is an estimated 2600 years old, making it more venerable than four of the five most widespread religions in the world (only Hinduism is older). It was a sapling when Pythagoras and Confucius taught, but a mere hundred years ago it almost became roof shingles: only the fact that settlers deemed its wood rotten inside saved it from the saw. To see it you need to take the **boat trip**, the earliest leaving at 10am from Puerto Limonao, 3km north of the intendencia, with another from Puerto Chucao at noon, halfway round the Lago Verde/Río Arrayanes trail loop that starts at the *pasarela*. The earlier sailing crosses Lago Futalaufquen and goes down Río Arrayanes to Puerto Mermoud followed by a thirty-minute walk across the isthmus to meet up with the noon sailing at Puerto Chucao. The excursion is guided, but in Spanish only; if you want an English translation, you'll need to organize a tour from Esquel rather than just turn up at the pier. Either way, you should book in advance – boats are generally full in peak season and go only when demand is sufficient in low season. Both boats are run by Brazo Sur (Ⓣ02945/471008, Ⓦwww.brazosur.com/safari.htm).

On the ninety-minute trip across the pristine blue waters of **Lago Menéndez** you get fine views of the Cerro Torrecillas glacier, which is receding fast and may last only another seventy years. To get to El Abuelo, a three-kilometre trail takes you through dense Valdivian temperate rainforest (*selva Valdiviana*), a habitat distinguished from the surrounding Patagonian forests by the presence of different layers to the canopy, in addition to the growth of lianas, epiphytes, surface roots and species more commonly found in Chile. Here a mass of vegetation is engaged in the eternal struggle of the jungle: height equals light. In addition to the *alerces*, you'll see fuchsia bushes and *arrayanes*, with trunks like rough-chiselled cinnamon sticks that are cold to the touch. Despite its name **Lago Cisne** is no longer home to any Black-necked Swans; they were wiped out by mink.

Trekking in the park

There are 130km of **public trails** in the park, which are generally well maintained and marked at intervals with red spots. As always, you are required to **register** with the nearest *guardaparque* before setting off (remember to check back in afterwards), and some treks – such as El Dedal – are not recommended in winter or for those under 10 years old. In times of drought, some trails are closed, while others (including El Dedal) can only be undertaken with a guide. Bring plenty of water, sun protection, and adequate clothing as the weather changes rapidly and unseasonal snowfalls occur in the higher regions. Insect repellent is worthwhile, especially after several consecutive hot days in December and January, as that's when the fierce horseflies (*tábanos*) come out.

The most difficult part of the pastoral 500m **Pinturas Rupestres** circuit is the spring-loaded gate at the beginning. You pass eroded indigenous geometric designs painted about 3000 years ago on a hulk of grey rock that's surrounded by *caña colihue* and *maitén* trees; the lookout from the top of the rock affords a fine view. Longer walks include the **Cinco Saltos**, **El Cocinero** and **Cerro Alto El Petiso** in the north of the park, which is best accessed from Lago Verde and provides sterling vistas of the northern lakes. Another worthwhile trip is to the *hostería* and campsite at the southern end of **Lago Krugger**. This can be reached in a fairly stiff day's trekking, returning the same way or by launch the next day (cost depends on number of passengers). However, it's better to make it into a three- or four-day excursion. You can break the outward-bound trek by putting up a tent by the beautiful beach at Playa Blanca (about 8hr from the intendencia), but you must have previously obtained permission at the visitors' centre. Fires are strictly prohibited and there are no facilities.

The **El Dedal Circuit** is one of the most popular and convenient hikes in the park. It involves some fairly stiff climbs but you'll be rewarded with some excellent panoramic views – ask the *guardaparque* about guides. Calculate on taking some six to seven hours (4hr up and 2–3hr down). Take the "Sendero Cascada" (which runs up behind the visitors' centre) for approximately 35 minutes through thick *maitén* and *caña colihue*, then take the signposted right-hand branch where the path forks. Further up, you enter impressive mature woodland. Approximately two hours into the walk, you climb above the tree line into an area of open, flattened scrub on the hilltop. From here you have a panoramic view of the scarified, rust-coloured **Las Monjitas** range opposite. If it's *tábano* season, though, you'll want to keep moving rather than enjoy the view. Climb up to the ridge and follow this northwest towards the craggy El Dedal massif above you. Up here you'll see delicate celeste and grey-blue *perezia* flowers, and possibly even condors. Do not follow the crest too far up though: look out for a short right-hand traverse after some 300m. The path then levels off for 100m. Below you is gorgeous **Lago Futalaufquen**, whose turquoise body is fringed, in places, by a frill of Caribbean-blue shallows. Bear left across a slight scoop of a valley, and you'll come to the lip of an impressive, oxide-coloured glaciated cwm (valley). From here, follow the thirty-degree slope down into the bowl. The path up the other side of the cwm is difficult to make out: follow the paint blotches, choosing the pale, broad band of scree and make the tiring scramble up the top of the ridge, which overlooks the *Hostería Futalaufquen* and Puerto Limonao. From the ridge, a poor path leads up left to the summit of **Cerro Alto El Dedal** (1916m), about forty minutes away; don't attempt it in poor weather. Descending from the ridge, it's about ninety minutes to the road by the port's prefectura and then another half-hour back to the intendencia.

Local cowboy Carlos Rosales offers guided horse-riding trips from mid-Nov to mid-April from his home. Follow the *cabalgata* sign from RP-71, 1.5km north of the village (☎02945/156-80315).

Travel details

Buses

The major bus companies operating in this region are: Albus (Ⓦwww.albus.com.ar), Andesmar (Ⓦwww.andesmar.com.ar), Cruceros del Norte (Ⓦwww.crucerosdelnorte.com.ar), El Valle (Ⓦwww.elvalle.com.ar), Via Bariloche (Ⓦwww.viabariloche.com.ar) and Via TAC (Ⓦwww.viatac.com.ar).

Aluminé to: Villa Pehuenia (3 daily; 1hr & 1hr 30min respectively); Zapala (3 daily; 2hr 30min).

Andacollo to: Chos Malal (2 daily; 1hr 30min–2hr); Las Ovejas (2 daily; 1hr).

Bariloche to: El Bolsón (14 daily; 2hr); Buenos Aires (7 daily; 23hr); Córdoba (2 daily; 22hr); Esquel (5–6 daily; 4hr 30min); Epuyén (5 weekly; 3hr); Junín de los Andes (1 daily; 4hr); Lago Puelo (3 daily; 2hr 20min); Mendoza (daily; 18hr 45min); Neuquén (12 daily; 5hr 30min–6hr); Puerto Madryn (daily; 14hr); Salta (2 daily; 39hr); San Martín de los Andes (2 daily; 6hr); Santa Rosa (3 daily; 15hr); Trelew (daily; 13–16hr); Villa La Angostura (3 daily in summer; 1hr); Villa Traful (daily–4 weekly; 1hr 45min–2hr 30min).

El Bolsón to: Bariloche (14 daily; 2hr); Esquel (6 daily); Lago Puelo (5–10 daily; 30min).

Caviahue to: Copahue (1 daily in high season; 45min); Las Lajas (3 daily; 1hr 45min–2hr 15min); Neuquén (2 daily; 5–6hr); Zapala (2 daily; 3hr–3hr 15min).

Cholila to: El Bolsón (daily; 1hr 40min–2hr); Esquel (3 daily or 5 weekly depending on season; 2hr 30min–3hr 45min).

Chos Malal to: Andacollo (2 daily; 1hr 30min–2hr); Las Ovejas (2 daily; 3hr); Neuquén (5 daily; 6hr); Zapala (5 daily; 3hr).
Copahue to: Caviahue (1 daily in high season; 45min).
Esquel to: Bariloche (15 daily; 4hr 30min); El Bolsón (15 daily; 2hr 30min); Cholila (3 daily or 5 weekly depending on season; 2hr 30min–3hr 45min); Trevelin (hourly Mon–Fri, every 2hr Sat–Sun; 30min).
Junín de los Andes to: Aluminé (3 weekly; 3hr); Buenos Aires (7 daily; 20hr); San Martín de los Andes (9 daily; 1hr); Zapala (16 daily; 3hr).
Lago Puelo to: El Bolsón (5 daily; 30min); Cholila (2 weekly; 2hr 45min).
Las Lajas to: Caviahue (3 daily; 1hr 45min–2hr 15min); Chos Malal (every 2hr; 2hr).
El Maitén to: El Bolsón (daily; 1hr); Esquel (4 weekly).
Moquehue to: Neuquén (3 weekly; 5hr 30min); Villa Pehuenia (5 weekly; 40min).
Neuquén to: Bariloche (21 daily mainly am; 5hr 30min–6hr); Buenos Aires (hourly; 15hr–16hr 30min); Caviahue (2 daily; 5–6hr); Chos Malal (2 daily; 6hr); Córdoba (7 daily; 18hr 30min); Mendoza (8 daily; 12hr–12hr 30min); Moquehue (1 daily; 5hr 30min); San Juan (3 daily; 12hr–12hr 30min); San Martín de los Andes (8 daily; 6hr); Villa Pehuenia (2 daily; 5hr); Zapala (hourly; 2hr 30min–3hr).
Las Ovejas to: Andacollo (2 daily; 1hr).
San Martín de los Andes to: Bariloche (3 daily; 6hr); Junín de los Andes (hourly; 1hr); Villa La Angostura (2 daily; 2hr 30min).
Trevelin to: Esquel (every 1–2hr; 30min).
Villa La Angostura to: Bariloche (approximately hourly; 1hr); San Martín de los Andes (5 daily; 2hr 30min).
Villa Pehuenia to: Aluminé (3 daily; 1hr & 1hr 30min respectively); Moquehue (5 weekly; 30min); Neuquén (3 weekly; 5hr); Zapala (3 daily; 2hr 30min).
Villa Traful to: Bariloche (daily; 1hr 45min–2hr 30min).
Zapala to: Aluminé (3 daily; 2hr 30min); Buenos Aires (7 daily; 17–18hr); Caviahue (3 daily; 3hr 30min); Chos Malal (7 daily; 3hr); Copahue (3 daily; 4hr); Cutral Có (every 30min; 1hr); Junín de los Andes (8 daily; 3hr); Neuquén (every 30min; 2hr 30min–3hr); Plaza Huincul (hourly; 1hr); San Martín de los Andes (4 daily; 4hr); Villa Pehuenia (3 daily; 2hr 15min).

International buses

Bariloche to: Osorno (4 daily; 4–5hr); Puerto Montt (3 daily; 7–8hr).
San Martín de los Andes and Junín de los Andes to: Pucón (daily; 4hr 45min and 4hr respectively).

Flights

Bariloche to: Buenos Aires (6–8 daily; 2hr); Córdoba (1 daily; 2hr); Esquel (5 weekly; 30min); Mendoza (1 daily; 1hr 30min); Puerto Madryn (2 weekly; 3hr); Trelew (2 weekly; 1hr 15min).
Chapelco to: Buenos Aires (daily during skiing season; 2hr).
Neuquén to: Buenos Aires (3 daily; 1hr 35min); Puerto Madryn (1 weekly; 4hr 30min); Trelew (1–2 daily; 5hr); Ushuaia (1 daily; 7hr 30min–8hr 30min).
Esquel to: Bariloche (5 weekly; 1hr); Buenos Aires (Wed–Fri 1–2 daily; 3hr); Trelew (Wed–Fri 1–2 daily; 2hr).

Trains

Bariloche to: Viedma (Mon & Fri 6pm; 16hr).
Viedma to: Bariloche (Sun & Thurs 6pm; 16hr).

8

Patagonia

BOLIVIA
PARAGUAY
BRAZIL
5
4
3
6
URUGUAY
Buenos Aires
1
CHILE
PACIFIC OCEAN
2
ATLANTIC OCEAN
7
8
N
9
0
500 km

CHAPTER 8

Highlights

* **Whale-watching** Getting a glimpse of southern right whales off Península Valdés ranks as one of the most memorable nature experiences on the planet. See p.667

* **Welsh tea** Don't miss afternoon tea and cakes in one of Argentina's Welsh villages. See p.674

* **Petrified forests** Phenomenally preserved fossilized trunks scatter the lunar landscapes of the Bosque Petrificado Sarmiento and Monumento Natural Bosques Petrificados. See p.678 & p.681

* **Asados** Lamb cooked over an open fire defines Patagonia almost as much as the open spaces and relentless winds. See p.688

* **Cueva de las Manos Pintadas** Ancient rock art dramatically sited in the heart of a scenic canyon. See p.694

* **Parque Nacional Los Glaciares** World-class trekking in the northern sector and huge, calving glaciers – including legendary Glaciar Perito Moreno – in the south. See p.703

△ Southern right whales, Península Valdés

8

Patagonia

"Why then, and this is not only my particular case, does this barren land possess my mind? I find it hard to explain...but it might partly be because it enhances the horizons of imagination."

Charles Darwin

A land of adventures and adventurers, of myths and fabulous reality, **Patagonia**'s geographical immensity is paralleled only by the size of its reputation. As a region of contrasts and extremes, it has few equals in the world: from the biting winds that howl off the **Hielo Continental Sur** (Southern Patagonian Icecap) to the comforting hearthside warmth of unforgettable, old-time Patagonian hospitality; from the lowest point on the South American continent, the **Gran Bajo de San Julián**, to the savage peaks of the **Fitz Roy massif**; from the sterile plains of the coastline to the astoundingly rich marine breeding grounds that abut them, among which **Península Valdés** is the crowned king. Linking them all are hundreds of kilometres of desert steppe, seemingly an infinity of space.

The term "Patagonia" was formerly used to refer to all lands on both sides of the Andes that lay south of the southernmost white settlement. On the Argentine side, this once signified any land below Buenos Aires, though as the whites moved further into indigenous territory, so Patagonia's frontiers pushed ever southwards. By the nineteenth century, the concept of Patagonia had begun to take on a more fixed location, one that is usually defined today as all lands south of Argentina's Río Colorado and Chile's Río Bio Bio. This chapter deals with all of Argentine Patagonia, with the exception of Tierra del Fuego (see Chapter 9) and the northwestern Lake District (see Chapter 7), and also includes a section on southern mainland Chilean Patagonia.

One of Argentine Patagonia's principal arteries, **RN-3**, runs from the historic town of **Carmen de Patagones** down to **Río Gallegos** and across to the border with Chile, providing access to the narrow fringe of Atlantic coastline and the vast central steppe. The principal highlight of this stretch is the wildlife, most notably at the marine reserve of **Península Valdés**, famous for its whale-watching, and at **Punta Tombo**, the continent's largest penguin colony, but also further south, in Santa Cruz Province, where colonies of seabirds perch on spectacular porphyry cliffs at **Puerto Deseado** and playful Commerson's dolphins frolic in the *ría*, or estuary, just outside the town. This is an area that was key in defining the Patagonian pioneering spirit: Welsh settlers landed on a beach just south of Península Valdés, at what is now the resort town of **Puerto Madryn**, and gradually ventured into the **Lower Chubut Valley** (see box, p.663). You can explore their cultural legacy in the villages of Gaiman and Dolavon, and at the town of **Trelew**. Further inland, worthy detours off RN-3 lead to a couple of

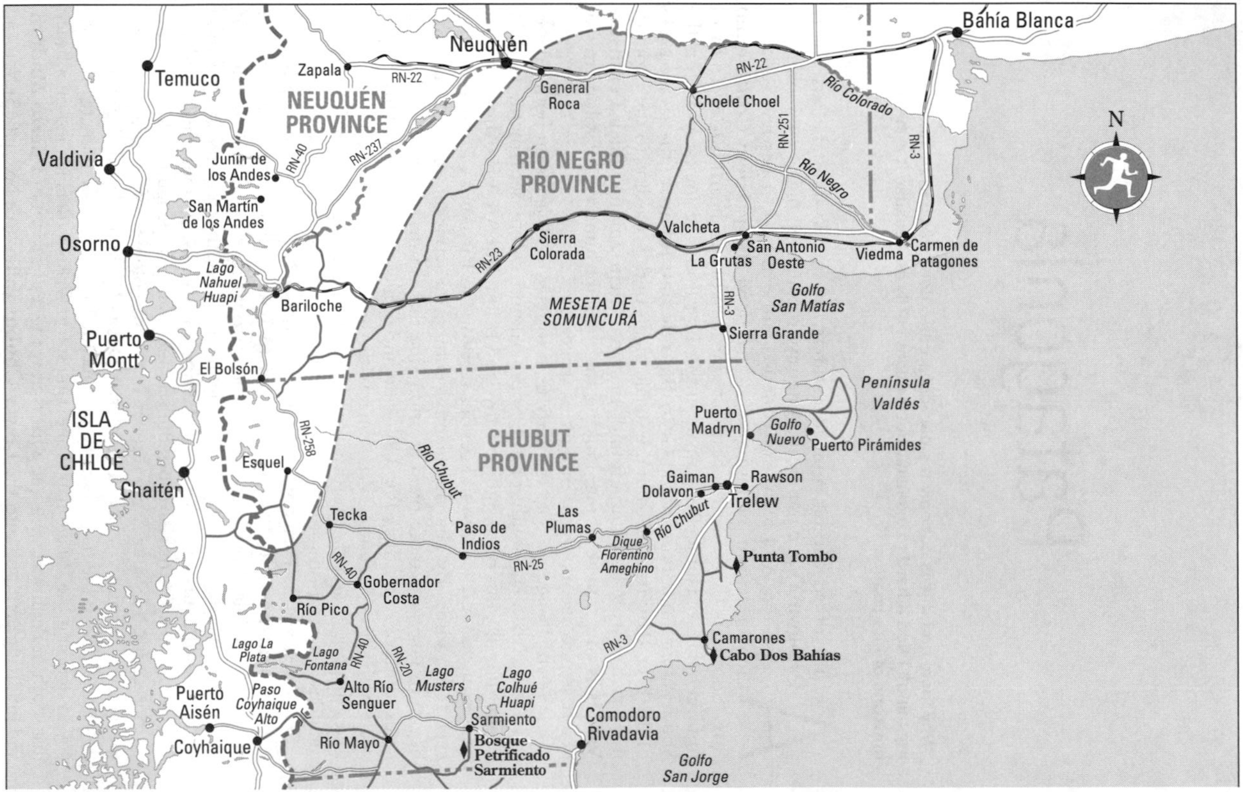

Bahía Blanca
Neuquén
Temuco
Zapala
RN-22
General Roca
Choele Choel
RN-22
Río Colorado
NEUQUÉN PROVINCE
RÍO NEGRO PROVINCE
RN-251
RN-3
N
Valdivia
Junín de los Andes
RN-40
RN-237
Río Negro
San Martín de los Andes
Osorno
Valcheta
Sierra Colorada
RN-23
San Antonio Oeste
La Grutas
Viedma
Carmen de Patagones
Lago Nahuel Huapi
Bariloche
MESETA DE SOMUNCURÁ
Golfo San Matías
RN-3
Sierra Grande
Puerto Montt
El Bolsón
Península Valdés
Puerto Madryn
Golfo Nuevo
Puerto Pirámides
ISLA DE CHILOÉ
RN-258
CHUBUT PROVINCE
Río Chubut
Esquel
Chaitén
Gaiman
Dolavon
Rawson
Trelew
Tecka
Las Plumas
Paso de Indios
Río Chubut
Dique Florentino Ameghino
RN-25
Punta Tombo
RN-40
Gobernador Costa
Río Pico
Camarones
Cabo Dos Bahías
RN-3
Lago La Plata
Lago Fontana
RN-40
RN-20
Lago Musters
Lago Colhué Huapi
Paso Coyhaique Alto
Alto Río Senguer
Puerto Aisén
Sarmiento
Comodoro Rivadavia
Coyhaique
Río Mayo
Bosque Petrificado Sarmiento
Golfo San Jorge

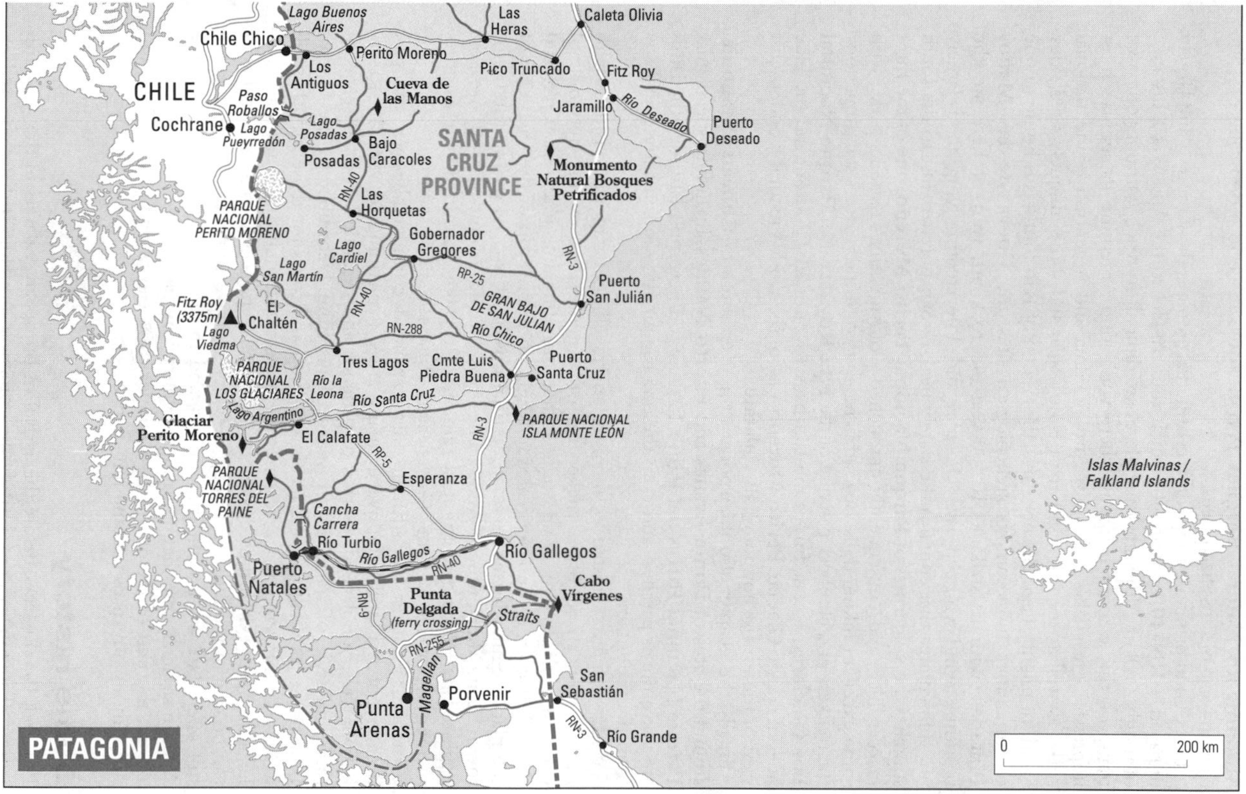
PATAGONIA
CHILE
Chile Chico
Lago Buenos Aires
Los Antiguos
Perito Moreno
Las Heras
Caleta Olivia
Pico Truncado
Fitz Roy
Jaramillo
Río Deseado
Puerto Deseado
Cueva de las Manos
Paso Roballos
Cochrane
Lago Pueyrredón
Lago Posadas
Posadas
Bajo Caracoles
SANTA CRUZ PROVINCE
Monumento Natural Bosques Petrificados
RN-40
Las Horquetas
PARQUE NACIONAL PERITO MORENO
Gobernador Gregores
Lago Cardiel
Lago San Martín
RP-25
RN-3
Puerto San Julián
GRAN BAJO DE SAN JULIAN
Fitz Roy (3375m)
El Chaltén
Lago Viedma
RN-288
Río Chico
Tres Lagos
Cmte Luis Piedra Buena
Puerto Santa Cruz
PARQUE NACIONAL LOS GLACIARES
Río la Leona
Río Santa Cruz
Lago Argentino
Glaciar Perito Moreno
El Calafate
PARQUE NACIONAL ISLA MONTE LEÓN
RP-5
Esperanza
PARQUE NACIONAL TORRES DEL PAINE
Cancha Carrera
Río Turbio
Río Gallegos
Puerto Natales
Cabo Vírgenes
RN-9
Punta Delgada
(ferry crossing)
Straits
RN-255
Magellan
San Sebastián
Porvenir
Punta Arenas
Río Grande
Islas Malvinas / Falkland Islands
0
200 km

incredible petrified forests: the **Bosque Petrificado Sarmiento**, accessed from the region's industrial hub, Comodoro Rivadavia, and, further south, the **Monumento Natural Bosques Petrificados**, an eerie moonscape of 150-million-year-old fossilized trees.

The second principal artery of Argentine Patagonia is the famous – and largely unpaved – **RN-40**, or Ruta 40, which runs parallel to the Andes, at a distance of roughly 90km. Although some places are difficult to reach without your own transport, this western fringe is where you'll find Argentine Patagonia's most impressive great lakes – Buenos Aires, Viedma and Argentino – and national parks, as well as the finest spit-roast lamb *asados* and some uniquely wild skies. South of mighty Lago Buenos Aires, the Cañon of Río Pinturas is home to one of Argentina's most famous archeological sites, the **Cueva de las Manos Pintadas**, with its striking, 10,000-year-old rock art; west of here are the beautiful, wind-whipped lakes Posadas and Pueyrredón, lying in a largely unexplored area that contains the stately peak of San Lorenzo. Just to the south stretches the wilderness of **Parque Nacional Perito Moreno**, one of the most inaccessible – and, consequently, untouched – of Argentina's national parks, with some excellent hiking trails. Beyond here are two of the region's star attractions: the trekkers' and climbers' paradise of the **Fitz Roy** sector of **Parque Nacional Los Glaciares**, accessed from the laid-back town of **El Chaltén**; and the blue hues of craggy **Glaciar Perito Moreno**, one of the world's natural wonders, just west of the tourist hotspot of **El Calafate**.

Finally, this chapter also incorporates the deep south of **Chilean Patagonia**, around the area of **Punta Arenas** and **Puerto Natales**, including spectacular **Parque Nacional Torres del Paine**. In these southernmost latitudes, the lands are not quite as parched, and even the odd tongue of woodland stretches away from the mountains.

With such huge distances involved in travelling Patagonia, visitors who have limited time often make use of Argentina's growing network of **domestic flights** to avoid some rather gruelling bus journeys. Overland travel, however, is the only real way to get an impression of the vast scale of the place; regular **buses** serve all destinations on RN-3, as well as the major towns along the southern Andes. The areas on and around RN-40 are best explored by **renting a car**. Just remember to take caution on the region's many gravel roads (see the *The legendary Ruta 40* colour section).

Patagonia's tourist infrastructure has expanded considerably over the past decade, but it is still primitive in many areas: if planning to visit the lesser-known sites, you'll need reserves of patience and flexibility, both in terms of time and style of travel. **High season** runs from December to the end of February – it's vital to book accommodation and tours for these months well in advance. November is a pleasant time to visit, although the winds that scour Patagonia are at their most unremitting, while the period from March to Easter can be one of the most rewarding in which to travel: most tourist services are still open, but you'll avoid the crowds, and the Patagonian forests along the Andean spine assume their autumnal colours. **Low season** runs from Easter to around the end of October, when temperatures can plummet to –25°C, and many mountain roads become impassable.

Some history

For over 10,000 years, before the arrival of European seafarers in the sixteenth century, Patagonia was exclusively the domain of nomadic **indigenous tribes**. It was Magellan who coined the name "Patagonia" on landing at the **Bahía San Julián**. The tales related by these early mariners awed and frightened their countrymen back home, mutating into myths of a godless region where death came easy.

Two centuries of sporadic attempts to colonize the inhospitable coastlands only partially ameliorated Patagonia's unwholesome aura. In 1779, the Spanish established **Carmen de Patagones**, which managed to survive as a trading centre on the Patagonian frontier. In doing so, it fared considerably better than other early settlements: **Puerto de los Leones**, near Camarones (1535); **Nombre de Jesús**, by the Magellan Straits (late 1580s); **Floridablanca**, near San Julián (1784); and **San José** on the Península Valdés, all failed miserably, the latter crushed by a Tehuelche attack in 1810 after braving it out for twenty years. Change was afoot, nevertheless. In 1848, Chile founded Punta Arenas on the Magellan Straits, and in 1865, fired by their visionary faith, a group of **Welsh Nonconformists** arrived in the Lower Chubut Valley. Rescued from starvation in the early years by **Tehuelche** tribespeople and Argentine government subsidies, they managed to establish a stable agricultural colony by the mid-1870s.

In the late nineteenth century, Patagonia changed forever with the introduction of **sheep**, originally brought across from the Islas Malvinas/Falkland Islands. The region's image shifted from one of hostility and hardship to that of an exciting frontier, where the "white gold" of wool opened the path to fabulous fortunes for pioneer investors. The transformation was complete within a generation: the plains were fenced in and roads were run from the coast to the cordillera. Native populations were booted out of their ancestral lands, while foxes and pumas were poisoned to make way for massive estancias. By the early 1970s, there were over sixteen million sheep grazing the fragile pastures on over a thousand estancias. Later, the region's confidence blossomed further with the discovery of oil, spurring the growth of industry in towns such as **Comodoro Rivadavia**.

Falling international wool prices and desertification, though, eventually brought sheep farming to its knees, a situation compounded by the eruption of Volcán Hudson in 1991, which buried immense areas of grazing land in choking ash (see box, p.692). To make matters worse, the oil industry also went through a massive downturn and shed thousands of jobs.

The corner has since been turned, however, and today the picture is far from bleak. Although there are hundreds of abandoned estancias in Santa Cruz alone, the Patagonian economy is once again booming – wool prices are on the rise and, perhaps more importantly for the region's future, so, too, are the numbers of **tourists**, as visitors come looking for a wild experience in an almost mythical land. This swelling interest has helped rekindle regional pride, and Spanish speakers will hear many locals boasting of being *NYC – Nacido Y Criado* ("Born and Bred") – in Patagonia.

The Atlantic seaboard

A hostile, cliff-lined coast, backed by an expanse of seemingly endless desolation – for at least three centuries after Magellan's voyage, this is what the word "Patagonia" conjured up in the imagination of the Western world. Today such spaces may seem most appealingly covered by air, but if you're committed to discovering what Patagonia is really about, steel yourself for the overland crossing: you can travel along the Atlantic seaboard all the way from the town of **Carmen de Patagones** to Río Gallegos in around 28 hours, though a more realistic estimate is to spend a week to ten days making the trip. This allows time to see the world-famous wildlife reserve at **Península Valdés**, usually accessed from the seaside town of **Puerto Madryn**; to investigate Patagonia's vaunted Welsh legacy in the villages of the Lower Chubut Valley near **Trelew**, the jumping-off point for seasonal trips to the huge Magellanic penguin colony at **Punta Tombo**; and to break the journey south with a stopover in beautiful **Puerto Deseado** or convenient **Puerto San Julián**, each with their own significant populations of marine wildlife and rich historical associations. If you have your own transport, you could also fit in a side-trip to the petrified forests of the **Monumento Natural Bosques Petrificados** or **Bosque Petrificado Sarmiento**.

Carmen de Patagones and Viedma

The RN-3 from Bahía Blanca reaches the Río Negro at **CARMEN DE PATAGONES**, a slow-paced town on a hill on the river's northern bank. Patagones was the second Spanish settlement created to fortify the Patagonian coast against incursions of English and Portuguese pirates, and the only one to survive in the long term. The first families came direct from Spain, many from the Maragatería region of León in Old Castile (the town's inhabitants are known to this day as Maragatos), and originally lived in caves excavated in the cliff-face – you can see evidence of these at the **Cuevas Maragatas** on Rivadavia, 250m northeast of the main square, **Plaza 7 de Marzo**.

Patagones has been the symbolic gateway to Patagonia since its founding by Francisco de Viedma in 1779, but the town's finest hour came on March 7, 1827, during the fledgling Argentine Republic's war with Brazil over the Banda Oriental (present-day Uruguay), when local militiamen outwitted a far superior force of Brazilian troops who tried to storm the town. The two vast standards they captured can be seen in the Neoclassical **Iglesia Parroquial Nuestra Señora de Carmen** (8am–noon & 4–9pm), on Plaza 7 de Marzo. Built between 1880 and 1885, this twin-towered edifice was the first Salesian church in Patagonia and replaced the fort's church. Of the original fort, only the stone watchtower, the **Torre del Fuerte**, survives; dating back to 1780, it's Patagonia's oldest building. Two blocks south of here, at J.J. Viedma 64, is the well-presented and informative **Museo Histórico Regional** (Mon–Fri 10am–noon & 2.30–4.30pm, Sat 5–7pm; $2), which contains some eight thousand documents and artefacts that help trace the town's extensive history.

Across the river from Patagones is its uninspiring sister town, **VIEDMA**, the capital of Río Negro province. In the 1980s, President Alfonsín's government declared that Viedma was to be the future federal capital of Argentina, replacing Buenos Aires; needless to say, the plan bombed, and the only reason to get the ferry over here today is to find a place to stay or a bite to eat, as, surprisingly, the options are better here than in Patagones.

Practicalities

The **airport** for Carmen de Patagones and Viedma lies 8km southeast of the latter (no bus; $15 by taxi). Patagones' **bus terminal** is on Calle Barbieri, less than ten minutes' walk from the centre of town: turn left out of the terminal,

The Tehuelche

Once spread throughout much of Patagonia, the **Tehuelche**, whose name, meaning "brave people", is derived from the language of the Chilean Araucanian groups, actually consisted of three different tribes – the Gününa'küna, Mecharnúek'enk and Aónik'enk – each of whom spoke a different language but shared common bonds of culture and similar ways of life. Great inter-tribal parliaments were held occasionally to discuss trade or common threats to the community, but any alliances formed would be temporary and shifting, and sporadic warfare occurred between the different tribes.

The Tehuelche's **nomadic culture** – centred on the hunting of rhea and guanaco, the skins of which they used to build shelters (*toldos*) – had probably existed for well over three thousand years by the time Magellan and the first Europeans landed on Patagonian soil, but contact with Europeans soon brought change. By 1580, Sarmiento de Gamboa had reported use of the horse by the Tehuelche around the Magellan Straits, and by the early eighteenth century the animal had become integral to Tehuelche life. Inter-tribal contact and intermarriage became more regular, and hunting techniques evolved, with **boleadoras** and lances increasingly preferred to the older bow and arrow. The *boleadora* consisted of two or three stones wrapped in guanaco hide and connected by long thongs made from the sinews of rheas or guanacos. Whirled around the head, these were thrown to ensnare animals at close quarters. *Boleadoras* are the only real physical legacy of Tehuelche culture in today's Argentina.

Tehuelche **religious beliefs** recognized a benign supreme god (variously named Kooch, Maipé or Táarken-Kets), but he did not figure greatly in any outward devotions and was always rather distant in normal life. In contrast, the malign spirit, **Gualicho**, was a much-feared figure who was the regular beneficiary of horse sacrifices and the object of shamanistic attentions; today, this spiritual legacy is recognized not just in Argentina, but also in parts of Bolivia, Brazil, Paraguay and Uruguay. The greatest of the Tehuelche divine heroes was **Elal**, the being who created man, gave him fire and established the sacred relationships that exist both between the sexes and between man and beasts.

The decline of **Tehuelche civilization** came fast: in 1870, the Victorian adventurer George Musters estimated that there were 1500 Tehuelche in Patagonia; a 1931 census in the province of Santa Cruz (which had the greatest population of Tehuelche) recorded only 350. As with other indigenous tribes in the south, the **causes** of the destruction of this civilization were complex and interrelated. Wars with the *huincas* (white men) were catastrophic – above all, Julio Roca's Conquest of the Desert in 1879 – and were exacerbated by inter-tribal conflicts between Tehuelche groups themselves and with the Araucanians. Contact with *huinca* civilization, even when conducted on a peaceful basis, led to severe problems: disease wiped out whole tribal groups, while alcohol abuse led whites to replace one misconception (that of the "noble savage") with another (the "moral delinquent"), enabling them spuriously to justify attempts to settle ancestral Tehuelche lands as part of a greater plan to "civilize the *indio*".

Following the capitulation of the last rebel group to Roca in December 1884, the remaining Tehuelche were pushed into increasingly marginal lands. Guanaco populations plummeted, and Tehuelche life, culturally dislocated, became one of dependency. Many found the closest substitute to the old way of life was to join the estancias that had displaced them as *peón* shepherds. In this way, they were absorbed into the rural underclass. Whereas Mapuche customs and language have managed, tenuously, to survive into the twenty-first century, Tehuelche populations were much more fragmented geographically, and so fell below that imprecise, critical number that is necessary for the survival of a cultural heritage. The last speaker of Gününa'küna died in 1960. The Aónik'enk language can be spoken, at least partially, by fewer than a dozen people.

walk three blocks northwest to Calle Bynon and turn left. This leads to Plaza 7 de Marzo, on the east side of which is the helpful **tourist office** (March–Nov Mon–Fri 7am–9pm, Dec–Feb Mon–Fri 7am–9pm, Sat & Sun 10am–1pm & 6–9pm; ⓣ02920/461777 ext 253). Continuing a couple of blocks downhill from here brings you to the pier, from where the passenger **ferry** to Viedma departs (daily 7am–11pm, every 5min; $1).

You can find **accommodation** in Patagones at the no-frills *Hotel Percaz*, Comodoro Rivadavia and Irigoyen (ⓣ02920/464104, ⓔhotel@hotelpercaz.com.ar; ⑤ with breakfast). Over in Viedma, try the welcoming *Hotel Spa*, 25 de Mayo 174 (ⓣ02920/430459; ④), which has tidy, good-value rooms, or the *Hotel Austral*, by the ferry pier at Villarino 292 (ⓣ02920/422615, ⓔviedma@hoteles-austral.com.ar; ⑥ with breakfast) – the slightly dated rooms enjoy good views across the river to Patagones. The best **place to eat** is also in Viedma: cosy *La Balsa* on Villarino serves great seafood and has a good list of provincial wines.

Puerto Madryn

Spread out along the beautiful sweep of the Golfo Nuevo, **PUERTO MADRYN**, 425km south of Viedma, is Argentina's diving capital. Though it makes a pleasant place to stay for a couple of nights, its real pull is as a base for trips to the ecological treasure trove of Península Valdés; indeed, the superb **Ecocentro** (see p.662), just east of town, makes a great introduction to the area's abundant marine life.

Though Puerto Madryn is the site where the Welsh first landed in Patagonia in 1865, it was not developed until the arrival of the railway from Trelew in 1889, when it began to act as the port for the communities in the Lower Chubut Valley. With the explosion of tourism, Madryn has experienced rapid growth, and the town's permanent population of 65,000 swells significantly early in the year, thanks to its popularity as a summer resort.

Arrival and information

Madryn's **airport** handles only a few LADE flights every week; most air travellers arrive at Trelew, 65km south (see p.671). Minibuses shuttle passengers to Madryn and will drop you off at any central address ($15). You can also take a *remise* into town ($95) or catch the hourly bus ($13) that runs to Madryn's **bus terminal**. Most of what you'll need in town is within three blocks in any direction of the first-rate **tourist office**, at Julio Roca 223 (April to mid-Dec Mon–Fri 7am–9pm, Sat & Sun 8am–9pm, mid-Dec to March Mon–Fri 7am–11pm, Sat & Sun 8am–11pm; ⓣ02965/453504 or 452148, ⓦwww.madryn.gov.ar), where you can pick up good maps and leaflets in English. The accommodating staff also have a list of independent guides who speak foreign languages, and will furnish timetables for the **tides** in the area (useful if heading to Península Valdés).

Diving trips that take in the area's offshore wrecks and abundant marine life are available through the experienced Madryn Buceo, on Boulevard Brown by the third roundabout in Balneario Nativo Sur (ⓣ02965/155-64422, ⓦwww.madrynbuceo.com); English-speaking instructors teach a range of courses (a five-day PADI Openwater course costs around $750). Scuba Duba, Boulevard Brown 893 (ⓣ02965/452699, ⓔscubaduba@infovia.com.ar), is another worthwhile option and there are numerous other outfits as well – expect to pay $150

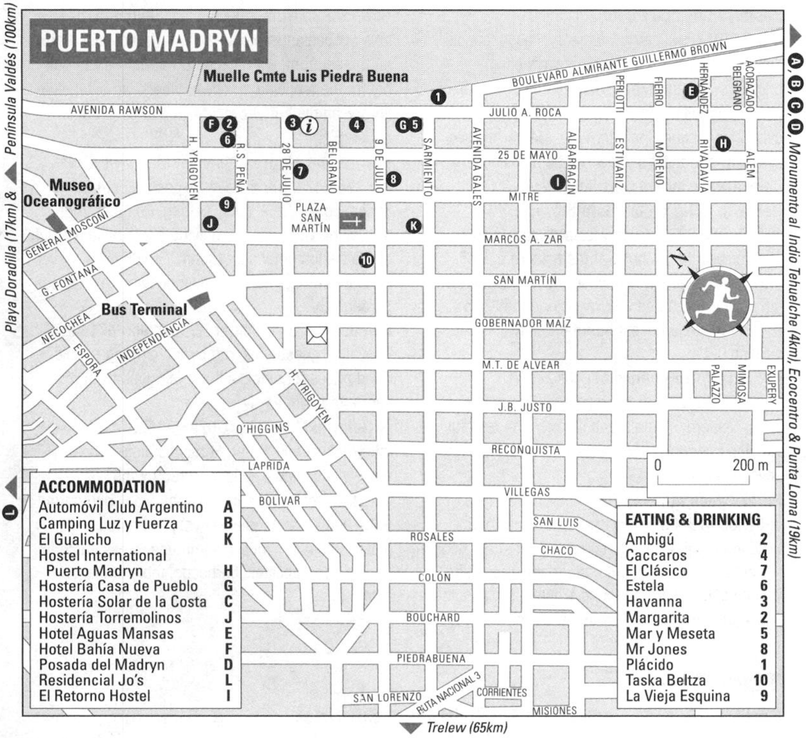

per excursion. **Mountain bikes** can be rented from Vernardino, Boulevard Brown 860 ($25 per day). There are a couple of good bike excursions within easy reach of town: north along the old Puerto Pirámides road to Playa Doradilla (17km from Madryn), where you can often see whales late in the afternoon between June and September, and to the sea-lion colony at Punta Loma (19km in other direction; $10).

Accommodation

Madryn has a wide range of **accommodation** options and good discounts are available in the off-season; high season, when prices jump significantly, starts around October due to the whale-watching. There are two **campsites** near the Monumento al Indio Tehuelche, round the bay (Linea #2 from the bus terminal or the main plaza will take you to within easy walking distance): *Automóvil Club Argentino* (☎02965/452952; $21 per person) and *Camping Luz y Fuerza*, beside Ecocentro (☎02965/457047; $10 per person).

El Gualicho Marcos Zar 480 ☎02965/454163, ⓦwww.elgualichohostel.com.ar. Fantastic hostel with a lovely garden and welcoming staff who arrange tours and diving trips. Has a good range of private rooms (❺) and four-, six- and eight-bed dorms ($30), each with breakfast included. Bike rental available.

Hostel International Puerto Madryn 25 de Mayo 1136 ☎02965/474426. Calm, clean hostel with a mixture of shared and en-suite doubles (❸) and bungalows (three, four or five people). It has kitchen and laundry facilities, plus a pleasant garden with a barbecue area. Closed May–Sept. Bungalows $20 per person.

Hostería Casa de Pueblo Roca 475 ⓣ02965/472500, ⓦwww.madryncasadepueblo.com.ar. Housed in one of the town's early buildings, this attractive seafront hotel maintains a pioneering yet homely feel. Bedrooms – overlooking either the internal garden or the sea – are cosy, and there's a lovely little first-floor terrace. Price includes breakfast. ❺

Hostería Solar de la Costa Brown 257 ⓣ02965/458822, ⓦwww.solardelacosta.com. Popular beachfront hotel at the eastern end of town, with tastefully furnished rooms – the doubles have good-sized beds – overlooking the Golfo Nuevo. Serves a decent buffet breakfast. Private parking. ❺

Hostería Torremolinos Marcos Zar 64 ⓣ02965/453215, ⓦwww.patagoniatorremolinos.com. Modern, intimate and stylish, with tasteful wooden interiors. Only five rooms, so book in advance in season. ❺

Hotel Aguas Mansas José Hernández 51 ⓣ02965/473103, ⓦwww.aguasmansas.com. Welcoming mid-range hotel on a quiet street near the beach, with small but comfortable rooms, an inviting salon centred around a huge fireplace and a tidy garden, complete with swimming pool. ❺

Hotel Bahía Nueva Roca 67 ⓣ02965/451677, ⓦwww.bahianueva.com.ar. Smart, red-brick hotel on the seafront, with standard rooms – try to get one of the few with an ocean view – an extensive library, ample buffet breakfasts and covered parking. ❻

Posada del Madryn Abraham Matthews 2951 ⓣ02965/474087, ⓦwww.la-posada.com.ar. Stylish posada in a lovely setting. Compact rooms are bright, while the large living areas have a touch of the design hotel about them. Breakfast is served in a glass-fronted annexe overlooking the spacious garden. ❻

Residencial Jo's Bolivar 75 ⓣ02965/471433. Cosy little guesthouse run by a charming couple. Good prices for singles, but a fair walk from the centre of town. ❸

El Retorno Mitre 798 ⓣ02965/456044, ⓦwww.elretornohostel.com.ar. Attractive place whose whitewashed exterior is mirrored by the spick-and-span rooms – four-, six- and eight-bed dorms ($20) and en-suite doubles (❹) – heated bathrooms and spotless communal areas. Kitchen and laundry facilities, barbecue, table tennis and bike rental.

The Town

Early in the morning, the **Golfo Nuevo** can be as still and glassy smooth as a lake, while at sunset there's a glorious view of the wide arc of the gulf back to the lights of town from the **Monumento al Indio Tehuelche**. Four kilometres south along the beach at **Punta Cuevas**, the statue marks the centenary of the arrival of the Welsh (see box opposite), and stands in homage to the Tehuelche, without whose help the settlement would probably have failed. Just before it sits the three-metre-square foundations of the very first houses built by the pioneers, right above the high-water mark.

Round the headland past the monument is Madryn's best attraction, the excellent **Ecocentro**, at Julio Verne 3784 (March–Aug Mon & Wed–Sun 3–7pm, Sept–April Mon & Wed–Sun 9am–7pm; $18; ⓣ02965/457470, ⓦwww.ecocentro.org.ar), reachable on Linea #2 from the bus terminal. An interactive museum set up to promote respect and understanding for marine ecosystems, it also houses a stunning life-size model of the orca Mel, famous for catching sea-lion pups and returning them to the shore unharmed. Be sure to go up the tower as well, to relax on one of the comfy sofas while enjoying panoramic views of the bay.

North of town, at D. Garcia and Menéndez, is the rather staid **Museo Oceanográfico y de Ciencias Naturales** (Mon–Fri 9am–1pm and 5–9pm, Sat 5–9pm; $6). It's not in the same league as Ecocentro, but the location – in the elegant, turreted Chalet Pujol – is grand and you can feel a whale's baleen and view relics from Welsh pioneering days in addition to more sombre photos of sea-lion massacres.

The arrival of the Welsh

In July 1865, after two months at sea, 153 **Welsh** men, women and children who had fled Britain to escape cultural and religious oppression disembarked from their clipper, the *Mimosa*, and took the first steps into what they believed was to be their Promised Land. Here they planned to emulate the Old Testament example of bringing forth gardens from the wilderness, but though the land around the Golfo Nuevo had the appearance of Israel, its parched harshness cannot have been of much comfort to those who had left the green valleys of Wales. Fired by Robert FitzRoy's descriptions of the Lower Chubut Valley, they explored south and, two months later, relocated – a piecemeal process during which some groups had, in the words of one of the leading settlers, Abraham Matthews, to live off "what they could hunt, foxes and birds of prey, creatures not permitted under Mosaic Law, but acceptable in the circumstances".

The immigrants were mostly miners or small merchants from southeast Wales and had little farming experience. Doubts and insecurities spread, with some settlers petitioning the British to rescue them, but when all avenues of credit seemed closed, vital assistance came from the Argentine government by way of provisions and substantial monthly subsidies. And despite initial mistrust of the **Tehuelche**, the Welsh learned survival and hunting skills from their native neighbours, which proved invaluable when the settlers' sheep died and the first three harvests failed. By the early 1870s, 44 settlers had abandoned the attempt, and sixteen had died, but optimists pointed to the fact that ten new settlers had since arrived, and 21 Welsh-Argentines had been born into the community. They decided to stick it out.

With increasing awareness of irrigation techniques, the pioneers began to coax their first proper yields from the Lower Chubut Valley, and recruitment trips to Wales and the US brought a much-needed influx of new settlers in 1874, the year in which Gaiman (see p.673) was founded. Yet, the best indicator of the settlement's progress was the international recognition received when samples of barley and wheat grown in Dolavon returned from major international expositions in Paris (1889) and the US (1892) with gold medals in their respective categories. The village's flour mill, built in the 1880s, still works.

Eating and drinking

Puerto Madryn is known for its seafood, and there are several beachfront **restaurants** that serve nothing else, including the town speciality, *arroz con mariscos* – a variant of paella that uses prawns, squid and clams.

Ambigú Roca and R.S. Peña. Good Spanish-style ham and melon, but the pizzas – arguably the best in town – are the real draw at this tasteful, warehouse-style spot.

Caccaros Roca 385. Stylish but unpretentious waterfront bistro with terrace seating and good tunes on the stereo. The menu includes a range of seafood and meat dishes, plus simpler sandwiches.

El Clásico 28 de Julio and 25 de Mayo. Large portions of affordable pasta and meat or a good-value *menú del día*, served in a fun café that's popular with locals.

Estela R.S. Peña 27. Warm, down-to-earth diner that prepares a juicy *parrilla* mixed grill for two. Closed Mon.

Havanna Roca and 28 de Julio. Relaxed central café/bar with a sea view, serving tasty *alfajores* to accompany the best espresso in town. Open till 2am Fri & Sat.

Margarita Roca and R.S. Peña. An attractive place to enjoy a pre- or post-dinner drink – most people plump for one of the potent cocktails. Live music on Thurs.

Mar y Meseta Roca 485 ⓣ02965/458740. Enjoy imaginative *raciones* like prawns in champagne or rabbit in chocolate sauce in the stylish dining room or out on the seafront terrace.

Mr Jones 9 de Julio 116. Buzzing little eatery, immensely popular with locals and young gringos alike. Most of the diners – who fill up the wooden benches and spill out onto the streetside tables – are here for the delicious picada menu.

Plácido Roca 506 ⓣ02965/455991. Elegant, intimate restaurant, directly overlooking the Golfo Nuevo, serving fine seafood, including delicious prawn kebabs with sweet-potato mash, and (cheaper) home-made pasta dishes. There's an excellent Argentine wine list. Open till 1am.

Taska Beltza 9 de Julio 345 ⓣ02965/474003. Unquestionably the best seafood restaurant in town, with reasonable prices. Ask for the daily special cooked by El Negro, the chef, or sample a few Basque tapas, followed by a mouthwatering *merluza*, washed down with a chilled chablis. Closed Mon.

La Vieja Esquina Mitre and R.S. Peña. Choice *asados* and great pasta prepared in a big corrugated building surreally decorated with hundreds of melted wine bottles and old typewriters.

Listings

Airlines Aerolíneas Argentinas, Roca 427 ⓣ02965/471463; LADE, Roca 117 ⓣ02965/451256.

Banks Plenty of ATMs, including at Banco de la Nación, 9 de Julio 117; Banco del Chubut, 25 de Mayo 154.

Books Re Creo, Roca and 28 de Julio.

Car rental Fiorasi Roca 165 ⓣ02965/456300; Localiza, Roca 536 ⓣ02965/456300.

Cinema 28 de Julio 129.

Hospital Emergencies ⓣ107; Hospital Subzonal, R Gomez 383 ⓣ02965/473445.

Internet access Abundant, including the Telefonica at Roca and 9 de Julio (daily 8am–midnight), which also has phones.

Laundry Servicios de Lavandería Morenas, Sarmiento and Marcos Zar. Closed Sun.

Pharmacy Farmacia Central, 25 de Mayo 272.

Police ⓣ101.

Post office Maiz and Belgrano.

Supermarket La Anónima, H. Yrigoyen 76.

Taxis Gales ⓣ471100; Patagonia ⓣ458300.

Tour agents Dozens of agencies organize day-trips to the Península Valdés, all charging around $115 (plus $35 entrance fee; whale-watching extra): some of the best-run are Tito Bottazzi, Boulevard Brown and Martín Fierro (ⓣ02965/474110; ⓦwww.titobottazzi.com); Argentina Vision, Roca 536 (ⓣ02965/451427, ⓦwww.argentinavision.com); Cuyun Co, Roca 165 (ⓣ02965/451845, ⓦwww.cuyunco.com); and Nievemar, Roca 549 (ⓣ02965/455544, ⓦwww.nievemartours.com.ar).

Península Valdés

PENÍNSULA VALDÉS, a sandy-beige, treeless hump of land connected to the mainland by a 35-kilometre isthmus, is one of the planet's most significant marine reserves and was designated a UNESCO World Heritage Site in 1999. It's an amazing place, evoked beautifully by writer Gerald Durrell in *The Whispering Land*: "It was almost as if the peninsula and its narrow isthmus was a cul-de-sac into which all the wildlife of Chubut had drained and from which it could not escape." Nothing prepares you for the astonishing richness of the marine environment that surrounds it – most notably the **southern right whales** that migrate here each year to frolic in the waters off the village of **Puerto Pirámides** – nor the immense animal colonies that live at the feet of the peninsula's steep, unstable cliffs.

The first attempt to establish a permanent settlement here was made in 1779 by Juan de la Piedra, who constructed a fort on the shores of the Golfo San José. A small number of settlers tried to scrape a living by extracting salt, but the colony was abandoned in 1810 after attacks by the local Tehuelche; an extremely limited salt-extraction industry exists to this day in the salt-pans at the bottom of Argentina's second deepest depression, the **Salina Grande**, 42m below sea level, in the centre of the peninsula. However, it is nature tourism that's the pot of gold now, with **Punta Delgada**, **Punta Cantor** and **Punta Norte**, along with **Caleta Valdés** bay, providing some of the best opportunities on the continent for viewing elephant seals and sea lions.

Visiting Península Valdés

Many people see Península Valdés in a day **tour** from Puerto Madryn (see p.660), following a fairly standard route that visits the lookout point for Isla de los Pájaros, Puerto Pirámides (whale trip costs from $60 extra) and Punta Cantor and Caleta Valdés and – depending on the operator – either Punta Norte or Punta Delgada. Be sure to find out exactly what sights you're visiting and how long you'll get in each place (most tours stay 1hr at each destination), whether the guide speaks English and the size of the group (some companies use large buses). Tours are long (10–12hr) so bring picnic provisions, though you can buy lunch in Puerto Pirámides.

If you want to visit the peninsula independently, the Mar y Valle **bus service** links Madryn with Puerto Pirámides (daily 9.30am, return 6pm; 1hr 15min; Jan/Feb second departure from Madryn 5pm, return 11am; $11 one way). This gives you the choice of going on more than one whale-watching trip, but it's difficult to organize trips from Pirámides to the rest of Península Valdés.

The **best way to see the peninsula**, however, is to **rent a car** from Puerto Madryn. This means you decide how long you want to spend wildlife-watching, and you can time your arrival at Punta Norte or Caleta Valdés for high tide, when there's the best chance of seeing orcas; it also gives you the freedom to stay at an estancia, recommended for a better appreciation of what makes the peninsula so special (see opposite). A word of warning, however: do not attempt to rush, especially if this is your first experience of driving on unsurfaced roads – serious crashes and fatalities happen with alarming regularity on the peninsula, especially after rain. When renting, check what happens if you break down or have a minor accident.

The whale-watching season runs from mid-June to mid-December, but the **best time to visit** the peninsula is September to November, when – in addition – elephant seals are active, the penguin colonies have returned to breed and, if you're lucky, you stand a chance of seeing orcas cruising behind the spit at Caleta Valdés.

The road to the peninsula

The reserve entrance ($35; pay at the gate) is in the middle of the isthmus, 43km from Madryn. Some 22km further, you pass a signposted turn-off north that takes you 5km to the lookout point for the **Isla de los Pájaros** (Bird Island), a strictly controlled area where access is only permitted for the purposes of scientific research. From the shore, telescopes enable you to spot seabirds in the nesting colonies 800m away. The most active months are between September and March, when you can spot egrets, herons, waders, ducks, cormorants, gulls and terns. Just past the turn-off is the **Centro de Interpretaciones** (daily 8am–8pm; free), poor by comparison with Madryn's Ecocentro, but with some interesting old photos and the skeleton of a young southern right whale that washed up at Caleta Valdés.

You should not collect your own shellfish in the area, due to the possibility of periodic red-tide outbreaks (see p.756), though shellfish served in restaurants are all checked and are safe for consumption.

Puerto Pirámides

At the end of the asphalt road, 105km from Madryn, lies the tiny settlement of **Puerto Pirámides**, one of the best places in the country for whale-watching: between mid-June and mid-December it's home to the most famous of all the peninsula's temporary residents, the **southern right whale**. Few experiences beat the thrill of seeing these massive and curious animals approaching your boat, breaching, or just jutting their tails above the water. Pirámides also has good **diving**

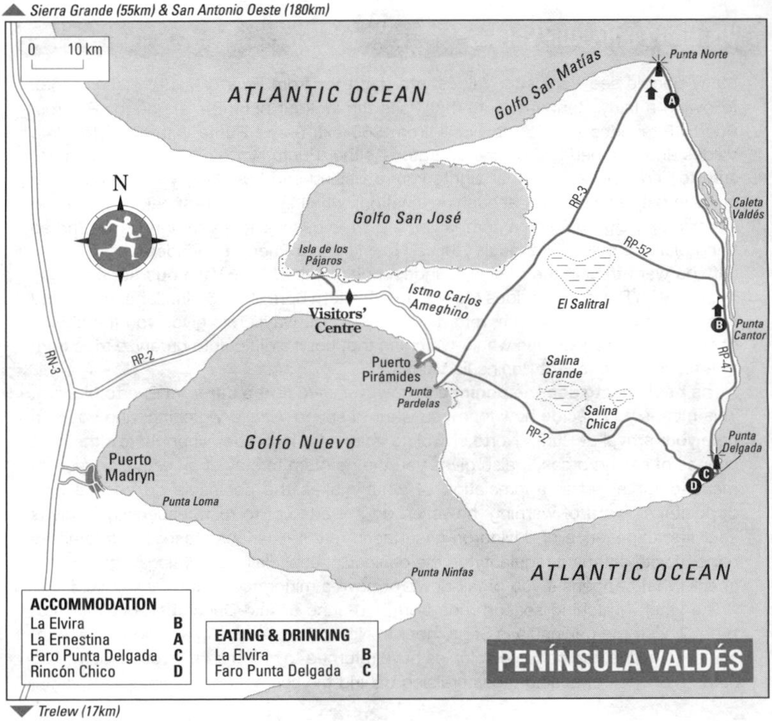

opportunities (see opposite), with some trips attracting the attention of sea lions and whales (it's officially illegal to dive with whales; instead, local parlance includes the euphemism "*excursiones especiales*"). You can walk to the **sea-lion colony** (Jan is the best time) at Punta Pirámides, 5km round the headland to the northwest.

Practicalities

With only three streets, the village's orientation is straightforward: the main one you come in on, Avenida de las Ballenas, runs parallel to the beach, with two perpendicular streets descending to the water (known as Primera Bajada and Segunda Bajada, respectively). There's **tourist information** on Primera Bajada (daily 8am–8pm; ⓣ02965/495084), and a Banco del Chubut **ATM** halfway up Avenida de las Ballenas.

Puerto Pirámides has plenty of **accommodation**, but book ahead in January and February. The most upmarket place is recently refurbished *Las Restingas*, on Primera Bajada (ⓣ02965/495101, ⓦwww.lasrestingas.com; US$281 half-board with sea view, US$214 without; closed mid-April to June), which enjoys a superb location, right on the beach; most of the bright, airy rooms have wonderful sea views. All other worthwhile options are on Avenida de las Ballenas. *Bahia Ballenas*, on the left side just inside the village (ⓣ02965/474110, ⓔreservas@bahiaballenas.com; $30 with breakfast), is an excellent little hostel, with a snug lounge, two tidy dorms and some of the cleanest bathrooms you'll ever see; the owners run Tito Bottazzi (see opposite) and offer guests discounts on their tours. Otherwise, there's the *ACA Motel*, opposite (ⓣ02965/495004; ⑤ with breakfast), which has clean and spacious but rather uninspired rooms, some with sea views; simple *La Posta*, on the corner of Ballenas and Primera Bajada (Ⓣ02965/495036, Ⓦwww.lapostapiramides.com.ar; $40 per person with breakfast), a staggered line of great-value apartments that come with kitchen and cable TV; or, at the far end of the village, on the corner of Ballenas and Segunda Bajada, *Hostería The Paradise* (Ⓣ02965/495030, Ⓦwww.hosteriaparadise.com.ar; US$180), which has smart but pricey rooms – including spacious Jacuzzi suites – in an attractive red-brick building. The huge **campsite** in the centre of the village can get severely overcrowded, but has direct access to the beach (Ⓣ02965/495098; $5 per person).

Hosterá The Paradise's **restaurant** is one of the best in Puerto Píramides, thanks to its tasty regional dishes, varied wine list and consistently friendly service. *Mammadeus*, also on Avenida de las Ballenas, is in a beautiful old building and serves excellent seafood, including a tremendous fish stew. *La Estación*, opposite the petrol station, has great home-made pastas and is also, with its laid-back vibe and mix of old-time memorabilia and rock iconography, one of the best **bars** in Patagonia.

Excursions from Puerto Pirámides

In season (mid-June to mid-Dec), you are almost guaranteed to come within a few metres of a southern right whale – or two, if you're here towards the end of the year, when you're likely to see mothers with calves. Outside these dates there are general boat trips, and dolphins and sea lions are the more standard sightings. A growing number of companies offer regular day (1hr; $60–75) and sunset (2hr; $120–150) whale-watching trips into the Golfo Nuevo, but recommended operators include Hydrosport (Ⓣ02965/495065, Ⓦwww.hydrosport.com.ar), Whales Argentina (Ⓣ02965/495015, Ⓦwww.whalesargentina.com.ar) and Tito Bottazzi (Ⓣ02965/495050, Ⓦwww.titobottazzi.com), all on Primera Bajada, and Jorge Schmid (Ⓣ02965/495012, Ⓦwww.puntaballena.com.ar), on Segunda Bajada. Services are pretty standard, but check what type of boat you'll be using, as the semi-rigid inflatable zodiacs allow you to get closer; remember, though, that boat operators are meant to observe strict regulations about keeping a respectful distance from the cetaceans.

For **diving**, Buceo Aventura (Ⓣ02965/495031, Ⓦwww.buceoaventura.com.ar) has decent equipment and friendly staff, as does Patagonia Scuba (Ⓣ02965/495030); both charge around $150 per dive. Steve Johnson (Ⓣ02965/15406755, Ⓔquilimbai@yahoo.com; ask for him at Patagonia Scuba), an American diver who has lived so long on the peninsula that he has forgotten most of his English, will take underwater photographs of your *excursion especial* and package them on a CD ($70).

Patagonian Brothers Expeditions on Avenida de las Ballenas (Ⓣ02965/15416843, Ⓦwww.patagoniaexplorers.com) runs excellent guided small-group **kayak** trips in both gulfs, from half-day paddles to nine-day expeditions.

Punta Pardelas and Punta Delgada

Just outside Puerto Pirámides, it's worth taking the short road down to **Punta Pardelas**, a delightful little spot right on the shore of Golfo Nuevo, from where you can often get spectacular close-up sightings of southern right whales as they make their way along the coast. From here, it's another 70km to **Punta Delgada**, at the southeasterly tip of the peninsula, past the pinky-white salt deposits of the **Salina Grande** and **Salina Chica** depressions. Punta Delgada itself is a headland topped by a lighthouse, part of the attractive *Faro Punta Delgada* **hotel** (Ⓣ02965/471910, Ⓦwww.puntadelgada.com; ❾ includes breakfast and excellent three-hour tour of nearby elephant-seal colony; closed

△ Elephant seal, Punta Delgada

April–July); perched on the cliff and buffeted by winds, it's an extremely atmospheric place to stay. The area affords excellent opportunities to view **sea lions** and, in high season, **elephant seals**. However, note that it is private property, and really only visited by Argentina Vision tours (see p.664) – who own the *Faro Punta Delgada*. Independent travellers are allowed to stop, but if you're not on a trip with Argentina Vision, you'll need to buy lunch at the hotel's restaurant in order to access the beach on a short guided tour (1pm, 2pm & 3pm; free).

Just southwest of Punta Delgada, there is more superb **accommodation** at *Rincón Chico* (Ⓣ02965/471733, Ⓦwww.rinconchico.com.ar; US$315 full board plus two excursions; closed Easter to mid-Aug), an estancia that blends traditional architecture with attractively furnished modern rooms. Guided walks visit the large colonies of marine wildlife (up to 3500 sea lions and 10,000 elephant seals) that gather on the estancia's private beach.

Punta Cantor and Caleta Valdés

Heading north along the coast from Punta Delgada are beaches replete with marine mammals. **Punta Cantor**, mid-way up the peninsula, is a colony of seven thousand elephant seals at the foot of a high cliff. Walk down the cliff-face of sedimentary deposits and fossilized oysters (aged 10 to 14 million years old) to the ridge just above the beach – don't try to climb down onto the beach, however, as it is strictly off-limits. The best time to visit is from late September until early November, when the bull elephant seals fight for females – a display of bloodied blubbery bulk. During the rest of the year, you will hear snorts and

Marine mammals of Valdés

Although diverse and significant populations of birds and terrestrial mammals exist on **Peninsúla Valdés**, it is the **marine mammals** here that are of particular interest. Pride of place goes to the **southern right whale** (*ballena franca austral*), which comes to the sheltered waters of the Golfo Nuevo and Golfo San José to breed. Weighing up to 50 tonnes and measuring up to 18m (the females are larger than the males), these gentle leviathans are filter-feeders, deriving nutrients from the plankton they sift from the seas with their baleen plates. Once favoured targets for the world's whalers – they were the "right" whales to harpoon, as they were slow, yielded copious quantities of oil and floated when killed – they have now been declared a National Natural Monument, and are protected from the moment they enter Argentine territorial waters. This foresight has enabled the present tourist industry to develop, reinforcing the economic value of keeping these creatures alive; their charming curiosity – a trait that once put them in danger – now makes them one of the most enjoyable cetaceans to view in the wild.

The **killer whale**, or orca, is not in fact a whale at all, but the largest member of the dolphin family – it displays the high levels of intelligence we associate with such creatures, if not their cuteness. This is amply demonstrated in their unique hunting behaviour at Caleta Valdés and Punta Norte, where orcas storm the shingle banks, beaching themselves in order to snap up their preferred prey: baby sea lions and young elephant seals. Male killer whales have been known to measure over nine metres, and weigh some eight tonnes, although the ones off Valdés do not reach these sizes; females are not quite as long and weigh considerably less. The dorsal fin on an adult male is the biggest in the animal kingdom, measuring 1.8m – the height of an average man – and its size and shape is one of the factors used to identify individual orcas, along with the shape of the saddle patch and colour variations; 23 have been tracked off Punta Norte. If you want to know more, contact Fundación Orca (ⓣ02965/454723, ⓦwww.fundorca.org.ar), a Madryn-based scientific organization dedicated to the study of this creature.

Sea lions (*lobo marino*) were once so numerous on the peninsula that 20,000 would to be culled annually for their skins and blubber – a figure that equals the entire population found here today, despite almost thirty years of protection. They are the most widely distributed of the Patagonian marine mammals and their anthropomorphic antics make them a delight to watch. It's easy to see the derivation of the name when you look at a 300-kilogram adult male, ennobled by a fine yellowy-brown mane.

As animals go, few come into the league of the southern **elephant seal** (*elefante marino*), a creature so large that Noah made him swim. Península Valdés is their only continental breeding ground and, as such, the only place you're ever likely to see them in the all-too-evident flesh. Weighing some three tonnes and measuring four to five metres, bull elephant seals mean business. Though the average size of a harem for a dominant male ranges between ten and fifteen females, some superstud tyrants get greedy. One macho male at Caleta Valdés amassed 131 consorts, fighting off love rivals in the process. October is the best month to see these noisy clashes of the titans, but be prepared for some gore, as tusk wounds are inevitable. Adult females, a fifth of the size of the vast males, are pregnant for eleven months of the year, giving birth from about mid-September. Pups weigh 40kg at birth, but then balloon on the rich milk of their mothers to weigh 200kg after only three weeks. The elephant seal's most remarkable attribute, however, is as the world's champion deep-sea diving mammal. Depths of over a thousand metres are not uncommon, and it is reckoned that some of these animals have reached depths of 1500m, staying submerged for a breathtaking two hours.

sneezes, see stretches, scratching and the odd fatty quiver like a waterbed being slapped, but otherwise the animals are content just to sleep.

Two kilometres north is a viewpoint over the shifting curves of the shingle spits of **Caleta Valdés** – from September to November, orcas may be spotted entering the *caleta*, or bay behind the spit, at high tide – and there's a colony of Magellanic penguins 3km further on. This road is also one of the best for sighting *maras*, *ñandús*, skunks and other terrestrial wildlife.

For **accommodation** there's *La Elvira*, a rather ugly modern block with somewhat attractively rustic rooms, near the Punta Cantor turn-off (Ⓣ02965/474248, Ⓦwww.laelvira.com.ar; US$295 full board including excursions; closed April–Aug); the restaurant's cheap, buffet-style food is popular with tours.

Punta Norte

Wild **Punta Norte**, the northernmost point of the peninsula, is famous for the **orca attacks** on baby sea lions that occur there during March and early April. In a spectacle rivalling anything in the natural world, the eight-tonne orcas beach themselves at up to 50km per hour and attempt to grab a pup; most efforts are unsuccessful, and an orca will sometimes settle for a snack of penguin. Attacks usually occur with the high tides, so if you're so inclined, check with the Centro de Interpretaciones (see p.665) for times and plan your arrival to coincide with the hour either side of high tide to stand the best chance of witnessing one. These aside, the sight of ominous black dorsal fins of a pod of killer whales cruising just off the coast is thrilling enough. Serious photographers can buy a permit to descend to the beach (US$300; contact the Secretaria de Turismo in Rawson Ⓣ02965/481113, Ⓔinfo@chubutur.gov.ar), but the general viewing area can be as good a vantage point as any.

On the slope above the beach there's a **café** where the personable owner prepares filling snacks, as well as an interesting **visitors' centre and museum** (free); inside, you can identify the distinguishing features of the different individual orcas. You can also **stay** up here, at the characterful but pricey *La Ernestina* (Ⓣ02965/471143, Ⓦwww.laernestina.com.ar; US$280 full board including drinks and excursions), whose excellent location, right on the beach, makes it a favourite haunt of wildlife photographers.

The Welsh heartland

If you're coming to Chubut Province looking for the villages of a Dylan Thomas play, think again. The **Welsh**, like the Tehuelche before them, have been absorbed almost seamlessly into Argentina's diverse cultural identity. Under the surface, though, there remain vestiges of their pioneering culture and a real pride in both the historical legacy – evident in the number of fine **Welsh chapels** dotted across the farmlands of the **Lower Chubut Valley** – and the current cultural connection that goes well beyond the touristy trappings.

Halting Welsh is still spoken by some of the third- or fourth-generation residents in the main towns of **Trelew**, **Gaiman** and **Dolavon**, even if it isn't the language of common usage, and whereas it once seemed doomed to die out, the tongue now appears to be enjoying a limited **renaissance**. In municipal schools today, young students have the option to study the language of their forebears: a team of **Welsh teachers** works in Chubut, and **cultural exchanges** with Cymru are thriving – two or three pupils are sent annually from Chubut to Welsh universities and numerous delegations from different associations ply across the Atlantic. It's not all one-way, either, since scholars have come from Wales to study the manuscripts left by pioneers and seek inspiration from what they pronounce to be the purity of the language that was preserved in Patagonia.

Trelew

With a population of 107,000, **TRELEW** is second only to Comodoro Rivadavia as an industrial and commercial centre in Chubut, though it's a more attractive place, with fewer high-rises and marked less by heavy industry. Home to a couple of excellent museums, the town's good transport connections make it a convenient base from which to explore the surrounding Welsh settlements of the **Lower Chubut Valley** and, to the south, the famous penguin colony at **Punta Tombo**.

Arrival and information

Trelew's **airport** (which also serves Puerto Madryn) is 5km northeast of town; there's a Banco de Chubut **ATM** and a simple **tourist office** counter that opens for flight arrivals. Several car-rental agencies serve the airport, though you'll get a better deal in Trelew itself; *remises* into town cost $8 (for details of getting to Puerto Madryn, see p.660). The **bus terminal** is within easy walking distance of the town centre; regular buses run to Gaiman, Dolavon and Rawson. The helpful main **tourist office** is at San Martín and Mitre (Mon–Fri 8am–8pm, Sat & Sun 9am–9pm; ⓣ2965/420139, ⓦwww.trelewpatagonia.gov.ar); the staff can provide you with a good leaflet on the various Welsh chapels of the Lower Chubut Valley.

Accommodation

With the exception of the historic *Hotel Touring Club*, Trelew's **hotels** are rather mundane; if you're visiting multiple Welsh towns, you'll find more homely accommodation in Gaiman. The nearest **campsite** is *Camping Patagonia* (ⓣ02965/15406907; $9 per person), 12km southeast of town along Ruta 7.

Galicia Hotel 9 de Julio 214 ⓣ02965/433802, ⓦwww.hotelgalicia.com.ar. Has a grand entrance and a lavish lobby but the rooms, while perfectly comfortable, are on the small side. ❺

Hotel Centenario San Martín 150 ⓣ02965/426111, ⓔhotelcentenario@yahoo.com.ar. Fairly standard but fuddy-duddy hotel – its name hints at the age of its decor – occupying a block near Plaza Independencia. ❺

Hotel Libertador Rivadavia 31 ⓣ02965/420220, ⓦwww.hotellibertadortw.com.ar. Another large, rather old-fashioned establishment, but the rooms are clean and the staff efficient and friendly. ❻

Hotel Rayentray San Martin 101 ⓣ02965/434702, ⓦwww.cadenarayentray.com.ar. The most upmarket option in town, with larger than normal rooms and a range of facilities, including a top-floor swimming pool. ❼

Hotel Touring Club Fontana 240 ⓣ02965/425790. Charming if slightly faded Art Deco historic monument (Butch Cassidy and the Sundance Kid once stayed here), with airy, spacious rooms, fronted by a tremendous high-ceilinged bar (see p.673). ❺

The Town

Trelew's name in Welsh means the "Village of Lewis", in honour of Lewis Jones, its founder. The settlement rose to prominence after the completion, in 1889, of the rail link to Puerto Madryn, which allowed easy export of the burgeoning agricultural yields. The railway has since disappeared, and the old station, on 9 de Julio and Fontana, is now home to the **Museo Regional Pueblo de Luis** (Mon–Fri 8am–8pm, Sat & Sun 2–8pm; $2). One of two fine museums in Trelew, it does a good job of tracing the area's **Celtic** history and also explores

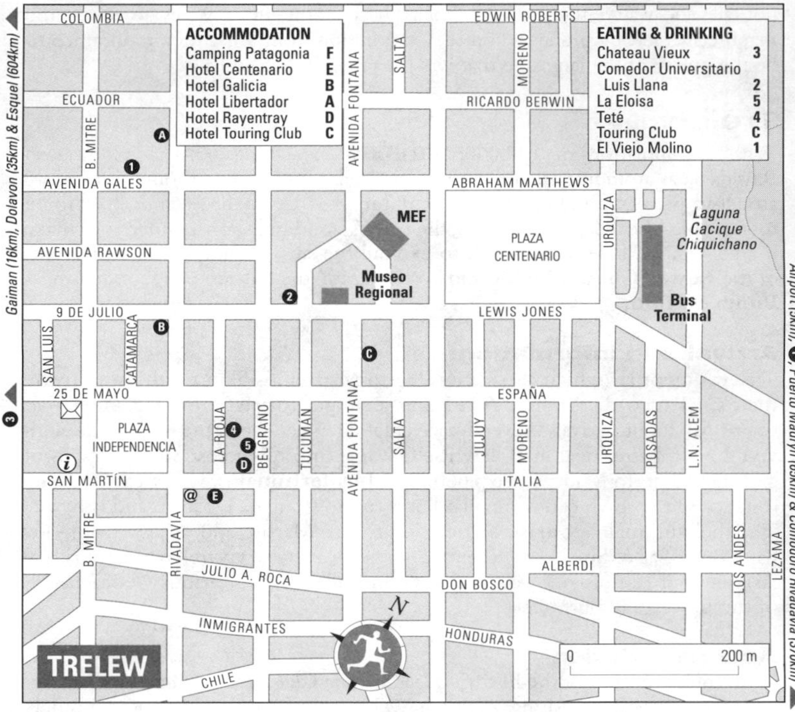

the coexistence of the Welsh and the Tehuelche as well as the eisteddfod (traditional annual Welsh) festivals. Across the road is the excellent modern **Museo Paleontológico Egidio Feruglio (MEF)**, Fontana and Lewis Jones (April–Aug Mon–Fri 10am–6pm, Sat & Sun 10am–8pm; Sept–March daily 9am–8pm; $15; Ⓦwww.mef.org.ar), one of South America's most important paleontological collections, which claims to describe "300 million years of history" and contains beautifully preserved clutches of dinosaur eggs and skeletons from the region, including a 95-million-year-old argentosaurus, one of the world's largest dinosaurs. Ask for an English guided tour (45min; free), if you need one.

Trelew's urban centrepiece is its beautiful main square, the **Plaza Independencia**, with flourishing trees and an elegant gazebo, built by the Welsh to honour the centenary of Argentine Independence; in September/October each year, the leafy plaza becomes the focus for the most important of the province's **eisteddfods**, when two prestigious awards are made: the *Sillón del Bardo* (The Bard's Chair), for the best poetry in Welsh, and the *Corona del Bardo* (The Bard's Crown), for the best in Spanish.

Eating and drinking

Most **eating** and **drinking** options in Trelew are open daily from noon till 3pm and 8pm till midnight, and all are within a few minutes' walk from the main square. You can stock up on food for day-trips at several **supermarkets** around town, including the Hiper Norte at Rivadavia and 9 de Julio.

Chateau Vieux 25 de Mayo and A.P. Bell ⓣ02965/425247. Fine Patagonian dining – lamb, rabbit and the like – and even finer wines in an atmospheric 1920s building.
Comedor Universitario Luis Llana Opposite the Museo Regional on Rivadavia. Simple but filling local fare at student prices. Open 10am–8pm.
La Eloisa Belgrano 351. A smart, formal restaurant, which, despite the impressive *asado* in the window, also does a good seafood à la carte menu. Open 7am–3am.
Teté La Rioja 326. Snug, minimalist *parrilla* that adds tasty grilled vegetables to the lamb and beef standards.
Touring Club Fontana 240. Characterful *confitería* and bar with touches of grandeur, offering *milanesas* – or something a little stronger from the terrifying array of dusty bottles lining the 1920s bar. Open 6.30am–midnight.
El Viejo Molino Avenida Gales 250. Excellent meat and fish dishes, including a novel *tabla de ahumados* (a mixed platter of smoked cold cuts), served in an old mill setting.

Listings

Airlines Aerolíneas Argentinas, 25 de Mayo 33 ⓣ02965/420170; LADE, 1st floor bus terminal ⓣ02965/435740.
Banks Banco del Chubut, Rivadavia and 25 de Mayo; Banco de la Nacion, Fontana and 25 de Mayo.
Car rental Fiorasi, Urquiza 310 ⓣ02965/435344; Rent a Car Patagonia, San Martín 129 ⓣ02965/420898.
Internet access San Martín 182.
Pharmacy Farmacia Patagónicas, Rivadavia 348.
Taxis Outside bus terminal, or call ⓣ02965/420404 or 424445.
Tour agencies In season (Sept–March), several agencies run half-day tours to the penguin colony at Punta Tombo ($90 plus $20 entrance fee), and full-day tours that also take in a Welsh tea in Gaiman and Commerson's dolphin-watching in nearby Playa Unión ($160 plus $20 entrance fee and $25 tea). Recommended outfits include Alcamar Travel, San Martín 146 (ⓣ02965/421213, ⓦwww.argentinapatagonia.com.ar); Explore Patagonia, Roca 297 (ⓣ02965/437860); and Nievemar Tours, Italia 98 (ⓣ02965/434114, ⓦwww.nievemartours.com.ar).

The Lower Chubut Valley

West of Trelew is the broad Lower Chubut Valley. Although flanked by low, brown hills, the valley itself is a fertile stretch, thanks to the Río Chubut, which flows through here from the Andes. The river derives its name from the Tehuelche word "*chupat*", meaning clean or transparent. The Welsh began using the Chubut to irrigate the valley in 1867, and it was dammed a hundred years later to ensure a more predictable flow to the farm plots, whilst also generating electricity for industrial development. A string of well-maintained **Welsh chapels** (*capillas galesas*) line the Chubut, including – just south of Trelew – the Cappila Moriah; dating from 1880, it's the oldest in Argentina, and many of the original settlers are buried in its cemetery. The small towns along the river's route are all charming and, though you won't exactly hear Welsh spoken in the streets, the legacy of pioneering times is never far beneath the surface.

Gaiman

GAIMAN, 16km west of Trelew along RN-25, sits amid lush pastures and poplar trees, making the place feel more like a Monet watercolour than Patagonia. The most eminently "Welsh" of the area's settlements, thanks to its numerous *casas de té*, or teahouses, and various monuments to the settlers, Gaiman is a pretty village made fascinating if you get the locals to talk about their Celtic roots – Gaiman hosts mini-**eisteddfods** in mid-September and the first week of May.

You can spend a pleasant hour or two taking in the village's various sights: the attractive brick **Capilla Bethel** from 1913, next to its late nineteenth-century predecessor; the squat stone **Primera Casa** (First House), dating from 1874, and looking as if it had been transplanted from Snowdonia; the appealing little plaza with its early bust commemorating Christopher Columbus; the old train station that now houses the **Museo Histórico Regional** (Tues–Sun 3–7pm; $2), with exhibits relating to the trials of pioneer life; and you can even walk through the abandoned 300-metre-long **railway tunnel** near the tourist office.

The main attraction, though, is working your way through a mountain of cakes over afternoon tea at one of the village's **casas de té**, some of which are owned and run by descendants of the original Welsh settlers. They open daily from around 2pm and serve similar arrays of cake, toast, scones and home-made jams ($20–25 per person); the most typical cake of all is the *torta negra* (Welsh black fruit cake), which was traditionally given at weddings, to be eaten on a couple's first anniversary. Ivy-clad *Tŷ Nain*, H. Irigoyen 283, is one of the most authentic, and bang in the centre, next to the plaza; take your tea surrounded by the owners' collection of tea- and Welsh-related artefacts. The warm welcome guests receive at *Plas y Coed*, east along Irigoyen, at no. 320, is mirrored in the generous portions served there, while at nearby *Tŷ Cymraeg*, Abraham Matthews 74, a descendant of the pioneers serves tea in the original family home.

For all its memorials to its Celtic heritage, Gaiman's most surprising monument has nothing whatsoever to do with tradition, Welsh or otherwise. **Parque El Desafío** ("The Challenge Park"; daily 10am–6pm; $10; Ⓦwww.eldesafiogaiman.com.ar), on Almirante Brown, is a backyard where **tin cans** and plastic bottles have been recycled and reincarnated. It's the work of octogenarian Joaquín Alonso, dubbed by the local media as the Dalí of Gaiman, whose constructions, such as the tower he erected "in homage to myself", stand alongside ironic mockeries of modern consumerist society.

Eight kilometres south of the village is the **Parque Paleontológico Bryn Gwyn** (daily: March–Sept 11am–5pm, Oct–Feb 10am–6pm; $8; Ⓦwww.mef.org.ar), where a 1.5-kilometre circuit takes you past stratified fossil beds dating back some forty million years.

Practicalities

Buses from Trelew stop outside the **tourist office** (Mon–Sat 9am–8pm, Sun 1–8pm; Ⓣ02965/491571; Ⓔinformes@gaiman.gov.ar) in the Casa de Cultura on the corner of Rivadavia and Belgrano, one block up from the modest main street, Avenida Tello. Alternatively, a **taxi** will cost around $25.

If you intend **to stay** here, try the *Plas y Coed* on Irigoyen 320 (Ⓣ02965/15697069, Ⓔgplasycoed@yahoo.com.ar; ❹ with a huge, and very sweet, breakfast). The owners have done a good job of recreating the homely atmosphere that pervaded their original property – the first teahouse in Gaiman – just around the corner, and there's a spacious living room for guests. The *Hostería Gwesty Tywi*, at Miguel Jones 342 (Ⓣ02965/491292, Ⓔgwestywi@yahoo.com.ar; ❹), is a clean, perfumed B&B whose owners speak Welsh and English, while the larger *Ty Gwen*, 9 de Julio 111 (Ⓣ02965/491009, Ⓔtygwyn@tygywn.com.ar; ❺), has compact wood-floored rooms with partial views of the Río Chubut. There's also a **campsite**, *Los Doce Nogales* ($10 per person) across the river to the southeast, near the *Tŷ Tě Caerdydd* teahouse.

For a more substantial meal than tea and cakes, head to *El Vieja Cuadra*, an inviting **restaurant** on the corner of Jones and Tello (Mon–Sat 8pm–midnight, Sun noon–3.30pm) that serves sizeable pizzas, or *El Angel*, at Rivadavia 241 (Ⓣ02965/491460; evenings only, closed Thurs), which is essentially someone's home, so you'll need to ring in advance.

Dolavon

DOLAVON, 19km west of Gaiman, is the most authentically Welsh of all the Chubut villages and that which best preserves the character of an early pioneering settlement – the original, whitened brick buildings are evocative of times gone by, and there's not a teashop in sight. In terms of specific sights, however, there's little to see apart from the **Molino Harinero** at Calle Maipú 61 (Old Flour Mill; daily 11am–7pm; free or $3 with a guide; ⓣ02965/492290). The original steam machinery, made in Kentucky in 1880 and brought here in 1903, was converted to electricity and is still in working order. Dishes served at *La Molienda*, the charming **restaurant** at the rear, use flour ground on site. The **bus** from Trelew stops at the compact terminal, near the disused train station. There's a free municipal **campsite** on the northern edge of the village but no other **accommodation**.

South of Trelew

From Trelew, it's around 360km south along paved roads to Comodoro Rivadavia. En route, it's worth making two side-trips to the coastal nature reserves of **Punta Tombo** and **Cabo Dos Bahías**. Alternatively, the first reserve, 107km south of Trelew down unpaved but well-maintained RP-1, makes an easy day-excursion.

Punta Tombo

Punta Tombo is the largest single colony of penguins on the continent, with a population of more than 500,000 birds. The noise from these black and white **Magellanic penguins** – slightly less glamorous versions of the larger king and emperor penguins, the yellow-throated birds that have so successfully cornered the brand image – is immense: it's an unmissable experience to wander around this scrubland avian metropolis amid a cacophony of braying, surrounded on all sides by waddling, tottering birds. The penguins nest behind the stony beach in scrapes underneath the bushes, with a close eye on approaching strangers. Get

The Magellanic penguin

The word "penguin", some maintain, derives from Welsh *pen gwyn* (white head), a name allegedly bestowed by a Welsh sailor passing these shores with Thomas Cavendish in the sixteenth century. In fact, a white head is not what you first associate with a **Magellanic penguin**, and it's far more likely that the name comes from the archaic Spanish *pingüe*, or fat. The birds were a gift to the early mariners, being the nearest equivalent at that time to a TV dinner.

Though they're not exactly nimble on land, in water these birds can keep up a steady 8km an hour, or several times that over short bursts. An adult bird stands 50 to 60cm tall and weighs a plump 4 to 5.5kg. Birds begin arriving at their ancestral Patagonian nesting sites – which can be up to 1km from the sea – from late August, and by early October nesting is in full swing. Parents share the task of incubation, as they do the feeding of the brood once the eggs start to hatch, in early November. By early January, chicks that have not been preyed upon by seabirds, foxes or armadillos make their first sorties into the water. During the twenty-day February moult, the birds do not swim, as they lose their protective layer of waterproof insulation; at this time, penguin sites are awash with fuzzy down and sneezing birds. In March and April, they begin to vacate the nesting sites. Although little is known of their habits while at sea, scientists do know that the birds migrate north, reaching as far as the coast off Rio de Janeiro, 3000km away.

too close and they'll indicate their displeasure by hissing or bobbing their heads from side to side like a dashboard dog – respect these warning signals, and remember that a penguin can inflict a good deal of pain with its sharp bill.

The **reserve** ($20; pay at the gate) is open between September and late March although late **November** to **January** is probably the best time to visit, as there are plenty of young chicks. The penguins are most active in the morning and early evening; tour agencies run morning trips from Trelew, allowing around one and a half hours with the birds. The nearby countryside is an excellent place to see **terrestrial wildlife**, such as guanacos, *choiques*, skunks, armadillos and *maras*.

Cabo Dos Bahías

The remote coastal reserve of **Cabo Dos Bahías** ($10; pay at the gate), stuck out on a headland 30km from the tiny fishing village of **Camarones**, is home to 55,000 Magellanic penguins and a colony of sea lions from August to April. It had the only continental colony of fur seals until they were turfed out during the Falklands War in 1982. The seals now live on Isla Moreno 3km off shore, and are difficult to see. Tame herds of guanacos are abundant in the park, which also has healthy populations of *ñandú* and *mara*. There is a **restaurant** at Caleta Sara, a small bay reached by taking the left fork shortly after the reserve entrance, where there is also basic but clean **accommodation** in converted five-metre-long freight containers ($12 per person); you can also pitch your tent for free by the *Club de YPF*. In Camarones, 72km off RN-3 down paved RP-30, there is decent enough accommodation at *Viejo Torino* near the harbour (Ⓣ0297/496-3003; ❻), or try the *Bahía del Sueño* cabins on the left as you approach the village (Ⓣ0297/496-3007; ❻ for four people).

Buses reach as far as Camarones but leave from Trelew only (Mon, Wed & Fri 8am, returns same day 4pm; 3hr), and you'll have to rely on bagging a lift from someone in Camarones (about $75) to the park. Alternatively, travel agents in Comodoro Rivadavia run regular **trips** to the reserve (see opposite).

Southern Chubut and northern Santa Cruz

Encompassing some pretty dreary towns – the former oil centres of **Comodoro Rivadavia** and **Caleta Oliva** among them – and some of the most desolate scenery in the whole of the country, the region along this stretch of RN-3 does, however, possess two natural gems: the **Ría Deseado estuary** at **Puerto Deseado**, with its beautiful porphyry cliffs and marvellous opportunities to view wildlife at close quarters, and the tremendous trunks of fossilized araucaria monkey puzzles in the **Monumento Natural Bosques Petrificados**. In addition, the inland agricultural town of **Sarmiento** has a different but equally detour-worthy petrified forest nearby, the **Bosque Petrificado Sarmiento**.

Comodoro Rivadavia

The second largest Patagonian town, with a population of 130,000, austere **COMODORO RIVADAVIA** is not a place you're likely to want to stay for longer than the time it takes to make your bus connection. Originally founded as a port to service the livestock industry, the town's fortunes were altered dramatically by the discovery of oil here in 1907. Following privatization of the petrol industry in the 1990s and the recession at the start of the new millennium, hopes for economic upturn now rest with the **Corredor Biocéanico**, 570km of road linking the town with the Pacific Ocean, at Puerto Chacabuco in Chile. This will be used to truck containers across the continent, thus obviating the need for slow-ship passages around Cape Horn – but the section between Río Mayo and the border has yet to be completed.

The centre of Comodoro is sandwiched between **Golfo San Jorge** and the bald, khaki-coloured ridge of **Cerro Chenque** (Tomb Hill). The best way of killing time is to visit the **Museo Nacional del Petróleo** (summer Tues–Fri 8am–1pm & 3–8pm, Sat & Sun 3–8pm; winter Tues–Fri 9am–6pm, Sat & Sun 2–6pm; $10) in the main northern suburb, Barrio General Mosconi (take bus #7 or #8 from the terminal), on the site where oil was first discovered in Argentina; the museum gets considerable mileage out of its subject, with displays on the oil-production cycle and a comprehensive model of the exploitation zone. Otherwise, head to the popular resort town of **Rada Tilly**, 15km south, where you can stroll along several kilometres of beach or visit the sea-lion colony at Punta Marqués, 4.5km to the southeast.

Practicalities

Comodoro's **airport**, 8km from the centre, is one of the region's busiest. *Colectivo* bus #8 connects it with the bus terminal, or it's $15 in a *remise*. The centrally located **bus terminal** has a tourist kiosk (Mon–Fri 8am–9pm, Sat & Sun 9am–9pm; ⓣ0297/447-3330 ext 267). Leaving the terminal, walk one block towards Cerro Chenque to reach the main thoroughfare, Avenida Rivadavia, where you'll find the municipal **tourist office**, half a block to the west at no. 430 (Mon–Fri 8am–3pm; ⓣ0297/446-2376).

Thanks to the oil industry, Comodoro is a good place to **rent cars** and 4WDs – try Dubrovnik, Moreno 941 (ⓣ0297/444-1844, ⓦwww.rentacardubrovnik.com), or Patagonia Sur Car, Rawson 1190 (ⓣ0297/446-6768, ⓦwww.patagoniasurcar.com.ar), one of the few Argentine car-rental agencies that has permission to cross into Chile. Unlimited-mileage deals make good sense for day-trips to the Bosque Petrificado Sarmiento (there are no car-rental agencies in Sarmiento itself). The Aónik'enk travel agency, Rawson 1190 (ⓣ0297/446-6768, ⓦwww.aonikenk.com.ar), runs excursions to Cabo Dos Bahías, as well as trips to the petrified forests near Sarmiento and Jaramillo (see p.678 & p.681), and along RN-40.

If you're unlucky with transport connections and need somewhere **to stay**, try *Hospedaje 25 de Mayo*, 25 de Mayo 989 (ⓣ0297/447-2350, ⓔhosp25demayo@uol.com.ar; ❷), a clean, inexpensive guesthouse close to the bus terminal, with a breezy courtyard area; *Hotel Victoria*, at Belgrano 585 (ⓣ0297/446-0725; ❺), also close to the bus terminal, with tidy rooms, some with bathtubs and sea views; or the considerably more upmarket *Luciano Palazzo*, Moreno 676 (ⓣ0297/449-9300, ⓦwww.lucania-palazzo.com; ❽), a grand but unstuffy business hotel with a gleaming lobby and bright, comfortable rooms.

Restaurants include *Peperonni*, Rivadavia 619, whose attentive staff serve an interesting – and unusual, for central Patagonia – selection of omelettes and home-made pastas, and *Los Tres Chinos*, a Chinese *tenedor libre*, Rivadavia 341, where you can refuel at the cheap, expansive buffet.

Sarmiento and around

Heading inland from Comodoro, it's 150km along paved RN-26 (later becoming RP-20) to Sarmiento. The road cuts through hilly steppe country, covered in *duraznillo* bushes and the nodding heads of hundreds of oil wells relentlessly probing the ground. The desiccated landscape improves as you approach Sarmiento, well irrigated by waters from the Río Senguer and the lakes it feeds, **Lago Colhué Huapi** and **Lago Musters**, the latter named after a famous English adventurer of the nineteenth century, Captain George Musters, who was the first white man to learn of its existence.

SARMIENTO itself is a farming community, originally founded by the Welsh, the Lithuanians and another well-known immigrant group, the **Boers**, who fled here at the beginning of the twentieth century in an effort to escape the British after the Boer War. Although the people are friendly, the town is completely without charm and attracts relatively few visitors, despite the presence of the intriguing petrified forest nearby (see below). The gimmicky **Parque Paleontológico** on Perito Moreno (accessible only on a guided visit; ask at the tourist office) is a poor man's MEF (see p.672); far more interesting is the **Museo Regional Desiderio Torres**, housed in the old train station round the corner at 20 de Junio (Tues–Sun 1–7pm; free), with its sizeable collection of indigenous artefacts and dinosaur bones, plus displays of indigenous Mapuche and Tehuelche weavings. Over the second weekend in February, the inhabitants celebrate the three-day **Festival Provincial de Doma y Folklore**, with horse-taming and racing in the afternoon and folk concerts in the evening, at the Club Deportivo on RP-20.

Practicalities

Sarmiento's main street, initially Avenida Regimiento de Infantería, later becoming Avenida San Martín, runs off RP-20 at a right angle. **Buses** pull into the terminal at the far end, at San Martín and Avenida 12 de Octubre. The eager **tourist office** (daily April to mid-Dec 9am–8pm, mid-Dec to March 8am–11pm; ⓣ0297/489-8220, ⓔturismo@coloniasarmiento.gov.ar) is at the entrance to town on Regimiento de Infantería 25, just before the water-tower that marks the beginning of Avenida San Martín. They have a useful tourist map of the town centre and surrounding region. The Banco del Chubut, San Martín 756, buys and sells **Chilean pesos**.

For **accommodation**, by far the best option is *Chacra Labrador*, 10km west of town on RP-20 (ⓣ0297/289-3329, ⓦwww.hosterialabrador.com.ar; ❺ with breakfast; dinner with wine $45; closed May–Sept). The congenial owners have modelled their farmhouse on a British-style B&B, and it has two charming rooms on a sixty-hectare estancia. In town, the best of a poor bunch is *Hotel Ismar*, Patagonia 248 (ⓣ0297/489-3293; ❸), which has clean, basic rooms off a courtyard. *Camping del Bulgaro* is the most attractive of the town's **campsites**, amongst a strand of poplars on the shores of Lago Musters (ⓣ0297/489-3114, ⓔelbulgaro@coopsar.com.ar; $10); there's a small shop selling provisions on site.

Despite the bland appearance, *El Rancho Grande*, on the corner of Estrada and San Martín (closed Mon), is a decent enough *parrilla*, while the steaks at *Oliver*, España 520 (Tues 7pm–midnight, Wed–Sun 9.30am–3pm & 7pm–midnight), are as good as dining gets in Sarmiento.

Bosque Petrificado Sarmiento

Two kilometres from the centre of town, a clearly signposted dirt track off RP-20 leads 29km to the **BOSQUE PETRIFICADO SARMIENTO** (daily April–Sept 9am–6pm; Oct–March 9am–9pm; $10). Here, perfectly preserved 65-million-year-old trunks are randomly strewn across a near-lunar setting with a stunning purple-and-orange cliff backdrop.

The petrified forest – formed by mineral-rich water permeating the wood over hundreds of thousands of years, effectively turning the trees into stone – has parallels with the Monumento Natural Bosques Petrificados in Santa Cruz Province (see p.681), but its bands of "painted desert" soils are more striking and erosion processes are much more visible here. Traversing the two-kilometre

△ Petrified tree, Bosque Petrificado Sarmiento

circuit is rather like walking around a sawmill, the ground covered by splinters of bark and rotten wood that chink under foot, except that these woodchips are Mesozoic. The *guardaparque* can take you to see the famous chunk of **hollow fossilized log** ($25; 30min).

Remises from the bus terminal will run you to the park and back for $70 including an hour's wait, although locals prefer that you go with a guide from the tourist office ($25, including transport), as visitors often stray from the paths, damaging the terrain. There are no services in the park. In bad weather or strong winds, check at the tourist office in Sarmiento that the park is open.

Caleta Olivia

CALETA OLIVIA makes an inauspicious introduction to the province of Santa Cruz. Never the most beautiful of towns, the place is made less attractive still by the sense of depression that's settled on it since the oil industry bottomed out in the 1990s, causing high levels of unemployment. It's all a far cry from the heady days of 1969, when the locals proudly raised **El Gorosito**, the thirteen-metre-high stucco statue of an oil worker that still dominates the town.

If you do find yourself having to **overnight** here, *Robert*, San Martín 2151 (Ⓣ0297/485-1452; ❸–❹, with a 10 percent cash discount) has clean rooms, with the more expensive ones getting more daylight and a sea view; its **restaurant**, *La Rosa*, is as good as any locally. The smaller *Granada* at San José Obrero 953 (Ⓣ0297/485-1512; ❷) has dull but passable rooms. The municipal **campsite**, a stony site on the Avenida Costanera by the beach (Ⓣ0297/485-0999), deems it prudent to offer 24-hour security, but is run by an amicable bunch.

Puerto Deseado and around

Easy-going **PUERTO DESEADO**, a straggly but engaging fishing port on the estuary (*ría*) of the Río Deseado, is blessed with spectacular coastal scenery and some remarkable colonies of marine wildlife that thrive within sight of town, most dramatically along the **estuary**, the only one of its kind in South America.

The town owes its name to the English privateer Thomas Cavendish, who baptized it **Port Desire**, in honour of his ship, when he put in here in 1586. Later expeditions had less success, and a sunken caravel from 1770, the *Swift*, was discovered in the port in 1982 – the **Museo Regional Mario Brozoski**, by the seafront (Mon–Fri 8am–5pm, Sat & Sun 3–7pm; free), displays items brought up from the ship, including gallon gin bottles. Modern-day Puerto Deseado, however, was shaped more by the Ferrocarril Nacional Patagónico, a cross-country cargo route that ran northwest to Las Heras; the town's fine, porphyry-coloured former train station, opposite the Salesian college, operated as the route's terminus from 1911 until 1979 and now functions as the **Museo de la Estación del Ferrocarril** (daily 4–7pm; free), housing train memorabilia.

Practicalities

Buses connect the town with Comodoro Rivadavia and Río Gallegos, via Caleta Olivia, but Deseado's **bus terminal** is inconveniently sited at the far end of town. Try to disembark in the centre or, if leaving town, flag down the bus as it passes along Avenida España. The main **tourist office** is at San Martín 1525 (daily April–Oct 9am–4pm, Nov–March 9am–8pm; ⓣ0297/487-0220, ⓔturismo@pdeseado.com.ar). There's an **ATM** at the Banco Santa Cruz, San Martín 1056, and several **Internet** and **phone** places on the corner of San Martín and Alte Brown.

The most inviting **accommodation** is *Los Acantilados* (ⓣ0297/487-2167, ⓔacantour@pdeseado.com.ar), occupying the bluff at España and Pueyrredón as you approach town, some of whose comfortable rooms have great estuary views (❻). The rooms facing the town are good value (❺) but get very noisy when there's a "night-time" show on in the downstairs bar. Cheaper options include *Isla Chaffers*, a very clean and welcoming hotel in the centre, on San Martín and Moreno (ⓣ&ⓕ0297/487-2246; ❺); and friendly *Residencial Los Olmos*, Gob. Gregores 849 (ⓣ&ⓕ0297/487-0077; ❹), meticulously well kept with good-value rooms. The windy municipal **campsite** on Avenida Marcelo Lotufo (ⓣ0297/156-252890; $10) occupies a large gravelly site facing the bay, and has trailers with four beds (❶).

Always full of locals, the best **restaurant** in town is *El Pingüino*, Piedrabuena 958 (closed Sun); the *platos del día* are excellent value, and there is a good fish and *parrilla* selection, though the service can get stretched at times. *Puerto Cristal* at España 1698 (closed Wed lunch) has all the atmosphere of a food mall but serves tasty pastas and grills and has good views of the port.

Ría Deseado

Stretching 45km inland from Puerto Deseado is the **RÍA DESEADO**, an astonishing sunken river valley, which, unlike other estuaries on the continent, is flooded by the sea. Opposite the town, its purple cliffs are smeared with guano from five species of **cormorant**, including the dapper, morning-suited Grey Cormorant (*cormorán gris*), whose dull-coloured body sets off its yellow bill and scarlet legs. These birds are seen in few other places, and nowhere else will you get such a sterling opportunity to photograph them. The estuary also hosts several penguin colonies, small flocks of Snowy Sheathbills (*palomas antárticas*), a colony of sea lions and an estimated fifty playful and photogenic **Commerson's dolphins** (*toninas averas*); the undisputed stars here, these beautiful creatures torpedo through the water to rollick in bow waves just feet from boats.

Darwin Expediciones, based beside the Gipsy dock on the approach to town (ⓣ0297/156-247554, ⓦwww.darwin-expeditions.com), runs three excellent

boat trips around the Ría Deseado and, if the tide is high, up the **Cañadon Torcida**, a narrow and steep-sided channel of the estuary: dolphin-spotting on the way to **Isla de los Pájaros**, where passengers can disembark and photograph the birdlife (departs 10am & 3pm; 2hr; $75); to **Isla Pingüino**, one of the few places outside of Antractica where Rockhopper Penguins (*pingüino de penacho amarillo*) can easily be spotted (departs 10am; 6hr; $275); and a trip up the estuary to the scenic **Miradores de Darwin**, retracing the scientist's 1833 journey and stopping to look at wildlife en route (departs 10am; 6hr; $275). Owners Javier and Ricardo also tailor trips to demand and will run excursions to see the rare fur seals at Cabo Blanco, 90km north of Puerto Deseado, as well as to the Monumento Natural Bosques Petrificados (see below). Los Vikingos, Estrada 1275 (Ⓣ0297/487-0020), runs similar tours.

Monumento Natural Bosques Petrificados

The **MONUMENTO NATURAL BOSQUES PETRIFICADOS** (sometimes called Bosque Petrificado de Jaramillo; daily: April–Sept 10am–5pm, Oct–March 9am–8pm; free) is down a branch road 50km off RN-3, some 256km from Puerto Deseado and 210km north of Puerto San Julián. It stretches the imagination to picture this desert covered with plant life, but a forest it once was – and quite some forest, too. The sheer magnitude of the **fossilized trunks** here is astonishing, measuring some 35m long and up to 3m across. They're strangely beautiful, especially at sunset, when their jasper-red expanses soak up the glow, as though they're heating up from within.

The primeval Jurassic forest grew here 150 million years ago – 60 million years before the Andean cordillera was forced up, forming the rain barrier that has such a dramatic effect on the scenery we know now. In Jurassic times, this area was still swept by moisture-laden winds from the Pacific, allowing the growth of araucaria trees. A cataclysmic blast from an unidentified volcano flattened these colossi and covered the fallen trunks with ash. The wood absorbed silicates in the ash and petrified, later to be revealed when erosion wore down the supervening strata.

Surrounding the trunks is a bizarre **moonscape** of arid basalt *meseta*, dominated by the 400-metre-tall **Cerro Madre e Hija** (Mother and Daughter Mount). Guanaco roam around, somehow managing to find sufficient subsistence from what plant life does exist. A two-kilometre trail, littered by shards of fossilized bark as if it were a woodchip path through a garden, leads from the administration past all the most impressive trunks.

Day-trips to the park are easiest if you have your own car but can be organized with travel agents from Comodoro Rivadavia or Puerto Deseado. There are fascinating fossils such as the araucaria pinecones in the small **museum**. Don't succumb to the temptation of picking up "souvenirs", and note that you're not permitted to pitch a tent in the park; the only **camping** nearby is at *La Paloma*, 24km before the administration ($15 per person).

RN-3: Puerto San Julián to Río Gallegos

Overland, **RN-3** runs for 330km between Puerto San Julián and Río Gallegos, the provincial capital. This stretch is home to little of interest, with the exception of **Puerto San Julián** itself, a historic town with access to one of the most conveniently situated penguin colonies in Patagonia. Nevertheless, you can break the distances into more manageable chunks by stopping at the fishing destination of **Comandante Luis Piedra Buena** or **Parque Nacional Monte León**, Argentina's first marine national park.

Puerto San Julián

The small port of **PUERTO SAN JULIÁN** makes a convenient place to break the enormous journey between Trelew and Río Gallegos. The town, treeless and barren, is rich in historical associations, due to its oddly shaped, shingle-banked **bay**, which was one of the few safe anchorages along the Patagonian coast for early mariners. Sadly, there's little visible evidence of the port's history, but it's a good place to go on one of various **tours**, including an extremely convenient trip to view the **marine life** of the bay (see opposite) – highly recommended, especially if you're unable to visit Ría Deseado. The penguins here live closer to human settlement than at any other site in the south, and are not afraid to assert ancestral privilege. Local radio has been known, not without irony, to put out appeals to remove penguins from the town hall.

One of the few traces of the past to be preserved, right in what passes for the town's main square, went unobserved for many years, until someone noticed that a paving slab he'd just walked on had been walked on before – by a dinosaur. The distinct, prehistoric prints of the **sauropod** (a crocodile-like reptile) were moved to the local **Museo Regional Rosa Novak** on Rivadavia and Vieytes (early March to mid-Dec Mon–Fri 9am–1pm & 2–5pm, mid-Dec to early March Mon–Fri 9am–1pm & 4–9pm, Sat & Sun 10am–1pm & 4–9pm; free). The museum also houses a few relics from **Floridablanca**, an ill-fated settlement founded by Antonio de Viedma in 1780, the scant ruins of which lie west of town, on an estancia owned by Italian clothing magnates Luciano and Carlo **Benetton**; they're usually only open to archeological digs but it's worth checking the latest situation with the tourist office. The 830,000-acre ranch is one of five estancias the family owns in Patagonia, which, at a combined total of over two million acres, makes the Italians the country's largest landowners. Consequently, you might hear some grumbles among the locals, as many lament that labour and supplies for the estancia are brought in from afar and the San Julián population benefits little.

Practicalities

Puerto San Julián lies 3km off RN-3, down a straight road that becomes Avenida San Martín, the town's main artery. The **tourist office** is at San Martin and Rivadavia (Mon–Fri 7am–9pm, Sat & Sun 9am–9pm; ⓣ02962/452353).

Patagonia's birthplace

Puerto San Julián can rightfully claim to be the **birthplace of Patagonia**. In 1520, during **Magellan**'s stay in the bay, the very first encounter occurred between the Europeans and the "giants" of this nameless land, when, it is believed, the explorer bestowed on them the name "*patgon*" (literally "big foot") in reference to their comparatively large build. As related by Antonio Pigafetta, the expedition's chronicler: "One day, without anyone expecting it, we saw a giant, who was on the shore of the sea, quite naked, and was dancing and leaping, and singing, and whilst singing he put sand and dust on his head... When he was before us he began to be astonished, and to be afraid, and he raised one finger on high, thinking that we came from heaven. He was so tall that the tallest of us only came up to his waist... The captain named this kind of people Patagon." On Palm Sunday, April 1, 1520, Magellan celebrated the first Mass on Argentine soil, near a site marked by a cross, down by the town's port.

For **accommodation**, breezy, seafront *Hostería Municipal*, 25 de Mayo 917 (ⓣ02962/452300, ⓔhosteria@sanjulian.gov.ar; ❺), has good views of the bay from its upstairs rooms, plus an extremely helpful manageress. *Hotel Bahía*, San Martín 1075 (ⓣ02962/454028, ⓦwww.hotelbahiasanjulian.com.ar; ❺), is the most upmarket option, having modern, well-furnished rooms with spacious bathrooms. At the other end of the scale, *La Casona*, on Avenida Costanera (ⓣ02962/452434; $60 per person), is a rustic corrugated-iron house with simple rooms. The municipal **campsite** next to the bay is stony but clean (ⓣ02962/452806; $3 per person), and gets very busy in January. The best seafood **restaurant** in town is *La Rural*, near the Museo Regional, at Ameghino 811 (ⓣ02962/454066; closed Tues) – aside from tasty snooks and *pejerrey*, their menu occasionally features local specialities such as seven-gill shark and elephant fish – although *Naso*, at 9 de Julio and Mitre, runs it a close second. *Casa Lara*, San Martín and Ameghino, is an excellent, informal **bar** in a historic early 1900s building.

Bahía de San Julián

The easiest tour from Puerto San Julián is also the best: a trip around the bay in a zodiac launch to see the most conveniently situated **penguin colony** in Patagonia and a wide variety of flying seabirds. In addition, you stand a good chance of spotting **Commerson's dolphins**, a graceful, fun-loving species that regularly play games with the boats. You'll also be taken to the protected island of **Banco Justicia** (Justice Bank) to see the cormorant colonies (Rock, Olivaceous, Guanay and Imperial), plus other seabirds, such as the dazzling-white Snowy Sheathbill, looking more suited to life in a dovecote than on stormy oceans. Banco Justicia is thought by some to be where, in the sixteenth century, Magellan, and later Francis Drake, executed members of their crews who had mutinied while in the bay, although others maintain it was at **Punta Horca** (Gallows Point), on the tongue of land that encloses the bay, opposite the town. You're not allowed to disembark at either, though you are allowed to get off at the misleadingly named **Banco Cormorán** to photograph its Magellanic penguins up close.

In season (Sept–April), good-value **trips** run by Excursiones Pinocho, Costanera and 9 de Julio (departs 8am; 2hr; $70, min four people; ⓣ02962/454600), leave from next door to *Muelle Viejo* on the seafront, with German and English commentary from volunteer biologists. The best month for seeing dolphins and cormorants is December (Jan to early April is also good), but the guide, Señor Pinocho, will always give a scrupulously honest appraisal of your chances.

Another possible excursion is to drive the **Circuito Costero** (Coastal Circuit), a 110-kilometre round-trip along the mainland side of the turquoise bay, which has some lovely coastal views and passes the **tomb of Lieutenant Robert Sholl**, who died here whilst on board the *Beagle*, during FitzRoy's first expedition of 1828. If you don't have your own transport, you can go in a *remise* (around $75); Sur Remise at San Martín and Sarsfield (ⓣ02962/452233) is reliable and can also take you to the Monumento Natural Bosques Petrificados (see p.681; around $450).

Comandante Luis Piedra Buena and Parque Nacional Monte León

Even the most ardent devotee of steppe scenery might be finding RN-3 a trifle tiring by now. Fifty kilometres south of Puerto San Julián, the desolate monotony is lifted, briefly, by the **Gran Bajo de San Julián**, whose Laguna del Carbón – 105m below sea level – is the lowest point in the entire South American continent. It's another 70km from here to **COMANDANTE LUIS PIEDRA BUENA**, a sleepy town 1km off RN-3, with little to detain visitors unless you've come specifically for the world-class **steelhead trout fishing** (licences available at the municipalidad, Av Gregorio Ibañez 388, just down from the bus terminal). The town is named after one of Argentina's most renowned nineteenth-century Patagonian explorers and mariners, the naval hero Piedra Buena, who was famed for his gentlemanly ways and determination to assert Argentine sovereignty in the south. In 1859, he made **Isla Pavón** (the island in the jade-coloured Río Santa Cruz) his home, building a diminutive house, from which he traded with the local Aónik'enk Tehuelche. You can visit a bare reconstruction of the house, the **Casa Histórica Luis Piedra Buena** (if closed, ask at the campsite for key; free). The island's **campsite** (Ⓣ02966/156-44956; $7 per pitch) gets extremely busy in summer, but is otherwise pleasant, with plenty of poplars. Nearby is one of the area's best **hotels**, the high-quality but homely *Hostería Isla Pavón* (Ⓣ02966/156-38380; ❹), which enjoys a stunning shoreside location with fantastic views. In town, *El Alamo*, Lavalle 8 (Ⓣ02962/497249; ❷), is well kept with a *confitería*, and basic *Huayén*, Belgrano 321 (02962/497265; ❷), is clean if not much else.

Heading south from Luis Piedra Buena, the Patagonian plateau continues with unabating harshness for 235km to Río Gallegos. An early detour, 33km out of Luis Piedra Buena, leads to **PARQUE NACIONAL MONTE LEÓN**, the country's newest – and first-ever coastal – national park. Established in October 2004, the magnificent 155,000-acre reserve – land donated by a conservation group run by American entrepreneur Kris Tompkins, founder of the Patagonia clothing company – encompasses sweeping cliffs, rocky islands and picturesque bays. Between September and April, the waters are awash with wildlife, including sea-lion and penguin colonies (the fourth largest in Argentina) and three types of cormorant. The rugged cliffs that dominate the landscape are indented with vast caverns and rock windows – at low tide, you can walk out to La Olla, an incredible cavern eroded by the sea, and to Isla Monte León itself; check with the *guardafauna* at the estancia 7km north of the park entrance on RN-3 for times. There are wild beaches and a free **campsite** (mid-Nov to mid-April) with drinking water and a toilet block, but no other services. The estancia itself is a glorious, if expensive, **place to stay**, offering a taste of simple, isolated country life; reservations must be made through their Buenos Aires office (Ⓣ011/4621-4780, Ⓦwww.monteleon-patagonia.com; US$320 full board; closed April–Oct).

Río Gallegos

Few people hang around long in **RÍO GALLEGOS**, heading out instead to El Calafate, south to Ushuaia or up the coast with as little delay as possible. If you find yourself waiting for a bus here, though, all is not lost – there are a couple of little museums, one or two attractive early twentieth-century buildings, and it's possible to take a day-excursion to the **penguin colony** at Cabo Vírgenes (see p.687).

One thing that does attract people to Gallegos from distant locales and keeps them here is its incredible **fly-fishing**. As with Río Grande in Tierra del Fuego (see p.771), **Río Gallegos** (the river that the town is named after) is the haunt of some of the most spectacularly sized, sea-going **brown trout** anywhere in the world. Take with you your licence ($30 a day; from the provincial tourist office), a guide and a camera for the glory shot, as it's considered particularly poor form to kill these leviathans.

Arrival and information

The **airport** is 7km west of town. There are no buses to the town centre – a taxi will cost around $15 – though, oddly enough, you *can* take a bus to El Calafate, some 300km away. There's also an **ATM**.

From the **bus terminal**, near the edge of town on RN-3, it's best to take a cab 2km into the centre; alternatively, buses #1 or #12 will drop you in Avenida Roca in the heart of town. Gallegos has two main **tourist offices** in the centre, both extremely helpful and efficient: the provincial office, at Roca 863 (Mon–Fri 9am–6pm, Sat 10am–4pm; ⓣ02966/438725), and the municipal office, at Roca and Córdoba (Mon–Fri 8am–8pm; ⓣ02966/436920, ⓔturismo@riogallegos.gov.ar). The municipal office also has a tiny booth in the bus terminal (daily May–Nov 8am–8pm, Dec–April 7am–9pm; ⓣ02966/442159). You can buy **Chilean pesos** at Thaler *casa de cambio*, San Martin 484 (Mon–Fri 9am–3pm).

Accommodation

Accommodation in Río Gallegos is mostly within walking distance of the centre, and does get busy during the tourist season so it's worth arriving early or booking a day or two ahead. For **campers**, there's *ATSA*, Asturias and Yugoslavia (ⓣ02966/442310; $7 per person), and *Chacra Daniel* (ⓣ02966/423970; $10 per tent plus $5 per person), 3km out of town on the road to Ushuaia.

Colonial Urquiza and Rivadavia ⓣ02966/422329. A pleasant budget choice for Gallegos, not far from the centre, and good for singles ($37). Rooms have shared bathrooms. ❸

Nevada Zapiola 480 ⓣ02966/425990. Excellent-value hotel with friendly owners, though you'll have to fight past the enormous plants at the front door. The slightly pricier, en-suite rooms are worth the money for the extra space – in both the bedroom and the bathroom. ❸

La Posada Ameghino 331 ⓣ02966/436445, ⓔmarianobertinat@hotmail.com. Welcoming B&B with a convivial dining area and good atmosphere. Attractive rooms are set around an internal garden. ❹

Sehuén Rawson 160 ⓣ02966/425683, ⓔreservas@hotelsehuen.com. Gallegos' best hotel, the Sehuén is a refreshing combination of bright, modern rooms and economical prices. It has en-suite bathrooms with bath and good shower. ❺

El Viejo Miramar Roca 1630 ⓣ02966/430401, ⓔhotelviejomiramar@yahoo.com.ar. Small family-run *hostería* with clean if rather petite and gloomy rooms. Off-street parking. ❺

The Town

The provincial capital is a bustling centre of commerce for the region, and the main shopping thoroughfare, **Avenida Roca**, is the focus of city life. The attractive main square, **Plaza San Martín**, is marked by a fine equestrian **statue** of General San Martín and the quaint white and green Salesian **cathedral**, Nuestra Señora de Luján (Mon–Fri 10am–5pm, Sat & Sun 2–6pm), a classic example of a pioneer church made from corrugated iron, and originally built in 1899 with a labour force composed of displaced indigenous Tehuelche.

The **Museo de Los Pioneros**, housed in a snug townhouse – the city's oldest – on the corner of Alberdí and Elcano (daily 10am–8pm; free), gives a good insight into life in the region a century ago. Apart from the usual collection of black-and-white photographs of pioneering families, there's a 1904 Victrola music cupboard on which the curators will play ancient, crackly discs. The eclectic **Museo Regional Padre Molina**, San Martín and Ramón and Cajal 51 (Mon–Fri 8am–8pm, Sat & Sun 11am–7pm; free), hosts temporary exhibitions of contemporary art, along with displays of Tehuelche artefacts, dinosaur remains and impressive reconstructions of Pleistocene mammals such as a megatherium, rearing up in Godzilla pose; there's also a weaving workshop selling handmade shawls, sweaters and the like.

Eating and drinking

Most **eating and drinking** options open daily for lunch from noon to 3pm, and then again between about 7.30pm and midnight.

Club Británico Roca 935. Well-priced and imaginative food, such as *pulpo en escabeche* (marinated octopus), served in formal style. A port of call for Bruce Chatwin, it has more than a hint of a gentleman's club about it and is still the favoured hangout for the declining community of those with British descent.

El Horreo Roca 862 ⓣ02966/426462. An attractive, fairly sophisticated place in the historic Sociedad Española building, with an original Spanish-inspired menu. Open till 1am.

Laguanacazul Lista and Sarmiento ⓣ02966/444114. The best restaurant in Gallegos, where the stylish setting is only bettered by the food: fresh Patagonian cuisine – principally seafood – that varies with the season but is never short of excellent.

Puesto Molino Roca 854. Buzzing, high-quality pizzeria with a busy wood-fired oven and communal wooden tables.

RoCo Roca 1157 ⓣ02966/420203. A fine, and consequently popular, *parrilla* with large servings of *lomo*, and a refreshingly wide selection of salads.

Cabo Vírgenes

Cabo Vírgenes, continental Argentina's most southerly point, was named by Magellan when he rounded it for the first time on the feast day of the Eleven Thousand Virgins, October 21, 1520. This bleak and inauspicious spot was the site of one of Patagonia's most miserable and tragic failures: Pedro Sarmiento de Gamboa's settlement of **Nombre de Jesús**, founded in 1584 and intended as a permanent base on the Magellan Straits to prevent a repetition of Drake's damaging raids of 1578–79. Of the 23 ships and 3500 settlers and soldiers that originally left Spain, only one ship, carrying three hundred people, reached this far. All bar one were to die either here or in the sister settlement of San Felipe (Puerto Hambre in Chile), killed partly in skirmishes with the local Tehuelche,

Moving on to Chilean Patagonia and Tierra del Fuego

It takes the best part of a day to get from Río Gallegos to Río Grande, the first major town in **Argentine Tierra del Fuego**, a journey that involves crossing two borders and the Magellan Straits. At the **Monte Aymond border crossing** (April–Oct 9am–11pm; Nov–March 24hr), 67km south of Gallegos, formalities are fairly straightforward, but don't try to bring fresh vegetables, fruit or meat products into Chile, as they'll be confiscated. On the **Chilean** side, the road improves and heads to **Punta Arenas** (see p.729), **Puerto Natales** (see p.733) and, down a turning at Kimiri Aike, 48km from the border, **Tierra del Fuego**. This road, RN-257, takes you to Punta Delgada and the Primera Angostura (First Narrows) of the Magellan Straits. The **ferry** that plies across them leaves from 7am to midnight, making the thirty-minute crossing roughly every 40min (CH$1400 per person, CH$12,000 for a car). As early mariners knew, the currents here can be ferocious, but they're unlikely to be as disruptive to your plans as they were to sea-goers in the past – only in extremely testy weather does the ferry not leave. Whilst crossing history's most famous straits, look out for Commerson's dolphins.

Heading for **Ushuaia**, the road then traverses Chilean Tierra del Fuego to the border settlement of San Sebastián (April–Oct 9am–11pm; Nov–March 24hr), 80km from Río Grande. Note that Chilean time is one hour behind Argentine from March to October.

Buses depart regularly from Río Gallegos for Punta Arenas (5hr), Río Grande (8hr) and Ushuaia (13hr); ferry crossings are included in the fare.

but mostly by depression, disease and starvation. No trace remains now, except for one shapeless concrete monument at the foot of the scarp on the Argentine side, and a cross over the border in Chile.

The Argentine Navy permits you to climb the **lighthouse** here, whose 400-watt light bulb throws its beam 40km out to sea, for an excellent view of the windswept coast. A couple of kilometres further south, is the second largest **penguin colony** in Patagonia, where up to 180,000 penguins come between October and March to nest amongst the perfumed, resinous-scented *mata verde* scrub. Entrance to see the colony is $7, and there's a small information centre staffed by an amicable *guardaparque* as well as a good *confitería*. **Camping** is permitted but there are no services. For more upmarket accommodation, you can stay at *Monte Dinero*, a working estancia 15km from Cabo Vírgines (Ⓣ02966/428922, Ⓦwww.montedinero.com.ar; US$280 full board including excursions), whose six comfortable rooms feature furniture salvaged from coastal shipwrecks.

In season (mid-Sept to April), **tours** to the penguin colony are run from Río Gallegos by Maco Tobiano at Roca 998 (departs 11am; $120; Ⓣ02966/434021), also taking in the lighthouse and Estancia Cóndor on the way (Sept–Dec & March $100, min five people). Otherwise, a *remise* with Co-operative Río Gallegos (Ⓣ02966/422879) will set you back $300 round trip.

Andean Patagonia

The western boundary of Argentine Patagonia is formed by the **Cordillera de los Andes**, the feature that draws most visitors to the region, luring them in with a chain of lakes and world-class national parks, which are home to some of the finest trekking – and most famous glaciers – on the continent. Much of this stretch – from Esquel to El Calafate – is completely barren, especially in the Andean foothills, but some slopes are densely cloaked in southern beech woods, with a narrow fringe of scrubland separating forest from steppe. It's in these areas that you stand your best chance of seeing condors, and perhaps even a puma or a highly endangered *huemul*.

The inland slice of Patagonia immediately east of the *cordillera* is dissected lengthwise by the nationally famous **RN-40**, the "Ruta Cuarenta", often simply called "La Cuarenta" (for more about this emblematic highway, see the *The legendary Ruta 40* colour section). The scenery here is predominately dry and flat; most brush looks fairly dreary and anonymous for the better part of the year, but some bushes liven up considerably in the spring: the thorny *calafate* (see box, p.717) blooms with a profusion of delicate yellow flowers, and the *lengua de fuego* produces gloriously bright orange flowers like clam shells. Prevalent throughout moister segments – particularly around the fishing lakes of the **Río Pico** area, the only diversion of any note between Esquel and the town of Perito Moreno – is *colapiche* (armadillos' tail), so named for its tough green fronds, which resemble armadillos' tails, and you're sure to see the grey *senecio miser*, the robust *mata negra*, the slender-leaved *duraznillo* and the aggressively spiked *molle*, peppered with spherical galls. The road also passes harsh *meseta*, blasted rocky outcrops, patches of desert and the occasional river valley, usually accompanied

Getting around Andean Patagonia

For many years, the south Patagonian cordillera was notoriously difficult to explore unless you had your own transport or time to hitch. This has changed somewhat with the introduction of a **public transport** service along RN-40. From November to the end of March, Andes Patagónicos (Mitre 125, Bariloche ⓣ02944/426809) operates a **bus** between Bariloche and Los Antiguos/Perito Moreno ($155/165), from where Chaltén Travel (El Calafate ⓣ02902/491833) and Itinerarios y Travesías (El Chaltén ⓣ02962/493088) continue the trip to El Chaltén/El Calafate ($188/215). The service gives a good picture of the immensity of Patagonia, though with the drawback of spending two long days (each about 13hr) in a bus without stopping to see the mountains or meet the locals. Another option is to take a **tour**: four-day trips are run by Chaltén Travel, with two days spent exploring the area around the Cueva de las Manos Pintadas, and Overland Patagonia (the travel agency of Bariloche's *Periko*'s and *Alaska* hostels ⓣ02944/437654, ⓦwww.overlandpatagonia.com; $950, including a night's accommodation at the end of your trip, in either Bariloche or El Calafate), which has overnight stops in Rio Mayo, *Estancia La Cueva de las Manos* and *Estancia Menelik* bordering Parque Nacional Perito Moreno.

Alternatively, and to truly appreciate the mystique of the area, you could **drive** yourself. RN-40 is just about passable in a normal sedan – if it doesn't rain, and if you don't mind having to drive at 30kph for fear of crunching the undercarriage – but whether you'll be able to rent one is another matter, as few agencies will lease you anything other than a 4WD once they know you're tackling *La Cuarenta*. Although the government is steadily tarmacking the road, large sections between Tecka and El Calafate are still *ripio*. These neglected stretches of gravel road require careful negotiating but add greatly to the sense of adventure; for more on driving techniques on the RN-40, see the *The legendary Ruta 40* colour section.

by boggy pasture and lined in places with emerald-green willows and poplars. Here you'll find the few people who live along the route, where old traditions (like the open-air *asado*), gaucho clothes and an unhurried pace reign.

A relaxed road tour of Andean Patagonia could take no more than four days, but to explore some of the little-visited spots near the cordillera, aim instead to spend one to two weeks. Most access roads run west from RN-40: to the Chilean border at the orchard town of **Los Antiguos**, near **Perito Moreno**; to the wild trekking areas around lakes **Posadas** and **Pueyrredón** and in **Parque Nacional Perito Moreno**; and, considerably further south, to a similarly scenic area around **Lago San Martín**.The exception is the incredible archeological site of the **Cueva de las Manos Pintadas**, which lies in the canyon of **Río de las Pinturas**, just to the east of RN-40. From Los Antiguos you can, in season, detour to Posadas before rejoining the highway, but in all other cases you must return to the road along the same track before continuing your journey. Eventually, you'll reach the far south and two of Argentina's supreme highlights: the mountainous **Fitz Roy** area near the village of **El Chaltén**, and the creaking **Glaciar Perito Moreno**, whose proximity to **El Calafate** has made the town *the* major destination for visitors to Santa Cruz Province.

Esquel to Perito Moreno

Between Esquel (see p.638) and the town of Perito Moreno lie a few rather depressing transit towns with little to detain you, except for the detour to the fishing region of Río Pico in the Andean foothills. RN-40 is paved for the first 96km as far as drab **Tecka**, from where *ripio* takes over. Seventy kilometres south of Tecka, by the Río Putrachoique, a consolidated road branches west off RN-40 to **RÍO PICO**, a **fishing** mecca in the damp pre-cordillera. Rich anglers pay hundreds of dollars a day to fish for specimens of the elusive brook trout, which here grows to sizes far exceeding those found in its native US. The friendly owners of the *Posada Tayaluz* (see below) will assist those who want to fish the same waters much more economically (permits $200). Bruce Chatwin fans can visit the cross that marks the grave of American bandits **Wilson and Evans**; Chatwin claimed, rather dubiously, that the Sundance Kid was actually one of the bodies buried here. The cross is 2km up a rutted track, which branches north off the road heading back to RN-40, about 4km east of Río Pico – a lone tree marks the junction, just before a small dip. Pass one gate, and continue up until the track is fenced off, where a small sign indicates the site of the grave, 100m to the left.

The best **accommodation** is *Posada Tayaluz*, an alpine-style building with large, airy rooms, which enjoys a peaceful setting just outside the village (ⓣ02945/492015, ⓔtajaluz@yahoo.com.ar; $45 per person), or one of the cabins scattered round the various nearby lakes – try *Cabañas La Bahía* at Lago Uno, 12km from Río Pico (ⓣ02945/492053; ❺ for six people).

The RN-40 splits the strung-out settlement of **Gobernador Costa**, 16km south of the Río Pico turn-off. Costa has two **fuel** stations with shops, an **ATM** and a *locutorio*, but unless your visit coincides with the annual **Fiesta Provincial del Caballo** (usually the third weekend in Feb), when locals perform feats of gaucho horsemanship, you won't want to stop. At a junction 54km south of the settlement, take paved RP-20 in preference to much slower, unpaved RN-40. RP-20 runs parallel to the Río Senguer before reaching a triangular junction where it peels off east towards the petrified forests near Sarmiento (see p.678) or west to rejoin RN-40 at **RÍO MAYO**, a ramshackle, charmless little place with regimented military barracks. On the second weekend in January, Río Mayo hosts the **Festival Nacional de la Esquila** to find the region's premier sheep-shearer. The town's best **hotel** is the faded *El Viejo Covadonga*, San Martín 573 (ⓣ02903/420020, ⓔelviejacovadonga@yahoo.com.ar; ❷ including breakfast), where the older rooms hint of a bygone, more prosperous age. Alternatively, there's the **campsite** *Labrador* at Belgrano and San Martín ($5 per person). There's a daily **bus** to Comodoro Rivadavia via Sarmiento, and twice-weekly service (Wed & Sat) to the **border crossings** at **Paso Huemules**, on the transcontinental route passing through Balmaceda (April–Nov 8am–9pm; Dec–March 7am–11pm). South of Río Mayo, RN-40 degenerates into an

Tourist estancias in Santa Cruz

In many people's minds, Argentina is composed of a vast patchwork of immense *latifundias* presided over by their *estanciero* owners. Although this image is no longer as true as it once was, landowning is still deeply embedded in the national consciousness, and an opportunity to stay at an **estancia** provides an excellent glimpse into this important facet of Argentine culture. The sheep-farming province of Santa Cruz is a perfect place to try this out. A group of estancia owners runs the **Estancias de Santa Cruz** (ⓦwww.estanciasdesantacruz.com), which produces an excellent booklet promoting their establishments, available from the head office at Suipacha 1120, Buenos Aires Capital Federal (ⓣ011/43253098), or the office in El Calafate at Libertador 1215 (ⓣ02902/4928580); the best of these are listed in the guide.

unsealed road that should be driven with care. After 112km, having crossed the **provincial boundary** from Chubut into Santa Cruz, you'll join paved RP-43, which heads west for 12km to Perito Moreno.

Perito Moreno and around

With four thousand inhabitants, **PERITO MORENO** is the most populous town in this part of the world. It's a typically featureless, spread-out Patagonian settlement and is of use to the visitor only as a base for excursions to places such as the Cueva de las Manos Pintadas (see p.694), or for its transport services to Posadas and to the border at Los Antiguos/Chile Chico. There is, though, a wildlife refuge (free) within town, the **Laguna de los Cisnes**, where Black-necked Swans and flamingoes pass their time – if there's enough water.

Practicalities

The **bus terminal** is just north of town on RP-43, by the Petrobras **fuel** station; from here, cross the road and walk down Avenida San Martín to reach the town centre in about ten minutes. Chaltén Travel **buses** stop outside the *Hotel Belgrano*, at the far end of San Martin, en route between Bariloche and El Chaltén, while El Guraño buses for Bajo Caracoles and Posadas (Tues around 5–6pm) leave from *Hotel Santa Cruz*, three blocks west of San Martín, at Belgrano 1565. For those heading south, Perito Moreno is the best place until El Calafate to **change money** – the Banco de Santa Cruz at San Martín 1493 has an **ATM** and sells Chilean pesos – or stock up on **food**, at one of several *panaderías* lining San Martin. The **tourist office** is at San Martín and Gendarmería Nacional (daily 7am–11pm; ⓣ02963/432732), and there's **Internet** at CTC, Perito Moreno 1062, and a *locutorio* at San Martin 1730.

Accommodation is neither good value nor abundant – if you're heading to Chile, it's better to push on to Los Antiguos or Chile Chico across the border. Even better, funds permitting, try one of the nearby tourist estancias, *La Serena* (see opposite), on the road to Los Antiguos, or *Telken*, to the south (see p.693). The best places in town are the homely *Posada del Caminante* at Rivadavia 937 (ⓣ02963/432204; ❸), which has large, comfortable rooms and a relaxing communal area, and the sociable municipal **campsite** ($7 per tent), on the shore of Laguna de los Cisnes, at Mariano Moreno and Paseo Julio A. Roca. The site also has a couple of small, six-person **cabins** for rent ($12 per person in cabin) – the cheapest option in town for those with a sleeping bag but no tent.

Tours from Perito Moreno

English-speaking Harry Nauta of Guanacóndor, at Perito Moreno 1087 (ⓣ02963/432303, ⓔjarinauta@yahoo.com.ar), runs a variety of trips to the **Cueva de las Manos Pintadas**, the best of which includes a three-hour walk down into the spectacular canyon floor ($85), as well as a recommended tour to **Arroyo Feo** (Ugly Stream; $100), another area of great beauty and archeological interest, 70km south of town; with its dramatic narrow canyon and important 9000-year-old cave-paintings, it offers a wilder alternative to the Cueva de las Manos. From December, Nauta also runs three-day trips ($350) that take in **RP-41**, a scenic road that skirts striking Monte Zeballos (see p.692). Zoyen Turismo, at San Martín and Saavedra (ⓣ02963/432207, ⓦwww.zoyenturismo.com.ar), runs similar tours.

None of Perito Moreno's **restaurants** is particularly special, but *Patagones* restaurant-bar, at San Martín and Mitre, has filling home-made burgers and a good taste in rock music, while *Nono's*, at 9 de Julio and Saavedra, does a decent attempt at pizza.

West to Los Antiguos

Leaving Perito Moreno, paved and well-maintained RP-43 sweeps towards the impressive expanse of **Lago Buenos Aires**, its ocean-blue waters in striking contrast with the dusty brown steppe and snowcapped peaks surrounding it. At several points, you can walk across the scrub from the road to the shore, but though the water looks wholly inviting, the temperature may douse your enthusiasm – it remains at about 10°C throughout the year.

This vast lake – the second largest in South America – was divided in half by the border commission in the early 1900s, and thus has two names: the Chileans call their half Lago General Carreras. The frontier marks an equally abrupt change of scenery, as the Argentine *meseta* slopes upwards into the cordillera. The distinctive, ash-grey pyramid **Cerro Pirámide**, dominating the north shore, is not, as it would seem, a volcanic cone, although infamous Volcán Hudson (see box, p.692) does lie in the range some 90km away behind it, out of sight. Some of the higher peaks that border Chile's Hielo Continental Norte (Northern Patagonian Icecap) are revealed by the broad U-shaped gap formed by the lake itself.

Sited near the lakeshore, 29km out of Perito Moreno, in a tousled clump of poplars and willows, is the tourist estancia *La Serena* (Ⓣ029715/621-7841, Ⓦwww.patagoniasouth.com; ⑧ half-board), with six simple but smart wooden cabins and an inviting dining room where classic Patagonian meals are dished up by a roaring fire. Home-made bread and jams are served for breakfast. Buses to and from Los Antiguos stop at the entrance.

Los Antiguos and around

The welcome sight of greenery as you approach the serene little town of **LOS ANTIGUOS**, 56km west of Perito Moreno, is your first indication of the spring-like microclimate that exists in this area of the pre-cordillera. High levels of sunshine and a sheltered position mean that, despite the southerly latitudes, it's an area well suited to fruit production, being famous for its succulent **cherries**. To visit some of the *chacras* (fruit farms), try **Chacra Don Neno** (strawberries), 600m on the main road north out of town, which has been reaping the benefits of the valley since the 1920s (open daily), or **Chacra El Paraíso** (cherries), 3km further on (daily 10am–1pm & 3–8pm); both sell a variety of delicious home-made jams, cakes and liqueurs. In the first weekend of January, the famous local crop is celebrated at the three-day **Fiesta de la Cereza** with music, dance and, of course, fresh, cheap cherries. Carnivores will enjoy the annual **Fiesta del Pueblo**, a vast orgy of free meat-eating, held on February 5.

Los Antiguos was one of the sacred places where elderly Tehuelche would come to spend their last days once advancing age had made a wandering lifestyle impossible – indeed, the town gets its name (The Ancients) from this legacy. Unfortunately, the **Tehuelche tombs**, little jumbles of blackened stones that used to line the road into town, have been desecrated by artefact hunters and only a few tombs on private land remain.

Running south from Los Antiguos, parallel to the poetic-sounding **Río Jeinemeni**, is stunningly scenic and desolate **RP-41**. This road, just about the only Patagonian route that runs alongside the border with Chile, passes the

When Hudson erupted

In early August 1991, Chile's **Volcán Hudson erupted**, sending a plume of ash and gases 18,000m up into the stratosphere. Due to the strength of the prevailing westerly winds, its effects were felt more keenly in Argentina than its homeland. **Ash** was deposited over a cone of land that, on the coast, stretched from Puerto Deseado to Puerto San Julián, while inland a crust of pumice formed like a scab on the surface of **Lago Buenos Aires**, turning its waters grey. The RN-3 from Buenos Aires was blocked in places by drifts of ash that reached depths of a metre and lasted for months, while several centimetres of ash fell even as far away as the Islas Malvinas/Falkland Islands. In all, over a million sheep died across the 25 million acres affected – for an already struggling sheep-farming industry, Hudson proved the last straw, as hundreds of estancias in Andean Patagonia were bankrupted and abandoned, changing the face of the countryside. Patagonia's strong winds continued to spread the dust for months afterwards, but the land itself recovered remarkably quickly: rivers loaded with sediment in the immediate aftermath had returned to their previous condition within a year, while soil incorporated the ash layers, prompting a fast revival of orchards by late 1993.

angular form of biscuit-coloured Monte Zeballos (2743m), on its way to **Lago Posadas**, or Cochrane in Chile by way of Paso Roballos, one of the possible locations of the fabled City of the Caesars, searched for by generations of gold hunters. It's passable only in summer (usually from Dec) and often closed because of landslides, and even then you'll need a high-clearance 4WD; check road conditions at the *gendarmería* on Avenida 11 de Julio before setting out (ask for the *informe de vialidad provincial*). Tours from Perito Moreno are probably an easier alternative (see box, p.690).

Practicalities

Buses from Perito Moreno will drop you at their respective offices in town. The friendly, helpful **tourist office** at 11 de Julio 432 (April–Nov 8am–8pm, Dec–March 8am–midnight; ⓣ02963/491261, ⓔlosantiguos@epatagonia.gov.ar) can point you towards four lookouts above town, for wonderful views of the lake and mountains. They can also help organize **bike rental** ($40 per day), a good way of getting round the *chacras*. The Banco Santa Cruz, at 11 de Julio 531, gives **cash advances** on credit cards and changes Chilean pesos.

The most expensive **accommodation** in Los Antiguos is at *Hostería Antigua Patagonia*, a group of institutional buildings down by Lago Buenos Aires on the way into town (ⓣ02963/491038, ⓦwww.antiguapatagonia.com.ar; ❼); it has a casino and a sauna and great lake and mountain views but the rooms are rather plain. Alternatively, there's the more basic but friendly *Argentino* at 11 de Julio 850 (ⓣ&ⓕ02963/491132; ❹ including a scrumptious breakfast). The lakeside municipal **campsite** is a ten-minute walk from the centre (ⓣ02963/491265; $2.50 per tent plus $3 per person) and also rents dirty **cabins** (❷ for four people; no bedding supplied), although in March these are likely to be booked by local fishermen.

For **food**, glass-fronted *Viva El Viento*, 11 de Julio 477, has a European-centric menu, while the suburban facade of *Restaurante Agua Grance*, 11 de Julio 875, belies an intimate interior in which tasty pasta dishes are served.

Crossing the border to Chile Chico

Daily minibuses (9am, noon & 2pm) run from the centre of Los Antiguos to the border (summer 8am–10pm, winter 9am–9pm). There are few border formalities, but you are prohibited from taking meat, fruit and vegetables into Chile. From town, it's 3km to Argentine immigration, a further 2km across the Río Jeinemeini no-man's land to Chilean immigration, and then 4km to **CHILE CHICO**. This welcoming little frontier town has excellent views across Lago Carreras and is a frequent jumping-off point for the verdant **Carretera Austral**, the single-track dirt road that is southern Chile's major artery. The **tourist office** (Mon–Sat 10am–5pm; ⓣ67/411123) is housed within the Casa de Cultura on the main street, O'Higgins.

Argentine pesos and US dollars can be exchanged until late at the Casa Loly phone centre at Pedro Antonio González 25, fronting the square. From Chile Chico, a **ferry** (Dec–Easter daily, Easter–Nov 5 weekly; 2hr 45min; CH$2650) crosses Lago Carreras to Puerto Ibáñez, from where frequent buses leave for Coyhaique. Acotrans minibuses run back to Los Antiguos, while Transportes Ales, Rosa Amelia 820, operates a twice-weekly bus service (Tues & Fri) west to the Carretera Austral and south to Cochrane. Several *casas de familia* offer basic **accommodation**, including the attractive *Residencial Aguas Azules*, at Balmaceda 10 (ⓣ67/411320; ❹). A more expensive alternative, in a charming old-fashioned house with a cosy atmosphere and comfortable rooms, is *Hostería de la Patagonia*, Chacra 3-A (ⓣ67/411337; ❺), on the road that links the immigration post to town. Opposite is *Casa Quinta Me Olvides* (ⓣ088/338006; ❸), which is popular with backpackers and has space to **camp** in its large orchard.

South of Perito Moreno

South of Perito Moreno, the landscape that best embodies most people's concept of Patagonia begins – kilometre after kilometre of sparsely populated or empty lands stretching to the horizon. From here it's *ripio* (unsurfaced road) for over 450km until you hit Tres Lagos. Thirty kilometres south of Perito Moreno is the turn-off to the excellent *Estancia Telken* (Oct–April ⓣ02963/432079 or in Buenos Aires ⓣ011/4797-7216, ⓔtelkenpatagonia @yahoo.com.ar; ❼ with breakfast; closed May–Sept). Hosts Coco and Petty Nauta are renowned for their hospitable welcome, and this is one of the best estancias to visit for a taste of what it means to live on a working ranch – idiosyncratic bedrooms are warmed by gas stoves and tales of old Patagonia are recounted around the family table. You can also **camp** here (US$5 per tent), eat well (home-cooked dinner with wine US$20), go bird-watching at Laguna del Clarke and reconnoitre the land on horseback.

Further on, RN-40 descends through a moonscape valley of stratified "paleo-dunes", where paleontologists have excavated dinosaur skeletons. Another 35km south you'll pass the turn-off to *Estancia La Cueva de las Manos* (formerly *Estancia Los Toldos*; ⓣ02963/432730 or in Buenos Aires ⓣ011/4901-0436, ⓦwww.cuevadelasmanos.net; ❼, dorms $48; closed May–Oct), a functional building 7km up a side track. Good meals are served and there are kitchen facilities as well. The incredible Cueva de las Manos Pintadas (see p.694) lies on their land and, if experienced, you can ride to it by horse; they also run 4WD trips to the *cueva* as well as to nearby Charcamata, a similar rock-art site. More basic, but also extremely friendly, is the *Casa de Piedra* (ⓣ02963/432199; ❹; closed April–Oct), set in a clump of willows and surrounded by the marshy pastures of the Río Ecker Valley, 80km south of Perito Moreno and 50km north of Bajo Caracoles. You can **camp** at this pleasant spot ($10 per tent), and the owners sell *gaseosas*, beers and, occasionally, snacks; they also offer excursions to the Cueva de las Manos.

South of *Casa de Piedra* along RN-40, weather permitting, the vast, recumbent hulk of San Lorenzo comes into view to the west – at 3706m the tallest peak

RN-40 to Parque Nacional Perito Moreno and beyond

The 338-kilometre stretch of **RN-40 between Bajo Caracoles and Tres Lagos** is the most rugged of the entire route. High crosswinds can make driving hazardous, so always keep your speed under control and take breaks. There is no recognized fuel station along this part of the journey, and you need to carry enough fuel for 600km of motoring if you plan to visit **Parque Nacional Perito Moreno** and continue south on RN-40 – more if you're going to explore around **Lago Cardiel**. The two estancias just outside and in the national park – *Estancia Menelik* and *Estancia La Oriental* – sell *super* and diesel, but *Menelik* is often out and *La Oriental*'s is intended for guests only; they will, however, help out in an emergency. There is also an YPF station in Gobernador Gregores (see p.701), southeast of the national park, but that involves a seventy-kilometre detour.

There is no **accommodation** along RN-40 until you reach *Estancia La Angostura*, 190km south of Bajo Caracoles, although you can get a drink in *Hotel Río Olnie*, a mere 30km into the leg.

in Argentine Patagonia south of Volcán Lanín. Approximately 10km north of Bajo Caracoles, rough roads turn off west to Paso Roballos on the Chilean border, and east to the Cueva de las Manos Pintadas, after which you reach the miserable settlement of **Bajo Caracoles** itself, only useful as a place to catch transport to Posadas (Tues around 8pm) and to **refuel** (if you're heading south, it's the last reliable petrol stop until Gobernador Gregores or Tres Lagos; see box above). There's the overpriced *Hotel Bajo Caracoles* (Ⓣ02963/490100; ❹), with an equally overpriced shop, a café, a **public phone** (the last one until Gobernador Gregores or El Chaltén) and a couple of simple rooms, but you'll be better off at *Hostel Ruta 40* (Ⓔhostel_ruta40@hotmail.com; ❸), a friendly place with dinky rooms, which also serves evening meals ($15).

Cueva de las Manos Pintadas

The **CUEVA DE LAS MANOS PINTADAS** (Cave of the Painted Hands) is one of South America's finest examples of rock-paintings. It can be approached either by road from Bajo Caracoles, or, better, by walking or riding up the canyon it overlooks, the impressive **Cañón de Río Pinturas**.

From the canyon rim, it's a spectacular two-hour **walk** to the cave-paintings. The path drops sharply to the flat valley bed, and continues to the right of the snaking river, nestling up against rock walls and pinnacles that display the region's geological history in bands of black basalt, slabs of rust-coloured sandstone and a layer of sedimentary rocks that range in hue from chalky white to mottled ochre. Bring binoculars for viewing the finches and birds of prey that inhabit the canyon, plus food, water, a hat and sunscreen.

At the point where the course of the Río Pinturas is diverted by a vast rampart of red sandstone, you start to climb the valley side again to reach the road from Bajo Caracoles and the **entrance building** to the protected area around the paintings (daily 9am–7pm; $15), where there's a modest display. Unfortunately, some parts of the site have been tarnished by tourists etching modern graffiti on the rock – hence the fence that now keeps visitors at a distance – and you can only access the cave accompanied by a *guardaparque* on a **guided walk** (1hr; June–Sept on demand, Oct–May every 90min).

The *cueva* itself is less a cave than a series of overhangs: natural cutaways at the foot of a towering ninety-metre cliff-face overlooking the canyon below, a vantage point from which groups of Palaeolithic hunter-gatherers would survey the valley floor for game. Despite the rather heavy-handed fence that now frames them, the collage of black, white, red and ochre **handprints**, mixed with gracefully flowing vignettes of guanaco hunts, still makes for an astonishing spectacle. Of the 829 handprints, most are male, and only 31 are right handed. They are all "negatives", being made by placing the hand on the rock face, and imprinting its outline by blowing pigments through a tube. Interspersed with these are human figures, as well as the outlines of puma paws and rhea prints, and creatures such as a scorpion.

The earliest paintings were made by the **Toldense** culture and date as far back as 9300 BC, but archeologists have identified four later cultural phases, ending with depictions by early Tehuelche groups – notably geometric shapes and zigzags – from approximately 1300 AD. The significance of the paintings is much debated: whether they represented part of the rite of passage for adolescents into the adult world, and were thus part of ceremonies to strengthen familial or tribal bonds, or whether they were connected to religious ceremonies that preceded the hunt will probably never be known. Other tantalizing mysteries involve theories surrounding the large number of heavily pregnant guanacos depicted, and whether these herds were actually semi-domesticated. One thing is for certain: considering their exposed position, it is remarkable how vivid some of the colours still are – the colours were made from the berries of *calafate* bushes, earth and charcoal, with guanaco fat and urine applied to create the waterproof coating that has preserved them so well.

From Bajo Caracoles, a rough 45-kilometre stretch of *ripio* runs to a car park, 600m from the entrance building. Alternatively, you can visit the *cueva*

△ Cueva de las Manos Pintadas

on a **tour** from Perito Moreno (see box, p.690), some of which involve walking up through the canyon. **Hikes** and **horse rides** can be arranged from *Estancia La Cueva de los Manos* or *Casa de Piedra* (see p.693); both can also organize **transport** to the canyon rim, saving hours, and making for a comfortable day-trip.

Posadas and around

Seventy-five kilometres west of Bajo Caracoles on RP-39, the seldom-visited area around turquoise **Lago Posadas** and lapis-blue **Lago Pueyrredón** are well worth the detour, but most places of interest around the lakes are accessible only to those with their own vehicle. The two lakes, just beyond the village of **Posadas**, are famous for their dramatic colour contrast – most notable in spring – and are separated by the narrowest of strips of land, the arrow-straight **La Península**, which looks for all the world like a man-made causeway. It was actually formed during a static phase of the last Ice Age, when an otherwise retreating glacier left an intermediate dump of moraine, now covered by sand dunes, which cut the shallow lagoon of Lago Posadas off from its grander and more tempestuous neighbour. Pueyrredón is the better of the two for fishing – rainbow and brown trout of up to 8kg can be found at the mouth of the Río Oro.

Posadas

The area's main village is listed on some maps as **Hipólito Irigoyen**, but is usually referred to by its old name of **POSADAS**, from the neighbouring lake. Though little more than a loosely grouped assemblage of modern houses, its inhabitants are amicable, and keen to promote the region. Three kilometres south of town, the low, rounded wedge of **Cerro de los Indios** lies beneath the higher scarp of the valley. Bruce Chatwin's description of this rock in *In Patagonia* is unerring: "a lump of basalt, flecked red and green, smooth as patinated bronze and fracturing in linear slabs. The Indians had chosen the place with an unfaltering eye for the sacred."

Indigenous **rock-paintings**, some almost 10,000 years old, mark the foot of the cliff, about two-thirds of the way along the rock to the left. The famous depiction of a "unicorn" – now thought to be a *huemul* – is rather faded; more impressive are the wonderful concentric circles of a hypnotic labyrinth design. The red blotches high up on the overhangs appear to have been the result of guanaco hunters firing up arrows tipped in pigment-stained fabric, perhaps in an ancient version of darts. However, the site's most remarkable feature is the polished shine on the rocks, which really do possess the patina and texture of antique bronze. There's also no ugly fence screening off the engravings and paintings here as at Cueva de las Manos Pintadas, leaving the site's magical aura uncompromised.

Practicalities

There are a couple of decent places to **stay**: *Los Pioneros*, shortly after you enter the village (Ⓣ02963/490209; ④), has tiny but tidy rooms, while more established *La Posada de Posadas* (Ⓣ02963/490250, Ⓦwww.delposadas.com.ar) has both an old hotel ($25 per person), with shared bathrooms around a courtyard, and a set of smart bungalows further towards Lago Posadas (⑥ including breakfast), with modern fittings and comfortable beds in rooms for two or three people. The owners of *La Posada*, Pedro and Susanna Fortuny, run the village's

The legendary Ruta 40

Argentines fondly refer to RN-40, or Ruta 40, the country's longest road, as La Cuarenta – The Forty. Stretching from Cabo Vírgenes, the southernmost point of the Argentine mainland, to northernmost Ciénaga, on the Bolivian border, it's more than just a highway. Like Route 66 in the US, the road has its own ethos – it has inspired songs, been the subject of books and caused arguments. Whatever you do, don't steer clear of Ruta 40 – it's as central to a visit to Argentina as a football match or a *milonga*.

▲ Andean landscape, Santa Cruz Province

A long and winding road

La Cuarenta runs a staggering 5224km from the tip of **Patagonia** to **Bolivia** – the distance from Amsterdam to Afghanistan. Partly to make it more attractive for tourists, the road's **itinerary** has been changed over the years. When it was created in 1935, distances were counted both north (to Jujuy Province) and south (to Río Gallegos) from the centre of Mendoza city; many road signs still use this old system. Ruta 40 now starts at the ocean at **Cabo Vírgenes** and winds up through eleven provinces, past twenty national parks and across 24 major rivers, before reaching the altiplano. There it breaks a record: the dizzying **Abra de Acay**, at 5061m, is the highest point on a national road anywhere in the world. Although sections of the route are relatively busy, notably around Bariloche and between Mendoza and San Juan cities, most of La Cuarenta runs through Argentina's magnificent **open spaces**, seldom more than 100km from the majestic peaks of the **Andes**. Many visitors are drawn by the road's rugged mystique – a result of its inaccessibility and frequently poor condition – while others are put off for the same reason. Currently only half its length is **tarmacked** but the good news – or the bad, depending on your point of view – is that the Argentine government has pledged to pave the entire road by the end of the decade.

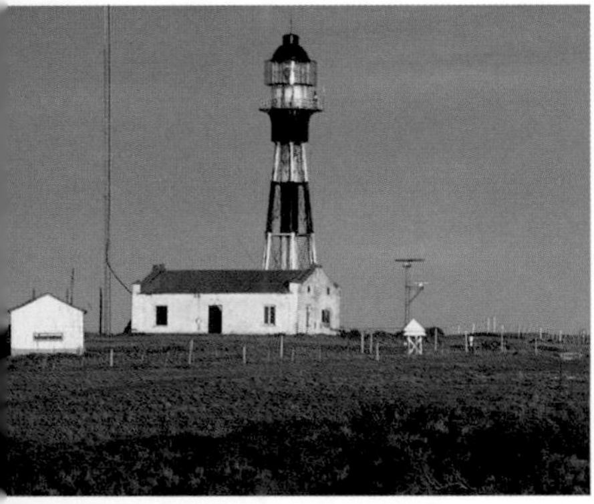

◀ Lighthouse, Cabo Virgenes

Highway highlights

On its great voyage from **south to north**, Ruta 40 takes you over, under and past some of the leading sights in the country – viaducts and volcanoes, mountain passes and lakeside estancias, Andean villages and crystalline lakes.

The south

A navy lighthouse at **Cabo Vírgenes**, Santa Cruz (see p.686), marks La Cuarenta's starting point, but the nearby penguin colony is more exciting. Between here and Chos Malal, in Neuquén Province, the road zigzags across the **Patagonian steppe**, a barren, windswept expanse thickly blanketed with snow during the winter. Consider splurging at **Estancia Lagos del Furioso**, in Santa Cruz (see p.697), where you'll find glorious views, excellent fishing and every creature comfort.

▲ Sierra de Famatina

The midlands

North of Neuquén Province, Ruta 40 enters the **Cuyo**, Argentina's western midlands. It meanders through little-visited **La Payunia**, in Mendoza Province (see p.547), a land of rosy lava and ebony gorges, deep karstic caves and flamingo-flecked lagoons, before passing near **Laguna Diamante** (see p.536). A visit to this all-but-inaccessible lagoon rewards the adventurous – enjoy a picnic on the banks of a crystalline brook as you admire the silhouette of Volcán Maipo. Further north, in La Rioja Province, the road skirts sunny valleys and hugs the **Cuesta de Miranda** (see p.576). Offering spectacular vistas of the Sierra de Famatina, the serpentine corniche winds through polychrome mountains that contrast with the verdant vegetation along the riverbanks below.

The north

Mostly dirt track, La Cuarenta's last – and highest – stretch cuts through the historic **Northwest**, a land of cold, starry nights and warm, sunny days. Rippling hills, herds of goats and crumbling adobe houses are typical sights here. For a top-notch poncho, stop off at **Belén**, in Catamarca (see p.494) – local methods of weaving have been maintained in this highland village since pre-Hispanic times. You'll also want to stop in **Cachi**, in Salta Province (see p.445), for a photo of the surrounding snow-topped sierras and valleys, where fields blaze red with drying paprika peppers in the autumn. Just before Ruta 40 reaches the Bolivian border, it is spanned by the mighty **La Polvorilla viaduct** (see p.440). It may look like something out of a model town in all the tourist brochures, but this fabulous feat of engineering is impressive whether you chug across it in the Train to the Clouds or look up at it from the road below.

◄ La Polvorilla

> Argentine rock group **La Renga** paid homage to La Cuarenta in a song entitled *Ruta 40*, on their 2006 album *Truenotierra*:
>
> Riding in the wind, headed north or south
> Whatever you do take the Ruta 40
> Straight tracks and bends, far, far it goes
> Towards other worlds stored in your head
> It seems to go round in circles
> Like a witch's spell in the desert

Hitting the road

By far the best way to approach Ruta 40 is to **hire a vehicle and drive yourself** – it's worth investing in a **4WD**, even for the paved sections. Special care is required, though, especially further south where strong crosswinds and poorly maintained gravel (*ripio*) roads make it extremely easy to flip over. Driving on gravel is much like driving on snow – fine in a straight line but difficult on bends or when braking. To keep safe, stick to the Highway Code and follow this **advice**:

- On unpaved sections follow the most recently used tracks and never exceed 70km/hr.
- Slow down and move as far right as possible when approaching an oncoming vehicle to avoid windscreen or headlight damage.
- Overtake with caution – dust and stones thrown up by your vehicle will obscure visibility.
- Go downhill in a low gear – the rear will skid if you go too fast.
- Slow down in strong winds, especially crosswinds – in a high-clearance 4WD the wind may get underneath – and be careful opening doors, as they can be wrenched from their hinges.
- Give help if you see someone has broken down: offering water or taking a message to the next town could be vital.
- Refuel whenever you see a pump – the next one may be hundreds of kilometres away.

▼ Sheep crossing Ruta 40, Santa Cruz Province

best **restaurant**, serving two-course Mediterranean-style meals ($30), and have excellent knowledge of local hikes and fishing. The village has an YPF **fuel** station and a public telephone. El Guraño **buses** leaves for Bajo Caracoles and Perito Moreno once a week (Tues around 7pm). Five kilometres east of Posadas, beautiful RP-41 runs north towards the Chilean border at Paso Roballos, and Los Antiguos (see p.691), though spring floods mean that it is usually only passable from mid-December to March.

Lago Posadas

Do not try to drive around the south shore of **LAGO POSADAS**, even though a road is marked on many maps: cars can easily get bogged down near the Río Furioso. Instead, take the route running around the north shore, which passes through a zone of blasted, bare humps, crisscrossed by lines of *duraznillo* bushes. Known as **El Quemado** (The Burnt One), it's one of the most ancient formations in Argentina, dating back 180 million years to the Jurassic age, and there are spectacular contrasts between minerals such as green olivina sandstone and porphyry iron oxides.

At the northwest end of Lago Posadas the road swings left, running along La Península before following the south bank of Lago Pueyrredón. Beautifully located at the southern end of La Península, the tourist estancia *Lagos del Furioso* (in Buenos Aires ⓣ011/4812-0959, ⓦwww.lagosdelfurioso.com; US$235, minimum two-night stay; closed Easter–Oct) rates as the most luxurious accommodation in the north of Santa Cruz. Purpose-built as a hotel, it doesn't provide the agrotourism opportunities of a working estancia, but the corresponding comforts are obvious: well-designed bungalows blanketed from the wind by a pocket of poplars, a sauna and an airy communal dining room where freshly prepared cuisine of an international standard is served, complemented by panoramic views of Lago Posadas and the striated Río Furioso canyon.

Lago Pueyrredón and the Río Oro Valley

Ambitious engineers have somehow managed to squeeze a dirt road between the southern shore of pristinely beautiful **LAGO PUEYRREDÓN** and the hills that press up against it, without having to resort to tiresome infill projects. This precarious arrangement is compromised only by the occasional spring flood (Sept is the worst month).

Just past the neat bridge over the **Río Oro**, a track wends its way up the mountainside and past the magnificent purple chasm of the **Garganta del Río Oro**. Fourteen kilometres from *Lagos del Furioso* are the more economical *Estancia Suyai* **cabins** (ⓣ02963/490242, ⓔestanciasuyai@speedy.com.ar; closed April–Sept; ⑦) and **camping** ($18 per person), set on a stunningly beautiful peninsula jutting out into the lake. Beyond the campsite, the track deteriorates and the Río Oro is normally only crossable by 4WD.

Further on, the road rises through the wild foothills of **Monte San Lorenzo** and towards the snowline. This is private land, and crossing the border here is illegal; climbers intending to ascend San Lorenzo from the Chilean side should cross over to Cochrane at one of the legitimate border posts further north and tackle the mountain from Padre de Agostini's base camp, owned by the mountain guide, Luís Soto de la Cruz. Alternatively, contact Pedro Fortuny (of *La Posada de Posadas*; see opposite), who can help organize an expedition up San Lorenzo ($600 per person for four people). The best **maps** available are those from the Instituto Geográfico Militar in Buenos Aires (see p.70: #4772-27 *Cerro Pico Agudo* and #4772-33 y 32 *Lago Belgrano*).

Parque Nacional Perito Moreno

Extreme isolation means that, despite being one of Argentina's first national parks, **PARQUE NACIONAL PERITO MORENO** is also one of its least visited. Though replete with glorious mountains and beautiful lakes, this is not a "sightseeing" park in the way that Nahuel Huapi is, nor does it have the obvious mountain highlights of the Fitz Roy massif or Torres del Paine in Chile, even though the peak of San Lorenzo looms just to the north. The bulk of the park's forested mountain scenery lies in its western two-thirds, which are reserved for **scientific study**, meaning that most of the area accessible to the public consists of arid steppe. Its tourist infrastructure is rudimentary, but what the park does offer those who have made the effort to get here is a solitude that few other places on the continent can match.

Though you can visit much of the park by car in a day or two, you could spend much longer trekking through the starkly beautiful high pampas, past virulently colourful lakes and near the imperious snowcapped hulk of San Lorenzo – and still miss out on many of its hidden wonders. In the absence of man, **wildlife** thrives here. Guanacos can be seen at close quarters, and their alarm call, a rasping laugh, can be startling. The luckiest visitors may glimpse a puma (or at least its tracks), or an endangered *huemul*, of which about one hundred are thought to live in the park. Condors are plentiful, and other **birdlife** includes the Chilean flamingo, Black-necked Swans, Steamer Ducks, Upland Geese (*cauquenes*), Buff-necked Ibises (*bandurrias*), *ñandús* and the powerful black-chested Buzzard Eagle (*águila mora*); in the *lenga* woods, you may come across the Austral Pygmy Owl (*cuburé grande*), a surprisingly tame and curious bird that you can approach to within a couple of metres. One of the park's most biologically interesting features are its **lakes**: introduced species of trout and salmon have devastated indigenous fish populations throughout Argentina, but the ones here have never been stocked with non-endemic species – they're now protected, and no fishing is allowed.

Just as much of the rest of Patagonia has experienced a recent surge in **visitors**, so, too, has the park. In 1992, just ninety people visited. In 2003, that number reached over a thousand for the first time.

Park practicalities

Reached by a ninety-kilometre *ripio* spur road, which meets RN-40 100km south of Bajo Caracoles, the park is **open year round** but between mid-March and the end of November it can be cut off by snow, sometimes for weeks on end. Bring warm, waterproof clothes, since the weather changes moods like a spoilt child. Temperatures are bracing all year, and can drop to –25°C in winter, even before the wind-chill is taken into account.

Without your own transport, **getting to the park** is an expensive affair: visitors to *La Oriental* (see opposite) can arrange a pick-up from RN-40 ($270 unless someone from there happens to be making the journey); a *remise* from Gobernador Gregores, where there is a park office at San Martín 882 (ⓣ02962/491477, ⓔperitomoreno@apn.gov.ar), costs around $450. Otherwise, several tour agencies, including Overland Patagonia (in Bariloche ⓣ02944/435674, ⓦwww.overlandpatagonia.com) and RN-40 (in Comodoro Rivadavia ⓣ0297/446-5337, ⓦwww.ruta-40.com), visit the national park on their RN-40 itineraries.

The **administration building** (daily 8am–8pm), where you are required to register and give an idea of where you're planning to explore, is 5km inside the

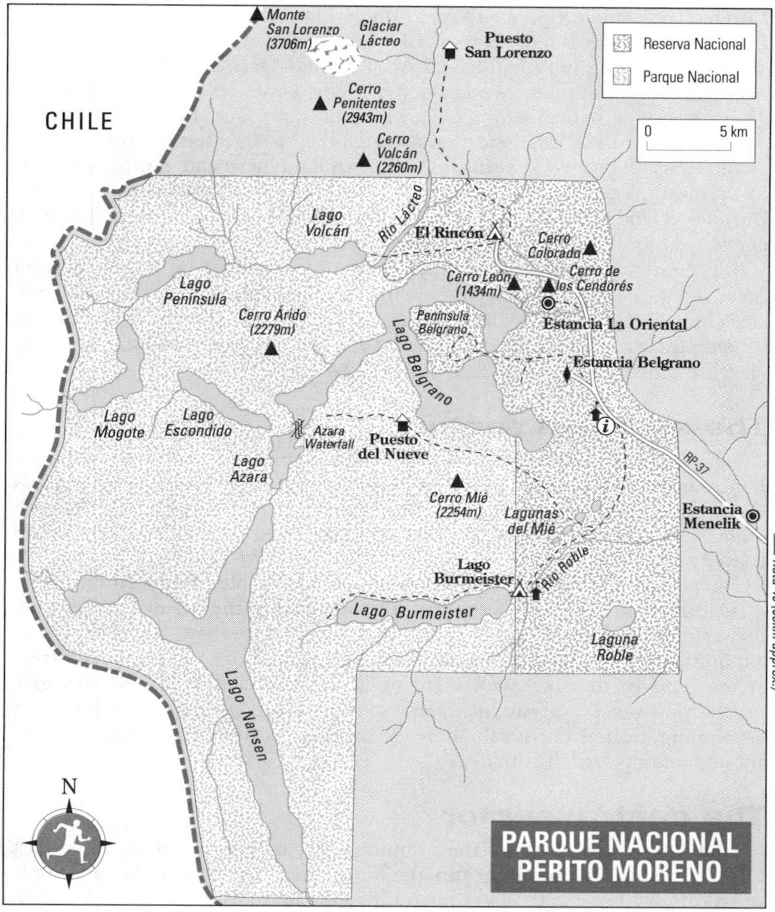

park. Here, you'll also be given a welcoming talk and leaflets on the trails and wildlife (some in English); there are creative educational displays in the small museum. You can refill water containers, but there are no other facilities. Anyone planning to head for the refuges at Puesto del Nueve and Puesto San Lorenzo must also register here.

The best **place to stay** in the park is *Estancia La Oriental*, a beautifully sited working estancia, looking out across the northern curl of Lago Belgrano about 7km north of the administration (in Buenos Aires ⓣ011/5237-4043, ⓦwww.estanciasdesantacruz.com; ⑧ half-board; closed April–Oct). A homely, down-to-earth feel pervades the ranch, befitting its day-job, though it also houses the park's only tourist beds in comfortable rooms. The owner cooks simple but hearty food and often serves delicious scones for breakfast. Facilities for **camping** are clean and sheltered, but it's a bit pricey ($45 per tent). There's fuel (*nafta* and *gasoil*), intended for guests only, as well as radio contact. **Horse-riding** ($50 for 3hr, plus $100 for a guide) here is fantastic.

An equally scenic option, though 10km outside the park, off RP-37, is *Estancia Menelik* (in Buenos Aires ⓣ011/4836-3502, ⓦwww.cielospatagonicos.com; ❼ including breakfast; closed April to mid-Oct), an English-style *casco viejo*, most of whose cosy, wood-floored rooms have views across the steppe. There is also a sixteen-bed refuge with hot water and firewood ($60 per person). You can buy fuel here, too, although they do run out periodically.

Otherwise, there are the **refugios** at Puesto del Nueve and, outside the park to the north, Puesto San Lorenzo, and a couple of free **campsites** – at Lago Burmeister and El Rincón – which, although distinctly lacking in facilities, enjoy great locations. Alternatively, pitch your tent wherever you please.

The sensitivity of this special area's environment should be respected at all times: do not light fires, do not remove any archeological artefact or fossil ammonite, do not fish, bury toilet waste and pack out all other rubbish. Walkers should note that, despite it being marked as a pass on several maps, it is strictly illegal to cross into Chile at Paso Cordoniz by Lago Nansen.

The southern sector

A clearly marked trail leads 8km south of the administration building to the **Lagunas del Mié**, a series of shallow lagoons in the stark plateau of the pampas that are the favoured feeding grounds of a rich variety of waterfowl. The path splits, with the right fork heading towards the Puesto del Nueve refuge and Lago Azara (see below).

Otherwise, continue south to the gorgeous marine-blue **Lago Burmeister** – curiously, the only lake in the park that drains into the Atlantic rather than the Pacific – squeezed into its wooded mountain valley, 16km from the administration. A well-sited **campsite** lies in a stand of southern beech trees at the head of the lake, with a latrine as its only facility. Windbreaks give protection from the persistent stormy gusts. Ask the *guardaparque* here about continuing around the north shore of the lake – there may be restrictions about camping further round.

The central sector

A kilometre or two north of the administration, at *Estancia Belgrano*, the track forks left towards **Lago Belgrano**, the most remarkable of the lakes accessible to visitors, with one of the most intensely gaudy turquoise colours anywhere in Patagonia. After 8km you reach the scrub-covered **Península Belgrano** – to all intents an island, except that Mother Nature has forgotten to cut its improbable umbilical attachment to the mainland. A leaflet in English is available from administration for a self-guided two-hour circular trail through the *mata negra* bushes, detailing the behaviour of its graceful guanaco inhabitants. Look out for the mounds of guanaco dung at the animals' communal toilets, and the piles of bones pumas have left behind. Although it only takes three to four hours to walk to the other side, you can **camp** on the peninsula allowing more time to take in the beauty – or worry about the predators.

A longer hike of two to three days can be made south of Lago Belgrano, accessed on a path that cuts through the Lagunas del Mié (see above), but you must ask permission from park administration first to use the old shepherd's refuge, **Puesto del Nueve**, as a base. From here, you can visit the ten-metre waterfall that drains Lago Belgrano and explore the region around beautiful **Lago Azara**, where you stand a slim chance of finding footprints or traces of *huemules*, the endangered Andean deer that is the park's symbol. You may cook on the small stove in the refuge, but should replace all firewood used.

Back on the main track, heading north from *Estancia Belgrano*, you reach the well-marked turn-off to *Estancia La Oriental*, which lies on the edge of a tranquil valley (see p.699). About 3km further north, on the other side of the valley, stands **Cerro de los Condorés**, a cliff-face stained by great white smears, indicating the presence of condors' nests. About thirty of the giant birds use the *condorera* regularly. To gain a similar perspective, you can climb nearby **Cerro León** (1434m; 4hr return), which affords excellent views of the heartland of the park, and which is one of the favoured habitats of a famous rodent: the *chinchillón gris* or *anaranjado* (a type of vizcacha found only in Santa Cruz, and bearing some resemblance to a chinchilla).

The northern sector

From *La Oriental*, the pass next to La Condorera leads 10km on to the *guardaparque*'s house at **El Rincón**, once one of the most isolated estancias in Argentina, where you can **camp**. Just before the buildings, a track branches west towards Chile. The first 3km can be covered by car, and from here it's a five-kilometre walk to the desolate shores of **Lago Volcán**, a milky-green glacial lake. Although a pass (Paso de la Balsa) is marked on some maps this is not a legal frontier crossing and you will be detained if caught.

From El Rincón, it's a stiff five- to six-hour walk to the **Puesto San Lorenzo** refuge, from where you can access the park's finest views of Monte San Lorenzo; if you speak Spanish, consult the helpful *guardaparque* about conditions ahead first. As a safety measure, you are required to register with him or at the administration. Take the winding track to the right of the house (traversable in a normal car for 5km, and then in a high-clearance 4WD a bit further), leaving the park's northern boundary. After one particularly tight hairpin down a small gravel scarp, you must ford two streams and pick up the track on the other side. Eventually, you reach a bluff with a steep moraine scarp, which is far as you can get with a vehicle (9km from El Rincón). From here, you have a fine view of the turbulent **Río Lácteo**, which you must keep on your left. The track drops down the bluff, passes a windbreak and then gives up entirely in the woods some 200m beyond. From here on, there's always a temptation to drop down onto the flat gravel bed of the Río Lácteo, but resist this and stay high, at least until you have passed the huge alluvial moraine fan that pushes the river far over to the eastern side of the valley. After this, the path drops down and wends its way through the marshy grassland that borders the river valley. A little further on, the tin shack of Puesto San Lorenzo is easily visible. A supply of firewood and a rustic stove await inside, but remember to replace the wood you use.

With care, you can ford the Río Lácteo here. Beyond, a path leads west up the valley towards **Glaciar Lácteo** and the two-thousand-metre fortress wall of **San Lorenzo's southeast face**, one of the most "Himalayan" sights in the Patagonian cordillera – if you are lucky enough, that is, to catch this notoriously temperamental mountain in one of its more benevolent moods.

South to Parque Nacional Los Glaciares

The RN-40 **south to Parque Nacional Los Glaciares** is at its most desolate and remote. Once past the turn-off for Parque Nacional Perito Moreno, there's nothing much along it for the next 60km until RP-25 branches off east to San Julián (see p.682) on the coast, passing through tiny **Gobernador Gregores**, where there's a YPF **fuel station** and basic **accommodation** at *Cañadón León*,

Roca 397 (ⓣ02962/491082; ❸), and *Hotel San Francisco*, San Martín 463 (ⓣ02962/491039; ❸).

Continuing along RN-40, you pass the *Estancia La Angostura* (ⓣ02962/491501, ⓦwww.estancialaangostura.com.ar; ❺ breakfast included; closed April–Sept), 190km south of Bajo Caracoles or 140km north of Tres Lagos and 4km off the road. This is very much a working estancia, and you'll get a real sense of the realities of life in the Patagonian interior. Accommodation is in the main house, in rather uninspiring rooms with sagging beds, but the welcome is warm and the atmosphere convivial, with evening meals ($30) taken around the family table; this is a good place to try a typical regional dish that's rarely available to the tourist: *liebre al escabeche* (hare in *escabeche*), which is prepared with a vinegar, carrot and onion marinade. Bird-watchers should keep their eyes open for possible sightings of the endangered, endemic Hooded Grebe (*macá tobiano*), which sometimes inhabits the pools of the wetlands that front the estancia.

Forty kilometres south, a track leads west to the shores of **Lago Cardiel**, a turquoise lake named after a Jesuit priest who explored the area in 1745. Geologists who have studied the lake have compared its depositional features to that of a cup of tea – the lake's current causes sediment to accumulate at its centre, in much the same way that tea leaves concentrate in the middle of a stirred cup – and though saline, its waters contain a proliferation of three-kilogram brook and rainbow trout. Thirty kilometres south of the turn-off is the roadside estancia *La Siberia* (❺ breakfast included; closed April–Oct), a poor alternative to *La Angostura* and only really worth considering if you don't have time to push on to El Chaltén; its lacklustre rooms, with dirty bathrooms, are in a fragile outbuilding. From the *casco*, you can descend to Lago Cardiel along a track, but don't go too far in a vehicle, as wheels tend to get stuck in the sand.

Tres Lagos

The RN-40 continues for 90km through one of its most barren stretches – so little used that some plants have fairly well taken root in the middle of the road – before reaching the YPF **fuel station** at a junction 2km east of the village of **TRES LAGOS**, a place that's not worth visiting in itself, but which has a free municipal **campsite**, shaded by cherry trees (take the first left and it's 100m down the road by a small stream). Other services include a couple of tyre-repair places (*gomerías*) and a supermarket. There's a barely functioning **hotel**, the *Sorsona's*, to the left of the main street (ⓣ02962/495033; $25 per person), but you've a better chance of a roof over your head at *Huentru Niyeu*'s newer, petite *cabañas*, just past the campsite (ⓣ02962/495006; $35 per person).

Two major routes lead out of Tres Lagos: west of the YPF station, RP-31, another gravel road, strikes out towards the area of **Lago San Martín**, 110km away; south of the junction, RN-40 – now paved – turns westwards and continues for 35km to the RP-23 turn-off towards **El Chaltén** (see opposite). Running parallel to the northern shore of Patagonia's third largest lake, Lago Viedma (see p.716), RP-23 speeds towards **Parque Nacional Los Glaciares**, and for the next 90km the park's iconic Fitz Roy massif grows and grows in front of you, pushing skyward out of the flat steppe.

Lago San Martín

The most erratically shaped of all the major Patagonian lakes, with its glacial fjords stretching across the border into Chile like the tentacles of some gigantic ice-blue squid, **LAGO SAN MARTÍN** is one of the region's most isolated attractions. It was named after Argentina's national hero but, symbolically in an area that has had more than its fair share of entrenched patriotic wrangles over the placement of the frontier, it transmutes into Lago O'Higgins on the Chilean side, in honour of Chile's founding father. Ironically, these two great generals were contemporaries and friends who united to fight a common cause in the struggle for independence from Spain.

Fortunately, cross-border co-operation is increasing these days, and the region is opening up to tourism, especially now that Chile's **Carretera Austral** (a single-track dirt road) reaches its frontier settlement of **Villa O'Higgins**. Nevertheless, the area's climate can be inhospitable, and furious winds frequently lash the lake's surface, making navigation on its waters a perilous enterprise. Very good **accommodation** is on the southern shores of the lake at the sheep-farming *Estancia La Maipú* (in Buenos Aires ⓣ011/4901-5591; ⓦwww.estancialamaipu.com.ar; ❽ including breakfast; closed May–Sept), a pretty, country-style cottage where juicy *asados* are roasted in a *quincho*, a traditional thatch-roofed barbecue hut. A nearby *condorera* offers great opportunities to view these birds in the wild, and the horse riding ($105 for a full day, plus $105 for a guide) is first-rate. Transport to and from Tres Lagos must be arranged in advance. Alternatively, in a sheltered poplar grove on the shore of Lago San Martín, there's the equally impressive *Estancia El Condor*, set in expansive lands characterized by snaking rivers, deep valleys and spectacular vistas (ⓣ011/4836-3502, ⓦwww.cielospatagonicos.com; ❼ including breakfast).

Parque Nacional Los Glaciares

Declared a "Patrimony of Humanity" by UNESCO in 1981, the wild expanse of **Parque Nacional Los Glaciares** encompasses environments ranging from enormous glaciers that flow down from the heights of the Hielo Continental Sur to thick, sub-Antarctic woodland of deciduous *lenga* and *ñire*, and evergreen *guindo* and *canelo*; and from savage, rain-lashed, unclimbed crags to dry, billiard-table Patagonian *meseta*. The vast majority of this is off-limits to the public, and most will visit only the **Fitz Roy** sector for superb trekking in the north and the sightseeing area in the south around the **Glaciar Perito Moreno**, one of the world's most famous glaciers. Serving as bases for these two areas are the villages of **El Chaltén**, in the north, and **El Calafate**, in the south, both of which cater well to a burgeoning influx of outdoor enthusiasts.

El Chaltén

Now that Fitz Roy is no longer an exclusive private paradise for climbers, the village of **EL CHALTÉN**, 90km from RN-40, has undergone a convulsive expansion. Established in 1985 in a (successful) attempt to claim the area from Chile, this thriving tourist centre regrettably shows signs of uncontrolled development, and whereas certain hotels have been – and continue to be – built in a style sympathetic to their surroundings, others would look more at ease in the beach resort of Mar del Plata. That said, the atmosphere in the village is pleasant and relaxed, with a friendly mix of young Argentines and foreign visitors.

Rearing up on the opposite bank of the **Río de las Vueltas** is the curiously stepped, dark-grey cliff-face of **Cerro Pirámide**, while you can glimpse the tips of the park's most daunting peaks, **Fitz Roy** and **Cerro Torre**, from the southern and eastern fringes of the village. Otherwise, in terms of specific sights, there is only the classically uncluttered alpine **chapel** on the western edge of the village. Built by Austrian craftsmen with Austrian materials, it's a fitting memorial to the climbing purist Toni Egger (see box, p.713), as well as to others who have lost their lives in the park.

As with most parks in Patagonia, autumn is a **good time to visit**: March and April are beautiful months, when the wind normally drops. The spring months of October and November are also good for avoiding the crowds, if not the winds. More than most tourist centres, El Chaltén shuts up shop for the **winter season** – many establishments close between Easter and October.

Arrival and information

Unless you ask otherwise, **buses** will drop you off at their offices or at hotel terminals: Cal Tur start and finish at the *Fitz Roy Inn*, Chaltén Travel at the *Albergue Rancho Grande* and TAQSA and Los Glaciares from their offices on M.M. Güemes 68 and San Martín and Lago del Desierto, respectively. Cal Tur, Chaltén Travel and TAQSA run daily services in season to El Calafate, while Los Glaciares' buses leaves three times a week (Tues, Thurs & Sat). In the summer months, a daily service runs to Perito Moreno and Los Antiguos: Itinerarios y Travesías, at Perito Moreno 152, heads north on even dates, Chaltén Travel on odd.

The **national park visitors' centre** (8am–6pm; ⓣ&ⓕ02962/493004), less than 1km south of the village, is a necessary point of call; helpful volunteers advise visitors of the park's regulations. Inside are wildlife exhibits, a message board and a useful information book for climbers, all of whom must register here, as should anyone planning to stay at the Laguna Toro refuge and campsite to the south. Fishing licences can be purchased at the desk, or in the Mercado Artesanal in the village. The **tourist office** is in the Comisión de Fomento, at M.M. Güemes 21 (March–Nov Mon–Fri 9am–6pm, Dec–Feb daily 8am–8pm; ⓣ02962/493011, ⓔcomfomelchalten@yahoo.com.ar); the staff are helpful, particularly if you're stuck for accommodation.

Accommodation

Generally, the **accommodation** in El Chaltén's centre has better views of the mountains, while the places on and around Avenida San Martín are more upmarket. Most places are closed between Easter and October; conversely, in high season, especially January, it is advisable to **book in advance**. Scenic *Campamento Madsen*, at the Fitz Roy trailhead north of town, is the best of the free **campsites**. It has no showers and only one latrine; you should only use fallen wood for fires. Two of the best paying sites in town are *El Refugio*, San

Organized trips from El Chaltén

Casa de Guias, on Avenida Costanera del Sur (ⓣ02962/493118, ⓦwww.casadeguias.com.ar), provides **guides** for the Parque Nacional Los Glaciares' numerous day-treks (from $25 per person) and also run one-day **rock-climbing** workshops ($20). The excellent Fitz Roy Expediciones, Lionnel Terray 212 (ⓣ02962/493017, ⓦwww.fitzroyexpediciones.com.ar), managed by legendary climber Alberto del Castillo, organizes both **trekking on Glaciar Torre** (teaching basic ice-climbing techniques; $250) and much more serious and expensive (up to US$1850) five- to nine-day expeditions onto the Hielo Continental Sur for experienced trekkers. Patagonia Magica, on San Martín (ⓣ02962/493066, ⓦwww.patagoniamagica.com), runs **mountain-biking trips** from Lago del Desierto back to El Chaltén, while Rodolfo Guerra, near *Rancho Grande* (ⓣ02962/493020), can arrange **horse-riding** excursions to Laguna Torre and Río Blanco (from $80 per person). South of El Chaltén, **boat trips** across Lago Viedma to **Glaciar Viedma** and mini-trekking near its flanks ($250 with transfer) are run by Patagonia Aventura, on Güemes (ⓣ02962/493110).

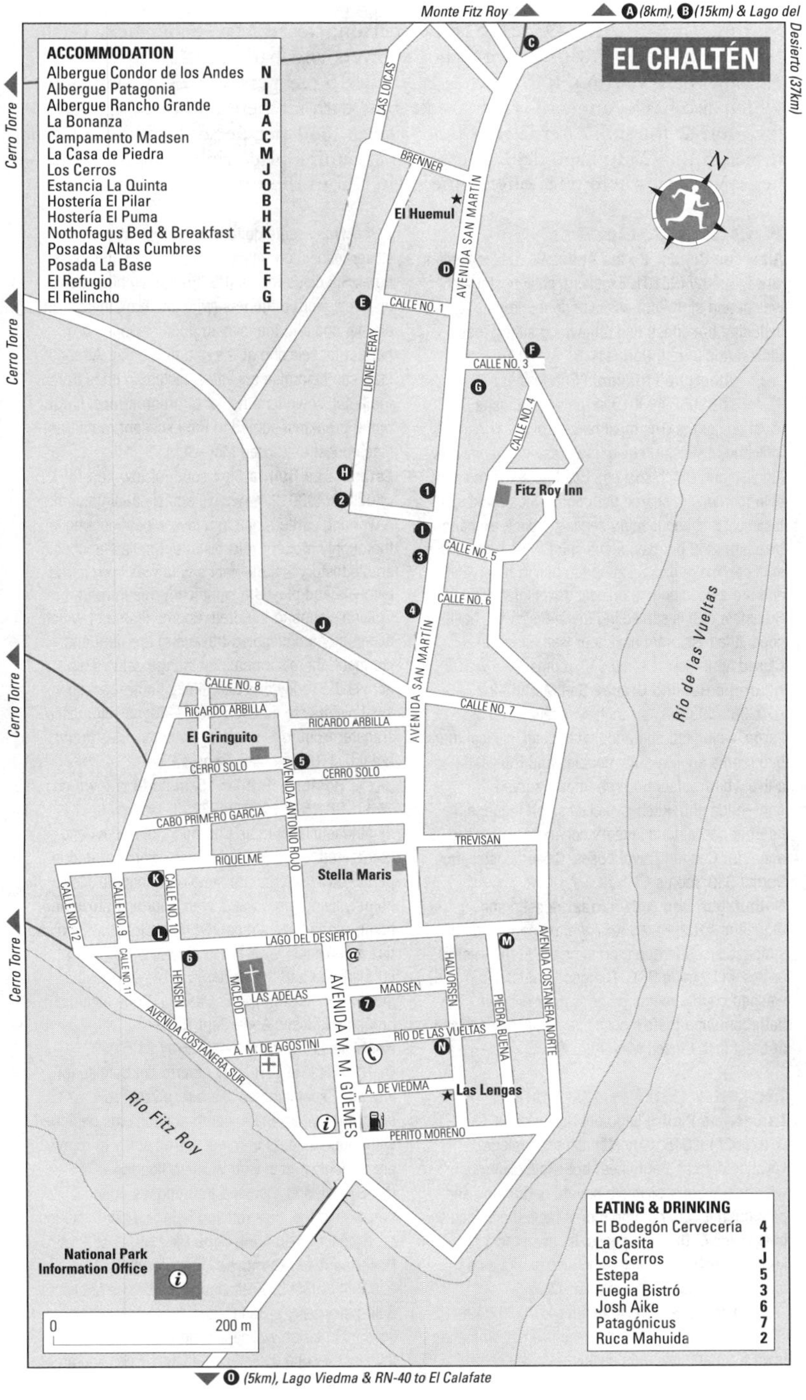

EL CHALTÉN
ACCOMMODATION
Albergue Condor de los Andes N
Albergue Patagonia I
Albergue Rancho Grande D
La Bonanza A
Campamento Madsen C
La Casa de Piedra M
Los Cerros J
Estancia La Quinta O
Hostería El Pilar B
Hostería El Puma H
Nothofagus Bed & Breakfast K
Posadas Altas Cumbres E
Posada La Base L
El Refugio F
El Relincho G
EATING & DRINKING
El Bodegón Cervecería 4
La Casita 1
Los Cerros J
Estepa 5
Fuegia Bistró 3
Josh Aike 6
Patagónicus 7
Ruca Mahuida 2
Monte Fitz Roy
A (8km), B (15km) & Lago del Desierto (37km)
O (5km), Lago Viedma & RN-40 to El Calafate
Cerro Torre
Cerro Torre
Cerro Torre
Cerro Torre
N
Río de las Vueltas
Río Fitz Roy
El Huemul
Fitz Roy Inn
El Gringuito
Stella Maris
Las Lengas
National Park Information Office
LAS LOICAS
BRENNER
AVENIDA SAN MARTÍN
CALLE NO. 1
LIONEL TERAY
CALLE NO. 3
CALLE NO. 4
CALLE NO. 5
CALLE NO. 6
CALLE NO. 7
CALLE NO. 8
RICARDO ARBILLA
RICARDO ARBILLA
CERRO SOLO
CERRO SOLO
AVENIDA ANTONIO ROJO
CABO PRIMERO GARCIA
TREVISAN
RIQUELME
CALLE NO. 12
CALLE NO. 9
CALLE NO. 10
LAGO DEL DESIERTO
CALLE NO. 11
HENSEN
MCLEOD
LAS ADELAS
AVENIDA M. M. GÜEMES
MADSEN
HALVORSEN
PIEDRA BUENA
AVENIDA COSTANERA NORTE
RÍO DE LAS VUELTAS
AVENIDA COSTANERA SUR
A. M. DE AGOSTINI
A. DE VIEDMA
PERITO MORENO
0
200 m

Martín s/n (☎02962/493221; $15 per person; closed May–Sept), next to the Río de las Vueltas, with 24-hour hot showers and barbecue facilities; and *El Relincho*, San Martín s/n (☎02962/493007; $15 per person; closed May–Sept), which also has a couple of good-sized cabins with kitchens and maid service (7 for four, 8 for six). Alternatively, *La Bonanza* ($14 per person), 8km north of town on RP-23 to Lago del Desierto, is a charming place right next to the Río de las Vueltas, where trees offer some shelter from the wind.

Hostels & B&Bs

Albergue Condor de los Andes Río de las Vueltas s/n ☎02962/493101. Excellent, cosy hostel with welcoming staff, four en-suite double rooms (5) including breakfast, and an inviting sitting area. Closed April–Sept. Dorms $35.

Albergue Patagonia San Martín 392 ☎02962/493019, ©patagoniahostel@yahoo.com.ar. The most homely of the YHA-affiliated hostels, run by a hard-working, genial crew (English and Dutch spoken). Has heated dorms and twin rooms with shared bathrooms, plus cooking facilities, a cheap laundry service, a book exchange, bike hire ($50 per day) and a snug living room. The staff can make excursion and transport reservations and are a good source of local travel information. Breakfast ($8) is served in *Fuegia Bistró*, the hostel's good little restaurant next door (see opposite). Closed April–Sept. Dorms $30, rooms 4

Albergue Rancho Grande San Martín 724 ☎02962/493005, ©rancho@cotecal.com.ar. Large, well-oiled operation with clean, clinical four-bed rooms and en-suite doubles and triples. It has a lively bar/restaurant area (meals served 6am–midnight), kitchen facilities, left luggage, Internet and a good laundry service. It's also the agent for Chaltén Travel buses. Closed Easter–Oct. Dorms $30, rooms 6

Nothofagus Bed & Breakfast Hensen and Riquelme ☎02962/493087. As the name would suggest, wood features prominently in the interior of this welcoming B&B. The good-value, sun-washed double rooms come with or without bathroom, and there's delicious home-made bread at breakfast. Closed May–Aug. 5–6

Hotels and estancias

La Casa de Piedra Lago del Desierto s/n ☎02962/493015, ©hosterialacasadepiedra@yahoo.com.ar. Rents neat but expensive rooms with comfy beds, sizeable private bathrooms and plentiful hot water; some rooms have the village's best views of the high peaks. Its owner is a knowledgeable geologist who also works as a guide. Price includes breakfast. 8

Los Cerros San Martín s/n ☎02962/493182, ®www.loscerrosdelchalten.com. Dominating town from an elevated position near the centre, *Los Cerros* seems quite incongruous at first but closer inspection reveals a welcoming first-class hotel. Spacious rooms (US$250) have huge beds and designer bathrooms (with Jacuzzi), there's an on-site spa and the inviting public lounges are perfect for relaxing at the end of the day. Attentive staff can help plan activities, including ones from the hotel's own lengthy list of programmes. Large buffet breakfast served in the excellent restaurant (see opposite). Closed May–Sept.

Estancia La Quinta 5km south of town off RP-23 ☎02962/493012, ®www.estancialaquinta.com.ar. A working cattle ranch in a lovely location whose thoroughly modern refurbishment belies its considerable history – the owner's wife was born in the estancia and played a significant role in refuting Chilean claims to the area. Rooms (some of which accommodate disabled travellers) are neat and compact, there's a peaceful lounge with views across the valley and beautifully home-cooked local dishes are served in the 100-year-old *casco*. Transfer from/to El Chaltén. Price includes buffet breakfast. Closed May–Sept. 9

Hostería El Pilar 15km north of town on RP-15 ☎02962/493002, ®www.hosteriaelpilar.com.ar. Charming, old-fashioned corrugated metal *casco*, delightfully decorated in period style. Rooms are snug and peaceful, the homely living room has a wood-burning stove and home-made tarts are served in the tearoom, which has an enviable view of Fitz Roy. There is a neat little garden and the owner is a knowledgeable guide. Transfer from/to El Chaltén. Price includes breakfast. Closed April–Sept. 8

Hostería El Puma Lionnel Terray 212 ☎02962/493095. Run by Alberto del Castillo (of Fitz Roy Expediciones; see box, p.704), this excellent, upper-end accommodation was designed with mountaineers in mind. Warm, softly lit rooms are stylishly rustic, with wooden flooring throughout, and there's a tremendous open fireplace in the cosy reading lounge. Price includes breakfast. Closed April–Sept. 8

Posadas Altas Cumbres Lionel Terray 342 ☎02962/493060, ©altascumbres22@hotmail.com. Split-personality posada – the dark, older rooms are covered in tartan wallpaper and fading fast, while the airy en-suite doubles in the new extension are bright, comfortable and incredibly spacious – whose cosy lounge has a great fire for relaxing in front of. Surprisingly, the bubbly host runs a no-children policy. Price includes breakfast. ❻

Posada La Base Hensen 16 ⓣ02962/493031, ⓦwww.elchaltenpatagonia.com.ar. Some of the best-value rooms (singles, doubles and triples) in El Chaltén, several with mountain views. Its owners are hospitable, and it has shared kitchen facilities (one for every two rooms), cheap laundry and free video showings in the attic sitting room. Closed May–Sept. ❺

Eating and drinking

El Chaltén has several very good **restaurants** (although prices are fairly high), as well as a growing number of great little **bars** in which to ease your aches and pains at the end of the day. The best-value food is to be had from the **supermarkets** (see below), or from the *El Charito* kiosk on Güemes, which offers fine home-baked bread and delicious tarts. Alternatively, most hotels and restaurants make up **lunchboxes** for day-treks (from $20).

El Bodegón Cervecería San Martín s/n. Excellent microbrewery whose crisp, clean pilsners provide relief after a day on the trail. Genial staff and the occasional music session add greatly to the convivial atmosphere.

La Casita San Martín s/n. Cosy, ever-popular confitería that makes a fine meeting-place. Avoid the doughy pizzas and go for the good-value *milanesas* and home-made pasta dishes. Sometimes changes US dollars.

Los Cerros San Martín s/n ⓣ02962/493182. Delicious two- or three-course meals are thoughtfully presented and skilfully served in this hotel restaurant, which specializes in *cocina patagónica*, particularly lamb and trout dishes. The views – spectacular panoramas of the Río de las Vueltas – are equally impressive, visible through wall-length windows. Lunch from $80, dinner from $100, including non-alcoholic drinks.

Estepa Cerro Solo and Antonio Rojo. Warm, welcoming restaurant/bar in an adobe-style building lying in the shadow of Fitz Roy. Good selection of lamb dishes ($35), as well as hearty calzones and pizzas ($25) from the wood-fired oven. Bar open until 1am.

Fuegia Bistró San Martín 493. Located in the *Albergue Patagonia*, and deservedly popular with the hostel's clientele. Serves a decent range of Patagonian-influenced meat dishes (around $30), as well as one or two interesting vegetarian options.

Josh Aike Lago Desierto 104. Funky little *chocolatería* in a two-storey wood cabin with stand-out views of Fitz Roy from the upstairs window seat. Fresh orange juice, coffee, cakes and, of course, chocolate – home-made and in a mouth-watering variety of calorific flavours. The bitter-sweet hot chocolate is worth the visit alone.

Patagónicus Güemes and Madsen. Terrific range of fine pizzas – the best in town – served up at chunky wooden tables in a social, friendly atmosphere.

Ruca Mahuida Lionnel Terray 104 ⓣ02962/493018. Tiny cabin that's home to the most imaginative and, with only four tables, exclusive dining in El Chaltén. The menu – the largest in town – covers regional and international dishes (from $60 for a three-course meal), including surprising options such as venison ragout and vegetarian risotto. Sheepskin-covered benches complete the homely ambience.

Listings

Banks and exchange There are no banks or official money-changing facilities in El Chaltén, but some restaurants will change US dollars.

Books and maps Marcopolo, Güemes and Madsen.

Camping equipment El Volcán on Av Güemes sells camping gas; Viento Oeste, at San Martín 898, rents climbing and trekking gear, including tents ($15–20) and sleeping bags ($10).

Fuel YPF station at the beginning of Güemes.

Hospital Puesto Sanitario, De Agostini ⓣ02962/493033.

Internet access At several Internet cafés including Chaltén Travel, Güemes and Lago del Desierto (daily 9am–10pm; $2.50 per 15min).

Laundry Wash and Go, San Martín 351 (daily 9am–1pm & 3–9pm).

Pharmacy Farmacia del Cerro, H. Halvorsen.

Police Río de las Vueltas s/n ⓣ02962/493003.

Post office In the Comisión de Fomento, at Güemes 21.

Supermarket Stella Maris, Av San Martín s/n; El Gringuito, Calle Antonio Rojo s/n.

Telephone Several, including the *locutorio* next door to El Volcán on Güemes (Mon–Fri 9am–11pm).

Los Glaciares: the northern sector

Northern Parque Nacional Los Glaciares' claim to be the trekking capital of Argentina is justified, and the closer you get to the mountains, the clearer their grandeur becomes. Early mornings are the best time for views and photography, both for the light and the weather, since the westerly winds tend to pick up from about 11am, bringing the clouds with them.

Adequate outdoor clothing is essential at all times of the year, as snowstorms are possible even in midsummer. Unlike in Torres del Paine (see p.736), one of the beauties of this park is that those with limited time, or not in peak fitness, can still make worthwhile **day-walks** using El Chaltén as a base. The shortest of these walks is to **Chorrillo del Salto**, a plunging twenty-metre waterfall, framed by a moss-green cliff and adorned by the skeletons of drowned *lenga* trees, ten minutes off RP-23, 3km past *Campamento Madsen* north of town.

For those who enjoy camping, the quintessential three-day **Fitz Roy/ Cerro Torre loop** at the centre of the park makes a good option, and can be done in either direction. The advantage of going anticlockwise is that you avoid the steep climb up to Lagunas Madre y Hija and you have the wind at your back when returning to El Chaltén. However, the biggest gamble is always what the weather will be like around Cerro Torre, so if this unpredictable peak is visible on day one, you might like to head for it first. The longer interlocking circuit to the north will add at least another two days. There are, of course, a variety of alternatives for those with more time, including the trek to **Laguna Toro** and the **Paso del Viento**. A certain degree of flexibility is desirable in all cases, again due to the likelihood of the weather playing havoc with the views.

There is a **ban on lighting campfires** in the park, so if you need your food hot, make careful use of gas stoves. Pack out all rubbish, and minimalize your impact on this highly sensitive environment by sticking to the marked trails, camping only where permitted, using only biodegradable detergents and being as sparing as possible in their use and the use of toothpaste, not going to the toilet near water sources and burying all toilet waste.

The best trekking **map** available is the 1:50,000 *Monte Fitz Roy & Cerro Torre* published by Zagier & Urruty, on sale in town ($25), which includes a 1:100,000 scale map of the Lago del Desierto area. The informative *Trekking in Chaltén and Lago del Desierto* by Miguel A. Alonso ($35) is also good.

The Fitz Roy sector

The northernmost section of Parque Nacional Los Glaciares, the **Fitz Roy sector**, contains some of the most breathtakingly beautiful mountain peaks on the planet. Two concentric jaws of jagged teeth puncture the Patagonian sky with the 3405-metre incisor of **Monte Fitz Roy** at the centre of the massif. This sculpted peak was known to the Tehuelche as El Chaltén, "The Mountain that Smokes" or "The Volcano", due to the almost perpetual presence of a scarf of cloud attached to its summit. It is not inconceivable, however, that the Tehuelche were using the term in a rather more metaphorical sense to allude to the fiery pink colour that the rock walls turn when struck by the first light of dawn. Francisco Moreno saw fit to name the pagan summit after the evangelical captain of the *Beagle*, who, with Charles Darwin, had viewed the Andes from a distance, after having journeyed up the Río Santa Cruz by whaleboat to within 50km of Lago Argentino. Alongside Monte Fitz Roy rise **Cerro Poincenot** and **Aguja Saint-Exupéry**, whilst set behind them is the forbidding needle of **Cerro Torre**, a finger that stands in bold defiance of all the elements that the Hielo Continental Sur hurls against it.

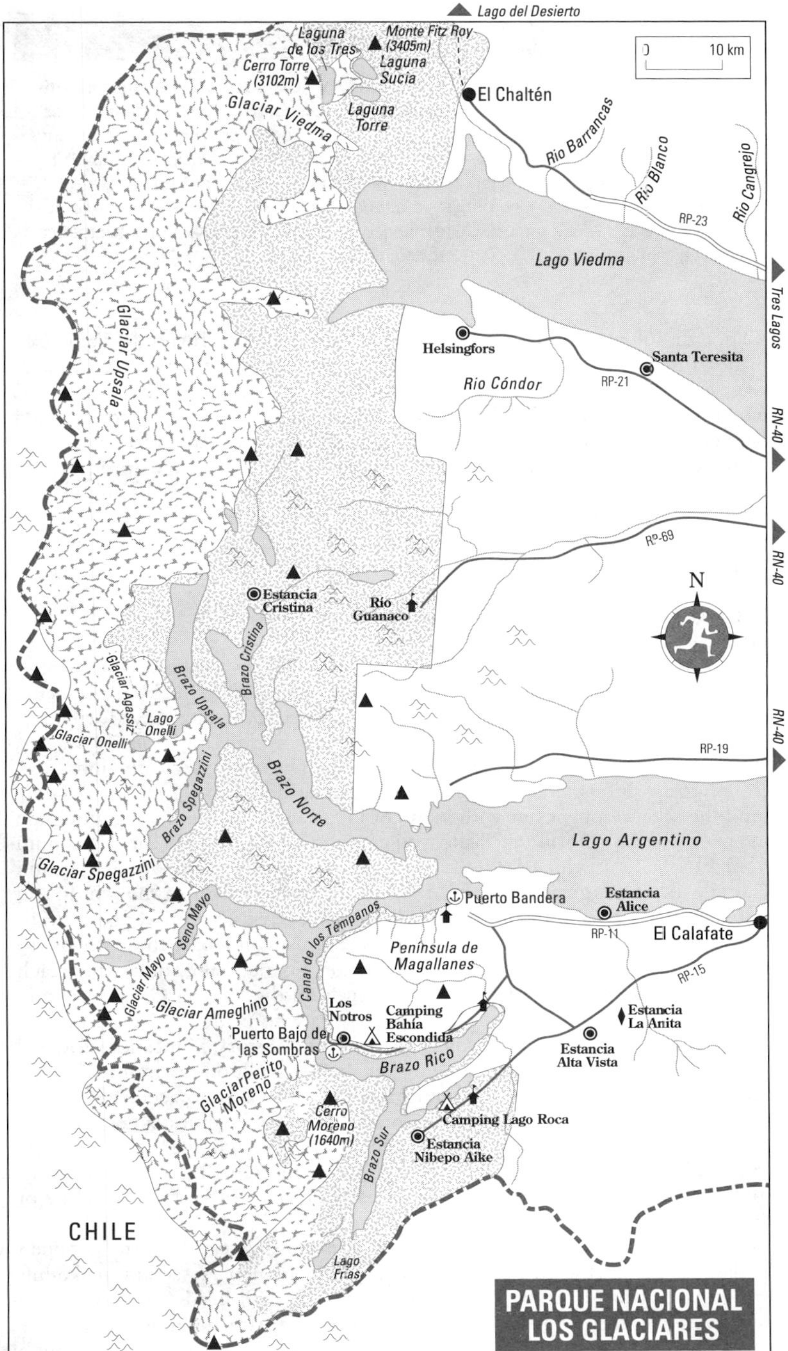
Lago del Desierto
0
10 km
Laguna de los Tres
Monte Fitz Roy (3405m)
Cerro Torre (3102m)
Laguna Sucia
Laguna Torre
El Chaltén
Glaciar Viedma
Río Barrancas
Río Blanco
Río Cangrejo
RP-23
Lago Viedma
Tres Lagos
Glaciar Upsala
Helsingfors
Santa Teresita
Río Cóndor
RP-21
RN-40
RP-69
Estancia Cristina
Río Guanaco
N
Brazo Upsala
Brazo Cristina
Glaciar Agassiz
Lago Onelli
Glaciar Onelli
Brazo Spegazzini
Brazo Norte
RP-19
Lago Argentino
Glaciar Spegazzini
Seno Mayo
Puerto Bandera
Estancia Alice
Canal de los Témpanos
RP-11
El Calafate
Península de Magallanes
RP-15
Glaciar Mayo
Glaciar Ameghino
Los Notros
Camping Bahía Escondida
Estancia La Anita
Puerto Bajo de las Sombras
Brazo Rico
Estancia Alta Vista
Glaciar Perito Moreno
Cerro Moreno (1640m)
Camping Lago Roca
Brazo Sur
Estancia Nibepo Aike
CHILE
Lago Frías
PARQUE NACIONAL LOS GLACIARES

The Hielo Continental Sur

Blanketing massive expanses of Parque Nacional Los Glaciares, the **Hielo Continental Sur** (Southern Patagonian Icecap) is the largest body of ice outside the poles. Estimates vary as to exactly how big it is but most studies put the figure at around 17,000 square kilometres, some seventy percent of which is in neighbouring Chile. What is certain is that it is suffering from the effects of global warming. In late 2003, the journal *Science Magazine* published a report claiming over sixteen cubic kilometres of ice was melting annually; Greenpeace puts the figure at 42 cubic kilometres annually, or "enough to fill 10,000 large football stadiums".

Though not as expansive or as famous globally as Chile's Torres del Paine (see p.736), this area still rivals it on most counts. Geologically, the two are in many ways sister parks, characterized by majestic spires of granite-like diorite, formed when the softer layers of rock that had covered these igneous intrusions eroded over eighteen million years (twelve million in the case of Paine) to reveal their polished bones. Like Paine, the Fitz Roy massif is afflicted by **unpredictable weather**, and many climbing expeditions have been foiled by the mountains' stubborn brew of sulky grey weather. When Darwin spoke of summits "occasionally peeping through their dusky envelope of clouds", he was conveying a generously pastoral effect.

El Chaltén to Laguna Capri, Campamento Poincenot and Laguna de los Tres

The trek from **El Chaltén to Laguna de los Tres** (13km; 3–4hr; 750m ascent), at the very foot of **Monte Fitz Roy**, is one of the park's most scenic trails, and can be hiked either as a return trip or part of the Fitz Roy/Torre loop. The starting point for this classic hike is the house overlooking *Camping Madsen*, at the northern end of Avenida San Martín. The path is clearly indicated, climbing up through the wooded slopes of Cerro Rosado and Cerro León, until the scenery opens out with views of Fitz Roy. After heading up alongside the ravine of the Chorillo del Salto, you come to a turn-off left (1hr–1hr 30min from El Chaltén), which leads after ten minutes to the **campsite** at **Laguna Capri** – there are great views, but the site is rather exposed to the winds, and water from the lake should be boiled or treated. Better, if you have the time, to push on down the main path, crossing one stream just past the turn-off to Laguna Madre, and another brook, the Chorrillo del Salto, until you reach **Campamento Poincenot** (1hr–1hr 15min from the Laguna Capri turn-off), named after one of the team of French climbers who made the victorious first ascent of Fitz Roy in 1952. According to the official story, Poincenot drowned whilst trying to cross the Río Fitz Roy before the assault on the mountain even took place, although another rumour hinted that this was no accident, but the work of a cuckolded estancia owner, enraged by his wife's infidelities with the dashing Gallic mountaineer. The campsite covers a sprawling area, set amongst *lenga* and *ñire* woodland on the eastern bank of the Río Blanco. Choose your spot well and you won't need to get out of your tent to see the rosy blaze of dawn on the cliffs of Fitz Roy.

From *Campamento Poincenot*, follow the crisscrossing paths to the wooden bridge that spans the main current of the Río Blanco. A second, makeshift bridge takes you to the far bank, from where the path heads up through the woods, passing the refuges of the **Río Blanco campsite** (intended for the use of climbers), before pushing on past the tree line. The next section is tough going as the eroded path ascends a steep gradient, but mercifully it's not long before you come to the top of the ridge, cross a boggy meadow and then climb the final hurdle: a moraine ridge that hides a breathtaking panorama – perhaps the finest in the entire park – on the other side.

You now stand in the cirque of the rich, navy-blue **Laguna de los Tres** (1hr–1hr 15min from *Campamento Poincenot*) fed by a concertinaed glacier and ringed by a giant's crown of granite peaks, including Aguja Saint-Exupéry (named after Antoine de Saint-Exupéry, who drew on his experiences as a pioneer of Patagonian aviation when writing the minor classic, *Vol de Nuit*), Cerro Poincenot, Fitz Roy and a host of other spikes. Round the small rocky

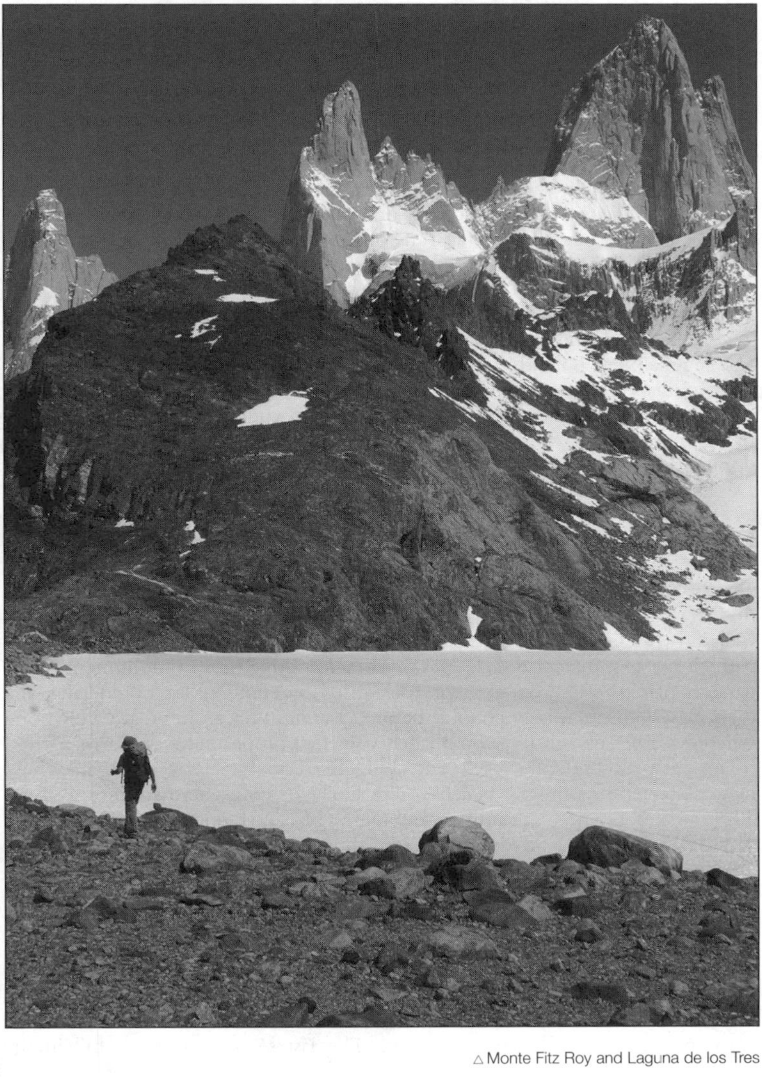

△ Monte Fitz Roy and Laguna de los Tres

outcrop to the left for even more impressive views: this ridge separates the basins of Laguna de los Tres and Laguna Sucia, some 200m below the level of the first lake. The **Glaciar Río Blanco**, hanging above Laguna Sucia, periodically sheds scales of ice and snow, which, though they look tiny at this distance, reveal their true magnitude by the ear-splitting reports they make as they hit the surface of the lake. Retrace your steps and follow the path on the western (right-hand) bank of the Río Blanco (40min from the *Río Blanco* campsite).

Lagunas Madre y Hija trail

From *Campamento Poincenot*, there are two other trails: one crosses the Río Blanco and follows its western bank northward towards the Río Eléctrico and Piedra del Fraile (see p.714), while the path from **Campamento Poincenot to Campamento De Agostini** (6km; 2–3hr; 100m descent), at the eastern end of Laguna Torre, leads past **Lagunas Madre y Hija** (Mother and Daughter Lagoons); to do this, you'll need to double back towards Laguna Capri a little way, before finding the signposted route.

Walk due south of the campsite to the Chorrillo del Salto and follow the stream's eastern bank until you see a signpost directing horse-riders left and hikers right. Take the right turning, which leads across a little bridge, and follow the boardwalk as it curves east to the turn-off to Laguna Madre, less than five minutes away. The route past the two lagoons makes for gentle walking and is easy to follow, pushing through knee-high bushes, and after a few hundred metres rising to and passing through the young forest to avoid the swampy ground for the most part. Look out for Upland Geese (*cauquenes*), which like to graze by the lakeshore. The path curls round to the right, squeezing between the far end of Laguna Hija and Laguna Nieta (Granddaughter Lagoon), and continues through mixed pasture and woodland before coming to the lip of the valley of Río Fitz Roy. Here, the path descends the steep slope and, if you look to your right, you may get your first glimpses of Cerro Torre through the *lenga* forest. Emerging from the trees, the slope levels out and you link up with the path from El Chaltén to *Campamento De Agostini* (see below), a forty-minute walk away.

El Chaltén to Campamento De Agostini and Laguna Torre

The most scenic route from **El Chaltén to Laguna Torre** (10km; 2hr 15min–3hr; 250m ascent), the silty lake in which – on perfect days – the imposing peak of **Cerro Torre** (3102m) is reflected, is reached by turning off Avenida San Martín by Viento Oeste, picking up the marked path at the base of the hill. This path climbs past the eerie skeleton of a large *lenga* tree (now a monument to the dangers of cigarettes), on to some rocks used by climbers for bouldering, and then weaves through hilly country before arriving, after an hour, at a viewpoint where, weather permitting, you'll catch your first proper view of Cerro Torre.

The path subsequently levels out along the Río Fitz Roy valley, in whose ragged stands of southern beech you're likely to come across wrens and the Thorn-tailed Rayadito, a diminutive foraging bird. A signposted turn-off on the right leads to Lagunas Madre y Hija (see above), which you'll need to return to if hiking the central circuit in clockwise fashion. This path soon starts to climb a steep, wooded hillside, before levelling out, running along the right-hand (eastern) side of the shallow lakes and continuing on to *Campamento Poincenot* (1hr 30min–2hr 15min from turn-off).

Sticking on the trail towards Laguna Torre, the path climbs to another viewpoint, before dropping down onto the valley floor – covered here in puddles that, in good weather, mirror Cerro Torre. You'll see an area that burned in 2003, apparently due to a discarded cigarette. The last section crosses a hill in the middle of the valley and a small stream before coming to blustery *Campamento De Agostini*, the closest **campsite** to the mountain for trekkers. Occupying a beautiful wooded site on the banks of the Río Fitz Roy, it also acts as the base camp for climbers and can get very busy (especially in Jan), so plan accordingly. The only good views of Cerro Torre from the campsite are from a rocky outcrop at the back of the wood, where there's one extremely exposed pitch. Otherwise, follow the path alongside the river, which brings you after about ten minutes to

The Cerro Torre controversy

Even members of the French team that first ascended Fitz Roy in 1952 thought that summitting **Cerro Torre** was an impossible task. The altitude wasn't the problem – at 3102m, it wouldn't reach even halfway up some Andean peaks – neither was the type of rock it was made out of – crystalline igneous diorite is perfect for climbing. Rather, it was the shape and the formidable weather: a terrifying spire dropping sheer for almost 2km into glacial ice, battered by winds of up to 200kph and temperatures so extreme that ice more than 20cm thick can form on rock faces. Not only that, but the peculiar glaciers – "mushrooms" of ice – which build up on the mountain's summit often shear off, depositing huge blocks of ice onto climbers below.

The Italian alpinist **Cesare Maestri** became the first to make a serious attempt on the summit. In 1959, he and Austrian climber **Toni Egger** worked their way up the northern edge. Caught in a storm, Egger was swept off the face and killed by an avalanche. Maestri somehow made it to the bottom, and announced that he had **conquered the summit** with Egger. The world, however, demanded proof, something that Maestri could not furnish – the camera, he claimed, lay entombed with Egger.

Angered by the doubters, Maestri vowed to return. This he did, in 1970, and it was clear that he meant business. Among the expedition equipment lay his secret weapon: a compressor weighing over 150kg for drilling bolts into the unforgiving rock. Torre couldn't resist in the face of such a determined onslaught, and Maestri's expedition reached the summit, making very sure that photos were snapped on top. A stake had been driven through Torre's Gothic heart.

Or had it? The climbing world was riven by dispute. Were Maestri's tactics in keeping with the aesthetic code of climbing or had the use of a machine invalidated his efforts? Did this represent a true ascent? On top of this, Maestri's photos revealed that although he had reached the top of the rock, he had not climbed the ice mushroom – the icing that topped the cake. The monster would not lie down and die.

Enter **Casimiro Ferrari**, another Italian climber. Using guile where Maestri had favoured strong-arm tactics, Ferrari sneaked up on the beast from behind, from the Hielo Continental Sur. In the space of two days, Ferrari achieved his goal, and, elatedly, his team brought down photos of them atop the summit, ice mushroom and all.

So, almost thirty years on, who does the climbing community take as the first to conquer the mountain? Toni Egger's body was recovered in 1975, but no camera was found with him (he is now commemorated in the name of a jagged peak alongside Cerro Torre and a simple chapel in El Chaltén). The compressor drill used by Maestri in 1970 still hangs near the top, a testament to his subjection of the mountain. And, despite the controversy at the time, the bolts drilled by Maestri are used to this day, forming the most common route to the summit.

Nevertheless, this irony is a bittersweet triumph for Maestri, who feels he has been cursed. In the 1990s, he reputedly voiced his hatred for the mountain, claiming that he wanted it razed to the ground. History has added its own weight to that of the doubters. The mountain has been scaled by routes of tremendous technical difficulty by modern climbers with modern equipment, culminating in the Slovenians Silvo Karo and Janez Jeglic's ascent of the south wall in 1988. No one, however, has ever been able to repeat the route that Maestri claimed he and Egger took in 1959.

the moraine at the end of **Laguna Torre**. On top of the moraine, you can gaze at the granite needles of Cerro Torre, **Aguja Egger** (2900m), and **Cerro Standhardt** (2800m). Here, too, you'll find a **cable crossing** of the river, used by climbers that go ice-trekking on **Glaciar Torre**. Although it looks easy enough to cross without a harness, be warned: a girl drowned here in 1998 while attempting to do just that – gusts of wind can be sudden and fierce.

You can get closer to the mountain by walking for forty minutes along the path that runs parallel to the northern shore of Laguna Torre to the **Mirador Maestri** lookout point, passing en route an expedition hut that contains moving commemorative dedications to climbers who never quite succeeded in their attempts on the various peaks (note that this is not a recognized camping spot). The *mirador* provides superb views of Cerro Torre and Cerro Grande, and the incredible peak-dotted ridge that runs between them.

Río Eléctrico, Piedra del Fraile and beyond

The area to the north of Fitz Roy, just outside the national park, makes for rewarding trekking and can be linked to the Fitz Roy/Torre circuit. Although much of this is private land, you are welcome as long as you observe the same regulations stipulated by the park and camp only in designated sites.

To get to the start of the trek from **RP-23 to Piedra del Fraile** (6km; 1hr 45min–2hr 15min; 80m ascent), take one of the buses for Lago del Desierto (daily 7am, 8.30am & 3pm; $20; see p.716) and get off right next to the bridge over the **Río Eléctrico**, a tempestuous river; this saves having to struggle for five to six hours against the prevailing winds that sweep down the valley from the north. The path starts to the left of the bridge, although its first section is imperilled every time the river is in spate. Soon you peel away from the river and, following the fairly inconspicuous cairns, cross the flat gravel floor of the Río Blanco valley. On the other side of the valley, the path joins the one heading south to Laguna Piedras Blancas and *Campamento Poincenot* (see p.710). Rather than turn south, aim right of the ridge ahead, into the valley of the Río Eléctrico, where you enter an enchanting, sub-Antarctic woodland, interspersed with grassy glades. Cross a brook and fifteen minutes further on you come to a gate in a ragged fence, followed shortly by another gate in another, equally dishevelled, fence. From the second gate, head right, towards the Río Eléctrico, and follow its bank. After approximately thirty-five minutes' gentle walk, you emerge from the woodland to be greeted with a terrific view of **Glaciar Marconi**; Piedra del Fraile is just five minutes' further on.

At **Piedra del Fraile**, you'll find the *Los Troncos refugio* and campsite ($14 per tent), scenically set alongside the swift-flowing Río Eléctrico and sheltered by a vast erratic boulder – the *piedra* of the name. The *fraile* (friar or priest) was Padre de Agostini (1883–1960), a Salesian priest who was one of Patagonia's most avid early mountaineers and explorers, and who lends his name to the campsite at Laguna Torre (see p.712). He was the first person to survey the area, and chose this site for his camp. There is a day-use *refugio* with kitchen and possibly the hottest shower in Patagonia. The cosy restaurant hut serves doorstep wedges of toasted sandwiches, unpretentious but filling meals, and chocolate and alcohol.

Two worthwhile treks lead from here, though you'll be charged $10 to continue your journey on through private land: the first, from **Piedra del Fraile to Glaciar Marconi** (10km return; 5hr–6hr 30min return; 35m ascent), takes you to the foot of the glacier, fording the Río Pollone and passing through the blasted scenery on the southern shore of Lago Eléctrico. There are fine views of the northern flank of Fitz Roy, especially from the Río Pollone valley, but be warned that the trail is unmarked once you cross the river; keep tight to the shore of Lago Eléctrico as it curves right, then continue due north past *Campamento La Playita*, following the Río Eléctrico Superior upstream to Laguna Marconi and its glacier. Glaciar Marconi itself sweeps down off the **Hielo Continental Sur** (see box, p.710), and forms the most frequently used point of access for expeditions heading onto this frigid expanse, by way of the windy **Paso Marconi** (1500m).

The second hike, from **Piedra del Fraile to the Paso del Cuadrado** (6km return; 7–9hr return; 1200m ascent), involves a much more difficult climb and should only be attempted by those with comprehensive mountaineering experience. From the camp, cross the small stream on the south side, walk through a wood and strike towards the gap between two streams, to the right of the wooded hillside. The path zigzags steeply up, though eventually levels out. After one-and-a-half to two hours, you pass an oddly shaped boulder with a tiny pool just above it and then the path peters out further up, once it reaches the scree. From here on you must make your own course, keeping the main stream to your right. When you reach the terminal moraine of the glacier, ford the river and work your way around the right-hand side of the col, two to two-and-a-half hours from the boulder. Cross the exposed area of rock on your right and then make the tiring thirty-minute climb up the snow to the pass, which is not immediately obvious but lies in the middle of the ridge. Expect a ferocious blast of wind at the top of Paso del Cuadrado (approximately 1700m), but hold onto your headgear and look out at one of the most dramatic views you're likely to come across in Patagonia. Weather permitting, you'll be able to see Fitz Roy's north face, across to the steeple of Cerro Torre, and down, across deeply crevassed glaciers, to the peaks of Aguja and Cerro Pollone, named after Padre de Agostini's home village in the Italian Alps.

Piedra del Fraile to Campamento Poincenot

You can head back east from **Piedra del Fraile to Campamento Poincenot** (11km; 3hr–3hr 30min; 200m ascent) to join up with the Fitz Roy/Torre loop. The path follows the Vallé Río Blanco south but can be difficult to pick up due to a number of false trails created by meandering cattle. Upon leaving the woods and emerging into the valley plain of the Río Blanco, head back towards RP-23 until you reach a stream (about 20min). Turn right and follow its course until you see a faint path that heads south along the tree line. After about half an hour, you enter back into the national park and eventually pick up the line of under-ambitious cairns that mark the path: follow these until you come to the confluence of the Piedras Blancas stream and Río Blanco.

This area is strewn with chunks of granite. It's worth making a short detour right (west) up this valley, scrambling across the boulders to see the **Glaciar Piedras Blancas** tumbling into its murky lake, backed by a partial view of Fitz Roy (20–30min one way). Otherwise, ford the Piedras Blancas stream a little way up from where it meets the Río Blanco and cross the moraine dump to regain the trail. From this point, it's less than an hour's walk along the deteriorated if fairly easy path to *Campamento Poincenot* (see p.710).

Laguna Toro and the Paso del Viento

South of El Chaltén, the trek from the **national park visitors' centre to Laguna Toro** (15km; 6–7hr; 460m ascent) affords views of both Fitz Roy and Cerro Torre as it wends its way through the valley of the Río Túnel and on towards the silty glacial lake of Laguna Toro. You need to register at the visitors' centre and ascertain what conditions are like before starting out. Park authorities will tell you there is no marked trail and you'll have to prove to them you're competent with a compass and are properly equipped if you want to go further. The route forms part of a more ambitious seven- to ten-day loop that crosses the **Paso del Viento** (1550m) to the treacherous Hielo Continental Sur, and comes out over Paso Marconi to the north (see p.715), a route that is suitable only for organized, properly equipped expeditions – for more information, contact Fitz Roy Expediciones (see box, p.704).

Lago del Desierto

Lago del Desierto (Lake of the Desert), 37km north of El Chaltén, is far less forbidding than its name suggests, being an alpine-style lake, surrounded by forested mountains. The area has opened to tourism considerably in the past few years, which in some ways is a shame, since its population of endangered *huemules* is bound to suffer. Day-trips are possible, allowing you to make the short walk from the southern end of the lake up to the **mirador** at **Laguna del Huemul** (1hr one way; $10 toll), with its excellent views of Fitz Roy. However, it's better to allow at least two days, so you can trek some of the longer trails, such as the eleven-kilometre track that runs along the eastern lakeshore to the Refugio Lago del Desierto at the northern end (5hr; $15).

Lago del Desierto became one of the *causes célèbres* of Argentine/Chilean **border disputes**, bringing the two countries to the brink of war in the 1960s. In 1995, an international commission awarded the area to Argentina, but the issue had repercussions: the Chilean military felt itself humiliated, and pushed claims over the Hielo Continental Sur. Eventually, in 1999, the Argentine Senate ratified a treaty conceding sovereignty over a chunk of land in the southeast of the Parque Nacional Los Glaciares, thus resolving the last outstanding border conflict. With better relations the norm nowadays, those with a spirit of adventure can **hike into Chile**. Get an exit stamp from the police at the northern end of Lago del Desierto and walk north to the border (2hr), from where it's another four hours or so to the Chilean *carabineros* at Lago O'Higgins; *Quetru*, the **boat** across the lake to Villa O'Higgins (Wed & Sat 5.30pm; 5hr; CH$17,5000), leaves from Puerto Candelario Mancilla, just south of here. You can **camp** near the port, at the *Estancia Candelario Mancilla*, on the lake's edge ($10 per person).

Practicalities

Las Lengas and El Huemel **minibuses** leave El Chaltén for **Lago del Desierto** at 7am, 8.30am and 3pm ($35; 1hr); a privately owned boat, *Viedma*, connects the two ends of the lake, running from the Puerta Sur in the south ($60). Several companies in El Chaltén, including Fitzroy Expediciones (see box, p.704), run El Chaltén–Villa O'Higgins trips, leaving Tuesdays and Fridays at 8.30am and arriving in Villa O'Higgins at 9pm the following day ($300, including all transportation, a guide and accommodation at *Estancia Candelario Mancilla*).

Lago Viedma and on to El Calafate

Just south of the turn-off to El Chaltén, RN-40, once again a *ripio* road, passes a track leading 2km to the shores of **Lago Viedma**, a lake named after the colonizer and explorer Antonio Viedma, the founder of Floridablanca (see p.657) and the first white man to see the body of water: looking for wood to build his new settlement, he explored its shores in 1782.

Fifteen kilometres further on, RN-40 crosses the **Río La Leona**, the sizeable, fast-flowing river that drains Lago Viedma. On the south side of the bridge is one of RN-40's original **wayside inns**, *Hotel La Leona*, worth stopping at for a slice of home-made lemon meringue and apple pie. Don't miss the opportunity to play the *juego de la argolla*, an old gaucho drinking game where you take turns to land a ring that's attached by a string to the ceiling over a hook mounted on the wall opposite: the first person to succeed wins a drink (try a sweet and inexpensive *caña ombú* or *caña quemada*).

Hotel La Leona marks the turn-off for two tourist estancias with tremendously privileged positions, occupying land on the southern shore of Lago Viedma. The extensive sheep-farming establishment of *Santa Teresita* (Ⓣ&Ⓕ02902/491732; ⑧ including breakfast; closed April–Nov), 48km from RN-40, has rooms for up to five people in the old *casco*, with fantastic views of Fitz Roy and Cerro Torre. A further 25km on, at the western end of the route, exclusive *Helsingfors* (in Buenos Aires Ⓣ011/4315-1222, Ⓦwww.helsingfors.com.ar; US$550 full board plus excursions and transfer from El Calafate; closed March–Sept), within the confines of the Parque Nacional Los Glaciares, is a plush estancia dedicated to upper-end tourism.

Back on RN-40 to **El Calafate**, the road shadows the course of the Río La Leona, passing beneath some fascinating desiccated crags on the far side, before coming to Lago Viedma's bigger sister, Lago Argentino. The RN-40 recrosses the Río La Leona at the point where it enters the lake, then over a bridge spanning the Río Santa Cruz, the river that drains this entire, massive basin; 5km from here, smooth and quick RP-11 leads 32km to El Calafate.

El Calafate

EL CALAFATE is the base for seeing **Glaciar Perito Moreno** and the other world-class attractions that occupy the southern sector of Parque National Los Glaciares and, as such, is one of the country's most-visited tourist destinations. These attractions cluster around **Lago Argentino**, the largest of all exclusively Argentine lakes, and the third biggest in all South America, with a surface area of 1600 square kilometres – it's so deep that its temperature remains almost constant at 8°C year round. Catch it on a cloudy day and you could be looking at a tarnished expanse of molten lead, while when the weather is brighter the lake soaks up the light of the Patagonian sky to reflect a glorious hue of polarized blue. Most of Lago Argentino is surrounded by harsh, rolling steppe, but the scenery becomes more interesting around its western tendrils: transitional scrub and southern beech woodland press up on its shores, and the snow-capped mountains that fringe the **Hielo Continental Sur** rear up behind.

Nowhere in Argentina has been more affected by the influx of tourism following the 2001 devaluation than here. In the mid-1980s, El Calafate was little more than a single street. By early 2007, there were over 140 places and more were being built to help cope with over 150,000 annual visitors. The

The calafate bush

Calafate, the indigenous name for what is known in English as the box-leaved barberry (*Berberis buxifolia*), is Patagonia's most famous plant. The bushes are protected by vindictive thorns, and the wood contains a substance known as *berberina*, which possesses medicinal properties and is used as a textile dye. From late October onwards, the bushes are covered with exquisite little bright yellow flowers. Depending on where they're growing, the berries mature between December and March. Once used by the indigenous populations for dye, they're nowadays often employed in appetizing home-made preserves. Sampling some on your toast should ensure you come back some day – if the oft-quoted saying that, "*El que come el calafate, volverá*" ("He who eats the calafate will return") is to be believed.

resulting space and labour shortage has led to considerable inflation, which you will find reflected in hotel and restaurant prices.

The best **times to visit** are spring and autumn (Nov to mid-Dec, and March–Easter), when there's a nice balance between having enough visitors to keep services running but not too many for the place to seem overcrowded. The advantage of high season (mid-Oct to Easter) is that you're sure to meet up with many friendly and exuberant Argentine holidaymakers. If you're planning to arrive any time outside winter, you're advised to book accommodation, and especially flights or car rental, well in advance.

Arrival and information

Calafate's international **airport** lies 15km east of town; in high season, there's a weekday flight to and from Puerto Natales in Chile (for tickets, contact DAP in Punta Arenas on ⓣ0056 61 223340 or at ⓦwww.aeroviasdap.cl). From the airport, taxis run into town ($28) or you can take the Aerobus ($10). All **buses** stop at the terminal on Avenida Julio Roca, on the hillside one block above the main thoroughfare, Avenida Libertador, to which it's connected by a flight of steps. The helpful **tourist office** is in the terminal (daily 8am–10pm; ⓣ02902/491090, ⓦwww.elcalafate.gov.ar); it has a list of hotels with daily availability and can help you track down a room in a *casa de familia* if everywhere else is full. The **national park information office**, Libertador 1302 (Mon–Fri 8am–7pm, Sat & Sun 9.30am–7pm; ⓣ02902/491545, ⓔapnglaciares@cotecal.com.ar), has some maps and sells fishing licences.

The town's biggest festival, the **Festival del Lago Argentino**, takes place in the week leading up to February 15, with music and a free *asado* on the final day.

Accommodation

Accommodation prices are considerably reduced in low season, when upper-end hotels become much more affordable. **Camping** options include the pleasant *Camping Municipal*, José Pantín s/n (ⓣ02902/493422; $10 per person), with restaurant and sparkling shower block, conveniently located one block behind the YPF station at the entrance to town; and *Jorgito Camping*, Gob. Moyano 943 (ⓣ02902/491323; $10 per person), in the owner's garden.

If you don't care to stay in the town itself, there are nearby tourist estancias, camping at Lago Roca (ⓣ02902/499500; $12 per person; two- and four-bed cabins ❸–❺; restaurant and bike hire) and, near Glaciar Perito Moreno, a luxury hotel, *Los Notros*, and a busy campsite, *Bahía Escondido* (ⓣ02902/493053; $15 per person, book in advance in Jan).

Hostels

Albergue Las Carretas Libertador 537 ⓣ02902/491015, ⓔalbeguelascarretas@hotmail.com. Small hostel near the Museo Regional with clean and airy dorms and some doubles (❺). The communal salon is light and bright, with gleaming wooden floors and spit-polished benches, and there are cooking facilities, laundry and lunchboxes ($20–30) provided daily. Dorms $20.

Albergue Mochilero 25 de Mayo 286 ⓣ02902/492006, ⓦwww.alberguenochilero.com.ar. Relaxing place with a simple social area, large kitchen and range of compact, comfortable rooms: four- and six-bed dorms and en-suite doubles and triples. Cheap laundry. Dorms $20–25, rooms ❺

America del Sur Puerto Deseado s/n ⓣ02902/493525, ⓦwww.americahostel.com.ar. Well-designed, spacious and friendly place with sensational views of Lago Argentino. Knowledgeable owners can help organize a wide range of trips. Four-bed dorms and doubles have under-floor heating. Free shuttle bus into centre. Dorms $30, rooms ❻

Calafate Hostel Gob. Moyano 1226 ⓣ02902/492450, ⓦwww.calafatehostels.com. Huge but friendly cabin-style hostel with kitchen,

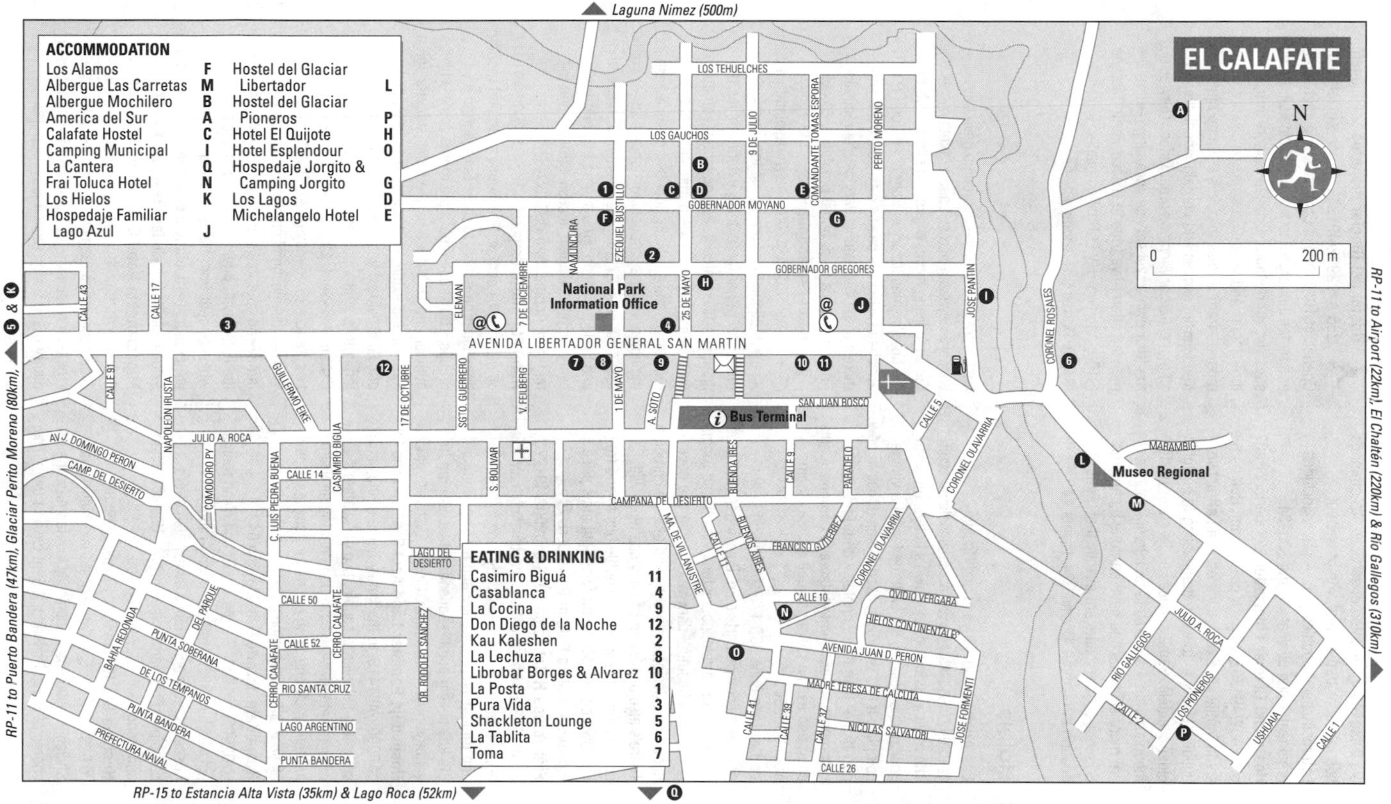
EL CALAFATE
ACCOMMODATION
Los Alamos F
Albergue Las Carretas M
Albergue Mochilero B
America del Sur A
Calafate Hostel C
Camping Municipal I
La Cantera Q
Frai Toluca Hotel N
Los Hielos K
Hospedaje Familiar Lago Azul J
Hostel del Glaciar Libertador L
Hostel del Glaciar Pioneros P
Hotel El Quijote H
Hotel Esplendour O
Hospedaje Jorgito & Camping Jorgito G
Los Lagos D
Michelangelo Hotel E
EATING & DRINKING
Casimiro Biguá 11
Casablanca 4
La Cocina 9
Don Diego de la Noche 12
Kau Kaleshen 2
La Lechuza 8
Librobar Borges & Alvarez 10
La Posta 1
Pura Vida 3
Shackleton Lounge 5
La Tablita 6
Toma 7
Laguna Nimez (500m)
RP-11 to Airport (22km), El Chaltén (220km) & Río Gallegos (310km)
RP-15 to Estancia Alta Vista (35km) & Lago Roca (52km)
RP-11 to Puerto Bandera (47km), Glaciar Perito Moreno (80km), 5 & K
National Park Information Office
Bus Terminal
Museo Regional
AVENIDA LIBERTADOR GENERAL SAN MARTIN
N
0
200 m

big living room and Internet services. Accommodation is in four-bed dorms, with or without bathrooms, and doubles (5) – prices include breakfast. Open all year. Dorms $30–34.

Hostel del Glaciar Libertador Av Libertador 587 ⓣ02902/491792, ⓦwww.glaciar.com. Run by the same family as *Hostel Pioneros*, in an attractive building closer to town, and appealing to a slightly older clientele. Same services as its sister hostel, though dorms – set around an internal courtyard – are more spacious and have en-suite bathrooms. Superior double rooms are exactly that. Central heating throughout. Dorms $34, rooms 7

Hostel del Glaciar Pioneros Los Pioneros 255 ⓣ02902/491243, ⓦwww.glaciar.com. Opened in 1987, this is Calafate's original hostel, and by far the largest in town. Multilingual, friendly staff, decent restaurant, cheap laundry, bright, three- four- and six-bed dorms, excellent en-suite rooms – from singles to quads – kitchen facilities, free Internet access and bargain lunchboxes ($14) all make *Glaciar Pioneros* great value. They also run their own travel service, including recommended alternative trips to Glaciar Perito Moreno ($158) and two-day El Chaltén glacier trekking ($428). Dorms $31, rooms 5–6

Hotels

Los Alamos Gob. Moyano and Bustillo ⓣ02902/491144, ⓦwww.posadalosalamos.com. The most luxurious of the town's hotels, modestly posing as a posada, but with the feel of a village complex. It has wood-panelled rooms (those in new part bigger than those in old), with bright bathrooms, an excellent restaurant, gardens, tennis court and even a Lilliputian golf course. Rooms from US$250.

La Cantera Calle 306 173 ⓣ02902/495998, ⓦwww.lacanteraaparts.com. Enjoying tremendous views of Lago Argentino, tastefully furnished rooms are set in a beautiful dark-wood cabin and have huge beds, designer couches and plush bathrooms. There's also a sizeable balcony scattered with comfy loungers and a free shuttle bus to and from the town centre. Minimum two-night stay; price includes transfers to/from the airport. 9

Frai Toluca Hotel Perón 1016 ⓣ02902/491773 or 491593, ⓔfraitolucahotel@cotecal.com.ar. Popular but quiet hotel with tidy rooms (doubles and triples), an airy lounge and reading room and – the key selling point – sensational views from its vantage point above town. Closed Easter–Aug. 7

Hospedaje Familiar Lago Azul Perito Moreno 83 ⓣ02902/491419. In the family home of the charming Echeverría couple, two of Calafate's original settlers, who have been putting up visitors in their spick-and-span rooms for decades. Open all year. $25 per person.

Hospedaje Jorgito Gob. Moyano 943 ⓣ02902/491323. Simple, bright and clean rooms (shared bathrooms only) in a long-running *hospedaje*; the eponymous owner also offers camping in his garden (see p.718). Use of kitchen and living room. $27 per person.

Hostería Los Hielos René Favaloro 3968 ⓣ02902/492965, ⓦwww.hosterialoshielos.com. Stylishly rustic hotel, scenically located near the shores of Bahía Redonda, 2.5km west of town. The light, attractive en-suite bedrooms have bay-window views out across Lago Argentino – as does the snug living room, where you can thumb through the hotel's small library in front of an open fire. The attached restaurant has its own *asado* pit, and there's a spa with sauna. Very helpful reception. Price includes a fresh buffet breakfast. 8–9

Hotel Esplendour Perón 1143 ⓣ011/5217-5700, ⓦwww.esplendour.com. Sharp boutique hotel on the hill that overlooks town. The rather forebidding exterior belies the light, sun-filled interior: a huge lobby – complete with antler chandeliers – a minimalist bar/restaurant, and rustically cool bedrooms awash in the colours of the Patagonian steppe. Corner suites (US$250) have 270-degree views of El Calafate and Lago Argentino. Free shuttle bus into town every 30min. Disabled access. Closed June to mid-Aug. Rooms from US$235.

Hotel El Quijote Gregores 1155 ⓣ02902/491017, ⓦwww.hielos.com.ar. Excellently sited and modern hotel catering mainly to older European tour groups. The double and triple rooms come with minibar and TV but are on the small side, though a forthcoming extension should push down their prices. Breakfast (included) is served next door at the hotel's appropriately named restaurant, *Sancho*. Closed May–Sept. 9

Los Lagos 25 de Mayo 120 ⓣ02902/491170, ⓦwww.loslagoshotel.com.ar. Extremely welcoming, family-run spot that's among the most affordable of the hotels with private bathrooms. Pleasant rooms, which benefit from the quiet location, are on the larger side, particularly the plusher ones in the new extension. Price includes breakfast. 5–6

Michelangelo Hotel Gob. Moyano and Cmte. Espora ⓣ02902/491045, ⓔmichelangelhotel@cotecal.com.ar. Heavy, 1970s log-cabin-style architecture outside, but comfortable interior, with plenty of hot water. Closed May–Sept. 7

Los Notros 80km west of El Calafate, in Buenos Aires ⓣ011/4814-3934, ⓦwww.losnotros.com. The only hotel close to the Glaciar Perito Moreno (and with views of its left flank). Tastefully designed "rustic" wooden lodge built on private land, with an excellent (if expensive) restaurant that prepares regional specialities. Much cheaper if you book in advance: check out the online offers on two- to four-day all-inclusive packages with full board, excursions and pick-up from the airport. Closed June to mid-Sept. US$800 per person full board including excursions for the minimum two-night stay.

Estancias

The office of *Estancias de Santa Cruz*, Libertador 1215 (ⓣ02902/492858, ⓦwww.estanciasdesantacruz.com) has leaflets and maps and can take reservations (see box, p.689).

Alice also known as *El Galpón del Glaciar* ⓣ02902/491793, ⓦwww.estanciaalice.com.ar. *Alice*, on the way to Puerto Bandera, 22km west of El Calafate, is nice enough, a welcoming homestead in a beautiful area, but high numbers of day-trippers may take off some of the charm. It also has an office in town at Libertador 1015 that books excursions to see agricultural displays such as sheep-shearing. Closed May–Sept. 8

Alta Vista 35km west of El Calafate on RP-15 ⓣ02902/491247 or in Buenos Aires ⓣ011/4343-8883, ⓦwww.hosteriaaltavista.com.ar. One of the more exclusive and expensive of the Santa Cruz tourist estancias, playing host to those seeking discretion and peace. Airy, intimate rooms have tasteful, restrained decor; the service is non-intrusive and professional; and there's a delightful garden filled with lupins. The excellent restaurant serves simple, classically prepared regional cuisine. Closed May–Sept. US$365 full board including excursions.

Cristina ⓣ02902/491034 or in Buenos Aires ⓣ011/4814-3934, ⓦwww.estanciacristina.com. Superbly located estancia hidden at the end of remote Bahía Cristina, accessible only by boat. Top-notch accommodation – in spacious, homely rooms benefiting from peak-framed views across the surrounding *meseta* – is part of a two-day package, which includes a boat trip to Glacier Upsala and hiking or horse-riding excursions. Can also be visited on a day-trip to Upsala (see p.726). Closed June to mid-Sept. US$790 full board including boat transfer and excursions.

Nibepo Aike ⓣ02966/422626, ⓦwww.nibepoaike.com.ar. Beautiful farmhouse dating from early last century set in a stunning valley south of Lago Roca, 60km from El Calafate. Delicious meals are prepared with home-grown produce; it's also a great place to try traditional lamb *asado*. Excellent hiking and horse-riding options on hand. Minimum two-night stay. Closed May–Sept. 8 half-board.

The Town

Once a staging post between the estancias and Río Gallegos, today El Calafate is made up of a hotchpotch of neo-pioneer architecture designed to appeal solely to tourists. Though not unpleasant, the main street is crowded with garish souvenir shops and, in high season (especially Jan & Feb) the place is invaded by everyone and their grandmother who come to marvel at the Glaciar Perito Moreno, some 80km away. If emerging from RN-40, arriving in Calafate can seem like coming to suckle at Mammon's very breast; if you've flown in from Buenos Aires, you'll be surprised at just how modest and dusty the place is, sprawled under its eponymous mountain. Apart from shopping or eating, however, there's little to do in town. The small **Museo Regional** (Mon–Fri 8am–7pm; free) in the Dirección de Cultura, Libertador 575, has the standard collection of pioneer family photos plus some indigenous artefacts, but isn't particularly inspiring.

A thirty-minute walk north of town along Calle Ezequel Bustillo, the bird reserve of **Laguna Nimez** (9am–9pm; $2) has Black-necked Swans, Upland Geese, Chilean Flamingoes, the Silvery Grebe (*macá plateado*) and other species of waterfowl. Though suffering from the effects of pollution, it still makes a pleasant spot for an evening walk.

Eating and drinking

Restaurants, most of which are clustered along or within a block of Avenida Libertador, tend to open from noon till 3pm, and then again in the evening from about 8pm to midnight or later. With a few exceptions, most are pricier than in other parts of the country.

Restaurants

Casimiro Biguá Grill & Rotisserie Libertador 993. Upmarket, but almost equally popular, alternative to *La Tablita*, serving fine cuts of prime Argentine beef and succulent Patagonian lamb in a slick but congenial atmosphere. Carries one of the best wine lists in town, including 250 vintages from Argentina alone.

La Cocina Libertador 1245. Cosy diner with a mouthwatering list of savoury pancakes and pastas but understaffed – the stressed waiters sweat to cover the room. From 7pm. Closed Tues.

La Lechuza Libertador and Primero de Mayo. Not to be confused with their branch on Espora that specializes in *panchos*, this deservedly popular place serves up a huge range of pizzas from its wood-fired oven, plus make-your-own salads and family-sized meat sandwiches.

La Posta In the grounds of *Los Alamos* hotel ⓣ02902/491144. Spacious dining room overlooks the manicured setting. Exotic international menu, with an inventive range of sauces and sympathetic use of local ingredients – the rolled lamb with rose-hip sauce is excellent. Well-chosen selection of Argentine wines.

Pura Vida Libertador 1876. Extremely friendly young owners provide traditional food with a modern touch in an A-frame cabin. Hearty stews and good vegetarian choices, such as baked pumpkin with corn, help make this a place not to be missed. Evenings only. Closed Wed.

La Tablita Cnel. Rosales 28 ⓣ02902/491065. Legendary *asador*, deservedly popular with locals and tour groups alike, who come here to gorge on delicious, serious-sized lamb or beef grills (the mixed *parrilla* could feed a small army), all served with suitable dignity. Sides are fairly expensive but the massive mains are good value. Closed Wed lunch & June–Aug.

Cafés and bars

Casablanca Libertador 1202. Buzzing café that serves some of the best coffee in town, as well as cool draught beer and tasty *lomitos*. Extensive jazz play-list. Open till 1am.

Don Diego de la Noche Libertador 1603. Well-established pub and restaurant (named after the bright yellow flower that grows locally) with a lively nightlife buzz, especially in high season – but don't turn up till late. Live folklore music sessions after 11pm and (overpriced) food served till late (5am).

Kau Kaleshen Gob. Gregores 1256. Charming but expensive *casa de té* frequented by locals and visitors alike and devoting itself to speciality coffees and home-made cakes. Open daily 5–10pm.

Librobar Borges y Alvarez Libertador 1005. Small café/bar that makes a relaxing spot from which to watch the comings and goings down on Avenida Libertador or pour over the extensive selection of local-interest books crammed onto overstacked shelves. There's a good range of coffees, and cocktails are served in the evenings.

Shackleton Lounge Libertador 3287. Smart, novel bar in huge wooden cabin 1km west of town – several of the town's hostels organize trips out here – offering fantastic views of Lago Argentino and playing cool tunes till late.

Toma Libertador 1359. Softly lit bar with a relaxing ambience and an excellent selection of Argentine wines.

Other excursions from El Calafate

Few people budget more time in El Calafate than it takes to see the glaciers (see pp.723–726), but there are a couple more excursions worth checking out if you're in town for longer. Andes Expeditions, Libertador 1341 (ⓣ02902/492075, ⓔprodriguez@cotecal.com.ar), runs day-trips to the **Bosque Petrificado La Leona**, a petrified forest south of Lago Viedma, about 100km from El Calafate ($185). Though not as extensive as those near Sarmiento or Jaramillo (see p.678 & p.681), there are fossilized trunks up to 1.5m in diameter and dinosaur bones strewn across the "painted" desert landscape.

Cerro Frias, Libertador 1857 (ⓣ02902/492808, ⓦwww.cerrofrias.com) runs twice-daily trekking, horse-riding or 4WD trips up **Cerro Frías** ($115 including barbecue lunch or dinner), from which there are views, weather permitting, of both Monte Fitz Roy to the north and Torres del Paine in the south. Closer to town, Calafate Extremo, Libertador 1185 (ⓣ02902/491095, ⓦwww.calafateextremo.com) has 4WD excursions that off-road up the so-called **Balcón del Calafate**, a hill behind town that offers fine views across Lago Argentino ($95 including lunch or dinner). Alternatively, Calbagatas del Glaciar (ⓣ02902/495447, ⓦwww.cabalgatasdelglaciar.com, book through Cal Tur; see p.727) offers recommended **horse-riding** trips to Glaciar Perito Moreno and Lago Roca ($180 including lunch), as well as two-day trips to Paso Zamora, at the border with Chile.

Listings

Airlines Aerolíneas Argentinas, 9 de Julio 57 ⓣ02902/492814; LADE, Roca 1004 ⓣ02902/491262.

Banks and exchange Several ATMs including the Banco de la Nacion, Libertador 1133, and Banco de Santa Cruz, Libertador 1285. Thaler, 9 de Julio, buys and sells Chilean pesos.

Bike rental HLS, Buenos Aires 173 ⓣ02902/493806 (1hr $8, half-day $30, full day $50).

Books and maps Boutique del Libro, Libertador 1033.

Bus connections Freddy Representaciones in the bus terminal (ⓣ02902/492127, ⓔfreddy@cotecal.com.ar) has forensic knowledge of national bus routes and timetables.

Car rental Dubrovnik, Padre Agostini 147 ⓣ02902/496222; Localiza, Libertador 687 ⓣ02902/491398; Servi Car, Libertador 695 ⓣ02902/492301; Wagen, Libertador 1341 T02902/492297.

Hospital Julio Roca 1487 ⓣ02902/491173.

Internet access Koonex, Cmte. Espora 44 ($5/hr; daily 9–3am).

Laundry Lava… Andina, Cmte. Espora 88 (daily 9am–1pm & 4–9pm).

Pharmacy El Calafate, Libertador 1192 (daily 7am–10.30pm).

Police Libertador 835 ⓣ02902/491824.

Post office Libertador 1133.

Supermarkets La Anónima, Libertador 902; Alas, 9 de Julio 59. Stock up here if heading north on RN-40.

Taxis Cóndor, 25 de Mayo 50 ⓣ02902/491655

Telephones COOP Telefónica, Libertador 1486 (7–2am).

Los Glaciares: the southern sector

The exalted glaciers in the **southern sector** of the park attract visitors from all over the world and it takes a bit of planning to find the magic and avoid the crowds. There are three main destinations in this portion of the park: the **Glaciar Perito Moreno**, which slams into the western end of **Península de Magallanes**; **Puerto Bandera**, from where boat trips depart to Upsala and the other northern glaciers; and, south down RP-15, the much less visited **Lago Roca** and the southern arm of Lago Argentino, the **Brazo Sur**.

Park entrance for the Glaciar Perito Moreno and Upsala trips is $30 for foreigners, which you must pay at the respective gates, but the Lago Roca area is free. Within the boundaries, be especially aware of the dangers of fire. Take care with cigarette butts and extinguish any campfire with plenty of water (earth is not as effective) – an area of forest near Glaciar Spegazzini that burnt in the 1930s still hasn't even remotely recovered. **Mammals** in the park include the *gato montés* wildcat, pumas and the endangered *huemul*, although you are highly unlikely to see any of these due to their scarcity and elusive nature. Instead, enjoy the **flora**, such as the *notro* bush, with its flaming red blooms between November and March, and **birds** such as the majestic black and red Magellanic Woodpecker (*carpintero patagónico*).

Glaciar Perito Moreno

Argentina's two greatest natural wonders couldn't contrast more: the sub-tropical waterfalls at Iguazú and the immense pack-ice of the **GLACIAR PERITO MORENO** (also called Ventisquero Perito Moreno). It's not the

Getting to the Glaciar Perito Moreno

Most people visit the **Glaciar Perito Moreno** on guided day-**tours**, which are offered by virtually all agencies in El Calafate and allow for around four hours at the ice face, the minimum required fully to appreciate the spectacle, and cost around $90, plus park entrance fee. Rather than having a fixed point of departure, companies tend to drive round town collecting passengers from hotels; to avoid having to get up much earlier than you need to, try to arrange that you're the last pick-up or that you go to the office just before the bus leaves. The trips with *Hostel del Glaciar Pioneros* (see p.720), Chaltén Travel (Libertador 1174 ⓣ02902/492212, ⓦwww.chaltentravel.com) and Rumbo Sur (Libertador 960 ⓣ02902/492155, ⓦwww.rumbosur.com.ar) are recommended for their knowledgeable, friendly guides and time spent at the glacier.

If you don't want to be restricted to a tour, Cal Tur runs a twice-daily **bus service** ($25 one way) departing at 8am and 3pm and returning 1pm and 8pm. If you get the 8am departure you'll probably be among the first to arrive at the glacier – it's worth the effort to beat the crowds and glimpse the early morning sun shining on the west-facing snout. Equally, the 3pm departure returns after most tours have long gone, but arrives at the glacier after the boat trips (see p.726) stop running. Alternatively, you could hire a **remise taxi** ($210 including four-hour wait at the glacier).

The other option is to **rent a car** (around $170/day), either down lesser-used RP-15 towards Lago Roca or along paved RP-11. The **RP-15** is *ripio* but by far the most picturesque. Leaving El Calafate, turn left at *Don Diego de la Noche*. After about 30km, the road passes historical Estancia Anita, the scene of one of Patagonia's most grisly episodes: in 1921, 121 men were executed here by an army battalion that had been sent to crush a rural strike and the related social unrest; a monument by the roadside commemorates the victims. Turn right just after the tourist estancia of *Alta Vista* (see p.721), and then left after another 12km to the park's main entrance.

The second route, along **RP-11**, heads straight down Avenida Libertador and along a paved road that lines the lakeshore, passing the tourist estancia *Alice* (see p.721) before dropping down to the park's main entrance; the right turning here, down RP-8, leads to Puerto Bandera (see p.727), for boat trips to Upsala and other glaciers.

The **park's main entrance** (24hr; $30) is as you enter the peninsula, and the trees nearby are a favourite evening roost of the rabble-rousing austral parakeet (*cachaña*), the most southerly of the world's parrots. From here it's a forty-minute drive (a little more than 30km) past picnic spots, a campsite and the exclusive *Los Notros* hotel (see p.721) to the boardwalks in front of the glacier. The *ripio* road is poor and very dusty in hot weather, but traversable by any family car; arrive early and/or leave late to avoid the inevitable congestion.

longest of Argentina's glaciers – nearby Glaciar Upsala is twice as long (60km) – and though the ice cliffs at its snout tower 50m to 60m high, the face of Glaciar Spegazzini can reach heights double that. However, such comparisons prove irrelevant when you stand on the **boardwalks** that face this monster. Perito Moreno has a star quality that none of the others rivals.

The glacier sweeps down off the icecap in a great motorway curve, a jagged mass of crevasses and towering, knife-edged seracs almost unsullied by the streaks of dirty moraine that discolour many of its counterparts. When it collides with the southern arm of Lago Argentino, the **Canal de los Témpanos** (Iceberg Channel), the show really begins: vast blocks of ice, some weighing hundreds of tonnes, detonate off the face of the glacier with the report of a small cannon and come crashing down into the waters below. These frozen depth-charges then surge back to the surface as icebergs, sending out a fairy ring of smaller lumps that form a protecting reef around the berg, which is left to float in a mirror-smooth pool of its own.

Along with the virtually inaccessible Pío XI in Chile, Perito Moreno is one of only two **advancing glaciers** in South America, and one of the very few on the planet, at a rate of about 7cm a day in winter. Above all, the glacier became famous for the way it periodically pushes right across the channel, forming a massive dyke of ice that cut off the Brazo Rico and Brazo Sur from the main body of Lago Argentino. Isolated from their natural outlet, the water in the *brazos* would build up against the flank of the glacier, flooding the surrounding area, until eventually the pressure forced open a passage into the canal once again. Happening over the course of several hours, such a **rupture** is, for those lucky enough to witness it, one of nature's most awesome spectacles. The glacier first reached the peninsula in 1917, having advanced some 750m in fifteen years, but the channel did not remain blocked for long and the phenomenon remained little known. This changed in 1939, when a vast area was flooded and planes made a futile attempt to break the glacier by bombing it. In 1950, water levels rose by 30m and the channel was closed for two years; in 1966, levels reached an astonishing 32m above their normal level. The glacier then settled into a fairly regular cycle, completely blocking the channel approximately every four years or so up to 1988; after that there was a sixteen-year gap until the more recent ruptures in 2004 and again in March 2006, when, during the night, tonnes of ice crashed from the face of the glacier into the chilly waters below.

That said, it's more likely you'll have to content yourself with the thuds, cracks, creaks and grinding crunches that the glacier habitually makes, as well as the wonderful variety of **colours of the ice**: marbled in places with streaks of muddy grey and copper-sulphate blue, whilst at the bottom the pressurized, de-oxygenated ice has a deep blue, waxy sheen. The glacier tends to be more active in sunny weather and in the afternoon, but early morning can also be beautiful, as the sun strikes the ice cliffs.

△ Glaciar Perito Moreno

Many species of the park's native **flora** next to the boardwalks are handily labelled; look out, too, for the **fauna**, such as the Crested Rufous-collared Sparrow (*chingolo*) and the brightly coloured Patagonian Sierra Finch (*fríngilo patagónico*), a little yellow and grey bird that has become semi-tame.

Practicalities

The park infrastructure was designed to support only a fraction of the two thousand or so tourists who visit the glacier daily and authorities are under pressure from El Calafate businesses to double the boardwalks and expand eating facilities. Currently, there are just a couple of **cafés** (which have the only toilet facilities). With the wind coming off the ice, the temperature at the glacier can be a lot colder than in El Calafate, so take extra clothes. Do not stray from the boardwalks: 32 people were killed between 1968 and 1988, either being hit by ricocheting ice or swept off the rocks by the subsequent wave surge.

An excellent way of seeing the ice-face from another angle is to take one of the hour-long **boat trips** that chug along near the towering heights of the ice wall: Safari Náutico heads to the southern face from Puerto Bajo de las Sombras (daily departures every hour 10.30am–3.30pm; $25), while Moreno Fiesta runs a similar trip to the northern side from near the ranger's house 2km before the boardwalks (daily departures every hour 10.30am–2.30pm; $38).

For an even closer look, you can **walk on the glacier** with Hielo y Aventura, Libertador 935 (Ⓣ02902/492205, Ⓦwww.hieloyaventura.com), which organizes daily "Mini Trekking" trips (departs El Calafate at 8am; 1hr 30min on the ice; $250 plus park entrance fee) and longer, more demanding "Big Ice" excursions (departs 7am; 4hr on the ice; $340 plus park entrance fee), which include a boat trip across to the glacier. This is **ice-trekking**, not ice-*climbing* (try El Chaltén for that): you do not need to be a peak-bagging mountain man to do it. You'll be issued crampons, but bring sunglasses, sun cream, gloves and a packed lunch, and wear warm, weatherproof clothes.

For **photos**, if you've got a SLR camera try underexposing some of the glacier shots by about a stop (third to half a stop if using slides) to bring out the blue in the ice.

Upsala, Spegazzini, Onelli and Agassiz glaciers

Glaciar Upsala is the undisputed heavyweight of the park: between 5km and 7km wide, with a sixty-metre-high snout and a length of 60km. It's still South America's longest glacier, despite massive retrocession over the last decade or so, and covers a total area three times larger than that of metropolitan Buenos Aires. Upsala played an important role in consolidating Argentine claims to its Antarctic territory – expedition teams used to acclimatize by living for months in a base on the glacier.

Navigating **Brazo Upsala** is a highlight in itself. Apart from the wooded shores, it could be Antarctica, as **icebergs** bob, grind and even turn occasional flips around you. As any good student of the *Titanic* will know, for every one part of iceberg above the surface, it has six to seven parts below, which gives an idea of the tremendous size of these blocks. Even in flat light, the icy blues shine as if lit by a neon strip-light – an eerie, incredible, cerulean glow.

Glaciar Spegazzini is some people's favourite glacier, with an imposing ice cascade to the right and the most dizzying snout of all the glaciers in the park (80–135m high). The **Onelli** and **Agassiz glaciers** are less impressive – but still beautiful – and are reached by an easy eight-hundred-metre walk to **Laguna Onelli**, a chilly lake dotted with small bergs. The walk itself is likely to appeal only to those who haven't had the opportunity to see Patagonian forest elsewhere, since the beauty of these woodlands is not enhanced by the presence of up to three hundred day-trippers.

Practicalities

Boat trips to see the Upsala, Spegazzini and Onelli glaciers are run as a park's concession from **Puerto Bandera** by René Fernández Campbell, Libertador 867 (ⓣ02902/49115, ⓦwww.fernandezcampbell.com.ar), using a fleet of modern catamarans and launches. When the weather's fine, the full-day excursions (8.30am–5.30pm; $195 plus park entrance fee) are definitely a memorable experience; when it's rough, they can be memorable for the wrong reasons – if badly affected by motion sickness, take precautionary seasickness tablets (*pastillas contra el mareo*). Dress in warm, waterproof and windproof clothing, and take spare film and food since prices on board are high. Before booking, remember that your scope for refunds is limited: the weather has to be exceptionally foul for the trip to be cancelled entirely, and the company fulfils its legal obligations if only one main part of the trip is completed; in windy weather especially, icebergs can block the channels, with Brazo Upsala being particularly prone. That said, the company is professional and tries hard to complete itineraries: in the event of cancellation, you will be offered a refund or a passage the next day.

A rather more expensive excursion, but one where you get to **stay overnight near the glaciers**, is "The Spirit of the Glaciers", run by Mar Patag (in Buenos Aires ⓣ011/5031-0756, ⓦwww.crucerosmarpatag.com); the two-day trip aboard the plush *Leal* takes in close-quarter views of the Upsala and Spegazzini glaciers – as well as Glacier Perito Moreno – anchoring at Puerto las Vacas, off the Brazo Spegazzini, for the night (July–May; US$420 full board, guided activities and transfers).

Alternatively, the long day-trip run by *Estancia Cristina* (book through their El Calafate office, 9 de Julio 69 ⓣ02902/491133, ⓦwww.estanciacristina.com) is one of the few ways of gaining access to the central sector of the park and the windswept, desolate **Bahía Cristina** area. Boats visit Glacier Upsala (breakfast onboard) before heading up Bahía Cristina to the isolated estancia (see p.721), a favoured point of entry for explorers of the icecap, including Padre de Agostini and Eric Shipton, the famous mountaineer and explorer of the 1960s. Lunch is at the estancia followed by a choice of excursion: 4WD, horse-riding or the recommended moderate trek to the Upsala lookout (May–Sept; US$150 plus transfer to/from Puerto Bandera and park entrance fee).

Lago Roca

Overshadowed by the nearby glaciers, **Lago Roca**, a southern branch of Lago Argentino, tends to be frequented mainly by keen fishermen. Lying 52km from El Calafate, it offers good horse-riding and trekking possibilities in stunning areas of open woodland and amongst the neighbouring hills of the Cordón de los Cristales; it also has examples of rock art dating back 3000 years. The rock art is along a signposted trail to the left of the main road just before Lago Roca campsite (see p.718); you can continue the four-hour hike to the summit of Cerro Cristales from where, weather permitting, there are fine views of Torres del Paine to the south.

Cal Tur runs **buses** to Lago Roca (Mon, Wed & Fri–Sun leaving El Calafate at 8.30am, returning 6pm; $50), while a *remise* from town costs about $160. Alternatively, you can take a day-trip with Leutz Turismo, Libertador 1341 (daily 9.30am; $125; ⓣ02902/492316, ⓦwww.leutzturismo.com.ar), which visits Estancia Anita (see box, p.724) and includes lunch at Lago Roca and a visit to the *Nibepo Aike* estancia (see p.721). You can arrange to return another day and stay at either of the above.

South from El Calafate

The zone southeast of El Calafate is one that you'll cross if heading to the **deep south of Chile**, including Puerto Natales and Parque National Torres del Paine, or across to Río Gallegos, the provincial capital of Santa Cruz, and RN-3 along the Atlantic coast. It's not the most interesting of areas from a visitor's perspective, and much of it is either blasted, flat steppe or industrial towns such as **Río Turbio**, although the southwestern area close to the Chilean border is richer in the way of grassland and has patches of dwarf southern beech woodland. You have several options in the way of horse riding, and the western reaches of the Río Gallegos offer some good fishing.

RP-5: El Calafate to Río Gallegos

There are two main routes from **El Calafate to Río Gallegos**: more scenic RN-40, which passes several crossing points into the far south of Chile as it curves around to Gallegos; and quicker RP-5, the busiest of the roads that cross the deep south of Santa Cruz Province, since it's paved and relatively well maintained – in the early twentieth century this journey took up to 45 days by ox-cart, but you can now do it in less than four hours.

The RP-5 is a continuation of the paved part of RN-40, beginning where (unpaved) RN-40 turns off south, 94km southeast of El Calafate. About 160km from El Calafate, you reach the hamlet of **La Esperanza**, where you can **refuel** and **eat**, and, if it's too late to push on, **stay** at the only hotel (Ⓣ02902/499200; $25 per person). Take RP-7 here if you're heading from Río Gallegos to the Chilean border at Cancha Carrera (see below). From La Esperanza, RP-5 continues east to Güer Aike and on to Río Gallegos.

Routes into Chile and RN-40 to Río Gallegos

Where it links up with paved RP-5, 94km southeast of El Calafate, RN-40 **branches south to the Chilean border** on its way to Río Gallegos, reverting to its unpaved state as it crosses the dry, barren *meseta*. In the far distance, you catch your first views of the Torres del Paine massif in Chile.

Forty-five kilometres south of Tapi Aike (a useful stop for its **fuel** station) you reach the steppe-land **border crossing** at **Cancha Carrera** (8am–10pm), the closest crossing to Parque Nacional Torres del Paine. Argentine border formalities are quite straightforward; meat, dairy products, fruit and fresh vegetables cannot be taken into Chile – you're likely to have your bags searched when you get to the immigration post at **Cerro Castillo** (same hours), a tiny settlement 7km further on, from where a *ripio* road leads 70km north to Parque Nacional Torres del Paine and 65km south to Puerto Natales. On the Argentine side, just south of the border post, is the tourist estancia *Cancha Carrera* (Ⓣ&Ⓕ02966/423236 or 424236; ❼ half-board; closed April–Sept), a beautiful old *casco antiguo* (main house) in a typically Anglo-Patagonian style from the early twentieth century with elegantly furnished rooms; buses from El Calafate to Puerto Natales pass close by.

Beyond here, RN-40 runs parallel to the international border, passing through the miserable mining town of **Río Turbio**, where you come face to face with the sorry scars left by Argentina's coal industry; the coal deposits here are the biggest in the country, but the industry has been hit by a severe depression. Just outside the town is the 24-hour **border crossing** of **Paso Mina Uno**. Chilean immigration is just the other side, and from here it's a straightforward 26-kilometre run to Puerto Natales.

Another 24-hour **border crossing**, more convenient for those travelling on RN-40 between Puerto Natales and Río Gallegos, is at Paso Casas Viejas/La Laurita, 35km south of Río Turbio, past its sister town of 28 de Noviembre. Beyond here, RN-40 continues eastwards for 250km of *ripio* road to Río Gallegos. After the first 20km, you come to the only recognized lodging on this route, the tourist **estancia** *Stag River* (ⓣ02966/424410 or 422466; US$200 full board including drinks; closed June–Sept), where there's good trout-fishing.

Chilean Patagonia

The great tourist lure in the **south** of mainland **Patagonia** is Chile's **Parque Nacional Torres del Paine**, a land of awesome natural beauty that's famous as a trekking Mecca. If you're planning to visit this park or if you're simply travelling overland between mainland Argentine Patagonia and Tierra del Fuego (or vice versa), you are likely to pass through the bustling city of **Punta Arenas** and **Puerto Natales**, the latter a base for trips to the park.

Since the Argentine peso's devaluation, Chile is no longer cheaper than its neighbour, apart from international postage rates. Entering Chile is straightforward, and you are given a ninety-day tourist card at the border. Everyone requires a passport that is valid for at least six months. No meat or dairy products may be brought into the country, nor any fresh fruit or vegetables. For more details, refer to the *Rough Guide to Chile*.

Punta Arenas and around

PUNTA ARENAS is a bustling port, characterized by its engaging monuments and statues. It is the most venerable of southern Patagonia's towns, dating back to 1848, and for decades was the only substantial trading centre in the region. The town's golden age lasted from the late nineteenth century until World War I, an era of sheep-farming barons and merchants who made enormous profits from supplying the marine traffic around Cape Horn. The opulence of

The **international dialling code** for Chile from Argentina is ⓣ0056. The **area code** for this portion of Chilean Patagonia is ⓣ61.

The **Chilean peso** (CH$) is the national currency. At the time of writing, the **exchange rate** was CH$960 to £1, CH$500 to US$1.

past times can be seen in the fine *belle époque* buildings dotted around **Plaza Muñoz Gamero**, with their mansard roofs, European furnishings and urban luxury, while the town's history is writ large in its fascinating **cemetery**. Attractions within striking distance of Punta Arenas are **Fuerte Bulnes**, the area's original settlement, and, closer to town, the more appealing penguin colony at **Isla Magdelana**.

Arrival, information and orientation

The **airport** lies 20km to the north of town; minibuses run from the offices of the main airlines in the city to connect with flights (CH$2500), while a *remise* to the centre will cost around CH$6000. All **buses** connecting with Río Gallegos or Puerto Natales arrive and depart along Avenida Bulnes. There is no central bus terminal, so each company arrives at its own office in the centre, all within a few blocks of the main plaza. The Transbordadora Austral Broom **ferry** to and from **Porvenir** in Chilean Tierra del Fuego uses the port 5km to the north of town at Bulnes 5075 (Tues–Sat 2pm & Sun 5pm; 2hr 20min; CH$4300 for foot passengers, CH$27000 with a car; ⓣ61/218100, ⓦwww.tabsa.cl). The company also runs an adventurous 34-hour service to **Puerto Williams** on Isla Navarino (Wed; from US$140). Taxis from the port to the centre cost CH$1500.

The best **tourist office** (Mon–Fri 8.15am–6pm & Sat 10am–1pm & 2.30–6pm; ⓣ61/241330) is the Sernatur at Magallenes 960, near the Plaza Muñoz Gamero. The helpful staff will give you a copy of the Comapa town plan, the best of the free **maps** available. The municipal **tourist office** is close by in the plaza (Mon–Fri 8am–6pm, Sat 8am–7pm & Sun 9.30am–2.30pm; ⓣ61/200610).

The city's main north–south artery is **Avenida Bulnes**, which leads straight into the centre from the north, before splitting into two parallel streets, Calle Bories (the principal shopping thoroughfare) and Calle Magallanes. These cross the wide, landscaped **Avenida Colón** – the main boulevard that runs westwards from the sea – before sandwiching the Plaza Muñoz Gamero two short blocks further on. Calle Lautaro Navarro, a busy commercial street lined with airline offices, travel agents and several accommodation options, runs parallel with Magallanes, one block to the east. North of the cemetery, Avenida Bulnes's street numbers are prefixed by an additional zero.

Accommodation

Punta Arenas has **accommodation** options to suit most budgets, with many of the best places within a couple of blocks of Plaza Muñoz Gamero.

Backpackers Paradise Ignacio Carrera Pinto 1022 ⓣ61/222554, ⓔbackpackersparadise@hotmail.com. A lively, busy hostel – the most popular in town – with thirty bunks in two open-plan (noisy) rooms. It has a well-equipped Internet café in its basement. Dorms CH$5000.

Hospedaje Huala Maipú 851 ⓣ61/244244. Relaxed and enjoyable *hospedaje*, run by hospitable, artistic owners. There are only two rooms, so you're guaranteed a quiet stay, but at seven blocks from the centre, it's a little too far out for some. ❹

Hostal Calafate 1 Lautaro Navarro 850 ⓣ61/248415, ⓦwww.calafate.tie.cl. A pleasant, meticulously clean townhouse with a commodious living room and personable owners who speak English. Some rooms have their own bathrooms and breakfast is included. ❺–❻

Hostal de la Patagonia O'Higgins 730 ⓣ61/249970, ⓦwww.ecotourpatagonia.com. A snug, friendly home that offers welcoming, spruce rooms with beds that have good mattresses. En-suite rooms cost more, but breakfast is included, and they offer hefty discounts May–Oct. ❻

Hostal La Estancia O'Higgins 765 ⓣ61/249130, ⓔreservas_laestancia@hotmail.com. Homely accommodation in high-ceilinged dorms on the ground floor, and bright rooms with shared bathroom upstairs. Breakfast included. Dorms CH$7500, rooms ⑤–⑥

Hotel José Nogueira Bories 959 ⓣ61/248840, ⓦwww.hotelnogueira.com. Boasting a prime location on the main plaza, the most stylish hotel in town takes up one half of the Palacio Sara Braun, a national monument from the late nineteenth century. The old-world elegance and luxury are only slightly marred by the piped music in reception, and it has a restaurant, the exquisite *Pergola*, in the conservatory (see p.732). Rooms start at US$190.

Hotel Panamericana Cabo de Hornos Plaza Muñoz Gamero 1025 ⓣ61/242134, ⓦwww.hch.co.cl. Lording it over the city centre, this top-end hotel has smart but rather business-like rooms, with scenic views of the main square and the sea from the third and fifth floors respectively, a good restaurant and a great bar. ⑧

The City

Punta Arenas's focus is its tranquil central plaza, the **Plaza Muñoz Gamero**, with an attractive mix of shady Chilean trees and a **statue of Magellan** standing above a pair of native inhabitants, one Selk'nam (Ona) and one Aónik'enk Tehuelche. Ironically, the statue was donated by the family of José Menéndez, the most powerful of the local land-owning magnates and a suspect for bankrolling the bounty hunters responsible for the genocide of the Selk'nam in Tierra del Fuego (see box, p.766). Kissing the shiny bronze **big toe** of one of the natives is reckoned to ensure you'll return to Punta Arenas.

Dominating the northwest corner of the plaza is the fine **Palacio Sara Braun** (Tues–Fri 10.30am–1pm & 5–8.30pm, Sat 10.30am–1pm & 8–10pm, Sun 11am–2pm; CH$1000), an impressive building constructed in 1895 by a French architect for Sara Braun, the widow of José Menéndez. It took nine years to build, during which time Braun spent much of the sheep baron's fortune filling the interior with materials from Europe, including hand-carved furniture from England, tapestries from Belgium and crystal chandeliers from France. Just off the plaza's northeast corner, at Magallanes 949, is another *palacio*, **Palacio Braun Menéndez**, housing the **Museo Regional Magallanes**

△ Punta Arenas cemetery

(May–Sept Mon–Sun 10.30am–2pm; Oct–April Mon–Sat 10.30am–5pm, Sun 10.30am–2pm; CH$1000, free on Sun); a place of stiff European opulence, heavily influenced by nineteenth-century French tastes, it has displays on the city's history, including some relics from Sarmiento de Gamboa's settlement of San Felipe (Puerto Hambre). Charlie Milward – the great-uncle of Bruce Chatwin, who figures prominently in Chatwin's *In Patagonia* – used to live in the sandstone Gothic house at Avenida España 959.

The best museum, however, is the Salesian religious order's eclectic **Museo Regional Salesiano Maggiorino Borgatello** at Bulnes 336, seven blocks north of the main plaza (Tues–Sun 10am–1pm & 2.30–6pm; CH$2000). It has a Victorian-style assemblage of mounted specimens of the region's wildlife, heavily dusted with borax, as well as some superb ethnographic material, including a remarkable bark canoe made by the native Alacalufes, and an exquisite, rare cape made from cormorant skins.

Two blocks north of the Museo Salesiano is the city's **cemetery** (daily: summer 7.30am–8pm; winter 8am–6pm; free), a magnificent ensemble of simple tombs and opulent mausoleums that chart the history of the city's settlement. Look out for José Menéndez's final resting place – a gargantuan take on Victor Emmanuel II's wedding-cake tomb in Rome.

More light-hearted entertainment can be had at the **Museo del Recuerdo**, a fun, open-air museum at the excellent Instituto Patagonia, 4km north of town along Avenida Bulnes (Mon–Fri 8.30–11.30am & 2.30–6.30pm, Sat 8.30am–12.30pm; CH$1000), with a variety of threshers, reapers and haymakers from a century ago, as well as rebuilt, typically Patagonian homes.

Eating and drinking

La Luna O'Higgins 1017. Fine fare with wonderfully friendly service make this one of the city's best – and most popular – eateries. The very tasty *chupe del centolla* is the pick of the seafood-heavy menu.

La Marmita Plaza Sampaio 678. Welcoming, rustic restaurant with a relaxed ambience. The emphasis is on vegetarian dishes and ethnic specialities – many of which are made using traditional Mapuche cooking methods – but there's also an interesting twist on a French classic: beaver bourguignon. Closed Sun eve.

El Mercado Mejicana 617, second floor. First-class seafood served 24 hours a day. Check out the size of the *centolla* (king crab) mounted on the wall before you tackle a whole one.

Pergola Bories 959 ⓣ61/248840. Beautiful restaurant in the *Hotel José Nogueira*'s vine-draped conservatory. Relax with a pisco sour or try the reasonably priced fillet steak in crab sauce.

Listings

Airlines Aerolíneas Argentinas, Pedro Montt 969 ⓣ61/221020; DAP, O'Higgins 891 ⓣ61/223340; LanChile, Lautaro Navarro 999 ⓣ61/241232.

Banks and exchange Banks are open Mon–Fri 9am–2pm. The best ones are grouped around the main plaza: Banco de Santiago, Citibank and Banco Edwards. *Cambios* (open until 5.30pm) include Stop, José Nogueira 1168, and Sur Cambios, Lautaro Navarro 1001.

Car rental International, Waldo Seguel 443 ⓣ61/228323; Magallenes, O'Higgins 949 ⓣ61/220780, ⓦwww.magallenesrentacar.cl.

Consulates Argentina, 21 de Mayo 1878 ⓣ61/261912; UK, Catarata de Niaguara 1325 ⓣ61/211535.

Hospital Hospital Regional, Angamos 180 ⓣ61/244040; alternatively, there's a private clinic: Clínica Magallanes, Bulnes and Kuzma Slavic ⓣ61/211527.

Internet access Many places including Hostal *Calafate II*, Magallanes 926.

Laundry Lavandería Record, O'Higgins 969.

Pharmacies Ahumada Bories 950.

Police Carabineros, Waldo Seguel 653 ⓣ61/222295; emergencies ⓣ133.

Post office Bories 911.

Taxis Navarino ⓣ61/621387; Ona ⓣ61/281544.

Telephones Several including at Lautaro Navarro 931 and Bories 801A.

Around Punta Arenas

Just 35km northeast of Punta Arenas, tiny **Isla Magdelana** is home to more than 120,000 Magellenic penguins, making it one of the largest **penguin colonies** in southern Chile. The birds return to the island around late September each year, to mate and raise their chicks, before heading out into the ocean again come April. Their nests are fenced off but you can get surprisingly close to them as they waddle their way through the tufts of grass that cover the island. In season, the *Melinka* **ferry** (see box, p.748) runs to Isla Magdelana three times a week (Dec–Feb Tues, Thurs & Sat 4pm); the five-hour round-trip includes one hour at the nest area (CH$20,000).

Sixty kilometres south of the city lie two reminders of the region's past: **Fuerte Bulnes**, a reconstructed fort on the site of Punta Arenas's original settlement, founded in September 1843 by British Captain John Williams on an expedition to pre-empt colonization from Europe; and **Puerto Hambre**, the tragic remains of one of the first two Spanish colonies on the Magellan Straits. There's less to see here, but the isolation and exposure make for an atmospheric spot. Virtually all travel agencies offer morning **tours** to Fuerte Bulnes, combined with a visit to the site of Puerto Hambre (tours depart 9.30am; CH$10,000); try Arka Patagonia, Magallenes 345 (Ⓣ61/248167, Ⓦwww.arkapatagonia.com) or Eco Tour Patagonia, O'Higgins 730 (Ⓣ61/249970, Ⓦwww.ecotourpatagonia.com).

Puerto Natales and Parque Nacional Torres del Paine

One of South America's most famous national parks, **Parque Nacional Torres del Paine** attracts visitors from all over the globe who come to enjoy the grandeur of its glaciers, lakes and, above all, its jagged mountain peaks. It is accessed from the unassuming little port town of **Puerto Natales**, which, with its mellow pace of life, makes an ideal base for trekkers.

Puerto Natales

PUERTO NATALES, attractively sited on the shores of Seno Ultima Esperanza ("Last Hope Sound"), has a contented small-town feel. There's not much to do in Natales itself, although it receives a steady stream of visitors on their way to the national park or heading north on the *Navimag* to Puerto Montt, one of Chile's great boat journeys.

Arrival and information

Natales is connected by frequent **buses** to Punta Arenas and El Calafate in Argentina; companies drop you at their respective offices in the centre. The **port** lies a block left (south) of the foot of Avenida Manuel Bulnes, from where the famous **Navimag** ferry sets sail on its 66-hour trip to Puerto Montt; the ticket office is in the Comapa agency at Bulnes 533 (departs Thurs; from US$355; Ⓣ61/414300, Ⓦwww.comapa.com). There's also a weekday morning DAP **flight** in high season from El Calafate (see p.717).

The municipal **tourist office** is at Bulnes 285, in the same building as the Museo Histórico Municipal (Mon–Fri 8am–7pm, Sat 10am–1pm & 3–7pm; Ⓣ061/411263). Turn right at the foot of Bulnes to get to the scenically,

if inconveniently, situated Sernatur **tourist office**, on the seafront at Pedro Montt 19 (Mon–Fri 8.15am–7pm, Sat 10am–1pm & 3–6pm; Ⓣ61/412125, Ⓔinfonatales@sernatur.cl); it has limited stocks of an excellent, free historical tourist **map** of the region.

Accommodation

Accommodation in Natales is not normally a problem, as the town has numerous, cosy *casas de familia*, whose owners "greet" you as soon as you get off the bus. These budget guesthouses usually offer breakfast in the room price, store luggage, have kitchen facilities and often provide a laundry service.

Altiplanico Sur Huerto Familiar 282 Ⓣ61/412525, Ⓦwww.altiplanico.cl. Bunker-like hotel sunk into a hillside 3km outside town and featuring grass-covered roofs, with great views of Seno Ultima Esperanza and Glacier Balmaceda. The minimalist decor – there's lots of bare stone and steel – is offset by sheep-skin throws in the bedrooms. Restaurant, cafeteria, bar, laundry and Internet. ⑨

Casa Cecilia Tomás Rogers 60 Ⓣ61/411797, Ⓔredcecilia@entelchile.net. Cosy, welcoming *hospedaje* whose modern rooms, grouped around a covered central courtyard, are kept to a high standard of hygiene, with crisp bed linen. The good breakfast includes tasty home-made bread. Bike rental available. ④–⑤

Casa Dickson Bulnes 307 Ⓣ61/411871. A well-heated lodging house, with a large kitchen open to guests. The newer en-suite rooms are worth the extra cost. Offers a minibus service to Torres del Paine. ④

Costaustralis Pedro Montt 262 Ⓣ61/412000, Ⓦwww.australis.com. The most luxurious hotel in town, excellently sited on the seafront, with modern rooms offering sea or (cheaper) city views. ⑧

Erratic Rock Baquedano 719, Ⓣ61/410355, Ⓦwww.erraticrock.com. A good, central location and friendly staff help make this cosy trekkers' hostel an ever-popular choice. It's also a good place to arrange half-, full- and multi-day trips. Dorms $35, rooms ④–⑤

Hospedaje Chila Carrera Pinto 442 ⓣ61/413981. Great-value, sociable lodging with a marvellously hospitable, helpful family. It has a spacious kitchen and good shared bathrooms, but some squeaky beds. ❸

Hotel Indigo Ladrilleros 105 ⓣ61/413609, ⓦwww.indigopatagonia.com. Trendy hotel whose beautifully renovated rooms, done out in floor-to-ceiling pine, have great views of the sound. The recent addition of a spa means you can now enjoy a soak in a terrace Jacuzzi overlooking the water. There's an attached restaurant and (popular) lounge bar (see below). ❽

Patagonia Adventure Tomás Rogers 179 ⓣ61/411028, ⓔpatagonia_adventure@terra.cl. Excellent hostel with small dorms and a couple of double rooms, and friendly young owners who are into hiking. Wonderful home-baked bread for breakfast, plus camping-gear rental and transfers. Dorms CH$5000, rooms ❹

The town and around

Civic pride is expressed in characteristically modest manner with a jaunty train engine in the pretty central square, **Plaza de Armas**, and painted rubbish bins welded into shapes such as a *milodón*, a giant ground sloth from the Pleistocene age that died out in the area some 10,000 years ago. Famously, rare freeze-dried remains of this creature were discovered in a cave, the **Cueva del Milodón** (daily: May–Sept 8.30am–6pm; Oct–April 8am–9pm; May–Sept CH$1500; Oct–April CH$3000), which lies some 25km northwest of town and can be visited by taxi or on a tour – the story forms the background for Bruce Chatwin's *In Patagonia*. In town, the best sight is the commendable little **Museo Histórico Municipal** at Bulnes 285 (same hours as municipal tourist office; CH$1000), with lovingly presented displays on the region's history and wildlife, including a collapsible boat that belonged to the resourceful Herman Eberhard, the region's first settler.

Eating and drinking

El Asador Patagónico Prat 158. The huge *parrilla* in the window promises much, and the excellent meat dishes, particularly the spit-roast lamb, don't disappoint.

Hotel Indigo Ladrilleros 105. Fine Patagonian cuisine features at the wooden-tiled restaurant attached to the hotel, while the second-floor *Lounge Bar* makes a great spot to enjoy a beer or two as the sun sets into the sound.

El Living Prat 156. Smart wooden tables, soothing decor and decent music make this an appealing place for a drink – yogurt shakes, tea, coffee, cocktails – or a light vegetarian meal.

El Maritimo Pedro Montt 214. Excellent seafront fish restaurant with enormous fresh portions of salmon and other dishes at remarkably low prices.

La Oveja Negra Tomás Rogers 169. Cheerful café on the main plaza serving typical Chilean dishes and decent pisco sours.

Listings

Airlines DAP, Bulnes 100 ⓣ61/415100.

Banks and exchange Plenty of ATMs, including at Banco Santiago, Bulnes 436, and several *cambios*, including Omega, 238 Blanco Encalada.

Camping equipment *Patagonia Adventure*, Tomás Rogers 179, has one of the widest selections.

Car rental EMSA, Bulnes 632 ⓣ61/241182; Ultima Esperanza, Blanco Encalada 206 ⓣ061/410461.

Internet access Various places including at Blanco Encalada 266.

Laundry Servilaundry, Bulnes 513.

Post office Eberhard 429.

Telephones Several including at Baquedano 270.

Tour operators Path@gone, Eberhard 595 (ⓣ61/413291, ⓦwww.pathgone.com), acts as a hub for the companies that run the *refugios* in Torres del Paine and consequently is the best place for national park info and accommodation reservations.

Parque Nacional Torres del Paine

Some 150km north of Natales is **PARQUE NACIONAL TORRES DEL PAINE** (daily 8.30am–8pm; summer CH$15,000; winter CH$7500), whose 2400 square kilometres were declared a UNESCO Biosphere Reserve in 1978. The stunning centrepiece of the park is the Paine massif, a prominent outcrop in the middle of the steppe that comprises several main mountain groups. These include the dramatic **Torres** ("Towers") themselves, which are incisor-shaped spires of smooth grey granite grouped around a central tarn; the **Cuernos** ("Horns"), jagged peaks of quite startling beauty, their dark upper caps of friable sedimentary rock contrasting with their pale igneous base; and **Cerro Paine Grande**, the tallest mountain in the park (3050m). Splayed around the foot of this massif are a startling collection of meltwater lakes whose colours range from Prussian blue to bright turquoise; glaciers streaming off the Hielo Continental Sur; forests of *Nothofagus* southern beech; and semi-wooded pastureland that joins with boggy river meadows and arid steppe.

The park sees over 150,000 visitors a year and, especially in high season (late Dec–Feb), you'll have to contend with some busy trails and coach-tour groups at the major lowland sites of interest. The **best times to visit** are the quieter periods, from November to early December, or in March and April – when it's less windy and the autumn leaves provide a stunning backdrop – though the park is extensive enough always to offer options for those who seek solitude. Although you can get a taste of Torres del Paine on a day-tour, the most rewarding treks take four to seven days. The park is also one of the best places to see guanaco up close, and there's a healthy condor population.

Arrival and information

Numerous regular public **buses** (depart 7–8am; CH$15,000 return-trip) leave daily from their respective companies' offices in Puerto Natales for the park; the return leg is open and you can be picked up by the same company at one of several spots along the park road. The main **park gate** is at **Laguna Amarga** (115km from Natales), from where several unsealed roads run further into the park. The principal route runs for 56km like a bent fishhook through the south of Paine to the southern end of **Lago Grey**, which is fed by the enormous icecap **glacier** of the same name. On the way, this road passes a short detour to the pretty waterfalls of Salto Grande (24km from the gate); the exceptionally beautiful turquoise **Lago Pehoé** (27km), with its splendid views of the Cuernos del Paine and a good **boat excursion**, which runs between the Pudeto and Lago Pehoé refugios (Nov to mid-March 9.30am, noon & 6pm, fewer rest of year; 30min one way; CH$11,000 or CHS$17,000 return, plus CH$4000 per bag); and the main **park administration** and **information centre** at Lago del Toro (40km). Another road from the main gate runs 7km west to the *Hostería Las Torres* and campsite, which is the starting point for the park's classic treks (see p.740); while a third runs north for a similar distance to the Cascada Paine, a low but impressively powerful waterfall in the gully of the Río Paine.

Trekkers must register at the park gate (bring your passport). The **weather** in this area of the world is extremely temperamental. You can get caught in snow blizzards even in mid-summer, so it is vital that you come fully prepared even if you're just doing a day-hike. The place is also famous for its unremitting **winds**, which – at speeds of up to 60kph between October and March – can blow hard enough to knock you off your feet. If you're just going for a day-trip, it may be worth phoning the park administration (daily 8.30am–8pm; ⓣ061/691931) to check what the weather is like, as it can be very different

Tours into Torres del Paine

Day-tours into **Torres del Paine** can be booked at most tourist agencies in Puerto Natales, stopping at all the major road-accessible spots in the park and visiting the Cueva del Milodón quickly on the way (depart around 7.30am; 12hr; CH$17,500 per person, plus park entrance). Servitur, Arturo Prat 353 (Ⓣ61/411858, Ⓦwww.servitur.cl), has a good reputation and specializes in running trips to the national park; Fortaleza Aventura, Arturo Prat 234 (Ⓣ061/410595), is owned by an active young crowd, and also offers a reliable, fun service; while Onas Patagonia, Eberhard 599 (Ⓣ61/412707; Ⓦwww.onaspatagonia.com), organizes tours into the south of the park via the **Glaciar Balmaceda** and **Río Serrano** (CH$70,000). Big Foot, Bories 206 (Ⓣ61/414611, Ⓦwww.bigfootpatagonia.com), sells ice-climbing and glacier-hiking packages (from CH$50,000 per day) and multi-day rafting options (three days on Río Serrano CH$305,000).

from that in Puerto Natales. The administration will normally store luggage, and buses leave here for Natales between noon and 6.30pm in season (check off-season times in Natales).

You are strongly advised to invest in a decent **map** (especially if trekking). These are sold in numerous outlets in Natales, and the best available is Mattassi's *Mapas* series, #13 *Torres del Paine* (CH$3500); it gives you plenty of information about the refuges and campsites in the park, which can be supplemented by chatting to fellow trekkers and the *guardaparques* to find out about the most recent situation concerning litter, mice and trail conditions.

Accommodation in the park

The park is well served by a network of **campsites** and **refuges** as well as more luxurious hotel accommodation; indeed, if you're tackling Paine after trekking in Parque Nacional Los Glaciares, the slickness of the operation – and the expense – will come as quite a shock. If visiting between December and February, it is essential to book as much in advance (ie months) as possible. The majority of places are run as short-term park concessions, and service varies depending on the concessionaire. The *refugios* (US$20–39 per person) and campgrounds (free–CH$8000 per person) are run by three operators: Andescape (Ⓣ61/412592, Ⓦwww.andescapetour.com) and Fantástico Sur (Ⓣ61/226054, Ⓦwww.lastorres.com) – who share the Path@gone office in Puerto Natales, at Eberhard 595 – and Comapa, Bulnes 533 (Ⓣ61/414300, Ⓦwww.comapa.com). These refuges are well-run, comfortable, thirty-bed outfits, and facilities include hot showers, kitchen, equipment rental, and a full meal service (dinner costs around CH$10,000); you can also buy very pricey groceries. The free *refugios*, such as the one at Pudeto jetty on Lago Pehoé, are not particularly clean and are generally worth avoiding. In high season, some of the more popular campsites fill up with litter (*Italiano* is notorious for this) and, although there is no hantavirus in the park, mice have been known to chew through tents to get at food; to avoid them getting at yours, store your supplies in a plastic bag and tie it to a tree branch. Note, *Lodge Paine Grande* (US$35) and its campsite (CH$18,000 per site with free hot showers) is beautifully sited but gets extremely busy.

Hotels and luxury campsite

The **hotels** in the park all tend to be expensive, but still need booking well in advance, particularly in the high season.

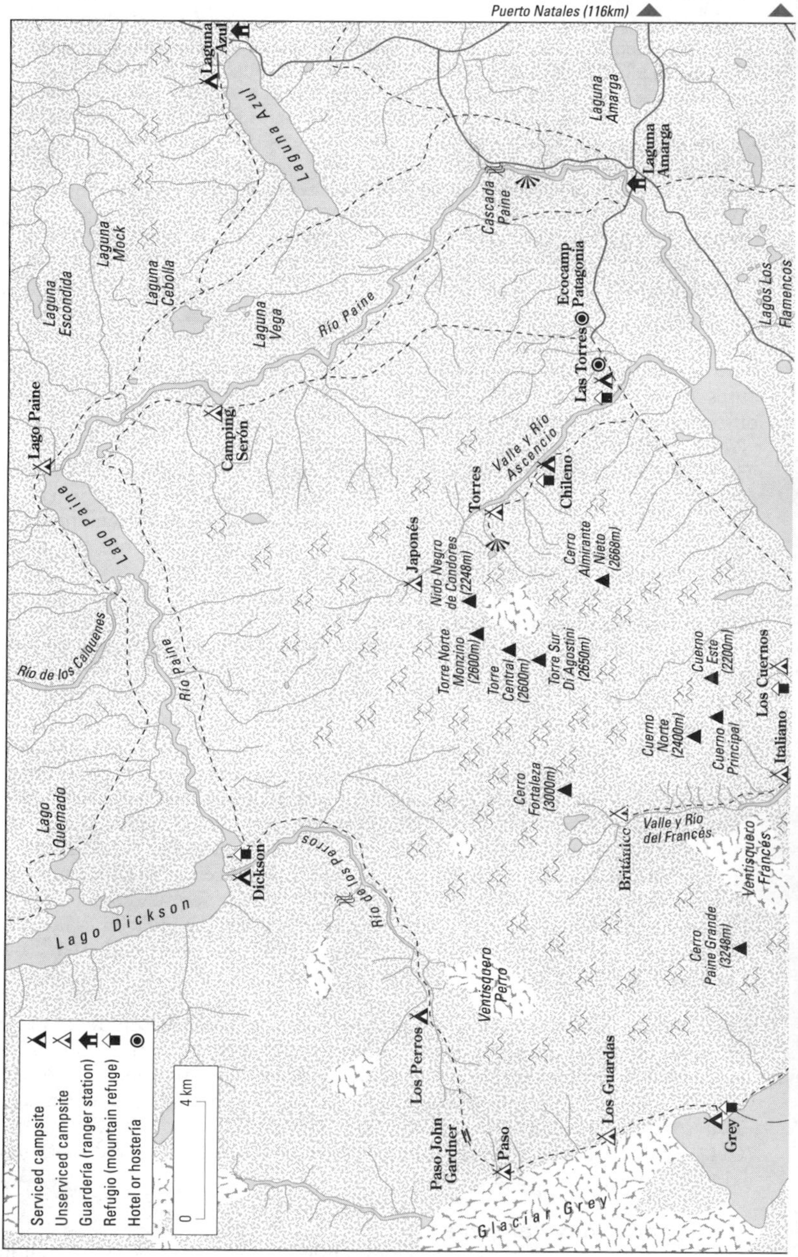
Puerto Natales (116km)
Serviced campsite
Unserviced campsite
Guardería (ranger station)
Refugio (mountain refuge)
Hotel or hostería
0
4 km
Laguna Azul
Laguna Azul
Laguna Amarga
Laguna Amarga
Cascada Paine
Laguna Mock
Laguna Escondida
Laguna Cebolla
Laguna Vega
Río Paine
Ecocamp Patagonia
Lagos Los Flamencos
Las Torres
Lago Paine
Lago Paine
Camping Serón
Valle y Río Ascencio
Torres
Chileno
Japonés
Nido Negro de Condores (2248m)
Cerro Almirante Nieto (2668m)
Río de los Calquenes
Río Paine
Torre Norte Monzino (2600m)
Torre Central (2600m)
Torre Sur Di Agostini (2650m)
Cuerno Este (2200m)
Los Cuernos
Cuerno Norte (2400m)
Cuerno Principal
Italiano
Lago Quemado
Cerro Fortaleza (3000m)
Británico
Valle y Río del Francés
Ventisquero Francés
Lago Dickson
Dickson
Río de los Perros
Ventisquero Perro
Cerro Paine Grande (3248m)
Los Perros
Los Guardas
Paso John Gardner
Paso
Grey
Glaciar Grey

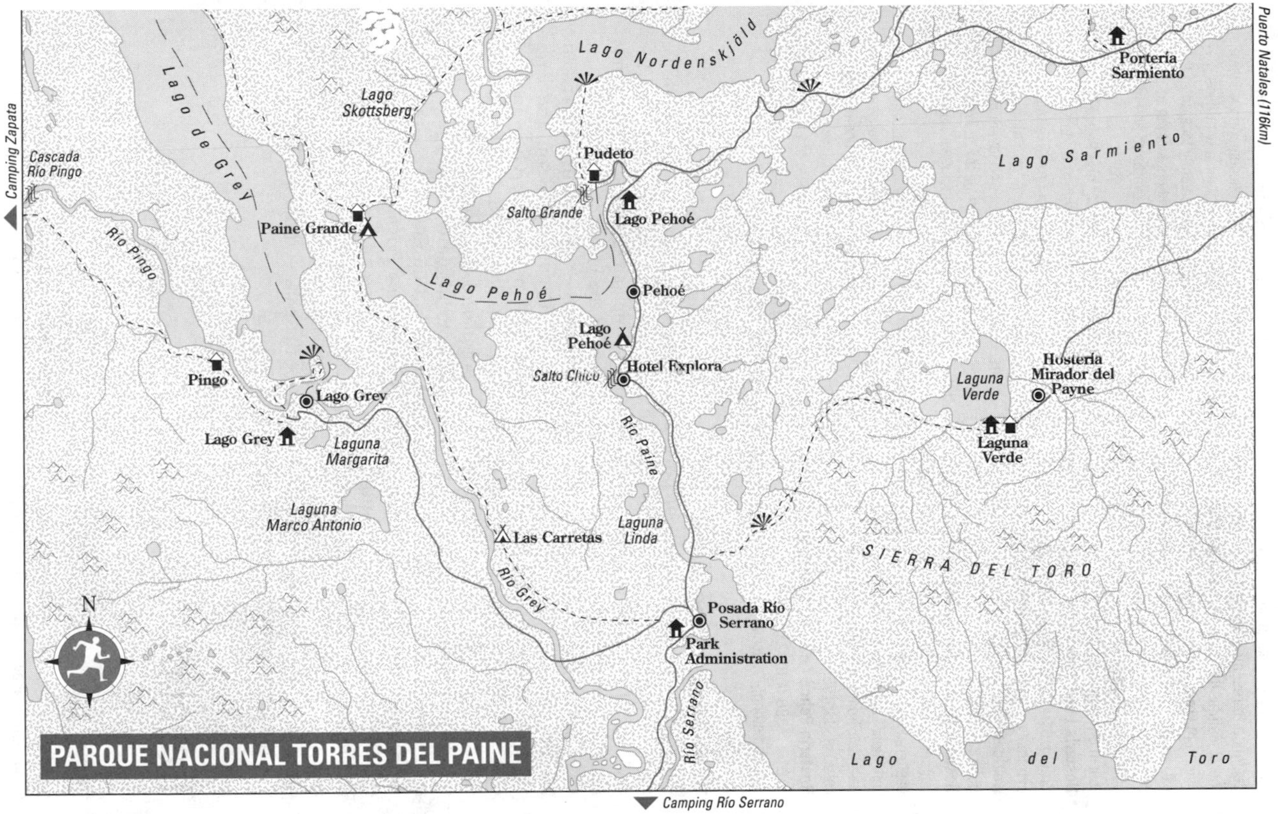
PARQUE NACIONAL TORRES DEL PAINE
Puerto Natales (116km)
Camping Zapata
Camping Río Serrano
Portería Sarmiento
Lago Sarmiento
Lago Nordenskjöld
Lago Skottsberg
Lago de Grey
Cascada Río Pingo
Río Pingo
Pingo
Paine Grande
Lago Pehoé
Pudeto
Salto Grande
Pehoé
Lago Pehoé
Hotel Explora
Salto Chico
Río Paine
Lago Grey
Laguna Margarita
Laguna Marco Antonio
Las Carretas
Laguna Linda
Río Grey
Posada Río Serrano
Park Administration
Río Serrano
Laguna Verde
Hostería Mirador del Payne
SIERRA DEL TORO
Lago del Toro
N

EcoCamp Patagonia In the centre of the park, near *Hostería Las Torres* ⓣ2/232-9878, ⓦwww.ecocamp.travel. Collection of novel pod tents, designed to resemble the igloo-shaped huts of the Alacalufe, the area's original inhabitants, run using only renewable energy sources. The extremely comfortable "pods" (doubles only) are connected by a series of raised wooden platforms. US$215 per person per night, four-night minimum stay.

Hostería Lago Grey At the southern end of Lago Grey ⓣ61/410220, ⓦwww.lagogrey.cl. Inviting, extremely popular place overlooking the lake, with well-designed, airy cabins and attentive service. US$180–200.

Hostería Mirador del Payne 61/228712, ⓦwww.miradordelpayne.com. Tucked away in the south-eastern corner of the park at the foot of the Sierra del Toro, near Laguna Verde; accommodation is in a verandah-fronted colonial-style house or eight cabañas. US$195.

Hostería Pehoé On an island in Lago Pehoé ⓣ61/411390 or 02/235-0252, ⓦwww.pehoe.cl. Superb setting – reached by an idyllic bridge and overlooking the Cuernos – but the rooms are rather basic for the price. ❽–❾

Hostería Las Torres In the centre of the park ⓣ61/710050, ⓦwww.lastorres.com. An exclusive, privately owned, sprawling estancia with good views up to the Torres; conveniently located at the end of the "W" circuit for trekkers looking to reward their feat. It runs its own tours and hires out horses. US$205.

Hotel Explora Just south of Lago Pehoé ⓣ61/411247, ⓦwww.explora.com. Luxury concept hotel, by far the most extravagant in the park, with jaw-dropping views from all the rooms, a gourmet restaurant and lavish added extras, including an open-air Jacuzzi. From US$2170 per person for all-inclusive four-night package.

Posada Río Serrano Near the administration building ⓣ61/410684, ⓦwww.baqueanozamora.com. The most atmospheric accommodation in Torres del Paine, set in an attractive, recently revamped old structure on the site of the park's first estancia. Rooms are tidy and the living area is snug. Rooms from US$190.

Trekking in the park

Though there are hundreds of possible options for trekking in this extensive park, the two most popular ones are the "**Circuit**" and the "**W**" (so called for the pattern the trail marks on the map), both of which are physically challenging but not particularly technical routes. The Circuit is the classic Paine trek, which takes around five to seven days to complete, and loops – customarily undertaken anticlockwise – around the entire massif via the Refugio Dickson, the Paso John Gardner (the highest point of the trail at 1241m), Glaciar Grey and the Cuernos del Paine, before finishing at *Hostería Las Torres*. The first leg of the more intense "W" hike, currently the more popular of the two, takes you up to the Torres themselves, and this is the best option for those who only have time for a **day-hike**. You then retrace your steps and head up the next major valley to the west, the Valle del Francés, as far as *Campamento Británico*, and complete the "W" by heading to Refugio Grey near the glacier of the same name. Pay particular attention at all times to responsible fire-lighting practices when camping – in February 2005, a month-long wildfire, caused by an overturned camp stove, damaged some 15,000 hectares of the park – and, especially on the Circuit, be prepared for very boggy sections.

Travel details

Buses

Some services do not operate out of season (Easter–Sept), above all along and around RN-40, whilst others are severely curtailed.

Bajo Caracoles to: Perito Moreno (every Tues; 2hr); Posadas (every Tues; 2hr).

Caleta Olivia to: Comandante Luis Piedra Buena (twice daily; 6hr); Comodoro Rivadavia (hourly; 1hr); Puerto Deseado (5 daily; 2hr 45min–3hr);

Puerto San Julián (twice daily; 4hr 30min); Río Gallegos (3 daily; 9hr).
Camarones to: Trelew (3 weekly; 3hr).
Carmen de Patagones to: Bahía Blanca (8–10 daily; 3hr 30min); Buenos Aires (3 daily; 12hr); Caleta Olivia (4 daily; 14hr); Comodoro Rivadavia (6 daily; 13hr); Mar del Plata (3 weekly; 9hr 30min); Puerto Madryn (6 daily; 6hr); Neuquén (daily; 10hr 15min); Trelew (6 daily; 6hr 40min); Viedma (every 30min; 15min).
Comandante Luis Piedra Buena to: Caleta Olivia (3 daily; 6hr); Comodoro Rivadavia (4 daily; 6hr 30min–8hr); Puerto San Julián (4 daily; 1hr 30min); Río Gallegos (6 daily; 3hr).
Comodoro Rivadavia to: Buenos Aires (3 daily; 24hr); Caleta Olivia (hourly; 1hr); Carmen de Patagones (6 daily; 13hr); Esquel (1–2 daily; 8hr); Puerto Madryn (10 daily; 6hr); Puerto San Julián (10 daily; 5hr–6hr 30min); Río Gallegos (10 daily; 10–12hr); Rio Mayo (daily; 4hr); Sarmiento (5 daily; 2hr 15min); Trelew (several hourly; 5hr 15min).
Dolavon to: Gaiman (8–13 daily; 25–35min); Trelew (8–13 daily; 55min–1hr 15min).
El Calafate to: El Chaltén (9–10 daily; 4hr); Perito Moreno (daily in summer; 13hr); Río Gallegos (4–5 daily; 4hr–4hr 30min); Río Turbio (2 daily; 4hr); Ushuaia (via Chile; Mon–Sat daily; 18hr).
El Chaltén to: El Calafate (9–10 daily; 4hr); Lago del Desierto (3 daily; 1hr); Perito Moreno (daily in summer; 13hr).
Gaiman to: Dolavon (8–13 daily; 25–35min); Trelew (11–18 daily; 25–35min).
Los Antiguos to: El Chaltén (daily in summer; 13hr); Perito Moreno (5–9 daily; 50min).
Perito Moreno to: Bajo Caracoles (every Tues; 2hr); Comodoro Rivadavia (2–3 daily; 5 hr); El Calafate (daily in summer; 13hr); El Chaltén (daily in summer; 13hr); Los Antiguos (5–9 daily; 50min); Posadas (every Tues; 4hr).
Posadas to: Bajo Caracoles (every Tues; 2hr); Perito Moreno (every Tues; 4hr).
Puerto Deseado to: Caleta Olivia (5 daily; 2hr 45min–3hr).
Puerto Madryn to: Bariloche (1–3 daily; 9hr); Buenos Aires (13–14 daily; 18hr); Carmen de Patagones (6 daily; 6hr); Comodoro Rivadavia (12 daily; 6hr); Puerto Pirámides (1–2 daily; 1hr 15min); Río Gallegos (5–7 daily; 16–19hr); Trelew (hourly; 1hr).
Puerto Natales to: Punta Arenas (hourly; 3hr).
Puerto Pirámides to: Puerto Madryn (1–2 daily; 1hr 15min); Trelew (daily in summer; 2hr 45min).
Puerto San Julián to: Comandante Luis Piedra Buena (4 daily; 1hr 30min); Comodoro Rivadavia (10 daily; 5hr–6hr 30min); Río Gallegos (hourly; 4–5hr); Trelew (5 daily; 10hr 30min).
Punta Arenas to: Puerto Natales (hourly; 3hr).
Río Gallegos to: Caleta Olivia (3 daily; 9hr); Comodoro Rivadavia (10 daily; 10–12hr); El Calafate (10–12 daily; 3hr 30min–4hr 30min); Puerto Madryn (7 daily; 18–19hr); Río Grande (via Chile; 6 weekly; 13hr); Puerto San Julián (hourly; 4–5hr); Trelew (4 daily; 15–16hr); Ushuaia (via Chile; 1–2 daily; 13hr).
Río Turbio to: El Calafate (2 daily; 4hr); Río Gallegos (4 daily; 5hr).
Sarmiento to: Comodoro Rivadavia (5 daily; 2hr 15min); Esquel (1–2 daily; 6hr); Río Mayo (daily; 3hr).
Trelew to: Bariloche (3 daily; 13hr); Buenos Aires (11 daily; 19–21hr); Camarones (3 weekly; 3hr); Comodoro Rivadavia (several hourly; 5hr 15min); Dolavon (11–18 daily; 55min–1hr 15min); Esquel (daily; 8hr 30min); Gaiman (11–18 daily; 25–35min); Puerto Madryn (hourly; 1hr); Puerto Pirámides (daily; 2hr 45min); Puerto San Julián (5 daily; 10hr–11hr 30min); Rawson (every 15min; 20min); Río Gallegos (4 daily; 15–16hr).
Viedma to: Carmen de Patagones (every 30min; 15min).

Trains

Bariloche to: Viedma (Thurs & Sun 5pm; 17hr).
Viedma to: Bariloche (Mon & Fri 6pm; 17hr).

Ferries

Puerto Natales to: Puerto Montt (weekly; 66hr).
Punta Arenas to: Porvenir (Tues–Sun daily; 2hr 20min); Puerto Williams (Nov–March weekly; 34hr).
Punta Delgada to: Bahía Azul, across the Magellan Straits (every 40min, no crossings at low tide; 30min).

Flights

Comodoro Rivadavia to: Buenos Aires (1–3 daily; 2hr); Perito Moreno (Mon; 1hr); Río Gallegos (2 daily; 1hr 15min); Trelew (daily; 45min).
El Calafate to: Bariloche (1–2 daily; 2hr); Buenos Aires (2–4 daily; 3hr); Puerto Natales (5 weekly; 1hr); Río Gallegos (4 weekly; 50min); Ushuaia (2–3 daily; 1hr 10min).
Puerto Madryn to: Buenos Aires (daily; 2hr); Ushuaia (irregular; 2hr). *See also* Trelew.
Perito Moreno to: Comodoro Rivadavia (Mon; 1hr).
Punta Arenas to: Porvenir (Mon–Sat 2–3 daily; 20min); Puerto Williams (Tues–Sun; 1hr 15min); Ushuaia (3 weekly; 1hr).
Río Gallegos to: Buenos Aires (2–3 daily; 3hr); Comodoro Rivadavia (2 daily; 1hr 15min);

El Calafate (daily; 50min); Río Grande (twice weekly; 1hr 15min); Ushuaia (daily 55min).
Trelew to: Buenos Aires (3–4 daily; 1hr 50min); Comodoro Rivadavia (daily; 1hr); Ushuaia (irregular; 2hr).

International buses

Chile Chico to: Los Antiguos (3 daily; 40min).
El Calafate to: Puerto Natales (1–2 daily; 5hr).
Los Antiguos to: Chile Chico (3 daily; 40min).
Río Gallegos to: Puerto Natales (1–2 daily; 7hr); Punta Arenas (daily; 5hr).
Río Turbio to: Puerto Natales (1–2 daily; 1hr).
Punta Arenas to: Río Gallegos (daily; 5hr); Río Grande (Mon–Sat daily; 9hr); Ushuaia (daily except Tues; 12hr).
Puerto Natales to: El Calafate (1–2 daily; 5hr); Río Gallegos (4 weekly; 4hr); Río Turbio (1–2 daily; 1hr); Ushuaia (4 weekly; 16hr).
Sarmiento to: Coyhaique (5 weekly; 12hr).

9

Tierra del Fuego

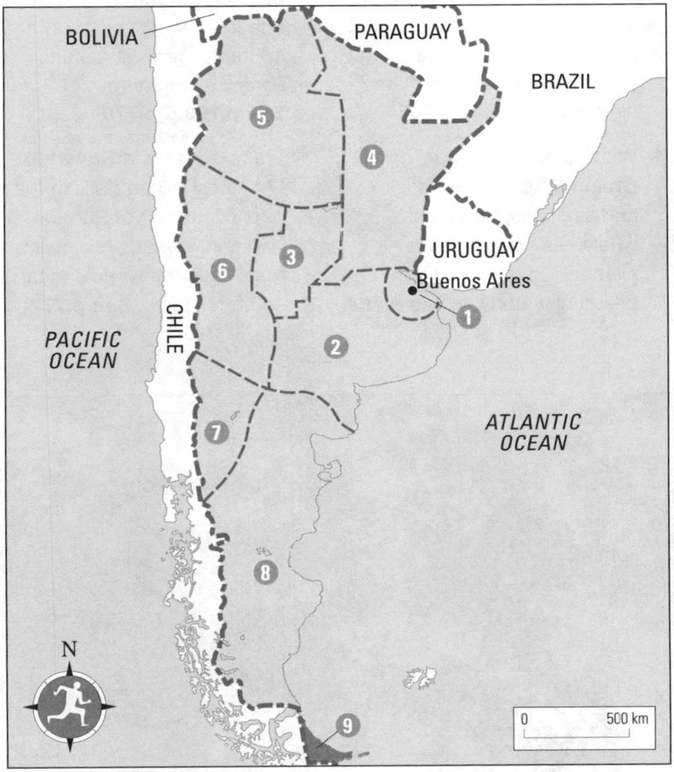

CHAPTER 9

Highlights

* **Arriving at Ushuaia by plane** The town's dramatic location – wedged between the tail-end of the Andes and the Beagle Channel – makes this a landing to remember. See p.748

* **Fresh king crab** Plucked straight from the Beagle Channel, *centolla* appears on all the best menus in Ushuaia, and is delicious served in soups, baked in its shell or simply grilled. See p.756

* **Wildlife in the Beagle Channel** Spot albatrosses and sea lions, terns and whales as you brave the elements in this stunningly beautiful waterway. See p.759

* **Parque Nacional Tierra del Fuego** Parakeets and hummingbirds are some of the surprising inhabitants of this precious forestland. See p.760

* **Estancia stays** Get away from it all at charming *Estancia Rivadavia*, or get a taste of working life on a Fuegian farm at historic *Estancia Viamonte*. See p.769 & p.770

* **Trekking on Isla Navarino** The finest hiking trails in the region lead out of Puerto Williams – what Chile claims to be truly the world's most southerly town. See p.777

△ Parque Nacional Tierra del Fuego

9

Tierra del Fuego

Across the Magellan Strait from mainland Patagonia, **TIERRA DEL FUEGO** is a land of windswept bleakness, whose settlements seem to huddle with their backs against the elements: cold winters, cool summers, gales in the spring, frost in the autumn. Yet this remote archipelago, tucked away at the foot of the South American continent, exercises a fascination over many travellers. Some look to follow in the footsteps of the region's famous explorers, such as navigator Ferdinand Magellan, naturalist Charles Darwin or more recently, author Bruce Chatwin. Others just want to see what it's like down here, at the very end of the world.

Though comprising a number of islands, it's more or less the sum of its most developed part, **Isla Grande**, the biggest island in South America. Its eastern section, roughly a third of the island, along with a few islets, belongs to Argentina – the rest is Chilean territory. The major destination for visitors is the Argentine city of **Ushuaia**, a year-round resort on the south coast. Beautifully located, backed by distinctive jagged mountains, it is *the* base for visiting the tremendous **Beagle Channel**, rich in marine wildlife, and the wild, forested peaks of the **Cordillera Darwin**. With the lakes, forests and tundra of **Parque Nacional Tierra del Fuego** just 12km to the west, and historic **Estancia Harberton**, home to descendants of Thomas Bridges, an Anglican missionary who settled here in 1871, a short excursion from the city, you could easily spend a week or so in the area.

Lago Fagnano, and the village of **Tolhuin** at its eastern end, are the main focus of the island's central area, which is of considerably greater interest than the windswept plains and scrubby *coirón* grasslands in the north. From Tolhuin to **Paso Garibaldi** – at 430m, the gateway to Ushuaia by road – you travel through patches of transitional Fuegian woodland, where lichen beards hanging from gnarled branches make it look as though a tickertape parade has just passed by. Much of the area's beauty, together with its isolated estancias, is only really accessible to those with their own transport. Try the loop along the RCf and RCh roads or, better still, the **RCa**, which winds through some rugged scenery along the eastern coastline. Connecting all of these minor roads is RN-3, which passes the bleak **Río Grande** – only really useful as an overnight stop for travellers entering the island by one of the ferry crossings – on its journey north to Buenos Aires.

The southeastern chunk of Isla Grande, **Península Mitre**, is one of Argentina's least accessible regions, a boggy wilderness with low scrub and next to no human habitation, while, to its east, lies the mysterious **Isla de los Estados**, known in English as Staten Island. It is another extremely difficult area to visit, even more than the great white continent of **Antarctica**, which can be reached from Ushuaia (see box, p.760), at a price.

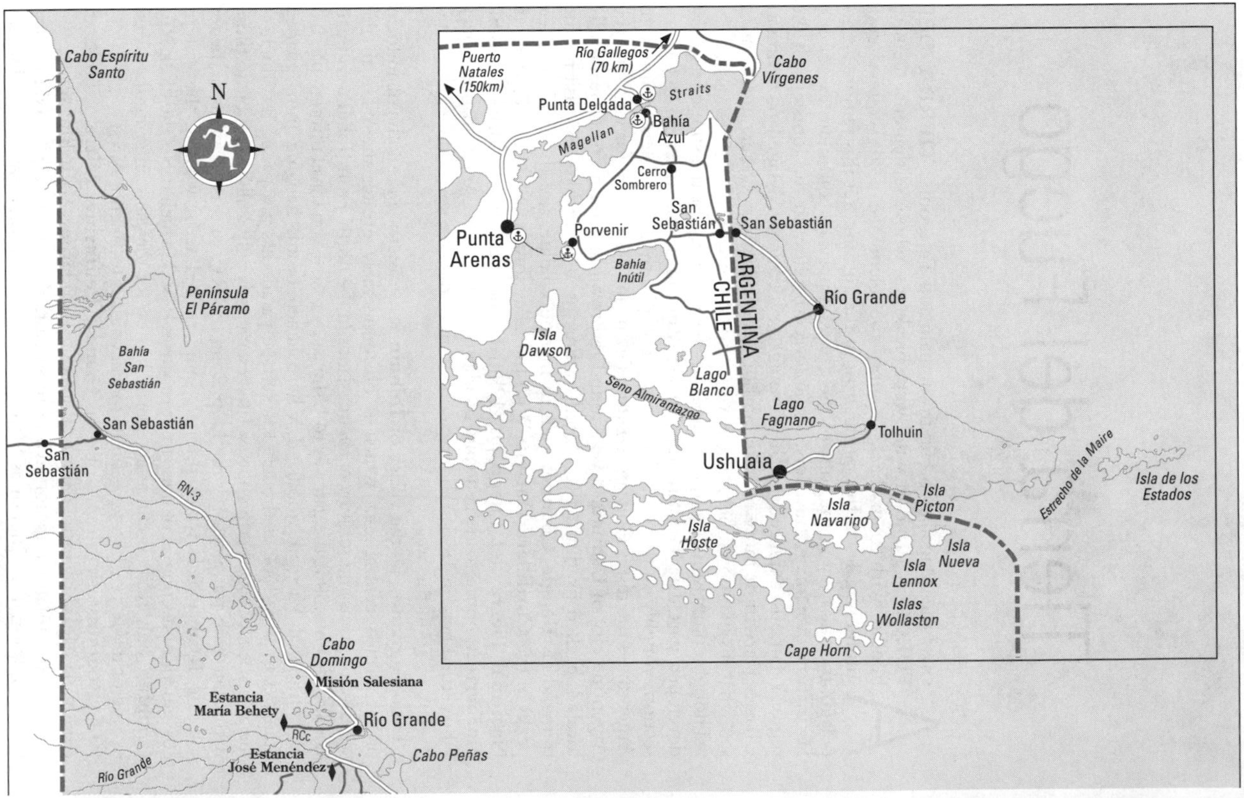
Cabo Espíritu Santo
N
Península El Páramo
Bahía San Sebastián
San Sebastián
San Sebastián
RN-3
Cabo Domingo
Misión Salesiana
Estancia María Behety
Río Grande
RCc
Estancia José Menéndez
Río Grande
Cabo Peñas
Puerto Natales (150km)
Río Gallegos (70 km)
Punta Delgada
Straits
Bahía Azul
Magellan
Cabo Vírgenes
Cerro Sombrero
San Sebastián
San Sebastián
Punta Arenas
Porvenir
Bahía Inútil
ARGENTINA
CHILE
Río Grande
Isla Dawson
Lago Blanco
Seno Almirantazgo
Lago Fagnano
Tolhuin
Ushuaia
Estrecho de la Maire
Isla de los Estados
Isla Picton
Isla Navarino
Isla Hoste
Isla Nueva
Isla Lennox
Islas Wollaston
Cape Horn

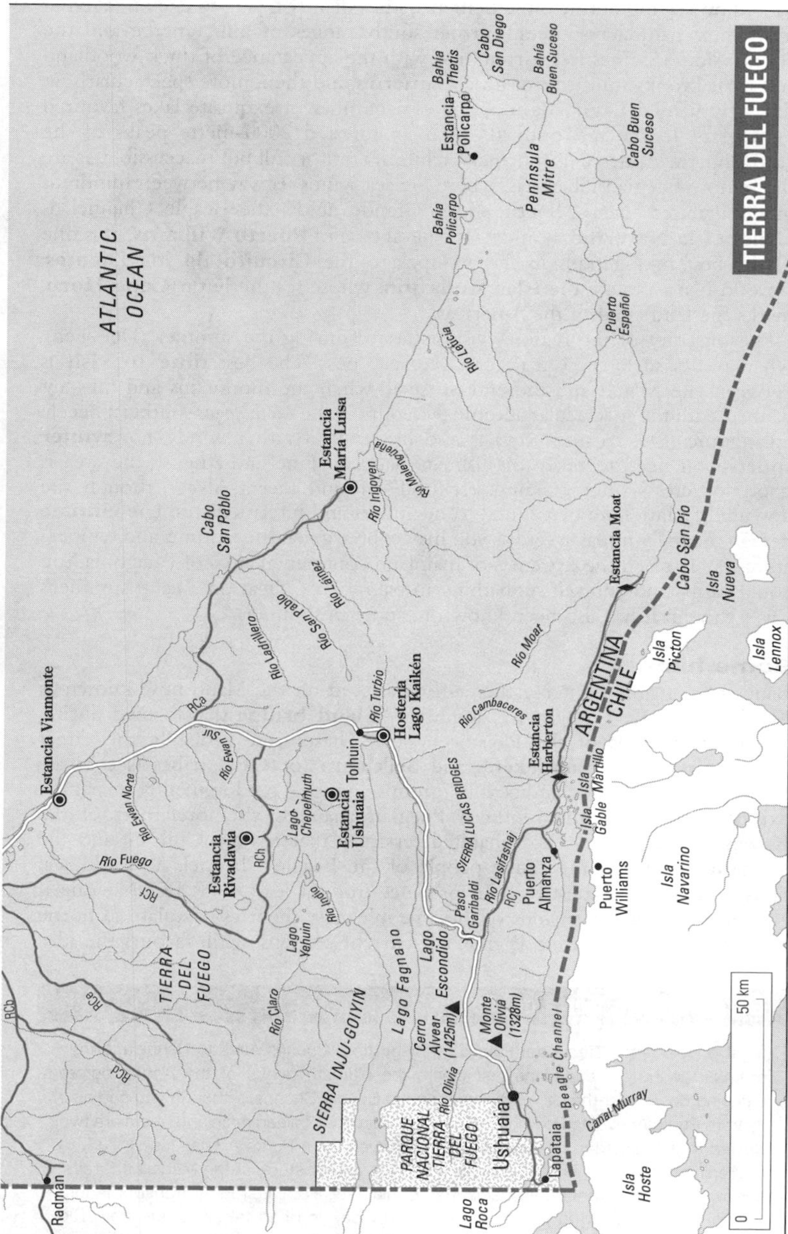
TIERRA DEL FUEGO
ATLANTIC OCEAN
Estancia Viamonte
Cabo San Pablo
Estancia María Luisa
Bahía Policarpo
Estancia Policarpo
Bahía Thetis
Cabo San Diego
Bahía Buen Suceso
Península Mitre
Cabo Buen Suceso
Puerto Español
Río Leticia
Río Irigoyen
Río Malengüena
Río Láinez
Río San Pablo
Río Ladrillero
Río Turbio
Hostería Lago Kaikén
Tolhuin
RCa
Río Ewan Sur
Río Ewan Norte
Estancia Ushuaia
Lago Chepelmuth
Estancia Rivadavia
RCh
Río Fuego
RCf
Río Indio
Lago Yehuin
TIERRA DEL FUEGO
RCb
RCe
RCd
Río Claro
Radman
SIERRA INJU-GOIYIN
Lago Fagnano
Lago Escondido
Cerro Alvear (1425m)
Monte Olivia (1328m)
Río Olivia
PARQUE NACIONAL TIERRA DEL FUEGO
Ushuaia
Lapataia
Lago Roca
Beagle Channel
Canal Murray
Isla Hoste
Paso Garibaldi
SIERRA LUCAS BRIDGES
Río Lasifashaj
RCj
Puerto Almanza
Puerto Williams
Isla Navarino
Isla Gable
Isla Martillo
Estancia Harberton
Río Cambaceres
Río Moat
ARGENTINA
CHILE
Estancia Moat
Cabo San Pío
Isla Nueva
Isla Picton
Isla Lennox
0
50 km

On the less-visited **Chilean side** of Tierra del Fuego, the main town is **Porvenir**, easily accessible from Punta Arenas by plane and ferry, and accompanied by a string of tiny oil settlements, still valiantly trying to eke out a living from their natural resources. Further south, ranges of hills emerge and the countryside becomes less barren, first with the appearance of thick woodland and clear brooks southeast of little **Camerón** and then, more spectacularly, at the aptly named **Lago Blanco**, one of a number of exquisite lakes favoured by anglers. In the far south, the densely forested 2000-metre peaks of the cordillera, the Andes' tail-end, make Chilean territory all but inaccessible, as are the remote Fuegian Channels, where the sea winds its way between hundreds of uninhabited islands. South of Isla Grande, across the Beagle Channel, is Chilean **Isla Navarino**, home to the naval base of **Puerto Williams**, plus one of the best hiking trails in the archipelago, the **Circuito de los Dientes**. Beyond Navarino are the **Islas Wollaston**, whose southerly tip, **Cape Horn**, marks the land's end of the Americas.

The majority of the region's visitors arrive during the summer (Dec–Feb), when places such as Ushuaia can get very busy. The best **time to visit** is between late March and the end of April, when the mountains and hills are daubed with the spectacular autumnal colours of the *Nothofagus* southern beech. Springtime (Oct to mid-Nov) is also beautiful, if rather windy. For **winter sports**, you need to head for Ushuaia between June and August; the area is good for cross-country skiing, especially around Sierra Alvear, though the downhill facilities are best suited to beginners and intermediates. The **climate** here is generally not as severe as you may expect given the latitude, and temperatures rarely reach the extremes of mainland continental areas of Patagonia. You could easily find yourself sunbathing in balmy 20°C heat on a calm summer's day – though it has also been known to snow in summer.

Some history

Bands of nomadic hunter-gatherers first arrived on the island now known as Isla Grande some 12,000 years ago across a **land bridge** that formed during glacial fluctuations of the Pleistocene era. These were probably the direct antecedents of the **Mannekenk** and **Selk'nam** (or **Ona**) tribes (see boxes, p.768 & p.770). Later, indigenous groups living a predominantly maritime existence colonized the southern Fuegian channels: the forefathers of the **Kawéskar** (Alacaluf) who inhabited territory that is now Chilean; and the **Yámana** (Yaghans), the canoe people of the Beagle Channel. Archeological finds near Ushuaia attest to their presence from at least 4000 BC. No one is certain about the provenance of these people: new theories postulate seaborne migrations from across the Pacific, but current consensus still favours the idea

The journey to Tierra del Fuego

Most people reach **Tierra del Fuego** by **flying** from Buenos Aires to Ushuaia, a truly dramatic journey – the plane just clears the ultimate peaks of the Andes before plunging down over the city and skimming the Beagle Channel – though you can also fly from Punta Arenas to Porvenir or Ushuaia. From the Chilean mainland, there are two **ferries** to Isla Grande: the *Barcaza Melinka* travels from Punta Arenas (see p.733) to Porvenir, while the *Bahía Azul* crosses the Primera Angostura, at the Magellan Straits' narrowest section, from Punta Delgada to Bahía Azul. Both are run by Transbordadora Austral Broom, based in Punta Arenas. Otherwise, you can take the **bus** from Río Gallegos, Puerto Natales or Punta Arenas to Río Grande and then on to Ushuaia.

that they evolved from the same ethnic base as the terrestrial groups, in spite of considerable ethnographic and linguistic differences.

In 1520, **Ferdinand Magellan**, as he sailed through the straits that were later named after him, espied clouds of smoke rising from numerous fires that the Selk'nam lit along the coast of Isla Grande and called the land Tierra del Humo ("Land of Smoke"); it was the king of Spain who thought Tierra del Fuego, or "Land of Fire", much more poetic. Early contact between indigenous groups and other **European explorers** was sporadic from the sixteenth century onwards, even with the advent of commercial whaling and sealing in the eighteenth century, but this changed dramatically in the latter half of the nineteenth century, with tragic results for the indigenous population. When FitzRoy came here in the *Beagle* in the 1830s, an estimated three to four thousand Selk'nam and Mannekenk were living in Isla Grande, with some three thousand each of Yámana and Kawéskar in the entire southern archipelago. By the 1930s, however, the Mannekenk were virtually extinct, and the other groups had been effectively annihilated.

White settlement came to Tierra del Fuego in three phases. Anglican **missionaries** began to catechize the Yámana in the south, and Thomas Bridges established the first permanent mission on Ushuaia Bay in 1871. From the late 1880s, the Italian Roman Catholic Salesian Order began a similar process to the north of the Fuegian Andes, consolidated with the foundation of their first mission near the Río Grande river in 1893. Alluvial **gold** was discovered on the island in 1879, and soon afterwards a Romanian-born adventurer, Julius Popper, established a fiefdom based around Bahía San Sebastián, which he ruled as a despot between 1887 and 1893, issuing his own coinage and periodically gunning down the indigenous inhabitants. From the mid-1890s came a new colonizing impetus: the inauspicious-looking northern plains proved to be ideal **sheep-farming** territory, and vast *latifundias* sprang up, owned by money-chasing magnates such as José Menéndez. Croat, Scottish, Basque, Italian and Galician immigrants, along with Chileans from across the border, arrived to work on the estancias and build up their own landholdings.

The issue of that international border has been a contentious one over the years, as it has been along other sections of the Argentina–Chile boundary. Frontier disputes at the end of the nineteenth century required the arbitration of Great Britain, who in 1902 awarded Argentina the eastern half of Tierra del Fuego; land squabbles were still going on over eighty years later, the two countries almost coming to war in 1984 over the Beagle Channel islands of Lennox, Nueva and Picton. This time it took the intervention of Pope John Paul II, who, possibly to even things up, gave the islands to Chile. A cordial peace has reigned since. In 1991, the Argentine sector gained full provincial status and is known as the **Provincia de Tierra del Fuego, Antártida e Islas del Atlántico Sur**. Its jurisdiction is seen to extend over all southern territories, including the Islas Malvinas/Falklands Islands (see box, pp.800–801), which lie 550km off the coast, and the Argentine segment of Antarctica.

Today, Tierra del Fuego's **economy** is dependent on the production of petroleum and natural gas, fisheries, forestry and technological industries such as television assembly plants, which were attracted to the area by its status as a duty-free zone. Luxury items are comparatively cheap, but basic items such as food are much more expensive than in other parts of the country, owing to the huge distances involved in importing them. Hopes run high for the fast-expanding tourist industry centred on Ushuaia.

Ushuaia and around

USHUAIA, the provincial capital and hub of tourism for the whole of Tierra del Fuego, lies in the far south of Isla Grande. Dramatically situated between the mountains – amongst them **Cerro Martial** and **Monte Olivia** – and the sea, the town tumbles, rather chaotically, down the hillside to the encircling arm of land that protects its bay from the southwesterly winds and occasional thrashing storms of the icy **Beagle Channel**. Ushuaia is primarily a convenient base for exploring the rugged beauty of the lands that border the channel, a historically important sea passage, but be warned that it exploits tourism to the full – prices can be high, but services are usually of a correspondingly good standard. Puerto Williams lies just across the channel, on the southern (Chilean) side of the straits, and there are other trips, too: to historic **Estancia Harberton**, and to Bahía Lapataia in Parque Nacional Tierra del Fuego (see p.757). In winter, there's decent skiing in the **Sierra Alvear** region north of town; this area, along with neighbouring Sierra Valdivieso and Chile's Isla Navarino (see p.775), are also the places to head for if you're looking for physically challenging **trekking**.

Every year on June 21 – the longest night of the year – the **Bajada de Las Antorchas** takes place, with the darkness celebrated by a torchlit ski descent of Cerro Martial's slopes, traditionally opening the season. Daylight lasts from about 9am till 4pm at this time of year. In mid-November, the town hosts the **Ushuaia Jazz Festival**, and between Christmas and New Year the municipality organizes various events, including live concerts, often with nationally famous bands.

Some history

In 1869, Reverend Waite Stirling became Tierra del Fuego's first white settler when he founded his **Anglican mission** amongst the Yámana here; the city takes its name from the Yámana tongue, and means something akin to "bay that stretches towards the west". Stirling stayed for six months, before being recalled to the Islas Malvinas/Falklands Islands to be appointed Anglican bishop for South America. Thomas Bridges, his assistant, took over the mission in 1871, after which time Ushuaia began to figure on mariners' charts as a place of refuge in the event of shipwreck. A modest **monument** to the achievements of the early missionaries can be found where the first mission stood, on the south side of Ushuaia Bay, and is reached by the modern causeway southwest of the town centre.

In 1884, Commodore Augusto Lasserre raised the Argentine flag over Ushuaia for the first time, formally incorporating the area into the Argentine Republic. From 1896, in order to consolidate its sovereignty and open up the region to wider colonization, the Argentine state established a **penal colony** here. Forced convict labour was used for developing the settlement's infrastructure and for logging the local forests to build the town (by 1910, 25km of railway had been constructed for this purpose), but the prison had a reputation as the Siberia of Argentina and Perón closed it in 1947.

Nowadays, Ushuaia has a quite different reputation: the most populous, and popular, town in Tierra del Fuego, it depends largely on its thriving tourist industry, capitalizing on the beauty of its natural setting. You'll soon catch on that this is the world's most southerly resort, allowing you to amass claims to fame galore – golf on the world's most southerly course, a ride on the world's most southerly train – but Ushuaia has plenty of sites worthy of a visit on their own merits, and not just for their unique geographical circumstance.

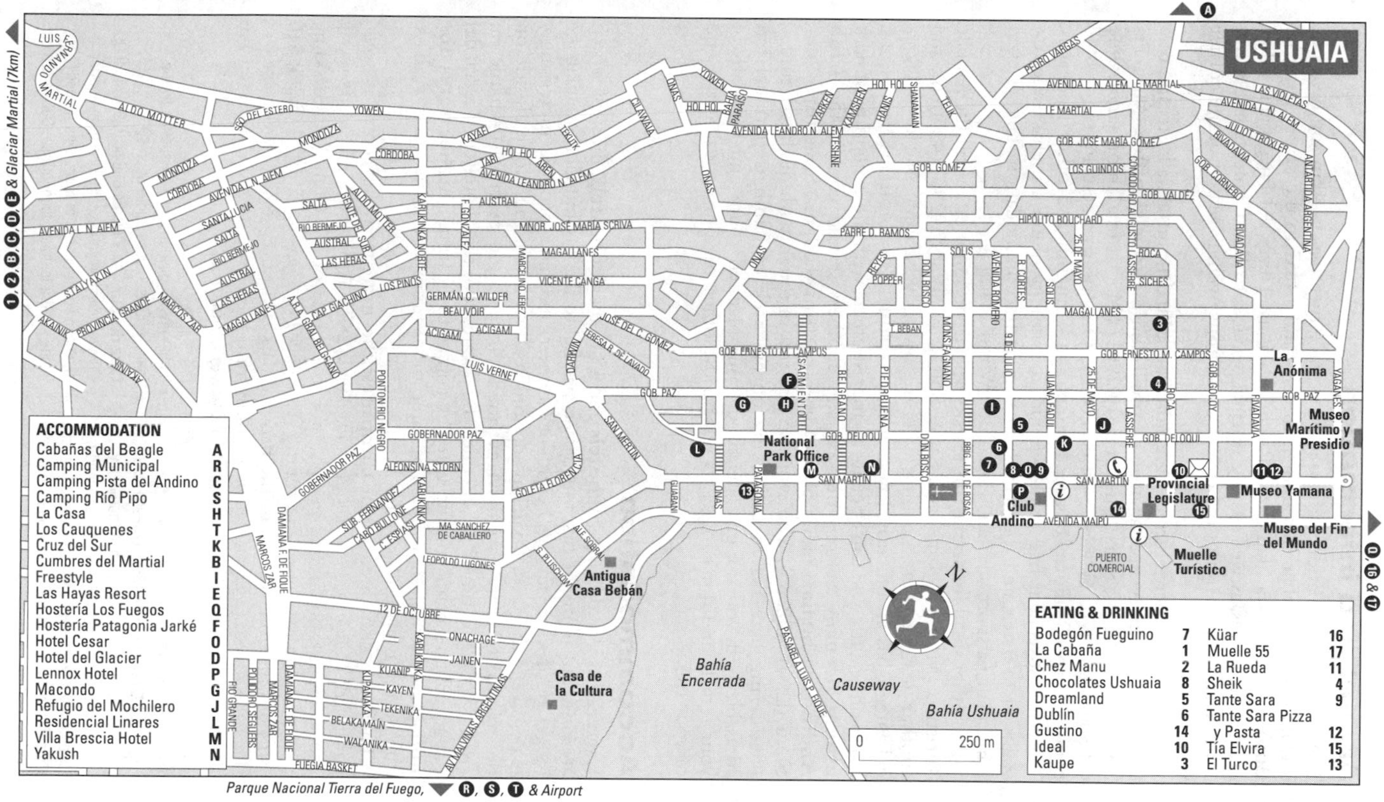

USHUAIA
ACCOMMODATION
Cabañas del Beagle A
Camping Municipal R
Camping Pista del Andino C
Camping Río Pipo S
La Casa H
Los Cauquenes T
Cruz del Sur K
Cumbres del Martial B
Freestyle I
Las Hayas Resort E
Hostería Los Fuegos Q
Hostería Patagonia Jarké F
Hotel Cesar O
Hotel del Glacier D
Lennox Hotel P
Macondo G
Refugio del Mochilero J
Residencial Linares L
Villa Brescia Hotel M
Yakush N
EATING & DRINKING
Bodegón Fueguino 7
La Cabaña 1
Chez Manu 2
Chocolates Ushuaia 8
Dreamland 5
Dublín 6
Gustino 14
Ideal 10
Kaupe 3
Küar 16
Muelle 55 17
La Rueda 11
Sheik 4
Tante Sara 9
Tante Sara Pizza y Pasta 12
Tía Elvira 15
El Turco 13
La Anónima
Museo Marítimo y Presidio
Museo Yamana
Provincial Legislature
Museo del Fin del Mundo
Muelle Turístico
Puerto Comercial
Club Andino
National Park Office
Antigua Casa Bebán
Casa de la Cultura
Bahía Encerrada
Bahía Ushuaia
Causeway
Pasarela Luis P. Fique
0 250 m
N
1, 2, B, C, D, E & Glaciar Martial (7km)
A
0, 16 & 17
Parque Nacional Tierra del Fuego, R, S, T & Airport

Arrival and information

The modern international **airport**, Malvinas Argentinas, is 4km southwest of town; there's no public transport to the city, and a **taxi** to the centre costs $5. **Buses** – to Estancia Harberton, Parque Nacional Tierra del Fuego and other nearby attractions, as well as long-distance services to Río Grande and beyond – arrive and depart from the car park on seafront Avenida Maipú, at the corner with Juan Fadul.

The main commercial street, **Avenida San Martín**, runs parallel to and one block uphill from Maipú; at no. 674, you'll find the **tourist office** (Mon–Fri 8am–10pm, Sat & Sun 9am–8pm; ⓣ02901/424550, free information line ⓣ0800/333-1476, ⓦwww.e-ushuaia.com). One of the best in the whole country, its well-informed, friendly staff speak English and other languages. They have excellent free printed guides to the region and a useful leaflet on walks in the area, and they can help you find accommodation. They'll even frank your passport with an "End of the World" stamp.

Two other small **information kiosks** operate in summer: one at the Muelle Turístico (Mon–Fri 8am–8pm, Sat & Sun 9am–8pm; ⓣ02901/437666), and another at the airport, opening when flights arrive. Parque Nacional Tierra del Fuego has an office in town, at San Martín 1395 (Mon–Fri 9am–4pm), but it offers little you can't get at the tourist office, with the exception of park **fishing licences**. Serious trekkers and climbers should contact the **Club Andino Ushuaia**, Fadul 50 (Mon–Fri 10am–9.30pm, Sat 10am–2pm; ⓣ&ⓕ02901/422335), who will also put you in touch with qualified guides. Registering here before embarking on any trek or climb is optional but advisable – if you do, give details of your planned route and the date of your return, and don't forget to inform the office of your arrival at the end of your trek.

Accommodation

Ushuaia has a wide range of **hotels** and a number of **hostels**, most of which are clustered along the first four streets parallel to the bay, but all these manage to get booked up in the height of summer, and have become increasingly expensive – the most luxurious options tend to be up the mountainside on the road to Glaciar Martial. Many hotels charge a ten-percent surcharge on credit cards and travellers' cheques. Be aware, too, that hotels in Tierra del Fuego are the main culprits when it comes to charging **higher rates for non-residents**, often as much as three times more – in such cases, we have quoted the non-resident rate.

There are also three useful **campsites**: the nearest to the centre is well-equipped *Camping Pista del Andino*, Alem 2873 (ⓣ02901/435890, ⓦwww.lapistaandino.com.ar; $12 per person), at the base of the Club Andino skiing piste (free transfer from the centre). *Camping Rió Pipo* (ⓣ02901/435796; $10 per person) is on the way to the national park, 5km from town by the river of the same name; *Camping Municipal*, 8km from the centre, near the Tren del Fin del Mundo train station, is basic (no showers) but free.

Hostels and B&Bs

La Casa Gob. Paz 1380 ⓣ02901/423202, ⓔcasalaga@satlink.com. A thoroughly inviting and distinctive B&B – it was designed by its architect owner – with fantastic views from the breakfast room. The six bedrooms share three bathrooms. English and French spoken by the friendly hosts. Closed June–Sept. ❺

Cruz del Sur Gob. Deloqui 636 ⓣ02901/434099, ⓦwww.xdelsur@yahoo.com. One of the better unofficial youth hostels in town, with a good kitchen and a laidback lounge area. Dorms are on the small side but are clean and each has a view. Free Internet; breakfast included in the price. Dorms $28.

Freestyle Gob. Paz 866 ⓣ02901/432874, ⓦwww.ushuaiafreestyle.com. Delightful place that is more boutique hotel than hostel, with spacious four- and six-bed dorms, modern, personable en-suites (2–4 people) and swish bathrooms. There's a beanbag-filled TV room, and the relaxing top-floor lounge, complete with pool table and comfy sofas, enjoys superb views across the bay. Breakfast included; free parking. Dorms $35, rooms ❻

Refugio del Mochilero 25 de Mayo 231 ⓣ02901/436129, ⓦwww.refugiodelmochilero.netfirms.com. A dark but friendly hostel, in a central location, with several kitchens, laundry facilities and Internet access. Dorms are spacious but bare; clean doubles (❹) have good bathrooms. Other amenities include cable TV, free coffee and *mate*. Dorms $25.

Residencial Linares Gob. Deloqui 1522 ⓣ02901/423594, ⓦwww.hosterilinares.com.ar. Welcoming B&B in a cosy, split-level house with sterling views of the Beagle Channel. There's free Wi-Fi Internet access, and a decent breakfast ❻

Yakush San Martín and Piedrabuena ⓣ02901/435807, ⓦwww.hostelyakush.com.ar. High-ceilinged hostel with a great location in the centre of town – the breakfast room overlooks busy San Martín – and a couple of good communal areas: an attic lounge room and a backyard with panoramic views. Free Internet. Dorms $30, rooms ❺

Cabañas, hosterías and hotels

Cabañas del Beagle Las Aljabas 375 ⓣ02901/432785, ⓦwww.cabaniasdelbeagle.com. Characterful, self-contained cottages beautifully constructed in local stone and wood, with floor-to-ceiling windows that make the most of their lofty location. Original fireplaces add to the cosiness, and there's under-floor heating throughout. Continental breakfast included in the price. Free transfer from/to airport. ❽

Los Cauquenes Reinamora, 7km out of town towards Parque Nacional Tierra del Fuego ⓣ02901/441300, ⓦwww.loscauquenesushuaia.com.ar. Ushuaia's latest luxury resort-style hotel dominates the hillside to the east of town. The 54 rooms are softly furnished though surprisingly small – those looking for more spacious accommodation will need to invest in one of the five suites, which come with two plasma TVs, a private terrace and swimming-pool-sized whirlpool. On-site spa has a lengthy list of massage treatments. ❾

Cumbres del Martial Luis Martial 3560 ⓣ02901/424779, ⓦwww.cumbresdelmartial.com.ar. Situated by the glacier chairlift, this excellent hotel combines its fabulous position, which affords amazing views of the city and the Beagle Channel, with tasteful charm, enticing decor and modern amenities, such as Jacuzzis and smart bathrooms. Standard and luxury accommodation, the latter in huge self-contained cabañas. Rooms US$175–270.

Las Hayas Resort Luis Martial 1650 ⓣ02901/430710, ⓦwww.tierradelfuego.org.ar/lashayas. Luxurious, quiet and high up, 4km from town on the road to the glacier, *Las Hayas Resort* was the town's first five-star hotel – most rooms have views of the Beagle Channel, which is just as well since the decor is atrocious. Singles are pricey and there are no triples, though there's a health club and indoor swimming pool. An hourly shuttle bus runs from the port (9.30am–8.15pm). Rooms from US$230.

Hostería Los Fuegos Perito Moreno 4960 ⓣ02901/430884, ⓦwww.hosterialosfuegos.com. Truly charming *hostería* set among *lenga* woods on the banks of the Río Olivia, on the far eastern outskirts of town; the warm, rustic rooms are sympathetically decorated, scrumptious teas are served in the teahouse and the highly personable owner is full of good advice. ❽

Hostería Patagonia Jarké Sarmiento 310 ⓣ02901/437245, ⓦwww.hosteriapatagoniaj.com. Bright, rambling, timber and glass building, enthusiastically bedecked by the congenial owner. The majority of the cosy rooms enjoy stunning views across the bay. Paying by credit card will increase the bill by a quarter. ❽

Hotel Cesar San Martín 753 ⓣ02901/421460, ⓦwww.hotelcesarhostal.com.ar. Centrally located, standard mid-range hotel whose smart lobby overshadows the rooms themselves, which are carpeted but rather plain. ❻

Hotel del Glaciar Luis Martial 2355 ⓣ02901/430636, ⓦwww.hoteldelglaciar.com. Huge, bunker-style edifice at the foot of the Glaciar Martial chairlift, 5km up the steep mountain from the city (free shuttle bus for guests). Rooms (singles to quintuples) have good-sized beds but seem to have been bypassed by style, though they do all come with mountain or (more expensive) sea views. ❾

Lennox Hotel San Martín 776 ⓣ02901/436430, ⓦwww.lennoxhotel.com. Smart boutique hotel, with the emphasis on rustic chic. Rooms are large and extremely comfortable – those at the front have mountain views from their balconies – and breakfast is taken directly overlooking the Bahía

Ushuaia. Popular with Antarctic expeditions. Rooms from US$190.

Macondo Gob. Paz 1410 ⓣ02901/437576, ⓦwww.macondohouse.com. Elegant little hotel creatively designed by its welcoming Barcelona-born owner. The seven minimalist doubles see plenty of natural light and have attractive stoneware bathrooms, and there are good vistas from the tasteful corner living room. The video room doubles as a kids' play area. ❼

Villa Brescia Hotel San Martín 1299 ⓣ02901/433222, ⓦwww.villabresciahotel.com.ar. Good-value, mid-range hotel, with bright rooms for two to four people, and wide-reaching views from the second floor, though there's a hefty twenty-percent surcharge on credit cards. ❼

The City

The best place to start wandering around Ushuaia is down by the pier, the **Muelle Turístico**, where an **obelisk** commemorates Augusto Lasserre's ceremony to assert Argentine sovereignty in this part of the world. Overlooking the sea from the other side of the street is the 1920s **Provincial Legislature**, one of the town's most stately buildings. Northeast of here at Maipú and Rivadavia is the small, worthwhile **Museo del Fin del Mundo** (daily 9am–8pm; $10), with exhibits on the region's history and wildlife, including the polychrome figurehead of the *Duchess of Albany*, an English ship wrecked on the eastern end of the island in 1883; a one-gram gold coin minted by Julius Popper in 1889; and a rare example of a Selk'nam–Spanish dictionary written by Salesian missionary José María Beauvoir.

You can visit the former **prison** to see the **Museo Marítimo y Presidio** (daily 9am–8pm; $30), two blocks further along the front and two more inland, at Yaganes and Gobernador Paz. This houses a motley collection of exhibits, the best of which are the meticulous scale-models of famous **ships** from the island's history, and a much cruder, if equally painstaking, reconstruction of a Yámana canoe. The prison building itself, though, is the main draw, its wings radiating out like spokes from a half-wheel. The bare cells are complete with gory details of the notorious criminals who occupied them, but the impact is diminished for those unable to read the information boards, which are mostly in Spanish. The most celebrated prisoner held here was early twentieth-century anarchist

△ Ushuaia harbour

Winter sports around Ushuaia

In order to boast that you have been to the end of the world to **ski** or **snowboard**, you'll need to visit between late May and early September – June to August are the most reliable months. The majority of runs are for beginners and intermediates, but several companies, such as Gotama Expediciones (ⓣ02901/15605301, ⓦwww.gotama-expediciones.com) offer guided back-country skiing for the more advanced. Equipment rental is reasonable and there are a couple of downhill (*esqui alpino*) pistes close to Ushuaia: the small Club Andino, 3km from town, and the more impressive one up by Glaciar Martial, 7km behind town. Better runs are to be had, however, in the Sierra Alvear, the resorts of which are accessed from RN-3 (see p.766). These include the modern Cerro Castor centre (ⓦwww.cerrocastor.com), 27km from town, with 15km of pistes in runs, including a few black ones, up to 2km long.

The Sierra Alvear is also an excellent area for **cross-country** skiing (*esqui de fondo* or *esqui nórdico*). In addition, there are several winter-sports centres (*centros invernales*) along the **Valle Tierra Mayor** where you can try out snowmobiles, snowshoes, ice-skating and dogsled trips (*trineos de perros*): Altos del Valle (see p.767), Solar del Bosque, Nunatak (see p.767), Tierra Mayor, Llanos del Castor, Valle Hermoso, Los Cotorras and Haruwen.

Simón Radowitzsky, whose miserable stay and subsequent brief escape in 1918 are recounted by Bruce Chatwin in *In Patagonia*. There's a free guided **tour** of the museum's collections (daily 10.30am), which is the only time you're allowed to enter the otherwise locked scale-reconstruction of the former lighthouse on the Isla de los Estados, the inspiration for Jules Verne's *Lighthouse at the End of the World*. Outside the museum is *La Coqueta*, a locomotive once used to transport the prisoners to their daily toil of logging the forests. If you just want a look at the prison interior without having to pay the stiff entrance fee, have a coffee in the public **café/restaurant** in the main exercise hall (open until midnight).

Ushuaia's other museum is the **Museo Yámana**, a charming little place in a converted house at Rivadavia 56 (daily 10am–8pm; $8) that charts the arrival of pre-Columbian and European settlers in the archipelago. Beautiful dioramas give an idea of the native habitats and way of life, but the displays go rather easy on the white invaders; excellent descriptions in Spanish and English, though, more than validate its claim to be an interpretation centre.

It's worth popping into the **Antigua Casa Beban**, at the southwestern end of town at Maipú and Plüschow, a lovely pavilion-style place with a steep roof and ornamental gabling that was prefabricated in Sweden in 1913. It hosts exhibitions of photos and artwork, as well as occasional films (Mon–Fri 10am–6pm, Sat & Sun 4–8pm; free), and is the venue for the **Ushuaia Jazz Festival** every November. Finally, for first-rate views of the Beagle Channel and the islands of Chile, you can head to the hanging **Glaciar Martial**, 7km behind town; walk up the steep Luis Martial road, or take a bus from the Muelle Turístico (half-hourly 9.30am–1pm; return hourly 1–6pm; $10 return), and then climb or take the **chairlift** ($25) from behind the *Cumbres del Martial*. Take sun protection: the effects of the ozone layer hole can result in fierce solar radiation at these latitudes. During the winter, Glaciar Martial offers the closest decent skiing to Ushuaia (see box above).

Eating, drinking and nightlife

Main-drag San Martín is lined with countless good places to eat or people-watch over a *café con leche*. Still, if you confine yourself to these venues you'll be missing out on some of Ushuaia's best **restaurants**, which are spread across town, often in locations with breathtaking views. The quality of cuisine in Ushuaia has rocketed in recent years and there are several places where you can splash out on a memorable meal and sample the local gastronomic pride, *centolla*, the emperor of crustaceans, known in English as **king crab**.

Bodegón Fueguino San Martín 895. Convivial place, its sheep-skin-covered benches packed with young gringos appreciating the home-brewed beer, interesting – and tasty – *picada* menu and good-value pasta dishes. Closed Mon.

La Cabaña Luis Martial 3560. Part of the *Cumbres del Martial* complex, this cosy mountain cabin serves tea, cakes, chocolate and delicious selections of cheese and smoked cold cuts in earnestly alpine style.

Chez Manu Luis Martial 2135 ⓣ02901/432253. Stunning panoramic views from huge windows and gourmet French food using local produce – *centolla*, of course, plus fish, melt-in-the-mouth lamb and seafood – make this one of the city's most sought-after dining spots, though it is a bit expensive.

Chocolates Ushuaia San Martín 783. Simple café and *chocolatería* serving a fair range of chunky sandwiches, though most patrons are here for the great hot chocolate, accompanied by an enormous slab of cake or two.

Dreamland 9 de Julio and Deoqui. Wood-cabin club with a good bar and a beanbag-filled corner for chilling in between DJ (mainly house) sets. Open from 3pm till late.

Dublín 9 de Julio 168. In theory, an Irish pub, serving good draught beer and Irish whiskey, its buzzing atmosphere attracting locals and gringos alike – but apart from the Guinness adverts, there isn't much in the way of Hibernian trappings. Open till late.

Gustino Maipú and Lasserre ⓣ02901/430003. Smart new restaurant attached to the *Hotel Albatros*, with full length-window views of the Beagle Channel, where you can wash down creative regional dishes with a glass of *vino* from the most comprehensive wine cellar in town.

Kaupe Roca 470 ⓣ02901/422704. Hands down the best restaurant in Ushuaia, *Kaupe*'s service is friendly, the food delicious and the decor unpretentious in what is just a family home with a fabulous view. Try the sea bass in black butter sauce with capers, or splash out on the excellent seafood *degustacíon* menu. Reservations essential.

Küar Perito Moreno 2232. Set in an attractive stone and timber building right on the seafront, on the road out towards Río Grande, this youthful bar/restaurant has stupendous views and a blazing fire, as well as unusual dishes and its own delicious home-brewed pale ale, amber ale and dark porter.

Muelle 55 Perito Moreno 255. The best venue in Ushuaia for after-dark entertainment, with regular DJ sets and a variety of themed "rock 'n' roll" nights.

La Rueda San Martín 193. The best of a cluster of *parrillas* at the western end of San Martín, serving generous portions of well-cooked lamb at

Southern shellfish

Though you may be tempted by the region's waterborne delicacies, do not collect your own **shellfish** in Tierra del Fuego, as it is occasionally affected by a deadly poisonous, colourless version of **red tide** (*marea roja*), a noxious algal bloom. Cooking only increases the virulence of red-tide toxins. Following a severe outbreak of red-tide-related poisonings in the early 1970s, both Chilean and Argentine authorities introduced strict shellfish controls. Testing is now carried out on all seafood deemed to be a potential risk to ensure it is safe for consumption, so you can tuck in to the area's delicious mussels (*cholgas*) in shops and restaurants without fear.

Unaffected by red tide is the undisputed prince of the palate, the **centolla** (king crab). The crab's spindly legs can measure over a metre from tip to tip, but the meat comes from the body, with an average individual yielding some 300g. The less savoury practice of catching them with traps baited with dolphin or penguin meat has almost been stamped out by the imposition of hefty fines by both Chilean and Argentine authorities, but despite controls on size limits, they are still subject to rampant over-fishing. Canned king crab is served off-season, but is bland and not worth the prices charged; frozen *centolla* is only slightly better, so always make sure it is fresh.

knockdown prices. Tackling the popular *tenedor libre* will satiate even the strongest carnivore cravings.
Sheik Gob. Paz and Roca. Rather cheesy, bright orange club playing a standard mix of mainstream pop tunes to a tourist crowd.
Tante Sara San Martín 175. Popular *confitería* and *panadería*, which does a fine line in fresh, oven-baked baguettes and rolls, in addition to simple coffees and teas.
Tante Sara Pizza y Pasta San Martín 137. Not to be confused with the *confitería* of the same name, this rather stark pizzeria is arguably the best in town, and also serves very commendable pasta.
Tía Elvira Maipú 349 ⓣ02901/424725. *Tía Elvira* specializes in fresh seafood, including excellent mussels and delicious *centolla*, and offers a respectable list of Argentine wines.
El Turco San Martín 1410. Local favourite, serving hearty portions of pizza, home-made pasta and empañadas by the dozen with good-humoured service. The lunch menu is unbeatable value. Closed Sun lunch time.

Listings

Airlines Aerolíneas Argentinas, Roca 116 ⓣ02901/421228; DAP, Deloqui 555 ⓣ02901/431110; LADE, San Martín 542 ⓣ02901/421123. Aeroclub Ushuaia (ⓣ02901/421717, ⓦwww.aeroclubushuaia.org.ar) flies to Puerto Williams on Chilean Isla Navarino three times weekly (Mon, Wed & Fri; US$100 one way).
Banks and exchange Banco Tierra del Fuego, San Martín and Roca; Banco de la Nación, San Martín 190. There's a *casa de cambio* at San Martín 877.
Books Boutique del Libro, 25 de Mayo 62.
Car rental Cinco Estrellas, San Martín 788 ⓣ02901/421450, ⓔcincoestrentacar@yahoo.com.ar; Crossing Patagonia, Maipú 857 ⓣ02901/430786, ⓦwww.crossingpatagonia.com; Europcar, Maipú 857 ⓣ02901/430786; Localiza, Sarmiento 81 ⓣ02901/430780, ⓦwww.localiza.com. Most companies do not permit you to take your rental car out of the Argentine part of the island. Roads are fairly reliable from Oct to early May; outside this period, carry snow chains and drive with caution.
Consulate Chile, Jainén 50 ⓣ02901/430909 or 430910.
Hospital Maipú and 12 de Octubre ⓣ02901/421439 or 421278; emergencies ⓣ107.
Internet access Available several places, including Cafe-Net, San Martín 565.
Laundry Qualis, Güiraldes 568. Open daily.
Pharmacy Andina, San Martín 638 (daily 8am–midnight).
Police Deloqui 492 ⓣ02901/421773; emergencies ⓣ101.
Post office San Martín and Godoy.
Shopping Renata Rafalak, Piedrabuena 51. The eponymous owner makes some of the finest craft items in southern Patagonia, her specialities being reproductions of the bark masks worn by the Selk'nam and Yámana in their Hain and Kina initiation ceremonies.
Supermarkets La Anonima, Gob. Paz and Rivadavia, also at San Martín and Onas.
Taxis Carlito's ⓣ02901/422222.
Travel agents All Patagonia, Juan Fadul 60 ⓣ02901/430725, ⓦwww.allpatagonia.com; Canal, 9 de Julio 118 ⓣ02901/437395 ⓦwww.canalfun.com; Rumbo Sur, San Martín 350 ⓣ02901/422275, ⓦwww.rumbosur.com.ar; Turismo de Campo, 25 de Mayo 64 ⓣ02901/437351, ⓔevt@turismodecampo.com.ar. For trips to Estancia Harberton and on the Beagle Channel, go to the Muelle Turístico and book direct.

Estancia Harberton and the RCj

The unsealed **RCj** is one of the two most interesting branch roads on the island, offering spectacular views of the Beagle Channel and the chance to visit Patagonia's most historic estancia, Harberton. The turn-off for the RCj is 40km northeast of Ushuaia on RN-3. Twenty-five kilometres from the turn-off, you emerge from the forested route by a delightful lagoon fringed by the skeletons of *Nothofagus* beeches, and can look right across the Beagle Channel to the Chilean town of Puerto Williams. A few hundred metres beyond here the road splits: take the left-hand fork heading eastwards across rolling open country and past a clump of **flag trees**, swept back in exaggerated quiffs by the unremitting wind.

Ten kilometres beyond the turn-off and 85km east of Ushuaia is **Estancia Harberton**, an ordered assortment of whitewashed buildings on the shores of a sheltered bay (daily 10am–7pm; $20; ⓣ02901/422742, ⓦwww.estanciaharberton.com). Though Harberton is assuredly scenic, it's the historical resonance of the place that fleshes out a visit: this farmstead – or more particularly the family that settled here – played a role out of all proportion to its size in the region's history. It was built by Reverend Thomas Bridges, the man who authored one of the two seminal Fuegian texts, the *Yámana–English Dictionary*, and was the inspiration for the other, Lucas Bridges' classic, *Uttermost Part of the Earth*. Apart from being a place where scientists and shipwrecked sailors were assured assistance, Harberton developed into a sanctuary of refuge for groups of Yámana and Mannekenk, and even the warlike Selk'nam would refrain from hostilities here.

Today, the estancia is owned by Tommy Goodall, a great-grandson of Thomas Bridges, and is open to **guided tours** only (Nov–April daily 10am–7pm, last tour 5.30pm; 1hr), which take in the copse on the hill, where you learn about the properties of the island's plant life, as well as authentic reconstructions of indigenous Yámana dwellings, the family cemetery and the old shearing shed. The *Mánacatush* **tearoom** is the only part of the main building open to the public: here you can enjoy afternoon tea, with large helpings of cake and delicious home-made jams or – if you book a couple of days in advance – a generous three-course lunch.

Housed in a building at the entrance to the farmstead is an impressive marine-mammal museum, **Museo Acatushún** (same hours as house; $10, plus estancia entrance fee; ⓦwww.acatushun.com), which is overseen by Tommy's American-born wife, Natalie, a renowned biologist. Mostly taken up by research laboratories, it displays the remains of all the main families of such animals – whales, dolphins, seals and the like – found in the surrounding waters. Highly informative guided tours explore the bones and skeletons of hundreds of the mammals – estimated at around half the world's collection.

You can stay the night, though the **accommodation** is hardly luxurious or inexpensive: choose between the old *Shepherd's House*, which has two triple rooms with private bath, a small shared kitchenette and a large porch ($240 per person, bed and breakfast, full occupancy); and the old *Cook's House*, with a double room and another bedroom with bunk-beds, a rustic bathroom, kitchenette and dining/sitting room ($180–210 per person). Alternatively, you could stay at one of the estancia's three **campsites**: all are free, but you must first register at the tearoom and obtain a permit. Choose between *Río Varela*, the closest site, 4km to the east, *Río Cambaceres*, 6km further east, and the beautiful *Río Lasifashaj*, 7km west of the estancia. All sites have abundant fresh water, but no other facilities.

While at Harberton you can also cross (twice daily in summer; 1hr 30min; $50) to the Reserva Yecapasela on **Isla Martillo**, which in addition to two species of penguin is also home to a large shag colony.

Beyond Harberton, the RCj runs for forty spectacular kilometres – accessible only with your own transport – to **Estancia Moat**, past the famous islands that guard the eastern mouth of the Beagle Channel: **Picton**, **Nueva** and **Lennox**. These uninhabited atolls have a controversial past, with both Chile and Argentina long claiming sovereignty over them. Simmering tensions threatened to boil over in the late 1970s, when manoeuvres by the military regimes of both countries brought the two to the brink of war. Arbitration was left to the UK's Queen Elizabeth II, harking back to the beginning of the twentieth century, when the British Crown mediated a settlement along the countries' Andean frontier. This time, the Crown ruled in favour of Chile, although Argentina refused to cede sovereignty until a further ruling, by the Vatican, in 1984. The track comes to an end at a naval outpost, beyond which Península Mitre (see p.769) stretches to Cabo San Diego, at the far tip of Tierra del Fuego.

Five companies run **buses** from Ushuaia to Harberton, departing between 9.30am and 3pm and returning hourly between 2 and 8pm (1hr 30min; $70–80 return).

Trips along the Beagle Channel

No trip to Ushuaia is complete without a voyage on the legendary **Beagle Channel**, the majestic, mountain-fringed sea passage south of the city. Most **boat excursions** start and finish in Ushuaia, and you get the best views of town looking back at it from the straits. Standard trips visit Isla Bridges, Isla de los Pájaros and Isla de los Lobo, looping around Faro Les Eclaireurs, sometimes erroneously called the Lighthouse at the End of the World – that title belongs to the beacon at the tip of Isla de los Estados – on their way back. Boats depart from the **Muelle Turístico**, where you'll find agents' booking huts: recommended vessels include the *Barracuda*, offering good-value, informative tours (daily 9.30am & 3pm; 3hr; $80), and the *Tres Marías* (daily 9.30am & 3pm; 4hr; $110, including hot drinks), a quiet motorized sailboat ideal for small groups, whose trip includes trekking on Islas "H", to see Yámana shell middens. Other companies offer catamaran and sailboat trips for $95 to $140.

Longer boat trips head further along the Beagle Channel: west to Bahía Lapataia in the national park; east to Estancia Harberton and the penguin colony on Isla Martillo; or south to Puerto Williams on Isla Navarino. Ideally, **Bahía Lapataia** is done as part of a combination tour, with one leg overland – a service offered by both Rumbo Sur and Tolkeyen, whose trips (daily 10.30am; 6hr; $125) visit the lighthouse and islands en route. Their boat-only return trips to the Magellanic and Gentoo **penguin colony on Isla Martillo** include a tour of Harberton (Tolkeyen Mon, Wed & Fri 9.30am; Rumbo Sur Tues, Thurs,

△ Magellanic penguins in the Beagle Channel

Antarctica and the Isla de los Estados

Ushuaia lies 1000km north of **Antarctica**, but is still the world's closest port to the white continent – and most tourists pass through the town to make their journey across Drake's Passage, the wild stretch of ocean that separates it from South America. The grandeur of Antarctica's pack ice, rugged mountains and phenomenal bird- and marine life will leave you breathless: whales, elephant seals, albatrosses and numerous species of penguins are just some of the species you can hope to see. Regular **cruise ships** depart from November to mid-March and most cruises last between eight and 22 days, some stopping at the **South Atlantic islands** (Islas Malvinas/Falklands, South Georgia, the South Orkneys, Elephant Island and the South Shetlands) en route. These trips are generally very expensive (around US$4500), but last-minute "bargains" can be snapped up in Ushuaia, especially on the newest ships, which are less likely to sell out their berths. Ushuaia's **Oficina Antártica** at the Muelle Turístico (Ⓣ02901/430015) has details of current sailings and can advise on what each trip involves; otherwise, try contacting Antarpply, at Gob. Paz 633 (Ⓣ02901/436747, Ⓦwww.antarpply.com), or Quark Expeditions (Ⓦwww.quarkexpeditions.com). The former is currently the only one to offer tours of the **Isla de los Estados**, known in English as Staten Island; almost perpetually swathed in mist and cloud, it is a land of deep fjords, swamps, scrubby sub-antarctic forests and craggy peaks, and had a black reputation amongst mariners of past centuries for the fierce currents that surround it.

Sat & Sun; 9hr; $170). Another trip runs between Bahía Ensenada and Lapataia in the national park (see p.763).

On boat trips, look out for **seabirds** such as the Black-browed Albatross, the thick-set Giant Petrel, Southern Skuas and the South American Tern, as well as **marine mammals** such as sea lions, Peale's dolphin (with a grey patch on its flank) and the occasional minke whale.

For an alternative perspective, Ushuaia Divers (Ⓣ02901/444701, Ⓦwww.ushuaiadivers.com.ar; $170 a day) runs **diving** trips into the channel to look for *centolla* and sea lions amongst the seaweed forests.

Parque Nacional Tierra del Fuego

PARQUE NACIONAL TIERRA DEL FUEGO, a mere 12km west of Ushuaia, is the easiest to access of southern Argentina's national parks. Protecting 630 square kilometres of jagged mountains, intricate lakes, southern beech forest, swampy peat bog, sub-antarctic tundra and verdant coastline, the park stretches along the frontier with Chile, from the Beagle Channel to the **Sierra Inju-Goiyin** (also called the Sierra Beauvoir) north of Lago Fagnano, but only the southernmost quarter of this is open to the public, accessed via RN-3 from Ushuaia. Fortunately, this area contains much of the park's most beautiful scenery, if also some of the wettest – bring rain gear. The quarter is broken down into three main sectors: Bahía Ensenada and Río Pipo in the east, close to the station for the Tren del Fin del Mundo; Lago Roca further west; and the Lapataia area south of Lago Roca, which includes Laguna Verde and, at the end of RN-3, Bahía Lapataia. You can get a good overview of the park in a day, but walkers will want to stay two to three days to appreciate the scenery and the **wildlife**, which includes birds such as Magellanic Woodpeckers (*carpintero patagónico*), condors, Steamer Ducks, Kelp Geese – the park's symbol – and

Buff-necked Ibises; and mammals such as the guanaco, the rare southern sea otter (*nutria marina*), the Patagonian grey fox and its larger cousin, the native Fuegian red fox, once heavily hunted for its pelt.

The park is also one of southern Argentina's easiest to walk around, and offers several relatively unchallenging though beautiful **trails** (*sendas*), many of which are completed in minutes rather than hours or days; the best is arguably the scenic Senda Costera (Coastal Path) connecting Bahía Ensenada with Lago Roca and Bahía Lapataia. The spectacular climb up Cerro Guanaco from Lago Roca is comparatively tough, though hardened trekkers will find sterner physical challenges in the Sierra Valdivieso and the Sierra Alvear (see p.766), or on Isla Navarino (see p.775). Obey the signs warning you to refrain from collecting shellfish (see box, p.756), and light fires only in permitted campsites, extinguishing them with water, not earth.

Park practicalities

The commonest and cheapest way to **access the park** is along the good dirt road from Ushuaia. A $20 entrance fee must be paid at the main park gate, payable in addition to any bus, boat or train tickets. Virtually all travel agencies in Ushuaia offer **tours** of the park ($70, plus entrance fee); most last four hours and stop at the major places of interest, including Bahía Lapataia. Four companies run regular **buses** (depart daily 8am–7pm, return 9am–8pm), which stop at various points in the park: the entrance or Bahía Ensenada ($10 one way), Lago Roca ($15) and Bahía Lapataia ($20).

You can also get to the park on a **boat trip** along the Beagle Channel from Ushuaia (see p.759) – services drop you at the jetty at Bahía Lapataia – or on the world's most southern railway, the **Tren del Fin del Mundo**

(9.30am, noon & 3pm; 40min; $60 one way; ⓣ02901/431600, ⓦwww.trendelfindelmundo.com.ar), which chugs its way through woodland meadows and alongside the Río Pipo to the **park station**, 2km from the main gate. It's little more than a tourist toy train, though, and you'll still need to get a bus to the main station, 8km west of Ushuaia on the road to the national park (depart 9am–2.30pm, return noon–5pm; $15 return).

There are four main areas for **camping** in the park: the two nearest the entrance, *Río Pipo* and *Bahía Ensenada*, are free, but you're better off heading to Lago Roca and Laguna Verde, in the more exciting western section of the park. *Camping Lago Roca* sits near picturesque Lago Roca, where it bottlenecks into the Río Lapataia (ⓣ02901/423409, ⓔlagoroca@speedy.com.ar; $8–12 per person), and has hot showers and a shop. The free sites further south, on the Archipiélago Comoranes – *Camping Las Bandurrias*, *Camping Laguna Verde* and *Camping Los Cauquenes* – just about edge it for beauty, though, set on grassy patches of land encircled by the Río Ovando, with lawn-like pitches kept trim by the resident rabbits.

Río Pipo and Bahía Ensenada

North of the train terminus is the pleasant wooded valley of Cañadón del Toro, through which runs the **Río Pipo**. A gentle four-kilometre walk along an unsealed road brings you to *Camping Río Pipo* (see above), and a couple of hundred metres on you come to an attractive **waterfall**. Although a through route north from here to Lago Fagnano is marked on some old maps, the area is now off-limits and you will be fined if caught there. If you're heading from Río Pipo back south to Bahía Ensenada, a more interesting alternative to walking between the two by road is to take the fairly demanding **Senda Pampa Alta** (5km; 1hr 30min), which is signposted off west on the way back to the train-station crossroads. This offers fine views from a lookout over the Beagle Channel as it crosses RN-3 towards Bahía Lapataia 3km west of the crossroads, and then drops to the coast on a poor path through thick forest.

Bahía Ensenada, 2km south of the crossroads, is a small bay with little of intrinsic interest. It does, however, have the jetty for boats to Bahía Lapataia and Isla Redonda, and is the trailhead for one of the park's most pleasant walks, the excellent **Senda Costera** (6.5km; 3hr). The route affords spectacular views from the Beagle Channel shoreline and takes you through dense coastal forest

Tierra del Fuego's surprising avian residents

Parrots and hummingbirds are two types of birds most visitors to South America quite naturally associate more with the steamy, verdant jungles of the Amazon than the frigid extremes of Tierra del Fuego. Nevertheless, don't go jumping to conclusions, as you can see both in the Parque Nacional Tierra del Fuego. The unmistakably garrulous **Austral Parakeet** is the world's most southerly parrot, inhabiting these temperate forests year-round. The Selk'nam christened it *Kerrhprrh*, in onomatopoeic imitation of its call. Once upon a time, according to their beliefs, all Fuegian trees were coniferous, and it was *Kerrhprrh* who transformed some into deciduous forests, painting them autumnal reds with the feathers of its breast. The tiny **Green-backed Firecrown** is the planet's most southerly hummingbird, and may be glimpsed – albeit rarely – flickering about flowering shrubs in summer. Known to the Selk'nam by the graceful name of *Sinu K-Tam* (Daughter of the Wind), this diminutive creature was, curiously, believed by them to be the offspring of *Ohchin*, the whale, and *Sinu*, the wind.

of evergreen beech, Winter's bark and *lenga*, some of their branches clad in *barba de viejo* (old man's beard), a hanging lichen that gives the trees a rather sorrowful appearance. Look out, too, for the *pan de Indio* (Indian bread), a bulbous orange fungus that clusters around the knots of branches. On the way, you'll pass grass-covered mounds that are the ancient campsite **middens** of the Yámana – these are protected archeological sites and should not be disturbed. In autumn, evergreen beech leaves carpet the pathway, a phenomenon that has become more prevalent in recent years, and which some believe is linked to damage caused by the hole in the ozone layer. Along the route, you stand a healthy chance of seeing birds such as the powerful Magellanic Woodpecker and the flightless Steamer Duck (*alacush*), which uses its wings in paddle-steaming fashion to hurry way from danger.

Lago Roca

Two kilometres after the Senda Costera rejoins RN-3, a turn-off to the right takes you across the lush meadows of the broad Río Lapataia to **Lago Roca** and its campsite. Just past the campsite buildings, there's a car park that looks out across the lake, which extends across the border into Chile. From here, the gentle **Senda Hito XXIV** (8km return; 3hr return) hugs the lake's northern shore and heads through majestic *lenga* forest to the Chilean border. Do not attempt to cross the border: it is under regular surveillance and you will be arrested if you try to do so.

A more spectacular but much more demanding trek is the tough climb up 970-metre-high **Cerro Guanaco** (4km one way; 4hr one way), the mountain ridge on the north side of Lago Roca. Take the Senda Hito XXIV from the car park at Lago Roca and after ten minutes you'll cross a small bridge over a stream. Immediately afterwards, take the right fork that leads up the forested mountainside to the *cerro*. The path crosses the Arroyo Guanaco at several points; it's not hazardous, but after rain you're sure to encounter some slippery tree roots and muddy patches. Above the tree line, the views are tremendous, but the path becomes increasingly difficult to follow in the boggy valley, especially after snowfalls. Cerro Guanaco itself is to the left on the ridge above you. Even if you can't make out the path, and as long as visibility is good, you can scramble your way to just about any point along the crest of the ridge with few problems. From here, the **views** of the angular landscape are superb: the swollen finger of Lago Roca, flanked by the spiky ridge of Cerro Cóndor, with the jagged Cordillera Darwin beyond; to the east, Ushuaia and its airport; and to the north, a vertiginous cliff plunges down to the Cañadón del Toro, and behind that are the inhospitable Valdivieso and Vinciguerra ranges obscuring the view to Lago Fagnano. Best of all, however, are the views to the south: the tangle of islands and rivers of the Archipiélago Cormoranes; Lapataia's sinuous curves; the Isla Redonda in the Beagle Channel; and across to the Chilean islands, Hoste and Navarino, separated by the Murray Channel. On a clear day, in the distance beyond the channel, you can make out the Islas Wollaston, the group of islands whose southernmost point is Cape Horn.

Note that the weather on Cerro Guanaco can turn capricious with little warning at any time of year, so bring adequate clothing, even if you set out in glorious sunshine.

The Lapataia area

The absorbing Lapataia area is accessed by way of the final four-kilometre stretch of RN-3, as it winds south from the Lago Roca junction, past **Laguna**

Verde, and on to **Lapataia** itself, on the bay of the same name. This is one of the most intriguing sections to explore: a kind of "park within a park". In the space of a few hours, you can take a network of short trails past an incredible variety of scenery, including peat bogs, river islets, wooded knolls and seacoast. A few hundred metres past the Lago Roca junction, you cross the Río Lapataia – over a bridge that's a favoured haunt of Ringed Kingfishers (*martín pescador grande*) – onto the **Archipiélago Cormoranes** (Cormorant Archipelago). Signposted left off the road here is a short circuit trail, the **Paseo de la Isla** (600m), a delightful walk through tiny, enchanting humped islets. Just past the trail, to the right of the main road, is *Las Bandurrias* campsite, popular with fishermen (see p.762).

Next you pass **Laguna Verde**, which is actually a sumptuous, sweeping bend of the Río Ovando, and makes a lovely setting for the two campsites here, *Camping Laguna Verde* and *Camping Los Cauquenes* (see p.762). From Laguna Verde, it's only 2km to Lapataia, but there are several easy nature trails along the way, which you can stroll along in half an hour or so, allowing time to stop and

Logging in Tierra del Fuego

At the end of 1993, a **US logging company**, Trillium Co, bought 670,000 acres of forest in the Chilean half of Isla Grande, and followed this up with a purchase, in 1994, of a further 170,000 acres in the Argentine half. Faced with ever-tightening environmental legislation at home, Trillium seemed to have found easy pickings in Tierra del Fuego: vast swathes of ancient temperate hardwood forest in an area with a tiny population and a young, emergent political structure. Their interest lay primarily in a wood ideal for the furniture industry: Patagonian **lenga** (high-deciduous beech).

The Río Condor Project, as Trillium called it, had all the hallmarks of a neo-colonial hit-and-run raid. No independent environmental-impact studies had been carried out; no system had been created for supervision of the company's logging practices; and no consideration had been given to the potential value of the forests as a tourist resource. Envisaging a repeat of the disastrous clearing of temperate forests that has occurred in mainland Chilean Patagonia, environmental groups **Defensores de los Bosques Chilenos**, on the Chilean side, and **Finis Terrae**, based in Ushuaia, resolved not to let Trillium steamroller local concerns. The groups scored several legal victories along the way, but permission to proceed with logging was nevertheless granted by Chile in 1999, albeit on a significantly reduced scale, and by Argentina the following year.

The campaigning had taken its toll, though, and financial difficulties forced Trillium to cede its entire holdings in Chile to its creditors, Goldman Sachs. In September 2004, the US bank donated all 670,000 acres to the Chilean government; the area is now under the administration of the World Conservation Society, which is in the process of establishing a **nature reserve** on the site. Unfortunately, Trillium has continued with its logging operations in Argentina, where campaigners worry **environmental damage** could be catastrophic. Soil erosion is a great fear: topsoils on Isla Grande are very thin, winds are strong and there's heavy rainfall. A diverse native forest ecosystem can absorb up to fifty times as much rainfall as agricultural land; with felling, run-off and wood pulp affect the purity of the island's lakes and streams. **Regeneration** takes at least thirty years, with most *lenga* trees taking over a hundred years to reach maturity.

Naturally, environmental groups would like to see the cessation of all logging if possible; however, if logging is to continue, the groups insist that it should at least be controlled, and that the local community benefits in some way, with wood being processed on the island for high-value manufactured items such as furniture parts, and not just exported as planks. For more information, see Ⓦ www.elbosquechileno.cl.

study the signs with ecological and botanical information (in Spanish). Leaving the campsites, you cross the Río Ovando bridge and, after a couple of hundred metres, come to the start of the **Senda Laguna Negra** (950m), a nature-trail loop to a shallow pond fringed by a peat bog. Insectivorous sundew plants grow by the lakeshore, but sadly few have taken to the area adjacent to the boardwalk, on which you must stay. A little further along RN-3 – about 1km from Laguna Verde – is a turn-off to Paseo Mirador (1km), which takes you down to Bahía Lapataia via an impressive lookout over the bay. This whole area to the left (east) of RN-3 is crisscrossed by trails through peat-bog scenery, including the **Paseo del Turbal** (Peat-Bog Walk; 2km), accessed a short way into the trail to Mirador Lapataia or from a left-hand turn-off further down RN-3.

Opposite the turn-off to Paseo del Turbal is the start of the **Senda Castorera**, going only a couple of hundred metres off the road to a **beaver dam**. Introduced from Canada in the 1940s in order to kick-start a fur-farming industry, beavers (*castores*) have destroyed large areas of the park, their dams flooding tree roots, "drowning" them in the process. You stand a good chance of spotting these rodents – which now number nearly 50,000 – if you arrive in the early morning or at dusk.

The RN-3 comes to its scenic end – a mere 3063km from Buenos Aires, and marked by a much-photographed sign – at Lapataia on the **Bahía Lapataia**. Deriving its name from the Yámana for "forested cove", it is a serenely beautiful bay studded with small islets. Near the car park here is the **jetty** for boat trips to Bahía Ensenada and Ushuaia, and the adjacent grassy knolls are Yámana shell middens (see box, p.766). For the best views of the bay, it's worth taking the five-minute walk up the **Paseo Mirador**, which runs east from the car park to the little wooded lookout hill at its head. A path on the western side of the bay, **Senda de la Baliza** (Beacon Trail; 1.5km), runs through meadows and crosses another active beaver colony, but do not stray beyond here, as it's off-limits.

Central and northern Tierra del Fuego

The second largest settlement in Tierra del Fuego, **Río Grande** is also the only town of significance in Isla Grande's **central** and **northern** sector. The sterile-looking plains that surround it harbour fields of petroleum and natural gas that generate over millions of dollars of wealth annually, with huge quantities of gas transported each year to Ushuaia and as far away as Buenos Aires. North of town, RN-3 runs through monotonous scenery towards San Sebastián, where you cross the border into Chile or continue north on a dead-end route to the mouth of the Magellan Straits at Cabo Espíritu Santo. On the way to Río Grande from Ushuaia, RN-3 winds up to **Paso Garibaldi**, where you have majestic views over **Lago Escondido**, and then bypasses **Tolhuin**, crossing the woodland scenery of the central region. This stretch is marked by a string of *ripio* branch roads, the **rutas complementarias**, which wiggle away from RN-3; those headed west take you to a couple of fine estancias, and those headed east into the **Península Mitre**, the windswept land that forms Isla Grande's desolate tip.

One of the northern region's principal tourist draws is its world-class **trout-fishing**, especially for sea-running brown trout, which on occasion swell to weights in excess of 14kg. The river, also named Río Grande, currently holds five of the fly-fishing world records for brown trout caught with various breaking strains of line. The mouths of the Río Fuego and Río Ewan can also

The Yámana: Fuegian seafarers

The **Yámana** (Yaghan) were a sea-going people who lived in the channels of the Fuegian archipelago. Their society was based on tribal groups of extended families, each of which lived for long periods aboard their equivalent of a houseboat: a canoe fashioned of *lenga* bark. Out on the ocean, work was divided between the sexes: the men hunted seals from the prow whilst the women – the only ones who could swim – took to the icy waters, collecting shellfish with only a layer of seal grease to protect them from the cold. When not at sea, the Yámana stayed in dwellings made of *guindo* evergreen beech branches, building conical huts in winter (to shed snow), and more aerodynamic dome-shaped ones in the summer (when strong winds blow). Favoured campsites were used over millennia, and, at these sites, **middens** of discarded shells would accumulate in the shape of a ring, since doors were constantly being shifted to face away from the wind.

The first Europeans to encounter the Yámana were members of a Dutch expedition that sailed near Cape Horn in 1624, but systematic contact only occurred once Robert FitzRoy "discovered" the Beagle Channel, with the subsequent efforts of the Anglican South American Missionary Society to evangelize these "savages". Yámana culture, which depended on a fine-tuned system of interaction with the environment, had few defences against these "civilizing" forces.

In the end, it was this "civilization" that wiped out the Yámana. The arrival of settlers in 1884 triggered a **measles epidemic** that killed approximately half the estimated one thousand remaining Yámana. However incomprehensible it would have seemed to Europeans, the Yámana certainly fared better before contact. Damp, dirty clothing – European cast-offs given by well-meaning missionaries – actually increased the risk of disease, which spread fast in the mission communities. Missionaries promoted a shift to sedentary agriculture, but the consequent change of diet, from one high in animal fats to one more reliant on vegetables, reduced the Yámana's resistance to the cold, further increasing the likelihood of disease. Outbreaks of scrofula, pneumonia and tuberculosis meant that by 1911 fewer than one hundred Yámana remained. Well before the 1930s, commentators wrote off their chances of survival, referring to them as one of the "races soon to be extinct". Abuela Rosa, the last of the Yámana to live in the manner of her ancestors, died in 1982. Nevertheless, a few Yámana descendants still live near Puerto Williams on Isla Navarino, among them Abuela Cristina, the sole surviving speaker of the Yámana tongue, who works with the community's children in an effort to keep the language alive.

be spectacularly fruitful, as can sections of the Malengüeña, Irigoyen, Claro and Turbio rivers and lakes Yehuin and Fagnano.

Ushuaia to Paso Garibaldi and the Sierra Alvear

The road from Ushuaia to **Paso Garibaldi** wends its way north and east through dramatic forested scenery, with great views of the valleys and savage mountain ranges that cross the southern part of the island. Many activity centres and refuges have sprung up along the route, primarily to cater to **winter-sports** enthusiasts (see box, p.755), though they often also make excellent bases for adventurous **trekking** or horse-riding. Above all, the rugged, serrated peaks of the **Sierra Valdivieso** and **Sierra Alvear ranges** make ideal bushwhacking territory. If rough-hiking independently, consult the Club Andino in Ushuaia (see p.752) and arm yourself with a copy of Zagier & Urruty's *Ushuaia Trekking Map*, but do not underestimate the need for orienteering skills or the unpredictable nature of the weather: blizzards can hit at any time. You must also be prepared to get thoroughly soaked when crossing bogs and streams, but you'll be rewarded by the sight of **beaver dams** up to two and a half metres high, as well, in all probability, as their destructive constructors.

Heading northeast from Ushuaia, RN-3 curls up around the foot of **Monte Olivia** and heads into the **Valle de Tierra Mayor**, a popular area for winter sports and a good spot for trekking in the Sierra Alvear. One of the first centres you come across, 18km out from Ushuaia, is Altos del Valle, a breeding centre for baying huskies (sled rides available) that offers rustic **accommodation** in a *refugio* (Ⓣ02901/422234, Ⓔgatocuruchet@hotmail.com; bring a sleeping bag; $50 per person plus $7 for breakfast). The *refugio* marks the start of a relatively clear trail to attractive **Laguna Esmeralda** (4.5km; 2hr), where you can camp, and a more challenging hike to **Glaciar Alvear** (another 3.5km; 2hr 30min), which feeds the lake below. A kilometre beyond Altos del Valle is the excellent Nunatak (Ⓣ02901/423240, Ⓦwww.nunatakadventure.com; $25 with basic breakfast), a clean *refugio* that offers tremendous views across the peat flatlands of the valley floor and up to both the pyramidal peak of Cerro Bonete (1100m) and Cerro Alvear (1425m). Nunatak has showers, a kitchen and even videos, and serves inexpensive meals, but bring your own sleeping bag. Ask about their tough but fascinating guided trek to **Lago Ojo del Albino** (10hr; guide, crampons and food included). Several companies in Ushuaia run **buses** to Altos del Valle and Nunatak, leaving town daily from 9.30am until 1pm, returning between 1 and 6pm ($20–30 return).

Lago Fagnano and Tolhuin

Cresting the **Paso Garibaldi** some 45km out of Ushuaia, RN-3 descends towards **Lago Escondido**, the first of the lowland lakes, reachable down a four-kilometre branch road to the north, before heading alongside the southern shore of **LAGO FAGNANO**. This impressive lake, also called Lago Kami from its Selk'nam name, is flanked by ranges of hills, and straddles the Chilean border at its western end. Most of its 105km are inaccessible to visitors, apart from dedicated anglers who can afford to rent a good launch. Travelling along RN-3 as it parallels the lake, you'll see several sawmills, denoted by their squat, conical brick chimneys, used for burning bark.

Near the eastern end of Lago Fagnano, the road splits: the left fork is the more scenic, old, unsealed RN-3 route, which cuts north across the lake along a splendid causeway; the right is the RN-3 bypass, the more direct route to **TOLHUIN**, the region's oddest little town. Created in the 1970s, Tolhuin was designed to provide a focus for the heartland of Isla Grande – indeed, the name means "heart-shaped" in Selk'nam – but as a place of unassuming houses that hangs together with little focus, it has an artificial commune-like feel. It does, however, make a useful halfway point to break the journey – as most buses do – between Ushuaia and Río Grande.

Practicalities

Daily **buses** from Ushuaia to lakes Escondido and Fagnano leave between 9.30am and 3pm, and return between 2 and 7.30pm ($60 return). At Lago Escondido, you can overnight at *Hostería Petrel* (Ⓣ02901/433569; ❾ including breakfast), a **lodge** built in a typically heavy-handed, solid 1960s style, but with soothing views of the lake. For budget accommodation, head to the eastern end of Lago Fagnano to windy *Camping Hain del Lago* (Ⓣ02964/425951), which has three types of **refugio** (from ❸) and a **campsite** ($13 per person), or adjacent *Cabañas Khami* (Ⓣ02964/15566045, Ⓔmingoranceo@hotmail.com.ar; ❺ for up to six people during the week, ❽ at weekends), with snug log

Hunters turned hunted: the Selk'nam

In 1580, Sarmiento de Gamboa became the first European to encounter the **Selk'nam**. He was impressed by these "Big People", with their powerful frames, guanaco robes and conical headgear. It was not long before their war-like, defiant nature became evident, though, and a bloody skirmish with a Dutch expedition in 1599 proved them to be superb fighters, a fact long known by the Yámana (see box, p.766), who feared the people they called the **Ona**.

Before the arrival of the Europeans, Selk'nam society revolved around the hunting of **guanaco**, which they relied on not just for meat – the skin was made into moccasins and capes, the bones were used for fashioning arrowheads and the sinews for bowstrings. Hunting was done on foot, and the Selk'nam used stealth and teamwork to encircle guanacos, bringing them down with bow and arrow, a weapon with which they were expert. These proved to be of limited use, however, in preventing the invasion of white settlers at the end of the nineteenth century.

A covert campaign of **systematic genocide** of the Selk'nam began with the **arrival of sheep farms in the late nineteenth century**. Hundreds of miles of wire fencing were erected, which the Selk'nam, unsurprisingly, resented, seeing it as an incursion into their ancestral lands; however, they soon acquired a taste for hunting the slow animals, which they referred to as "white guanaco". For the settlers, this was an unpardonable crime, representing a drain on their investment. The Selk'nam were painted as "barbarous savages" who constituted an obstacle to settlement and progress, and isolated incidents of attack and retaliation soon escalated into bloody conflict. In a gruesome inversion of the contemporary white prejudice, the whites assumed the role of **headhunters**. Reliable sources point to prices being paid to bounty hunters on receipt of grisly invoices: a pair of severed ears (later to be modified to the whole head, after earless Selk'nam were seen roaming the countryside), with bonuses paid for pregnant women. The headhunters were paid £1 sterling per "trophy" – the same price as for a puma – and some purchasers made a handsome profit selling the heads to Europe's museums. Sheep and whale carcasses were laced with strychnine to poison unsuspecting Selk'nam, and there were reports of hunting with trained dogs and even of injecting captured children with infectious diseases.

The assault on Selk'nam culture, too, was abrupt and devastating, led by the "civilizing" techniques of the **Salesian missions**, who were paid £5 sterling by landowners for each Selk'nam that they "rehoused" in one of their missions. In 1881, at the beginning of the colonizing phase of Tierra del Fuego's history, some 3500 Selk'nam lived on Isla Grande. Fifteen hundred were forced into the Misión Salesiana Nuestra Señora de la Candelaria in Río Grande in 1897, and many were then deported from their homeland to the mission on **Isla Dawson**, south of Punta Arenas. By 1911, an estimated three hundred Selk'nam remained, but a measles epidemic in 1925 proved the tribe's death knell. The survivors had no alternative to succumb to acculturization, and by the late 1920s there were probably no indigenous Selk'nam living as their forefathers had done. In the *Uttermost Part of the Earth*, Lucas Bridges writes of the unparalleled skill of the Selk'nam as shepherds and shearers, but comments that: "Those Indians who avoided hard work soon became 'poor whites'." When pure-blooded Lola Kiepje and Esteban Yshton passed away in 1966 and 1969, respectively, Selk'nam culture died with them.

cabins intended primarily for fishermen. At the far end of the causeway, 7km from Tolhuin and just before the old RN-3 links up with the new, is the refurbished *Hostería Kaikén* (Ⓣ02901/492208, Ⓦwww.hosteriakaiken.com.ar; ❼), a plush but pleasant hotel that commands fine views of the lake, especially from its restaurant. Ushuaia–Río Grande buses stop in Tolhuin at the quirky *Panadería La Unión*, a bakery and **restaurant** that acts as the hub of village life, not only selling delicious breads and other goodies, but also housing a cybercafé, *locutorio* and clean toilets.

Tolhuin to Río Grande: RN-3 and the rutas complementarias

The main route between Tolhuin and Río Grande is fast, paved RN-3, but if you have the time it's worth exploring one or more of the unsealed **rutas complementarias** (RC) that branch off it – alphabetized roads that provide access to the heartland of Argentine Tierra del Fuego but are only really accessible to those with their own transport. The **RCh**, which branches off RN-3 22km north of Tolhuin, and the connecting **RCf**, which joins RN-3 some 10km south of the bridge over the Río Grande, form a 120-kilometre loop that passes through swathes of transitional Fuegian woodland and grassy pasture-meadows (*vegas*) populated by sheep. Along RCh you'll see cone-shaped Mount Yakush and pyramid-like Mount Atukoyak to the south before the road joins the RCf by **Lago Yehuin**, a popular fishing locale and a good place for spotting **condors**, which nest on Cerro Shenolsh between the lake and its shallow neighbour, **Lago Chepelmut**. Two excellent **places to stay** are located just off the RCh: *Estancia Ushuaia* (Ⓣ02901/431663, Ⓦwww.estanciaushuaia.com.ar; ⑨ full board), a rebuilt farmhouse set among marvellously bucolic land, which offers horse rides across the plains or up a nearby hill for fantastic views, and the more upmarket *Estancia Rivadavia* (Ⓣ02901/492186, Ⓦwww.estanciarivadavia.com; US$360 full board), a hospitable boutique hotel with delightful rooms, where you can ride horses and trek across the estancia's 160 square kilometres of land, which include the deep azure waters of Lago Yehuin and Lago Chepelmut.

Some 40km north of Tolhuin, the most beautiful of the central *rutas complementarias*, the **RCa**, branches east through golden pastureland, rimmed by *lengas* and flaming red *ñires*, towards the coast and the knobbly protrusion of **Cabo San Pablo**. A wonderful panorama stretches out from the south side of Cabo San Pablo, encompassing the wreck of the *Desdémona*, grounded during a storm in the early 1980s – at low tide, you can walk out to the ship – but the area is mainly of interest to fishermen, who can choose from several excellent **fishing** spots in the estuaries of nearby Río San Pablo and, just to the north, the Río Ladrillero. Beyond the cape, the road continues for 17km through wetlands and burnt-out "tree cemeteries" and past the odd beaver dam to the *Estancia Fueguina*, from where you'll need a high-clearance 4WD to progress any further. The public track eventually fizzles out at *Estancia María Luisa*, 18km further on, just beyond which run the famous fishing rivers, Irigoyen and Malengüeña, but the rights are strictly private and only organized trips are allowed – contact the *Hotel Villa* in Río Grande (Ⓣ02964/424998, Ⓔhotelvillarg@hotmail.com). This is the beginning of the **Península Mitre**, the bleak toe of land that forms the southeast extremity of Tierra del Fuego. This semi-wilderness – primarily swampy moorland and thickets fringed by rugged coastal scenery – was once the territory of the indigenous Mannekenk (see box, p.770), whose presence is attested to by old shell middens. Before the 1850s, the only white men who came ashore were sailors and scientists, such as FitzRoy and Darwin, as well as shipwreck victims; the remains of many wrecks line the shore, including the late nineteenth-century *Duchess of Albany*, near **Bahía Policarpo**. Apart from a few gauchos, the peninsula is now effectively uninhabited, and the only way to explore the area is on guided **horse-riding** excursions with Centro Hípico Ushuaia (Ⓣ02901/1556-8278, Ⓦwww.centrohipicoushuaia.com.ar), which runs eight-day trips down the Costa de los Naufragios, from *Estancia María Luisa* to *Estancia Policarpo* and back (US$795).

Heading **north along RN-3** from the RCa turn-off leads, after some 37km, to the extremely atmospheric *Estancia Viamonte* (ⓣ02964/430861, ⓦwww.estanciaviamonte.com; US$360 full board and excursions). Established against the odds by Lucas Bridges with the help of his Selk'nam friends – and still run by his descendants – this is one of the island's most historic farms and figures prominently in his epic work, *Uttermost Part of the Earth*. The rooms are simple but thoughtfully furnished and the welcome warm; it's a great place to gain a real insight into life on a working estancia – farm activities are included in the price.

The scenery north of *Estancia Viamonte* undergoes an abrupt transition, from scraggly clumps of Fuegian woodland to the forlorn, bald landscape of the steppe. South of the town of Río Grande, a few kilometres before you cross the Río Grande itself, you pass the turn-off for the **RCb**, worth detouring along for 1km to see the tiny village of **Estancia José Menéndez**, whose shearing shed is emblazoned by the head of a prize ewe, its face obscured by an over-effusive wig of curls. The estancia was founded as Estancia Primera Argentina in 1896 by sheep magnate Menéndez. The most notorious of its first managers was a hard-drinking Scotsman by the name of MacLennan, who earned himself the sobriquet of "Red Pig" for taking pleasure in gunning down the Selk'nam. The RCb continues across the steppe for 70km to the Chilean frontier at **Radman**, where there's a little-used **border crossing**, known as Bella Vista (Nov–March 8am–9pm), which allows access to Lago Blanco, an excellent fishing destination, as well as providing an alternative route west to Porvenir (in Chile; see p.773).

Península Mitre's extinct race: the Mannekenk

Modern knowledge of the **Mannekenk** (also known as the Haush or Aush), a relatively small ethnic group that was confined to the Península Mitre, is decidedly sketchy in comparison with other Fuegian tribes. Their culture was a mix of the Yámana and the Selk'nam ways, and intermarriage occurred with both these groups.

Like the Yámana, the Mannekenk were heavily dependent on the sea for food, although they did not have canoes. However, they were more similar, both physiologically and culturally, to the Selk'nam, and it has been suggested that they were a related ancestral group, pushed into the less hospitable corner of the island by their more warlike cousins. And though their languages were unrelated, the Selk'nam adopted several Mannekenk terms in their sacred Hain ceremony, which may itself have originated in part from a Mannekenk initiation rite. "Haush" derives from a Yámana term meaning "seaweed-eaters", but Lucas Bridges tells us the Yámana called the Mannekenk "Etalum Ona", meaning "Eastern Ona", which suggests that the canoe-folk viewed them as related to the Selk'nam.

The first record we have of the Mannekenk came from a Spanish expedition in 1619. They were certainly acquainted with Europeans and their goods by the time Captain Cook arrived, and he reported that they already had some Western trinkets (possibly salvaged off shipwrecks). In the late nineteenth century, sealers and Eastern European goldminers made forays into their territory, bringing death through disease and sporadic skirmishing. In 1890, Lucas Bridges estimated that there were only perhaps sixty left, a figure that had dropped to five in 1911. By the 1930s, the Mannekenk were just a memory – all that remains now is their shell middens.

Río Grande and around

RÍO GRANDE is a drab, sprawling city that grew up on the river of the same name as a port for José Menéndez's sheep enterprises. The treacherous tides along this stretch of the coast can reach over 15m at the spring equinox, and low tide exposes a shelf of mudflats better for seabirds than boats. The port, therefore, has virtually ceased to exist, having been superseded by the vastly superior one at Ushuaia. And in spite of the people's friendliness, the atmosphere here is as flat as the landscape: it's a place to pass through quickly, unless you're a trout fisherman, in which case it's a functional starting-point for exploring the region's fruitful rivers – the wonderful **Monumento a la Trucha**, a statue of a giant brown trout on RN-3, leaves you with no doubt about what the town is famous for. The only sight worth visiting hereabouts is the **Misión Salesiana Nuestra Señora de la Candelaria**, a mission turned agricultural school 11km north of town, whose museum traces attempts to convert the local Selk'nam. If you're looking to kill time, you might consider taking a **city tour** (see below), a convenient way of visiting the town's scattered subsidiary sites that are otherwise awkward to reach, including the **Estancia María Behety**, one of the island's largest and oldest sheep-farming establishments, dating from 1897, 17km due west of town along the RCc.

Practicalities

Río Grande's **airport** is 5km out of town ($10 by taxi). **Buses** drop passengers off at their offices, most of which are a couple of blocks from the main avenue, Almirante Brown. The helpful provincial **tourist office** is on Plaza Almirante Brown, at Rosales 350 (Dec–March Mon–Fri 9am–9pm, Sat & Sun 2–9pm, April–Nov Mon–Fri 9am–5pm, Sat & Sun 2–5pm; Ⓣ02964/422887, Ⓔrg-turismo@netcombbs.com.ar). **Fishing licences** and information on fishing can be obtained from the Asociación de Pesca con Mosca at Montilla 1040. For **city tours**, lasting about three hours and costing around $45, contact Shelk'nam Viajes, Belgrano 1122 (Ⓣ02964/426278, Ⓔshelknam@netcombbs.com.ar).

Accommodation in Río Grande, catering mostly to anglers with big pockets, is generally overpriced. The most comfortable option is the restful *Posada de los Sauces*, El Cano 839 (Ⓣ02964/432895, Ⓦwww.posadadelossauces.com.ar; ❻), across the road from the bus terminal, with well-decorated rooms, a relaxed lounge bar and an appealing *á la carte* restaurant. *Hotel Federico Ibarra*, Rosales 357 (Ⓣ02964/430071, Ⓦwww.federicoibarrahotel.com.ar; ❻), has good-sized rooms, though those overlooking the plaza tend to absorb noise, while *Hotel Argentino*, San Martín 64 (Ⓣ02964/422546, Ⓔhotelargentino@hotmail.com; dorms $31, rooms ❸), is the best budget option in town, an amicable hostel with kitchen facilities and an airy dining area.

The best spot to grab something to **eat** is *La Nueva Colonial*, Belgrano and Laserre, a popular spot where the convivial owner spoons out large portions of home-cooked pasta with hearty sauces. Most Argentine towns seem to have a *parrilla* called *La Rueda*, and Río Grande is no exception. In fact, it's a step ahead of the competition, with two: the main one at Islas Malvinas 998, and a smaller branch at Moreno and 9 de Julio; both serve fish and barbecued meat dishes, accompanied by a salad buffet bar.

Misión Salesiana Nuestra Señora de la Candelaria

Eleven kilometres north of the centre of Río Grande on RN-3 stands the **Misión Salesiana Nuestra Señora de la Candelaria**, a collection of whitewashed buildings grouped around a modest but elegant chapel. Río Grande's

Border crossings

The main land **border crossing** between the Chilean and Argentine halves of Tierra del Fuego's Isla Grande is at **San Sebastián**, in the north of the island. The respective customs posts (April–Oct 9am–11pm, Nov–March 24hr) are several hundred metres apart, some 15km west of the Argentine village of the same name. Formalities are straightforward, if somewhat lengthy at times. You may not take any fresh fruit, meat or dairy products into Chile, and Argentine officers sometimes reciprocate. Note that Argentina is one hour ahead of Chile from March to October.

first mission, it was founded in 1893 by two of Patagonia's most influential Salesian fathers, Monseñor Fagnano and Padre Beauvoir, but their first township burnt down in 1896, and was relocated to its present site. Originally, it was built with the purpose of catechizing the island's Selk'nam, but in effect, it acted as part refuge and part prison, since local sheep magnates would round up the indigenous peoples on their land and pay the Salesians for their "conversion". In 1942, with virtually no Selk'nam remaining, the mission became an agricultural school, a role it has retained to this day. The **Museo Monseñor Fagnano** (Mon–Sat 10am–1.30pm & 3–7pm, Sun 3–7pm; $2; ⓣ02964/430667) is in the building to the left of the chapel as you enter the compound. There's a medley of exhibits on local flora and fauna but more interesting are the homages to Don Bosco, the founder of the Salesian movement, amongst which you'll find some first-rate Fuegian indigenous items and a kerosene-lit projector that was used to entertain, and no doubt indoctrinate, the Selk'nam. Across the road is a fenced **cemetery** with some vandalized tombs of Salesian fathers and unmarked crosses indicating Selk'nam graves, testaments to a culture that had been completely depersonalized. To reach the mission from town, take the Línea B **bus** "Misión" from Avenida San Martín (hourly; 25min; $3).

North to San Sebastián and the Chilean border

North of the Misión Salesiano rears **Cabo Domingo**, and beyond that, the unforgiving plains of Patagonian shingle begin again, dotted by shallow saline lagoons that sometimes host feeding flamingoes. The RN-3 is paved as far as the **San Sebastián border post**, 82km north of Río Grande (see box above), on the bay of the same name. The Bahía San Sebastián itself is famous for its summer populations of migratory waders and shorebirds and is a vital part of the **Hemisphere Reserve for Shorebirds**, designed to protect migratory birds along the coasts and interior wetlands of the Americas. Spare a thought for birds such as the Hudsonian Godwit (*becasa de mar*) and the Red Knot (*playero rojizo*): they've travelled over 17,000km to get here.

Chilean Tierra del Fuego

Compared with the Argentine side of Tierra del Fuego's main island, there really isn't much to see in the **Chilean** sector: just the principal town of **Porvenir** and the inevitable string of oil settlements. Evidence of the importance of oil is everywhere, from pipelines that follow the road to the remains of windscreens shattered by the stones kicked up by enormous oil trucks. The northern half of the island is a wasteland of windswept steppe, but the hills gradually become higher and less barren as you move south, culminating eventually in the Cordillera Darwin, a craggy range of forest-clad peaks. Beneath these mountains, glaciers meander through narrow valleys, then break up in the Beagle Channel. Facing Ushuaia across the channel, but part of Chilean Tierra del Fuego, is picturesque **Isla Navarino**, home to some of the best trekking in the far south.

Public **transport** is next to non-existent and traffic's very light, so travelling without your own car is difficult.

Porvenir

A collection of brightly painted corrugated-iron houses set in a narrow bay of the same name, **PORVENIR** (optimistically meaning "future"), 35km east of Punta Arenas across the Magellan Straits and 147km west of the border crossing at San Sebastián, serves as a brief stopover-point for most travellers, who hurry through on their way to Ushuaia or Punta Arenas.

The town started life in 1883 as a police outpost in the days of the Fuegian gold rush, and has since been settled by foreigners. First came the British managers of sheep farms, and then refugees from Croatia after World War II. You can read the history of the town in the names of the dead in the **cemetery** (daily 8am–6pm), four blocks north of Plaza de Armas: Mary Montgomery Mackenzie lies opposite Rosenda Manquemilla Muñoz, who lies beside Juan Senkovic Restovich. It's not only the names that are fascinating here, though – at the far end of the trees there's the tomb of the Mimica Scarpa family, designed to resemble a miniature mosque, complete with a scaled-down minaret. The only other site of interest in Porvenir is the **Museo Provincial Fernando Cordero Rusque** on the north corner of the plaza (Mon–Thurs 9am–5pm, Fri 9am–4pm, Sat & Sun 11am–2pm & 3–5pm; CH$500; ⓣ61/580098), with photographs of miners and machinery from the gold-rush years, a collection of cameras from the early days of Chilean film and the usual assortment of stuffed animals. The museum also doubles as a tourist office of sorts.

Practicalities

Ferries from Punta Arenas arrive at Bahía Chilota, 5km west of Porvenir along the bay, from where a taxi into town will cost CH$2500 and a *colectivo* CH$500. The **aerodrome** is 5km north of town; DAP flights are met by taxis that charge CH$3000 to take you into Porvenir. You can buy ferry and plane **tickets** back to Punta Arenas from a kiosk on Calle Señoret (Mon–Fri 9am–noon & 2–6.30pm, Sat 9am–noon & 3–6pm). If that's shut, the restaurant at Bahía Chilota sells tickets for the ferry an hour before it leaves (departures Tues–Sat 2pm & Sun 5pm; 2hr 20min). DAP's offices (ⓣ61/580089) are at Señoret and Muñoz Gamero. **Buses** run to Río Grande in Argentina (daily except Mon; noon) from the corner of Riobo and Sampaio, a couple of blocks northeast of the immaculate Plaza de Armas; you can get a connection in Río Grande to Ushuaia or Buenos Aires.

The **international dialling code** for Chile from Argentina is ⓣ0056. The **area code** for Chilean Tierra del Fuego is ⓣ61. The **Chilean peso** (CH$) is the national currency. One pound sterling buys around CH$960, one US dollar CH$500.

You can **change money** at the Banco del Estado, Philippi 265, and there's **Internet** access available further down the main street, at no. 375. There's also a **post office** on the plaza.

There are a number of reasonable **places to stay**. Modern *Hostal Patagonia*, Jorge Schythe 230 (Ⓣ61/580371; ❹), has good-quality en-suite rooms, while friendly *Residential Colón*, Riobo 198 (Ⓣ61/580593; ❸), offers bed-and-breakfast accommodation with a large, bright dining room; guests may use the kitchen, and you can also camp outside (CH$2500). The best accommodation options, though, are *Hotel España*, Croacia 698 (Ⓣ61/580160, Ⓦwww.hotelespana.cl; ❹–❺), a deceptively large old building run by a formidable woman, offering both basic rooms with shared bathrooms and plush en-suite doubles in the newer, brighter section, and cosy *Hotel Rosas*, Philippi 296 (Ⓣ&Ⓕ61/580088; ❺), whose owner is a fund of information on the area.

The best of the few **places to eat** in town is *Club Croata*, Señoret 542, which serves well-prepared Chilean fare. The restaurant in *Hotel Rosas* serves up generous portions of seafood, or there's *Hotel España*, which does good sandwiches and set meals.

Northeast to Cerro Sombrero and Bahía Azul

The first 20km heading north out of Porvenir is lined with large shallow lakes that range in colour from turquoise to sapphire and are often adorned with dazzling pink flamingoes. After that excitement, there's not much for the next 86km until you reach the turn-off on the right that leads to Chilean Tierra del Fuego's other town, **CERRO SOMBRERO**, a small oil settlement looming up out of the moonscape, snugly ensconced on the top of a small flat hill and bristling with TV aerials like something out of *Mad Max*. It's not worth travelling to the end of the earth to visit, but it's friendly enough – and makes a good place to stop if you need petrol or just want a break. Thanks to its natural resources, Cerro Sombero is not short of heating, and the Plaza de Armas is blessed with a plant-filled conservatory. The best **place to stay**, should you need to, is *Hostería Tunkelen*, a pleasant truck stop at the bottom of the hill (Ⓣ61/212757; ❹). Run by a hospitable family, it features a good-quality en-suite room in the main house, a block of rooms with a shared bathroom and, best of all, an efficient water-heating system.

Forty-three kilometres north of Cerro Sombrero (139km from Porvenir), the **ferry** that crosses the Primera Angostura departs from **Bahía Azul** (often marked as "Puerto Espora" on maps), where you can grab a quick snack at the terminal while you wait for the boat.

South to Lago Blanco

While the north of Chilean Isla Grande is bleak wasteland, in the south, around the beautiful, but mostly ignored, **Lago Blanco**, there are areas of forest where you can trek, fish and camp. The prettiest road towards the lake follows the coast, starting along the northern shore of **Bahía Inutil**, a wide bay that got its name through being a useless anchorage for sailing ships. After 99km you reach a crossroads; turn south, and just past the village of Onaisin is a little **English cemetery**. The desolate landscape is at stark odds with the English gravestones, which carry inscriptions that hint at tragic stories: "killed by Indians", "accidentally drowned" and "died in a storm".

The coast road then skirts around the south of Bahía Inutil, giving beautiful views across to **Isla Dawson** and passing the occasional small cluster of fishermen's huts – keep an eye out for the windlasses with which they draw up their small boats out of the reach of the sea, but be careful of taking photos here, as the whole area is a military zone. When the tide's out, you can see a more ancient means of catching fish – underwater stone *corrals* (pens) built by the Selk'nam to trap fish when the tide turned. Just before the village of **Camerón**, the road turns inland and leaves the bay. Camerón, built on either side of the Río Shetland, was once a thriving Scottish settlement – hence the names – the centre of the largest sheep farm on the island, but nowadays all that's left are some little workers' houses and a shearing shed.

From here, the land begins to lose its Patagonian severity, and as you travel inland it becomes densely forested. After 37km, you pass another rusting reminder of the gold rush – a 1904 dredge, now preserved as a national monument. Some 20km later, the road forks north to San Sebastián, and south to a place called Sección Río Grande, where an iron bridge crosses the river; from here, it's 21km to **LAGO BLANCO** itself, majestic and brooding, encompassed by steeply forested hills and snow-covered mountains. The lake is being developed, with *cabañas* springing up around its edge and a romantic fishing lodge on an island in the middle. In a few years' time, it might resemble some of the over-developed resorts of the Lake District, but at the moment it's a place of isolation and escape. Arranging somewhere to stay is difficult, since there are no telephones down here, only radio phones. Two lodges share a contact number in Punta Arenas and charge similar high-end rates: *Tierra del Fuego Lodge*, in nearby Río Rassmusen, and *Refugio Isla Victoria*, in Lago Blanco itself (Ⓣ61/241197; both closed Sept–March; US$150–300).

With no public transport and little traffic down here, the only realistic means of travelling is in a rental car, though an erratic bus service does (sometimes) run between Porvenir and Camerón.

Isla Navarino

Apart from tiny **Puerto Williams**, a quirky naval base that is truly the world's southernmost settlement, and a few estancias along the northern coast, **ISLA NAVARINO**, the largish island south of Isla Grande, is an uninhabited wilderness studded with barren peaks and isolated valleys. Covering about 4000 square kilometres, virtually unspoilt and mostly inaccessible, Navarino is dominated by a dramatic range of peaks, **Los Dientes del Navarino**, through which weaves a superb seventy-kilometre hiking trail – the **Circuito de los Dientes**. A sign of the island's remoteness is the fact that this trail is more the result of wandering guanacos than of man. What has spoilt some of the landscape, especially the woodland, however, is the devastation brought about by **beavers**, introduced from Canada. Once protected but now hunted extensively – and sold for their meat and their pelts – these cuddly-looking but destructive animals have gnawed through countless tree trunks, and their dams cause terrible flooding.

Getting there

The most reliable way to get to Isla Navarino is to **fly** – with DAP from Punta Arenas, or by making the short hop across the Beagle Channel with Aeroclub Ushuaia (see p.757). Transbordadora Austral Broom runs a weekly **ferry** from Punta Arenas (34hr; from US$140 one way; Ⓦwww.tabsa.cl), or you can take a **semi-rigid craft** across with Ushuaia Boating (daily

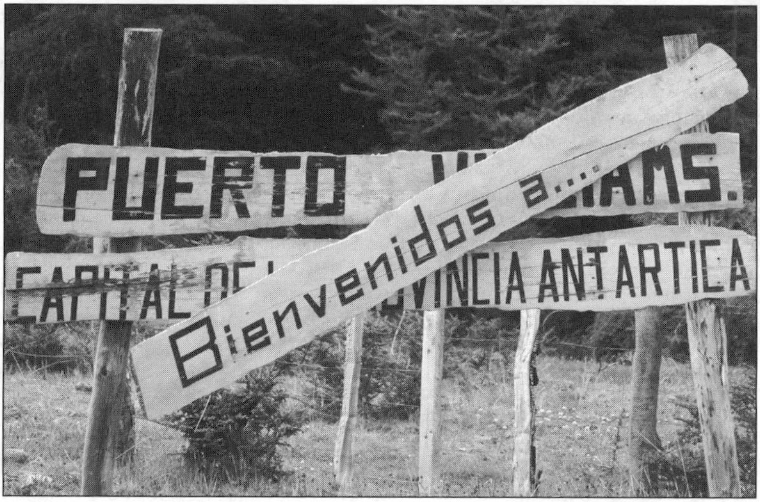

△ Puerto Williams sign, Isla Navarino

depending on weather; US$100 one way including transfer from Puerto Navarino; ⓣ02901/436193, ⓦwww.ushuaiaboating.com.ar), an exciting but expensive journey that is often sandwiched between interminable delays of days rather than hours.

Puerto Williams

Nestled in a small bay on the north shore of Isla Navarino, 82km due east and ever so slightly south of Ushuaia along the Beagle Channel, is **PUERTO WILLIAMS**. "Williams" is something of a thorn in Argentina's toe, since despite all the publicity and hype about Ushuaia being **the most southerly town in the world**, that dubious privilege actually belongs to Puerto Williams. Founded as a military outpost and officially the capital of Chilean Antarctica, the town looks tranquil and idyllic on a fine day, with colourful roofs surrounded by the jagged peaks of **Los Dientes**.

Arrival and information

If you arrive at the midget **airport**, you'll be met by at least one private car acting as a taxi that will take you into town; the trip is further than it looks, as the peninsula on which the airfield is built is separated from Puerto Williams by a long, narrow channel. **Ferries** dock at the Muelle Guardian Brito, just south of the centre, while Ushuaia Boating lands at Puerto Navarino, 54km along a *ripio* road to the west.

There's no **tourist information** office in town, but the owners of *Café Angelus* (see p.778) are good sources of local info. There's an **ATM** at the Banco de Chile, just behind the main plaza, the ambitiously titled "Centro Comercial", where there is also a **post office** and a Telefonica **telephone centre**. The main **tour agencies** are SIM, also on the Centro Comercial (ⓣ61/621150, ⓦwww.simltd.com), and Victory Cruises, a couple of blocks uphill, at Teniente Muñoz 118 (ⓣ61/621010, ⓦwww.victory.cruises.com). Ask for details of treks around the island and boat trips to Cape Horn. DAP has offices in the Centro Comercial (ⓣ61/621114).

Accommodation

Accommodation in Puerto Williams is mostly basic but reasonable, and is mainly clustered around the centre. The best place to stay on the island is *Hotel Lakutaía* (Ⓣ61/621733, Ⓦwww.lakutaia.cl; US$250 full board including guided excursions), an upmarket establishment that enjoys a beautiful setting overlooking Seno Lauta, 2km west of town. The comfortable rooms have smart bathrooms and beds you can get lost in, and the large, naturally furnished lounge affords glorious views of the sound and the Beagle Channel. The extremely friendly owners organize horse-riding and canoeing trips and can take you to see a nearby beaver dam. You could also try simple but warm *Hostal Pusaki*, Piloto Pardo 222 (Ⓣ61/621116, Ⓔpattypusaki@yahoo.es; ❻), with shared bathrooms, where use of the kitchen is free, within reason, and delicious meals are laid on for overnight guests; *Hostal Coirón*, Maragaño 168 (Ⓣ61/621227, Ⓔreservas@hostalcoiron.cl; ❺), which has shared rooms with bunks, a kitchen open to guests and space for camping; or cosy, colourful *Patagonia*, Yelcho 230 (Ⓣ61/621294, Ⓔpedroortiz@chilesat.net; ❺).

The Town

Known as "Puerto Luisa" until 1956 and as "Uspashun" to the native Yámana, Puerto Williams is a tiny place, with a centre not much bigger than a single square kilometre. Although the first things you notice on your approach by sea or air are likely to be the Chilean Navy's black gunboats, the town is extremely relaxed and welcoming. The true purpose of any visit to Williams, however, is to fulfil a desire to come this far south and this far away from "civilization"; indeed, the only thing to visit as such is the **Museo Martín Gusinde**, at the far western end of town, on Comandante Aragay 1 (Mon–Thurs 9am–1pm & 2.30–7.15pm, Sat & Sun 2.30–6.30pm; free), where well-laid-out photographs and maps chart the history and exploration of the region, from the days of the Fuegian Indians, through the gold rush, to the commercial shipping of today. There's also a collection of knick-knacks donated by kayakers who've paddled around Cape Horn, not far south of here, and an informative display of the island's flora and fauna illustrated by the usual array of stuffed creatures and dried vegetation.

Eating and drinking

One of the most interesting **places to eat** is *Patagonia*, at Yelcho 230, where the hotel's owners serve up regional dishes including *castor* (beaver), a rich, pungent red meat. Otherwise, there's *Los Dientes del Navarino*, a small, friendly

Los Dientes del Navarino

The seventy-kilometre – but wholly worthwhile – **Circuito de los Dientes** that circumnavigates the Cordón de los Dientes, usually referred to as **Los Dientes del Navarino**, leaves from the statue of the Virgin Mary, about one kilometre west of town on the road to the airport. There you'll find a turning uphill, which leads to a waterfall and a dammed stream, to the left of which is a marked trail. The tough climb to the lookout on **Cerro Bandera** can be done as a day-hike (4hr return), and affords spectacular views along the Beagle Channel to Ushuaia. Allow at least five days to complete the whole, clockwise circuit, taking plentiful supplies and outdoor gear and anticipating bad weather, even snow in summer; and remember to inform people in town before leaving. Alternatively, you can tackle the circuit on an organized trek with one of the agencies in town (see opposite).

Getting to Cape Horn

Having come this far south, many travellers like to go the whole hog and "round the Cape", erroneously translated into Spanish as *Cabo de Hornos* ("Ovens Cape"). Ask around in Puerto Williams – SIM travel agency (see p.782) is a good place to start – about **boat trips** to the most southerly point of the world's landmass, barring Antarctica. Weather permitting, you disembark on a shingle beach, climb a rickety ladder and visit the tiny Chilean naval base, lighthouse and chapel; there's not much to do otherwise and it's all quite desolate. DAP and Aeroclub Ushuaia (see p.757) also run not terribly expensive thirty-minute **flights** from Punta Arenas, Puerto Williams and Ushuaia, which make a loop over the headland and return without landing. These air excursions treat you to incredible views of Isla Navarino and the Darwin peaks, but, again, weather is a vital factor.

restaurant in the Centro Comercial, where you'll probably have to go into the kitchen and point out what you want, or the warm and welcoming *Café Angelus*, also on the main plaza, which has a small menu of more recognizable fare – soups, pastas and the like. At the excellent Supermercado Simón y Simón, opposite *Hostal Pusaki*, you can buy delicious bread, empañadas and amazingly good wine, along with picnic fixings. There is no **nightlife** as such here: the only place to while away your evening is the ★ *Club de Yates Micalvi*, an ex-Navy supply ship with a markedly "old salt" atmosphere and a well-stocked bar where you can chat and drink as long as the last man's standing.

Around Puerto Williams

Four kilometres **west** of town is the experimental **Parque Etnobotánico Omora** (daylight hours; donation suggested), named for the world's southernmost hummingbird. A part-state, part-private enterprise, the park is intended to play an educational and environmental role, protecting the *ñire* and *lenga* forest by, among other things, encouraging locals to cull beavers for their meat. Native birds, including the red-headed Magellanic Woodpecker (*lana*) and the Ruffed-Legged Owl (*kujurj*), are monitored, along with other endangered species of flora and fauna. You can find out more, including details about the park's trail, at the visitors' centre near the entrance.

Further west along the coast are numerous picturesque little bays and islands with an abundance of birdlife, both along the shore and in the edge of the forest, one of which, **Bahía Virginia**, has large middens of mussel and clam shells left by what must once have been a large settlement of Yámana.

An easy stroll 2km **east** of Puerto Williams is the straggly hamlet of **Ukika**, a small collection of houses where fifty or so people of Yámana descent – including Abuela Cristina (see box, p.766) – live. You can buy reed baskets and replica canoes, but do not take photographs unless invited to do so. Beyond, the road continues, giving beautiful views across the Beagle Channel before ducking into the forest and heading inland. It emerges once again at **Puerto Eugenia**, the end of the last road in South America, looking out at **Picton Island** and beyond, into the endless seas of the Atlantic Ocean.

Travel details

Below are the summer season timetables; out of season, services are reduced drastically.

Buses

Río Grande to: Porvenir (Tues–Sun daily; 5hr); Punta Arenas (Mon–Sat daily; 9hr); Tolhuin (11–15 daily; 1hr 30min); Río Gallegos (Mon–Sat daily; 10hr); Ushuaia (12–16 daily; 3hr 30min–4hr).
Porvenir to: Río Grande (Tues–Sun daily; 5hr).
Tolhuin to: Río Grande (11–15 daily; 1hr 30min); Ushuaia (11–15 daily; 1hr 30min).
Ushuaia to: El Calafate (Mon–Sat daily; 18hr); Puerto Natales (4 weekly; 16hr); Punta Arenas (daily except Tues; 12hr); Río Gallegos (1–2 daily; 13hr); Río Grande (12–16 daily; 3hr 30min–4hr); Tolhuin (11–15 daily; 1hr 30min).

Ferries

Bahía Azul to: Punta Delgada (every 30min, no crossings at low tide; 30min).
Porvenir to: Punta Arenas (Tues–Sun daily; 2hr 20min).
Punta Arenas to: Porvenir (Tues–Sun daily; 2hr 20min); Puerto Williams (weekly; 34hr).
Punta Delgada to: Bahía Azul (every 40min, no crossings at low tide; 30min).
Puerto Williams to: Porvenir (weekly; 34hr).

Flights

Porvenir to: Punta Arenas (Mon–Sat 2–3 daily; 20min).
Punta Arenas to: Puerto Williams (Tues–Sun daily; 1hr 15min).
Puerto Williams to: Punta Arenas (Tues–Sun daily; 1hr 15min); Ushuaia (3 weekly; 20min).
Río Grande to: Buenos Aires (daily; 3hr 30min); Río Gallegos (twice weekly; 1hr 5min); Ushuaia (twice weekly; 35min).
Ushuaia to: Buenos Aires (Ezeiza and Aeroparque; 9–12 daily; 3hr 30min); El Calafate (4 daily; 1hr 10min); Puerto Madryn (irregular; 2hr); Punta Arenas (3 weekly; 1hr); Puerto Williams (3 weekly; 20min); Río Gallegos (daily; 55min); Río Grande (2 weekly; 35min); Trelew (irregular; 2hr).

Contexts

Contexts

History

Argentina's past might best be summed up as "chequered". The modern nation is a product of Spanish colonialism and immigration from all corners of Europe and the Middle East during the late nineteenth and early twentieth centuries. Relatively little of its pre-Columbian civilizations has survived, other than archeological finds, though there is more of an indigenous influence on present-day Argentine culture than initially meets the eye. After independence, Argentina repeatedly took one step forward to progressive democracy and two steps back into corrupt lawlessness. Twentieth-century Argentina produced its fair share of international icons – with Evita and Che Guevara leading the way, followed closely by Maradona – and was often in the news for the wrong reasons. A series of nasty dictatorships culminated in the late 1970s with the Dirty War, a regime that relied on inhuman terror tactics only to be brought down in 1982, in part by the Falklands/Malvinas fiasco. Argentina again hit the international headlines for the wrong reasons when social unrest and recession lurched into chaos in late 2001. In 2003, Néstor Kirchner became president, overseeing an economic recovery and a period of relative calm.

Pre-Columbian Argentina

The earliest records for human presence in the territory that is now Argentina can be dated back to around 10,000 BC. Over the millennia that preceded the arrival of Europeans, widely varying cultures developed. From around 4000 BC, distinct nomadic cultures like that of the **Yámana** (see box, p.766) emerged in the Fuegian archipelago. Other groups, such as the **Guaraní** peoples of the subtropical northeast, evolved semi-nomadic lifestyles dependent on hunter-gathering and slash-and-burn agriculture.

The most complex cultures emerged, however, in the **Andean northwest**, where sedentary agricultural practices developed from about 500 BC. Irrigation permitted the intensive cultivation of crops like maize, quinoa, squash and potatoes and this, combined with the domestication of animals like the llama, facilitated the growth of rich material cultures. The most important early sedentary culture was the **Tafí**, whose people sculpted intriguing stone menhirs. Later, this period saw the development of Catamarca's **Condorhuasi** culture, renowned for its distinctive, beautifully patterned ceramics. From about 600 AD, metallurgical technologies developed, and bronze was used for items such as ceremonial axes and chest-plates, perhaps best by the **Aguada** civilization, also centred on Catamarca. The increasing organization of Andean groups after 850 AD is demonstrated by the appearance of fortified urban settlements. Three important **Diaguita** cultures emerge: Sanagasta, Belén and **Santa María**, whose overlapping zones of influence stretched from Salta to San Juan, and which are notable for their painted ceramics, anthropomorphic funeral urns and superb metalwork.

Trade networks vastly increased once the area came under the sway of pan-Andean empires: first that of Bolivia's great city, **Tiahuanaco**, which probably influenced Condorhuasi culture; and, from 1480, that of the **Inca**, who incorporated the area into Kollasuyo, their southernmost administrative region.

Incredibly well-preserved finds, such as **three ritually sacrificed mummies** at the summit of 6739-metre Cerro Llullaillaco – the world's highest archeological discovery (see p.430) – are helping to reveal the extent of this influence in terms of customs, religion and dress.

In the early sixteenth century, before the arrival of Europeans, Argentina's **indigenous population** was probably around half a million, an estimated two-thirds of whom lived in the Northwest. Other relatively densely settled areas included the central sierras of Córdoba and San Luis, where the **Comechingones** and the Sanavirones lived. The Cuyo region was home to semi-sedentary Huarpe; while south and east of them lived various Tehuelche tribes (see box, p.659), often referred to generically by the Spanish as Pampas Indians or, further south, Patagones. Tierra del Fuego was inhabited by Selk'nam and Mannekenk, as well as Yámana (see box, p.766). The Gran Chaco region (see box, pp.402–403) was home to many nomadic groups, including Chiriguano, Lule-Vilela, Wichí and groups of the Guaycurú nation, like the Abipone and Qom. The northeastern areas of El Litoral and Mesopotamia were inhabited by Kaingang, Charrúa and Guaraní groups.

The first group to encounter the Spanish were probably the nomadic **Querandí** of the Pampas region. They lived in temporary shelters and hunted guanaco and rhea with *boleadores*. Though they put up determined resistance to the Spanish for several decades, their culture was eliminated during the subsequent colonial period – a fate shared by many others.

Early Spanish settlement

In 1516, Juan Díaz de Solís, a Portuguese mariner in the employ of the Spanish Crown, led a small crew to the shores of the River Plate in the search of a trade route to the Far East. He was killed by either the Querandí or the Charrúa, who inhabited what is now Uruguay. Another brief exploration of the region was made in 1520 by Ferdinand Magellan, who continued his epic voyage south to discover the famous straits that now bear his name, and the next significant expedition to this part of the world was made by an explorer of Italian descent, **Sebastian Cabot** (see box below).

Cabot – Argentina's unwitting baptizer

Explorer **Sebastian Cabot** reached the River Plate in 1526 and built a small, short-lived fort near modern Rosario. He misleadingly christened the river the Río de la Plata ("River of Silver"), after finding bullion and believing there to be deposits nearby. Ironically, the metal had probably been brought here by a Portuguese adventurer, Aleixo Garcia. In 1524, Garcia had reached the eastern fringes of the Inca empire, but was killed with his Andean booty on his return journey.

Cabot's silver had its most lasting legacy in the word "Argentina" itself, which derives from the metal's Latin name, **argentum**. Its first recorded use was in a Venetian atlas of the New World produced in the middle of the sixteenth century. Martín del Barco Centenera, member of a later expedition, published an epic poem in 1602 called *La Argentina*. The name also appeared in Ruy Díaz de Guzmán's 1612 book *Historia del descubrimiento, población y conquista del Río de la Plata* (History of the discovery, population and conquest of the River Plate), where he referred to the territory as Tierra Argentina, or "Land of Silver". However, "Argentina" was not adopted as the name of the Republic until the middle of the nineteenth century.

In 1535, Pedro de Mendoza was authorized by the Spanish Crown to colonize the River Plate in an effort to pre-empt Portuguese conquest. In February 1536, he founded Buenos Aires, naming it Ciudad de la Santísima Trinidad y Puerto de Santa María de los Buenos Ayres, after the sailors' favourite saint, the provider of fair winds. However his plans soon went awry, as it proved impossible to subjugate the local nomadic Querandí. Mendoza was forced to send Pedro de Ayolas upstream to find a more suitable site for settlement, and in August 1537, Ayolas founded **Nuestra Señora de la Asunción del Paraguay** (Asunción). Mendoza died at sea on the way back to Spain, and authority for the colony devolved to Domingo de Irala, who, after almost constant struggle with the Querandí, finally ordered the evacuation of Buenos Aires in 1541. By this time, Spanish interest in colonizing this area of the world had decreased significantly anyway, mainly as a result of **Pizarro**'s spectacular conquest, in 1535, of Inca Peru.

From 1543, the new Viceroyalty of Peru, with its capital at Lima, was given authority over all of southern Spanish South America. The northwest region of Argentina was first tentatively explored in the mid-1530s, but the impulse for colonizing this region really came with the discovery, in 1545, of enormous **silver deposits** in **Potosí**, in Alto Peru (modern-day Bolivia). This led to the establishment of the **Governorship of Tucumán**, covering a region that embraced most of today's Northwest. Conquistadors crossed the Andes seeking to press the locals into labour and find an overland route to the Potosí mines. Francisco de Aguirre founded Santiago del Estero, Argentina's earliest continually inhabited town, in 1553, while other settlements were established at Mendoza (1561), San Juan (1562), Córdoba (1573), Salta (1582), La Rioja (1591) and San Salvador de Jujuy (1593).

Meanwhile, the Spanish in Asunción sent an expedition under the command of Juan de Garay down the River Paraná, founding Santa Fe in 1573 and **resettling Buenos Aires** in 1580 – this time, for good. Settlers benefited from one vital legacy of the Mendoza settlement – the feral **horses and cattle** that had multiplied in the area. Few then realized the significance these animals would have on most of Argentina's future.

Colonial developments

Buenos Aires and its surrounds were largely overlooked by the Spanish Crown until the late eighteenth century. Direct trade with Spain from the River Plate was prohibited from 1554, and all imported and exported goods traded via Lima, which restricted growth of the port, but encouraged **contraband** imports. The governorship's potential was limited: there was no market in pre-industrial Europe for agricultural produce, and the indigenous populations could not easily be yoked into the **encomienda** system of forced labour. It was the Society of Jesus – the Jesuits – that effectively pioneered Spanish colonization of this region (see box, p.786).

More important than the River Plate at this point was the Governorship of Tucumán. The *encomienda* system was more effective here and in the central Córdoban sierras, as they were more densely settled. Though some trade from this area was directed towards Buenos Aires, the local economy was run so as to provide the Potosí mine with mules, sugar, cotton textiles and wheat. Indigenous resistance to the colonizers erupted on occasion, as with the Diaguita rebellion of 1657, which was actually led by a Spanish rebel, Pedro Bohórquez.

The Jesuit missions

The **Jesuits** first arrived in the region of the upper Paraná during the late sixteenth century, initially prospering under the protection of the Crown. The first **missions** to the Guaraní were established in the upper Paraná from 1609 (see box, pp.352–353). Though the Jesuits tried to evangelize other parts of the country over the next 150 years, it was in the subtropical Upper Paraná where they had their greatest success. After raids in the region by roaming **Portuguese slavers** in the 1630s, the Jesuits established their own indigenous militias for protection. Thereafter, Jesuit activity thrived: there were as many as thirty missions here by the beginning of the eighteenth century. The Guaraní who lived in the missions had the benefit of Jesuit education and skills, and were exempt from forced labour in silver mines, but this was no earthly paradise: coercion and violence were not unknown, and epidemics ravaged these communities on a periodic basis.

In the seventeenth century, the Crown revoked its tax concessions to the Jesuits, forcing their communities to enter the colonial economy. They did so with vigour, exporting **yerba mate** (see box, pp.392–393), sugar and tobacco. However, their success aroused jealousy. Some missions housed more than 4000 indigenous people and this **monopolization of labour**, together with the economic and political influence of the Jesuits in Córdoba (see box, p.285), stirred the resentment of nearby settlers. In the 1720s, secular settlers rebelled, urging the Crown to curb the domination of the Jesuits. In and around Asunción and Corrientes, they subjected Jesuit communities to **raids**, and other acts of violoence. Though it survived that threat, the mission experiment succumbed soon afterwards, a victim of power politics in Europe, lobbying from interests bent on exploiting native labour and **King Carlos III**'s perception that the existence of a powerful Jesuit community was a threat to secular royal authority. In 1767, he ordered the **Jesuits' expulsion** from all Spanish territories, an order carried out the following year. The remaining communities were subsequently entrusted to the Franciscans, whose mismanagement led to their being plundered and to many Guaraní being led away to slavery.

The rebellion was brutally crushed in 1659 and survivors were displaced from their decimated communities and forcibly resettled as workers on haciendas. By the second half of the eighteenth century, demand for labour from both Potosí and the towns of Tucumán was so great that it led to the importation of **black slave labour**. It is estimated that by 1778 one in ten of Tucumán's regional population was a slave, while well over a quarter were of pure indigenous blood. Racial divisions were strongly demarcated, and the rights of whites to control land and political offices were reinforced by a dress code and a weapons ban for the non-white castes.

As with Tucumán, the economies of Buenos Aires, Santa Fe, Entre Ríos and Corrientes engendered strife with the native peoples. Mounted raids by indigenous tribes from the Gran Chaco, such as the Abipone, terrorized the northeastern provinces well into the eighteenth century, and Buenos Aires, dependent on its round-ups of wild cattle (*vaquerías*) for its **hide and tallow industries**, frequently came into conflict both with groups of Tehuelche and, increasingly from the eighteenth century, Mapuche (Araucanians). These peoples relied on the same feral cattle and horses, driving vast herds of them to the northern Patagonian Andes for the purpose of trading with Chileans, both white settlers and other indigenous groups. The seventeenth and eighteenth centuries also saw the emergence and apogee of **gauchos**, nomadic horsemen, often of mestizo origins, who roamed in small bands and lived off the wild herds of livestock.

The Viceroyalty of the River Plate

By the late eighteenth century, the British controlled the Caribbean and were blocking the Lima sea routes, so the establishment of another route to Potosí became vital. The River Plate seemed the logical choice, and the growing value of Buenos Aires as a market and strategic post gained the recognition of the Spanish Crown, which, in 1776, made it the capital of the new **Viceroyalty of the River Plate**, whose jurisdiction included Alto Peru (modern Bolivia), Paraguay and the Governorship of Montevideo. Commercial restrictions were gradually loosened, and trade permitted with ports in Spain and Spanish America, but the Crown still clung to its monopoly on colonial commerce, prohibiting the sale of silver to foreign powers.

Tensions between **monopolist traders** and those who advocated **free trade** were becoming entrenched. Thanks to the European wars of the late eighteenth century the Crown was forced to further loosen its control, and in 1797, allowed its colonies to trade with neutral countries. To the dismay of monopolists, cheap European manufactures flowed freely into Buenos Aires courtesy of contraband merchants. Monopolists trading on the traditional Cádiz route suffered, and exports to Spain plummeted. It became increasingly difficult to reinstate restrictions, and attempts to do so caused anger amongst merchants, such as **Manuel Belgrano**, who argued for free trade with all nations, but not rebellion against the Crown. Although the ideas of the French Revolution and the American Declaration of Independence circulated among Buenos Aires' elite, there was not yet any significant revolutionary feeling against Spain. The **British**, however, caught wind of the commercial tensions in Buenos Aires, and, mistakenly interpreting them as revolutionary, **invaded** the city in 1806 (see box below).

Other changes in the economy of Buenos Aires became increasingly apparent during the Viceroyalty. Rich merchants (*comerciantes*) helped finance the growth of **estancias** (ranches) in the province, a shift away from the earlier practice of *vaquerías* – Wild West-style round-ups. By the end of the eighteenth century, these estancias had become highly profitable enterprises. Bolstered by immigration from peninsular Spain and by Creole Spanish Americans from the interior, the Buenos Aires population stood at over 40,000 by 1810. Despite the increased importance of the region, the territory that was to become Argentina

The British invasions

In **June 1806**, a force of 1600 men led by **General William Beresford** stormed into Buenos Aires hoping to assert British imperial control over the entire Viceroyalty. The Viceroy, the **Marqués de Sobremonte**, fled the city, and the remaining Spanish authorities grudgingly swore allegiance to the British Crown. Among the ordinary inhabitants, though, there was a sense of offended honour at the way such a tiny force had been allowed to overrun the city's defences.

The locals regrouped under a new commander-in-chief, the French-born **Santiago Liniers**, and ousted their invaders during the **Reconquista** of August 12. Undaunted, the British captured Montevideo, from where they launched a second assault on a better-prepared Buenos Aires in July 1807. This battle led to the surrender of the British and came to be known as **La Defensa**, a name imbued with the bravura of Liniers' hastily assembled militia, whose cannon- and musket-fire peppered the enemy, while women poured boiling oil from the tops of the city's buildings on the hapless British soldiers.

was still sparsely populated, however, and, as late as 1810, half of its estimated 360,000 inhabitants were indigenous Amerindians.

The May revolution and independence

One consequence of the victory over the British was to make the people of Buenos Aires aware of the extent to which they could manage their own affairs and how little they could rely on the viceregal authorities. This was the first time that they had fought in unison against a foreign invader and in certain sectors the feeling of pride carried over into a stance of defiance against the monarchy.

In 1808, **Napoleon Bonaparte** invaded the Iberian Peninsula, forced the Spanish king, Carlos IV, to **abdicate**, and installed his brother, Joseph Bonaparte, on the throne. This had massive repercussions in the Latin American colonies, ushering in two decades of upheaval. A new viceroy, Viscount Balthasar de Cisneros, arrived to replace Sobremonte, and scrapped most of the free-trade initiatives Liniers had issued. The ban on trading in silver was reinstated, causing free-trade activists such as Belgrano to begin planning a revolution. On May 25, the people of Buenos Aires gathered in front of the Cabildo, wearing rosettes of sky-blue and white ribbons, the colours that were later to make up the **Argentine flag**. Inside, Cisneros was ousted and the **Primera Junta** sworn in. However, deposition of the viceroy and the establishment of self-government did not necessarily mean advocating republicanism, and many members of government proclaimed loyalty to Ferdinand VII, imprisoned heir to Carlos IV.

The Primera Junta was headed by **Cornelio Saavedra**, one of those who proclaimed a token loyalty to the Spanish Crown, and who believed in sharing power with the provinces. Other members of the Junta, including Belgrano and **Mariano Moreno**, were less moderate free-trade enthusiasts, intent on bringing the rest of the territory under the control of Buenos Aires. Moreno's views came to represent what was to be the position of the **Unitarists** (or **Azules** – "Blues") who favoured centralism, while Saavedra's contained the first seeds of the ideas of **Federalists** (the **Colorados** or Rojos – "Reds"), promoting the autonomy of the provinces within the framework of a confederation. This dispute was to dominate Argentine politics of the nineteenth century, causing bitter division and **civil war**. While the Junta's internal disputes prevented unity in Buenos Aires, the May Revolution also failed to mark a break from the motherland. Royalists under the leadership of Martín de Alzaga continued to press for the return of a viceroyalty.

As Unitarist and Federalist interests continued to battle for control of the capital, clashes between pro-royalist forces and pro-independence forces flared up across the old viceroyalty. After 1810, in the interior these struggles saw the emergence of Federalist **caudillos**, powerful local warlords. They recruited – or, rather, press-ganged – militias from among the slaves, indigenous peoples and gauchos of the countryside. The most famous *caudillos* were Estanislao López in Santa Fe and Francisco Ramírez in Entre Ríos. Back in Buenos Aires, the royalist factions were effectively crushed by 1812, and a *criollo* front led by **José de San Martín** (see box opposite), the Sociedad Patriótica, sought full emancipation from foreign powers.

José de San Martín

It's impossible to stay for even a short time in Argentina without coming across the name of national hero **José de San Martín** – he's as ubiquitous as Washington in the US or de Gaulle in France, and has countless villages, barrios, streets, plazas, public buildings and even a mountain named after him, as well as innumerable statues in his honour. He's often simply referred to as **El Libertador** (The Liberator) and is treated with saint-like reverence. It's ironic, therefore, that he didn't even take part in the country's initial liberation from the Spanish Crown, that he actually helped to free Chile – Argentina's traditional rival – and that he spent the last 23 years of his life in self-imposed exile in France. Even this last fact is celebrated, though, with streets and whole barrios named after **Boulogne-sur-Mer**, the northern French town where he died on August 17, 1850. A slightly larger-than-original replica of his Parisian mansion, Grand Bourg, built on the edge of leafy Palermo Chico, is now the Instituto Sanmartiniano, a library-cum-study-centre given over to research into the great man.

San Martín was born into a humble family – he was the son of a junior officer – in 1778 in the former Jesuit mission settlement of Yapeyú, Corrientes Province. He was packed off to the academy in Buenos Aires and then to military school in Spain, and later served in the royal army, taking part in the Spanish victories against the Napoleonic invasions in 1808–11. He even lived in Westminster for a few weeks at the end of 1811. He returned to his homeland soon afterwards, and assisted in training the rag-bag army that was trying to resist Spain's attempt to cling onto its South American empire. After replacing Manuel Belgrano as leader of the independence forces in 1813, he became increasingly active in politics, as a conservative, and attended the Tucumán Congress in 1816. He then formed his own army, known popularly as the **Ejército de los Andes**, basing himself in Mendoza, where he was governor for several years, and in San Juan. From there he crossed the Andes and obliterated royalist troops at Chacabuco, thereby **freeing Chile** from the imperialist yoke – though his friend and comrade-in-arms Bernardo O'Higgins got most of the credit – finally mopping up the remaining royalist resistance at Maipú in 1818, before moving on to Lima, Peru.

San Martín was not at all interested in personal political power, but was in favour of setting up a constitutional monarchy in the emerging South American states. In 1821, he signed the so-called Punchanca agreement with the viceroy of Peru to put a member of the Spanish royal family on the Peruvian throne, but the royalists did not respond and, ultimately, he declared Peru's independence on July 12, 1821. Unable to hold the country together in the face of royalist resistance, he called upon **Simón Bolívar**, the liberator of Venezuela, to come to his assistance. The only meeting between the two occurred in Guayaquil, Ecuador, in 1822. Bolívar's radical republican ideals clashed with San Martín's conservative mindset, and, though no one knows what exactly was said in this encounter, San Martín opted to withdraw from Peru. Frustrated by a nascent Argentina that was neither the new-style kingdom he yearned for nor the democratic modern nation-state Bolívar had advocated, but, instead, a patchwork of disunited provinces led by brutish *caudillos*, San Martín took off to **France**. He never returned to Argentina during his lifetime, and, in his self-imposed exile, he slipped into obscurity; all this changed after his death, however, and the national hero's bodily remains were repatriated later that century. He now lies buried in Buenos Aires' Metropolitan Cathedral, where his tomb is a national monument. His death is commemorated every year with a national holiday on the Monday nearest to August 17.

Two congresses were convened to discuss the future of the former viceroyalty, but these were dominated by Unitarists and failed to produce a cohesive plan for the country. However, at the second, held on **July 9, 1816** in the city of Tucumán, the independence of the **United Provinces of the River Plate** was formally declared, a title first adopted by Buenos Aires in 1813. The date, July 9, has since come to be recognized as Argentina's official **independence day**.

Later that year, San Martín led five thousand men across the Andes to attack the Spanish in Chile, in one of the defining moments of Latin America's struggle against its colonial rulers. During this time, he was assisted in the north by another hero of Argentine independence, **Martín Miguel de Güemes**, an anti-royalist, Federalist *caudillo* whose gaucho army eventually liberated Salta. Though *caudillos* such as Güemes were in favour of independence, many resented the heavy taxes imposed to fund the struggle for autonomy, and tensions remained high. Men like López and Ramírez defeated the attempt to impose a Unitarist constitution in 1819.

Caudillismo and civil war

The 1820s began with infighting amongst *caudillo* groups. In 1826, **Bernardino Rivadavia**, a Unitarist admirer of European ideals, became the first outright president of what was then called the United Provinces of South America. He proposed a new constitution, which was rejected by the provinces, who objected to the call for dissolution of their militia and the concession of land to the national government. At the same time, conflict with Brazil over Uruguay led to a blockade of the River Plate and caused a financial crisis. These two

Rosas – the "Caligula of the River Plate"

Rosas, one of the most controversial figures of Argentine history, was born into an influential cattle-ranching family, and was respected by his gauchos for his riding skills and personal bravery. He was an avowed Federalist, but his particular brand of Federalism had more to do with opposing intellectual Unitarism, with its gravitation towards foreign, European influence, than it did in respecting provincial autonomy per se. As it turned out, his platform was more about centralizing power in his own province, Buenos Aires.

He left office at the end of his term in 1832 but returned as dictator in 1835 as the country teetered on the brink of fresh civil war after the assassination of an ally of his, the *caudillo* of La Rioja, **Juan "Facundo" Quiroga**. For seventeen years Rosas ruthlessly consolidated power using the army and his own brutal police force, the **Mazorca**. The Mazorca used a network of spies and assassins to keep resistance in check. During this time, many opponents and intellectuals fled to Uruguay and Europe.

Rosas sought to improve his network of **patronage** through the expansion of territories available for farming in the Pampas. His **Desert Campaign** of 1833 against the indigenous peoples was the precursor to Roca's genocidal Conquest of the Desert of the late 1870s (see p.792). The vast landholdings that Rosas dealt out to "conquerors" ensured he retained powerful allies.

However, Rosas managed to alienate many of the interior provinces by not permitting free trade along the Paraná, by increasing taxes on provincial trade and by allowing the import of cheap foreign produce, such as French wine, into Buenos Aires. Rosas' bloody regime was brought to an end in 1852, at the Battle of Caseros. Defeat came at the hands of a one-time ally, the powerful *caudillo* governor of Entre Ríos, **Justo José de Urquiza**, who was backed by a coalition of interests that desired free trade on the Paraná, including the Brazilians, British and French. After defeat, Rosas left for England to become a farmer in Southampton, where he died in 1877.

issues brought Rivadavia's presidency to its knees by 1827. The bitter Unitarist/Federalist fighting that ensued only ceased when a *caudillo* from Buenos Aires, **General Juan Manuel de Rosas**, emerged victorious (see box opposite). In 1829, he became governor of Buenos Aires, with power over the newly titled Confederation of the River Plate or Argentine Confederation.

The creation of Argentina

The thirty years that followed the defeat of Rosas saw the foundations laid for the **modern Argentine state**. Economic expansion and the triumph of Unitarism ensured the conditions for the boom that followed, Buenos Aires was finally to emerge supreme from its struggles with the provinces and territorial conquest began in earnest, resulting in the subjugation of the most important of the unconquered indigenous groups: those of the south.

Urquiza's attempt to establish a constitution sympathetic to Federalist interests foundered when Buenos Aires proved unwilling to renounce its privileged trading terms or submit to his rule. The province refused to approve the **1853 constitution**, which led to the creation of two republics: one in Buenos Aires and the other, the Argentine Confederation, centred on Entre Ríos and headed by Urquiza. This situation changed in 1861, when the governor of Buenos Aires, **Bartolomé Mitre**, defeated Urquiza. The 1853 constitution was then, with a few significant amendments, ratified by Buenos Aires, and the basic structure of Argentine government was set. In 1862, Mitre was elected the first president of the new **Argentine Republic**. Constitutional provisions included ending trade restrictions throughout the country and promoting the colonization of the interior, a result of which was the small Welsh settlement in Patagonia (see box, p.663).

Mitre aimed for the rapid **modernization** of the country, focusing particularly on the capital. His achievements included the creation of a national army and postal system, and the expansion of a **railway network**. These initiatives were financed by foreign investment from Britain, which contributed the capital to build railways, and by greater export earnings, the result, particularly, of the important expanding trade in **wool**. The other significant event of Mitre's presidency was the **War of the Triple Alliance** (1865–70), a conflict that had its origins in the expansionist ambitions of Paraguay's insane dictator Mariscal Francisco Solano López, in addition to disputes over navigation rights in the Paraná and River Plate. In it, Argentina allied with Uruguay and Brazil to defeat Paraguay, though much of the fighting, some of it farcical yet brutal, was left to the Brazilians, whose military ineptitude resulted in a prolonged campaign. Argentina secured control of the upper Paraná and the territory (now Province) of Misiones.

The end of the war overlapped with the presidency of **Domingo Sarmiento**, the man most identified with the drive to "Europeanize" Argentina in the nineteenth century. Sarmiento was an opponent of *caudillismo* and famous for pillorying the likes of Rosas, Quiroga, López and Ramírez. He believed that his age represented a "barbaric" era in Argentine history, its legacy holding the country back from contemporary North American and European notions of progress and civilization. These theories of progress impacted heavily on the remaining indigenous populations of Argentina, as they sponsored those who believed in "civilizing the Indian", and helped underpin the doctrine of the so-called "Generation of the Eighties" (the 1880s) who subscribed to imposing the nation-state by force. Sarmiento is also remembered for his highly ambitious **education policy** and for encouraging European immigration on a grand scale.

The Conquest of the Desert

With the near disappearance of wild herds of livestock and the movement of settlers into the Pampas, Mapuche and Tehuelche groups found it increasingly difficult to maintain their way of life. Indigenous raids – called **malones** – on estancias and white settlements became more frequent, and debate raged in the 1870s as to how to solve the "Indian Problem". Two main positions crystallized. The one propounded by Minister of War **Alsina** consisted of containment, and aimed at a gradual integration of the indigenous tribes. The second, propounded by his successor, **General Julio Roca**, advocated uncompromising conquest and subjugation – Argentina could then concentrate on territorial expansion to the south. Indeed, the likes of Roca believed that was where the future of the Argentine nation lay.

Roca led an army south in 1879, and his brutal **Conquest of the Desert** was effectively over by the following year, leaving over 1300 indigenous dead and the whole of Patagonia effectively open to settlement. Roca was swept to victory in the 1880 presidential election on the back of his success. He believed strongly in a highly centralized government and consolidated his power base by using the vast new tracts of land as a system of patronage. With the southern frontier secure, he could, from the mid-1880s, back campaigns to defeat indigenous groups in the **Gran Chaco**, and thus stabilize the country's northern frontier with Paraguay.

Social and economic change: 1850–1914

Agriculture and infrastructure continued to expand, benefiting from massive British investment. The first **railway**, built in 1854, connected Buenos Aires to the farms and estancias in its vicinity. By 1880, the railway network carried over three million passengers and over one million tonnes of cargo, and between 1857 and 1890, nearly 10,000km of track were built. **Wool production** became such a strong sector of the economy in the second half of the nineteenth century that sheep outnumbered people, thirty to one. The rise in number of sheep farms – small, privately owned or rented family concerns – saw the growth of a strong middle class in the provinces. Also transforming the countryside was the boom in **export crops** such as wheat, oats and linseed. Another development of importance was the invention of **refrigerator ships** in 1876, which enabled Argentina to start exporting meat to the urban centres of Britain and Europe. In Buenos Aires and other areas, the age of **latifundismo** had begun as huge tracts of land were bought up by Argentine speculators hoping to profit by their sale to railway companies. In the meanwhile, they were rented out to sheep farmers and sharecroppers.

At the same time, European immigration to Argentina was on the rise. Significant numbers of French people arrived in the 1850s, followed later by groups of Italians, Swiss and Germans. Many came in search of land but settled for work either as sharecroppers in estancias and *latifundios* or as shepherds, labourers and artisans. Between 1880 and World War I, six million **immigrants** came to Argentina. Half of these were Italians and a quarter Spaniards, while other groups included French, Portuguese, Russians, Ottoman subjects (mostly Syrians and Lebanese), Irish and Welsh. In 1895, immigrants represented nearly one-third of the population of Buenos Aires city, which had grown from 90,000 in 1869 to 670,000 in 1895. This convulsive influx caused occasional resentment, particularly during periods of economic depression, which were usually sparked by events abroad. Growth depended largely on foreign investment and the country was susceptible to economic slumps like the one that affected Britain in the 1870s, prompting occasional debate about **protectionism**. Immigrant participation in politics was not encouraged, and few took up Argentine citizenship on arrival, because citizens were obliged to perform military service. Generally, though, immigrants were welcomed as part of the drive towards economic expansion and colonization of the countryside.

The age of Radicalismo

By the early years of the twentieth century, pressure for political change was increasing. Power still rested in the hands of the landed and urban elite, a tiny minority, leaving the rapidly expanding urban professional and working classes unrepresented. From 1890, a new party, the **Radical Civic Union** (Unión Cívica Radical or UCR), agitated for reform but was excluded from power. A sea change came with the introduction of **universal manhood suffrage** and secret balloting in 1912 by reformist conservative president, Roque Sáenz Peña. In 1916, this saw the victory of the first radical president, **Hipólito Yrigoyen**, ushering in thirteen unbroken years of radicalism, under him and his associate, **Marcelo T. de Alvear**. After World War I, economic growth picked up again, with the expansion of manufacturing industries, but its benefits were far from equally distributed. Confrontations between police and strikers in Buenos Aires led to numerous deaths in the **Semana Trágica** – or Tragic Week – of 1919. This was followed by the 1920–21 **workers' strikes** in southern Patagonia. Most strikers were immigrant peón farmhands from the impoverished Chilean island of Chiloe but there were also a few labour activists, Bolsheviks and anarchists. A first strike in 1920 was sparked by the fact that peones had been unable to cash in or exchange the tokens with which they were paid by sheep barons. The protest expanded to include a raft of other grievances concerning working rights and conditions, and radical factions latched onto what was, at root, a fairly conservative phenomenon. Shaken, estancia owners promised to arrange payment, but when this was not forthcoming, a second strike was unleashed, this time releasing more in the way of pent-up anger and frustration. Incidents of **violent lawlessness** were used by opponents of the strike to panic the authorities, now better prepared, into **brutal repression**. The final tragedy came with the massacre in cold blood of 121 men by an army battalion at Estancia Anita. Later, the radicals introduced social security and pro-labour reforms.

By the end of the 1920s, Argentina was the **seventh richest nation in the world**, and confidence was sky-high. Britain remained the country's major investor and market – as revealed in a confidential report by Sir Malcolm Robertson, ambassador to Argentina, in 1929: "Argentina must be regarded as an essential part of the British Empire. We cannot get on without her, nor she without us." This was a nation that people predicted would challenge the United States in economic power. Within a few decades, however, Argentina had fallen to the status of a Third World state. This loss of a golden dream of prosperity has haunted and perplexed the Argentine conscience ever since. The decline in status was not constant, but the **world depression** that followed the Wall Street Crash of 1929 marked one of the first serious blows. The effects of the crash and the collapse of export markets left the radical regime reeling and precipitated a **military takeover** in 1930 – an inauspicious omen of events later in the century. The military restored power to the oligarchic elite, who ruled through a succession of coalition governments that gained a reputation for fraud and electoral corruption. By the late 1930s, the value of the manufactured goods overtook that of agriculture for the first time. Immigration continued apace, with one important group being Jews fleeing persecution in Germany.

The rise and fall of Perón

The first watershed of the twentieth century was the rise of **Juan Domingo Perón**, a charismatic military man of relatively modest origins who had risen through the ranks during the 1930s to the status of colonel. The outbreak of **World War II** had repercussions in Argentina, though it stayed neutral: a split developed in the armed forces, with one faction favouring the Allies and another larger one, the Axis powers.

Perón's involvement with politics intensified after a **military coup** in 1943, in which the army replaced a conservative coalition government that had come to be seen as self-serving and which was veering towards a declaration of support for the Allies. Perón was appointed Secretary for Labour, and he used this minor post as a platform to cultivate links with trade unions. His popularity alarmed his military superiors, who arrested him in 1945. However, this move backfired: Perón's second wife, **Evita** (see box opposite) helped to organize mass demonstrations that secured his release, generating the momentum that swept him to the **presidency** in the 1946 elections. His first term in government signalled a programme of radical social and political change, but his philosophy of government, known as Peronism, defies easy definition (see box, p.797).

Controversy surrounds many aspects of Perón's regime. Dissident opinion had no place in his scheme: these years were marked by a **suppression of the press**, increasingly heavy-handed control over institutions of higher education and the use of violent intimidation. Though it is unclear to what extent he was personally involved, Perón's apparent willingness to provide a haven for Nazi refugees has also done little for his or Argentina's international reputation. Adolf Eichmann (see box, p.113) was one of the most notorious war criminals to settle here and, much more recently, Erich Priebke was extradited from Bariloche to Italy to face trial for atrocities committed in wartime Rome. A recent report has revealed that fewer Nazis actually fled to Argentina than thought, listing the number as 180, most of whom were Croats, not Germans – though others suggest that various regimes including Carlos Menem's (see p.803) had records relating to this period destroyed.

In 1949, Perón secured a constitutional amendment that allowed him to run for a **second term**. Though he won by a landslide in the 1951 elections, his position was severely weakened by the death of Evita, who had been a principal political asset. It was becoming clear that his administration, and the cult of personality that had swept him to power and fed his reputation, was losing political impetus.

Evita Perón

Evita Perón, in true rags-to-riches style, began life humbly. She was born **María Eva Duarte** in 1919, the fifth illegitimate child of Juana Ibarguren and Juan Duarte, a landowner in the rural interior of Buenos Aires. She was raised in poverty by her mother, Duarte having abandoned the family before Evita reached her first birthday. At the age of 15, she headed to the capital to pursue her dream of becoming an actress, and managed to scrape a living from several minor roles in radio and TV before working her way into higher-profile leading roles through the influence of well-connected lovers. Her life changed dramatically in 1944 when she met Juan Perón. She became his mistress and married him a year later, shortly before his election to the presidency.

As First Lady, Evita was in her element. She championed the rights of the working classes and underprivileged poor, whom she named her **descamisados** ("shirtless ones"), and immersed herself in populist politics and programmes of social aid. In person, she would receive petitions from individual members of the public, distributing favours on a massive scale through her powerful and wealthy instrument of patronage, the Social Aid Foundation. She played the role of the devoted wife, but was, in many ways, a pioneering feminist of Argentine society, and has been credited with assuring that women were finally granted suffrage in 1947. She yearned to legitimize her political role through direct election, but resentment amongst the military forced her to pull out of running for the position of vice-president to her husband in the election of 1951.

Another role she revelled in was that of **ambassador** for her country, captivating a star-struck press and public during a 1948 tour of post-war Europe, during which she was granted an audience with the Pope. Hers was the international face of Argentina, dressed in Dior and Balenciaga, which assuredly compounded the jealousy of Europhile upper-class women at home. She was detested by the Argentine elite as a vulgar upstart who respected neither rank nor customary protocol. They painted her as a whore and as someone who was more interested in feeding her own personality cult than assisting the *descamisados*. Evita, for her part, seemed to revel in antagonizing the oligarchic establishment, whipping up popular resentment towards an "anti-Argentine" class.

Stricken by **cancer of the uterus**, she died in 1952, at the age of only 33. Her death was greeted with mass outpourings of grief never seen in Argentina before or since. Eight people were crushed to death in the crowds of mourners that gathered, and over two thousand needed treatment for injuries. In death, Evita led an even more rarefied existence than she had in life. After the military coup of 1955, the military made decoy copies of her **embalmed corpse** and spirited the original away to Europe, all too aware of its power as an icon and focus for political dissent. There followed a truly bizarre series of burials, reburials and even allegations of necrophilia, before she was repatriated in 1974, during Perón's third administration and, later, afforded a decent burial in Recoleta Cemetery. To this day, Evita retains saint-like status amongst many traditionalist, working-class Peronists, some of whom maintain altars to her. Protests and furious graffiti greeted the casting of Madonna, fresh from a series of pornographic photo shoots, to portray her in the Alan Parker film musical, *Evita*. For many, this was sacrilege – an insult to the memory of the most important woman of Argentine history.

He faced dissent within the army, resentful at what they saw as the subordination of their role during Evita's lifetime. He had also incited the wrath of the powerful Catholic Church, whose privileges he had attacked. In addition, his successful wealth-redistribution policies had alienated wealthy sectors of society while raising the expectations of the less well-off – expectations that he found

△ Mural of Evita, Buenos Aires

increasingly difficult to fulfil. Agriculture had been allowed to stagnate in favour of industrial development, resulting in inflation and economic recession. Against a background of strikes and civil unrest, factions within the military rebelled in 1955, with the tacit support of a broad coalition of those interests that Perón had alienated. In the **Revolución Libertadora**, or Revolution of Liberation, Perón was ousted from power and went into **exile**.

Defining Peronism

Perón's brand of fierce **nationalism**, combined with an **authoritarian cult** of the leader, bore many of the hallmarks of Fascism. Nevertheless, he assumed power by overwhelming democratic vote, and was seen by the poor as a saviour. Perón's scheme involved a type of "corporatism" that offered genuine improvements to the lives of the workers while making it easier to control them for the smooth running of the capitalist system. Perón saw strong **state intervention** as a way of melding the interests of labour and capital, and propounded the doctrine of **justicialismo**, or social justice, which soon began to be identified as **Peronism**. His administration passed a comprehensive programme of social welfare legislation that, among other things, granted workers a minimum wage, paid holidays (often at specially built hotels) and pension schemes, and established house-building programmes.

Perón also supported nationalization and **industrialization**, in an attempt to render Argentina less dependent on foreign capital. One of the most significant acts of his administration was, in 1947, to nationalize the country's railway system, compensating its British owners to the tune of £150 million. In so doing, he also capitalized on popular anti-British sentiment, which had been fostered over preceding generations by the disproportionate commercial influence wielded by the tiny class of British farming and industrial oligarchs. Nevertheless, some believe that he paid over the odds for outdated stock.

Military governments and guerrilla activity: 1955–73

The initial backlash against Peronism was swift: General Aramburu banned it as a political movement, Peronist iconography and statues were stripped from public places and even mention of his name was forbidden. There followed eighteen years of alternate military and short-lived civilian regimes that lurched from one crisis to another. Civilian administrations were dependent on the backing of the military, which itself was unsure of how to align itself with the Peronist legacy and the trade unions. Much of the 1960s was characterized by economic stagnation, strikes, wage freezes and a growing disillusionment of the populace with the government. Throughout this time, Perón hovered in the background, in exile in Spain, providing a focus for opposition to the military.

In 1966, a **military coup** led by General Juan Carlos Onganía saw the imposition of austere measures to stabilize the economy, and repression to keep a tight rein on political dissent. This was not without consequences, and, in the city of radical politics, Córdoba, tension eventually exploded into violence in May 1969. In what has become known as the **Cordobazo**, left-wing student protesters and trade unionists sparked off a spree of general rioting that lasted for two days, and left many people dead and the authorities profoundly shaken. Onganía's position became less and less tenable and, with unrest spreading throughout the country and an economic crisis that provoked devaluation, he was deposed by the army.

It was about this time that society saw the emergence of **guerrilla** organizations, which crystallized, over the course of the early 1970s, into two main groups: the People's Revolutionary Army (Ejército Revolucionario del Pueblo or **ERP**), a movement committed to radical international revolution in the style of Trotsky or Che Guevara; and the **Montoneros**, a more urban movement that espoused revolution on a more distinctly national model, extrapolated from left-wing traits within Peronism. Multinationals, landed oligarchics and the security forces were favoured Montonero targets.

The return of Perón and the collapse of democracy

By 1973, the army seemed to have recognized that its efforts to engineer some sort of national unity had failed. The economy continued to splutter, guerrilla violence was spreading and incidences of military repression were rising. Army leader General Lanusse, decided to risk calling an election, and in an attempt to heal the long-standing national divide permitted the Peronist party – but not Perón himself – to stand. Perón, then living in Spain, nominated a proxy candidate, **Héctor José Cámpora**, to stand in his place. Cámpora emerged victorious in the June elections and forced a reluctant military to allow Perón himself to return to stand in new elections.

By this time, Perón had come to represent all things to all men. Left-wing Montoneros saw themselves as true Peronists – the natural upholders of the type of Peronism that championed the rights of the *descamisados* and freedom from imperialist domination. Likewise, some members of conservative landed groups saw him as a symbol of stability in the face of anarchy. Any illusion that Perón was going to be the balm for the nation's ills dissipated before touchdown at Ezeiza International Airport. Like a group of unsuspecting wives assembled to greet a secret polygamist, his welcoming party dissolved into a violent melee, with rival groups in the crowd of 500,000 shooting at each other. It's not known how many people died in the fracas; the total is thought to be in three figures, though the official figure is 25.

Cámpora resigned and handed power to Raúl Lastiri (speaker of the House of Deputies and son-in-law of José López Rega, Perón's private secretary), who called new elections in September 1973. Perón was allowed to stand this time and as his running mate he chose his third wife, María Estela Martínez de Perón, a former dancer from La Rioja, commonly known by her stage name, **Isabelita**. They had met at a night-club in Panama (where Perón was first exiled), in circumstances that were later the cause of much speculation, lived together in Venezuela and then in Spain, where they married.

Perón was 78, and his health was failing; though he won the elections with ease, his third term lasted less than nine months, ending with his death in July 1974. Power devolved to Isabelita, who became the world's first woman president. She managed to make a bitterly divided nation agree on at least one thing: her regime was a catastrophic failure. Rudderless, out of her depth and with no bedrock of support, Isabelita clung increasingly desperately to the advice of her Minister for Social Welfare, Rega, a shadowy figure who had been Péron's secretary and became known as the "Wizard", even being compared to Rasputin. Rega's prime notoriety stems from having founded the much feared right-wing **death squads** (the Triple "A", or Alianza Argentina Anticomunista) that targeted intellectuals and guerrilla sympathizers. The only boom industry, it seemed, was corruption, and with hyperinflation and spiralling violence, the country was gripped by paralysis.

Totalitarianism: the Proceso, or Dirty War

The long-expected **military coup** finally came on March 24, 1976 (now commemorated every year as a national holiday). Ousted President Perón (Isabelita) was imprisoned and later returned to exile in Spain. Under **General Jorge Videla**, a military junta initiated what it termed the Process of National Reorganization (usually known as the **Proceso**), which is more often referred to as the Guerra Sucia, or **Dirty War**. In the minds of the military, there was only one response to opposition: an iron fist. Any attempt to combat it through the normal judicial process was seen as sure to result in failure. The constitution was therefore suspended, and a campaign of systematic violence backed by the full apparatus of the state was unleashed. In the language of chauvinistic patriotism, they invoked the Doctrine of National Security to justify what they saw as part of the war against international Communism. These events were set against the background of **Cold War politics**, and the generals received covert CIA support. Apart from guerrillas and anyone suspected of harbouring guerrilla sympathies, those targeted included liberal intellectuals, journalists, psychologists, Jews, Marxists, trade unionists, atheists and anyone who, in the words of Videla, "spreads ideas that are contrary to Western and Christian civilization".

The most notorious tactic was to send hit squads to make people "disappear". Once seized, these **desaparecidos** simply ceased to exist – no one knew who had taken them or where they had gone. In fact, the *desaparecidos* were taken to secret detention camps – places like the infamous **Navy Mechanics School** (ESMA), now a national memorial – where they were subjected to torture, rape and, usually, execution. Many were taken up in planes and thrown, drugged and weighted with concrete, into the River Plate. Most victims were between their late teens and thirties, but no one was exempt, even pregnant women and the handicapped. Jacobo Timerman, in *Prisoner Without a Name, Cell Without a Number* (1981), an account of his experiences in a torture centre, gives an insight into the mind of one of his interrogators, who told him: "Only God gives and takes life. But God is busy elsewhere, and we're the ones who must undertake this task in Argentina."

In the midst of this, the armed forces had the opportunity to demonstrate the "success" of their regime to the world, by hosting the **1978 World Cup**. Though victory of the Argentine team in the final stoked national pride, few observers saw this as a reflection of the achievements of the military. Indeed, the event backfired on the military in other ways. The vast expense of hosting the tournament compounded the regime's economic problems. In addition, it provided a forum for human-rights advocates, including a courageous group called the **Madres de Plaza de Mayo** (see box, p.103), to bring the issue of the *desaparecidos* to the attention of the international media. The Madres of the Plaza de Mayo were one of the few groups to challenge the regime directly, organizing weekly demonstrations in Buenos Aires' central square. Their protests continued until January 2006, when their leader said that they no longer had an enemy in the Casa Rosada.

A slight softening of Videla's extremist stance came when **General Roberto Viola** took control of the army in 1978 and then the presidency of the junta in 1981, but he was forced out later the same year by hardliners under **General Leopoldo Galtieri**. The military's grip on the country, by this time, was

A historical dispute: the Falkland Islands/Islas Malvinas

Any British person travelling around Argentina is certain to become involved, at some point, in a discussion on the islands known to the British as the **Falklands**, and to Argentines as **Las Malvinas**. In the vast majority of cases, these conversations are polite and usually very interesting; only on extremely rare occasions is the issue raised antagonistically. From the cradle – and with a fervour little short of indoctrination – Argentines are taught that the islands are Argentine. At every point of entry to the country, visitors are greeted with a sign declaring *Las Malvinas Son Argentinas* – "the Malvinas belong to Argentina" – and, in 1999, a poll by newspaper *Clarín* showed that only 14 percent of Argentines believe that solving the "Malvinas problem" is not important, though that figure seems to have dropped since the economic crisis of 2001.

The islands lie some 12,500km from Britain and 550km off the coast of Argentina. Disputes have raged as to who first discovered them, but the first verifiable sighting comes from a Dutch sailor, Seebald de Weert, who sailed past them in 1600. In 1690, Captain John Strong discovered the strait that divides the two major islands in the group, and christened the archipelago the "Falkland Islands", after Viscount Falkland, the commissioner of the British Admiralty at the time.

French sailors from St Malo made numerous expeditions to the islands from 1698, naming them the **Iles Malouines**, from which derives the Argentine name "Malvinas". The first serious attempt at settlement came when a French expedition established a base at Port St Louis in 1764. A year later, claiming ignorance of the French settlement, a party of British sailors settled **Port Egmont**, and claimed the islands for George III. The Spanish, at this time, also believed they had legal title to the area dating from the 1494 Treaty of Tordesillas, arranged by the papacy, which divided the Americas between Spain and Portugal. (The British later claimed the treaty was invalid, as it rested on an authority they no longer recognized.) Reluctant to come to blows with an ally, the French negotiated a settlement, and, in 1767, Port St Louis was surrendered to Spain. In 1774, the British were persuaded to abandon their colony (although not, they would later maintain, their claims to sovereignty), while Spain agreed to cede control of Florida.

In 1820, the newly independent Argentine federation asserted what it saw as its right to inherit the sovereign Spanish title to the islands. This was not, initially, contested by the British, but in the late 1820s Britain started to make noises about reasserting its sovereignty claim. The Argentine federation, paralysed by internal disputes, was powerless to prevent Britain from establishing a base on the islands, and its colony developed significantly after the founding, in 1851, of the **Falkland Islands Company** and with the beginnings of serious commercial exploitation: from the mid-1860s with sheep farming and, as the century wore on, the boom in whaling and animal oil (elephant seal and penguin) industries. By 1871, eight hundred people were living in Port Stanley.

In April 1982, faced with severe domestic unrest, rampant inflation and high unemployment, General Galtieri saw the opportunity to divert attention away from his junta's failed policies by organizing a military crusade to liberate the islands. The

nonetheless increasingly shaky, with the economy in recession, skyrocketing interest rates and the first mass demonstrations against the regime since its imposition in 1976. Galtieri, with no other cards left to play, chose April 2, 1982 to play his trump: **an invasion of the Falkland Islands**, or **Islas Malvinas** as they are known to Argentines. Nothing could have been more certain to bring a sense of purpose to the nation, and the population reacted with delight. This, however, soon turned to dismay when people realized that the British government was prepared to go to war. The Argentine forces were defeated by mid-June (see box above).

British actually contributed to Galtieri's mood of optimism by making preparations for the scrapping of HMS *Endurance*, the UK's only naval presence in the South Atlantic, an event interpreted by Galtieri as signalling that Britain was preparing to withdraw from the region. Galtieri, whose regime was backed by the Reagan administration, mistakenly believed he could count on US support. However, a more serious misjudgement was the belief that Britain would acquiesce in the face of an invasion.

Following the arrival of the **British Task Force**, the conflict was mercifully short. The struggle was unequal: poorly equipped, inadequately trained Argentine teenagers on military service, many from subtropical provinces like Corrientes and Misiones, were expected to combat professional paratroopers more than capable of withstanding a harsh South Atlantic winter. The Air Force was the only branch of the Argentine armed forces that acquitted itself well, sinking several British ships with the help of French missiles. However, in what proved the worst atrocity of the war, the *General Belgrano* was torpedoed outside the British-imposed naval exclusion zone, leading to the death of nearly four hundred Argentine sailors. Whatever their position on sovereignty and the validity of the war, this single event is still viewed with bitterness amongst Argentines.

More than a thousand people perished in the 74-day war, and negotiations on the sovereignty issue were set back decades. At the time of the invasion, the islands were essentially a forgotten British colony that had long suffered a dearth of development. Indeed, what infrastructure projects there had been in the 1970s had been built by the Argentines, including the airport. This process of gradual integration into the Argentine economic sphere, encouraged by the British, stopped abruptly with the war.

Whether Britain would like to engage in talks on sovereignty or not, the issue has been a non-starter since 1982, owing to the oft-stated primacy of the islanders' desire to remain allied to Britain (**"self-determination"**). However, the subject will not simply disappear. Options have been put forward that attempt to bridge the gap between the islanders' right to determine their own future and Argentina's historical case for recognition of sovereignty. And, in many respects, the relationship between the islanders and the Argentines is getting closer. Economic treaties have been signed that pave the way for co-operation with regards to prospecting for suspected offshore oil deposits, and in the exploitation of fishing grounds. In July 1999, Britain and Argentina signed an accord renewing flight links between Argentina and the islands and permitting Argentine civilians to visit war graves without special permission. There are plans to dedicate some kind of war memorial to the Argentine casualties of the conflict.

As yet, there is no change on the respective position of the two countries as regards the issue of sovereignty, but both are determined that dialogue and co-operation, and not the politics of confrontation, should be the way forward. For too long, the islands have been used as a political football: a *cause célèbre* in Argentine domestic politics that has frequently been abused for the sake of posturing, and an issue whose complexities have been clouded by ignorance on both sides.

The military had proved themselves incapable of mastering politics and disastrous stewards of the economy, and now they had suffered ignominious failure doing what they were supposed to be specialists at: fighting. Perhaps the only positive thing to come out of this futile war was that it was the final spur for Argentines to throw off the shackles of the regime. While the junta prepared to hand over to civilian control, **General Reynaldo Bignone**, successor to Galtieri, issued a decree that pronounced an amnesty for all members of the armed forces for any alleged human rights atrocity.

Alfonsín and the restoration of democracy

Democracy was restored with the elections of October 1983, won by the radical **Raúl Alfonsín** – the first time in its four decades of existence that the Peronist party was defeated at the polls. Alfonsín, a lawyer much respected for his record on human rights, inherited a precarious political panorama. He faced two great challenges: the first, to build some sort of national concord after the bitter divisions of the 1970s; and the second, to restore a shattered economy, where inflation was running at over 400 percent and the foreign debt was over US$40,000 million. In the midst of this, he solved a politically sensitive border dispute with Chile over three islands in the Beagle Channel – **Picton**, **Nueva and Lennox**. Papal arbitration had awarded the islands to Chile, but Alfonsín ensured, in 1984, that the mechanism for approving this was by public referendum.

The issue of prosecuting those responsible for crimes against humanity during the dictatorship proved an intractable one. Alfonsín set up a **National Commission on Disappeared People** (CONADEP), chaired by the respected writer Ernesto Sabato, to investigate the alleged atrocities. Their report, *Nunca Más* – or "Never Again" – documented nine thousand cases of torture and disappearance, although it is generally accepted that the figure for the number of deaths during the Dirty War was actually closer to thirty thousand. It recommended that those responsible be brought to **trial**. Those convicted in the first wave of trials included the reviled Videla, Viola, Galtieri, and Admiral Emilio Massera, one of the most despised figures of the junta. All were sentenced to life imprisonment.

Military sensibilities were offended by the trials: defeat in the South Atlantic War had discredited them but they could still pose considerable danger to the fragile democracy and Alfonsín couldn't risk full confrontation. In 1986, he caved in to military pressure and passed *Punto Final*, or "End Point", legislation, which put a final date for the submission of writs for human rights crimes. However, in a window of two months, the courts were flooded with such writs, and, for the first time, the courts indicted officers still in active service.

Several short-lived uprisings forced Alfonsín to pull back from pursuing widespread prosecutions. In 1987, the **Law of Due Obedience** (*Obediencia Debida*) was passed, granting an amnesty to all but the leaders for atrocities committed during the dictatorship. At a stroke, this reduced the number of people facing charges from 370 to fewer than fifty. This incensed the victims' relatives, who saw notorious Proceso torturers escape prosecution, including the "Angel of Death", **Alfredo Astiz**, who attained international notoriety for the brutal murder of two French nuns and a young girl.

Alfonsín managed to secure some respite regarding the economy by restructuring the national debt and, in 1985, introducing a platform of stringent austerity measures, which were received with disappointed bitterness by many sectors of the population. These measures, named the **Plan Austral** in reference to the new currency that was introduced, were nonetheless essential, with inflation running at well over a thousand percent annually. The government continued to be crippled by **hyperinflation**, however, even after the introduction of a second raft of belt-tightening measures, the *australito*, in 1987. The inflationary crisis turned to meltdown in 1989, when the World Bank suspended all loans: many shops remained closed, preferring to keep their stock rather than selling it for a currency whose value disappeared before their eyes. In supermarkets, purchasers would have to listen to the tannoy to hear the latest prices, which would often change in the time it took to take an item from the shelf to the checkout. Elections were called in 1989, but, with severe **civil unrest** breaking out across the country, Alfonsín called a state of siege and stood down early, handing control to his elected successor, **Carlos Saúl Menem**. This was the first time since 1928 that power had transferred, after a free election, from one civilian government to another.

Menem's Presidency: 1989–99

The 1990s were dominated by Peronist leader Carlos Menem – the son of Syrian immigrants – and characterized by radical reforms and controversy. Menem had been governor of La Rioja at the outbreak of military rule in 1976 and he had spent most of the dictatorship in detention. His **Justicialist Party** (*Partido Justicialista* or PJ) was Peronist in name but – once elected in 1989 – he was to embark on a series of sweeping **neo-liberal reforms**.

His first major achievement was to destroy **inflation**. Backed by international finance organizations, Menem and his finance minister, **Domingo Cavallo**, introduced the Convertibility Plan (*Plan de Convertibilidad*), which pegged a new currency (the Argentine peso, worth 10,000 australes) at parity with the US dollar, and guaranteed its value by prohibiting the Central Bank from printing money it couldn't cover with federal reserves. Inflation fell to an annual rate of eight percent by 1993 and remained in single figures throughout the 1990s.

Menem also abandoned the Peronist principle of state ownership and the dogma of state intervention. His presidency saw the **privatization** of all the major utilities and industries: electricity, gas, telephones, Aerolíneas Argentinas and even the profitable YPF, the state-owned petroleum company, were sold off. Investment came primarily from European, mainly Spanish and French, corporations, and the sales often benefited individuals rather than the state. Free-market development policies also saw the cessation of all Federal railway subsidies in 1993 and the introduction of massive **public spending cuts**. In 1995, many regional trade barriers fell, as a consequence of the full implementation of the **Mercosur** trading agreement, creating a **free-trade block** of Southern Cone countries – Brazil, Argentina, Uruguay and Paraguay, with Chile and Venezuela developing close ties later on. Unemployment rates rocketed and acute financial hardship resulted in strikes and sporadic civil unrest, as more people fell beneath the bread line.

One thing about Menem's brand of Peronism that stayed faithful to the original was his style of government. A cavalier **populist**, Menem never stopped trying to develop the "cult of the leader". He modelled his image, mutton-chop sideburns and all, on that of provincial *caudillos* such as Facundo Quiroga, the La Rioja warlord of the 1830s. Not known for his modesty, he preached austerity while developing a penchant for the life of a playboy.

The president increasingly became associated with trying to rule by **decree**. One of the most controversial aspects of this policy was the issuing of executive **amnesties** in 1989 to those guilty of atrocities during the 1970s. Although the amnesty included ex-guerrillas, public outrage centred on the release of former members of the junta, including all the leading generals. To Menem it was the pragmatic price to pay to secure the military's cooperation; to virtually all the rest of the country, it was a flagrant moral capitulation. His apparent failure to launch a serious investigation into two terrorist attacks that targeted the **Jewish community** in 1992 and 1994 (see box, p.113) also showed him in a very poor light.

In August 1994, he secured a **constitutional amendment** that allowed a sitting president to stand for a second term, although the mandate was reduced from six years to four. The voters, trusting Menem's economic record, elected him to a second term the following year. But in 1996, he sacked his finance minister, Domingo Cavallo, who formed a new political party, the Acción por la República, which, though never gaining much of a power base, served to highlight the issue of government corruption.

Human rights issues continued to surface on the front-line agenda. One of the most important developments was the start of a campaign to prosecute those guilty of having **"kidnapped"** babies of *desaparecidos* born in detention, in order to give them up for adoption to childless military couples. Recognition of this crime, not covered by the Punto Final legislation of Alfonsín's years, resulted in the successful interrogation and detention of many of the leading members of the old junta, including Videla and Massera. In the mid-1990s, the armed forces acknowledged their role in the atrocities of the dictatorship, making a **public apology** – a symbolic act that was followed by similar repentance by the Catholic Church.

Austerity measures seemed to apply to anyone not in government, and foreign debt continued to balloon. When, at the beginning of 1999, Brazil's currency lost half of its value, the government had to resist acute pressure to devalue the peso. Convertibility held, but Menem announced that Argentina ought seriously to consider the "**dollarization**" of the economy – an issue that would have had severe ramifications on national pride.

As the end of his second term approached, Menem mooted the possibility of running for a third consecutive term of office. He argued that, although his own constitutional amendment allowed a sitting president to stand for re-election only once, he had enjoyed only one full term of government since that amendment had been passed. Apparently his ploy was designed to alienate voters and scupper the chances of fellow member of the Justicialist Party, **Eduardo Duhalde**, in the forthcoming presidential election. Duhalde, as governor of Buenos Aires province, was the favoured candidate to replace Menem and lead the election fight. However, Menem, who increasingly treated the party as his own fief, apparently preferred the Justicialists to lose the election so that he could stand again in 2003. The tactic certainly seemed to work: the shenanigans of his supporters, the so-called "re-re-eleccionistas", alienated the populace still further, in the run-up to the vote in 1999.

Fernando De la Rúa, Córdoba-born mayor of the city of Buenos Aires, had won the candidacy of the **Alianza**, a coalition of the radicals (UCR), of which he was leader, and **FREPASO**, itself a coalition party of left-wingers and disaffected Peronists. With the desire for change palpable across the country, De la Rúa won a clear mandate. Duhalde, embittered, vowed to continue his personal vendetta against Menem.

The De la Rúa government: hope followed by disaster

Known for his stolid reliability rather than his charisma – he admitted to being as dull as ditch water – De la Rúa was a complete contrast to his predecessor.

Upon taking office in 1999 he seemed to represent the **fiscal and moral probity** that Argentines, tired of the excesses of the Menem administration, felt their country – already starting to show signs of its worst-ever recession – needed. Once in charge, though, the Alianza coalition was hit by severe infighting. Press reports that the government had bribed senators to approve a reform to the country's strict labour legislation triggered a political crisis. FREPASO leader **Carlos "Chacho" Alvarez**, the head of the Senate and vice-president, quit in October 2000, claiming De la Rúa had not properly investigated the allegation. A few months later, De la Rúa's finance minister, José Luis Machinea, reached an agreement with the **IMF** to meet stiff budgetary targets in exchange for a "financial shield." When he resigned in March 2001, **Ricardo López Murphy**, took over his portfolio. The new minister announced wide-ranging budget cuts that hit education hardest, sparking the wrath of progressive sectors of the Radical Party, traditional defenders of the country's university system. Murphy was forced to resign within a fortnight, following massive street demonstrations, and in a surprise move De la Rúa summoned **Domingo Cavallo** to replace him.

Menem's erstwhile finance minister announced an unrealistic "zero deficit" drive to meet stiff IMF targets and protect convertibility, but the country still wasn't pulling out of recession, with industrial production and exports dismally low owing to the phoney exchange rate, unemployment rising rapidly and financial confidence on the wane. Then, in the national elections of October 2001, the Peronists gained control of both houses of Congress. Soon afterwards private depositors began to pull their money out of banks, afraid the peso-dollar peg would be abolished. Under severe pressure to abandon convertibility and devalue the peso, Cavallo stood firm. In early December 2001, in a desperate bid to avoid devaluation and stop the cash drain from banks, he announced restrictions severely limiting access to private peso deposits, including salaries. This measure, known as the **corralito**, or "playpen", understandably riled Argentines of all classes, though the wealthiest managed to get their money out in dollars and into accounts abroad. To cap it all, shortly afterwards, the IMF announced the withdrawal of support on grounds of lack of confidence that Argentina could meet its targets.

On December 13, a general strike was staged against the *corralito* by the Peronist-controlled unions and acts of looting were reported in Greater Buenos Aires, a Peronist bastion. Despite De la Rúa's announcement of a state of siege to deal with the crisis, on the evening of 19 December tens of thousands of protestors bashing pots and pans (the first of many noisy "**cacerolazos**", or saucepan protests) marched on the Plaza de Mayo. Although the police dispersed the huge crowd, more demonstrations took place the following day. Pleading desperately for the support of the Peronist governors, De la Rúa found himself politically isolated, while brutal police efforts to clear the Plaza de Mayo and halt **demonstrations** in other cities ended in a bloodbath, with at least 25 people dead nationwide. De la Rúa left office, ignominiously fleeing Government House by helicopter.

The interregnum

After a series of farcically disastrous, short-lived appointments, the provincial assembly finally opted for **Eduardo Duhalde**, the Peronist candidate defeated by De la Rúa in 1999, who was sworn in on January 1, 2002. He heavily

Piqueteros and cartoneros – the tougher side of Argentine life

Piqueteros – from the English "picketers" - first came to notice around the time of the 2001 crisis and still occasionally turn nasty, staging violent protests outside the houses of former junta members or banks and businesses, blockading roads and major access points to cities, in order to draw attention to social injustices such as hospital closures or poor conditions in factories. The most notorious groups of *piqueteros* belong to the Movimiento Patriótico Revolucionario, or Patriotic Revolutionary Movement, better known as **Quebracho**, after a virtually indestructible sub-tropical timber. This Marxist movement formed in the late 1990s sees itself as the natural heir to 1970s guerrillas, such as the Montoneros, and its stated goal is to abolish poverty and all forms of ownership with it. It deliberately attacks the forces of law and order and holds confrontational demonstrations when foreign dignitaries come to Buenos Aires, especially US politicians or representatives of international financial institutions. Their hatred of the US is so strong that they have publicly voiced support for Iran just out of spite. Quebracho's leader, Fernando Esteche, was arrested and jailed after he allegedly masterminded a violent clash with the police to coincide with a visit to Buenos Aires by Rodrigo Rato, the head of the IMF, in August 2006.

A new phenomenon for the new millennium, the **cartonero**, is now a common sight on the streets of the capital. *Cartoneros* are poor people who effectively act as semi-official refuse recyclers. They rummage through garbage bags, salvaging paper and cardboard to sell for scrap value. The sight of whole families, including young children, sorting out rubbish on the city pavements, does not exactly make for a good image and will be a challenge faced by the new city administration.

devalued the peso within days and then spent most of the year trying to negotiate a new agreement with the IMF to avoid a humiliating default with international lending agencies. After militant jobless groups known as *piqueteros* (see box above) clashed with police, leaving two people dead, in June 2002 he announced early **presidential elections** at some time in 2003, promising that he and his colleagues would not stand for office.

Once the worst of the crisis had subsided, Duhalde's unflappable finance minister, **Roberto Lavagna**, was credited with calming financial markets, avoiding hyperinflation and stabilizing the US dollar exchange rate at just over three pesos, after a peak of nearly four. He also reached a short-term agreement with the IMF and, by early 2003, signs of economic recovery – in particular, increased exports and productivity – began to show. The downside to this was a **sharp rise in poverty** across the country, as the price of basic products and imports soared.

April 27 was chosen as the date for presidential elections, with a second, run-off round expected on May 18. The Peronists, meanwhile, failed to unite, allowing the warring factions to field three separate contenders: former presidents Menem and Rodríguez Saá (one of the short-lived heads of state – he had lasted only one week) and Duhalde's protégé, **Néstor Kirchner**, who enjoyed a narrow lead in opinion polls. Memories of the disastrous De la Rúa administration meant that none of the opposition parties seemed likely to oust the Peronists from power. In the event, **Menem** came first, with just under a quarter of the vote – a victory some opponents attributed to the purchase of votes – with Kirchner going through to the second round, only a couple of percentage points behind. But, as the run-off approached, opinion polls unanimously suggested that only three voters in ten would back Menem – who unexpectedly withdrew from the race to avoid ignominious defeat and, it was said, to deprive Kirchner of an overwhelming victory.

Kirchner: taking Argentina into the new millennium

Despite being a lacklustre public speaker with an unfortunate speech defect, and something of a political nobody from a far-off provincial backwater, President **Néstor Kirchner** has proved a surprisingly powerful force in Argentine politics. Since 2003, he and his entourage, including his family, especially his strong-willed wife, **Cristina Fernández de Kirchner** (see box, p.809), have come to dominate the country to an extent that many Argentines talk of a "penguin" takeover. The president, often known simply as **"K"** – easier on the tongue than his Swiss-German surname – is nicknamed "Pingüino", both for his bird-like appearance and his Patagonian origins.

Kirchner is decidedly one of the new generation of **South American leaders**, set on forging regional independence and inter-dependence, strengthening Mercosur, limiting the influence of multinationals, defying the IMF and generally thumbing his nose at Washington DC. He has forged a relationship with Brazil's Lula, kept on good terms with Chile's Bachelet and even cosied up to Venezuela's **Chávez** and Bolivia's Morales, without espousing total hero worship of Castro or, so far at least, showing dangerously autocratic or

An Argentina for the twenty-first century – the 2010 Bicentennial

Argentina will observe its **bicentennial** in 2010: two hundred years ago, on May 25, 1810, locals gathered in Buenos Aires' Plaza de Mayo to demand the withdrawal of the Spanish viceroy and to form the **Primera Junta**, the first move in throwing off the yoke of Spanish rule and creating an independent nation.

In 1910, the centennial anniversary was cause for great celebration. In its first hundred years Argentina had gone from being a fairly small colonial backwater to one of the world's richest countries, still in the throes of an unprecedented immigration and building boom, and bursting with confidence that it was destined to be a great country, challenging US hegemony in the Western Hemisphere – a view shared by outsiders. Several foreign nations gifted statues and other monuments, many of which are still standing in Buenos Aires, including the Torre Monumental (Britain; see p.129) and the Monumento de los Españoles (Spain; see p.139).

Now, a century further on, Argentina hasn't exactly lived up to that heady promise, but its citizens are still bound to put lots of enthusiasm (and, doubtlessly, endless reflection) into the bicentennial celebrations. José Nun, Secretary of Culture, said in March 2007: "The Bicentennial will become that great moment of collective enthusiasm which allows us to change our way of constructing reality and definitively break the sequence of innumerable crises that we have suffered and which still affect us."

The main post office building in Buenos Aires, the Correo Central at Sarmiento 189, will be the centre of festivities. Other plans in the capital (though not all yet confirmed) include: **exhibitions** at the new Casa del Bicentenario at Riobamba 983; a **regatta** of navy school boats from around the world; the part **pedestrianization** and remodelling of the Plaza de Mayo, with lighting designed to show the historical development of the plaza; free **Wi-Fi** throughout the city; a new **park**, the Parque del Bicentenario, near the Reserva Ecológica; and bilateral events with **Chile**, which also celebrates its bicentennial in 2010 (as do Colombia and Mexico). For the latest information on the festivities, contact the Buenos Aires tourist office or the Casa del Bicentenario (ⓣ011/4129-2400, ⓦwww.bicentenario.gov.ar).

anti-democratic tendencies. If Kirchner has one thing in common with Carlos Menem it is a much-criticized over-dependence on ruling by **decree**, even though he has a Congress so behind him that usually even the Radical opposition rubberstamps his policies.

This said, Kirchner is no flamboyant playboy, and treats international diplomacy and media relations with an indifference verging on contempt. Having initially kept Lavagna at the helm of the country's treasury, he sacked him in 2005, in spite of his prudent management of the economy – no doubt partly because Lavagna's own presidential ambitions had begun to emerge. In the meantime Argentina has pulled swiftly out of recession, since 2003 registering one of the world's highest **GDP growth rates** (averaging over eight percent a year), though this showed signs of slowing down in 2007, after a gas shortage caused an energy crisis. Exports have shot up, resulting in a bumper trade surplus; imports have grown at a healthy rate; industrial production has rocketed; national tax revenues have broke records; and even the joblessness figures have started to drop, dipping below ten percent for the first time in a decade in 2007 (8.5 percent in July). Argentina has also had a string of record years for **international tourism**, matched with huge numbers of Argentine holidaymakers forced to discover their own country owing to the exchange rate and inaccessible airfares. The country is now preparing for the celebration of its Bicentennial in 2010 (see box, p.807), which, if the high returns continue, will certainly be cause for celebration.

As tax revenues have swelled, the president – who describes himself as left of centre and an opponent of neo-liberal capitalism – has been able to honour many of his election pledges, namely to reverse years of spending cuts in the education, welfare and public-service sectors. Acute **poverty** has also been reduced but remains widespread – witness, for example, the *cartoneros* on the streets of the capital (see box, p.806). Despite rapid growth, many economic aggregates are still far lower than in the late 1990s. Skilful macroeconomic management was certainly a factor, but the government was also lucky as commodity and agriculture prices (especially **soya**) reached all-time highs, the dollar dropped in value against major currencies like the euro and yen and global interest rates remained extremely low. As market confidence rose, the value of the peso edged towards the 3.10–3.20 to the dollar mark, keeping export levels high.

All of this has made Kirchner the most popular resident of the Casa Rosada for years, with an approval rating at times as high as eighty percent. Seldom seen in a suit and tie, he is also down-to-earth, although the presidential couple have been criticized for making too many flights to their home base of Santa Cruz in the official presidential jet. Further criticism has been levelled at him from within his own, still-divided Peronist party, not least because he has never mentioned the Peróns once by name. His response has been that he focuses on the social justice aspect of **justicialismo**, rather than looking to specific personalities and the past, but he has certainly taken a leaf or two out of the founding father's populist book – he prefers attending an inauguration of **subsidized housing projects** to a night at the opera or a reception for visiting dignitaries. He has also risked the wrath of sections of his party, as well as the military, by repealing the **amnesty laws** that made it impossible to prosecute those who committed human rights atrocities, including members of the last junta. Moreover, he closed the **Escuela Mecánica de la Armada** (Navy Mechanics School) so it could be turned into a monument to the dictatorship, and excluded some Peronist politicians with a dubious past from a memorial ceremony for the disappeared.

In general there have been few foreign policy problems of note, but 2005 saw a diplomatic war of words begin with Argentina's neighbour and traditional ally, Uruguay, over the construction of massive paper-pulp plants, or **papeleras** (see box, pp.324–325). Owing to local fears of destructive pollution in the Río Uruguay, the case went to the International Court in The Hague and still remains unresolved. Huge demonstrations by Argentine residents have frequently led to blockades of the road bridges linking the countries.

However, not all has been plain sailing. The government has faced an upsurge in the number of violent **crimes** in the capital and other large cities – some of them directly involving the corrupt police force. A huge demonstration was held in 2004 in reaction to the barbaric murder of a 23-year-old student, **Axel Blumberg**, who had been kidnapped in a wealthy suburb of Buenos Aires. **Felisa Miceli** replaced her former mentor, Roberto Lavagna, as finance minister in November 2005, and generally did a good job but, in early 2007, \$100,000 and US\$30,000 in banknotes were found in a bag in the toilet next to her office; she claimed the money was a loan from her brother to buy a house (real-estate transactions are often conducted in cash in Argentina) but not everyone was convinced, and media pressure led to her resignation in July 2007. Previously, she had been receiving a lot of flak over the way in which the rate of **inflation** is measured in Argentina. The state statistical office **INDEC** was accused of

Cristina – the new Evita?

In July 2007, it was announced that **Cristina Fernández de Kirchner** would stand for the presidency in October of that year, as the candidate of the ruling **Frente para la Victoria** (Victory Front, or FPV). Born in 1953, she is senator for Buenos Aires Province and, since 2003, has been the country's First Lady – or, as she prefers it, "First Female Citizen". Cristina, or **CFK**, as she is generally known, is a political animal. She began as an activist while studying law in her native La Plata, in the 1970s. She met Néstor Kirchner through politics, and after they married the two moved back to his native **Santa Cruz Province** where they practised law and began their political careers; her first successful election to Congress was in 1989. Glamorous and extremely photogenic, she has a forthright manner and a sharp tongue – in the early years of her husband's presidency she famously scowled (rather than smiled) at cameras.

Her popularity with the working classes and her high-profile **ambassadorial trips** to Europe and the US – together with a fashionable wardrobe – have led to inevitable comparisons with **Evita**. She famously said in a newspaper interview – perhaps tongue-in-cheek – that she would replace Evita in history because she is both more intelligent and more beautiful. She has taken a firm and progressive stand on issues such as **equality**, human rights, especially justice for the victims of the dictatorship, combating anti-Semitism and the need for South America to assert itself on the world stage.

Opinion polls since the announcement of her candidacy have shown her likely to score forty to fifty percent in the first round of voting, with her nearest rival barely scraping fifteen percent. Many experts believe that the Kirchners' long-term strategy is to alternate the next three elections, giving husband and wife a total of four terms, or sixteen years, in office, while avoiding the frequent lame-duck syndrome. At the time of writing, it looks improbable that Cristina will *not* become Argentina's second woman president and the first to be elected in her own right. As for the comparisons with Evita, more serious observers tend to liken her instead to **Hillary Clinton** – another clever, tough politician not afraid to make enemies. But in another press interview Cristina dismissed that too, saying that Hillary only became a force in national politics because she was married to Bill. She, on the other hand, is very much her own boss.

massaging the figures – the official annual rate stood at around twelve percent in early 2007, but independent press surveys put the real rate much higher. The latest in a row of scandals broke in August 2007, when the opposition called for the resignation of Planning Minister **Julio de Vido**, after officials in his ministry allegedly tried to bring US$800,000 into the country illegally.

Meanwhile, former president **Menem** has remained in the news, going into exile in Chile with his former beauty-queen second wife. Two extradition demands by Argentine authorities in 2004 were bungled, but he later returned in the knowledge he was virtually safe from prosecution on corruption charges. His political ambitions remain alive – he has been a vitriolic critic of Kirchner – but his wings were severely clipped in mid-2007 when he was overwhelmingly defeated in provincial elections on his home turf of **La Rioja**, losing to a Kirchnerist candidate. *Pagina 12* declared him to be pensioned off for good. Former president **Isabelita Perón** has also been in the news; in January 2007 she was arrested and held under house arrest in Spain, after a federal judge in Argentina issued an extradition request so she could face trial for the disappearance of a student in 1976.

Even so, Kirchner's faction has had mixed results in elections in the months leading to the next presidential polls. The biggest electoral debacle came in June 2007 when the populist president of Boca Juniors football club, **Mauricio Macri**, easily won the second round of mayoral elections in Buenos Aires; he beat high-spending incumbent Jorge Telerman and Education Minister Daniel Filmus whom the President had gone out of his way to back. Nonetheless, **Cristina Fernández de Kirchner** (see box, p.809), seems guaranteed a resounding victory in the presidential election in October 2007 – the year's bad electoral and economic news just can't seem to dent her lead in the opinion polls.

Environment and wildlife

Argentina's natural wonders are some of its chief joys. Its remarkable diversity of habitats, ranging from subtropical jungles to sub-antarctic icesheets, is complemented by an unexpected juxtaposition of species: parrots foraging alongside glaciers, or shocking-pink flamingoes surviving bitter sub-zero temperatures on the stark Andean altiplano. Though the divisions are too complicated to list fully here, we've covered Argentina's most distinctive habitats below, along with the species of flora and fauna typical to each.

Despite the protection afforded by a relatively well-managed national park system, the country's precious environmental heritage remains under threat. As ever, by far and away the most pressing issue is **habitat loss**. The chaco is a good case in point. Previously, the lack of water in the *Impenetrable* was the flora and fauna's best asset. Nowadays, climate change has seen rainfall levels increase, and irrigation projects are fast opening up areas of the *Impenetrable* to settlement and agriculture, with a poorly controlled exploitation of mature woodland for timber or charcoal and **land clearance** (*desmonte*) for crops such as cotton. Forestry in other areas of the country – notably Misiones and Tierra del Fuego – is worrying as well. **Hydroelectric projects** in the northeast have destroyed valuable habitats along the Uruguay and Paraná rivers, and **overfishing** has also severely depleted stocks in the latter. The phenomenal rise of **genetically modified soya** production in Argentina has also alarmed environmental campaigners. While genetic modification does not provoke the same "Frankenstein food" outcry as in Europe, there is concern about the effects of monoculture on the country's biodiversity.

That said, environmental consciousness is slowly gaining ground (especially among the younger generation). Greenpeace is self-financing in Argentina, with thousands of paying members; the national parks system is expanding with the help of international loans; and committed national and local pressure groups such as the Fundación de Vida Silvestre and Asociación Ornitológica del Plata (both based in Buenos Aires), Proyecto Lemú (based in Epuyén) and Fundación Orca (based in Puerto Madryn) are ensuring that ecological issues are not ignored.

Pampas grassland and the espinal

The vast alluvial plain that centres on Buenos Aires Province and radiates out into eastern Córdoba, southern Santa Fe and northeast La Pampa provinces, was once pampas grassland, famous for its clumps of brush-tailed *cortadera* grass. However, its deep, extremely fertile soil has seen it become the agricultural heart of modern Argentina, and this original habitat has almost entirely disappeared, transformed by cattle grazing and intensive arable farming, and by the planting of introduced trees such as eucalyptus. It's still possible to find a few vestiges of marshlands and grasslands, such as the area of tall *stipa* grassland around Médanos, southwest of Bahía Blanca.

Bordering the pampas to the north and west, across the centre of Corrientes, Entre Ríos, Santa Fe, Córdoba and San Luis provinces, is a semicircular fringe of **espinal woodland**, a type of open wooded "parkland". Common species of tree include **acacia** and, in the north, the ñandubay and **ceibo**, Argentina's national tree, which in spring produces a profusion of scarlet blooms. In the north, espinal scenery mixes in places with the swamps and marshes of Mesopotamia, and in the south with monte desert.

The only type of habitat endemic to Argentina is the so-called **monte scrub** found in the arid intermontane valleys that lie in the rainshadow of the central Andes. It runs from northern Patagonia through the Cuyo region and northwards as far as Salta Province, where in some places it separates the humid *yungas* from the high-mountain *puna*. Monte scrub is characterized by thorny *jarilla* bushes, which flower yellow in spring. In the Andean foothills and floodplains of the Mendoza region, much of this desert monte has been irrigated and replaced with vineyards. It's an interesting habitat from a wildlife point of view for a high number of endemic bird species, such as the **Carbonated Sierra Finch**, the **Sandy Gallito** – a wren-like bird with a pale eye-stripe – and the **Cinammon Warbling Finch** (*moneterita canela*).

Once, these plains were the home of **pampas deer** (*venado de las pampas*), but habitat change and overhunting have brought the species to the edge of extinction, and today only a few hundred individuals survive, mainly in Samborombón and Campos del Tuyú in Buenos Aires Province. Standing 70cm at the shoulder, the deer is easily identified by its three-pronged antler.

The **coypu** (*coipo* or *falsa nutria*) is a large rodent commonly found in the region's wetlands, especially in the central east of Buenos Aires Province and the Paraná Delta. The great vizcacha dens (*vizcacheras*) described in the nineteenth century by famous natural history writer W.H. Hudson have all but disappeared, but you may see an endemic bird named after the writer, Hudson's Canastero, along with **Greater Rheas**, **Burrowing Parrots** (*loro barranquero*), and **Ovenbirds** (*horneros*). Named after the domed, concrete-hard mud nests they build on posts, Ovenbirds have always been held in great affection by gauchos and country folk.

Mesopotamian grassland

The humid Mesopotamian grasslands extend across much of Corrientes and Entre Ríos provinces and into southernmost Misiones. Here you will find *yatay* palm savannah and some of Argentina's most important **wetlands**, most notably the Esteros de Iberá and the Parque Nacional Mburucuyá, which make for some of the country's most productive nature safaris.

The wetlands have a remarkable diversity of birdlife, including numerous species of ducks, rails, ibises and herons. Some of the most distinctive species are the **Wattled Jacana** (*jacana*), which tiptoes over floating vegetation; the **Southern Screamer** (*chajá*), a hulking bird the size of a turkey; the unmistakable **Scarlet-headed Blackbird** (*federal*); filter-feeding **Roseate Spoonbills** (*espátula rosada*); the **Rufescent Tiger Heron** (*hocó colorado*); and jabirus (*yabirú*), the largest variety of stork, measuring almost 1.5m tall, with a bald head, shoehorn bill and red ruff. Up above fly **Snail Kites** (*caracoleros*), which use their bills to prise freshwater *caracoles* from their shells.

In the shallow swamps, amongst reedbeds and long grasses, you will find the **marsh deer** (*ciervo de los pantanos*), on the list of endangered species. Standing 1.3m tall, it is South America's largest native deer, easily identifiable by its size and its multi-horned antlers. One of the most common wetland animals is the

capybara (*carpincho*), the world's biggest rodent, weighing up to 50kg. Though most active at night, it is easy to see in the day, frequently half-submerged. **Reptiles** include the **black cayman** (*yacaré negro* or *yacaré hocico angosto*), which grows up to 2.8m in length, and is the victim of illegal hunting; and snakes like the *lampalagua* **boa** (up to 5m in length) and the *curiyú* **yellow anaconda** (which can grow over 3m), both of which are non-poisonous, relying on constriction to kill their prey.

Subtropical Paraná forest

Subtropical Paraná forest (*Selva Paranaense*) is Argentina's most biologically diverse ecosystem, a dense mass of vegetation that conforms to most people's idea of a jungle. The most frequently visited area of Paraná forest is Parque Nacional Iguazú, but it is also found in patches across the rest of Misiones, with small remnant areas in the northeast of Corrientes Province. It has over two hundred tree species, amongst which figure the **palo rosa** (one of the highest canopy species, at up to 40m); the **strangler fig** (*higuerón bravo*); the **lapacho**, with its beautiful pink flowers; and the **Misiones cedar** (*cedro misionero*), a fine hardwood species that has suffered heavily from logging. Upland areas along the Brazilian border still preserve stands of **Paraná pine**, a type of rare araucaria monkey puzzle related to the more famous species found in northern Patagonia. Lower storeys of vegetation include the wild **yerba mate** tree, first cultivated by the Jesuits in the seventeenth century; the **palmito** palm, whose edible core is exploited as palm heart; and endangered prehistoric **tree ferns**. Festooning the forest are lianas, mosses, ferns and epiphytes, including several hundred varieties of **orchid**.

More than five hundred species of bird inhabit the Paraná forest, and you stand a good chance of seeing the **Toco Toucan** (*tucán grande*), with its bright orange bill, along with other smaller members of the same family. Rarities include the magnificent **Harpy Eagle** (*harpía*), one of the world's most powerful avian predators, and the **Bare-faced Curassow** (*muitú*).

This part of the country is one of the few places you might just see the highly endangered **jaguar** (*yaguareté* or *tigre*). Weighing up to 160kg, this beast is the continent's most fearsome predator. The beautiful spotted **ocelot** (*gato onza*) is similarly elusive and almost as endangered, having suffered massive hunting for its pelt during the 1970s.

The wet chaco

The habitat described as wet chaco is found in the eastern third of Chaco and Formosa provinces and the northeast of Santa Fe. It consists of small patches of gallery forest (not unlike the Paraná forest) growing by rivers and ox-bow lakes; savannah grasslands studded with *caranday* palms; "islands" of mixed scrub woodland (*isletas de monte*); and wetland environments similar to the Mesopotamian grasslands. The key tree species is the **quebracho colorado chaqueño**, one of Argentina's four *quebracho* species, whose name means "axe-breaker" in Spanish, though it has always been valued more for its tannin than for its hard wood. It can reach the height of 24m, and the most venerable specimens can be anything from

300 to 500 years old. Other common trees are the *urunday*, the *timbó colorado*, the *lapacho negro* and the intriguing **crown of thorns** tree (*espina corona*), with dramatic spikes jutting out from its trunk. On the savannahs, graceful **caranday** palms (*palmares*) reach heights of up to 15m. They are extremely resilient, surviving both flooding and the regular burning of the grasslands in order to stimulate new growth for cattle pasture.

The wetland swamps are often choked with rafts of **camalote**, a waterlily with a lilac flower, or with the large pads of another distinctive waterlily, the *flor de Irupé*, whose name comes from the Guaraní word for "plate on the water". *Pirí*, looking like papyrus horsetail, and *pehuajó*, with leaves like a banana palm, form reed beds where the water is shallower.

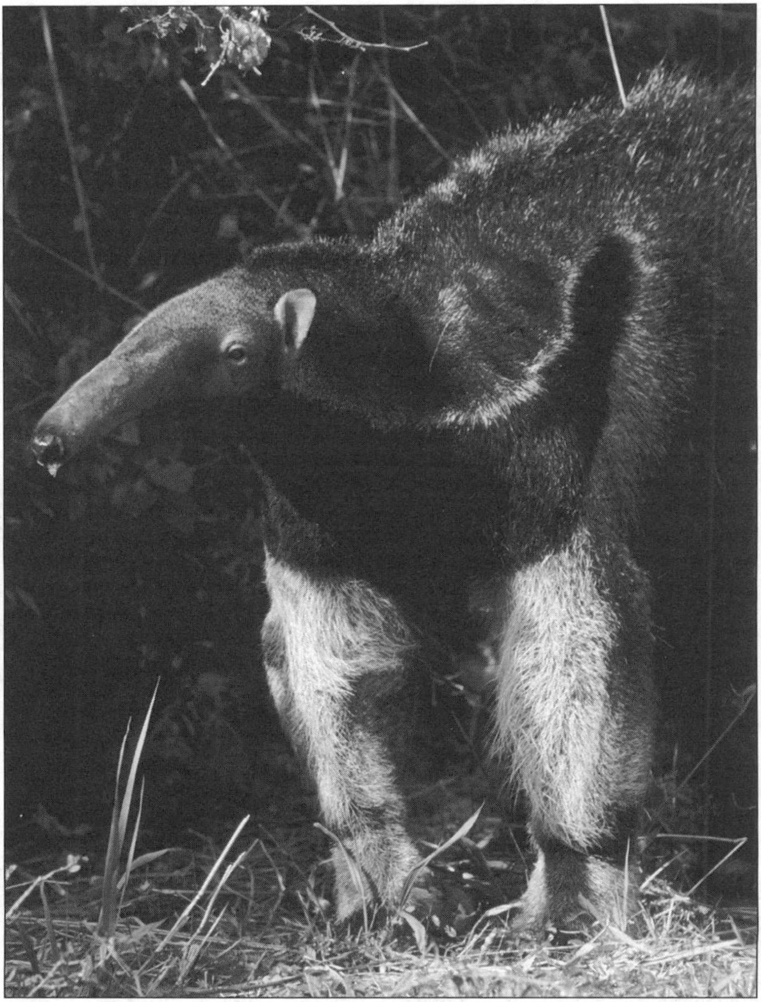

△ Anteater

The birdlife of the wet chaco is similar to that of the Mesopotamian swamps. You're likely to see the **Greater Rhea** (called *suri* in this region more often than *ñandú*); **Fork-tailed Flycatchers** (*tijereta*), with overlong tailfeathers; **Monk Parakeets** (*cotorras*), which build huge communal nests in *caranday* palms; **Red-legged Seriemas** (*chuña de patas rojas*), long-legged roadrunner-type birds; and two birds that are trapped for the pet trade – the **Red-crested Cardinal** (*cardenal común*), and the **Turquoise-fronted Amazon** (*loro hablador*), an accomplished ventriloquist parrot.

One of the most beautiful, and rarest, animals in the wet chaco is the solitary, nocturnal **maned wolf** (*aguará guazú* or *lobo de crin*). To this day it is persecuted for fear that it's a werewolf (*lobizón*), and the legend that its glance can kill a chicken hardly endears it to farmers. The coppery auburn beast, standing almost a metre tall and weighing up to 25kg, actually eats birds' eggs, armadillos, rodents and fruit. This part of Argentina is the southernmost limit of its natural habitat.

One of the most curious-looking denizens of the region is the **giant anteater** (*oso hormiguero, oso bandera* or *yurumí*). Its sense of smell is forty times better than humans', to make up for its poor eyesight. It breaks open rock-hard termite mounds with its strong claws, and scours them out with its tongue. Much smaller is the **collared anteater** (*oso melero* or *tamanduá*), a perplexed-looking creature with a black and orange-yellow coat. It can be found on the ground, but its prehensile tail makes it better suited to climbing trees. The region's primates behave similarly: the **black howler monkey** (*carayá* or *mono aullador negro*), one of South America's biggest monkeys; the black-capped or **tufted capuchin** (*caí*); and the endangered **mirikiná** (*mono de noche*), Argentina's smallest primate (only 60–70cm long, including its tail), and the world's only nocturnal monkey.

The dry chaco

The dry chaco refers to the parched plain of thorn scrub that covers most of central and western Chaco and Formosa provinces, northeastern Salta and much of Santiago del Estero. To early explorers and settlers, much of this area was known simply as the **Impenetrable** for its aridity. The habitat was once more varied, but deforestation and the introduction of cattle have standardized the vegetation. Everything, it seems, is defensive: the *vinal* shrub, for instance, is dreaded by riders for its brutal spikes, up to 20cm long. In places, there is a dense undergrowth of **chaguar** and **caraguatá**: robust, yucca-like plants that the Wichí process to make fibre for their *yica* bags.

The tallest trees in the dry chaco are the *quebrachos*, notably the **quebracho colorado santiagueño** (up to 24m tall and 1.5m diameter), exploited for tannin. The bark of the **quebracho blanco** – cracked into thick "scales", not dissimilar to cork-oak bark – has antimalarial properties. Several other species also reach imposing heights, such as the two types of **carob tree**, the *algarrobo blanco* and *algarrobo negro*, both of which play an integral role in the life of the Wichí and other indigenous groups. The beautiful **guayacán**, with hard wood, flaky, olive-green bark and leaves somewhat like a mimosa, is used for furniture. Perhaps the hardest wood is that of the endangered, slow-growing **palo santo** (meaning "holy stick"). Its fragrant, green-tinged wood can be burnt as an insect repellent. Finally, the **palo borracho** (or *yuchán*) is the most distinctive tree of all, with a bulbous, porous trunk to store water; the tree protects itself, especially when young, with rhino-horned spikes.

Creepers such as the famous medicinal **uña de gato** (or *garabato*) are quite common. **Cacti** are some of the very few plants here that grow straight: predominantly the candelabra *cardón* (a different species from that which grows in the Andes), which grows to the size of a tree, and its cousin, the *ucle*.

Commonly associated with dry-chaco habitat are birds like the **Black-legged Seriema** (*chuña de patas negras*), which is rather like an Argentine roadrunner; and the **Chaco Chachalaca** (*charata*). More excitingly, the dry chaco holds forty percent of Argentina's mammal species (143 types). Though it's not easy to give an exact number, it's thought about two hundred **jaguars** hang on in these lands, as do a handful of **ocelots**. Less threatened are the **puma** and the **Geoffroy's cat** (*gato montés*). One of three species of native Argentine wild pig, the famous **Chacoan peccary** (*chancho quimilero*) was thought to be extinct until rediscovered in Paraguay in 1975, and later in a few isolated areas of the Argentine dry chaco. Another high-profile living fossil is the nocturnal **giant armadillo** (*tatú carreta*). Up to 1.5m long and weighing as much as 60kg, a full-grown one is strong enough to carry a man. Smaller but equally interesting are the **coatimundi** (*coatí*) and the **crab-eating raccoon** (*aguará popé* or *osito lavador*). One of the most frequently sighted animals is the **brown brocket deer** (*corzuela pardo* or *guazuncho*).

Of the Gran Chaco's numerous types of snake, the venomous (but generally unaggressive) **coral snake** (*coral*) and the innocuous **false coral snake** (*falsa coral*) are often confused. Both are similarly patterned in red, black and white – the poisonous species has two white bands between a group of three black, and the imposter has a single white band between two black – and are best left alone. More dangerous are **vipers**: the diamond-back rattlesnake (*cascabel*), the *yarará de la cruz*, and the *yarará común*, all of which have an extensive range in northern and central Argentina.

The yungas

Yungas is the term applied to the subtropical band of the Argentine Northwest that lies between the chaco and the Andean precordillera, from the Bolivian border through Jujuy, Salta, Tucumán and into Catamarca. Abrupt changes of altitude give rise to radical changes in the flora here, creating wildly different ecosystems. All are characterized by fairly high year-round precipitation, but have distinct seasons, with winter being drier. The lowest altitudes are home to transitional woodland and lowland jungle (*selva pedemontana*), up to about 600m. Most of the trees and shrubs in these lower levels are deciduous and have showy blossoms: jacaranda, fuchsia, *pacará*, *palo blanco* and *amarillo*, *lapacho* (or *tabebuia*), *timbó colorado* (the black-eared tree), *palo borracho* (*chorisia* or *yuchán*) and the **ceibo**. Much of this forest has been hard-hit by clearance, with 78 plant species under threat.

Above 600m starts the most famous *yungas* habitat, the **montane cloud-forests** (*selva montaña* or *nuboselva*), best seen in the national parks of Calilegua, Baritú and El Rey. The *selva montaña* is split into two categories: lower montane forest (*selva basal*), which rises to about 1000m; and true cloudforest, which is found as high as 2200m. These forests form a gloomy canopy of tall evergreens – dominated by laurels and acacia-like tipas at lower levels, and *yunga* cedars, *horco molle*, *nogal* and myrtles higher up – beneath which several varieties of cane and bamboo compete for sunlight. The tree trunks are covered in moss and lichen, lianas hang in a tangle, epiphytes and orchids flourish and bromeliads, heliconias, parasites and succulents all add to the dank atmosphere. On the tier above the cloudforest, you'll find typically single-species woods of alder, *nogal* or mountain pine at 1500–2400m. Above this begins the pre-*puna* highland meadows (*prados*) of *queñoa* trees, reeds and different *puna* grasses.

More than three hundred varieties of **bird** inhabit the *yungas* forests. Species include the **Toco Toucan** (the official symbol of Parque El Rey); the rare **Black-and-chestnut Eagle** (*águila poma*); the **King Vulture** (*jote real* or *cuervo rey*), with a strikingly patterned head; dusky-legged **Red-faced Guans** (*pava de monte común* and *alisera*); numerous varieties of **hummingbird**; **Mitred** and **Green-cheeked parakeets** (*loro de cara roja* and *chiripepé de cabeza gris* respectively); and the Torrent Duck (*pato de los torrentes*) and Rufous-throated **Dipper** (*mirlo de aqua*).

Like the flora, the **fauna** in the *yungas* changes with altitude. The streams are favourite haunts of southern river **otters** and crab-eating **raccoons** (called *mayuatos* here). Other mammals found close to the water include South America's largest native terrestrial mammal, the **Brazilian tapir** (*tapir*, *anta* or *mborevi*), a Shetland pony-sized creature with a trunk-like stump of a nose. The strange **tree-porcupine** (*coendú*) clambers around the canopy with the help of its tail, as do capuchins and black howler **monkeys**, while the **three-toed sloth** (*perezoso*), which virtually never descends from the trees, depends on its sabre-like claws for locomotion. Felines are represented by **jaguars**, **margays**, **pumas** and **Geoffroy's cats**, but you will be lucky to see anything other than their tracks. This also applies to the most famous regional creature of all: the **taruca**, a stocky native Andean deer. Traditionally hunted by locals, it was brought to the brink of extinction in Argentina and is now one of only three animals protected by the status of Natural Monument. It grazes in small herds just below the tree line in winter, and on high rocky pastures such as those above Calilegua in summer.

The puna

The pre-*puna* and higher **puna** of the Andean Northwest encompass harsh, arid habitats that range from *cardón* cactus valleys to bleak altiplanic vegetation. Everything that grows here must be able to cope with impoverished soils and a huge difference in day- and night-time temperatures. Pre-*puna* habitat usually refers to the sparsely vegetated rocky gullies and highland meadows (*prados*) of the cordillera, and is found at altitudes of 2000 to 3500m. The most distinctive Pre-*puna* plant is the **cardón cactus** (also called *pasakán*), which indigenous folklore holds to be the reincarnated form of ancestors. These grow in a fairly restricted range centred on the Valle Calchaquíes, and take a century to reach their full height of 10m.

The *puna* is found above 3400m, and is characterized by spongy wetlands (*bofedales*) around shallow high-mountain lagoons and sun-scorched flat altiplano pastures. On the higher slopes, you'll find **lichens** and a type of rock-hard cushion-shaped prehistoric moss called **yacreta** that grows incredibly slowly – perhaps a millimetre a year – but lives for hundreds of years. It has been heavily exploited – partly for making medicinal teas, but mainly because it is the only fuel found at these altitudes.

Of the fauna, birds are the most prolific: you can see all three varieties of **flamingo** wading or flying together, especially on the banks of Laguna de los Pozuelos. They are, in decreasing size, the Andean Flamingo (*parina grande*; with yellow legs), Chilean Flamingo (*flamenco austral*; with bluish-grey legs) and Puna or James' Flamingo (*parina chica*; with red legs). The Lesser Rhea (*ñandú petizo*, *choique* or *suri*), a flightless bird, is shy and will sprint away from you. Binoculars can also be trained on **Giant Coots** (*gallareta gigante*) and its rare relative, the **Horned Coot** (*gallareta cornuda*), **Andean Avocets**, **Puna Plovers** (*chorlito puñeno*), **Andean Geese** (*guayata*), **Andean Lapwings** (*tero serrano*), and all kinds of grebes, teals and other ducks. The most common bird you'll hear is the **Grey-breasted Seedsnipe**, but listen, too, for the entrancing whistle of the wading **Tawny-throated Dotterel**.

The animals most people associate with the Andean *puna* are the four species of South American camelids, especially the **llama**, a domesticated species. The local people use llamas as beasts of burden, as well as for meat and wool. The other domesticated camelid is the slightly smaller **alpaca**, which varies in colour from white to black. Alpacas produce finer wool, and one thick fleece, harvested every two years, may weigh as much as 5kg. You're only likely to see them in the Antofagasta de la Sierra area.

The two other South American camelids are both wild. The short-haired antelope-like **guanaco** inhabits a wide area, from the northwest *puna* to the mountains and steppe of Tierra del Fuego. Listen for their eerie, rasping call. The guanaco population is still relatively healthy, although it is hunted for its meat and skin. The guanaco's diminutive cousin, the **vicuña**, is the most graceful, shy and – despite its appearance – hardy of the four camelids, capable of living at the most extreme altitudes. It's usually found between 3500 and 4600m, as far south as northern San Juan Province, although the biggest flocks are in Catamarca Province. Like rodents, they have incisors that continually grow, enabling them to munch on spiny altiplano vegetation. They faced extinction after thousands were shot for their pelts in the 1950s and 1960s, but protection measures have helped ensure that their numbers have risen to safe levels. This has allowed a carefully monitored experiment in Jujuy's Valle Calchaquíes, whereby their valuable fur (the second finest natural fibre in the world after silk) is exploited on a controlled, sustainable commercial level.

Other mammals spotted in the *puna* include the nearly extinct **royal chinchilla** and several varieties of armadillo. Mountain **vizcachas**, looking like large rabbits with curly, long tails, can often be seen nodding off in the sun near watering-places. You're unlikely to see the **puma**, silently prowling around the region.

Patagonian steppe

Typified by brush scrub and wiry grassland, the Patagonian steppe (*estepa*) covers the greatest extent of any Argentine ecosystem. This vast expanse of semi-desert lies south of the pampas, east of the Andean cordillera and as far south as Tierra del Fuego. Vegetation is stunted by gravelly soils, high winds and lack of water, except along rivers, where you find marshlands (*mallines*) and startlingly green willows (*sauces*). Just about the only trees, apart from the willows, are non-native Lombardy poplars, planted to shelter estancias. The habitat itself can be broadly grouped into **brush steppe**, which frequently forms part of the transitional zone between more barren lands to the east and cordillera forests; and **grass steppe**, typified by yellowy-brown *coirón* grass.

Much of the scrubby brush is composed of monochrome *mata negra*, but in places you'll come across the resinous, perfumed *mata verde*, or the ash-grey *mata guanaco*, which blooms with dazzling orange flowers. You'll also see spiky **calafate** bushes, and the *duraznillo*, which has dark green, tapered leaves. One of the largest bushes is the **molle**, covered with thorns and parasitic galls. *Molle* sap was once utilized by indigenous peoples to attach arrowheads and scrapers to wooden shafts, but nowadays the most common use for this bush is as firewood for an *asado*. Smaller shrubs include the silver-grey *senecio miser*; spiky *neneo* plants; and the *lengua de fuego*, a grey shrub with red flowers. In moister areas, you'll find the *colapiche*, whose name ("armadillo's tail") comes from the appearance of its smooth, leafless fronds.

Your best chance of sighting some of the steppe's key species is in places such as Chubut's Peninsula Valdés and Punta Tombo. **Guanacos** abound here. Look out too for the **mara** (Patagonian hare), the largest of Argentina's endemic mammals. This long-legged rodent, the size of a small dog, is becoming ever more rare. The **zorro gris** (grey fox) is regularly found around national park gates, waiting for scraps thrown by tourists. The only time you're likely to come across its larger, more elusive cousin, the **zorro colorado** (red fox), is on a barbed-wire fence – it having bitten something altogether less savoury, by way of poisoned bait or a bullet. Grey foxes regularly suffer the same fate, but are rather more astute at distinguishing friends. *Pichi* and *peludo* **armadillos** are often seen scampering across the plains. Even more regularly, they are spotted at the side of the road, forming the diet of a natty **Southern Crested Caracara** (*carancho*) or a dusty-brown **Chimango Caracara** (*chimango*), both scavenging birds.

Another characteristic bird of prey is the Black-chested Buzzard-Eagle (*águila mora*), a powerful flier with broad wings and splendid plumage. The classic bird of the steppe, though, is the Lesser or Darwin's Rhea (*ñandú petiso* or *choique*). These ashy-grey birds lay their eggs in communal clutches, and in spring you'll see them with their broods of young.

The Patagonian **Sierra Finch** (*fríngilo patagónico*) is an attractive yellow and slate-grey bird often found near humans, as is the **Rufous-collared Sparrow** (*chingolo*). On lagoons and lakes, you'll find the **Black-necked Swan** (*cisne de cuello negro*). Also look out for **Chilean Flamingoes**; the beautiful, endangered **Hooded Grebe** (*macá tobiano*), discovered in 1974 and endemic to Santa Cruz; the **Great Grebe** (*huala*); all four types of *chorlito* seedsnipes; **Upland Geese** (*cauquén* or *avutarda*), which migrate as far north as southern Buenos Aires Province; **Buff-necked Ibises** (*bandurrias*), who amble around in small bands, honking, as they probe wetland pastures with their curved bills; and the **Southern Lapwing** (*tero*), a bird that mates for life and whose plaintive cries and insistent warning shrieks will be familiar to trekkers.

Patagonian cordillera forests

The eastern slopes of the Patagonian cordillera are cloaked, for most of their length, in forests of **Nothofagus southern beech**. Two species run from northern Neuquén to Tierra del Fuego: the **lenga** (upland beech); and the **ñire** (lowland or antarctic beech). At lower altitudes, the *lenga* is taller, but closer to the tree line the two intermingle as dwarf shrubs. The *lenga*, capable of flourishing on incredibly thin topsoils, tends to form the tree line. The *ñire*, which rarely grows more than 15m tall, tends to be found near water; and though in autumn both species turn a variety of hues, the *ñire* is more vibrant. Compare leaves to distinguish between the two species: *lenga* leaves are veiny, with each band between veins having a uniform double lobe; *ñire* leaves have fewer veins, and each band has a less regular edge with several lobes. Associated with *lenga* and *ñire* are three intriguing plant species: false mistletoe (*farolito chino*), a semi-parasitic plant; verdigris-coloured **lichen beards** (*barba del indio* or *toalla del indio*); and **llao llao** tree fungus, also called *pan de indio* ("Indian's bread"). The *llao llao* produces brain-like knots on trunks and branches that are beloved of local artisans. *Lenga* and *ñire* are the only species that occur at all latitudes where you can find Patagonian Andean forest.

The next most prominent tree species are two related evergreen beeches, the **coihue** and the **guindo** (or *coihue de Magallanes*), found mainly in Tierra del Fuego. Both have fairly smooth bark and laurel-green leaves that are small, shiny and tough, with a rounded shape and serrated edge. Both trees grow only in damp zones near lakes or, in the case of Tierra del Fuego, by the shores of the Beagle Channel.

One of Argentina's most remarkable trees, the **araucaria monkey puzzle**, grows in central Neuquén on volcanic soils, in widely spaced pure forests or, more normally, mixed with species of *Nothofagus*. The forests of Parque Nacional Lanín contain two species of broad-leafed *Nothofagus* not found elsewhere: the **roble pellín** (named for its oak-like leaves), and the **raulí** (with more oval leaves). Also confined to the area is the **radal**, a shrubby tree with greyish wood that is valued by craftsmen for its speckled vein.

The most diverse type of forest in the region is the rare **Valdivian temperate rainforest** (*selva Valdiviana*), found in patches of the central Patagonian Andes from Lanín to Los Alerces, usually around low passes where rainfall is heaviest. It requires extremely high precipitation (3000–4000mm annually), and it is marked out from the rest of the forest by several factors: different layers of canopy, thick roots breaking the surface of the soil and both epiphytes and lianas. Two other tree species found only in the central Patagonian Lake District are the **arrayán** myrtle, always next to water; and the mighty **alerce**, or Patagonian cypress, which resembles a Californian redwood and is one of the world's oldest and grandest species.

The understorey of the forests is dominated in most places by dense thickets of a bamboo-like plant, **caña colihue**, a mixed Spanish and Mapudungun term that means "tree of the place of water". The most stunning shrub, if you catch it in bloom (late spring or autumn), is the **notro firebush** (or *ciruelillo*). Another native to these parts, the **fuchsia**, has conquered the world as a garden favourite. Growing in Tierra del Fuego, and looking rather like a glossy rhododendron, the evergreen **canelo** takes its name from the fleeting cinnamon taste of its bark. In English it is known as Winter's bark, after a Captain Winter of Francis Drake's expedition, who discovered that its leaves helped treat scurvy. The native **wild holly** (*muérdago silvestre*) has glossy, dark-green leaves and, in spring, clusters of yellow-orange blooms. Of forest flowers, two of the most brightly coloured are the **amancay**, a golden-orange lily, and the yellow **lady's slipper** (*zapatilla de la Virgen*), whose blooms bob on delicate stems in spring. **Lupins** (*lupinos*), introduced by the British, have spread through parks like Lanín, and, though considered a plague, they do put on a glorious show from late December to January.

As you move away from the mountains towards the drier steppe, you'll often find a zone of **transitional woodland**. In northern and central Patagonia, it's normally composed of species like the mountain **cypress** (*ciprés de la cordillera*), or the *retamo*, which has pale-violet blooms. Found on mountain-valley floors or just above the tree line are peaty **sphagnum moors** (*turbales*) and bogs (*mallines*). Here you'll see *chaura* prickly heath, whose waxy, pinky-red berries you can eat. **Creeping diddle dee** (*murtilla*) is a common upland plant. On rocky soils, look out for the blue perezia (*perezia azul*), whose mauve flowers have a double rosette of spatula-shaped petals.

Many of the birds that inhabit the steppe are also found in the cordillera. Typical woodland species include the world's most southerly parrot, the **Austral Parakeet** (*cachaña* or *cotorra*); the **Green-backed Firecrown** (*picaflor rubí*); the hyperactive **Thorn-tailed Rayadito**; two secretive ground birds, the **Chucao Tapaculo** and **Chestnut-throated Huet-Huet**, that are both more often heard than seen; and two birds that allow you to get surprisingly close – the **Magellanic Woodpecker** (*carpintero negro gigante*), and the **Austral Pygmy Owl** (*caburé*). Finally, if any bird has a claim to symbolizing South America, it's the **Andean Condor**. With eyesight eight times better than human's, and the longest wingspan of any bird of prey (reaching up to 3.10m), it's the undisputed lord of the skies from Venezuela to Tierra del Fuego. Until fairly recently, this imperious bird was poisoned and shot. It's now protected in Argentina, with a stable population.

The principal predator of cordillera mammals is the **puma**. Commonly known as *león* (lion) by country-dwellers, this cat is no pussy. Though chances are that a puma will sight you and make itself scarce well before you sight it, there are extremely infrequent cases of attacks on humans. In the highly unlikely event of being faced with an aggressive puma, do not run, but make yourself appear as big as possible, and, facing it at all times, back off slowly, shouting loudly. The law confers protection on pumas, but even conservationists recognize that this is hard to enforce outside national parks: on private land they are seen as fair game. A smaller feline, the **Geoffroy's cat** (*gato montés*), tends to run before you've even seen it.

Perhaps the most endangered creature is the **huemul**, a thick-set native deer, of which fewer than two thousand remain. It is a relative of the *taruca* of the northwestern Andes, and has likewise been named a Natural Monument. Almost as endangered is the **pudú**, the world's smallest deer, measuring 40cm at the shoulder. It has small, single-pointed horns, and is difficult to spot, as it inhabits the dense undergrowth of the central cordillera forests. Also hard to spot are the **opossum** (*comadreja común*) and another interesting marsupial, the **monito de monte**, both being localized and nocturnal; your best chance of seeing one is in Nahuel Huapi or the southern part of Lanín. The endangered *culebra valdiviana* is a poisonous (but not mortally) woodland **snake** that's confined pretty much to this range, too.

The European **red deer** (*ciervo colorado*) and **wild boar** (*jabalí*) have reached plague proportions in some parts of the central Lake District. The **beaver** (*castor*), introduced to Tierra del Fuego in an attempt to start a fur-farming industry, has had devastating effects on the environment. The rodents have chewed their way through valuable woodland and blocked streams with dams, flooding mountain valleys, flatlands and pasture. Year-round, no-limits hunting has been permitted to combat this public enemy, but some now believe that hunting can actually increase populations, since they simply give birth to larger broods. Other non-native species have had deleterious effects too: **muskrats** (*ratas almizcleras*), introduced at the same time as the beaver; **rabbits** (*conejos*) crossed into the northern plains from Chile during the 1930s, invading the southern region after escaping from a fur farm in Ushuaia in the 1950s; and the **mink** (*visón*), the principal threat to the southern river otter, or *hullin*.

The Atlantic seaboard

Argentina has 4725km of **Atlantic coastline**, comprising three main types of habitat. From the mouth of the estuary of the Río de la Plata to just beyond the southern limit of Buenos Aires Province, the shoreline is mainly flat, fringed by dunes, sandy beaches and pampas grass. South of Viedma begin endless stretches of Patagonian cliffs (*barrancas*), such as those fronting Península Valdés, broken in places by gulfs and estuaries, but almost entirely devoid of vegetation. The third section of coastline is that found south of Tierra del Fuego's Río Grande, where you see, in succession, patches of woodland, bleak moorland tundra and the rich southern beech forests of the Beagle Channel, exemplified by those in Parque Nacional Tierra del Fuego.

Several coastal areas, notably those of the Bahía San Antonio, Bahía San Sebastián and the Estuario del Río Gallegos, have been integrated into the Western Hemisphere Shorebird Reserve Network, designed to protect migrant waders across the Americas. Birds like the **Hudsonian Godwit** (*becasa de mar*) and the **Red Knot** (*playero rojizo*) migrate from Alaska as far as Tierra del Fuego – over 17,000km. Other coastal species are **Magellanic Penguins** (*pingüino magallánico*), whose major continental breeding colony is at Punta Tombo, but which are also found at Valdés, Puerto Deseado, San Julián and Cabo Vírgenes; **Chilean flamingoes**; and the South American **Tern** (*gaviotín sudamericano*). At Deseado, you can see all four different types of **cormorant** (*cormorán*) including the Blue-eyed (*imperial*) and the uncommon Red-legged Cormorant (*gris*). Look out for the dove-like **Snowy Sheathbill** (*paloma antártica*); and several types of duck, including the **Crested Duck** (*pato juarjual* or *crestón*) and the flightless **Steamer Duck** (*quetro no volador* or *alacush*), which uses its wings in paddle-steaming fashion to hurry from danger. On the open sea, especially in the far south, you stand a good chance of seeing **Black-browed Albatrosses**, and **Giant Petrels**, both skilful fliers.

Península Valdés is the main destination for marine fauna. Its twin bays, Golfo Nuevo and Golfo San José (Latin America's first marine park), are where as much as a quarter of the world's population of **southern right whales** (*ballena franca austral*) breed annually. The peninsula also hosts a 40,000-strong and growing colony of **southern elephant seals** (*elefante marino*). Other sightings might include **sea lions** (*lobos del mar*), found in colonies along the whole Atlantic coast, and possibly even a **killer whale** (*orca*). Further down the coast at Cabo Blanco, you can see the endangered **fur seal** (*lobo de dos pelos*); while Puerto Deseado and San Julián are fine places to catch the energetic, piebald **Commerson's dolphins** (*toninas overas*). Sea trips on the Beagle Channel offer a slim chance of seeing **Peale's dolphins** or a **minke whale**, or even perhaps an endangered **marine otter** (*nutria marina* or *chungungo*).

Music

With the obvious exception of **tango**, Argentina's music has a fairly low international profile. True to its image as the continent's odd man out, the country has a tradition that doesn't quite fit the popular concept of "Latin American" music: there is little of the exhilarating tropical rhythms of, say, Brazil, nor is there much of the pan-pipe sound associated with Andean countries. Within Latin America, however, Argentina is famed for its rock music, known simply as **rock nacional** – a term which embraces an eclectic bunch of groups and musicians, from the heavy rock of Pappo, to the sweet poppy rock of Fito Páez, to ska- and punk-influenced Los Fabulosos Cadillacs. Folk music, known as **folklore** in Argentina, is also popular throughout the country and provides a predominantly rural counterpoint to the essentially urban tango. The genre has also produced two internationally renowned stars; Mercedes Sosa and Atahualpa Yupanqui.

Tango

The great Argentine writer Jorge Luis Borges was a tango enthusiast and something of a historian of the music. "My informants all agree on one fact," he wrote, "the Tango was born in the brothels." Borges' sources were a little presumptuous, perhaps, for no one can exactly pinpoint **tango**'s birthplace, but it certainly had roots in Buenos Aires. Early tango was a definitively urban music: a product of the melting-pot of European immigrants, *criollos*, blacks and natives, drawn together when the city became the country's capital in 1880. Tango was thus forged from a range of musical influences that included Andalucían flamenco, southern Italian melodies, Cuban habanera, African candombé and percussion, European polkas and mazurkas, Spanish contradanse and, closer to home, the *milonga* – the song of the gaucho. In this early form, tango became associated with the bohemian life of bordello brawls and *compadritos* – knife-wielding, womanizing thugs. By 1914 there were over 100,000 more men than women in Buenos Aires, and machismo and violence were part of the culture. Men would dance together in cafés and bars, practising new steps and keeping in shape while waiting for their women, often the *minas* of the bordellos. Their dances tended to have a showy yet predatory quality, often revolving around a possessive relationship between two men and one woman. In these surroundings, the *compadrito* danced the tango into existence.

The original **tango ensembles** were trios of violin, guitar and flute, but around the end of the nineteenth century the **bandoneón**, the tango accordion, arrived from Germany, and the classic tango orchestra was born. The box-shaped button accordion, now inextricably linked with Argentine tango, was invented around 1860 in Germany to play religious music in organless churches. One Heinrich Band reworked an older portable instrument nicknamed the "asthmatic worm", giving his new instrument the name "Band-Union", a combination of his and his company's names. Mispronounced as it travelled the world, it became the *bandoneón*.

In Argentina, an early pioneer of the instrument was **Eduardo Arolas**, remembered as the "Tiger of the Bandoneón". He recognized its immediate affinity with the tango – indeed, he claimed it was an instrument made to play tango, with a deep melancholy feeling that suited immigrants. It is not, however,

△ Tango orchestra, Buenos Aires

an easy instrument to play, demanding a great deal of skill, with its seventy-odd buttons each producing one of two notes depending on whether the bellows are being compressed or expanded.

Vicente Greco (1888–1924) is credited as the first bandleader to standardize the form of a tango group, with his **Orquesta Típica Criolla** of two violins and two *bandoneones*. There were some larger bands but the instrumentation remained virtually unchanged until the 1940s.

First tango in Paris

By the first decade of the twentieth century, the tango was an intrinsic part of the popular culture of Buenos Aires, played on the streets by organ grinders and danced in tenement courtyards. Its association with whorehouses and the low-down Porteño lifestyle, plus its saucy, sometimes obscene and fatalistic lyrics, didn't endear it to the aristocratic families of Buenos Aires, though, and they did their best to protect their children from the new dance, but it was a losing battle.

A number of upper-class playboys, such as poet and writer **Ricardo Güiraldes**, enjoyed mixing with the *compadritos* and emulating their lifestyle – from a debonair distance. It was Güiraldes who, on a European grand tour in 1910, was responsible for bringing the dance to Europe. In 1911 he wrote a poem called *Tango*, in its honour: "... hats tilted over sardonic sneers. The all-absorbing love of a tyrant, jealously guarding his dominion, over women who have surrendered submissively, like obedient beasts...". The following year Güiraldes gave an impromptu performance in a Paris salon to a fashionable audience, for whom tango's risqué sexuality ("the vertical expression of horizontal desire", as one wag dubbed it) was highly attractive. Despite the local archbishop's admonition that Christians should not in good conscience tango, they did, and in large numbers. Tango was thus the first of many Latin dances to conquer Europe. And, once it was embraced in French salons, its credibility at home greatly increased. Back in Argentina, from bordello to ballroom, everyone was soon dancing the tango.

And then came **Rudolph Valentino**. The tango fitted his image to a T. Hollywood wasted no time in capitalizing on the superstar's charisma, the magnetism of the tango and the public's attraction to both. Valentino and Tango! Tango and Valentino! The combination was irresistible to cinema moguls, who added a tango scene to his latest film, *The Four Horsemen of the Apocalypse* (1926). The fact that in the film Valentino was playing a gaucho – and gauchos don't tango – didn't deter them for a moment. Valentino was a special gaucho and this gaucho could tango. And why not? The scene was incredible: Valentino, dressed in a gaucho's wide trousers and leather chaps in the middle of the pampas, with a carnation between his lips and a whip in his hand; his partner, a Spanish señorita, kitted out with headscarf and hair comb plus the strongest pair of heels this side of the Río de la Plata.

Predictably enough, the tango scene was the hit of the film, and, travesty though it was, it meant the dance was now known all over the world. Tango classes and competitions were held in Paris, and tango teas in England, with young devotees togged up as Argentine gauchos. Even the greatest tango singer of all time, **Carlos Gardel**, when he became the darling of Parisian society, and later starred in Hollywood films, was forced to perform dressed as a gaucho. To this day, this image remains many people's primary perception of tango.

Tango's golden age

Back in Argentina, in the 1920s, the tango moved out of the cantinas and bordellos and into cabarets and theatres, entering a classic era under bandleaders like **Roberto Firpo**, **Julio de Caro** and **Francisco Canaro**. With their *orquestas típicas* they took the old line-up of Vicente Greco (two *bandoneones*, two violins, a piano and flute) and substituted a double bass for the flute, thereby adding sonority and depth. This combination continued for the next twenty years, even in the larger ensembles common after the mid-1930s. It was during this period that some of the most famous of all tangos were written, including Uruguayan **Gerardo Hernán Matos Rodríguez**'s *La Comparsita* in 1917.

Early **tango-canciónes** (tango songs) used the language of the ghetto and celebrated the life of ruffians and pimps. **Angel Villoldo** and **Pascual Contursi** introduced the classic lyric of a male perspective, placing the blame for heartache firmly on the shoulders of a fickle woman, with Contursi putting lyrics to Samuel Castriota's tune *Lita*: "Woman who left me, in the prime of my life, wounding my soul, and driving thorns into my heart... Nothing can console me now, so I am drowning my sorrows, to try to forget your love...". Typical of tango songs, male behaviour itself was beyond reproach, with the man a victim of women's capriciousness.

In its **dance**, tango consolidated a contradictory mix of earthy sensuality and middle-class kitsch. It depended on an almost violent and dangerous friction of bodies, which collided often in a passion that seemed controlled by the dance itself. A glittering respectability hid darker undercurrents in the obvious macho domination of the male over the female in a series of intricate steps and in the close embraces, which were highly suggestive of the sexual act. The cut and thrust of intricate and interlacing fast leg movements between a couple imitated the movement of blades in a knife fight.

Carlos Gardel

Carlos Gardel (1887–1935) was – and still is – a legend in Argentina. He was a huge influence in spreading the popularity of tango round the world, and came to be seen as a symbol of the fulfilment of the dreams of poor Porteño workers.

In Argentina, it was Gardel above all who transformed tango from an essentially low-down dance form to a song style popular among widely differing social classes. He actually started out as a variety act singing traditional folk and country music, and although he enjoyed great success with this it was his recording of Contursi's *Mi noche triste* (My sorrowful night) in 1917 that was to change the course of his future. Everything about Gardel – his suavity, his arrogance and his natural machismo – spelt tango. The advent of radio, recording and film all helped his career, but nothing helped him more than his own voice – a voice that was born to sing tango and which became the model for all future singers of the genre.

His arrival on the scene coincided with the first period of tango's golden age and the development of *tango-canción* in the 1920s and 1930s. During his life, Gardel recorded some nine hundred songs and starred in numerous films, notably *The Tango on Broadway* in 1934. He was tragically killed in an aircrash in Colombia at the height of his fame, and his legendary status was confirmed. His image is still everywhere in Buenos Aires, on plaques and huge murals, and in record-store windows, while admirers pay homage to his life-sized, bronze statue in Chacarita cemetery (see p.154).

After Gardel, the split between the **evolutionists**, who wanted to develop new forms of tango, and the **traditionalists**, who thought it was fine as it was, became more pronounced. Bands, as elsewhere in the world during this period, became larger, in the mode of small orchestras, and a mass following for tango was enjoyed through dance halls, radio and recordings until the end of the golden age around 1950.

Tango politics

As an expression of the working classes, the progression of the tango has inevitably been linked with social and political developments in Argentina. The music declined a little in the 1930s as the army took power and suppressed what was seen as a potentially subversive force. Even so, the figure of **Juan D'Arienzo**, violinist and bandleader, looms large from the 1930s on. With a sharp, staccato rhythm, and prominent piano, his orchestra was the flavour of those years. His recording of *La Comparsita* at the end of 1937 is considered one of the greatest of all time.

Tango fortunes revived again in the 1940s when certain political freedoms returned, and the music enjoyed a second golden age with the rise of Perón and his emphasis on nationalism and popular culture. This was the era of a new generation of bandleaders. Alongside D'Arienzo at the top were **Osvaldo Pugliese**, **Hector Varela** and the innovative **Aníbal Troilo**. Of all *bandoneón* players, it was Troilo who expressed most vividly, powerfully and tenderly the nostalgic sound of the instrument. When he died in 1975 half a million people followed his funeral procession.

By the late 1940s Buenos Aires was a city of five or six million, and each barrio boasted ten or fifteen amateur tango orchestras, while the established orchestras played in the cabarets and nightclubs in the city centre. Sometime in this era, however, tango began to move away from working class and into middle class and intellectual milieus. It became a sort of collective reminiscence of a world that no longer existed – essentially nostalgia. As a popular lyric, *Tango de otros tiempos* (Tango of Other Times), put it:

Tango, you were the king
In one word, a friend
Blossoming from the bandoneón music of Arolas

Tango, the rot set in
When you became sophisticated
And with your airs and graces
You quit the suburbs where you were born
Tango, it saddens me to see
How you've deserted the mean dirt-streets
For a carpeted drawing-room
In my soul I carry a small piece
Of that happy past!
But the good old times are over
In Paris you've become Frenchified
And today, thinking of what's happened
A tear mars your song.

In the 1950s, with the end of Peronism and the coming of rock 'n' roll, tango slipped into the shadows once again.

Astor Piazzolla and tango nuevo

Astor Piazzolla (see box, p.828) dominates the recent history of tango, much as Carlos Gardel was the key figure of its classic era. From 1937, Piazzolla played second *bandoneón* in the orchestra of Aníbal Troilo, where he developed his feel for arrangements. (The first *bandoneón* takes the melody, and the second *bandoneón* the harmony.)

Troilo left Piazzolla his *bandoneón* when he died, and Piazzolla went on to ensure that tango would never be the same again. Piazzolla's idea was that tango could be a serious music to listen to, not just for dancing, and for many of the old guard this was a step too far. As he explained: "Musicians hated me. I was taking the old tango away from them. The old tango, the one they loved, was dying. And they hated me, they threatened my life hundreds of times. They waited for me outside my house, two or three of them, and gave me a good beating. They even put a gun at my head once. I was in a radio station doing an interview, and all of a sudden the door opens and in comes this tango singer with a gun. That's how it was." In the 1970s, Piazzolla was out of favour with Argentina's military regime and he and his family moved to Paris, returning to Argentina only after the fall of the junta. His influence, however, had spread, and his experiments – and international success – opened the way for other radical transformations.

Chief among these, in 1970s Buenos Aires, was the fusion of **tango-rockero** – tango rock. This replaced the flexible combination of *bandoneón*, bass and no drums, as favoured by Piazzolla, with a rock-style rhythm section, electric guitars and synthesizers. It was pioneered by **Litto Nebbia**, whose album, *Homage to Gardél and Le Péra*, is one of the most successful products of this fusion, retaining the melancholy of the traditional form in a rock format. Tango moved across to jazz, too, through groups such as the trio **Siglo XX**, while old guard figures like **Roberto "Polaco" Goyeneche** and **Osvaldo Pugliese** kept traditional tango alive.

These days in Argentina, the tango scene is a pretty broad one, with rock and jazz elements, along with the more traditional sound of acoustic groups. There is no shortage of good *tangueros* and they know each other well and jam together often. Big tango orchestras, however, are a thing of the past, and tango bands have returned to their roots, to an intimate era of trios, quartets and quintets – a sextet is serious business. Two of the best sextets, the **Sexteto Mayor** and **Sexteto Berlingieri**, joined together in the 1980s to play for the show *Tango Argentino*, and subsequent shows which revived an interest in tango

Astor Piazzolla

Astor Piazzolla (1921–92) brought the tango a long way from when it was first danced in Buenos Aires a century ago by two pimps on a street corner. In his hands this backstreet dance acquired a modernist "art music" gloss.

Born in Mar de Plata and raised in New York, Piazzolla's controversial innovations came from his classical music studies in Paris with **Nadia Boulanger**, who thought his classical compositions lacked feeling – but upon hearing his tango *Triunfal* apparently said, "Don't ever abandon this. This is your music. This is Piazzolla."

Piazzolla returned to Mar de Plata in 1937, moving to Buenos Aires two years later, where he joined **Aníbal Troilo's orchestra** as *bandoneonista* and arranger. In 1946 he formed his own group, and in 1960 his influential **Quinteto Nuevo Tango**. With this group, he experimented audaciously, turning tango inside out, introducing unexpected chords, chromatic harmony, differently emphasized rhythms and a sense of dissonance. Traditional tango captures the dislocation of the immigrant, the disillusionment with the dream of a new life, transmuting these raw emotions onto a personal plane of betrayal and triangular relationships. Piazzolla's genius comes from the fact that, within the many layers and changing moods and pace of his pieces, he never betrays this essence of tango – its sense of fate, its core of hopeless misery, its desperate sense of loss.

Piazzolla translated the philosophy expounded by tango poets like Enrique Santos Discépolo – who, in *El cambalache* (The Junkshop) concludes that the twentieth-century world is an insolent display of blatant wickedness – onto the musical plane. A Piazzolla piece can change from the personal to the epic so that a cry from a violin or cello becomes a wailing city siren as if following a shift from personal misery to a larger, more menacing urban canvas. In Piazzolla's tangos, passion and sensuality still walk side by side with sadness, but emotions, often drawn out to a level of almost unbearable intensity, are suddenly subsumed in a disquieting sense of inevitability. If you close your eyes while listening to his work, you can exploit the filmic dimension of the music: create your own movie, walk Buenos Aires alone at Zero Hour, visit clubs and bars, pass through empty streets shadowed by the ghosts of a turbulent history. Piazzolla always said that he composed for the new generations of Porteños, offering a music that allowed them to live an often dark and difficult present while absorbing their past.

Piazzolla's own ensembles turned tango into concert music. "For me," he said, "tango was always for the ear rather than the feet." This process escalated in the 1960s, when he started to work with poet **Horacio Ferrer**. Their first major work was a little opera called *María de Buenos Aires* (1967) but it was the seminal *Balada para un loco* (Ballad for a madman) which pushed the borders of tango lyrics far from those of thwarted romance and broken dreams of traditional tango songs. Surreal and witty, the ballad's lyrics reveal the tortured mental state and condition of a half-dancing, half-flying bowler-hatted apparition on the streets of Buenos Aires. While it appalled traditional *tangueros*, the song inspired new aficionados at home and abroad, particularly among musicians.

Elected "Distinguished Citizen of Buenos Aires" in 1985, Piazzolla's commitment to tango was unequivocal. A prolific composer of over 750 works, including concertos, theatre and film scores, he created some atmospheric "classical" pieces, including a 1979 concerto for *bandoneón* and orchestra, which combines the flavour of tango with a homage to Bach, and, in 1989, "Five Tango Sensations", a series of moody pieces for *bandoneón* and string quartet. These are thrilling pieces, as indeed are all of his last 1980s concert performances, released posthumously on CD.

across Europe and the US, with each group going its own way in Buenos Aires. The Sexteto Mayor, founded in 1973 and starring the virtuoso *bandoneonistas* **José Libertella** and **Luís Stazo**, is one of the best tango ensembles in Argentina today.

In a more modern idiom, singers like **Susana Rinaldi** and **Adriana Varela**, working with Litto Nebbia, are successfully renovating and re-creating tango, both at home and abroad, Varela particularly in Spain. They are names to look out for along with *bandoneonistas* **Osvaldo Piro**, **Carlos Buono** and **Walter Ríos** (Ríos has also worked with folk singer Mercedes Sosa); violinist **Antonio Agri** who worked with Piazzolla and more recently with Paco de Lucía; *bandoneonista*, arranger and film-score composer **Néstor Marconi**; singer **José Angel Trelles**; pianist and composer **Gustavo Fedel**; and **Grupo Volpe Tango Contemporáneo**, led by Antonio Volpe.

Latterly, tango is enjoying an upsurge of popularity in Argentina and other parts of the world, with young bohemians such as Buenos Aires' Parakultural outfit once again reinventing tango for a new generation.

Discography

Tango can increasingly be found in the world-music section of major record stores throughout the globe, most commonly in collections of variable quality aimed at dancers, closely followed by the works of Carlos Gardel and Astor Piazzolla. A worldwide mail-order service is offered by the Buenos Aires' tango store Zivals, accessed through their website Ⓦwww.tangostore.com.

The following recordings offer a good introduction to tango's major stars, both old and new.

The Rough Guide to Tango and **The Rough Guide to Tango Nuevo** With tracks from twenty of the greatest tango musicians – from Gardel and Piazzolla to more contemporary artists – *The Rough Guide to Tango* is one of the best introductions to the genre, while the *Tango Nuevo* disc features nineteen tracks from contemporary figures such as Adriana Varela and Juan Carlos Caceres.

Carlos Gardel *20 Grandes Éxitos*. One of the best of the innumerable collections of Gardel's finest recordings, packed with his unmistakable renderings of iconic classics such as *El día me quieras*, *Volver*, *Caminito* and *Cuesta Abajo*.

Roberto Goyeneche *Maestros del Tango*. A superb compilation of hits from one of tango's most beloved characters; includes his classic interpretations of *Malena*, the seductive *Naranjo en Flor* and the wonderful *Sur*, an elegy to the south of Buenos Aires, tango's true home.

Tita Merello *La Merello*. Classic compilation by one of tango's early and most famous female stars, including her own composition, the bittersweet *Se dice de mí*.

Astor Piazzolla *Noches del Regina*. The master of modern tango interprets classics, such as the polemical *Cambalache* and the inimitable *Balada para un loco*. For his most characteristic, avant-garde compositions, check out *Adios Nonino,* titled after perhaps his most famous composition, or *A Rough Guide to Astor Piazzolla*, a compilation of his best tracks.

Osvaldo Pugliese *Tangos Famosos*. Classic recordings by the maestro of the "Generación del 40", displaying his towering talent as both composer and pianist.

Susana Rinaldi *Cantando*. One of tango's major contemporary female stars, noted for her powerful voice – occasionally a little strident but rich and expressive at its best. Includes classics such as *Cafetín de Buenos Aires*, *Madame Ivonne* and the gorgeous *María* by Cátulo Castillo.

Edmundo Rivero *En Lunfardo*. The charismatic singer interprets classic tangos such as *El Chamuyo* and

Atentí, Pebeta, infused with Buenos Aires' street slang, *lunfardo*.

Sexteto Mayor *Trottoirs de Buenos Aires.* This largely instrumental album of classic tangos by Argentina's premier tango ensemble is thrilling, with Adriana Varela unleashing her husky voice on four songs. Unashamedly emotional and utterly convincing.

Julio Sosa *El Varón del Tango.* The self-styled "macho" of tango and last of the "old-style" singers interprets classics such as *Sus ojos se cerraron* and the world-famous *La Comparsita*. Look out too for his version of *La Casita de mis viejos* for an insight into tango's almost mawkish attachment to the parental home – and in particular the mother.

Aníbal Troilo *Obra Completa.* Known affectionately as "pichuco", *bandoneonista* Aníbal Troilo led one of Argentina's most successful tango orchestras and composed many classics such as *Sur* and *Barrio de Tango*. His trademark *Che, bandoneón*, with lyrics by one of tango's great poets, Homero Manzi, is a sweet, sad elegy to the *bandoneón* itself.

Adriana Varela *Maquillaje.* One of tango's most successful contemporary singers, offering a very distinctive, throaty interpretation of classic tangos and compositions by *rock nacional* superstars Fito Páez and Litto Nebbia.

Text courtesy of Jan Fairley, with a discography by Lucy Phillips

Rock nacional

Listened to passionately throughout the country, Argentina's homegrown rock music – known simply as **rock nacional** – has something for just about everyone among its numerous charismatic performers.

Rock nacional began to emerge in the 1960s with groups such as **Almendra**, one of whose members, **Luis Alberto Spinetta**, went on to a solo career and is still one of Argentina's most successful and original musicians, and **Los Gatos**, who in 1967 had a massive hit with the eloquent *La Balsa* and two of whose members – Litto Nebbia and Pappo – also went on to solo careers. From a sociological point of view, though, the significance of *rock nacional* really began to emerge under the military dictatorship of 1976–83. At the very beginning of the dictatorship, there was an upsurge in rock concerts, during which musicians such as **Charly García**, frontman of the hugely popular **Serú Girán** and now a soloist, provided a subtle form of resistance with songs such as *No te dejes desanimar* (Don't be discouraged), which helped provoke a collective sense of opposition amongst fans. It wasn't long, however, before the military rulers clamped down on what it saw as the subversive atmosphere generated at such concerts. In a famous 1976 speech, Admiral Massera referred to "suspect youths", whose immersion in the "secret society" of clothes, music and drugs associated with rock music made them potential guerrilla material. The clampdown began in 1977–78, with police repression and government-issued recommendations that stadium owners should not let their premises be used for rock concerts. Attempts to move the rock scene to smaller venues were equally repressed, and by the end of the 1970s many bands had split up or gone into exile.

By 1980, cracks had begun to appear in the regime: a growing recession saw powerful economic groups withdrawing their support, while the military leaders themselves were riven by internal conflict, and a subtle freeing-up of the public sphere began. The slow resurgence of rock concerts followed. In

December 1980, a concert by Serú Girán attracted 60,000 fans to La Rural in Palermo: led by Charly García, the fans began to shout, in full view of the television cameras "no se banca más" (We won't put up with it anymore).

Without abandoning their previous repressive measures, the military regime, under the leadership of General Viola, began to employ different tactics to deal with rock's subversive tendencies, producing its own, non-threatening rock magazine, and inaugurating a "musical train" which travelled around the country with some of Argentina's most famous rock musicians on board. Under Galtieri, however, there was a return to a more direct, authoritarian approach – though by then it was proving increasingly difficult to silence the opposition to the military. By 1982, the rock movement was a loudly cynical voice, creating massively popular songs such as **Fito Páez**'s self-explanatory *Tiempos difíciles* (Difficult Times), Charly García's *Dinosaurios*, whose title is a clear reference to the military rulers and *Maribel* by Argentina's finest rock lyricist, Spinetta, dedicated to the Madres de Plaza de Mayo. When the Malvinas/Falkland Islands conflict broke out, **León Gieco**'s *Sólo le pido a Dios* expressed antiwar sentiment and suspicion of the government's motives in lines such as "I only ask of God/ not to be indifferent to war/ it's a giant monster and it stamps hard/ on the poor innocence of the people". The song has become a modern popular classic, recorded by several artists since and sung with gusto at football games.

After the dictatorship ended, rock returned to a more apolitical role, typified by the lighthearted approach of 1984's most popular group, **Los Abuelos de la Nada**. One of the founding members of Los Abuelos, **Pappo**, went on to a solo career in heavy rock, appealing to a predominantly working-class section of society who felt that their lot had improved little with democracy; Pappo's music seemed to sum up their frustrations. One of the most popular groups of the 1980s was **Sumo**, fronted by charismatic **Luca Prodan**, an Italian raised in the UK who had come to Argentina in an attempt to shake off his heroin addiction (an uncharacteristically sensitive recording of Sumo's is a version of the Velvet Underground's *Heroin*). Sumo made sometimes surreal, noisy, reggae-influenced tracks, expressing distaste for the frivolous attitudes of Buenos Aires' upper-middle-class youth on tracks such as *Rubia tarada* (Stupid Blonde); a minority of their tracks are in English, such as the melancholic *Just Like London*. Luca Prodan ultimately died of a heroin overdose in 1987, but is still idolized by Argentine rock fans.

Like Sumo, the strangely named and massively popular **Patricio Rey y sus Redonditos de Ricota** (literally: Patricio Rey and the little balls of ricotta; they're abbreviated to Los Redondos) made noise with enigmatic tracks such as *Aquella vaca solitaria cubana* (That solitary Cuban cow), often touching on the dissatisfactions felt by many young Argentines in the aftermath of the dictatorship. Another success story of the 1980s and 1990s – albeit in a very different vein – was **Fito Páez**, whose 1992 album *El Amor después del amor*, with its sweet melodic tunes – one of them inspired by the film *Thelma and Louise* – sold millions throughout Latin America. Páez also made an anthemic recording *Dale alegría a mi corazón* (Bring happiness to my heart), inspired by Diego Maradona. One of Argentina's most original bands also emerged in the 1980s – **Los Fabulosos Cadillacs**, with their diverse and often frenetic fusion of rock, ska, dub, punk and rap. An irreverent and ironic sense of humour often underlies their politicized lyrics, all belted out by their charismatic, astringently voiced lead singer, Vincentico, and backed up with a tight horn section and driving Latin percussion. Their classic album is *El León* (1992), on which you'll find their most famous anthem, *Matador*, a savage indictment of the military dictatorship.

Rock nacional's most enduring figures are still Charly García – whose wild exploits fill the pages of gossip magazines – and other old timers such as

Fito Paéz, Los Fabulosos Cadillacs, León Gieco and Luis Alberto Spinetta. Newcomers to the scene – who regularly play in the country – include the internationally popular "sonic rock" band **Babasónicos**, experimental **Catupechu Machu**, punky **Attaque 77**, **Las Pelotas**, incorporating former Sumo members, and the tropical rock sound of **Bersuit Vergarabat**.

Chamamé, cuarteto and folklore

Tango aside, Argentine music is mostly rooted in the rural dance traditions of the countryside, an amalgam of Spanish and immigrant Central European styles with indigenous music. Many of these dances – *rancheras*, *milongas*, *chacareras* and more – are shared with the neighbouring countries of Chile, Peru and Bolivia, while others like **chamamé** are particularly Argentine. This short article focuses on the music of chamamé and **cuarteto**, and on rural folk music (**folklore**). Argentina, however, also has Amerindian roots, a music explored from the 1930s on by Atahualpa Yupanqui, which grew new shoots in the politicized *nueva canción* (new song) movement.

Chamamé

Chamamé is probably Argentina's most popular roots music. It has its origins in the rural culture of Corrientes – an Amerindian area which attracted nineteenth-century settlers from Czechoslovakia, Poland, Austria and Germany. These immigrants brought with them Middle European waltzes, mazurkas and polkas, which over time merged with music from the local Guaraní Amerindian traditions, and African rhythms from the music of the region's slaves. Thus emerged chamamé, a music of poor rural mestizos, many of whom looked more Indian than European, and whose songs used both Spanish and the Indian Guaraní languages.

Chamamé's melodies have a touch of the melancholy attributed to the Guaraní, while its history charts the social, cultural and political relationships of mestizo migrants. Until the 1950s, it was largely confined to Corrientes, but during that decade many rural migrants moved to Buenos Aires, bringing their music and dances with them. Chamamé began to attract wider attention – in part, perhaps, because it was a rare folk dance in which people dance in cheek-to-cheek embrace.

The essential sound of chamamé comes from its key instrument – the large **piano accordion** (on occasion the *bandoneón*). It sweeps through tunes which marry contrasting rhythms, giving the music an immediate swing. Its African influences may have contributed to the music's accented weak beats so that bars blend and swing together. The distinctive percussive rhythms to the haunting, evocative melodies are the music's unique, compelling feature.

Argentina's reigning king of chamamé is **Raúl Barboza**, an artist who has also notched up a certain degree of success in Europe. He followed in the footsteps of his Corrientes-born father Adolfo, who founded his first group in 1956. Barboza's conjunto features a typical chamamé line-up of one or two accordions, a guitar (occasionally two guitars whose main job is to mark the rhythm) and *guitarrón* (bass guitar). Perhaps one of the best-known chamamé artists internationally is **Chango Spasiuk**, an Argentine of Ukrainian heritage, who has been successful in producing a sort of chamamé-rock crossover, with a more modern feel that still preserves the music's essence.

Cuarteto

The Argentine dance style known as cuarteto first became popular in the 1940s. Named after the original **Cuarteto Leo** who played it, its line-up involved a solo singer, piano, accordion and violin, and its dance consisted of a huge circle, moving counter-clockwise, to a rhythm called *tunga-tunga*. In the 1980s it underwent a resurgence of interest in the working-class "tropical" dancehalls of Buenos Aires, where it was adopted alongside Colombian *guarachas*, Dominican merengue and Latin salsa. It slowly climbed up the social ladder to reach a middle-class market, notching up big record sales. The most famous contemporary singer of cuarteto is **Carlos "La Mona" Jiménez**.

Folklore

In a movement aligned to *nueva canción*, dozens of folklore singers and groups emerged in the 1960s and 1970s – their music characterized by tight arrangements and four-part harmonies. Alongside *nueva canción* star **Mercedes Sosa**, leading artists of these decades included the groups **Los Chalchaleros**, **Los Fronterizos** and **Los Hermanos Abalos**; and guitarists **Eduardo Falú**, **Ramón Ayala**, **Ariel Ramírez** (notable for his *zambas* and his Creole Mass), **Suma Paz** and **Jorge Cafrune**.

The 1980s saw the emergence of new folklore composers including **Antonio Tarragó Ros** and **Peteco Carabajal**, while in more recent years groups have come through experimenting and re-evaluating the folk dance traditions of *zamba*, *chacareras*, *cuecas* and the like, with a poetic emphasis. Among this new wave are **Los Trovadores**, **Los Huanca Hua**, **Cuarteto Zupuy**, **El Grupo Vocal Argentino** and **Opus 4**. The best place to see folklore music is at the annual **Cosquín national folklore festival** (see p.289), which has been a fixture since the 1960s.

Discography

Raúl Barboza *Raúl Barboza*. With guitar, bass, harp, percussion and second accordion, Barboza leads a compelling concert set of quintessential chamamé on this recording: typical rasguido dobles and polkas that sound like nothing you've ever heard in Europe.

Before The Tango: ***Argentina's Folk Tradition 1905–1936*** A fascinating collection of recordings which map the folk music of the country from the beginning of the twentieth century. It moves from improvising verses of *payadores*, through blind harpists to paso dobles, to *cuecas* and a Galician *muineras*: music from the interior of the country brought by immigrants from Spain, Italy and other parts of the world.

Chamamé A compilation featuring a number of small bands playing chamamé instrumentals and songs or poetic texts. Includes Los Zorzales del Litoral, Hector Ballario, Grupo Convicción and pick of the bunch, singer and accordionist Favio Salvagiot in a band with two dynamic accordions.

Rudy and Nini Flores *Chamamé – Music of the Paraná*. The Flores are two young brothers from Corrientes Province playing instrumental chamamé: Rudy on guitar and Nini on accordion. This superb collection of their work is an intimate disc of great artistry. A sharp, poignant and mischievous accordion sound that sustains the interest in nineteen chamamé duos.

Books

Argentina's 95 percent literacy rate is one of the highest in the world and its many bookshops, especially the splendidly monumental ones in Buenos Aires, are a reflection of the considerable interest in what is written in both Argentina and the outside world. There are a fair number of books about Argentina available in English, ranging from academic publications to travelogues. In Argentina itself, there are many coffee-table books produced that focus on subjects such as Buenos Aires, Patagonia, gauchos and indigenous peoples. These vary in quality, but generally consist of good, glossy photos and dubious text.

You can track down most of the works listed below fairly easily via the Internet – Amazon (Ⓦwww.amazon.co.uk or Ⓦwww.amazon.com) is a good starting-point. The term o/p denotes that a book is currently out of print, but is still generally available through secondhand bookstores or the Internet; similarly, if a book is currently only published in the UK or US that fact is indicated in parentheses after the title.

A 🏃 preceding a title means that it is highly recommended.

Travel

🏃 **Bruce Chatwin** *In Patagonia.* For many travellers, *the Argentine travel book* – in fact, the book that broke the mould for travel writing in general. Written in the 1970s, it's really a series of self-contained tales (most famously of the Argentine adventures of Butch Cassidy and the Sundance Kid) strung together by their connection with Patagonia. This idiosyncratic book has even inspired a "Chatwin trail", although his rather cold style and literary embellishments on the region's history have their detractors too.

Bruce Chatwin and Paul Theroux *Patagonia Revisited* (o/p), published in the US as *Nowhere is a Place* (o/p). The two doyens of Western travel writing combine to explore the literary associations of Patagonia. Wafer-thin and thoroughly enjoyable, this book throws more light on the myths of this far-flung land than it does on the place itself.

Dereck Foster & Richard Tripp *Food and Drink in Argentina.* Foster has been the *Buenos Aires Herald*'s food and drink columnist for forty years, and in this slim and useful guide, co-authored with Richard Tripp, he provides both general information to whet the appetite of first-time visitors and a detailed pictorial glossary to enable veteran travellers to tell *medialunas* from *moñitos*.

Miranda France *Bad Times in Buenos Aires.* Despite the title and the critical (some might say patronizing) tone, this journal penned during the height of the Menem era brings Porteños to life, and you can't help feeling the author secretly loves the place. Highlights include a near-miss with Menem's toupee.

🏃 **Che Guevara** *The Motorcycle Diaries.* Ernesto "Che" Guevara's own account of his epic motorcyle tour around Latin America, beginning in Buenos Aires and heading south to Patagonia and then up through Chile. Che undertook the tour when he was just 23 and the resulting diary is an intriguing blend of travel anecdotes and an insight into the mind of a nascent revolutionary. The 2004 movie version, starring Mexican Gael García Bernal as Che, has done its part to inspire a new generation to read the book.

George Chaworth Musters *At Home with the Patagonians.* The amazing 1869 journey of Musters as he rode with the Aónik'enk from southern Patagonia to Carmen de Patagones, becoming in the process the first outsider to be accepted into Tehuelche society and the first white man to traverse the region south to north. This book is our prime source for information on the Tehuelche, and gives a portrait of a culture about to be exterminated.

Eric Shipton *Tierra del Fuego: the Fatal Lodestone* (o/p). An involved and passionate account of the discovery and exploration of the southernmost archipelago, recounted by a hardened adventurer and mountaineer who had more insight into these lands than most. A riveting read.

Paul Theroux *The Old Patagonian Express.* More tales about trains by the tireless cynic. In the four chapters on Argentina, which he passed through just before the 1978 World Cup, he waxes lyrical about cathedral-like Retiro station and has a surreal dialogue with Borges.

A.F. Tschiffely *Tschiffely's Ride.* An account of a truly adventurous horseback ride – described as the "longest and most arduous on record ever made by man and horse" – made by Tschiffely from Buenos Aires to Washington DC in the 1920s. The first forty pages deals with his trip to the Bolivian border in Jujuy and, though his style is rather pedestrian, it provides an insight into rural Argentina at the time.

History, politics and society

Rita Arditti *Searching for Life.* The story of the *abuelas* (grandmothers), of the Plaza de Mayo and their long-running investigation into the whereabouts of the hundreds of children who disappeared during the military dictatorship. A moving yet positive account of the grandmothers' ongoing search, which remains a controversial issue in the country.

Paul Blustein *And the Money Kept Rolling In (and Out); Wall Street, the IMF, and the Bankrupting of Argentina.* The definitive account of the Argentine economic crisis of 2001. *Washington Post* journalist Blustein contends that, though Argentina's fate was always in the hands of its own politicians, the IMF worsened the situation by indulging their emerging market "poster child" long beyond the point when the debt burden had become unsustainable, while the unrestricted flows of the global finance market had their role to play, too. Authoritative, and a cracking read.

Lucas Bridges *The Uttermost Part of the Earth.* Returned to publication in 2007, the genius of this classic text on pioneering life in Tierra del Fuego in the late nineteenth century lies less in its literary attributes than in the extraordinary tales of an adventurous young man's relationship with the area's indigenous groups, and the invaluable ethnographic knowledge he imparts about a people whose culture was set to disappear within his lifetime.

Jimmy Burns *The Hand of God.* A compelling read in which Anglo-Argentine journalist Burns charts the rise and fall of Argentina's bad-boy hero of football, Diego Maradona. Burns also wrote *The Land that Lost its Heroes*, a thoroughly researched account of the Falklands/Malvinas conflict.

Ian Fletcher *The Waters of Oblivion; the British Invasion of the Rio de la Plata 1806–1807*. The only dedicated account in English of the abortive attempt by the British to invade Buenos Aires in 1807, explaining how the mighty British army was routed by a local militia. Good for fans of military history.

Uki Goñi *The Real Odessa*. This is the definitive account of the aid given by Perón (and the Vatican) to Nazi war criminals; hundreds settled in Argentina. The Argentine government and Peronist party in particular has done little to address its sheltering of these men – indeed, Goñi finds evidence that incriminating documents were being burnt as late as 1996.

Simon Kuper *Football Against the Enemy*, published in the US as *Soccer Against the Enemy*. A collection of essays on how politics is all too frequently the unwelcome bedfellow of football, including an insightful chapter on the murky 1978 World Cup campaign in Argentina, and revelations about ex-president Menem's priorities in government: football comes first.

Daniel K. Lewis *The History of Argentina*. Reasonable brief, chronological account of the country's history. Strongest and most detailed on the Perón years and their aftermath.

Richard Llewellyn *Down Where the Moon is Small* (o/p). The concluding part of a trilogy that started with *How Green Was My Valley*, this book examines the themes of faith, righteousness, exile and toil in the pioneering Welsh community of Trevelin around the end of the nineteenth century. Well-researched and evocative, it examines the failure of the early Welsh dream to be masters of their own land, the realities of incorporation into a nation-state and the supplanting of the earlier indigenous culture.

John Lynch *Massacre in the Pampas, 1872: Britain and Argentina in the Age of Migration*. A well-researched examination of nineteenth-century immigration to Argentina and its unsettling influence on sections of the *criollo* population, culminating in the bloody Tata Dios revolt in the town of Tandil. Lynch is a major Latin American scholar; his numerous books on the region include an essential biography of nineteenth-century dictator Rosas and a new biography of independence hero Simón Bolivar.

Alberto Manguel *With Borges*. Accomplished Argentine writer Manguel recounts the time as a young man he spent reading to Borges. Absolutely charming essay, with the kind of gentle humour, subtle poetry and sharp insights into Buenos Aires life that characterize the great man's own work.

Lucio V. Mansilla *A Visit to the Ranquel Indians*. Taking the form of letters home to Buenos Aires, its anthropological descriptions are mingled with personal insights of a Porteño colonel exposed for the first time to the country's outposts and indigenous peoples. Clouded in places by self-obsession and frustrated ambition, it nevertheless provides an interesting counterpoint to the dominant theme, the "Indian problem".

Tony Mason *Passion of the People? Football in South America* (o/p). An analytical account of the developments and popularity of football in South America, largely concentrating on Brazil and Argentina. An interesting read that manages to interweave sport, culture and politics.

Michael McCaughan *True Crimes: Rodolfo Walsh* (UK). The life and work of one of Argentina's most important journalists, Rodolfo Walsh, assassinated by the military government in 1977 for his involvement with the Montoneros guerrillas and his continued criticism of the dictatorship. The text alternates Walsh's own work, including his acclaimed short stories, with a biography that illuminates the period from a left-wing perspective.

Gabriella Nouzeilles and **Graciela Montaldo** (eds) *The Argentina Reader.* Compendium of essays and stories on Argentina's history and culture, with the majority of the pieces written by Argentines. An excellent starting-point for further reading, though a bit hefty for lugging around.

Nunca Más (o/p). The 1984 report by CONADEP, Argentina's National Commission on the Disappeared, headed by novelist Ernesto Sabato, that was appointed to investigate the fate of those who disappeared during the 1976–83 military dictatorship. Not comfortable reading, but essential for anyone who wishes to understand more about what happened in those years; if you can't stomach the first-hand accounts, at least read the excellent prologue by Sabato. You can also find it in English online at Ⓦwww.nuncamas.org.

Alicia Partnoy *The Little School: Tales of Disappearance and Survival in Argentina.* An account of the time spent by the author in one of Argentina's most notorious detention centres during the 1970s. A bleak tale, though leavened by its portrayal of the human spirit's ability to survive adversity.

Domingo F. Sarmiento *Facundo, or Civilization and Barbarism.* Probably the most influential of all books written in Latin America in the nineteenth century, this essay defines one of Argentina's major cultural peculiarities – the battle between the provinces seeking decentralized power and a sophisticated metropolis more interested in what is going on abroad than in its vast hinterland. Written in the form of the biography of a gaucho thug named Facundo Quiroga, it attacks the arbitrary rule of provincial strongmen such as Rosas, Sarmiento's arch-enemy. Sarmiento was obsessed with the idea that Argentina was condemned to backwater status unless it shook off the "uncivilized" leadership of men such as Rosas and instead imported education and democracy from the US and culture from Europe.

Nicholas Shumway *The Invention of Argentina.* A sterling treatment of nineteenth-century intellectual impulses behind the formation of the modern Argentine nation-state and the development of a national identity. Though the subject matter would seem weighty, the book reads extremely well, with rich cultural detail throughout.

Richard W. Slatta *Gauchos and the Vanishing Frontier.* Scholarly work that is the perfect cerebral accompaniment to the coffee-table tomes sold on the subject. Slatta charts the rise, fall and rise again of the gaucho, his lifestyle, his maltreatment by the upper classes and the myths that grew around him.

Jacobo Timerman *Prisoner Without A Name, Cell Without A Number* (US). A gruelling tale of detention under the 1976–83 military dictatorship, as endured by Timerman, then the editor of leading liberal newspaper of the time, *La Opinión.* The author is Jewish, and his experiences lead to a wider consideration of anti-Semitism and the nature of totalitarian regimes.

Horacio Verbitsky *The Flight: Confessions of an Argentine Dirty Warrior.* A respected investigative journalist, Verbitsky tells the story of

Francisco Silingo, a junior naval officer during the Dirty War, involved in the horrific practice of pushing drugged prisoners out of planes over the Atlantic Ocean and the River Plate. A meticulously researched account of a dark episode in Argentina's history.

Nature and wildlife

Charles Darwin *The Voyage of the Beagle.* Very readable account of Darwin's famous voyage, which takes him through Patagonia and the pampas. Filled with observations on the flora, fauna, landscape and people (including the dictator Rosas) that Darwin encounters, all described in the scientist's methodical yet evocative style.

Gerald Durrell *The Whispering Land.* A lighthearted read detailing Durrell's observations while animal-collecting in Peninsula Valdés, the Patagonian steppe and the *yungas.* Enduring good value, despite what now comes across as a colonial tone: his capacity for making animals into characters is unsurpassed. See also *The Drunken Forest* (o/p), about his trip to the Chaco.

W.H. Hudson *Far Away and Long Ago.* A nostalgic and gently ambling portrait of childhood and rural tranquillity in the Argentine pampas in Rosas' time. An early environmentalist, the author regrets the expansion of agriculture and the destruction of habitat variety in the pampas in the course of his lifetime. In the US it is out of copyright and can be downloaded free at Ⓦwww.gutenberg.org.

Martín R. de la Peña and **Maurice Rumboll** *Birds of Southern South America and Antarctica.* The best field guide currently available on Argentine ornithology, and a useful companion for even the non-specialist bird-watcher. It would benefit from some indication of frequency and a few illustrations could do with more detail, but overall thoroughly recommended.

The arts

Simon Collier (ed) *Tango! The Dance, the Song, the Story.* A glossy coffee-table book with a lively account of the history of tango and its key protagonists, well illustrated with colour and black-and-white photos.

David Elliott (ed) *Art from Argentina: 1920–1994* (UK). Comprehensive illustrated account of the development of twentieth-century Argentine art, composed of a series of focused essays and monographs of major figures. Indispensable to anyone with a serious interest in the subject.

John King and **Nissa Torrents** (eds) *Garden of the Forking Paths: Argentine Cinema* (o/p). Authoritative collection of essays on Argentine cinema, compiled by two experts in the field. An excellent introduction to Argentina's film industry.

Fiction

César Aira *The Hare.* A witty novel about an English naturalist in nineteenth-century Argentina by Borges' literary heir, a truly prolific and original writer at the forefront of contemporary Argentine literature.

Roberto Arlt *The Seven Madmen.* Until his tragically early death, Roberto Arlt captured the lot of the poor immigrant with his gripping, if idiosyncratic, novels about anarchists, whores and other marginal characters in 1920s Buenos Aires. *The Seven Madmen* is the pick of his works – dark and at times surreal, it's filled with images of the frenetic and alienating pace of urban life as experienced by the novel's tormented protagonist, Remo Erdosain.

Jorge Luis Borges *Labyrinths.* Not only Argentina's greatest writer, but one of the world's finest and most influential. His prose is highly original, witty and concise; rather than novels, he introduces his ideas through short stories and essays – ideal for dipping into – and *Labyrinths* is a good introduction to these, with selections from his major collections. It includes many of his best-known and most enigmatic tales, including *Library of Babel*, an analogy of the world as a never-ending library, and *Death and the Compass*, an erudite detective story.

Julio Cortázar *Hopscotch.* Cortázar is probably second only to Borges in the canon of Argentine writers and *Hopscotch* is a major work, published in the 1960s and currently being reappraised as the first "hypertext" novel. In this fantastically complex book, Cortázar defies traditional narrative structure, inviting the reader to "hop" between chapters (hence the name), which recount the lives of a group of friends in Paris and London. Cortázar is also well regarded for his enigmatic short stories – try *Blow Up and Other Stories.*

Edgardo Cozarinsky *The Bride from Odessa.* A collection of short stories focusing on exile, bouncing back and forth (like Cozarinsky himself) between Argentina and Europe. The best tale is saved for last, with a young man in Lisbon tracking down the truth behind his grand-parents' move to Argentina.

Graham Greene *The Honorary Consul.* A masterful account of a farcical kidnapping attempt that goes tragically wrong. Set in the city of Corrientes and dedicated to Argentine literary doyenne Victoria Ocampo, with whom Greene spent time in San Isidro and Mar del Plata.

Ricardo Güiraldes *Don Segundo Sombra* (o/p). A tender and nostalgic evocation of past life on the pampas, chronicling the relationship between a young boy and his mentor, the novel's eponymous gaucho. Written in 1926, some decades after the gaucho era had come to a close, it was a key text in changing the image of the Argentine cowboy from that of a violent undesirable to a strong, independent man with simple tastes, at the heart of Argentina's national identity.

José Hernández *Martín Fierro.* The classic gaucho novel – actually a verse of epic proportions, traditionally learnt by heart by many Argentines. Written as a protest against the corrupt authorities, it features a highly likeable gaucho outlaw on the run, who rails against the country's weak institutional structures and dictatorial rulers. Its rhyming verse and liberal use of gaucho lingo make translation difficult; one version is the classic Walter Owen translation from the 1930s, available in Argentine bookshops.

Tomás Eloy Martínez *The Perón Novel* and *Santa Evita* (both o/p). Darting between fact and fiction, Tomás Eloy Martínez intersperses his account of the events surrounding Perón's return to Argentina in 1973 with anecdotes from his past. The companion volume *Santa Evita* recounts the morbid and at times farcical true story of Evita's life and – more importantly – afterlife, during which her corpse was hijacked and smuggled abroad. Martínez' latest work is *The Tango Singer*, an evocative tale set in the *milongas* of Buenos Aires.

Manuel Puig *Kiss of the Spider-woman* (US). Arguably the finest book by one of Argentina's most original twentieth-century writers, distinguished by a style that mixes film dialogue and popular culture with more traditional narrative. Set during the 1970s dictatorship, this is an absorbing tale of two cellmates, worlds apart on the outside but drawn together by gay protagonist Molina's recounting of films to his companion, left-wing guerrilla Valentín.

Horacio Quiroga *The Decapitated Chicken and Other Stories.* Wonderful, if sometimes disturbing gothic tales of love, madness and death. Includes the spine-chilling "Feather Pillow", in which the life is slowly sucked from a young bride by a hideous blood-sucking beast, found engorged after her death within her feather pillow.

Ernesto Sábato *The Tunnel* (o/p). Existential angst, obsession and madness are the themes of this supremely accomplished novella, which tells the story of a tormented painter's destructive fixation with a sad and beautiful woman.

Colm Toibin *The Story of the Night.* A moving tale of a young Anglo-Argentine trying to come to terms both with his sexuality and existential dilemmas in the wake of the South Atlantic conflict, and getting caught up in an undercover plot by the CIA to get Carlos Menem elected president.

Painting and sculpture

The comprehensive catalogue published in 1994 for the exhibition of "Art from Argentina 1920–1994", held at the Museum of Modern Art, Oxford, claimed to be the first book on twentieth-century Argentine art ever to appear in Europe. The exhibition organizers put this down to the fact that, while Argentina is the Latin American country that appears to be most like Europe, the reality is more alien: that of a new, fast-growing but isolated nation, searching for an identity against a background of permanent insecurity, political violence, entrenched conservatism and generalized chaos. Surprisingly little has yet to be written in English-speaking countries, even the US, about the plastic arts in Argentina, despite the country's massive, sometimes innovative and often fascinating production.

The search for an identity

It has been said that Argentina's artistic creativity was not "decolonized" until the **1920s**, when it showed signs, albeit hesitantly, of no longer drawing its inspiration exclusively from European countries. Under Marcelo T. de Alvear, a relatively progressive president from 1922 to 1928, a relaxed climate of creativity and prosperity began to emerge. Xul Solar and Emilio Pettoruti came back to Argentina after long stays in Europe. The *Martín Fierro* magazine, a vaguely patriotic publication interested in *criollo* and "neo-*criollo*" culture as a means of

△ Drago, by Xul Solar

achieving a strictly non-chauvinistic brand of "Argentinidad" in all fields of artistic creation, first went on sale in 1924.

Of all the early "post-colonial" artists, **Xul Solar**, born Oscar Agustín Alejandro Schulz Solari (1887–1963), stands out, both technically and for his originality; he is one of the few artists in Argentina to have a museum to himself, the fantastic **Museo Xul Solar** (see p.140). Solar was an eccentric polymath, born just outside Buenos Aires to a German-speaking Latvian father and a Genoese mother. After abandoning his architectural studies in the capital he set sail for Hong Kong but jumped ship in London, stayed in Europe for twelve years and began working as an artist. Returning to Buenos Aires, he experimented with new styles and influences and, in 1939, fascinated by astrology and Buddhism, he founded the **Pan Klub**, a group of artists and intellectuals sharing his utopian pacifist credo. Some of his more disturbing pictures evoke the ruins left by World War II.

Xul Solar worked mainly with watercolour and tempera, preferring their fluidity and pastel colours. While many influences are visible, his closest soul mate, both artistically and philosophically, is undoubtedly Klee, though artists as varied as Bosch, Braque, Chagall and Dalí evidently provided inspiration as well. His paintings essentially work on two levels: a magical, almost infantile universe of fantasy, depicted in bright colours and immediately appealing forms, and a far more complex philosophy of erudite symbolism and allegory, in which zodiac and cabalistic signs predominate, along with a repetition of snake and ladder motifs. His adopted name is not only a deformation of his real surnames but also "Lux" (light) backwards, while "solar" suggests his obsession with the planets. Octavio Paz's maxim "painting has one foot in architecture and the other in dreams" has often been applied to Solar – his early architectural training comes across unmistakably in his paintings.

You can see a particularly fine watercolour, *Pupo*, one of Xul Solar's earlier works (1918), at Buenos Aires' **Museo Nacional de Bellas Artes (MNBA)**, the country's biggest and richest collection of nineteenth- and twentieth-century painting and sculpture. In the same museum you can see a very fine painting – *Arlequín* (1928) – by Solar's friend and contemporary, **Emilio Pettoruti** (1892–1971), whose major exhibition in 1924 sent ripples across the conservative capital. This event is widely interpreted as the beginning of the modern era in Argentine painting. Pettoruti transferred into painting and collage his personal and, for some, Argentine, vision of Cubism.

The MNBA not only houses a beautiful collection of art, but it also traces in a concrete form the history of the country's painting and sculpture since independence. In colonial times Argentina relied on two main sources to satisfy the growing demand for artwork: the craftsmen of Peru and Bolivia, especially those of the **Cusco School**, who churned out mostly religious paintings and objects that added a mestizo touch to European baroque themes and styles; and artisans and artists from Brazil, whose different techniques and inspiration provided some variety among the objects on offer. As a gaucho identity began to emerge, a more specific creativity appeared, in the form of mostly silver and leather "*motivos*" – *mate* vessels, saddles, knives, guns. A major collection of these objects is housed at the **Museo Hernández** in Palermo, Buenos Aires. But as a middle class and wealthy land-owning aristocracy became firmly established, they heaped scorn upon this "vulgar sub-culture" and many would have nothing in their homes but fashionable European and European-style art. Not until 1799 did Buenos Aires have its own **art school**, the Escuela de Dibujo, but it was shut down upon the orders of King Carlos IV only three years later. After independence, an

Lola Mora

Dolores Mora Vega de Hernández – better known as **Lola Mora** – was born on November 17, 1866, at El Tala, a tiny village in Salta Province very close to the Tucumán border. She completed her studies in Italy and took to working in **marble**, a medium used for much of her prolific oeuvre of statues and monuments. In addition to works in various towns and cities around the country, she is best known for her invaluable contribution to the Monumento a la Bandera in Rosario (see p.377); the magnificent Nereidas fountain adorning the Costanera Sur in Buenos Aires (see p.116); and the voluptuous set of allegorical figures – Peace, Progress, Justice, Freedom and Labour – intended for the National Congress building (see p.110) but never placed there, as they were considered too shocking. Instead the five naked forms can be admired at the Casa de Gobierno in Jujuy (see p.452). Hailed as the country's foremost **sculptress**, Lola had a tragic life, losing her parents at an early age, enduring a turbulent marriage and facing social rejection owing to her bohemian lifestyle and her predilection for portraying shapely female forms (leading to comparisons with Camille Claudel). Towards the end of her life, she suffered from ill health and psychological problems. She died in poverty, on June 7, 1936, shortly after reconciliation with her husband after seventeen years of estrangement and only a few months after the national government agreed to grant her a pension.

academy of fine art was founded, but all the teachers came from Europe and it too was closed down, for lack of funding, in the 1830s.

Carlos Morel (1813–94), one of the first recognized Argentine artists, had trained there; firmly entrenched in the Romantic tradition of early nineteenth-century France, his oils of urban and rural scenes and military episodes are exquisitely executed. You can see a particularly fine example, *Carga de Caballería del Ejército Federal* (exact date unknown), at the MNBA.

All eyes on Europe

Nearly the entire ground floor of the MNBA is taken up by paintings and sculpture from France, Italy, Holland and Spain, plus later works by artists from the US. Virtually every Argentine artist worth his or her salt studied in Europe and slavishly imitated European styles, such as naturalism and Impressionism – and their work has been "relegated" to the upper floor. These include **Prilidiano Pueyrredón**'s (1823–70) *Un alto en la pulpería* (*c.*1860); **Eduardo Sívori**'s (1847–1918) *El despertar de la criada* (1887); **Martín Malharro**'s (1865–1911); *Las parvas* (1911); **Fernando Fader**'s (1882–1935) *Los mantones de Manila* (1914); and **Valentín Thibon de Libian**'s (1889–1931) *La fragua* (1916). One of the country's greatest-ever sculptors **Rogelio Yrurtia** (1879–1950), heavily influenced by Rodin, was chosen to create a number of rather bombastic monuments across Buenos Aires, and his house in Belgrano is now a museum (see p.153).

Despite the "decolonization" that the likes of Xul Solar had led in the 1920s, most of Argentina's artists continued to fix their gaze on Europe throughout the 1930s – the so-called *década infama*, a period of political repression, economic depression and general melancholy – and increasingly on the US, for inspiration. Two of the greatest Argentine artists active in that period were **Antonio Berni** (1905–81), whose *Primeros pasos* (1937) is on display at the MNBA, and **Lino Enea Spilimbergo** (1896–1964) – seek out his *Figura*

(1937) hanging nearby. Both were taught by the now much-overlooked French Surrealist André Lhote (1885–1962), as shows clearly in their paintings, which aimed to depict the social reality of an Argentina in economic and political turmoil without espousing any political cause – Berni was hailed as the leader of the so-called *Arte Político*. His incredibly moving *La Torre Eiffel en la Pampa* (1930) single-handedly seems to sum up the continuing dilemma among Argentine artists – are they nostalgic for Paris while in Argentina or for Buenos Aires and the pampas when in Europe?

Breaking away and drifting back

The big break with European artistic traditions came towards the end of World War II. *Arturo*, an abstract art review seen as a pioneer in world art circles, was first published in 1944. Argentine artists, many of whom were born in Europe, often in the Central and Eastern European countries most affected by the war, rejected what they saw as an unjustifiable hegemony, led from countries that had just indulged in such acts of barbarism that they could teach the New World no lessons, either in politics or in art. **Abstract** art was a way of indirectly protesting against reactionary politics. Just after Perón came to power, a number of ground-breaking exhibitions were staged in Buenos Aires, including that of the Asociación Arte Concreto-Invención and Arte Madí, both in 1942. Three major art manifestos were published that year or the following: the Manifiesto Intervencionista, by Tomás Maldonado and his friends, the Manifiesto Madí, signed by Hungarian-born **Gyula Kosice** (born 1924) and his colleagues, and the Manifiesto Blanco, issued by members of the Academia Altamira, which wanted to create a new art form based on "matter, colour and sound in perpetual movement".

The last of the three was primarily instigated by **Lucio Fontana** (1899–1968), indisputably one of the twentieth century's key artists and founder of the Informalist movement. Fontana may have done most of his work in Italy, but he was born in Argentina, in Rosario, the son of an Italian immigrant and an Argentine actress of Italian origin. He was dispatched to Italy for his education, where he studied architecture. A hero during World War I, he returned to Argentina in 1940, after churning out a number of monuments for Mussolini's regime, though he never espoused fascism. In Argentina he worked for his father's firm sculpting funerary monuments, a job he quickly gave up in favour of teaching art in the capital. A co-founder of both the Altamira School and the Escuela Libre de Artes Plásticos in Recoleta, he never recovered from being runner-up in the competition to design the flag monument in his native city. Perhaps a case of sour grapes, he later described the years spent in Rosario and Buenos Aires, as "una vita da coglione" (a shitty existence), and he decided to leave the country "as a more positive alternative to committing suicide". Back in Italy in 1947, he developed his own theory of art – enshrined in the **Spatialist Manifesto** issued that year – and his now unmistakable style: a series of monochrome canvases, slashed or pierced, apparently evocative of restrained violence or simply representing an "exploration of space". Known somewhat irreverently in the art world as "Lucio the Slasher" or "Lucio the Ripper", he has been the subject of a couple of major exhibitions in Buenos Aires in recent years, suggestive of a rehabilitation, but the rest of the world still thinks of him as an Italian creator. Nonetheless a couple of his works, including the somewhat unrepresentative *Concepto espacial*, are displayed inside the entrance to the MNBA.

Meanwhile in Argentina other **avant-garde** artists seemed more intent on theory than practice, but nonetheless produced some work that is still regarded as significant. **Madí**, probably a nonsense word like Dada, but sometimes said to be derived from "materialismo dialéctico", was decidedly political in its aims of creating a classless society. One of the movement's most radical ideas, cooked up in the 1970s, was to build a series of "Hydrospatial Cities" suspended in space over water, starting with the River Plate, where the urban environment would be so radically different from those previously created that there would be no need for art. Back in 1946 Kosice produced a series of works using neon lighting, thought to be the first of their kind, and he later experimented with glass, plexiglass, acrylic, cork, aluminium and bone – his *Dispersión del aire* (1967), at the MNBA, is one such work. His articulated wooden sculpture *Röyi*, dating from 1944, is also regarded as revolutionary, as it is both abstract and lathed rather than "sculpted". Another member of the movement, Kosice's wife **Diyi Laañ** (born 1927), created works such as her *Pintura sobre el marco recortado* (1948) on a structured frame in an abstract, hollow shape. **Rhod Rothfuss** (1920–69) was the Uruguayan leader of Madí, and his enamel paintings on wood, created in the 1940s, were highly influential in Argentina.

Rivals of the Madí group, the Asociación Arte Concreto-Invención or Intervencionistas, were far more radical politically, espousing solidarity with the Soviet Union largely as a means of protesting against US interference in Latin American affairs. Artistically, though. they were more conventional than the Madí lot, and tended to produce paintings in traditionally shaped frames; they drew much of their inspiration from artists like Mondrian, Van Doesburg and Malevich. Members included the leading theorist **Tomás Maldonado** (born 1922), Claudio Girola, Lidy Prati and Gregorio Vardánega, but the most acclaimed artists in the movement are **Enio Iommi** (born 1926), **Alfredo Hlito** (1923–93) and **Raúl Lozza** (1911–2007). The first of the three is generally regarded as one of Argentina's greatest-ever artists and he stands out from the other Intervencionistas in part because he works in three dimensions. His exquisite sculptures in stainless steel – such as *Torsión de planos* (1964), at the MNBA – wood, bronze and aluminium, express his personal "spatialist" credo that in many ways link him closely to Fontana. More recently Iommi underwent an about-turn and began producing objects with emphasis on the material, using industrial and household refuse – his 1977 Retiro exhibition entitled *Adiós a una época* marked his switch to *arte povera*, after decades of using "noble" materials. Hlito, meanwhile, was a more "mainstream" Intervencionista, whose work displays the influences of people like Mondrian and Max Bill, and even Seurat and Cézanne – though it was their use of colour and brushstrokes that most interested him. A very typical work, *Lineas tangentes* (1955), is on show at the MNBA. Lozza, on the other hand, became so obsessed with the intricacies of colour, form and representation in art that he formed his own movement in 1949, called Perceptismo, according to which paintings must be sketched obeying certain architectural rules before the colour can be filled in. His watershed work *Pintura Numero 153* (1948), executed just before he left the Intervencionistas, is on show at the MNBA.

Reactionary politics and artistic responses

The 1950s to 1970s were once again times of turmoil in Argentina; Peronism was replaced by short-lived democratic governments and military dictatorships that shared only one ruthless aim: eliminating Peronism. Since 1983, following the South Atlantic conflict, Argentina has been unshakeably if imperfectly democratic. All of these ups and downs have been reflected in the country's post-war art as much as, if not more than, in its literature, cinema and music. The reactionary politics of virtually everyone who held power in Argentina from 1944 to 1983 were either rebelled against by mainly leftist, *engagé* artists or dictated by a more conservative approach, often based on mainstream artistic schools in Europe.

Raquel Forner (1902–87) came to the fore in the 1950s – even though she had begun to paint in the 1920s as a student of Spilimbergo – mainly because she was unmistakably influenced by Picasso. This comes through in her style – in which human figures are amalgamated with symbolic images – and subject matter. She painted two series of haunting oils about the Spanish Civil War and World War II: *España* (1937–39) and *El drama* (1939–46); the spine-chilling *Retablo de dolor* (1944), at the MNBA, which belongs to the second group, also reveals her interest in the religious paintings of El Greco. She set herself apart in the 1960s by concentrating on the theme of the human conquest of space, as exemplified by her 1968 *Conquest of Moon Rock*.

Unusual Italian-born sculptor **Libero Badii** (1916-2001), some of whose work, including later paintings, is displayed at the Fundación Banco Francés, Buenos Aires, won a national prize in 1953 with a sensually organic marble figure, *Torrente*, which can be seen at the MNBA. Arp and Brancusi are easily detectable influences on his earlier works.

From 1955 to 1963, **Jorge Romero Brest** was director of the MNBA. Politics had its dictators and so did the art world – this staunchly anti-Peronist guru of Argentine art went on to direct the highly influential and virtually monopolistic Centro de Artes Visuales at the capital's wealthy Instituto Torcuato di Tella, where he had the power to make or break artists, until 1970. Essentially a democrat, however, he staged increasingly subversive exhibitions by avant-garde artists after General Juan Onganía's mob seized totalitarian power in 1966, purportedly to combat both Marxism and Peronism. Romero Brest's most famous achievement while in charge of the MNBA was the discovery of four artists who went under the label of Otra Figuración, after a revolutionary exhibition of that name held in Buenos Aires in 1961.

Part German-style Expressionism, part Dubuffet, part de Kooning and quite a lot of Rauschenberg, these young artists dominated Argentine painting throughout the rest of the decade. **Ernesto Deira** (1928–86), **Jorge de la Vega** (1930–71), **Rómulo Macció** (born 1931) and **Luis Felipe Noé** (born 1933) all produced highly acclaimed work, though Vega is usually regarded as the most original. Deira's *Homenaje a Fernand Léger* (1963) at the MNBA speaks for itself; heavy neo-figurative shades of Francis Bacon are detectable in Macció's *Vivir un poco cada día* (1963), also at the MNBA; while Noé's Ensoresque masterpiece *Introducción a la esperanza* (1963), at the same museum, illustrates his theory of "*cuadro dividido*", in which several paintings are chaotically assembled to make one work. Vega's *Intimidades de un tímido* (1960s), at the Museo Nacional, is typical of his vast canvases, brimming with vitality but largely mysterious in their imagery. Of the four, his work is hardest to pigeonhole. Similarly, while **Alberto Heredia** (born 1924), admirer of Marcel Duchamp, was closely related to the Otra Figuración, he also has a lot in common with both Surrealism and Pop Art. His now famous *Camembert Boxes* (1961–63), filled with day-to-day junk, are seen as a breakthrough in Argentine sculpture, while his later *Los amordazamientos* (1972–74), at the MNBA, is apocalyptic in its depiction of human despair.

Worldwide, the 1960s were marked by the new artistic phenomenon of Happenings, and what Argentine artists called Ambientaciones; despite their often massive scale and laborious preparations, they were by nature ephemeral events, and all we have left now are photographic documents. Argentina's answer to Andy Warhol, **Marta Minujín** (born 1941), whose colourful *Colchón* (1964) can be seen at the MNBA, has been a leading exponent. Her two key works in 1965, *La menesunda* and *El batacazo*, both staged at the Centro de Artes Visuales, were labyrinths meant to excite, delight, disturb and attack the visitor's five senses, and caused both scandal and wonderment. She continued to perform into the 1970s, poking fun at national icons like Carlos Gardel and the ovenbird, Argentina's national bird; after creating *Obelisco acostado* in 1978, the following year she constructed a thirty-metre-high *Obelisco de pan dulce*, a half-scale model of Buenos Aires' famous phallic symbol clad with thousands of plastic-wrapped raisin breads, erected at the cattle-raisers' temple, the Sociedad Rural in Palermo. To celebrate the return to democracy in 1983, her *Partenón de libros* was a massive monument covered in books – many publications had been banned or burned under the junta – also raised outdoors in the capital. In recent years her output has continued, including performance art over the Internet and, since 2006, a sculpture on display at the Salentein winery in Mendoza.

Contemporary Argentine art: back to square one

The 1970s and early 1980s saw many Argentine artists leave the country, out of justifiable fear for their lives. Some preferred to stay, using indirect means of criticizing the government. In 1971, the Centro de Arte y Comunicación (CAYC) was founded by art critic Jorge Glusberg (director of the MNBA from 1994 until 2004, when he was eased out under a cloud of scandal), and took over where the disbanded Centro de Artes Visuales and Romero Brest had left off – though in those days Glusberg was less dictatorial in his approach. Two figures stand out during this period: **Pablo Suárez** (1937-2006) whose *La terraza* (1983) at the MNBA is typical of his black humour and anti-Argentinidad credo, being a sardonically cruel pastiche of the Sunday *asado*; and his contemporary **Víctor Grippo** (born 1936), whose *Analogía I* (1970–71) at the MNBA comprises forty potatoes in pigeonholes with electrodes attached, seen retrospectively as a horrific premonition of the military's torture chambers. Suárez had first had to rebel against his aristocratic *estanciero* family, which he did as an adolescent by fashioning erotic sculptures. Much of his later work is also sexually provocative, while poking fun at sacrosanct aspects of the Argentine way of life. His grotesque *Monumento a Mate* (1987) hits a raw nerve of the Argentine psyche, the national drink of *mate*, while his oyster-shaped sculpture *La Perla: retrato de un taxi-boy* (1992) depicts a naked adolescent reclining in the place of a pearl – *taxi-boy* is the Porteño term for a rent-boy, so-called because male prostitutes in the capital demand the "taxi-fare home" rather than payment. As for Grippo, his most famous work is *Analogía IV* (1972), again featuring potatoes, highly symbolic as they are native to South America and imported into North America, Europe and the rest of the world. In this seminal work a white table-top is laid with a china plate, metal cutlery and three potatoes, while another, black in colour, is laid with identical crockery and cutlery in transparent plastic – this mirror image of "real" and "fake" apparently represents military puppet President General Alejandro Lanusse's humiliating invitation to recall Perón from exile in 1973. Another contemporary of theirs, **Antonio Seguí** (born 1934), is also out on an artistic limb: his comic-like paintings, such as the untitled acrylic (1987) on show at the MNBA, depict a somewhat sinister, behatted figure in countless different poses, representing urban alienation. Younger artist **Alfredo Prior** (born 1952) – whose *En cada sueño habita una pena* (1985) at the MNBA, is one of the most horrific yet beautiful Argentine paintings produced in recent years – deliberately kept himself apart from artistic circles, rarely exhibiting his work. Minimalism and Japanese art are strong influences, along with Turner in his use of colour, as in *Paraíso* (1988). The style of **Ricardo Cinalli** (born 1948), who lives in London, has been described as post-modern Neoclassicism, and his *Blue Box* (1990) is a prime example of his original use of layers of tissue paper upon which he colours in pastel. **Mónica Girón** (born 1959) takes her inspiration from her native Patagonia and her environmental concerns to produce innovative works like *Trousseau for a Conqueror* (1993) which features a pullover specially knitted for a Buff-necked Ibis, putting her undeniably in the same school, despite her different style, as Marta Minujín.

Guillermo Kuitca (born 1961) is without a doubt Argentina's most successful contemporary artist – his paintings sell for six-figure sums at auction – and in many ways he encapsulates what Argentine art has become, the way it has turned full circle. Argentina remains a country of mostly European immigrants and their descendants who, however hard they try, cannot sever the umbilical cord that links them culturally to their parents' and grandparents' homelands. Above all, Kuitca's work is highly original, in other words individual, and makes no attempt to create something nationally Argentine – as witnessed by his beautiful painting at the MNBA, *La consagración de la primavera* (1983) – but it is no coincidence that his series of maps, such as those printed onto a triptych of mattresses (1989), are largely of Germany and Central Europe, where his own roots are. The 1986 novel *The Lost Language of Cranes*, by David Leavitt, in which the son's favourite pastime is drawing maps of non-existent places, was the main inspiration for this theme, while the choreography of German creator Pina Bausch is another source of ideas. Argentine artists seem finally to have given up trying to forge the Argentinidad that Borges and his colleagues were set on inventing in the 1920s, and have acknowledged instead that, in the global village of constant interaction, personal styles and talent are more important than an attempt to create an artificial national identity through art.

The way in which Argentine art fits into that of Latin America as a whole is another important issue, addressed in concrete fashion by the fabulous **MALBA** museum in Buenos Aires (see p.146). Various other institutions have also seen light of day, mostly in the capital, but also in provincial cities such as Salta and Rosario, offering excitingly groundbreaking spaces for exhibiting Argentina's contemporary art.

Language

Language

Argentine Spanish

You'll find it very useful to have at least a decent smattering of Spanish in Argentina. Though you'll frequently come across English-speakers, especially in big cities, you can't rely on there always being someone there when you need them, and, in general, Argentines are appreciative of visitors who make the effort to communicate in **castellano** (as Spanish is nearly always called here, rather than *español*). Any basic Spanish course will give you a good grounding before you go. A good pocket **dictionary**, such as Collins, is a vital accessory, while of the bigger dictionaries Collins, Oxford and Larousse are all good – make sure your choice covers Latin American usage. If you really want to refine your grasp of the subtleties of the language, a comprehensive grammar such as *A New Reference Grammar of Modern Spanish* by John Butt and Carmen Benjamin (Edward Arnold, London 1988) is a good investment.

Argentine Spanish is one of the most distinctive varieties of the language. Dominating the country's linguistic identity is the unmistakable Porteño accent, characterized by an expressive, almost drawling intonation, peppered with colloquialisms. This linguistic influence spreads out for several hundred kilo-metres around Buenos Aires (and is often known as "Rioplatense", after the River Plate); beyond this, subtle regional variations take hold, though certain constructions and words apply for the whole country. If you've learnt Spanish in **Spain**, the most obvious difference you will encounter is the absence of the lisping *th* sound in words like *cielo* ("sky"; pronounced SYE-lo in Argentina) and *zorro* ("fox"; it sounds a bit like the English word "sorrow"

The voseo

The use of **vos** as the second-person pronoun, a usage known as the **voseo**, is common to nearly the whole of Argentina (and also parts of Central America and local dialects, plus Ladino). Though you will be understood perfectly if you use the *tú* form, you should familiarize yourself with the *vos* form, if only in order to understand what is being said to you.

The easiest way to form the present-tense verb endings employed with *vos* is to take the infinitive and replace the final -r with an -s, adding an accent to the final vowel to retain final stress. Thus, *venir* (you come) becomes Argentine *vos venís*; the main exception to this rule is the verb *ser* (to be) - *vos sos*. The imperative is formed by dropping the final -s: *¡vení!* - the only exception being *¡andá!*, from *ir* (to go). Past, conditional, subjunctive and future forms used with *vos* are the same as the *tú* forms.

Some examples:

¿querés salir?	do you want to go out?
¿hablás inglés?	do you speak English?
¿dónde vivís?	where do you live?
¡tomá!	take!
¡comé!	eat!
¡seguí!	carry on!

but with a Scottish-style trilled *r*). In Buenos Aires, in particular, you will also be struck by the strong consonantal pronunciation of "y" and "ll", as in *yo* and *calle* (see p.853 & p.856), a completely different sound to that used in Spain and much of Latin America (where it sounds like the "y" in "yes"). Another notable difference is the use of *vos* as the second-person pronoun, in place of *tú*, with correspondingly different verb endings (see box, p.851). *Ustedes* is used as the second-person pronoun (the plural of "you"), never *vosotros*, and it takes the third-person plural *(ellos)* form of the verb. In general, Latin American speech is slightly more formal than that found in Spain, and the polite *usted* is used far more often. A good guideline is that *vos* is always used for children and usually between strangers under about 30; though within circles who regard themselves as politically progressive *vos* is used as a mark of shared values.

Argentine vocabulary is often quite different to other forms of Spanish, too (see box, pp.854–855). The use of "che" (used when addressing someone; it loosely translates to "hey mate") in particular is so much identified with Argentina that other Latin Americans sometimes refer to Argentines as "*Los che*". The word was most famously applied as a nickname of Ernesto Guevara, who was popularly and universally known as "Che" Guevara.

Pronunciation

The Spanish pronunciation system is remarkably straightforward, with only five pure vowel sounds. Just a few sounds tend to cause problems for English-speakers, most notably the rolled double (or initial) R and the single R which, though not rolled, is trilled more than its English counterpart. Another characteristic of Spanish is that there is no audible gap between words within a breath group; thus Buenos Aires is pronounced "BWEnoSAIres" and not "BWE-nos-AI-res". Failure to observe this produces very stilted Spanish.

Vowels

Spanish vowel sounds do not exactly correspond to any sound in standard British or American English, though approximate sounds exist for all of them. In general, English vowel sounds tend to be formed by a combination of two vocalic sounds: English "close", for example, is really a combination of "o" and "oo". Spanish has no such tendency, representing such sounds with two written vowels.

A is pronounced somewhere between the "a" of "father" and that of "back".

E is similar to the "e" in English "get" or "ten", with some of the openness of English "day" (though much shorter).

I is similar to the sound in "meet", though much shorter.

O is more open or rounded than in English "hot", though shorter than in "dose".

U is similar to the "oo" of "boot", though much shorter. A close equivalent can be found in the French word *coup*. In the combinations "gue" (as in *guerra*, pronounced "GE-rra"); gui (*guiso*, pronounced "GI-so"); que (*queso*, pronounced "KE-so"); and *qui* (Quito, the Ecuadorean capital, pronounced "KI-to"), the U is silent. A diaeresis (like the German umlaut) preserves the U, producing a "w" sound in words such as Güemes, pronounced GWEmes.

Diphthongs

A diphthong is basically a combination of two vocalic sounds. Common diphthongs in Spanish include AU, as in *jaula* (cage), pronounced "HOW-la" and EI or EY as in *ley* (law) pronounced very like the English word "lay". The rarer EU, as in Europa (pronounced ayoo-RO-pa) and the very uncommon OU, as in the GOU (Grupo de Oficiales Unidos, the group of officers from which Perón emerged in the 1940s, pronounced like the English "go") take a bit of getting used to.

Consonants

Consonants not covered below are pronounced virtually the same as in standard British English.

B (*b larga*) and V (*b corta*) are pronounced the same in Spanish. At the beginning of a breath group (e.g. *¿Venís a mi casa?* – "Are you coming to my house?"), or after M or N (e.g. *envidia*, "envy"), it is a hard sound, similar to the "b" in the English "bell". In all other positions, it is a much softer sound, heading a little towards the English "v" in "ever". There is no English equivalent, so the best way to learn the sound is by listening carefully to native pronunciation of phrases such as "soy de Buenos Aires" or "me gusta el vino."

C has two pronunciations; before E and I, it is pronounced as an S, as in *cero* (zero, pronounced "SE-ro"). Before A, O and U, it is pronounced as an English "k": *casa* (house) is a good example.

D follows more or less the same pattern as B/V: at the beginning of a breath group or after L or N it is a hard sound, similar to the English "d" of "dog". In all other positions it is a softer sound, heading towards the "th" in the English word "other". Between vowels and at the end of words it is pronounced very softly and sometimes not at all.

G follows a similar pattern to C: before E and I it is rather like the English "h", though a hint more guttural, heading towards the "ch" in the Scottish "loch" (but far less explosive in Latin America than in Spain). Thus *general* is pronounced "he-ne-RAL". Before A, O and U, G has two possible sounds: at the beginning of a breath group or after N (for example, in "tango"), it is pronounced as in the English "gone". In other positions, G is pronounced like a "g" but slightly guttural: listen for the pronunciation of the word *lago* (lake).

H is silent.

J is a guttural sound.

L is pronounced as in the English "leaf" but not the swallowed English sound in "will" or "bell".

LL is pronounced in Buenos Aires, and much of the rest of the country, rather like the "j" in French *jour*, or the "g" in beige, or the "s" in pleasure; some people make a softer sound, almost like "sh", but this may be considered vulgar; thus *calle* (street) is pronounced "KA-je". In parts of the country, notably the north, it is closer to the "y" sound used in the rest of the continent and in Spain ("KA-ye"). In Corrientes, it is often pronounced as a "ly" sound.

Ñ is pronounced with the tongue flat against the roof of the mouth. Try pronouncing an "n" followed very quickly by a "y", in a similar way to the "ni" sound in the word "onion"; thus *mañana* is like "ma-NYA-na".

Q only occurs before UE and UI, and is pronounced like English "k".

R is pronounced in one of two ways; at the beginning of a word, and after L, N or S it is rolled as for RR, below. Between vowels, or at the end of a word it is a single "flapped" R, produced by a single tap of the tongue on the roof of the mouth immediately behind the teeth. This is actually quite difficult for English-speakers to master; words like *pero* and *cara* are probably the best tests of a gringo accent.

Argentine Spanish vocabulary

In addition to the voseo and various different pronunciations, those who have learnt Spanish elsewhere will need to become accustomed to some different vocabulary in Argentina. In general, Peninsular Spanish terms are recognized, but a familiarity with Argentine equivalents will smooth things along. Though few terms used in Spain are actually rejected in Argentina, there is one major exception, which holds for much of Latin America. The verb *coger*, used in Spain for everything from "to pick up" or "fetch" to "to catch (a bus)" is never used in this way in Argentina, where it is the equivalent of "to fuck". This catch-all Spanish verb is replaced in Argentina by terms such as *tomar* (to take) as in *tomar el colectivo* (to catch the bus) and *agarrar* (to take hold of or grab) as in *agarrá la llave* (take the key). Less likely to cause problems, but still one to watch is *concha*, which in Spain is a perfectly innocent word meaning seashell, but in Argentina is usually used to refer to the female genitals. The words *caracol* or *almeja* are always used instead for shells and Argentines never tire of finding the Spanish woman's name Conchita (short for Inmaculada Concepción) hilarious (it sounds like "little cunt").

el almacén	grocery shop/store	*el living*	living room
el auto	car	*la manteca*	butter
la birome	biro/ballpoint pen	*las medias*	socks
el boliche	nightclub; also sometimes bar/ store/shop in rural areas	*el negocio*	shop (in general)
		el nene/la nena	child
		la palta	avocado
		la papa	potato
las bombachas	knickers	*la pollera*	skirt
la cartera	handbag/purse	*el pomelo*	grapefruit
la carpa	tent	*la remera*	T-shirt
chico/a	small (also boy/girl)	*el suéter*	sweater
el colectivo	bus	*el tapado*	coat (usually woman's)
el durazno	peach		
estacionar	park (verb)	*la vereda*	pavement
la lapicera	pen	*la vidriera*	shop window

Colloquial speech and lunfardo

Colloquial speech in Argentina, particularly in Buenos Aires, is extremely colourful, and it's good fun to learn a bit of the local lingo. There's a clear Italian influence in some words. Many colloquial expressions and words also derive from a form of slang known as lunfardo, originally the language of the Buenos Aires underworld (hence the myriad terms in *lunfardo* proper for police, pimps and prostitutes). There's also a playful form of speech, known as vesre, in which words are pronounced backwards (vesre is revés – reverse, backwards) – a few of these words, such as *feca* (see opposite) have found their way into everyday speech. Though these expressions will sound odd coming from the mouth of a less-than-fluent foreigner, knowing a few of them will help you get the most out of what's being said around you. *Lunfardo* is also an important part of the repertoire of tango lyrics. Another feature to listen for is the widespread use of the prefix "re-", to mean "really" or "totally". *Re-lindo/a* means really good-looking; *re-malo/a* is really bad. *Recontra-* is even stronger: something that is *recontra-barato* is really, really inexpensive, or on sale at a rock-bottom price.

Words listed below that are marked with an asterisk (*) should be used with some caution; those marked with a double asterisk (**) are best avoided until you are really familiar with local customs and language.

afanar	to rob
bancar	to put up with; *no me lo banco* "I can't stand it/him"
bárbaro/a	great!

la barra brava	hardcore football supporters; each club has its own *barra brava*
la birra	beer
el boludo/pelotudo	idiot (equivalent to prat, jerk etc.)**
el bondi	bus
la bronca	rage, as in *me da bronca* "he/she/it makes me angry"
el cana	police officer (cop)*
canchero	sharp-witted, (over)confident
el chabón	boy/lad
el chamuyo	conversation/chat
el chancho	ticket inspector*
el chanta	braggart, unreliable person*
el chorro	thief
chupar	to drink (alcohol)*
copado	cool, good
el despelote	mess
estar en pedo	to be drunk*
el faso	cigarette
el feca	coffee (from *café*)
la fiaca	tiredness/laziness, eg *tengo fiaca*
el forro	condom/idiot**
el gil	idiot*
la guita/la plata	money*
el hinchapelotas	irritating person**
laburar	to work
la luca	one thousand (pesos)
mamado	drunk* (*un mamado*** means a blow-job)
el mango	peso/monetary unit as in *no tengo un mango* "I don't have a penny"
manyar	to eat
una maza	something cool, as in *es una maza* "it's/he's/she's really cool'
el milico	member of the military*
la mina	woman/girl
morfar	to eat
onda	atmosphere/character, as in *tiene buena onda* "it's got a good atmosphere" or "she's good-natured"
el palo	one million (pesos); *un palo verde* is a million US dollars (greenbacks)
la patota	gang
el pendejo	kid (mostly used derogatorily)**
petiso	small, also small person
el pibe	kid
pinta	"it looks good"
la pinta	appearance, as in *tiene pinta* or *tiene buena pinta*
piola	cool, smart
el pucho	cigarette
el quilombo	mess*
el tacho	taxi (*tachero* is taxi driver)
el tano/la tana	Italian*
el telo	short-stay hotel where couples go to have sex*
trucho	fake, phoney
la vieja/el viejo	mum/dad
zafar	to get away with*

RR is written "rr", or "r" in the positions detailed above, and is a strongly trilled sound, produced in the same way as R, but with several rapid taps of the tongue. Some people (native Spanish-speakers included) find it impossible to produce this sound, but it is important for differentiating words such as *pero* (but) and *perro* (dog), or the potentially embarrassing *foro* (forum) and *forro* (slang for "condom" or "idiot"). There are regional variations: in much of Córdoba and the Northwest, especially La Rioja, it is commonly pronounced like a cross between "sh" and "r".

S between vowels or at the beginning of a word is basically as in English "sun". Before consonants it is commonly aspirated in Argentina; meaning that it sounds something like a soft English H: thus *las calles* (the streets) sounds like lah-KA-jes. You don't need to worry about replicating this sound yourself, but familiarizing yourself with it will make it easier to understand what's being said around you. In some regions, S at the end of a word is weakened or even dropped.

Y (*i griega*, in Spanish) between vowels (*playa*, beach) or at the beginning of a word (*yo*, I) is pronounced as LL (see p.853). Otherwise it is pronounced as I (see p.852), as in *y*, the Spanish word for "and".

Z is pronounced the same as S, and is never lisped.

Stress

Familiarizing yourself with Spanish stress rules will make it easy to work out on which syllable the emphasis falls (shown throughout this section as block capitals). Basically, any vowel marked with an accent is stressed; thus *andén* (platform) is an-DEN; the Venezuelan Independence hero Bolívar is bo-LEE-var and María is ma-REE-a. If there is no written accent, then there are two possibilities. If the word ends in a vowel, N or S, it is stressed on the second to last syllable: thus *desayuno* (breakfast) is de-sa-JOO-no, *comen* (they eat) is KO-men and *casas* (houses) is KA-sas. If the word ends in any other consonant, then it is automatically stressed on the last syllable: thus *ciudad* (city) is ciu-DA(D), *comer* (to eat) is ko-MER and Uruguay is oo-roo-GWAY.

Also note that some words that are feminine in Spanish can be masculine in Argentine; eg *vuelto* – change, *llamado* – (telephone) call.

Useful expressions and vocabulary

Basics

sí, no	yes, no
por favor, gracias	please, thank you
dónde, cuándo	where, when
qué, cuánto	what, how much
acá, allá	here, there
esto, eso	this, that
ahora, más tarde/luego	now, later
abierto/a, cerrado/a	open, closed
con, sin	with, without
buen(o)/a, mal(o)/a	good, bad
gran(de)	big
chico/a	small
más, menos	more, less
poco, mucho	a little, a lot
muy	very
hoy, mañana, ayer	today, tomorrow, yesterday
alguien	someone
algo	something
nada, nunca	nothing, never
pero	but
entrada, salida	entrance, exit
tire, empuje	pull, push
Australia	Australia
Canadá	Canada
Inglaterra	England

Gran Bretaña	Great Britain
Irlanda	Ireland
Nueva Zelanda	New Zealand
Sudáfrica	South Africa
Reino Unido	United Kingdom
Estados Unidos	United States
Escocia	Scotland
Gales	Wales

Greetings and responses

hola, chau (*adiós* is used too, but is more formal)	hello, goodbye
buen día	good morning
buenas tardes	good afternoon
buenas noches	good night
hasta luego	see you later
¿cómo está(s)? ¿cómo anda/andás?	how are you?
(muy) bien gracias, ¿y vos/usted?	(very) well, thanks, and you?
de nada	not at all
(con) permiso	excuse me
perdón, disculpe (me)	sorry
¡salud!	cheers!

Useful phrases and expressions

Note that when two verb forms are given, the first corresponds to the familiar *vos* form and the second to the formal *usted* form.

(no) entiendo	I (don't) understand
¿Hablás inglés or **(usted) habla inglés?**	Do you speak English?
(no) hablo castellano	I (don't) speak Spanish
me llamo . . .	My name is . . .
¿cómo te llamás/cómo se llama (usted)?	What's your name?
soy británico/a	I'm British/
. . . soy inglés(a)	. . . English
. . . estadounidense or **norteamericano/a**	. . . American
. . . australiano/a	. . . Australian
. . . canadiense	. . . Canadian
. . . irlandés(a)	. . . Irish
. . . escocés(a)	. . . Scottish
. . . galés(a)	. . . Welsh
. . . neocelandés/a	. . . a New Zealander
. . . sudafricano(a)	. . . South African
¿cómo se dice en castellano?	What's the Spanish for this?
tengo hambre	I'm hungry
tengo sed	I'm thirsty
tengo sueño	I'm tired
no me siento bien	I'm ill
qué pasa?	What's up?
no (lo) sé	I don't know
¿qué hora es?	What's the time?

Hotels and transport

Hay un hotel/banco cerca (de aquí)?	Is there a hotel/bank nearby?
Cómo hago para llegar a...?	How do I get to...?
doblá/doble a la izquierda/derecha, a la izquierda/derecha	Turn left/right, on the left/right
seguí/siga derecho	Go straight on
una cuadra, dos cuadras	one block/two blocks
¿Dónde está . . . ?	Where is . . . ?
la terminal de omnibus	the bus station
la estación de ferrocarril	the train station
el baño	the toilet
Quiero un pasaje dos (de ida y vuelta) para . . .	I want a (return) ticket to . . .
¿de dónde sale el micro para . . . ?	Where does the bus for . . . leave from?
¿a qué hora sale?	What time does it leave?
¿cuánto tarda?	How long does it take?
¿usted pasa por . . . ?	Do you go past . . . ?
lejos, cerca	far, near
lento, rápido	slow, quick
quiero/quería . . .	I want/would like . . .
hay (¿hay?) descuento para estudiantes (?)	there is (is there?) a discount for students(?)
¿hay agua caliente?	is there hot water available?

¿sabe . . . ?	Do you know . . . ?
¿tenés/tiene . . . ? una habitación (single/doble)	Do you have . . . ? a (single, double) room
. . .con dos camas	. . .with two beds
. . .con cama matrimonial	. . .with a double bed
con baño privado	with a private bathroom
con desayuno	with breakfast
es para una persona/ una noche/dos semanas	it's for one person/ one night/two weeks
¿cuánto es/cuánto sale?	How much is it?
está bien	it's fine
es demasiado caro	it's too expensive
¿hay algo más barato?	do you have anything cheaper?
¿hay descuento por pago en efectivo?	Is there a discount for cash?
ventilador, aire acondicionado, calefacción	fan, air-conditioning, heating
¿se puede acampar aquí?	Is camping allowed here?

Numbers, days and months

cero	0
uno/una	1
dos	2
tres	3
cuatro	4
cinco	5
seis	6
siete	7
ocho	8
nueve	9
diez	10
once	11
doce	12
trece	13
catorce	14
quince	15
dieciséis	16
diecisiete	17
dieciocho	18
diecinueve	19
veinte	20
veintiuno/a	21
treinta	30
treinta y uno/una	31
cuarenta	40
cincuenta	50
sesenta	60
setenta	70
ochenta	80
noventa	90
cien/ciento	100
ciento uno/una	101
doscientos/as	200
mil	1000
cien mil	100,000
un millón	1,000,000
dos mil	2000
dos mil ocho	2008
lunes	Monday
martes	Tuesday
miércoles	Wednesday
jueves	Thursday
viernes	Friday
sábado	Saturday
domingo	Sunday
enero	January
febrero	February
marzo	March
abril	April
mayo	May
junio	June
julio	July
agosto	August
se(p)tiembre	September
octubre	October
noviembre	November
diciembre	December

An Argentine menu reader

Basics

aceite de maíz	corn oil
aceite de oliva	olive oil
agregado	side order *or* garnish
ají	chilli
ajo	garlic
almuerzo	lunch
arroz	rice
azúcar	sugar
carta/menú	menu
cena	dinner
comedor	diner *or* dining room
copa	glass (for wine)
cuchara	spoon
cuchillo	knife
cuenta	bill
desayuno	breakfast
guarnición	side dish
harina	flour
huevos	eggs
lata/latita	can or tin
manteca	butter
mayonesa	mayonnaise
menú del día	set meal
mermelada/dulce	jam
mostaza	mustard
pan (francés)	bread (baguette *or* French stick)
pebete	sandwich in a bun *or* bread-roll
pimienta	pepper
pimentón dulce	paprika
plato	plate *or* dish
queso	cheese
sal	salt
sanduich	sandwich (usually made with very thinly sliced bread: *sanduich de miga*)
servilleta	napkin
taza	cup
tenedor	fork
vaso	glass (for water)
vegetariano	vegetarian
vinagre	vinegar

Culinary terms

parrilla	barbecue
asado	roasted *or* barbecued; *un asado* is a barbecue
a la plancha	grilled
ahumado	smoked
al horno	baked/roasted
al natural	canned (of fruit)
al vapor	steamed
crudo	raw
frito	fried
picante	hot (spicy)
puré	puréed *or* mashed potatoes
relleno	stuffed

Meat (carne) and poultry (aves)

bife	steak
bife de chorizo	prize steak cut
cabrito	goat (kid)
carne vacuna	beef
cerdo	pork
ciervo	venison
codorniz	quail
conejo	rabbit
cordero	lamb
chivito	kid *or* goat
chuleta	chop
churrasco	grilled beef
fiambres	cured meats – hams, salami, etc
filete	fillet steak
jabalí	wild boar
jamón	ham
lechón/cochinillo	suckling pig
lomo	tenderloin steak
milanesa	breaded veal escalope
oca	goose
paletilla	shoulder of lamb
panceta	Italian-style bacon
pato	duck
pavo	turkey

pollo	chicken
ternera	grass-fed veal
tocino/beicon	bacon

Offal (achuras)

bofes	lights (lungs)
corazón	heart
criadillas	testicles
chinchulines	small intestine
chorizo (blanco)	meaty sausage (not spiced like Spanish chorizo – chorizo colorado)
hígado	liver
lengua	tongue
mollejas	sweetbreads (thymus gland)
mondongo	cow's stomach
morcilla	blood sausage
orejas	ears
patas	feet *or* trotters
riñones	kidneys
sesos	brains
tripa gorda	tripe (large intestine)
ubre	udder

Typical dishes (platos)

arroz con pollo	a kind of chicken risotto
bife a caballo	steak with a fried egg on top
bife a la criolla	steaks braised with onions, peppers and herbs
brochetas	kebabs
carbonada	a filling meat stew
cazuela de marisco	a seafood casserole
cerdo a la riojana	pork cooked with fruit
fainá	baked chickpea dough traditionally served with pizza
guiso	basic meat stew
locro	stew based on maize, beans and meat, often including tripe
matambre relleno	cold stuffed flank steak (normally filled with vegetables and hard-boiled eggs, and sliced; literally means "stuffed hunger killer")
matambrito	pork, often simmered in milk until soft
milanesa napolitana	breaded veal escalope topped with ham, tomato and melted cheese
milanesa de pollo	breaded chicken breast
mondongo	stew made of cow's stomach with potatoes and tomatoes
pastel de papa	shepherd's pie
provoletta	thick slice of provolone cheese grilled on a barbecue
puchero	a rustic stew, usually of chicken (*puchero de gallina*), made with potatoes and maize or whatever vegetable is to hand
vittel tonné	the Argentine starter par excellence: slices of cold roast beef in mayonnaise mixed with tuna

Fish (pescado)

abadejo	cod
atún	tuna
boga	large, flavoursome fish caught in the Río de la Plata
caballa	mackerel
corvina	sea bass
dorado	a large freshwater fish, with mushy flesh and loads of bones
lenguado	sole
lisa de río	oily river fish
manduví	river fish with delicate, pale flesh
manguruyú	oily river fish (best grilled)
merluza	hake

pacú	firm-fleshed river fish
pejerrey	popular inland-water fish
pirapitanga	salmon-like river fish
sábalo	oily-fleshed river fish
salmón	salmon
surubí	kind of catfish
trucha (arco iris)	(rainbow) trout
vieja	white, meaty-fleshed river-fish

Seafood (mariscos)

camarones	shrimps *or* prawns
cangrejo	crab
centolla	king crab
mejillones	mussels
ostras	oysters
vieira	scallop

Vegetables (verduras)

aceitunas	olives
acelga	chard (like spinach but tougher and more bitter)
albahaca	basil
alcauciles	artichokes
apio	celery
arvejas	peas
aspárragos	asparagus
berenjena	aubergine/eggplant
berro	watercress
cebolla	onion
champiñon	mushroom
chauchas	runner beans
choclo	maize *or* sweetcorn
chucrút	sauerkraut
coliflor	cauliflower
ensalada	salad
espinaca	spinach
garbanzo	chickpea
habas	broad beans
hinojo	fennel
hongos (silvestres)	(wild) mushrooms
lechuga	lettuce
lentejas	lentils
morrón (dulce/rojo/verde)	(sweet/red/green) pepper
palmito	palm heart
palta	avocado
papa	potato
papas fritas	chips/French fries
papines	small potatoes eaten whole
perejil	parsley
pimiento	green pepper
poroto	bean
puerro	leek
remolacha	beetroot
rúcula	rocket
tomate	tomato
tomillo	thyme
zanahoria	carrot
zapallo	pumpkin
zapallito	gem squash – small green pumpkins that are a favourite throughout the country, usually baked stuffed with rice and meat

Fruit and nuts (fruta y frutos secos)

almendra	almond
almíbar	syrup
ananá	pineapple
arándano	cranberry/blueberry
avellana	hazelnut
banana	banana
batata	sweet potato
castaña	chestnut
cayote	spaghetti squash
cereza	cherry
ciruela (seca)	plum (prune)
dátiles	dates
damasco	apricot
durazno	peach
frambuesa	raspberry
frutilla	strawberry
higo	fig
lima	lime
limón	lemon
maní	peanut
manzana	apple
melón	melon

membrillo	quince
mora	mulberry
mosqueta	rose hip
naranja	orange
nuez	walnut
pasa (de uva)	dried fruit (raisin)
pera	pear
pomelo (rosado)	(pink) grapefruit
quinoto	kumquat
sandía	watermelon
uva	grape(s)
zarza mora	blackberry

Desserts (postres)

arroz con leche	rice pudding
budín de pan	bread pudding
crema	custard *or* cream
dulce de leche	thick caramel made from milk and sugar, a national religion (see box, p.45)
dulce	sweet in general; candied fruit *or* jam
ensalada de fruta	fruit salad
flan	crème caramel
helado medialuna	ice cream
(dulce/salado)	(sweet/plain) croissant-like pastry, more like the Italian "cornetto"
miel (de abeja)	honey
miel (de caña)	molasses
panqueque/crepe	pancake
sambayón	zabaglione (custard made with egg yolks and wine, a popular ice-cream flavour)
torta	tart *or* cake
tortilla/tortita	breakfast pastry

Drinks (bebidas)

agua	water
agua mineral (con gas/sin gas)	mineral water (sparkling/still)
aguardiente	brandy-like spirit
botella	bottle
cacheteado	Coke and red wine spritzer (very popular in Córdoba)
café (con leche)	coffee (with milk)
cerveza	beer
champán	sparkling wine, usually Argentine, *or* champagne
chocolate caliente /submarino	hot chocolate (often a slab of chocolate melted in hot milk, served in a tall glass)
chopp	draught beer
cortado	espresso coffee "cut" with a little steaming milk (similar to macchiato)
Fernet (branca)	Italian-style digestive drink, popularly mixed with Coke (the gaucho drink par excellence)
gaseosa	fizzy drink
jugo (de naranja)	(orange) juice
lata	can
leche	milk
licuados	juice-based drinks *or* milkshakes
liso	small draught beer (Litoral)
mate cocido	infusion made with *mate*, sometimes heretically with a tea-bag
sidra	cider
soda	fizzy water, sometimes in a siphon
té	tea
vino (tinto/blanco /rosado)	wine (red/white/rosé)

A glossary of Argentine terms and acronyms

ACA (Automóvil Club Argentino) National motoring organization (pronounced A-ka).

Acampar To camp.

Aduana Customs post.

Aerosilla Chairlift.

Agreste Wild or rustic (often used to describe a campsite with very basic facilities).

Alerce Giant, slow-growing Patagonian cypress, similar to the Californian redwood.

Almacén Small grocery store, which in the past often functioned as a bar too.

Altiplano High Andean plateau.

Aónik'enk The southern group of Tehuelche (q.v.), the last of whose descendants live in the province of Santa Cruz.

Araucaria Monkey puzzle tree.

Arepa Flat maize bread.

Arroba The @ sign on a computer keyboard.

Arroyo Stream or small river.

Autopista Motorway.

Bailanta Dance club, where the predominant sound is *cumbia* (see p.165).

Balneario Bathing resort; also a complex of sunshades and small tents on the beach, often with a bar and shower facilities, for which users pay a daily, weekly or monthly rate.

Banda negativa Airline tariff bracket, where a percentage of seats is sold at heavily discounted rates.

Baqueano Mountain or wilderness guide.

Barrio Neighbourhood.

Bofedal Spongy Altiplano wetland.

Boleadoras/bolas Traditional hunting implement, composed of stone balls connected by thick cord, thrown to entangle legs or neck of prey. Traditionally used by gauchos, who inherited it from Argentina's indigenous inhabitants.

Boletería Ticket office.

Boleto Travel ticket.

Bombachas (de campo) Baggy gaucho trousers for riding.

Bombilla Straw-like implement, usually of metal, used for drinking *mate* from a gourd.

Bonaerense Adjective relating to or person from Buenos Aires Province.

Bondi Colloquial term in Buenos Aires for a bus.

Botiquín Medicine kit.

C/ The abbreviation of *calle* (street); only rarely used.

Cabildo Colonial town hall; now replaced by Municipalidad.

Cabina telefónica Phone booth.

Cacique Generic term for the head of a Latin American indigenous community or people, either elected or hereditary.

Cajero automático Cashpoint machine (ATM).

Calafate Type of thorny Patagonian bush, famous for its delicious blue berries.

Camioneta Pick-up truck.

Campesino Country-dweller; sometimes used to refer to someone with indigenous roots.

Campo de hielo Ice cap or ice-field.

Caña colihue Native Patagonian plant of the forest under-storey; resembles bamboo.

Cancha Football stadium.

Cantina Traditional restaurant, usually Italian.

Característica Telephone code.

Carretera Route or highway.

Cartelera Agency for buying discounted tickets for cinemas, theatres and concerts.

Casa de té Tearoom.

Casco Main building of estancia; the homestead.

Cataratas Waterfalls, usually used to refer specifically to Iguazú Falls.

Caudillo Regional military or political leader, usually with authoritarian overtones.

Cebar (mate) To brew (*mate*).

Ceibo Tropical tree with a twisted trunk, whose bright-red or pink blossom is the national flower of Argentina, Uruguay and Paraguay.

Cerro Hill, mountain peak.

Chaco húmedo Wet chaco habitat.

Chaco seco Dry chaco habitat.

Chacra Small farm.

Chamamé Folk music from the Litoral region, specifically Corrientes Province.

Chango Common term in the Northwest for a young boy; often used in the sense of "mate"/"buddy".

Chaqueño Someone from the Gran Chaco.

Chata Slang term for pick-up truck.

China A gaucho girl or woman.

Choique Common term, deriving from Mapudungun, for the smaller, southern Darwin's rhea of Patagonia.

Churro Strip of fried dough, somewhat similar to a doughnut, often filled with *dulce de leche*.

Colectivo Urban bus.

Combi Small minibus that runs urban bus routes.

Comparsa Carnival "school".

Confitería Café and tearoom, often with patisserie attached.

Conventillo Tenement building.

Cordillera Mountain range; usually used in Argentina to refer to the Andes.

Cortadera Pampas grass.

Costanera Riverside avenue.

Country Term for exclusive out-of-town residential compound or sports and social club.

Criollo Historically an Argentine-born person of Spanish descent. Used today in two ways: as a general term for Argentine (as in *comida criolla*, traditional Argentine food) and used by indigenous people to refer to those of non-indigenous descent.

Cuadra The distance from one street corner to the next, usually 100 metres (see also *manzana*).

Cuchilla Regional term for low hill in Entre Ríos.

Cuesta Slope or small hill.

Cumbia Popular Argentine "tropical" rhythm, inspired by Colombian cumbia.

Departamento Administrative district in a province; also an apartment.

Descamisados Term meaning "the shirtless ones," popularized by Juan and Evita Perón to refer to the working-class masses and dispossessed.

Despensa Shop (particularly in rural areas).

Día de campo Day spent at an estancia where traditional *asado* and empanadas are eaten and guests are usually given a display of gaucho skills.

Dique Dock; also dam.

E/ The abbreviation of *entre* (between), used in addresses.

Empalme Junction of two highways.

Encomienda Package, parcel; also historical term for form of trusteeship bestowed on Spaniards after conquest, granting them rights over the native population.

Entrada Ticket (for football match, theatre etc).

Estancia Argentine farm, traditionally with huge areas of land.

Estanciero An owner of an estancia.

Estepa Steppe.

Estero A shallow swampland, commonly found in El Litoral and Gran Chaco areas.

Facón Gaucho knife, usually carried in a sheath.

Federalists Nineteenth-century term for those in favour of autonomous power being given to the provinces; opponents of Unitarists (see p.867).

Feria artesanal/de artesanías Craft fair.

Ferretería Hardware shop (often useful for camping equipment).

Ferrocarril Railway.

Ficha Token.

Fogón Place for a barbecue or camp fire; bonfire.

Fonda Simple restaurant.

Galería Small shopping arcade.

Gaseosa Soft drink.

Gaucho The typical Argentine "cowboy", or rural estancia worker.

Gendarmería Police station.

Gomería Tyre repair centre.

Gomero Rubber tree.

Gringo Any white foreigner, though often specifically those from English-speaking countries; historically, European immigrants to Argentina (as opposed to *criollos*), as in *pampa gringa*, the part of the pampas settled by Europeans.

Guanaco Wild camelid of the llama family.

Guaraní Indigenous people and language, found principally in Misiones, Corrientes and Paraguay.

Guardaequipaje Left-luggage office.

Guardafauna Wildlife ranger.

Guardaganado Cattle grid.

Guardaparque National park ranger.

Gününa'küna The northern group of the Tehuelche (q.v.), now extinct.

Hacer dedo To hitchhike.

Humedal Any wetland swampy area.

IGM (Instituto Geográfico Militar) The national military's cartographic institution.

Impenetrable Term applied historically to the area of the dry chaco with the most inhospitable conditions for white settlement, due to lack of water; the name of a zone of northwestern Chaco Province.

Intendencia Head office of a national park.

Intendente Administrative chief of a national park.

Interno Telephone extension number.

Isleta de monte Clump of scrubby mixed woodland found in savannah or flat agricultural land, typically in the Gran Chaco and the northeast of the country.

IVA (*impuesto de valor agregado*) Value-added tax or sales tax.

Jacarandá Tropical tree with trumpet-shaped mauvish blossom.

Jarilla Thorny, chest-high bush.

Junta Military government coalition.

Kiosko Newspaper stand or small store selling cigarettes, confectionery and some foodstuffs.

Kolla Andean indigenous group predominant in the northwestern provinces of Salta and Jujuy.

Lancha Smallish motor boat.

Lapacho Tropical tree typical of the Litoral region and distinguished by bright-pink blossom.

Leña Firewood.

Lenga Type of *Nothofagus* southern beech common in Patagonian forests.

El litoral Littoral, shore – used to refer to the provinces of Entre Ríos, Corrientes, Misiones, Santa Fe and sometimes Eastern Chaco and Formosa.

Litoraleño Inhabitant of the Litoral (see above).

Locutorio Call centre, where phone calls are made from cabins and the caller is charged after the call has been made.

Lomo de burro Speed bump.

Lonco Head or *cacique* (see p.863) of a Mapuche community.

Madrejón A swampy ox-bow lake.

Mallín Swamp, particularly in upland moors.

Manzana City block; the square bounded by four *cuadras* (see opposite).

Mapuche One of Argentina's largest indigenous groups, whose ancestors originally came from Chilean Patagonia and whose biggest communities are found in the provinces of Chubut, Río Negro and especially Neuquén.

Mapudungun The language of the Mapuche.

Marcha Commercial dance music.

Mataco See *Wichí*.

Mate Strictly the *mate* gourd or receptacle, but used generally to describe the national "tea" drink.

Menú del día Standard set menu.

Menú ejecutivo Set menu. Tends to be more expensive than the *menú del día* (q.v.), though not always that executive.

Mesopotamia The three provinces of Entre Ríos, Corrientes and Misiones, by analogy with the ancient region lying between the rivers Tigris and Euphrates, in modern-day Iraq.

Micro Long-distance bus.

Microcentro The area of a city comprising the central square and neighbouring streets.

Milonga Style of folk-guitar music usually associated with the pampa region; also a tango dance and a subgenre of tango, more uptempo than tango proper. Also a tango dancing event, often with tuition (see box, p.170).

Mirador Scenic lookout point or tower.

Monte Scrubby woodland, often used to describe any uncultivated woodland area. Also used to refer to the desertified ecosystem that lies in the rainshadow of the central Andes around the Cuyo region.

Mozarabic Spanish architectural style, originally dating from the ninth to thirteenth centuries and characterized by a fusion of Romanesque and Moorish styles.

Muelle Pier or jetty.

Municipalidad Municipality building or town hall.

Ñandú A common name, derived from Guaraní, for the Greater Rhea, but also used to refer to its smaller cousin, the Darwin's Rhea.

Ñire Type of *Nothofagus* southern beech tree common in Patagonian forests.

Ñoqui Argentine spelling of the Italian *gnocchi*, a small potato dumpling. Used to refer to phoney employees who appear on a company's payroll but don't actually work there; also slang for a punch.

Nothofagus Genus of Patagonian trees commonly called southern beech (includes *lenga* and *ñire* q.v.).

Ombú Large shade tree, originally from the Mesopotamia region and now associated with the pampas where it was introduced in the eighteenth century.

Paisano Meaning "countryman"; sometimes loosely used as equivalent to gaucho and often used by people of indigenous descent to refer to themselves, thus avoiding the sometimes pejorative *indio* (Indian).

Palmar Palm grove.

Palo borracho Tree associated especially with the dry-chaco habitat of northern Argentina; its name (literally "drunken stick") is derived from its swollen trunk in which water is stored.

Palometa Piranha/piraña.

Pampa(S) The broad flat grasslands of central Argentina.

Parquímetro Parking meter.

Parrillada The meat barbecued on a *parrilla*.

Pasaje Narrow street.

Paseaperro Professional dog walker.

Pastizal Grassland, often used for grazing.

Pato The Argentine national sport; similar to handball on horseback.

Payada Traditional improvised musical style, often performed as a kind of dialogue between two singers (*payadores*) who accompany themselves on guitars.

Peaje Road toll.

Peatonal Pedestrianized street.

Pehuén Mapuche term for monkey puzzle tree.

Peña Circle or group (usually of artists or musicians); a *peña folklórica* is a folk-music club.

Peón Farmhand.

Picada A roughly marked path; also a plate of small snacks eaten before a meal, particularly cheese, ham or smoked meats.

Planta baja Ground floor (first floor, US).

Playa Beach.

Playa (de estacionamiento) Parking area; garage.

Plazoleta/plazuela Small town square.

Porteño Someone from Buenos Aires city.

Prefectura Naval prefecture for controlling river and marine traffic.

Puesto Small outpost or hut for shepherds or *guardaparques*.

Pukará Pre-Columbian fortress.

Pulpería A type of traditional general-provisions store that doubles up as a bar and rural meeting-point.

Puna High Andean plateau (alternative term for *altiplano*, see p.863).

Puntano Someone from San Luis.

Quebrada Ravine, gully.

Querandí Original indigenous inhabitants of the pampa region.

Quinta Suburban or country house with a small plot of land, where fruit and vegetables are often cultivated.

Qom An indigenous group, living principally in the east of Formosa and Chaco provinces. The word means "people" in their language.

Rancho Simple countryside dwelling, typically constructed of adobe.

Rastra Gaucho belt, typically ornamented with silver.

RC (Ruta Complementaria) Subsidiary, unsealed road in Tierra del Fuego.

Recargo Surcharge on credit cards.

Recova Arcade around the exterior of a building or courtyard, typical of colonial-era buildings.

Reducción Jesuit mission settlement.

Refugio Trekking refuge or hut.

Remise/remís Taxi or chauffeur-driven rental car, booked through a central office.

Remise colectivo Shared cab that runs fixed inter-urban routes.

Represa Dam; also reservoir.

Río River.

Rioplatense Referring to people or things (including language) from the region around the River Plate (Río de la Plata) – Buenos Aires Province, Santa Fe Province and Uruguay, plus slightly further afield.

Ripio Gravel; usually used to describe an unsurfaced gravel road.

RN (Ruta Nacional) Major route, usually paved.

RP (Ruta Provincial) Provincial road, sometimes paved.

Ruta Route or road.

Salto Waterfall.

Sapucay Bloodcurdling shriek characteristic of chamamé (see p.864).

Selk'nam Nomadic, indigenous guanaco-hunters from Tierra del Fuego, whose last members died in the 1960s. Also called Ona, the Yámana (q.v.) name for them.

Sendero Path or trail.

S/N Used in addresses to indicate that there's no house number (*sin número*).

Soroche Altitude sickness.

Sortija Display of gaucho skill in which the galloping rider must spear a small ring hung from a thread.

Subte Buenos Aires' underground railway.

Suri A type of rhea indigenous to Argentina.

Tanguería Tango club.

Tasa de terminal Terminal tax.

Taxímetro Taxi meter.

Tehuelche Generic term for the different nomadic steppe tribes of Patagonia, whom early European explorers named "Patagones".

Teleférico Gondola or cable car.

Tenedor libre All-you-can-eat buffet restaurant.

Tereré Common drink in the subtropical north of the country and Paraguay, composed of *yerba mate* served with wild herbs (*yuyos*) and ice-cold water or lemonade.

Terminal de ómnibus Bus terminal.

Terrateniente Landowner.

Tipa Acacia-like tree often found in northern *yungas*.

Toba See Qom.

Truco Argentina's national card game, in which the ability to outbluff your opponents is of major importance.

Unitarists Nineteenth-century centralists, in favour of power being centralized in Buenos Aires; opponents of Federalists (see p.865).

Villa Short for *villa miseria*, a shanty town.

Wichí Semi-nomadic indigenous group, living predominantly in the dry central and western areas of Chaco and Formosa provinces, and in the far east of Salta. Sometimes referred to pejoratively as Mataco.

Yahganes See *Yámana*.

Yámana Nomadic indigenous canoe-going people who lived in the islands and channels south of Tierra del Fuego, and whose culture died out in Argentina in the early twentieth century.

Yerba mate The dried and cured leaves of the plant used to brew *mate*.

YPF (Yacimientos Petroleros Fiscales) The principal Argentine petroleum company, now privatized and owned by Spanish firm REPSOL. It is usually used to refer to the company's fuel stations, which act as landmarks in the less populated areas of Patagonia in particular.

Zona franca Duty-free zone.

Travel store

Small print and
Index

A Rough Guide to Rough Guides

Published in 1982, the first Rough Guide – to Greece – was a student scheme that became a publishing phenomenon. Mark Ellingham, a recent graduate in English from Bristol University, had been traveling in Greece the previous summer and couldn't find the right guidebook. With a small group of friends he wrote his own guide, combining a highly contemporary, journalistic style with a thoroughly practical approach to travellers' needs.

The immediate success of the book spawned a series that rapidly covered dozens of destinations. And, in addition to impecunious backpackers, Rough Guides soon acquired a much broader and older readership that relished the guides' wit and inquisitiveness as much as their enthusiastic, critical approach and value-for-money ethos.

These days, Rough Guides include recommendations from shoestring to luxury and cover more than 200 destinations around the globe, including almost every country in the Americas and Europe, more than half of Africa and most of Asia and Australasia. Our ever-growing team of authors and photographers is spread all over the world, particularly in Europe, the USA and Australia.

In the early 1990s, Rough Guides branched out of travel, with the publication of Rough Guides to World Music, Classical Music and the Internet. All three have become benchmark titles in their fields, spearheading the publication of a wide range of books under the Rough Guide name.

Including the travel series, Rough Guides now number more than 350 titles, covering: phrasebooks, waterproof maps, music guides from Opera to Heavy Metal, reference works as diverse as Conspiracy Theories and Shakespeare, and popular culture books from iPods to Poker. Rough Guides also produce a series of more than 120 World Music CDs in partnership with World Music Network.

Visit www.roughguides.com to see our latest publications.

Rough Guide travel images are available for commercial licensing at www.roughguidespictures.com.

Rough Guide credits

Text editor: Ella Steim
Layout: Jessica Subramanian
Cartography: Alakananda Bhattacharya, Maxine Repath
Picture editor: Nicole Newman
Production: Vicky Baldwin
Proofreader: Jennifer Speake
Cover design: Chloë Roberts
Photographer: Greg Roden
Editorial: **London** Kate Berens, Claire Saunders, Ruth Blackmore, Alison Murchie, Karoline Densley, Andy Turner, Keith Drew, Edward Aves, Alice Park, Lucy White, Jo Kirby, James Smart, Natasha Foges, Róisín Cameron, Emma Traynor, Emma Gibbs, Kathryn Lane, Joe Staines, Duncan Clark, Peter Buckley, Matthew Milton, Tracy Hopkins, Ruth Tidball; **New York** Andrew Rosenberg, Steven Horak, AnneLise Sorensen, Amy Hegarty, April Isaacs, Anna Owens, Joseph Petta, Sean Mahoney; **Delhi** Madhavi Singh, Karen D'Souza
Design & Pictures: **London** Scott Stickland, Dan May, Diana Jarvis, Mark Thomas, Chloë Roberts, Sarah Cummins; **Delhi** Umesh Aggarwal, Ajay Verma, Ankur Guha, Pradeep Thapliyal, Sachin Tanwar, Anita Singh, Nikhil Agarwal
Production: Rebecca Short
Cartography: **London** Ed Wright, Katie Lloyd-Jones; **Delhi** Jai Prakash Mishra, Rajesh Chhibber, Ashutosh Bharti, Rajesh Mishra, Animesh Pathak, Jasbir Sandhu, Karobi Gogoi, Amod Singh, Swati Handoo
Online: Narender Kumar, Rakesh Kumar, Amit Verma, Rahul Kumar, Ganesh Sharma, Debojit Borah
Marketing & Publicity: **London** Liz Statham, Niki Hanmer, Louise Maher, Jess Carter, Vanessa Godden, Vivienne Watton, Anna Paynton, Rachel Sprackett; **New York** Geoff Colquitt, Megan Kennedy, Katy Ball; **Delhi** Ragini Govind
Manager India: Punita Singh
Series Editor: Mark Ellingham
Reference Director: Andrew Lockett
Publishing Coordinator: Helen Phillips
Publishing Director: Martin Dunford
Commercial Manager: Gino Magnotta
Managing Director: John Duhigg

Publishing information

This third edition published January 2008 by
Rough Guides Ltd,
80 Strand, London WC2R 0RL
345 Hudson St, 4th Floor,
New York, NY 10014, USA
14 Local Shopping Centre, Panchsheel Park,
New Delhi 110017, India
Distributed by the Penguin Group
Penguin Books Ltd,
80 Strand, London WC2R 0RL
Penguin Group (USA)
375 Hudson Street, NY 10014, USA
Penguin Group (Australia)
250 Camberwell Road, Camberwell,
Victoria 3124, Australia
Penguin Books Canada Ltd,
10 Alcorn Avenue, Toronto, Ontario,
Canada M4V 1E4
Penguin Group (NZ)
67 Apollo Drive, Mairangi Bay, Auckland 1310,
New Zealand
Cover concept by Peter Dyer.

Typeset in Bembo and Helvetica to an original design by Henry Iles.

Printed and bound in China

888pp includes index

A catalogue record for this book is available from the British Library

ISBN: 978-1-84353-844-8

3 5 7 9 8 6 4 2

Help us update

We've gone to a lot of effort to ensure that the third edition of **The Rough Guide to Argentina** is accurate and up to date. However, things change – places get "discovered", opening hours are notoriously fickle, restaurants and rooms raise prices or lower standards. If you feel we've got it wrong or left something out, we'd like to know, and if you can remember the address, the price, the hours, the phone number, so much the better.

Please send your comments with the subject line "**Rough Guide Argentina Update**" to ⓔmail@roughguides.com, or by post to the address above. We'll credit all contributions and send a copy of the next edition (or any other Rough Guide if you prefer) for the very best emails.

Have your questions answered and tell others about your trip at ⓦcommunity.roughguides.com.

Acknowledgements

Andrew Benson wishes to thank: all my friends around Argentina. At the risk of omitting anyone, I'd like to single out: Alberto; Elsa and her wonderful staff and family; China; my exemplary hosts in Esquina; Charlie and the whole gang in Colón; all the people who helped me in Jujuy Province; my dear friends Nanny and Ricardo; all my wonderful friends in Salta, San Lorenzo and the rest of the province; all those who showed me around Rosario; the fabulous people I met and danced with in Santiago; the maize-field guard who helped me change a wheel; my kind hosts in Tucumán; and Juan Pablo and his family; Constanza and all at Marina; Josefina and the family and staff at Don Numas; Marjan and her family, Martasu, Patricia, Sandrine, Soraya, Carlos, David, Eugenio, Gastón, Gustavo A. and Gustavo M., Ignacio, Mario, Miguel, Peter W., Ricardo, Robert, Rubén and Thierry; Andrea and Cristina for a great day in Colonia; Laura, Jackie and Peter M. for being great travel companions; and Fernando – despite some difficult moments. Last but not least, many thanks to Rosalba for being an incredibly cooperative and loyal colleague, and to Ella for her keen eye and flexible stance throughout a very long process.

Rosalba O'Brien wishes to thank: Ines Buzzetti, Kate and Andrew, Pepe el peronista and Irene, Jessica and Diego, Isabel at NA Concepts, Mimi, Carolina, Amalia and Sebastian, Andrew who shares my passion for Argentina, Ella for her eagle-eyed editing and most of all Esteban Fernandez Balbis for patience, explanations and Arwen Fernandez O'Brien.

Keith Drew wishes to thank: all the individuals who were so quick to help along the way, effortlessly enhancing Patagonia's deserved reputation for hospitality. Particular praise is due to: Ana Chiabrando, for much-needed tea and cakes in Gaiman; Petty and Coco; Verónica Sisti, first in El Calafate and then again in Ushuaia; Desirée Sauervein, for rescuing our laundry from the brink; and Paulina Fredes and her little Agustín, for tremendous hospitality on Isla Navarino. Thanks, also, to Gabriel Retamozo, Annelies Gerritsen and Nicholas Ayling, Martín Molina, Pedro and Susana Fortuny, Rita Agote, Alfredo and Patricia, Andrea Lagunas, Lorena Kemp, Flavia Raffo, Ricardo Perez, Carolina and Simon Goodall, Paloma, Rafael and Captain Ben Garrett. The greatest gratitude, though, goes to KLB, my treasured travelling companion, not just in Argentina but also in life. She drove 600km down a bleak gravel track in a Vauxhall Corsa and spent four days marooned at the end of the world but never lost that incredible smile. Without her, the trip, like the last 14 years, just wouldn't have quite cut it.

Paul Smith wishes to thank: Horacio Matarasso for showing me where to see condors and Delia for rescuing me in Pehuenia. At Rough Guides thanks to Ella for her dedication and patience. Special thanks to Mum and Dad and my wife Carol for their love, help and support.

The editor wishes to thank: Andrew, Rosalba, Keith and Paul for all their hard work. Many thanks also to Jessica Subramanian for patiently putting it all together; the cartographers – Alaknanda and everyone at RG Delhi, and Maxine; Nicole Newman, for picture research; Jennifer Speake for proofreading; Amy Hegarty; and AnneLise Sorensen, Steve Horak and Andrew Rosenberg for guidance throughout.

Readers' letters

Thanks to all the readers who have taken the time to write in with comments and suggestions (and apologies if we've inadvertently omitted or misspelt an yone's name):

Christine Airala, Richard Andrews, Francesco Arneodo, Ilona Carroll, Eddy le Couvreur, Bart de Boer, George Duncan, Eric Eisenhandler, Giorgio Genova, Dominic Gibson, Vanessa Hadley, Abigail Holt, Mark Hunter, Igor Kucera, Fritz Lanz, Huw Lewis, Lucia Linares, Margaret Lobley, Patricio Lopez, William Lucas, Philip Luther, Alicia Mianda, Caroline Moats, Helen Read, Oliver Reinhard, Martin Rester, Clifford and Maryke Roberts, Armand Schouten, Hannah Seger, Nicki Spencer, Majella Stack, Alicia Torres, Paul Whitfield, Roland Wirth and Andrew Young.

Photo credits

All photos © Rough Guides except the following:

Title page
Street musicians, Buenos Aires © Ozonas/Masterfile

Full page
Paprikas drying, Cachi © Andrew Benson

Introduction
Cowboy belt buckle © Barnabas Bosshart/Corbis
Quilmes ruins © Florian von der Fecht
Monte Fitz Roy, Parque Nacional Los Glaciares © Art Wolfe/Getty
Whale-watching © Florian von der Fecht
Lago Belgrano © Javier Etcheverry/Alamy
Gaucho on an estancia, Patagonia © Jeremy Hoare/Alamy

Things not to miss
01 Ruta de los Siete Lagos © Florian von der Fecht
03 El Carnaval del Pais, Gualeguaychú © Enrique Marcarian/Reuters/Corbis
04 Snowboarding © Florian von der Fecht
05 Dinosaur femur bone, Neuquén © Javier Etcheverry/Alamy
06 Guanaco © Gabriel Rojo/Nature Picture Library
07 Ushuaia © photolibrary
10 Chaco wildlife © Nature Picture Library
11 Gaucho in the Pampas © ImageState/Alamy
12 Aconcagua © Michael Lewis/Corbis
14 Colonia del Sacramento, Uruguay © Lemarco/Alamy
15 Rutini Pinot Noir 1999, Bodega La Rural © Per Karlsson/Alamy
17 Estancia, Tierra del Fuego © Nicolas Russell/Getty Images
18 Cueva de las Manos Pintadas © Keith Drew
19 Tigre Delta © Robert Fried/Alamy
20 Iguazú Falls © Florian von der Fecht
22 Capilla de Candonga, Córdoba © Florian von der Fecht
23 Glaciar Perito Moreno © Frank Krahmer/Zefa/Corbis
24 Polo match © Reuters
25 Teatro Colón © Michael Lewis/Corbis
26 Birdlife, Esteros del Iberá © Greg Roden
27 Handicrafts © Florian von der Fecht
28 Argentine football fans © Shaun Best/Reuters
29 Cerro de los Siete Colores, Quebrada de Humahuaca © Florian von der Fecht

Colour section: Criollo culture
Gaucho drinking mate © Marco Simoni/Robert Harding
Gauchos at barbecue © Peter Adams/Getty Images
Locro (a meat stew) © Gareth McCormack/Alamy
Gaucho belt © Florian von der Fecht
Gaucho sword case © Barnabas Bosshart/Corbis
Gaucho rides unbroken horse © Reuters/Andres Stapff
San Antonio de Areco © Andrea Booher/Getty Images

Colour section: Sports and outdoor activities
Cerro Pissis © Getty Images/Science Faction
Trekking in Santa Cruz Province © Aurora/Getty Images
Trail signposts, Parque Nacional Los Glaciares © Keith Drew
Fly-fishing in Neuquén Province © Florian von der Fecht
Pato © Frederic Cholin/Alamy
La Bombonera, Buenos Aires © Marcos Brindicci/Reuters/Corbis
Diego Maradona © Bongarts/Getty Images

Colour section: The legendary Ruta 40
Road sign, Chubut © Florian von der Fecht
Santa Cruz Province © Florian von der Fecht
Lighthouse, Santa Cruz © Florian von der Fecht
La Rioja Province © Florian von der Fecht
Viaducto La Polvorilla © Javier Etcheverry/Alamy
Sheep crossing Ruta 40, Santa Cruz © Keith Drew

Black and whites
p.187 Museo del Arte Tigre © Greg Roden
p.200 Gauchos drinking yerba mate © Peter Adams/Getty Images
p.210 Museo de Ciencias Naturales, La Plata © Louie Psihoyos/Corbis
p.233 Mar del Plata © photolibrary
p.242 Basílica Nuestra Señora De Luján © Sarah Murray/Masterfile
p.261 Black Vulture, Parque Nacional Lihué Calel © Gabriel Rojo/Nature Picture Library
p.266 Hang-gliding, Córdoba Province © Greg Roden
p.277 Cabildo and Cathedral, Córdoba © JTB Photo Communications, Inc/Alamy
p.286 Jesús María National Jesuitical Museum, Córdoba © Sarah Murray/Masterfile
p.291 Hotel Edén, La Falda © A. Parada/Alamy
p.298 Museo Casa Ernesto "Che" Guevara, Alta Gracia © Miguel Rojo/AFP/Getty Images
p.316 Ruins at San Ignacio Miní © photolibrary
p.322 El Carnaval del Pais, Gualeguaychú © Enrique Marcarian/Reuters/Corbis

p.338 Capybaras in the Esteros del Iberá © Joe McDonald/Corbis
p.345 Cathedral, Posadas © Richard Wareham Fotografie/Alamy
p.363 Iguazú Falls © photolibrary
p.378 Parque Indepencia, Rosario © Richard Wareham Fotografie/Alamy
p.383 Victoria bridge © Alfredo Celoria/Reuters/Corbis
p.391 Swimmers preparing for race, Paraná © Rob Howard/Corbis
p.404 Indigenous woman, Chaco Province © Pixonnet.com/Alamy
p.416 Pukará de Tilcara, Quebrada de Humahuaca © Florian von der Fecht
p.428 Plaza 9 de Julio, Salta © photolibrary
p.447 Vineyard, Calchaquíes Valley © Cézaro De Luca/EFE/Corbis
p.453 Lola Mora statue, Jujuy © Andrew Benson
p.466 Espina del Diablo, Jujuy © Florian von der Fecht
p.482 Museo Pacahamama, Amaicha © Andrew Benson
p.495 Shinkal ruins © Andrew Benson
p.504 Trekking towards Mount Aconcagua © John Warburton-Lee
p.519 Plaza España, Mendoza © Magical Andes
p.527 Vineyard, Mendoza © Cephas Picture Library/Alamy
p.542 Skiing, Las Leñas © Sergio De Divitiis/Getty Images/SambaPhoto
p.560 Rock formations, Parque Provincial Ischigualasto © Greg Roden
p.580 La Trochita (Old Patagonian Express) © Aurora/Getty Images
p.594 Monkey puzzle tree © Craig Lovell/Corbis
p.606 Volcán Lanín © Kevin Schafer/Alamy
p.613 Nahuel Huapi National Park © Swerve/Alamy
p.627 San Carlos de Bariloche © Craig Lovell/Corbis
p.637 Gauchos herding cows, Cholila © STR New/Reuter
p.652 Southern right whale, Puerto Pirámides © Keith Drew
p.668 Female elephant seal, Punta Delgada © Keith Drew
p.679 Bosque Petrificado Sarmiento © Keith Drew
p.695 Hand paintings, Cueva de las Manos Pintadas © Keith Drew
p.711 Hiking, Laguna de los Tres and Monte Fitz Roy, Parque Nacional Los Glaciares © Keith Drew
p.725 Glaciar Perito Moreno © Carlos Corvalan/Intendecia El Calafate/Reuters/Corbis
p.731 Municipal cemetery, Punta Arenas © Simon Vine/Alamy
p.744 Parque Nacional Tierra del Fuego © Martin Harvey/Corbis
p.754 Ushuaia harbour © Aurora/Getty Images
p.759 Magellanic Penguins in the Beagle Channel © Steve Allen Travel Photography/Alamy
p.776 Puerto Williams town sign, Isla Navarino © Keith Drew
p.814 Giant anteater, Chaco © Gabriel Rojo/Nature Picture Library
p.841 Xul Solar painting © Foundation Pan Klub, Xul Solar Museum

Index

Map entries are in colour.

C

D

E

M

Map symbols

maps are listed in the full index using coloured text

– – – ·	Chapter division boundary		Ranger station
▬ ▪ ▬ ▪ ▪	International border		Guardaparque HQ/park ranger HQ
▬ ▪ ▪	Provincial boundary		Serviced campsite
- · — · -	Barrios		Unserviced campsite
▬	Motorway		Refuge
═	Major road	▣	Accommodation
═	Minor road	◉	Restaurant/café
▬	Pedestrianized street	P	Parking
—	Unpaved road	⊞	Hospital
- - - - -	Path	ⓘ	Tourist office
	Steps	✆	Telephone
—	Railway	@	Internet
● - - - ●	Cable car and stations	✉	Post office
— —	Ferry route		Ski area
⊠—⊠	Gate		Golf course
······	River		Lighthouse
	Bridge		Vineyard
	Waterfall		Museum
	Rocks	⊙	Statue
	Mountains		Monument
	Volcano	✡	Synagogue
▲	Peak	‡	Church (regional maps)
	Spring/spa		Mosque/Muslim monument
	Cave		Church (city maps)
♦	Place of interest	□	Market
∩	Arch	■	Building
	Viewpoint	⬭	Stadium
∴	Ruin	+ + +	Christian cemetery
✈	International airport		Park
	Domestic airport		Swamp
★	Bus stop		Glacier
Ⓜ	Metro stop		Salt flat
⚓	Ferry/boat station		Beach